Child Development

SEVENTH EDITION

Laura E. Berk

Illinois State University

PEARSON

BOSTON   NEW YORK   SAN FRANCISCO

MEXICO CITY   MONTREAL   TORONTO   LONDON   MADRID   MUNICH   PARIS

HONG KONG   SINGAPORE   TOKYO   CAPETOWN   SYDNEY

In loving memory of my parents,
Sofie and Philip Eisenberg

Development Editors: Judy Ashkenaz, Maxine Effenson Chuck, Susan Messer
Development Manager: Judith H. Hauck
Editorial Assistant: Andrea Phiambolis
Executive Marketing Manager: Pamela Laskey
Composition Buyer: Linda Cox
Manufacturing Manager: Megan Cochran
Senior Production Editor: Elizabeth Gale Napolitano
Cover Director: Linda Knowles
Photo Researcher: Sarah Evertson—ImageQuest
Electronic Composition: Schneck-DePippo Graphics
Copyeditor: Connie Day
Proofreader: Bill Heckman

For related titles and support materials, visit our online catalog at www.ablongman.com

Library of Congress Cataloging-in-Publication Data
Berk, Laura E.
    Child development / Laura Berk.—7th ed.
        p. cm.
    Includes bibliographical references and index.
    ISBN 0-205-44913-1 (alk. paper)
    1. Child development. I. Title
    HQ767.9.B464 2003
    305.231—dc21   2005026002

Printed in the United States of America

10 9 8 7 6 5 4 3 2 1   VHP   09 08 07 06 05

ABOUT THE AUTHOR

Laura E. Berk is a distinguished professor of psychology at Illinois State University, where she has taught child development to both undergraduate and graduate students for more than three decades. She received her bachelor's degree in psychology from the University of California, Berkeley, and her master's and doctoral degrees in early childhood development and education from the University of Chicago. She has been a visiting scholar at Cornell University, UCLA, Stanford University, and the University of South Australia.

Berk has published widely on the effects of school environments on children's development, the development of private speech, and most recently the role of make-believe play in development. Her research has been funded by the U.S. Office of Education and the National Institute of Child Health and Human Development. It has appeared in many prominent journals, including *Child Development, Developmental Psychology, Merrill-Palmer Quarterly, Journal of Abnormal Child Psychology, Development and Psychopathology,* and *Early Childhood Research Quarterly.* Her empirical studies have attracted the attention of the general public, leading to contributions to *Psychology Today* and *Scientific American.*

Berk has served as a research editor for *Young Children* and consulting editor for *Early Childhood Research Quarterly* and the *Journal of Cognitive Education and Psychology.* She is a frequent contributor to edited volumes on early childhood development, having recently authored chapters on the importance of parenting, on make-believe play and self-regulation, and on the kindergarten child. She has also written the chapter on the extracurriculum for the *Handbook of Research on Curriculum* (American Educational Research Association), the chapter on development for *The Many Faces of Psychological Research in the Twenty-First Century* (Society for Teachers of Psychology), the article on Vygotsky for the *Encyclopedia of Cognitive Science,* and a chapter on storytelling as a teaching strategy for *Voices of Experience: Memorable Talks from the National Institute on the Teaching of Psychology* (American Psychological Society).

Berk's books include *Private Speech: From Social Interaction to Self-Regulation, Scaffolding Children's Learning: Vygotsky and Early Childhood Education,* and *Landscapes of Development: An Anthology of Readings.* In addition to *Child Development,* she is author of the best-selling texts *Infants, Children, and Adolescents* and *Development Through the Lifespan,* published by Allyn and Bacon. Her book for parents and teachers is *Awakening Children's Minds: How Parents and Teachers Can Make a Difference.*

Berk is active in work for children's causes. In addition to service in her home community, she is a member of the national board of directors of Jumpstart, a nonprofit organization that provides early literacy intervention to thousands of poverty-stricken preschoolers across the United States, using college and university students as interveners.

BRIEF CONTENTS

LIST OF FEATURES

⊚ CONTENTS

A PERSONAL NOTE TO STUDENTS

My more than thirty years of teaching child development have brought me in contact with thousands of students like you—students with diverse college majors, future goals, interests, and needs. Some are affiliated with my own department, psychology, but many come from other child-related fields—education, sociology, anthropology, family studies, social service, and biology, to name just a few. Each semester, my students' aspirations have proven to be as varied as their fields of study. Many look toward careers in applied work with children—teaching, caregiving, nursing, counseling, social work, school psychology, and program administration. Some plan to teach child development, and a few want to do research. Most hope someday to have children, whereas others are already parents who come with a desire to better understand and rear their own children. Almost all arrive with a deep curiosity about how they themselves developed from tiny infants into the complex human beings they are today.

My goal in preparing this seventh edition of *Child Development* is to provide a textbook that meets the instructional goals of your course as well as your personal interests and needs. To achieve these objectives, I have grounded this book in a carefully selected body of classic and current theory and research. In addition, the text highlights the interacting contributions of biology and environment to the developing child, explains how the research process helps solve real-world problems, illustrates commonalities and differences between ethnic groups and cultures, discusses the broader social contexts in which children develop, and pays special attention to policy issues that are crucial for safeguarding children's well-being in today's world. I have also provided a unique pedagogical program that will assist you in mastering information, integrating various aspects of development, critically examining controversial issues, and applying what you have learned.

I hope that learning about child development will be as rewarding for you as I have found it over the years. I would like to know what you think about both the field of child development and this book. I welcome your comments; please feel free to send them to me at Department of Psychology, Box 4620, Illinois State University, Normal, IL 61790, or care of the publisher, who will forward them to me.

Laura E. Berk

PREFACE FOR INSTRUCTORS

My decision to write *Child Development* was inspired by a wealth of professional and personal experiences. First and foremost were the interests and needs of hundreds of students of child development with whom I have worked in more than three decades of college teaching. I aimed for a text that is intellectually stimulating, that provides depth as well as breadth of coverage, that portrays the complexities of child development with clarity and excitement, and that is relevant and useful in building a bridge from theory and research to children's everyday lives.

Today, *Child Development* reaches around the globe, with editions published in five languages: English, Chinese, Japanese, Russian, and Spanish. Instructor and student enthusiasm for the book not only has been among my greatest sources of pride and satisfaction, but also has inspired me to rethink and improve each edition. I am honored and humbled to have entrusted to me the awesome responsibility of introducing the field of child development to so many students.

The seventeen years since *Child Development* first appeared have been a period of unprecedented expansion and change in theory and research. This seventh edition represents these rapid transformations, with a wealth of new content and teaching tools:

- *Diverse pathways of change are highlighted.* Investigators have reached broad consensus that variations in biological makeup, everyday tasks, and the people who support children in mastery of those tasks lead to wide individual differences in children's paths of change and resulting competencies. This edition pays more attention to variability in development and to recent theories—including ecological, sociocultural, and dynamic systems—that attempt to explain it. Multicultural and cross-cultural findings, including international comparisons, are enhanced throughout the text.

- *The complex, bidirectional relationship between biology and environment is given greater attention.* Accumulating evidence on development of the brain, motor skills, cognitive and language competencies, temperament, and developmental problems underscores the way biological factors emerge in, are modified by, and share power with experience. The interconnection between biology and environment is revisited throughout the text narrative and in the Biology and Environment boxes with new and updated topics.

- *Inclusion of interdisciplinary research is expanded.* The move toward viewing thoughts, feelings, and behavior as an integrated whole, affected by a wide array of influences in biology, social context, and culture, has motivated developmental researchers to strengthen their ties

with other fields of psychology and with other disciplines. Topics and findings included in this edition increasingly reflect the contributions of educational psychology, social psychology, healthy psychology, clinical psychology, neuropsychology, biology, pediatrics, sociology, anthropology, social welfare, and other fields.

- *The links between theory, research, and applications—a theme of this book since its inception—are strengthened.* As researchers intensify their efforts to generate findings relevant to real-life situations, I have placed even greater weight on social policy issues and sound theory- and research-based practices. Further applications are provided in the Applying What We Know tables, which give students concrete ways of building bridges between their learning and the real world.

- *Expanded coverage of Canadian content offers an integrated North American representation of the field.* With its contemporary North American perspective, the text greatly expands students' opportunity to learn more about social and cultural contexts for development and the powerful impact of public policies— especially in the realms of health and education—on children's lives. Canadian research and examples are included throughout the text.

- *The role of active student learning is made more explicit. Ask Yourself* questions at the end of each major section have been thoroughly revised and expanded to promote four approaches to engaging actively with the subject matter: *Review, Apply, Connect,* and *Reflect.* The new *Reflect* questions help make the study of child development personally meaningful by encouraging students to take well-reasoned stands on controversial issues and to relate theory and research to their own lives.

Text Philosophy

The basic approach of this book has been shaped by my own professional and personal history as a teacher, researcher, and parent. It consists of seven philosophical ingredients that I regard as essential for students to emerge from a course with a thorough understanding of child development:

1. **An understanding of major theories and the strengths and shortcomings of each.** The first chapter begins by emphasizing that only knowledge of multiple theories can do justice to the richness of child development. In each topical domain, I present a variety of theoretical perspectives, indicate how each highlights previously overlooked facets of development, and discuss research that evaluates it. If one or two theories have emerged as especially prominent in a particular area, I

indicate why, in terms of the theory's broad explanatory power. Consideration of contrasting theories also serves as the context for an evenhanded analysis of many controversial issues throughout the text.

2. **An appreciation of research strategies for investigating child development.** To evaluate theories, students need a firm grounding in research methods and designs. I devote an entire chapter to a description and critique of research strategies. Throughout the book, numerous studies are discussed in sufficient detail for students to use what they have learned to critically assess the findings, conclusions, and implications of research.

3. **Knowledge of both the sequence of child development and the processes that underlie it.** Students are provided with a description of the organized sequence of development along with processes of change. An understanding of process—how complex combinations of biological and environmental events produce development—has been the focus of most recent research. Accordingly, the text reflects this emphasis. But new information about the timetable of change has also emerged. In many ways, children have proved to be far more competent than they were believed to be in the past. Current evidence on the sequence and timing of development, along with its implications for process, is presented throughout the book.

4. **An appreciation of the impact of context and culture on child development.** A wealth of research indicates that children live in rich physical and social contexts that affect all aspects of development. In each chapter, the student travels to distant parts of the world as I review a growing body of cross-cultural evidence. The text narrative also discusses many findings on socioeconomically and ethnically diverse children within the United States and Canada, and children with varying abilities and disabilities. Besides highlighting the role of immediate settings, such as family, neighborhood, and school, I underscore the impact of larger social structures—societal values, laws, and government programs—on children's well being.

5. **An understanding of the joint contributions of biology and environment to development.** The field recognizes more powerfully than ever before the interaction of hereditary/constitutional and environmental factors—that these contributions to development combine in complex ways and cannot be separated in a simple manner. Numerous examples of how biological dispositions can be maintained as well as transformed by social contexts are presented throughout the book.

6. **A sense of the interdependency of all aspects of development—physical, cognitive, emotional, and social.** Every chapter takes an integrated approach to understanding children. I show how physical, cognitive, emotional, and social development are interwoven. Within the text narrative and in a special series of Ask Yourself *Connect* questions at the end of major sections, students are referred to other parts of the book to deepen their grasp of relationships among various aspects of change.

7. **An appreciation of the interrelatedness of theory, research, and applications.** Throughout this book, I emphasize that theories of child development and the research stimulated by them provide the foundation for sound, effective practices with children. The links between theory, research, and applications are reinforced by an organizational format in which theory and research are presented first, followed by practical implications. In addition, a current focus in the field—harnessing child development knowledge to shape social policies that support children's needs—is reflected in every chapter. The text addresses the current condition of children in the United States, Canada, and around the world, and shows how theory and research have sparked successful interventions.

New Coverage in the Seventh Edition

In this edition I continue to represent a rapidly transforming contemporary literature with theory and research from more than 1,800 new citations. Cutting-edge topics throughout the text underscore the book's major themes. Here is a sampling:

- **Chapter 1:** Introduction to emerging adulthood, a new period of development that extends adolescence • New historical findings on childhood as a separate phase of life in medieval Europe • Updated Biology and Environment box on resilience • Updated consideration of Vygotsky's view of development • Revised section on child development and social policy • Updated indicators on the status of children in the United States and Canada • New Social Issues box on welfare reform, poverty, and child development, illustrating the role of research in designing policies that safeguard children's well-being

- **Chapter 2:** New examples of systematic observation, including the time-sampling method of collecting data • Enhanced consideration of the strengths of structured interviews • Revised discussion of the validity of research designs, including internal and external validity • New examples of correlational research • New Biology and Environment box with a field experiment addressing the influence of musical experiences on children's intelligence • New example of a natural, or quasi-, experiment • Updated section on ethics in research on children

- **Chapter 3:** • Updated discussion of basic genetics • Enhanced consideration of fragile X syndrome • Updated Social Issues box on the pros and cons of reproductive technologies, including new techniques and related ethical concerns • Updated consideration of the implications of the Human Genome Project for development • New findings on the relationship of prenatal activity level to childhood temperament • New Biology and Environment box on the prenatal environment and health in later life • New evidence on long-term consequences of emotional stress during pregnancy • New findings on older maternal age and prenatal and birth complications • New evidence on developmental consequences of anoxia at birth • Updated discussion of preterm and low-birth-weight infants • Enhanced discussion of environmental influences on gene expression

● **Chapter 4:** Updated Social Issues box on sudden infant death syndrome • Enhanced section on infant crying • Revised and updated section on habituation • New evidence on infants' attraction to motion and persisting memory for the movements of objects and people • New findings on newborn imitation in humans and chimpanzees • Recent evidence that babies reach with their feet before they reach with their hands • New findings on infant pain perception • Updated findings on development of balance • Revised and expanded section on hearing, including infants as statistical analyzers of the speech stream • New evidence on how intermodal stimulation supports infants' efforts to make sense of language • Expanded consideration of early face perception • Revised and updated section on object perception

● **Chapter 5:** Enhanced consideration of sex differences in motor skills • New section on consequences of participation in youth sports programs • Enhanced discussion of cultural variations in physical growth • Expanded attention to brain plasticity, including a new Biology and Environment box with insights from research on children and adults with brain damage • Introduction to the field of developmental cognitive neuroscience • Updated section on breastfeeding • New findings on causes and consequences of obesity • New evidence on adolescents' sleep "phase delay" • New findings on the long-term consequences of early pubertal timing • New From Research to Practice box on parents' discussions with teenagers about sexual issues • Expanded consideration of factors related to adolescent parenthood • New evidence on sex education, including findings on abstinence-only programs

● **Chapter 6:** New evidence on infants' understanding of object permanence • New evidence on toddlers' capacity to engage in deferred imitation • Updated findings on the development of categorization in early childhood • Updated consideration of the development of cognitive maps, including cultural variations • Expanded treatment of the consequences of abstract thought, including development of decision making in adolescence • Expanded discussion of the core knowledge perspective • New Biology and Environment box on children's understanding of death • New Cultural Influences box on how children learn by observing and participating in adult work

● **Chapter 7:** Revised From Research to Practice box on speech–gesture mismatches as an indicator of readiness for learning • Revised Biology and Environment box on

children with attention-deficit hyperactivity disorder • New findings on gains in cognitive inhibition, including related changes in brain functioning • New research on cultural tools and adult assistance that support children's planning • Updated research on age-related changes in use of memory strategies • New research on the relationship between script and taxonomic categorization • New Biology and Environment box on infantile amnesia • New section on children's eyewitness memory, with increased attention to factors influencing children's suggestibility • Updated findings on development of emergent literacy • New findings on preschoolers' understanding of number concepts and counting • New research on the role of metacognition in development of scientific reasoning in adolescence

● **Chapter 8:** Updated description of Sternberg's triarchic theory of successful intelligence • New section on commonalities and differences between intelligence tests, aptitude tests, and achievement tests • New research on culture, communication styles, and children's mental test performance • New evidence on the impact of stereotype threat on the test taking of ethnic minority children • New Social Issues box on high-stakes testing • Enhanced consideration of the impact of early intervention for poverty-stricken children, with emphasis on long-term outcomes • Consideration of cultural variations in creativity

● **Chapter 9:** New Biology and Environment box on deaf children inventing language • Updated information on language areas in the brain • Revised and updated evidence on a sensitive period for language development • Revised and expanded section on the interactionist perspective, including information-processing and social interactionist theories • New research on infants' sensitivity to language sound patterns • New findings on the influence of phonological memory on word learning • New evidence on gradual mastery of grammar during the preschool years • New research indicating that parents provide preschoolers with many reformulations of grammatically incorrect expressions • New section on development of narratives • Revised and updated section on bilingualism, including a new Social Issues box on bilingual education in Canada and the United States

● **Chapter 10:** Enhanced discussion of the development of discrete emotional expressions in infancy • New findings on cultural variations in self-conscious emotions • Expanded treatment of emotional self-regulation • New findings on infants' social referencing using the parent's voice • Revised and updated consideration of the stability of temperament • New findings on the temperamental dimension of effortful control • New findings on the influence of the nonshared environment on temperament, with special emphasis on parents' tendency to emphasize differences between their children • Enhanced consideration of culture, maternal sensitivity, and attachment • New Cultural Influences box on the powerful role of paternal warmth in development • Expanded discussion of the influence of attachment security in infancy on later development • Updated evidence on the quality of American and Canadian child care

- **Chapter 11:** Expanded and updated discussion of the development of self-awareness • New findings on children's theory of mind, including development of second-order false belief in middle childhood • Updated Biology and Environment box on mindblindness and autism • Updated research on the relationship of self-esteem to competence at various activities • New findings on factors that support identity development, including family and peer influences • Updated Cultural Influences box on identity development among ethnic minority adolescents • Revised and updated Social Issues box on adolescent suicide, including incidence in industrialized nations and ethnic variations in the United States and Canada • New research on development of ethnic prejudices in childhood, including ways to reduce prejudice

- **Chapter 12:** Updated research on the impact of harsh punishment on development • New Cultural Influences box on ethnic differences in the consequences of physical punishment • Enhanced consideration of Kohlberg's stages as an extension of Piaget's theory of the development of moral judgment • New findings on cultural variations in care-based moral reasoning • Updated From Research to Practice box on the development of civic responsibility • New section on religious involvement and moral development • New Cultural Influences box on children's understanding of God • Revised and updated section on challenges to Kohlberg's theory • Updated research on development of morally relevant self-control • Revised consideration of types of aggression, including distinctions between physical, verbal, and relational forms • New findings on relational aggression, including sex differences and implications for continuing conduct problems • Updated research on the implications of early-onset aggressive behavior for serious antisocial behavior and delinquency in adolescence

- **Chapter 13:** Updated Cultural Influences box on Sweden's commitment to gender equality • New From Research to Practice box on how children learn about gender through mother–child conversations • New findings on long-term consequences of parents' gender-typed judgments of children's abilities • Updated evidence on gender-segregated peer groups for children's gender-typed attitudes and behaviors • New section on cultural variations in same-sex peer interactions • Updated research on cognitive contributions

to gender constancy • New findings on development of gender identity in middle childhood • New research on declining sex differences in mathematical abilities

- **Chapter 14:** Enhanced consideration of the influence of neighborhood conditions on parenting and children's adjustment • Updated From Research to Practice box on the transition to parenthood • New evidence on the harmful impact of parental psychological control on children and youths • Expanded discussion of the bidirectional relationship between parenting and children's attributes • Revised and updated section on parenting and adolescent autonomy • New section on adjustment problems of children and adolescents of affluent families • Updated section on ethnic variations in parenting beliefs and practices • New research on sibling relationships in middle childhood and adolescence • Revised and updated section on children of gay and lesbian families • New findings on children in never-married single-parent families • Updated consideration of long-term consequences of divorce and interventions for divorcing parents that help protect children's well-being • New evidence on maternal employment and children's adjustment, with special attention to the impact of workplace stressors • Updated section on child maltreatment, including the success of home visitation prevention programs

- **Chapter 15:** • Enhanced consideration of development of peer sociability in early childhood, including the consequences of nonsocial play for adjustment • New findings on development of rough-and-tumble play and its relationship to aggression in adolescent boys • Revised and updated section on parenting and children's peer relations • New findings on peer acceptance, including implications of peer-acceptance categories for bullying and victimization • New section on dating, including contributions of parent–child relationships and friendships to romantic ties and factors linked to dating violence • Revised and updated sections on television and computers, including benefits and risks for development • Revised and updated section on educational philosophies, including constructivist and social constructivist classrooms, and the community of learners approach • New evidence on relationships between children's characteristics and teacher–student interactions, with implications for educational self-fulfilling prophecies • Updated research on homogeneous grouping and tracking in schools • Revised and updated consideration of the effectiveness of mainstreaming and full inclusion for children with learning difficulties • New evidence on international comparisons of academic achievement in industrialized nations, with special attention to societal, school, and family factors that support high achievement in top-performing nations

Pedagogical Features

Maintaining a highly accessible writing style—one that is lucid and engaging without being simplistic—continues to be one of my major goals. I frequently converse with students, encouraging them to relate what they read to their own lives. In doing so, I hope to make the study of child development involving and pleasurable.

● **Chapter Introductions and End-of-Chapter Summaries.** To provide a helpful preview, I include an outline and overview of chapter content in each chapter introduction. Especially comprehensive end-of-chapter summaries, organized according to the major divisions of each chapter and highlighting important terms, remind students of key points in the text discussion. Review questions are included in the summaries to encourage active study.

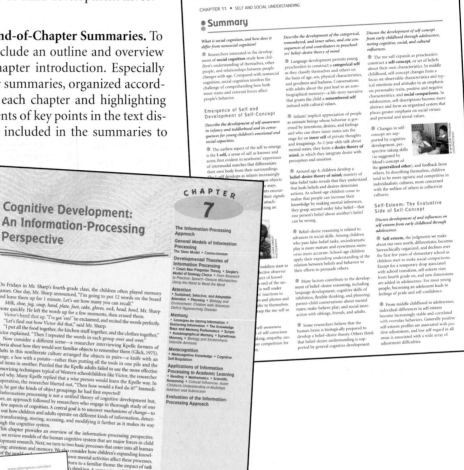

● **Ask Yourself Questions.** Active engagement with the subject matter is also supported by study questions at the end of each major section. Four types of questions prompt students to think about child development in diverse ways: **Review** questions help students recall and comprehend information they have just read. **Apply** questions encourage the application of knowledge to controversial issues and problems faced by children, parents, and professionals who work with them. **Connect** questions help students build an image of the whole child by integrating what they have learned across age periods and domains of development. **Reflect** questions help make the study of child development personally meaningful by asking students to reflect on their own development. An icon indicates that each question is answered on the text's companion website (*http://www.ablongman.com/berk*). Students may compare their reasoning to a model response.

Four types of thematic boxes accentuate the philosophical themes of this book:

- **Biology and Environment** boxes highlight the growing attention to the complex, bidirectional relationship between biology and environment during development. Examples include *Brain Plasticity: Insights from Research on Brain-Damaged Children and Adults; Do Infants Have Built-In Numerical Knowledge?; Language Development in Children with Williams Syndrome;* and *Bullies and Their Victims.*

- **From Research to Practice** boxes integrate theory, research, and applications on such topics as *The Pros and Cons of Reproductive Technologies; Parents and Teenagers (Don't) Talk About Sex; Development of Civic Responsibility;* and *Children Learn About Gender Through Mother–Child Conversations.*

- **Cultural Influences** boxes have been expanded and updated to deepen attention to culture threaded throughout the text. They emphasize both multicultural and cross-cultural variations— for example, *The Powerful Role of Paternal Warmth in Development; Children in Village and Tribal Cultures Observe and Participate in Adult Work; Identity Development Among Ethnic Minority Adolescents;* and *Children's Understanding of God.*

- **Social Issues** boxes discuss the impact of social conditions on children and emphasize the need for sensitive social policies to ensure their well-being. Topics related to both education and health are addressed and include *Welfare Reform, Poverty, and Child Development; A Cross-National Perspective on Health Care and Other Policies for Parents and Newborn Babies; High-Stakes Testing;* and *Two Approaches to Bilingual Education: Canada and the United States.*

● **Applying What We Know Tables.** In this new feature, I present succinct, research-based applications on many issues, speaking directly to students as parents or future parents and to those pursuing child- and family-related careers or areas of study, such as teaching, health care, counseling, or social work.

● **Milestones Tables.** Milestones tables summarize major developments within each topical area, providing a convenient overview of the chronology of development. In this edition, they are beautifully illustrated with many photos of the attainments of infants, children, and adolescents.

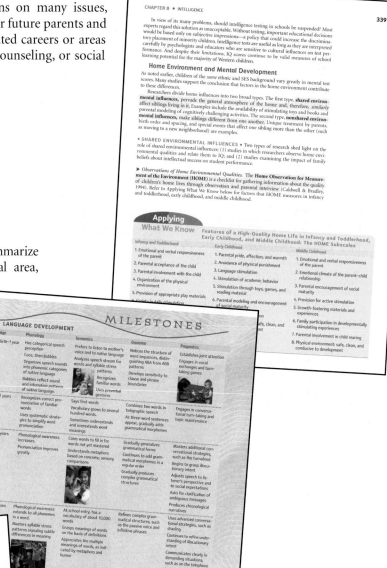

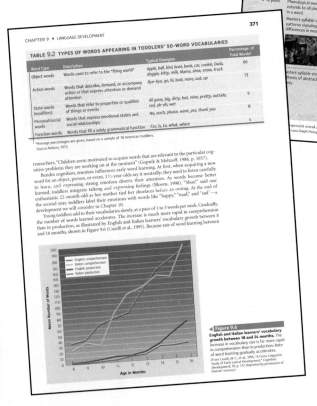

● **Additional Tables.** Attractively designed tables are liberally included to help readers grasp essential points in the text narrative and extend information on a topic.

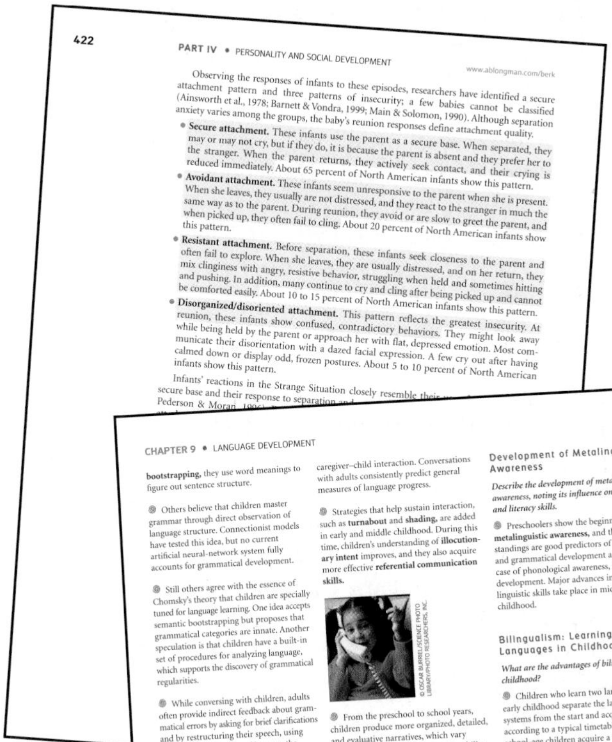

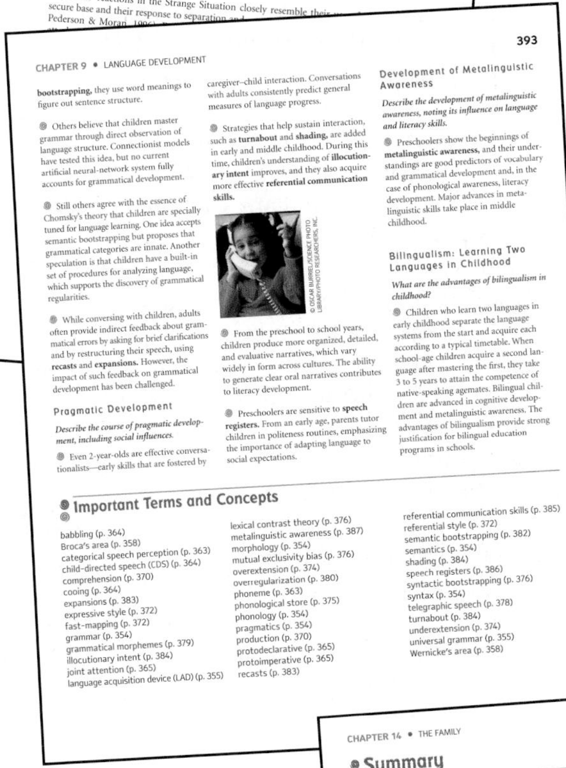

● **In-Text Key Terms with Definitions, End-of-Chapter Term List, and End-of-Book Glossary.** Mastery of terms that make up the central vocabulary of the field is promoted through new in-text highlighting of key-term and concept definitions, which encourages students to review the terminology of the field in greater depth by rereading related information. Key terms also appear in an end-of-chapter page-referenced term list and an end-of-book page-referenced glossary.

● **Enhanced Art and Photo Program.** A thoroughly revised art style presents concepts and research findings with clarity and attractiveness, thereby greatly aiding student understanding and retention. The illustration program also nearly doubles the number of photos in the previous edition, with each carefully selected to help teach theory, research, and applications in child development.

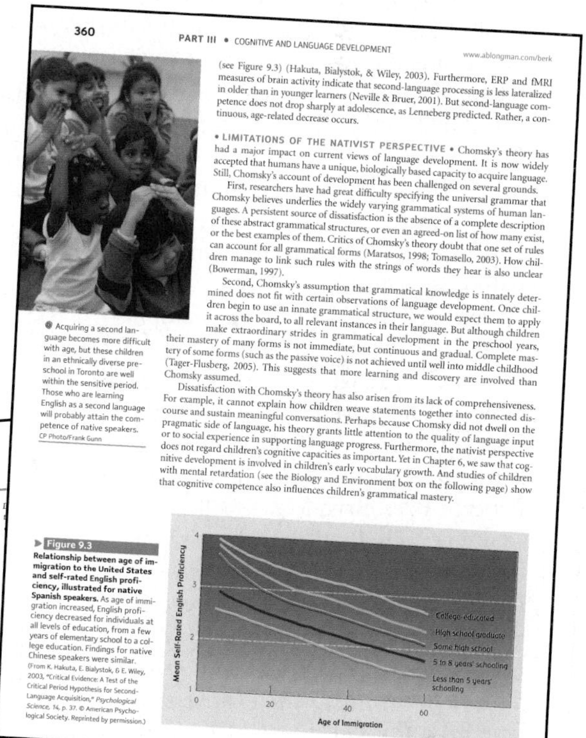

Sample page 422

422   PART IV • PERSONALITY AND SOCIAL DEVELOPMENT   www.ablongman.com/berk

Observing the responses of infants to these episodes, researchers have identified a secure attachment pattern and three patterns of insecurity; a few babies cannot be classified (Ainsworth et al., 1978; Barnett & Vondra, 1999; Main & Solomon, 1990). Although separation anxiety varies among the groups, the baby's reunion responses define attachment quality.

● **Secure attachment.** These infants use the parent as a secure base. When separated, they may or may not cry, but if they do, it is because the parent is absent and they prefer her to the stranger. When the parent returns, they actively seek contact, and their crying is reduced immediately. About 65 percent of North American infants show this pattern.

● **Avoidant attachment.** These infants seem unresponsive to the parent when she is present. When she leaves, they usually are not distressed, and they react to the stranger in much the same way as to the parent. During reunion, they avoid or are slow to greet the parent, and when picked up, they often fail to cling. About 20 percent of North American infants show this pattern.

● **Resistant attachment.** Before separation, these infants seek closeness to the parent and often fail to explore. When she leaves, they are usually distressed, and on her return, they mix clinginess with angry, resistive behavior, struggling when held and sometimes hitting and pushing. In addition, many continue to cry and cling after being picked up and cannot be comforted easily. About 10 to 15 percent of North American infants show this pattern.

● **Disorganized/disoriented attachment.** This pattern reflects the greatest insecurity. At reunion, these infants show confused, contradictory behaviors. They might look away while being held by the parent or approach her with flat, depressed emotion. Most communicate their disorientation with a dazed facial expression. A few cry out after having calmed down or display odd, frozen postures. About 5 to 10 percent of North American infants show this pattern.

Infants' reactions in the Strange Situation closely resemble their secure base and their response to separation and ... Pederson & Moran, 199...

Sample page 393

393

CHAPTER 9 • LANGUAGE DEVELOPMENT

bootstrapping, they use word meanings to figure out sentence structure.

● Others believe that children master grammar through direct observation of language structure. Connectionist models have tested this idea, but no current artificial neural-network system fully accounts for grammatical development.

● Still others agree with the essence of Chomsky's theory that children are specially tuned for language learning. One idea accepts semantic bootstrapping but proposes that grammatical categories are innate. Another speculation is that children have a built-in set of procedures for analyzing language, which supports the discovery of grammatical regularities.

● While conversing with children, adults often provide indirect feedback about grammatical errors by asking for clarifications and by restructuring their speech, using **recasts** and **expansions.** However, the impact of such feedback on grammatical development has been challenged.

Pragmatic Development

Describe the course of pragmatic development, including social influences.

● Even 2-year-olds are effective conversationalists—early skills that are fostered by

caregiver–child interaction. Conversations with adults consistently predict general measures of language progress.

● Strategies that help sustain interaction, such as **turnabout** and **shading,** are added in early and middle childhood. During this time, children's understanding of **illocutionary intent** improves, and they also acquire more effective **referential communication skills.**

● From the preschool to school years, children produce more organized, detailed, and evaluative narratives, which vary widely in form across cultures. The ability to generate clear oral narratives contributes to literacy development.

● Preschoolers are sensitive to **speech registers.** From an early age, parents tutor children in politeness routines, emphasizing the importance of adapting language to social expectations.

Development of Metalinguistic Awareness

Describe the development of metalinguistic awareness, noting its influence on language and literacy skills.

● Preschoolers show the beginnings of **metalinguistic awareness,** and their understandings are good predictors of vocabulary and grammatical development and, in the case of phonological awareness, literacy development. Major advances in metalinguistic skills take place in middle childhood.

Bilingualism: Learning Two Languages in Childhood

What are the advantages of bilingualism in childhood?

● Children who learn two languages in early childhood separate the language systems from the start and acquire each according to a typical timetable. When school-age children acquire a second language after mastering the first, they take 3 to 5 years to attain the competence of native-speaking agemates. Bilingual children are advanced in cognitive development and metalinguistic ability. The advantages of bilingualism provide strong justification for bilingual education programs in schools.

■ Important Terms and Concepts

babbling (p. 364)
Broca's area (p. 358)
categorical speech perception (p. 363)
child-directed speech (CDS) (p. 364)
comprehension (p. 370)
cooing (p. 364)
expansions (p. 383)
expressive style (p. 372)
fast-mapping (p. 372)
grammar (p. 354)
grammatical morphemes (p. 379)
illocutionary intent (p. 384)
joint attention (p. 365)
language acquisition device (LAD) (p. 355)

lexical contrast theory (p. 376)
metalinguistic awareness (p. 387)
morphology (p. 354)
mutual exclusivity bias (p. 375)
overextension (p. 374)
overregularization (p. 380)
phoneme (p. 363)
phonological store (p. 375)
phonology (p. 354)
pragmatics (p. 354)
production (p. 370)
protodeclarative (p. 365)
protoimperative (p. 365)
recasts (p. 383)

referential communication skills (p. 385)
referential style (p. 372)
semantic bootstrapping (p. 382)
semantics (p. 354)
shading (p. 384)
speech registers (p. 386)
syntactic bootstrapping (p. 376)
syntax (p. 354)
telegraphic speech (p. 378)
turnabout (p. 384)
underextension (p. 374)
universal grammar (p. 355)
Wernicke's area (p. 358)

Sample page 360

360   PART III • COGNITIVE AND LANGUAGE DEVELOPMENT   www.ablongman.com/berk

● Acquiring a second language becomes more difficult with age, but these children in an ethnically diverse preschool in Toronto are well within the sensitive period. Those who are learning English as a second language will probably attain the competence of native speakers.
CP Photo/Frank Gunn

(see Figure 9.3) (Hakuta, Bialystok, & Wiley, 2003). Furthermore, ERP and fMRI measures of brain activity indicate that second-language processing is less lateralized in older than in younger learners (Neville & Bruer, 2001). But second-language competence does not drop sharply at adolescence, as Lenneberg predicted. Rather, a continuous, age-related decrease occurs.

• **LIMITATIONS OF THE NATIVIST PERSPECTIVE** • Chomsky's theory has had a major impact on current views of language development. It is now widely accepted that humans have a unique, biologically based capacity to acquire language. Still, Chomsky's account of development has been challenged on several grounds.

First, researchers have had great difficulty specifying the universal grammar that Chomsky believes underlies the widely varying grammatical systems of human languages. A persistent source of dissatisfaction is the absence of a complete description of these abstract grammatical structures, or even an agreed-on list of how many exist, or the best examples of them. Critics of Chomsky's theory doubt that one set of rules can account for all grammatical forms (Maratsos, 1998; Tomasello, 2003). How children manage to link such rules with the strings of words they hear is also unclear (Bowerman, 1997).

Second, Chomsky's assumption that grammatical knowledge is innately determined does not fit with certain observations of language development. Once children begin to use an innate grammatical structure, we would expect them to apply it across the board, to all relevant instances in their language. But although children make extraordinary strides in grammatical development in the preschool years, their mastery of many forms is not immediate, but continuous and gradual. Complete mastery of some forms (such as the passive voice) is not achieved until well into middle childhood (Tager-Flusberg, 2005). This suggests that more learning and discovery are involved than Chomsky assumed.

Dissatisfaction with Chomsky's theory has also arisen from its lack of comprehensiveness. For example, it cannot explain how children weave statements together into connected discourse and sustain meaningful conversations. Perhaps because Chomsky did not dwell on the pragmatic side of language, his theory grants little attention to the quality of language input or to social experience in supporting language progress. Furthermore, the nativist perspective does not regard children's cognitive capacities as important. Yet in Chapter 6, we saw that cognitive development is involved in children's early vocabulary growth. And studies of children with mental retardation (see the Biology and Environment box on the following page) show that cognitive competence also influences children's grammatical mastery.

▶ **Figure 9.3**
Relationship between age of immigration to the United States and self-rated English proficiency, illustrated for native Spanish speakers. As age of immigration increased, English proficiency decreased for individuals at all levels of education, from a few years of elementary school to a college education. Findings for native Chinese speakers were similar.
(From K. Hakuta, E. Bialystok, & E. Wiley, 2003, "Critical Evidence: A Test of the Critical Period Hypothesis for Second-Language Acquisition," *Psychological Science,* 14, p. 37. © American Psychological Society. Reprinted by permission.)

[Graph: Mean Self-Rated English Proficiency vs. Age of Immigration — curves labeled College educated, High school graduate, Some high school, 5 to 8 years' schooling, Less than 5 years' schooling]

● When families experience stressors that accompany poverty, parents become depressed, irritable, and distracted. As a result, parents become less involved in child rearing, hostile family interactions increase, children experience depleted home learning environments, and their cognitive and emotional well-being suffers profoundly.

● Chinese, Hispanic, Asian Pacific Island, and African-American parents tend to be highly controlling. When combined with warmth, high control can be adaptive. Among African-American children, it is associated with cognitive and social competence. But when control becomes excessive, resulting in an authoritarian child-rearing style, it impairs children's adjustment.

● **Extended-family households,** in which one or more adult relatives live with the parent–child **nuclear family unit,** are common among ethnic minorities. Extended-family support helps protect children from the stress and disorganization of poverty.

Sample page — Chapter 14

CHAPTER 14 • THE FAMILY

● Summary

Evolutionary Origins

Discuss the evolutionary origins and adaptive value of the family among our hunting-and-gathering ancestors.

● The human family in its most common form can be traced to our hunting-and-gathering ancestors. When bipedalism evolved and arms were freed to carry things, our ancestors found it easier to cooperate and share, especially in providing food for the young. A man and woman assumed special responsibility for their own children because that arrangement enhanced survival. Kinship groups expanded, offering greater success at competing with other humans for resources.

Functions of the Family

Cite the functions modern families perform for society.

● Responsibilities of contemporary families are largely restricted to reproduction, socialization, and emotional support. As societies became more complex, other institutions developed to assist with certain functions, such as educating children and ensuring societal order.

The Family as a Social System

Describe the social systems perspective on family functioning, including its view of family interaction and the influence of surrounding social contexts.

● Contemporary researchers view the family from a **social systems perspective**—as a complex set of interacting relationships affected by the larger social context. Bidirectional influences exist whereby the behaviors of each family member affect those of others—an interplay of forces that most constantly adapt to the development of individual family members. Connections to the community—through formal organizations and informal social networks—grant parents and children social support, thereby promoting effective family interaction and children's development.

Socialization Within the Family

Discuss the features that differentiate major child-rearing styles, and explain how effective parents adapt child rearing to children's growing competence during middle childhood and adolescence.

● Three features differentiate major child-rearing styles: (1) acceptance of the child and involvement to establish emotional connection; (2) control of the child to promote mature behavior; and (3) autonomy granting to promote self-reliance. The **authoritative style** is high in acceptance and involvement, emphasizes firm control with explanations, and includes gradual, appropriate autonomy granting. It promotes cognitive, emotional, and social competence from early childhood into adolescence.

● The **authoritarian style** is low in acceptance and involvement, is high in both coercive and **psychological control,** and restricts instead of grants autonomy. It is associated with anxious, withdrawn, dependent child behavior, especially among girls, and with high rates of anger, defiance, and aggression, especially among boys. The **permissive style** is high in acceptance, low in control, and lax rather than appropriate in autonomy granting. Children who experience it typically show poor self-control and achievement and, in adolescence, are defiant and antisocial. The **uninvolved style** combines low acceptance and involvement with little control or effort to grant autonomy. When it begins early, it disrupts virtually all aspects of development.

● Authoritative child rearing promotes maturity and adjustment in children of diverse temperaments. But because of their dispositions, some children require more emphasis on certain authoritative features. Over time, the relationship between parent and children's attributes becomes increasingly bidirectional.

● In middle childhood, effective parents engage in **coregulation,** exerting parental oversight while permitting children to be in charge of moment-by-moment decision making. During adolescence, mature **autonomy** is fostered by parenting that grants young people independence in accord with their readiness, while maintaining a warm, supportive relationship.

Acknowledgments

The dedicated contributions of many individuals helped make this book a reality and contributed to refinements and improvements in each edition. An impressive cast of reviewers provided many helpful suggestions, constructive criticisms, and encouragement and enthusiasm for the organization and content of the book. I am grateful to each one of them.

● **REVIEWERS FOR THE FIRST THROUGH SIXTH EDITIONS** ●

Martha W. Alibali, University of Wisconsin, Madison
Daniel Ashmead, Vanderbilt University
Margarita Azmitia, University of California, Santa Cruz
Catherine L. Bagwell, University of Richmond
Lynne Baker-Ward, North Carolina State University
Carole R. Beal, University of Massachusetts
Rebecca S. Bigler, University of Texas, Austin
Dana W. Birnbaum, University of Maine at Orono
Kathryn N. Black, Purdue University
James H. Bodle, College of Mount Saint Joseph
Cathryn L. Booth, University of Washington
J. Paul Boudreau, University of Prince Edward Island
Sam Boyd, University of Central Arkansas
Celia A. Brownell, University of Pittsburgh
M. Michele Burnette, Community College of Allegheny County
Toni A. Campbell, San Jose State University
Beth Casey, Boston College
Robert Cohen, University of Memphis
John Condry, Cornell University
Rhoda Cummings, University of Nevada, Reno
James L. Dannemiller, University of Wisconsin, Madison
Zoe Ann Davidson, Alabama A & M University
Darlene DeSantis, West Chester University
Rebecca Eder, Bryn Mawr College
Claire Etaugh, Bradley University
Bill Fabricius, Arizona State University
Beverly Fagot, University of Oregon
Francine Favretto, University of Maryland
Larry Fenson, San Diego State University
James Garbarino, Cornell University
Jane F. Gaultney, University of North Carolina, Charlotte
John C. Gibbs, The Ohio State University
Peter Gordon, University of Pittsburgh
Katherine Green, Millersville University
Craig H. Hart, Brigham Young University
Kenneth Hill, Saint Mary's University, Halifax
Alice S. Honig, Syracuse University
Janis Jacobs, Pennsylvania State University
Scott Johnson, Cornell University
Katherine Kipp, University of Georgia
Paul Klaczynski, The Pennsylvania State University
Mareile Koenig, George Washington University Hospital
Claire Kopp, Claremont Graduate School

Beth Kurtz-Costes, University of North Carolina, Chapel Hill
Gary W. Ladd, Arizona State University
Daniel Lapsley, Ball State University
Frank Laycock, Oberlin College
Elise Lehman, George Mason University
Mary D. Leinbach, University of Oregon
Richard Lerner, Tufts University
Robert S. Marvin, University of Virginia
Tom McBride, Princeton University
Carolyn J. Mebert, University of New Hampshire
Gary B. Melton, University of Nebraska, Lincoln
Mary Evelyn Moore, Illinois State University
Lois Muir, University of Wisconsin, La Crosse
John P. Murray, Kansas State University
Bonnie K. Nastasi, State University of New York at Albany
Larry Nucci, University of Illinois at Chicago
Peter Ornstein, University of North Carolina
Randall Osbourne, Indiana University East
Carol Pandey, Pierce College, Los Angeles
Thomas S. Parish, Kansas State University
B. Kay Pasley, Colorado State University
Kathy Pezdek, Claremont Graduate School
Ellen F. Potter, University of South Carolina at Columbia
Kimberly K. Powlishta, Northern Illinois University
Kathleen Preston, Humboldt State University
Bud Protinsky, Virginia Polytechnic Institute and State University
Daniel Reschly, Iowa State University
Rosemary Rosser, University of Arizona
Alan Russell, Flinders University
Jane Ann Rysberg, California State University, Chico
Phil Schoggen, Cornell University
Maria E. Sera, University of Iowa
Beth Shapiro, Emory University
Linda Siegel, University of British Columbia
Robert Siegler, Carnegie Mellon University
Gregory J. Smith, Dickinson College
Robert J. Sternberg, Yale University
Harold Stevenson, University of Michigan
Ross A. Thompson, University of Nebraska, Lincoln
Barbara A. Tinsley, University of Illinois at Urbana–Champaign
Kim F. Townley, University of Kentucky
Janet Valadez, Pan American University
Amye R. Warren, University of Tennessee at Chattanooga

● **REVIEWERS FOR THE SEVENTH EDITION** ●

Lorraine Bahrick, Florida International University
David Baskind, Delta College
Rebecca S. Bigler, University of Texas, Austin
Paul Bloom, Yale University
Darlene A. Brodeur, Acadia University
Robert Coplan, Carelton University
Nancy Digdon, MacEwan University
Richard Ely, Boston University

Jayne Gackenbach, MacEwan University
John C. Gibbs, Ohio State University
Craig H. Hart, Brigham Young University
Joyce A. Hemphill, University of Wisconsin, Madison
Carla L. Hudson Kam, University of California, Berkeley
Scott Johnson, New York University
Wilma M. Marshall, Douglas College
Ashley E. Maynard, University of Hawaii
David A. Nelson, Brigham Young University
Susan Siaw, California State Polytechnic University
Barbara B. Simon, Midlands Technical College
Daniel Swingley, University of Pennsylvania
Doug Symons, Acadia University
Ross A. Thompson, University of California, Davis
Tracy Vaillancourt, McMaster University
Susan K. Walker, University of Maryland
Yiyuan Xu, University of Hawaii

I would like to extend special thanks to Stuart Shanker, York University, for invaluable assistance in preparing a new edition that speaks to both American and Canadian students. For many long months, Stuart regularly took time from his demanding schedule to provide me with information on the current status of children and families in Canada and on public policies and programs aimed at protecting and supporting the development of Canadian children. Stuart's contributions have greatly enriched the cultural and public policy content of the text. It has been a pleasure to get to know and work with him.

Colleagues and students at Illinois State University aided my research and contributed significantly to the text's supplements. Richard Payne, Department of Politics and Government, Illinois State University, is a kind and devoted friend with whom I have shared many profitable discussions about the writing process, the condition of children and families, and other topics that have significantly influenced my perspective on child development and social policy. My appreciation to Richard for having telephoned at crucial moments during many months of intense work on this project.

Sara Harris joined me in preparing the Instructor's Resource Manual, the Child Development in Action Observation Video Guide, A Window on Child Development Video Guide, and the VideoWorkshop Instructor's Teaching Guide and Student Learning Guide, bringing to these tasks enthusiasm, imagination, depth of knowledge, and impressive writing skill. JoDe Paladino's outstanding, dedicated work in conducting literature searches and in revising the Grade Aid Workbook are much appreciated. Kristy Barnes, Jennifer Naese, and Jennie Sullivan spent countless hours gathering and organizing library materials.

The supplements package also benefited from the talents and diligence of several other individuals. Gillian Wark of Simon Fraser University and Anoosha Aghakhani of the University of Calgary adapted several features of the Instructor's Resource Manual for its Canadian edition.

Kristine Anthis of Southern Connecticut State University and David Hibbard and Gail Walton of Illinois Wesleyan University also contributed to the Instructor's Resource Manual. Gabrielle Principe of Ursinus College and Naomi Tyler of Vanderbilt University authored a superb Test Bank and set of Practice Tests.

Judy Ashkenaz, development editor, worked closely with me as I wrote each chapter, making sure that every thought and concept would be precisely expressed and well developed. Her keen writing and editing skills and her impressive knowledge of children's issues made the editing an exceptional learning experience and pleasure. I am grateful, also, for Susan Messer's fine contributions to the photo captions, Judy Hauck's keen eye for enhancing the artwork, and Maxine Chuck's prerevision suggestions.

Liz Napolitano, Senior Production Editor, coordinated the complex production tasks that resulted in an exquisitely beautiful seventh edition. Liz's exceptional aesthetic sense, attention to detail, flexibility, efficiency, thoughtfulness, and interest in child development have left their mark on every page, and I look forward to a continuing partnership with her in future editions. I thank Sarah Evertson for obtaining the photographs that so aptly illustrate the text narrative. Connie Day and Bill Heckman provided outstanding copyediting and proofreading.

A final word of gratitude goes to my family, whose love, patience, and understanding have enabled me to be wife, mother, teacher, researcher, and text author at the same time. My sons, David and Peter, grew up with my child development texts, passing from childhood to adolescence and then to adulthood as successive editions were written. David has a special connection with the books' subject matter as an elementary school teacher, and Peter is now an experienced attorney. Both continue to enrich my understanding through reflections on events and progress in their own lives. My husband, Ken, willingly made room for yet another time-consuming endeavor in our life together and communicated his belief in its importance in a great many unspoken, caring ways.

Laura E. Berk

About the Cover and Chapter-Opening Art

I would like to extend grateful acknowledgments to the International Museum of Children's Art, Oslo, Norway, for the cover image and chapter opening art, which depict the talents, concerns, and viewpoints of child and adolescent artists from around the world. I was privileged to visit the museum in 2001, and I was profoundly moved by the endless variety and imaginativeness of the works gracing its walls. They express family, school, and community themes; good times and personal triumphs; profound appreciation for beauty; and great depth of emotion. I am pleased to share this journey into children's creativity, insightfulness, sensitivity, and compassion with readers of *Child Development.*

Supplementary Materials

• **INSTRUCTOR SUPPLEMENTS** • A variety of teaching tools are available to assist instructors in organizing lectures, planning demonstrations and examinations, and ensuring student comprehension.

Instructor's Resource Manual (IRM). This thoroughly revised IRM contains additional material to enrich your class presentations. For each chapter, the IRM provides a Chapter-at-a-Glance grid, Brief Chapter Summary, detailed Lecture Outline, Lecture Enhancements, Learning Activities, Ask Yourself questions with answers, Suggested Student Readings, Transparencies listing, and Media Materials. The Media Materials include descriptions that connect the Observation and Windows videos to chapter content, and detailed descriptions of other media materials relevant to the chapter.

Test Bank. The test bank contains over 2,000 multiple-choice questions, each of which is page-referenced to chapter content and classified by type (factual, applied, or conceptual). Each chapter also includes a selection of essay questions and sample answers.

Computerized Test Bank. This computerized version of the test bank, in easy-to-use software, lets you prepare tests for printing as well as for network and online testing. It has full editing capability. Test items are also available in CourseCompass, Blackboard, and WebCT formats.

Transparencies. Updated for this edition, over two hundred full-color transparencies taken from the text and other sources are referenced in the Instructor's Resource Manual for the most appropriate use in your classroom presentations.

Child Development in Action Observation Video Program. This revised and expanded real-life videotape is over two hours in length and contains hundreds of observation segments that illustrate theories, concepts, and milestones of child development. New additions include attachment, early development of compliance and self-control, understanding of false belief, moral reasoning in middle childhood, adolescent dating, and emerging adulthood. The videotape and Observation Guide are free to instructors who adopt the text and are available to students at a discount when packaged with the text.

A Window on Child Development Running Observational Footage Video. This video complements the Observation Program described above through two hours of unscripted footage on many aspects of child development. A revised Video Guide is also available. The videotape and the viewing guide are free to instructors who adopt the text.

PowerPoint™ CD-ROM. A PowerPoint™ CD-ROM contains outlines of key points and illustrations from each chapter.

Digital Media Archive. This collection of media products—including charts, graphs, tables, figures, audio, and video clips—assists you in meeting your classroom goals.

MyDevelopmentLab. This interactive and instructive multimedia resource can be used as a supplement to a classroom course or to completely administer an online course. Prepared in collaboration with Laura Berk, this product makes use of extensive video footage, multimedia simulations, biographies of major figures in the field, and interactive activities that are unique to this textbook. In addition to the features just mentioned, MyDevelopmentLab includes a variety of controlled assessments that enable continuous evaluation of students' learning. The power of MyDevelopmentLab lies in its design as an all-inclusive teaching and learning tool. For a sampling of its rich content, contact your Allyn and Bacon publisher's representative.

• **STUDENT SUPPLEMENTS** • Beyond the study aids found in the textbook, Allyn and Bacon offers a number of supplements for students:

Grade Aid Workbook with Practice Tests. This helpful guide offers Chapter Summaries, Learning Objectives, Study Questions organized according to major headings in the text, Suggested Student Readings, Crossword Puzzles for mastering important terms, and two multiple-choice Practice Tests per chapter

Emerging Adulthood Booklet. This mini-chapter details the most current theory and research on this new period of development, which intervenes between adolescence and full assumption of adult roles. It is also available as an appendix to the text on MyDevelopment Lab.

Biographies of Key Contributors to the Field of Child Development. This booklet includes historic and contemporary biographies that personalize major advances in theory and research, thereby expanding students' appreciation of both the traditions and current status of the field. It is also available on MyDevelopment Lab.

Milestones Study Cards. Adapted from the popular Milestones Tables featured in the text, these colorfully illustrated study cards outline key developmental attainments in an easy-to-use, chronological organization that assists students in integrating the various domains of development and constructing a vision of the whole child.

Companion Website. The companion website, *http://www.ablongman.com/berk* offers support for students through chapter-specific learning objectives, annotated web resources, flashcard vocabulary building activities, practice tests, and Ask Yourself questions that also appear in the text along with model answers.

Video Workshop. This complete teaching and learning system includes quality video footage on an easy-to-use CD-ROM plus a Student Learning Guide and an Instructor's Teaching Guide—both with text-specific correlation grids. Video Workshop is available free when packaged with the text. Contact your Allyn & Bacon sales representative for additional details and ordering information or visit *http://www.ablongman.com/videoworkshop.*

Allyn & Bacon Tutor Center. The Tutor Center provides students free, one-on-one, interactive tutoring from qualified instructors on all material in the text. Tutors offer help with understanding major developmental principles and suggest effective study techniques. Tutoring assistance is available by phone, FAX, Internet, or e-mail during Tutor Center hours. An access code is required. For more details and ordering information, please contact your Allyn & Bacon publisher's representative or visit *http://www.aw.com/tutorcenter.*

ResearchNavigator™. Through three exclusive databases, this intuitive search interface provides extensive help with the research process, allowing students to make the most of their research time. EBSCO's *ContentSelect* Academic Journal Database permits a discipline-specific search through professional and popular journals. Also featured are the *New York Times* Search-by-Subject Archive, and *Best of the Web* Link Library. (A required access code is contained in *ResearchNavigator* Guide.) Visit *http://www. researchnavigator.com.*

ResearchNavigator Guide: Human Development, with Research Navigator access code, is designed to help students select and evaluate research from the Web. This booklet contains a practical discussion of search engines, detailed information on evaluating online sources, citation guidelines for Web resources, additional Web activities and links for human development, and an access code and guide to *ResearchNavigator* (available only when packaged with the text).

Child Development

"My City"
Priyanka Anandjiwala
Age 13, India

This portrayal of life in a complex urban environment captures a diversity of sensations and impressions related to history, commerce, transportation, resources, and culture. As the multiplicity of theories reviewed in this chapter reveal, a similarly complex blend of genetic, family, school, community, and societal forces influence child development.

Reprinted with permission from the International Museum of Children's Art, Oslo, Norway.

History, Theory, and Applied Directions

Not long ago, I left my Midwestern home to live for a year near the small city in northern California where I spent my childhood. One morning, I visited the neighborhood where I grew up—a place I had not seen since I was 12 years old.

I stood at the entrance to my old schoolyard. Buildings and grounds that had looked large to me as a child now seemed strangely small. I peered through the window of my first-grade classroom. The desks were no longer arranged in rows but grouped in intimate clusters. Computers rested against the far wall, near where I once sat. I walked my old route home from school, the distance shrunken by my longer stride. I stopped in front of my best friend Kathryn's house, where we once drew sidewalk pictures, crossed the street to play kick ball, and produced plays in the garage. In place of the small shop where I had purchased penny candy stood a child-care center, filled with the voices and vigorous activity of toddlers and preschoolers.

As I walked, I reflected on early experiences that contributed to who I am and what I am like today—weekends helping my father in his downtown clothing shop, the year my mother studied to become a high school teacher, moments of companionship and rivalry with my sister and brother, Sunday outings to museums and the seashore, and visits to my grandmother's house, where I became someone extra special.

As I passed the homes of my childhood friends, I thought of what I knew about their present lives. Kathryn, star pupil and president of our sixth-grade class—today a successful corporate lawyer and mother of two. Shy, withdrawn Phil, cruelly teased because of his cleft lip—now owner of a thriving chain of hardware stores and member of the city council. Julio, immigrant from Mexico who joined our class in third grade—today director of an elementary school bilingual education program and single parent of an adopted Central American boy. And finally, my next-door neighbor Rick, who picked fights at recess, struggled with reading, repeated fourth grade, dropped out of high school, and (so I heard) moved from one job to another over the following 10 years.

As you begin this course in child development, perhaps you, too, are wondering about some of the same questions that crossed my mind during that nostalgic neighborhood walk:

• In what ways are children's home, school, and neighborhood experiences the same today as they were in generations past, and in what ways are they different?

• How is the infant's and young child's perception of the world the same as the adult's, and how is it different?

• What determines the features that humans have in common and those that make each of us unique—physically, mentally, and behaviorally?

- How did Julio, transplanted to a new culture at 8 years of age, master its language and customs and succeed in its society, yet remain strongly identified with his ethnic community?

- Why do some of us, like Kathryn and Rick, retain the same styles of responding that characterized us as children, whereas others, like Phil, change in essential ways?

- How does cultural change—employed mothers, child care, divorce, smaller families, and new technologies—affect children's characteristics and skills?

These are central questions addressed by **child development,** a field devoted to understanding constancy and change from conception through adolescence. Child development is part of a larger discipline known as **developmental psychology,** or, in its interdisciplinary sense, **human development,** which includes all changes we experience throughout the lifespan. Great diversity characterizes the interests and concerns of investigators who study child development. But all have a common goal: to describe and identify those factors that influence the consistencies and changes in young people during the first two decades of life.

The Field of Child Development

Look again at the questions just listed, and you will see that they are not just of scientific interest. Each is of *applied,* or practical, importance as well. In fact, scientific curiosity is just one factor that has led child development to become the exciting field of study it is today. Research about development has also been stimulated by social pressures to better the lives of children. For example, the beginning of public education in the early part of the twentieth century led to a demand for knowledge about what and how to teach children of different ages. Pediatricians' interest in improving children's health required an understanding of physical growth and nutrition. The social service profession's desire to treat children's anxieties and behavior problems required information about personality and social development. And parents have continually asked for advice about child-rearing practices and experiences that would promote the well-being of their child.

Our large storehouse of information about child development is *interdisciplinary.* It has grown through the combined efforts of people from many fields. Because of the need for solutions to everyday problems concerning children, researchers from psychology, sociology, anthropology, biology, and neuroscience have joined forces with professionals from education, family studies, medicine, public health, and social service, to name just a few. The field of child development, as it exists today, is a monument to the contributions of these many disciplines. Its body of knowledge is not just scientifically important but relevant and useful.

Domains of Development

To make the vast, interdisciplinary study of human constancy and change more orderly and convenient, development often is divided into three broad domains: *physical, cognitive,* and *emotional and social.* Refer to Figure 1.1 for a description and illustration of each. In this book, we will largely consider the domains of development in the order just mentioned. Yet we must keep in mind that they are not really distinct. Instead, they combine in an integrated, holistic fashion to yield the living, growing child. Furthermore, each domain influences and is influenced by the others. For example, in Chapter 4, you will see that new motor capacities, such as reaching, sitting, crawling, and walking (physical), contribute greatly to infants' understanding of their surroundings (cognitive). When babies think and act more competently, adults stimulate them more with games, language, and expressions of delight at the child's new achieve-

◉ Child development involves such vast changes that researchers divide it into age periods. Members of this large family of the Republic of Congo, West Africa, represent each of those periods: toddlerhood (far left), early childhood (center, unhappy about having his picture taken), middle childhood (standing, center, and standing, far right), adolescence (sitting, right), and emerging adulthood (far left).
(c) Uwe Ommer/
Families/Taschen ed.

Emotional and Social Development
Changes in emotional communication, self-understanding, knowledge about other people, interpersonal skills, friendships, intimate relationships, and moral reasoning and behavior

Physical Development
Changes in body size, proportions, appearance, functioning of body systems, perceptual and motor capacities, and physical health

Cognitive Development
Changes in intellectual abilities, including attention, memory, academic and everyday knowledge, problem solving, imagination, creativity, and language

© DENNIS MACDONALD/PHOTOEDIT

© JOSE LUIS PELAEZ, INC./CORBIS

© CHRIS BARTLETT/GETTY IMAGES/TAXI

▲ **Figure 1.1**

Major domains of development. The three domains are not really distinct. Rather, they overlap and interact.

ments (emotional and social). These enriched experiences, in turn, promote all aspects of development.

You will encounter instances of the interwoven nature of all domains on almost every page of this book. Also, look for the *Ask Yourself* feature at the end of major sections. Within it, I have included *Review* questions, which help you recall and think about information you have just read; *Apply* questions, which encourage you to apply your knowledge to controversial issues and problems faced by parents, teachers, and children; *Connect* questions, which help you form a coherent, unified picture of child development; and *Reflect* questions, which invite you to reflect on your own development and that of people you know well. The questions are designed to deepen your understanding and inspire new insights.

Periods of Development

Besides distinguishing and then integrating the three domains, another dilemma arises in discussing development: how to divide the flow of time into sensible, manageable parts. Researchers usually segment child development into the following five periods. Each brings new capacities and social expectations that serve as important transitions in major theories:

1. *The prenatal period: from conception to birth.* This 9-month period is the most rapid time of change, during which a one-celled organism is transformed into a human baby with remarkable capacities for adjusting to life in the surrounding world.

2. *Infancy and toddlerhood: from birth to 2 years.* This period brings dramatic changes in the body and brain that support the emergence of a wide array of motor, perceptual, and intellectual capacities; the beginnings of language; and first intimate ties to others. Infancy

spans the first year; toddlerhood spans the second, during which children take their first independent steps, marking a shift to greater autonomy.

3. *Early childhood: from 2 to 6 years.* The body becomes longer and leaner, motor skills are refined, and children become more self-controlled and self-sufficient. Make-believe play blossoms and supports all aspects of psychological development. Thought and language expand at an astounding pace, a sense of morality becomes evident, and children establish ties with peers.

4. *Middle childhood: from 6 to 11 years.* Children learn about the wider world and master new responsibilities that increasingly resemble those they will perform as adults. Improved athletic abilities, participation in organized games with rules, more logical thought processes, mastery of basic literacy skills, and advances in self-understanding, morality, and friendship are hallmarks of this period.

5. *Adolescence: from 11 to 18 years.* This period initiates the transition to adulthood. Puberty leads to an adult-size body and sexual maturity. Thought becomes abstract and idealistic, and schooling becomes increasingly directed toward preparation for higher education and the world of work. Young people begin to establish autonomy from the family and define personal values and goals.

For many contemporary youths, especially those in industrialized nations, the transition to adult roles has became increasingly prolonged, resulting in a new period of development called *emerging adulthood,* which spans ages 18 to 25. Although emerging adults have moved beyond adolescence, they have not yet fully assumed adult roles. Instead, they intensify their exploration of options in love, career, and personal values prior to making enduring commitments. Because the period of emerging adulthood surfaced only during the past few decades, researchers have just begun to study it (Arnett, 2000; 2003). Very likely, it is *your* period of development. In later chapters, we will touch on milestones of emerging adulthood, which build on adolescent attainments. To find out more about this period, consult the mini-chapter entitled Emerging Adulthood, available as a supplement to this text.

With this introduction in mind, let's turn to some basic issues that have captivated, puzzled, and sparked debate among child development theorists. Then our discussion will trace the emergence of the field and survey major theories.

◎ Basic Issues

Research on child development is a relatively recent endeavor. It did not begin until the late nineteenth and early twentieth centuries. Nevertheless, ideas about how children grow and change have existed for centuries. As these speculations combined with research, they inspired the construction of *theories* of development. A **theory** is an orderly, integrated set of statements that describes, explains, and predicts behavior. For example, a good theory of infant–caregiver attachment would (1) *describe* the behaviors of babies around 6 to 8 months of age as they seek the affection and comfort of a familiar adult, (2) *explain* how and why infants develop this strong desire to bond with a caregiver, and (3) *predict* the consequences of this emotional bond for future relationships.

Theories are vital tools for two reasons. First, they provide organizing frameworks for our observations of children. In other words, they *guide and give meaning* to what we see. Second, theories that are verified by research often serve as a sound basis for practical action. Once a theory helps us *understand* development, we are in a much better position *to know how to improve* the welfare and treatment of children.

As we will see later, theories are influenced by cultural values and belief systems of their times. But theories differ in one important way from mere opinion and belief: A theory's continued existence depends on *scientific verification.* In other words, all theories must be tested using a fair set of research procedures agreed on by the scientific community. (We will consider research strategies in Chapter 2.)

The field of child development contains many theories with very different ideas about what children are like and how they change. The study of child development provides no ulti-

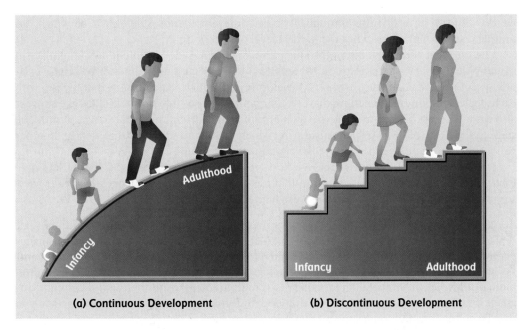

(a) Continuous Development   (b) Discontinuous Development

◄ Figure 1.2

Is development continuous or discontinuous? (a) Some theorists believe that development is a smooth, continuous process. Children gradually add more of the same types of skills. (b) Other theorists think that development takes place in discontinuous stages. Children change rapidly as they step up to a new level of development and then change very little for a while. With each step, the child interprets and responds to the world in a qualitatively different way.

mate truth because investigators do not always agree on the meaning of what they see. In addition, children are complex beings; they change physically, cognitively, emotionally, and socially. As yet, no single theory has been able to incorporate and explain all these aspects. However, the existence of many theories helps advance knowledge as researchers continually try to support, contradict, and integrate these different points of view.

Although there are many theories, almost all take a stand on three basic issues: (1) Is the course of development continuous or discontinuous? (2) Does one course of development characterize all children, or are there many possible courses? (3) Are genetic or environmental factors more important in influencing development? Let's look closely at each of these issues.

Continuous or Discontinuous Development?

Recently, the mother of 20-month-old Angelo reported to me with amazement that her young son had pushed a toy car across the living room floor while making a motorlike sound, "Brmmmm, brmmmm," for the first time. When he hit a nearby wall with a bang, Angelo let go of the car, exclaimed, "C'ash," and laughed heartily.

"How come Angelo can pretend, but he couldn't a few months ago?" queried his mother. "And I wonder what 'Brrmmmm, brmmmm' and 'Crash!' mean to Angelo? Is his understanding of motorlike sounds and collision similar to mine?"

Angelo's mother has raised a puzzling issue about development: How can we best describe the differences in capacities and behavior between small infants, young children, adolescents, and adults? As Figure 1.2 illustrates, major theories recognize two possibilities.

One view holds that infants and preschoolers respond to the world in much the same way as adults do. The difference between the immature and mature being is simply one of *amount* or *complexity*. For example, little Angelo's thinking might be just as logical and well organized as our own. Perhaps (as his mother reports) he can sort objects into simple categories, recognize whether he has more of one kind than another, and remember where he left his favorite toy at child care the week before. Angelo's only limitation may be that he cannot perform these skills with as much information and precision as we can. If this is so, then Angelo's development is **continuous**—a process that consists of gradually adding more of the same types of skills that were there to begin with.

According to a second view, Angelo's thoughts, emotions, and behavior differ considerably from those of adults. If so, then his development is **discontinuous**—a process in which new ways of understanding and responding to the world emerge at specific times. From this perspective, Angelo is not yet able to organize objects or remember and interpret experiences as we do. Instead, he will move through a series of developmental steps, each of which has unique features, until he reaches the highest level of functioning.

Theories that accept the discontinuous perspective regard development as taking place in **stages**—qualitative changes in thinking, feeling, and behaving that characterize specific periods of development. In stage theories, development is much like climbing a staircase, with each step corresponding to a more mature, reorganized way of functioning. The stage concept also assumes that children undergo periods of rapid transformation as they step up from one stage to the next, followed by plateaus during which they stand solidly within a stage. In other words, change is fairly sudden rather than gradual and ongoing.

Does development actually occur in a neat, orderly sequence of stages? For now, let's note that this is a very ambitious assumption that has faced significant challenges. We will review some influential stage theories later in this chapter.

One Course of Development or Many?

Stage theorists assume that children everywhere follow the same sequence of development. For example, in the domain of cognition, a stage theorist might try to identify the common biological and environmental factors that lead children to represent their world through language and make-believe play in early childhood, to think more logically and systematically in middle childhood, and to reason abstractly in adolescence.

At the same time, the field of child development is becoming increasingly aware that children grow up in distinct **contexts,** or unique combinations of genetic and environmental circumstances that can result in different paths of change. For example, a shy child who fears social encounters develops in very different contexts from those of a sociable agemate who readily seeks out other people (Kagan, 2003). Children in non-Western village societies encounter experiences in their families and communities that differ sharply from those of children in large Western cities. These different circumstances result in markedly different cognitive capacities, social skills, and feelings about the self and others (Rogoff, 2003; Shweder et al., 1998).

As you will see, contemporary theorists regard the contexts that shape development as many-layered and complex. On the personal side, these include heredity and biological makeup. On the environmental side, they include immediate settings, such as home, child-care center, school, and neighborhood, as well as circumstances more remote from children's everyday lives—community resources, societal values and priorities, and historical time period. Finally, a special interest in culture has led child development researchers to be more conscious than ever before of diversity in development.

Relative Influence of Nature and Nurture?

In addition to describing the course of development, each theory takes a stand on a major question about its underlying causes: Are genetic or environmental factors more important? This is the age-old **nature–nurture controversy.** By *nature,* we mean inborn biological givens—the hereditary information we receive from our parents at the moment of conception. By *nurture,* we mean the complex forces of the physical and social world that influence our biological makeup and psychological experiences before and after birth.

Although all theories grant at least some role to both nature and nurture, they vary in emphasis. For example, consider the following questions: Is the older child's ability to think in more complex ways largely the result of an inborn timetable of growth? Or is it primarily influenced by stimulation from parents and teachers? Do children acquire language because they are genetically predisposed to do so or

Ⓢ Will this 15-month-old's tantrums extend into a lifelong pattern of difficult behavior? Theorists emphasizing stability—that she will remain hard to manage—typically stress the importance of heredity. Others regard stability as due to early experiences—the way the mother handles her child's emotional outbursts. Still others believe that change is possible if new experiences support it.

© Laura Dwight Photography

because parents intensively teach them from an early age? And what accounts for the vast individual differences among children—in height, weight, physical coordination, intelligence, personality, and social skills? Is nature or nurture more responsible?

A theory's position on the roles of nature and nurture affects how it explains individual differences. Some theorists emphasize *stability*—that children who are high or low in a characteristic (such as verbal ability, anxiety, or sociability) will remain so at later ages. These theorists typically stress the importance of *heredity*. If they regard environment as important, they usually point to *early experiences* as establishing a lifelong pattern of behavior. Powerful negative events in the first few years, they argue, cannot be fully overcome by later, more positive ones (Bowlby, 1980; Johnson, 2000; Sroufe, Egeland, & Kreutzer, 1990). Other theorists are more optimistic. They believe that *change* is possible and likely if new experiences support it (Greenspan & Shanker, 2004; Masten & Reed, 2002; Nelson, 2002).

Throughout this book, you will see that investigators disagree, often sharply, on the question of *stability or change.* The answers they provide are of great practical significance. If you believe that development is largely due to nature, then providing experiences aimed at promoting change would seem to be of little value. If, on the other hand, you are convinced of the supreme importance of early experience, then you would intervene as soon as possible, offering high-quality stimulation and support to ensure that children develop at their best. Finally, if you think that environment is profoundly influential throughout development, you would provide assistance any time children or adolescents face difficulties, believing that, with the help of favorable life circumstances, they can recover from early negative events.

A Balanced Point of View

So far, we have discussed the basic issues of child development in terms of extremes—solutions on one side or the other. As we trace the unfolding of the field in the rest of this chapter, you will see that the positions of many theorists have softened. Contemporary ones, especially, recognize the merits of both sides. Some theorists believe that both continuous and discontinuous changes occur. And some acknowledge that development can have both universal features and features unique to the individual and his or her contexts. Furthermore, an increasing number of investigators regard heredity and environment as inseparably interwoven, each affecting the potential of the other to modify the child's traits and capacities (Huttenlocher, 2002; Reiss, 2003; Rutter, 2002). We will discuss these new ideas about nature and nurture in Chapter 3.

Finally, as you will see later in this book, the relative impact of early and later experiences varies greatly from one domain of development to another and even (as the Biology and Environment box on pages 10–11 indicates) across individuals! Because of the complex network of factors contributing to human change and the challenge of isolating the effects of each, many theoretical viewpoints have gathered research support. Although debate continues, this circumstance has also sparked more balanced visions of child development.

Ask Yourself

REVIEW	Why are there many theories of child development? Cite three basic issues on which almost all theories take a stand.
APPLY	A school counselor advises a parent, "Don't worry about your teenager's argumentative behavior. It shows that she understands the world differently than she did as a young child." What stance is the counselor taking on the issue of continuous or discontinuous development? Explain.
CONNECT	Provide an example of how one domain of development (physical, cognitive, or emotional/social) can affect development in another domain.
REFLECT	Cite an aspect of your development that differs from a parent's or grandparent's when he or she was your age. How might contexts explain this difference?

BIOLOGY AND ENVIRONMENT

Resilient Children

John and his best friend Gary grew up in a run-down, crime-ridden inner-city neighborhood. By age 10, each had experienced years of family conflict followed by parental divorce. Reared for the rest of childhood and adolescence in mother-headed households, John and Gary rarely saw their fathers. Both dropped out of high school and were in and out of trouble with the police.

Then John and Gary's paths diverged. By age 30, John had fathered two children with women he never married, had spent time in prison, was unemployed, and drank alcohol heavily. In contrast, Gary had returned to finish high school, studied auto mechanics at a community college, and became manager of a gas station and repair shop. Married with two children, he had saved his earnings and bought a home. He was happy, healthy, and well adapted to life.

A wealth of evidence shows that environmental risks—poverty, negative family interactions, parental divorce, job loss, mental illness, and drug abuse—predispose children to future problems (Masten &

Coatsworth, 1998). Why did Gary "beat the odds" and come through unscathed?

New evidence on **resilience**—the ability to adapt effectively in the face of threats to development—is receiving increasing attention because investigators want to find ways to protect young people from the damaging effects of stressful life conditions (Masten & Powell, 2003). This interest has been inspired by several long-term studies on the relationship of life stressors in childhood to competence and adjustment in adolescence and adulthood (Fergusson & Horwood, 2003; Garmezy, 1993; Masten et al., 1995; Werner & Smith, 1992). In each study, some individuals were shielded from negative outcomes, whereas others had lasting problems. Four broad factors seemed to offer protection from the damaging effects of stressful life events.

Personal Characteristics of Children

A child's biologically endowed characteristics can reduce exposure to risk or lead to experiences that compensate for early stressful events. High intelligence and socially valued talents (in music or athletics, for example)

are protective factors. They increase the chances that a child will have rewarding experiences in school and in the community that offset the impact of a stressful home life. Temperament is particularly powerful. Children with easy-going, sociable dispositions have an optimistic outlook on life and a special capacity to adapt to change—qualities that elicit positive responses from others. In contrast, emotionally reactive, irritable, and impulsive children often tax the patience of people around them (Masten & Reed, 2002; Masten et al., 1999). For example, both John and Gary moved several times during their childhoods. Each time, John became anxious and angry. Gary looked forward to making new friends and exploring a new neighborhood.

A Warm Parental Relationship

A close relationship with at least one parent who provides warmth, appropriately high expectations, monitoring of the child's activities, and an organized home environment fosters resilience. But note that this factor (as well as the next one) is not inde-

Historical Foundations

Contemporary theories of child development are the result of centuries of change in Western cultural values, philosophical thinking about children, and scientific progress. To understand the field as it exists today, we must return to its beginnings—to influences that long preceded scientific child study. We will see that early ideas about children linger as important forces in current theory and research.

Medieval Times

Historical artifacts and writings show that childhood was regarded as a separate period of life as early as medieval Europe—the sixth through the fifteenth centuries. Medieval painters often depicted children as childlike—dressed in loose, comfortable gowns while playing games and looking up to adults. Written texts contained terms that distinguished children under age 7 or 8 from other people and that recognized even young teenagers as not fully mature (Lett, 1997). Archeological digs have unearthed small bowls and eating utensils, toys, dolls, and other objects, which reveal that adults were sensitive to children's physical limitations and psychological needs.

pendent of children's personal characteristics. Children who are relaxed, socially responsive, and able to deal with change are easier to rear and more likely to enjoy positive relationships with parents and other people. At the same time, some children may develop more attractive dispositions as a result of parental warmth and attention (Conger & Conger, 2002).

Social Support Outside the Immediate Family

The most consistent asset of resilient children is a strong bond to a competent, caring adult, who need not be a parent. A grandparent, aunt, uncle, or teacher who forms a special relationship with the child can promote resilience (Masten & Reed, 2002). Gary received support in adolescence from his grandfather, who listened to Gary's concerns and helped him solve problems. In addition, Gary's grandfather had a stable marriage and work life and handled stressors skillfully. Consequently, he served as a model of effective coping.

Associations with rule-abiding peers who value school achievement are also linked to resilience. But children who have positive relationships with adults are far more likely to establish these supportive peer ties.

Community Resources and Opportunities

Community supports—good schools, convenient and affordable health care and social services, libraries, and recreation centers—foster both parents' and children's well-being. In addition, opportunities to participate in community life help older children and adolescents overcome adversity. Extracurricular activities at school, religious youth groups, scouting, and other organizations teach important social skills, such as cooperation, leadership, and contributing to others' welfare. As a result, participants gain in self-esteem, responsibility, and community commitment. As a high school student, Gary volunteered for Habitat for Humanity, a nonprofit organization that builds affordable housing in low-income neighborhoods. Community involvement offered Gary additional opportunities to form meaningful relationships and develop new competencies, which further strengthened his resilience (Seccombe, 2002).

Research on resilience highlights the complex connections between heredity and environment. Armed with positive characteristics, which stem from innate endowment, favorable rearing experiences, or both, children and adolescents take action to reduce stressful situations.

Nevertheless, when many risks pile up, they are increasingly difficult to overcome (Quyen et al., 1998). Therefore, interventions must reduce risks and enhance relationships at home, in school, and in the community that inoculate children against the negative effects of risk. This means attending to both the person and the environment—strengthening children's capacities as well as reducing hazardous experiences.

▲ This girl's special relationship with her grandfather provides the social support she needs to cope with stress and solve problems constructively. A warm tie with a person outside the immediate family can promote resilience. © Alan Hicks/ Getty Images/ Stone

By the fourteenth century, manuals offering advice on many aspects of child care, including health, feeding, clothing, games, and participation in family life, had become common (Alexandre-Bidon & Lett, 1997). Laws recognized that children needed protection from people who might mistreat them. And courts exercised leniency with lawbreaking youths because of their tender years (Hanawalt, 1993).

In sum, in medieval times, if not before, clear awareness existed of children as vulnerable beings and of childhood as a distinct developmental period. Religious writings, however, contained contradictory beliefs about children's basic nature. Sometimes infants were portrayed as possessed by the devil and in need of purification through exorcism and baptism. At other times, they were characterized as innocent and close to angels (Hanawalt, 2003). Both ideas foreshadowed views of childhood in succeeding centuries.

The Reformation

In the sixteenth century, a revised image of childhood sprang from the Puritan belief in original sin. According to Puritan doctrine, children were born evil and stubborn and had to be civilized (Shahar, 1990). Harsh, restrictive child-rearing practices were recommended to tame the depraved child. Children were dressed in stiff, uncomfortable clothing that held them in adultlike postures, and disobedient students were routinely beaten by their schoolmasters.

⊚ As far back as medieval times, adults regarded childhood as a distinct developmental period and were sensitive to children's needs. In this fourteenth-century image painted in a book of songs, children play a lively game of Blind Man's Bluff in a garden, dressed in loose, comfortable gowns.

© The Art Archive/Bibliothèque Universitaire de Mèdecine, Montpellier/Dagli Orti

Although punitiveness was the prevailing child-rearing philosophy, love and affection for their children prevented many Puritan parents from exercising extremely repressive measures (Moran & Vinovskis, 1986).

As the Puritans emigrated from England to America, they brought the belief that child rearing was one of their most important obligations. Although they continued to regard the child's soul as tainted by original sin, they tried to encourage their sons and daughters to use reason so they could separate right from wrong (Clarke-Stewart, 1998). The Puritans were the first to devise special reading materials for children that instructed them in religious and moral ideals. As they trained their children in self-reliance and self-control, Puritan parents gradually adopted a moderate balance between severity and permissiveness (Pollock, 1987).

Philosophies of the Enlightenment

The seventeenth-century Enlightenment brought new philosophies of reason and emphasized ideals of human dignity and respect. Conceptions of childhood were more humane than those of centuries past.

• **JOHN LOCKE** • The writings of John Locke (1632–1704), a leading British philosopher, served as the forerunner of a twentieth-century perspective that we will discuss shortly: behaviorism. Lock viewed the child as a **tabula rasa.** Translated from Latin, this means a "blank slate." According to this idea, children are, to begin with, nothing at all, and all kinds of experiences can shape their characters. Locke (1690/1892) described parents as rational tutors who can mold the child in any way they wish, through careful instruction, effective example, and rewards for good behavior. He was ahead of his time in recommending child-rearing practices that present-day research supports. For example, Locke suggested that parents reward children not with money or sweets but with praise and approval. He also opposed physical punishment: "The child repeatedly beaten in school cannot look upon books and teachers without experiencing fear and anger." Locke's philosophy led to a change from harshness toward children to kindness and compassion.

Look carefully at Locke's ideas, and you will see that he regarded development as *continuous*; adultlike behaviors are gradually built up through the warm, consistent teachings of parents. Furthermore, his view of the child as a tabula rasa meant that he championed *nurture*—the power of the environment to shape the child. And his faith in nurture suggests the possibility of *many courses of development* and of *change at later ages* due to new experiences.

Finally, Locke's philosophy characterizes children as doing little to influence their own destiny, which is written on "blank slates" by others. This vision of a passive child has been discarded. All contemporary theories view children as active, purposeful beings who make sense of their world and contribute substantially to their own development.

• **JEAN-JACQUES ROUSSEAU** • In the eighteenth century, French philosopher Jean-Jacques Rousseau (1712–1778) introduced a new view of childhood. Children, Rousseau (1762/1955) claimed, are not blank slates and empty containers to be filled by adult instruction. Instead, they are **noble savages,** naturally endowed with a sense of right and wrong and with an innate plan for orderly, healthy growth. Unlike Locke, Rousseau thought children's built-in moral sense and unique ways of thinking and feeling would only be harmed by adult training. His was a child-centered philosophy in which adults should be receptive to the child's needs at each of four stages: infancy, childhood, late childhood, and adolescence.

Rousseau's philosophy includes two influential concepts. The first is the concept of *stage,* which we discussed earlier. The second is the concept of **maturation,** which refers to a genetically determined, naturally unfolding course of growth. In contrast to Locke, Rousseau saw children as determining their own destinies. And he took a different stand on basic developmental issues. He saw development as a *discontinuous, stagewise* process that follows a *single, unified course* mapped out by *nature*.

Darwin: Forefather of Scientific Child Study

A century after Rousseau, British naturalist Charles Darwin (1809–1882) joined an expedition to distant parts of the world, where he observed infinite variation among plant and animal species. He also saw that within a species, no two individuals are exactly alike. From these observations, he constructed his famous *theory of evolution*.

The theory emphasized two related principles: *natural selection* and *survival of the fittest*. Darwin explained that certain species survive in particular parts of the world because they have characteristics that fit with, or are adapted to, their surroundings. Other species die off because they are not as well suited to their environments. Individuals within a species who best meet the survival requirements of the environment live long enough to reproduce and pass their more beneficial characteristics to future generations. Darwin's emphasis on the adaptive value of physical characteristics and behavior eventually found its way into important twentieth-century theories (Cairns, 1998).

During his explorations, Darwin discovered that the early prenatal growth of many species is strikingly similar. Other scientists concluded from Darwin's observation that the development of the human child follows the same general plan as the evolution of the human species. Although this belief eventually proved inaccurate, efforts to chart parallels between child growth and human evolution prompted researchers to make careful observations of all aspects of children's behavior. Out of these first attempts to document an idea about development, scientific child study was born.

Scientific Beginnings

Research on child development evolved quickly during the late nineteenth and early twentieth centuries. Early observations of children were soon followed by improved methods and theories. Each advance contributed to the firm foundation on which the field rests today.

• **THE BABY BIOGRAPHIES** • Imagine yourself as a forerunner in the field of child development, confronted with studying children for the first time. How might you go about this challenging task? Scientists of the late nineteenth and early twentieth centuries did what most of us would probably do—they selected a child of their own or of a close relative. Then, beginning in early infancy, they jotted down day-by-day descriptions and impressions of the child's behavior. By the 1890s, these baby biographies were being published regularly. In the following excerpt from one, the author reflects on the birth of her young niece:

> Its first act is a cry, not of wrath, . . . nor a shout of joy, . . . but a snuffling, and then a long, thin tearless á—á, with the timbre of a Scotch bagpipe, purely automatic, but of discomfort. With this monotonous and dismal cry, with its red, shriveled, parboiled skin . . ., it is not strange that, if the mother . . . has not come to love her child before birth, there is a brief interval occasionally dangerous to the child before the maternal instinct is fully aroused.

> It cannot be denied that this unflattering description is fair enough, and our baby was no handsomer than the rest of her kind. . . . Yet she did not lack admirers. I have never noticed that women (even those who are not mothers) mind a few little aesthetic defects, . . . with so many counterbalancing charms in the little warm, soft, living thing. (Shinn, 1900, pp. 20–21)

Can you tell from this passage why the baby biographies have sometimes been upheld as examples of how *not* to study children? These first investigators tended to be emotionally invested in the infants they observed, and they seldom began with a clear idea of what they wanted to find out. Not surprisingly, many of their records were eventually discarded as biased.

Nevertheless, the baby biographies were a step in the right direction. Two nineteenth-century theorists, Darwin (1877) and German biologist William Preyer (1882/1888), contributed to these early records of children's behavior. Preyer, especially, set high standards for making observations, recording what he saw immediately and checking the accuracy of his notes against those of a second observer (Cairns, 1998). These are the same standards that today's researchers use when observing children. As a result of the biographers' pioneering efforts, the child became a common focus of scientific research.

• **THE NORMATIVE PERIOD** • G. Stanley Hall (1844–1924), one of the most influential American psychologists of the early twentieth century, is generally regarded as the founder of the child study movement (Hogan, 2003). Inspired by Darwin's work, Hall and his well-known student, Arnold Gesell (1880–1961), developed theories based on evolutionary ideas. These early leaders regarded child development as a *maturational process*—a genetically determined series of events that unfolds automatically, much like a blooming flower (Gesell, 1933; Hall, 1904).

Hall and Gesell are remembered less for their one-sided theories than for their intensive efforts to describe all aspects of child development. This launched the **normative approach,** in which measures of behavior are taken on large numbers of individuals, and age-related averages are computed to represent typical development. Using this procedure, Hall constructed elaborate questionnaires asking children of different ages almost everything they could tell about themselves—interests, fears, imaginary playmates, dreams, friendships, everyday knowledge, and more (White, 1992). And through careful observations and interviews with parents, Gesell obtained detailed normative information on infants' and young children's motor achievements, social behaviors, and personality characteristics.

Gesell was also among the first to make knowledge about child development meaningful to parents by informing them of what to expect at each age. If, as he believed, the timetable of development is the product of millions of years of evolution, then children are naturally knowledgeable about their needs. His child-rearing advice, in the tradition of Rousseau, recommended sensitivity to children's cues (Thelen & Adolph, 1992). Along with Benjamin Spock's famous *Baby and Child Care,* Gesell's books became a central part of a rapidly expanding child development literature for parents (see the From Research to Practice box on page 15).

• **THE MENTAL TESTING MOVEMENT** • While Hall and Gesell were developing their theories and methods in the United States, French psychologist Alfred Binet (1857–1911) was also taking a normative approach to child development, but for a different reason. In the early 1900s, Binet and his colleague Theodore Simon were asked by Paris school officials to find a way to identify children with learning problems who needed to be placed in special classes. The first successful intelligence test, which they constructed for this purpose, grew out of practical educational concerns.

Binet's effort was unique in that he began with a well-developed theory. In contrast to earlier views, which reduced intelligence to simple elements of reaction time and sensitivity to physical stimuli, Binet captured the complexity of children's thinking. He defined intelligence as good judgment, planning, and critical reflection (Sternberg & Jarvin, 2003). Then he selected test items appropriate for each age that directly measured these abilities.

In 1916, Binet's test was adapted for use with English-speaking children at Stanford University. Since then, the English version has been known as the *Stanford-Binet Intelligence Scale.* Besides providing a score that could successfully predict school achievement, the Binet test sparked tremendous interest in individual differences in development. Comparisons of the intelligence test scores of children who vary in gender, ethnicity, birth order, family background, and other characteristics became a major focus of research. Intelligence tests also rose quickly to the forefront of the nature–nurture controversy.

• **JAMES MARK BALDWIN: EARLY DEVELOPMENTAL THEORIST** • A final important figure, overlooked in the history of child development for decades, is American psychologist James Mark Baldwin (1861–1934), who carried out his innovative work in both Canada and the United States. Both a theorist and a keen observer of children's behavior, Baldwin's (1897) rich interpretations of development are experiencing a revival today. He believed that children's understanding of their physical and social worlds develops through a sequence of stages, beginning with the simplest behavior patterns of the newborn infant and concluding with the adult's capacity to think abstractly and reflectively (Cairns, 1992, 1998).

Yet Baldwin regarded neither the child nor the environment as in control of development. Instead, he granted nature and nurture equal importance. Children, he argued, actively revise

Social Change and the Popular Literature on Parenting

Almost all parents—especially new ones—feel a need for sound advice on how to rear their children. To meet this need, experts have long been communicating with the general public through a wide variety of popular books and magazines. Prior to the 1970s, publications emphasized the central role of mothers in healthy child development. In the 1980s, fathers were encouraged to share in the full range of child-rearing responsibilities as research revealed that they influence all aspects of psychological development. Around that time, information about nonparental child care appeared. Experts reassured employed mothers that their babies did not require their continuous presence and offered advice on how to select good child care (Young, 1990).

From the mid-1990s to the present, an increasing number of books responded to concerns over the consequences of social change for parents' and children's well-being. More working parents complained of overly demanding lives and reported spending less time with their children in joint mealtimes, conversations, and leisure activities (Hofferth & Sandberg, 1999). At the same time, many parents reported worrisome changes in their children, including reduced engagement in school and increases in emotional and behavior problems (Vandivere, Gallagher, & Moore, 2004). And in one nationally representative survey of American parents, more than half judged the job that they were doing in rearing their children as "fair" or "poor." Many of these respondents believed that parents of previous generations had done better (Public Agenda, 2002). Few felt that they knew what to do to rear their children effectively.

In *Awakening Children's Minds*, Laura Berk (2001a) points out that parents' efforts to rear competent, well-adjusted children are complicated by both unfavorable cultural influences (such as scarcity of high-quality child care and harmful media messages) and a contradictory parenting-advice literature. Whereas some parenting manuals argue that parents are all-powerful, others grant supremacy to children's biological makeup. In the face of these incompatible messages, many parents come to doubt their own importance and retreat from involvement with their children. Berk argues that in view of the many factors in American society that threaten children's development, parenting today not only matters, but matters more than ever.

In a similar vein, James Garbarino and Claire Bedard (2001), in *Parents under Siege*, address youth antagonism and violence, including the recent spate of heinous crimes resulting in family and school maimings and murders. Because multiple factors—including an impulsive, explosive temperament; unfavorable school experiences; and antisocial peer influences—contribute to these tragedies, parents are not to blame for them. But, Garbarino and Bedard emphasize, parents nevertheless bear considerable responsibility. They often are unaware of everyday experiences that lead their youngster down the path to violence.

In terms of solutions, most experts writing for parents affirm the need for greater adult involvement in children's lives. Berk (2001a) shows how essential cognitive, moral, and social capacities emerge from parent–child communication in such seemingly mundane pursuits as a bedtime story, a homework assignment, or a family dinner. Garbarino and Bedard (2001) make a case for "empowered parenting," in which parents consider their youngster's strengths and limitations while closely monitoring and, when necessary, intervening in the social environment. They also admonish parents to provide a "moral compass of character" by insisting that children meet standards for personal achievement and caring for others. And in *The Ten Basic Principles of Good Parenting*, Laurence Steinberg (2004) aims to restore in parents a philosophy of good child rearing by outlining ten research-based parenting strategies that help children become kind, secure, and competent. These include: be loving,

▲ Experts writing for contemporary parents often emphasize the importance of increased adult involvement in children's lives. Much research shows that parents, while not all-powerful, profoundly influence their children's development.
(c) Nancy Sheehan/ Index Stock

establish rules and set limits, treat your child with respect, and foster independence by helping your child think through decisions.

Yet increasingly, popular advice has underscored that parents cannot do the job alone; they need the help of a caring community and society. As you study child development, read one or more popular books on parenting and evaluate their advice on the basis of what you have learned. How is the growing agreement of experts with the African proverb, "It takes a village to raise a child," consistent with the focus of current theories on *contexts* for development, described later in this chapter?

their ways of thinking about the world, but they also learn through habit, or by copying others' behaviors. As development proceeds, the child and her social surroundings influence each other, forming an inseparable, interwoven network.

Consider these ideas, and you will see why Baldwin (1895) argued that heredity and environment should not be viewed as distinct, opposing forces. Instead, he claimed, most human characteristics are "due to both causes working together" (p. 77). As we turn now to an overview of modern theories of child development, you will find Baldwin's ideas represented in several, especially the more recent ones.

Ask Yourself

REVIEW	Imagine a debate between John Locke and Jean-Jacques Rousseau on the nature–nurture controversy. Summarize the argument each historical figure is likely to present.
CONNECT	What do the ideas of Rousseau, Darwin, and Hall have in common?
REFLECT	Find out if your parents read Gesell, Spock, or other parenting advice books when you were growing up. What questions about child rearing most concerned them? Do you think today's parents have concerns that differ from those of your parents? Explain.

 ## Mid-Twentieth-Century Theories

In the mid-twentieth century, the field of child development expanded into a legitimate discipline. Specialized research centers and professional societies devoted to the scientific study of children were founded. A leader among these is the Society for Research in Child Development, established in 1933 to promote interdisciplinary research, dissemination of information, and applications of research findings. The society's inaugural membership of 425 grew rapidly. Today, approximately 5,500 researchers, applied professionals, and students from more than 50 countries are members.

As child development attracted increasing interest, a variety of mid-twentieth-century theories emerged, each of which continues to have followers today. In these theories, the European concern with the child's inner thoughts and feelings contrasts sharply with the focus of American academic psychology on scientific precision and concrete, observable behavior.

The Psychoanalytic Perspective

By the 1930s and 1940s, parents increasingly sought help from professionals to deal with children suffering from emotional stress and behavior problems. The earlier normative movement had answered the question, What are children like? But now another problem had to be addressed: How and why do children become the way they are? To treat psychological problems, psychiatrists and social workers turned to an emerging approach to personality development that emphasized the unique history of each child.

According to the **psychoanalytic perspective,** children move through a series of stages in which they confront conflicts between biological drives and social expectations. The way these conflicts are resolved determines the person's ability to learn, to get along with others, and to cope with anxiety. Although many individuals contributed to the psychoanalytic perspective, two have been especially influential: Sigmund Freud, founder of the psychoanalytic movement, and Erik Erikson.

• **FREUD'S THEORY** • Freud (1856–1939), a Viennese physician, saw patients in his practice with a variety of nervous symptoms, such as hallucinations, fears, and paralyses, that appeared to have no physical basis. Seeking a cure for these troubled adults, Freud found that their symptoms could be relieved by having patients talk freely about painful events of their childhoods. Working with these remembrances, Freud examined the unconscious motivations of his patients and constructed his **psychosexual theory.** It emphasized that how parents

TABLE 1.1 FREUD'S PSYCHOSEXUAL STAGES

Psychosexual Stage	Approximate Age	Description
Oral	Birth–1 year	The new ego directs the baby's sucking activities toward breast or bottle. If oral needs are not met appropriately, the individual may develop such habits as thumb sucking, fingernail biting, and pencil chewing in childhood and overeating and smoking later in life.
Anal	1–3 years	Young toddlers and preschoolers enjoy holding and releasing urine and feces. Toilet training becomes a major issue between parent and child. If parents insist that children be trained before they are ready or make too few demands, conflicts about anal control may appear in the form of extreme orderliness and cleanliness or messiness and disorder.
Phallic	3–6 years	Id impulses transfer to the genitals, and the child finds pleasure in genital stimulation. Freud's Oedipus conflict for boys and Electra conflict for girls arise, and young children feel a sexual desire for the other-sex parent. To avoid punishment, they give up this desire and, instead, adopt the same-sex parent's characteristics and values. As a result, the superego is formed. The relations between id, ego, and superego established at this time determine the individual's basic personality.
Latency	6–11 years	Sexual instincts die down, and the superego develops further. The child acquires new social values from adults outside the family and from play with same-sex peers.
Genital	Adolescence	Puberty causes the sexual impulses of the phallic stage to reappear. If development has been successful during earlier stages, it leads to mature sexuality, marriage, and the birth and rearing of children.

manage their child's sexual and aggressive drives in the first few years is crucial for healthy personality development.

▶ *Three Parts of the Personality.* In Freud's theory, three parts of the personality—id, ego, and superego—become integrated during five stages, summarized in Table 1.1. The *id,* the largest portion of the mind, is the source of basic biological needs and desires. The *ego,* the conscious, rational part of personality, emerges in early infancy to redirect the id's impulses so they are discharged in acceptable ways. For example, aided by the ego, the hungry baby of a few months of age stops crying when he sees his mother warm a bottle or unfasten her clothing for breastfeeding. And the more competent preschooler goes into the kitchen and gets a snack on her own.

Between 3 and 6 years of age, the *superego,* or conscience, develops from interactions with parents, who insist that children conform to the values of society. Now the ego faces the increasingly complex task of reconciling the demands of the id, the external world, and conscience (Freud, 1923/1974). For example, when the ego is tempted to gratify an id impulse by hitting a playmate to get an attractive toy, the superego may warn that such behavior is wrong. The ego must decide which of the two forces (id or superego) will win this inner struggle or work out a compromise, such as asking for a turn with the toy. According to Freud, the relations established between the id, ego, and superego during the preschool years determine the individual's basic personality.

▶ *Psychosexual Development.* Freud (1938/1973) believed that during childhood, sexual impulses shift their focus from the oral to the anal to the genital regions of the body. In each stage, parents walk a fine line between permitting too much or too little gratification of their child's basic needs. If parents strike an appropriate balance, then children grow into well-adjusted adults with the capacity for mature sexual behavior, investment in family life, and rearing of the next generation.

Freud's psychosexual theory highlighted the importance of family relationships and early experiences for children's development. But Freud's perspective was eventually criticized. First, the theory overemphasized the influence of sexual feelings in development. Second, because it was based on the problems of sexually repressed, well-to-do adults, it did not apply in cultures differing from nineteenth-century Victorian society. Finally, Freud had not studied children directly.

TABLE 1.2   ERIKSON'S PSYCHOSOCIAL STAGES, WITH CORRESPONDING PSYCHOSEXUAL STAGES INDICATED

(c) Olive Pierce/ Black Star

Erik Erikson

Psychosocial Stage	Period of Development	Description
Basic trust versus mistrust (Oral)	Birth–1 year	From warm, responsive care, infants gain a sense of trust, or confidence, that the world is good. Mistrust occurs when infants have to wait too long for comfort and are handled harshly.
Autonomy versus shame and doubt (Anal)	1–3 years	Using new mental and motor skills, children want to choose and decide for themselves. Autonomy is fostered when parents permit reasonable free choice and do not force or shame the child.
Initiative versus guilt (Phallic)	3–6 years	Through make-believe play, children experiment with the kind of person they can become. Initiative—a sense of ambition and responsibility—develops when parents support their child's new sense of purpose. The danger is that parents will demand too much self-control, which leads to overcontrol, meaning too much guilt.
Industry versus inferiority (Latency)	6–11 years	At school, children develop the capacity to work and cooperate with others. Inferiority develops when negative experiences at home, at school, or with peers lead to feelings of incompetence.
Identity versus identity confusion (Genital)	Adolescence	The adolescent tries to answer the question, Who am I, and what is my place in society? Self-chosen values and vocational goals lead to a lasting personal identity. The negative outcome is confusion about future adult roles.
Intimacy versus isolation	Emerging adulthood	Young people work on establishing intimate ties to others. Because of earlier disappointments, some individuals cannot form close relationships and remain isolated.
Generativity versus stagnation	Adulthood	Generativity means giving to the next generation through child rearing, caring for other people, or productive work. The person who fails in these ways feels an absence of meaningful accomplishment.
Integrity versus despair	Old age	In this final stage, individuals reflect on the kind of person they have been. Integrity results from feeling that life was worth living as it happened. Old people who are dissatisfied with their lives fear death.

• **ERIKSON'S THEORY** • Several of Freud's followers took what was useful from his theory and improved on his vision. The most important of these neo-Freudians for the field of child development is Erik Erikson (1902–1994).

Although Erikson (1950) accepted Freud's basic psychosexual framework, he expanded the picture of development at each stage. In his **psychosocial theory,** Erikson emphasized that the ego does not just mediate between id impulses and superego demands. It is also a positive force in development. At each stage, the ego acquires attitudes and skills that make the individual an active, contributing member of society. A basic psychosocial conflict, which is resolved along a continuum from positive to negative, determines whether healthy or maladaptive outcomes occur at each stage. As Table 1.2 shows, Erikson's first five stages parallel Freud's stages, but Erikson added three adult stages. He was one of the first to recognize the lifespan nature of development.

Finally, unlike Freud, Erikson pointed out that normal development must be understood in relation to each culture's life situation. For example, in the 1940s, he observed that Yurok Indians of the northwest coast of the United States deprived babies of breastfeeding for the first 10 days after birth and instead fed them a thin soup from a small shell. At age 6 months, infants were abruptly weaned—if necessary, by having the mother leave for a few days. These experiences, from our cultural vantage point, seem cruel. But Erikson explained that the Yurok lived in a world in which salmon fill the river just once a year, a circumstance that requires the development of considerable self-restraint for survival. In this way, he showed that child rearing can be understood only by making reference to the competencies valued and needed by the child's society.

• CONTRIBUTIONS AND LIMITATIONS OF THE PSYCHOANALYTIC PERSPECTIVE •
A special strength of the psychoanalytic perspective is its emphasis on the individual's unique life history as worthy of study and understanding (Emde, 1992). Consistent with this view, psychoanalytic theorists accept the *clinical,* or *case study, method,* which synthesizes information from a variety of sources into a detailed picture of the personality of a single child. (We will discuss this method further in Chapter 2.) Psychoanalytic theory has also inspired a wealth of research on many aspects of emotional and social development, including infant–caregiver attachment, aggression, sibling relationships, child-rearing practices, morality, gender roles, and adolescent identity.

Despite its extensive contributions, the psychoanalytic perspective is no longer in the mainstream of child development research (Cairns, 1998). Psychoanalytic theorists may have become isolated from the rest of the field because they were so strongly committed to in-depth study of each child that they failed to consider other methods. In addition, many psychoanalytic ideas, such as psychosexual stages and ego functioning, are so vague that they are difficult or impossible to test empirically (Thomas, 2000; Westen & Gabbard, 1999).

Behaviorism and Social Learning Theory

As psychoanalytic theory gained in prominence, the child study was also influenced by a very different perspective. According to **behaviorism,** directly observable events—stimuli and responses—are the appropriate focus of study. North American behaviorism began with the work of psychologist John Watson (1878–1958) in the early twentieth century. Watson wanted to create an objective science of psychology and rejected the psychoanalytic concern with the unseen workings of the mind (Horowitz, 1992).

• TRADITIONAL BEHAVIORISM • Watson was inspired by Russian physiologist Ivan Pavlov's studies of animal learning. Pavlov knew that dogs release saliva as an innate reflex when they are given food. But he noticed that his dogs were salivating before they tasted any food—when they saw the trainer who usually fed them. The dogs, Pavlov reasoned, must have learned to associate a neutral stimulus (the trainer) with another stimulus (food) that produces a reflexive response (salivation). As a result of this association, the neutral stimulus by itself could bring about a response resembling the reflex. Eager to test this idea, Pavlov successfully taught dogs to salivate at the sound of a bell by pairing it with the presentation of food. He had discovered *classical conditioning.*

Watson wanted to find out if classical conditioning could be applied to children's behavior. In a historic experiment, he taught Albert, an 11-month-old infant, to fear a neutral stimulus—a soft white rat—by presenting it several times with a sharp, loud sound, which naturally scared the baby. Little Albert, who at first had reached out eagerly to touch the furry rat, began to cry and turn his head away when he caught sight of it (Watson & Raynor, 1920). In fact, Albert's fear was so intense that researchers eventually questioned the ethics of studies like this one. Consistent with Locke's tabula rasa, Watson concluded that environment is the supreme force in development. Adults can mold children's behavior, he thought, by carefully controlling stimulus–response associations. And development is a continuous process, with the number and strength of these associations increasing with age.

B. F. Skinner (1904–1990), another noted American psychologist, is responsible for *operant conditioning theory.* According to Skinner, the frequency of a child's behavior can be increased by following it with a wide variety of *reinforcers,* such as food, drink, praise, a friendly smile, or a new toy. A behavior can also be decreased through *punishment,* such as withdrawal of privileges, parental disapproval, or being sent to one's room. As a result of Skinner's work, operant conditioning became a broadly applied learning principle in child psychology. We will consider these conditioning principles further when we explore the infant's learning capacities in Chapter 4.

• SOCIAL LEARNING THEORY • Psychologists quickly became interested in whether behaviorism might explain the development of children's social behavior better than the less precise concepts of psychoanalytic theory. This sparked the emergence of approaches that built on the principles of conditioning, offering expanded views of how children and adults acquire new responses.

Social learning theory recognizes that children acquire many skills through modeling. By observing and imitating her mother's behavior, this Vietnamese pre-schooler is becoming a skilled user of chopsticks.
© Margot Granitsas/The Image Works

Several kinds of **social learning theory** emerged. The most influential, devised by Canadian-born psychologist Albert Bandura, emphasized *modeling,* otherwise known as *imitation* or *observational learning,* as a powerful source of development. The baby who claps her hands after her mother does so, the child who angrily hits a playmate in the same way that he has been punished at home, and the teenager who wears the same clothes and hair-style as her friends at school are all displaying observational learn-ing. By the 1950s, social learning theory had become a major force in child development research.

Bandura's work continues to influence much research on chil-dren's social development. However, like the field of child devel-opment as a whole, today his theory stresses the importance of *cognition,* or thinking. Bandura has shown that children's ability to listen, remember, and abstract general rules from complex sets of observed behaviors affects their imitation and learning. In fact, Bandura's most recent revision of his theory (1992, 2001) places such strong emphasis on how children think about themselves and other people that he calls it a *social-cognitive* rather than a social learning approach.

According to Bandura's revised view, children gradually become more selective in what they imitate. From watching others engage in self-praise and self-blame and through feedback about the worth of their own actions, children develop *personal standards* for behavior and a *sense of self-efficacy*—the belief that their own abilities and characteristics will help them suc-ceed. These cognitions guide responses in particular situations (Bandura, 1999, 2001). For example, imagine a parent who often remarks, "I'm glad I kept working on that task, even though it was hard," who explains the value of persistence, and who encourages it by saying, "I know you can do a good job on that homework!" Soon the child starts to view herself as hardworking and high achieving and selects people with these characteristics as models. In this way, as children acquire attitudes, values, and convictions about themselves, they control their own learning and behavior.

• **CONTRIBUTIONS AND LIMITATIONS OF BEHAVIORISM AND SOCIAL LEARNING THEORY** • Behaviorism and social learning theory have had a major impact on practices with children. **Behavior modification** consists of procedures that combine conditioning and modeling to eliminate undesirable behaviors and increase desirable responses. It has been used to relieve a wide range of serious developmental problems, such as persistent aggression, language delays, and extreme fears (Pierce & Epling, 1995; Wolpe & Plaud, 1997). It is also effective in dealing with common, everyday difficulties, including poor time management; unwanted habits, such as nail biting and thumb sucking; disruptive behavior; and anxiety over such recurrent events as test taking and dental treatments. In one study, researchers reduced 4- and 5-year-olds' unruliness in a preschool classroom by reinforcing them with tokens (which they could exchange for candy) when they behaved appropriately and punishing them by taking away tokens when they screamed, threw objects, attacked other children, or refused to comply with a teacher's request (Conyers et al., 2004). In another investigation, children's anxious reactions during dental visits declined after an adult gave them small toys for answer-ing questions about a story she read to them while the dentist worked (Stark et al., 1989). Because the children could not listen to the story and cry at the same time, their resistance subsided.

Nevertheless, many theorists believe that behaviorism and social learning theory do not provide a complete account of development. They argue that these approaches offer too nar-row a view of important environmental influences, which extend beyond immediate rein-forcement, punishment, and modeled behaviors to children's rich physical and social worlds. In addition, behaviorism and social learning theory have been criticized for neglecting chil-dren's contributions to their own development. In emphasizing cognition, Bandura is unique among theorists whose work grew out of the behaviorist tradition in granting children an active role in their own learning.

TABLE 1.3 PIAGET'S STAGES OF COGNITIVE DEVELOPMENT

© Bettmann/ CORBIS

Stage	Period of Development	Description
Sensorimotor	Birth–2 years	Infants "think" by acting on the world with their eyes, ears, hands, and mouth. As a result, they invent ways of solving sensorimotor problems, such as pulling a lever to hear the sound of a music box, finding hidden toys, and putting objects in and taking them out of containers.
Preoperational	2–7 years	Preschool children use symbols to represent their earlier sensorimotor discoveries. Development of language and make-believe play takes place. However, thinking lacks the logic of the two remaining stages.
Concrete operational	7–11 years	Children's reasoning becomes logical. School-age children understand that a certain amount of lemonade or play dough remains the same even after its appearance changes. They also organize objects into hierarchies of classes and subclasses. However, thinking falls short of adult intelligence. It is not yet abstract.
Formal operational	11 years and older	The capacity for abstraction permits adolescents to reason with symbols that do not refer to objects in the real world, as in advanced mathematics. They can also think of all possible outcomes in a scientific problem, not just the most obvious ones.

Jean Piaget

Piaget's Cognitive-Developmental Theory

If one individual has influenced the contemporary field of child development more than any other, it is Swiss cognitive theorist Jean Piaget (1896–1980). North American investigators had been aware of Piaget's work since 1930. However, they did not grant it much attention until the 1960s, mainly because Piaget's ideas and methods of studying children were very much at odds with behaviorism, which dominated North American psychology during the middle of the twentieth century (Zigler & Gilman, 1998). Piaget did not believe that children's learning depends on reinforcers, such as rewards from adults. According to his **cognitive-developmental theory,** children actively construct knowledge as they manipulate and explore their world.

• **PIAGET'S STAGES** • Piaget's view of development was greatly influenced by his early training in biology. Central to his theory is the biological concept of *adaptation* (Piaget, 1971). Just as structures of the body are adapted to fit with the environment, so structures of the mind develop to better fit with, or represent, the external world. In infancy and early childhood, Piaget claimed, children's understanding is different from adults'. For example, he believed that young babies do not realize that an object hidden from view—a favorite toy or even the mother—continues to exist. He also concluded that preschoolers' thinking is full of faulty logic. For example, children younger than age 7 commonly say that the amount of milk or lemonade changes when it is poured into a differently shaped container. According to Piaget, children eventually revise these incorrect ideas in their ongoing efforts to achieve an *equilibrium*, or balance, between internal structures and information they encounter in their everyday worlds.

In Piaget's theory, as the brain develops and children's experiences expand, they move through four broad stages, each characterized by qualitatively distinct ways of thinking. Table 1.3 provides a brief description of Piaget's stages. In the *sensorimotor stage*, cognitive development begins with the baby's use of the senses and movements to explore the world. These action patterns evolve into the symbolic but illogical thinking of the preschooler in the *preoperational stage*. Then cognition is transformed into the more organized, logical reasoning of the school-age child in the *concrete operational stage*. Finally, in the *formal operational stage*, thought becomes the complex, abstract reasoning system of the adolescent and adult.

◉ In Piaget's preoperational stage, preschool children represent their earlier sensorimotor discoveries with symbols. Language and make-believe play develop rapidly. These 4-year-olds create an imaginative play scene with dress-up clothes and the assistance of a cooperative family pet.
© Tom McCarthy/ImageState

◉ In Piaget's concrete operational stage, school-age children think in an organized, logical fashion about concrete objects. This 6-year-old girl and 7-year-old boy understand that the amount of milk remains the same after being poured into a differently shaped container, even though its appearance changes.
© Bob Daemmrich/The Image Works

• **PIAGET'S METHODS OF STUDY** • Piaget devised special methods for investigating how children think. In the early part of his career, he carefully observed his three infant children and presented them with everyday problems, such as an attractive object that could be grasped, mouthed, kicked, or searched for. From their responses, Piaget derived his ideas about cognitive changes during the first 2 years. In studying childhood and adolescent thought, Piaget took advantage of children's ability to describe their thinking. He adapted the clinical method of psychoanalysis, conducting open-ended *clinical interviews* in which a child's initial response to a task served as the basis for the next question Piaget would ask. We will look more closely at this technique in Chapter 2.

• **CONTRIBUTIONS AND LIMITATIONS OF PIAGET'S THEORY** • Piaget's cognitive-developmental perspective convinced the field that children are active learners whose minds consist of rich structures of knowledge. Besides investigating children's understanding of the physical world, Piaget explored their reasoning about the social world. His stages have sparked a wealth of research on children's conceptions of themselves, other people, and human relationships. Practically speaking, Piaget's theory encouraged the development of educational philosophies and programs that emphasize discovery learning and direct contact with the environment.

Despite Piaget's overwhelming contributions, his theory has been challenged. Research indicates that Piaget underestimated the competencies of infants and preschoolers. We will see in Chapter 6 that when young children are given tasks that are scaled down in difficulty and made relevant to their everyday experiences, their understanding appears closer to that of the older child and adult than Piaget assumed. This discovery has led many researchers to conclude that the maturity of children's thinking may depend on their familiarity with the task presented and the complexity of knowledge sampled. Furthermore, many studies show that children's performance on Piagetian problems can be improved with training—findings that call into question Piaget's assumption that discovery learning rather than adult teaching is the best way to foster development (Caracciolo, Moderato, & Perini, 1988; Klahr & Nigam, 2004). Finally, critics point out that Piaget's stagewise account pays insufficient attention to social and cultural influences—and the resulting wide variation in thinking that exists among children of the same age.

Today, the field of child development is divided over its loyalty to Piaget's ideas. Those who continue to find merit in Piaget's approach accept a modified view—one in which changes in the quality of children's thinking take place more gradually than Piaget believed (Case, 1998; Demetriou et al., 2002; Fischer & Bidell, 1998). Others have turned to an approach that emphasizes continuous gains in children's cognition: information processing. And still others have been drawn to theories that focus on the role of children's social and cultural contexts. We take up these approaches in the next section.

Ask Yourself

REVIEW	Cite similarities and differences between Freud's and Erikson's views of development.
REVIEW	What aspect of behaviorism made it attractive to critics of the psychoanalytic perspective? How does Piaget's theory respond to a major limitation of behaviorism?
APPLY	A 4-year-old becomes frightened of the dark and refuses to go to sleep at night. How would a psychoanalyst and a behaviorist differ in their views of how this problem developed?
CONNECT	Although social learning theory focuses on social development and Piaget's theory on cognitive development, each has enhanced our understanding of other domains. Mention an additional domain addressed by each theory.

Recent Theoretical Perspectives

New ways of understanding children are constantly emerging—questioning, building on, and enhancing the discoveries of earlier theories. Today, a burst of fresh approaches and research emphases is broadening our understanding of children's development.

Information Processing

During the 1970s, researchers turned to the field of cognitive psychology for ways to understand the development of children's thinking. The design of digital computers that use mathematically specified steps to solve problems suggested to psychologists that the human mind might also be viewed as a symbol-manipulating system through which information flows—a perspective called **information processing** (Klahr & MacWhinney, 1998). From the time information is presented to the senses at *input* until it emerges as a behavioral response at *output,* information is actively coded, transformed, and organized.

Information-processing researchers often use flowcharts to map the precise steps individuals use to solve problems and complete tasks, much like the plans devised by programmers to get computers to perform a series of "mental operations." Let's look at an example to clarify the usefulness of this approach. In a study of children's problem solving, a researcher provided a pile of blocks varying in size, shape, and weight and asked 5- to 9-year-olds to build a bridge across a "river" (painted on a floor mat) that was too wide for any single block to span (Thornton, 1999). Figure 1.3 shows one solution to the problem: Two plank-like blocks span the water, each held in place by the counterweight of heavy blocks on the bridge's towers. Whereas many children age 7 and older built successful bridges, only one 5-year-old did. Careful tracking of her efforts revealed that she repeatedly tried unsuccessful strategies, such as pushing two planks together and pressing down on their ends to hold them in place. But eventually, her experimentation triggered the idea of using the blocks as counterweights. Her mistaken procedures helped her understand why the counterweight approach worked. The findings show how a child's actions within a task can facilitate problem solving. This child had no prior understanding of counterweight and balance. Yet she arrived at just as effective a solution as older children, who came with considerable task-relevant knowledge.

A variety of information-processing models exist. Some, like the one just considered, track children's mastery of one or a few tasks. Others describe the human cognitive system as a whole (Atkinson & Shiffrin, 1968; Lockhart & Craik, 1990). These general models are used as guides for asking questions about broad age changes in children's thinking. For example, does a child's ability to search the environment for information needed to solve a problem become more organized and "planful" with age? What strategies do younger and older children use to remember new information, and how do those strategies affect children's recall?

The information-processing approach is also being used to clarify the processing of social information. For example, flowcharts exist that track the steps children use to solve social

▼ **Figure 1.3**

Information-processing flowchart showing the steps that a 5-year-old used to solve a bridge-building problem. Her task was to use blocks varying in size, shape, and weight, some of which were planklike, to construct a bridge across a "river" (painted on a floor mat) too wide for any single block to span. The child discovered how to counterweight and balance the bridge. The arrows reveal that even after building a successful counterweight, she returned to earlier, unsuccessful strategies, which seemed to help her understand why the counterweight approach worked. (Adapted from Thornton, 1999.)

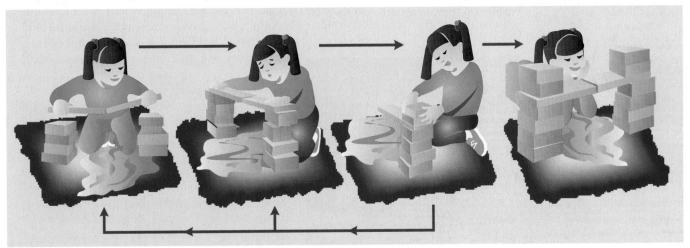

problems (such as how to enter an ongoing play group) and acquire gender-linked preferences and behaviors (Crick & Dodge, 1994; Liben & Bigler, 2002). If we can identify how social problem solving and gender stereotyping arise in childhood, then we can design interventions that promote more favorable social development.

Like Piaget's theory, the information-processing approach views children as actively making sense of their experiences and as modifying their own thinking in response to environmental demands (Halford, 2002; Klahr & MacWhinney, 1998). But unlike Piaget's theory, there are no stages of development. Rather, the thought processes studied—perception, attention, memory, categorization of information, planning, problem solving, and comprehension of written and spoken prose—are regarded as similar at all ages but present to a lesser or greater extent. Therefore, the view of development is one of continuous change.

A great strength of the information-processing approach is its commitment to careful, rigorous research methods. Because it has provided precise accounts of how children of different ages engage in many aspects of thinking, its findings have led to teaching interventions that help children solve problems in more advanced ways (Geary, 1994; Siegler, 1998). But information processing has fallen short in some respects. Although good at analyzing thinking into its components, it has difficulty putting them back together into a comprehensive theory. In addition, aspects of cognition that are not linear and logical, such as imagination and creativity, are all but ignored by this approach (Lutz & Sternberg, 1999). Furthermore, much information-processing research has been conducted in laboratories rather than real-life situations. Recently, investigators have addressed this concern by focusing on more realistic materials and activities. Today, they study children's conversations, stories, memory for everyday events, and academic problem solving.

An advantage of having many theories is that they encourage one another to attend to previously neglected dimensions of children's lives. A unique feature of the final four perspectives we will discuss is a focus on *contexts* for development—the way children's biological makeup combines with environmental circumstances to affect pathways of change. The first of these views emphasizes that the development of many capacities is influenced by our long evolutionary history.

Ethology and Evolutionary Developmental Psychology

Ethology is concerned with the adaptive, or survival, value of behavior and its evolutionary history (Dewsbury, 1992; Hinde, 1989). Its roots can be traced to the work of Darwin. Two European zoologists, Konrad Lorenz (1952) and Niko Tinbergen (1973), laid its modern foundations. Watching diverse animal species in their natural habitats, Lorenz and Tinbergen observed behavior patterns that promote survival. The best known of these is *imprinting,* the early following behavior of certain baby birds that ensures that the young will stay close to the mother and be fed and protected from danger. Imprinting takes place during an early, restricted period of development. If the mother goose is not present during this time, but an object resembling her in important features is, young goslings may imprint on it instead.

Observations of imprinting led to a major concept in child development: the *critical period*. It refers to a limited time during which the child is biologically prepared to acquire certain adaptive behaviors but needs the support of an appropriately stimulating environment. Many researchers have conducted studies to find out whether complex cognitive and social behaviors must be learned during certain periods. For example, if children are deprived of adequate food or physical and social stimulation during their early years, will their intelligence be impaired? If language is not mastered during early childhood, is the child's capacity to acquire it reduced?

In later chapters, we will discover that the term *sensitive period* applies better to human development than the strict notion of a critical period (Bornstein, 1989). A **sensitive period** is a time that is optimal for certain capacities to emerge and in which the individual is especially responsive to environmental influences. However, its boundaries are less well defined than those of a critical period. Development can occur later, but it is harder to induce.

Ⓖ Konrad Lorenz was one of the founders of ethology and a keen observer of animal behavior. He developed the concept of imprinting. Here, young geese that were separated from their mother and placed in the company of Lorenz during an early, critical period show that they have imprinted on him. They follow him as he swims through the water, a response that promotes survival.
© Nina Leen/Time & Life Pictures/Getty Images

Inspired by observations of imprinting, British psychoanalyst John Bowlby (1969) applied ethological theory to the understanding of the human infant–caregiver relationship. He argued that infant smiling, babbling, grasping, and crying are built-in social signals that encourage the caregiver to approach, care for, and interact with the baby. By keeping the parent near, these behaviors help ensure that the infant will be fed, protected from danger, and provided with stimulation and affection necessary for healthy growth. The development of attachment in human infants is a lengthy process that leads the baby to form a deep affectionate tie with the caregiver (van den Boom, 2002). It is far more complex than imprinting in baby birds. In Chapter 10, we will consider how infant, caregiver, and family context contribute to attachment and will examine the impact of attachment on later development.

Observations by ethologists have shown that many aspects of children's social behavior, including emotional expressions, aggression, cooperation, and social play, resemble those of our primate relatives. Recently, researchers have extended this effort in a new area of research called **evolutionary developmental psychology.** It seeks to understand the adaptive value of species-wide cognitive, emotional, and social competencies as those competencies change with age. Evolutionary developmental psychologists ask such questions as, What role does the newborn's visual preference for facelike stimuli play in survival? Does it support older infants' capacity to distinguish familiar caregivers from unfamiliar people? Why do children play in sex-segregated groups? What do they learn from such play that might lead to adult gender-typed behaviors, such as male dominance and female investment in caregiving?

As these examples suggest, evolutionary psychologists are not just concerned with the genetic and biological roots of development. They recognize that the extended childhood of humans resulted from the need to master an increasingly complex social and technological environment, so they are also interested in how children learn (Blasi & Bjorklund, 2003). And they realize that today's lifestyles differ so radically from those of our evolutionary ancestors that certain evolved behaviors (such as life-threatening risk taking in adolescents and male-to-male violence) are no longer adaptive (Bjorklund & Pellegrini, 2000, 2002). By clarifying the origins and development of such behaviors, evolutionary developmental psychology may help spark more effective interventions.

In sum, the interests of evolutionary psychologists are broad. They want to understand the entire *organism–environment system*. The next contextual perspective we will discuss, Vygotsky's sociocultural theory, serves as an excellent complement to the evolutionary viewpoint because it highlights the social and cultural dimensions of children's experiences.

Vygotsky's Sociocultural Theory

In recent decades, the field of child development has seen a dramatic increase in studies addressing the cultural context of children's lives. Investigations that make comparisons across cultures, and between ethnic groups within cultures, provide insight into whether developmental pathways apply to all children or are limited to particular environmental conditions. As a result, cross-cultural and multicultural research helps untangle the contributions of biological and environmental factors to the timing, order of appearance, and diversity of children's behaviors (Greenfield, 1994).

In the past, researchers focused on broad cultural differences in development—for example, whether children in one culture are more advanced in motor development or do better on intellectual tasks than children in another culture. However, this approach can lead us to conclude incorrectly that one culture is superior in enhancing development, whereas another is deficient. In addition, it does not help us understand the precise experiences that contribute to cultural differences in children's behavior.

Today, more research is examining the relationship of *culturally specific practices* to development. The contributions of Russian psychologist Lev Vygotsky (1896–1934) have played a major role in this trend. Vygotsky's (1934/1987) perspective is called **sociocultural theory.** It focuses on how *culture*—the values, beliefs, customs, and skills of a social group—is transmitted to the next generation. According to Vygotsky, *social interaction*—in particular, cooperative dialogues between children and more knowledgeable members of society—is necessary for children to acquire the ways of thinking and behaving that make up a community's culture (Rowe & Wertsch, 2002). Vygotsky believed that as adults and more-expert peers help children master culturally meaningful activities, the communication between them becomes part of children's

⑥ Vygotsky, pictured here with his daughter, believed that many cognitive processes and skills are socially transferred from more knowledgeable members of society to children. Vygotsky's sociocultural theory helps us understand the wide variation in cognitive competencies from culture to culture.

Courtesy of James V. Wertsch, Washington University in St. Louis

thinking. As children internalize the features of these dialogues, they use the language within them to guide their own thought and actions and to acquire new skills (Berk, 2003). The young child instructing herself while working a puzzle or preparing a table for dinner has started to produce the same kind of guiding comments that an adult previously used to help her master important tasks.

Vygotsky's theory has been especially influential in the study of children's cognition. Vygotsky agreed with Piaget that children are active, constructive beings. But unlike Piaget, who emphasized children's independent efforts to make sense of their world, Vygotsky viewed cognitive development as a *socially mediated process*—as dependent on the assistance that adults and more-expert peers provide as children tackle new challenges.

In Vygotsky's theory, children undergo certain stagewise changes. For example, when they acquire language, their ability to participate in dialogues with others is greatly enhanced, and mastery of culturally valued competencies surges forward. When children enter school, they spend much time discussing language, literacy, and other academic concepts—experiences that encourage them to reflect on their own thinking (Kozulin, 2003). As a result, they gain dramatically in reasoning and problem solving.

At the same time, Vygotsky stressed that dialogues with experts lead to continuous changes in cognition that vary greatly from culture to culture. Consistent with this view, a major finding of cross-cultural research is that cultures select different tasks for children's learning (Rogoff & Chavajay, 1995). Social interaction surrounding those tasks leads to competencies essential for success in a particular culture. For example, in industrialized nations, teachers can be seen helping people learn to read, drive a car, or use a computer. Among the Zinacanteco Indians of southern Mexico, adult experts guide young girls as they master complicated weaving techniques (Greenfield, Maynard, & Childs, 2000). In Brazil and other developing nations, child candy sellers with little or no schooling develop sophisticated mathematical abilities as the result of buying candy from wholesalers, pricing it in collaboration with adults and experienced peers, and bargaining with customers on city streets (Saxe, 1988). And as the research reported in the Cultural Influences box on the following page indicates, adults encourage culturally valued skills in children at a remarkably early age.

Vygotsky's theory, and the research stimulated by it, reveal that children in every culture develop unique strengths. At the same time, Vygotsky's emphasis on culture and social experience led him to neglect the biological side of development. Although he recognized the importance of heredity and brain growth, he said little about their role in cognitive change. Furthermore, Vygotsky's focus on social transmission of knowledge meant that he placed less emphasis than other theorists on children's capacity to shape their own development. Followers of Vygotsky stress that children actively participate in the conversations and social activities from which their development springs. From these joint experiences, they not only acquire culturally valued practices but also modify and transform those practices (Rogoff, 1998, 2003). Contemporary sociocultural theorists grant the individual and society balanced, mutually influential roles.

⑥ Through the guidance of her grandmother, a Navajo girl learns to use a vertical weaving loom. According to Vygotsky's sociocultural theory, social interaction between children and more knowledgeable members of their culture leads to ways of thinking and behaving essential for success in that culture.

© Paul Conklin/Photoedit

Ecological Systems Theory

Urie Bronfenbrenner is responsible for an approach that has moved to the forefront of the field because it offers the most differentiated and complete account of contextual influences on children's development. **Ecological systems theory** views the child as developing within a complex *system* of relationships affected by multiple levels of the surrounding environment. Since the child's biologically influenced dispositions join with environmental forces to mold development, Bronfenbrenner recently characterized his perspective as a *bioecological model* (Bronfenbrenner & Evans, 2000).

CULTURAL INFLUENCES

!Kung Infancy: Acquiring Culture

Interactions between caregivers and infants take different forms in different cultures. Through those interactions, adults start to transmit their society's values and skills to the next generation, channeling the course of future development.

Focusing on a culture very different from our own, researchers studied how caregivers respond to infants' play with objects among the !Kung, a hunting-and-gathering society living in the desert regions of Botswana, Africa (Bakeman et al., 1990). Daily foraging missions take small numbers of adults several miles from the campground, but most obtain enough food to contribute to group survival by working only 3 out of every 7 days. A mobile way of life also prevents the !Kung from collecting many possessions that require extensive care and maintenance. Adults have many free hours to relax around the campfire, and they spend it in intense social contact with one another and with children (Draper & Cashdan, 1988).

In this culture of intimate social bonds and minimal property, objects are valued as things to be shared, not as personal possessions. This message is conveyed to !Kung children at a very early age. Between 6 and 12 months, grandmothers start to train babies in the importance of exchanging objects by guiding them in handing beads to relatives. The child's first words generally include *i* ("Here, take this") and *na* ("Give it to me").

In !Kung society, no toys are made for infants. Instead, natural objects, such as twigs, grass, stones, and nutshells, are always available, along with cooking implements. However, adults do not encourage babies to play with these objects. In fact, adults are unlikely to interact with infants while they are exploring objects independently. But when a baby offers an object to another person, adults become highly responsive, encouraging and vocalizing much more than at other times. Thus, the !Kung cultural emphasis on the interpersonal rather than physical aspects of existence is reflected in how adults interact with the very youngest members of their community.

When you next have a chance, observe the conditions under which parents in your own society respond to infants' involvement with objects. How is parental responsiveness linked to cultural values? How does it compare with findings on the !Kung?

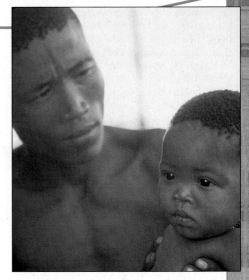

▲ !Kung children grow up in a hunting-and-gathering society in which possessions are a burden rather than an asset. From an early age, children experience warm social contact with adults and are taught the importance of sharing.
© Irven Devore/Anthro-Photo

Bronfenbrenner envisions the environment as a series of nested structures that includes but extends beyond home, school, and neighborhood settings in which children spend their everyday lives (see Figure 1.4 on page 28). Each layer of the environment is viewed as having a powerful impact on development.

• **THE MICROSYSTEM** • The innermost level of the environment is the **microsystem,** which consists of activities and interaction patterns in the child's immediate surroundings. Bronfenbrenner emphasizes that to understand child development at this level, we must keep in mind that all relationships are *bidirectional.* That is, adults affect children's behavior, but children's biologically and socially influenced characteristics—their physical attributes, personalities, and capacities—also affect adults' behavior. For example, a friendly, attentive child is likely to evoke positive and patient reactions from parents, whereas an irritable or distractible youngster is more likely to be a target of parental impatience, restriction, and punishment. When these reciprocal interactions occur often over time, they have an enduring impact on development (Collins et al., 2000; Crockenberg & Leerkes, 2003a).

At the same time, *third parties*—other individuals in the microsystem—affect the quality of any two-person relationship. If they are supportive, then interaction is enhanced. For example, when parents encourage one another in their child-rearing roles, each engages in

▶ **Figure 1.4**

Structure of the environment in ecological systems theory. The *microsystem* concerns relations between the child and the immediate environment; the *mesosystem,* connections among immediate settings; the *exosystem,* social settings that affect but do not contain the child; and the *macrosystem,* the values, laws, customs, and resources of the culture that affect activities and interactions at all inner layers. The *chronosystem* (not pictured) is not a specific context. Instead, it refers to the dynamic, ever-changing nature of the person's environment.

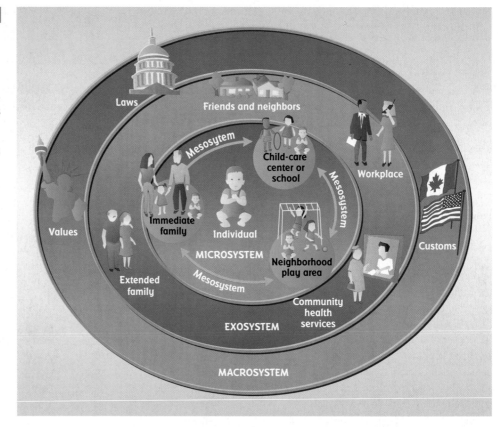

Ⓢ Family–neighborhood connections, at the level of the mesosystem in ecological systems theory, enhance development. A young girl proudly carries the Canadian flag in the Chinese New Year parade in the Chinatown district of Vancouver, British Columbia. The event fosters self-confidence, cooperation, and identification with her community and culture.
© Annie Griffiths Belt/Corbis

more effective parenting. In contrast, when a marriage is tense and hostile, parents often interfere with one another's child-rearing efforts, are less responsive to children's needs, and criticize, express anger, and punish (Cox, Paley, & Harter, 2001; McHale et al., 2002). Similarly, children can affect their parents' relationship in powerful ways. For example, as Chapter 14 will reveal, divorce is often associated with lasting emotional problems. Yet research reveals that long before the marital breakup, some children were impulsive and defiant. These behaviors may have contributed to, as well as been caused by, their parents' marital problems (Hetherington & Stanley-Hagan, 1999; Shaw, Winslow, & Flanagan, 1999).

• **THE MESOSYSTEM** • The second level of Bronfenbrenner's model, the **mesosystem,** encompasses connections between microsystems, such as home, school, neighborhood, and child-care center. For example, a child's academic progress depends not just on activities that take place in classrooms. It is also promoted by parent involvement in school life and the extent to which academic learning is carried over into the home (Epstein & Sanders, 2002). Similarly, parent–child interaction at home is likely to affect caregiver–child interaction in the child-care setting, and vice versa. Each relationship is more likely to support development when there are links, in the form of visits and cooperative exchanges of information, between home and child care.

Family–neighborhood connections are especially important for economically disadvantaged children. Affluent families are not as dependent on their immediate surroundings for social support, education, and leisure pursuits. They can afford to reach beyond the streets near their homes, transporting their children to lessons and entertainment and, if necessary, to better-quality schools in distant parts of the community (Elliott et al., 1996). In low-income neighborhoods, after-school programs that provide families with child care and offer children art, music, sports, scouting, and other special experiences are linked to improved school performance and psychological adjustment in middle childhood (Posner & Vandell, 1994; Vandell & Posner, 1999). Neighborhood organizations, such as religious youth groups and special-interest clubs, contribute to favorable development in adolescence, including self-confidence, school achievement, educational aspirations, and responsible social behavior (Gonzales et al., 1996; Kerestes & Youniss, 2003).

• **THE EXOSYSTEM** • The **exosystem** is made up of social settings that do not contain children but nevertheless affect their experiences in immediate settings. These can be formal organizations, such as parents' workplaces, their religious institutions, and health and welfare services in the community. For example, flexible work schedules and paid leave for childbirth and child illness are ways that work settings can help parents rear children and, indirectly, enhance development. Exosystem supports can also be informal, such as parents' social networks—friends and extended-family members who provide advice, companionship, and even financial assistance. Research confirms the negative impact of a breakdown in exosystem activities. Families who are socially isolated because they have few personal or community-based ties or who are affected by unemployment show increased rates of conflict and child abuse (Emery & Laumann-Billings, 1998).

• **THE MACROSYSTEM** • The outermost level of Bronfenbrenner's model, the **macrosystem,** consists of cultural values, laws, customs, and resources. The priority that the macrosystem gives to children's needs affects the support they receive at inner levels of the environment. For example, in countries that require high-quality standards for child care and workplace benefits for employed parents, children are more likely to have favorable experiences in their immediate settings. As you will see in greater detail later in this chapter and in other parts of this book, such programs are far less available in the United States than in Canada and other industrialized nations (Children's Defense Fund, 2004; Kamerman, 2000).

• **AN EVER-CHANGING SYSTEM** • According to Bronfenbrenner, the environment is not a static force that affects children in a uniform way. Instead, it is ever-changing. Important life events, such as the birth of a sibling, the beginning of school, or parents' divorce, modify existing relationships between children and their environment, producing new conditions that affect development. In addition, the timing of environmental change affects its impact. The arrival of a new sibling has very different consequences for a homebound toddler than for a school-age child with many relationships and activities beyond the family.

Bronfenbrenner refers to the temporal dimension of his model as the **chronosystem** (the prefix *chrono-* means "time"). Changes in life events can be imposed on the child, as in the examples just given. Alternatively, they can arise from within the child, since as children get older they select, modify, and create many of their own settings and experiences. How they do so depends on their physical, intellectual, and personality characteristics and their environmental opportunities. Therefore, in ecological systems theory, development is neither controlled by environmental circumstances nor driven by inner dispositions. Instead, children are both products and producers of their environments, so both children and the environment form a network of interdependent effects. Notice how our discussion of resilient children on page 10 illustrates this idea. We will see many more examples throughout this book.

New Directions: Development as a Dynamic System

Today, researchers recognize both consistency and variability in child development and want to do a better job of explaining variation. Consequently, a new wave of theorists has adopted a **dynamic systems perspective.** According to this view, the child's mind, body, and physical and social worlds form an *integrated system* that guides mastery of new skills. The system is *dynamic,* or constantly in motion. A change in any part of it—from brain growth to physical and social surroundings—disrupts the current organism–environment relationship. When this happens, the child actively reorganizes her behavior so that the components of the system work together again but in a more complex, effective way (Fischer & Bidell, 1998; Spencer & Schöner, 2003; Thelen & Smith, 1998).

Researchers adopting a dynamic systems perspective try to find out just how children attain new levels of organization by studying their behavior while they are in transition (Thelen & Corbetta, 2002). For example, when presented with an attractive toy, how does a 3-month-old baby who shows many, varied movements discover how to reach for it? On hearing a new word, how does a 2-year-old figure out the category of objects or events to which it refers?

Ⓢ Although these children are about the same age, they vary widely in competencies. The dynamic systems perspective aims to explain this variation by examining how the child's mind, body, and physical and social worlds form an integrated system that guides mastery of new skills.
© Michael Newman/PhotoEdit

Dynamic systems theorists acknowledge that a common human genetic heritage and basic regularities in children's physical and social worlds yield certain universal, broad outlines of development. But biological makeup, everyday tasks, and the people who support children in mastery of those tasks vary greatly, leading to wide individual differences in specific skills. Even when children master the same skills, such as walking, talking, or adding and subtracting, they often do so in unique ways. And because children build competencies by engaging in real activities in real contexts, different skills vary in maturity within the same child. From this perspective, development cannot be characterized as a single line of change. As Figure 1.5 shows, it is more like a web of fibers branching out in many directions, each of which represents a different skill area that may undergo continuous and stagewise transformations (Fischer & Bidell, 1998).

The dynamic systems view has been inspired by other scientific disciplines, especially biology and physics. In addition, it draws on information-processing and contextual theories—evolutionary developmental psychology, sociocultural theory, and ecological systems theory. At present, dynamic systems research is in its early stages. The perspective has largely been applied to children's motor and cognitive skills, but some investigators have drawn on it to explain emotional and social development as well (Fogel, 2000; Lewis, 2000). Consider the young teenager, whose body and reasoning powers are changing massively and who is also confronting the challenges of secondary school. Researchers following parent–child interaction over time found that the transition to adolescence disrupted family communication. It became unstable and variable for several years—a mix of positive, neutral, and negative exchanges. Gradually, as parent and adolescent devised new, more mature ways of relating to one another, the system reorganized and stabilized. Once again, interaction became predictable and mostly positive (Granic et al., 2003).

As dynamic systems research illustrates, today investigators are tracking and analyzing development in all its complexity. In doing so, they hope to move closer to an all-encompassing approach to understanding change.

▶ **Figure 1.5**

The dynamic systems view of development. Rather than envisioning a single line of stagewise or continuous change (refer to Figure 1.2 on page 7), dynamic systems theorists conceive of development as a web of fibers branching out in many directions. Each strand in the web represents a skill within the major domains of development—physical, cognitive, and emotional/social. The differing directions of the strands signify possible variations in paths and outcomes as the child masters skills necessary to participate in diverse contexts. The interconnections of the strands at each row of "hills" portray stagelike changes—periods of major transformation in which various skills work together as a functioning whole. As the web expands, skills become more numerous, complex, and effective.
(Adapted from Fischer & Bidell, 1998.)

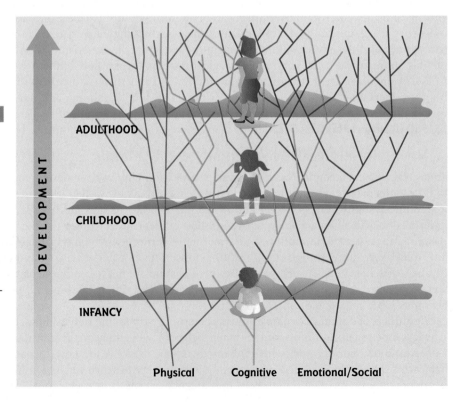

Ask Yourself

REVIEW	What features of Vygotsky's sociocultural theory distinguish it from Piaget's cognitive-developmental theory and from information processing?
REVIEW	Explain how each recent theoretical perspective regards children as active contributors to their own development.
APPLY	Return to the Biology and Environment box on page 10. How does the story of John and Gary illustrate bidirectional influences within the microsystem, as described in ecological systems theory?
REFLECT	To illustrate the chronosystem in ecological systems theory, select an important event from your childhood, such as a move to a new neighborhood, a class with an inspiring teacher, or parental divorce. How did the event affect you? How might its impact have differed had you been 5 years younger? How about 5 years older?

Comparing Child Development Theories

In the preceding sections, we reviewed major theoretical perspectives in child development research. They differ in many respects. First, they focus on different domains of development. Some, such as the psychoanalytic perspective and ethology, emphasize emotional and social development. Others, such as Piaget's cognitive-developmental theory, information processing, and Vygotsky's sociocultural theory, stress changes in thinking. The remaining approaches—behaviorism, social learning theory, evolutionary developmental psychology, ecological systems theory, and the dynamic systems perspective—discuss many aspects of children's functioning. Second, every theory contains a point of view about development. As we conclude our review of theoretical perspectives, identify the stand each theory takes on the controversial issues presented at the beginning of this chapter. Then check your analysis against Table 1.4 on page 32.

Finally, we have seen that theories have strengths and limitations. Perhaps you found that you are attracted to some theories, but you have doubts about others. As you read more about child development in later chapters, you may find it useful to keep a notebook in which you test your theoretical likes and dislikes against the evidence. Don't be surprised if you revise your ideas many times, just as theorists have done throughout this century. By the end of this course, you will have built your own personal perspective on child development. Very likely, it will be an *eclectic position,* or blend of several theories, since every viewpoint we have considered has contributed to what we know about children.

Applied Directions: Child Development and Social Policy

In recent years, the field of child development has become increasingly concerned with applying its vast knowledge base to solving pressing social problems. At the dawn of a new millennium, we know much more than ever before about family, school, and community contexts that foster physically healthy and cognitively and socially competent children. Yet a nation's values, policies, and programs powerfully affect children's experiences in these immediate contexts.

Social policy is any planned set of actions by a group, institution, or governing body directed at attaining a social goal. When widespread social problems arise, nations attempt to solve them through a special type of social policy called **public policy**—laws and government programs aimed at improving current conditions. Return to Bronfenbrenner's ecological systems theory, and note how the concept of the macrosystem suggests that sound public policies are essential for protecting children's well-being. For example, when poverty increases and families become homeless, a country might decide to build more low-cost housing, raise the minimum wage, and increase welfare benefits. When reports indicate that many children are not

TABLE 1.4   STANCES OF MAJOR THEORIES ON BASIC ISSUES IN CHILD DEVELOPMENT

Theory	Continuous or Discontinuous Development?	One Course of Development or Many?	Nature or Nurture as More Important?
Psychoanalytic perspective	*Discontinuous:* Psychosexual and psychosocial development takes place in stages.	*One course:* Stages are assumed to be universal.	*Both nature and nurture:* Innate impulses are channeled and controlled through child-rearing experiences. *Early experiences* set the course of later development.
Behaviorism and social learning theory	*Continuous:* Development involves an increase in learned behaviors.	*Many possible courses:* Behaviors reinforced and modeled may vary from child to child.	*Emphasis on nurture:* Development results from conditioning and modeling. *Both early and later experiences* are important.
Piaget's cognitive-developmental theory	*Discontinuous:* Cognitive development takes place in stages.	*One course:* Stages are assumed to be universal.	*Both nature and nurture:* Development occurs as the brain matures and children exercise their innate drive to discover reality in a generally stimulating environment. *Both early and later experiences* are important.
Information processing	*Continuous:* Children gradually improve in perception, attention, memory, and problem-solving skills.	*One course:* Changes studied characterize most or all children.	*Both nature and nurture:* Children are active, sense-making beings who modify their thinking as the brain matures and they confront new environmental demands. *Both early and later experiences* are important.
Ethology and evolutionary developmental psychology	*Both continuous and discontinuous:* Children gradually develop a wider range of adaptive behaviors. Sensitive periods occur, in which qualitatively distinct capacities emerge fairly suddenly.	*One course:* Adaptive behaviors and sensitive periods apply to all members of a species.	*Both nature and nurture:* Evolution and heredity influence behavior, and learning lends greater flexibility and adaptiveness to it. In sensitive periods, *early experiences* set the course of later development.
Vygotsky's sociocultural theory	*Both continuous and discontinuous:* Language acquisition and schooling lead to stagewise changes. Dialogues with more expert members of society also lead to continuous changes that vary from culture to culture.	*Many possible courses:* Socially mediated changes in thought and behavior vary from culture to culture.	*Both nature and nurture:* Heredity, brain growth, and dialogues with more expert members of society jointly contribute to development. *Both early and later experiences* are important.
Ecological systems theory	*Not specified.*	*Many possible courses:* Children's characteristics join with environmental forces at multiple levels to mold development in unique ways.	*Both nature and nurture:* Children's characteristics and the reactions of others affect each other in a bidirectional fashion. Layers of the environment influence child-rearing experiences. *Both early and later experiences* are important.
Dynamic systems perspective	*Both continuous and discontinuous:* Change in the system is always ongoing. Stagelike transformations occur as children reorganize their behavior so components of the system work as a functioning whole.	*Many possible courses:* Biological makeup, everyday tasks, and social experiences vary, yielding wide individual differences in specific skills.	*Both nature and nurture:* The child's mind, body, and physical and social surroundings form an integrated system that guides mastery of new skills. *Both early and later experiences* are important.

achieving well in school, federal and state or provincial governments might grant more tax money to school districts, strengthen teacher preparation, and make sure that help reaches children who need it most.

American and Canadian public policies that safeguard children and youths have lagged behind policies in other developed nations. A striking indicator is that about 16 percent of

American and Canadian children are poor—rates that climb to 32 percent for Native-American children, 34 percent for African-American and Hispanic children, and 60 percent for Canadian Aboriginal children.[1] Families hit hardest are parents under age 25 with young children. For single mothers with infants and preschoolers, the poverty rate in both countries is nearly 50 percent (Canada Campaign 2000, 2003b, 2004; U.S. Census Bureau, 2004b).

Of all Western nations, the United States has the highest percentage of extremely poor children. More than 6 percent of American children live in deep poverty (well below the poverty threshold, the income level judged necessary for a minimum living standard), compared with 2.5 percent of Canadian children. However, these circumstances are worrisome in both countries because the earlier poverty begins, the deeper it is, and the longer it lasts, the more devastating are its effects. Children of poverty are more likely than other children to suffer from lifelong poor physical health, persistent deficits in cognitive development and academic achievement, high school dropout, mental illness, and antisocial behavior (Children's Defense Fund, 2004; Poulton et al., 2002; Seccombe, 2002).

As Table 1.5 on page 34 reveals, the United States does not rank well on any key measure of children's health and well-being. Canada fares somewhat better, devoting considerably more of its resources to education and health. For example, Canada grants all its citizens government-funded health care. In contrast, approximately 12 percent of American children—most of them in low-income families—have no health insurance, making children the largest segment of the U.S. uninsured population (Children's Defense Fund, 2004).

The problems of children extend beyond the indicators included in the table. For example, the United States and Canada have been slow to move toward national standards and funding for child care. In both countries, affordable child care is in short supply, and much of it is substandard in quality (Goelman et al., 2000; NICHD Early Child Care Research Network, 2000). In families affected by divorce, weak enforcement of child support payments heightens poverty in mother-headed households. By the time they finish high school, many North American non-college-bound young people do not have the vocational preparation they need to contribute fully to society. And about 11 percent of U.S. and Canadian adolescents leave high school without a diploma (Bushnik, Barr-Telford, & Bussiére, 2004; U.S. Department of Education, 2004b). Most are from low-income families and have a long history of poor academic achievement, lack of interest in schoolwork, and low academic self-esteem. Dropouts who do not return to finish their education are at risk for lifelong poverty.

Why have attempts to help children and youths in the United States and (to a lesser extent) Canada been difficult to realize? A complex set of cultural, political, and economic forces is involved.

Texas third graders from low-income families attend a run-down, overcrowded, underequipped elementary school classroom. Poverty threatens all aspects of children's well-being. Along with their underprivileged home lives, unfavorable conditions at school increase these children's chances of failing academically and developing behavior problems.
© Bob Daemmrich/The Image Works

Culture and Public Policies

Each semester, I ask my students to think about the question, Who should be responsible for rearing young children? Here are some typical answers: "If parents decide to have a baby, then they should be ready to care for it." "Most people want to rear their own children and are not happy about others intruding into family life." These statements reflect a widely held opinion

---

[1]Aboriginal peoples in Canada include three groups: (1) First Nations, or Native Canadian peoples; (2) Inuit, most of whom live in northern Canada; and (3) Métis, or mixed-blood people of both Native Canadian and European descent.

TABLE 1.5   HOW DO THE UNITED STATES AND CANADA COMPARE TO OTHER NATIONS ON INDICATORS OF CHILDREN'S HEALTH AND WELL-BEING?

Indicator	U.S. Rank[a]	Canadian Rank[a]	Some Countries the United States and Canada Trail
Childhood poverty[b] (among 23 industrialized nations considered)	19th	19th	Australia, Czech Republic, Germany, Norway, Sweden, Spain
Infant deaths in the first year of life (worldwide)	26th	16th	Hong Kong, Ireland, Singapore, Spain
Teenage pregnancy rate (among 28 industrialized nations considered)	28th	21st	*For Canada:* Australia, Czech Republic, Denmark, Poland, Netherlands *For the U.S.:* Iceland, Portugal, Hungary, Slovak Republic
Public expenditures on education as a percentage of gross domestic product (among 22 industrialized nations considered)	10th	6th	*For Canada:* Israel, Sweden *For the U.S.:* Australia, France, New Zealand, Sweden
Public expenditures on health as a percentage of gross domestic product[c] (among 22 industrialized nations considered)	16th	4th	*For Canada:* France, Iceland, Switzerland *For the U.S.:* Austria, Australia, Hungary, New Zealand

[a]1 = highest, or best, rank

[b]The U.S. and Canadian childhood poverty rates of 16 percent greatly exceed those of any of these nations. For example, the rate is 12 percent in Australia, 6 percent in the Czech Republic, 4 percent in Norway, and 2.5 percent in Sweden.

[c]Gross domestic product is the value of all goods and services produced by a nation during a specified time period. It provides an overall measure of a nation's wealth.

Sources: Perie et al., 2000; United Nations Children's Fund, 2000, 2001; U.S. Census Bureau, 2004a; U.S. Department of Education, 2004a.

in North America—that the care and rearing of young children, and paying for that care, are the duty of parents, and only parents. This view has a long history—one in which independence, self-reliance, and the privacy of family life emerged as central North American values (Halfon & McLearn, 2002). It is one reason that the public has been slow to endorse government-supported benefits for all families, such as high-quality child care. And it has also contributed to the large number of American and Canadian children who remain poor, despite the fact that their parents are gainfully employed (Pohl, 2002; Zigler & Hall, 2000).

Consider our discussion so far, and you will see that it reflects cultural variation in values that strongly influence public policies: the extent to which *individualism* versus *collectivism* prevails. In **individualistic societies,** people think of themselves as separate entities and are largely concerned with their own personal needs. In **collectivist societies,** people define themselves as part of a group and stress group goals over individual goals (Triandis, 1995). Although individualism tends to increase as cultures become more complex, cross-national differences remain. The United States is strongly individualistic, and Canada falls in between the United States and most Western European nations, which lean toward collectivism.

Furthermore, less consensus exists among North American than among European citizens on issues of child and family policy, resulting in fewer and more limited programs—ones that target only the most economically disadvantaged and leave many needy children unserved (Ripple & Zigler, 2003). And good social programs are expensive; they must compete for a fair share of a country's economic resources. Children can easily remain unrecognized because they cannot vote or speak out to protect their own interests, as adult citizens do (Zigler & Finn-Stevenson, 1999). Instead, they must rely on the goodwill of others to make them an important government priority.

Without vigilance from child advocates, policies directed at solving one social problem can work at cross-purposes with children's well-being, leaving them in dire straits or worsening their condition. Consider, for example, welfare reforms aimed at returning welfare recipients to the work force. As the Social Issues box on the following page makes clear, these policies can help or harm children, depending on whether they lift a family out of poverty.

SOCIAL ISSUES

Welfare Reform, Poverty, and Child Development

In the mid-1990s, the United States and Canada recast their welfare policies, putting in place welfare-to-work programs that ended decades of guaranteed government financial aid to needy families. In these new systems, recipients must go to work or face reduced or terminated benefits. The goal is to encourage welfare families to become self-sufficient. The U.S. program is strictly time limited. A family can be on welfare for only 24 continuous months, with a lifetime limit of 60 months, and the states can further restrict these benefits. For example, a state can prevent payments from increasing if recipients have more children, and it can deny teenage single mothers any benefits. Canadian welfare policies, while strongly employment focused, are not as stringent. In Ontario, for example, welfare recipients must actively look for a job, engage in community volunteer work while acquiring work skills, and take any paid work offered that they are physically capable of performing. If these criteria are not met, eligibility for welfare ends. However, unlike the U.S. policy, a family's benefits increase if family size increases while the family is on welfare. Nevertheless, several provinces have reduced these payments (National Forum on Welfare to Work, 2004).

Until recently, most government-sponored evaluations of welfare-to-work focused on declines in the number of families on the welfare rolls. By these standards, welfare-to-work seemed to be a resounding success. But as researchers looked more closely, they found that in the years after welfare reform, some people made successful transitions to financial independence—typically, those who had more schooling and fewer mental health problems. Others, however, had difficulty meeting work requirements, lost their benefits, and fell deeper into poverty. Consequently, as welfare caseloads declined, the incomes of the poorest single-mother families dropped sharply (Lindsey & Martin, 2003; Primus et al., 1999).

Designers of welfare-to-work assumed that it would have positive benefits for children. But moving off welfare without increasing family income poses serious risks to child development. In one study, mothers who left welfare and also left poverty engaged in more positive parenting and had preschoolers who showed more favorable cognitive development, compared with working mothers whose incomes remained below the poverty threshold. Among these mothers, harsh, coercive parenting remained high (Smith et al., 2001). In additional research, families who moved from welfare to a combination of welfare and work experienced a greater reduction in young children's behavior problems than families who moved to total reliance on work (Dunifon, Kalil, & Danziger, 2003; Gennetian & Morris, 2003). Why was the welfare–work combination so beneficial? Most welfare recipients must take unstable jobs with erratic work hours and minimal or no benefits. Working while retaining some welfare support probably gave mothers an added sense of economic stability. In the United States, it also sustained government-provided health insurance (Medicaid), a major source of American parents' worry about leaving welfare (Kalil, Schweingruber, & Seefeldt, 2001). The resulting lessening of financial anxiety seemed to enhance children's adjustment.

In sum, welfare reform promotes children's development only when it results in a more adequate standard of living. Punitive aspects of welfare-to-work that reduce or cut off benefits push families deeper into poverty, with destructive consequences for children's well-being. Because of a shortage of affordable child care, mothers on welfare who have infants and preschoolers are least able to earn enough by working. Yet poverty is most harmful to development when it occurs early in life (see page 33).

Welfare policies in other Western nations do not just encourage parents to be better providers. They also protect children from

▲ This mother, who works as a nurse's aide at a Missouri children's hospital, earns barely more than minimum wage. She depends on supplemental welfare benefits to make ends meet. If the state of Missouri slashes those benefits, her capacity to engage in effective parenting and her two daughters' development are likely to suffer.
AP/ Wide World Photos

the damaging effects of poverty. France, for example, guarantees most of its citizens a modest minimum income. Single parents receive an extra amount during their child's first 3 years—a benefit that acknowledges a special need for income support during this period. Government-funded, high-quality child care begins at age 3, enabling mothers to go to work knowing that their children's development is supported (Duncan & Brooks-Gunn, 2000).

Canada offers working parents more generous tax refunds than are available in the United States. Still, widespread poverty in both nations underscores the need for more effective poverty prevention policies—ones that help poor families rear children while they transition to financial independence.

Contributions of Child Development Research

As the evidence in the Social Issues box suggests, for a policy to be effective in meeting children's needs, research must guide it at every step—during design, implementation, and evaluation of the program. Events of the 1960s and 1970s initiated the current trend toward greater involvement of child development researchers in the policy process (Zigler & Finn-Stevenson, 1999).

For example, in 1965, research on the importance of early experiences for children's intellectual development played a major role in the founding of Project Head Start, the largest educational and family-services intervention program for poverty-stricken preschool children in the United States. In Chapter 8, we will see that several decades of research on the long-term benefits of Head Start helped the program survive, contributed to recent increased government support, and inspired the Aboriginal Head Start Program in Canada. In another instance, findings on the severe impact of malnutrition on early brain development stimulated government-sponsored supplemental food programs. Since the 1970s, the U.S. Special Supplemental Food Program for Women, Infants, and Children (WIC) and the Canadian Prenatal Nutrition Program (CPNP) have supplied poverty-stricken women and their young children with food packages, nutrition education, breastfeeding support, and referral to health and social services.

As researchers examined the impact of child and family services, they saw how settings remote from children's daily lives affect their well-being. As a result, investigators broadened their focus to include wider social contexts, such as workplace, community, mass media, and government. They also addressed the impact of societal changes on children, including high rates of poverty, divorce, family violence, teenage parenthood, and maternal employment. All these efforts have helped to refine existing policies, inspire new initiatives, and expand our understanding of child development. The field of child development now recognizes that sound public policy is among the most powerful tools for preventing developmental problems and enhancing children's quality of life.

Looking Toward the Future

Policies aimed at fostering children's development can be justified on two grounds. The first is that children are the future—the parents, workers, and citizens of tomorrow. Investing in children yields valuable returns to a nation's economy and quality of life. In contrast, failure to invest in children results in "economic insufficiency, loss of productivity, shortages in needed skills, high health care costs, growing prison costs, and a nation that will be less safe, less caring, and less free" (Heckman & Masterov, 2004; Hernandez, 1994, p. 20).

Second, child-oriented policies can be defended on humanitarian grounds—children's basic rights as human beings. In 1989, the United Nations General Assembly, with the assistance of experts from many child-related fields, drew up the *Convention on the Rights of the Child,* a legal agreement among nations that commits each cooperating country to work toward guaranteeing environments that foster children's development, protect them from harm, and enhance their community participation and self-determination. Examples of rights include the highest attainable standard of health; an adequate standard of living; free and compulsory education; a happy, understanding, and loving family life; protection from all forms of abuse and neglect; and freedom of thought, conscience, and religion, subject to appropriate parental guidance and national law. Canada's Parliament ratified the Convention in 1991, shortly after the United Nations completed it. Although the United States played a key role in drawing up the Convention, it is one of only two countries in the world whose legislature has not yet ratified it. (The other nation is Somalia, which currently does not have a recognized national government.) American individualism has stood in the

⊚ The Children's Defense Fund is the most vigorous interest group working for the well-being of children in the United States. It released this poster expressing outrage that millions of American children, most living in poverty or near-poverty, have no health insurance, making children the largest segment of the U.S. uninsured population.

Permission granted by the Children's Defense Fund

way. Opponents of the Convention maintain that its provisions would shift the burden of child rearing from the family to the state (Woodhouse, 2001).

Despite the worrisome condition of many children and families, efforts are being made to improve their condition. Throughout this book, we will discuss many successful programs that could be expanded. Also, growing awareness of the gap between what we know and what we do to better children's lives has led experts in child development to join with concerned citizens as advocates for more effective policies. As a result, several influential interest groups devoted to the well-being of children have emerged.

In the United States, the most vigorous of these groups is the Children's Defense Fund. This private, nonprofit organization founded by Marian Wright Edelman in 1973 engages in research, public education, legal action, drafting of legislation, congressional testimony, and community organizing. Each year, it publishes *The State of America's Children,* which provides a comprehensive analysis of children's condition, including government-sponsored programs that serve children and families and proposals for improving those programs. To learn more about the Children's Defense Fund, visit its website at *www.childrensdefense.org*

In 1991, Canada initiated a public education movement, called Campaign 2000, to build nationwide awareness of the extent and consequences of child poverty and to lobby government representatives for improved policies benefiting children. Diverse organizations—including professional, religious, health, and labor groups at national, provincial, and community levels—have joined forces to work toward campaign goals. These include raising basic living standards so no child lives in poverty, ensuring each child affordable, appropriate housing, and strengthening child care and other community resources that assist families in rearing children. Consult *www.campaign2000.ca* to explore the work of Campaign 2000, including its annual *Report Card on Child Poverty in Canada.*

Finally, more researchers are collaborating with community and government agencies to enhance the social relevance of their investigations. They are also doing a better job of disseminating their findings to the public, through television documentaries, newspaper stories, magazine articles, websites, and direct reports to government officials. As a result, they are helping to create the sense of immediacy about the condition of children and families that is necessary to spur a society into action.

Ⓢ Campaign 2000 is Canada's public education movement aimed at building national awareness of the extent of child poverty and the need to improve policies benefiting children. This Campaign 2000 poster calls for strengthening a diverse array of community resources that assist families in rearing children.
Courtesy of Campaign 2000

Ask Yourself

REVIEW	Explain why both strong advocacy and policy-relevant research are vital for designing and implementing public policies that meet children's needs.
APPLY	Check your local newspaper or one or two national news magazines to see how often articles on the condition of children and families appear. Why is it important for researchers to communicate with the general public about children's needs?
CONNECT	Give an example of how cultural values and economic decisions affect child-oriented public policies. What level of Bronfenbrenner's ecological systems theory contains these influences?
REFLECT	Do you agree with the widespread North American sentiment that government should not intrude in family life? Explain.

Summary

The Field of Child Development

What is the field of child development, and what factors stimulated expansion of the field?

Child development is an interdisciplinary field devoted to the study of human constancy and change from conception through adolescence. It is part of a larger discipline known as **developmental psychology,** or **human development,** which includes the entire lifespan. Child development research has been stimulated by both scientific curiosity and social pressures to better the lives of children.

How is child development typically divided into manageable domains and periods?

Child development often is divided into three domains: (1) physical development, (2) cognitive development, and (3) emotional and social development. These domains are not really distinct; they form an integrated whole.

Researchers generally segment child development into five periods, each of which brings with it new capacities and social expectations that serve as important transitions in major theories: (1) the prenatal period, (2) infancy and toddlerhood, (3) early childhood, (4) middle childhood, and (5) adolescence. Many contemporary youths experience an additional period of development called emerging adulthood, in which they engage in further exploration prior to assuming adult roles.

Basic Issues

Identify three basic issues on which child development theories take a stand.

Almost all child development **theories** take a stand on the following controversial issues: (1) Is development a **continuous** process, or does it follow a series of **discontinuous stages**? (2) Does one general course of development characterize all children, or do many possible courses exist, depending on the **contexts** in which children grow up? (3) Is development primarily influenced by **nature** or **nurture,** and is it stable or open to change?

More recent theories take a balanced stand on these issues. And contemporary researchers realize that answers may vary across domains of development and even, as research on **resilience** illustrates, across individuals.

Historical Foundations

Describe major historical influences on current theories of child development.

Contemporary theories of child development have roots extending far into the past. As early as medieval times, childhood was regarded as a separate phase of life. In the sixteenth and seventeenth centuries, the Puritan conception of original sin led to a harsh philosophy of child rearing.

The Enlightenment brought new ideas favoring more humane treatment of children. Locke's notion of the **tabula rasa** provided the philosophical basis for twentieth-century behaviorism, and Rousseau's idea of the **noble savage** foreshadowed the concepts of stage and **maturation.** A century later, Darwin's theory emphasized the adaptive value of physical characteristics and behavior and stimulated scientific child study.

Efforts to observe children directly began in the late nineteenth and early twentieth centuries with baby biographies. Soon after, Hall and Gesell introduced the **normative approach,** which produced a large body of descriptive facts about children. Binet and Simon constructed the first successful intelligence test, which sparked interest in individual differences in development and led to a heated controversy over nature versus nurture. Baldwin's theory was ahead of its time in granting nature and nurture equal importance and regarding children and their social surroundings as mutually influential.

Mid-Twentieth-Century Theories

What theories influenced the study of child development in the mid-twentieth century?

In the 1930s and 1940s, psychiatrists and social workers turned to the **psychoanalytic perspective** for help in treating children's emotional and behavior problems. In Freud's **psychosexual theory,** children move through five stages, during which three parts of the personality—id, ego, and superego—become integrated. Erikson's **psychosocial theory** builds on Freud's theory by emphasizing the ego as a positive force in development, the development of culturally relevant attitudes and skills, and the lifespan nature of development.

As the psychoanalytic perspective gained in prominence, **behaviorism** and **social learning theory** emerged, emphasizing principles of conditioning and modeling and practical procedures of **behavior modification** to eliminate undesirable behaviors and increase desirable responses. But behaviorism and social learning theory have been criticized for offering too narrow a view of important environmental influences and disregarding children's contributions to their own development.

Piaget's **cognitive-developmental theory** emphasizes that children actively construct knowledge as they manipulate and explore their world. According to Piaget, children move through four stages, beginning with the baby's sensorimotor action patterns and ending with the elaborate, abstract reasoning system of the adolescent and adult. Piaget's theory has stimulated a wealth of research on children's thinking and encouraged educational programs that emphasize discovery learning. Nevertheless, his stagewise view of development has been challenged for underestimating the competencies of young children and for paying insufficient attention to social and cultural influences.

© PETE BYRON/PHOTOEDIT

Recent Theoretical Perspectives

Describe recent theoretical perspectives on child development.

Information processing views the mind as a complex, symbol-manipulating system, much like a computer. This approach helps researchers achieve a detailed understanding of what children of different ages do when faced with tasks and problems. Information processing has led to teaching interventions that help children approach tasks in more advanced ways. As yet, however, it has not generated a comprehensive theory of development.

Four perspectives emphasize contexts for development. **Ethology** stresses the evolutionary origins and adaptive value of behavior and inspired the **sensitive period** concept. In **evolutionary developmental psychology,** researchers have extended this emphasis, seeking to understand the adaptiveness of species-wide competencies as they change over time.

© STEVEN RUBIN/THE IMAGE WORKS

Vygotsky's **sociocultural theory** has enhanced our understanding of cultural influences, especially in the domain of cognitive development. Through cooperative dialogues with more knowledgeable members of society, children come to use language to guide their own thought and actions and acquire culturally relevant knowledge and skills. But Vygotsky's emphasis on culture and social experience led him to neglect the biological side of development.

In **ecological systems theory,** nested layers of the environment—**microsystem, mesosystem, exosystem,** and **macrosystem**—are seen as major influences on children's well-being. The **chronosystem** represents the dynamic, ever-changing nature of children and their experiences.

Inspired by ideas in other sciences and recent perspectives in child development, a new wave of theorists has adopted a **dynamic systems perspective** to account for wide variation in development. According to this view, the mind, body, and physical and social worlds form an integrated system that guides mastery of new skills. A change in any part of the system prompts the child to reorganize her behavior so the various components work together again, but in a more complex, effective way.

Comparing Child Development Theories

Identify the stand taken by each major theory on the basic issues of child development.

Theories that are major forces in child development research vary in their focus on different domains of development, in their view of development, and in their strengths and limitations. (For a full summary, see Table 1.4 on page 32.)

AP/ WIDE WORLD PHOTOS

Applied Directions: Child Development and Social Policy

Explain the importance of social policies for safeguarding children's well-being, and cite factors that affect the policy-making process, noting the role of child development research.

The field of child development has become increasingly concerned with applying its vast knowledge base to solving pressing social problems. When widespread problems arise, nations attempt to solve them through a special type of **social policy** called **public policy.** Favorable laws and government programs are essential for safeguarding children's well-being. American and (to a lesser extent) Canadian public policies favoring children and youths have lagged behind policies in other developed nations.

Many factors influence supportive public policies, including cultural values that stress **collectivism** over **individualism,** a nation's economic resources, and organizations and individuals that advocate for children's needs. Policy-relevant research helps refine existing policies, forge new policy directions, and expand our understanding of child development.

Important Terms and Concepts

behavior modification (p. 20)
behaviorism (p. 19)
child development (p. 4)
chronosystem (p. 29)
cognitive-developmental theory (p. 21)
collectivist society (p. 34)
contexts (p. 8)
continuous development (p. 7)
developmental psychology (p. 4)
discontinuous development (p. 7)
dynamic systems perspective (p. 29)
ecological systems theory (p. 26)
ethology (p. 24)

evolutionary developmental psychology (p. 25)
exosystem (p. 29)
human development (p. 4)
individualistic society (p. 34)
information processing (p. 23)
macrosystem (p. 29)
maturation (p. 12)
mesosystem (p. 28)
microsystem (p. 27)
nature–nurture controversy (p. 8)
noble savage (p. 12)
normative approach (p. 14)

psychoanalytic perspective (p. 16)
psychosexual theory (p. 16)
psychosocial theory (p. 18)
public policy (p. 31)
resilience (p. 10)
sensitive period (p. 24)
social learning theory (p. 20)
social policy (p. 31)
sociocultural theory (p. 25)
stage (p. 8)
tabula rasa (p. 12)
theory (p. 6)

"Cocoon"
Duval-Rohee Julien
Age 9, France.

The small face looks out from within the protective layers of a cocoon—an apt image for the care and security that children need to develop. Research strategies provide insights into the conditions that enable children to thrive—how best to protect, nourish, and encourage them as they grow.

Research Strategies

One afternoon, my colleague Ron crossed the street between his academic department and our laboratory school, the expression on his face reflecting a deep sense of apprehension. After weeks of planning, Ron was ready to launch his study on the development of children's peer relations. Thinking back to his own school years, he recalled the anguish of several classmates, who were repeatedly taunted and shunned by peers. Ron wanted to help rejected children, many of whom go on to lead troubled lives. In view of the importance of his research, Ron was puzzled by a request from the school's research committee that he appear before them.

At the meeting, Ron met with teachers and administrators charged with evaluating research proposals for their ethical integrity. A third-grade teacher spoke up:

"Ron, I see the value of your work, but frankly, I'm concerned about your asking my students to indicate which classmates they like most and which they like least. I've got a couple of kids who are soundly disliked, and I'm doing my best to keep the lid on the situation. There's also an immigrant West Indian child who's new to my classroom, and she's being ostracized because of the way she dresses and speaks. If you come in and start sensitizing my class to whom they like and dislike, the children are going to share these opinions. Unfortunately, I think your study is likely to promote conflict and negative interaction!"

Imagine Ron's dismay at hearing someone suggest that he might have to abandon his research. This chapter takes a close look at the research process—the many challenges investigators face as they plan and implement studies of children. Ron had already traveled a long and arduous path before he arrived at the door of the laboratory school, prepared to collect his data. First, he had spent many weeks developing a researchable idea, based on theory and prior knowledge of children's peer relations. Next, he had chosen an appropriate research strategy, which involved two main tasks. First, he had selected from a variety of *research methods*—the specific activities of participants, such as taking tests, answering questionnaires, responding to interviews, or being observed. Second, he had decided on a *research design*—an overall plan for his study that would permit the best test of his research idea. Finally, Ron had scrutinized his procedures for any possible harm they might cause to participants.

Still, as Ron approached a committee charged with protecting the welfare of research participants, he faced an ethical dilemma. Research, whether on animals or humans, must meet certain standards that protect participants from stressful treatment. Because of children's immaturity and vulnerability, extra precautions must be taken to ensure that their rights are not violated. In the final section of this chapter, you will find out how Ron resolved the committee's earnest challenge to the ethical integrity of his research.

From Theory to Hypothesis

In Chapter 1, we saw how theories structure the research process by identifying important research concerns and, occasionally, preferred methods for collecting data. We also discussed how theories guide the application of findings to real-life circumstances and practices with children. In fact, research usually begins with a prediction drawn from a theory, called a **hypothesis.** Think back to the various child development theories presented in Chapter 1. Many hypotheses can be drawn from any one of them that, once tested, would reflect on the accuracy of the theory.

Sometimes research pits a hypothesis taken from one theory against a hypothesis taken from another. For example, a theorist emphasizing the role of maturation in development would predict that adult encouragement will have little effect on the age at which children utter their first words, learn to count, or tie their shoes. A sociocultural theorist, in contrast, would speculate that these skills can be promoted through adult teaching.

At other times, research tests predictions drawn from a single theory. For example, ecological systems theory suggests that providing isolated, divorced mothers with social supports will lead them to be more patient with their children. An ethologist might hypothesize that an infant's cry will stimulate strong physiological arousal in adults who hear it, motivating them to soothe and protect a suffering baby.

Occasionally, little or no theory exists on a topic of interest. In these instances, the investigator may start with a *research question,* such as, Have recent world events—the U.S war on Iraq and a global rise in terrorism—heightened children's fears and anxieties? Which teenagers are heavy users of Internet communication—e-mail, instant messaging, and chat rooms? Are they sociable young people with many friends, or lonely individuals with few in-person social supports? Hypotheses and research questions offer investigators vital guidance as they settle on research methods and research designs.

At this point, you may be wondering, Why learn about research strategies? Why not leave these matters to research specialists and concentrate on what is already known about the child and how that knowledge can be applied? There are two reasons. First, each of us must be a wise and critical consumer of knowledge. Knowing the strengths and limitations of various research strategies is important in separating dependable information from misleading results. Second, individuals who work directly with children may be in a unique position to build bridges between research and practice by conducting studies, either on their own or in partnership with experienced investigators. Currently, community agencies such as schools, mental health facilities, and parks and recreation programs are collaborating with researchers in designing, implementing, and evaluating interventions aimed at enhancing children's development (Lerner, Fisher, & Weinberg, 2000). To broaden these efforts, a basic understanding of the research process is essential.

Common Methods Used to Study Children

How does a researcher choose a basic approach to gathering information about children? Common methods include systematic observation, self-reports, psychophysiological measures, clinical or case studies, and ethnographies of the life circumstances of a specific group of children. As you read about these methods, you may find it helpful to refer to Table 2.1, which summarizes the strengths and limitations of each.

Systematic Observation

Observations of the behavior of children, and of the adults who are important in their lives, can be made in different ways. One approach is to go into the field, or the natural environment, and record the behavior of interest, a method called **naturalistic observation.**

A study of preschoolers' responses to their peers' distress provides a good example of this technique (Farver & Branstetter, 1994). Observing 3- and 4-year-olds in child-care centers, the researchers recorded each instance of crying and the reactions of nearby children—whether

TABLE 2.1   STRENGTHS AND LIMITATIONS OF COMMON INFORMATION-GATHERING METHODS

Method	Description	Strengths	Limitations
Systematic Observation			
Naturalistic observation	Observation of behavior in natural contexts	Reflects participants' everyday behaviors.	Cannot control conditions under which participants are observed. Accuracy of observations may be reduced by observer influence and observer bias.
Structured observation	Observation of behavior in a laboratory, where conditions are the same for all participants	Grants each participant an equal opportunity to display the behavior of interest. Permits study of behaviors rarely seen in everyday life.	May not yield observations typical of participants' behavior in everyday life. Accuracy of observations may be reduced by observer influence and observer bias.
Self-Reports			
Clinical interview	Flexible interviewing procedure in which the investigator obtains a complete account of the participant's thoughts	Comes as close as possible to the way participants think in everyday life. Great breadth and depth of information can be obtained in a short time.	May not result in accurate reporting of information. Flexible procedure makes comparing individuals' responses difficult.
Structured interview, questionnaires, and tests	Self-report instruments in which each participant is asked the same questions in the same way	Permits comparisons of participants' responses and efficient data collection. Researchers can specify answer alternatives that participants might not think of in an open-ended interview.	Does not yield the same depth of information as a clinical interview. Responses are still subject to inaccurate reporting.
Psychophysiological Methods	Methods that measure the relationship between physiological processes and behavior	Reveals which central nervous system structures contribute to development and individual differences in certain competencies. Helps infer the perceptions, thoughts, and emotions of infants and young children, who cannot report them clearly.	Cannot reveal with certainty the meaning of autonomic or brain activity. Many factors besides those of interest to the researcher can influence a physiological response.
Clinical, or Case Study, Method	A full picture of one individual's psychological functioning, obtained by combining interviews, observations, test scores, and sometimes psychophysiological assessments	Provides rich, descriptive insights into factors that affect development.	May be biased by researchers' theoretical preferences. Findings cannot be applied to individuals other than the participant.
Ethnography	Participant observation of a culture or distinct social group; by making extensive field notes, the researcher tries to capture the culture's unique values and social processes	Provides a more complete description than can be derived from a single observational visit, interview, or questionnaire.	May be biased by researchers' values and theoretical preferences. Findings cannot be applied to individuals and settings other than the ones studied.

they ignored, watched, or commented on the child's unhappiness; scolded or teased; or shared, helped, or expressed sympathy. Caregiver behaviors, such as explaining why a child was crying, mediating conflict, or offering comfort, were noted to see if adult sensitivity was related to children's caring responses. A strong relationship emerged. The great strength of naturalistic observation is that investigators can see directly the everyday behaviors they hope to explain.

⊚ In naturalistic observation, the researcher goes into the field and records the behavior of interest. This researcher, who is observing children at a summer camp, might be focusing on their playmate choices, cooperation, helpfulness, or conflicts. A limitation of this method is that some children may have more opportunities than others to display certain behaviors in everyday life.
© Bob Daemmrich/The Image Works

Naturalistic observation also has a major limitation: Not all children have the same opportunity to display a particular behavior in everyday life. In the study just mentioned, some children might have witnessed a child crying more often than others or been exposed to more cues for positive social responses from caregivers. For this reason, they might have displayed more compassion.

Researchers commonly deal with this difficulty by making **structured observations,** in which the investigator sets up a laboratory situation that evokes the behavior of interest so that every participant has an equal opportunity to display the response. In one study, 2-year-olds' emotional reactions to harm that they thought they had caused were observed by asking them to take care of a rag doll that had been modified so its leg would fall off when the child picked it up. To make the child feel at fault, once the leg detached, an adult "talked for" the doll by saying, "Ow!" Researchers recorded children's facial expressions of sadness and concern for the injured doll, efforts to help the doll, and body tension—responses that indicated remorse and a desire to make amends for the mishap. In addition, mothers were asked to engage in brief conversations about emotions with their children (Garner, 2003). Mothers who more often explained the causes and consequences of emotions had toddlers who expressed more concern for the injured doll.

Structured observation permits greater control over the research situation than does naturalistic observation. In addition, the method is especially useful for studying behaviors—such as parent–child and friendship interactions—that investigators rarely have an opportunity to see in everyday life. For example, to compare friendship quality of aggressive and nonaggressive children, researchers had nearly one hundred 10-year-old boys come with their best friend to a laboratory, where the pairs played a board game and jointly solved scrambled-word puzzles. Aggressive boys and their friends were more likely to violate game rules, to cheat while working on the puzzles by looking at an answer key, and to encourage each other to engage in these dishonest acts. In addition, observers rated these boys' interactions as less emotionally positive, more intensely angry, and less reciprocal than the interactions of nonaggressive boys and their friends (Bagwell & Coie, 2004). The researchers concluded that instead of being warm and supportive, aggressive boys' close peer ties provide a context in which they practice hostility and other negative behaviors, which may contribute to increased antisocial behavior.

In this study, antisocial boys' laboratory interactions were probably similar to their natural behaviors. The boys acted negatively even though they knew they were being observed. Of course, the great disadvantage of structured observations is that most of the time, we cannot be certain that participants behave in the laboratory as they do in their natural environments.

• COLLECTING SYSTEMATIC OBSERVATIONS • The procedures used to collect systematic observations vary, depending on the research problem posed. Occasionally investigators choose to record the entire stream of behavior—everything the participant says and does. In one of my own studies, I wanted to find out how sensitive, responsive, and verbally stimulating caregivers were when they interacted with children in child-care centers (Berk, 1985). In this case, everything each caregiver said and did—even the amount of time she spent away from the children, taking coffee breaks and talking on the phone—was important.

In other studies, information on only one or a few kinds of behavior is needed, permitting more efficient procedures. In these instances, a common approach is **event sampling,** in which the observer records all instances of a particular behavior during a specified time period. In the study of preschoolers' responses to their peers' distress reported earlier, the researchers used event sampling by recording each instance in which a child cried, followed by other children's reactions.

Another way to observe efficiently is **time sampling.** In this procedure, the researcher records whether certain behaviors occur during a sample of short intervals. First, a checklist of the target behaviors is prepared. Then the observation period is divided into a series of brief time segments. For example, a half-hour observation period might be divided into 120 fifteen-second intervals. The observer watches the target person and checks off behaviors during each interval, repeating this process until the observation period is complete. Recently, my collaborators and I used time sampling to find out how parents and children spent time while visiting a community children's museum. Our observers followed more than one hundred parent–child pairs for 10 minutes each, checking off parent and child behaviors during 20 thirty-second intervals. Findings revealed that, on average, parents and children were jointly engaged in the museum's exhibits during 45 percent of the intervals. And during an additional 30 percent, parents remained nearby, closely observing their children's activities (Mann, Braswell, & Berk, 2005). The museum afforded parents many opportunities to interact with and learn about their child.

Researchers have devised ingenious ways of observing children's difficult-to-capture behaviors. For example, to record instances of bullying, a group of investigators set up video cameras overlooking a classroom and a playground and had fourth to sixth graders wear small, remote microphones and pocket-sized transmitters (Craig, Pepler, & Atlas, 2000). Results revealed that bullying occurred often—at rates of 2.4 episodes per hour in the classroom and 4.5 episodes per hour on the playground. Yet only 15 to 18 percent of the time did teachers take steps to stop the harassment. We will return to the topic of bullying in Chapter 15.

• **LIMITATIONS OF SYSTEMATIC OBSERVATION** • A major problem with systematic observation is **observer influence**—the effects of the observer on the behavior studied. The presence of a watchful, unfamiliar individual may cause children and adults to react in unnatural ways. For children under age 7 or 8, observer influence is generally limited to the first session or two. Young children cannot stop "being themselves" for long, and they quickly get used to the observer's presence. Older children and adults often engage in more socially desirable behavior when they know that they are being observed. In these instances, researchers can take participants' responses as an indication of the best behavior they can display under the circumstances.

Researchers can minimize observer influence. Adaptation periods, in which observers visit the research setting so participants can get used to their presence, are helpful. Another approach is to ask individuals who are part of the child's natural environment to do the observing. For example, in several studies, parents have been trained to record their children's behavior. Besides reducing the impact of an unfamiliar observer, this method limits the amount of time needed to gather observations, as some information can take a long time to obtain. In one such study, researchers wanted to know how preschool and young school-age children's TV watching affected their other home activities (Huston et al., 1999). To find out, every other month they telephoned parents for a detailed report of children's time use during the previous 24 hours. Findings indicated that the more children watched entertainment TV (cartoons and general-audience programs), the less time they spent reading, doing educational activities (such as art, music, and puzzles), and interacting with adults and peers.

In addition to observer influence, **observer bias** is a serious danger. When observers are aware of the purposes of a study, they may see and record what is expected rather than what participants actually do. Therefore, people who have no knowledge of the investigator's hypotheses—or who at least have little personal investment in them—are best suited to collect the observations.

Finally, although systematic observation provides invaluable information on how children and adults behave, it conveys little about the thinking that underlies behavior. For this kind of information, researchers must turn to self-report techniques.

Self-Reports: Interviews and Questionnaires

Self-reports ask research participants to provide information on their perceptions, thoughts, abilities, feelings, attitudes, beliefs, and past experiences. They range from relatively unstructured clinical interviews, the method used by Piaget to study children's thinking, to highly structured interviews, questionnaires, and tests.

Ⓖ Using the clinical interview, this researcher asks a mother to describe her child's development. The method permits large amounts of information to be gathered in a relatively short period. However, a major drawback is that participants do not always report information accurately.

© Tony Freeman/PhotoEdit

• **CLINICAL INTERVIEWS** • In a **clinical interview,** a flexible, conversational style is used to probe for the participant's point of view. Consider the following example, in which Piaget questioned a 3-year-old child about his understanding of dreams:

> *Where does the dream come from?*—I think you sleep so well that you dream.—*Does it come from us or from outside?*—From outside.—*When you are in bed and you dream, where is the dream?*—In my bed, under the blanket. I don't really know. If it was in my stomach, the bones would be in the way and I shouldn't see it.—*Is the dream there when you sleep?*—Yes, it is in the bed beside me. (Piaget, 1926/1930, pp. 97–98)

Notice how Piaget used a flexible, conversational style to encourage the child to expand his ideas. Although a researcher interviewing more than one child would typically ask the same first question to ensure a common task, individualized prompts provide a fuller picture of each child's reasoning (Ginsburg, 1997).

The clinical interview has two major strengths. First, it permits people to display their thoughts in terms that are as close as possible to the way they think in everyday life. Second, the clinical interview can provide a large amount of information in a fairly brief period. For example, in an hour-long session, we can obtain a wide range of child-rearing information from a parent—much more than we could capture by observing parent–child interaction for the same amount of time.

• **LIMITATIONS OF CLINICAL INTERVIEWS** • A major limitation of the clinical interview has to do with the accuracy with which people report their thoughts, feelings, and experiences. Some participants, desiring to please the interviewer, may make up answers that do not represent their actual thinking. And because the clinical interview depends on verbal ability and expressiveness, it may underestimate the capacities of individuals who have difficulty putting their thoughts into words. Skillful interviewers minimize these problems by wording questions carefully. They also watch for cues indicating that the participant may not have clearly understood a question or may need extra time to feel comfortable in the interview situation.

Interviews on certain topics are particularly vulnerable to distortion. In a few instances, researchers have been able to compare parents' and children's descriptions of events with information gathered years earlier, at the same time the events occurred. Reports of psychological states and family processes obtained on the two occasions showed little or no agreement (Henry et al., 1994). Parents often recall their child's development in glowing terms, reporting faster progress, fewer childhood problems, and child-rearing practices more in line with current expert advice than with records of behavior (Yarrow, Campbell, & Burton, 1970). Interviews that focus on current rather than past information and on specific characteristics rather than global judgments show a better match with observations and other sources of information. Even so, parents are far from perfect in describing their practices and their children's personalities, preferences, and cognitive abilities (Miller & Davis, 1992; Rothbart & Bates, 1998; Waschbusch, Daleiden, & Drabman, 2000).

Finally, as mentioned in Chapter 1, the clinical interview has been criticized because of its flexibility. When participants are asked different questions, their varied responses may be due to the manner of interviewing rather than to real differences in the way people think about a topic. A second self-report method, the structured interview, reduces this problem.

• **STRUCTURED INTERVIEWS, TESTS, AND QUESTIONNAIRES** • In a **structured interview,** each individual is asked the same set of questions in the same way. This approach eliminates the possibility that an interviewer might press and prompt some participants more than others. In addition, structured interviews are much more efficient than clinical interviews.

Answers are briefer, and researchers can obtain written responses from an entire class of children or group of parents at the same time Also, by listing answer alternatives, researchers can specify the activities and behaviors they are interested in—ones that participants might not think of in an open-ended clinical interview. For example, when parents were asked what they considered "the most important thing for children to prepare them for life," 62 percent checked "to think for themselves" when this alternative appeared on a list. Yet only 5 percent thought of it during a clinical interview (Schwarz, 1999).

Nevertheless, structured interviews do not yield the same depth of information as a clinical interview. And they can still be affected by the problem of inaccurate reporting.

Psychophysiological Methods

Researchers' desire to uncover the biological bases of perceptual, cognitive, and emotional responses has led to the use of **psychophysiological methods,** which measure the relationship between physiological processes and behavior. Investigators who rely on these methods want to find out which central nervous system structures contribute to development and individual differences. Psychophysiological methods also help investigators infer the perceptions, thoughts, and emotions of infants and young children, who cannot report their psychological experiences clearly.

Involuntary activities of the autonomic nervous system[1]—changes in heart rate, blood pressure, respiration, pupil dilation, electrical conductance of the skin, and stress hormone levels—are highly sensitive to psychological state. For example, heart rate can be used to infer whether an infant is staring blankly at a stimulus (heart rate is stable), processing information (heart rate slows during concentration), or experiencing distress (heart rate rises). Heart rate variations are also linked to certain emotions, such as interest, anger, and sadness (Fox & Card, 1998). And as Chapter 10 will reveal, distinct patterns of autonomic activity are related to aspects of temperament, such as shyness and sociability (Kagan & Saudino, 2001).

Autonomic indicators have also been enriched by measures of brain functioning. In an *electroencephalogram (EEG)*, researchers tape electrodes to the scalp to record the electrical activity of the brain. EEG brain waves are linked to different states of arousal, from deep sleep to alert wakefulness, permitting researchers to see how these states change with age. EEG patterns also vary with emotional states—whether children are upbeat and happy or distressed (Jones et al., 1997). At times, investigators study *event-related potentials (ERPs),* or EEG waves that accompany particular events. For example, different wave patterns appear when 3-month-olds from English-speaking homes hear passages in English, Italian, and Dutch, suggesting that the infants could discriminate the intonation patterns of the three languages and indicating the brain regions involved (Shafer, Shucard, & Jaeger, 1999).

Functional brain-imaging techniques, which yield three-dimensional pictures of brain activity, provide the most precise information on which brain regions are specialized for certain capacities. *Functional magnetic resonance imaging (fMRI)* is the most promising of these methods because it does not depend on X-ray photography, which requires injection of radioactive substances. Instead, when a child is shown a stimulus, changes in blood flow within the brain are detected magnetically, producing a computerized image of active areas. Currently, fMRI is being used to study age-related changes in brain organization and the brain functioning of children with learning and emotional problems (Gaillard et al., 2004; Pine, 2001; Thomas & Casey, 2003).

Despite their virtues, psychophysiological methods have limitations. First, interpreting physiological responses involves a high degree of inference. Even though a stimulus produces a consistent pattern of autonomic or brain activity, investigators cannot be certain that an infant or child has processed it in a certain way. Second, many factors can influence a physiological response. A researcher who takes a change in heart rate, respiration, or brain activity

---

[1]The autonomic nervous system regulates involuntary actions. It is divided into two parts: (1) the *sympathetic nervous system,* which mobilizes energy to deal with threatening situations (as when your heart rate rises in response to a fear-arousing event), and (2) the *parasympathetic nervous system,* which acts to conserve energy (as when your heart rate slows as you focus on an interesting stimulus).

 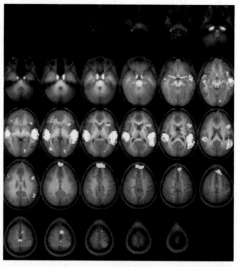

This 9-year-old, who has a reading disability, is undergoing functional magnetic resonance imaging (fMRI). Researchers peer inside his brain in an effort to learn what happens when he tries to process written information and whether certain teaching methods can help his brain "rewire" itself to read better. On the right are fMRI images of brain areas activated while the boy listened to a story.

Left: AP/Wide World Photos

Right: Scott K. Holland

as an indicator of information processing must make sure that the change was not due instead to hunger, boredom, fatigue, or body movements (Fox, Schmidt, & Henderson, 2000). Third, children often do not perform as well while lying in an fMRI scanner as they do outside the scanner. And the enclosed environment sometimes induces them to fall asleep! Finally, a child's fearful reaction to the equipment affects physiological measures. Preparing children by taking them through a simulated experience eases their apprehension (Rosenberg et al., 1997). Without such efforts, detection of correspondences between physiological and psychological reactions is difficult or impossible.

The Clinical, or Case Study, Method

An outgrowth of psychoanalytic theory, the **clinical, or case study, method** brings together a wide range of information on one child, including interviews, observations, test scores, and sometimes psychophysiological measures. The aim is to obtain as complete a picture as possible of that child's psychological functioning and the experiences that led up to it.

The clinical method is well suited to studying the development of certain types of individuals who are few in number but vary widely in characteristics. For example, the method has been used to find out what contributes to the accomplishments of *prodigies*—extremely gifted children who attain adult competence in a field before age 10 (Gardner, 1998b). Consider Adam, a boy who read, wrote, and composed musical pieces before he was out of diapers. By age 4, Adam was deeply involved in mastering human symbol systems—French, German, Russian, Sanskrit, Greek, the computer programming language BASIC, ancient hieroglyphs, music, and mathematics. Adam's parents provided a home rich in stimulation and reared him with affection, firmness, and humor. They searched for schools in which he could both develop his abilities and form rewarding social relationships. He graduated from college at age 18 and continued to pursue musical composition. Would Adam have realized his potential without the chance combination of his special gift and nurturing, committed parents? Probably not, researchers concluded (Goldsmith, 2000).

The clinical method yields richly detailed case narratives that offer valuable insights into the many factors that affect development. Nevertheless, like all other methods, it has drawbacks. Information often is collected unsystematically and subjectively, permitting too much leeway for researchers' theoretical preferences to bias their observations and interpretations. In addition, investigators cannot assume that their conclusions apply, or generalize, to anyone other than the child studied (Stanovich, 2004). Even when patterns emerge across several cases, it is wise to confirm them with other research strategies.

Methods for Studying Culture

To study the impact of culture, researchers adjust the methods just considered or tap procedures specially devised for cross-cultural and multicultural research. Which approach investigators choose depends on their research goals (Triandis, 1998).

Sometimes researchers are interested in characteristics believed to be universal but that vary in degree from one society to the next. These investigators might ask, Are parents warmer or more directive in some cultures than in others? How strong are gender stereotypes in different nations? In each instance, several cultural groups will be compared, and all participants must be questioned or observed in the same way. Therefore, researchers draw on the self-report and observational procedures we have already considered, adapting them through translation so they can be understood in each cultural context. For example, to study cultural variation in parenting practices, the same questionnaire, asking for ratings on such items as "I often hug and kiss my child" or "I scold my child when his/her behavior does not meet my expectations," is given to all participants (Wu et al., 2002).

At other times, researchers want to uncover the *cultural meanings* of children's and adults' behaviors by becoming as familiar as possible with their way of life. To achieve this goal, researchers rely on a method borrowed from the field of anthropology—**ethnography.** Like the clinical method, ethnographic research is a descriptive, qualitative technique. But instead of aiming to understand a single individual, it is directed at understanding a culture or a distinct social group through *participant observation.* Typically, the researcher spends months and sometimes years in the cultural community, participating in its daily life. Extensive field notes are made, consisting of a mix of observations, self-reports from members of the culture, and careful interpretations by the investigator (Miller, Hengst, & Wang, 2003; Shweder, 1996). Later, these notes are put together into a description of the community that tries to capture its unique values and social processes.

The ethnographic method assumes that by entering into close contact with a social group, researchers can understand the beliefs and behaviors of its members in a way not possible with an observational visit, interview, or questionnaire. In some ethnographies, investigators focus on many aspects of children's experience, as one researcher did in describing what it is like to grow up in a small town. Others focus on one or a few settings, such as home, school, or neighborhood life (LeVine et al., 1994; Peshkin, 1978, 1997; Valdés, 1998). And still others are limited to a particular practice, such as uncovering the cultural and religious influences on children's make-believe play. For example, ethnographic findings reveal that East Indian Hindu parents encourage preschoolers to communicate with "invisible" characters. They regard this activity as linked to *karma* (the cycle of birth and death) and believe that the child may be remembering a past life. In contrast, Christian fundamentalist parents often discourage children from pretending to be unreal characters. They believe that such play promotes dangerous spiritual ideas and deceitful behavior (Taylor & Carlson, 2000). Researchers may supplement traditional self-report and observational methods with ethnography if they suspect that unique meanings underlie cultural differences, as the Cultural Influences box on page 50 reveals.

Ethnographers strive to minimize their influence on the culture they are studying by becoming part of it. Nevertheless, as with clinical studies, investigators' cultural values and theoretical commitments sometimes lead them to observe selectively or misinterpret what they see. Finally, the findings of ethnographic studies cannot be assumed to generalize beyond the people and settings in which the research was originally conducted.

◎ This Western ethnographer is spending months living among the Efe people of the Republic of Congo. Here he observes a group of young children sharing food. Among the Efe, cooperation and generosity are highly valued and encouraged at an early age.
(c) Ed Tronick/ Anthro-Photo

Ask Yourself

REVIEW	Why might a researcher choose structured observation over naturalistic observation? How about the reverse? What might lead the researcher to opt for clinical interviewing over systematic observation?
REVIEW	What strengths and limitations do the clinical (or case study) method and ethnography have in common?
APPLY	A researcher wants to study the thoughts and feelings of children who have a parent serving in the military in Iraq. Which method is best suited for investigating this question?

Immigrant Youths: Amazing Adaptation

During the past quarter century, a rising tide of immigrants has come to North America, fleeing war and persecution in their homelands or otherwise seeking better life chances. Today, one-fifth of the U.S. youth population has foreign-born parents; nearly one-third of these youths are foreign born themselves. Similarly, immigrant youths are the fastest-growing segment of the Canadian population (Fuligni, 2001; Statistics Canada, 2000). They are ethnically diverse. In the United States, most come from Asia and Latin America; in Canada, from Asia, the Middle East, Africa, and Europe. Latin American immigrants to Canada, although fewer in number than other immigrant groups, are increasing rapidly. To find out how well immigrant youths are adapting to their new country, researchers draw on multiple methods, including academic testing, questionnaires assessing psychological adjustment, and in-depth ethnographic research.

Academic Achievement and Adjustment

Although educators and laypeople often assume that the transition to a new country has a negative impact on psychological well-being, recent evidence reveals that children of immigrant parents from diverse countries adapt amazingly well. Students who are first generation (foreign born) and second generation (American or Canadian born, with immigrant parents) achieve in school as well as or better than students of native-born parents (Fuligni, 1997; Rumbaut, 1997; Saucier et al., 2002). Their success is evident in many academic subjects, including language and literature, even though most speak their native language at home.

Findings on psychological adjustment resemble those on achievement. Compared with their agemates, adolescents from immigrant families are less likely to commit delinquent and violent acts, to use drugs and alcohol, or to have early sex. They are also in better health—less likely to be obese or to have missed school because of illness. And in terms of self-esteem, they feel as positively about themselves as young people with native-born parents, and they report less emotional distress. These successes do not depend on having extensive time to adjust to a new way of life. The school performance and psychological well-being of immigrant high school students who recently arrived in North America are as high as—and sometimes higher than—those of students who come at younger ages (Fuligni, 1998; Saucier et al., 2002).

The outcomes just described are strongest for Chinese, Japanese, Korean,

and East Indian youths, less dramatic for other ethnicities (Fuligni, 1997; Kao & Tienda, 1995; Louie, 2001). Variations in parental education and income account for these differences. Still, even first- and second-generation youths from ethnic groups that face considerable economic hardship (such as Mexican and Vietnamese) are remarkably successful (Fuligni & Yoshikawa, 2003). Factors other than income are responsible.

Family and Community Influences

Ethnographies provide insight into why most immigrant youths adapt well. Uniformly, immigrant parents express the belief that education is the surest way to improve life chances. Consequently, they place a high value on their children's academic achievement (Goldenberg et al., 2001; Louie, 2001). Aware of the challenges their children face, immigrant parents underscore the importance of trying hard. They remind their children that educational opportunities were not available in their native countries and, as a result, they themselves are often limited to menial jobs.

Adolescents from immigrant families internalize their parents' valuing of education, endorsing it more strongly than agemates with native-born parents (Asakawa, 2001; Fuligni, 1997). Because minority ethnicities usually stress allegiance to family and community over individual goals, first- and second-generation young people spend much time with their families and feel a strong sense of obligation to their parents. They view school success as one of the most important ways they can repay their parents for the hardships they endured in coming to a new land (Fuligni, Yip, & Tseng, 2002; Suárez-Orozco & Suárez-Orozco, 2001). Both family relationships and school achievement protect these youths from risky behaviors, such as delinquency, early pregnancy, and drug use (refer to the Biology and Environment box on resilient children on page 10 of Chapter 1).

Immigrant parents typically develop close ties to an ethnic community. It exerts additional control through a high consensus on values and constant monitoring of young people's activities. The following comments capture the power of these family and community forces:

A New York City cab driver from Ghana, father of a three teenage boys who later enrolled at prestigious universities: I make sure I know my children's friends and if they want to come to my house they have to follow my rules . . . And I never let my children work . . . Who knows what influences they will be exposed

▲ Immigrant youths from central and south Asia to Toronto, Canada, enjoy lunch together in their school cafeteria. Cultural values that foster allegiance to family and community and that emphasize the importance of achievement play a vital role in immigrant youths' academic success and favorable psychological adjustment.
CP PHOTO/ Adrian Wyld

to? (Suárez-Orozco & Suárez-Orozco, 2001, p. 89)

Thuy Trang, age 14, from Vietnam, middle-school Student of the Year: When my parents first emigrated from Vietnam, they spent every waking hour working hard to support a family. They have sacrificed for me, and I am willing to do anything for them.

Elizabeth, age 16, from Vietnam, straight-A student, like her two older sisters: My parents know pretty much all the kids in the neighborhood. . . . Everybody here knows everybody else. It's hard to get away with much. (Zhou & Bankston, 1998, pp. 93, 130)

Immigrant youths' experiences are not problem-free. Interviews with adolescents who had arrived in Canada within the previous 5 years revealed that the majority found their first year "very difficult" because they did not yet speak one of the country's two official languages (English and French) and felt homesick and socially isolated (Hanvey & Kunz, 2000). In addition, tensions between family values and the new culture often create identity conflicts—challenges we will take up in Chapter 11. And many immigrants encounter ethnic prejudices among their native-born peers. But family and community cohesion, supervision, and expectations for academic and social maturity powerfully shape long-term favorable outcomes for these young people.

Reliability and Validity: Keys to Scientifically Sound Research

Once investigators choose their research methods, they must ensure that their procedures provide trustworthy information. To be acceptable to the scientific community, self-reports, observations, and physiological measures must be both *reliable* and *valid*—two keys to scientifically sound research.

Reliability

Suppose you go into an elementary school classroom and record how attentive and cooperative each child is, but your research partner, in simultaneously rating the same children, comes up with very different judgments. Or you question a group of children about their interests, but a week later, when you ask them again, their answers are very different. **Reliability** refers to the consistency, or repeatability, of measures of behavior. To be reliable, observations and evaluations of peoples' actions cannot be unique to a single observer. Instead, observers must agree on what they see. And an interview, test, or questionnaire, when given again within a short time (before participants can reasonably be expected to change their opinions or develop new responses), must yield similar results on both occasions.

Researchers determine the reliability of data in different ways. In observational research, observers are asked to evaluate the same behaviors, and agreement between them—called *inter-rater reliability*—is obtained. Reliability of self-report and psychophysiological data can be demonstrated by comparing children's responses to the same measures on separate occasions, an approach called *test–retest reliability*. In the case of self-reports, researchers can also compare children's answers on different forms of the same test or questionnaire. And if necessary, reliability can be estimated from a single testing session by comparing children's answers on different halves of the test.

Because clinical and ethnographic studies do not yield quantitative scores that can be matched with those of another observer or test form, the reliability of these methods must be determined with other procedures. After examining the qualitative records, one or more judges can see if they agree with the researcher that the patterns and themes identified are grounded in evidence and are plausible (McGrath & Johnson, 2003).

Validity

For research methods to have high **validity,** they must accurately measure characteristics that the researcher set out to measure. Think about this idea, and you will see that reliability is essential for valid research. Methods that are implemented carelessly, unevenly, and inconsistently cannot possibly represent what an investigator originally intended to study.

But researchers must go further to guarantee validity. They often examine the contents of observations and self-reports to make sure the behaviors of interest are included. For example, a test intended to measure fifth-grade children's knowledge of mathematics would not be valid if it contained addition problems but no subtraction, multiplication, or division problems (Miller, 1998). Another approach is to see how effective a method is in predicting behavior we would reasonably expect it to predict. If scores on a math test are valid, they should be related to how well children do on their math assignments in school or even to how quickly and accurately they can make change in a game of Monopoly.

As we turn now to research designs, you will discover that the concept of validity can also be applied more broadly: to the overall accuracy of research findings and conclusions. In setting up an investigation, researchers must safeguard two types of validity. The first, **internal validity,** is the degree to which *conditions internal to the design of the study* permit an accurate test of the researcher's hypothesis or question. If, during any phase of the investigation—selecting participants, choosing research settings and tasks, and implementing procedures—factors unrelated to the hypothesis influence participants' behavior, then the accuracy of the results is in doubt. Second, researchers must consider

To relax this child before a research session, an adult encouraged him to draw a picture and build with LEGOs—activities the boy enjoys greatly. In taking these steps, the researchers hoped to increase the validity of their findings. Making the boy feel at ease helps ensure internal validity, the accuracy of research findings. It may also foster external validity, the extent to which findings generalize to other situations, such as home or preschool.

(c) Kevin Leigh/ Index Stock

external validity, the degree to which their *findings generalize to settings and participants outside the original study.* Ensuring that samples, tasks, and contexts for conducting research represent the real-world people and situations that the investigator aims to understand is key to this type of accuracy.

Ask Yourself

REVIEW	Explain why a research method must be reliable to be valid, yet reliability *does not guarantee* validity.
APPLY	In studying the development of attention in school-age children, a researcher wonders whether to make naturalistic observations or structured observations. Which approach is best for ensuring internal validity? How about external validity? Why?
CONNECT	Why is it better for a researcher to use multiple methods rather than just one method to test a hypothesis or answer a research question?

General Research Designs

In deciding on a research design, investigators choose a way of setting up a study that permits them to test their hypotheses with the greatest certainty possible. Two main types of designs are used in all research on human behavior: correlational and experimental.

Correlational Design

In a **correlational design,** researchers gather information on individuals, generally in natural life circumstances, without altering their experiences. Then they look at relationships between participants' characteristics and their behavior or development. Suppose we want to answer such questions as, Do parents' styles of interacting with their children have any bearing on children's intelligence? Does spending more time in child care interfere with a secure attachment bond between parent and child? How does children's self-esteem affect their academic performance and peer relations? In these and many other instances, the conditions of interest are difficult or impossible to arrange and control and must be studied as they currently exist.

The correlational design offers a way of looking at relationships between variables. But correlational studies have one major limitation: We cannot infer cause and effect. For example, if we were to find that parental interaction is related to children's intelligence, we would not know whether parents' behavior actually *causes* intellectual differences among children. In fact, the opposite is possible. The behaviors of highly intelligent children may be so attractive that they cause parents to interact more favorably. Or a third variable that we did not even consider, such as the amount of noise and distraction in the home, may cause changes in both maternal interaction and children's intelligence.

In correlational studies and in other types of research designs, investigators often examine relationships between variables by using a **correlation coefficient,** a number that describes how two measures, or variables, are associated with one another. Although other statistical approaches to examining relationships also exist, we will encounter the correlation coefficient in discussing research findings throughout this book. So let's look at what it is and how it is interpreted. A correlation coefficient can range in value from +1.00 to –1.00. The *magnitude, or size, of the number* shows the *strength of the relationship.* A zero correlation indicates no relationship; but the closer the value is to +1.00 or –1.00, the stronger the relationship (see Figure 2.1). For instance, a correlation of –.78 is high, –.52 is moderate, and –.18 is low. Note, however, that correlations of +.52 and –.52 are equally strong. The *sign of the number* (+ or –) refers to the *direction of the relationship.* A positive sign (+) means that as one variable *increases,* the other also *increases.* A negative sign (–) indicates that as one variable *increases,* the other *decreases.*

Let's look at some examples of how a correlation coefficient works. One researcher reported a +.55 correlation between a measure of maternal language

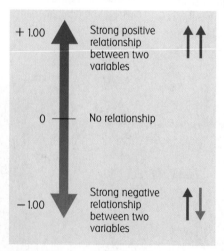

▼ **Figure 2.1**

The meaning of correlation coefficients. The magnitude of the number indicates the *strength* of the relationship. The sign of the number (+ or –) indicates the *direction* of the relationship.

stimulation and the size of children's vocabularies at age 2 years (Hoff, 2003b). This is a moderate correlation, which indicates that mothers who verbalized more had children who were more advanced in language development. In two other studies, child-rearing practices were related to toddlers' compliance in consistent ways. First, the extent to which mothers were warm and sensitive during a play session correlated positively with children's willingness to follow their mother's directive to clean up the toys, at +.34 (Feldman & Klein, 2003). And second, the extent to which mothers ignored their 10-month-olds' bids for attention correlated negatively with children's compliance 1 year later—at −.46 for boys and −.36 for girls (Martin, 1981). These moderate correlations revealed that the more mothers expressed affection and support, the more their children cooperated. And the more mothers ignored their children, the less the children cooperated (see Figure 2.2 for visual portrayals of these relationships).

All these investigations found correlations between parenting and young children's behavior. Are you tempted to conclude that the maternal behaviors influenced children's responses? Although the researchers suspected this was so, in none of the studies could they be sure about cause and effect. But finding a relationship in a correlational study suggests that tracking down its cause—with a more powerful experimental strategy, if possible—would be worthwhile.

◉ Do parents' styles of interacting with their children affect their children's academic performance and peer relations? A correlational design can be used to examine the relationship between parenting styles and children's development, but it does not permit researchers to infer cause and effect.
© Ed Bock/ CORBIS

Experimental Design

An **experimental design** permits inferences about cause and effect because researchers use an evenhanded procedure to assign people to two or more treatment conditions. In an experiment, the events and behaviors of interest are divided into two types: independent and dependent variables. The **independent variable** is the one the investigator expects to cause changes in another variable. The **dependent variable** is the one the investigator expects to be influenced by the independent variable. Cause-and-effect relationships can be detected because the researcher directly *controls* or *manipulates* changes in the independent variable by

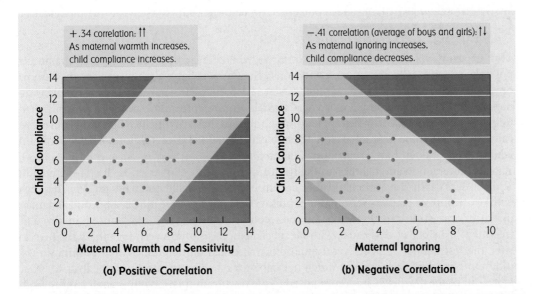

(a) Positive Correlation

+.34 correlation: ↑↑
As maternal warmth increases, child compliance increases.

(b) Negative Correlation

−.41 correlation (average of boys and girls): ↑↓
As maternal ignoring increases, child compliance decreases.

▶ **Figure 2.2**

A positive and a negative correlation. A researcher reported that maternal warmth and sensitivity were *positively* correlated with children's willingness to comply with their mother's directive to clean up toys (a). A second researcher reported that maternal ignoring of their infants was *negatively* correlated with children's compliance 1 year later (b). Each dot represents a participant's score on the two variables—maternal behavior and child compliance. Both correlations are moderate in strength because the pattern of dots deviates from a straight line, which would be a perfect correlation. Notice how in the positive correlation, as maternal warmth *increases,* child compliance tends to *increase.* In the negative correlation, as maternal ignoring increases, child compliance tends to *decrease.* If a pattern of dots shows no upward or downward trend, then the correlation is near zero, indicating little or no relationship between the two variables.

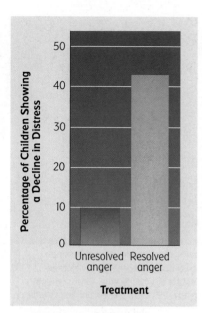

▲ Figure 2.3

Does the way adults end their angry encounters affect children's emotional reactions? A laboratory experiment revealed that when adults resolve their disputes by apologizing and compromising, children are more likely to show less distress when witnessing subsequent adult conflicts than when adults leave their arguments unresolved. Note in this graph that only 10 percent of children in the unresolved-anger treatment declined in distress (see bar on left), whereas 42 percent of children in the resolved-anger treatment did so (see bar on right). (Adapted from El-Sheikh, Cummings, & Reiter, 1996.)

exposing participants to treatment conditions. Then the researcher compares their performance on measures of the dependent variable.

In one **laboratory experiment,** researchers explored the impact of adults' angry interactions on children's adjustment (El-Sheikh, Cummings, & Reiter, 1996). They hypothesized that the way angry encounters end (independent variable) affects children's emotional reactions (dependent variable). Four- and 5-year-olds were brought one at a time to a laboratory, accompanied by their mothers. One group was exposed to an *unresolved-anger treatment,* in which two adult actors entered the room and argued but did not work out their disagreements. The other group witnessed a *resolved-anger treatment,* in which the adults ended their disputes by apologizing and compromising. As Figure 2.3 shows, while witnessing a follow-up adult conflict, more children in the resolved-anger treatment showed a decline in distress, as measured by fewer anxious facial expressions, less freezing in place, and less seeking of closeness to their mothers. The experiment revealed that anger resolution can reduce the stressful impact of adult conflict on children.

In experimental studies, investigators must take special precautions to control for participants' characteristics that could reduce the internal validity of their findings. For example, in the study just described, if a greater number of children from homes high in parental conflict ended up in the unresolved-anger treatment, we could not tell whether the independent variable or the children's backgrounds produced the results. Parental conflict and treatment conditions would be **confounding variables**—so closely associated that their effects on an outcome cannot be distinguished. To protect against this problem, researchers engage in **random assignment** of participants to treatment conditions. By using an unbiased procedure, such as drawing numbers out of a hat or flipping a coin, investigators increase the chances that participants' characteristics will be equally distributed across treatment groups.

Sometimes researchers combine random assignment with another technique called **matching.** In this procedure, participants are measured ahead of time on the factor in question—in our example, parental conflict. Then children high and low on that factor are assigned in equal numbers to each treatment condition. In this way, the experimental groups are deliberately matched, or made equivalent, on characteristics likely to distort the results.

Modified Experimental Designs

Most experiments are conducted in laboratories, where researchers can achieve the maximum possible control over treatment conditions. But, as we have already indicated, findings obtained in laboratories often have limited external validity: They may not apply to everyday situations. In **field experiments,** researchers capitalize on opportunities to randomly assign participants to treatment conditions in natural settings. In the experiment we just considered, we can conclude that the emotional climate established by adults affects children's behavior in the laboratory. But does it also do so in daily life?

Another study helps answer this question (Yarrow, Scott, & Waxler, 1973). This time, the research was carried out in a child-care center. A caregiver deliberately interacted differently with two groups of preschoolers. In one condition (the *nurturant treatment*), she modeled many instances of warmth and helpfulness. In the second condition (the *control,* since it involved no treatment), she behaved as usual, with no special emphasis on concern for others. Two weeks later, the researchers created several situations that called for helpfulness. For example, a visiting mother asked each child to watch her baby for a few moments, but the baby's toys had fallen out of the playpen. Children exposed to the nurturant treatment were much more likely than those in the control condition to return toys to the baby.

See the Biology and Environment box on the following page for an additional example of field research, with important implications for how best to foster children's intelligence. Often researchers cannot randomly assign participants and manipulate conditions in the real world, as these investigators were able to do. Sometimes they can compromise by conducting **natural, or quasi-, experiments.** Treatments that already exist, such as different family environments, schools, child-care centers, and preschool programs, are compared. These studies differ from correlational research only in that groups of people are carefully chosen to ensure

Can Musical Experiences Enhance Intelligence?

In a 1993 experiment, researchers reported that college students who listened to a Mozart sonata for a few minutes just before taking a test of spatial reasoning abilities did better on the test than students who took the test after listening to relaxation instructions or sitting in silence (Rauscher, Shaw, & Ky, 1993). Strains of Mozart, the investigators concluded, seem to induce changes in the brain that "warm up" neural connections, thereby improving thinking. But the gain in performance—widely publicized as the "Mozart effect"—lasted only 15 minutes and proved difficult to replicate. Rather than involving a real change in ability, Mozart seemed to improve arousal and mood, yielding better concentration on the test (Husain, Thompson, & Schellenberg, 2002; Thompson, Schellenberg, & Husain, 2001).

Despite mounting evidence that the Mozart effect was uncertain at best, the media and politicians were enthralled with the idea that a brief exposure of the brain to classical music in infancy, when neural connections are forming rapidly, might yield lifelong intellectual benefits. In 1996, the governor and legislature of the state of Georgia mandated that a CD containing the Mozart sonata and other classical music be given to every newborn baby leaving the hospital. Yet no studies of the Mozart effect have ever been conducted on infants! And

an experiment with school-age children failed to yield any intellectual gains as a result of simply listening to music (McKelvie & Low, 2002).

Research suggests that to produce lasting gains in mental-test scores, interventions must be long lasting and involve children's active participation. Consequently, Glenn Schellenberg (2004) wondered, Can music lessons enhance intelligence? Children who take music lessons must practice regularly, exhibit extended focused attention, read music, memorize lengthy musical passages, understand diverse musical structures, and master technical skills. These experiences might foster cognitive processing, particularly during childhood, when regions of the brain are taking on specialized functions and are highly sensitive to environmental influences.

Schellenberg conducted a field experiment involving 132 6-year-olds—children just old enough for formal lessons. First, the children took an intelligence test and were rated for social maturity, allowing researchers to see whether music lessons affect some aspects of development but not others. Next, the children were randomly assigned to one of four treatments. Two were music groups; one received piano lessons and the other voice lessons. The third group took drama lessons—a condition that shed light on whether intellectual gains were unique to musical experiences. The fourth group—a no-lessons control—was offered music lessons the following year. Music and drama instruction took place at the prestigious Royal Conservatory of Music in Toronto, where highly trained, experienced teachers taught the children in small groups. After 36 weeks of lessons, the children's intelligence and social maturity were assessed again.

▲ When children take music lessons over many weeks, they gain in mental test performance compared to children who take drama lessons or who receive no lessons at all. To make music, children must engage in diverse intellectual skill, including extended focused attention, reading musical notation, memorizing lengthy passages, analyzing musical structures, and mastering technical skills. © Zephyr Picture/ Index Stock

All four groups showed gains in mental-test performance, probably because the participants had just entered grade school, which usually leads to an increase in intelligence test scores (see Chapter 8). But the two music groups consistently gained more than the control groups (see Figure 2.4). Their advantage, though just a few points, extended across many mental abilities, including verbal and spatial skills and speed of thinking. At the same time, only the drama group improved in social maturity; the music and no-lesson control groups showed no change.

In sum, active, sustained musical experiences can lead to small increases in intelligence among 6-year-olds that do not arise from comparable drama lessons. But other enrichment activities with similar properties, such as reading, science, math, and chess programs, may confer similar benefits. All demand that children invest far more time and effort than they would in listening to a Mozart sonata. Nevertheless, music companies persist in selling CDs entitled "Tune Your Brain with Mozart" and "Mozart for Newborns: A Bright Beginning."

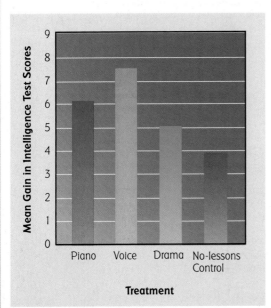

◀ **Figure 2.4**

Music lessons promote gains in intelligence. In a field experiment comparing 36 weeks of piano and voice lessons with drama lessons and a no-lesson control, children in the two groups receiving music lessons showed slightly greater gains in intelligence test performance. (Adapted from Schellenberg, 2004.)

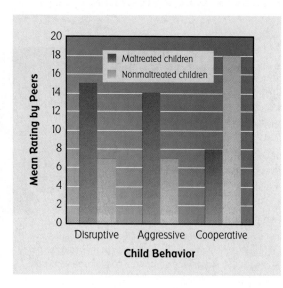

▶ **Figure 2.5**

A natural, or quasi-, experiment on the relationship of child maltreatment to children's social adjustment. Researchers brought maltreated and nonmaltreated children together at a summer camp so they could be observed under similar conditions. After only a short time together, peers consistently rated maltreated children as less well adjusted—more disruptive, more aggressive, and less cooperative. (Adapted from Shields, Ryan, & Cicchetti, 2001.)

that their characteristics are as much alike as possible. Occasionally, the same participants experience both treatments. In this way, investigators do their best to avoid confounding variables and alternative explanations for treatment effects.

Natural experiments permit researchers to examine the impact of many conditions that cannot be experimentally manipulated for ethical reasons—for example, the influence of premature birth, grade retention, or child maltreatment on development (Sameroff & MacKenzie, 2003). In one such study, maltreated and nonmaltreated 8- to 12-year-olds were enrolled in the same summer camp and, therefore, were observed and questioned under similar social conditions. When asked to complete stories about parenting that tapped themes of conflict, discipline, autonomy, and affection, maltreated children gave responses that were less elaborate and more negative than those of their nonmaltreated counterparts. Furthermore, peers rated maltreated children as more disruptive, more aggressive, and less cooperative (see Figure 2.5). Not surprisingly, peers strongly disliked these youngsters. Finally, children who represented their parents negatively in stories were especially likely to display maladaptive social behaviors (Shields, Ryan, & Cicchetti, 2001). The investigators concluded that maltreated children's internalized, unfavorable parenting images probably contribute to their poor social adjustment. And their poor adjustment reduces their access to the healing effects of warm, enjoyable relationships with peers. Despite intriguing findings like these, natural experiments cannot achieve the precision and rigor of true experimental research.

To help you compare the correlational and experimental designs we have discussed, Table 2.2 summarizes their strengths and limitations. Now let's take a close look at designs for studying development.

TABLE 2.2 STRENGTHS AND LIMITATIONS OF GENERAL RESEARCH DESIGNS

Design	Description	Strengths	Limitations
Correlational design	The investigator obtains information on participants without altering their experiences.	Permits study of relationships between variables.	Does not permit inferences about cause-and-effect relationships.
Laboratory experiment	Under controlled laboratory conditions, the investigator manipulates an independent variable and looks at its effect on a dependent variable; requires random assignment of participants to treatment conditions.	Permits inferences about cause-and-effect relationships.	Findings may not generalize to the real world.
Field experiment	The investigator randomly assigns participants to treatment conditions in natural settings.	Permits generalization of experimental findings to the real world.	Control over the treatment is generally weaker than in a laboratory experiment.
Natural, or quasi-, experiment	The investigator compares already existing treatments in the real world, carefully selecting groups of participants to ensure that their characteristics are as much alike as possible.	Permits study of many real-world conditions that cannot be experimentally manipulated.	Findings may be due to variables other than the treatment.

Ask Yourself

REVIEW	Why can we infer a cause-and-effect relationship in laboratory experiments but not in correlational studies?
REVIEW	Why are natural experiments less precise than laboratory and field experiments?
APPLY	A researcher compares children who went to summer leadership camps with children who attended athletic camps. She finds that those who attended leadership camps are friendlier. Should the investigator tell parents that sending children to leadership camps will cause them to be more sociable? Why or why not?
CONNECT	Reread the description of the study of aggressive boys and their friendships on page 44. What type of design did the researchers use, and why?

Designs for Studying Development

Scientists interested in child development require information about the way research participants change over time. To answer questions about development, they must extend correlational and experimental approaches to include measurements at different ages. Longitudinal and cross-sectional designs are special *developmental research* strategies. In each, age comparisons form the basis of the research plan.

The Longitudinal Design

In a **longitudinal design,** participants are studied repeatedly, and changes are noted as they get older. The time spanned may be relatively short (a few months to several years) or very long (a decade or even a lifetime).

• **ADVANTAGES OF THE LONGITUDINAL DESIGN** • The longitudinal approach has two major strengths. First, since it tracks the performance of each person over time, researchers can identify common patterns as well as individual differences in development. Second, longitudinal studies permit investigators to examine relationships between early and later events and behaviors. Let's illustrate these ideas.

A group of researchers wondered whether children who display extreme personality styles—either angry and explosive or shy and withdrawn—retain the same dispositions when they become adults. In addition, the researchers wanted to know what kinds of experiences promote stability or change in personality and what consequences explosiveness and shyness have for long-term adjustment. To answer these questions, the researchers delved into the archives of the Guidance Study, a well-known longitudinal investigation initiated in 1928 at the University of California, Berkeley, and continued over several decades (Caspi, Elder, & Bem, 1987, 1988).

Results revealed that the two personality styles were moderately stable. Between ages 8 and 30, a good number of individuals remained the same, whereas others changed substantially. When stability did occur, it appeared to be due to a "snowballing effect," in which children evoked responses from adults and peers that acted to maintain their dispositions. Explosive youngsters were likely to be treated with anger, whereas shy children were apt to be ignored. As a result, the two types of children came to view their social worlds differently. Explosive children regarded others as hostile; shy children regarded them as unfriendly (Caspi & Roberts, 2001). Together, these factors led explosive children to sustain or increase their unruliness and shy children to continue to withdraw.

Persistence of extreme personality styles affected many areas of adult adjustment. For men, the results of early explosiveness were most apparent in their work lives, in the form of conflicts with supervisors, frequent job changes, and unemployment. Since few women in this sample of an earlier generation worked after marriage, their family lives were most affected. Explosive girls grew up to be hotheaded wives and mothers who were especially prone to divorce. Sex differences in the long-term consequences of shyness were even greater. Men who had been withdrawn in childhood were delayed in marrying, becoming fathers, and developing careers. However, because a withdrawn, unassertive style was socially acceptable for females, women who had shy personalities showed no special adjustment problems.

• **PROBLEMS IN CONDUCTING LONGITUDINAL RESEARCH** • Despite their strengths, longitudinal investigations pose a number of problems that can compromise both internal and external validity. **Biased sampling**—the failure to enlist participants who represent the population of interest—is a common problem. People who willingly participate in research that requires them to be observed and tested over many years are likely to have unique characteristics—at the very least, a special appreciation for the scientific value of research. As a result, we cannot easily generalize from them to the rest of the population. Furthermore, longitudinal samples generally become more biased as the investigation proceeds because of **selective attrition.** Participants may move away or drop out for other reasons, and the ones who remain are likely to differ in important ways from the ones who do not continue.

The very experience of being repeatedly observed, interviewed, and tested can also interfere with a study's validity. Children and adults may gradually be alerted to their own thoughts, feelings, and actions, think about them, and revise them in ways that have little to do with age-related change. In addition, with repeated testing, participants may become "test-wise." Their performance may improve because of **practice effects**—better test-taking skills and increased familiarity with the test—not because of factors commonly associated with development.

The most widely discussed threat to the validity of longitudinal findings is cultural–historical change, or what are commonly called **cohort effects.** Longitudinal studies examine the development of *cohorts*—children developing in the same time period who are influenced by particular cultural and historical conditions. Results based on one cohort may not apply to children developing at other times. For example, unlike the findings on female shyness described in the previous section, which were gathered more than a half-century ago, today's shy young women tend to be poorly adjusted—a difference that may be due to changes in gender roles in Western societies. Shy adults, whether male or female, feel more depressed, have fewer social supports, and may do less well in educational and career attainment than their agemates (Caspi, 2000; Caspi et al., 2003). Similarly, a longitudinal study of social development would probably result in quite different findings, depending on whether it was carried out in the first decade of the twenty-first century, around the time of World War II, or during the Great Depression of the 1930s (see the Cultural Influences box on the following page).

Cohort effects don't just operate broadly on an entire generation. They also occur when specific experiences influence some children but not others in the same generation. For example, children who witnessed the terrorist attacks of September 11, 2001, either because they were near Ground Zero or because they saw injury and death on TV, were far more likely than other children to display persistent emotional problems, including intense fear, anxiety, and depression (Saylor et al., 2003). A study of one New York City sample suggested that as many as one-fourth of the city's children were affected (Hoven, Mandell, & Duarte, 2003).

Finally, changes occurring within the field of child development may create problems for longitudinal research covering an extended time period. Theories and methods constantly change, and those that first inspired a longitudinal study may become outdated. For this reason, as well as the others just mentioned, many recent longitudinal studies span only a few months or years. Although short-term longitudinal research does not yield the same breadth of information as long-term studies, researchers are spared at least some formidable obstacles.

The Cross-Sectional Design

The length of time it takes for many behaviors to change, even in limited longitudinal studies, has led researchers to turn to a more convenient strategy for studying development. In the **cross-sectional design,** groups of people differing in age are studied at the same time.

• **ADVANTAGES OF THE CROSS-SECTIONAL DESIGN** • The cross-sectional design is an efficient strategy for describing age-related trends. And because participants are measured only once, researchers need not be concerned about such difficulties as selective attrition, practice effects, or changes in the field that might make the findings obsolete by the time the study is complete.

An investigation in which students in grades 3, 6, 9, and 12 filled out a questionnaire asking about their sibling relationships provides a good illustration (Buhrmester & Furman, 1990). Findings revealed that sibling interaction was characterized by greater equality and less power assertion with age. Also, feelings of sibling companionship declined during adolescence. The researchers thought that several factors contributed to these age differences. As later-born

CULTURAL INFLUENCES

Impact of Historical Times on Development: The Great Depression and World War II

Cataclysmic events, such as economic disaster, war, and rapid social change, shake the foundations of life, inducing shared adaptations among people born at the same time (Rogler, 2002). Glen Elder (1999) capitalized on the hardships that families experienced during the Great Depression of the 1930s to study its influence on development. He delved into the vast archives of two major longitudinal studies: (1) the Oakland Growth Study, an investigation of individuals born in the early 1920s, who were adolescents when the Depression took its toll; and (2) the Guidance Study, whose participants were born in the late 1920s and were young children when their families faced severe financial losses.

In both cohorts, relationships changed when economic deprivation struck. As unemployed fathers lost status, mothers took greater control over family affairs. This reversal of traditional gender roles often sparked conflict. Fathers sometimes became explosive and punitive toward their children. At other times, they withdrew into passivity and depression. Mothers often became frantic with worry over their family's well-being and sought work to make ends meet (Elder, Liker, & Cross, 1984).

Outcomes for Adolescents

Although unusual burdens were placed on them as family lives changed, the Oakland Growth Study cohort—especially the boys—weathered economic hardship quite well. As adolescents, they were too old to be wholly dependent on their highly stressed parents. Boys spent less time at home as they searched for part-time jobs, and many turned toward adults and peers outside the family for emotional support. Girls took over

responsibility for household chores and caring for younger siblings. Their greater involvement in family affairs exposed them to more parental conflict and unhappiness. Consequently, adolescent girls' adjustment in economically deprived homes was somewhat less favorable than that of adolescent boys (Elder, Van Nguyen, & Caspi, 1985).

These changes had major consequences for adolescents' future aspirations and adult lives. As girls focused on home and family, they were less likely to think about college and careers and more likely to marry early. Boys learned that economic resources could not be taken for granted, and they tended to make an early commitment to an occupational choice. And the chance to become a parent was especially important to men whose lives had been disrupted by the Depression. Perhaps because they believed that a rewarding career could not be guaranteed, they viewed children as the most enduring benefit of their adult lives.

Outcomes for Children

Unlike the Oakland Growth Study cohort, the Guidance Study participants were within the years of intense family dependency when the Depression struck. For young boys (who, as you will see in later chapters, are especially prone to adjustment problems in the face of family stress), the impact of economic strain was severe.

They showed emotional difficulties and poor attitudes toward school and work that persisted through the teenage years (Elder & Caspi, 1988).

But as the Guidance Study sample became adolescents, another major historical event occurred: World War II. As a result, thousands of men left their communities for military bases, leading to dramatic life changes. Some combat veterans came away with symptoms of emotional trauma that persisted for decades. Yet for most young soldiers, war mobilization broadened their range of knowledge and experience. It also granted time out from civilian responsibilities, giving many soldiers a chance to consider where their lives were going. And the GI Bill of Rights, which provided government subsidies for college education, enabled veterans to acquire new knowledge and skills after the war. By middle adulthood, the Guidance Study veterans had reversed the early negative impact of the Great Depression. They were more successful educationally and occupationally than their counterparts who had not entered the service (Elder & Hareven, 1993).

Clearly, cultural-historical change does not have a uniform impact on development. Outcomes can vary considerably, depending on the pattern of historical events and the age at which people experience them.

▶ Historical time period can profoundly affect development. The Great Depression of the 1930s left this farm family without a steady income. Children were more negatively affected than adolescents, who were no longer entirely dependent on their highly stressed parents. © Corbis

children become more competent and independent, they no longer need, and are probably less willing to accept, direction from older siblings. In addition, as adolescents move from psychological dependence on the family to greater involvement with peers, they may have less time and emotional need to invest in siblings. These intriguing ideas about the development of sibling relationships, as we will see in Chapter 14, have been confirmed in subsequent research.

• **PROBLEMS IN CONDUCTING CROSS-SECTIONAL RESEARCH** • Despite its convenience, cross-sectional research does not provide evidence about development at the level at which it actually occurs: the individual (Kraemer et al., 2000). For example, in the cross-sectional study of sibling relationships just discussed, comparisons are limited to age-group averages. We cannot tell if important individual differences exist. Indeed, longitudinal findings reveal that adolescents vary considerably in the changing quality of their sibling relationships. Although many become more distant, others become more supportive and intimate, and still others become more rivalrous and antagonistic (Branje et al., 2004; Dunn, Slomkowski, & Beardsall, 1994).

Cross-sectional studies—especially those that cover a wide age span—have another problem. Like longitudinal research, they can be threatened by cohort effects. For example, comparisons of 5-year-old cohorts and 15-year-old cohorts—groups born and reared in different years—may not really represent age-related changes. Instead, they may reflect unique experiences associated with the time period in which the age groups were growing up.

Improving Developmental Designs

Researchers have devised ways of building on the strengths and minimizing the weaknesses of longitudinal and cross-sectional approaches. Several modified developmental designs have resulted.

• **COMBINING LONGITUDINAL AND CROSS-SECTIONAL APPROACHES** • In the **sequential design,** researchers merge longitudinal and cross-sectional strategies by following a sequence of samples (two or more age groups), collecting data on them at the same points in time. For example, suppose we select three samples—sixth, seventh, and eighth graders—and track them for 2 years. That is, we observe each sample this year and next year, as follows: Sample 1 from grades 6 to 7; Sample 2 from grades 7 to 8; and Sample 3 from grades 8 to 9.

The design has three advantages: (1) We can find out whether cohort effects are operating by comparing children of the same age (or grade in school) who were born in different years. Using our example, we can compare children from different samples at grades 7 and 8. If they do not differ, then we can rule out cohort effects. (2) We can make both longitudinal and cross-sectional comparisons. If outcomes are similar, then we can be especially confident about the accuracy of our findings. (3) The design is efficient. In our example, we can find out about change over a 4-year period by following each cohort for just 2 years.

A study of adolescents' gender-stereotyped beliefs included the sequential features just described (Alfieri, Ruble, & Higgins, 1996). The researchers focused on stereotype flexibility—young people's willingness to say that "masculine" traits (such as *strong*) and "feminine" traits (such as *gentle*) characterize both males and females. As Figure 2.6 reveals, Samples 2 and 3 showed a sharp longitudinal decline in stereotype flexibility and had similar scores when measured at grade 8. But Sample 1, on reaching seventh grade, scored much lower than seventh graders in Sample 2.

The reason, the researchers discovered, was that Sample 1 remained in the same school from sixth to seventh grade, whereas Samples 2 and 3 had transitioned from elementary to junior high school. Entry into junior high sparked a temporary rise in gender-stereotype flexibility, perhaps because of exposure to a wide range of older peers, some of whom challenged stereotypes. Over time, stereotype flexibility decreased in Samples 2 and 3. The researchers speculated that these young junior high students were responding to social pressures to conform to traditional gender roles—a topic we will take up in Chapter 13.

Notice how the developmental trend shown in Figure 2.6—high gender-stereotype flexibility at grade 7 that drops off steeply—characterizes only adolescents who moved to a self-contained junior high school. Researchers have become increasingly interested in identifying such cohort effects because they help explain diversity in development.

• **EXAMINING MICROCOSMS OF DEVELOPMENT** • In all the examples of developmental research we have discussed, observations of children are fairly widely spaced. When we observe

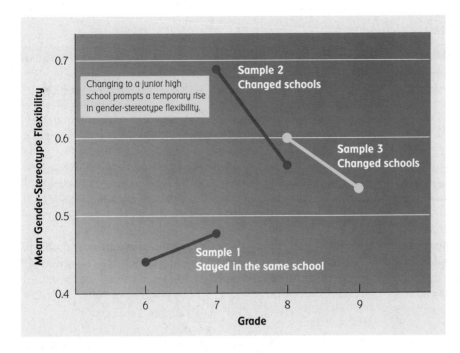

Figure 2.6

A longitudinal-sequential study of the development of the gender-stereotyped beliefs during adolescence. Three samples were followed longitudinally from one school year to the next. The researchers compared Sample 1 with Sample 2 at grade 7 and Sample 2 with Sample 3 at grade 8. The scores of Samples 1 and 2 did not match! The reason, the investigators discovered from additional evidence, was that a cohort effect—transition to junior high school—prompts a temporary rise in gender-stereotype flexibility. Because the scores of Samples 2 and 3 were similar at grade 8, the researchers were confident that gender-stereotype flexibility declines sharply in the years following transition to junior high school. (Adapted from Alfieri, Ruble, & Higgins, 1996.)

once a year or every few years, we can describe change, but we have little opportunity to capture the processes that produce it. The **microgenetic design,** an adaptation of the longitudinal approach, presents children with a novel task and follows their mastery over a series of closely spaced sessions. Within this "microcosm" of development, researchers observe how change occurs (Kuhn, 1995; Siegler & Crowley, 1991). The microgenetic design is especially useful for studying cognitive development. For example, researchers can examine the strategies children use to acquire new knowledge in reading, mathematics, and science (Siegler, 1996, 2002). As you will see in Chapter 4, the microgenetic design has also been used to trace infants' mastery of motor skills.

Nevertheless, microgenetic studies are difficult to carry out. Researchers must pore over hours of recorded information, analyzing each participant's behavior many times. In addition, the time required for children to change is hard to anticipate. It depends on a careful match between the child's capabilities and the demands of the task. Finally, as in other longitudinal research, practice effects can distort microgenetic findings. As a check, researchers can compare microgenetic with cross-sectional observations. If new behaviors that emerge microgenetically reflect typical development, they should match the behaviors displayed by more advanced participants in cross-sectional studies, who are observed only once (Kuhn, 1995). When researchers overcome the challenges of microgenetic research, they reap the benefits of seeing development as it takes place.

• **COMBINING EXPERIMENTAL AND DEVELOPMENTAL DESIGNS** • Perhaps you noticed that all the examples of longitudinal and cross-sectional research we have considered permit only correlational, and not causal, inferences. Yet causal information is desirable, both for testing theories and for finding ways to improve children's lives. If a developmental design indicates that children's experiences and behavior are related, in some instances we can explore the causal link by experimentally manipulating the experiences. If, as a result, development is enhanced, then we have strong evidence for a causal association between experiences and behavior. Today, research that combines an experimental strategy with either a longitudinal or a cross-sectional approach appears with increasing frequency. These designs help investigators move beyond correlated variables to a causal account of development. For a summary of the strengths and limitations of developmental research designs, refer to Table 2.3 on page 62.

In a block-gluing project, 5-year-olds experiment with balance, observe the results with rapt attention, and—if the structure tumbles—take corrective steps. What strategies do the children use, and how do they become proficient? Because a microgenetic design permits researchers to follow children's mastery of a challenging task, it is uniquely suited to answering these questions.

© Ellen Senisi/The Image Works

TABLE 2.3   STRENGTHS AND LIMITATIONS OF DEVELOPMENTAL RESEARCH DESIGNS

Design	Description	Strengths	Limitations
Longitudinal design	The investigator studies the same group of participants repeatedly at different ages.	Permits study of common patterns and individual differences in development and relationships between early and later events and behaviors.	Age-related changes may be distorted because of biased sampling, selective attrition, practice effects, and cohort effects. Theoretical and methodological changes in the field can make findings obsolete.
Cross-sectional design	The investigator studies groups of participants differing in age at the same time.	More efficient than the longitudinal design. Not plagued by selective attrition, practice effects, or theoretical and methodological changes in the field.	Does not permit study of individual developmental trends. Age differences may be distorted because of cohort effects.
Sequential design	The investigator follows a sequence of samples (two or more age groups), collecting data on them at the same points in time.	Permits both longitudinal and cross-sectional comparisons. Reveals cohort effects. Permits tracking of age-related changes more efficiently than the longitudinal design.	May have the same problems as longitudinal and cross-sectional strategies, but the design itself helps identify difficulties.
Microgenetic design	The investigator presents children with a novel task and follows their mastery over a series of closely spaced sessions.	Offers insights into processes of development.	Requires intensive study of participants' moment-by-moment behaviors; the time required for participants to change is difficult to anticipate; practice effects may distort developmental trends.

Ask Yourself

REVIEW	Explain how cohort effects can distort the findings of both longitudinal and cross-sectional studies. How does the sequential design reveal cohort effects?
REVIEW	What design is best suited to studying processes of change, and why? When researchers use this design, what factors can threaten the internal validity of their findings?
APPLY	A researcher wants to know whether children enrolled in child-care centers in the first few years of life do as well in school as those who are not in child care. Which developmental design is appropriate for answering this question? Explain.
REFLECT	Suppose a researcher asks you to enroll your baby in a 10-year longitudinal study. What factors would lead you to agree and stay involved? Do your answers shed light on why longitudinal studies often have biased samples? Explain.

Ethics in Research on Children

Research into human behavior creates ethical issues because, unfortunately, the quest for scientific knowledge can sometimes exploit people. When children take part in research, the ethical concerns are especially complex. Children are more vulnerable than adults to physical and psychological harm. In addition, immaturity makes it difficult or impossible for children to evaluate for themselves what participation in research will mean. For these reasons, special ethical guidelines for research on children have been developed by the federal government, by funding agencies, and by research-oriented associations such as the American Psychological Association (2002), the Canadian Psychological Association (2000), and the Society for Research in Child Development (1993).

Table 2.4 presents a summary of children's basic research rights. Once you have examined them, think back to the ethical controversy faced by my colleague Ron, described at the beginning of this chapter. Then read the following research situations, each of which poses an additional ethical dilemma. What precautions do you think should be taken in each instance? Is either so threatening to children's well-being that it should not be carried out?

- In a study of moral development, a researcher wants to assess children's ability to resist temptation by videotaping their behavior without their knowledge. She promises 7-year-olds a prize for solving difficult puzzles but tells them not to look at a classmate's correct solutions, which are deliberately placed at the back of the room. Informing children ahead of time that cheating is being studied or that their behavior is being monitored will destroy the purpose of the study.

- A researcher is interviewing fifth graders about their experiences with bullying. A girl describes being victimized by an older sibling, but the behavior is not severe enough to warrant a report of abuse to child welfare authorities. Although the girl is unhappy, she wants to handle the problem on her own. If the researcher alerts the girl's parents to provide protection and help, he will violate his promise to keep participants' responses private.

Did you find it difficult to evaluate these examples? Virtually every organization that has devised ethical principles for research has concluded that conflicts arising in research situations cannot be resolved with simple right-or-wrong answers. The ultimate responsibility for the ethical integrity of research lies with the investigator. However, researchers are advised—and often required—to seek advice from others. Committees for this purpose (like the one that evaluated Ron's research) exist in colleges, universities, and other institutions. These *institutional review boards (IRBs)* assess proposed studies on the basis of a **risks-versus-benefits ratio.** This involves weighing the costs to participants in terms of inconvenience and possible psychological or physical injury against the study's value for advancing knowledge and improving conditions of life.

Ron's procedures, the school's research committee claimed, might not offer children sufficient **protection from harm.** If there are any risks to the safety and welfare of participants that the research does not justify, then preference is always given to the research participants. Vulnerability to harm, as the From Research to Practice box on page 64 reveals, varies with children's age and characteristics. Occasionally, further inquiry can help resolve perplexing ethical dilemmas. In Ron's case, he provided the research committee with findings showing that asking

TABLE 2.4 CHILDREN'S RESEARCH RIGHTS

Research Right	Description
Protection from harm	Children have the right to be protected from physical or psychological harm in research. If in doubt about the harmful effects of research, investigators should seek the opinion of others. When harm seems possible, investigators should find other means for obtaining the desired information or abandon the research.
Informed consent	All research participants, including children, have the right to have explained to them, in language appropriate to their level of understanding, all aspects of the research that may affect their willingness to participate. When children are participants, informed consent of parents as well as others who act on the child's behalf (such as school officials) should be obtained, preferably in writing. Children, and the adults responsible for them, have the right to discontinue participation in the research at any time.
Privacy	Children have the right to concealment of their identity on all information collected in the course of research. They also have this right with respect to written reports and any informal discussions about the research.
Knowledge of results	Children have the right to be informed of the results of research in language that is appropriate to their level of understanding.
Beneficial treatments	If experimental treatments believed to be beneficial are under investigation, children in control groups have the right to alternative beneficial treatments if they are available.

Sources: American Psychological Association, 2002; Canadian Psychological Association, 2000; Society for Research in Child Development, 1993.

FROM RESEARCH TO PRACTICE

Children's Research Risks: Developmental and Individual Differences

Researchers interested in children face formidable challenges in defining their ethical responsibilities. Compared with adults, children are less capable of benefiting from research experiences. Furthermore, most risks children encounter are psychological rather than physical (as in medical research) and therefore difficult to anticipate and even detect (Thompson, 1992). Consider, for example, 7-year-old Henry, who did not want to answer a researcher's questions about how he feels about his younger brother, who has physical disabilities. Since Henry's parents told him they had given permission for his participation, he did not feel free to say no. Or take 11-year-old Isabelle, who tried to solve a problem unsuccessfully. Despite the researcher's assurances that the task was set up to be impossible, Isabelle ended up doubting her own competence.

How can we make sure that children are subjected to the least research risk possible? One valuable resource is our expanding knowledge of age-related capacities and individual differences. Research risks vary with development in complex ways. Some risks decrease with age, others increase, and still others occur at many or all ages (Thompson, 1990b). And because of their personal characteristics and life circumstances, some children are more vulnerable to harm than others.

Age Differences

Research plans for younger children typically receive the most scrutiny because their limited cognitive competencies restrict their ability to make reasoned decisions and resist violations of their rights. In addition, as Henry's predicament illustrates, young children's limited social power can make it hard to refuse participation. In research that examined children's understanding of research procedures, 9-year-olds had great difficulty identifying their research rights and recognizing violations of those rights. Even 12-year-olds struggled to grasp their rights to decline participation, be protected from harm, and

be given the study's results (Bruzzese & Fisher, 2003). And regardless of age, most children and adolescents thought that withdrawing from a study would have negative consequences and felt external pressure to continue. For example, they believed the researcher would be unhappy if they stopped (Ondrusek et al., 1998). But if researchers briefly name and explain each research right, comprehension improves, especially among adolescents.

Whereas young children often fail to comprehend the research process, older children are more susceptible to procedures that threaten the way they view themselves. As middle childhood brings greater sensitivity to others' evaluations, giving false feedback or inducing failure (as happened to Isabelle) is more stressful. In adolescence, when questioning of authority is common, young people may be better at sizing up and rejecting researchers' deceptive evaluations (Thompson, 1992).

Children's Unique Characteristics

At times, children's backgrounds and experiences introduce vulnerabilities. For example, in certain ethnic minority communities, where deference to authority, maintaining pleasant relationships, and meeting the needs of a guest (the researcher) are highly valued, children and parents may be likely to consent when they would rather not do so (Fisher et al., 2002). In other circumstances, such as child maltreatment, parents are not necessarily good advocates for their children's rights. The consent of an additional adult invested in the child's welfare — a relative, teacher, or therapist — may be necessary to protect the child. And in some cases, such as teenagers who are substance abusers or delinquents, parents may be so eager to get them into contact with professionals that they are willing to agree to almost any research, with little forethought (Drotar et al., 2000).

Finding ways to reconcile the risks-versus-benefits conflicts we have considered

▲ Although this 9-year-old boy cooperates with a researcher's requests, he may not know why he was asked to participate, or realize that he may withdraw at any time without negative consequences. Because children have difficulty understanding the research process, extra steps must be taken to ensure their research rights.
© Will & Deni McIntyre/ CORBIS

is vital because research on children is of great value to society. As institutional review boards evaluate each study, participants' age and unique characteristics should be central to the discussion. Children and adolescents need clear, age-appropriate explanations of their rights, reminders of those rights as the research proceeds, and invitations to ask questions about anything they do not understand. And their decision should be the final word in most investigations, even though this standard is not mandatory in current guidelines.

elementary school children to identify disliked peers does not cause them to interact less frequently or more negatively with those children (Bell-Dolan, Foster, & Sikora, 1989). At the same time, Ron agreed to take special precautions when requesting such information. He promised to ask all the children to keep their comments confidential. He also arranged to conduct the study at a time when classmates have limited opportunity to interact with one another—just before a school vacation (Bell-Dolan & Wessler, 1994). With these safeguards in place, the committee approved Ron's research.

The ethical principle of **informed consent**—people's right to have all aspects of a study explained to them that might affect their willingness to participate—requires special interpretation when individuals cannot fully appreciate the research goals and activities. Parental consent is meant to protect the safety of children whose ability to decide is not yet fully mature. Besides obtaining parental consent, researchers should seek agreement of others who act on children's behalf, such as institutional officials when research is conducted in schools, child-care centers, or hospitals. This is especially important when studies include special groups whose parents may not represent their best interests (refer again to the From Research to Practice box on the preceding page).

As soon as children are old enough to appreciate the purpose of the research, and certainly by 7 years of age, their own informed consent should be obtained in addition to parental consent. Around age 7, changes in children's thinking permit them to better understand simple scientific principles and the needs of others. Researchers should respect and enhance these new capacities by providing school-age children with a full explanation of research activities in language they can understand (Fisher, 1993). Careful attention to informed consent helps resolve dilemmas about revealing children's responses to parents, teachers, or other authorities because those responses suggest that the child's welfare is in danger. Children can be told in advance that if they report that someone is harming them, then the researcher will tell an appropriate adult to take action to ensure the child's safety (Mishna, Antle, & Regehr, 2004).

Finally, young children rely on a basic faith in adults to feel secure in unfamiliar situations. For this reason, some types of research may be particularly disturbing to them. All ethical guidelines advise that special precautions be taken in the use of deception and concealment, as occurs when researchers observe children from behind one-way mirrors, give them false feedback about their performance, or do not tell them the truth regarding what the research is about. When these kinds of procedures are used with adult participants, **debriefing,** in which the researcher provides a full account and justification of the activities, occurs after the research session is over. Debriefing should also be done with children, but it rarely works as well. Despite explanations, children may leave the research situation with their belief in the honesty of adults undermined. Ethical standards permit deception in research with children if investigators satisfy institutional committees that such practices are necessary. Nevertheless, because deception may have serious emotional consequences for some youngsters, many child development specialists believe that researchers should come up with other research strategies when children are involved.

Ask Yourself

REVIEW	Explain why researchers must consider children's age-related capacities to ensure that they are protected from harm and have freely consented to research.
APPLY	When a researcher engaged in naturalistic observation of preschoolers' play, a child said, "Stop watching me!" Using the research rights in Table 2.4, indicate how the researcher should respond, and why.
CONNECT	Review the experiment on music lessons and intelligence reported in the Biology and Environment box on page 55. Why was it ethically important for the researchers to offer music lessons to the no-lessons control group during the year after completion of the study?
REFLECT	Suppose you want to conduct clinical interviews with school-age children, each of whom has a parent with AIDS, to elicit their thoughts and feelings about living with a parent who has a chronic, stigmatizing illness. After obtaining parental consent to ask about this sensitive, private topic, what steps would you take throughout the interview to ensure that you have the children's informed consent?

◉ Summary

From Theory to Hypothesis

Describe the role of theories, hypotheses, and research questions in the research process.

◉ Research usually begins with a **hypothesis,** or prediction about behavior drawn from a theory. When little or no theory exists on a topic of interest, investigators begin with a research question. On the basis of the hypothesis or question, the investigator selects research methods (specific activities of participants) and a research design (overall plan for the study).

Common Methods Used to Study Children

Describe research methods commonly used to study children, noting strengths and limitations of each.

◉ **Naturalistic observations,** gathered in children's everyday environments, permit researchers to see directly the everyday behaviors they hope to explain. In contrast, **structured observations** take place in laboratories, where every participant has an equal opportunity to display the behaviors of interest.

◉ Depending on the researcher's purpose, observations can preserve participants' entire stream of behavior, or they can be limited to one or a few behaviors, as in **event sampling** and **time sampling. Observer influence** and **observer bias** can reduce the accuracy of observational findings.

◉ Self-report methods can be flexible and open-ended like the **clinical interview,** which permits participants to express their thoughts in ways similar to their thinking in everyday life. Alternatively, **structured interviews,** tests, and questionnaires are more efficient and permit researchers to specify activities and behaviors that participants might not think of in an open-ended interview. Both approaches depend on participants' ability and willingness to engage in accurate reporting.

◉ **Psychophysiological methods** measure the relation between physiological processes and behavior. They help researchers uncover the biological bases of children's perceptual, cognitive, and emotional responses. Nevertheless, these methods involve a high degree of inference; researchers cannot be sure that certain patterns of autonomic or brain activity signal particular cognitive processes.

◉ Investigators rely on the **clinical,** or **case study, method** to obtain an in-depth understanding of a single child. In this approach, interviews, observations, test scores, and sometimes psychophysiological assessments are synthesized into a complete description of the participant's development and psychological functioning. But the method risks unsystematic and subjective collection of information, and researchers cannot generalize to anyone other than the child studied.

◉ A growing interest in the impact of culture has prompted child development researchers to adapt observational and self-report methods to permit direct comparisons of cultures. To uncover the cultural meanings of children's and adults' behaviors, they rely on **ethnography.** It uses participant observation to understand the unique values and social processes of a culture or distinct social group. But investigators' cultural values and theoretical commitments sometimes lead them to observe selectively or misinterpret what they see.

© JORGEN SCHYTTE / PETER ARNOLD, INC.

© BOB DAEMMRICH/THE IMAGE WORKS

Reliability and Validity: Keys to Scientifically Sound Research

Explain how reliability and validity apply to research methods and to the overall accuracy of research findings and conclusions.

◉ To be acceptable to the scientific community, research methods must be both reliable and valid. **Reliability** refers to the consistency, or repeatability, of observational, self-report, and psychophysiological measures. In the case of clinical and ethnographic research, reliability involves assessing whether the patterns and themes identified by the researcher are grounded in evidence and are plausible.

◉ A method has high **validity** if, after examining its content and relationships with other measures of behavior, the researcher finds that it reflects what it was intended to measure. The concept of validity can also be applied more broadly, to the overall accuracy of research findings and conclusions. In designing a study, investigators must take special precautions to ensure **internal validity**—that conditions internal to the study's design permit an accurate test of the hypothesis or question. They must also consider **external validity**—the degree to which findings generalize to settings and participants outside the original study.

General Research Designs

Distinguish correlational and experimental research designs, noting strengths and limitations of each.

◉ The **correlational design** examines relationships between variables as they happen to occur, without altering people's experiences. The **correlation coefficient** often is used to measure the association between variables. Correlational studies do not permit inferences about cause and effect. However, their use is justified when it is difficult or impossible to control the variables of interest.

An **experimental design** permits inferences about cause and effect. Researchers manipulate an **independent variable** by exposing groups of participants to two or more treatment conditions. Then they determine what effect this variable has on a **dependent variable. Random assignment** and **matching** ensure that characteristics of participants and treatment conditions do not operate as **confounding variables** that reduce the internal validity of experimental findings.

Laboratory experiments usually achieve high degrees of control, but their findings may not apply to everyday life. To overcome this problem, researchers sometimes conduct **field experiments,** in which they randomly assign participants to treatment conditions in the real world. When this is impossible, investigators may compromise and conduct **natural,** or **quasi-, experiments,** in which already existing treatments, involving groups of people whose characteristics are as much alike as possible, are compared. This approach, however, is less precise and rigorous than a true experimental design.

Designs for Studying Development

Describe designs for studying development, noting strengths and limitations of each.

The **longitudinal design** permits study of common patterns as well as individual differences in development and the relationship between early and later events and behaviors.

Researchers face a variety of problems in conducting longitudinal research, including **biased sampling, selective attrition, practice effects,** and changes in accepted theories and methods during long-term studies. But the most widely discussed threat to the validity of longitudinal findings is **cohort effects**—difficulty generalizing to children growing up during different time periods.

The **cross-sectional design,** in which groups of participants differing in age are studied at the same time, offers an efficient approach to studying development. Although not plagued by such problems as selective attrition, practice effects, or theoretical and methodological changes in the field, it is limited to comparisons of age-group averages. Like longitudinal research, cross-sectional studies can be threatened by cohort effects, especially when they cover a wide age span.

Modified developmental designs overcome some of the limitations of longitudinal and cross-sectional research. By combining the two approaches in the **sequential design,** researchers can test for cohort effects, make longitudinal and cross-sectional comparisons, and gather information about development efficiently. In the **microgenetic design,** researchers track change as it occurs to gain insights into the processes of development. However, the time required for children to change is hard to anticipate, and practice effects can bias findings. When researchers combine experimental and developmental

© LAURA DWIGHT PHOTOGRAPHY

designs, they can examine causal influences on development.

Ethics in Research on Children

What special ethical issues arise in doing research on children?

Because of their immaturity, children are especially vulnerable to harm and often cannot evaluate the risks and benefits of research. Ethical principles and institutional review boards (IRBs) that weigh research in terms of a **risks-versus-benefits ratio** help ensure that children's rights are safeguarded and that they are afforded **protection from harm.** In addition to parental consent and agreement of others who act on children's behalf, researchers should seek the **informed consent** of children age 7 and older by explaining, in language the child can understand, all aspects of the research procedures and the child's rights. The use of deception in research with children is especially risky, since **debriefing** can undermine their basic faith in the trustworthiness of adults.

Important Terms and Concepts

biased sampling (p. 58)
clinical interview (p. 46)
clinical, or case study, method (p. 48)
cohort effects (p. 58)
confounding variables (p. 54)
correlation coefficient (p. 52)
correlational design (p. 52)
cross-sectional design (p. 58)
debriefing (p. 65)
dependent variable (p. 53)
ethnography (p. 49)
event sampling (p. 44)
experimental design (p. 54)

external validity (p. 52)
field experiment (p. 54)
hypothesis (p. 42)
independent variable (p. 53)
informed consent (p. 65)
internal validity (p. 52)
laboratory experiment (p. 54)
longitudinal design (p. 57)
matching (p. 54)
microgenetic design (p. 61)
natural, or quasi-, experiment (p. 54)
naturalistic observation (p. 42)
observer bias (p. 45)

observer influence (p. 45)
practice effects (p. 58)
protection from harm (p. 63)
psychophysiological methods (p. 47)
random assignment (p. 54)
reliability (p. 51)
risks-versus-benefits ratio (p. 63)
selective attrition (p. 58)
sequential design (p. 60)
structured interview (p. 46)
structured observation (p. 44)
time sampling (p. 45)
validity (p. 51)

"Pregnant Mummy"
Eliska Kocová
Age 5, Czech Republic

This portrait of a new being, safe within its mother's womb and surrounded by an optimistic world, captures the myriad influences on children's development. From the very beginning, a complex blend of genetic and environmental forces underlies children's growth, advancing capacities, and well-being.

Reprinted with permission from the International Museum of Children's Art, Oslo, Norway.

Biological Foundations, Prenatal Development, and Birth

"It's a girl," announces the doctor, who holds up the squalling little creature, while her new parents gaze with amazement at their miraculous creation. "A girl! We've named her Sarah!" exclaims the proud father to eager relatives waiting by the telephone for word about their new family member.

As we join these parents in thinking about how this wondrous being came into existence and imagining her future, we are struck by many questions. How could this baby, equipped with everything necessary for life outside the womb, have developed from the union of two tiny cells? What ensures that Sarah will, in due time, roll over, walk, talk, make friends, imagine, and create—just like every other normal child born before her? Why is she a girl and not a boy, dark-haired rather than blond, calm and cuddly instead of wiry and energetic? What difference will it make that Sarah lives in one family, community, nation, and culture rather than another?

We begin our discussion of these questions by considering genetic foundations. Because nature has prepared us for survival, all humans have features in common. Yet each human being is also unique. Take a moment to think about several children you know well. Jot down the most obvious physical and behavioral similarities between them and their parents. Did you find that one child shows combined features of both parents, another resembles just one parent, whereas a third is not like either parent? These directly observable characteristics are called **phenotypes.** They depend in part on the individual's **genotype**—the complex blend of genetic information that determines our species and influences all our unique characteristics. But phenotypes, as our discussion will show, are also affected by environmental influences—ones that begin even before conception.

Next, we trace prenatal development, the most rapid period of growth, during which complex transactions between heredity and environment profoundly affect children's health and well-being. Then we turn to the drama of birth and to the problems of infants who are born underweight or too early.

As our discussion proceeds, some findings about the influence of nature and nurture may surprise you. For example, many people believe that when children inherit unfavorable characteristics, not much can be done to help them. Others are convinced that the damage done to a child by a harmful environment can easily be corrected. We will see that neither of these assumptions is true. In the final section of this chapter, we take up the question of how nature and nurture work together to shape the course of development.

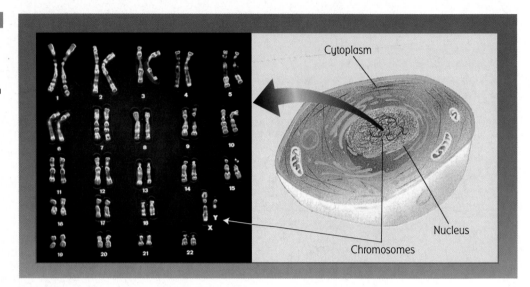

© CNRI/Science Photo Library/Photo Researchers

▶ **Figure 3.1**

A karyotype, or photograph, of human chromosomes. The 46 chromosomes shown on the left were isolated from a human cell, stained, greatly magnified, and arranged in pairs according to decreasing size of the upper "arm" of each chromosome. Note the twenty-third pair, XY. The cell donor is a male. In a female, the twenty-third pair would be XX.

Genetic Foundations

Each of us is made up of trillions of units called *cells*. Inside every cell is a control center, or *nucleus*, containing rodlike structures called **chromosomes**, which store and transmit genetic information. Their number varies from species to species—48 for chimpanzees, 64 for horses, 40 for mice, and 46 for human beings. Human chromosomes come in 23 matching pairs (an exception is the XY pair in males, which we will discuss shortly). Each member of a pair corresponds to the other in size, shape, and genetic functions, with one chromosome inherited from the mother and the other from the father (see Figure 3.1).

The Genetic Code

Chromosomes are made up of a chemical substance called **deoxyribonucleic acid,** or **DNA.** As Figure 3.2 shows, DNA is a long, double-stranded molecule that looks like a twisted ladder. Each rung of the ladder consists of a pair of chemical substances called bases. Although the bases always pair up in the same way across the ladder rungs—A with T, C with G—they can occur in any order along its sides. It is this sequence of base pairs that provides genetic instructions. A **gene** is a segment of DNA along the length of the chromosome. Genes can be of different lengths—perhaps 100 to several thousand ladder rungs long. An estimated 20,000 to 25,000 genes lie along the human chromosomes (International Human Genome Sequencing Consortium, 2004).

We share some of our genetic makeup with even the simplest organisms, such as bacteria and molds, and most of it with other mammals, especially primates. Between 98 and 99 percent of chimpanzee and human DNA is identical. This means that only a small portion of our heredity is responsible for the traits that make us human, from our upright gait to our extraordinary language and cognitive capacities. And the genetic variation from one human to the next is even less! Individuals around the world are about 99.1 percent genetically identical (Gibbons, 1998; Gibbons et al., 2004). Only a tiny quantity of DNA contributes to human variation in traits and capacities.

A unique feature of DNA is that it can duplicate itself through a process called **mitosis.** This special ability permits a single cell, formed at conception, to develop into a complex human being composed of a great many cells. Refer again to Figure 3.2, and you will see that during mitosis, the chromosomes copy themselves. As a result, each new body cell contains the same number of chromosomes and the identical genetic information.

Genes accomplish their task by sending instructions for making a rich assortment of proteins to the *cytoplasm,* the area surrounding the cell nucleus. Proteins, which trigger chemical reactions throughout the body, are the biological foundation on which our characteristics are

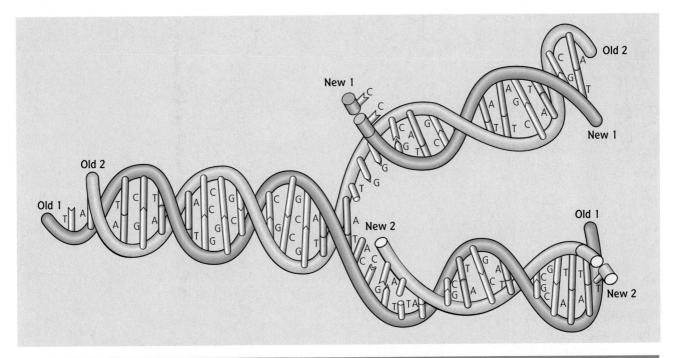

◀ **Figure 3.2**

DNA's ladderlike structure. This figure shows that the pairings of bases across the rungs of the ladder are very specific: Adenine (A) always appears with thymine (T), and cytosine (C) always appears with guanine (G). Here, the DNA ladder duplicates by splitting down the middle of its ladder rungs. Each free base picks up a new complementary partner from the area surrounding the cell nucleus.

built. How do humans, with far fewer genes than scientists once thought (only one-third more than the worm or fly), manage to develop into such complex beings? The answer lies in the proteins our genes make, which break up and reassemble in staggering variety—about 10 to 20 million altogether. Simpler species have far fewer proteins. Furthermore, the communication system between the cell nucleus and cytoplasm, which fine-tunes gene activity, is more intricate in humans than in simpler organisms. Within the cell, a wide range of environmental factors modify gene expression (Strachan & Read, 2004). So, even at this microscopic level, biological events are the result of *both* genetic and nongenetic forces.

The Sex Cells

New individuals are created when two special cells called **gametes,** or sex cells—the sperm and ovum—combine. A gamete contains only 23 chromosomes, half as many as a regular body cell. Gametes are formed through a cell division process called **meiosis,** which halves the number of chromosomes normally present in body cells. When sperm and ovum unite at fertilization, the cell that results, called a **zygote,** will again have 46 chromosomes.

Meiosis takes place according to the steps in Figure 3.3 on page 72. First, chromosomes pair up within the original cell, and each one copies itself. Then a special event called **crossing over** occurs, in which chromosomes next to each other break at one or more points along their length and exchange segments, so that genes from one are replaced by genes from another. This shuffling of genes creates new hereditary combinations. Next, the chromosome pairs separate into different cells, but chance determines which member of each pair will gather with others and end up in the same gamete. Finally, each chromosome leaves its partner and becomes part of a gamete containing only 23 chromosomes instead of the usual 46.

These events make the chances extremely low—about 1 in 700 trillion—that nontwin offspring of the same two parents will be genetically identical (Gould & Keeton, 1996). Therefore, meiosis helps us understand why siblings differ, even though they also have features

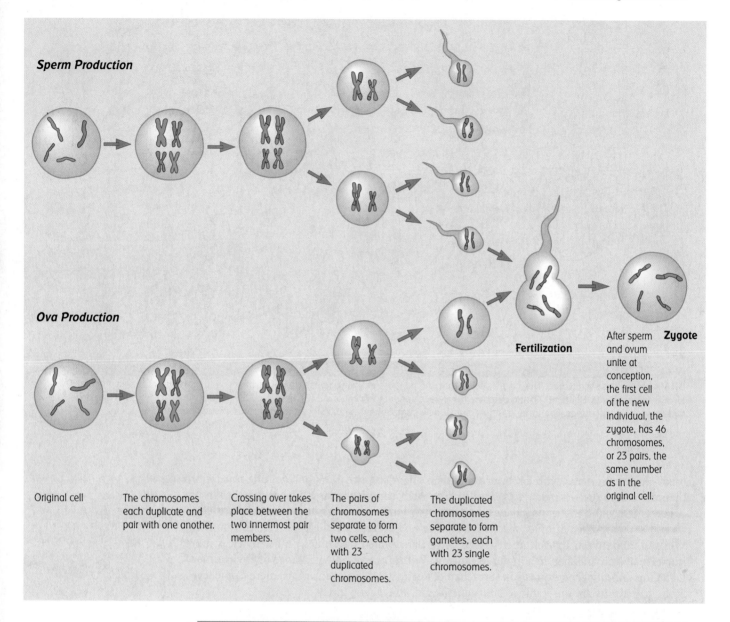

Sperm Production

Ova Production

After sperm and ovum unite at conception, the first cell of the new individual, the zygote, has 46 chromosomes, or 23 pairs, the same number as in the original cell.

Fertilization   **Zygote**

Original cell

The chromosomes each duplicate and pair with one another.

Crossing over takes place between the two innermost pair members.

The pairs of chromosomes separate to form two cells, each with 23 duplicated chromosomes.

The duplicated chromosomes separate to form gametes, each with 23 single chromosomes.

▲ **Figure 3.3**

The cell division process of meiosis, leading to gamete formation. (Here, original cells are depicted with 2 rather than the full complement of 23 pairs.) Meiosis creates gametes with only half the usual number of chromosomes. When sperm and ovum unite at conception, the first cell of the new individual (the zygote) has the correct, full number of chromosomes.

in common. The genetic variability produced by meiosis is adaptive: It increases the chances that at least some members of a species will cope with ever-changing environments and survive.

In the male, four sperm are produced when meiosis is complete. Also, the cells from which sperm arise are produced continuously throughout life. For this reason, a healthy man can father a child at any age after sexual maturity. In the female, meiosis results in just one ovum. In addition, the female is born with all her ova already present in her ovaries, and she can bear children for only three to four decades. Still, there are plenty of female sex cells. About 1 to 2 million are present at birth, 40,000 remain at adolescence, and approximately 350 to 450 will mature during a woman's childbearing years (Moore & Persaud, 2003).

Boy or Girl?

Return to Figure 3.1 and note the 22 matching pairs of chromosomes, which geneticists number from longest (1) to shortest (22). These are called **autosomes** (meaning *not* sex chromosomes). The twenty-third pair consists of **sex chromosomes.** In females, this pair is called XX; in males, it is called XY. The X is a relatively large chromosome, whereas the Y is short and carries little genetic material. When gametes form in males, the X and Y chromosomes separate into different sperm cells. The gametes that form in females all carry an X chromosome. Therefore, the sex of the new organism is determined by whether an X-bearing or a Y-bearing sperm fertilizes the ovum. In fact, scientists have isolated three genes on the Y chromosome that are crucial for male sexual development—one that switches on the production of male hormones and two involved in the formation of male sex organs. But they also know that other genes, yet to be discovered, are involved in the development of sexual characteristics (Cotinot et al., 2002).

Multiple Offspring

Sometimes a zygote that has started to duplicate separates into two clusters of cells that develop into two individuals. These are called **identical,** or **monozygotic, twins** because they have the same genetic makeup. The frequency of identical twins is the same around the world—about 1 in every 285 births (Zach, Pramanik, & Ford, 2001). Animal research has uncovered a variety of environmental influences that prompt this type of twinning, including temperature changes, variation in oxygen levels, and late fertilization of the ovum.

Fraternal, or **dizygotic, twins,** the most common type of multiple birth, results from the release and fertilization of two ova. Genetically fraternal twins are no more alike than ordinary siblings. Table 3.1 summarizes genetic and environmental factors that increase the chances of giving birth to fraternal twins. Older maternal age, fertility drugs, and in vitro fertilization (to be discussed shortly) are major causes of the doubling of fraternal twinning and the even greater rise in other multiple births in North America since 1970 (Russell et al., 2003; SOGC, 2003). Currently, fraternal twins account for 1 in every 38 births in the United States and 1 in every 85 births in Canada (Statistics Canada, 2004a; U.S. Department of Health and Human Services, 2004b).

◉ These identical, or monozygotic, twins were created when a duplicating zygote separated into two clusters of cells, and two individuals with the same genetic makeup developed.
© Laura Dwight Photography

TABLE 3.1	MATERNAL FACTORS LINKED TO FRATERNAL TWINNING
Factor	**Description**
Ethnicity	Occurs in 4 per 1,000 births among Asians, 8 per 1,000 births among whites, 12 to 16 per 1,000 births among blacks[a]
Family history of twinning	Occurs more often among women whose mothers and sisters gave birth to fraternal twins
Age	Rises with maternal age, peaking between 35 and 39 years, and then rapidly falls
Nutrition	Occurs less often among women with poor diets; occurs more often among women who are tall and overweight or of normal weight as opposed to slight body build
Number of births	Is more likely with each additional birth
Fertility drugs and in vitro fertilization	Is more likely with fertility hormones and in vitro fertilization (see page 82), which also increase the chances of triplets to quintuplets

[a]Worldwide rates, not including multiple births resulting from use of fertility drugs.

Source: Bortolus et al., 1999; Mange & Mange, 1998.

Patterns of Genetic Inheritance

Two forms of each gene occur at the same place on the chromosomes, one inherited from the mother and one from the father. Each form of a gene is called an **allele.** If the alleles from both parents are alike, the child is **homozygous** and will display the inherited trait. If the alleles differ, then the child is **heterozygous,** and relationships between the alleles determine the trait that will appear.

• **DOMINANT–RECESSIVE RELATIONSHIPS** • In many heterozygous pairings, **dominant–recessive inheritance** occurs: Only one allele affects the child's characteristics. It is called *dominant;* the second allele, which has no effect, is called *recessive.* Hair color is an example. The allele for dark hair is dominant (we can represent it with a capital *D*), whereas the one for blond hair is recessive (symbolized by a lowercase *b*). A child who inherits a homozygous pair of dominant alleles (*DD*) and a child who inherits a heterozygous pair (*Db*) will both be dark-haired, even though their genotypes differ. Blond hair can result only from having two recessive alleles (*bb*). Still, heterozygous individuals with just one recessive allele (*Db*) can pass that trait to their children. Therefore, they are called **carriers** of the trait.

Some human characteristics and disorders that follow the rules of dominant–recessive inheritance are listed in Table 3.2 and Table 3.3, respectively. As you can see, many disabilities and diseases are the product of recessive alleles. One of the most frequently occurring recessive disorders is *phenylketonuria,* or *PKU,* which affects the way the body breaks down proteins contained in many foods. Infants born with two recessive alleles lack an enzyme that converts one of the basic amino acids that make up proteins (phenylalanine) into a by-product essential for body functioning (tyrosine). Without this enzyme, phenylalanine quickly builds to toxic levels that damage the central nervous system. By 1 year, infants with PKU are permanently mentally retarded.

Despite its potentially damaging effects, PKU provides an excellent illustration of the fact that inheriting unfavorable genes does not always lead to an untreatable condition. All U.S. states and Canadian provinces require that each newborn be given a blood test for PKU. If the disease is found, doctors immediately place the baby on a diet low in phenylalanine. Children who receive this treatment nevertheless show mild deficits in certain cognitive skills, such as memory, planning, and problem solving, because even small amounts of phenylalanine interfere with brain functioning. Cognitive deficits increase in severity with greater phenylalanine exposure (Antshel, 2003; Luciana, Sullivan, & Nelson, 2001). But as long as dietary treatment begins early and continues, children with PKU usually attain an average level of intelligence and have a normal lifespan.

In dominant–recessive inheritance, if we know the genetic makeup of the parents, we can predict the percentage of children in a family who are likely to display or carry a trait. Figure 3.4 on page 76 illustrates this for PKU. Notice that for a child to inherit the condition, each parent must have a recessive allele (*p*). As the figure also shows, a single gene can affect more than one trait. Because of their inability to convert phenylalanine into tyrosine (which is responsible for pigmentation), children with PKU usually have light hair and blue eyes. Furthermore, children vary in the degree to which phenylalanine accumulates in their tissues and in the extent to which they respond to treatment. This is due to the action of **modifier genes,** which enhance or dilute the effects of other genes.

Only rarely are serious diseases due to dominant alleles. Think about why this is so. Children who inherit the

---

TABLE 3.2   EXAMPLES OF DOMINANT AND RECESSIVE CHARACTERISTICS

Dominant	Recessive
Dark hair	Blond hair
Normal hair	Pattern baldness
Curly hair	Straight hair
Nonred hair	Red hair
Facial dimples	No dimples
Normal hearing	Some forms of deafness
Normal vision	Nearsightedness
Farsightedness	Normal vision
Normal vision	Congenital eye cataracts
Normally pigmented skin	Albinism
Double-jointedness	Normal joints
Type A blood	Type O blood
Type B blood	Type O blood
Rh-positive blood	Rh-negative blood

Note: Many normal characteristics that were previously thought to result from dominant–recessive inheritance, such as eye color, are now regarded as due to multiple genes. For the characteristics listed here, most experts agree that the simple dominant–recessive relationship holds.

Source: McKusick, 1998.

TABLE 3.3   EXAMPLES OF DOMINANT AND RECESSIVE DISEASES

Disease	Description	Mode of Inheritance	Incidence	Treatment
Autosomal Diseases				
Cooley's anemia	Pale appearance, retarded physical growth, and lethargic behavior begin in infancy.	Recessive	1 in 500 births to parents of Mediterranean descent	Frequent blood transfusion; death from complications usually occurs by adolescence.
Cystic fibrosis	Lungs, liver, and pancreas secrete large amounts of thick mucus, leading to breathing and digestive difficulties.	Recessive	1 in 2,000 to 2,500 Caucasian births; 1 in 16,000 births to North Americans of African descent	Bronchial drainage, prompt treatment of respiratory infection, dietary management. Advances in medical care allow survival with good life quality into adulthood.
Phenylketonnuria (PKU)	Inability to metabolize the amino acid phenylalanine, contained in many proteins, causes severe central nervous system damage in the first year of life.	Recessive	1 in 8,000 births	Placing the child on a special diet results in average intelligence and normal lifespan. Subtle difficulties with planning and problem solving are often present.
Sickle cell anemia	Abnormal sickling of red blood cells causes oxygen deprivation, pain, swelling, and tissue damage. Anemia and susceptibility to infections, especially pneumonia, occur.	Recessive	1 in 600 births to North Americans of African descent	Blood transfusions, painkillers, prompt treatment of infection. No known cure; 50 percent die by age 20.
Tay-Sachs disease	Central nervous system degeneration, with onset at about 6 months, leads to poor muscle tone, blindness, deafness, and convulsions.	Recessive	1 in 3,600 births to Jews of European descent and to French Canadians	None. Death by 3 to 4 years of age.
Huntington disease	Central nervous system degeneration leads to muscular coordination difficulties, mental deterioration, and personality changes. Symptoms usually do not appear until age 35 or later.	Dominant	1 in 18,000 to 25,000 births	None. Death occurs 10 to 20 years after symptom onset.
Marfan syndrome	Tall, slender build; thin, elongated arms and legs. Heart defects and eye abnormalities, especially of the lens. Excessive lengthening of the body results in a variety of skeletal defects.	Dominant	1 in 20,000 births	Correction of heart and eye defects sometimes possible. Death from heart failure in young adulthood is common.
X-Linked Diseases				
Duchenne muscular dystrophy	Degenerative muscle disease. Abnormal gait, loss of ability to walk between 7 and 13 years of age.	Recessive	1 in 3,000 to 5,000 male births	None. Death from respiratory infection or weakening of the heart muscle usually occurs in adolescence.
Hemophilia	Blood fails to clot normally. Can lead to severe internal bleeding and tissue damage.	Recessive	1 in 4,000 to 7,000 male births	Blood transfusions. Safety precautions to prevent injury.
Diabetes insipidus	Insufficient production of the hormone vasopressin results in excessive thirst and urination. Dehydration can cause central nervous system damage.	Recessive	1 in 2,500 male births	Hormone replacement.

Note: For recessive disorders, carrier status can be detected in prospective parents through a blood test or genetic analyses. For all disorders listed, prenatal diagnosis is available (see page 81).

Sources: Behrman, Kliegman, & Arvin, 1996; Chodirker et al., 2001; Gott, 1998; Grody, 1999; Knoers et al., 1993; McKusick, 1998; Schulman & Black, 1997.

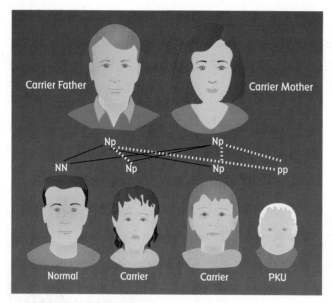

▲ **Figure 3.4**

Dominant–recessive mode of inheritance, as illustrated by PKU. When both parents are heterozygous carriers of the recessive gene (*p*), we can predict that 25 percent of their offspring are likely to be normal (*NN*), 50 percent are likely to be carriers (*Np*), and 25 percent are likely to inherit the disorder (*pp*). Notice that the PKU-affected child, in contrast to his siblings, has light hair. The recessive gene for PKU affects more than one trait. It also leads to fair coloring.

dominant allele always develop the disorder. They seldom live long enough to reproduce, so the harmful dominant allele is eliminated from the family's heredity in a single generation. Some dominant disorders, however, do persist. One is *Huntington disease,* a condition in which the central nervous system degenerates. Why has this disorder endured? Its symptoms usually do not appear until age 35 or later, after the person has passed on the dominant gene to his or her children.

• **CODOMINANCE** • In some heterozygous circumstances, the dominant–recessive relationship does not hold completely. Instead, we see **codominance,** a pattern of inheritance in which both alleles influence the person's characteristics.

The *sickle cell trait,* a heterozygous condition present in many black Africans, provides an example. *Sickle cell anemia* (see Table 3.3 on page 75) occurs in full form when a child inherits two recessive alleles. They cause the usually round red blood cells to become sickle (crescent moon) shaped, especially under low-oxygen conditions. The sickled cells clog the blood vessels and block the flow of blood, causing intense pain, swelling, and tissue damage. Thirty years ago, only half of affected children reached adulthood; today, 85 percent do. But even with better medical treatment, North Americans with sickle cell anemia have an average life expectancy of only 55 years (Quinn, Rogers, & Buchanan, 2004; Wierenga, Hambleton, & Lewis, 2001). Heterozygous individuals are protected from the disease under most circumstances. However, when they experience oxygen deprivation—for example, at high altitudes or after intense physical exercise—the single recessive allele asserts itself, and a temporary mild form of the illness occurs.

The sickle cell allele is common among black Africans for a special reason. Carriers of it are more resistant to malaria than are individuals with two alleles for normal red blood cells. In Africa, where malaria is common, these carriers survived and reproduced more frequently than others, leading the gene to be maintained in the black population. In regions of the world where the risk of malaria is low, the frequency of the gene is declining. For example, compared with 20 percent of black Africans, only 8 percent of African Americans are carriers. The carrier rate is believed to be slightly higher in Canada than in the United States because a greater proportion of African Canadians are recent immigrants (Goldbloom, 2004).

• **X-LINKED INHERITANCE** • Males and females have an equal chance of inheriting recessive disorders carried on the autosomes, such as PKU and sickle cell anemia. But when a harmful allele is carried on the X chromosome, **X-linked inheritance** applies. Males are more likely to be affected because their sex chromosomes do not match. In females, any recessive allele on one X chromosome has a good chance of being suppressed by a dominant allele on the other X. But the Y chromosome is only about one-third as long and therefore lacks many corresponding alleles to override those on the X. A well-known example is *hemophilia,* a disorder in which the blood fails to clot normally. Figure 3.5 shows its greater likelihood of inheritance by male children whose mothers carry the abnormal allele.

Besides X-linked disorders, many other sex differences reveal the male to be at a disadvantage. Rates of miscarriage, infant and childhood deaths, birth defects, learning disabilities, behavior disorders, and mental retardation all are higher for boys (Halpern, 1997). It is possible that these sex differences can be traced to the genetic code. The female, with two X chromosomes, benefits from a greater variety of genes. Nature, however, seems to have adjusted for the male's disadvantage. Worldwide, about 105 boys are born for every 100 girls, and judging from miscarriage and abortion statistics, a still greater number of boys are conceived (Pyeritz, 1998).

Nevertheless, in recent decades, the proportion of male births has declined in many industrialized countries, including the United States, Canada, and European nations (Jongbloet et al., 2001). Some researchers attribute the trend to a rise in stressful living conditions, which heighten spontaneous abortions, especially of male fetuses. In one test of this hypothesis, male-to-female-birth ratios in East Germany were examined over the 54-year period between 1946 and 1999. The ratio was lowest in 1991, the year that the country's economy collapsed (Catalano, 2003).

• **GENETIC IMPRINTING** • More than 1,000 human characteristics follow the rules of dominant–recessive and codominant inheritance (McKusick, 1998). In these cases, whichever parent contributes a gene to the new individual, the gene responds in the same way. Geneticists, however, have identified some exceptions. In **genetic imprinting,** alleles are *imprinted,* or chemically *marked,* so that one pair member (either the mother's or the father's) is activated, regardless of its makeup. The imprint is often temporary; it may be erased in the next generation, and it may not occur in all individuals (Everman & Cassidy, 2000).

Imprinting helps us understand certain puzzling genetic patterns. For example, children are more likely to develop diabetes if their father, rather than their mother, suffers from it. And people with asthma or hay fever tend to have mothers, not fathers, with the illness. Imprinting is involved in several childhood cancers and in *Prader-Willi syndrome,* a disorder with symptoms of mental retardation and severe obesity (Buiting et al., 2003). It may also explain why Huntington disease, when inherited from the father, tends to emerge at an earlier age and progress more rapidly (Navarrete, Martinez, & Salamanca, 1994).

Genetic imprinting can also operate on the sex chromosomes, as *fragile X syndrome*—the most common inherited cause of mental retardation—reveals. In this disorder, an abnormal repetition of a sequence of DNA bases occurs in a special spot on the X chromosome, damaging a particular gene. The defective gene at the fragile site is expressed only when it is passed from mother to child. Because the disorder is X-linked, males are more severely affected than females (Reiss & Dant, 2003). Females usually have a normally functioning gene on their other X chromosome (inherited from the father) that partially compensates for the abnormal gene.

The intellectual deficits of fragile X syndrome range from mild learning disabilities to severe mental retardation. Certain physical features, such as enlarged ears, a long face with a prominent chin, and (in males) enlarged testicles are common. Fragile X has also been linked to 2 to 3 percent of cases of *autism,* a serious disorder usually diagnosed in early childhood that involves impaired social interaction, delayed or absent language and communication, narrow and overly intense interests, and repetitive motor behavior (Hagerman & Hagerman, 2002).

Approximately 1 in 250 females and 1 in 800 males are carriers of fragile X. They typically have an abnormal DNA repeat that is too short to produce symptoms. But as females pass the

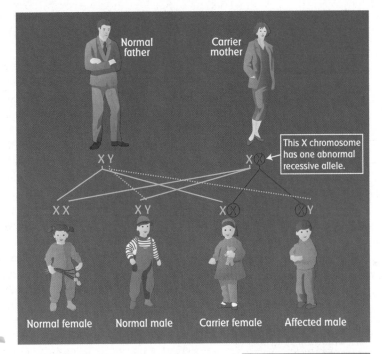

Normal father   Carrier mother

This X chromosome has one abnormal recessive allele.

Normal female   Normal male   Carrier female   Affected male

▲ **Figure 3.5**

X-linked inheritance. In the example shown here, the allele on the father's X chromosome is normal. The mother has one normal and one abnormal recessive allele on her X chromosomes. By looking at the possible combinations of the parents' alleles, we can predict that 50 percent of these parents' male children are likely to have the disorder and 50 percent of their female children are likely to be carriers of it.

A boy with fragile X syndrome works in the classroom. The disorder, tied to gene damage on the X chromosome, can produce a range of deficits—from mild learning disabilities to severe mental retardation.
© Laura Dwight Photography

gene to their offspring, the repeat often destabilizes and enlarges (Oostra & Willemsen, 2002). Consequently, with each generation, the chances increase that offspring will inherit the disorder.

• MUTATION • How are harmful genes created in the first place? The answer is **mutation, a sudden but permanent change in a segment of DNA.** A mutation may affect only one or two genes, or it may involve many genes, as in the chromosomal disorders we will discuss shortly. Some mutations occur spontaneously, simply by chance. Others are caused by hazardous environmental agents.

Although nonionizing forms of radiation—electromagnetic waves and microwaves—have no demonstrated impact on DNA, ionizing (high-energy) radiation is an established cause of mutation. Women who receive repeated doses before conception are more likely to miscarry or to give birth to children with hereditary defects. Genetic abnormalities, such as physical malformations and childhood cancer, are also higher in children whose fathers are exposed to radiation in their occupation. However, infrequent and mild exposure to radiation does not cause genetic damage (Jacquet, 2004). It takes high doses over a long period to impair DNA.

Less than 3 percent of pregnancies result in the birth of a baby with a hereditary abnormality. Nevertheless, these children account for about 20 percent of infant deaths and contribute substantially to lifelong impaired physical and mental functioning (U.S. Department of Health and Human Services, 2004a). Progress in preventing and treating genetic diseases still lags far behind that for nongenetic diseases, although (as we will see shortly) great strides are being made.

• POLYGENIC INHERITANCE • So far, we have discussed patterns of inheritance in which people either display a trait or do not. These cut-and-dried individual differences are much easier to trace to their genetic origins than are characteristics that vary on a continuum among people, such as height, weight, intelligence, and personality. These traits are due to **polygenic inheritance,** in which many genes determine the characteristic in question. Polygenic inheritance is complex, and much about it is still unknown. In the final section of this chapter, we will discuss how researchers infer the influence of heredity on human attributes when they do not know the precise patterns of inheritance.

Chromosomal Abnormalities

Besides harmful recessive alleles, abnormalities of the chromosomes are a major cause of serious developmental problems. Most chromosomal defects result from mistakes occurring during meiosis, when the ovum and sperm are formed. A chromosome pair does not separate properly, or part of a chromosome breaks off. Because these errors involve far more DNA than problems due to single genes, they usually produce many physical and mental symptoms.

◉ The facial features of the 9-year-old boy on the right are typical of Down syndrome. Here he collaborates with his normally developing 4-year-old brother in making won ton dumplings.
© Laura Dwight Photography

• DOWN SYNDROME • The most common chromosomal abnormality, occurring in 1 out of every 800 live births, is *Down syndrome.* In 95 percent of cases, it results from a failure of the twenty-first pair of chromosomes to separate during meiosis, so the new individual inherits three of these chromosomes rather than the normal two. For this reason, Down syndrome is sometimes called *trisomy 21.* In other, less frequent forms, an extra broken piece of a twenty-first chromosome is attached to part of another chromosome (called a *translocation* pattern). Or an error occurs during the early stages of mitosis, causing some but not all body cells to have the defective chromosomal makeup (called a *mosaic* pattern) (Tocci, 2000). Because less genetic material is involved in the mosaic type, symptoms of the disorder are usually less extreme.

The consequences of Down syndrome include mental retardation, memory and speech problems, limited vocabulary, and slow motor development. Affected individuals also have distinct physical features—a short, stocky build, a flattened face, a protruding tongue, almond-shaped eyes, and an unusual crease running across the palm of the hand. In addition, infants with Down syndrome are often born with eye cataracts, hearing loss, and heart and intestinal defects. Because of medical advances, fewer individuals with Down syndrome die early than was the case in the past.

Many survive into their fifties, and a few into their sixties to eighties (Roizen & Patterson, 2003). Although this lengthening of life expectancy is cause for celebration, many affected individuals who live past age 40 show symptoms of Alzheimer's disease, the most common form of dementia (Head & Lott, 2004). Genes on chromosome 21 are linked to this disorder.

Parents face extra challenges in caring for a baby with Down syndrome. Facial deformities often lead to breathing and feeding difficulties. Also, these infants smile less readily, show poor eye-to-eye contact, and explore objects less persistently. But when parents encourage them to become engaged in their surroundings, Down syndrome children develop more favorably (Sigman, 1999). They also benefit from infant and preschool intervention programs, although emotional, social, and motor skills improve more than intellectual performance (Carr, 2002). Clearly, environmental factors affect how well children with Down syndrome fare.

As Table 3.4 shows, the risk of bearing a Down syndrome baby rises dramatically with maternal age. Why is this so? Geneticists believe that the ova, present in the woman's body since her own prenatal period, weaken over time. As a result, chromosomes do not separate properly as they complete the process of meiosis at conception. But in about 5 to 10 percent of cases, the extra genetic material originates with the father. The reasons for this mutation are unknown. Some studies suggest a role for advanced paternal age, whereas others show no age effects (Fisch et al., 2003; Muller et al., 2000; Savage et al., 1998).

• **ABNORMALITIES OF THE SEX CHROMOSOMES** • Disorders of the autosomes other than Down syndrome usually disrupt development so severely that miscarriage occurs. When such babies are born, they rarely survive beyond early childhood. In contrast, abnormalities of the sex chromosomes usually lead to fewer problems. In fact, sex chromosome disorders often are not recognized until adolescence when, in some of the deviations, puberty is delayed. The most common problems involve the presence of an extra chromosome (either X or Y) or the absence of one X in females (see Table 3.5).

A variety of myths about individuals with sex chromosome disorders have been discredited by research. For example, as is evident from Table 3.5, males with *XYY syndrome* are not necessarily more aggressive and antisocial than XY males. And most children with sex chromosome disorders do not suffer from mental retardation. Instead, their intellectual problems

TABLE 3.4	RISK OF GIVING BIRTH TO A BABY WITH DOWN SYNDROME BY MATERNAL AGE
Maternal Age	**Risk**
20	1 in 1,900 births
25	1 in 1,200
30	1 in 900
33	1 in 600
36	1 in 280
39	1 in 130
42	1 in 65
45	1 in 30
48	1 in 15

Note: The risk of giving birth to a baby with Down syndrome after age 35 has increased slightly over the past 20 years, due to improved medical interventions during pregnancy and consequent greater likelihood of a Down syndrome fetus surviving to be liveborn.

Source: Adapted from Halliday et al., 1995; Meyers et al., 1997.

TABLE 3.5	SEX CHROMOSOMAL DISORDERS		
Disorder	**Description**	**Incidence**	**Treatment**
XYY syndrome	Extra Y chromosome. Above-average height, large teeth, and sometimes severe acne. Intelligence, male sexual development, and fertility are normal.	1 in 1,000 male births	No special treatment necessary.
Triple X syndrome (XXX)	Extra X chromosome. Tallness and impaired verbal intelligence. Female sexual development and fertility are normal.	1 in 500 to 1,250 female births	Special education to treat verbal ability problems.
Klinefelter syndrome (XXY)	Extra X chromosome. Tallness, body fat distribution resembling females, incomplete development of sex characteristics at puberty, sterility, and impaired verbal intelligence.	1 in 900 male births	Hormone therapy at puberty to stimulate development of sex characteristics; special education to treat verbal ability problems.
Turner syndrome (XO)	Missing X chromosome. Short stature, webbed neck, incomplete development of sex characteristics at puberty, sterility, and impaired spatial intelligence.	1 in 2,500 to 8,000 female births	Hormone therapy in childhood to stimulate physical growth and at puberty to promote development of sex characteristics; special education to treat spatial ability problems.

Sources: Geerts, Steyaert, & Fryns, 2003; Moore & Persaud, 2003; Simpson et al., 2003; Rovet et al., 1996.

usually are very specific. Verbal difficulties—for example, with reading and vocabulary—are common among girls with *triple X syndrome* and boys with *Klinefelter syndrome*, both of whom inherit an extra X chromosome. In contrast, girls with *Turner syndrome*, who are missing an X, have trouble with spatial relationships—for example, drawing pictures, telling right from left, following travel directions, and noticing changes in facial expressions (Geschwind et al., 2000; Lawrence et al., 2003; Simpson et al., 2003). These findings tell us that adding to or subtracting from the usual number of X chromosomes results in particular intellectual deficits. At present, geneticists do not know why.

Ask Yourself

REVIEW Explain the genetic origins of PKU and Down syndrome. Cite evidence indicating that both heredity and environment contribute to the development of children with these disorders.

REVIEW Using your knowledge of genetic imprinting and X-linked inheritance, explain how fragile X syndrome is passed from parent to child, and why its symptoms are more severe in males than females.

APPLY Gilbert's genetic makeup is homozygous for dark hair. Jan's is homozygous for blond hair. What proportion of their children are likely to be dark-haired? Explain.

CONNECT Referring to ecological systems theory (Chapter 1, pages 26–29), explain why parents of children with genetic disorders often experience increased stress. What factors, within and beyond the family, can help these parents support their children's development?

Reproductive Choices

In the past, many couples with genetic disorders in their families chose not to have children rather than risk the birth of an abnormal baby. Today, genetic counseling and prenatal diagnosis help people make informed decisions about conceiving or carrying a pregnancy to term.

Genetic Counseling

Genetic counseling is a communication process designed to help couples assess their chances of giving birth to a baby with a hereditary disorder and choose the best course of action in view of risks and family goals (Shiloh, 1996). Individuals likely to seek counseling are those who have had difficulties bearing children—for example, repeated miscarriages—or who know that genetic problems exist in their families. In addition, women who delay childbearing past age 35 are candidates for genetic counseling. After this age, the overall rate of chromosomal abnormalities rises sharply, from 1 in every 190 to as many as 1 in every 20 pregnancies at age 43 (Wille et al., 2004).

If a family history of mental retardation, physical defects, or inherited diseases exists, the genetic counselor interviews the couple and prepares a *pedigree,* a picture of the family tree in which affected relatives are identified. The pedigree is used to estimate the likelihood that parents will have an abnormal child, using the genetic principles discussed earlier in this chapter. For many disorders, blood tests or genetic analyses can reveal whether the parent is a carrier of the harmful gene. Carrier detection is possible for all the recessive diseases listed in Table 3.3 on page 75, as well as others, and for fragile X syndrome.

When all the relevant information is in, the genetic counselor helps people consider appropriate options. These include taking a chance and conceiving, adopting a child, or choosing from a variety of reproductive technologies (see the From Research to Practice box on pages 82 and 83), or adopting a child.

Prenatal Diagnosis and Fetal Medicine

If couples who might bear an abnormal child decide to conceive, several **prenatal diagnostic methods**—medical procedures that permit detection of problems before birth—are available (see Table 3.6). Women of advanced maternal age are prime candidates for *amniocentesis* or *chorionic villus sampling* (see Figure 3.6 on page 84). Except for *ultrasound* and *maternal blood analysis*, however, prenatal diagnosis should not be used routinely, since other methods have some chance of injuring the developing organism.

Prenatal diagnosis has led to advances in fetal medicine. For example, by inserting a needle into the uterus, doctors can administer drugs to the fetus. Surgery has been performed to repair such problems as heart, lung, and diaphragm malformations, urinary tract obstructions, neural defects, and tumors of the tailbone. Fetuses with blood disorders have been given blood transfusions. And those with immune deficiencies have received bone marrow transplants that succeeded in creating a normally functioning immune system (Flake, 2003).

These techniques frequently result in complications, the most common being premature labor and miscarriage (James, 1998). Yet parents may be willing to try almost any option, even one with only a slim chance of success. Currently, the medical profession is struggling with how to help parents make informed decisions about fetal surgery.

Advances in *genetic engineering* also offer new hope for correcting hereditary defects. As part of the Human Genome Project—an ambitious, international research program aimed at deciphering the chemical makeup of human genetic material (genome)—researchers have mapped the sequence of all human DNA base pairs. Using that information, they are "annotating" the genome—identifying all its genes and their functions, including their protein products and what these products do. A major goal is to understand the estimated 4,000 human disorders, both those due to single genes and those resulting from a complex interplay of multiple genes and environmental factors.

TABLE 3.6 PRENATAL DIAGNOSTIC METHODS

Method	Description
Amniocentesis	The most widely used technique. A hollow needle is inserted through the abdominal wall to obtain a sample of fluid in the uterus. Cells are examined for genetic defects. Can be performed by the fourteenth week after conception; 1 to 2 more weeks are required for test results. Small risk of miscarriage.
Chorionic villus sampling	A procedure that can be used if results are desired or needed very early in pregnancy. A thin tube is inserted into the uterus through the vagina, or a hollow needle is inserted through the abdominal wall. A small plug of tissue is removed from the end of one or more chorionic villi, the hairlike projections on the membrane surrounding the developing organism. Cells are examined for genetic defects. Can be performed by the ninth week after conception, and results are available within 24 hours. Entails a slightly greater risk of miscarriage than amniocentesis. Also associated with a small risk of limb deformities, which increases the earlier the procedure is performed.
Fetoscopy	A small tube with a light source at one end is inserted into the uterus to inspect the fetus for defects of the limbs and face. Also allows a sample of fetal blood to be obtained, permitting diagnosis of such disorders as hemophilia and sickle cell anemia, as well as neural defects (see below). Usually performed between 15 and 18 weeks after conception, but can be done as early as 5 weeks. Entails some risk of miscarriage.
Ultrasound	High-frequency sound waves are beamed at the uterus; their reflection is translated into a picture on a video screen that reveals the size, shape, and placement of the fetus. By itself, permits assessment of fetal age, detection of multiple pregnancies, and identification of gross physical defects. Also used to guide amniocentesis, chorionic villus sampling, and fetoscopy. When used five or more times, may increase the chances of low birth weight.
Maternal blood analysis	By the second month of pregnancy, some of the developing organism's cells enter the maternal bloodstream. An elevated level of alpha-fetoprotein may indicate kidney disease, abnormal closure of the esophagus, or neural tube defects, such as *anencephaly* (absence of most of the brain) and *spina bifida* (bulging of the spinal cord from the spinal column). Isolated cells can be examined for genetic defects, such as Down syndrome.
Preimplantation genetic diagnosis	After in vitro fertilization and duplication of the zygote into a cluster of about eight cells, one cell is removed and examined for hereditary defects. Only if that cell is free of detectable genetic disorders is the fertilized ovum implanted in the woman's uterus. Permits parents at high risk of bearing offspring with a genetic disorder and women of advanced childbearing age to avoid implantation of most abnormal embryos.

Sources: Kumar & O'Brien, 2004; Moore & Persaud, 2003; Newnham et al., 1993; Sermon, Van Steirteghem, & Liebaers, 2004.

FROM RESEARCH TO PRACTICE

The Pros and Cons of Reproductive Technologies

Some couples decide not to risk pregnancy because of a history of genetic disease. Many others—in fact, one-sixth of all couples who try to conceive—discover that they are sterile. And some never-married adults and gay and lesbian partners want to bear children. Today, increasing numbers of individuals are turning to alternative methods of conception—technologies that, although they fulfill the wish of parenthood, have become the subject of heated debate.

Donor Insemination and In Vitro Fertilization

For several decades, *donor insemination*—injection of sperm from an anonymous man into a woman—has been used to overcome male reproductive difficulties. In recent years, it has also enabled women without a heterosexual partner to become pregnant. Donor insemination is 70 to 80 percent successful, resulting in about 30,000 to 50,000 births in North America each year (Reynolds et al., 2003; Wright et al., 2004).

In vitro fertilization is another reproductive technology that has become increasingly common. Since the first "test tube" baby was born in England in 1978, 1 percent of all North American children—about 40,000 babies in the United States and 3,500 in Canada—have been conceived through this technique annually (Jackson, Gibson, & Wu, 2004; Sutcliffe, 2002). With in vitro fertilization, hormones are given to a woman, stimulating the ripening of several ova. These are removed surgically and placed in a dish of nutrients, to which sperm are added. Once an ovum is fertilized and begins to duplicate into several cells, it is injected into the mother's uterus.

By mixing and matching gametes, pregnancies can be brought about when either or both partners have a reproductive problem. Usually, in vitro fertilization is used to

treat women whose fallopian tubes are permanently damaged. But a recently developed technique permits a single sperm to be injected directly into an ovum, thereby overcoming most male fertility problems. And a "sex sorter" method helps ensure that couples who carry X-linked diseases (which usually affect males) have a daughter. Fertilized ova and sperm can even be frozen and stored in embryo banks for use at some future time, thereby guaranteeing healthy zygotes should age or illness lead to fertility problems.

The overall success rate of in vitro fertilization is about 30 percent. However, success declines steadily with age, from 40 percent in women younger than age 35 to 7 percent in women age 43 and older (Wright et al., 2004). Furthermore, the resulting children may be genetically unrelated to one or both of their parents. In addition, most parents who used in vitro fertilization do not tell their children about their origins, even though health professionals usually encourage them to do so. Does lack of genetic ties or secrecy surrounding these techniques interfere with parent–child relationships? Perhaps because of a strong desire for parenthood, caregiving tends to be somewhat warmer for young children conceived through donor insemination or in vitro fertilization. And in vitro infants are as securely attached to their parents, and in vitro children and adolescents as well adjusted, as their counterparts who were naturally conceived (Golombok & MacCallum, 2003).

Although donor insemination and in vitro fertilization have many benefits, serious questions have arisen about their use. Most U.S. states and Canadian provinces have few legal guidelines for these procedures. As a result, donors are not always screened for genetic or sexually transmit-

ted diseases. In many countries, including Canada, Denmark, Great Britain, Norway, and the United States, donors remain anonymous, and doctors are not required to keep records of their characteristics. Canada, however, retains a file on donor identities, permitting contact only in cases of serious disease, where knowledge of the child's genetic background might be helpful for medical reasons (Bioethics Consultative Committee, 2003). Another concern is that the in vitro "sex sorter" method will lead to parental sex selection, thereby eroding the moral value that boys and girls are equally precious.

Finally, more than 50 percent of in vitro procedures result in multiple births. Most are twins, but 9 percent are triplets and higher-order multiples. Consequently, among in vitro babies, the rate of low birth weight is 2.6 times higher than in the general population (Jackson, Gibson, & Wu, 2004). Risk of major birth defects also doubles because of many factors, including drugs used to induce ripening of ova and to maintain the pregnancy and delays in fertilizing ova outside the womb (Hansen et al., 2002). In sum, in vitro fertilization poses greater risks than natural conception to infant survival and healthy development.

Surrogate Motherhood

An even more controversial form of medically assisted conception is *surrogate motherhood*. Typically in this procedure, sperm from a man whose wife is infertile are used to inseminate a woman, called a surrogate, who is paid a fee for her childbearing services. In return, the surrogate agrees to turn the baby over to the man (who is the natural father). The child is then adopted by his wife.

Although most of these arrangements proceed smoothly, those that end up in court highlight serious risks for all concerned. In one case, both parties rejected the infant with severe disabilities that resulted from the pregnancy. In several others, the surrogate mother wanted to keep the baby or the couple changed their minds during the pregnancy. And in still another case, a couple who had arranged a surrogate birth later divorced and tried to walk away from their baby, until the courts intervened (Schwartz, 2003). These children came into the world in the midst of conflict that threatened to last for years.

Because surrogacy favors the wealthy as contractors for infants and the less economically advantaged as surrogates, it may promote exploitation of financially needy women (Sureau, 1997). In addition, most surrogates already have children of their own, who may be deeply affected by the pregnancy. Knowledge that their mother would give away a baby for profit may cause these children to worry about the security of their own family circumstances.

New Reproductive Frontiers

Reproductive technologies are evolving faster than societies can weigh the ethics of these procedures. Doctors have used donor ova from younger women in combination with in vitro fertilization to help postmenopausal women become pregnant. Most recipients are in their forties, but several women in their fifties and sixties have given birth. Even though candidates for postmenopausal-assisted childbirth are selected on the basis of good health, serious questions arise about bringing children into the world whose parents may not live to see them reach adulthood. Based on U.S. life expectancy data, 1 in 3 mothers and 1 in 2 fathers having a baby at age 55 will die before their child enters college (U.S. Census Bureau, 2004b).

Currently, experts are debating other reproductive options. In once instance, a woman with a busy stage career who could have conceived naturally chose to combine in vitro fertilization (using her own ova and her husband's sperm) and surrogate motherhood. This permitted the woman to continue her career while the surrogate carried her biological child (Wood, 2001). At donor banks, customers can select ova or sperm on the basis of physical characteristics and even IQ. Some worry that this practice is a dangerous step toward selective breeding through "designer babies" — controlling offspring characteristics by manipulating the genetic makeup of fertilized ova.

Finally, scientists have successfully cloned (made multiple copies of) fertilized ova in sheep, cattle, and monkeys, and they are working on effective ways to do so in humans. By providing extra ova for injection, cloning might improve the success rate of in vitro fertilization. But it also opens the possibility of mass-producing genetically identical people. Therefore, it is widely condemned (Fasouliotis & Schenker, 2000).

Although reproductive technologies permit many barren couples to rear healthy newborn babies, laws are needed to regulate such practices. In Australia, New Zealand, Sweden, and Switzerland, individuals conceived with donated gametes have a right to information about their genetic origins (Frith, 2001). Pressure from those working in the field of assisted reproduction may soon lead to similar policies in the United States and Canada.

In the case of surrogate motherhood, the ethical problems are so complex that 18 U.S. states have sharply restricted the practice, and Australia, Canada, and many European nations have banned it, arguing that the status of a baby should not be a matter of

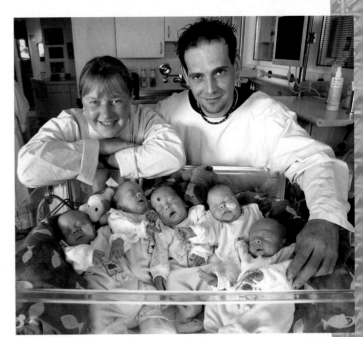

▲ Fertility drugs and in vitro fertilization often lead to multiple fetuses. This German couple has given birth to quintuplets. The babies were very small at birth, averaging 2 pounds, or 940 grams, each. Although they are now in good condition, reproductive technologies can pose grave ethical dilemmas. When three or more fetuses fill the uterus, pregnancy complications are often so severe that doctors recommend aborting one or more to save the others.
© AP/ Wide World Photos

commercial arrangement, and that a part of the body should not be rented or sold (Chen, 2003; McGee, 1997). Denmark, France, and Great Britain have prohibited in vitro fertilization for women past menopause (Bioethics Consultative Committee, 2003). At present, nothing is known about the psychological consequences of being a product of these procedures. Research on how such children grow up, including what they know and how they feel about their origins, is important for weighing the pros and cons of these techniques.

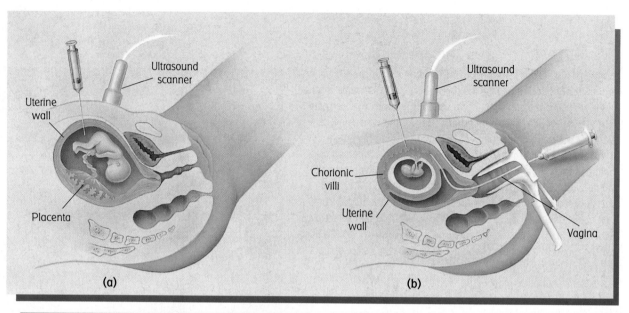

▲ **Figure 3.6**

Amniocentesis and chorionic villus sampling.   Today, hundreds of defects and diseases can be detected before birth using these two procedures. (a) In amniocentesis, a hollow needle is inserted through the abdominal wall into the uterus during the fourteenth week after conception, or later. Fluid is withdrawn and fetal cells are cultured, a process that takes 1 to 2 weeks. (b) Chorionic villus sampling can be performed much earlier in pregnancy, at 9 weeks after conception, and results are available within 24 hours. Two approaches to obtaining a sample of chorionic villus are shown: inserting a thin tube through the vagina into the uterus, and inserting a needle through the abdominal wall. In both amniocentesis and chorionic villus sampling, an ultrasound scanner is used for guidance. (From K. L. Moore & T. V. N. Persaud, 2003, *Before We Are Born*, 6th ed., Philadelphia: Saunders, p.87. Adapted by permission of the publisher and author.

Already, thousands of genes have been identified, including those involved in hundreds of diseases, such as cystic fibrosis, Duchenne muscular dystrophy, Huntington disease, Marfan syndrome, sickle cell anemia, and many forms of cancer (National Institutes of Health, 2004). As a result, new treatments are being explored, such as *gene therapy*—correcting genetic abnormalities by delivering DNA carrying a functional gene to the cells. In recent experiments, gene therapy relieved symptoms in hemophilia patients and in patients with severe immune system dysfunction. A few, however, experienced serious side effects (Relph, Harrington, & Pandha, 2004). In another approach, called *proteomics,* scientists modify gene-specified proteins involved in disease (Banks, 2003).

Genetic treatments are still some distance in the future for most single-gene defects and far off for genes that combine in complex ways with one another and the environment. Fortunately, 95 percent of fetuses examined through prenatal diagnosis are normal (Moore & Persaud, 2003). Because of such tests, many individuals whose family history would have caused them to avoid pregnancy are having healthy children.

Ask Yourself

REVIEW	Why is genetic counseling called a *communication process?* Who should seek it?
REVIEW	Describe the ethical pros and cons of fetal surgery, surrogate motherhood, and postmenopausal-assisted childbearing.
REFLECT	Put yourself in the place of a woman who is a carrier of fragile X syndrome but who wants to have children. Would you become pregnant, adopt, use a surrogate mother, or give up your desire for parenthood? Explain. If you became pregnant, would you opt for prenatal diagnosis? Why or why not?

Prenatal Development

The sperm and ovum that unite to form the new individual are uniquely suited for the task of reproduction. The ovum is a tiny sphere, measuring $\frac{1}{175}$ of an inch in diameter, that is barely visible to the naked eye as a dot the size of the period at the end of this sentence. But in its microscopic world, it is a giant—the largest cell in the human body. The ovum's size makes it a perfect target for the much smaller sperm, which measure only $\frac{1}{500}$ of an inch.

Conception

About once every 28 days, in the middle of a woman's menstrual cycle, an ovum bursts from one of her *ovaries,* two walnut-sized organs deep inside her abdomen, and is drawn into one of two *fallopian tubes*—long, thin structures that lead to the hollow, soft-lined uterus (see Figure 3.7). While the ovum travels, the spot on the ovary from which it was released, now called the *corpus luteum,* secretes hormones that prepare the lining of the uterus to receive a fertilized ovum. If pregnancy does not occur, the corpus luteum shrinks, and the lining of the uterus is discarded 2 weeks later with menstruation.

The male produces sperm in vast numbers—an average of 300 million a day. In the final process of maturation, each sperm develops a tail that permits it to swim long distances, upstream in the female reproductive tract, through the *cervix* (opening of the uterus), and into the fallopian tube, where fertilization usually takes place. The journey is difficult, and many sperm die. Only 300 to 500 reach the ovum, if one happens to be present. Sperm live for up to

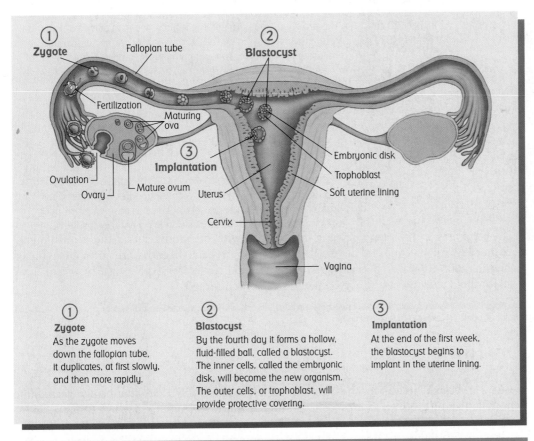

▲ **Figure 3.7**

Female reproductive organs, showing fertilization, early cell duplication, and implantation.

(Adapted from K. L. Moore and T. V. N. Persaud, 2003, *Before We Are Born,* 6th ed., Philadelphia: Saunders, p. 36. Reprinted by permission of the publisher and authors.)

MILESTONES

PRENATAL DEVELOPMENT

Trimester	Period	Weeks	Length and Weight	Major Events
First	Zygote	1		The one-celled zygote multiplies and forms a blastocyst.
		2		The blastocyst burrows into the uterine lining. Structures that feed and protect the developing organism begin to form—amnion, chorion, yolk sac, placenta, and umbilical cord.
	Embryo	3–4	¼ inch (6 mm)	A primitive brain and spinal cord appear. Heart, muscles, ribs, backbone, and digestive tract begin to develop.
		5–8	1 inch (2.5 cm); ⅐ ounce (4 g)	Many external body structures (face, arms, legs, toes, fingers) and internal organs form. The sense of touch begins to develop, and the embryo can move.
	Fetus	9–12	3 inches (7.6 cm); less than 1 ounce (28 g)	Rapid increase in size begins. Nervous system, organs, and muscles become organized and connected, and new behavioral capacities (kicking, thumb sucking, mouth opening, and rehearsal of breathing) appear. External genitals are well formed, and the fetus's sex is evident.
Second		13–24	12 inches (30 cm); 1.8 pounds (820 g)	The fetus continues to enlarge rapidly. In the middle of this period, fetal movements can be felt by the mother. Vernix and lanugo keep the fetus's skin from chapping in the amniotic fluid. Most of the brain's neurons are present by 24 weeks. Eyes are sensitive to light, and the fetus reacts to sound.
Third		25–38	20 inches (50 cm); 7.5 pounds (3,400 g)	The fetus has a chance of survival if born during this time. Size increases. Lungs mature. Rapid brain development causes sensory and behavioral capacities to expand. In the middle of this period, a layer of fat is added under the skin. Antibodies are transmitted from mother to fetus to protect against disease. Most fetuses rotate into an upside-down position in preparation for birth.

Source: Moore & Persaud, 2003.

Photos: (from top to bottom) © Claude Cortier/Photo Researchers, Inc.; © G. Moscoso/Photo Reserachers, Inc.; © John Watney/Photo Researchers, Inc.; © James Stevenson/Photo Researchers, Inc.; © Lennart Nilsson/A Child is Born/Bonniers

6 days and can lie in wait for the ovum, which survives for only 1 day after being released into the fallopian tube. However, most conceptions result from intercourse during a 3-day period—on the day of ovulation or during the 2 days preceding it (Wilcox, Weinberg, & Baird, 1995).

With conception, the story of prenatal development begins to unfold. The vast changes that take place during the 38 weeks of pregnancy are usually divided into three periods: (1) the period of the zygote, (2) the period of the embryo, and (3) the period of the fetus. As we look at what happens in each, you may find it useful to refer to the Milestones table above.

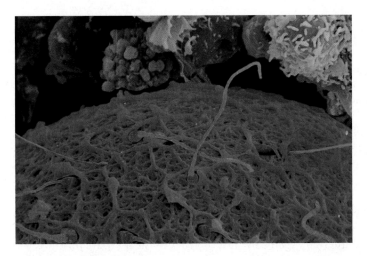

◎ In this photo taken with the aid of a powerful microscope, sperm have completed their journey up the female reproductive tract and are beginning to penetrate the surface of the enormous-looking ovum, the largest cell in the human body. When one of the sperm is successful at fertilizing the ovum, the resulting zygote will begin to duplicate. © Jack Burns/Ace/Phototake

◎ **Period of the zygote: seventh to ninth day.** The fertilized ovum duplicates at an increasingly rapid rate, forming a hollow ball of cells, or blastocyst, by the fourth day after fertilization. Here the blastocyst, magnified thousands of times, burrows into the uterine lining between the seventh and ninth day. © Lennart Nilsson, *A Child Is Born*/Bonniers

The Period of the Zygote

The period of the zygote lasts about 2 weeks, from fertilization until the tiny mass of cells drifts down and out of the fallopian tube and attaches itself to the wall of the uterus. The zygote's first cell duplication is long and drawn out; it is not complete until about 30 hours after conception. Gradually, new cells are added at a faster rate. By the fourth day, 60 to 70 cells exist that form a hollow, fluid-filled ball called a *blastocyst* (refer again to Figure 3.7). The cells on the inside, called the *embryonic disk,* will become the new organism; the outer ring of cells, termed the *trophoblast,* will provide protective covering and nourishment.

• **IMPLANTATION** • Between the seventh and ninth days, *implantation* occurs: The blastocyst burrows deep into the uterine lining where, surrounded by the woman's nourishing blood, it starts to grow in earnest. At first, the trophoblast (protective outer layer) multiplies fastest. It forms a membrane, called the **amnion,** that encloses the developing organism in *amniotic fluid.* The amnion helps keep the temperature of the prenatal world constant and provides a cushion against any jolts caused by the woman's movement. A *yolk sac* emerges that produces blood cells until the developing liver, spleen, and bone marrow are mature enough to take over this function (Moore & Persaud, 2003).

The events of these first 2 weeks are delicate and uncertain. As many as 30 percent of zygotes do not survive this period. In some, the sperm and ovum do not join properly. In others, for some unknown reason, cell duplication never begins. By preventing implantation in these cases, nature eliminates most prenatal abnormalities (Sadler, 2000).

• **THE PLACENTA AND UMBILICAL CORD** • By the end of the second week, cells of the trophoblast form another protective membrane—the **chorion,** which surrounds the amnion. From the chorion, tiny hairlike *villi,* or blood vessels, emerge.[1] As these villi burrow into the uterine wall, a special organ called the *placenta* starts to develop. By bringing the embryo's and mother's blood close together, the **placenta** will permit food and oxygen to reach the organism and waste products to be carried away. A membrane forms that allows these substances to be exchanged but prevents the the blood of the mother and that of the embryo from mixing directly.

---

[1]Recall from Table 3.6 on page 81 that *chorionic villus sampling* is the prenatal diagnostic method that can be performed earliest, by 6 to 8 weeks after conception. In this procedure, tissues from the ends of the villi are removed and examined for genetic abnormalities.

The placenta is connected to the developing organism by the **umbilical cord.** In the period of the zygote, the cord first appears as a primitive body stalk; during the course of pregnancy, it will grow to a length of 1 to 3 feet. The umbilical cord contains one large vein, which delivers blood loaded with nutrients, and two arteries, which remove waste products. The force of blood flowing through the cord keeps it firm, much like a garden hose, so it seldom tangles while the embryo, like a space-walking astronaut, floats freely in its fluid-filled chamber (Moore & Persaud, 2003).

By the end of the period of the zygote, the developing organism has found food and shelter in the uterus. Already, it is a complex being. These dramatic beginnings take place before most mothers know they are pregnant.

The Period of the Embryo

The period of the **embryo** lasts from implantation through the eighth week of pregnancy. During these brief 6 weeks, the most rapid prenatal changes take place, as the groundwork is laid for all body structures and internal organs. Because all parts of the body are forming, the embryo is especially vulnerable to interference with healthy development. But the short time span of embryonic growth helps limit opportunities for serious harm.

• **LAST HALF OF THE FIRST MONTH** • In the first week of this period, the embryonic disk forms three layers of cells: (1) the *ectoderm,* which will become the nervous system and skin; (2) the *mesoderm,* from which will develop the muscles, skeleton, circulatory system, and other internal organs; and (3) the *endoderm,* which will become the digestive system, lungs, urinary tract, and glands. These three layers give rise to all parts of the body.

At first, the nervous system develops fastest. The ectoderm folds to form a *neural tube,* or primitive spinal cord. At 3½ weeks, the top of the neural tube swells to form a brain. Production of *neurons* (nerve cells that store and transmit information) begins deep inside the

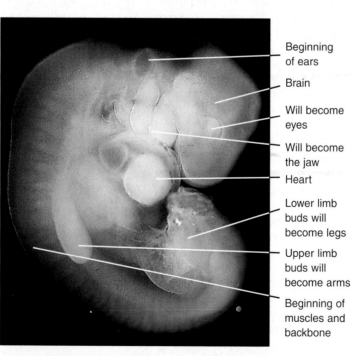

Beginning of ears

Brain

Will become eyes

Will become the jaw

Heart

Lower limb buds will become legs

Upper limb buds will become arms

Beginning of muscles and backbone

◉ **Period of the embryo: fourth week.** In actual size, this 4-week-old embryo is only ¼ inch long, but many body structures have begun to form.
© Lennart Nilsson, *A Child Is Born*/Bonniers

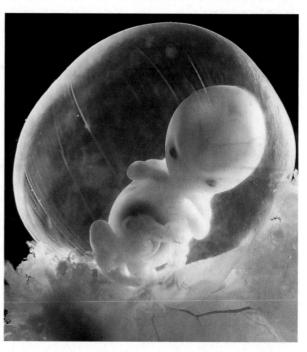

◉ **Period of the embryo: seventh week.** The embryo's posture is more upright. Body structures—eyes, nose, arms, legs, and internal organs—are more distinct. An embryo of this age responds to touch. It also can move, although at less than one inch long and an ounce in weight, it is still too tiny to be felt by the mother.
© Lennart Nilsson, *A Child Is Born*/Bonniers

neural tube at the astounding pace of more than 250,000 per minute. Once formed, neurons travel along tiny threads to their permanent locations, where they will form the major parts of the brain (Huttenlocher, 2002).

While the nervous system is developing, the heart begins to pump blood, and muscles, backbone, ribs, and digestive tract appear. At the end of the first month, the curled embryo—only ¼ inch long—consists of millions of organized groups of cells with specific functions.

• **THE SECOND MONTH** • Growth continues rapidly in the second month, when the eyes, ears, nose, jaw, and neck form. Tiny buds become arms, legs, fingers, and toes. Internal organs are more distinct: The intestines grow, the heart develops separate chambers, and the liver and spleen take over production of blood cells so the yolk sac is no longer needed. Changing body proportions cause the embryo's posture to become more upright. Now 1 inch long and ¹/₇ of an ounce in weight, the embryo can sense its world. It responds to touch, particularly in the mouth area and on the soles of the feet. And it can move, although its tiny flutters are still too light to be felt by the mother (Moore & Persaud, 2003).

The Period of the Fetus

The period of the **fetus,** lasting until the end of pregnancy, is the longest prenatal period. During this "growth and finishing" phase, the organism increases rapidly in size, especially from the ninth to the twentieth week.

• **THE THIRD MONTH** • In the third month, the organs, muscles, and nervous system start to become organized and connected. The brain signals and, in response, the fetus kicks, bends its arms, forms a fist, curls its toes, opens its mouth, and even sucks its thumb. The tiny lungs begin to expand and contract in an early rehearsal of breathing movements (Joseph, 2000). By the twelfth week, the external genitals are well formed, and the sex of the fetus can be detected with ultrasound. Other finishing touches appear, such as fingernails, toenails, tooth buds, and eyelids that open and close. The heartbeat is now stronger and can be heard through a stethoscope.

Prenatal development is often divided into *trimesters,* or three equal time periods. At the end of the third month, the first trimester is complete.

• **THE SECOND TRIMESTER** • By the middle of the second trimester, between 17 and 20 weeks, the new being has grown large enough that the mother can feel its movements. A white, cheeselike substance called **vernix** covers the skin, protecting it from chapping during the long months spent in the amniotic fluid. White, downy hair called **lanugo** also covers the entire body, helping the vernix stick to the skin.

At the end of the second trimester, many organs are quite well developed. And a major milestone is reached in brain development in that, of the billions of neurons that populate the mature brain, nearly all are in place; few will be produced after this time. However, *glial cells,* which support and feed the neurons, continue to increase at a rapid rate throughout the remaining months of pregnancy, as well as after birth. Consequently, brain weight increases tenfold from the 20th week until birth (Roelfsema et al., 2004).

Brain growth means new behavioral capacities. The 20-week-old fetus can be stimulated as well as irritated by sounds. And if a doctor looks inside the uterus with fetoscopy (refer again to Table 3.6), fetuses try to shield their eyes from the light with their hands, indicating that sight has begun to emerge (Nilsson & Hamberger, 1990). Still, a fetus born at this time cannot survive. Its lungs are too immature, and the brain cannot yet control breathing and body temperature.

• **THE THIRD TRIMESTER** • During the final trimester, a fetus born early has a chance for survival. The point at which the baby can first survive, called the **age of viability,** occurs sometime between 22 and 26 weeks (Moore & Persaud, 2003). If born between the seventh and eighth months, however, the baby usually needs oxygen assistance to breathe. Although the

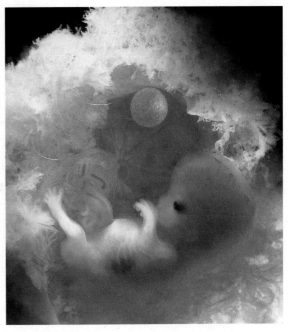

Ⓖ **Period of the fetus: eleventh week.** The brain and muscles are better connected. The fetus can kick, bend its arms, open and close its hands and mouth, and suck its thumb. Notice the yolk sac, which shrinks as pregnancy advances. The internal organs have taken over its function of producing blood cells.

© Lennart Nilsson, *A Child Is Born/* Bonniers

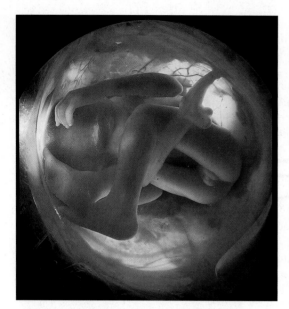

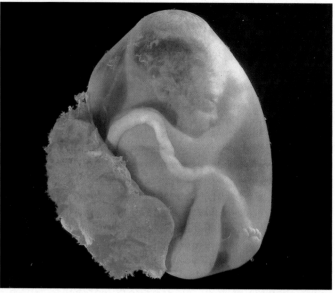

◉ **Period of the fetus: twenty-second week.** This fetus is almost a foot long and weighs slightly more than a pound. Its movements can be felt easily by the mother and other family members who place a hand on her abdomen. The fetus has reached the age of viability; if born, it has a slim chance of surviving.
© Lennart Nilsson, *A Child Is Born*/Bonniers

◉ **Period of the fetus: thirty-sixth week.** This fetus fills the uterus. To support its need for nourishment, the umbilical cord and placenta have grown large. Notice the vernix (cheeselike substance) on the skin, which protects it from chapping. The fetus has accumulated a layer of fat to assist with temperature regulation after birth. In 2 more weeks, it would be full term.
© Lennart Nilsson, *A Child Is Born*/Bonniers

respiratory center of the brain is now mature, tiny air sacs in the lungs are not yet ready to inflate and exchange carbon dioxide for oxygen.

The brain continues to make great strides during the last 3 months. The *cerebral cortex*, the seat of human intelligence, enlarges. Grooves and convolutions in its surface appear, permitting a dramatic increase in surface area without extensive increase in head size. As a result, maximum prenatal brain growth takes place, yet the full-term baby's head is not too large to pass through the birth canal. As cortical folds become more apparent and neurological organization improves, the fetus spends more time awake. At 20 weeks, the fetal heart rate reveals no periods of alertness. But by 28 weeks, fetuses are awake about 11 percent of the time, a figure that rises to 16 percent just before birth (DiPietro et al., 1996).

By the end of pregnancy, the organism takes on the beginnings of a personality. Higher fetal activity in the last weeks predicts a more active infant in the first month of life—a relationship that, for boys, persists into early childhood (Groome et al., 1999). Fetal activity is linked in other ways to infant temperament. In one study, more active fetuses during the third trimester became 1-year-olds who could better handle frustration and 2-year-olds who were less fearful, in that they more readily interacted with toys and with an unfamiliar adult in a laboratory (DiPietro et al., 2002). Perhaps fetal activity level is an indicator of healthy neurological development, which fosters adaptability in childhood. The relationships just described, however, are only modest. As you will see in Chapter 10, sensitive caregiving can modify the temperaments of children who have difficulty adapting to new experiences.

During the final 3 months, the fetus gains more than 5 pounds and grows 7 inches. As it fills the uterus, it gradually moves less often. In addition, brain development, which permits the organism to inhibit behavior, contributes to a decline in physical activity (DiPietro et al., 1996). In the eighth month, a layer of fat is added to assist with temperature regulation. The fetus also receives antibodies from the mother's blood to protect against illnesses, since the newborn's own immune system will not work well until several months after birth. In the last weeks, most fetuses assume an upside-down position, partly because of the shape of the uterus and also because the head is heavier than the feet. Growth slows, and birth is about to take place.

Ask Yourself

REVIEW	Why is the period of the embryo regarded as the most dramatic prenatal phase? Why is the period of the fetus called the "growth and finishing" phase?
APPLY	Amy, 2 months pregnant, wonders how the developing organism is being fed. "I don't look pregnant yet, so does that mean not much development has occurred?" she asks. How would you respond to Amy?
CONNECT	How is brain development related to fetal behavior? What implications do individual differences in fetal behavior have for the baby's temperament after birth?

Prenatal Environmental Influences

Although the prenatal environment is far more constant than the world outside the womb, many factors can affect the embryo and fetus. In the following sections, you will see that there is much that parents—and society as a whole—can do to create a safe environment for development before birth.

Teratogens

The term **teratogen** refers to any environmental agent that causes damage during the prenatal period. It comes from the Greek word *teras*, meaning "malformation" or "monstrosity." Scientists selected this label because they first learned about harmful prenatal influences from cases in which babies had been profoundly damaged. Yet the harm done by teratogens is not always simple and straightforward. It depends on the following factors:

- *Dose.* As we discuss particular teratogens, you will see that larger doses over longer time periods usually have more negative effects.

- *Heredity.* The genetic makeup of the mother and that of the developing organism play an important role. Some individuals are better able than others to withstand harmful environments.

- *Other negative influences.* The presence of several negative factors at once, such as poor nutrition, lack of medical care, and additional teratogens, can worsen the impact of a single harmful agent.

- *Age.* The effects of teratogens vary with the age of the organism at time of exposure.

We can best understand this last idea if we think of the *sensitive period* concept introduced in Chapter 1. A sensitive period is a limited time span in which a part of the body or a behavior is biologically prepared to develop rapidly. During that time, it is especially sensitive to its surroundings. If the environment is harmful, then damage occurs, and recovery is difficult and sometimes impossible.

Figure 3.8 on page 92 summarizes prenatal sensitive periods. Look at it carefully, and you will see that some parts of the body, such as the brain and eye, have long sensitive periods. Other sensitive periods, such as those for the limbs and palate, are much shorter. Figure 3.8 also indicates that we can make some general statements about the timing of harmful influences:

- In the *period of the zygote*, before implantation, teratogens rarely have any impact. If they do, the tiny mass of cells is usually so damaged that it dies.

- The *embryonic period* is the time when serious defects are most likely to occur because the foundations for all body parts are being laid down.

- During the *fetal period*, teratogenic damage is usually minor. However, organs such as the brain, eye, and genitals can still be strongly affected.

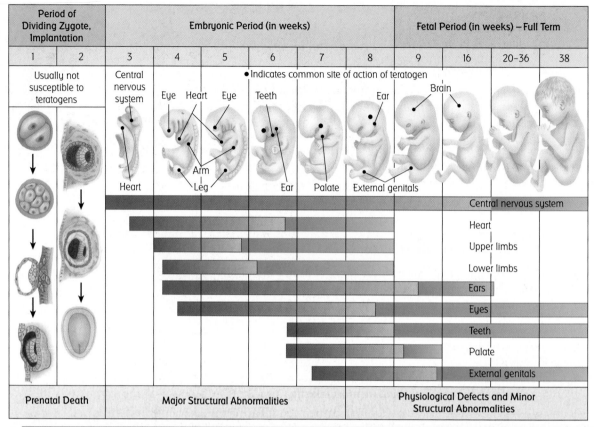

Period of Dividing Zygote, Implantation		Embryonic Period (in weeks)						Fetal Period (in weeks) – Full Term			
1	2	3	4	5	6	7	8	9	16	20–36	38

▲ **Figure 3.8**

Sensitive periods in prenatal development. Each organ or structure has a sensitive period, during which its development may be disturbed. Blue horizontal bars indicate highly sensitive periods. Green horizontal bars indicate periods that are somewhat less sensitive to teratogens, although damage can occur. (Adapted from K. L. Moore & T. V. N. Persaud, 2003, *Before We Are Born,* 6th ed., Philadelphia: Saunders, p. 130. Reprinted by permission of the publisher and authors.)

The effects of teratogens are not limited to immediate physical damage. Some health outcomes are subtle and delayed. As the Biology and Environment box on pages 94 and 95 illustrates, they may not show up for decades. Furthermore, psychological consequences may occur indirectly, as a result of physical damage. For example, a defect resulting from drugs the mother took during pregnancy can change reactions of others to the child as well as the child's ability to explore the environment. These experiences, in turn, can have far-reaching consequences for cognitive, emotional, and social development.

Notice how an important idea about development discussed in Chapter 1 is at work here—that of *bidirectional influences* between child and environment. Now let's look at what scientists have discovered about a variety of teratogens.

• **PRESCRIPTION AND NONPRESCRIPTION DRUGS** • In the early 1960s, the world learned a tragic lesson about drugs and prenatal development. At that time, a sedative called *thalidomide* was widely available in Canada, Europe, and South America. When taken by mothers 4 to 6 weeks after conception, thalidomide produced gross deformities of the embryo's developing arms and legs and, less frequently, damage to the ears, heart, kidneys, and genitals. About 7,000 infants worldwide were affected (Moore & Persaud, 2003). As children exposed to thalidomide grew older, many scored below average in intelligence. Perhaps the drug damaged the central nervous system directly. Or the conditions in which these severely deformed youngsters were reared may have impaired their intellectual development.

Another medication, a synthetic hormone called *diethylstilbestrol (DES),* was widely prescribed between 1945 and 1970 to prevent miscarriages. As daughters of these mothers reached adolescence and young adulthood, they showed unusually high rates of cancer of the vagina, malformations of the uterus, and infertility. When they tried to have children, their pregnancies more often resulted in prematurity, low birth weight, and miscarriage than those of non-DES-exposed women. Sons of these mothers showed an increased risk of genital abnormalities and cancer of the testes (Hammes & Laitman, 2003; Palmer et al., 2001).

Currently, a vitamin A derivative called *Accutane,* used to treat severe acne (also known by the generic name *isotretinoin),* is the most widely used potent teratogen. Exposure during the first trimester of pregnancy results in extensive damage to the developing organism, including eye, ear, skull, brain, heart, and immune system abnormalities. Hundreds of thousands of American and Canadian women of childbearing age take Accutane, and their numbers are increasing. Accutane's packaging warns users to avoid pregnancy by using two methods of birth control, but many women do not heed this advice (Honein, Paulozzi, & Erickson, 2001). Although the number of babies born with Accutane-caused malformations is not known, more than 150 documented U.S. cases exist (Accutane Action Group Forum, 2003).

Indeed, any drug with a molecule small enough to penetrate the placental barrier can enter the embryonic or fetal bloodstream. Nevertheless, many pregnant women continue to take over-the-counter medications without consulting their doctors. Aspirin is one of the most common. Several studies suggest that regular aspirin use is linked to low birth weight, infant death around the time of birth, poorer motor development, and lower intelligence test scores in early childhood, although other research fails to confirm these findings (Barr et al., 1990; Hauth et al., 1995; Streissguth et al., 1987). Coffee, tea, cola, and cocoa contain another frequently consumed drug, caffeine. Heavy caffeine intake (more than 3 cups of coffee per day) is associated with low birth weight, miscarriage, and newborn withdrawal symptoms, such as irritability and vomiting (Gilbert-Barnes, 2000; Klebanoff et al., 2002; Vik et al., 2003). And antidepressant medication taken during the third trimester is linked to increased risk of birth complications, including respiratory distress (Costei et al., 2002).

Because children's lives are involved, we must take findings like these seriously. At the same time, we cannot be sure that these frequently used drugs actually cause the problems mentioned. Often mothers take more than one substance. If the prenatal organism is injured, it is hard to tell which might be responsible or whether other factors correlated with drug taking are at fault. Until we have more information, the safest course for pregnant women is to cut down on or avoid such drugs entirely.

• **ILLEGAL DRUGS** • The use of highly addictive mood-altering drugs, such as cocaine and heroin, has become more widespread, especially in poverty-stricken inner-city areas, where these drugs provide a temporary escape from a daily life of hopelessness. As many as 3 to 7 percent of American and Canadian infants born in large cities, and 1 to 2 percent of all North American newborns, have been exposed to cocaine prenatally (British Columbia Reproductive Care Program, 2003; Lester et al., 2001).

Babies born to users of cocaine, heroin, or methadone (a less addictive drug used to wean people away from heroin) are at risk for a wide variety of problems, including prematurity, low birth weight, physical defects, breathing difficulties, and death at or around the time of birth (Behnke et al., 2001; Walker, Rosenberg, & Balaban-Gil, 1999). In addition, these infants are born drug addicted. They often are feverish and irritable and have trouble sleeping (Friedman & Polifka, 1998). When mothers with many problems of their own must take care of these babies, who are difficult to calm down, cuddle, and feed, behavior problems are likely to persist.

Throughout the first year, heroin- and methadone-exposed infants are less attentive to the environment than nonexposed babies, and their motor development is slow. After infancy, some children get better, whereas others remain jittery and inattentive. The kind of parenting they receive may explain why problems last for some but not for others (Cosden, Peerson, & Elliott, 1997).

Evidence on cocaine suggests that some prenatally exposed babies have lasting difficulties. Cocaine constricts the blood vessels, causing oxygen delivery to the

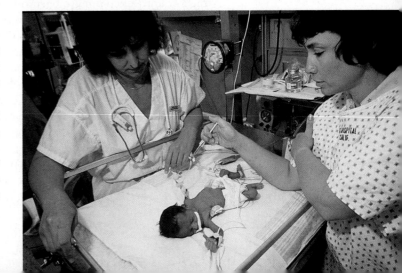

◉ This baby, whose mother took crack during pregnancy, was born many weeks before his due date. He breathes with the aid of a respirator, and his central nervous system may be damaged.
© Chuck Nacke/Woodfin Camp & Associates

BIOLOGY AND ENVIRONMENT

The Prenatal Environment and Health in Later Life

When Michael entered the world 55 years ago, 6 weeks premature and weighing only 4 pounds, the doctor delivering him wasn't sure he would make it. Michael not only survived but enjoyed good health until his mid-forties, when, during a routine medical checkup, he was diagnosed with high blood pressure and adult-onset diabetes. Michael had no apparent risk factors for these conditions: He wasn't overweight, didn't smoke, and didn't eat high-fat foods. Nor did the illnesses run in his family. Could the roots of Michael's health problems date back to his prenatal development?

Increasing evidence suggests that pre-natal environmental factors—ones not toxic (like tobacco or alcohol) but rather fairly subtle, such as the flow of nutrients and hormones across the placenta—can affect an individual's health decades later (Wheeler, Barker, & O'Brien, 1999).

Low Birth Weight and Heart Disease, Stroke, and Diabetes

Carefully controlled animal experiments reveal that a poorly nourished, underweight fetus experiences changes in body structure and function that result in cardiovascular disease in adulthood (Franco et al., 2002). To explore this relationship in humans,

researchers tapped public records, gathering information on the birth weights of 15,000 British men and women and the occurrence of disease in middle adulthood. Those weighing less than 5 pounds at birth had a 50 percent greater chance of dying of heart disease and stroke, after income, education, and a variety of health risks were controlled. The connection between birth weight and cardiovascular disease was strongest for people whose weight-to-length ratio at birth was very low—a sign of prenatal growth stunting (Godfrey & Barker, 2000; Martyn, Barker, & Osmond, 1996).

In other large-scale studies, a consistent link between low birth weight and heart disease, stroke, and diabetes in middle adulthood emerged—for both sexes and in several countries, including Finland, India, Jamaica, and the United States (Barker et al., 2002; Forsén et al., 2000; Godfrey & Barker, 2001). Smallness itself does not cause later health problems; rather, researchers believe, complex factors associated with it are involved.

Some speculate that a poorly nourished fetus diverts large amounts of blood to the brain, causing organs in the abdomen, such as the liver and kidney (involved in control-ling cholesterol and blood pressure), to be undersized (Hales & Ozanne, 2003). The

result is heightened future risk for heart disease and stroke. In the case of diabetes, inadequate prenatal nutrition may perma-nently impair functioning of the pancreas, leading glucose intolerance to rise as the person ages (Rich-Edwards et al., 1999). Yet another hypothesis, supported by both ani-mal and human research, is that the mal-functioning placentas of some expectant mothers permit high levels of stress hor-mones to reach the fetus. These hormones retard fetal growth, increase fetal blood pres-sure, and promote hyperglycemia (excess blood sugar), predisposing the developing person to later disease (Osmond & Barker, 2000). Finally, as Chapter 5 will make clear, prenatally growth-stunted babies often gain excessive weight in childhood, once they have access to plentiful food. This excess weight usually persists, greatly mag-nifying the risk of diabetes in midlife (Hyppönen, Power, & Smith, 2003).

High Birth Weight and Breast Cancer

The other prenatal growth extreme—high birth weight—is related to breast cancer, the most common malignancy in adult women (Andersson et al., 2001; Vatten et al., 2002). In one study, the mothers of 589 nurses with invasive breast cancer

developing organism to fall for 15 minutes following a high dose. Cocaine also alters the pro-duction and functioning of neurons and the chemical balance in the fetus's brain. These effects may contribute to an array of cocaine-associated physical defects, including eye, bone, genital, urinary tract, kidney, and heart deformities; brain hemorrhages and seizures; and severe growth retardation (Covington et al., 2002; Espy, Kaufmann, & Glisky, 1999; Mayes, 1999). Several studies report perceptual, motor, attention, memory, and language problems in infancy that persist into the preschool years (Lester et al., 2003; Richardson et al., 1996; Singer et al., 2002a, 2002b).

But other investigations reveal no major negative effects of prenatal cocaine exposure (Frank et al., 2001; Zuckerman, Frank, & Mayes, 2002). These contradictory findings indicate how dif-ficult it is to isolate the precise damage caused by illegal drugs. Cocaine users vary greatly in the amount, potency, and purity of the cocaine they ingest. Also, they often take several drugs, dis-play other high-risk behaviors, suffer from poverty and other stresses, and engage in insensitive caregiving (Lester, 2000). The joint impact of these factors worsens outcomes for children

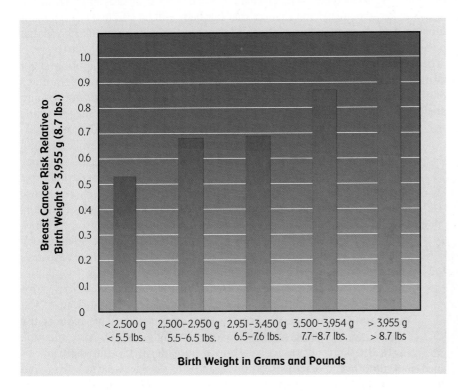

Figure 3.9

Relationship of birth weight to breast cancer risk in adulthood. In a study of 589 nurses with invasive breast cancer and 1,569 nurses who did not have breast cancer, birth weight predicted breast cancer incidence after many other prenatal and postnatal health risks were controlled. The breast cancer risk was especially high for women whose birth weights were greater than 3,955 grams, or 8.7 pounds. (Adapted from Michels et al., 1996.)

and 1,569 nurses who did not have breast cancer were asked to provide their daughter's birth weights, early life exposures (for example, smoking during pregnancy), and a family health history (such as relatives diagnosed with breast cancer). The nurses themselves provided information on their adult health. After other risk factors were controlled, high birth weight—especially more than 8.7 pounds—emerged as a clear predictor of breast cancer (see Figure 3.9) (Michels et al., 1996). Researchers speculate that the culprit is an overweight expectant mother, who releases an excess of estrogens (female sex hormones). Estrogens promote large fetal size and alter the makeup of breast tissue so that it may readily become malignant in adulthood.

Prevention

The relationships between prenatal development and later-life illnesses emerging in research do not mean that the illnesses are inevitable. Prenatal environmental conditions *influence* adult health, but the steps people take to protect their health can prevent risks from becoming reality. Researchers advise individuals who were low-weight at birth to get regular medical checkups and to be attentive to diet, weight, fitness, and stress—controllable factors that contribute to heart disease and adult-onset diabetes. And high-birth-weight women should be conscientious about breast self-exams and mammograms, which permit early detection—and, in many instances, cure—of breast cancer.

Both low birth weight and high birth weight are linked to economic disadvantage. Nations must address the social and economic factors that increase these prenatal risks to a healthy, long life.

(Alessandri, Bendersky, & Lewis, 1998; Carta et al., 2001). But researchers have yet to determine exactly what accounts for findings of cocaine-related damage in some studies but not in others.

Another illegal drug, marijuana, is used more widely than heroin and cocaine. Studies examining its relationship to low birth weight and prematurity reveal mixed findings (Fried, 1993). Several researchers have linked prenatal marijuana exposure to smaller head size (a measure of brain growth), to sleep, attention, and memory difficulties in childhood, and to poorer problem-solving performance in adolescence (Dahl et al., 1995; Fried, Watkinson, & Gray, 2003; Fried, 2000a, 2000b). As with cocaine, however, lasting consequences are not well established. Overall, the effects of illegal drugs are far less consistent than the impact of two legal substances to which we now turn: tobacco and alcohol.

• **TOBACCO** • Although smoking has declined in Western nations, an estimated 12 percent of American women and 19 percent of Canadian women smoke during their pregnancies (Health Canada, 2001; Ventura et al., 2003). The most well-known effect of smoking during pregnancy is low birth weight. But the likelihood of other serious consequences, such as miscarriage, prematurity, impaired heart rate and breathing during sleep, infant death, and asthma and cancer later in childhood, is also increased (Franco et al., 2000; Jaakkola & Gissler, 2004). The more cigarettes a mother smokes, the greater the chances that her baby will be affected. If a pregnant woman stops smoking at any time, even during the third trimester, she reduces the likelihood that her infant will be born underweight and suffer from future problems (Klesges et al., 2001).

Even when a baby of a smoking mother appears to be born in good physical condition, slight behavioral abnormalities may threaten the child's development. Newborns of smoking mothers are less attentive to sounds, display more muscle tension, are more excitable when touched and visually stimulated, and more often have colic (persistent crying)—findings that suggest subtle

negative effects on brain development (Law et al., 2003; Sondergaard et al., 2002). Furthermore, an unresponsive, restless baby may not evoke the kind of interaction from adults that promotes healthy psychological development. Some studies report that prenatally exposed youngsters have shorter attention spans, poorer memories, lower mental test scores, and more behavior problems in childhood and adolescence, after many other factors have been controlled (Cornelius et al., 2001; Fried, Watkinson, & Gray, 2003; Thapar et al., 2003). However, factors associated with smoking, such as lower maternal education and income, may contribute to these outcomes (Ernst, Moolchan, & Robinson, 2001).

Exactly how can smoking harm the fetus? Nicotine, the addictive substance in tobacco, constricts blood vessels, lessens blood flow to the uterus, and causes the placenta to grow abnormally. This reduces the transfer of nutrients, so the fetus gains weight poorly. Also, nicotine raises the concentration of carbon monoxide in the bloodstreams of both mother and fetus. Carbon monoxide displaces oxygen from red blood cells, damaging the central nervous system and slowing body growth in the fetuses of laboratory animals (Friedman, 1996). Similar effects may occur in humans.

From one-third to one-half of nonsmoking pregnant women are "passive smokers" because their husbands, relatives, or co-workers use cigarettes. Passive smoking is also related to low birth weight, infant death, and possible long-term impairments in attention and learning (Dejin-Karlsson et al., 1998; Makin, Fried, & Watkinson, 1991). Clearly, expectant mothers should avoid smoke-filled environments.

● **ALCOHOL** ● In a moving story, Michael Dorris (1989), a Dartmouth University anthropology professor, described what it was like to rear his adopted son Adam, whose biological mother drank heavily throughout pregnancy and died of alcohol poisoning shortly after his birth. A Sioux Indian, Adam was born with a condition called **fetal alcohol syndrome (FAS).** Mental retardation; impaired motor coordination, attention, memory, and language; and overactivity are typical of children with this disorder (Connor et al., 2001; Sokol, Delaney-Black, & Nordstrom,

Ⓒ (Top) The mother of these twin baby girls drank heavily during pregnancy. Their widely spaced eyes, thin upper lip, and short eyelid openings are typical of fetal alcohol syndrome (FAS). (Bottom) The adolescent girl shown here also has symptoms of FAS. © George Steinmetz

2003). Distinct physical symptoms also accompany FAS, including slow physical growth and a particular pattern of facial abnormalities: widely spaced eyes, short eyelid openings, a small upturned nose, a thin upper lip, and a small head, indicating that the brain has not developed fully. Other defects—of the eyes, ears, nose, throat, heart, genitals, urinary tract, or immune system—may also be present.

In all babies with FAS, the mother drank heavily through most or all of her pregnancy. A related condition, known as **fetal alcohol effects (FAE),** is seen in individuals whose mothers generally drank alcohol in smaller quantities. FAE children display only some of the abnormalities associated with FAS. The particular defects vary with the timing and length of alcohol exposure during pregnancy (Goodlett & Johnson, 1999; Mattson et al., 1998).

Even when provided with enriched diets, FAS babies fail to catch up in physical size during infancy and childhood. Mental impairment is also permanent: In his teens and twenties,

Adam had trouble concentrating and keeping a routine job. He also suffered from poor judgment. For example, he might buy something and not wait for change, or wander off in the middle of a task. The more alcohol consumed by a woman during pregnancy, the poorer the child's motor coordination, speed of information processing, reasoning, and intelligence and achievement test scores during the preschool and school years (Korkman, Kettunen, & Autti-Raemoe, 2003; Streissguth et al., 1994). In adolescence, FAS is associated with poor school performance, trouble with the law, inappropriate sexual behavior, alcohol and drug abuse, and lasting mental health problems (Baer et al., 2003; Kelly, Day, & Streissguth, 2000).

How does alcohol produce its devastating effects? First, it interferes with cell duplication and migration in the primitive neural tube. Psychophysiological measures, such as fMRI and EEGs, reveal structural damage, arrested brain growth, and abnormalities in brain functioning, including the electrical and chemical activity involved in transferring messages from one part of the brain to another (Bookstein et al., 2002; Goodlett & Horn, 2001). Second, the body uses large quantities of oxygen to metabolize alcohol. A pregnant woman's heavy drinking draws away oxygen that the developing organism needs for cell growth.

About 25 percent of American and Canadian mothers reported drinking at some time during their pregnancies. As with heroin and cocaine, alcohol abuse is higher in poverty-stricken women (Health Canada, 2003b; U.S. Department of Health and Human Services, 2003a). On some Native American and Canadian First Nations reservations, the incidence of FAS is as high as 10 percent (Silverman et al., 2003). Unfortunately, when affected girls later become pregnant, the poor judgment caused by the syndrome often prevents them from understanding why they should avoid alcohol themselves. Thus, the tragic cycle is likely to be repeated in the next generation.

How much alcohol is safe during pregnancy? Even mild drinking, less than one drink per day, is associated with FAS-like facial features and reduced head size and body growth among children followed into adolescence (Astley et al., 1992; Day et al., 2002). Recall that other factors—both genetic and environmental—can make some fetuses more vulnerable to teratogens. Therefore, no amount of alcohol is safe, and pregnant women should avoid it entirely.

• **RADIATION** • Earlier we saw that ionizing radiation can cause mutation, damaging the DNA in ova and sperm. When mothers are exposed to radiation during pregnancy, additional harm can come to the embryo or fetus. Defects due to radiation were tragically apparent in the children born to pregnant Japanese women who survived the atomic bombing of Hiroshima and Nagasaki during World War II. Similar abnormalities surfaced in the 9 months following the 1986 Chernobyl, Ukraine, nuclear power plant accident. After each disaster, the incidence of miscarriage, small head size (indicating an underdeveloped brain), physical deformities, and slow physical growth rose dramatically (Hoffmann, 2001; Schull, 2003).

Even when a radiation-exposed baby seems normal, problems may appear later. For example, low-level radiation, resulting from industrial leakage or medical X-rays, can increase the risk of childhood cancer (Fattibene et al., 1999). In middle childhood, prenatally exposed Chernobyl children showed abnormal EEG brain-wave activity, lower intelligence test scores, and rates of language and emotional disorders two to three times greater than those of nonexposed Russian children (Kolominsky, Igumnov, & Drozdovitch, 1999; Loganovskaja & Loganovsky, 1999).

• **ENVIRONMENTAL POLLUTION** • An astounding number of potentially dangerous chemicals are released into the environment in industrialized nations. More than 100,000 are in common use, and many new pollutants are introduced each year.

Mercury is an established teratogen. In the 1950s, an industrial plant released waste containing high levels of mercury into a bay providing food and water for the town of Minamata, Japan. Many children born at the time displayed physical deformities, mental retardation, abnormal speech, difficulty in chewing and swallowing, and uncoordinated movements. Prenatal mercury exposure disrupts production and migration of neurons, causing widespread brain damage (Clarkson, Magos, & Myers, 2003).

⑤ This child's mother was just a few weeks pregnant during the Chernobyl nuclear power plant disaster. Radiation exposure probably is responsible for his limb deformities.
© Sergei Guneyev/Time & Life Pictures/Getty Images

Another teratogen, *lead,* is present in paint flaking off the walls of old buildings and in certain materials used in industrial occupations. High levels of lead exposure are consistently related to prematurity, low birth weight, brain damage, and a wide variety of physical defects (Dye-White, 1986). Even low levels seem to be dangerous. Affected babies show slightly poorer mental and motor development (Dietrich, Berger, & Succop, 1993; Wasserman et al., 1994).

For many years, *polychlorinated biphenyls (PCBs)* were used to insulate electrical equipment, until research showed that (like mercury) they found their way into waterways and entered the food supply. In Taiwan, prenatal exposure to very high levels of PCBs in rice oil resulted in low birth weight, discolored skin, deformities of the gums and nails, brain-wave abnormalities, and delayed cognitive development (Chen & Hsu, 1994; Chen et al., 1994). Steady, low-level PCB exposure is also harmful. Compared with those who ate little or no fish, women who frequently ate PCB-contaminated fish had infants with lower birth weights, smaller heads, more intense physiological reactions to stress, and less interest in their surroundings (Jacobson et al., 1984; Stewart et al., 2000). Follow-ups in early and middle childhood revealed persisting attention and memory difficulties and lower intelligence test scores (Jacobson & Jacobson, 2003; Walkowiak et al., 2001).

• **MATERNAL DISEASE** • Five percent of women catch an infectious disease while pregnant. Most of these illnesses, such as the common cold, seem to have no impact on the embryo or fetus. However, as Table 3.7 indicates, certain diseases can cause extensive damage.

▶ *Viruses. Rubella* (3-day German measles) is a well-known teratogen. In the mid-1960s, a worldwide epidemic of rubella led to the birth of more than 20,000 North American babies with serious defects. Consistent with the sensitive period concept, the greatest damage occurs when rubella strikes during the embryonic period. More than 50 percent of infants whose mothers become ill during that time show eye cataracts; deafness; heart, genital, urinary, and intestinal abnormalities; and mental retardation (Eberhart-Phillips, Frederick, & Baron, 1993). Infection during the fetal period is less harmful, but low birth weight, hearing loss, and bone defects may still occur. And the brain abnormalities resulting from prenatal rubella increase the

TABLE 3.7   EFFECTS OF SOME INFECTIOUS DISEASES DURING PREGNANCY

Disease	Miscarriage	Physical Malformations	Mental Retardation	Low Birth Weight and Prematurity
Viral				
Acquired immune deficiency syndrome (AIDS)	o	?	+	?
Chicken pox	o	+	+	+
Cytomegalovirus	+	+	+	+
Herpes simplex 2 (genital herpes)	+	+	+	+
Mumps	+	?	o	o
Rubella (German measles)	+	+	+	+
Bacterial				
Syphilis	+	+	+	?
Tuberculosis	+	?	+	+
Parasitic				
Malaria	+	o	o	+
Toxoplasmosis	+	+	+	+

+ = established finding, o = no present evidence, ? = possible effect that is not clearly established.

Sources: Behrman, Kliegman, & Jenson, 2000; O'Rahilly & Müller, 2001; Jones, Lopez, & Wilson, 2003.

risk of severe mental illness, especially schizophrenia, in adulthood (Brown & Susser, 2002).

Since 1996, infants and young children have been routinely vaccinated against rubella; therefore, prenatal cases today are far fewer than they were a generation ago. Still, 10 to 20 percent of women in North America and Western Europe lack the rubella antibody, so new disease outbreaks are possible (Health Canada, 2002; Pebody et al., 2000).

The *human immunodeficiency virus (HIV)*, which can lead to *acquired immune deficiency syndrome (AIDS)*, a disease that destroys the immune system, has infected increasing numbers of teenage girls and women over the past decade. Currently, females account for about one-fourth of newly diagnosed AIDS victims in the United States and Canada (Health Canada, 2004d; U.S. Department of Health and Human Services, 2004c). Although the incidence of AIDS has declined in industrialized nations, the disease is rampant in developing countries, where 95 percent of new infections occur, more than half of which affect women. In South Africa, for example, one-fourth of all pregnant women are HIV-positive (United Nations, 2004a). They pass the deadly virus to the developing organism 20 to 30 percent of the time.

AIDS progresses rapidly in infants. By 6 months, weight loss, diarrhea, and repeated respiratory illnesses are common. The virus also causes brain damage. Most prenatal AIDS babies survive for only 5 to 8 months after the appearance of these symptoms (O'Rahilly & Müller, 2001). The antiviral drug zidovudine (ZDV) reduces prenatal AIDS transmission by as much as 95 percent, with no harmful consequences of drug treatment for children (Culnane et al., 1999). Although ZDV has led to a dramatic decline in prenatally acquired AIDS in Western nations, it is not widely available in impoverished regions of the world.

As Table 3.7 reveals, the developing organism is especially sensitive to the family of herpes viruses, for which no vaccine or treatment exists. Among these, *cytomegalovirus* (the most frequent prenatal infection, transmitted through respiratory or sexual contact) and *herpes simplex 2* (which is sexually transmitted) are especially dangerous. In both, the virus invades the mother's genital tract. Babies can be infected either during pregnancy or at birth.

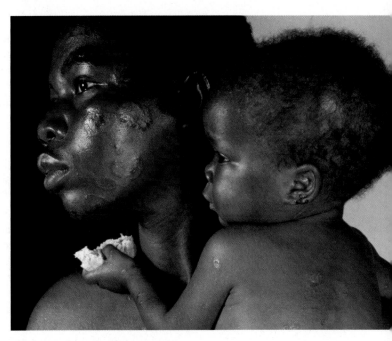

◉ This South African mother and infant have AIDS. Both have extensive ringworm skin rashes. Their weakened immune systems make normally harmless infections life threatening. Because AIDS progresses rapidly in infants, the baby may live only a few more months.
© Dr. M. A. Ansary/Photo Researchers, Inc.

▶ *Bacterial and Parasitic Diseases.* Table 3.7 also includes several bacterial and parasitic diseases. Among the most common is *toxoplasmosis,* caused by a parasite found in many animals. Pregnant women may become infected from eating raw or undercooked meat or from contact with the feces of infected cats. About 40 percent of women who have the disease transmit it to the developing organism. If it strikes during the first trimester, it is likely to cause eye and brain damage. Later infection is linked to mild visual and cognitive impairments. And about 80 percent of affected newborns with no obvious signs of damage develop learning or visual disabilities in later life (Jones, Lopez, & Wilson, 2003). Expectant mothers can avoid toxoplasmosis by making sure that the meat they eat is well cooked, having pet cats checked for the disease, and turning over care of litter boxes to other family members.

Other Maternal Factors

Besides teratogens, maternal exercise, nutrition, and emotional well-being affect the embryo and fetus. In addition, many expectant parents wonder about the impact of a woman's age on the course of pregnancy. We examine each of these influences in the following sections.

• **EXERCISE** • In healthy, physically fit women, regular moderate exercise, such as walking, swimming, biking, or an aerobic workout, is related to increased birth weight (Leiferman & Evenson, 2003). However, very frequent, vigorous exercise—working up a sweat for more than 30 minutes, four or five days a week, especially late in pregnancy—results in lower birth weight than in healthy controls (Clapp et al., 2002; Pivarnik, 1998). Pregnant women with health problems, such as circulatory difficulties or a history of miscarriage, should consult their doctors before beginning or continuing a physical fitness routine.

During the last trimester, when the abdomen grows very large, mothers often must cut back on exercise. In most cases, a mother who has remained fit during the earlier months is likely to experience fewer physical discomforts, such as back pain, upward pressure on the chest, and difficulty breathing.

• **NUTRITION** • During the prenatal period, when children are growing more rapidly than at any other time, they depend totally on the mother for nutrients. A healthy diet that results in a maternal weight gain of 25 to 30 pounds (10 to 13.5 kilograms) helps ensure the health of mother and baby.

▶ *Consequences of Prenatal Malnutrition.* During World War II, a severe famine occurred in the Netherlands, giving scientists a rare opportunity to study the impact of nutrition on prenatal development. Findings revealed that the sensitive period concept operates with nutrition, just as it does with teratogens. Women affected by the famine during the first trimester were more likely to have miscarriages or give birth to babies with physical defects. When women were past the first trimester, fetuses usually survived, but many were born underweight and had small heads (Stein et al., 1975).

We now know that prenatal malnutrition can cause serious damage to the central nervous system. The poorer the mother's diet, the greater the loss in brain weight, especially if malnutrition occurred during the last trimester. During that time, the brain is increasing rapidly in size; for it to reach its full potential, the mother must have a diet high in all the basic nutrients (Morgane et al., 1993). An inadequate diet during pregnancy can also distort the structure of other organs, including the liver, kidney, and pancreas, resulting in lifelong health problems (refer again to the Biology and Environment box on pages 94–95).

Because poor nutrition suppresses development of the immune system, prenatally malnourished babies frequently catch respiratory illnesses (Chandra, 1991). In addition, they are often irritable and unresponsive to stimulation. In poverty-stricken families, these effects quickly combine with a stressful home life. With age, low intelligence test scores and serious learning problems become more apparent (Pollitt, 1996).

▶ *Prevention and Treatment.* Many studies show that providing pregnant women with adequate food has a substantial impact on the health of their babies. Yet the growth demands of the prenatal period require more than just increased quantity of food. Vitamin–mineral enrichment is also crucial.

For example, taking a folic acid supplement around the time of conception reduces by more than 70 percent abnormalities of the neural tube, such as *anencephaly* and *spina bifida* (see Table 3.6 on page 81) (MCR Vitamin Study Research Group, 1991). In addition, adequate folic acid intake during the last 10 weeks of pregnancy cuts in half the risk of premature delivery and low birth weight (Scholl, Heidiger, & Belsky, 1996). Because of these findings, U.S. and Canadian government guidelines recommend that all women of childbearing age consume at least 0.4 but not more than 1 milligram of folic acid per day (excessive intake can be harmful). Currently, bread, flour, rice, pasta, and other grain products are being fortified with folic acid.

Other vitamins and minerals also have established benefits. Enriching women's diets with calcium helps prevent maternal high blood pressure and low birth weight. Adequate magnesium and zinc reduce the risk of many prenatal and birth complications (Christian et al., 2003; Facchinetti et al., 1992; Jameson, 1993). Fortifying table salt with iodine virtually eradicates *cretinism,* a disorder in which disrupted growth of the thyroid gland causes stunted growth and mental retardation (Mathews, Yudkin, & Neil, 1999). And sufficient vitamin C and iron beginning early in pregnancy promote growth of the placenta and healthy birth weight (Christian, 2003; Mathews, Yudkin, & Neil, 1999). Nevertheless, a supplement program should complement, not replace, efforts to improve maternal diets during pregnancy. For women who get too little food or an inadequate variety of foods, multivitamin tablets are a necessary but not sufficient intervention.

When poor nutrition continues throughout pregnancy, infants usually require more than dietary improvement. Their tired, restless behavior leads mothers to be less sensitive and stimulating. In response, babies become even more passive and withdrawn. Successful interventions must break this cycle of apathetic mother–baby interaction. Some do so by teaching parents how to interact effectively with their infants, whereas others focus on stimulating infants to promote active engagement with their physical and social surroundings (Grantham-McGregor et al., 1994; Zeskind & Ramey, 1978, 1981).

Although prenatal malnutrition is highest in poverty-stricken regions of the world, it is not limited to developing countries. The U.S. Special Supplemental Food Program for Women, Infants, and Children (WIC) provides food packages and nutrition education to poverty-stricken pregnant women, reaching about 90 percent of those who qualify because of their extremely low incomes (U.S. Department of Agriculture, 2004). But many American women who need nutrition intervention are not eligible for WIC. The Canadian Prenatal Nutrition Program (CPNP) is open to all pregnant women in need, regardless of income—including those who are adolescents, who abuse alcohol or drugs, or who live with violence. CPNP also makes a special effort to serve immigrant, First Nations, and Inuit communities. As a result, it reaches nearly 10 percent of expectant mothers in Canada (Health Canada, 2004b).

⑤ A Canadian obstetrician discusses dietary issues with a new mother and an expectant mother. During the prenatal period, the brain increases rapidly in size; for it to reach its full potential, the mother must have a diet high in all the basic nutrients.
CP Photo/DEREK OLIVER

• **EMOTIONAL STRESS** • When women experience severe emotional stress during pregnancy, their babies are at risk for a wide variety of difficulties. Intense anxiety is associated with a higher rate of miscarriage, prematurity, low birth weight, and infant respiratory illness and digestive disturbances (Mulder et al., 2002; Wadhwa, Sandman, & Garite, 2001). It is also related to prenatal growth delays and certain physical defects, such as cleft lip and palate, heart deformities, and pyloric stenosis (tightening of the infant's stomach outlet, which must be treated surgically) (Carmichael & Shaw, 2000). Follow-ups reveal that maternal prenatal stress predicts greater irritability and poorer motor and mental development through age 3, as well as higher rates of emotional and behavior problems in early childhood (De Weerth, van Hees, & Buitelaar, 2003; Graham et al., 1999; O'Connor et al., 2002).

When we experience fear and anxiety, stimulant hormones released into our bloodstream cause us to be "poised for action." Large amounts of blood are sent to parts of the body involved in the defensive response—the brain, the heart, and muscles in the arms, legs, and trunk. Blood flow to other organs, including the uterus, is reduced. As a result, the fetus is deprived of a full supply of oxygen and nutrients. Stress hormones also cross the placenta, causing a dramatic rise in fetal heart rate and activity level. They may also alter fetal neurological functioning, thereby heightening reactivity to stressors later in life (Graham et al., 1999; Monk et al., 2003). Finally, pregnant women who experience long-term anxiety are more likely to contract infectious diseases (due to a weakened immune system) and to smoke, drink, eat poorly, and engage in other harmful behaviors.

But stress-related prenatal complications are greatly reduced when mothers have husbands, other family members, and friends who offer support (McLean et al., 1993; Nuckolls, Cassel, & Kaplan, 1972). The link between social support and positive pregnancy outcomes is particularly strong for low-income women, who often lead highly stressful lives (Hoffman & Hatch, 1996).

• **MATERNAL AGE AND PREVIOUS BIRTHS** • Over the past quarter century, first births to women in their thirties have increased more than threefold, and those to women in their early forties have doubled. Many more couples are putting off childbearing until their careers

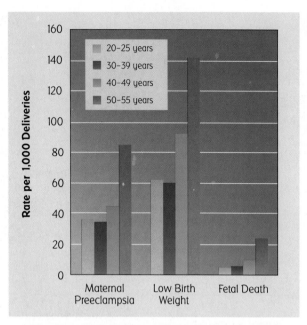

▲ **Figure 3.10**

Relationship of maternal age to prenatal and birth complications. Complications increase after age 45, with a sharp rise between 50 and 55 years. *Preeclampsia* is a serious disorder of the second and third trimesters involving high blood pressure, sudden weight gains, headaches, and swelling of the face, hands and feet. Without immediate treatment, the condition progresses rapidly and is a leading cause of maternal and infant illness and death. Similarly, low birth weight greatly increases the risk of infant death and health problems. (Adapted from Salihu et all., 2003).

are well established and they know they can support a child. Recall that women who delay having children face increased risk of infertility, miscarriage, and babies born with chromosomal defects. Are other pregnancy complications more common among older mothers? For many years, scientists thought so. But healthy women in their thirties and early forties have about the same rates of prenatal and birth complications as those in their twenties (Bianco et al., 1996; Dildy et al., 1996; Prysak, Lorenz, & Kisly, 1995). Thereafter, as Figure 3.10 shows, complication rates increase, with a sharp rise among women age 50 to 55 (an age at which, because of menopause and aging reproductive organs, few women can conceive naturally) (Salihu et al., 2003).

In the case of teenage mothers, does physical immaturity cause prenatal problems? Research shows that a teenager's body is large enough and strong enough to support pregnancy. In fact, as we will see in Chapter 5, nature tries to ensure that once a girl can conceive, she is physically ready to carry and give birth to a baby. Infants of teenagers are born with a higher rate of problems, but not directly because of maternal age. Most pregnant teenagers come from low-income backgrounds, where stress, poor nutrition, and health problems are common. Also, many are afraid to seek medical care or, in the United States, do not have access to such care because they lack health insurance (U.S. Department of Health and Human Services, 2003c).

As we conclude our discussion of the prenatal environment, refer to Applying What We Know on page 103, which summarizes "do's and "don'ts" for a healthy pregnancy. Public education about these vital precautions can greatly reduce prenatal health problems and their long-term negative consequences. The Canadian Institute of Child Health, a national nonprofit organization devoted to improving the health of Canada's children and youths, disseminates information to the public on how to foster prenatal health. It also advocates for safe, supportive care during childbirth—our next topic.

Ask Yourself

REVIEW	Why is it difficult to determine the effects of many environmental agents, such as drugs and pollution, on the embryo and fetus?
APPLY	Nora, pregnant for the first time, has heard about the teratogenic impact of alcohol and tobacco. Nevertheless, she believes that a few cigarettes and a glass of wine a day won't be harmful. Provide Nora with research-based reasons for not smoking or drinking.
CONNECT	List teratogens and other maternal factors that affect brain development during the prenatal period. Using Figure 3.8 on page 92, explain why the central nervous system is often affected when the prenatal environment is compromised.
REFLECT	A recent survey reported that only 24 percent of women of childbearing age knew that taking a daily folic acid supplement around the time of conception reduces the incidence of neural tube defects (March of Dimes, 2004). Were you aware of the prenatal effects of folic acid? If you could publicize five influences in a campaign aimed at safeguarding prenatal development, which ones would you choose, and why?

Applying
What We Know   Do's and Don'ts for a Healthy Pregnancy

Do	Don't
Do make sure that, before you get pregnant, you have been vaccinated against infectious diseases that are dangerous to the embryo and fetus, such as rubella. Most vaccinations are unsafe during pregnancy.	Don't take any drugs without consulting your doctor.
Do see a doctor as soon as you suspect that you are pregnant, and continue to get regular medical checkups throughout pregnancy.	Don't smoke. If you are a smoker, cut down or, better yet, quit. Avoid secondhand smoke. If other members of your family smoke, ask them to quit or to smoke outside.
Do eat a well-balanced diet and take vitamin–mineral supplements, as prescribed by your doctor, both prior to and during pregnancy. Gain 25 to 30 pounds gradually.	Don't drink alcohol from the time you decide to get pregnant.
Do keep physically fit through moderate exercise. If possible, join an exercise class for expectant mothers.	Don't engage in activities that might expose the developing organism to environmental hazards, such as radiation or pollutants.
Do avoid emotional stress. If you are a single expectant mother, find a relative or friend on whom you can count for emotional support.	Don't eat undercooked meat, handle cat litter, or garden in areas frequented by cats—behaviors that increase the risk of toxoplasmosis.
Do get plenty of rest. An overtired mother is at risk for complications.	Don't choose pregnancy as a time to go on a diet.
Do obtain literature from your doctor, library, or bookstore about prenatal development, and ask your doctor about anything that concerns you.	Don't gain too much weight during pregnancy. An excessive weight gain is associated with complications.
Do enroll in a prenatal and childbirth education class with your partner or other companion. When you know what to expect, the 9 months before birth can be one of the most joyful times of life.	

Childbirth

It is not surprising that childbirth is often referred to as *labor*. It is the hardest physical work that a woman may ever do. A complex series of hormonal exchanges between mother and fetus initiates the process, which divides naturally into three stages (see Figure 3.11 on page 104):

1. *Dilation and effacement of the cervix.* This is the longest stage of labor, lasting an average of 12 to 14 hours in a first birth and 4 to 6 hours in later births. Contractions of the uterus gradually become more frequent and powerful, causing the cervix, or uterine opening, to widen and thin to nothing, forming a clear channel from the uterus into the birth canal, or vagina.

2. *Delivery of the baby.* Once the cervix is fully open, the baby is ready to be born. This second stage is much shorter than the first, lasting about 50 minutes in a first birth and 20 minutes in later births. Strong contractions of the uterus continue, but the mother also feels a natural urge to squeeze and push with her abdominal muscles. As she does so with each contraction, she forces the baby down and out.

3. *Birth of the placenta.* Labor comes to an end with a few final contractions and pushes. These cause the placenta to separate from the wall of the uterus and be delivered in about 5 to 10 minutes.

The Baby's Adaptation to Labor and Delivery

At first glance, labor and delivery seem like a dangerous ordeal for the baby. The strong contractions expose the head to a great deal of pressure, and they squeeze the placenta and the umbilical cord repeatedly. Each time, the baby's supply of oxygen is temporarily reduced.

Fortunately, healthy babies are well equipped to withstand these traumas. The force of the contractions causes the infant to produce high levels of stress hormones. Unlike during the

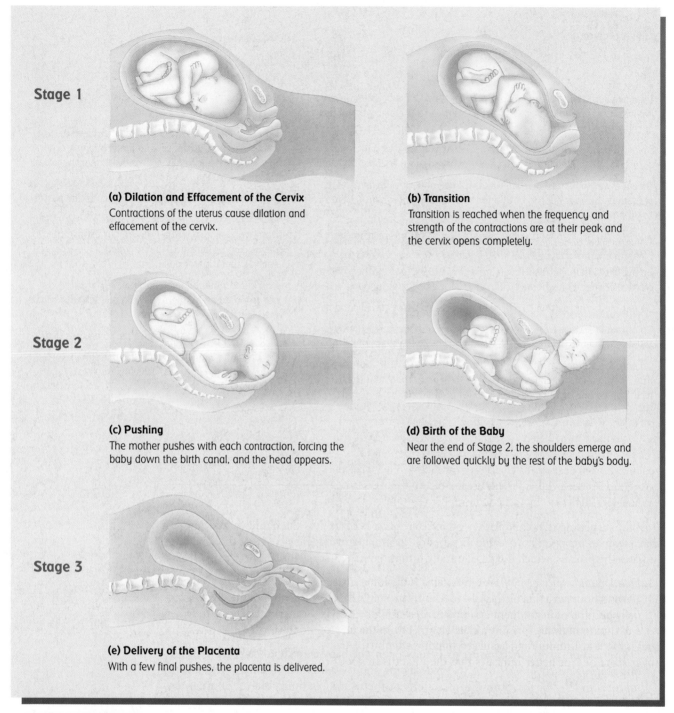

Stage 1

(a) Dilation and Effacement of the Cervix
Contractions of the uterus cause dilation and
effacement of the cervix.

(b) Transition
Transition is reached when the frequency and
strength of the contractions are at their peak and
the cervix opens completely.

Stage 2

(c) Pushing
The mother pushes with each contraction, forcing the
baby down the birth canal, and the head appears.

(d) Birth of the Baby
Near the end of Stage 2, the shoulders emerge and
are followed quickly by the rest of the baby's body.

Stage 3

(e) Delivery of the Placenta
With a few final pushes, the placenta is delivered.

▲ **Figure 3.11**

The three stages of labor.

pregnancy, the baby's production of stress hormones during childbirth is adaptive. It helps the
infant withstand oxygen deprivation by sending a rich supply of blood to the brain and heart.
In addition, stress hormones prepare the baby to breathe by causing the lungs to absorb any
remaining fluid and by expanding the bronchial tubes (passages leading to the lungs). Finally,
stress hormones arouse infants into alertness so they are born wide awake, ready to interact
with their world (Lagercrantz & Slotkin, 1986).

The Newborn Baby's Appearance

Parents are often surprised at the odd appearance of the newborn—a far cry from the storybook image many had in their minds before birth. The average newborn is 20 inches long and

TABLE 3.8　THE APGAR SCALE

Sign[a]	Score		
	0	1	2
Heart rate	No heartbeat	Under 100 beats per minute	100 to 140 beats per minute
Respiratory effort	No breathing for 60 seconds	Irregular, shallow breathing	Strong breathing and crying
Reflex irritability (sneezing, coughing, and grimacing)	No response	Weak reflexive response	Strong reflexive response
Muscle tone	Completely limp	Weak movements of arms and legs	Strong movements of arms and legs
Color	Blue body, arms, and legs	Body pink with blue arms and legs	Body, arms, and legs completely pink

[a]To remember these signs, you may find it helpful to use a technique in which the original labels are reordered and renamed as follows: color = **A**ppearance, heart rate = **P**ulse, reflex irritability = **G**rimace, muscle tone = **A**ctivity, and respiratory effort = **R**espiration. Together, the first letters of the new labels spell Apgar.

Source: Apgar, 1953.

weighs 7½ pounds; boys tend to be slightly longer and heavier than girls. The head is large in relation to the trunk and legs, which are short and bowed. This combination of a large head (with its well-developed brain) and a small body means that human infants learn quickly in the first few months of life. Unlike most mammals, however, they cannot get around on their own until much later.

Even though newborn babies may not match parents' idealized image, some features do make them attractive. Their round faces, chubby cheeks, large foreheads, and big eyes make adults feel like picking them up and cuddling them (Berman, 1980; Lorenz, 1943).

Assessing the Newborn's Physical Condition: The Apgar Scale

Infants who have difficulty making the transition to life outside the uterus require special help at once. To assess the baby's physical condition, doctors and nurses use the **Apgar Scale.** As Table 3.8 shows, a rating of 0, 1, or 2 on each of five characteristics is made at 1 minute and again at 5 minutes after birth. An Apgar score of 7 or better indicates that the infant is in good physical condition. If the score is between 4 and 6, the baby requires special help in establishing breathing and other vital signs. If the score is 3 or below, the infant is in serious danger, and emergency medical attention is needed. Two Apgar ratings are given because some babies have trouble adjusting at first but are doing well after a few minutes (Apgar, 1953).

To accommodate the well-developed brain, a newborn's head is large in relation to the trunk and legs. In addition, the round face, with its chubby cheeks and big eyes, induces adults to approach, pick up, and cuddle the newborn.
© SIU/Peter Arnold, Inc.

Approaches to Childbirth

Childbirth practices, like other aspects of family life, are molded by the society of which mother and baby are a part. In many village and tribal cultures, expectant mothers are well acquainted with the childbirth process. For example, anthropologists such as Margaret Mead reported that the Jarara of South America and the Pukapukans of the Pacific Islands treat birth as a vital part of daily life. The Jarara mother gives birth in full view of the entire community. The Pukapukan

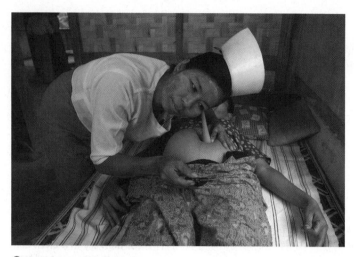

In Myanmar (Burma), a midwife examines a pregnant woman, using an instrument to listen for the heartbeat of the fetus. The mother will give birth at home, supported by family members throughout labor and delivery.
© SHEHZAD NOORANI/Peter Arnold, Inc.

girl is so familiar with the events of labor and delivery that she frequently can be seen playing at it. Using a coconut to represent the baby, she stuffs it inside her dress, imitates the mother's pushing, and lets the nut fall at the proper moment. Although they may not be attended by medical personnel, most women in nonindustrialized cultures are assisted by someone during childbirth. Among the Mayans of the Yucatán, the mother leans against a woman called the "head helper," who supports her weight and breathes with her during each contraction (Jordan, 1993; Mead & Newton, 1967).

In large Western nations, childbirth has changed dramatically over the centuries. Before the late 1800s, birth usually took place at home and was a family-centered event. The industrial revolution brought greater crowding to cities, along with new health problems. As a result, childbirth moved from home to hospital, where the health of mothers and babies could be protected. Once doctors assumed responsibility for childbirth, women's knowledge of it declined, and relatives and friends no longer participated (Borst, 1995).

By the 1950s and 1960s, women were starting to question the medical procedures that came to be used routinely during labor and delivery. Many felt that routine use of strong drugs and delivery instruments had robbed them of a precious experience and often were neither necessary nor safe for the baby. Gradually, a natural childbirth movement arose in Europe and spread to North America. Its purpose was to make hospital birth as comfortable and rewarding for mothers as possible. Today, most hospitals offer birth centers that are family centered and homelike. Freestanding birth centers, which permit greater maternal control over labor and delivery, including choice of delivery positions, presence of family members and friends, and early contact between parents and baby, also exist. However, they offer less backup medical care than hospitals. And a small number of North American women reject institutional birth entirely and choose to have their babies at home.

Natural, or Prepared, Childbirth

Natural, or **prepared, childbirth** consists of a group of techniques aimed at reducing pain and medical intervention and making childbirth as rewarding an experience as possible. Although many natural childbirth programs exist, most draw on methods developed by Grantly Dick-Read (1959) in England and Ferdinand Lamaze (1958) in France. These physicians recognized that cultural attitudes had taught women to fear the birth experience. An anxious, frightened woman in labor tenses muscles, turning the mild pain that sometimes accompanies strong contractions into intense pain.

In a typical natural childbirth program, the expectant mother and a companion (a partner, a relative, or a friend) participate in three activities:

1. *Classes.* The expectant mother and her companion attend a series of classes in which they learn about the anatomy and physiology of labor and delivery. Knowledge about the birth process reduces a mother's fear.

2. *Relaxation and breathing techniques.* Expectant mothers are taught relaxation and breathing exercises aimed at counteracting the pain of uterine contractions.

3. *Labor coach.* The companion learns how to help during childbirth by reminding the mother to relax and breathe, massaging her back, supporting her body, and offering encouragement and affection.

• **SOCIAL SUPPORT AND NATURAL CHILDBIRTH** • Social support is important to the success of natural childbirth techniques. In Guatemalan and American hospitals that routinely isolated patients during childbirth, some mothers were randomly assigned a trained companion who stayed with them throughout labor and delivery, talking to them, holding their hands, and rubbing their backs to promote relaxation. These mothers had fewer birth complications, and their labors were several hours shorter than those of women who did not have supportive companionship. Guatemalan mothers who received support also interacted more positively with their babies after delivery, talking, smiling, and gently stroking (Kennell et al., 1991; Sosa et al., 1980). Other studies indicate that mothers who are supported during labor and delivery less often have cesarean (surgical) deliveries, and their babies' Apgar scores are higher (Sauls, 2002).

The continuous rather than intermittent support of a trained companion strengthens these outcomes. It is particularly helpful during a first childbirth, when mothers are more anxious (DiMatteo & Kahn, 1997; Scott, Berkowitz, & Klaus, 1999). And this aspect of natural childbirth makes Western hospital birth customs more acceptable to women from parts of the world where assistance from family and community members is the norm (Granot et al., 1996).

• **POSITIONS FOR DELIVERY** • With natural childbirth, mothers often give birth in the upright, sitting position shown in Figure 3.12 rather than lying flat on their backs with their feet in stirrups (the traditional hospital delivery room practice). When mothers are upright, labor is shortened because pushing is easier and more effective. The baby benefits from a richer supply of oxygen because blood flow to the placenta is increased (Davidson et al., 1993). Because the mother can see the delivery, she can track the effectiveness of each contraction in pushing the baby out of the birth canal (Kelly, Terry, & Naglieri, 1999). This helps her work with the doctor or midwife to ensure that the baby's head and shoulders emerge slowly, which reduces the chances of tearing the vaginal opening.

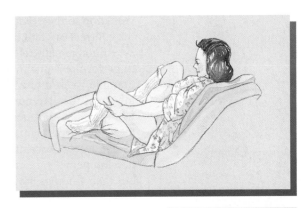

▲ **Figure 3.12**

Sitting position often used for delivery in a birth center or at home. It facilitates pushing during the second stage of labor; increases blood flow to the placenta, which grants the baby a richer supply of oxygen; and permits the mother to see the delivery, enabling her to track the effectiveness of each contraction.

Home Delivery

Home birth has always been popular in certain industrialized nations, such as England, the Netherlands, and Sweden. The number of North American women choosing to have their babies at home increased during the 1970s and 1980s but remains small, at about 1 percent (Curtin & Park, 1999). These mothers want birth to be an important part of family life. In addition, most want to avoid unnecessary medical procedures. And they want greater control over their own care and that of their babies than hospitals permit (Wickham, 1999). Although some home births are attended by doctors, many more are handled by certified nurse-midwives, who have degrees in nursing and additional training in childbirth management.

Is it just as safe to give birth at home as in a hospital? For healthy women who are assisted by a well-trained doctor or midwife, it seems so, since complications rarely occur (Janssen et al., 2002; Vedam, 2003). However, if attendants are not carefully trained and prepared to handle emergencies, the rate of infant death is high (Mehlmadrona & Madrona, 1997). When mothers are at risk for any kind of complication, the appropriate place for labor and delivery is the hospital, where life-saving treatment is available.

Labor and Delivery Medication

Although natural childbirth techniques lessen or eliminate the need for pain-relieving drugs, some form of medication is used in more than 80 percent of North American births (Sharma & Leveno, 2003). *Analgesics* are drugs used to relieve pain. When they are given during labor, the dose is usually mild and intended to help a mother relax. *Anesthetics* are a stronger type of painkiller that blocks sensation. Currently, the most common approach to controlling pain during labor is *epidural analgesia*, in which a regional pain-relieving drug is delivered continuously through a catheter into a small space in the lower spine. Rather than numbing the lower half of the body, as older spinal block procedures do, epidural analgesia limits pain

⑥ As the midwife and grandmother look on, a mother and father ecstatically greet their newborn baby. The birth took place at home, where the mother used a birthing tub, which permitted her to relax in a soothing bath during labor and delivery. AP/Wide World Photos

reduction to the pelvic region. Because the mother retains the capacity to feel the pressure of the contractions and move her trunk and legs, she can push during the second stage of labor.

Although pain-relieving drugs assist women in coping with childbirth and enable doctors to perform essential medical interventions, they also cause problems. Epidural analgesia, for example, weakens uterine contractions. As a result, labor is prolonged. And because drugs rapidly cross the placenta, exposed newborns tend to have lower Apgar scores, to be sleepy and withdrawn, to suck poorly during feedings, and to be irritable when awake (Caton et al., 2002; Eltzschig, Lieberman, & Camann, 2003; Emory, Schlackman, & Fiano, 1996).

Do heavy doses of childbirth medication have a lasting impact on physical and mental development? Some researchers have claimed so (Brackbill, McManus, & Woodward, 1985), but their findings have been challenged (Golub, 1996). Use of medication may be related to other risk factors that could account for the long-term consequences in some studies. More research is needed to sort out these effects. Meanwhile, the negative impact of these drugs on the newborn's adjustment supports the current trend to limit their use.

Ask Yourself

REVIEW	Describe the features and benefits of natural childbirth. What aspect contributes greatly to favorable outcomes, and why?
APPLY	On seeing her newborn baby for the first time, Caroline exclaimed, "Why is she so out of proportion?" What observations prompted Caroline to ask this question? Explain why her baby's appearance is adaptive.
CONNECT	How might use of epidural analgesia during labor and delivery negatively affect the parent–newborn relationship? Does your answer illustrate bidirectional influences between parent and child? Explain.
REFLECT	If you were an expectant parent, would you choose home birth? Why or why not?

Birth Complications

We have seen that some babies—in particular, those whose mothers are in poor health, do not receive good medical care, or have a history of pregnancy problems—are especially likely to experience birth complications. Inadequate oxygen, a pregnancy that ends too early, and a baby who is born underweight are serious risks to development that we have touched on many times. Let's look at the impact of each complication on later development.

Oxygen Deprivation

A small number of infants experience *anoxia*, or inadequate oxygen supply, during the birth process. Sometimes the problem results from a failure to start breathing within a few minutes. Healthy newborns can survive periods of little or no oxygen longer than adults can; they reduce their metabolic rate, thereby conserving the limited oxygen available. Nevertheless, brain damage is likely if regular breathing is delayed more than 10 minutes (Parer, 1998).

At other times, anoxia occurs during labor. A common cause is squeezing of the umbilical cord, a condition that is especially likely when infants are in **breech position**—turned in such a way that the buttocks or feet would be delivered first (1 in every 25 births). Because of this danger, breech babies often experience a cesarean (surgical) delivery. An additional cause of oxygen deprivation is *placenta abruptio*, or premature separation of the placenta (about 1 in every 250 births), a life-threatening event that requires immediate delivery (Matsuda, Maeda, & Kouno, 2003). Although the reasons for placenta abruptio are not well understood, teratogens that cause abnormal development of the placenta, such as cigarette smoking, are related to it.

Still another condition that can lead to anoxia is **Rh factor incompatibility** between the mother's and baby's blood types. When the mother is Rh negative (lacks the Rh protein) and the father is Rh positive (has the Rh protein), the baby may inherit the father's Rh-positive blood type. If even a little of a fetus's Rh-positive blood crosses the placenta into the Rh-negative mother's bloodstream, she begins to form antibodies to the foreign protein. If these enter the fetus's system, they destroy red blood cells, reducing the supply of oxygen. Mental retardation, miscarriage, heart damage, and infant death can occur. It takes time for the mother to produce antibodies, so first-born children are rarely affected. The danger increases with each pregnancy. Fortunately, Rh incompatibility can be prevented in most cases. After the birth of each Rh-positive baby, Rh-negative mothers are given a vaccine to prevent the buildup of antibodies.

How do children who experience anoxia during labor and delivery fare as they get older? Research suggests that the greater the oxygen deprivation, the poorer children's cognitive and language skills in early and middle childhood (Hopkins-Golightly, Raz, & Sander, 2003; Porter-Stevens, Raz, & Sander, 1999). Still, many children with mild to moderate anoxia improve over time (Raz, Shah, & Sander, 1996).

When development is severely impaired, the anoxia was probably extreme. Perhaps it was caused by prenatal insult to the baby's respiratory system or occurred because the infant's lungs were not yet mature enough to breathe. For example, babies born more than 6 weeks early commonly have *respiratory distress syndrome* (otherwise known as *hyaline membrane disease*). Their tiny lungs are so poorly developed that the air sacs collapse, causing serious breathing difficulties. Today, mechanical respirators keep many such infants alive. In spite of these measures, some babies suffer permanent brain damage from lack of oxygen, and in other cases their delicate lungs are harmed by the treatment itself. Respiratory distress syndrome is only one of many risks for babies born too soon, as we will see in the following section.

Preterm and Low-Birth-Weight Infants

Babies born 3 weeks or more before the end of a full 38-week pregnancy or who weigh less than $5\frac{1}{2}$ pounds (2,500 grams) have for many years been referred to as "premature." A wealth of research indicates that premature babies are at risk for many problems. Birth weight is the best available predictor of infant survival and healthy development. Many newborns who weigh less than $3\frac{1}{2}$ pounds (1,500 grams) experience difficulties that are not overcome, an effect that becomes stronger as birth weight decreases. Frequent illness, inattention, overactivity, language delays, low intelligence test scores, deficits in school learning, and emotional and behavior problems are some of the difficulties that persist through childhood and adolescence and into adulthood (Bhutta et al., 2002; Hack et al., 2002; Johnson et al., 2003).

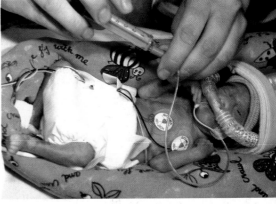

Ⓖ This baby was born 12 weeks before her due date and weighs little more than 2 pounds. Because her lungs are too immature to function independently, she breathes with the aid of a respirator. Her survival and development are seriously at risk.
© Knut Mueller/Das Fotoarchiv/Peter Arnold, Inc.

About 1 in 13 American infants and 1 in 18 Canadian infants are born underweight. Although the problem can strike unexpectedly, it is highest among poverty-stricken women (Children's Defense Fund, 2004; Statistics Canada, 2004d). These mothers, as indicated earlier, are more likely to be undernourished and to be exposed to harmful environmental influences. In addition, they often do not receive adequate prenatal care.

Prematurity is also common when mothers are carrying twins. Twins are usually born about 3 weeks early. Because space inside the uterus is restricted, they gain less weight than singletons after the twentieth week of pregnancy.

• **PRETERM VERSUS SMALL FOR DATE** • Although low-birth-weight infants face many obstacles to healthy development, most go on to lead normal lives; half of those who weighed only a couple of pounds at birth have no disability (see Figure 3.13 on page 110). To better understand why some babies do better than others, researchers divide them into two groups. **Preterm infants** are those born several weeks or more before their due date. Although they are small, their weight may still be appropriate, based on time spent in the uterus. **Small-for-date infants** are below their expected weight considering length of the pregnancy. Some small-for-date infants are actually full term. Others are preterm babies who are especially underweight.

Of the two types of babies, small-for-date infants usually have more serious problems. During the first year, they are more likely to die, catch infections, and show evidence of brain damage. By middle childhood, they have lower intelligence test scores, are less attentive, achieve more poorly in school, and are socially immature (Minde, 2000; O'Keefe et al., 2003). Small-for-date infants probably experienced inadequate nutrition before birth. Perhaps their

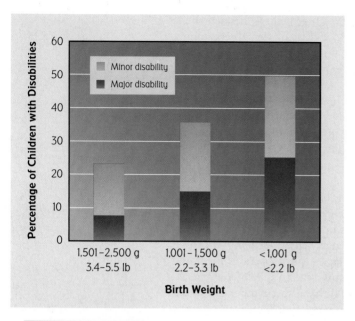

▲ **Figure 3.13**

Incidence of major and minor disabilities by birth weight, obtained from studies of low-birth-weight children at school age. *Major disabilities* include cerebral palsy, mental retardation, and vision and hearing impairments. *Minor disabilities* include slightly below-average intelligence, learning disabilities (usually in reading, spelling, and math), mild difficulties in motor control, and behavior problems (including poor attention and impulse control, aggressiveness, noncompliance, depression, passivity, anxiety, and difficulty separating from parents). (Adapted from D'Agostino & Clifford, 1998.)

mothers did not eat properly, the placenta did not function normally, or the babies themselves had defects that prevented them from growing as they should.

• **CONSEQUENCES FOR CAREGIVING** • Imagine a scrawny, thin-skinned infant whose body is only a little larger than the size of your hand. You try to play with the baby by stroking and talking softly, but he is sleepy and unresponsive. When you feed him, he sucks poorly. He is usually irritable during the short, unpredictable periods in which he is awake.

The appearance and behavior of preterm babies can lead parents to be less sensitive and responsive in caring for them. Compared with full-term infants, preterm babies—especially those who are very ill at birth—are less often held close, touched, and talked to gently. At times, mothers of these infants resort to interfering pokes and verbal commands, in an effort to obtain a higher level of response from the baby (Barratt, Roach, & Leavitt, 1996). This may explain why preterm babies as a group are at risk for child abuse. When they are born to isolated, poverty-stricken mothers who cannot provide good nutrition, health care, and parenting, the likelihood of unfavorable outcomes increases (Bacharach & Baumeister, 1998). In contrast, parents with stable life circumstances and social supports usually can overcome the stresses of caring for a preterm infant. In these cases, even some sick preterm babies have a good chance of catching up in development by middle childhood (Ment et al., 2003).

These findings suggest that how well preterm infants develop has a great deal to do with the parent–child relationship. Consequently, interventions directed at supporting both sides of this tie are more likely to help these infants recover.

• **INTERVENTIONS FOR PRETERM INFANTS** • A preterm baby is cared for in a special Plexiglas-enclosed bed called an *isolette*. Temperature is carefully controlled because these infants cannot yet regulate their own body temperature effectively. To help protect the baby from infection, air is filtered before it enters the isolette. When a preterm infant is fed through a stomach tube, breathes with the aid of a respirator, and receives medication through an intravenous needle, the isolette can be very isolating indeed! Physical needs that otherwise would lead to close contact and other human stimulation are met mechanically.

▶ *Special Infant Stimulation.* At one time, doctors believed that stimulating such a fragile baby could be harmful. Now we know that in proper doses, certain kinds of stimulation can help preterm infants develop. In some intensive care nurseries, preterm babies can be seen rocking in suspended hammocks or lying on waterbeds designed to replace the gentle motion they would have received while still in the mother's uterus. Other forms of stimulation have also been used—for example, an attractive mobile or a tape recording of a heartbeat, soft music, or the mother's voice. These experiences promote faster weight gain, more predictable sleep patterns, and greater alertness (Marshall-Baker, Lickliter, & Cooper, 1998; Standley, 1998).

Touch is an especially important form of stimulation. In baby animals, touching the skin releases certain brain chemicals that support physical growth—effects believed to occur in humans as well. When preterm infants were massaged several times each day in the hospital, they gained weight faster and, at the end of the first year, were advanced in mental and motor development over preterm infants not given this stimulation (Field, 2001; Field, Hernandez-Reif, & Freedman, 2004).

In developing countries where hospitalization is not always possible, skin-to-skin "kangaroo care," in which the preterm infant is tucked close to the chest and peers over the top of the caregiver's clothing, is encouraged. The technique is used in Western nations as a supplement to hospital intensive care. It fosters improved oxygenation of the baby's body, temperature regulation, breathing, feeding, and infant survival (Anderson, 1999; Feldman & Eidelman,

2003). In addition, mothers and fathers practicing kangaroo care interact more sensitively and affectionately with their babies, who develop more favorably (Feldman et al., 2002, 2003).

Some very small or sick babies, however, are too weak for much stimulation. The noise, bright lights, and constant medical monitoring of the intensive care nursery are already overwhelming, triggering irritability and withdrawal. When doctors and nurses carefully adjusted the amount and kind of stimulation to fit babies' individual needs, EEG and fMRI measures revealed more organized brain functioning by 2 weeks of age. Such infants also scored higher in motor, cognitive, and emotional maturity when reassessed 9 months later (Als et al., 2004).

▶ *Training Parents in Infant Caregiving Skills.* Interventions that support parents of preterm infants generally teach them about the infant's characteristics and promote caregiving skills. For parents with the economic and personal resources to care for a preterm infant, just a few sessions of coaching in recognizing and responding to the baby's needs are linked to steady gains in mental test performance that, after several years, equal those of full-term children (Achenbach et al., 1990). Warm parenting that helps preterm infants sustain attention (for example, gently commenting on and showing the baby interesting features of a toy) is especially helpful in promoting early cognitive and language development (Smith et al., 1996).

When preterm infants live in stressed, low-income households, long-term intervention is required to reduce developmental problems. In the Infant Health and Development Program, preterm babies born into poverty received a comprehensive intervention that combined medical follow-up, weekly parent training sessions, and enrollment in cognitively stimulating child care from 1 through 3 years of age. Compared with controls receiving only medical follow-up, more than four times as many intervention 3-year-olds were within normal range in intelligence, psychological adjustment, and physical growth (Bradley et al., 1994). In addition, mothers in the intervention group were more affectionate and more often encouraged play and cognitive mastery in their children—a reason their 3-year-olds may have been developing so favorably (McCarton, 1998).

At ages 5 and 8, children who had attended the child-care program regularly—for more than 350 days over the 3-year period—continued to show better intellectual functioning. And the more they attended, the higher they scored, with greater gains for those whose birth weights were higher—between 4½ and 5½ pounds (2,001–2,500 grams) (see Figure 3.14). In contrast, children who attended only sporadically gained little or lost ground (Hill, Brooks-Gunn, & Waldfogel, 2003). These findings confirm that babies who are both preterm and economically disadvantaged require *intensive* intervention. And special strategies, such as extra adult–child interaction, may be necessary to help children with the lowest birth weights develop.

Finally, the high rate of underweight babies in the United States—one of the worst in the industrialized world—could be

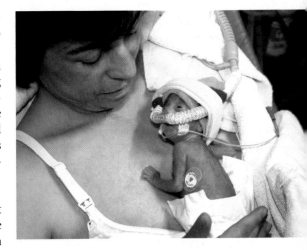

◉ This mother practices "kangaroo care" with her preterm baby in the intensive care nursery. By holding the infant close to her chest, she promotes oxygenation of the baby's body, temperature regulation, feeding, alertness, and more favorable development. At the same time, she gains confidence in her ability to meet her fragile newborn's needs. © Knut Mueller/Das Fotoarchiv/Peter Arnold, Inc.

▶ **Figure 3.14**

Influence of intensity of early intervention for low-income, preterm babies on intellectual functioning at age 8. Infants born preterm received cognitively stimulating child care from 1 through 3 years of age. Those who attended the program sporadically gained little in intellectual functioning (heavier-weight babies) or lost ground (light-weight babies). The more children attended, the greater their intellectual gains. Heavier babies consistently gained more than light babies. But boosting the intensity of intervention above 400 days led to a dramatic increase in the performance of the light-weight group. (Adapted from Hill, Brooks-Gunn, & Waldfogel, 2003.)

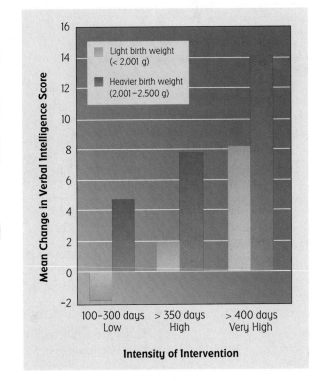

SOCIAL ISSUES

A Cross-National Perspective
on Health Care and Other Policies for Parents and Newborn Babies

Infant mortality is an index used around the world to assess the overall health of a nation's children. It refers to the number of deaths in the first year of life per 1,000 live births. The United States has the most up-to-date health care technology in the world, including a newborn intensive care capacity per number of births that far exceeds that of other industrialized nations (Thompson, Goodman, & Little, 2002). Nevertheless, it has made less progress in reducing infant deaths. Over the past three decades, it has slipped in the international rankings, from seventh in the 1950s to twenty-sixth in 2002. Members of America's poor ethnic minorities are at greatest risk. African-American and Native-American babies are twice as likely as white infants to die in the first year of life (U.S. Census Bureau, 2004b). Canada, in contrast, has achieved one of the lowest infant mortality rates in the world. It

ranks sixteenth and falls only slightly behind top-ranked countries. Still, infant mortality among Canada's lowest-income groups is much higher than the national figure. First Nations babies die at twice the rate, and Inuit babies at three times the rate, of Canadian babies in general (Smylie, 2001; Statistics Canada, 2004d).

Neonatal mortality, the rate of death within the first month of life, accounts for 67 percent of the infant death rate in the United States and 80 percent in Canada. Two factors are largely responsible for neonatal mortality. The first is serious physical defects, most of which cannot be prevented. The percentage of babies born with physical defects is about the same in all ethnic and income groups. The second leading cause of neonatal mortality is low birth weight, which is largely preventable. African-American, Native-American, and Canadian Aboriginal babies are more than twice as likely as white infants to be born early and underweight (Health Canada, 2003c; Martin et al., 2003).

Widespread poverty and, in the United States, weak health

care programs for mothers and young children are largely responsible for these trends. Each country in Figure 3.15 that outranks the United States in infant survival provides all its citizens with government-sponsored health care benefits. And each takes extra steps to make sure that pregnant mothers and babies have access to good nutrition, high-quality medical care, and social and economic supports that promote effective parenting.

For example, all Western European nations guarantee women a certain number of prenatal visits at very low or no cost. After a baby is born, a health professional routinely visits the home to provide counseling about infant care and to arrange continuing medical services. Home assistance is especially extensive in the Netherlands. For a token fee, each mother is granted a specially trained maternity helper, who assists with infant care, shopping, housekeeping, meal preparation, and the care of other children during the days after delivery (Bradley & Bray, 1996; Kamerman, 1993).

Paid, job-protected employment leave is another vital societal intervention for new parents. Canadian mothers are eligible for 15 weeks maternity leave at 55 percent of prior earnings, and Canadian mothers or fathers are eligible for an additional

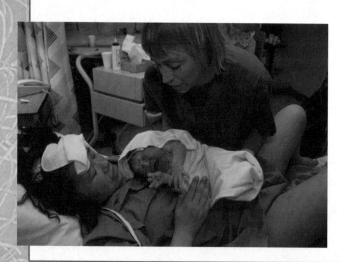

◀ This Inuit mother, from Baffin Island in northernmost Canada, experienced pregnancy complications and had to be flown 190 miles to deliver her son. Limited access to health care and social services in remote areas compromise the futures of many Inuit newborns. © Joanna B. Pinneo/AURORA

greatly reduced by improving the health and social conditions described in the Social Issues box above. Fortunately, today we can save many preterm infants, but an even better course of action would be to prevent this serious threat to infant survival and development before it happens.

Birth Complications, Parenting, and Resilience

In the preceding sections, we considered a variety of birth complications. Now let's try to put the evidence together. Can any general principles help us understand how infants who survive

▶ **Figure 3.15**

Infant mortality in 29 nations. Despite its advanced health care technology, the United States ranks poorly. It is twenty-sixth in the world, with a death rate of 6.6 infants per 1,000 births. Canada provides all its citizens with government-funded health care and ranks fifteenth. Its infant death rate is 4.8 per 1,000 births. (Adapted from U.S. Census Bureau, 2004b.)

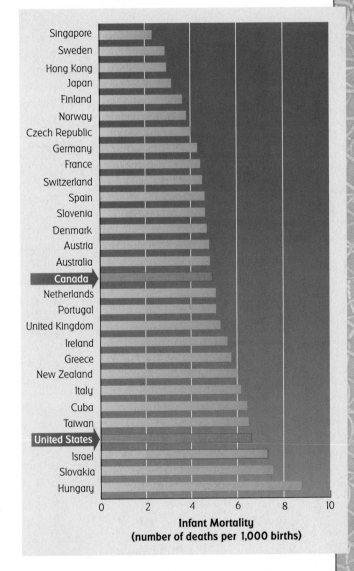

Infant Mortality
(number of deaths per 1,000 births)

35 weeks at the same rate. Paid leave is widely available in other industrialized nations as well. Sweden has the most generous parental leave program in the world. Parents have the right to birth leave of 2 weeks for fathers plus 18 months of leave to share between them—the first 12 months at 80 percent of prior earnings, the next 3 months at a modest flat rate, and the final 3 months unpaid (Seward, Yeats, & Zottarelli, 2002). Even less-developed nations offer parental leave benefits. For example, in the People's Republic of China, a new mother is granted 3 months' leave at regular pay. Furthermore, many countries supplement basic paid leave. In Germany, for example, after a fully paid 3-month leave, a parent may take 2 more years at a flat rate and a third year at no pay (Waldfogel, 2001).

Yet in the United States, the federal government mandates *only 12 weeks of unpaid leave* for employees in companies with at least 50 workers. Most women, however, work in smaller businesses, and even those who work in large-enough companies may be unable to afford to take unpaid leave (Hewlett, 2003). In 2002, California became the first state to guarantee a mother or father paid leave—up to 6 weeks at half salary, regardless of the size of the company. Nevertheless, research indicates that 6 weeks of childbirth leave is too short. When a family is stressed by a baby's arrival, leaves of 6 weeks or less are linked to increased maternal anxiety, depression, marital dissatisfaction, sense of role overload (conflict between work and family responsibilities), and negative interactions with the baby. Longer leaves of 12 weeks or more predict favorable maternal mental health and sensitive, responsive caregiving (Clark et al., 1997; Hyde et al., 1995, 2001). Single women and their babies are most hurt by the absence of a generous national paid-leave policy. These mothers are usually the sole source of support for their families and can least afford to take time from their jobs.

In countries with low infant mortality rates, expectant mothers need not wonder how or where they will get health care and other resources to support their baby's development. The powerful impact of universal, high-quality health care, generous parental leave, and other social services on maternal and infant well-being provides strong justification for these policies.

a traumatic birth are likely to develop? A landmark study carried out in Hawaii provides answers to this question.

In 1955, Emmy Werner and Ruth Smith began to follow nearly 700 infants on the island of Kauai who had experienced mild, moderate, or severe birth complications. Each was matched, on the basis of SES and ethnicity, with a healthy newborn (Werner & Smith, 1982). Findings revealed that the likelihood of long-term difficulties increased if birth trauma was severe. Among mildly to moderately stressed children, however, the best predictor of how well they did in later years was the quality of their home environments. Children growing up in stable families did almost as well on measures of intelligence and psychological adjustment as those with no birth problems. Those exposed to poverty, family disorganization, and mentally ill parents often developed serious learning difficulties, behavior problems, and emotional disturbance.

The Kauai study tells us that as long as birth injuries are not overwhelming, a supportive home environment can restore children's growth. But the most intriguing cases in this study were the handful of exceptions. A few children with both fairly serious birth complications and troubled families grew into competent adults who fared as well as controls in career attainment and psychological adjustment. Werner and Smith found that these children relied on factors outside the family and within themselves to overcome stress. Some had attractive personalities that caused them to receive positive responses from relatives, neighbors, and peers. In other instances, a grandparent, aunt, uncle, or babysitter provided the needed emotional support (Werner, 1989, 2001; Werner & Smith, 1992).

Do these outcomes remind you of the characteristics of resilient children, discussed in Chapter 1? The Kauai study—and other similar investigations—reveal that the impact of early biological risks often wanes as children's personal characteristics and social experiences increasingly contribute to their functioning (Laucht, Esser, & Schmidt, 1997; Resnick et al., 1999). In sum, when the overall balance of life events tips toward the favorable side, children with serious birth problems can develop successfully. But when negative factors outweigh positive ones, even a sturdy newborn can become a lifelong casualty.

Ask Yourself

REVIEW	Sensitive care can help preterm infants recover, but they are less likely than full-term newborns to receive such care. Explain why.
APPLY	Cecilia and Adena each gave birth to a 3-pound baby 7 weeks preterm. Cecilia is single and on welfare. Adena and her husband are happily married and earn a good income. Plan an intervention for helping each baby develop.
CONNECT	List factors discussed in this chapter that increase the chances that an infant will be born underweight. How many of these factors could be prevented by better health care for expectant mothers?
REFLECT	Many people object to the use of extraordinary medical measures to save extremely low-birth-weight babies (less than 1½ pounds, or 1,000 grams) because most who survive develop serious physical, cognitive, and emotional problems. Do you agree or disagree? Explain.

Heredity, Environment, and Behavior: A Look Ahead

Throughout this chapter, we have discussed a wide variety of genetic and early environmental influences, each of which has the power to alter the course of development. When we consider them together, it may seem surprising that any newborn babies arrive intact. Yet the vast majority—over 90 percent in North America—do. Born healthy and vigorous, these developing members of the human species vary greatly in behavior. Some are outgoing and sociable; others are shy and reserved. By school age, one child loves to read, another is attracted to mathematics, while a third excels at music. **Behavioral genetics** is a field devoted to uncovering the contributions of nature and nurture to this diversity in human traits and abilities. We have already seen that researchers have just begun to understand the genetic and environmental events preceding birth that affect the child's potential. How, then, do they unravel the roots of the many characteristics that emerge later?

All contemporary researchers agree that both heredity and environment are involved in every aspect of development. But for polygenic traits (those due to many genes), such as intelligence and personality, scientists are a long way from knowing precisely what hereditary influences are involved. They must study the impact of genes on these characteristics indirectly.

Some believe that it is useful and possible to answer the question of *how much each factor contributes* to differences among children. A growing consensus, however, regards that question as unanswerable. These investigators believe that heredity and environment are insepa-rable. The important question, they maintain, is *how nature and nurture work together.* Let's consider each position in turn.

The Question, "How Much?"

Behavioral geneticists use two methods—heritability estimates and concordance rates—to infer the role of heredity in complex human characteristics. Let's look closely at the information these procedures yield, along with their limitations.

• **HERITABILITY** • **Heritability estimates** measure the extent to which individual differences in complex traits in a specific population are due to genetic factors. We will take a brief look at heritability findings on intelligence and personality here and will return to them in later chapters, when we consider these topics in greater detail. Heritability estimates are obtained from **kinship studies,** which compare the characteristics of family members. The most common type of kinship study compares identical twins, who share all their genes, with fraternal twins, who share only some. If people who are genetically more alike are also more similar in intelligence and personality, then the researcher assumes that heredity plays an important role.

Kinship studies of intelligence provide some of the most controversial findings in the field of child development. Some experts claim a strong genetic influence, whereas others believe that heredity is barely involved. Currently, most kinship findings support a moderate role for heredity. When many twin studies are examined, correlations between the scores of identical twins are con-sistently higher than those of fraternal twins. In a summary of more than 10,000 twin pairs, the correlation for intelligence was .86 for identical twins and .60 for fraternal twins (Plomin & Spinath, 2004).

Researchers use a complex statistical procedure to compare these correlations, arriving at a heritability estimate ranging from 0 to 1.00. The value for intelligence is about .50 for child and adolescent samples in Western industrialized nations. This suggests that differences in genetic makeup explain half the variation in intelligence. Adopted children's intelligence is more strongly related to their biological parents' scores than to those of their adoptive parents, offering further support for the role of heredity (Plomin et al., 1997).

Heritability research also reveals that genetic factors are important in personality. For fre-quently studied traits, such as sociability, emotional expressiveness, agreeableness, and activ-ity level, heritability estimates obtained on child, adolescent, and emerging adult twins are moderate, at .40 to .50 (Bouchard & McGue, 2003; Rothbart & Bates, 1998).

• **CONCORDANCE** • A second measure used to infer the contribution of heredity to com-plex characteristics is the **concordance rate.** It refers to the percentage of instances in which both twins show a trait when it is present in one twin. Researchers typically use concordance to study emotional and behavior disorders, which can be judged as either present or absent.

A concordance rate ranges from 0 to 100 percent. A score of 0 indicates that if one twin has the trait, the other twin never has it. A score of 100 means that if one twin has the trait, the other one always has it. When a concordance rate is much higher for identical twins than for fraternal twins, heredity is believed to play a major role. As Figure 3.16 on page 116 reveals, twin studies of schizophrenia (a disorder involving delusions and hallucinations, difficulty distinguishing fantasy from reality, and irrational and inappropriate behaviors) and severe depression show this pattern. Look carefully at the figure, and you will see that the influence of heredity on antisocial behavior and criminality, though apparent, is less strong. In that case, the difference between the concordance rates for identical and fraternal twins is smaller. Again, adoption studies support these results. Biological relatives of schizophrenic and depressed adoptees are more likely than adoptive relatives to share the disorder (Plomin et al., 2001; Tienari et al., 2003).

◎ Adriana and Tamara, identi-cal twins born in Mexico, were separated at birth and adopted into different homes in the New York City area. They were unaware of each other until a mutual acquaintance noted resemblances between them. At age 20, they decided to meet and discovered that they were similar in many ways: Both like the same styles of clothing, were B students, prefer to stay up late at night, and love to dance. The study of identical twins reared apart reveals that heredity con-tributes to many psychological characteristics. Nevertheless, not all separated twins match up as well as this pair, and generalizing from twin evi-dence to the population is controversial.
© Jacquie Hemmerdinger/
The New York Times

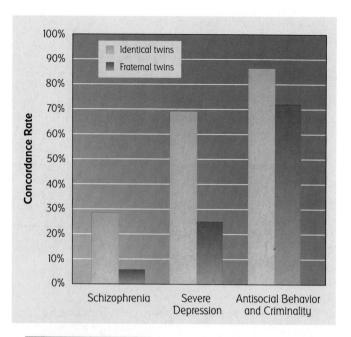

▲ Figure 3.16

Concordance rates for schizophrenia, severe depression, and antisocial behavior and criminality. We know that heredity plays some role in schizophrenia and is even more influential in severe depression because the concordance rate is much higher for identical than for fraternal twins. Heredity contributes less to antisocial behavior and criminality because the difference between identical and fraternal twins' concordance rates is smaller.

(From Gottesman, 1991; McGuffin & Sargeant, 1991; Torrey et al., 1994.)

Taken together, concordance and adoption research suggests that the tendency for schizophrenia, depression, and criminality to run in families is partly due to genetic factors. However, we also know that environment is involved: If heredity were the only influence, the concordance rate for identical twins would be 100 percent.

• LIMITATIONS OF HERITABILITY AND CONCORDANCE • Serious questions have been raised about the accuracy of heritability estimates and concordance rates. First, each value refers only to the particular population studied and its unique range of genetic and environmental influences. For example, imagine a country in which all children's home, school, and neighborhood experiences are very similar. Under these conditions, individual differences in behavior would be largely genetic, and heritability estimates would be close to 1.00. Conversely, the more environments vary, the greater their opportunity to account for individual differences, and the lower heritability estimates are likely to be.

Second, the accuracy of heritability estimates and concordance rates depends on the extent to which the twin pairs used reflect genetic and environmental variation in the population. Yet most twins studied are reared together under highly similar conditions. Even when separated twins are available for study, social service agencies have often placed them both in advantaged homes that are alike in many ways (Rutter et al., 2001). Because the environments of most twin pairs are less diverse than those of the general population, heritability estimates are likely to exaggerate the role of heredity.

Heritability estimates are controversial because they can easily be misapplied. For example, high heritabilities have been used to suggest that ethnic differences in intelligence, such as the poorer performance of black children compared to white children, have a genetic basis (Jensen, 1969, 1985, 1998). Yet this line of reasoning is widely regarded as incorrect. Heritabilities computed on mostly white twin samples do not tell us what is responsible for test score differences between ethnic groups. We have already seen that large economic and cultural differences are involved. In Chapter 8, we will discuss research indicating that when black children are adopted into economically advantaged homes at an early age, their scores are well above average and substantially higher than those of children growing up in impoverished families.

Perhaps the most serious criticism of heritability estimates and concordance rates has to do with their limited usefulness. They are interesting statistics but give us no precise information on how intelligence and personality develop or how children might respond to environments designed to help them develop as far as possible (Rutter, 2002; Wachs, 1999). Indeed, the heritability of intelligence increases as parental education and income increase—that is, as children grow up in conditions that allow them to make the most of their genetic endowment. In disadvantaged environments, children are prevented from realizing their potential. Consequently, enhancing their experiences through interventions—such as parent education and high-quality preschool or child care—has a greater impact on development (Bronfenbrenner & Morris, 1998; Turkheimer et al., 2003).

According to one group of experts, heritability estimates have too many problems to yield any firm conclusions about the relative strength of nature and nurture (Collins et al., 2000). Although these statistics confirm that heredity contributes to complex traits, they do not tell us how environment can modify genetic influences.

The Question, "How?"

Today, most researchers view development as the result of a dynamic interplay between heredity and environment. How do nature and nurture work together? Several concepts shed light on this question.

• **REACTION RANGE** • The first of these ideas is **range of reaction,** each person's unique, genetically determined response to the environment (Gottesman, 1963). Let's explore this idea in Figure 3.17. Reaction range can apply to any characteristic; here it is illustrated for intelligence. Notice that when environments vary from extremely unstimulating to highly enriched, Ben's intelligence test score increases steadily, Linda's rises sharply and then falls off, and Ron's begins to increase only after the environment becomes modestly stimulating.

Reaction range highlights two important points. First, it shows that because each of us has a unique genetic makeup, we respond differently to the same environment. Notice in Figure 3.17 how a poor environment results in similarly low scores for all three children. But Linda is by far the best-performing child when environments provide an intermediate level of stimulation. And when environments are highly enriched, Ben does best, followed by Ron, both of whom now outperform Linda. Second, sometimes different genetic–environmental combinations can make two children look the same! For example, if Linda is reared in a minimally stimulating environment, her score will be about 100—average for children in general. Ben and Ron can also obtain this score, but to do so they must grow up in a fairly enriched home. In sum, range of reaction reveals that unique blends of heredity and environment lead to both similarities and differences in children's behavior (Wahlsten, 1994).

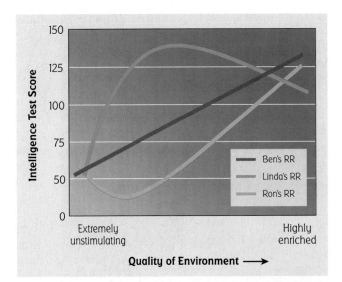

▲ **Figure 3.17**

Intellectual ranges of reaction (RR) for three children in environments that vary from extremely unstimulating to highly enriched. Each child, due to his or her genetic makeup, responds differently as quality of the environment changes. Ben's intelligence test score increases steadily, Linda's rises sharply and then falls off, and Ron's begins to increase only after the environment becomes modestly stimulating.
(Adapted from Wahlsten, 1994.)

• **CANALIZATION** • The concept of canalization provides another way of understanding how heredity and environment combine. **Canalization** is the tendency of heredity to restrict the development of some characteristics to just one or a few outcomes. A behavior that is strongly canalized follows a genetic growth plan, and only strong environmental forces can change it (Waddington, 1957). For example, infant perceptual and motor development seems to be strongly canalized: All normal human babies eventually roll over, sit up, crawl, and walk. It takes extreme conditions to modify these behaviors. In contrast, intelligence and personality are less strongly canalized, since they vary much more with changes in the environment.

When we look at the behaviors constrained by heredity, we can see that canalization is highly adaptive. Through it, nature ensures that children will develop certain species-typical skills under a wide range of rearing conditions, thereby promoting survival.

• **GENETIC–ENVIRONMENTAL CORRELATION** • A major problem in trying to separate heredity and environment is that they are often correlated (Plomin et al., 2001; Scarr & McCartney, 1983). According to the concept of **genetic–environmental correlation,** our genes influence the environments to which we are exposed. The way this happens changes with age.

▶ *Passive and Evocative Correlation.* At younger ages, two types of genetic–environmental correlation are common. The first is called *passive* correlation because the child has no control over it. Early on, parents provide environments influenced by their own heredity. For example, parents who are good athletes emphasize outdoor activities and enroll their children in activities like swimming and gymnastics. Besides being exposed to an "athletic environment," the children may have inherited their parents' athletic ability. As a result, they are likely to become good athletes for both genetic and environmental reasons.

The second type of genetic–environmental correlation is *evocative.* Children evoke responses that are influenced by the child's heredity, and these responses strengthen the child's original style. For example, an active, friendly baby is likely to receive more social stimulation than a passive, quiet infant. And a cooperative, attentive child probably receives more patient and sensitive interactions from parents than an inattentive, distractible child. In support of this idea, the less genetically alike siblings are, the more their parents treat them differently, in both warmth and negativity. Thus, parents' treatment of identical twins is highly similar, whereas their treatment

◎ This mother is an accomplished skier who exposes her children to skiing. In addition, the children may have inherited their mother's athletic talent. When both heredity and environment foster a particular capacity, the two influences cannot be separated from each other. © Mitch Wojnarowicz/ The Image Works

of fraternal twins and nontwin biological siblings is only moderately so. And little resemblance exists in parents' warm and negative interactions with unrelated stepsiblings (Reiss, 2003).

▶ *Active Correlation.* At older ages, *active* genetic–environmental correlation becomes common. As children extend their experiences beyond the immediate family and are given the freedom to make more choices, they actively seek environments that fit with their genetic tendencies. The well-coordinated, muscular child spends more time at after-school sports, the musically talented youngster joins the school orchestra and practices his violin, and the intellectually curious child is a familiar patron at her local library.

This tendency to actively choose environments that complement our heredity is called **niche-picking** (Scarr & McCartney, 1983). Infants and young children cannot do much niche-picking because adults select environments for them. In contrast, older children and adolescents are much more in charge of their environments. The niche-picking idea explains why identical twins reared apart during childhood and later reunited may find, to their great surprise, that they have similar hobbies, food preferences, and vocations—a trend that is especially marked when twins' environmental opportunities are similar (Plomin, 1994). Niche-picking also helps us understand why identical twins become somewhat more alike, and fraternal twins and adopted siblings less alike, in intelligence with age (Loehlin, Horn, & Willerman, 1997). The influence of heredity and environment is not constant but changes over time. With age, genetic factors may become more important in influencing the environments we experience and choose for ourselves.

• **ENVIRONMENTAL INFLUENCES ON GENE EXPRESSION** • Notice how, in the concepts just considered, heredity is granted priority. In range of reaction, it *limits* responsiveness to varying environments. In canalization, it *restricts* the development of certain behaviors. Similarly, some theorists regard genetic–environmental correlation as entirely driven by genetics (Harris, 1998; Rowe, 1994). They believe that children's genetic makeup causes them to receive, evoke, or seek experiences that actualize their inborn tendencies.

Others argue that heredity does not dictate children's experiences or development in a rigid way. For example, parents and other caring adults can *uncouple* adverse genetic–environmental correlations. They often provide children with positive experiences that modify the expression of heredity, yielding favorable outcomes (see the Biology and Environment box on the following page). Other research shows that parents' unequal treatment of siblings is not simply the result of children's heredity but is partly due to aspects of family life. In large families, single-parent families, low-income families, and families with unhappy marriages, siblings receive more differential treatment from parents (Jenkins, Rasbash, & O'Connor, 2003). When parents are under stress, perhaps they concentrate their limited energies on one child.

Accumulating evidence reveals that the relationship between heredity and environment is not a one-way street, from genes to environment to behavior. Rather, like other system influences considered in this and the previous chapter, it is *bidirectional:* Genes affect children's behavior and experiences, but their experiences and behavior also affect gene expression (Gottlieb, 2000, 2003). Stimulation—both *internal* to the child (activity within the cytoplasm of the cell, release of hormones into the bloodstream) and *external* to the child (home, neighborhood, school, and community)—triggers gene activity.

Researchers call this view of the relationship between heredity and environment the *epigenetic framework* (Gottlieb, 1992, 1998). It is depicted in Figure 3.19 on page 120. **Epigenesis** means development resulting from ongoing, bidirectional exchanges between heredity and all levels of the environment. To illustrate, providing a baby with a healthy diet increases brain growth, which translates into new connections between nerve cells, which transform gene expression. This opens the door to new gene–environment exchanges—for example, advanced exploration of objects and interaction with caregivers, which further enhance brain

BIOLOGY AND ENVIRONMENT

Uncoupling Genetic-Environmental Correlations for Mental Illness and Antisocial Behavior

Diagnosed with schizophrenia, Lars's and Sven's biological mothers had such difficulty functioning in everyday life that each gave up her infant son for adoption. Lars had the misfortune of being placed with adoptive parents who, like his biological mother, were mentally ill. His home life was chaotic, and his parents were punitive and neglectful. Sven's adoptive parents, in contrast, were psychologically healthy and reared him with love, patience, and consistency.

Lars displays a commonly observed genetic–environmental correlation: a predisposition for schizophrenia coupled with maladaptive parenting. Will he be more likely than Sven, whose adoption *uncoupled* this adverse genotype–environment link, to develop mental illness? In a large Finnish adoption study, nearly 200 adopted children of schizophrenic mothers were followed into adulthood (Tienari et al., 1994, 2003). Those (like Sven) who were reared by healthy adoptive parents showed little mental illness—no more than a control group with healthy biological and adoptive parents. In contrast, psychological impairments piled up in adoptees (like Lars) whose biological and adoptive parents were both disturbed. These children were considerably more likely to develop mental illness than were controls whose biological parents were healthy but who

were being reared by severely disturbed adoptive parents.

Similar findings emerged in American, British, and Swedish studies addressing genetic and environmental contributions to antisocial behavior. Adopted infants whose biological mothers were imprisoned criminal offenders displayed a high rate of antisocial behavior in adolescence only when reared in unfavorable homes, as indicated by adoptive parents or siblings with severe adjustment problems. In families free of psychological disturbance, adoptees with a predisposition to criminality did not differ from adoptees without this genetic background (Bohman, 1996; Yates, Cadoret, & Troughton, 1999).

In another investigation that tracked the development of 5-year-old identical twins, pair members tended to resemble each other in antisocial behavior. And the more antisocial behavior they displayed, the more criticism and hostility their mothers expressed toward them (a genetic–environmental correlation). Nevertheless, some mothers treated their twins differently. As Figure 3.18 shows,

when followed up at age 7, twins who had been targets of more maternal negativity tended to display more antisocial behavior. In contrast, their better-treated, genetically identical counterparts were shielded from this spiraling, antisocial course of development (Caspi et al., 2004). Asked why they treated their identical twins differently, some mothers reported that one child had been ill and more diffcult to care for; illness led some mothers to be more negative and others to be less negative. Mothers also reported feeling closer to one twin than the other, and they treated their twins accordingly.

In sum, the chances that genes for psychological disorder will be expressed are far greater when child rearing is maladaptive. Healthy-functioning families seem to promote healthy development in children, despite genetic risk for mental illness or antisocial behavior.

▶ Figure 3.18

Relationship of maternal negativity (criticism and hostility) to antisocial behavior among identical twins. Twins who were targets of more maternal negativity at age 5 were rated as more antisocial by their classroom teachers at age 7, after controlling for any behavioral differences between twin-pair members at age 5. (Adapted from Caspi et al., 2004).

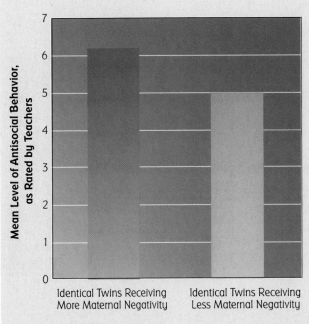

▶ **Figure 3.19**

The epigenetic framework.
Development takes place through ongoing, bidirectional exchanges between heredity and all levels of the environment. Genes affect behavior and experiences. Experiences and behavior also affect gene expression.
(Adapted from Gottlieb, 2000.)

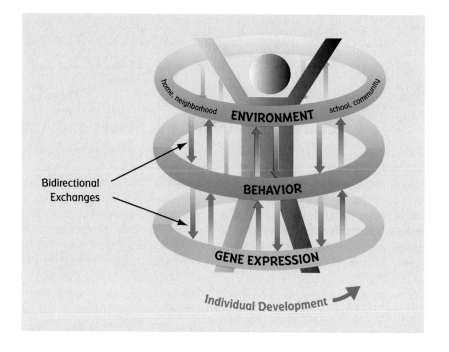

growth and gene expression. These ongoing, bidirectional influences foster cognitive and social development. In contrast, harmful environments can dampen gene expression, at times so profoundly that later experiences can do little to change characteristics (such as intelligence and personality) that were flexible to begin with.

A major reason that researchers are interested in the nature–nurture issue is that they want to improve environments so that children can develop as far as possible. The concept of epigenesis reminds us that development is best understood as a series of complex exchanges between nature and nurture. Although children cannot be changed in any way we might desire, environments can modify genetic influences. The success of any attempt to improve development depends on the characteristics we want to change, the genetic makeup of the child, and the type and timing of our intervention.

Ask Yourself

REVIEW	What is epigenesis, and how does it differ from range of reaction and genetic–environmental correlation? Provide an example of epigenesis.
APPLY	Bianca's parents are accomplished musicians. At age 4, Bianca began taking piano lessons. By age 10, she was accompanying the school choir. At age 14, she asked if she could attend a special music high school. Explain how genetic–environmental correlation promoted Bianca's talent.
CONNECT	The discussion of range of reaction on page 117 illustrates that unique blends of heredity and environment lead to both similarities and differences in behavior. How do findings discussed in the Biology and Environment box on page 119 illustrate this idea for psychological disorders?
REFLECT	What aspects of your own development—for example, interests, hobbies, college major, or vocational choice—are probably due to niche-picking? Explain.

◎ Summary

Genetic Foundations

What are genes, and how are they transmitted from one generation to the next?

◎ Each individual's **phenotype,** or directly observable characteristics, is a product of both **genotype** and environment. **Chromosomes,** rodlike structures within the cell nucleus, contain our hereditary endowment. Along their length are **genes,** segments of **DNA** that send instructions for making a rich assortment of proteins to the cytoplasm of the cell—a process that makes us distinctly human and influences our development and characteristics.

◎ **Gametes,** or sex cells, are produced through the process of cell division known as **meiosis. Crossing over** and independent assortment of chromosomes ensure that each gamete receives a unique set of genes from each parent. Once sperm and ovum unite, the resulting **zygote** starts to develop into a complex human being through cell duplication, or **mitosis.**

◎ **Fraternal,** or **dizygotic, twins** result when two ova are released from the mother's ovaries and each is fertilized. **Identical,** or **monozygotic, twins** develop when a zygote divides in two during the early stages of cell duplication. If the fertilizing sperm carries an X chromosome, the child will be a girl; if it contains a Y chromosome, a boy will be born.

© ELLEN SENISI/THE IMAGE WORKS

Describe various patterns of genetic inheritance.

◎ **Dominant–recessive inheritance** and **codominance** are patterns of inheritance that apply to traits controlled by single genes. In dominant–recessive inheritance,

heterozygous individuals with one recessive **allele** are **carriers** of the recessive trait. **Modifier genes** enhance or dilute the effects of other genes.

◎ When recessive disorders are **X-linked** (carried on the X chromosome), males are more likely to be affected. **Genetic imprinting** is a pattern of inheritance in which one parent's allele is activated, regardless of its makeup.

◎ Unfavorable genes arise from **mutations,** which can occur spontaneously or be induced by hazardous environmental agents.

◎ Human traits that vary continuously, such as intelligence and personality, are **polygenic,** or influenced by many genes. Since the genetic principles involved are unknown, scientists must study the influence of heredity on these characteristics indirectly.

Describe major chromosomal abnormalities, and explain how they occur.

◎ Most chromosomal abnormalities are due to errors in meiosis. The most common chromosomal disorder is Down syndrome, which results in physical defects and mental retardation. Disorders of the **sex chromosomes**—XYY, triple X, Klinefelter, and Turner syndromes—are milder than defects of the **autosomes.**

Reproductive Choices

What procedures can assist prospective parents in having healthy children?

◎ **Genetic counseling** helps couples at risk for giving birth to children with hereditary defects consider appropriate reproductive options. **Prenatal diagnostic methods** make early detection of abnormalities possible. Although reproductive technologies—such as donor insemination, in vitro fertilization, surrogate motherhood, and postmenopausal-assisted childbirth—permit many individuals to become parents who otherwise would not, they also raise serious legal and ethical concerns.

Prenatal Development

List the three periods of prenatal development, and describe the major milestones of each.

◎ The period of the zygote lasts about 2 weeks, from fertilization until the blastocyst becomes deeply implanted in the uterine lining. During this time, structures that will support prenatal growth begin to form. The embryonic disk is surrounded by the trophoblast, which forms structures that protect and nourish the organism. The **amnion** fills with amniotic fluid to regulate temperature and cushion against the mother's movements. From the **chorion,** villi emerge that burrow into the uterine wall, and the **placenta** starts to develop. The developing organism is connected to the placenta by the **umbilical cord.**

◎ The period of the **embryo** lasts from implantation through the eighth week of pregnancy, during which the foundations for all body structures are laid down. In the first week of this period, the neural tube forms, and the nervous system starts to develop. Other organs follow and grow rapidly. At the end of this period, the embryo responds to touch and can move.

◎ The period of the **fetus,** lasting from the ninth week until the end of pregnancy, involves a dramatic increase in body size and completion of physical structures. By the middle of the second trimester, the mother can feel movement. The fetus becomes covered with **vernix,** which protects the skin from chapping. White, downy hair called **lanugo** helps the vernix stick to the skin. At the end of the second trimester, most neurons in the brain are in place.

◎ The **age of viability** occurs at the beginning of the final trimester, sometime between 22 and 26 weeks. The brain continues to develop rapidly, and new sensory and behavioral capacities emerge. Gradually, the lungs mature, the fetus fills the uterus, and birth draws near.

Prenatal Environmental Influences

Cite factors that influence the impact of teratogens on the developing organism, noting agents that are known teratogens.

◎ **Teratogens** are environmental agents that cause damage during the prenatal period. Their effects conform to the sensitive period concept. The organism is especially vulnerable during the embryonic period, when body structures emerge rapidly.

◉ The impact of teratogens varies as a result of the amount and length of exposure, the genetic makeup of mother and fetus, the presence or absence of other harmful agents, and the age of the organism at time of exposure. The effects of teratogens are not limited to immediate physical damage. Some health consequences appear later in development. Psychological consequences may occur indirectly, as a result of physical defects.

◉ Drugs (such as thalidomide, diethylstilbestrol, and Accutane), tobacco, alcohol, radiation, environmental pollution, and certain infectious diseases are teratogens that can endanger the developing organism. Maternal alcohol consumption can lead to **fetal alcohol syndrome (FAS),** a disorder characterized by mental retardation and impaired motor coordination, or to a milder form of the disorder known as **fetal alcohol effects (FAE).**

Describe the impact of additional maternal factors on prenatal development.

◉ In healthy, physically fit women, regular moderate exercise is related to increased birth weight. However, very frequent, vigorous exercise results in lower birth weight.

◉ When the mother's diet is inadequate, low birth weight and damage to the brain and other organs are major concerns. Vitamin–mineral supplementation beginning early in pregnancy can improve maternal health and prevent certain prenatal and birth complications. Severe emotional stress is associated with many pregnancy complications; its impact can be reduced by providing mothers with social support.

◉ Aside from the risk of chromosomal abnormalities in older women, maternal age through the early forties is not a major cause of prenatal problems. Poor health and environmental risks associated with poverty are the strongest predictors of pregnancy complications in both teenagers and older women.

Childbirth

Describe the three stages of childbirth, the baby's adaptation to labor and delivery, and the newborn baby's appearance.

◉ In the first stage of childbirth, contractions widen and thin the cervix. In the second

© DAVID YOUNG-WOLFF/PHOTOEDIT

stage, the mother feels an urge to push the baby through the birth canal. In the final stage, the placenta is delivered. During labor, infants produce high levels of stress hormones, which help them withstand oxygen deprivation, clear the lungs for breathing, and arouse them into alertness at birth.

◉ Newborn babies have large heads, small bodies, and facial features that make adults feel like picking them up and cuddling them. The **Apgar Scale** is used to assess the newborn baby's physical condition at birth.

Approaches to Childbirth

Describe natural childbirth and home delivery, and explain the benefits and risks of using pain-relieving drugs during labor and delivery.

◉ **Natural,** or **prepared, childbirth** involves (1) classes that provide information about labor and delivery, (2) relaxation and breathing techniques to counteract pain, and (3) coaching by a companion. Social support, a vital part of natural childbirth, reduces the length of labor and the incidence of birth complications.

◉ Home birth reduces unnecessary medical procedures and permits greater maternal control over the birth experience. As long as mothers are healthy and assisted by a well-trained doctor or midwife, giving birth at home is just as safe as giving birth in a hospital.

◉ The use of analgesics and anesthetics during childbirth can prolong labor and cause newborns to be withdrawn and irritable and to feed poorly. The negative impact of pain-relieving drugs on newborn adjustment is reason to limit their use.

Birth Complications

What risks are associated with oxygen deprivation and with preterm and low-birth-

weight infants, and what factors can help infants who survive a traumatic birth develop normally?

◉ Anoxia can result when breathing fails to start immediately after delivery, the umbilical cord is squeezed because the baby is in **breech position,** or **Rh factor incompatibility** leads to destruction of the baby's red blood cells. Oxygen deprivation is a serious birth complication that can damage the brain and other organs. As long as anoxia is not extreme, most affected children catch up in development by the school years.

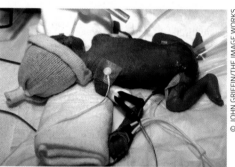

© JOHN GRIFFIN/THE IMAGE WORKS

◉ The incidence of premature births is high among low-income pregnant women and mothers of twins. Compared with **preterm infants** whose weight is appropriate for time spent in the uterus, **small-for-date infants** usually have longer-lasting difficulties. Some interventions provide special stimulation in the intensive care nursery; others teach parents how to care for and interact with their babies. When preterm infants live in stressed, low-income households, long-term, intensive intervention is necessary. A major cause of **infant mortality** is low birth weight.

◉ When infants experience birth trauma, a supportive family environment or relationships with other caring adults can help restore their growth. Even infants with serious birth complications can recover with the help of positive life events.

Heredity, Environment, and Behavior: A Look Ahead

Explain the various ways heredity and environment may combine to influence complex traits.

◉ **Behavioral genetics** is a field devoted to discovering the contributions of nature and nurture to complex traits. Some researchers believe that it is useful and possible to determine how much each factor contributes to differences. These investigators compute **heritability estimates** and **concordance rates** from **kinship studies.** Although these measures show that genetic factors contribute to such traits as intelligence and personality, their accuracy and usefulness have been challenged.

Most researchers view development as the result of a dynamic interplay between nature and nurture and investigate how these forces work together. According to the concepts of **range of reaction** and **canalization,** heredity influences children's responsiveness to varying environments.

In **genetic–environmental correlation** and **niche-picking,** children's genes affect the environments to which they are exposed. **Epigenesis** reminds us that development is best understood as a series of complex exchanges between nature and nurture.

Important Terms and Concepts

age of viability (p. 89)
allele (p. 74)
amnion (p. 87)
Apgar Scale (p. 105)
autosomes (p. 73)
behavioral genetics (p. 114)
breech position (p. 108)
canalization (p. 117)
carrier (p. 74)
chorion (p. 87)
chromosomes (p. 70)
codominance (p. 76)
concordance rate (p. 115)
crossing over (p. 71)
deoxyribonucleic acid (DNA) (p. 70)
dominant–recessive inheritance (p. 74)
embryo (p. 88)
epigenesis (p. 118)
fetal alcohol effects (FAE) (p. 96)

fetal alcohol syndrome (FAS) (p. 96)
fetus (p. 89)
fraternal, or dizygotic, twins (p. 73)
gametes (p. 71)
gene (p. 70)
genetic counseling (p. 80)
genetic–environmental correlation (p. 117)
genetic imprinting (p. 77)
genotype (p. 69)
heritability estimate (p. 115)
heterozygous (p. 74)
homozygous (p. 74)
identical, or monozygotic, twins (p. 73)
infant mortality (p. 112)
kinship studies (p. 115)
lanugo (p. 89)
meiosis (p. 71)
mitosis (p. 70)

modifier genes (p. 74)
mutation (p. 78)
natural, or prepared, childbirth (p. 106)
neonatal mortality (p. 112)
niche-picking (p. 118)
phenotype (p. 69)
placenta (p. 87)
polygenic inheritance (p. 78)
prenatal diagnostic methods (p. 80)
preterm infants (p. 109)
range of reaction (p. 117)
Rh factor incompatibility (p. 108)
sex chromosomes (p. 73)
small-for-date infants (p. 109)
teratogen (p. 91)
umbilical cord (p. 88)
vernix (p. 89)
X-linked inheritance (p. 76)
zygote (p. 71)

"Mother with Child"
Ma Hninn Moe Htwe
Age 12, Myanmar

Lifted by his mother into a world of wonders, the baby responds with joy, determined to master his world. Research confirms that infants are remarkably capable beings who rapidly make sense of constantly changing sounds, shapes, patterns, and surfaces in their surroundings.

Infancy: Early Learning, Motor Skills, and Perceptual Capacities

Enthralled with their new baby, Yolanda and Jay came to my child development class when Joshua was 4 weeks old to share their reactions to new parenthood. Holding little Joshua over his shoulder while patting him gently, Jay remarked, "When we first saw him—a tiny bundle with his arms and legs all scrunched up, so helpless looking—we worried, 'How will we ever figure out how to meet his needs?' To our surprise, almost immediately, Joshua was able to help us!"

Yolanda demonstrated by speaking softly to Joshua. "Look," she said, "at the sound of our voices, his face perks up, and he turns toward us with rapt attention." She touched his palm and continued, "Look at how his tiny hand grasps whatever comes near it—our fingers or the folds of our clothing—and how tightly he holds on."

As Joshua snuggled against Jay's chest, Jay noted, "When he's unhappy, we hold him close so he can feel our heartbeats." Joshua whimpered, so Jay began to walk around the room, "When he's bored, we carry him to a new place and sing to him, and often that's enough to quiet him. His cry is becoming a language we can understand."

Jay placed Joshua on his tummy on a blanket-covered table. "See," he announced proudly, "he lifts his head and shows off his strength with these shaky half push-ups." When Jay turned Joshua on his back, the baby stared at Yolanda's bright pink blouse, his face utterly absorbed. Lifting Joshua and giving him a kiss, Jay exclaimed, "We marvel at his determination to master his world!"

As Yolanda's and Jay's observations confirm, our view of infancy—the period of development that spans the first year of life—has changed drastically over the past century. At one time, the newborn, or *neonate*, was considered a passive, incompetent being whose world was, in the words of turn-of-the-twentieth-century psychologist William James, "a blooming, buzzing confusion." Careful observations of infants' behavior and more refined methods enabling researchers to test babies' capacities confirm that, from the outset, infants are skilled, capable beings who display many complex abilities.

Infant development proceeds at an astonishing pace. Excited relatives who visit just after the birth and then return a few months later often remark that the baby does not seem like the same individual! Although researchers agree that infants are competent beings, fervent debates continue over questions like these: What capacities are present from the very beginning? Which mature with the passage of time? And which result from the baby's constant interaction with her physical and social worlds? In this chapter, we explore the infant's remarkable capabilities—early reflexes, ability to learn, motor skills, and perceptual capacities—and the debates that surround them.

CHAPTER 4

The Organized Newborn

The newborn baby, as we saw in Chapter 3, is homely looking, with a head that appears too large in relation to the potbellied trunk and bowlegged lower body. In addition, the baby's skin is usually wrinkled and "parboiled" in appearance. Yet a few hours spent with a neonate reveal a wide variety of capacities that are crucial for survival and that evoke care and attention from adults. In relating to their physical and social worlds, babies are active from the very start.

Reflexes

A **reflex** is an inborn, automatic response to a particular form of stimulation. Reflexes are the neonate's most obvious organized patterns of behavior. A father, changing his newborn baby's diaper, bumps the side of the table. The infant flings her arms wide and then brings them back toward her body. A mother softly strokes her infant's cheek, and the baby turns his head in her direction. Table 4.1 lists the major newborn reflexes. See if you can identify the ones described here and in Joshua's behavior in the introduction to this chapter. Then let's consider the meaning and purpose of these curious behaviors.

• **ADAPTIVE VALUE OF REFLEXES** • Some reflexes have survival value. The rooting reflex helps a breastfed baby find the mother's nipple. Babies display it only when hungry and

TABLE 4.1 SOME NEWBORN REFLEXES

Reflex	Stimulation	Response	Age of Disappearance	Function
Eye blink	Shine bright light at eyes or clap hand near head	Infant quickly closes eyelids	Permanent	Protects infant from strong stimulation
Rooting	Stroke cheek near corner of mouth	Head turns toward source of stimulation	3 weeks (becomes voluntary head turning at this time)	Helps infant find the nipple
Sucking	Place finger in infant's mouth	Infant sucks finger rhythmically	Replaced by voluntary sucking after 4 months	Permits feeding
Swimming[a]	Place infant face down in pool of water	Baby paddles and kicks in swimming motion	4–6 months	Helps infant survive if dropped into water
Moro	Hold infant horizontally on back and let head drop slightly, or produce a sudden loud sound against surface supporting infant	Infant makes an "embracing" motion by arching back, extending legs, throwing arms outward, and then bringing arms in toward the body	6 months	In human evolutionary past, may have helped infant cling to mother
Palmar grasp	Place finger in infant's hand and press against palm	Spontaneous grasp of finger	3–4 months	Prepares infant for voluntary grasping
Tonic neck	Turn baby's head to one side while infant is lying awake on back	Infant lies in a "fencing position." One arm is extended in front of eyes on side to which head is turned, other arm is flexed	4 months	May prepare infant for voluntary reaching
Stepping	Hold infant under arms and permit bare feet to touch a flat surface	Infant lifts one foot after another in stepping response	2 months in infants who gain weight quickly; sustained in lighter infants	Prepares infant for voluntary walking
Babinski	Stroke sole of foot from toe toward heel	Toes fan out and curl as foot twists in	8–12 months	Unknown

[a]Placing infants in a pool of water is dangerous. See discussion on page 127.

Sources: Knobloch & Pasamanick, 1974; Prechtl & Beintema, 1965; Thelen, Fisher, & Ridley-Johnson, 1984.

touched by another person, not when they touch themselves (Rochat & Hespos, 1997). And if newborns could not suck, our species would be unlikely to survive for a single generation! At birth, babies adjust their sucking pressure to how easily milk flows from the nipple (Craig & Lee, 1999). The swimming reflex helps a baby who is accidentally dropped into water stay afloat, increasing the chances of retrieval by the caregiver.

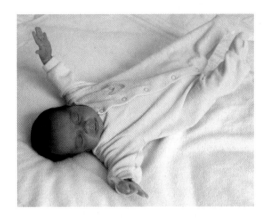

Ⓢ In the Moro reflex, loss of support or a sudden loud sound causes a baby to make an "embracing" motion, extending legs and throwing arms outward.
© Laura Dwight Photography

Other reflexes probably helped babies survive during our evolutionary past. For example, the Moro, or "embracing," reflex is believed to have helped infants cling to their mothers when they were carried about all day. If the baby happened to lose support, the reflex caused the infant to embrace and, along with the powerful grasp reflex (so strong during the first week that it can support the baby's entire weight), regain its hold on the mother's body (Kessen, 1967; Prechtl, 1958).

Several reflexes help parents and infants establish gratifying interaction. A baby who searches for and successfully finds the nipple, sucks easily during feedings, and grasps when her hand is touched encourages parents to respond lovingly and feel competent as caregivers. Reflexes can also help parents comfort the baby because they permit infants to control distress and amount of stimulation. As any new mother who remembers to bring a pacifier on an outing with her young baby knows, sucking helps quiet a fussy infant.

• **REFLEXES AND THE DEVELOPMENT OF MOTOR SKILLS** • A few reflexes form the basis for complex motor skills that will develop later. For example, the tonic neck reflex may prepare the baby for voluntary reaching. When babies lie on their backs in this "fencing position," they naturally gaze at the hand in front of their eyes. The reflex may encourage them to combine vision with arm movements and, eventually, reach for objects (Knobloch & Pasamanick, 1974).

Ⓢ The palmar grasp reflex is so strong during the first week after birth that many infants can use it to support their entire weight.
© Laura Dwight Photography

Certain reflexes—such as the palmar grasp, swimming, and stepping—drop out of the infants' behavioral repertoire early, but the motor functions involved are renewed later. The stepping reflex, for example, looks like a primitive walking response. In infants who gain weight quickly in the weeks after birth, the stepping reflex drops out because thigh and calf muscles are not strong enough to lift the baby's increasingly chubby legs. But if the lower part of the infant's body is dipped in water, the reflex reappears because the buoyancy of the water lightens the load on the baby's muscles (Thelen, Fisher, & Ridley-Johnson, 1984). When the stepping reflex is exercised regularly, babies display more spontaneous stepping movements and gain muscle strength. Consequently, they tend to walk several weeks earlier than if stepping is not practiced (Zelazo et al., 1993). However, there is no special need for infants to practice the stepping reflex because all normal babies walk in due time.

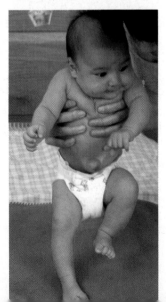

Ⓢ When held upright under the arms, newborn babies show reflexive stepping movements, which form the basis for later walking.
© Laura Dwight Photography

In the case of the swimming reflex, trying to build on it is risky. Although young babies placed in a swimming pool will paddle and kick, they swallow large amounts of water. This lowers the concentration of salt in the baby's blood, which can cause brain swelling and seizures. Despite this remarkable reflex, swimming lessons are best postponed until at least 3 years of age.

• THE IMPORTANCE OF ASSESSING REFLEXES • Look at Table 4.1 again, and you will see that most newborn reflexes disappear during the first 6 months. Researchers believe that this is due to a gradual increase in voluntary control over behavior as the cerebral cortex develops. Pediatricians test reflexes carefully, especially if a newborn has experienced birth trauma, because reflexes can reveal the health of the baby's nervous system. Weak or absent reflexes, overly rigid or exaggerated reflexes, and reflexes that persist beyond the point in development when they should normally disappear can signal damage to the cerebral cortex (Schott & Rossor, 2003; Zafeiriou, 2000). However, individual differences in reflexive responses exist that are not cause for concern. An observer must assess newborn reflexes along with other characteristics to distinguish normal from abnormal central nervous system functioning (Touwen, 1984).

States

Throughout the day and night, newborn infants move in and out of five **states of arousal,** or degrees of sleep and wakefulness, described in Table 4.2. During the first month, these states alternate frequently. The most fleeting is quiet alertness, which usually moves quickly toward fussing and crying. Much to the relief of their fatigued parents, newborns spend the greatest amount of time asleep—about 16 to 18 hours a day (Davis, Parker, & Montgomery, 2004).

Between birth and 2 years, the organization of sleep and wakefulness changes substantially. The decline in total sleep time is not great; the average 2-year-old still needs 12 to 13 hours per day. The greatest changes are that periods of sleep and wakefulness become fewer but longer, and the sleep–wake pattern increasingly conforms to a *circadian rhythm,* or 24-hour schedule. Although at birth babies sleep more at night than during the day, their sleep–wake cycles are determined mostly by fullness–hunger (Goodlin-Jones, Burnham, & Anders, 2000). By 2 to 3 months, infants respond more to darkness–light. Babies of this age who are exposed to more bright sunlight—for example, through regular, early afternoon stroller rides—sleep better at night (Harrison, 2004) Between 6 and 9 months, daytime sleep typically declines to two naps. By 1½ years, most infants take just one nap. And around 4 to 5 years, napping subsides (Iglowstein et al., 2003).

Although these changing arousal patterns are due to brain development, they are affected by the social environment as well. In most Western nations, parents usually succeed in getting their babies to sleep through the night around 4 months of age by offering an evening feeding before putting them down in a separate, quiet room. In this way, they push young infants to the limits of their neurological capacities. Not until the middle of the first year is the secretion of *melatonin,* a hormone within the brain that promotes drowsiness, much greater at night than during the day (Sadeh, 1997).

As the Cultural Influences box on the following page reveals, the practice of isolating infants to promote sleep is rare elsewhere in the world. When babies sleep with their parents,

TABLE 4.2 INFANT STATES OF AROUSAL

State	Description	Daily Duration in Newborn
Regular, or NREM, sleep	The infant is at full rest and shows little or no body activity. The eyelids are closed, no eye movements occur, the face is relaxed, and breathing is slow and regular.	8–9 hours
Irregular, or REM, sleep	Gentle limb movements, occasional stirring, and facial grimacing occur. Although the eyelids are closed, occasional rapid eye movements can be seen beneath them. Breathing is irregular.	8–9 hours
Drowsiness	The infant is either falling asleep or waking up. Body is less active than in irregular sleep but more active than in regular sleep. The eyes open and close; when open, they have a glazed look. Breathing is even but somewhat faster than in regular sleep.	Varies
Quiet alertness	The infant's body is relatively inactive, with eyes open and attentive. Breathing is even.	2–3 hours
Waking activity and crying	The infant shows frequent bursts of uncoordinated body activity. Breathing is very irregular. Face may be relaxed or tense and wrinkled. Crying may occur.	1–4 hours

Source: Wolff, 1966.

CULTURAL INFLUENCES

Cultural Variation in Infant Sleeping Arrangements

While awaiting the birth of a new baby, North American parents typically furnish a room as the infant's sleeping quarters. For decades, child-rearing advice from experts has strongly encouraged the nighttime separation of baby from parent. For example, the most recent edition of Benjamin Spock's *Baby and Child Care* recommends that babies be moved into their own room by 3 months of age, explaining, "By 6 months, a child who regularly sleeps in her parents' room may become dependent on this arrangement" (Spock & Needlman, 2004, p. 60).

Yet parent–infant "cosleeping" is the norm for approximately 90 percent of the world's population. Cultures as diverse as the Japanese, the Guatamalan Maya, the Inuit of northwestern Canada, and the !Kung of Botswana, Africa, practice it. Japanese and Korean children usually lie next to their mothers throughout infancy and early childhood, and many continue to sleep with a parent or other family member until adolescence (Takahashi, 1990; Yang & Hahn, 2002). Among the Maya, mother–infant cosleeping is interrupted only by the birth of a new baby, at which time the older child is moved next to the father or to another bed in the same room (Morelli et al., 1992). Cosleeping is also common in some North American groups. African-American children frequently fall asleep with their parents and remain with them for part or all of the night (Brenner et al., 2003). Appalachian children of eastern Kentucky typically sleep with their parents for the first 2 years (Abbott, 1992).

Cultural values—specifically, *collectivism versus individualism* (see Chapter 1, page 34)—strongly influence infant sleeping arrangements. In one study, researchers interviewed Guatemalan Mayan mothers and American middle-SES mothers about their sleeping practices. Mayan mothers stressed a collectivist perspective, explain-

ing that cosleeping builds a close parent–child bond, which is essential for children to learn the ways of people around them. In contrast, American mothers conveyed an individualistic perspective, mentioning the importance of instilling early independence, preventing bad habits, and protecting their own privacy (Morelli et al., 1992).

Perhaps because more mothers are breastfeeding, during the past decade cosleeping increased from 6 to 13 percent among North American mothers and their infants (McKenna, 2002; Willinger et al., 2003). Research suggests that bedsharing evolved to protect infants' survival and health. During the night, cosleeping babies breastfeed three times longer than infants who sleep alone. Because infants arouse to nurse more often when sleeping next to their mothers, some researchers believe that cosleeping may help safeguard babies at risk for sudden infant death syndrome (SIDS) (see From Research to Practice on page 132). In Asian cultures where cosleeping is the norm, including Cambodia, China, Japan, Korea, Thailand, and Vietnam, SIDS is rare (McKenna, 2002; Mosko, Richard, & McKenna, 1997a). And contrary to popular belief, mothers' total sleep time is not decreased by cosleeping, although they experience a greater number of brief awakenings, which permit them to check on their baby (Mosko, Richard, & McKenna, 1997b).

Infant sleeping practices affect other aspects of family life. For example, sleep problems are not an issue for Mayan parents. Babies doze off in the midst of ongoing family activities and are carried to bed by their mothers. In contrast, for many North American parents, getting young children ready for bed often requires an elaborate ritual that takes a good part of the evening. Perhaps bedtime struggles, so common in North American homes but rare elsewhere in the world, are related to the stress young children feel when they

are required to fall asleep without assistance (Latz, Wolf, & Lozoff, 1999).

Critics worry that cosleeping children will develop emotional problems, especially excessive dependency. Yet a longitudinal study following children from the end of pregnancy through age 18 showed that young people who had bedshared in the early years were no different from others in any aspect of adjustment (Okami, Weisner, & Olmstead, 2002). Another concern is that infants might become trapped under the parent's body or in soft covers and suffocate. Parents who are obese or who smoke while bedsharing do pose a serious risk to their babies, as does the use of quilts and comforters (Willinger et al., 2003). But with appropriate precautions, parents and infants can cosleep safely. In cultures where cosleeping is widespread, parents and infants usually sleep with light covering on hard surfaces (such as firm mattresses, floor mats, and wooden planks), or infants sleep in a wicker basket placed between the parents or in a cradle or hammock next to the parents' bed (McKenna, 2001, 2002; Nelson, Schiefenhoevel, & Haimerl, 2000).

▼ This Cambodian father and child sleep together—a practice common in their culture and around the globe. Many parents who practice cosleeping believe that it helps build a close parent–child bond.
© Stephen L. Raymer/National Geographic Image Collection

their average sleep period remains constant at 3 hours from 1 to 8 months of age. Only at the end of the first year, as REM sleep (the state that usually prompts waking) declines, do infants move in the direction of an adultlike sleep–waking schedule (Ficca et al., 1999).

Even after infants sleep through the night, they continue to wake occasionally. In sleep observations and in surveys of parents in Australia, Israel, and the United States, night wakings increased around 6 months and again between 1½ and 2 years (Armstrong, Quinn, & Dadds, 1994; Scher, Epstein, & Tirosh, 2004; Scher et al., 1995). Around the middle of the first year, many infants encounter changes in caregiving routines, such as the mother's return to work. And as Chapters 10 and 11 will reveal, the challenges of toddlerhood—the ability to range farther from the familiar caregiver and increased awareness of the self as separate from others—often prompt anxiety, evident in disturbed sleep and clinginess. When parents offer comfort, these behaviors subside.

Although arousal states become more organized with age, striking individual differences in daily rhythms exist that affect parents' attitudes toward and interactions with the baby. A few infants sleep for long periods at an early age, increasing the energy their well-rested parents have for sensitive, responsive care. Other babies cry a great deal, and their parents must exert great effort to soothe them. If these parents do not succeed, they may feel less competent and positive toward their infant. Babies who spend more time alert probably receive more social stimulation and opportunities to explore and, therefore, may be slightly advantaged in mental development (Gertner et al., 2002).

Of the states listed in Table 4.2, the two extremes of sleep and crying have been of greatest interest to researchers. Each tells us something about normal and abnormal early development.

• **SLEEP** • Sleep is made up of at least two states. The expression "sleeping like a baby" was probably not meant to describe irregular, or **rapid-eye-movement (REM) sleep,** in which electrical brain-wave activity, measured with the EEG, is remarkably similar to that of the waking state. The eyes dart beneath the lids; heart rate, blood pressure, and breathing are uneven; and slight body movements occur. In contrast, during regular, or **non-rapid-eye-movement (NREM) sleep,** the body is almost motionless, and heart rate, breathing, and brain-wave activity are slow and regular.

Like children and adults, newborns alternate between REM and NREM sleep. However, as Figure 4.1 shows, they spend far more time in the REM state than they ever will again. REM sleep accounts for 50 percent of the newborn baby's sleep time. By 3 to 5 years, it has declined to an adultlike level of 20 percent (Louis et al., 1997).

Why do young infants spend so much time in REM sleep? In older children and adults, the REM state is associated with dreaming. Babies probably do not dream, at least not in the same way we do. But researchers believe that the stimulation of REM sleep is vital for growth of the central nervous system. Young infants seem to have a special need for this stimulation because they spend so little time in an alert state, when they can get input from the environment. In support of this idea, the percentage of REM sleep is especially great in the fetus and in preterm babies, who are even less able than full-term newborns to take advantage of external stimulation (DiPietro et al., 1996; de Weerd & van den Bossche, 2003).

Whereas the brain-wave activity of REM sleep safeguards the central nervous system, the rapid eye movements protect the health of the eye. Eye movements cause the vitreous (gelatin-like substance within the eye) to circulate, thereby delivering oxygen to parts of

▼ **Figure 4.1**

Changes in REM sleep, NREM sleep, and the waking state from the prenatal period to middle childhood. REM sleep declines steadily over the prenatal period and the first few years of life. Between 3 and 5 years, it accounts for about the same percentage of sleep time as it does in adulthood.

(Adapted from de Weerd & van den Bossche, 2003; Roffwarg, Muzio, & Dement, 1996.)

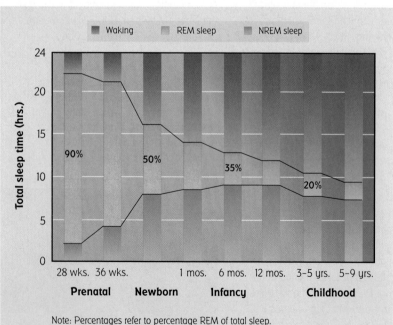

Note: Percentages refer to percentage REM of total sleep.

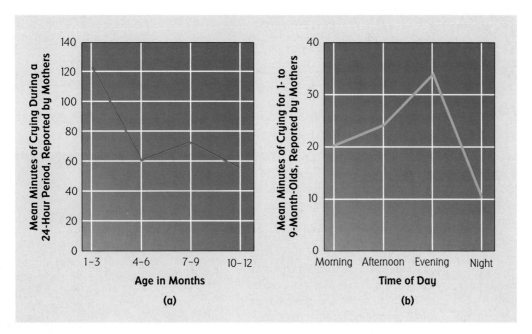

◀ **Figure 4.2**

Crying patterns during the first year of life. A sample of 400 mothers answered questions about how much time their infants spent crying. (a) Crying was greatest during the first 3 months but declined with age. The largest drop occurred after 3 months. (b) During the first 9 months, crying peaked in the evening. (Adapted from St James-Roberts & Halil, 1991.)

the eye that do not have their own blood supply. During sleep, when the eye and the vitreous are still, visual structures are at risk for anoxia. As the brain cycles through REM-sleep periods, rapid eye movements stir up the vitreous, ensuring that the eye is fully oxygenated (Blumberg & Lucas, 1996).

Because the normal sleep behavior of the newborn baby is organized and patterned, observations of sleep states can help identify central nervous system abnormalities. In infants who are brain damaged or who have experienced birth trauma, disturbed sleep cycles are often present, generally in the form of disorganized transitions between REM and NREM sleep that cannot be identified as a specific state. Babies with poor sleep organization are likely to be behaviorally disorganized and, therefore, to have difficulty learning and eliciting caregiver interactions that enhance their development (de Weerd & van den Bossche, 2003; Groome et al., 1997). And the brain-functioning problems that underlie newborn sleep irregularities may culminate in sudden infant death syndrome, a major cause of infant mortality (see the From Research to Practice box on page 132).

• **CRYING** • Crying is the first way that babies communicate, letting parents know that they need food, comfort, and stimulation. During the weeks after birth, all babies have some fussy periods when they are difficult to console. But most of the time, the nature of the cry, combined with the experiences leading up to it, helps guide parents toward its cause. The baby's cry is a complex auditory stimulus that varies in intensity, from a whimper to a message of all-out distress (Gustafson, Wood, & Green, 2000). As early as the first few weeks of life, individual infants can be identified by the unique vocal "signature" of their cries, which helps parents locate the baby from a distance (Gustafson, Green, & Cleland, 1994).

Young infants usually cry because of physical needs, most commonly hunger, but babies may also cry in response to temperature change when undressed, a sudden noise, or a painful stimulus. An infant's state also affects proneness to cry. A baby who, when quietly alert, regards a colorful or noise-making object with interest may burst into tears when confronted with the same object while in a state of mild discomfort. And newborns (as well as older infants) often cry at the sound of another crying baby (Dondi, Simion, & Caltran, 1999). Some researchers believe that this response reflects an inborn capacity to react to the suffering of others. Furthermore, as Figure 4.2 shows, crying typically increases during the early weeks, peaks at about 6 weeks, and then declines. Because this pattern appears in many cultures with vastly different infant care practices, researchers believe that normal readjustments of the central nervous system underlie it (Barr, 2001).

FROM RESEARCH TO PRACTICE

The Mysterious Tragedy of Sudden Infant Death Syndrome

Millie awoke with a start one morning and looked at the clock. It was 7:30, and Sasha had missed her night waking and early morning feeding. Wondering if she was all right, Millie and her husband Stuart tiptoed into the room. Sasha lay still, curled up under her blanket. She had died silently during her sleep.

Sasha was a victim of **sudden infant death syndrome (SIDS),** the unexpected death, usually during the night, of an infant younger than 1 year of age that remains unexplained after thorough investigation. In industrialized nations, SIDS is the leading cause of infant mortality between 1 week and 12 months of age. It accounts for one-third of these deaths in the United States and one-fourth in Canada (Health Canada, 2002b; Martin et al., 2003).

Although the precise cause of SIDS is not known, its victims usually show physical problems from the very beginning. Early medical records of SIDS babies reveal higher rates of prematurity and low birth weight, poor Apgar scores, and limp muscle tone. Abnormal heart rate and respiration and disturbances in sleep–wake activity are also involved (Daley, 2004; Kato et al., 2003). At the time of death, many SIDS babies have a mild respiratory infection (Samuels, 2003). This seems to increase the chances of respiratory failure in an already vulnerable baby.

One hypothesis about the cause of SIDS is that problems in brain functioning prevent these infants from learning how to respond when their survival is threatened—for example, when respiration is suddenly interrupted. Between 2 and 4 months, when SIDS is most likely to occur, reflexes decline and are replaced by voluntary, learned responses. Respiratory and muscular weaknesses may stop SIDS babies from acquiring behaviors that replace defensive reflexes (Lipsitt, 2003). As a result, when breathing difficulties occur during sleep, the infants do not wake up, shift their position, or cry out for help. Instead, they simply give in to oxygen

deprivation and death. In support of this interpretation, autopsies reveal that SIDS babies, more often than other infants, show structural and chemical abnormalities in brain centers controlling breathing (Kinney et al., 2003; Sawaguchi et al., 2003).

In an effort to reduce the occurrence of SIDS, researchers are studying environmental factors related to it. Maternal cigarette smoking, both during and after pregnancy, as well as smoking by other caregivers, strongly predicts the disorder. Babies exposed to cigarette smoke have more respiratory infections and are two to four times as likely as nonexposed infants to die of SIDS (Sundell, 2001). Prenatal abuse of drugs that depress central nervous system functioning (opiates and barbiturates) increases the risk of SIDS tenfold (Kandall et al., 1993). SIDS babies also are more likely to sleep on their stomachs than on their backs, and they more often lie on soft bedding and are wrapped warmly in clothing and blankets (Hauck et al., 2003).

Researchers suspect that nicotine, depressant drugs, excessive body warmth, and respiratory infection all lead to physiological stress, which disrupts the normal sleep pattern. When sleep-deprived infants experience a sleep "rebound," they sleep more deeply, which results in loss of muscle tone in the airway passages. In at-risk babies, the airway may collapse, and the infant may fail to arouse sufficiently to reestablish breathing (Simpson, 2001). In other cases, healthy babies sleeping face down on soft bedding may die from continually breathing their own exhaled breath.

Quitting smoking, changing an infant's sleeping position, and removing a few bedclothes can reduce the incidence of SIDS. For example, if women refrained from smoking while pregnant, an estimated 30 percent of SIDS would be prevented. Over the past decade, public education campaigns that discourage parents from putting babies down on their stomachs have cut the inci-

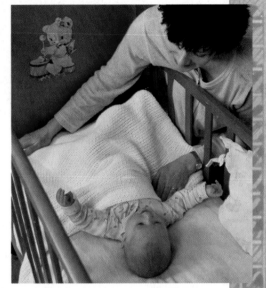

▲ Having babies sleep on their backs with only a light covering has dramatically reduced the incidence of sudden infant death syndrome (SIDS). If an infant's face becomes trapped in blankets, excessive body warmth can lead to physiological stress followed by deeper sleep. Under these conditions, at-risk babies may fail to arouse and reestablish respiration.
© Chris Priest/Photo Researchers, Inc.

dence of SIDS in half in many Western nations (Byard & Krous, 2003). Nevertheless, compared with white infants, SIDS rates are two to six times as high in poverty-stricken minority groups, where parental stress, substance abuse, reduced access to health care, and lack of knowledge about safe sleep practices are widespread (Kinney et al., 2003; Unger et al., 2003).

When SIDS does occur, surviving family members require a great deal of help to overcome a sudden and unexpected death. As Millie commented 6 months after Sasha died, "It's the worst crisis we've ever been through. What's helped us most are the comforting words of others who've experienced the same tragedy."

▶ *Adult Responsiveness to Infant Cries.* The next time you hear a baby cry, notice your own reaction. The sound stimulates strong feelings of arousal and discomfort in men and women, parents and nonparents alike (Murray, 1985). This powerful response is probably innately programmed in all humans to make sure that babies receive the care and protection they need to survive.

Although parents do not always interpret the baby's cry correctly, their accuracy improves with experience. As babies get older, parents react to more subtle cues in the cry—not just intensity but also whimpering and calling sounds (Thompson & Leger, 1999). These cues, together with the context of the cry, help them figure out what is wrong. If the baby has not eaten for several hours, she is likely to be hungry. If a period of wakefulness and stimulation preceded the cry, the infant may be tired. A sharp, piercing, sustained cry usually means the baby is in pain and prompts caregivers to rush to the infant. Very intense cries are rated as more unpleasant and produce greater physiological arousal in adults (Crowe & Zeskind, 1992). These adaptive reactions help ensure that an infant in danger will quickly get help.

At the same time, parents vary widely in responsiveness. In one laboratory study, parents viewed videotapes of an infant moving from fussing to vigorous crying. Some said they would respond within 20 seconds, whereas others indicated they would wait several minutes. Parents who scored high in empathy (ability to take the perspective of others in distress) and who held "child-centered" attitudes toward infant care (for example, believed that babies cannot be spoiled by being picked up) were more likely to respond quickly to infant crying (Zeifman, 2003). In another study, mothers who believed that they could easily control the crying of an artificial baby (whose quieting was unrelated to the mother's behavior) had difficulty detecting changes in cry sounds, engaged in less sensitive infant care, and had babies who developed into uncooperative toddlers (Donovan, Leavitt, & Walsh, 1997, 2000). The internal state of these mothers—who reacted defensively when they couldn't calm the artificial baby—seemed to interfere with their ability to cope effectively with infant crying.

▶ *Soothing a Crying Infant.* Fortunately, there are many ways to soothe a crying baby when feeding and diaper changing do not work (see Applying What We Know on page 134). The technique that Western parents usually try first, lifting the infant to the shoulder and rocking or walking, is most effective.

Another common soothing method is swaddling—wrapping the baby snugly in a blanket. The Quechua, who live in the cold, high-altitude desert regions of Peru, dress young babies in several layers of clothing and blankets that cover the head and body. The result—a warm pouch placed on the mother's back that moves rhythmically as she walks—reduces crying and promotes sleep. It also allows the baby to conserve energy for early growth in the harsh Peruvian highlands (Tronick, Thomas, & Daltabuit, 1994).

Will reacting promptly and consistently to infant cries give babies a sense of confidence that their needs will be met and, over time, reduce fussing and complaining? Or will it strengthen crying behavior and produce a miniature tyrant? Answers are contradictory.

According to *ethological theory,* parental responsiveness is adaptive in that it ensures that the infant's basic needs will be met (see Chapter 1, pages 24–25). At the same time, it brings the baby into close contact with the caregiver, who encourages the infant to communicate through means other than crying. In support of this view, two studies showed that mothers who were slow or failed to respond to their young baby's cries had infants who cried more at the end of the first year (Bell & Ainsworth, 1972; Hubbard & van IJzendoorn, 1991). Furthermore, in many tribal and village societies and non-Western developed nations, infants are in physical contact with their caregivers nearly continuously. Among the !Kung of Botswana, Africa, mothers sling their babies on their hips, so the infants can see their surroundings and nurse at will. Japanese mothers and infants also spend much time in close body contact (Small, 1998). Infants in these cultures show shorter bouts of crying than North American babies (Barr, 2001).

In responding to her crying baby's needs, this mother holds her infant upright against her gently moving body. © Laura Dwight Photography

Applying
What We Know   Soothing a Crying Baby

Technique	Explanation
Lift the baby to the shoulder and rock or walk.	This provides a combination of physical contact, upright posture, and motion. It is the most effective soothing technique, causing young infants to become quietly alert.
Swaddle the baby.	Restricting movement and increasing warmth often soothe an infant.
Offer a pacifier, preferably sweetened with a sugar solution.	Sucking helps babies control their own level of arousal. Sucking a sweetened pacifier relieves pain and quiets a crying infant.
Talk softly or play rhythmic sounds.	Continuous, monotonous, rhythmic sounds (such as a clock ticking, a fan whirring, or peaceful music) are more effective than intermittent sounds.
Take the baby for a short car ride or a walk in a baby carriage; swing the baby in a cradle.	Gentle, rhythmic motion of any kind helps lull the baby to sleep.
Massage the baby's body.	Stroke the baby's torso and limbs with continuous, gentle motions. This technique is used in some non-Western cultures to relax the baby's muscles.
Combine several methods just listed.	Stimulating several of the baby's senses at once is often more effective than stimulating only one.
If these methods do not work, let the baby cry for a short period.	Occasionally, a baby responds well to just being put down and will, after a few minutes, fall asleep.

Sources: Blass, 1999; Campos, 1989; Lester, 1985; Reisman, 1987.

But not all research indicates that rapid parental responsiveness reduces infant crying (van IJzendoorn & Hubbard, 2000). The conditions that prompt crying are complex, and parents must make reasoned choices about what to do on the basis of culturally accepted practices, the suspected reason for the cry, and the context in which it occurs—for example, in the privacy of their own home or while having dinner at a restaurant. Fortunately, with age, crying declines and occurs more often for psychological (demands for attention, expressions of frustration) than physical reasons. Virtually all researchers agree that parents can lessen older babies' need to cry by encouraging more mature ways of expressing their desires, such as gestures and vocalizations.

▶ *Abnormal Crying.* Like reflexes and sleep patterns, the infant's cry offers a clue to central nervous system distress. The cries of brain-damaged babies and those who have experienced prenatal and birth complications are often shrill, piercing, and shorter in duration than those of healthy infants (Boukydis & Lester, 1998; Green, Irwin, & Gustafson, 2000). Even neonates with a fairly common problem—*colic,* or persistent crying—tend to have high-pitched, harsh-sounding cries (Zeskind & Barr, 1997). Although the cause of colic is unknown, certain newborns, who react especially strongly to unpleasant stimuli, are susceptible. Because their crying is intense, they have more difficulty calming down than other babies. Colic generally subsides between 3 and 6 months (Barr & Gunnar, 2000; St James-Roberts et al., 2003).

Most parents try to respond to a crying baby's call for help with extra care and attention, but sometimes the cry is so unpleasant and the infant so difficult to soothe that parents become frustrated, resentful, and angry. Preterm and ill babies are more likely to be abused by highly stressed parents, who sometimes mention a high-pitched, grating cry as one factor that disrupted their empathic feelings and caused them to lose control and harm the baby (Zeskind & Lester, 2001). We will discuss a host of additional influences on child abuse in Chapter 14.

Neonatal Behavioral Assessment

A variety of instruments enable doctors, nurses, and researchers to assess the organized functioning of newborn babies. The most widely used of these tests, T. Berry Brazelton's **Neonatal Behavioral Assessment Scale (NBAS),** evaluates the baby's reflexes, state changes, responsiveness to physical and social stimuli, and other reactions (Brazelton & Nugent, 1995). A major goal is to understand each infant's capacity to initiate caregiver support and to adjust his or her behavior to avoid being overwhelmed by stimulation.

The NBAS has been given to many infants around the world. As a result, researchers have learned a great deal about individual and cultural differences in newborn behavior and how child-rearing practices can maintain or change a baby's reactions. For example, NBAS scores of Asian and Native-American babies reveal that they are less irritable than Caucasian infants. Mothers in these cultures often encourage their babies' calm dispositions through swaddling, close physical contact, and nursing at the first signs of discomfort (Chisholm, 1989; Freedman & Freedman, 1969; Murett-Wagstaff & Moore, 1989). In contrast, maternal care quickly changes the poor NBAS scores of undernourished infants in Zambia, Africa. The Zambian mother carries her baby about all day, providing a rich variety of sensory stimulation. As a result, a once unresponsive newborn becomes an alert, contented 1-week-old (Brazelton, Koslowski, & Tronick, 1976).

Can you tell from these examples why a single NBAS score is not a good predictor of later development? Because newborn behavior and parenting styles combine to influence development, *changes in NBAS scores* over the first week or two of life (rather than a single score) provide the best estimate of the baby's ability to recover from the stress of birth. NBAS "recovery curves" predict normal brain functioning (as assessed by EEG and fMRI), intelligence, and absence of emotional and behavior problems with moderate success well into the preschool years (Brazelton, Nugent, & Lester, 1987; Ohgi et al., 2003a, 2003b).

The NBAS also has been used to help parents get to know their infants. In some hospitals, health professionals discuss with or demonstrate to parents the newborn capacities assessed by the NBAS. Parents of both preterm and full-term newborns who participate in these programs interact more effectively with their babies (Eiden & Reifman, 1996). In one study, Brazilian mothers who experienced a 50-minute NBAS-based discussion a few days after delivery were more likely than controls who received only health care information to establish eye contact, smile, vocalize, and soothe in response to infant signals a month later (Wendland-Carro, Piccinini, & Millar, 1999). Although lasting effects on development have not been demonstrated, NBAS interventions are useful in helping the parent–infant relationship get off to a good start.

⊚ This mother of the El Molo people of northern Kenya carries her baby about all day, providing close physical contact, a rich variety of stimulation, and ready feeding.
© Jeffrey L. Rotman/Corbis

Learning Capacities

Learning refers to changes in behavior as the result of experience. Babies come into the world with built-in learning capacities that permit them to profit from experience immediately. Infants are capable of two basic forms of learning, which were introduced in Chapter 1: classical and operant conditioning. In addition, they learn through their natural preference for novel stimulation. Finally, shortly after birth, babies learn by observing others; they can soon imitate the facial expressions and gestures of adults.

• **CLASSICAL CONDITIONING** • Newborn reflexes make **classical conditioning** possible in the young infant. In this form of learning, a neutral stimulus is paired with a stimulus that leads to a reflexive response. Once the baby's nervous system makes the connection between the two stimuli, the new stimulus will produce the behavior by itself.

Classical conditioning is of great value to human infants because it helps them recognize which events usually occur together in the everyday world. As a result, they can anticipate what is about to happen next, and the environment becomes more orderly and predictable. Let's take a closer look at the steps of classical conditioning.

Imagine a mother who gently strokes her infant's forehead each time she settles down to nurse the baby. Soon the mother notices that each time the baby's forehead is stroked, he makes active sucking movements. The infant has been classically conditioned. Here is how it happened (see Figure 4.3 on page 136):

● Before learning takes place, an **unconditioned stimulus (UCS)** must consistently produce a reflexive, or **unconditioned, response (UCR).** In our example, the stimulus of sweet breast milk (UCS) resulted in sucking (UCR).

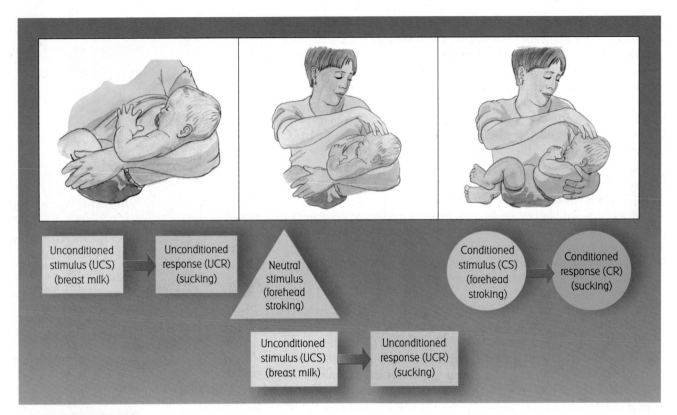

▲ **Figure 4.3**

The steps of classical conditioning. The example here shows how a mother classically conditioned her baby to make sucking movements by stroking his forehead at the beginning of feedings.

- To produce learning, a *neutral stimulus* that does not lead to the reflex is presented at about the same time as the UCS. Ideally, the neutral stimulus should occur just before the UCS. The mother stroked the baby's forehead as each nursing period began. The stroking (neutral stimulus) was paired with the taste of milk (UCS).

- If learning has occurred, the neutral stimulus by itself produces a response similar to the reflexive response. The neutral stimulus is then called a **conditioned stimulus (CS),** and the response it elicits is called a **conditioned response (CR).** We know that the baby has been classically conditioned because stroking his forehead outside the feeding situation (CS) results in sucking (CR).

If the CS is presented alone enough times, without being paired with the UCS, the CR will no longer occur, an outcome called **extinction.** In other words, if the mother strokes the infant's forehead again and again without feeding him, the baby will gradually stop sucking in response to stroking.

Young infants can be classically conditioned most easily when the association between two stimuli has survival value. Thus they learn quickly in the feeding situation, since learning which stimuli regularly accompany feeding improves the infant's ability to get food and survive (Blass, Ganchrow, & Steiner, 1984). In contrast, some responses, such as fear, are very difficult to classically condition in young babies. Until infants have the motor skills to escape unpleasant events, they have no biological need to form these associations. After 6 months of age, however, fear is easy to condition, as seen in the famous example of little Albert, conditioned by John Watson to withdraw and cry at the sight of a furry white rat. Return to Chapter 1, page 19, to review this well-known study. Then test your knowledge of classical conditioning by identifying the UCS, UCR, CS, and CR in Watson's study. In Chapter 10, we will discuss the development of fear, as well as other emotional reactions.

• **OPERANT CONDITIONING** • In classical conditioning, babies build expectations about stimulus events in the environment, but their behavior does not influence the stimuli that occur. In **operant conditioning,** infants act (or *operate)* on the environment, and the stimuli that follow their behavior change the probability that the behavior will occur again. A stimulus that increases the occurrence of a response is called a **reinforcer.** For example, sweet liquid *reinforces* the sucking response in newborn babies. Removing a desirable stimulus or presenting an unpleasant one to decrease the occurrence of a response is called **punishment.**

Because the young infant can control only a few behaviors, successful operant conditioning in the early weeks is limited to head-turning and sucking responses. But many stimuli besides food can serve as reinforcers. For example, researchers have created special laboratory conditions in which the baby's rate of sucking on a nipple produces a variety of interesting sights and sounds. Newborns will suck faster to see visual designs or to hear music and human voices (Floccia, Christophe, & Bertoncini, 1997). Even preterm babies will seek reinforcing stimulation. In one study, they increased their contact with a soft teddy bear that "breathed" at a rate reflecting the infant's respiration, whereas they decreased their contact with a nonbreathing bear (Thoman & Ingersoll, 1993). As these findings suggest, operant conditioning has become a powerful tool for finding out what stimuli babies can perceive and which ones they prefer.

As infants get older, operant conditioning includes a wider range of responses and stimuli. For example, researchers have hung mobiles over the cribs of 2- to 6-month-olds. When the baby's foot is attached to the mobile with a long cord, the infant can, by kicking, make the mobile turn. Under these conditions, it takes only a few minutes for the infant to start kicking vigorously. This technique has yielded important information about infant memory. In a series of studies, Carolyn Rovee-Collier found that 3-month-olds remembered how to activate the mobile 1 week after training. By 6 months, memory increases to 2 weeks (Rovee-Collier, 1999; Rovee-Collier & Bhatt, 1993). Around the middle of the first year, babies can manipulate switches or buttons to control stimulation. When 6- to 18-month-olds pressed a lever to make a toy train move around a track, duration of memory continued to increase with age; 13 weeks after training, 18-month-olds still remembered how to press the lever (Hartshorn et al., 1998b). Figure 4.4 shows this dramatic rise in retention of operant responses over the first year and a half.

Even after 3- to 6-month-olds forget an operant response, they need only a brief prompt—an adult who shakes the mobile—to reinstate the memory (Hildreth & Rovee-Collier, 2002). And when 6-month-olds are given a chance to reactivate the response themselves for just a couple of minutes—jiggling the mobile by kicking or moving the train by lever-pressing—their memory not only returns but extends further, to about 17 weeks (Hildreth, Sweeney, & Rovee-Collier, 2003). Perhaps permitting the baby to generate the previously learned behavior strengthens memory because it re-exposes the child to more aspects of the original learning situation.

At first, infants' memory for operant responses is highly *context dependent.* If 2- to 6-month-olds are not tested in the same situation in which they were trained—with the same mobile and crib bumper and in the same room—they remember poorly (Boller, Grabelle, & Rovee-Collier, 1995; Hayne & Rovee-Collier, 1995). After 9 months, the importance of context declines. Older infants and toddlers remember how to make the toy train move even when its features are altered and testing takes place in a different room (Hartshorn et al., 1998a; Hayne, Boniface, & Barr, 2000). As babies move on their own and experience frequent changes in context, their memory for responses that lead to interesting consequences becomes increasingly *context free.* They apply those responses more flexibly, generalizing them to relevant new situations.

As Chapter 6 will make clear, operant conditioning has also been used to study babies' ability to group similar stimuli into categories. It plays a vital role in the formation of social relationships as well. As the baby gazes into the adult's eyes, the adult looks and smiles back, and then the infant looks and smiles again. The behavior of each partner reinforces the other, and both continue their pleasurable interaction. In Chapter 10, we will see that this contingent responsiveness contributes to the development of infant–caregiver attachment.

▼ Figure 4.4

Increase in retention of operant responses in two tasks from 2 to 18 months of age. Two- to 6-month-olds were trained to make a kicking response that turned a mobile. Six- to 18-month-olds were trained to press a lever that made a toy train move around a track. Six-month-olds learned both responses and retained them for an identical length of time, indicating that the tasks are comparable. Consequently, researchers could plot a single line tracking gains in retention of operant responses from 2 to 18 months of age. The line shows that memory improves dramatically. (From C. Rovee-Collier & R. Barr, 2001, "Infant Learning and Memory," in G. Bremner & A. Fogel, eds., *Blackwell Handbook of Infant Development,* Oxford, U.K.: Blackwell, p. 150. Reprinted by permission.)

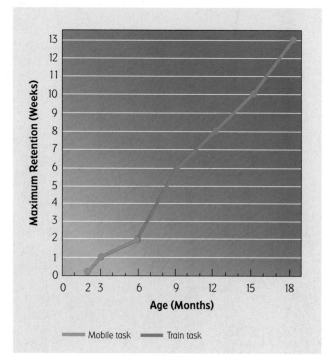

Mobile task   Train task

• **HABITUATION** • At birth, the human brain is set up to be attracted to novelty. Infants tend to respond more strongly to a new element that has entered their environment. **Habituation** refers to a gradual reduction in the strength of a response due to repetitive stimulation. Looking, heart rate, and respiration rate may all decline, indicating a loss of interest. Once this has occurred, a new stimulus—a change in the environment—causes the habituated response to return to a high level, an increase called **recovery.** For example, when you walk through a familiar space, you notice things that are new or different—a recently purchased picture on the wall, a piece of furniture that has been moved. Habituation and recovery make learning more efficient by enabling us to focus our attention on those aspects of the environment we know least about.

▶ *Window into Early Attention, Memory, and Knowledge.* More than any other learning capacity, researchers rely on habituation and recovery to explore infants' understanding of the world. For example, a baby who first *habituates* to a visual pattern (a photo of a baby), then *recovers* to a new one (a photo of a bald man), appears to remember the first stimulus and perceive the second one as new and different from it. This method of studying infant attention, perception, and memory, illustrated in Figure 4.5a, can be used with newborn babies, even those who are preterm. It has even been used to study the fetus's sensitivity to external stimuli—for example, by measuring changes in fetal heart rate when various repeated sounds are presented (Hepper, 1997).

Preterm and newborn babies require a long time to habituate and recover to novel visual stimuli—about 3 or 4 minutes. But by 4 or 5 months, they require as little as 5 to 10 seconds to take in a complex visual stimulus and recognize it as different from a previous one. Yet a fascinating exception to this trend exists. Two-month-olds actually take longer to habituate to novel visual forms than do newborns and older infants (Colombo, 2002). Later we will see that 2 months is also a time of dramatic gains in visual perception. Perhaps when young babies are first able to perceive certain information, they require more time to take it in. Another contributor to the long habituation times of young babies is their difficulty disengaging attention from a stimulus. By 4 months, attention becomes more flexible—a change believed to be due to development of brain structures controlling eye movements (Johnson, 1996). (Nevertheless, as will be apparent shortly, a few babies continue to have trouble shifting attention.)

Recovery, or novelty preference, assesses infants' *recent memory.* Think about what happens when you return to a place you have not seen for a long time. Instead of attending to novelty, you are likely to focus on aspects that are familiar, remarking, "I recognize that. I've been here before!" Similarly, with passage of time, infants *shift from a novelty preference to a familiarity preference.* That is, they recover to the familiar stimulus rather than to a novel stimulus (see Figure 4.5b) (Bahrick & Pickens, 1995; Courage & Howe, 1998). By capitalizing on that shift, researchers can use habituation to assess *remote memory,* or memory for stimuli to which infants were exposed weeks or months earlier.

Habituation studies show that from the constantly changing flow of objects, actions, and events in their surroundings, infants detect and remember an extraordinarily wide range of stimuli. They are especially attentive to the movements of objects and people, and they retain such information over many weeks. In one study, 5½-month-old babies habituated to a video in which they saw the face of a woman performing an action (either brushing teeth, blowing bubbles, or brushing

▼ **Figure 4.5**

Using habituation to study infant memory and knowledge. In the habituation phase, infants view a photo of a baby until their looking declines. In the test phase, infants are again shown the baby photo, but this time it appears alongside a photo of a bald-headed man. (a) When the test phase occurs soon after the habituation phase (within minutes, hours, or days, depending on the age of the infants), participants who remember the baby face and distinguish it from the man's face show a *novelty preference;* they recover to the new stimulus. (b) When the test phase is delayed for weeks or months, infants who continue to remember the baby face shift to a *familiarity preference;* they recover to the familiar baby face rather than to the novel man's face.

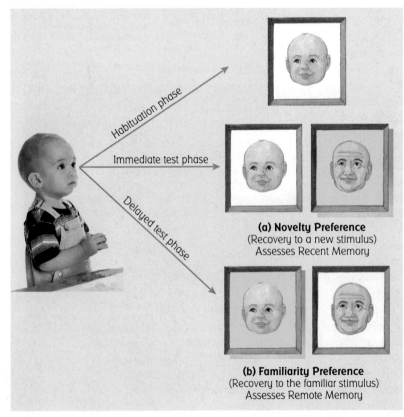

Habituation phase

Immediate test phase

Delayed test phase

(a) Novelty Preference
(Recovery to a new stimulus)
Assesses Recent Memory

(b) Familiarity Preference
(Recovery to the familiar stimulus)
Assesses Remote Memory

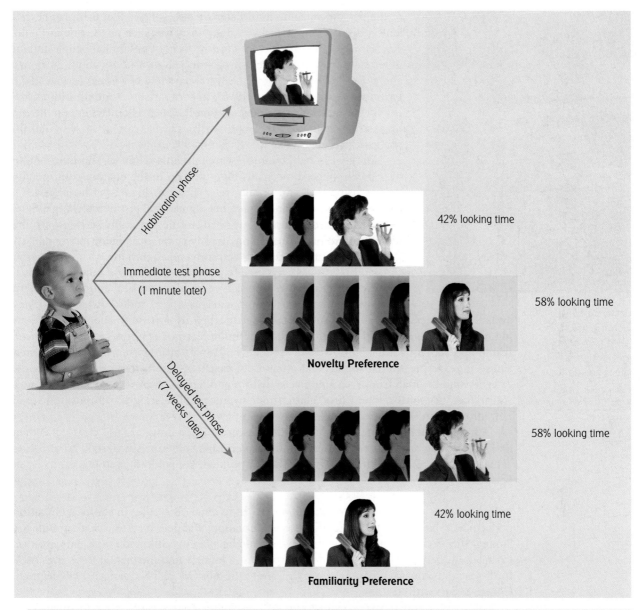

42% looking time

58% looking time

Novelty Preference

58% looking time

42% looking time

Familiarity Preference

Habituation phase

Immediate test phase
(1 minute later)

Delayed test phase
(7 weeks later)

▲ **Figure 4.6**

Infants' recent and remote memory for human actions. Infants 5¹/₂ months old habituated to a video that showed the face of a woman while she performed an action, such as brushing teeth. In two test phases, they saw the familiar video next to a novel video, in which the action changed—for example, to brushing hair—while the woman's face remained the same. In the *immediate test phase* (1 minute later), which assessed *recent memory,* infants displayed a *novelty preference;* they looked longer at the novel action than the familiar action. In the *delayed test phase* (7 weeks later), which assessed *remote memory,* infants showed a *familiarity preference;* they looked longer at the familiar action than the novel action. These findings reveal that young infants remember human actions for an impressively long time. (Adapted from Bahrick, Gogate, & Ruiz, 2002.)

hair) (Bahrick, Gogate, & Ruiz, 2002). In a test phase 1 minute later and again after a 7-week delay, infants watched the familiar video next to a novel video, in which the action changed while the woman's face remained the same. As Figure 4.6 indicates, infants clearly remembered the action. At 1 minute, most showed a *novelty preference,* looking longer at the new action than the old action. But at 7 weeks, most showed a *familiarity preference,* looking longer at the familiar action than the new action. In fact, the babies were so attentive to the woman's action that they ignored her face! In an additional test phase that assessed face recognition in a novel video (the woman's face changed while her original action remained the same), infants showed no facial preference.

These findings, and others in this chapter, confirm that infants find motion especially captivating—so much so that they attend to and remember an action far better than the features

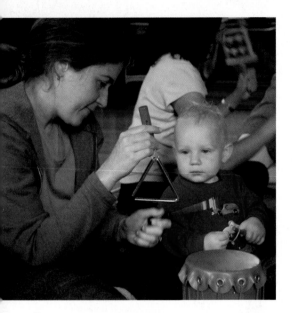

Ⓢ Infants are captivated by people's actions, as is this fully engaged baby who watches his mother strike the triangle in an infant music class.

© Geri Engberg/The Image Works

of the person engaging in it! Later we also will see that babies are excellent at discriminating faces in static displays (such as the one in Figure 4.5). However, infants' memory for the faces of unfamiliar people and for other static patterns is short-lived—at 3 months, only about 24 hours, and at the end of the first year, several days to a few weeks (Fagan, 1973; Pascalis, de Haan, & Nelson, 1998). In comparison, 3-month-olds' memory for the unusual movements of objects (such as a metal nut on the end of a string swinging back and forth) persists for at least 3 months (Bahrick, Hernandez-Reif, & Pickens, 1997).

Note that in habituation research, infants retain certain information over much longer time spans than they do in the operant conditioning studies using the crib mobile (refer again to Figure 4.4 on page 137). Clearly, infants learn and remember a great deal just by watching objects and events around them. They need not be physically active to acquire new information (although, as will become clear later, motor activity facilitates certain aspects of perception and cognition).

Habituation has been used to assess a wide range of infant perceptual and cognitive capacities—speech perception, musical and visual pattern perception, object perception, categorization, and knowledge of many aspects of the social world. These studies reveal yet another disparity with operant conditioning research: When assessed through habituation, infant learning is not as *context dependent.* In this and subsequent chapters, we will see many examples of infants' *detection of relationships*—for example, speech sounds that often occur together, objects that belong to the same category, and the match between an object's rhythm and tempo of movement and its sounds. As early as 3½ months, infants use their current awareness of relationships to make sense of new information (Bahrick, 2002).

Despite the many strengths of habituation research, its findings are not clear-cut. When looking, sucking, or heart rate declines and recovers, it is sometimes uncertain what babies actually know about the stimuli to which they responded. We will return to this difficulty in Chapter 6.

▶ *Habituation and Later Mental Development.* Individual differences in babies' habituation performance have long-term significance. Habituation and recovery to visual stimuli are among the earliest available predictors of intelligence in childhood and adolescence. Correlations between the speed of these responses in infancy and the mental test scores of 3- to 18-year-olds consistently range from the .30s to the .60s (McCall & Carriger, 1993; Sigman, Cohen, & Beckwith, 1997).

Habituation and recovery seem to be an especially effective early index of intelligence because they assess quickness and flexibility of thinking, which underlie intelligent behavior at all ages. Compared with infants who habituate and recover quickly, infants who are "long lookers" on these tasks have difficulty redirecting their attention from one spot to another. Instead of taking in the overall arrangement of a stimulus followed by its finer details, they get stuck on certain small features. As a result, they process much less information (Colombo, 2002; Colombo et al., 2004). When researchers induced 5-month-old long lookers to take in a complex design by successively illuminating each of its parts with a red light, the babies changed their approach and scanned visual stimuli just as "short lookers" do. As a result, their capacity to discriminate and remember visual stimuli in habituation tasks improved (Jankowski, Rose, & Feldman, 2001). Investigators have yet to explore the impact of such early intervention on intellectual development.

So far, we have considered only one type of memory—*recognition.* It is the simplest form of memory: All the baby has to do is indicate (by looking, kicking, or pressing a lever) whether a new stimulus is identical or similar to a previous one. *Recall* is a second, more challenging form of memory that involves remembering something not present. Can infants engage in recall? By the end of the first year, they can, as indicated by their ability find hidden objects and imitate the actions of others hours or days after they observed the behavior. We will take up recall in Chapter 7.

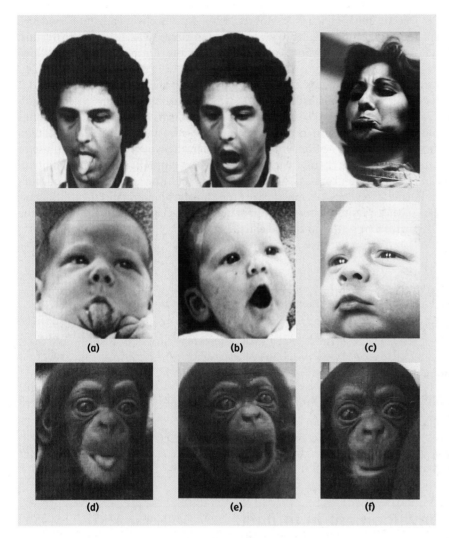

◀ **Figure 4.7**

Imitation by human and chimpanzee newborns. The human infants in the center row imitating (a) tongue protrusion and (b) mouth opening are 2 to 3 weeks old. The human infant imitating (c) lip protrusion is 2 days old. The chimpanzee imitating all three facial expressions, (d), (e), and (f), is 2 weeks old.

(From A. N. Meltzoff & M. K. Moore, 1977, "Imitation of Facial and Manual Gestures by Human Neonates," *Science, 198*, p. 75; T. M. Field et al., 1992, "Discrimination and Imitation of Facial Expressions by Neonates," *Science, 218*, p. 180; and M. Myowa-Yamakoshi et al., 2004, "Imitation in neonatal chimpanzees (Pan troglodytes)," *Developmental Science, 7*, p. 440. Copyright 1997 and 1982 by the AAAS, copyright 2004 by Blackwell Publishing Ltd. Reprinted by permission.)

(a)   (b)   (c)

(d)   (e)   (f)

• **NEWBORN IMITATION** • Newborn babies come into the world with a primitive ability to learn through **imitation**—by copying the behavior of another person. Figure 4.7 shows infants from 2 days to several weeks old imitating adult facial expressions (Field et al., 1982; Meltzoff & Moore, 1977). The human newborn's capacity to imitate extends to certain gestures, such as head movements, and has been demonstrated in many ethnic groups and cultures (Meltzoff & Kuhl, 1994). As the figure reveals, even the newborns of chimpanzees, our closest evolutionary ancestors, imitate some facial expressions: tongue protrusion, mouth opening, and lip protrusion (Myowa-Yamakoshi et al., 2004).

But a few studies have failed to reproduce the human findings (see, for example, Anisfeld et al., 2001). And imitation is more difficult to induce in babies 2 to 3 months old than just after birth. Therefore, some investigators regard the capacity as little more than an automatic response that declines with age, much like a reflex. Others claim that newborns imitate a variety of facial expressions and head movements with apparent effort and determination, even after short delays—when the adult is no longer demonstrating the behavior. Furthermore, these investigators argue, imitation does not decline, as reflexes do. Human babies several months old often do not imitate an adult's behavior right away because they try to play social games they are used to in face-to-face interaction—mutual gazing, cooing, smiling, and waving their arms. When an adult models a gesture repeatedly, older human infants soon get down to business and imitate (Meltzoff & Moore, 1994). Similarly, imitation declines in baby chimps around 9 weeks of age, when mother–baby mutual gazing and other face-to-face exchanges increase.

According to Andrew Meltzoff, newborns imitate in much the same way older children and adults do—by actively trying to match body movements they *see* with ones they *feel* themselves make (Meltzoff & Decety, 2003; Meltzoff & Moore, 1999). Later we will encounter evidence that young infants are surprisingly good at coordinating information across sensory systems. Still, Meltzoff and Moore's view of newborn imitation as a flexible, voluntary capacity remains controversial.

As we will see in Chapter 6, infants' capacity to imitate improves greatly over the first 2 years. But however limited it is at birth, imitation may reflect the baby's deep-seated need to communicate (Blasi & Bjorklund, 2003). It is also a powerful means of learning. Using imitation, infants explore their social world, getting to know people by matching behavioral states with them. In the process, babies notice similarities between their own actions and those of others and start to find out about themselves. Furthermore, by tapping into infants' ability to imitate, adults can get infants to express desirable behaviors; once they do, adults can encourage these further. Finally, caregivers take great pleasure in a baby who imitates their facial gestures and actions. Newborn imitation clearly seems one of those capacities that helps get the infant's relationship with parents off to a good start.

Ask Yourself

REVIEW	What functions does REM sleep serve in young infants? Can sleep and crying tell us about the health of the baby's central nervous system? Explain.
REVIEW	Provide an example of classical conditioning, of operant conditioning, and of habituation in young infants. Why is each type of learning useful? Cite differences between operant conditioning and habituation findings on infant memory.
APPLY	After a difficult birth, 2-day-old Kelly scores poorly on the NBAS. How would you address her mother's concern that Kelly might not develop normally?
CONNECT	How do the diverse capacities of newborn babies contribute to their first social relationships? List as many examples as you can.

Motor Development in Infancy

Virtually all parents eagerly await mastery of new motor skills, recording with pride when their infants hold up their heads, reach for objects, sit by themselves, and walk alone. Parents' enthusiasm for these achievements makes perfect sense. With each new motor skill, babies master their bodies and the environment in a new way. For example, sitting upright gives infants an entirely different perspective on the world. Reaching enables babies to find out about objects by acting on them. And when infants can move on their own, their opportunities for exploration multiply.

Babies' motor achievements have a powerful impact on their social relationships. Once infants can crawl, parents start to restrict their activities by saying "no" and expressing mild anger and impatience. Walking often brings the first "testing of wills" (Biringen et al., 1995). Despite her parents' warnings, one newly walking 12-month-old continued to pull items from shelves that were off limits. "I said not to do that!" her mother remarked as she repeatedly took the infant by the hand and redirected her activities.

At the same time, parents increase their expressions of affection and playful activities as their independently moving baby seeks them out for greetings, hugs, and a gleeful game of hide-and-seek (Campos, Kermoian, & Zumbahlen, 1992). Certain motor skills, such as reaching and pointing, permit infants to communicate more effectively. Finally, babies' delight—laughing, smiling, and babbling—as they work on new motor competencies triggers pleasurable reactions in others, which encourage infants' efforts further (Mayes & Zigler, 1992). Motor skills, emotional and social competencies, cognition, and language develop together and support one another.

The Sequence of Motor Development

Gross motor development refers to control over actions that help infants get around in the environment, such as crawling, standing, and walking. In contrast, *fine motor development* has to

MILESTONES

GROSS AND FINE MOTOR DEVELOPMENT IN THE FIRST TWO YEARS

Motor Skill	Average Age Achieved	Age Range in Which 90 Percent of Infants Achieve the Skill
When held upright, holds head erect and steady	6 weeks	3 weeks–4 months
When prone, lifts self by arms	2 months	3 weeks–4 months
Rolls from side to back	2 months	3 weeks–5 months
Grasps cube	3 months, 3 weeks	2–7 months
Rolls from back to side	4½ months	2–7 months
Sits alone	7 months	5–9 months
Crawls	7 months	5–11 months
Pulls to stand	8 months	5–12 months
Plays pat-a-cake	9 months, 3 weeks	7–15 months
Stands alone	11 months	9–16 months
Walks alone	11 months, 3 weeks	9–17 months
Builds tower of two cubes	11 months, 3 weeks	10–19 months
Scribbles vigorously	14 months	10–21 months
Walks up stairs with help	16 months	12–23 months
Jumps in place	23 months, 2 weeks	17–30 months
Walks on tiptoe	25 months	16–30 months

Note: These milestones represent overall age trends. Individual differences exist in the precise age at which each milestone is attained.

Sources: Bayley, 1969, 1993.

Photos: (top) © Bob Daemmrich/The Image Works; (center) © Myrleen Ferguson Cate/PhotoEdit; (bottom) © Barbara Peacock/Getty Images/Taxi

do with smaller movements, such as reaching and grasping. The Milestones table above shows the average ages at which infants and toddlers achieve a variety of gross and fine motor skills.

Notice that this table also presents the age ranges during which the majority of infants accomplish each skill. Although the *sequence* of motor development is fairly uniform, large individual differences exist in *rate* of motor progress. Also, a baby who is a late reacher is not necessarily going to be a late crawler or walker. We would be concerned about a child's development only if many motor skills were seriously delayed.

Look at the table once more, and you will see organization and direction in infants' motor achievements. A **cephalocaudal trend,** or head-to-tail sequence, is evident: Motor control of the head comes before control of the arms and trunk, which comes before control of the legs. You can also see a **proximodistal trend,** meaning from the center of the body outward: Head, trunk, and arm control is advanced over coordination of the hands and fingers. Physical growth follows a cephalocaudal and proximodistal course during the prenatal period, infancy, and childhood (see Chapter 5). The similarities between physical and motor development suggest a genetic contribution to motor progress. As we will see, however, some motor milestones deviate sharply from these trends.

We must be careful not to think of motor skills as unrelated accomplishments that follow a fixed maturational timetable. Instead, each skill is a product of earlier motor attainments and a contributor to new ones. Furthermore, children acquire motor skills in highly individual ways. For example, most babies crawl before they pull to a stand and walk. Yet one infant I know, who disliked being placed on her tummy but enjoyed sitting and being held upright, pulled to a stand and walked before she crawled!

Many influences—both internal and external to the child—support the vast transformations in motor competencies of the first 2 years. The *dynamic systems perspective*, introduced in Chapter 1 (see page 29), helps us understand how motor development takes place.

Motor Skills as Dynamic Systems

According to **dynamic systems theory of motor development**, mastery of motor skills involves acquiring increasingly complex *systems of action*. When motor skills work as a *system*, separate abilities blend together, each cooperating with others to produce more effective ways of exploring and controlling the environment. For example, control of the head and upper chest are combined into sitting with support. Kicking, rocking on all fours, and reaching combine to become crawling. Then crawling, standing, and stepping unite into walking (Thelen, 1989).

Each new skill is a joint product of the following factors: (1) central nervous system development, (2) movement capacities of the body, (3) the goal the child has in mind, and (4) environmental supports for the skill. Change in any element makes the system less stable, and the child starts to explore and select new, more effective motor patterns.

The factors that induce change vary with age. In the early weeks of life, brain and body growth are especially important as infants achieve control over the head, shoulders, and upper torso. Later, the baby's goals (getting a toy or crossing the room) and environmental supports (parental encouragement, objects in the infant's everyday setting) play a greater role. Characteristics of the broader physical world also profoundly influence motor skills. For example, if children were reared in the moon's reduced gravity, they would prefer jumping to walking or running!

When a skill is first acquired, infants must refine it. For example, one baby, just starting to crawl, often collapsed on her tummy and moved backward instead of forward. Soon she figured out how to propel herself forward by alternately pulling with her arms and pushing with her feet. As she experimented, she perfected the crawling motion (Adolph, Vereijken, & Denny, 1998). In mastering walking, toddlers practice six or more hours a day, traveling the length of 29 football fields! Gradually their small, unsteady steps change to a longer stride, their feet move closer together, their toes point to the front, and their legs become symmetrically coordinated (Adolph, Vereijken, & Shrout, 2003). As movements are repeated thousands of times, they promote new connections in the brain that govern motor patterns.

Look carefully at dynamic systems theory, and you will see why motor development cannot be genetically determined. Because it is motivated by exploration and the desire to master new tasks, heredity can map it out only at a general level. Instead of behaviors being *hardwired* into the nervous system, they are *softly assembled*, and different paths to the same motor skill exist (Hopkins & Butterworth, 1997; Thelen & Smith, 1998).

• **DYNAMIC MOTOR SYSTEMS IN ACTION** • To study infants' mastery of motor milestones, researchers have conducted *microgenetic studies* (see Chapter 2, page 63), following babies from their first attempts at a skill until it becomes smooth and effortless. Using this research strategy, James Galloway and Esther Thelen (2004) held sounding toys alternately in front of infants' hands and feet, from the time they first showed interest until they engaged in well-coordinated reaching and grasping. In a violation of the cephalocaudal trend, infants first contacted the toys with their feet—as early as 8 weeks of age! These were not accidental contacts. The babies explored deliberately, spending longer times with their feet in contact with the toys than they spent moving their feet in the area where the toys had been offered (see Figure 4.8).

Infants' foot reaching preceded their hand reaching by at least a month. Why did they reach "feet first"? Because the hip joint constrains the legs to move less freely than the shoulder constrains the arms, infants could more easily control their leg movements. When they first tried reaching with their hands, their arms

Ⓢ This baby inches toward a goal—a colorful ball—problem solving all the while. A strong desire to explore and control the environment motivates her efforts to perfect the crawling motion in her own individual way.
© Laura Dwight Photography

actually moved away from the object! Consequently, hand reaching required far more practice than foot reaching. As these findings confirm, rather than following a strict, predetermined cephalocaudal pattern, the order in which motor skills develop depends on the anatomy of the body part being used, the surrounding environment, and the baby's efforts.

• **CULTURAL VARIATIONS IN MOTOR DEVELOPMENT** • Cross-cultural research further illustrates how early movement opportunities and a stimulating environment contribute to motor development. Nearly a half-century ago, Wayne Dennis (1960) observed infants in Iranian orphanages who were deprived of the tantalizing surroundings that induce infants to acquire motor skills. The Iranian babies spent their days lying on their backs in cribs, without toys to play with. As a result, most did not move on their own until after 2 years of age. When they finally did move, the constant experience of lying on their backs led them to scoot in a sitting position rather than crawl on their hands and knees. Because babies who scoot come up against objects such as furniture with their feet, not their hands, they are far less likely to pull themselves to a standing position in preparation for walking. Indeed, by 3 to 4 years of age, only 15 percent of the Iranian orphans were walking.

Cultural variations in infant-rearing practices affect motor development. Ask this question of several parents you know: Should sitting, crawling, and walking be deliberately encouraged? Answers vary widely from culture to culture. Japanese mothers and mothers from rural India, for example, believe that such efforts are unnecessary. They say that children "just learn" (Seymour, 1999). Among the Zinacanteco Indians of southern Mexico, rapid motor progress is actively discouraged. Babies who walk before they know enough to keep away from cooking fires and weaving looms are viewed as dangerous to themselves and disruptive to others (Greenfield, 1992).

In contrast, among the Kipsigis of Kenya and the West Indians of Jamaica, babies hold their heads up, sit alone, and walk considerably earlier than North American infants. Kipsigi parents deliberately teach these motor skills. In the first few months, babies are seated in holes dug in the ground, and rolled blankets are used to keep them upright. Walking is promoted by frequently bouncing babies on their feet (Super, 1981). As Figure 4.9 shows, West Indian mothers use a highly stimulating, formal handling routine. They believe that exercise helps

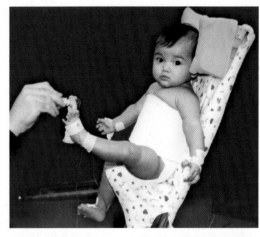

▲ **Figure 4.8**
Reaching "feet first." When sounding toys were held in front of babies' hands and feet, they reached with their feet as early as 8 weeks of age, a month or more before they reached with their hands—a clear violation of the cephalo-caudal pattern. Reduced freedom of movement in the hip joint makes leg movements easier to control than arm movements. This 2½-month-old skillfully explores an object with her foot.

© Dexter Gormley/Courtesy of Cole Galloway, Ph.D.

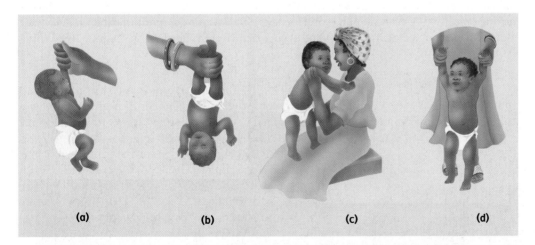

(a)   (b)   (c)   (d)

▲ **Figure 4.9**
West Indians of Jamaica use a formal handling routine with their babies. Exercises practiced in the first few months include (a) stretching each arm while suspending the baby and (b) holding the infant upside-down by the ankles. Later in the first year, the baby is (c) "walked" up the mother's body and (d) encouraged to take steps on the floor while supported. (Adapted from B. Hopkins & T. Westra, 1988, "Maternal Handling and Motor Development: An Intracultural Study," *Genetic, Social and General Psychology Monographs, 14,* pp. 385, 388, 389. Reprinted by permission of the Helen Dwight Reid Educational Foundation. Published by Heldref Publications, 1319 Eighteenth St., N.W., Washington, DC 20036-1802.)

infants grow strong, healthy, and physically attractive (Hopkins & Westra, 1988).

From the evidence we have discussed so far, we must conclude that early motor development results from complex transactions between nature and nurture. As dynamic systems theory suggests, heredity establishes the broad outlines of change. But the precise sequence and rate of progress result from an ongoing dialogue between the brain, the body, and the physical and social environment.

Fine Motor Development: Reaching and Grasping

Of all motor skills, reaching may play the greatest role in infant cognitive development because it opens up a whole new way of exploring the environment (Bushnell & Boudreau, 1993). By grasping things, turning them over, and seeing what happens when they are released, infants learn a great deal about the sights, sounds, and feel of objects.

The development of reaching and grasping, illustrated in Figure 4.10, provides an excellent example of how motor skills start out as gross, diffuse activity and move toward mastery of fine movements. Newborns make well-aimed but poorly coordinated swipes or swings, called **prereaching,** toward an object dangled in front of them. Because they cannot control their arms and hands, they seldom contact the object (von Hofsten, 1982). Nevertheless, newborns try hard to bring their hand within the visual field and seem to reach to attain a goal: touching things (van der Meer, van der Weel, & Lee, 1995; von Hofsten, 2004). Like newborn reflexes, prereaching drops out—around 7 weeks of age. Yet these early behaviors suggest that babies are biologically prepared to coordinate hand with eye in the act of exploring (Thelen, 2001).

• **DEVELOPMENT OF REACHING AND GRASPING** • At about 3 months, as infants develop the necessary eye-gaze and head and shoulder postural control, reaching reappears and improves in accuracy (Bertenthal & von Hofsten, 1998; Spencer et al., 2000). By 4 months, infants reach for a glowing object in the dark. And at 5 to 6 months, they reach for an object they can no longer see (one that has been darkened during the reach by switching off the lights)—a skill that improves over the next few months (Clifton et al., 1993, 1994; McCarty & Ashmead, 1999). These findings indicate that reaching does not require babies to use vision to guide their arms and hands. Instead, reaching is largely controlled by *proprioception,* our sense of movement and location in space, arising from stimuli within the body. When vision is freed from the basic act of reaching, it can focus on more complex adjustments, such as fine-tuning actions to fit the distance and shape of objects.

Reaching improves as depth perception advances and as infants gain greater control of body posture and arm and hand movements. Four-month-olds aim their reaches ahead of a moving object so they can catch it (von Hofsten, 1993). Around 5 months, babies reduce their efforts when an object is moved beyond their reach (Robin, Berthier, & Clifton, 1996). By 7

▼ **Figure 4.10**

Some milestones of voluntary reaching. The average age at which each skill is attained is given. (Ages from Bayley, 1969; Rochat, 1989.)

Prereaching	Reaching with ulnar grasp	Transfer object from hand to hand	Pincer grasp

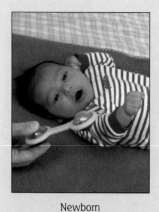   

Newborn	3–4 months	4–5 months	9 months

Photos: (left, middle left, middle right, and right) © Laura Dwight Photography

months, their arms become more independent: They reach for objects with one arm, rather than extending both (Fagard & Pezé, 1997). During the next few months, infants become better at reaching for moving objects—ones that spin, change direction, or move closer or farther away (Wentworth, Benson, & Haith, 2000).

Individual differences in movement styles affect how reaching is perfected (Thelen, Corbetta, & Spencer, 1996). Babies with large, forceful arm movements must make them less vigorous to reach for a toy successfully. Those with quiet, gentle actions must use more muscle power to lift and extend their arms (Thelen et al., 1993). Each infant builds the act of reaching uniquely by exploring the match between current movements and those demanded by the task.

Once infants can reach, they start to modify their grasp. When the grasp reflex of the newborn period weakens at 3 to 4 months, it is replaced by the **ulnar grasp,** a clumsy motion in which the fingers close against the palm. Still, even 3-month-olds readily adjust their grasp to the size and shape of an object—a capacity that improves over the first year (Newman, Atkinson, & Braddick, 2001). Around 4 to 5 months, when infants begin to sit up, they no longer need their arms to maintain body balance. This frees both hands to explore objects. Babies of this age can hold an object in one hand while the other scans it with the tips of the fingers, and they frequently transfer objects from hand to hand (Rochat & Goubet, 1995). By the end of the first year, infants use the thumb and index finger opposably in a well-coordinated **pincer grasp.** After that, the ability to manipulate objects greatly expands. The 1-year-old can pick up raisins and blades of grass, turn knobs, and open and close small boxes.

Between 8 and 11 months, reaching and grasping are well practiced. As a result, attention is freed from the motor skill to events that occur before and after obtaining the object. For example, 10-month-olds easily adjust their reach to anticipate their next action. They reach for a ball faster when they intend to throw it than when they intend to drop it carefully through a narrow tube (Claxton, Keen, & McCarty, 2003). Around this time, too, infants begin to solve simple problems that involve reaching, such as searching for and finding a hidden toy.

 This 3-month-old looks at patterns hung over his crib. A moderate amount of stimulation, tailored to his level of visual development, will lead to earlier reaching than would very little or excessive stimulation. © Julie O'Neil/Index Stock

• **EARLY EXPERIENCE AND REACHING** • Like other motor milestones, early experience affects reaching. In a well-known study, institutionalized infants given a moderate amount of visual stimulation—at first, simple designs; later, a mobile hung over their cribs—reached for objects 6 weeks earlier than infants given nothing to look at. A third group given massive stimulation—patterned crib bumpers and mobiles at an early age—also reached sooner than the unstimulated babies. But this heavy enrichment took its toll. These infants looked away and cried a great deal, and they were not as advanced in reaching as the moderately stimulated group (White & Held, 1966). These findings remind us that more stimulation is not necessarily better. Trying to push infants beyond their current readiness to handle stimulation can undermine the development of important motor skills. We will return to this theme at the end of this chapter, and in Chapter 5, where we consider brain development.

Ask Yourself

REVIEW	Cite evidence that motor development is not genetically programmed but rather is a joint product of biological, psychological, and environmental factors.
APPLY	Roseanne hung mobiles and pictures above her newborn baby's crib, hoping that this would stimulate her infant's motor development. Is Roseanne doing the right thing? Why or why not?
CONNECT	Provide several examples of how motor development influences infants' social experiences. How do social experiences, in turn, influence motor development?
REFLECT	Do you favor early training of infants in motor skills, such as crawling, standing, walking, and stair climbing? Why or why not?

◉ Perceptual Development in Infancy

Think back to White and Held's study, described at the end of the previous section. It illustrates the close link between perception and action in discovering new skills. To reach for objects, maintain balance, or move across various surfaces, infants must continually coordinate their motor behavior with perceptual information. Acting and perceiving are not separate aspects of experience. Instead, motor activity provides infants with a vital means for exploring and learning about the world, and improved perception brings about more effective motor activity. The union of perceptual and motor information is basic to our nervous systems, and each domain supports development of the other (Bertenthal & Clifton, 1998; von Hofsten, 2004).

What can young infants perceive with their senses, and how does perception change with age? Researchers have sought answers to these questions for two reasons. First, studies of infant perception reveal in what ways babies are biologically prepared to perceive their world, and how brain development and experience expand their capacities. Second, infant perception is of interest because it sheds light on other aspects of development. For example, because touch, vision, and hearing permit us to interact with others, they are basic to emotional and social development. Through hearing, language is learned. And because knowledge of the world is first gathered through the senses, perception provides the foundation for cognitive development.

Studying infant perception is especially challenging because babies cannot describe their experiences. Fortunately, investigators can make use of a variety of nonverbal responses that vary with stimulation, such as looking, sucking, head turning, facial expressions, and reaching. As noted earlier, researchers also rely on operant conditioning and habituation to find out whether infants can make certain discriminations. And psychophysiological measures, such as stimulus-induced changes in respiration, heart rate, and EEG brain waves (event-related potentials, or ERPs), are sometimes used. We will see examples of these methods as we explore the baby's sensitivity to touch, taste, smell, sound, and visual stimulation.

Touch

Touch is a fundamental means of interaction between parents and babies. Within the first few days, mothers can recognize their own newborn by stroking the infant's cheek or hand (Kaitz et al., 1993). Touch helps stimulate early physical growth (see Chapter 3), and it is vital for emotional development. Therefore, it is not surprising that sensitivity to touch is well developed at birth. The reflexes listed in Table 4.1 on page 126 reveal that the newborn baby responds to touch, especially around the mouth, on the palms, and on the soles of the feet. During the prenatal period, these areas, along with the genitals, are the first to become sensitive to touch (Humphrey, 1978).

At birth, infants are quite sensitive to pain. If male newborns are circumcised, anesthesia is sometimes not used because of the risks associated with giving pain-relieving drugs to a very young infant. Babies often respond to pain with a high-pitched, stressful cry and a dramatic rise in heart rate, blood pressure, palm sweating, pupil dilation, and muscle tension (Jorgensen, 1999; Warnock & Sandrin, 2004). Recent research establishing the safety of certain local anesthetics for newborns promises to ease the pain of these procedures. Offering a nipple that delivers a sugar solution is also helpful; it quickly reduces crying and discomfort in young babies, preterm and full-term alike. And combining the sweet liquid with gentle holding by the parent lessens pain even more. Research on infant mammals indicates that physical touch releases *endorphins*—painkilling chemicals in the brain (Gormally et al., 2001; Nelson & Panksepp, 1998). Allowing a baby to endure severe pain overwhelms the nervous system with stress hormones, which can disrupt the child's developing capacity to handle common, everyday stressors. The result is heightened pain sensitivity, sleep disturbances, feeding problems, and difficulty calming down when upset (Mitchell & Boss, 2002).

Touching that is pleasurable enhances babies' responsiveness to the environment. An adult's soft caresses induce infants to smile and become more attentive to the adult's face (Stack & Muir, 1992). And

◉ The mohel, a highly trained specialist who performs Jewish circumcisions, prepares to remove the foreskin of this 8-day-old baby while a relative gives the baby a taste of something sweet—possibly red wine—to reduce the pain of the procedure.
© Bill Aron/PhotoEdit

even newborns use touch to investigate their world. They habituate to an object placed in their palms (by reducing their holding) and recover to a novel object, indicating that they can use touch to distinguish object shapes (Streri, Lhote, & Dutilleul, 2000). As reaching develops, babies frequently mouth novel objects, running their lips and tongue over the surface, after which they remove the object to look at it. Exploratory mouthing peaks in the middle of the first year as hand–mouth contact becomes more accurate (Lew & Butterworth, 1997). Then it declines in favor of more elaborate touching with the hands, in which infants turn, poke, and feel the surface of things while looking at them intently (Ruff et al., 1992).

Taste and Smell

At birth, facial expressions reveal that babies can distinguish several basic tastes. Like adults, they relax their facial muscles in response to sweetness, purse their lips when the taste is sour, and show a distinct archlike mouth opening when it is bitter (Steiner, 1979; Steiner et al., 2001). These reactions are important for survival. The food that best supports the infant's early growth is the sweet-tasting milk of the mother's breast. In contrast, many toxic substances are bitter tasting. Not until age 4 months do babies prefer a salty taste to plain water, a change that may prepare them to accept solid foods (Mennella & Beauchamp, 1998).

Nevertheless, newborns can readily learn to like a taste that at first evoked either a neutral or a negative response. For example, babies allergic to cow's-milk formula who are given a soy or other vegetable-based substitute (typically very strong and bitter-tasting) soon prefer it to regular formula. A taste previously disliked can come to be preferred when it is paired with relief of hunger (Harris, 1997).

As with taste, certain odor preferences are present at birth. For example, the smell of bananas or chocolate causes a relaxed, pleasant facial expression, whereas the odor of rotten eggs makes the infant frown (Steiner, 1979). During pregnancy, the amniotic fluid is rich in tastes and smells that vary with the mother's diet. These early experiences influence newborns' preferences. In a study carried out in the Alsatian region of France, where anise is frequently used to flavor foods, researchers tested newborns for their reaction to the anise odor (Schaal, Marlier, & Soussignan, 2000). The mothers of some babies had regularly consumed anise-flavored foods and drinks during the last 2 weeks of pregnancy; the other mothers had never consumed anise. On the day of birth, the two groups of infants responded similarly to a control odor (paraffin oil). When presented with the anise odor, babies of the anise-consuming mothers spent more time mouthing and turning toward the odor. In contrast, infants of non-anise-consuming mothers were far more likely to turn away and display negative facial expressions (see Figure 4.11). These responses were still apparent 4 days later, even though all mothers had refrained from consuming anise during this time.

In many mammals, the sense of smell plays an important role in protecting the young from predators by helping mothers and babies identify each other. Although smell is less well developed in humans, traces of its survival value remain. Newborns given a choice between the smell of their own mother's amniotic fluid and that of another mother spend more time oriented toward the familiar fluid (Marlier, Schaal, & Soussignan, 1998). The smell of the mother's amniotic fluid is comforting; babies exposed to it cry less than babies who are not (Varendi et al., 1998).

Immediately after birth, infants placed face down between their mother's breasts spontaneously latch on to a nipple and begin sucking within an hour. If one breast is washed to remove its natural scent, most newborns grasp the unwashed breast, indicating that they are guided by smell (Varendi & Porter, 2001). At 4 days of age, breastfed babies prefer the smell of their own mother's breast to that of an unfamiliar lactating mother (Cernoch & Porter, 1985). Bottle-fed babies orient to the smell of any lactating woman over the smells of formula or a nonlactating woman

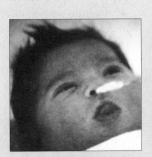

(a) Responses by newborns of anise-consuming mothers

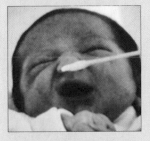
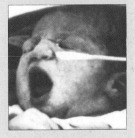

(b) Responses by newborns of non-anise-consuming mothers

▼ **Figure 4.11**

Examples of facial expressions of newborns exposed to the odor of anise whose mothers differed in anise consumption during late pregnancy. (a) Babies of anise-consuming mothers spent more time turning toward the odor and mouthing (sucking, licking, and chewing). (b) Babies of non-anise-consuming mothers more often turned away and displayed negative facial expressions, such as wrinkling their brows and noses, raising their upper lips, lowering the corners of their lips, and closing their eyes. (From B. Schaal, L. Marlier, & R. Soussignan, 2000, "Human Foetuses Learn Odours from Their Pregnant Mother's Diet," *Chemical Senses, 25,* p. 731. Reprinted by permission of the authors.)

(Marlier & Schaal, 1997; Porter et al., 1992). Newborn infants' dual attraction to the odors of their mother and of the lactating breast helps them locate an appropriate food source and, in the process, begin to distinguish their caregiver from other people.

Balance

To take in and make sense of their surroundings, infants must be able to balance the body, adjusting their movements so they remain in a steady position relative to the surface on which they are sitting or standing. Making these postural changes is so important that three sources of sensory information signal a need to adapt body position: (1) *proprioceptive stimulation*, arising from sensations in the skin, joints, and muscles; (2) *vestibular stimulation*, arising from the semicircular canals of the inner ear; and (3) *optical-flow stimulation*, arising from movements in the visual field.

Research focuses largely on **optical flow**—visually detected movements in the surrounding environment—because it can be manipulated easily. Consider how you use optical-flow information. You sense that you are in motion when the entire visual field moves, and you make postural adjustments in accord with its direction and speed. For example, imagine yourself standing on a train pulling out of the station. Scenery flowing past you signals that you are moving. Your perceived direction (forward) is opposite the direction of optical flow, so you compensate by swaying backward to remain upright.

Even newborns adapt their head movements to optical flow (Jouen & Lepecq, 1989). As motor control improves, postural adjustments become more precise. In a series of studies, researchers placed 5- to 13-month-olds in a seat with pressure-sensitive receptors in the "moving room" shown in Figure 4.12. When the front and side walls of the room oscillated forward and backward, all infants displayed appropriate body movements. Between 5 and 9 months, as infants perfected sitting without support, their back-and-forth sway became more finely tuned to the optical-flow changes produced by oscillating walls of the moving room (Bertenthal, Rose, & Bai, 1997; Rose & Bertenthal, 1995).

Clearly, newborn babies have a sense of balance that they refine with motor control and experience. Like those of adults, infants' postural adjustments to self-movement take place unconsciously, freeing their attention for exploration (Bertenthal & Clifton, 1998). But to support actions effectively, many postural adjustments must occur in advance of behavior. By the end of the first year, infants *anticipate* loss of balance. Researchers had 10- to 17-month-olds open a cabinet drawer to retrieve toys and then doubled the drawer's resistance against their pull (Witherington et al., 2002). Between 13 and 16 months, when walking improves, babies increasingly tensed their arm and abdominal muscles prior to opening the drawer, thereby preventing a fall when they let go. Experience with walking may motivate toddlers to make these adjustments. As they repeatedly tumble over, perhaps they realize the need for preventive action.

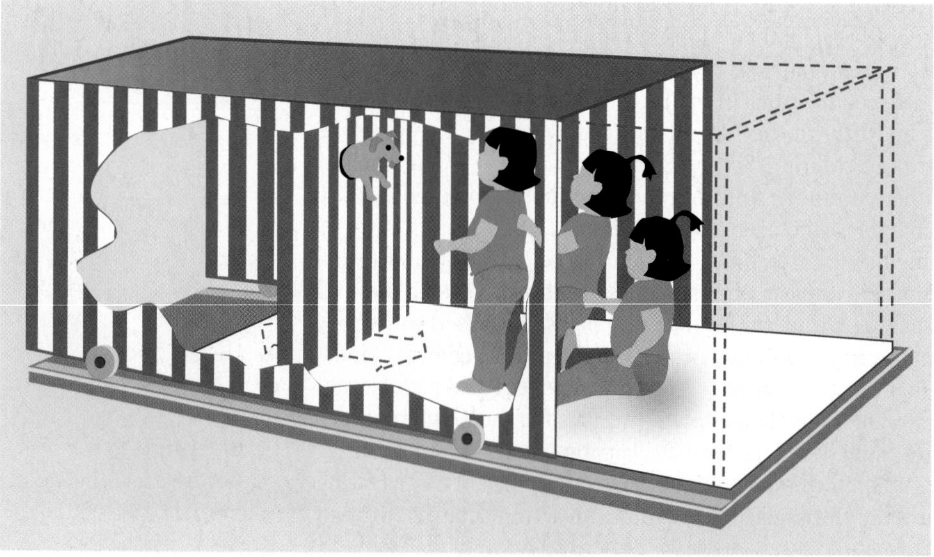

▼ **Figure 4.12**

The "moving room" used to test infants' sensitivity to balance and self-movement. The front and side walls are mounted on wheels that roll on a track. This permits systematic variation of optical flow by moving the walls back and forth at different speeds. To make sure the infant faces forward, a box containing a mechanical dog who "comes alive" is located on the front wall. The figure shows a child falling backward as the front and side walls move toward her. This postural compensation occurs if the child perceives the optical flow as a forward sway of her body. To test 5- to 13-month-olds, a seat with pressure-sensitive receptors is used that measures backward and forward body sway. (From B. I. Bertenthal, J. L. Rose, & D. L. Bai, 1997, "Perception–Action Coupling in the Development of Visual Control of Posture," *Journal of Experimental Psychology: Human Perception and Performance, 23*, p. 1632. Copyright © 1997 by the American Psychological Association. Reprinted by permission.)

Hearing

Newborn infants can hear a wide variety of sounds, although their sensitivity improves greatly over the first few months (Tharpe & Ashmead, 2001). At birth, infants prefer complex sounds, such as noises and voices, to pure tones. And babies only a few days old can tell the difference between a few sound patterns—a series of tones arranged in ascending versus descending order; utterances with two versus three syllables; the stress patterns of words, such as ma-ma versus ma-ma; and happy-sounding speech as opposed to speech with negative or neutral emotional qualities (Mastropieri & Turkewitz, 1999; Sansavini, Bertoncini, & Giovanelli, 1997; Trehub, 2001).

Over the first year, infants organize sounds into increasingly elaborate patterns. Between 4 and 7 months, they have a sense of musical phrasing. They prefer Mozart minuets with pauses between phrases to those with awkward breaks (Krumhansl & Jusczyk, 1990). At the end of the first year, infants recognize the same melody when it is played in different keys. And when the tone sequence is changed only slightly, they can tell that the melody is no longer the same (Trehub, 2001).

Responsiveness to sound provides support for the young baby's exploration of the environment. Infants as young as 3 days old turn their eyes and head in the general direction of a sound. The ability to identify the precise location of a sound improves greatly over the first 6 months and shows further gains into the second year (Litovsky & Ashmead, 1997).

• **SPEECH PERCEPTION** • Young infants listen longer to human speech than structurally similar nonspeech sounds (Vouloumanos & Werker, 2004). And they can detect the sounds of any human language. Newborns make fine-grained distinctions between many speech sounds—"ba" and "ga," "ma" and "na," and the short vowel sounds "a" and "i," to name just a few. For example, when given a nipple that turns on the "ba" sound, babies suck vigorously and then habituate. When the sound switches to "ga," sucking recovers, indicating that infants detect this subtle difference. Using this method, researchers have found only a few speech sounds that newborns cannot discriminate. Their ability to perceive sounds not found in their own language is more precise than an adult's (Aldridge, Stillman, & Bower, 2001; Jusczyk, 1995).

Listen carefully to yourself the next time you talk to a young baby. You will probably speak in ways that highlight important parts of the speech stream—use a slow, clear, high-pitched, expressive voice with a rising tone at the end of speech segments, and pause before continuing. Adults probably communicate this way because they notice that infants are more attentive when they do so. Indeed, newborns prefer human speech with these characteristics (Aslin, Jusczyk, & Pisoni, 1998). In addition, newborns will suck more on a nipple to hear a recording of their mother's voice than that of an unfamiliar woman, and to hear their native language as opposed to a foreign language (Moon, Cooper, & Fifer, 1993; Spence & DeCasper, 1987). These preferences may have developed from hearing the muffled sounds of the mother's voice before birth.

Over the first year, infants learn much about the organization of sounds in their native language. As they listen to the talk of people around them, they learn to focus on meaningful sound variations. ERP brain-wave recordings reveal that around 5 months, they become sensitive to syllable stress patterns in their own language (Weber et al., 2004). Between 6 and 8 months, they start to "screen out" sounds not used in their native tongue (Anderson, Morgan, & White, 2003; Polka & Werker, 1994). Soon after, they focus on larger speech units: They recognize familiar words in spoken passages, listen longer to speech with clear clause and phrase boundaries, and begin to divide the speech stream into wordlike units (Jusczyk, 2002; Jusczyk & Hohne, 1997; Soderstrom et al., 2003).

• **ANALYZING THE SPEECH STREAM** • How do infants make such rapid progress in perceiving the structure of language? Research shows that babies are impressive *statistical analyzers* of the speech stream. In one set of studies, researchers had 8- and 9-month-olds listen to a continuous sequence of nonsense syllables. Then they gave the babies brief, new syllable sequences; some conformed to the syllable patterns in the original sequence and some did not. The babies quickly inferred syllable structure: They preferred to listen to new speech that preserved the original syllable patterns. In other words, they listened for statistical regularities, discriminating syllables that often occur together (indicating that they belong to the same word) from syllables that seldom occur together (signaling a word boundary). To cite an English example, consider the word sequence *pretty#baby*. After listening to the speech stream for just 1 minute (about 60 words), babies can distinguish a word-internal syllable pair

ⓢ Mothers often name objects—for example, saying "doggie"—while moving the toy and, sometimes, having the toy touch the infant. This multisensory stimulation helps infants associate words with objects.
© David Young-Wolff/PhotoEdit

(pretty) from a word-external syllable pair *(ty#ba)* (Saffran, Aslin, & Newport, 1996; Saffran & Thiessen, 2003).

Infants don't just notice syllable patterns; they also attend to regularities in word sequences. In a study using nonsense words, 7-month-olds discriminated the ABA structure of "ga ti ga" and "li na li" from the ABB structure of "wo fe fe" and "ta la la" (Marcus et al., 1999). The infants seemed to detect simple word-order rules—a capacity that may help them figure out the basic grammar of their language.

Clearly, babies have a powerful ability to extract regularities from continuous, complex verbal stimulation. Some researchers believe that infants are innately equipped with a general learning mechanism for detecting structure in the environment, which they also apply to visual stimulation (Kirkham, Slemmer, & Johnson, 2002). Indeed, because communication is often multisensory (simultaneously verbal, visual, and tactile), infants receive much support from other senses in analyzing speech. Perhaps you have observed mothers name objects while demonstrating for their babies—for example, saying "doll" while moving a doll and, sometimes, having the doll touch the infant. Research confirms that when mothers speak to 5- to 8-month-olds, they provide a great deal of temporal synchrony between words, object motions, and touch (Gogate, Bahrick, & Watson, 2000). In doing so, they create a supportive learning environment: In two studies, 7-month-olds remembered associations between sounds and objects only when they heard the sound and saw the object move at the same time (Gogate & Bahrick, 1998, 2001).

Finally, infants' special responsiveness to speech encourages parents to talk to their baby. As they do so, both readiness for language and the emotional bond between caregiver and child are strengthened. At first, infants depend on the union of auditory and visual stimuli to pick up emotional information. Three- and 4-month-olds can distinguish happy- from sad-sounding speech, but only while looking at people's faces. Later, babies can discriminate positive from negative emotion in each sensory modality, first in voices and then in faces (Walker-Andrews, 1997).

Before we turn to visual development, consult the Milestones table on the following page for a summary of the perceptual capacities we have just considered.

Vision

For active exploration of the environment, humans depend on vision more than any other sense. Yet vision is the least mature of the newborn baby's senses. Visual structures in the eye and the brain continue to develop after birth. For example, cells in the *retina*, the membrane lining the inside of the eye that captures light and transforms it into messages that are sent to the brain, are not as mature or densely packed at birth as they will be several months later. Likewise, the optic nerve and other pathways that relay these messages, and the visual centers in the brain that receive them, will not be adultlike for several years. Furthermore, the muscles of the *lens*, which permit us to adjust our focus to varying distances, are weak (Atkinson, 2000).

Because visual structures are immature, newborn babies cannot focus their eyes well, and their **visual acuity,** or fineness of discrimination, is limited. At birth, infants perceive objects at a distance of 20 feet about as clearly as adults do at 600 feet (Slater, 2001). In addition, unlike adults (who see nearby objects most clearly), newborn babies see unclearly across a wide range of distances (Banks, 1980; Hainline, 1998). As a result, images such as the parent's face, even from close up, look like the blurry image in Figure 4.13. And despite their prefer-

(a) Newborn View

(b) Adult View

◀ **Figure 4.13**

View of the human face by the newborn and the adult. The newborn baby's limited focusing ability and poor visual acuity lead the mother's face, even when viewed from close up, to look more like the fuzzy image in (a) than the clear image in (b). Also, newborn infants have some color vision, although they have difficulty discriminating colors. Researchers speculate that colors probably appear similar, but less intense, to newborns than to older infants and adults. (From Hainline, 1998; Slater, 2001.)

MILESTONES

DEVELOPMENT OF TOUCH, TASTE, SMELL, BALANCE, AND HEARING

Age	Touch	Taste and Smell	Balance	Hearing
Birth	Is responsive to touch and pain Can distinguish objects placed in palm	Distinguishes sweet, sour, and bitter tastes; prefers sweetness Distinguishes odors; prefers those of sweet-tasting foods Prefers smell of own mother's amniotic fluid and the lactating breast	Adapts head movements to optical flow	Prefers complex sounds to pure tones Can distinguish some sound patterns Recognizes differences between almost all speech sounds Turns in the general direction of a sound
1–6 months	Frequently engages in exploratory mouthing of objects	Prefers salt solution to plain water Taste preferences are easily changed through experience	As motor control improves, postural adjustments to optical flow become more precise	Organizes sounds into more complex patterns, such as musical phrases Can identify the location of a sound more precisely By the end of this period, is sensitive to syllable stress patterns in own language
7–12 months			Makes anticipatory postural adjustments to avoid loss of balance	"Screens out" sounds not used in own language Perceives larger speech units crucial to understanding meaning

Note: These milestones represent overall age trends. Individual differences exist in the precise age at which each milestone is attained.

Photos: (clockwise from top) © Laura Dwight Photography, © Fredrik Naumann/Panos Pictures, © Laura Dwight Photography, © Michael Newman/PhotoEdit.

ence for colored over gray stimuli, newborn babies are not yet good at discriminating colors. But by 2 months, infants can discriminate colors across the entire spectrum (Teller, 1998).

Although they cannot yet see well, newborns actively explore their environment by scanning it for interesting sights and tracking moving objects. However, their eye movements are slow and inaccurate. The visual system develops rapidly over the first few months. Around 2 months, infants can focus on objects about as well as adults can. Visual acuity increases steadily, reaching a near-adult level of about 20/20 by 6 months (Slater, 2001). Scanning and tracking improve over the first half-year as infants see more clearly and eye movements come under voluntary control (von Hofsten & Rosander, 1998). In addition, as young infants build an organized perceptual world, they scan more thoroughly and systematically, strategically picking up important information and anticipating with their eye movements what they expect to happen next in a series of events (Haith, 1994; Johnson, Slemmer, & Amso, 2004). Consequently, scanning enhances perception, and perception enhances scanning, in bidirectional fashion.

As infants explore the visual field more adeptly, they figure out the characteristics of objects and how they are arranged in space. We can best understand how they do so by examining the development of three aspects of vision: depth, pattern, and object perception.

• **DEPTH PERCEPTION** • *Depth perception* is the ability to judge the distance of objects from one another and from ourselves. It is important for understanding the layout of the environment and for guiding motor activity. To reach for objects, babies must have some sense of

▲ **Figure 4.14**

The visual cliff. Plexiglas covers the deep and shallow sides. By refusing to cross the deep side and showing a preference for the shallow side, this infant demonstrates the ability to perceive depth.
© Mark Richards/PhotoEdit

depth. Later, when infants crawl, depth perception helps prevent them from bumping into furniture and falling down stairs.

Figure 4.14 shows the well-known **visual cliff,** designed by Eleanor Gibson and Richard Walk (1960) and used in the earliest studies of depth perception. It consists of a Plexiglas-covered table with a platform at the center, a "shallow" side with a checkerboard pattern just under the glass, and a "deep" side with a checkerboard several feet below the glass. The researchers found that crawling babies readily crossed the shallow side, but most reacted with fear to the deep side. They concluded that around the time that infants crawl, most distinguish deep from shallow surfaces and avoid drop-offs.

The research of Gibson and Walk shows that crawling and avoidance of drop-offs are linked, but it does not tell us how they are related or when depth perception first appears. To better understand the development of depth perception, recent research has looked at babies' ability to detect specific depth cues, using methods that do not require that they crawl.

▶ *Emergence of Depth Perception.* How do we know when an object is near rather than far away? To find out, try these exercises: Pick up a small object (such as your cup) and move it toward your face, then away. Did its image grow larger as it approached and smaller as it receded? Next time you take a car or bike ride, notice that nearby objects move past your field of vision more quickly than those far away.

Kinetic depth cues, created by movements of the body or of objects in the environment, are the first to which infants are sensitive. Babies 3 to 4 weeks old blink their eyes defensively when an object moves toward their face as if it is going to hit (Nánez & Yonas, 1994). As they are carried about and as people and things turn and move before their eyes, infants learn more about depth. For example, by the time they are 3 months old, motion has helped them figure out that objects are not flat but three-dimensional (Arterberry, Craton, & Yonas, 1993).

Binocular depth cues arise because our two eyes have slightly different views of the visual field. In a process called *stereopsis,* the brain blends these two images, resulting in perception of depth. To study infants' sensitivity to binocular cues, researchers project two overlapping images before the baby, who wears special goggles to ensure that each eye receives one of the images. If babies use binocular cues, they will perceive and visually track an organized, three-dimensional form rather than seeing random dots. Results reveal that binocular sensitivity emerges between 2 and 3 months and improves rapidly over the first year (Birch, 1993; Brown & Miracle, 2003). Infants soon make use of binocular cues in their reaching, adjusting arm and hand movements to match the distance of objects.

Last to develop are **pictorial depth cues**—the ones artists use to make a painting look three-dimensional. Examples include receding lines that create the illusion of perspective, changes in texture (nearby textures are more detailed than faraway ones), and overlapping objects (an object partially hidden by another object is perceived to be more distant). Studies in which researchers observe whether babies reach toward the closer-appearing parts of images containing pictorial cues reveal that 7-month-olds are sensitive to these cues, although 5-month-olds are not (Sen, Yonas, & Knill, 2001; Yonas et al., 1986).

Why does perception of depth cues emerge in the order just described? Researchers speculate that motor development is involved. For example, control of the head during the early weeks of life may help babies notice motion and binocular cues. And around 5 to 6 months, the ability to turn, poke, and feel the surface of objects may promote perception of pictorial cues as infants pick up information about size, texture, and shape (Bushnell & Boudreau, 1993). Indeed, as we will see next, research shows that one aspect of motor progress—independent movement—plays a vital role in refinement of depth perception.

▶ *Crawling and Depth Perception.* A mother I know described her newly crawling 9-month-old as a "fearless daredevil." "If I put April down in the middle of our bed, she crawls right over the edge," the mother exclaimed. "The same thing's happened by the stairs."

Will April become more wary of the side of the bed and the staircase as she becomes a more experienced crawler? Research suggests that she will. Infants with more crawling experience (regardless of when they start to crawl) are far more likely to refuse to cross the deep side of the visual cliff (Bertenthal, Campos, & Barrett, 1984; Campos, 2000).

What do infants learn from crawling that promotes this sensitivity to depth information? Research suggests that from extensive everyday experience, babies gradually figure out how to use depth cues to detect the danger of falling. But because the loss of postural control that leads to falling differs greatly for each body position, babies must undergo this learning separately for each posture. In one study, 9-month-olds, who were experienced sitters but novice crawlers, were placed on the edge of a shallow drop-off that could be widened (Adolph, 2000). While in the familiar sitting position, infants avoided leaning out for an attractive toy at distances likely to result in falling. But in the unfamiliar crawling posture, they headed over the edge, even when the distance was extremely wide! As infants discover how to avoid falling in diverse postures and situations, their understanding of depth expands.

Crawling experience promotes other aspects of three-dimensional understanding. For example, seasoned crawlers are better than their inexperienced agemates at remembering object locations and finding hidden objects (Bai & Bertenthal, 1992; Campos et al., 2000). Why does crawling make such a difference? Compare your experience of the environment when you are driven from one place to another as opposed to walking or driving yourself. When you move on your own, you are much more aware of landmarks and routes of travel, and you take more careful note of what things look like from different points of view. The same is true for infants. In fact, crawling promotes a new level of brain organization, as indicated by more organized EEG brain-wave activity in the cerebral cortex. Perhaps crawling strengthens certain neural connections, especially those involved in vision and understanding of space (Bell & Fox, 1996). As the Biology and Environment box on page 156 reveals, the link between independent movement and spatial knowledge is also evident in a population with very different perceptual experience: infants with severe visual impairments.

Crawling promotes three-dimensional understanding, such as wariness of drop-offs. In addition, as this baby crawls about, he learns how to get from place to place, where objects are in relation to himself and to other objects, and what they look like from various points of view.

© Bob Daemmrich/Stock Boston, LLC.

• **PATTERN PERCEPTION** • Even newborns prefer to look at patterned as opposed to plain stimuli—for example, a drawing of the human face or one with scrambled facial features rather than a black-and-white oval (Fantz, 1961). As infants get older, they prefer more complex patterns. For example, 3-week-olds look longest at black-and-white checkerboards with a few large squares, whereas 8- and 14-week-olds prefer those with many squares (Brennan, Ames, & Moore, 1966).

▶ *Contrast Sensitivity.* A general principle, called **contrast sensitivity,** explains early pattern preferences (Banks & Ginsburg, 1985). *Contrast* refers to the difference in the amount of light between adjacent regions in a pattern. If babies *are sensitive to* (can detect) the contrast in two or more patterns, they prefer the one with more contrast. To understand this idea, look at the checkerboards in the top row of Figure 4.15. To us, the one with many small squares has more contrasting elements. Now look at the bottom row, which shows how these checkerboards appear to infants in the first few weeks of life. Because of their poor vision, very young babies cannot resolve the small features in more complex patterns, so they prefer to look at the large, bold

▶ **Figure 4.15**

The way two checkerboards differing in complexity look to infants in the first few weeks of life. Because of their poor vision, very young infants cannot resolve the fine detail in the *complex checkerboard.* It appears blurred, like a gray field. The large, *bold checkerboard* appears to have more contrast, so babies prefer to look at it. (Adapted from M. S. Banks & P. Salapatek, 1983, "Infant Visual Perception," in M. M. Haith & J. J. Campos [Eds.], *Handbook of Child Psychology: Vol. 2. Infancy and Developmental Psychobiology* [4th ed.], New York: Wiley, p. 504. Copyright © 1983 by John Wiley & Sons. Reprinted by permission.)

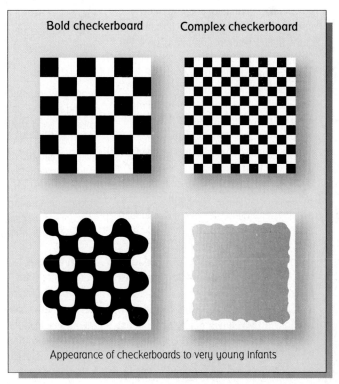

Bold checkerboard   Complex checkerboard

Appearance of checkerboards to very young infants

BIOLOGY AND ENVIRONMENT

Development of Infants with Severe Visual Impairments

Research on infants who can see little or nothing at all dramatically illustrates the interdependence of vision, motor exploration, social interaction, and understanding of the world. In a longitudinal study, infants with a visual acuity of 20/800 or worse—that is, they had only dim light perception or were blind—were followed through the preschool years. Compared to agemates with less severe visual impairments, they showed serious delays in all aspects of development. Motor and cognitive functioning suffered the most; with age, performance in both domains became increasingly distant from that of other children (Hatton et al., 1997).

What explains these profound developmental delays? Minimal or absent vision can alter the child's experiences in at least two crucial, interrelated ways.

Impact on Motor Exploration and Spatial Understanding

Infants with severe visual impairments attain gross and fine motor milestones many months later than their sighted counterparts (Levtzion-Korach et al., 2000). For example, on average, blind infants do not reach for and manipulate objects until 12 months, crawl until 13 months, and walk until 19 months (compare these averages to the motor norms given in the Milestones table on page 143). Why is this so?

Infants with severe visual impairments must rely on sound to identify the where-abouts of objects. But sound does not function as a precise clue to object location until much later than vision—around the middle of the first year (Litovsky & Ashmead, 1997). And because infants who cannot see have difficulty engaging their caregivers, adults may not provide them with rich early exposure to sounding objects. As a result, the baby comes to understand relatively late that there is a world of tantalizing objects to explore.

Until "reaching on sound" is achieved, infants with severe visual impairments are not motivated to move independently. Because of their own uncertainty coupled with parents' protectiveness and restraint to prevent injury, blind infants are typically tentative in their movements. These factors delay motor development further.

Motor and cognitive development are closely linked, especially for infants with little or no vision. These babies build an understanding of the location and arrangement of objects in space only after reaching and crawling (Bigelow, 1992). As these children get older, inability to imitate the motor actions of others presents additional challenges, contributing to declines in motor and cognitive progress relative to peers with better vision (Hatton et al., 1997).

Impact on the Caregiver–Infant Relationship

Infants who see poorly have great difficulty evoking stimulating caregiver interaction. They cannot make eye contact, imitate, or pick up nonverbal social cues. Their emotional expressions are muted; for example, their smile is fleeting and unpredictable. And because they cannot gaze in the same direction as a partner, they are greatly delayed in establishing a shared focus of attention on objects as the basis for play (Bigelow, 2003). Consequently, these infants may receive little adult attention and other stimulation vital for all aspects of development.

When a visually impaired child does not learn how to participate in social interaction during infancy, communication is compromised in early childhood. In an observational study of blind children enrolled in preschools with sighted agemates, the blind children seldom initiated contact with peers and teachers. When they did interact, they had trouble interpreting the meaning of others' reactions and responding appropriately (Preisler, 1991, 1993).

Interventions

Parents, teachers, and caregivers can help infants with minimal vision overcome early developmental delays through stimulating, responsive interaction. Until a close emotional bond with an adult is forged, visually impaired babies cannot establish vital links with their environments.

▲ As a result of complications from prematurity, this 2-year-old experienced nearly complete detachment of her retinas and has only minimal light perception. By guiding the child's exploration of a zither through touch and sound, a caregiver helps prevent the developmental delays often associated with severely impaired vision. Courtesy of Rich Kenney, Foundation for Blind Children

Techniques that help infants become aware of their physical and social surroundings include heightened sensory input through combining sound and touch (holding, touching, or bringing the baby's hands to the adult's face while talking or singing), engaging in many repetitions, and consistently reinforcing the infant's efforts to make contact. Manipulative play with objects that make sounds is also vital.

Finally, rich language stimulation can compensate for visual loss (Conti-Ramsden & Pérez-Pereira, 1999). It grants young children a ready means of finding out about objects, events, and behaviors they cannot see. Once language emerges, many children with limited or no vision show impressive rebounds. Some acquire a unique capacity for abstract thinking, and most master social and practical skills that permit them to lead productive, independent lives (Warren, 1994).

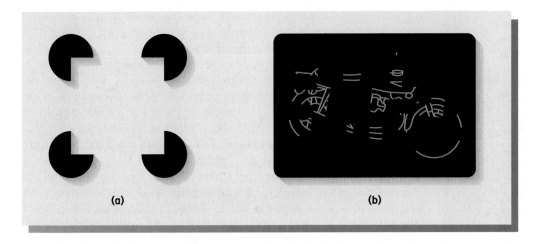

(a)   (b)

◀ **Figure 4.16**

Subjective boundaries in visual patterns. (a) Do you perceive a square in the middle of the figure on the left? By 4 months of age, infants do, too. (b) What does the image on the right, missing two-thirds of its outline, look like to you? By 12 months, infants detect the image of a motor-cycle. After habituating to the incomplete motorcycle image, they were shown an intact motorcycle figure paired with a novel form. Twelve-month-olds recovered to (looked longer at) the novel figure, indicating that they recognized the motorcycle pattern on the basis of very little visual information. (Adapted from Ghim, 1990; Rose, Jankowski, & Senior, 1997.)

checkerboard. Around 2 months of age, when detection of fine-grained detail has improved considerably, infants become sensitive to the greater contrast in complex patterns and spend more time looking at them. Contrast sensitivity continues to improve during infancy and childhood (Gwiazda & Birch, 2001).

▶ *Combining Pattern Elements.* In the early weeks of life, infants respond to the separate parts of a pattern. They stare at single, high-contrast features and have difficulty shifting their gaze away toward other interesting stimuli (Hunnius & Geuze, 2004a, 2004b). In exploring drawings of human faces, for example, 1-month-olds often limit themselves to the edges of the stimulus and focus on the hairline or chin. At 2 to 3 months, when contrast sensitivity improves and infants can better control their scanning, they thoroughly explore a pattern's internal features, pausing briefly to look at each salient part (Bronson, 1994). (Recall from page 140 that some babies continue to focus on small features and, therefore, take in less information.)

At the same time, babies' scanning varies with pattern characteristics. When exposed to dynamic stimuli, such as the mother's nodding, smiling face, 6-week-olds fixate more on internal features (the mouth and eyes) than on edges. Furthermore, when stimuli are dynamic, development of scanning takes place over a longer period; thorough inspection of the entire stimulus emerges only after 4 months of age (Hunnius & Geuze, 2004b). Exploring complex moving patterns seems to be more demanding than exploring stationary patterns—a difference we must keep in mind as we examine research on pattern perception, which is based largely on static stimuli.

Once babies take in all aspects of a pattern, they integrate them into a unified whole. Around 4 months, they are so good at detecting organization in static patterns that they even perceive subjective boundaries that are not really present. For example, they perceive a square in the center of Figure 4.16a, just as you do (Ghim, 1990). Older infants carry this responsiveness to subjective form even further. For example, 9-month-olds show a special preference for an organized series of moving lights that resembles a human being walking, in that they look much longer at this display than at upside-down or scrambled versions (Bertenthal, 1993). At 12 months, infants detect objects represented by incomplete drawings, even when as much as two-thirds of the drawing is missing (see Figure 4.16b) (Rose, Jankowski, & Senior, 1997). By the end of the first year, a suggestive image is all that babies need to recognize a familiar form. As these findings reveal, infants' increasing knowledge of objects and actions supports pattern perception. As we turn now to perception of the human face, we will see additional examples of this idea.

• **FACE PERCEPTION** • Infants' tendency to search for structure in a patterned stimulus applies to face perception. Newborns prefer to look at simple, facelike stimuli with features arranged naturally (upright) rather than unnaturally (upside down or sideways) (see Figure 4.17a on page 158) (Mondloch et al., 1999). They also track a facelike pattern moving across their visual field farther than they track other stimuli (Johnson, 1999). And although their ability to distinguish real faces on the basis of inner features is limited, shortly after birth babies prefer photos of faces with eyes open and a direct gaze. Yet another amazing capacity is their tendency to look longer at faces judged by adults as attractive, compared with less

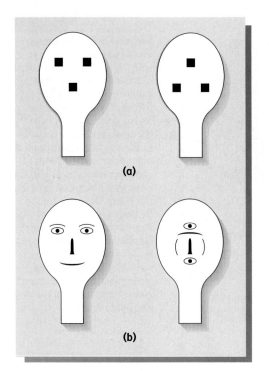

(a)

(b)

▲ **Figure 4.17**

Early face perception. (a)
Newborns prefer to look at
the simple pattern resembling
a face on the left over the
upside-down version on the
right. (b) When the complex
drawing of a face on the left
and the equally complex,
scrambled version on the right
are moved across newborns'
visual field, they follow the
face longer. But if the two
stimuli are stationary, infants
show no preference for the
face until 2 to 3 months of
age. (From Johnson, 1999;
Mondloch et al., 1999.)

attractive ones—a preference that may be the origin of the widespread
social bias favoring physically attractive people (Slater et al., 2000).

Some researchers claim that these behaviors reflect a built-in capacity to
orient toward members of one's own species, just as many newborn animals
do (Johnson, 2001a; Slater & Quinn, 2001). In support of this view, the
upright face preference occurs only when newborns view stimuli in the
periphery of their visual field—an area of the retina governed by primitive
brain centers (Cassia, Simion, & Umiltá, 2001). Others refute the claim that
newborns have a special sensitivity to the facial pattern. Instead, they assert,
newborns prefer any stimulus in which the most salient elements are
arranged horizontally in the upper part of a pattern—like the "eyes" in
Figure 4.17a. Indeed, newborns do prefer nonfacial patterns with these characteristics over other nonfacial arrangements (Simion et al., 2001; Turati,
2004). Possibly, however, a bias favoring the facial pattern promotes such
preferences. Still other researchers argue that newborns are exposed to faces
more often than to other stimuli—early experiences that could quickly
"wire" the brain to detect faces and prefer attractive ones (Nelson, 2001).

Although newborns respond to a general, facelike structure, they cannot discriminate a complex, static image of the human face from other,
equally complex configurations (see Figure 4.17b). Nevertheless, from
repeated exposures to their mother's face, they quickly learn to prefer her
face to that of an unfamiliar woman, although they are sensitive only to its
broad outlines, not its fine-grained features. Babies quickly apply their tendency to search for pattern to face perception. Around 2 months, when they can scan an entire
stimulus and combine its elements into an organized whole, they recognize and prefer their
mothers' facial features (Bartrip, Morton, & de Schonen, 2001). And they prefer a drawing of
the human face to other stimulus arrangements (Dannemiller & Stephens, 1988).

Around 3 months, infants make fine distinctions between the features of different faces.
For example, they can tell the difference between the photos of two strangers, even when the
faces are moderately similar (Morton, 1993). At 5 months—and strengthening over the second half of the first year—infants perceive emotional expressions as meaningful wholes. They
treat positive faces (happy or surprised) as different from negative ones (sad or fearful), even
when the expressions are demonstrated in varying ways by different models (Bornstein &
Arterberry, 2003; Ludemann, 1991).

Extensive face-to-face interaction between infants and their caregivers undoubtedly contributes to the refinement of face perception. As we will see in Chapter 10, babies' developing
sensitivity to the human face supports their earliest social relationships and helps regulate
exploration of the environment in adaptive ways.

• **OBJECT PERCEPTION** • Research on pattern perception involves only two-dimensional
stimuli, but our environment is made up of stable, three-dimensional objects. Do young
infants perceive a world of independently existing objects—knowledge essential for distinguishing the self, other people, and things?

▶ *Size and Shape Constancy.* As we move around the environment, the images objects cast
on our retina constantly change in size and shape. To perceive objects as stable and unchanging, we must translate these varying retinal images into a single representation.

Size constancy—perception of an object's size as stable, despite changes in the size of its
retinal image—is evident in the first week of life. To test for it, researchers capitalized on the
habituation response, using procedures described and illustrated in Figure 4.18. Perception of
an object's shape as stable, despite changes in the shape projected on the retina, is called **shape
constancy.** Habituation research reveals that it, too, is present within the first week of life, long
before babies can actively rotate objects with their hands and view them from different angles
(Slater & Johnson, 1999).

In sum, both size and shape constancy appear to be built-in capacities that help babies
detect a coherent world of objects. Yet they provide only a partial picture of young infants'
object perception.

(a) Habituation Phase

(b) Test Phase

Figure 4.18

Testing newborns for size constancy. (a) Infants are habituated to a small black-and-white cube at varying distances from the eye. In this way, researchers hope to desensitize them to changes in the cube's retinal image size and direct their attention to its actual size. (b) Next, the small cube and a new, large cube are presented together, but at different distances so they cast retinal images of the same size. All babies recover to (look longer at) the novel, large cube, indicating that they distinguish objects on the basis of actual size, not retinal image size. (Adapted from Slater, 2001.)

▶ *Perception of Object Identity.* As adults, we distinguish an object from its surroundings by looking for a regular shape and uniform texture and color. Very young infants, however, are not sensitive to these indictors of an object's boundaries. At first, they rely heavily on motion and spatial arrangement to identify objects (Jusczyk et al., 1999; Spelke & Hermer, 1996). When two objects are touching and either move in unison or stand still, babies younger than 4 months cannot distinguish between them. Infants, as we saw earlier in this chapter, are fascinated by moving objects. As they observe objects' motions, they pick up additional information about objects' boundaries, such as shape, color, and texture.

For example, as Figure 4.19 reveals, around 2 months of age, babies first realize that a moving rod whose center is hidden behind a box is a complete rod rather than two rod pieces. Motion, a textured background, alignment of the top and bottom of the rod, and a small box (so most of the rod is visible) are necessary for young infants to infer object unity. They cannot do so without all these cues to heighten the distinction between objects in the display

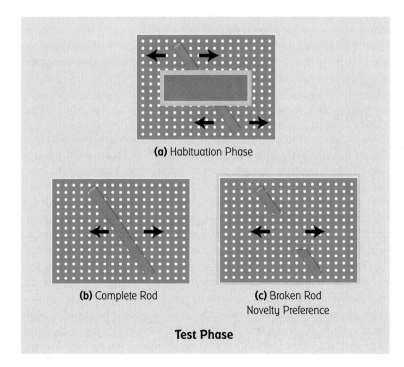

(a) Habituation Phase

(b) Complete Rod

(c) Broken Rod
Novelty Preference

Test Phase

Figure 4.19

Testing infants' ability to perceive object unity. (a) Infants are habituated to a rod moving back and forth behind a box against a textured background. Next, they are shown two test displays in alternation: (b) a complete rod, and (c) a broken rod with a gap corresponding to the location of the box. Each stimulus is moved back and forth against the textured background, in the same way as the habituation stimulus. Infants 2 months of age and older typically recover to (look longer at) the broken rod than the complete rod. Their novelty preference suggests that they perceive the rod behind the box in the first display as a single unit. (Adapted from Johnson, 1997.)

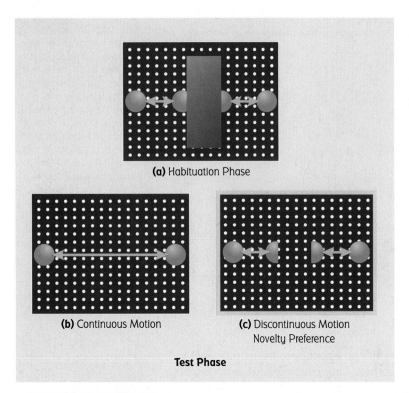

(a) Habituation Phase

(b) Continuous Motion

(c) Discontinuous Motion
Novelty Preference

Test Phase

▲ Figure 4.20

Testing infants' ability to perceive an object's path of movement. (a) Infants are habituated to a ball moving back and forth behind a screen. Next, they are shown two test displays in alternation: (b) a ball undergoing continuous back-and-forth motion, with its full trajectory visible, and (c) a ball undergoing discontinuous motion, out of and back into view just as in the habituation stimulus, but without moving behind a visible screen. As long as the ball is out of sight only briefly in the habituation display, 4-month-olds typically recover to (look longer at) the discontinuous motion than the continuous motion. Their novelty preference suggests that they perceive the motion of the ball behind the screen in the first display as continuous.

(From S P. Johnson et al., 2003, "Infants' Perception of Object Trajectories," *Child Development, 74,* pp. 98, 101. © The Society for Research in Child Development, Inc. Reprinted by permission.)

(Johnson, 2004; Johnson et al., 2002). As infants become familiar with many objects and can integrate each object's diverse features into a unified whole, they rely more on shape, color, and texture and less on motion (Cohen & Cashon, 2001). Babies as young as $4\frac{1}{2}$ months can discriminate two touching objects on the basis of their features in simple, easy-to-process situations. And prior exposure to one of the test objects enhances $4\frac{1}{2}$-month-olds' ability to discern the boundary between two touching objects—a finding that highlights the role of experience (Needham, 2001; Dueker, Modi, & Needham, 2003). In the second half of the first year, the capacity to distinguish objects on the basis of their features extends to increasingly complex displays of objects.

In everyday life, objects frequently move in and out of sight. In addition to discerning objects by their features, infants must keep track of their disappearance and reappearance to perceive their identity. To find out if infants can register an object's path of movement without seeing the entire path, researchers habituated babies to a ball moving back and forth behind a screen (see Figure 4.20). Recovery to test events revealed that as long as the ball was out of view only briefly, 4-month-olds (but not younger infants) perceived the ball's path as continuous rather than broken (Johnson et al., 2003). Once again, experience—in particular, watching objects move in out of view—contributes to perception of a moving object's path (Johnson, Amso, & Slemmer, 2003). Between 4 and 5 months, infants can monitor increasingly intricate paths of objects. As indicated by their anticipatory eye movements (looking ahead to where they expect an object to appear from behind a barrier), 5-month-olds even keep track of an object that travels on a curvilinear course at varying speeds (Rosander & von Hofsten, 2004).

Notice that perception of *object unity* in the rod-and-box task (Figure 4.19) is mastered before perception of the *continuity of an object's path of movement* (Figure 4.20). Tracking a disappearing and reappearing object seems to pose extra challenges. We will revisit these attainments when we take up infants' mastery of object permanence (understanding that an object still exists when hidden from view) in Chapter 6.

The Milestones table on the following page provides an overview of the vast changes that take place in visual perception during the first year. Up to this point, we have considered the sensory systems one by one. Now let's examine their coordination.

Intermodal Perception

We live in a world that provides us with a rich, continuous flux of *intermodal stimulation*—simultaneous input from more than one modality, or sensory system. In **intermodal perception,** we make sense of these running streams of light, sound, tactile, odor, and taste information by perceiving unitary objects and events. We know, for example, that the shape of an object is the same whether we see it or touch it, that lip movements are closely coordinated with the sound of a voice, that breaking a glass causes a sharp, crashing sound, and that the patter of footsteps signals the approach of a person. How do infants, who begin life with no prior knowledge to guide them, figure out which strands of sensory stimulation go together, and which do not?

Recall that in the first few days of life, babies turn in the general direction of a sound and reach for objects in a primitive way. These behaviors suggest that infants expect sight, sound, touch to go together. Research reveals that babies perceive input from different sensory systems in a unified way by detecting **amodal sensory properties,** information that is not specific to a single modality but that overlaps two or more sensory systems, such as rate, rhythm, duration, intensity, and (for vision and hearing) temporal synchrony. Consider the sight and sound

MILESTONES

VISUAL DEVELOPMENT IN INFANCY

Age	Acuity, Color Perception, Focusing, and Exploration	Depth Perception	Pattern Perception	Object Perception
Birth–1 month	Visual acuity is 20/600 Scans the visual field and tracks moving objects	Responds to kinetic depth cues	Prefers large, bold patterns Scans the edges of a static pattern and focuses on single features Prefers simple, facelike stimuli Prefers attractive faces to less attractive ones	Displays size and shape constancy
2–3 months	Has adultlike focusing ability Perceives colors across entire spectrum Scans more thoroughly and systematically	Responds to binocular depth cues	Prefers patterns with finer details Thoroughly scans internal pattern features Begins to perceive overall pattern structure Prefers complex, static image of a face Recognizes mother's face and distinguishes features of different faces	Uses motion and spatial arrangement to identify objects
4–5 months		Sensitivity to binocular depth cues improves	Detects subjective boundaries in patterns	Uses shape, color, and texture to identify objects Perceives an object's path of movement without seeing the entire path
6–9 months	Visual acuity improves to near 20/20 Scans visual field and tracks moving objects more efficiently	Responds to pictorial depth cues Avoids crawling over deep side of visual cliff	Perceives patterns (such as human walking movements and facial expressions of emotion) as meaningful wholes	
10-12 months			Can extract pattern information in the absence of a full image (from a moving light or partial picture)	

Note: These milestones represent overall age trends. Individual differences exist in the precise age at which each milestone is attained.

Photos: (top) © Laura Dwight/PhotoEdit; (three other photos) © Laura Dwight Photography

of a bouncing ball or the face and voice of a speaking person. In each event, visual and auditory information are conveyed simultaneously and with the same rate, rhythm, duration, and intensity.

Early on, both animal and human babies are impressive perceivers of amodal properties (Lickliter & Bahrick, 2000). In one study, bobwhite quail embryos were exposed to a light flashing in synchrony with the rate and rhythm of a typical maternal call during the 24 hours before they hatched. After birth, the intermodally stimulated chicks developed a preference for the familiar call over a novel call four times faster than chicks exposed to only the call or the

◉ Babies quickly learn associations between the sights, sounds, and feel of toys, as this 3-month-old is doing, assisted by her mother. Within the first half-year, infants master a remarkable range of intermodal relationships.
© Laura Dwight Photography

flashing light. Clearly, the embryos responded to amodal information, which influenced their later learning (Lickliter, Bahrick, & Honeycutt, 2002). Similarly, human newborns are highly sensitive to amodal properties in audiovisual stimulation. For example, after just one exposure, they quickly learn associations between the sights and sound of toys, such as a rhythmically jangling rattle (Morrongiello, Fenwick, & Chance, 1998).

Within the first half-year, infants master a remarkable range of intermodal relationships. For example, they match the motions of a wide array of objects with their appropriate sounds. In one such study, 3- and 4-month-olds watched two films side by side, one with two blocks banging and the other with two sponges being squashed together. At the same time, the sound track for only one of the films (either a sharp, banging noise or a soft, squishing noise) could be heard. Infants looked at the film that went with the sound track (Bahrick, 1983). In similar research, infants matched faces with voices on the basis of lip–voice synchrony, emotional expression, and even age and gender of the speaker (Bahrick, Netto, & Hernandez-Reif, 1998; Walker-Andrews, 1997). Furthermore, recall that 5- to 6-month olds will reach for an object in a room that has been darkened during their reach—a behavior that illustrates the union of sight and touch. They also will reach for a sounding object in the dark, displaying union of sound and touch (Clifton et al., 1994).

In addition to detecting amodal properties, babies gradually learn many intermodal associations that are arbitrary, such as the relation between a person's face and the particular sound of his or her voice or between the appearance of an object and its verbal label. The detection of amodal relations precedes and seems to provide a basis for differentiation of these more specific intermodal matches (Bahrick, 2001).

Indeed, young infants' intermodal sensitivity is crucial for perceptual development. In the early months, infants detect amodal properties only when exposed to intermodal stimulation. For example, 3-month-olds discriminated a change in the rhythm of a toy hammer tapping from an audiovisual display, but not from a purely auditory presentation (just hearing the tapping) or a purely visual presentation (just seeing the hammer move) (Bahrick, Flom, & Lickliter, 2003). Intermodal stimulation makes amodal properties (such as rhythm) stand out. As a result, inexperienced perceivers notice a meaningful unitary event (the hammer's intricate tapping) and are not diverted to momentarily irrelevant aspects of the situation, such as the hammer's color or orientation. In contrast, young infants notice changes in purely visual properties, such as color, orientation, and pattern, only when exposed to purely visual information (Bahrick, Lickliter, & Flom, 2004). With experience, perceptual capacities become more flexible. In the second half of the first year, infants can discriminate amodal properties in both intermodal and unimodal (sights or sounds alone) stimulation. But early on, when much input is unfamiliar and confusing, intermodal stimulation helps babies selectively attend to and make sense of their surroundings.

In addition to easing infants' perception of the physical world, intermodal stimulation facilitates social and language processing, as evidence reviewed earlier in this chapter illustrates. Recall that an adult's gentle touch induces infants to attend to her face (see page 148). And as infants gaze at an adult's face, they initially require both vocal and visual input to distinguish positive from negative emotional expressions. Furthermore, in their earliest efforts to make sense of language, infants profit from temporal synchrony between a speech sound and the motion of an object (page 152).

In sum, intermodal perception is a fundamental ability that fosters all aspects of psychological development. In animals, the intermodal stimulation arising out of early social interaction—for example, the mother's simultaneous touch, smell, vocalizations, and gestures—is vital for normal development of both intermodal and unimodal perceptual responsiveness (Lickliter & Bahrick, 2000). The same is likely to be true for human infants.

Understanding Perceptual Development

Now that we have reviewed the development of infant perceptual capacities, how can we put together this diverse array of amazing achievements? Widely accepted answers come from the work of Eleanor and James Gibson. According to the Gibsons' **differentiation theory,** infants actively search for **invariant features** of the environment—those that remain stable—in a constantly changing perceptual world. For example, in pattern perception, at first babies are confronted with a confusing mass of stimulation. Very quickly, however, they search for features that stand out along the border of a stimulus and orient toward images that crudely represent a face. Soon they explore internal features and notice *stable relationships* between those features. As a result, they detect patterns, such as complex designs and faces. The development of intermodal perception also reflects this principle. Babies seek out invariant relationships— for example, amodal properties, such as rhythm—in concurrent sights and sounds. Gradually, they perceive more detailed intermodal associations. And, eventually, they can distinguish amodal properties in unimodal stimulation.

The Gibsons use the word *differentiation* (which means analyzing or breaking down) to describe their theory because, over time, the baby detects finer and finer invariant features among stimuli. In addition to pattern perception and intermodal perception, differentiation applies to depth and object perception. Recall how, in each, sensitivity to motion precedes detection of detailed stationary cues. So one way of understanding perceptual development is to think of it as a built-in tendency to search for order and consistency, a capacity that becomes increasingly fine-tuned with age (Gibson, 1970; Gibson, 1979).

Acting on the environment is vital in perceptual differentiation. According to the Gibsons, perception is guided by discovery of **affordances**—the action possibilities that a situation offers an organism with certain motor capabilities (Gibson, 2000, 2003). By moving about and exploring the environment, babies figure out which objects can be grasped, squeezed, bounced, or stroked and whether a surface is safe to cross or presents the possibility of falling. Sensitivity to these affordances makes our actions future oriented and largely successful rather than reactive and blundering. Consequently, we spend far less time correcting ineffective actions than we otherwise would.

To illustrate, let's consider how infants' changing capabilities for independent movement affect their perception. When babies crawl, and again when they walk, they gradually realize that a steeply sloping surface *affords the possibility* of falling (see Figure 4.21). With added weeks of practicing each skill, they hesitate to crawl or walk down a risky incline. Experience in trying to keep their balance on various surfaces seems to make crawlers and walkers more aware of the consequences of their movements. Crawlers come to detect when surface slant places so

◀ **Figure 4.21**

Acting on the environment plays a major role in perceptual differentiation. Crawling and walking change the way babies perceive a steeply sloping surface. The newly crawling infant on the left plunges headlong down a steeply sloping surface. He has not yet learned that it affords the possibility of falling. The toddler on the right, who has been walking for more than a month, approaches the slope cautiously. Experience in trying to remain upright but frequently tumbling over has made him more aware of the consequences of his movements. He perceives the incline differently than he did at a younger age.

(Photos courtesy of Karen Adolph, Emory Unitversity)

much body weight on their arms that they will fall forward, and walkers come to sense when an incline shifts body weight so their legs and feet can no longer hold them upright (Adolph, 1997; Adolph & Eppler, 1998, 1999). Each skill leads infants to perceive surfaces in new ways that guide their movements. As a result, they act more competently. Can you think of other links between motor milestones and perceptual development described in this chapter?

At this point, it is only fair to note that some researchers believe that babies do more than make sense of experience by searching for invariant features and discovering affordances. They also *impose meaning* on what they perceive, constructing categories of objects and events in the surrounding environment. We have seen the glimmerings of this *cognitive* point of view in this chapter. For example, older babies *interpret* a familiar face as a source of pleasure and affection and a pattern of blinking lights as a moving human being. We will save our discussion of infant cognition for later chapters, acknowledging that this cognitive perspective also has merit in understanding the achievements of infancy. In fact, many researchers combine these two positions, regarding infant development as proceeding from a perceptual to a cognitive emphasis over the first year of life.

Ask Yourself

REVIEW	Using examples, explain why intermodal stimulation is vital for all aspects of infant psychological development.
APPLY	After several weeks of crawling, Ben learned to avoid going headfirst down a steep incline. Now he has started to walk. Can his mother trust him not to try walking down the steep surface? Explain, using the concept of affordances.
CONNECT	According to differentiation theory, perceptual development reflects infants' active search for invariant features. Provide examples from research on hearing, pattern perception, and intermodal perception.
REFLECT	Are young infants more competent than you thought they were before you read this chapter? Cite examples of capacities that most surprised you.

Early Deprivation and Enrichment: Is Infancy a Sensitive Period of Development?

Throughout this chapter, we have discussed how a variety of early experiences affect the development of motor and perceptual skills. In view of the findings already reported, it is not surprising that many investigations have found that stimulating physical surroundings and warm caregiving that is responsive to infants' self-initiated efforts promote active exploration of the environment and earlier attainment of developmental milestones (see, for example, Belsky & Fearon, 2002; Bendersky & Lewis, 1994).

The powerful effect of early experience is dramatically apparent in infants who lack the rich, varied stimulation of normal homes. Babies reared in severely deprived family situations or in institutions remain substantially below average in physical and psychological development and display emotional and behavior problems throughout childhood (Johnson, 2000). These findings indicate that early experience has a profound impact, but they do not tell us whether infancy is a *sensitive period*. That is, if babies do not experience appropriate stimulation of their senses in the first year or two of life, can they ever fully recover? This question is controversial. Recall from Chapter 1 that some theorists argue that early experience leaves a lasting imprint on the child's competence. Others believe that most developmental delays resulting from events in the first few years of life can be overcome.

The existence of sensitive periods has been amply demonstrated in studies of animals exposed to extreme forms of sensory deprivation. For example, rich and varied visual experiences must occur during a specific time for the visual centers of a kitten's brain to develop normally. If a month-old kitten is deprived of light for as brief a time as 3 or 4 days, these areas of the brain degenerate. If the kitten is kept in the dark during the fourth week of life and beyond, the damage is severe and permanent (Crair, Gillespie, & Stryker, 1998). Furthermore, the general quality of the early environment affects overall brain growth. When animals reared from birth in physically and socially stimulating surroundings are compared with those reared in isolation, the brains of the stimulated animals are larger (Greenough & Black, 1992).

For ethical reasons, we cannot deliberately deprive some infants of normal rearing experiences and observe the impact on their brains and competencies. The best available test of whether infancy is a sensitive period comes from natural experiments, in which children were victims of deprived early environments but were later exposed to stimulating, sensitive care. If the sensitive period hypothesis is correct, then the effects of deprivation during infancy should persist, even when children are moved into enriched settings.

Research on children from Eastern European orphanages consistently shows that the earlier infants are removed from deprived rearing conditions, the greater their catch-up in development. In one study, Michael Rutter and his colleagues (1998, 2004; O'Connor et al., 2000) followed the progress of a large sample of children transferred between birth and 3½ years from Romanian orphanages to adoptive families in Great Britain. On arrival, most were malnourished, prone to infection, and impaired in all domains of development. By the preschool years, catch-up in height and weight was dramatic. Although cognitive catch-up was also impressive, it was not as great for children adopted after 6 months of age. These adoptees were far more likely to display cognitive impairment and behavior problems at 6 years than were Romanian or British children adopted in the first 6 months of life. The longer infants were institutionalized, the more severe and persistent their deficits; those adopted after 2 years of age were profoundly affected (see Figure 4.22). Finally, even among babies who arrived in Great Britain adequately nourished, a major correlate of both time spent in the institution and poor cognitive functioning was below-average head size. These findings suggest that early lack of stimulation damaged the brain.

An investigation of Romanian babies adopted into Canada yielded findings consistent with the British study: Children who spent 2 or more years in institutions showed severe cognitive, emotional, and social deficits that were still apparent at age 9 (Ames & Chisholm, 2001; MacLean, 2003). In sum, exposing babies to deprived institutional care for 2 years seems to undermine permanently all aspects of their psychological development.

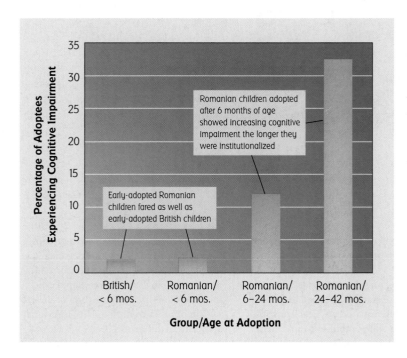

◀ **Figure 4.22**

Relationship of age at adoption to incidence of cognitive impairment at age 6 years among British and Romanian adoptees. Children transferred from Romanian orphanages to British adoptive homes in the first 6 months of life fared as well as British early-adopted children, suggesting that they had fully recovered from extreme early deprivation. Romanian children adopted after 6 months of age showed an increasing incidence of cognitive impairment with time spent institutionalized. Those adopted after 2 years of age were profoundly affected; 30 percent scored below 80 on an intelligence test. (Adapted from Rutter et al., 2004.)

This child has spent her life in an orphanage in Tula, Russia, with little adult contact and little stimulation. The longer she remains in this barren environment, the more she will withdraw and wither and display permanent impairments in all domains of development.

© Peter Turnley/CORBIS

Among institutionalized infants, abnormal development in one domain often impedes progress in others. For example, adoptive parents of children from orphanages often report visual impairments. A frequent problem is *strabismus* (commonly known as "crossed eyes"), in which the eyes, because of muscle weakness, do not converge on the same point in space. Untreated infants, for whom strabismus persists longer than a few months, show abnormalities in the brain's visual structures and permanent deficits in visual acuity, depth perception, tracking of moving objects, and perception of the spatial layout of the environment (Tychsen, 2001). Also, the bland, colorless rooms where orphanage infants spend their days, rarely touched or spoken to, lead to deficits in intermodal perception (Cermak & Daunhauer, 1997). Children who have trouble integrating information across modalities tend to be overwhelmed by stimulation, reacting to it with disorganized behavior or withdrawal. As a result, motor, cognitive, and social development suffers.

Unfortunately, many infants reared in underprivileged environments—whether homes or institutions—continue to be affected by disadvantaged conditions during their childhood years. As we will see in later chapters, interventions that break this pattern with warm, stimulating caregiver interaction and environmental enrichment have lasting cognitive and social benefits. One of the most important outcomes is that withdrawn, apathetic babies become active, alert beings with the capacity to evoke positive interactions from caregivers and to initiate stimulating play and exploration for themselves.

Finally, in addition to impoverished environments, ones that overwhelm children with expectations beyond their current capacities also undermine development. In recent years, expensive early learning centers have sprung up, in which infants are trained with letter and number flash cards, and slightly older toddlers are given a full curriculum of reading, math, science, art, gym, and more. There is no evidence that these programs yield smarter, better "superbabies" (Hirsh-Pasek & Golinkoff, 2003). Instead, trying to prime infants with stimulation for which they are not ready can cause them to withdraw, threatening their spontaneous interest and pleasure in learning and creating conditions much like those of stimulus deprivation! We will return to this theme when we take up brain development in Chapter 5.

Ask Yourself

REVIEW   Explain why either too much stimulation or too little stimulation for an extended time has adverse effects on infant development.

CONNECT   What implications do findings on children from Eastern European orphanages have for the controversy over the lasting impact of early experiences on development (see Chapter 1, page 9)?

REFLECT   Do you think infancy is a sensitive period? Explain, using research evidence.

Summary

The Organized Newborn

Explain the functions of newborn reflexes, and describe changing states of arousal during infancy, emphasizing sleep and crying.

Reflexes are the newborn baby's most obvious organized patterns of behavior. Some have survival value, others help parents and infants establish gratifying interaction, and still others provide the foundation for voluntary motor skills.

Although newborns alternate frequently between five **states of arousal,** they spend most of their time asleep. Sleep consists of at least two states: **rapid-eye-movement (REM)** and **non-rapid-eye-movement (NREM) sleep.** REM sleep time is greater during the prenatal and newborn periods than at any later age. It provides young infants with stimulation essential for central nervous system development. Rapid eye movements ensure that structures of the eye remain oxygenated during sleep. Individual and cultural differences in sleep–wake patterns are evident in early infancy. Disturbed REM–NREM cycles are a sign of central nervous system abnormalities, which may contribute to **sudden infant death syndrome (SIDS).**

⚙ A crying baby stimulates strong feelings of discomfort in nearby adults. The intensity of the cry and the experiences that led up to it help parents identify what is wrong. Once feeding and diaper changing have been tried, lifting the baby to the shoulder and rocking or walking is the most effective soothing technique. According to ethological research, prompt parental responsiveness to infant crying results in a baby who cries less over time. A shrill, piercing cry is an indicator of central nervous system distress.

Why is neonatal behavioral assessment useful?

⚙ The most widely used instrument for assessing the organized functioning of newborn infants is Brazelton's **Neonatal Behavioral Assessment Scale (NBAS).** It has helped researchers understand individual and cultural differences in newborn behavior. Sometimes it is used to teach parents about their baby's capacities—knowledge that can help parents interact more confidently and sensitively.

Describe infant learning capacities, the conditions under which they occur, and the unique value of each.

⚙ **Classical conditioning** permits infants to recognize which events usually occur together in the everyday world. In this form of learning, a neutral stimulus is paired with an **unconditioned stimulus (UCS)** that produces a reflexive, or **unconditioned, response (UCR).** Once learning has occurred, the neutral stimulus, now called the **conditioned stimulus (CS),** by itself elicits a similar response, called the **conditioned response (CR). Extinction** occurs when the conditional stimulus is presented enough times without the unconditioned stimulus to result in a decline of the conditioned response. Young infants can be classically conditioned when the pairing of a UCS with a CS has survival value.

⚙ **Operant conditioning** helps infants explore and control their surroundings. In addition to food, interesting sights and sounds serve as effective **reinforcers,** increasing the occurrence of a preceding behavior. **Punishment** involves removing a desirable stimulus or presenting an unpleasant one to decrease the occurrence of a response. With age, operant conditioning expands to include a wider range of stimuli and responses. The technique has yielded important information about infant memory—that retention of operant responses increases dramatically over the first year and a half.

⚙ **Habituation** and **recovery** reveal that at birth, babies are attracted to novelty. With age, infants habituate and recover more quickly. Novelty preference (recovery to a novel stimulus) assesses infants' recent memory, whereas familiarity preference (greater responsiveness to a familiar stimulus) assesses infants' remote memory. Habituation research reveals that young infants are especially attracted to motion and that they remember the movements of objects and people for weeks to months. Speed of habituation and recovery in infancy are among the best early predictors of intelligence in childhood and adolescence.

⚙ Newborn infants have a primitive ability to **imitate** the facial expressions and gestures of adults. Some researchers regard newborn imitation as little more than an automatic response to specific stimuli. Others believe that it is a flexible, voluntary capacity that contributes to self- and social awareness and the early parent–infant relationship.

Motor Development in Infancy

Describe the course of gross and fine motor development during the first 2 years, along with factors that influence it.

⚙ Overall, motor development follows the **cephalocaudal** and **proximodistal trends.** But some dramatic exceptions exist; for example, infants reach with their feet before they reach with their hands. According to **dynamic systems theory of motor development,** new motor skills develop as existing skills combine into increasingly complex systems of action. Each new skill is a joint product of central nervous system development, movement possibilities of the body, the goal the child has in mind, and environmental supports for the skill.

⚙ Movement opportunities and a stimulating environment profoundly affect motor development, as shown by research on infants raised in institutions. Cultural values and child-rearing customs also contribute to the emergence and refinement of motor skills.

⚙ During the first year, infants gradually perfect their reaching and grasping. The poorly coordinated **prereaching** of the newborn period eventually drops out. As depth perception and control of body posture and the arms and hands improve, reaching and grasping become more flexible and accurate. Gradually, the clumsy **ulnar grasp** is transformed into a refined **pincer grasp.**

Perceptual Development in Infancy

Describe the newborn baby's senses of touch, taste, smell, and hearing, noting changes during infancy.

⚙ Newborns are highly sensitive to touch and pain. They have a preference for a sweet taste and certain sweet odors; a liking for the salty taste emerges later and probably supports acceptance of solid foods. The taste preferences of young infants can be easily modified. The mother's diet during pregnancy, through its impact on the amniotic fluid, influences newborns' odor preferences. Newborns orient toward the odor of their own mother's amniotic fluid and the lactating breast—responses that help them identify their caregiver and locate an appropriate food source.

⚙ As responsiveness to **optical flow** reveals, newborn babies have a sense of balance that is fundamental to everything they learn through exploration. Postural adjustments take place unconsciously and improve with experience and motor control. By the end of the first year, infants anticipate loss of balance, thereby preventing falls.

⚙ Newborns can distinguish almost all speech sounds. They are especially responsive to slow, clear, high-pitched expressive voices, to their own mother's voice, and to speech in their native language. Over the first year, babies organize sounds into more complex patterns. By the middle of the first year, they become more sensitive to the sounds of their own language.

⊚ Soon babies use their remarkable ability to statistically analyze the speech stream to detect meaningful speech units. They also attend to regularities in word sequences, detecting simple word-order rules. Multi-sensory communication—mothers' tendency to label an object while demonstrating—supports infants' language learning.

Describe the development of vision in infancy, placing special emphasis on depth, pattern, and object perception.

⊚ Vision is the least mature of the new-born baby's senses. As the eye and visual centers in the brain develop during the first few months, focusing ability, **visual acuity,** scanning, tracking, and color perception improve rapidly. And as infants build an organized perceptual world, they scan more thoroughly and systematically.

⊚ Research on depth perception reveals that responsiveness to **kinetic depth cues** appears by the end of the first month, followed by sensitivity to **binocular depth cues** between 2 and 3 months. Perception of **pictorial depth cues** emerges last, around 7 months of age.

⊚ Experience in crawling facilitates coordination of action with depth information, although babies must learn to avoid drop-offs, such as the deep side of the **visual cliff,** for each body posture. Crawling promotes other aspects of three-dimensional understanding and results in a new level of brain organization.

⊚ **Contrast sensitivity** accounts for infants' early pattern preferences. At first, babies stare at single, high-contrast features and often limit themselves to the edges of a static pattern. At 2 to 3 months, they explore a pattern's internal features and combine its elements into a unified whole. In the second

half of the first year, they discriminate increasingly complex, meaningful patterns. By 12 months, they extract meaningful patterns from very little information, such as an incomplete drawing with as much as two-thirds missing.

⊚ Newborns prefer to look at and track simple, facelike stimuli. However, researchers disagree on whether they have an innate tendency to orient toward human faces. At 2 months, infants recognize and prefer their mothers' facial features, and they prefer a drawing of the human face to other stimulus arrangements. By 3 months, infants make fine distinctions between the features of different faces; at 5 months, and strengthening over the second half of the first year, babies perceive emotional expressions as organized, meaningful wholes.

⊚ At birth, **size** and **shape constancy** assist infants in building a coherent world of three-dimensional objects. Initially, infants depend on motion and spatial arrangement to identify objects. After 4 months, they rely increasingly on other features, such as distinct color, shape, and texture. At about this time, infants begin to register the continuous path of movement of an object that moves in and out of sight.

© CHRISTINA KENNEDY/PHOTOEDIT

Describe infants' capacity for intermodal perception, and explain differentiation theory of perceptual development.

⊚ Infants have a remarkable capacity to engage in **intermodal perception.** Newborn babies are highly sensitive to **amodal sensory properties** (such as rate, rhythm, duration, intensity, and temporary synchrony), which enable them to perceive input from different sensory systems in a unified way. Babies quickly master many intermodal associations, often after just one exposure to a new situation. Detection of amodal relations precedes and may provide a basis for detecting other intermodal matches.

⊚ Intermodal stimulation helps young babies selectively attend to meaningful unitary events. It is a fundamental ability that fosters all aspects of psychological development, including perception of the physical world and social and language processing.

⊚ According to **differentiation theory,** perceptual development is a matter of detecting increasingly fine-grained, **invariant features** in a constantly changing perceptual world. Perception is guided by discovery of **affordances**—the action possibilities a situation offers the individual.

Early Deprivation and Enrichment: Is Infancy a Sensitive Period of Development?

Explain how research on early deprivation and enrichment sheds light on the question of whether infancy is a sensitive period of development.

⊚ Natural experiments on children from Eastern European orphanages placed in adoptive families at various ages support the view that infancy is a sensitive period. The later children are removed from deprived rearing conditions, the less favorably they develop. When children spend the first 2 years or more in unstimulating institutions, they display severe and persistent impairments in all domains of development. Environments that overwhelm infants with stimulation beyond their current capacities also undermine development.

◎ Important Terms and Concepts

affordances (p. 163)
amodal sensory properties (p. 160)
binocular depth cues (p. 154)
cephalocaudal trend (p. 143)
classical conditioning (p. 135)
conditioned response (CR) (p. 136)
conditioned stimulus (CS) (p. 136)
contrast sensitivity (p. 155)
differentiation theory (p. 163)
dynamic systems theory of motor
    development (p. 144)
extinction (p. 136)
habituation (p. 138)
imitation (p. 141)

intermodal perception (p. 160)
invariant features (p. 163)
kinetic depth cues (p. 154)
Neonatal Behavioral Assessment Scale
    (NBAS) (p. 134)
non-rapid-eye-movement (NREM) sleep
    (p. 130)
operant conditioning (p. 136)
optical flow (p. 150)
pictorial depth cues (p. 154)
pincer grasp (p. 147)
prereaching (p. 146)
proximodistal trend (p. 143)
punishment (p. 137)

rapid-eye-movement (REM) sleep (p. 130)
recovery (p. 138)
reflex (p. 126)
reinforcer (p. 137)
shape constancy (p. 158)
size constancy (p. 158)
states of arousal (p. 128)
sudden infant death syndrome (SIDS)
    (p. 132)
ulnar grasp (p. 147)
unconditioned response (UCR) (p. 135)
unconditioned stimulus (UCS) (p. 135)
visual acuity (p. 152)
visual cliff (p. 154)

"Sweetness"
Viraya Jeayee
Age 12, Thailand

Like the flowers in a field, young children grow and blossom, experiencing joy in their increasingly able bodies. Unlike flowers, however, children undergo a prolonged period of physical growth, granting them time to acquire the knowledge and skills they need for life in a complex social world.

Physical Growth

On Sabrina's eleventh birthday, her friend Joyce gave her a surprise party, but Sabrina seemed somber during the celebration. Although Sabrina and Joyce had been close friends since third grade, their relationship was faltering. Sabrina was a head taller and some 20 pounds heavier than most girls in her sixth-grade class. Her breasts were well developed, her hips and thighs had broadened, and she had begun to menstruate. In contrast, Joyce still had the short, lean, flat-chested body of a school-age child. Ducking into the bathroom while the other girls put candles on the cake, Sabrina looked herself over in the mirror and whispered, "Gosh, I feel so big and heavy." At church youth group on Sundays, Sabrina broke away from Joyce and spent time with the eighth-grade girls, around whom she didn't feel so awkward.

Once a month, parents gathered at Sabrina's and Joyce's school for discussions about child-rearing concerns. Sabrina's parents, Franca and Antonio, attended whenever they could. "How you know they are becoming teenagers is this," volunteered Antonio. "The bedroom door is closed, and they want to be alone. Also, they contradict and disagree. I say something to Sabrina, and the next moment she is arguing with me."

"All our four children were early developers," Franca added. "The three boys, too, were tall by age 12 or 13, but it was easier for them—it made them feel big and important. Sabrina is moody, she doesn't want to be with her old friends, and she thinks about boys instead of her studies. As a little girl, she was skinny, but now she says she is too fat, and she wants to diet. I try to be patient with her," reflected Franca sympathetically.

During the first two decades of life, the human body changes continuously and dramatically. The average individual's height multiplies more than threefold, and weight increases as much as fifteen- to twenty-fold. The top-heavy, chubby infant, whose head represents a quarter of the body's total length, gradually becomes the better-proportioned child and eventually the taller, broader, more muscular teenager. This chapter traces the course of human growth, along with biological and environmental factors that regulate and control it.

As Sabrina's behavior indicates, physical and psychological development are closely linked. But just how the child's transforming body is related to cognitive, emotional, and social changes has puzzled philosophers and scientists for centuries. In particular, they have pondered this question with respect to *puberty*. Ask several parents of young children what they expect their sons and daughters to be like as teenagers, and you may get answers like these: "Rebellious and reckless," "Full of rages and tempers" (Buchanan & Holmbeck, 1998).

This widespread view dates back to eighteenth-century philosopher Jean-Jacques Rousseau (see Chapter 1), who believed that a natural outgrowth of the biological upheaval of puberty was heightened emotionality, conflict, and defiance of adults. In the twentieth century, major theorists picked up this perspective. The most influential was G. Stanley Hall, who described adolescence as a cascade of instinctual passions, a phase of growth so turbulent that it resembled the period in which human beings evolved from savages into civilized beings.

Were Rousseau and Hall correct in this image of adolescence as a period of biologically engendered storm and stress? Or do social and cultural factors combine with biology to influence psychological development? In our discussion, we will see what contemporary research says about this issue.

The Course of Physical Growth

Compared with other animals, primates (including humans) experience a prolonged period of physical growth. Among mice and rats, only a few weeks—about 2 percent of the lifespan—intervene between birth and puberty. By contrast, in chimpanzees, which are closest to humans in the evolutionary hierarchy, growth is extended to about 7 years, or 16 percent of the lifespan. Physical immaturity is even more exaggerated in humans, who devote about 20 percent of their total years to growing. This prolonged physical immaturity has clear adaptive value: By ensuring that children remain dependent on adults, it gives them added time to acquire the knowledge and skills essential for life in a complex social world.

Changes in Body Size

The most obvious signs of physical growth are changes in the overall size of the child's body. During infancy, these changes are rapid—faster than at any other time after birth. By the end of the first year, a typical infant's height is 50 percent greater than it was at birth, and by 2 years, it is 75 percent greater. Weight shows similar dramatic gains. By 5 months of age, birth weight has doubled, at 1 year it has tripled, and at 2 years it has quadrupled. If children kept growing at the rate they do during the early months of life, by age 10 they would be 10 feet tall and weigh over 200 pounds! Fortunately, growth slows in early and middle childhood. Children add about 2 to 3 inches in height and 5 pounds in weight each year. Then, puberty brings a sharp acceleration. On average, adolescents gain nearly 10 inches in height and about 40 pounds in weight.

Two types of growth curves are used to track overall changes in body size. The first, shown in Figure 5.1a, is a **distance curve,** which plots the average size of a sample of children at each age. It indicates typical yearly progress toward maturity. The figure shows gains in height;

▼ **Figure 5.1**

Distance and velocity curves for height. (a) The *distance curve* plots average size at each age and shows typical yearly progress toward maturity. (b) The *velocity curve* plots average amount of growth at each yearly interval and reveals the timing of growth spurts. The curves are based on cross-sectional height measurements taken on thousands of U.S. children. Canada does not have a system for collecting nationally representative growth information and commonly relies on the U.S. norms. (Dietitians of Canada et al., 2004; U.S. Department of Health and Human Services, 2000.)

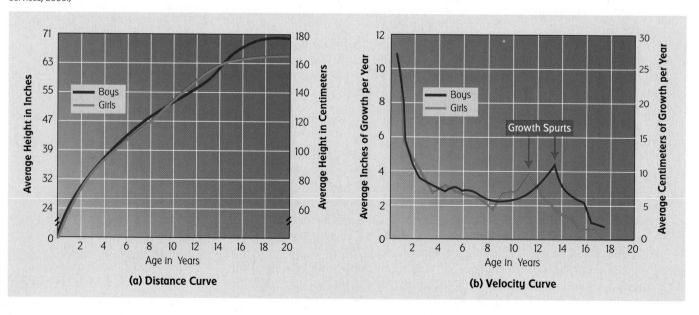

(a) Distance Curve   (b) Velocity Curve

gains in weight follow a similar trend. Notice how during infancy and childhood the two sexes are similar, with the typical girl just slightly shorter (and lighter) than the typical boy. Around age 10 to 11, the typical North American and European girl becomes taller (and heavier) for a time because her pubertal growth spurt takes place 2 years earlier than the boy's. But this advantage is short-lived (Bogin, 2001). At age 14, she is surpassed by the typical boy, whose growth spurt has started, whereas hers is almost finished. Growth in height is complete for most North American and European girls by age 16, for boys by age 17½.

A second type of growth curve is the **velocity curve,** depicted in Figure 5.1b. It plots the average amount of growth at each yearly interval. As a result, it reveals the exact timing of growth spurts. Note the rapid but decelerating growth in infancy; a slower, constant rate during early and middle childhood; and a sharp increase in early adolescence, followed by a swift decrease as the body approaches its adult size.

Changes in Body Proportions

As the child's overall size increases, parts of the body grow at different rates. Recall from Chapter 3 that during the prenatal period, the head develops first from the primitive embryonic disk, followed by the lower part of the body. After birth, the head and chest continue to have a growth advantage, but the trunk and legs gradually pick up speed. Do you recognize the familiar *cephalocaudal trend,* discussed in Chapter 4 and depicted in Figure 5.2? Physical growth during infancy and childhood also follows the *proximodistal trend,* from the center of the body outward. The head, chest, and trunk grow first, followed by the arms and legs, and finally the hands and feet.

During puberty, growth proceeds in the reverse direction. At first, the hands, legs, and feet accelerate, and then the torso, which accounts for most of the adolescent height gain (Sheehy et al., 1999). This pattern of development helps explain why young adolescents often appear awkward and out of proportion—long-legged, with giant feet and hands.

Although girls' and boys' body proportions are similar in infancy and childhood, large differences appear during adolescence, caused by the action of sex hormones on the skeleton. Boys' shoulders broaden relative to the hips, whereas girls' hips broaden relative to the waist. Of course, boys also end up larger than girls, and their legs are longer in relation to the rest of the body. The major reason is that boys have 2 extra years of preadolescent growth, when the legs are growing the fastest.

Changes in Muscle-Fat Makeup

Body fat (most of which lies just beneath the skin) increases in the last few weeks of prenatal life and continues to do so after birth, reaching a peak at about 9 months of age. This early rise in "baby fat" helps the small infant keep a constant body temperature. During the second

Ⓢ Toddlers and 5-year-olds have very different body shapes. During early childhood, body fat declines, the torso enlarges to better accommodate the internal organs, and the spine straightens. Compared to her younger brother, this girl looks more streamlined. Her body proportions resemble those of an adult.
© Bob Daemmrich/Stock Boston, LLC.

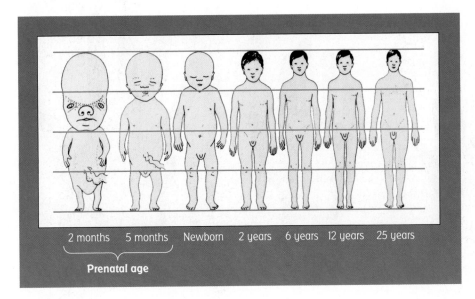

2 months   5 months   Newborn   2 years   6 years   12 years   25 years

Prenatal age

◀ **Figure 5.2**

Changes in body proportions from the early prenatal period to adulthood. This figure illustrates the cephalocaudal trend of physical growth. The head gradually becomes smaller, and the legs longer, in proportion to the rest of the body.

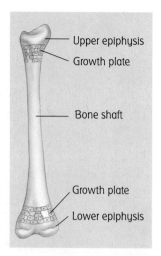

▲ Figure 5.3

Diagram of a long bone showing upper and lower epiphyses. Cartilage cells are produced at the growth plates of the epiphyses and gradually harden into bone.

(From J. M. Tanner, *Foetus into Man* [2nd ed.], Cambridge, MA: Harvard University Press, p. 32. Copyright © 1990 by J. M. Tanner. All rights reserved. Reprinted by permission of the publisher and author.)

year, most toddlers slim down, a trend that continues into middle childhood (Fomon & Nelson, 2002). At birth, girls have slightly more body fat than boys, a difference that persists into the early school years and then magnifies. Around age 8, girls start to add more fat on their arms, legs, and trunk; they continue to do so throughout puberty. In contrast, the arm and leg fat of adolescent boys decreases (Siervogel et al., 2000).

Muscle accumulates slowly throughout infancy and childhood, then rises dramatically at adolescence. Although both sexes gain muscle at puberty, this increase is 150 percent greater in boys, who develop larger skeletal muscles, hearts, and lung capacity (Rogol, Roemmich, & Clark, 2002). Also, the number of red blood cells—and therefore the ability to carry oxygen from the lungs to the muscles—increases in boys but not in girls. Altogether, boys gain far more muscle strength than girls, a difference that contributes to boys' superior athletic performance during the teenage years (Ramos et al., 1998).

Skeletal Growth

Children of the same age differ in *rate* of physical growth. As a result, researchers have devised methods for measuring progress toward physical maturity that are useful for studying the causes and consequences of these individual differences. The best way of estimating a child's physical maturity is to use **skeletal age,** a measure of development of the bones of the body. The embryonic skeleton is first formed out of soft, pliable tissue called *cartilage.* In the sixth week of pregnancy, cartilage cells begin to harden into bone, a gradual process that continues throughout childhood and adolescence (Tanner, Healy, & Cameron, 2001).

Just before birth, special growth centers in the bones, called **epiphyses,** appear at the two extreme ends of each of the long bones of the body (see Figure 5.3). Cartilage cells continue to be produced at the growth plates of these epiphyses, which increase in number throughout childhood and then, as growth continues, get thinner and disappear. Once this has occurred, no further growth in bone length is possible. As Figure 5.4 shows, skeletal age can be estimated by X-raying the bones to see how many epiphyses there are and the extent to which they are fused.

When skeletal ages are examined, African-American children tend to be slightly ahead of Caucasian-American children. In addition, girls are considerably ahead of boys. At birth, the difference between the sexes is about 4 to 6 weeks, a gap that widens over infancy and childhood (Humphrey, 1998). Girls are advanced in development of other organs as well. Their physical maturity may contribute to their greater resistance to harmful environmental influences. Recall from Chapter 3 that girls experience fewer developmental problems than boys, and also have lower infant and childhood mortality rates.

▶ Figure 5.4

X-rays of a girl's hand, showing skeletal maturity at three ages. Notice how, at age 2½, wide gaps exist between the wrist bones and at the ends of the finger and arm bones. By age 6½, these have filled in considerably. At age 14½ (when this girl reached her adult size), the wrist and long bones are completely fused.

(From J. M. Tanner, M. J. R. Healy, & N. Cameron, 2001, *Assessment of Skeletal Maturity and Prediction of Adult Height [TW3 Method],* 3rd ed., Philadelphia: Saunders, p. 86. Reprinted by permission.)

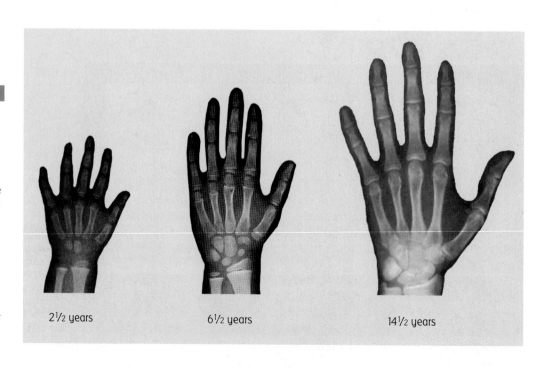

2½ years   6½ years   14½ years

MILESTONES

GROSS MOTOR DEVELOPMENT IN EARLY AND MIDDLE CHILDHOOD

Age		Gross Motor Skills
2–3 years		Walks more rhythmically; hurried walk changes to run. Jumps, hops, throws, and catches with rigid upper body. Pushes riding toy with feet; little steering.
3–4 years		Walks up stairs, alternating feet, and down stairs, leading with one foot. Jumps and hops, flexing upper body. Throws and catches with slight involvement of upper body; still catches by trapping ball against chest. Pedals and steers tricycle.
4–5 years		Walks down stairs, alternating feet; runs more smoothly. Gallops and skips with one foot. Throws ball with increased body rotation and transfer of weight on feet; catches ball with hands. Rides tricycle rapidly; steers smoothly.
5–6 years		Increases running speed to 12 feet per second. Gallops more smoothly; engages in true skipping and sideways stepping. Displays mature, whole-body throwing and catching pattern; increases throwing speed. Rides bicycle with training wheels.
7–12 years		Increases running speed to more than 18 feet per second. Displays continuous, fluid skipping and sideways stepping. Increases vertical jump from 4 to 12 inches and broad jump from 3 to over 5 feet; accurately jumps and hops from square to square. Increases throwing and kicking accuracy, distance, and speed. Involves the whole body in batting a ball; batting increases in speed and accuracy. Dribbling changes from awkward slapping of the ball to continuous, relaxed, even stroking.

Note: These milestones represent overall age trends. Individual differences exist in the precise age at which each milestone is attained.

Sources: Cratty, 1986; Malina & Bouchard, 1991; Newborg, Stock, & Wnek, 1984; Roberton, 1984.

Photos: (top) © Lawrence Migdale/Photo Researchers, Inc.; (top middle) © Tony Freeman/PhotoEdit; (bottom middle) © Bob Daemmrich/The Image Works; (bottom) © David Young Wolff/PhotoEdit

Gains in Gross Motor Skills

Changes in size, proportions, and muscle strength support an explosion of new gross motor skills. As the body becomes more streamlined and less top-heavy, the center of gravity shifts downward, toward the trunk. As a result, balance improves greatly, paving the way for new motor skills involving large muscles.

• ADVANCES IN EARLY AND MIDDLE CHILDHOOD • By age 2, preschoolers' gaits become smooth and rhythmic—secure enough that they soon leave the ground, at first by running and jumping and then, between 3 and 6 years, by hopping, galloping, and skipping. Eventually, upper and lower body skills combine into more effective actions (Getchell & Roberton, 1989). For example, 2- and 3-year-olds throw a ball rigidly, using only the arms. By ages 4 and 5, they involve the shoulders, torso, trunk, and legs in a smooth, flexible motion that makes the ball travel faster and farther.

During the school years, improved balance, strength, agility, and flexibility support refinements in running, jumping, hopping, and ball skills. Children sprint across the playground, engage in intricate patterns of hopscotch, kick and dribble soccer balls, and swing bats at balls pitched by their classmates. Increased body size and muscle at adolescence bring continued motor gains. The Milestones table above summarizes gross motor achievements in early and middle childhood.

Sex Differences in Gross Motor Development

Sex differences in gross motor development are present as early as the preschool years, increase during middle childhood, and are large at adolescence. What underlies this expanding gender gap, and how can we ensure that both boys and girls have opportunities that optimize both skill and enjoyment of athletics?

Early and Middle Childhood

In early childhood, boys are slightly advanced over girls in abilities that emphasize force and power. By age 5, they can broad-jump slightly farther, run slightly faster, and throw a ball about 5 feet farther. During middle childhood, these differences intensify. For example, on average, a 12-year-old boy can throw a ball 43 feet farther than a 12-year-old girl. Boys are also more adept at batting, kicking, dribbling, and catching. Girls have an edge in fine motor skills and in gross motor capacities that require a combination of good balance and foot movement, such as hopping and skipping (Cratty, 1986; Fischman, Moore, & Steele, 1992). Boys' slightly greater muscle mass and (in the case of throwing) longer forearms may contribute to their skill advantages. And girls' greater overall physical maturity may be partly responsible for their better balance and precision of movement.

At the same time, from an early age, boys and girls are usually encouraged into different physical activities. For example, fathers often play catch with their sons but seldom do so with their daughters. As children get older, differences in motor skills between boys and girls get larger, although sex differences in physical capacity remain small throughout childhood. These trends suggest that social pressures for boys, more than girls, to be active and physically skilled exaggerate small, genetically based sex differences. In support of this view, boys can throw a ball much father than girls only when using their dominant hand. When they use their nondominant hand, the sex difference is minimal (Williams, Haywood, & Painter, 1996). This suggests that practice is largely responsible for boys' superior throwing.

Research confirms that parents hold higher expectations for boys' athletic performance, and children absorb these social messages at an early age. From first through twelfth grades, girls are less positive than boys about the value of sports and their own sports ability—differences explained in part by parental beliefs (Fredricks & Eccles, 2002). In one study, boys more often stated that it was vital to their parents that they participate in athletics. These attitudes affected children's self-confidence and behavior. Girls saw themselves as having less talent at sports, and by sixth grade they devoted less time to athletics than their male classmates did (Eccles & Harold, 1991). At the same time, girls and older school-age children regard boys' advantage in sports as unjust. They indicate, for example, that coaches should spend equal time with children of each sex and that female sports should command just as much public attention as male sports (Solomon & Bredemeier, 1999).

▶ Because these soccer-playing girls are encouraged by parents and coaches, they are likely to evaluate their own sports ability positively and maintain their interest in soccer, thereby narrowing the gender gap in athletic participation, skill, and enjoyment.
© David Young Wolff/PhotoEdit

The same principle that governs motor development during the first 2 years continues to operate in childhood and adolescence. Children integrate previously acquired skills into more complex, *dynamic systems of action*. (Return to Chapter 4, page 144, to review this concept.) Then they revise each skill as their bodies become larger and stronger, their central nervous systems become better developed, their interests and goals become clearer, and their environments present new challenges. Sex differences in motor skills, present as early as the preschool years, illustrate these multiple influences. Although size and strength contribute to boys' superior athletic performance in adolescence, physical growth cannot fully account for boys' childhood advantage. As the Social Issues box above reveals, the social environment plays a prominent role.

• **ORGANIZED YOUTH SPORTS** • Partly because of parents' concerns about safety and the availability and attractions of TV, computer games, and the Internet, today's school-age children devote less time to outdoor, informal physical play than children in previous generations. At the same time, organized sports, such as Little League baseball and soccer and hockey leagues, have expanded tremendously, filling many hours that children used to spend gather-

Adolescence

Not until puberty do sharp sex-related differences in physical size and muscle strength account for large differences in athletic ability. During adolescence, girls' gains in gross motor performance are slow and gradual, leveling off by age 14. In contrast, boys show a dramatic spurt in strength, speed, and endurance that continues through the teenage years, widening the gender gap. By midadolescence, very few girls perform as well as the average boy in running speed, broad-jump length, and throwing distance, and practically no boys score as low as the average girl (Malina & Bouchard, 1991).

In 1972, the U.S. federal government required schools receiving public funds to provide equal opportunities for males and females in all educational programs, including athletics. Since then, girls' high school extracurricular sports participation has increased in both the United States and Canada. Still, as Figure 5.5 shows, girls' involvement falls short of boys'. Physical activity declines during high school for both sexes, but the drop is more than twice as great for girls. These trends parallel reductions in school physical education requirements—measures largely taken to conserve costs. Attendance drops off with each grade, especially for girls (Canadian Fitness and Lifestyle Research Institute, 2003; U.S. Department of Health and Human Services, 2001). By high school, only 52 percent of U.S. and 65 percent of Canadian students are enrolled in any physical education.

Interventions

Besides improving motor performance, sports and exercise influence cognitive and social development. Interschool and intramural athletics provide important lessons in teamwork, problem solving, assertiveness, and competition. And regular, sustained physical activity is associated with healthier dietary habits and improved psychological well-being in adolescence, as indicated by a reduction in use of alcohol, cigarettes, and illegal drugs and in sexual activity (Donnelly & Kidd, 2004; Pate et al., 2000).

Clearly, steps must be taken to raise girls' confidence that they can do well at athletics. Educating parents about the minimal differences between school-age boys' and girls' physical capacities and sensitizing them to unfair biases against promotion of athletic ability among girls may prove helpful. In addition, greater emphasis on skill training for girls, along with increased public attention to their athletic achievements, is likely to improve their participation and performance. As a positive sign, many more girls are participating in individual and team sports in their communities, such as gymnastics and soccer, than was the case a generation ago (National Council of Youth Sports, 2002; Sport Canada, 2003).

Finally, daily physical education in school, with an emphasis on enjoyable games and individual exercise rather than competition, is particularly motivating for girls and is associated with lasting positive consequences (Weinberg et al., 2000). In a long-term study, participating in team or individual sports at age 14 predicted high rates of physical activity at age 31. Endurance sports, such as running and cycling, were especially likely to carry over into adulthood (Tammelin et al., 2003). These activities can easily be performed on one's own time, without expensive equipment or special facilities. And the stamina they require fosters high *physical self-efficacy*—belief in one's ability to sustain an exercise program (Motl et al., 2002).

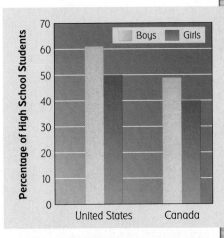

▲ **Figure 5.5**

Involvement of American and Canadian high school students in extracurricular school sports. In both nations, more boys than girls participate. Nevertheless, girls' participation has increased greatly over the past several decades. (From Canadian Fitness and Lifestyle Research Institute, 2004; National Federation of State High School Associations, 2004.)

ing spontaneously on sidewalks and playgrounds. About half of North American youngsters—60 percent of boys and 40 percent of girls—participate in organized sports at some time between ages 5 and 14 (National Council of Youth Sports, 2002; Sport Canada, 2003).

Research indicates that for most children, playing on a community athletic team is associated with greater social competence (Fletcher, Nickerson, & Wright, 2003). But the arguments of critics—that youth sports overemphasize competition and substitute adult control for children's natural experimentation with rules and strategies—are valid in some cases. Children who join teams so early that the necessary skills are beyond their capabilities soon lose interest. And coaches who criticize rather than encourage and who react angrily to defeat can prompt intense anxiety in some children. Similarly, high parental pressure for performance is linked to children's emotional difficulties and early athletic dropout, not elite performance (Marsh & Daigneault, 1999; Tofler, Knapp, & Drell, 1998).

Sports-related injuries are another concern. Perhaps because organized sports specify health and safety rules, injuries tend to be infrequent and mild, except in football, which has a high rate of serious injury (Radelet et al., 2002). Nevertheless, in any sport, frequent, intense practice can

Only about 40 percent of girls engage in sufficient physical activity for good health, but these sixth graders are in that group—fortunate enough to know the pleasure that vigorous exercise can bring.
© David Young Wolff/PhotoEdit

▼ Figure 5.6

Cross section of the human brain, showing the location of the hypothalamus and pituitary gland. Also shown are three additional structures—the cerebellum, the reticular formation, and the corpus callosum—that we will discuss in a later section.

lead to painful "overuse" injuries, sometimes fracturing the soft cartilage in the epiphyses of the long bones, leading to premature closure and arrested growth (Matheson, 2001).

When parents and coaches emphasize effort, improvement, and teamwork and permit children to contribute to rules and strategies, young athletes enjoy sports more, gain in self-esteem, and persist in sports longer, through community or school programs (Stryer, Tofler, & Lapchick, 1998). Such parents and coaches also help curb the high physical inactivity rates among North American youths. Among U.S. and Canadian 5- to 17-year-olds, only about 50 percent of boys and 40 percent of girls engage in enough regular, vigorous aerobic activity for good health (Canadian Fitness and Lifestyle Research Institute, 2003; U.S. Department of Health and Human Services, 2004f).

Hormonal Influences on Physical Growth

The endocrine glands control the vast physical changes of childhood and adolescence. They manufacture *hormones*, chemical substances secreted by specialized cells in one part of the body that pass to and influence cells in another.

The most important hormones for human growth are released by the **pituitary gland,** located at the base of the brain near the **hypothalamus,** a structure that initiates and regulates pituitary secretions (see Figure 5.6). Once pituitary hormones enter the bloodstream, they act directly on body tissues to induce growth, or they stimulate the release of other hormones from endocrine glands located elsewhere in the body. The hypothalamus contains special receptors that detect hormone levels in the bloodstream. Through a highly sensitive feedback loop, it instructs the pituitary gland to increase or decrease the amount of each hormone. In this way, growth is carefully controlled. You may find it useful to refer to Figure 5.7 as we review major hormonal influences.

Growth hormone (GH) is the only pituitary secretion produced continuously throughout life. It affects development of all tissues except the central nervous system and the genitals. GH production doubles during puberty, contributing to rapid gains in body size, and then decreases after final adult height is reached. It acts directly on the body and also stimulates the liver and epiphyses of the skeleton to release another hormone, *somatomedin,* which triggers cell duplication in the bones. Although GH does not seem to affect prenatal growth, it is necessary for physical development from birth on. Children who lack it attain an average mature height of only 4 feet, 4 inches. When treated early with injections of synthetic GH, such children show catch-up growth and then grow at a normal rate, reaching a height much greater than they would have without treatment (Saenger, 2003).

Together, the hypothalamus and pituitary gland prompt the thyroid gland (in the neck) to release **thyroxine,** which is necessary for brain development and for GH to have its full impact on body size. Infants born with a deficiency of thyroxine must receive it at once, or they will be mentally retarded. At later ages, children with too little thyroxine grow at a below-average rate, but the central nervous system is no longer affected because the most rapid period of brain development is complete. With prompt treatment, such children eventually reach normal size (Salerno et al., 2001).

Sexual maturation is controlled by pituitary secretions that stimulate the release of sex hormones. Although we think of **estrogens** as female hormones and **androgens** as male hormones, both types are present in each sex, but in different amounts. The boy's testes

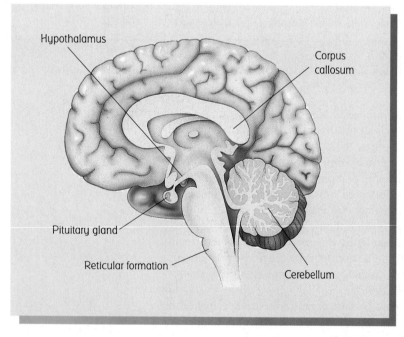

Hypothalamus

Corpus callosum

Pituitary gland

Reticular formation

Cerebellum

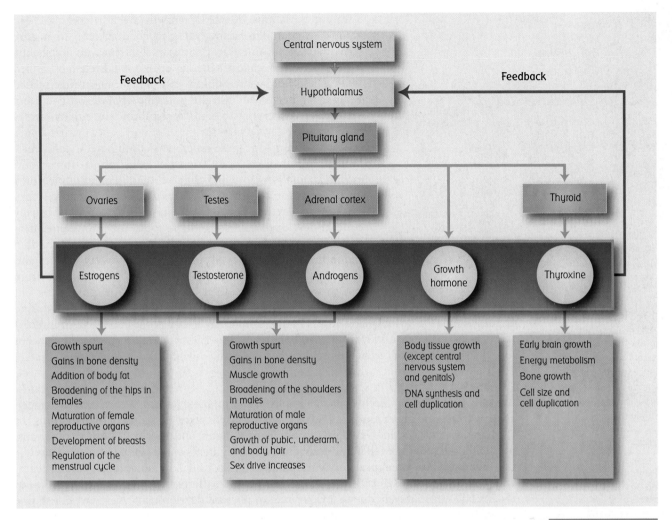

▲ Figure 5.7

Hormonal influences on postnatal growth. The hypothalamus stimulates the pituitary gland to release hormones that either induce growth directly or stimulate other endocrine glands to release growth-inducing hormones (red lines). A highly sensitive feedback loop exists in which the hypothalamus detects hormone levels in the bloodstream and instructs the pituitary gland to increase or decrease the amount of each hormone accordingly (blue lines).

release large quantities of the androgen *testosterone,* which leads to muscle growth, body and facial hair, and other male sex characteristics. Androgens (especially testosterone for boys) exert a GH-enhancing effect, contributing greatly to gains in body size. The testes secrete small amounts of estrogen as well; as a result, 50 percent of boys experience temporary breast enlargement. In both sexes, estrogens also increase GH secretion, adding to the growth spurt and, in combination with androgens, stimulating gains in bone density, which continue into adulthood (Delemarre-van de Waal, van Coeverden, & Rotteveel, 2001; Styne, 2003).

Estrogens released by girls' ovaries cause the breasts, uterus, and vagina to mature, the body to take on feminine proportions, and fat to accumulate. Estrogens also contribute to regulation of the menstrual cycle. *Adrenal androgens,* released from the adrenal glands located on top of each kidney, influence girls' height spurt and stimulate growth of underarm and pubic hair. They have little impact on boys, whose physical characteristics are influenced mainly by androgen and estrogen secretions from the testes.

Worldwide Variations in Body Size

A glance into almost any school classroom reveals wide individual differences in physical size. This diversity is even more apparent when comparing children of different nations. Worldwide, a 9-inch gap exists between the smallest and the largest 8-year-olds. The shortest children, who tend to be found in South America, Asia, the Pacific Islands, and parts of Africa, include such ethnic groups as Colombian, Burmese, Thai, Vietnamese, Ethiopian, and Bantu. The tallest reside in Australia, northern and central Europe, Canada, and the United States and come from Czech, Dutch, Latvian, Norwegian, Swiss, and African populations (Meredith, 1978).

© Body size is sometimes the result of evolutionary adaptations to a particular climate. These boys of the Sudan, who live on the hot African plains, have long, lean physiques, which permit the body to cool easily.
© Betty Press/Woodfin Camp & Associates

Ethnic variations in rate of growth are also common. For example, African-American and Asian children tend to mature faster than North American Caucasian children, who are slightly ahead of European children (Berkey et al., 1994; Eveleth & Tanner, 1990). These findings remind us that *growth norms* (age-related averages for height and weight) must be applied with caution, especially in countries with high immigration rates and many ethnic minorities.

What accounts for these differences? Both heredity and environment are involved. Body size sometimes results from evolutionary adaptations to a particular climate. For example, long, lean physiques are typical in hot, tropical regions and short, stocky ones in cold, Arctic areas. Also, children who grow tallest usually reside in developed countries, where food is plentiful and infectious diseases are largely controlled. In contrast, small children tend to live in less developed regions, where poverty, hunger, and disease are common (Bogin, 2001). When families move from poor to wealthy nations, their children not only grow taller but also change to a longer-legged body shape. (Recall that during childhood, the legs are growing fastest.) For example, American-born school-age children of immigrant Guatemalan Mayan parents are, on average, 4½ inches taller and nearly 3 inches longer-legged than their agemates in Guatemalan Mayan villages (Bogin et al., 2002).

Secular Trends

Over the past 150 years, **secular trends in physical growth**—changes in body size and rate of growth from one generation to the next—have taken place in industrialized nations. In Australia, Canada, Japan, New Zealand, the United States, and nearly all European nations, most children today are taller and heavier than their parents and grandparents were as children. The secular gain appears early in life, increases over childhood and early adolescence, and then declines as mature body size is reached. This pattern suggests that the larger size of today's children is mostly due to a faster rate of physical development. As Figure 5.8 shows, age of first menstruation declined steadily from 1900 to 1970, by about 3 to 4 months per decade. Boys, as well, have reached puberty earlier in recent decades (Karpati et al., 2002).

▶ **Figure 5.8**

Secular trend in age at menarche in six industrialized nations. Age of menarche declined from 1900 to 1970. Thereafter, a few countries showed a modest, continuing decline due to rising rates of overweight and obesity. Others leveled off or underwent a slight reversal. (From S. M. P. F. de Muinck Keizer-Schrama & D. Mul, 2001, "Trends in Pubertal Development in Europe," *Human Reproduction Update, 7*, p. 289. Reprinted by permission.)

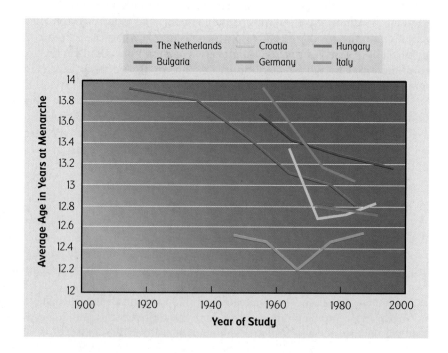

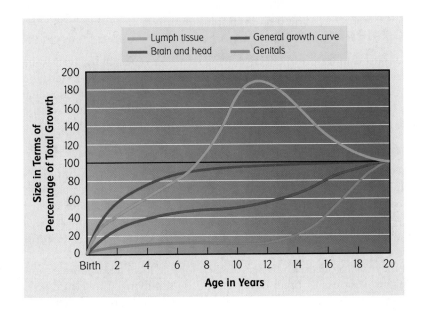

▶ **Figure 5.9**

Growth of three different organ systems and tissues contrasted with the body's general growth. Growth is plotted in terms of percentage of change from birth to 20 years. Note that the growth of lymph tissue rises to nearly twice its adult level by the end of childhood. Then it declines. (Reprinted by permission of the publisher from J. M. Tanner, 1990, *Foetus into Man,* 2nd ed., Cambridge, MA: Harvard University Press, p. 16. Copyright © 1990 by J. M. Tanner. All rights reserved.)

Improved health and nutrition are largely responsible for these growth gains. Secular trends are smaller for low-income children, who have poorer diets and are more likely to suffer from growth-stunting illnesses. And in regions of the world with widespread poverty, famine, and disease, either no secular change or a secular decrease has occurred (Barnes-Josiah & Augustin, 1995; Cole, 2000).

In most industrialized nations, the secular gain in height has slowed, and the trend toward earlier first menstruation has stopped. As you will see later, however, overweight and obesity have contributed to a continuing secular trend toward earlier first menstruation in North America and a few European countries, such as Denmark, Finland, and the Netherlands (Parent et al., 2003).

Asynchronies in Physical Growth

Body systems differ in their unique, carefully timed patterns of growth. As Figure 5.9 shows, physical growth is *asynchronous*. Body size (as measured by height and weight) and a variety of internal organs follow the **general growth curve:** rapid growth during infancy, slower gains in early and middle childhood, and rapid growth again during adolescence. The genitals develop slowly from birth to age 4, change little throughout middle childhood, and then grow rapidly during adolescence. In contrast, the lymph glands grow at an astounding pace in infancy and childhood, and then their rate of growth declines in adolescence. The lymph system helps fight infection and assists with the absorption of nutrients, thereby supporting children's health and survival (Malina & Bouchard, 1991).

Figure 5.9 illustrates another growth trend: During the first few years, the brain grows faster than any other body structure.

Ask Yourself

REVIEW	What factors account for boys' childhood advantage over girls in athletic skills?
APPLY	Nine-year-old Allison thinks she isn't good at sports, and she doesn't like physical education class. Suggest some strategies her teacher can use to improve her involvement and pleasure in physical activity.
CONNECT	Relate secular trends in physical growth to the concept of cohort effects, discussed on page 59 of Chapter 2.
REFLECT	Did you participate in organized sports as a child? If so, what kind of climate for learning did coaches and parents create? How do you think your experiences influenced your development?

Brain Development

The human brain is the most elaborate and effective living structure on earth today. Despite its complexity, it reaches its adult size earlier than any other organ. We can best understand brain growth by looking at it from two vantage points: (1) the microscopic level of individual brain cells, and (2) the larger level of the cerebral cortex, the most complex brain structure and the one responsible for the highly developed intelligence of our species.

Development of Neurons

The human brain has 100 to 200 billion **neurons,** or nerve cells, that store and transmit information, many of which have thousands of direct connections with other neurons. Neurons differ from other body cells in that they are not tightly packed together. Between them are tiny gaps, or **synapses,** where fibers from different neurons come close together but do not touch (see Figure 5.10). Neurons send messages to one another by releasing chemicals called **neurotransmitters,** which cross synapses.

The basic story of brain growth concerns how neurons develop and form this elaborate communication system. Major milestones of brain development are summarized in Figure 5.11. During the prenatal period, neurons are produced in the primitive neural tube of the embryo. From there, they migrate to form the major parts of the brain, traveling along threads produced by a network of guiding cells. By the end of the second trimester of pregnancy, production and migration of neurons are largely complete (see Chapter 3, page 89).

Once neurons are in place, they differentiate, establishing their unique functions by extending their fibers to form synaptic connections with neighboring cells. During infancy and early childhood, growth of neural fibers increases at an astounding pace (Huttenlocher, 1994; Moore & Persaud, 2003). Because neurons require space for these connective structures, a surprising aspect of brain growth is **programmed cell death:** As synapses form, many surrounding neurons die—20 to 80 percent, depending on the brain region (de Haan & Johnson, 2003b; Stiles, 2001a). Fortunately, during embryonic growth, the neural tube produces far more neurons than the brain will ever need.

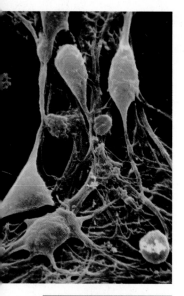

▲ **Figure 5.10**

Neurons and their connective fibers. This photograph of several neurons, taken with the aid of a powerful microscope, shows the elaborate synaptic connections that form with neighboring cells.
© ASAP/CNRI/Science Source/Photo Researchers, Inc.

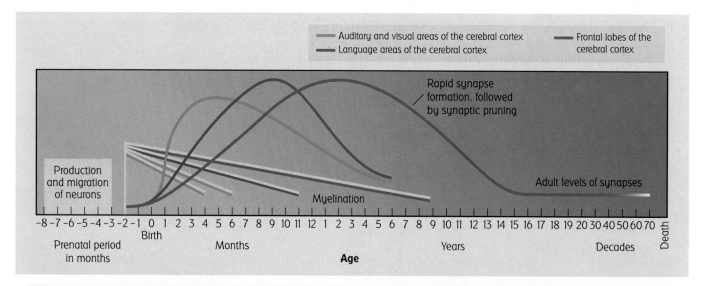

▲ **Figure 5.11**

Major milestones of brain development. Formation of synapses is rapid during the first 2 years of life, especially in the auditory, visual, and language areas of the cerebral cortex. The frontal lobes, responsible for thought, undergo more extended synaptic growth. In each area, overproduction of synapses is followed by synaptic pruning as stimulation strengthens needed connections and returns neurons not needed at the moment to an uncommitted state so that they can support future skills. The frontal lobes are among the last regions to attain adult levels of synaptic connections—in mid- to late adolescence. Myelination occurs at a dramatic pace during the first 2 years and then at a slower pace through childhood and adolescence. The multiple yellow lines indicate that the timing of myelination varies among different brain areas. For example, neural fibers continue to myelinate over a longer period in the language areas, and especially in the frontal lobes, than in the visual and auditory areas. (Adapted from Thompson & Nelson, 2001).

As neurons form connections, *stimulation* becomes vital to their survival. Neurons that are stimulated by input from the surrounding environment continue to establish synapses, forming increasingly elaborate systems of communication that support more complex abilities. Neurons that are seldom stimulated soon lose their synapses, a process called **synaptic pruning.** Pruning returns neurons not needed at the moment to an uncommitted state so they can support future development. In all, about 40 percent of synapses are pruned during childhood and adolescence to reach the adult level (refer again to Figure 5.11). (Webb, Monk, & Nelson, 2001). Notice how, for this process to go forward, appropriate stimulation of the child's brain is vital during periods in which the formation of synapses is at its peak (Greenough et al., 1993; Huttenlocher, 2002).

If few new neurons are produced after the prenatal period, what causes the dramatic increase in brain size during infancy and early childhood? About half the brain's volume is made up of **glial cells,** which are responsible for **myelination,** the coating of neural fibers with an insulating fatty sheath (called *myelin*) that improves the efficiency of message transfer. Glial cells multiply rapidly from the fourth month of pregnancy through the second year of life, a process that continues at a slower pace through adolescence. Dramatic increases in neural fibers and myelination are responsible for the swift gain in overall size of the brain. At birth, the brain is nearly 30 percent of its adult weight; by age 2, it reaches 70 percent, and at 6 years, 90 percent (Thatcher et al., 1996).

In sum, brain development can be compared to molding a "living sculpture." After neurons and synapses are overproduced, cell death and synaptic pruning sculpt away excess building material to form the mature brain—a process jointly influenced by genetically programmed events and the child's experiences. The resulting sculpture is a set of interconnected regions, each with specific functions—much like countries on a globe that communicate with one another (Johnston et al., 2001). This "geography" of the brain permits researchers to study its organization with various psychophysiological measures. EEG brain-wave patterns can be examined for stability and coherence—signs of mature brain functioning Also, recall from Chapter 2 that as a child processes a stimulus, ERPs detect the location of brain-wave activity, and fMRI the location of changes in blood flow. Both techniques identify active areas, with fMRI doing so especially precisely (see page 47). We will encounter these measures as we turn now to the development of the cerebral cortex.

Development of the Cerebral Cortex

The **cerebral cortex** surrounds the brain, looking much like a half-shelled walnut. It is the largest, most complex brain structure—accounting for 85 percent of the brain's weight, containing the greatest number of neurons and synapses, and making possible the unique intelligence of our species. Because the cerebral cortex is the last brain structure to stop growing, it is sensitive to environmental influences for a much longer period than any other part of the brain.

• **REGIONS OF THE CEREBRAL CORTEX** • Figure 5.12 shows specific functions of regions of the cerebral cortex, such as receiving information from the senses, instructing the body to move, and thinking. The general order in which cortical regions develop corresponds to the emergence of these capacities in the infant and child. For example, ERP and fMRI measures reveal a burst of activity (signifying synaptic growth and myelination) in the auditory and visual cortexes and in areas responsible for body movement over the first year—a period of dramatic gains in auditory and visual perception and mastery of motor skills (Johnson, 1998). Language areas are especially active from late infancy through the preschool years. Areas dedicated to spatial abilities increase in activity throughout early and middle childhood, with a slight spurt between ages 8 and 10 (Thatcher, Walker, & Giudice, 1987; Thompson et al., 2000).

The cortical regions with the most extended period of development are the *frontal lobes*, which are responsible for

▼ **Figure 5.12**

The left side of the human brain, showing the cerebral cortex. The cortex is divided into different lobes, each of which contains a variety of regions with specific functions. Some major regions are labeled here.

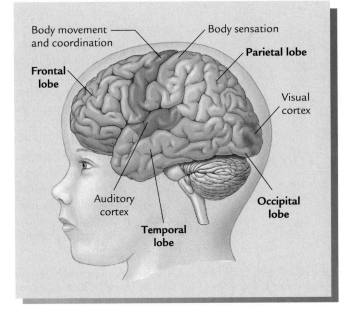

thought—in particular, consciousness, attention, inhibition of impulses, integration of information, and regulation of behavior through planning. From age 2 months on, these areas function more effectively than before, continuing their rapid synapse formation well into middle childhood (Nelson, 2002; Thompson et al., 2000). Myelination of the frontal lobes persists into adolescence, supporting refinement of complex cognitive capacities (Sowell et al., 2002).

• **LATERALIZATION OF THE CEREBRAL CORTEX** • The cerebral cortex has two *hemispheres,* or sides—left and right—that differ in their functions. Some tasks are done mostly by one hemisphere and some by the other. For example, each hemisphere receives sensory information from one side of the body and controls only that side—the one opposite to it.[1] For most of us, the left hemisphere is largely responsible for verbal abilities (such as spoken and written language) and positive emotion (for example, joy). The right hemisphere handles spatial abilities (judging distances, reading maps, and recognizing geometric shapes) and negative emotion (such as distress) (Banish & Heller, 1998; Nelson & Bosquet, 2000). This pattern may be reversed in left-handed people, but more often, the cortex of left-handers is less clearly specialized than that of right-handers.

Specialization of the two hemispheres is called **lateralization.** Why are behaviors and abilities lateralized? fMRI studies reveal that the left hemisphere is better at processing information in a sequential, analytic (piece-by-piece) way, a good approach for dealing with communicative information—both verbal (language) and emotional (a joyful smile). In contrast, the right hemisphere is specialized for processing information in a holistic, integrative manner, ideal for making sense of spatial information and regulating negative emotion (Banish, 1998). A lateralized brain is certainly adaptive: It permits a wider array of functions to be carried out effectively than if both sides processed information exactly the same way.

▶ *Brain Plasticity.* Researchers are interested in when brain lateralization occurs because they want to know more about **brain plasticity.** In a highly *plastic* cerebral cortex, many areas are not yet committed to specific functions. Consequently, the cortex has a high capacity for learning. In addition, if a part of the brain is damaged, other parts can take over tasks it would have handled. But once the hemispheres lateralize, damage to a specific region means that the abilities it controls cannot be recovered to the same extent or with the same ease that they could earlier.

At birth, the hemispheres have already begun to specialize. For example, most newborns favor the right side of the body in their head position and reflexive reactions (Grattan et al., 1992; Rönnqvist & Hopkins, 1998). Most also show greater ERPs (brain-wave activity) in the left hemisphere while listening to speech sounds and displaying positive emotion. In contrast, the right hemisphere reacts more strongly to nonspeech sounds and to stimuli (such as a sour-tasting fluid) that evoke negative emotion (Davidson, 1994; Fox & Davidson, 1986).

Nevertheless, dramatic evidence for substantial plasticity in the young brain comes from research on brain-damaged children, summarized in the Biology and Environment box on pages 186–187. Furthermore, early experience greatly influences the organization of the cerebral cortex. For example, deaf adults who, as infants and children, learned sign language (a spatial skill) depend more than hearing individuals on the right hemisphere for language processing (Neville & Bruer, 2001). Also, toddlers who are advanced in language development show greater left-hemispheric specialization for language than their more slowly developing agemates (Mills, Coffey-Corina, & Neville, 1997). Similarly, while performing motor and cognitive tasks, children show diffuse fMRI activity in the cerebral cortex relative to adolescents and adults, for whom activity is concentrated in certain cortical areas (Casey et al., 2002; Luna et al., 2001). Apparently, the very process of acquiring motor, cognitive, and language skills promotes lateralization.

In sum, the brain is more plastic during the first few years than at any later time of life (Nelson, 2000). Although the cortex is programmed from the start for hemispheric specialization, experience greatly influences the rate and success of its advancing organization. An overabundance of synaptic connections supports plasticity of the young brain, ensuring that the

---

[1]The eyes are an exception. Messages from the right half of each retina go to the right hemisphere; messages from the left half of each retina go to the left hemisphere. Thus, visual information from *both* eyes is received by *both* hemispheres.

child can acquire certain capacities even if some areas are damaged. fMRI evidence reveals that by age 4, many parts of the cortex have overproduced synapses. Around this time, cerebral blood flow peaks, signifying a high energy need (Huttenlocher, 2002; Johnson, 1998). With further stimulation, some neural fibers become more elaborate, synaptic pruning and death of surrounding neurons occur, and plasticity of the brain declines. By ages 8 to 10, energy consumption of most cortical regions drops to near-adult levels. This process takes longer in the frontal lobes, which recede to an adult level of synapses during adolescence (Nelson, 2002).

▶ *Lateralization and Handedness.* A expanding literature on handedness supports the joint contributions of nature and nurture to brain lateralization. By the end of the first year, infants typically display a hand preference in grasping and exploring objects that gradually extends to a wider range of skills, such as eating with utensils, throwing and catching, drawing, and writing (Hinojosa, Sheu, & Michel, 2003).

Handedness reflects the greater capacity of one side of the brain—often referred to as the individual's **dominant cerebral hemisphere**—to carry out skilled motor action. Other important abilities may be located on the dominant side as well. For right-handed people, who make up 90 percent of the population in Western nations, language is housed with hand control in the left hemisphere. For the remaining left-handed 10 percent, language is often shared between the hemispheres (Knecht et al., 2000). This indicates that the brains of left-handers tend to be less strongly lateralized than those of right-handers. Consistent with this idea, many left-handed individuals are also *ambidextrous*. Although they prefer their left hand, they sometimes use their right hand skillfully as well (McManus et al., 1988).

Researchers disagree on whether heredity influences handedness. Left-handed parents show only a weak tendency to have left-handed children. One genetic theory proposes that most children inherit a gene that *biases* them for right-handedness and a left-dominant cerebral hemisphere, but that the bias is not strong enough to overcome environmental pressures that might sway children toward a left-hand preference (Annett, 2002). Indeed, experiences that take place as early as prenatal life may profoundly affect handedness. Both identical and fraternal twins are more likely than ordinary siblings to differ in hand preference, probably because twins usually lie in opposite orientations in the uterus (Derom et al., 1996). The way most singleton fetuses orient—toward the left—is believed to promote greater control over movements on the body's right side (Previc, 1991).

◉ Twins typically lie in the uterus in opposite orientations during the prenatal period, which may explain why, like the twins in the photo, they are more often opposite-handed than are ordinary siblings.

© Laura Dwight Photography

Handedness also involves practice. Newborns' bias in head position causes them to spend more time looking at and using one hand, which contributes to greater skill development in that hand (Hinojosa, Sheu, & Michel, 2003) Also, wide cultural variation exists in rates of handedness. For example, in Tanzania, Africa, children are physically restrained and punished for favoring the left hand. Less than 1 percent of adult Tanzanians are left-handed (Provins, 1997).

You may have heard that left-handedness is especially prevalent among severely retarded and mentally ill people. Although this is true, recall that correlation between two variables does not mean that one causes the other. Atypical lateralization is probably not responsible for the problems of these individuals. Instead, they may have suffered early damage to the left hemisphere, which both caused their disabilities and led to a shift in handedness. In support of this idea, left-handedness is associated with prenatal and birth difficulties that can result in brain damage, including prolonged labor, prematurity, Rh factor incompatibility, and breech delivery (O'Callaghan et al., 1993; Powls et al., 1996).

Only a small number of left-handers show developmental problems. In fact, unusual lateralization may have certain advantages. Left- and mixed-handed young people are more likely than their right-handed agemates to develop outstanding verbal and mathematical talents (Flannery & Liederman, 1995). More even distribution of cognitive functions across both hemispheres may be responsible.

BIOLOGY AND ENVIRONMENT

Brain Plasticity: Insights from Research on Brain-Damaged Children and Adults

In the first few years of life, the brain is highly plastic. It can reorganize areas committed to specific functions in ways that the mature brain cannot. Consistently, adults who suffered brain injuries in infancy and early childhood show fewer cognitive impairments than adults with later-occurring injuries (Huttenlocher, 2002). Nevertheless, the young brain is not totally plastic. When it is injured, its functioning is compromised. The extent of plasticity depends on several factors, including age at time of injury, site of damage, and skill area.

Brain Plasticity in Infancy and Early Childhood

In a large study of children with injuries to the cerebral cortex that occurred before birth or in the first 6 months of life, language and spatial skills were assessed repeatedly into adolescence (Akshoomoff et al., 2002; Stiles, 2001a). All of the children had experienced early brain seizures or hemorrhages. fMRI and other brain-imaging techniques revealed the precise site of damage.

Regardless of whether injury occurred in the left or right cerebral hemisphere, the children showed delays in language development that persisted until about 3½ years of age. That damage to either hemisphere affected early language competence indicates that at first, language functioning is broadly distributed in the brain. But by age 5, the children caught up in vocabulary and grammatical skills. Undamaged areas—in either the left or the right hemisphere—had taken over these language functions.

Compared with language, spatial skills were more impaired after early brain injury. When preschool through adolescent-age youngsters were asked to copy designs, those with early right-hemispheric damage had trouble with holistic processing—accurately representing the overall shape. In contrast, those with left-hemispheric damage captured the basic shape but omitted fine-grained details (see Figure 5.13). Neverthe-less, the children showed improvement in their drawings with age—gains that do not occur in brain-injured adults (Akshoomoff et al., 2002; Stiles et al., 2003).

Clearly, recovery after early brain injury is greater for language than for spatial skills. Why is this so? Researchers speculate that spatial processing is the older of the two capacities in our evolutionary history and, therefore, more lateralized at birth (Stiles, 2001b; Stiles et al., 2002). But early brain injury has far less impact than later injury on *both* language and spatial skills. In sum, the young brain is remarkably plastic.

▶ This 8-year-old, who experienced brain damage in infancy, has well-developed language skills but has difficulty with spatial tasks. Still, because of early, high brain plasticity, he has been spared massive impairments. The boy's teachers strengthen his spatial skills by providing him with activities in which he copies and creates designs.
Courtesy of the Cotting School

Other Advances in Brain Development

In addition to the cerebral cortex, other areas of the brain make strides during infancy and childhood. As you will see, these changes involve establishing links between parts of the brain, increasing the coordinated functioning of the central nervous system. (To see where the structures we are about to discuss are located, turn back to Figure 5.6 on page 178.)

At the rear and base of the brain is the **cerebellum,** a structure that aids in balance and control of body movement. Fibers linking the cerebellum to the frontal and parietal lobes of the cerebral cortex grow and myelinate from birth through the preschool years. This change contributes to dramatic gains in visual-motor coordination, so that by the time they start school, children can play hopscotch, throw and catch a ball with a well-coordinated set of

The Price of High Plasticity in the Young Brain

Despite impressive recovery of language and (to a lesser extent) spatial skills, children with early brain injuries show deficits in a wide variety of complex mental abilities during the school years. For example, their progress in reading and math is slow. And when asked to tell stories, they produce simpler narratives than their agemates without early brain injuries (Reilly, Bates, & Marchman, 1998). Furthermore, the more brain tissue destroyed in infancy or early childhood, the poorer children score on intelligence tests (Levine et al., 1987).

High brain plasticity, researchers explain, comes at a price. When healthy brain regions take over the functions of damaged areas, a "crowding effect" occurs: Multiple tasks must be done by a smaller than usual volume of brain tissue. Consequently, the brain processes information less quickly and accurately than it would if it were intact. Complex mental abilities of all kinds suffer because performing them well requires considerable space in the cerebral cortex (Huttenlocher, 2002).

Later Plasticity

Plasticity is not restricted to early childhood. Although it is far more limited, reorganization in the brain can occur later, even in adulthood. For example, adult stroke victims often display some recovery, especially in response to stimulation of language and motor skills. Brain-imaging techniques reveal that structures adjacent to the permanently damaged area or in the opposite cerebral hemisphere reorganize to support the impaired ability (Bach-y-Rita, 2001; Hallett, 2000).

In infancy and childhood, the goal of brain growth is to form neural connections that ensure mastery of essential skills. Plasticity is greatest while the brain is forming many new synapses (Kolb & Gibb, 2001). At older ages, specialized brain structures are in place, but after injury they can still reorganize to some degree. Recent research reveals that the adult brain can produce a small number of new neurons (Gould et al., 1999). And when an individual practices relevant tasks, the brain strengthens existing synapses and generates new ones. Plasticity seems to be a basic property of the nervous system. Researchers hope to discover how experience and brain plasticity work together throughout life so they can help people of all ages—with and without brain injuries—develop at their best.

Shape Child Was Asked to Copy

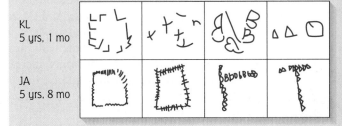

Early Right-Hemispheric Damage

KL
5 yrs, 1 mo

JA
5 yrs, 8 mo

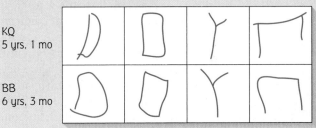

Early Left-Hemispheric Damage

KQ
5 yrs, 1 mo

BB
6 yrs, 3 mo

▲ **Figure 5.13**

Impairments in spatial skills in 5- and 6-year-olds who had experienced brain injury before birth or in the first 6 months of life. Compared with language skills, spatial skills are more impaired after early brain injury. When researchers had children copy designs, those with right-hemispheric damage had difficulty representing the overall shape. Those with left-hemispheric damage captured the basic shape but omitted fine-grained details. Although drawings improved over the school years, difficulties with spatial processing remained. (Adapted from J. Stiles, 2001, "Neural Plasticity and Cognitive Development," *Developmental Neuropsychology, 18,* p. 261. Reprinted by permission.)

movements, and print letters of the alphabet. Connections between the cerebellum and cerebral cortex also support higher cognitive processes (Diamond, 2000). Consequently, children with disorders involving the cerebellum usually display both motor and cognitive deficits, including problems with memory, planning, and language (Noterdaeme et al., 2002; Riva & Giorgi, 2000).

The **reticular formation,** a structure in the brain stem that maintains alertness and consciousness, generates synapses and myelinates throughout early childhood. Neurons in the reticular formation send out fibers to many other areas of the brain. A large number go to the frontal lobes of the cerebral cortex, contributing to improvements in sustained, controlled attention.

The **corpus callosum** is a large bundle of fibers that connects the two cortical hemispheres. Production of synapses and myelination of the corpus callosum increase at the end of the first year, peak between 3 and 6 years, and continue at a slower pace through adolescence (Thompson et al., 2000). The corpus callosum supports smooth coordination of movements on both sides of the body and integration of many aspects of thinking, including perception, attention, memory, language, and problem solving. The more complex the task, the more critical is communication between the hemispheres.

Finally, in many brain regions, sensitivity of neurons to certain chemical messages readjusts in adolescence. As humans and other mammals become sexually mature, neurons become more responsive to excitatory neurotransmitters. As a result, adolescents react more strongly to stressful events; they also experience pleasurable stimuli more intensely (Spear, 2003). These changes are believed to play a prominent role in teenagers' drive for novel experiences, including experimentation with drugs. Restructuring of neurotransmitter activity may also be involved in adolescents' increased susceptibility to certain disorders, such as eating disturbances, which we address in a later section, and depression, which we take up in Chapter 11.

Sensitive Periods in Brain Development

We have seen that stimulation of the brain is vital during periods in which it is growing most rapidly—when formation of synapses is at a peak. Animal studies, as noted in Chapter 4, reveal that early, extreme sensory deprivation results in permanent brain damage and loss of functions—findings that confirm the existence of sensitive periods in brain development. Recall, also, the findings of research on children adopted from Eastern European orphanages—that 2 years or more in deprived institutional care results in reduced brain size and impairments in all domains of psychological development (see page 165 of Chapter 4). Much evidence confirms that the brain is particularly spongelike during the first few years, so that children acquire new skills easily and quickly. How, then, can we characterize appropriate stimulation during this time? To answer this question, researchers distinguish between two types of brain development.

The first, **experience-expectant brain growth,** refers to the young brain's rapidly developing organization, which depends on ordinary experiences—opportunities to see and touch objects, to hear language and other sounds, and to move about and explore the environment. As a result of millions of years of evolution, the brains of all infants, toddlers, and young children *expect* to encounter these experiences and, if they do, grow normally.

The second type of brain development—**experience-dependent brain growth**—extends throughout our lives. It consists of additional growth and refinement of established brain structures as a result of specific learning experiences that vary widely across individuals and cultures (Greenough & Black, 1992). Reading, playing computer games, weaving an intricate rug, composing poetry, and practicing the violin are examples. The brain of a violinist differs in certain ways from the brain of a poet because each has exercised different brain regions for a long time (Thompson & Nelson, 2001).

Experience-expectant brain development takes place early and naturally, as caregivers offer babies and preschoolers age-appropriate play materials and engage them in enjoyable daily routines—a shared meal, a game of peek-a-boo, a bath before bed, a picture book to talk about, a song to sing, or an outing to the grocery store. The resulting growth provides the foundation for later-occurring, experience-dependent development (Huttenlocher, 2002; Shonkoff & Phillips, 2001). In Chapter 4, we indicated that not just understimulation but also overstimulation—overwhelming children with tasks and expectations for which they are not yet ready—can threaten their development. No evidence exists for a sensitive period in the first 5 or 6 years for mastering skills that depend on extensive training, such as reading, musical performance, or gymnastics (Bruer, 1999).

In previous chapters, you encountered evidence that the young, rapidly growing brain is vulnerable in many ways—to hazardous drug exposure, environmental toxins, poor diet, and chronic stress. Researchers speculate that rushing early learning also harms the brain by overwhelming its neural circuits, thereby reducing the brain's sensitivity to the everyday experiences it needs for a healthy start in life. In addition, when "mind-building" lessons do not produce young geniuses, they can lead to disappointed parents who view their children as failures at a tender age.

Ⓖ Relaxed participation with adults that ensures opportunities to see and touch objects, to hear language and other sounds, and to explore the environment are best for promoting brain growth during the early years. In contrast, overstimulating babies with academic training and other lessons can impede brain development and the child's desire to learn.

© Jose Luis Pelaez, Inc./Corbis

An Emerging Field: Developmental Cognitive Neuroscience

The findings just reviewed are the product of an exciting new field of research called *developmental cognitive neuroscience*. It brings together researchers from multiple disciplines, including psychology, biology, neuroscience, and medicine, in a common endeavor: expanding our knowledge of the relationship between brain growth and the child's behavioral capacities.

At one time, heredity was thought to be largely responsible for brain development, with experience merely fine-tuning the brain's functioning. In this and the previous chapter, we have seen numerous examples of how the child's activity and learning greatly influence changes in the brain. Current evidence suggests that babies come into the world with biases to process certain information—for example, social stimuli (such as faces), the movements of objects and people, and the sounds of language (see Chapter 4). These experiences seem to shape neural circuits, giving rise to a brain that can interact with others, explore the physical world, and attend, remember, and solve problems (Johnson, 2001b). Engaging in these activities, in turn, ensures adaptive specialization of brain regions.

The long period of human brain growth means that adults can greatly influence the child's brain through stimulation and teaching. Developmental cognitive neuroscientists are making rapid progress in identifying the types of experiences to which the brain is sensitive at various times. They are also clarifying the brain bases of many learning and behavior disorders and contributing to the design of more powerful interventions by examining their impact on both behavior and brain functioning (Munakata, Casey, & Diamond, 2004). Although much remains to be discovered, developmental cognitive neuroscience is already transforming our understanding of development, with major implications for practice and social policy.

Ask Yourself

REVIEW	How does stimulation affect early brain development? Cite evidence both at the level of neurons and at the level of the cerebral cortex.
REVIEW	Lucia experienced damage to the left hemisphere of her cerebral cortex shortly after birth. As a first grader, she shows impressive recovery of language and spatial skills, but her academic progress remains slow relative to her noninjured classmates. What accounts for her recovery of skills? How about her cognitive deficits?
APPLY	Which infant enrichment program would you choose: one that emphasizes gentle talking and touching, exposure to sights and sounds, and simple social games, or one that includes reading and number drills and classical music lessons? Explain.
CONNECT	What stance on the nature–nurture issue does evidence on development of handedness support? Document your answer with research findings.

Factors Affecting Physical Growth

Physical growth, like other aspects of development, results from the continuous and complex interplay between genetic and environmental factors. In the following sections, we take a closer look at this familiar theme.

Heredity

Because identical twins are much more alike in body size than fraternal twins, we know that heredity is an important factor in physical growth. When diet and health are adequate, height and rate of physical growth (as measured by skeletal age and timing of first menstruation) are largely determined by heredity. In fact, as long as negative environmental influences, such as poor nutrition or illness, are not severe, children and adolescents typically show **catch-up growth**—a return to a genetically influenced growth path once conditions improve. Still, many internal organs, ranging from the brain to the heart and digestive system, may be permanently compromised (Hales & Ozanne, 2003). (Recall the consequences of inadequate prenatal nutrition for long-term health, discussed on pages 94–95 of Chapter 3.)

Genes influence growth by controlling the body's production of and sensitivity to hormones. Mutations can disrupt this process, leading to deviations in physical size. Occasionally, a mutation becomes widespread in a population. Consider the Efe of the Republic of Congo, who normally grow to an adult height of less than 5 feet. During early childhood, the growth of Efe children tapers off. By age 5, the average Efe child is shorter than over 97 percent of North American 5-year-olds. For genetic reasons, growth hormone (GH) has less effect on Efe youngsters than on other children (Bailey, 1990). The Efe's small size probably evolved because it reduced their caloric requirements in the face of food scarcity in the rain forests of Central Africa and permitted them to move easily through the dense forest underbrush.

Genetic makeup also affects body weight, as seen in the weights of adopted children, which correlate more strongly with those of their biological than of their adoptive parents (Sørensen, Holst, & Stunkard, 1998). As far as weight is concerned, however, environment—in particular, nutrition—plays an especially important role.

Nutrition

Nutrition is important at any time of development, but it is especially crucial during the first 2 years because the brain and body are growing so rapidly. Pound for pound, an infant's energy needs are twice those of an adult. Twenty-five percent of their total caloric intake is devoted to growth, and infants need extra calories to keep rapidly developing organs of the body functioning properly (Trahms & Pipes, 1997).

• **BREASTFEEDING VERSUS BOTTLE-FEEDING** • Babies not only need enough food but also the right kind of food. In early infancy, breastfeeding is ideally suited to their needs, and bottled formulas try to imitate it. Refer to Applying What We Know on the following page, which summarizes the major nutritional and health advantages of breast milk.

Because of these benefits, breastfed babies in poverty-stricken regions of the world are much less likely than bottle-fed babies to be malnourished and 6 to 14 times more likely to survive the first year of life. The World Health Organization recommends breastfeeding until age 2 years, with solid foods added at 6 months—practices that, if widely followed, would save the lives of more than a million infants annually. Even breastfeeding for just a few weeks offers some protection against respiratory and intestinal infections, which are devastating to young children in developing countries. And because a mother is less likely to get pregnant while she is nursing, breastfeeding helps increase spacing between siblings, a major factor in reducing infant and childhood deaths in nations with widespread poverty (Darnton-Hill & Coyne, 1998). (Note, however, that breastfeeding is not a reliable method of birth control.)

Yet many mothers in the developing world do not know about the benefits of breastfeeding. In Africa, the Middle East, and Latin America, fewer than 40 percent of mothers breastfeed exclusively, and fewer than 60 percent partially, during the first 6 months. Furthermore, 30 to 60 percent of these mothers stop breastfeeding during the second year (Lauer et al., 2004). Many give their babies commercial formula or low-grade nutrients, such as rice water or highly diluted cow or goat milk. Contamination of these foods as a result of poor sanitation is common and often leads to illnesses. The United Nations has encouraged all hospitals and maternity units in developing countries to promote breastfeeding as long as mothers do not have viral or bacterial infections (such as HIV or tuberculosis) that can be transmitted to the baby. Today, most developing countries have banned the practice of giving free or subsidized formula to new mothers.

Partly as a result of the natural childbirth movement, over the past two decades, breastfeeding has become more common in industrialized nations, especially among well-educated women. Today, 68 percent of American and 73 percent of Canadian mothers breastfeed. However,

Ⓖ Breastfeeding is especially important in developing countries, where infants are at risk for malnutrition and early death due to widespread poverty. This baby from Gambia is likely to grow normally during the first year because his mother decided to breast-feed.

© Sean Sprague/The Image Works

Applying

What We Know   Reasons to Breastfeed

Nutritional and Health Advantages	Explanation
Provides the correct balance of fat and protein.	Compared with the milk of other mammals, human milk is higher in fat and lower in protein. This balance, as well as the unique proteins and fats contained in human milk, is ideal for a rapidly myelinating nervous system.
Ensures nutritional completeness.	A mother who breastfeeds need not add other foods to her infant's diet until the baby is 6 months old. The milks of all mammals are low in iron, but the iron contained in breast milk is much more easily absorbed by the baby's system. Consequently, bottle-fed infants need iron-fortified formula.
Helps ensure healthy physical growth.	In the first few months, breastfed infants add weight and length slightly faster than bottle-fed infants, who catch up by the end of the first year. One-year-old breastfed babies are leaner (have a higher percentage of muscle to fat), a growth pattern that may help prevent later overweight and obesity.
Protects against many diseases.	Breastfeeding transfers antibodies and other infection-fighting agents from mother to child and enhances functioning of the immune system. As a result, compared with bottle-fed infants, breastfed babies have far fewer allergic reactions and respiratory and intestinal illnesses. Components of human milk that protect against disease can be added to formula, but breastfeeding provides superior immunity.
Protects against faulty jaw development and tooth decay.	Sucking the mother's nipple instead of an artificial nipple helps avoid malocclusion, a condition in which the upper and lower jaws do not meet properly. It also protects against tooth decay due to sweet liquid remaining in the mouths of infants who fall asleep while sucking on a bottle.
Ensures digestibility.	Because breastfed babies have a different kind of bacteria growing in their intestines than do bottle-fed infants, they rarely suffer from constipation or other gastrointestinal problems.
Smoothes the transition to solid foods.	Breastfed infants accept new solid foods more easily than bottle-fed infants, perhaps because of their greater experience with a variety of flavors, which pass from the maternal diet into the mother's milk.

Sources: Fulham, Collier, & Duggan, 2003; Kramer et al., 2002, 2003; Kramer & Kakuma, 2002.

about two-thirds of breastfeeding American mothers and nearly half of Canadian mothers stop after a few months (Ahluwalia et al., 2003; Health Canada, 2002a). Breast milk is so easily digestible that a breastfed infant becomes hungry quite often—every 1½ to 2 hours, compared to every 3 to 4 hours for a bottle-fed baby. This makes breastfeeding inconvenient for many employed women. Not surprisingly, mothers who return to work sooner wean their babies from the breast earlier (Arora et al., 2000).

Mothers who cannot be with their babies all the time can still combine breastfeeding with bottle-feeding. American and Canadian national health agencies advise exclusive breastfeeding for the first 6 months. In the United States, recommendations also suggest that breast milk be included in the baby's diet until at least 1 year; in Canada, until 2 years and beyond (Health Canada, 2004c; Satcher, 2001).

Women who cannot or do not want to breastfeed sometimes worry that they are depriving their baby of an experience essential for healthy psychological development. Yet breastfed and bottle-fed children in industrialized nations do not differ in emotional adjustment (Fergusson & Woodward, 1999). Some studies report a small advantage in intelligence test performance for children and adolescents who were breastfed, after controlling for many factors, but other studies find no cognitive benefits (Gómez-Sanchiz et al., 2003; Jain, Concat, & Leventhal, 2002). Notice in Applying What We Know above that breast milk provides nutrients ideally suited for early rapid brain development.

• **NUTRITION IN CHILDHOOD AND ADOLESCENCE** • Around 1 year, infants' diets should include all the basic food groups. As children approach age 2, their appetites become unpredictable. Preschoolers eat well at one meal but barely touch their food at the next, and many become picky eaters. This decline in appetite occurs because growth has slowed. Furthermore, preschoolers' wariness of new foods is adaptive. Sticking to familiar foods means that they are less likely to swallow dangerous substances when adults are not around to protect them (Birch & Fisher, 1995). Parents need not worry about variations in amount eaten from meal to meal. Over the course of a day, preschoolers will compensate for a meal in which they eat little by eating more at a later meal (Hursti, 1999).

Children tend to imitate the food choices and eating practices of people they admire—adults as well as peers. For example, mothers who drink milk or soft drinks tend to have 5-year-old daughters with a similar beverage preference (Fisher et al., 2001). In Mexico, where children see family members delighting in the taste of peppery foods, preschoolers enthusiastically eat chili peppers, whereas American children reject them (Birch, Zimmerman, & Hind, 1980).

Repeated exposure to a new food (without direct pressure to eat it) also increases children's acceptance. Serving broccoli or tofu increases children's liking for these healthy foods. In contrast, offering sweet fruit or soft drinks promotes "milk avoidance" (Black et al., 2002). Although children's healthy eating depends on a wholesome food environment, too much parental control over eating limits children's opportunities to develop self-control. Some parents offer bribes ("Finish your vegetables, and you can have an extra cookie"), a practice that causes children to like the healthy food less and the treat more (Birch, Fisher, & Davison, 2003).

Once puberty arrives, rapid body growth leads to a dramatic rise in food intake. This increase in nutritional requirements comes at a time when eating habits are the poorest. Of all age groups, adolescents are the most likely to skip breakfast (a practice linked to obesity), consume empty calories, and eat on the run (Videon & Manning, 2003). Although fast-food restaurants, which are favorite teenage gathering places, now offer some healthful menu options, adolescents need guidance in choosing these alternatives. Fast-food eating and school à la carte food purchases (from snack bars and vending machines) are strongly associated with consumption of high-fat foods and soft drinks, indicating that teenagers often make unhealthy food selections (Bowman et al., 2004; Kubik et al., 2003).

The most common nutritional problem of adolescence is iron deficiency. A tired, listless, irritable adolescent may be suffering from anemia rather than unhappiness and should have a medical checkup. Most teenagers do not get enough calcium, and they are also deficient in riboflavin (vitamin B$_2$)and magnesium (both of which support metabolism) (Cavadini, Siega-Riz, & Popkin, 2000).

Frequency of family meals is strongly associated with healthy eating—greater intake of fruits, vegetables, grains, and calcium-rich foods—in teenagers (Neumark-Sztainer et al., 2003). Compared to families with children, however, those with adolescents eat fewer meals together. Finding ways to arrange family meals, despite busy schedules, could greatly improve teenagers' diets.

• **MALNUTRITION** • In developing countries and war-torn areas, where food resources are limited, malnutrition is widespread. Recent evidence indicates that about one-third of the world's children suffer from malnutrition before age 5 (UNICEF, 2004). The 4 to 7 percent who are severely affected suffer from two dietary diseases.

Marasmus is a wasted condition of the body caused by a diet low in all essential nutrients. It usually appears in the first year of life when a baby's mother is too malnourished to produce enough breast milk and bottle-feeding is also inadequate. The starving baby becomes painfully thin and is in danger of dying.

Kwashiorkor is caused by an unbalanced diet very low in protein. The disease usually strikes after weaning, between 1 and 3 years of age. It is common in areas of the world where children get just enough calories from starchy foods, but protein resources are scarce. The child's body responds by breaking down its own protein reserves. Soon the belly enlarges, the feet swell, the hair falls out, and a rash appears on the skin. A once bright-eyed, curious youngster becomes irritable and listless.

Children who survive these extreme forms of malnutrition are growth stunted—much smaller than average in all body dimensions (Galler, Ramsey, & Solimano, 1985). When their diets improve, however, they often gain excessive weight. Studies in many poverty-stricken regions of the world reveal that growth-stunted children are far more likely to be overweight than their nonstunted agemates (Branca &

The swollen abdomen and listless behavior of this Honduran child are classic symptoms of kwashiorkor, a nutritional illness that results from a diet very low in protein.
© Bob Daemmrich/The Image Works

Ferrari, 2002). A malnourished body protects itself by establishing a low basal metabolism rate, which may endure after nutrition improves. Also, malnutrition may disrupt appetite control centers in the brain, causing the child to overeat when food becomes plentiful.

Learning and behavior are also seriously affected. One long-term study of marasmic children revealed that an improved diet did not result in catch-up in head size (Stoch et al., 1982). The malnutrition probably interfered with growth of neural fibers and myelination, causing a permanent loss in brain weight. These children score low on intelligence tests, show poor fine motor coordination, and have difficulty paying attention (Galler et al., 1990; Liu et al., 2003). They also display a more intense stress response to fear-arousing situations, perhaps caused by the constant, gnawing pain of hunger (Fernald & Grantham-McGregor, 1998).

Recall from our discussion of prenatal malnutrition in Chapter 3 that the passivity and irritability of malnourished children worsen the impact of poor diet. These behaviors may appear even when protein-calorie deprivation is only mild to moderate. They also accompany *iron-deficiency anemia,* a condition common among poverty-stricken infants and children that interferes with many central nervous system processes. Withdrawal and listlessness reduce the nutritionally deprived child's ability to pay attention, explore, and evoke sensitive caregiving from parents, whose lives are already disrupted by poverty and stressful living conditions (Grantham-McGregor & Ani, 2001; Lozoff et al., 1998). For this reason, interventions for malnourished children must improve the family situation as well as the child's nutrition. Even better are efforts at prevention—providing high-quality food and medical care before the dire effects of malnutrition run their course.

Inadequate nutrition is not confined to developing countries; it is a national and international crisis. Because government-sponsored supplementary food programs do not reach all families in need, an estimated 13 percent of Canadian children and 16 percent of American children suffer from *food insecurity*—uncertain access to enough food for a healthy, active life. Food insecurity is especially high among single-parent families (30 percent) and low-income ethnic minority families—for example, Hispanic and African Americans (22 percent) and Canadian Aboriginals (31 percent) (U.S. Department of Agriculture, 2003; Government of Canada, 2004b). Although few of these children have marasmus or kwashiorkor, their physical growth and ability to learn are still affected.

• **OBESITY** • Today, about one-third of North American children and adolescents are overweight, half or more extremely so. Nearly 15 percent of Canadian and 16 percent of American youngsters suffer from **obesity,** a body weight greater than 20 percent over the average for the child's age, sex, and physical build (U.S. Department of Health and Human Services, 2004d; Willms, Tremblay, & Katzmarzyk, 2003). During the past several decades, a rise in overweight and obesity has occurred in many Western nations, with dramatic increases in Canada, Finland, Greece, Great Britain, Ireland, New Zealand, and especially the United States. Smaller increases have occurred in other industrialized nations, including Australia, Germany, Israel, the Netherlands, and Sweden. Obesity rates are also increasing rapidly in developing countries, as urbanization shifts the population toward sedentary lifestyles and diets high in meats and refined foods (World Press Review, 2004; Wrotniak et al., 2004).

Overweight and obesity rise with age; 80 percent of affected youngsters become overweight adults. Besides serious emotional and social difficulties, obese children are at risk for lifelong health problems. High blood pressure, high cholesterol levels, and respiratory abnormalities begin to appear in the early school years—symptoms that are powerful predictors of heart disease, adult-onset diabetes, liver and gallbladder disease, sleep and digestive disorders, most forms of cancer, and early death (Calle et al., 2003; Krebs & Jacobson, 2003). Indeed, "adult-onset" diabetes, which until recently was rare in childhood, is rising rapidly among overweight children, making the early appearance of other health problems more likely as well (Bobo et al., 2004).

Causes of Obesity. Not all children are equally at risk for excessive weight gain. Overweight children tend to have overweight parents, and concordance for obesity is higher in identical than in fraternal twins. But heredity accounts only for a tendency to gain weight (Salbe et al., 2002a). Environment is powerfully important, as seen in the consistent relationship between low SES and overweight and obesity in industrialized nations, with especially high rates

ⓖ These children at a county fair are eating cheesy fries—a high-fat, high-salt food—with joyous abandon. If such high-calorie, fatty foods are prominent in their family diet, and if their parents are overweight or obese, these children too may become overweight, as environment is a powerful predictor of obesity. © Jeff Greenberg/The Image Works

among low-income, ethnic minorities, including African-American, Hispanic, Native-American, and Canadian Aboriginal children and adults (Anand et al., 2001; Kim et al., 2002). Factors responsible include lack of knowledge about a healthy diet; a tendency to buy high-fat, low-cost foods; and family stress, which prompts some individuals to overeat. Recall, also, that children who were malnourished early in life are at increased risk for becoming overweight later.

Parental feeding practices also contribute to childhood obesity. Overweight children are more likely to eat larger quantities of high-calorie, sugary and fatty foods, perhaps because these foods are prominent in the diets offered by their parents, who also tend to be overweight. Interviews with more than 3,000 American parents revealed that many served their 4- to 24-month-olds French fries, pizza, candy, sugary fruit drinks, and soda on a daily basis. On average, infants consumed 20 percent and toddlers 30 percent more calories than they needed (Briefel et al., 2004). Some parents anxiously overfeed, interpreting almost all their child's discomforts as a desire for food. Others are overly controlling, restricting when, what, and how much their child eats and worrying that the child will gain too much weight (Birch, Fisher, & Davison, 2003; Spruijt-Metz et al., 2002). In each case, parents fail to help children learn to regulate their own food intake. Also, parents of overweight children often use food to reinforce other behaviors—a practice that leads children to attach great value to the treat (Sherry et al., 2004).

Because of these experiences, obese children soon develop maladaptive eating habits. They are more responsive to external stimuli associated with food—taste, sight, smell, time of day, and food-related words—and less responsive to internal hunger cues than are normal-weight individuals (Braet & Crombez, 2003; Jansen et al., 2003). They also eat faster and chew their food less thoroughly, a behavior pattern that appears as early as 18 months of age (Drabman et al., 1979).

Overweight children are less physically active than their normal-weight peers, and their parents are similarly inactive (Davison & Birch, 2002). Inactivity is both cause and consequence of excessive weight gain. Research reveals that the rise in childhood obesity is due in part to the many hours North American children spend watching television. In a study that tracked children's TV viewing from ages 4 to 11, the more TV children watched, the more body fat they added, with children who devoted more than 3 hours per day to TV accumulating 40 percent more fat than those devoting less than 1¾ hours (see Figure 5.14) (Proctor et al., 2003). Watching TV greatly reduces time spent in physical exercise, and TV ads encourage children to eat fattening, unhealthy snacks. As children get heavier, they increasingly

▶ **Figure 5.14**

Relationship of television viewing to gains in body fat from ages 4 to 11. Researchers followed children longitudinally, collecting information on hours per day of television viewing and on body fat, measured in millimeters of skinfold thickness at five body sites (upper arms, shoulders, abdomen, trunk, and thighs). The more TV children watched, the greater the gain in body fat. At ages 10 to 11, the difference between children watching less than 1¾ hours and those watching more than 3 hours had become large.
(Adapted from M. H. Proctor et al., 2003, "Television Viewing and Change in Body Fat from Preschool to Early Adolescence: The Framingham Children's Study," *International Journal of Obesity, 27,* p. 831. © Nature Publishing Group. Adapted by permission.)

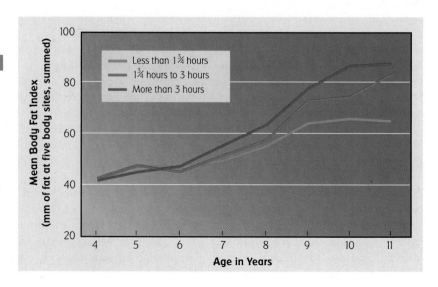

replace active play with sedentary pursuits, including eating, and gain still more weight (Salbe et al., 2002b).

Finally, the broader food environment affects the incidence of obesity. The Pima Indians of Arizona, who recently changed from a traditional diet of plant foods to a high-fat, typically American diet, have one of the highest rates of obesity in the world. Compared with descendants of their ancestors living in the remote Sierra Madre region of Mexico, the Arizona Pima have body weights 50 percent higher. Half the population has diabetes (eight times the national average), with many in their twenties and thirties already disabled by the disease—blind, in wheelchairs, and on kidney dialysis (Gladwell, 1998). Although the Pima have a genetic susceptibility to overweight, it emerges only under Western dietary conditions.

⑥ This Pima medicine man of Arizona is obese. By the time his daughters reach adolescence, they are likely to follow in his footsteps. Because of a high-fat diet, the Pima residing in the Southwestern United States have one of the highest rates of obesity in the world.
© Stephen Trimble

▶ *Consequences of Obesity.* Unfortunately, physical attractiveness is a powerful predictor of social acceptance in Western societies. Both children and adults rate obese youngsters as unlikable, stereotyping them as lazy, sloppy, ugly, stupid, self-doubting, and deceitful. In school, obese children are often socially isolated (Kilpatrick & Sanders, 1978; Strauss & Pollack, 2003). By middle childhood, obese children report more emotional, social, and school difficulties and display more behavior problems than their normal-weight agemates. Persistent obesity from childhood into adolescence predicts serious disorders, including defiance and aggression as well as severe depression (Mustillo et al., 2003; Schwimmer, Burwinkle, & Varni, 2003). As unhappiness and overeating contribute to one another, the child remains overweight.

The psychological consequences of obesity combine with continuing discrimination to result in reduced life chances. By young adulthood, overweight individuals have completed fewer years of schooling, have lower incomes, and are less likely to marry than are individuals with other chronic health problems. These outcomes are particularly strong for females (Gortmaker et al., 1993).

▶ *Treating Obesity.* Childhood obesity is difficult to treat because it is a family disorder. In a British study, only one-fourth of overweight parents judged their overweight children to have a weight problem (Jeffrey, 2004). The most effective interventions for obesity are family based and focus on changing attitudes and behaviors. In one study, both parent and child revised eating patterns, exercised daily, and reinforced each other with praise and points for progress, which they exchanged for special activities and times together. The more weight parents lost, the more their children lost—an outcome confirming the effectiveness of a family-based approach (Wrotniak et al., 2004). Weight loss was greater when treatments focused on both dietary and lifestyle changes, including regular, vigorous exercise. Follow-ups after 5 and 10 years showed that children maintained weight loss more effectively than adults (Epstein, Roemmich, & Raynor, 2001). Intervening early is essential for lifelong change.

Schools can help reduce obesity by ensuring regular physical education and serving healthier meals. The makeup of school lunches and snacks can greatly affect body weight because children consume one-third of their daily energy intake at school. As one example, in Singapore, school interventions consisting of nutrition education, low-fat food choices, and daily physical activity led child and adolescent obesity to decline from 14 to 11 percent (Schmitz & Jeffery, 2000).

Infectious Disease

Among well-nourished youngsters, ordinary childhood illnesses have no effect on physical growth. But when children are poorly fed, disease interacts with malnutrition in a vicious spiral, and the consequences can be severe.

• INFECTIOUS DISEASE AND MALNUTRITION • In developing nations where a large proportion of the population lives in poverty, illnesses such as measles and chicken pox, which typically do not appear until after age 3 in industrialized nations, occur much earlier. Poor diet depresses the body's immune system, making children far more susceptible to disease. Worldwide, of the 10 million annual deaths of children under age 5, 98 percent are in developing countries and 70 percent are due to infectious diseases (World Health Organization, 2003).

Disease, in turn, is a major contributor to malnutrition, thereby hindering physical growth and cognitive development. Illness reduces appetite, and it limits the body's ability to absorb foods. These outcomes are especially severe among children with intestinal infections. In developing countries, diarrhea is widespread, and it increases in early childhood as a result of unsafe water and contaminated foods, leading to 2½ million childhood deaths each year (Tharpar & Sanderson, 2004). Studies carried out in the slums and shantytowns of Brazil and Peru reveal that the more persistent diarrhea is in early childhood, the shorter children are in height and the lower they score on mental tests during the school years (Checkley et al., 2003; Niehaus et al., 2002).

Most growth retardation and deaths due to diarrhea can be prevented with nearly cost-free *oral rehydration therapy (ORT),* in which sick children are given a glucose, salt, and water solution that quickly replaces fluids the body loses. Since 1990, public health workers have taught nearly half of families in the developing world how to administer ORT. Also, supplements of zinc, a mineral essential for immune system functioning that costs only 30 cents for a month's supply, substantially reduce the incidence of severe and prolonged diarrhea (Bhandari et al., 2002). The lives of millions of children are being saved annually through these interventions.

• **IMMUNIZATION** • In industrialized nations, childhood diseases have declined dramatically during the past half-century, largely as a result of widespread immunization of infants and young children. Nevertheless, about 20 percent of American infants and toddlers are not fully immunized. Of the 80 percent who receive a complete schedule of vaccinations in the first 2 years, some do not receive the immunizations they need in early childhood. Overall, 23 percent of American preschoolers lack essential immunizations, a rate that rises to 40 percent for poverty-stricken children (U.S. Department of Health and Human Services, 2003b). In contrast, fewer than 10 percent of preschoolers lack immunizations in Denmark and Norway, and fewer than 7 percent in Canada, Great Britain, the Netherlands, and Sweden (Health Canada, 2000; United Nations, 2002).

How have these countries managed to achieve higher rates of immunization than the United States? In earlier chapters, we noted that compared to other Western nations, many more U.S. children do not have access to the health care they need. In 1994, all medically uninsured children in the United States were guaranteed free immunizations, a program that has led to a steady improvement in immunization rates.

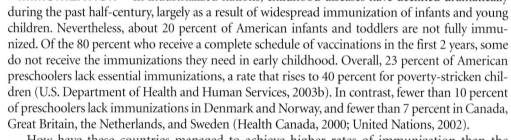

⊚ These families wait their turn for immunizations at a crowded public health clinic—the only option for people who lack private health insurance. Unfortunately, not all parents have schedules that allow them to endure the long waits, so their children go unvaccinated. © Spencer Grant/PhotoEdit

Inability to pay for vaccines, however, is only one cause of inadequate immunization. Parents with stressful daily lives or without health benefits of their own often fail to schedule vaccination appointments. Others without a primary care physician do not want to endure long waits in crowded U.S. public health clinics (Dombrowski, Lantz, & Freed, 2004; Hughes & Ng, 2003). Misconceptions also contribute—for example, the notion that vaccines do not work or that they weaken the immune system. Some parents have been influenced by media reports suggesting that the measles–mumps–rubella vaccine has contributed to a rise in the number of children diagnosed with autism, although large-scale studies show no association between immunization and autism (Dales, Hammer, & Smith, 2001; Stehr-Green et al., 2003). In areas where many parents have refused to immunize their children, new outbreaks of whooping cough, which is life-threatening to infants, have occurred (Tuyen & Bisgard, 2003). Public education programs directed at increasing parental knowledge about the importance and safety of timely immunizations are badly needed.

Emotional Well-Being

We may not think of love and stimulation as necessary for healthy physical growth, but they are just as vital as food. **Nonorganic failure to thrive,** a growth disorder that results from lack of parental love, is usually present by 18 months of age. Infants who have it show all the signs of marasmus—their bodies look wasted, and they are withdrawn and apathetic. But no organic (or biological) cause for the baby's failure to grow can be found. The baby is offered enough food and has no serious illness. The behavior of infants with failure to thrive provides a strong clue to its diagnosis. These infants keep their eyes on nearby adults, anxiously watching their every move. They rarely smile when the mother comes near or cuddle when picked up (Steward, 2001).

Family circumstances surrounding failure to thrive help explain these typical reactions. During feeding, diaper changing, and play, mothers of these infants seem cold and distant, at other times controlling, impatient, and hostile (Hagekull, Bohlin, & Rydell, 1997). In response, babies try to protect themselves by keeping track of the threatening adult's where-abouts and, when she approaches, avoiding her gaze. Often an unhappy marriage or parental psychological disturbance contributes to these serious caregiving problems (Drotar, Pallotta, & Eckerle, 1994; Duniz et al., 1996). Sometimes the baby is irritable and displays abnormal feeding behaviors, such as poor sucking or vomiting—circumstances that further stress the parent–child relationship (Wooster, 1999). When treated early, by helping parents or placing the baby in a caring foster home, failure-to-thrive infants show quick catch-up growth. But if the disorder is not corrected in infancy, most children remain small and show lasting cognitive and emotional difficulties (Wooster, 2000).

Extreme emotional deprivation can interfere with the production of GH and lead to **psychosocial dwarfism,** a growth disorder that usually appears between 2 and 15 years of age. Typical characteristics include very short stature, decreased GH secretion, immature skeletal age, and serious adjustment problems, which help distinguish psychosocial dwarfism from normal shortness (Doeker et al., 1999; Voss, Mulligan, & Betts, 1998). When such children are removed from their emotionally inadequate environments, their GH levels quickly return to normal, and they grow rapidly. But if treatment is delayed, the dwarfism can be permanent.

Ask Yourself

REVIEW	Explain how breastfeeding can have lifelong consequences for the development of babies born in poverty-stricken regions of the world.
APPLY	Ten-month-old Shaun is below average in height and painfully thin. He has one of two serious growth disorders. Name them, and indicate what clues you would look for to tell which one Shaun has.
CONNECT	How are bidirectional influences between parent and child involved in the impact of malnutrition on psychological development?
REFLECT	In rearing a child, what steps would you take to prevent obesity? List some feeding practices you would use and some you would avoid.

Puberty: The Physical Transition to Adulthood

During **puberty,** young people attain an adult-sized body and become capable of producing offspring. Accompanying rapid body growth are changes in physical features related to sexual functioning. Some, called **primary sexual characteristics,** involve the reproductive organs directly (ovaries, uterus, and vagina in females; penis, scrotum, and testes in males). Others, called **secondary sexual characteristics,** are visible on the outside of the body and serve as additional signs of sexual maturity (for example, breast development in females, and the appearance of underarm and pubic hair in both sexes). As the Milestones table on page 198 shows, these characteristics develop in a fairly standard sequence, although the ages at which each begins and is completed vary greatly. Typically, pubertal development takes 4 years, but some adolescents complete it in 2 years, whereas others take 5 to 6 years. And as you will soon see, puberty profoundly affects psychological development and social relationships.

Sexual Maturation in Girls

Menarche, from the Greek word *arche,* meaning "beginning," is the scientific name for first menstruation. Most people view it as the major sign of puberty in girls, but menarche actually occurs late in the sequence of pubertal events. Female puberty begins with the budding of the breasts, the growth spurt, and pubic hair. Menarche typically happens around age 12½ for North American girls and age 13 for Western European girls. But the age range is wide, extending from 10½ to 15½. Following menarche, breast and pubic hair growth are completed, and underarm hair appears (Rogol, Roemmich, & Clark, 2002).

MILESTONES

PUBERTAL DEVELOPMENT IN NORTH AMERICAN BOYS AND GIRLS

Girls	Average Age Attained	Age Range
Breasts begin to "bud"	10	(8–13)
Height spurt begins	10	(8–13)
Pubic hair appears	10.5	(8–14)
Peak strength spurt	11.6	(9.5–14)
Peak height spurt	11.7	(10–13.5)
Menarche (first menstruation) occurs	12.5	(10.5–14)
Peak weight spurt	12.7	(10–14)
Adult stature reached	13	(10–16)
Breast growth completed	14	(10–16)
Pubic hair growth completed	14.5	(14–15)

Boys	Average Age Attained	Age Range
Testes begin to enlarge	11.5	(9.5–13.5)
Pubic hair appears	12	(10–15)
Penis begins to enlarge	12	(10.5–14.5)
Height spurt begins	12.5	(10.5–16)
Spermarche (first ejaculation) occurs	13.5	(12–16)
Peak height spurt	14	(12.5–15.5)
Peak weight spurt	14	(12.5–15.5)
Facial hair begins to grow	14	(12.5–15.5)
Voice begins to deepen	14	(12.5–15.5)
Penis and testes growth completed	14.5	(12.5–16)
Peak strength spurt	15.3	(13–17)
Adult stature reached	15.5	(13.5–17.5)
Pubic hair growth completed	15.5	(14–17)

Sources: Chumlea et al., 2003; Rogol, Roemmich, & Clark, 2002; Wu, Mendola, & Buck, 2002.
Photos: (left) © Aaron Haupt/Photo Researchers, Inc.; (right) © Bill Aron/PhotoEdit

Notice in the Milestones table that nature delays sexual maturity until the girl's body is large enough for childbearing; menarche takes place after the peak of the height spurt. As an extra measure of security, for 12 to 18 months following menarche, the menstrual cycle often occurs without an ovum being released from the ovaries (Bogin, 2001). However, this temporary period of sterility does not occur in all girls, and it cannot be relied on for protection against pregnancy.

Sexual Maturation in Boys

The first sign of puberty in boys is the enlargement of the testes (glands that manufacture sperm), accompanied by changes in the texture and color of the scrotum. Pubic hair emerges soon after, about the same time the penis begins to enlarge (Rogol, Roemmich, & Clark, 2002).

Refer again to the Milestones table above, and you will see that the growth spurt occurs much later in the sequence of pubertal events for boys than for girls. Also, boys' height gain is more intense and longer lasting (Bogin, 2001). When it reaches its peak (at about age 14), enlargement of the testes and penis is nearly complete, and underarm hair appears soon after. Facial and body hair also emerge just after the peak in body growth and increase gradually for several years. Another landmark of male physical maturity is the deepening of the voice as the larynx enlarges and the vocal cords lengthen. (Girls' voices also deepen slightly.) Voice change usually occurs at the peak of the male growth spurt and often is not complete until puberty is over.

While the penis is growing, the prostate gland and seminal vesicles (which together produce semen, the fluid in which sperm are bathed) enlarge. Then, around age 13½, **spermarche,** or first ejaculation, occurs (Rogol, Roemmich, & Clark, 2002). For a while, the semen contains few living sperm. So, like girls, boys have an initial period of reduced fertility.

Individual and Group Differences in Pubertal Growth

Heredity contributes substantially to the timing of puberty; identical twins generally reach menarche within a month or two of each other, whereas fraternal twins differ by about 12 months (Kaprio et al., 1995). Nutrition and exercise also make a difference. In females, a sharp rise in body weight and fat may trigger sexual maturation. Fat cells release a protein called *leptin,* which is believed to signal the brain that girls' energy stores are sufficient for puberty—a likely reason that breast and pubic hair growth and menarche occur earlier for heavier and, especially, obese girls. In contrast, girls who begin rigorous athletic training at young ages or who eat very little (both of which reduce the percentage of body fat) usually experience later puberty (Anderson, Dallal, & Must, 2003; Delemarre-van de Waal, 2002).

Variations in pubertal growth also exist between regions of the world and between income and ethnic groups. Physical health plays a major role. In poverty-stricken regions where malnutrition and infectious disease are common, menarche is greatly delayed. In many parts of Africa, it does not occur until age 14 to 16. Within developing countries, girls from higher-income families consistently reach menarche 6 months to 3 years earlier than those from economically disadvantaged homes (Parent et al., 2003).

But in industrialized nations where food is abundant, the joint roles of heredity and environment in pubertal growth are apparent. For example, breast and pubic hair growth begin, on average, around age 9 in African-American girls—a year earlier than in Caucasian-American girls. And African American girls reach menarche about 6 months earlier, around age 12. Although widespread overweight and obesity in the black population contribute, a genetically influenced faster rate of physical maturation is also involved. Black girls usually reach menarche before white girls of the same age and body weight (Anderson, Dallal, & Must, 2003; Chumlea et al., 2003).

Early family experiences may also contribute to the timing of puberty. One theory suggests that humans have evolved to be sensitive to the emotional quality of their childhood environments. When children's safety and security are at risk, it is adaptive for them to reproduce early. Several studies indicate that girls exposed to family conflict tend to reach menarche early, whereas those with warm family ties reach menarche relatively late (Ellis & Garber, 2000; Ellis et al., 1999; Romans et al., 2003). But critics of this theory claim that the process through which parental behavior affects timing of menarche is unclear. According to an alternative, genetic hypothesis, an X-linked gene that predisposes fathers to engage in family fighting, when passed to daughters, accelerates puberty. In a study involving DNA analysis, presence of this gene was linked to aggressive behavior in men and to earlier age of menarche in women (Comings et al., 2002).

Sex differences in pubertal growth are obvious in these sixth graders. Although the girl is the same age as the boy in the striped shirt, the girl is taller and far more mature than the boy.
© Mary Kate Denney/PhotoEdit

 ## The Psychological Impact of Pubertal Events

Think back to your late elementary school and junior high days. As you reached puberty, how did your feelings about yourself and your relationships with others change? Were your reactions similar to those predicted by Rousseau and Hall, described at the beginning of this chapter?

Is Puberty Inevitably a Period of Storm and Stress?

Recent research suggests that the notion of adolescence as a biologically determined period of storm and stress is greatly exaggerated. A number of problems, such as eating disorders, depression, suicide (see Chapter 11), and lawbreaking (see Chapter 12), occur more often in adolescence than earlier. But the overall rate of serious psychological disturbance rises only slightly (by about 2 percent) from childhood to adolescence, when it is the same as in the adult population—about 20 percent (Costello & Angold, 1995). Although some teenagers encounter serious difficulties, emotional turbulence is not a routine feature of adolescence.

The first researcher to point out the wide variability in adolescent adjustment was anthropologist Margaret Mead (1928). She traveled to the Pacific islands of Samoa and returned with a startling conclusion: Because of the culture's relaxed social relationships and openness toward sexuality, adolescence "is perhaps the pleasantest time the Samoan girl (or boy) will ever know" (p. 308). In Mead's alternative view, the social environment is entirely responsible for the range of teenage experiences, from erratic and agitated to calm and stress-free.

Later researchers found that adolescence was not as smooth and untroubled as Mead had assumed (Freeman, 1983). Still, Mead's work had an enormous impact. Today we know that the experience of adolescence is a product of both biological and social forces. Simpler societies have a shorter transition to adulthood, but adolescence is not absent (Weisfield, 1997). A study of 186 tribal and village cultures revealed that almost all had an intervening phase, however brief, between childhood and full assumption of adult roles (Schlegel & Barry, 1991).

In industrialized nations, where successful participation in economic life requires many years of education, young people face additional years of dependence on parents and postponement of sexual gratification. As a result, adolescence is greatly extended, and teenagers confront a wider array of psychological challenges. In the following sections, we will see many examples of how biological and social forces combine to affect teenagers' adjustment.

Reactions to Pubertal Changes

Two generations ago, menarche was often traumatic. Today, girls commonly react with surprise, undoubtedly due to the sudden onset of the event. Otherwise, they typically report a mixture of positive and negative emotions. Yet wide individual differences exist, depending on prior knowledge and support from family members. Both are influenced by cultural attitudes toward puberty and sexuality.

For girls who have no advance information, menarche can be shocking and disturbing. In the 1950s, up to 50 percent received no prior warning, and of those who did, many were given negative, "grin-and-bear-it" messages (Costos, Ackerman, & Paradis, 2002; Shainess, 1961). Today, few girls are uninformed, a shift that is probably due to contemporary parents' greater willingness to discuss sexual matters and to the spread of health education classes (Omar, McElderry, & Zakharia, 2003). Almost all girls get some information from their mothers. And girls whose fathers know about their daughters' pubertal changes adjust especially well. Perhaps a father's involvement reflects a family atmosphere that is highly understanding and accepting of physical and sexual matters (Brooks-Gunn & Ruble, 1980, 1983).

Like girls' reactions to menarche, boys' reactions to spermarche reflect mixed feelings. Virtually all boys know about ejaculation ahead of time, but many say that no one spoke to them before or during puberty about physical changes (Omar, McElderry, & Zakharia, 2003). Usually they get information from reading material. But even those with advance knowledge often say that their first ejaculation occurred earlier than they expected and that they were unprepared for it. As with girls, the better prepared boys feel, the more positively they react (Stein & Reiser, 1994). In addition, whereas almost all girls tell a friend that they are menstruating, far fewer boys tell anyone about spermarche (Downs & Fuller, 1991). Overall, boys seem to get less social support than girls for the physical changes of puberty. This suggests that boys might benefit, especially, from opportunities to ask questions and discuss feelings with a sympathetic parent or health professional.

The experience of puberty is affected by the larger cultural context. Many tribal and village societies celebrate its onset with an *adolescent initiation ceremony,* a ritualized announcement to the community that marks an important change in privilege and responsibility. Consequently, young people know that reaching puberty is honored and valued in their culture. In contrast, Western societies grant little formal recognition to movement from childhood to adolescence or from adolescence to adulthood. Certain religious ceremonies, such as the Jewish bar or bat mitzvah and, in Hispanic communities, the Catholic Quinceañera (celebrating a 15-year-old girl's journey to adulthood), resemble initiation ceremonies. But they usually do not lead to a meaningful change in social status.

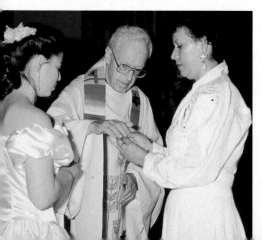

◎ Quinceañera, the traditional Hispanic fifteenth birthday celebration, is a rite of passage honoring a girl's journey from childhood to maturity and emphasizing the importance of family and community responsibility. It usually begins with a mass in which the priest blesses gifts presented to the girl, followed by a reception for family and friends. This girl receives a ring, symbolizing the unending circle of life and the emergence of her contributions to society.
© Robert Fried/Stock Boston, LLC

Instead, Western adolescents are confronted with many ages at which they are granted partial adult status—for example, different ages for starting employment, for driving, for leaving high school, for voting, and for drinking. In some contexts (on the highway and at work), they may be treated like adults. In others (at school and at home), they may still be regarded as children. The absence of a widely accepted marker of physical and social maturity makes the process of becoming an adult especially confusing.

Pubertal Change, Emotion, and Social Behavior

In the preceding section, we considered adolescents' reactions to their sexually maturing bodies. Puberty can also affect emotional state and social behavior. A common belief is that pubertal change triggers adolescent moodiness and the desire for greater physical and psychological separation from parents.

• **ADOLESCENT MOODINESS** • Although research reveals that higher sex hormone levels are related to greater moodiness, these relationships are not strong (Buchanan, Eccles, & Becker, 1992). What else might contribute to the common observation that adolescents are moody? In cross-sectional and longitudinal research, the moods of children, adolescents, and adults were monitored by having them carry electronic pagers. Over a one-week period, they were beeped at random intervals and asked to write down what they were doing, whom they were with, and how they felt.

As expected, adolescents reported less favorable moods than school-age children and adults (Larson et al., 2002; Larson & Lampman-Petraitis, 1989). But negative moods were linked to a greater number of negative life events, such as difficulties getting along with parents, disciplinary actions at school, and breaking up with a boyfriend or girlfriend. Negative events increased steadily from childhood to adolescence, and teenagers also reacted to them with greater emotion than children (Larson & Ham, 1993). (Recall the changes in brain neurotransmitter activity during adolescence, which heighten stress reactivity.)

Compared with the moods of adults, those of younger adolescents (ages 12 to 16) were less stable, often varying from cheerful to sad and back again. These mood swings were strongly related to situational changes. High points of adolescents' days were times spent with friends and in self-chosen leisure activities. Low points tended to occur in adult-structured settings: class, job, school halls, school library, and religious services.

Not surprisingly, adolescents' emotional high points were Friday and Saturday evenings, especially after they entered high school (see Figure 5.15). As teenagers transition to high school, frequency of going out with friends and romantic partners increases dramatically, so much so that it becomes a "cultural script" for what is *supposed* to happen. Teenagers who fall short of the script—who spend weekend evenings at home—often experience profound loneliness (Larson & Richards, 1998).

Yet another contributor to adolescent moodiness is change in sleep schedules. Although teenagers need almost as much sleep as they did in middle childhood (about 9 hours), they go to bed much later than they did as children. Biological changes may underlie this sleep "phase delay" because it strengthens with pubertal maturation. But today's teenagers—with more evening social activities, part-time jobs, and bedrooms equipped with televisions, telephones, computers—are more sleep-deprived than those of previous generations (Carskadon et al., 2002; Fins & Wohlgemuth, 2001). Because insufficient sleep impairs regulation of attention, emotion, and behavior, sleep-deprived adolescents are more likely to suffer from depressed mood, achieve poorly in school, and engage in high-risk behaviors, including drinking and reckless driving. Later school start times ease sleep loss but do not eliminate it (Dahl & Lewin, 2002).

Fortunately, frequent reports of negative mood subside after age 18 (Larson et al., 2002; Holsen, Kraft, & Vittersø, 2000). In sum, biological and situational forces combine to make adolescence a time of deeper valleys and higher peaks in emotional experience than the periods that surround it—a conclusion that is consistent with the balanced view presented earlier in this chapter.

• **PARENT–CHILD RELATIONSHIPS** • Recall the observations of Sabrina's father in the introduction to this chapter—that as children enter adolescence, they often resist spending

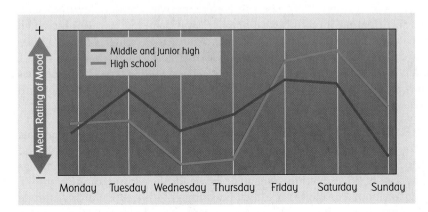

◀ **Figure 5.15**

Younger and older adolescents' emotional experiences across the week. Adolescents' reports revealed that emotional high points are on Fridays and Saturdays. Mood drops on Sunday, before returning to school, and during the week, as students spend much time in adult-structured settings in school. (From R. Larson & M. Richards, 1998, "Waiting for the Weekend: Friday and Saturday Night as the Emotional Climax of the Week." In A. C. Crouter & R. Larson [Eds.], *Temporal Rhythms in Adolescence: Clocks, Calendars, and the Coordination of Daily Life.* San Francisco: Jossey-Bass, p. 41. Reprinted by permission.)

Compared with children and adults, adolescents often seem moody. But young people's negative moods are linked to negative life events, which increase from childhood to adolescence. Frequent disagreements with parents might be responsible for this teenager's unhappy frame of mind. © Tony Freeman/PhotoEdit

time with the family and become more argumentative. Many studies show that puberty is related to a rise in parent–child conflict. During this time, both parents and teenagers report feeling less close to one another (Laursen, Coy, & Collins, 1998; Steinberg & Morris, 2001). Frequency of conflict is surprisingly similar across North American subcultures. It occurs about as often in families of European descent as in immigrant Chinese, Filipino, and Mexican families, whose traditions respect parental authority (Fuligni, 1998).

Why should a youngster's more adultlike appearance trigger these disputes? According to an evolutionary view, the association has adaptive value. Among nonhuman primates, the young typically leave the family around the time of puberty. The same is true in many nonindustrialized cultures (Caine, 1986; Schlegel & Barry, 1991). Departure of young people discourages sexual relations between close blood relatives. But because children in industrialized societies remain economically dependent on parents long after they reach puberty, they cannot leave the family. Consequently, a modern substitute for physical departure seems to have emerged: psychological distancing.

In later chapters, you will see that adolescents' new powers of reasoning may also contribute to a rise in family tensions. In addition, friction increases because children have become physically mature and demand to be treated in adultlike ways. Parent–adolescent disagreements focus largely on mundane, day-to-day matters, such as driving, dating partners, and curfews (Adams & Laursen, 2001). But beneath these disputes lie serious concerns—parental efforts to protect their teenagers from substance use, auto accidents, and early sex. The larger the gap between parents' and adolescents' views of teenagers' readiness to take on developmental tasks, the more quarreling (Deković, Noom, & Meeus, 1997).

Most disputes are mild, although a gender difference exists. Because parental restriction is greater for girls, parent–daughter conflict tends to be more intense (Allison & Schultz, 2004). This disparity varies with culture; for example, it is less evident in Canada than in Italy, where gender-role values are more traditional (Claes et al., 2003). Nevertheless, only a small minority of parents and older teenagers experience continuing friction. In reality, parents and adolescents display both conflict and affection, and usually they agree on important values, such as honesty and education (Arnett, 1999). Although separation from parents is adaptive, both generations benefit from warm, protective family bonds throughout the lifespan.

Early versus Late Pubertal Timing

In addition to dramatic physical change, the timing of puberty has a major impact on psychological adjustment. Findings of several studies indicate that both adults and peers viewed early maturing boys as relaxed, independent, self-confident, and physically attractive. Popular with agemates, they held leadership positions in school and tended to be athletic stars. In contrast, late-maturing boys were not well liked. Peers and adults viewed them as anxious, overly talkative, and attention seeking (Brooks-Gunn, 1988; Clausen, 1975; Jones, 1965). However, early maturing boys, though viewed as well adjusted, report slightly more psychological stress than their later-maturing agemates (Ge, Conger, & Elder, 2001b).

In contrast, early maturing girls were found to be unpopular, withdrawn, lacking in self-confidence, and anxious, and they held few leadership positions (Ge, Conger, & Elder, 1996; Graber et al., 1997; Jones & Mussen, 1958). These girls were more involved in deviant behavior (getting drunk, participating in early sexual activity) and achieved less well in school (Caspi et al., 1993; Dick et al., 2000). In contrast, their late-maturing counterparts were especially well off—regarded as physically attractive, lively, sociable, and leaders at school.

Two factors largely account for these trends: (1) how closely the adolescent's body matches cultural ideals of physical attractiveness, and (2) how well young people fit in physically with their agemates.

• **THE ROLE OF PHYSICAL ATTRACTIVENESS** • Flip through the pages of your favorite popular magazine. You will see evidence for our society's view of an attractive female as thin and long legged and a good-looking male as tall, broad shouldered, and muscular. The female image is a girlish shape that favors the late developer; the male image fits the early maturing boy.

As girls move from childhood to adolescence, their **body image**—conception of and attitude toward their physical appearance—becomes increasingly negative. Most want to be thinner

(Rosen, 2003). Early maturing girls are more dissatisfied with their body image than their on-time and late-maturing agemates. Among boys, the opposite occurs: Early pubertal timing is linked to a positive body image, whereas late maturation predicts dissatisfaction with the physical self (Alsaker, 1995). Although the difference between early and late-maturing boys disappears as the late maturers reach puberty, early maturing girls' negative body image worsens. Young people's satisfaction with their appearance strongly affects their self-esteem and psychological well-being (Usmiani & Daniluk, 1997).

• **THE IMPORTANCE OF FITTING IN WITH PEERS** • Physical status in relation to peers also explains differences in adjustment between early and late maturers. From this perspective, early maturing girls and late-maturing boys have difficulty because they fall at the extremes in physical development. Recall that Sabrina felt "out of place" when with her agemates. Not surprisingly, adolescents feel most comfortable with peers who match their own level of biological maturity (Stattin & Magnusson, 1990).

Because few agemates of the same pubertal status are available, early maturing adolescents of both sexes seek out older companions, sometimes with unfavorable consequences. Older peers often encourage them into activities they are not yet ready to handle emotionally, including sexual activity, drug and alcohol use, and minor delinquent acts (Ge et al., 2002). Perhaps because of such involvements, early maturers of both sexes report feeling depressed and show declines in academic performance (Graber, 2003; Kaltiala-Heino, Kosunen, & Rimpelä, 2003).

• **LONG-TERM CONSEQUENCES** • Do the effects of pubertal timing persist? Follow-ups reveal that early maturing girls, especially, are prone to lasting difficulties. In one study, early maturing boys' depression had subsided between ages 11 and 13; puberty seemed to be a temporary stressor. In contrast, depressed early maturing girls remained depressed (Ge at al., 2003). In another study that tracked young people from ages 14 to 24, early maturing boys again showed relatively good adjustment. Early maturing girls, however, displayed continuing problems, reporting poorer-quality relationships with family and friends, smaller social networks, and lower life satisfaction into emerging adulthood than their on-time maturing counterparts (Graber et al., 2004). Other evidence indicates that early maturing girls' achievement and substance use difficulties also persist into emerging adulthood, in the form of greater alcohol abuse and lower educational attainment (Andersson & Magnusson, 1990; Stattin & Magnusson, 1990).

Researchers believe that impaired social relationships play a major role in these long-term negative outcomes (Graber, 2003). Recall that childhood family conflict tends to be associated with early menarche (see page 199). Consequently, many early maturing girls may enter adolescence with emotional and social difficulties. As the stresses of puberty interfere with school performance and lead to unfavorable peer pressures, poor adjustment extends and deepens. Clearly, interventions that target at-risk early maturing youngsters are needed. These include educating parents and teachers and providing adolescents with counseling and social supports so they will be better prepared to handle the widening array of challenges that accompany adolescence.

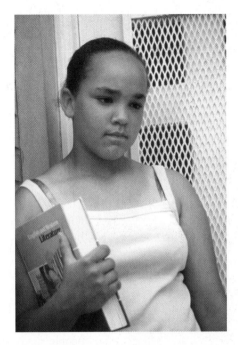

Ⓢ Because she falls at an extreme of physical development, this early maturing girl may feel out of place with both girls and boys her age. She may be drawn to friendships with physically similar, older adolescents, even though the emotional match with them may be uncomfortable or detrimental.
© CLEO PHOTOGRAPHY/PhotoEdit

Ask Yourself

REVIEW	Summarize the consequences of pubertal timing for adolescent development.
APPLY	After having been home on Friday and Saturday nights for three weekends in a row, 15-year-old Paul was despondent. His parents attributed his gloomy mood to the "storm and stress" of adolescence. Provide another, more likely explanation.
CONNECT	How might adolescent moodiness contribute to the psychological distancing between parents and children that accompanies puberty? (*Hint:* Think about bidirectional influences in parent–child relationships.)
REFLECT	Think back to your own reactions to the physical changes of puberty. Are they consistent with research findings? Explain.

◎ Puberty and Adolescent Health

The arrival of puberty is accompanied by new health concerns. Eating disturbances appear in many young people who worry about falling short of their idealized image of attractiveness and fitness. Homosexual teenagers face formidable challenges in forging an open, positive sexual identity. And sexual activity brings with it the risk of sexually transmitted disease and early pregnancy.

As adolescents are granted greater autonomy, their personal decision making becomes important, in health as in other areas. Yet none of the health concerns we are about to discuss can be traced to a single cause. Instead, biological, psychological, family, and cultural factors jointly contribute.

Eating Disorders

Girls who reach puberty early, who are very dissatisfied with their body image, and who grow up in homes where concern with weight and thinness is high are at risk for eating problems. Recall from the introduction to this chapter that Sabrina's mother worried about Sabrina's desire to lose weight when she reached puberty. Severe dieting is the strongest predictor of an eating disorder in adolescence (Patton et al., 1999). The two most serious eating disorders are anorexia nervosa and bulimia nervosa.

• **ANOREXIA NERVOSA** • **Anorexia nervosa** is a tragic eating disturbance in which young people starve themselves because of a compulsive fear of getting fat. Slightly less than 1 percent of North American and Western European teenage girls are affected. During the past half-century, cases have increased sharply, fueled by cultural admiration of female thinness. Asian-American, Caucasian-American, and Hispanic girls are at greater risk than African-American girls, who tend to be more satisfied with their size and shape (Fairburn & Harrison, 2003; Wildes, Emery, & Simons, 2001). Boys make up some 10 percent of anorexic cases. About half of these are homosexual or bisexual young people who are uncomfortable with a strong, muscular appearance (Robb & Dadson, 2002). Anorexia nervosa is equally common in all SES groups (Rogers et al., 1997).

Anorexics have an extremely distorted body image. Even after they have become severely underweight, they perceive themselves as too heavy. Most go on a self-imposed diet so strict that they struggle to avoid eating in response to hunger. To enhance weight loss, they exercise strenuously.

In their attempt to reach "perfect" slimness, anorexics lose between 25 and 50 percent of their body weight. Because a normal menstrual cycle requires about 15 percent body fat, either menarche does not occur or menstrual periods stop. Malnutrition causes pale skin, brittle discolored nails, fine dark hairs all over the body, and extreme sensitivity to cold. If it continues, the heart muscle can shrink, the kidneys can fail, and irreversible brain damage and loss of bone mass can occur. About 6 percent die of the disorder, as a result of either physical complications or suicide (Schmidt, 2000).

Forces within the person, the family, and the larger culture give rise to anorexia nervosa. The disorder tends to run in families, and concordance is higher in identical than in fraternal twins, indicating a genetic influence (Klump, Kaye, & Strober, 2001). Also, problem eating behavior in early childhood—persistently refusing to eat or eating very little—is linked to anorexia in adolescence (Rosen, 2003). As we have seen, the societal image of "thin is beautiful" contributes to the poor body image of many girls—especially early maturing girls, who are at greatest risk for anorexia nervosa (Tyrka, Graber, & Brooks-Gunn, 2000). In addition, many anorexics have extremely high standards for their own behavior and performance, are emotionally inhibited, and avoid forming intimate ties outside the family. Consequently, these girls are often excellent students who are responsible and well behaved—ideal daughters in many respects.

Yet parent–adolescent interactions reveal problems related to autonomy. Often the mothers of these girls have high expectations for physical appearance, achievement, and social acceptance and are overprotective and controlling. Fathers tend to be emotionally distant. Instead of rebelling openly, anorexic girls seem to do so covertly—by fiercely pursuing perfection in achievement, respectable behavior, and thinness (Bruch, 2001). Nevertheless, it remains unclear whether maladaptive parent–child relationships precede the disorder, emerge as a response to it, or both.

◎ Gennifer, an anorexia nervosa patient, is shown in the top photo in the hospital, where she received life-saving treatment for malnutrition. After prolonged family therapy, she recovered. She appears in the bottom photo at home, 2 years after her hospital stay. Only 50 percent of young people with anorexia fully overcome the disorder.
© Ed Quinn/Corbis

Because anorexic girls typically deny that any problem exists, treating the disorder is difficult. Hospitalization is often necessary to prevent life-threatening malnutrition. Family therapy, aimed at changing parent–child interaction and expectations, is the most successful treatment (Patel, Pratt, & Greydanus, 2003). As a supplementary approach, behavior modification—in which hospitalized anorexics are rewarded with praise, social contact, and opportunities for exercise when they eat and gain weight—is helpful. Still, less than 50 percent of anorexics fully recover (Seinhausen, 2002). For many, eating problems continue in less extreme form. About 10 percent show signs of a less severe, but nevertheless debilitating, disorder: bulimia nervosa.

• **BULIMIA NERVOSA** • In **bulimia nervosa,** young people (again, mainly girls, but homosexual and bisexual boys are also vulnerable) engage in strict dieting and excessive exercise accompanied by binge eating, often followed by deliberate vomiting and purging with laxatives. Bulimia is more common than anorexia nervosa, affecting about 2 to 3 percent of teenage girls, only 5 percent of whom have previously been anorexic.

Twin studies show that bulimia, like anorexia, is influenced by heredity (Klump, Kaye, & Strober, 2001). Personal factors that increase the risk include overweight and early puberty. Some bulimics, like anorexics, are perfectionists. Others, lacking self-control not just in eating but also in other areas of their lives, may engage in petty shoplifting and alcohol abuse. And although bulimics share with anorexics pathological anxiety about gaining weight, they may have experienced their parents as disengaged and emotionally unavailable rather than as overcontrolling (Fairburn & Harrison, 2003; Fairburn et al., 1997).

Bulimics differ from anorexics in that they are aware of their abnormal eating habits, feel depressed and guilty about them, and usually are desperate for help. As a result, bulimia is usually easier to treat through therapy focused on support groups, nutrition education, and revising eating habits and thoughts about food.

Sexuality

With the arrival of puberty, hormonal changes—in particular, the production of androgens in young people of both sexes—lead to an increase in sex drive (Halpern, Udry, & Suchindran, 1997). In response, adolescents become very concerned about how to manage sexuality in social relationships. New cognitive capacities involving perspective taking and self-reflection affect their efforts to do so. Yet, like the eating behaviors we have just discussed, adolescent sexuality is heavily influenced by the young person's social context.

• **THE IMPACT OF CULTURE** • When did you first learn the "facts of life"? Was sex discussed openly in your family, or was the subject treated with secrecy? Exposure to sex, education about it, and efforts to restrict the sexual curiosity of children and adolescents vary widely around the world. At one extreme are a number of Middle Eastern peoples, who murder girls if they lose their virginity before marriage. At the other extreme are several Asian and Pacific Island groups with highly permissive sexual attitudes and practices. For example, among the Trobriand Islanders of Papua New Guinea, older companions provide children with instruction in sexual practices, and adolescents are expected to engage in sexual experimentation with a variety of partners (Weiner, 1988).

Despite the publicity granted to the image of a sexually free adolescent, sexual attitudes in North America are relatively restrictive. Many parents give children little or no information about sex, discourage sex play, and rarely talk about sex in their presence. When young people become interested in sex, only about half report getting information from parents about intercourse, pregnancy prevention, and sexually transmitted disease (see the From Research to Practice box on pages 206–207). The majority learn about sex from friends, books, magazines, movies, TV, and the Internet (Jaccard, Dodge, & Dittus, 2002; Sutton et al., 2002). On prime-time TV shows, which adolescents watch more than other TV offerings, 80 percent of programs contain sexual content. Most depict partners as spontaneous and passionate, taking no steps to avoid pregnancy or sexually transmitted disease, and experiencing no negative consequences (Cope-Farrar & Kunkel, 2002).

◎ Cultural admiration of extreme female thinness, evident in the fashion and movie industries, has accompanied the rise in anorexia nervosa over the past half century. These emaciated models encourage young girls to feel dissatisfied with an average body weight and to go on highly restrictive diets to achieve this "perfect" body image. © Petre Buzoianu/Corbis

◎ Adolescence is an especially important time for the development of sexuality, as these two young people demonstrate, but North American teenagers receive contradictory and confusing messages about the appropriateness of sex.
© Jeff Greenberg/PhotoEdit

Parents and Teenagers (Don't) Talk About Sex

When a researcher asked a father of two girls and a boy to reflect on communication about sexual issues in his family, he replied,

> I've never had to talk to my children . . . about these issues because . . . my wife's already done it . . . I feel almost guilty for not partaking. The other thing, of course, is I don't know how—it's not an excuse, it's a fact. I don't know how comfortable they would be, me trying to talk to them about these topics . . . So I guess it's a bit of a coward's way out, to save embarrassment by both parties. . . . (Kirkman, Rosenthal, & Feldman, 2002, p. 60)

Warm communication, in which parents provide information on sex and contraception and convey their values, is associated with teenagers' adoption of parents' views

and with reduced teenage sexual risk taking (Jaccard, Dodge, & Dittus, 2003; Miller, Forehand, & Kotchick, 1999). But many parents fail to discuss sex, birth control, and negative consequences of pregnancy with their teenagers. On average, only 50 percent of adolescents report such conversations (Jaccard, Dodge, & Dittus, 2002).

As this father's remarks suggest, parents steer clear of meaningful discussions with teenagers about sex out of fear of embarrassment. They also express concern that the adolescent will not take them seriously. Because teenagers frequently tell parents they already know everything they need to know, parents often conclude that talking about sex is unnec-

essary (Jaccard, Dittus, & Gordon, 2000). But adolescents' perceptions of their knowledge are only weakly related to their actual knowledge (Radecki & Jaccard, 1995).

When parents do initiate discussions, teenagers may be reluctant to participate. They complain that parents do not treat them as equals, know little about contemporary teenage lifestyles, and are not sufficiently open, supportive, and empathic. Perhaps because of their better communication skills, mothers talk to adolescents about sex and birth control more than fathers do.

▶ Few parents discuss sexual matters with their adolescents. Among those who do, sympathetic listening, as demonstrated by the mother in this photo, along with respectful discussion and provision of accurate information, are associated with favorable results: teenagers who adopt their parents' values and take fewer sexual risks. © Ariel Skelley/Corbis

---

Consider the contradictory messages delivered by these sources. On one hand, adults emphasize that sex at a young age and outside marriage is wrong. On the other hand, the social environment extols the excitement and romanticism of sex. North American teenagers are left bewildered, poorly informed about sexual facts, and with little sound advice on how to conduct their sex lives responsibly.

• **ADOLESCENT SEXUAL ATTITUDES AND BEHAVIOR** • Although differences between subcultural groups exist, the sexual attitudes of North American adolescents and adults have become more liberal over the past 40 years. Compared with a generation ago, more people believe that sexual intercourse before marriage is all right, as long as two people are emotionally committed to each other (Michael et al., 1994). Recently, a slight swing back in the direction of conservative sexual beliefs has occurred, largely due to the risk of sexually transmitted disease, especially AIDS, and to teenage sexual abstinence programs sponsored by schools and religious organizations (Ali & Scelfo, 2002; Cope-Farrar & Kunkel, 2002).

Trends in the sexual activity of adolescents are consistent with their attitudes. Rates of extramarital sex among American and Canadian young people

Applying

What We Know — Communicating with Adolescents About Sexual Issues

Strategy	Explanation
Foster open communication.	Let the teenager know you are a willing and trustworthy resource by stating that you are available when questions arise and will answer fully and accurately.
Use correct terms for body parts.	Correct vocabulary provides the young person with a basis for future discussion and also indicates that sex is not a secretive topic.
Use effective discussion techniques.	Listen, encourage the adolescent to participate, ask open-ended rather than yes/no questions, and give supportive responses. Avoid dominating and lecturing, which cause teenagers to withdraw. If questions arise that you cannot answer, collaborate with the teenager in gathering further information.
Reflect before speaking.	When the adolescent asks questions or offers opinions about sex, remain nonjudgmental. If you differ with the teenager's views, convey your perspective in a nonthreatening manner, emphasizing that although you disagree, you are not attacking his or her character. Trying to dictate the young person's behavior generally results in alienation.
Keep conversations going.	Many parents regard their job as finished once they have had the "big talk" in early adolescence. But young people are more likely to be influenced by an accumulation of smaller discussions. If open communication is sustained, the teenager is more likely to return with thoughts and questions.

Source: Berkowitz, 2004.

Mothers more often dominate conversations about sexual than everyday matters, especially when talking to sons (Lefkowitz et al., 2002). When parents dominate, teenagers withdraw, reporting fewer sexual discussions and less knowledge (Lefkowitz, Sigman, & Au, 2000). Overall, balanced, mutual interaction and thorough consideration of sexual topics occur more often with daughters than with sons (Raffaeli, Bogenschneider, & Flood. 1998).

Parent-based sex education has many advantages. Parents can discuss topics in ways consistent with their own values, and they can tailor their delivery of information to their youngster's personality and current life circumstances in ways that school classes cannot. Clearly, however, parents need help communicating effectively about sexual issues. In one study, mothers who received training in talking with teenagers about sex, compared with a no-training control group, engaged in more give-and-take, asked more open-ended questions, were less judgmental, and discussed dating and sexuality more extensively. And their teenagers reported increased comfort with conversations and more consideration of birth control (Lefkowitz, Sigman, & Au, 2000). See Applying What We Know for qualities of successful communication.

rose for several decades but have declined since 1990 (Dryburgh, 2001; U.S. Department of Health and Human Services, 2004f). Nevertheless, a substantial minority of boys and girls are sexually active quite early, by age 15 (see Figure 5.16 on page 208). Males tend to have their first intercourse earlier than females.

The overall rates of teenage sexual activity in the United States, Canada, and other Western nations are similar, but the quality of sexual experiences differs to some degree. American youths, compared with their Canadian and Western European counterparts, begin sexual activity at a younger age (Boyce et al., 2003; U.S. Department of Health and Human Services, 2004f). Because early intercourse is linked to shorter and more sporadic sexual relationships, American teenagers are also more likely to have multiple sexual partners. For example, about 12 percent of adolescent boys in the United States, compared to 8 percent in Canada, have had relations with three or more partners in the past year (Alan Guttmacher Institute, 2004; Darroch, Frost, & Singh, 2001). Still, these teenagers are in the minority; most adolescents have had only one or two sexual partners. Contrary to popular belief, a runaway sexual revolution is not under way.

• **CHARACTERISTICS OF SEXUALLY ACTIVE ADOLESCENTS** • Early and frequent sexual activity is linked to personal, family, peer, and educational characteristics. These include early pubertal timing, parental divorce, single-parent and stepfamily homes, large family size, little

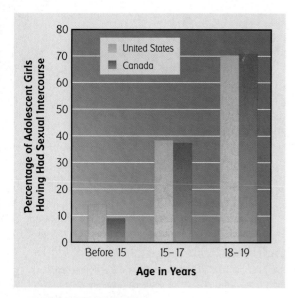

▲ **Figure 5.16**

Adolescent girls in the United States and Canada reporting ever having had sexual intercourse. A greater percentage of American than of Canadian girls engage in sexual activity before age 15. Otherwise, rates of sexual activity are similar in the two countries and resemble those of Western European nations. Boys' sexual activity rates are 3 to 6 percent higher than the rates for girls shown here.
(Adapted from Darroch, Frost, & Singh, 2001; Maticka-Tyndale, 2001.)

or no religious involvement, weak parental monitoring, disrupted parent–child communication, sexually active friends and older siblings, poor school performance, lower educational aspirations, and tendency to engage in norm-violating acts, including alcohol and drug use and delinquency (Anaya, Cantwell, & Rothman-Borus, 2003; Howard & Wang, 2004).

Because many of these factors are associated with growing up in a low-income family, it is not surprising that early sexual activity is more common among young people from economically disadvantaged homes. Living in a hazardous neighborhood—one high in physical deterioration, crime, and violence—also increases the likelihood that teenagers will be sexually active (Ge et al., 2002). In such neighborhoods, social ties are weak, adults exert little oversight and control over adolescents' activities, and negative peer influences are widespread. In fact, the high rate of sexual activity among African-American teenagers—67 percent report having had sexual intercourse, compared with 51 percent of all American young people—is largely accounted for by widespread poverty in the black population (Darroch, Frost, & Singh, 2001).

In two studies, one in the United States and the other in New Zealand, early and prolonged father absence predicted higher rates of intercourse and pregnancy among adolescent girls, after many family background and personal characteristics were controlled (Ellis et al., 2003). Perhaps father absence exposes young people to the dating and sexual behaviors of their mothers, who serve as models for their physically maturing children. An alternative, evolutionary account proposes that fathers' investment in parenting encourages daughters to delay sexual activity in favor of seeking a similarly committed male partner to ensure their offspring's well-being. Because father-absent girls view male commitment as uncertain, they may readily enter into casual sexual relationships.

• **CONTRACEPTIVE USE** • Although adolescent contraceptive use has increased in recent years, 27 percent of sexually active teenagers in the United States and 13 percent in Canada are at risk for unintended pregnancy because they do not use contraception consistently (Alan Guttmacher Institute, 2002; Manlove, Ryan, & Franzetta, 2003). Why do these youths fail to take precautions? As we will see in Chapter 6, adolescents can consider many more possibilities when faced with a problem, but they often fail to apply this reasoning to everyday situations. When asked to explain why they did not use contraception, teenagers often give answers like these: "I was waiting until I had a steady boyfriend." "I wasn't planning to have sex."

One reason for these responses is that advances in perspective taking—the capacity to imagine what others may be thinking and feeling—lead teenagers, for a time, to be extremely concerned about others' opinions of them. Furthermore, in the midst of everyday social pressures, adolescents often overlook the consequences of engaging in risky behaviors (Beyth-Marom & Fischhoff, 1997). The social environment also contributes to adolescents' reluctance to use contraception. Those who lack the rewards of meaningful education and work are especially likely to engage in irresponsible sex, sometimes within relationships characterized by exploitation. About 12 percent of North American girls and 6 percent of boys say they were pressured to have intercourse when they did not want to (Boyce et al., 2003; U.S. Department of Health and Human Services, 2004f).

In contrast, teenagers who report good relationships with parents and who talk openly with them about sex and contraception are more likely to use birth control (Kirby, 2002a). But few adolescents believe their parents would be understanding and supportive. And too many leave sex education classes with incomplete or factually incorrect knowledge. Some do not know where to get birth control counseling and devices. When they do, they often worry that a doctor or family planning clinic might not keep their visits confidential (American Academy of Pediatrics, 1999).

• **SEXUAL ORIENTATION** • Up to this point, our discussion has focused only on heterosexual behavior. About 3 to 6 percent of young people discover that they are lesbian or gay (see the Biology and Environment box on the following page). An as-yet-unknown but significant

Homosexuality: Coming Out to Oneself and Others

Cultures vary as much in their acceptance of homosexuality as in their approval of extramarital sex. In North America, homosexuals are stigmatized, as shown by the degrading language often used to describe them. This makes forming a sexual identity a much greater challenge for gay and lesbian youths than for their heterosexual counterparts.

Wide variations in sexual identity formation exist, depending on personal, family, and community factors. Yet interviews with homosexual adolescents and adults reveal that many (though not all) move through a three-phase sequence in coming out to themselves and others.

Feeling Different

Many gay men and lesbians say that they felt different from other children when they were young. Typically, this first sense of their biologically based sexual orientation appears between ages 6 and 12, in play interests more like those of the other gender (Rahman & Wilson, 2003). Boys may find that they are less interested in sports, drawn to quieter activities, and more emotionally sensitive than other boys, girls that they are more athletic and active than other girls.

By age 10, many such children start to engage in *sexual questioning*—trying to make sense of their inner feelings and wondering why the typical heterosexual orientation does not apply to them. Often, they experience their sense of being different as deeply distressing. They worry, for example, about "being normal" and being "found out" by family members and friends. Compared with children confident of their homosexuality, sexual-questioning children report increased anxiety about peer relationships, greater dissatisfaction with their biological gender, and greater gender nonconformity in personal traits and activities over time (Carver, Egan, & Perry, 2004).

Confusion

With the arrival of puberty, feeling different clearly encompasses feeling sexually different. In research on ethnically diverse gay, lesbian, and bisexual youths, awareness of a same-sex physical attraction occurred, on average, between ages 11 and 12 for boys and 14 and 15 for girls, perhaps because adolescent social pressures toward heterosexuality are particularly intense for girls (Diamond, 1998; Herdt & Boxer, 1993).

Realizing that homosexuality has personal relevance generally sparks additional confusion. A few adolescents resolve their discomfort by crystallizing a gay, lesbian, or bisexual identity quickly, with a flash of insight into their sense of being different. But most experience an inner struggle and a deep sense of isolation—outcomes intensified by lack of role models and social support (D'Augelli, 2002).

Some throw themselves into activities they have come to associate with heterosexuality. Boys may go out for athletic teams; girls may drop softball and basketball in favor of dance. Homosexual youths typically try heterosexual dating, sometimes to hide their sexual orientation and at other times to develop intimacy skills that they later apply to same-sex relationships (Dubé, Savin-Williams, & Diamond, 2001). Others are so bewildered, guilt ridden, and lonely that they escape into alcohol and drug abuse and suicidal thinking. Suicide attempts are unusually high among gay, lesbian, and bisexual young people (Anhalt & Morris, 1999; McDaniel, Purcell, & D'Augelli, 2001).

Self-Acceptance

By the end of adolescence, the majority of gay, lesbian, and bisexual teenagers accept their sexual identity. Then they face another crossroad: whether to tell others. Powerful stigma against homosexuality leads some youths to decide that no disclosure is possible. As a result, they self-define but otherwise "pass" as heterosexual (Savin-Williams, 2001). When homosexual youths do come out, they often face intense hostility from peers. In a study of over 500 gay, lesbian, and bisexual youths in Canada, New Zealand, and the United States, 75 percent reported being verbally abused, and 15 percent physically attacked, because of their sexual orientation (D'Augelli, 2002).

Nevertheless, many young people eventually acknowledge their sexual orientation publicly, usually by telling trusted friends first. Once teenagers establish a same-sex sexual or romantic relationship, many come out to parents—generally the mother first, either because she asks or because youths feel closer to her. Few parents respond with severe rejection; most are either positive or slightly negative and disbelieving (Savin-Williams & Ream, 2003a). This is an encour-

aging outcome because parental understanding is the strongest predictor of favorable adjustment among homosexual youths (Savin-Williams, 2003).

When people are accepting, coming out strengthens the adolescent's view of homosexuality as a valid, meaningful, and fulfilling identity. Contact with other gays and lesbians is important for reaching this phase, and changes in society permit many adolescents in urban areas to attain it earlier than they did several decades ago. Gay and lesbian communities exist in large cities, along with specialized interest groups, social clubs, religious groups, newspapers, and periodicals. Increasing numbers of favorable media images also are helpful. Small towns and rural areas remain difficult places to meet other homosexuals and to find a supportive environment. Teenagers in these locales have a special need for caring adults and peers who can help them find self- and social acceptance.

Gay and lesbian youths who succeed in coming out to themselves and others integrate their sexual orientation into a broader sense of identity, a process we will address in Chapter 11. As a result, they no longer need to focus so heavily on their homosexual self, and energy is freed for other aspects of psychological growth. In sum, coming out can foster many aspects of adolescent development, including self-esteem, psychological well-being, and relationships with family and friends.

▼ Teenagers from around Boston join in the annual Gay/Straight Youth Pride March. When family members and peers react with acceptance, coming out strengthens the young person's view of homosexuality as a valid, meaningful, and fulfilling identity.
© Marilyn Humphries/The Image Works

number—more women than men—are bisexual (Bailey, Dunne, & Martin, 2000; Michael et al., 1994). Adolescence is an equally crucial time for the sexual development of these individuals, and societal attitudes, once again, loom large in how well they fare.

Recent evidence indicates that heredity makes an important contribution to homosexuality. Identical twins of both sexes are more likely than fraternal twins to share a homosexual orientation; the same is true for biological as opposed to adoptive relatives (Kirk et al., 2000; Kendler et al., 2000). Furthermore, male homosexuality tends to be more common on the maternal than on the paternal side of families. This suggests that it might be X-linked (see Chapter 3). Indeed, one gene-mapping study found that among 40 pairs of homosexual brothers, 33 (82 percent) had an identical segment of DNA on the X chromosome. One or several genes in that region might predispose males to become homosexual (Hamer et al., 1993).

How might heredity lead to homosexuality? According to some researchers, certain genes affect the level or impact of prenatal sex hormones, which modify brain structures in ways that induce homosexual feelings and behavior (Bailey et al., 1995; LeVay, 1993). Keep in mind, however, that both genetic and environmental factors can alter prenatal hormones. Girls exposed prenatally to very high levels of androgens or estrogens—because of either a genetic defect or drugs given to the mother to prevent miscarriage—are more likely to become homosexual or bisexual (Meyer-Bahlburg et al., 1995). Furthermore, homosexual men tend to be later in birth order and have a higher-than-average number of older brothers (Bogaert, 2003). One possibility is that mothers with several male children sometimes produce antibodies to androgens, which reduce the prenatal impact of male sex hormones on the brains of later-born boys.

So far, efforts to identify early social experiences that promote homosexuality have turned up very little. Looking back at their childhoods, both male and female homosexuals describe their same-sex parent as cold, rejecting, or distant (Bell, Weinberg, & Hammersmith, 1981; McConaghy & Silove, 1992). But this does not mean that parents cause their youngsters to become homosexual. Rather, for some children, an early biological bias away from traditional gender-role behavior may prompt alienation from same-sex parents and peers. According to one theory, this alienation may lead the child to view same-sex peers as "exotic" and, therefore, to be sexually attracted to them (Bem, 1996). Critics, however, note that childhood parental and peer alienation cannot explain lesbianism because masculine interests and "tomboyish" behavior are socially acceptable for girls (Peplau et al., 1998).

Although definitive conclusions must await further research, the evidence to date suggests that genetic and prenatal biological influences are largely responsible for homosexuality. In our evolutionary past, homosexuality may have served the adaptive function of reducing aggressive competition for other-sex mates, thereby promoting the survival of group members (Rahman & Wilson, 2003).

Sexually Transmitted Disease

Sexually active adolescents, both homosexual and heterosexual, are at risk for sexually transmitted diseases (STDs). Adolescents have the highest incidence of STDs of all age groups. Despite a recent decline, the United States exceeds all other developed nations in incidence of STDs. Each year, 1 out of every 60 American teenagers contracts an STD, a rate three times higher than that of Canada. Canada, however, exceeds many Western European nations in incidence of the most common STDs, such as chlamydia and herpes (Maticka-Tyndale, 2001; Weinstock, Berman, & Cates, 2004). When STDs are left untreated, sterility and life-threatening complications can result. The teenagers in greatest danger of contracting STDs are the same ones most likely to engage in irresponsible sexual behavior: poverty-stricken young people who feel a sense of hopelessness about their lives (Niccolai et al., 2004).

The most serious STD is AIDS. In contrast to Canada, where the incidence of AIDS among people younger than 30 is low, one-fifth of U.S. AIDS cases occur between ages 20 and 29. Nearly all originate in adolescence, since AIDS symptoms typically take 8 to 10 years to emerge in an HIV-infected person. Drug-abusing and homosexual teenagers account for most cases, but heterosexual spread of the disease has increased, especially among teenagers who have had more than one partner in the previous 18 months (Kelley et al., 2003).

As a result of school courses and media campaigns, about 60 percent of junior high school students and 90 percent of high school students in Canada and the United States are aware of basic facts about AIDS. But most have limited understanding of other STDs and their consequences, underestimate their own susceptibility, and are poorly informed about how to protect themselves (Boyce et al., 2003; Coholl et al., 2001; Ethier et al., 2003). Concerted efforts are needed to educate young people about the full range of STDs.

Adolescent Pregnancy and Parenthood

An estimated 900,000 teenage girls in the United States—20 percent of those who have had sexual intercourse—become pregnant annually; 30,000 of them are younger than age 15. Despite a steady decline since 1991, the U.S. adolescent pregnancy rate is higher than that of most other industrialized countries (see Figure 5.17). Although the Canadian rate has also declined and is currently about half the U.S. rate, teenage pregnancy in Canada remains a problem. Three factors heighten the incidence of adolescent pregnancy: (1) effective sex education reaches too few teenagers; (2) convenient, low-cost contraceptive services for adolescents are scarce; and (3) many families live in poverty, which encourages young people to take risks without considering the implications of their behavior.

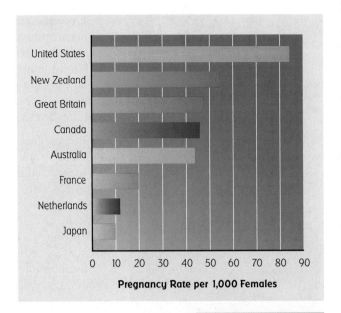

▲ **Figure 5.17**

Pregnancy rates among 15- to 19-year-olds in eight industrialized nations. American teenagers have the highest pregnancy rate. The pregnancy rate in Canada is about half the U.S. rate but much higher than that in Western European nations and Japan. (Adapted from Alan Guttmacher Institute, 2001; Singh & Darroch, 2000.)

Because 40 percent of U.S. and 50 percent of Canadian teenage pregnancies end in abortion, the number of North American teenage births is actually lower than it was 30 years ago (Maticka-Tyndale, 2001; U.S. Department of Health and Human Services, 2004f). But teenage parenthood is a much greater problem today because adolescents are far less likely to marry before childbirth. In 1960, only 15 percent of teenage births were to unmarried females; today, 85 percent are (Child Trends, 2001). Increased social acceptance of single motherhood, along with the belief of many teenage girls that a baby might fill a void in their lives, has meant that only a small number give up their infants for adoption.

• **CORRELATES AND CONSEQUENCES OF ADOLESCENT PARENTHOOD** • Becoming a parent is challenging for anyone, but it is especially difficult for adolescents. Teenage parents have not yet established a clear sense of direction for their own lives. They have both life conditions and personal attributes that interfere with their ability to parent effectively (Jaffee et al., 2001).

As we have seen, adolescent sexual activity is linked to economic disadvantage. Teenage parents are many times more likely to be poor than agemates who postpone childbearing. Their backgrounds often include low parental warmth and involvement, domestic violence and child abuse, repeated parental divorce and remarriage, adult models of single motherhood, and residence in neighborhoods where other adolescents display these risks. In terms of personal characteristics, girls at risk for early pregnancy do poorly in school, engage in alcohol and drug use, have a childhood history of aggressive and antisocial behavior, associate with deviant peers, and experience high rates of depression (Elfenbein & Felice, 2003; Hillis et al., 2004). Many of these young people seem to turn to early parenthood as a way to move into adulthood when educational and career avenues are unavailable.

The lives of pregnant teenagers are troubled in many ways. After the baby is born, their circumstances tend to worsen in at least three respects:

- *Educational attainment.* Giving birth before age 18 reduces the likelihood of finishing high school. Only about 50 percent of adolescent mothers graduate, compared with 96 percent of girls who wait to become parents (Fergusson & Woodward, 2000; Hotz, McElroy, & Sanders, 1997).

- *Marital patterns.* Teenage motherhood reduces the chances of marriage. When these mothers do marry, they are more likely to divorce than are their peers who delay childbearing (Moore et al., 1993). Consequently, teenage mothers spend more of their parenting years as single parents.

⑤ Early childbearing reduces the chances that this teenage mother will finish high school, marry, and enter a satisfying, well-paid vocation. Because of stressful life conditions, this baby is at risk for poor parenting.

© David Young-Wolff/PhotoEdit

- *Economic circumstances.* Because of low educational attainment, marital instability, and poverty, many teenage mothers are on welfare. If they are employed, their limited education restricts them to unsatisfying, low-paid jobs. Many adolescent fathers, as well, are unemployed or work at unskilled jobs. Usually they do not earn enough to provide their children with basic necessities. An estimated 50 percent have committed illegal offenses resulting in imprisonment (Elfenbein & Felice, 2003).

Because many pregnant teenage girls have inadequate diets, smoke, use alcohol and other drugs, and do not receive early prenatal care, their babies often experience pregnancy and birth complications—especially low birth weight (Dell, 2001). And compared with adult mothers, adolescent mothers know less about child development, have unrealistically high expectations of infants, perceive their babies as more difficult, and interact less effectively with them (Moore & Florsheim, 2001; Pomerleau, Scuccimarri, & Malcuit, 2003). Their children tend to score low on intelligence tests, achieve poorly in school, and engage in disruptive social behavior.

Furthermore, teenage parents tend to pass on their personal attributes and to create unfavorable child-rearing conditions. Consequently, their offspring are at risk for irresponsible sexual activity when they reach puberty. Adolescent parenthood frequently is repeated in the next generation (Brooks-Gunn, Schley, & Hardy, 2002; Jaffee et al., 2001). Even when children born to teenage mothers do not become early childbearers, their development is often compromised, in terms of likelihood of high school graduation, adulthood financial independence, and physical and mental health (Moore, Morrison, & Green, 1997).

Still, how well adolescent parents and their children fare varies. If the teenager finishes high school, avoids additional births, and finds a stable marriage partner, long-term disruptions in her own and her child's development will be less severe.

- **PREVENTION STRATEGIES** • Preventing teenage pregnancy means addressing the many factors underlying early sexual activity and lack of contraceptive use. Too often, sex education courses are given too late (after sexual activity has begun), last only a few sessions, and are limited to a catalogue of facts about anatomy and reproduction. Sex education that goes beyond this minimum does not encourage early sex, as some opponents claim (Kirby, 2002c). It does improve awareness of sexual facts—knowledge that is necessary for responsible sexual behavior.

Knowledge, however, is not sufficient to influence teenagers' behavior. Sex education must help them build a bridge between what they know and what they do. Today, effective sex education programs combine the following key elements:

- They teach skills for handling sexual situations through creative discussion and role-playing techniques.
- They promote the value of abstinence to teenagers not yet sexually active.
- They provide information about contraceptives and ready access to them.

The results of many studies reveal that sex education with these components can delay the initiation of sexual activity, increase contraceptive use, and reduce pregnancy rates (Kirby, 2002b).

Proposals to increase the availability of contraceptives are the most controversial aspect of adolescent pregnancy prevention efforts. Many adults argue that placing birth control pills or condoms in the hands of teenagers is equivalent to saying that early sex is okay. Consequently, the U.S. federal government is investing heavily in *abstinence-only programs,* which do not address skill-building and contraception but, instead, encourage teenagers to abstain from sex. Yet evaluations reveal that abstinence education prevents sexual activity only among sexually inexperienced adolescents; it is not effective with teenagers who have had intercourse (Aten et al., 2002; DiCenso et al., 2002). In Canada and Western Europe, where community and school-based clinics offer adolescents contraceptives and where universal health insurance helps pay for them, teenage sexual activity is no higher than in the United States, but pregnancy, childbirth, and abortion rates are much lower (Alan Guttmacher Institute, 2001).

Efforts to prevent adolescent pregnancy and parenthood must go beyond improving sex education. Building academic and social competence is also key. In one study, researchers randomly assigned at-risk high school students to either a year-long community service class, called Teen Outreach, or regular classroom experiences in health or social studies. In Teen Outreach, adolescents participated in at least 20 hours per week of volunteer work tailored to their interests. They returned to school for discussions that focused on enhancing their community service skills and their ability to cope with everyday challenges. At the end of the school year, pregnancy, school failure, and school suspension were substantially lower in the group enrolled in Teen Outreach, which fostered social skills, connection to the community, and self-respect (Allen et al., 1997).

Finally, school involvement is linked to delayed initiation of sexual activity and to reduced teenage pregnancy, perhaps because it increases interaction with and attachment to adults who discourage risk taking, and it strengthens belief in a promising future (Lammers et al., 2000). We will take up factors that promote adolescents' commitment to school in Chapter 15.

◉ Learning carpentry skills as part of the Summer of Service Teen Volunteer Program in Washington, DC, will allow these at-risk high school students to play a constructive role in their communities. Building competence through community service reduces rates of adolescent pregnancy and school failure.
© Mark Richards/PhotoEdit

• **INTERVENING WITH ADOLESCENT PARENTS** • The most difficult and costly way to deal with adolescent parenthood is to wait until it has happened. Young mothers need health care, encouragement to stay in school, job training, instruction in parenting and life-management skills, and high-quality, affordable child care. School programs that provide these services reduce the incidence of low-birth-weight babies, increase mothers' educational success, and prevent additional childbearing (Barnet et al., 2004; Seitz & Apfel, 1993, 1994).

Adolescent mothers also benefit from relationships with family members and other adults who are sensitive to their developmental needs. Older teenage mothers display more effective parenting when they establish their own residence with the help of relatives—an arrangement that provides the adolescent with a balance of autonomy and support (East & Felice, 1996). In one study, adolescent mothers with a long-term "mentor" relationship—an aunt, neighbor, or teacher who provided emotional support and guidance—were more than three times likelier than those without a mentor to stay in school and graduate (Klaw, Rhodes, & Fitzgerald, 2003).

Programs focusing on fathers are attempting to increase their emotional and financial commitment to the baby (Coley & Chase-Lansdale, 1998). Although nearly half of young fathers visit their children during the first few years after birth, contact usually diminishes. Teenage mothers who receive financial and child-care assistance and emotional support from the child's father are less distressed and more likely to sustain a relationship with him (Cutrona et al., 1998; Gee & Rhodes, 2003). And infants with lasting ties to their teenage fathers receive warmer, more stimulating caregiving and show better long-term adjustment (Furstenberg & Harris, 1993).

A Concluding Note

Because puberty prompts rapid and complex physical and psychological changes, teenagers are vulnerable to certain problems. Yet the unhealthy behaviors of the adolescent years are not an irrational response to inner turmoil, as theorists once believed. Instead, every level of the ecological system affects teenagers' well-being.

Furthermore, adolescent risks are interconnected; we have seen that teenagers with one problem frequently display others—a co-occurrence that you will encounter again when we look at delinquency, depression, suicide, substance abuse, and school underachievement and failure. In designing more powerful interventions, researchers must deal with simultaneous risks and multiple factors that contribute to them. Think back to the successful intervention efforts discussed in the preceding sections, and notice how they employ several strategies, target multiple behaviors, and involve several contexts.

Finally, adolescence is not just a time of risk; it is also a time of tremendous opportunity. Teenagers gain a better understanding of how the world works, greater control over their own social contexts, broader access to social support, and increased ability to avoid or alter risky behaviors. Families, schools, communities, and nations must create conditions that permit adolescents to exercise their expanding capacity for positive health practices. This is a theme we will revisit in later chapters.

Ask Yourself

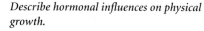

REVIEW	Compare risk factors for anorexia nervosa and bulimia nervosa. How do treatments and outcomes differ for the two disorders?
REVIEW	Describe unfavorable life experiences and personal attributes associated with early and frequent sexual activity.
APPLY	At age 17, Veronica gave birth to Ben. When her parents told her they didn't have room for the baby, Veronica dropped out of school and moved in with her boyfriend, Todd. A few months later, Todd left Veronica; he explained that he couldn't stand being tied down with the baby. Why are Veronica and Ben likely to experience lasting hardships?
REFLECT	Describe sex education classes that you experienced in school. Did they help you postpone early sex and engage in more responsible sexual behavior? Explain.

◎ Summary

The Course of Physical Growth

Describe the course of physical growth, including changes in body size, proportions, muscle–fat makeup, and skeleton, and their relationship to gains in gross motor skills.

◉ Compared with other animal species, humans experience a prolonged period of physical growth. **Distance and velocity curves** show the overall pattern of change: Gains in height and weight are rapid during infancy, slower during early and middle childhood, and rapid again during puberty.

◉ In childhood, physical growth follows cephalocaudal and proximodistal trends. During puberty, growth proceeds in the reverse direction, and sex differences in body proportions appear. Body fat is laid down quickly during the first 9 months, then rapidly again at adolescence for girls. In contrast, muscle development is slow and gradual until puberty, when it rises dramatically, especially for boys.

◉ **Epiphyses,** or bone growth centers, appear just before birth and increase in number throughout childhood. **Skeletal age,** a measure based on the number of epiphyses and the extent to which they are

fused, is the best way to estimate the child's overall physical maturity. Girls are advanced over boys, a gap that widens over infancy and childhood.

◉ In early childhood, body growth causes the child's center of gravity to shift toward the trunk, and balance improves, paving the way for new gross motor skills. During the school years, improved balance, strength, agility, and flexibility support refinements in running, jumping, hopping, and ball skills. Increased body size and muscle strength lead to continued motor gains in adolescence. Children continue to integrate previously acquired motor skills into more complex, dynamic systems of action.

◉ In childhood, parental expectations and practice are largely responsible for boys' advantage over girls in many gross motor skills. Sex differences in size and strength play a greater role in adolescence.

© RACHEL EPSTEIN/THE IMAGE WORKS

Describe hormonal influences on physical growth.

◉ Physical growth is controlled by hormones released by the **pituitary gland,** located at the base of the brain near the **hypothalamus,** which initiates and regulates pituitary secretions. **Growth hormone (GH)** affects the development of almost all body tissues. **Thyroxine,** released by the thyroid gland, influences brain growth and body size. Sexual maturation is controlled by the sex hormones—**estrogens** and **androgens.**

Discuss factors that contribute to worldwide variations, secular trends, and asynchronies in physical growth.

◉ Worldwide variations in body size are the combined result of heredity and environment, including evolutionary adaptations to climatic conditions, availability of food resources, and prevalence of disease. **Secular trends in physical growth** have occurred in industrialized nations. Because of improved health and nutrition, many children are growing larger and reaching physical maturity earlier than their ancestors.

◉ Physical growth is an asynchronous process. The **general growth curve** refers to change in overall body size. Other systems of the body, such as the genitals, the lymph tissue, and the brain, have their own unique timetables.

Brain Development

Cite major milestones in brain development, at the level of individual brain cells and at the level of the cerebral cortex.

◉ During the first few years, the human brain grows faster than any other organ. Once **neurons** are in place, they form **synapses** at a rapid rate. To communicate, neurons release **neurotransmitters,** which cross synapses. During the peak period of synaptic growth in any brain area, **programmed cell death** makes room for growth of neural fibers that form synaptic connections.

◉ Stimulation determines which neurons will continue to establish new synapses and which will lose their connective fibers through **synaptic pruning. Glial cells,** which are responsible for **myelination,** multiply dramatically through the second year, continuing to do so at a slower pace through adolescence. Myelination contributes greatly to childhood gains in brain size.

◉ Regions of the **cerebral cortex** develop in the order in which various capacities emerge in the infant and child, with the frontal lobes among the last to develop. **Lateralization** refers to specialization of the cerebral hemispheres. Some lateralization exists at birth, but during the first few years, **brain plasticity** is high. Both heredity and early experience contribute to brain organization.

◉ Hand preference reflects the individual's **dominant cerebral hemisphere.** It first appears in infancy and extends to a wider range of skills—a sign of strengthening lateralization. According to one theory, most children inherit a gene that biases them for right-handedness, but experience can sway children toward a left-hand preference. Body

position during the prenatal period and practice can affect handedness.

Describe changes in other brain structures, and discuss evidence on sensitive periods of brain development.

◉ During infancy and early childhood, connections are established between brain structures. Fibers linking the **cerebellum** to the cerebral cortex myelinate, enhancing children's balance and motor control and supporting higher cognitive processes. The **reticular formation,** responsible for alertness and consciousness, and the **corpus callosum,** which connects the two cerebral hemispheres, also develop rapidly.

◉ In many brain regions, sensitivity of neurons to excitatory neurotransmitters increases in adolescence. These changes are believed to contribute to teenagers' heightened drive for novel experiences, reactivity to stress, and susceptibility to certain psychological disorders.

◉ Animal and human evidence confirms the existence of sensitive periods in which appropriate stimulation is necessary for the brain to develop at its best. **Experience-expectant brain growth** characterizes the early years of rapidly developing brain organization. It takes place naturally as caregivers provide age-appropriate play materials and stimulating, enjoyable daily routines. **Experience-dependent brain growth**— additional growth and refinement of established brain structures as a result of specific learning—builds on this foundation and takes place later, continuing throughout life.

Factors Affecting Physical Growth

How do heredity, nutrition, infectious disease, and affection and stimulation contribute to physical growth and, as a result, affect other aspects of development?

◉ Twin and adoption studies reveal that heredity contributes to body size and rate of physical growth. As long as negative factors are not severe, children and adolescents who lag behind in body size show **catch-up growth** under improved environmental conditions.

◉ Breastfeeding is ideally suited to infants' growth needs and is crucial for protecting their health in the developing world. As growth slows in early childhood, appetite declines, and children become picky eaters.

Repeated exposure to a new food (without direct pressure to eat it) increases acceptance. During puberty, food intake rises dramatically, yet of all age groups, adolescents have the poorest eating habits. Family mealtimes increase healthy eating.

◉ **Marasmus** and **kwashiorkor** are diseases caused by malnutrition that affect many children in developing countries. If these conditions continue, body growth and brain development can be permanently stunted.

◉ **Obesity** is a growing problem in both industrialized and developing nations. Although heredity accounts for a tendency to gain weight, more powerful influences are parental feeding practices, maladaptive eating habits, lack of exercise, and Western high-fat diets. Obese children are often socially isolated and display more emotional, social, and school difficulties and behavior problems than their normal-weight peers.

◉ Malnutrition can combine with infectious disease to undermine healthy physical growth. In developing countries, diarrhea claims millions of young lives. Teaching families how to administer oral rehydration therapy (ORT) and providing zinc supplements can prevent most of these deaths.

◉ **Nonorganic failure to thrive** and **psychosocial dwarfism** are growth disorders that result from lack of parental affection and stimulation. Without an emotionally adequate environment early in life, growth retardation and psychological problems can be permanent.

Puberty: The Physical Transition to Adulthood

Describe sexual maturation in girls and boys, noting genetic and environmental influences on pubertal timing.

◉ Accompanying rapid changes in body size and proportions at **puberty** are changes in **primary** and **secondary sexual characteristics. Menarche** occurs late in the girl's sequence of pubertal events, after the growth spurt. In the following year, growth of the breasts and pubic hair is completed, and underarm hair appears. As the boy's body and sex organs enlarge and pubic and underarm hair appears, **spermarche** and deepening of the voice take place, followed by growth of facial and body hair.

◉ Heredity, nutrition, and overall health contribute to the timing of puberty.

Menarche is delayed in poverty-stricken regions of the world where malnutrition and infectious disease are widespread. In industrialized nations, both heredity and environment contribute to ethnic variations—for example, earlier menarche in African-American than in Caucasian-American girls.

The Psychological Impact of Pubertal Events

What factors influence adolescents' reactions to the physical changes of puberty?

◉ Puberty is not a biologically determined period of storm and stress. Adjustment varies widely and is a product of both biological and social forces.

◉ Girls generally react to menarche with surprise and mixed emotions. Whether their feelings are more positive or negative depends on the advance information and support they receive from family members. Similarly, boys, who receive less social support for the physical changes of puberty than girls, respond to spermarche with mixed feelings. In Western societies, the absence of a widely accepted marker for physical and social maturity, comparable to the adolescent initiation ceremonies of tribal and village societies, makes the process of becoming an adult especially confusing.

◉ In addition to higher hormone levels, other factors associated with adolescent moodiness are negative life events, adult-structured situations, and sleep loss. Puberty is accompanied by psychological distancing between parent and child, a reaction that may be a modern substitute for physical departure from the family, which typically occurs at puberty among primates. Parent–adolescent conflict also reflects teenagers' new powers of reasoning and parents' efforts to protect teenagers from risky situations.

Describe the impact of pubertal timing on adolescent adjustment, noting sex differences.

◉ Early maturing boys and late-maturing girls, whose appearance closely matches cultural standards of

physical attractiveness, have a more positive **body image** and usually adjust well in adolescence. In contrast, early maturing girls and late-maturing boys, who fit in least well physically with peers, experience emotional and social difficulties. For early maturing girls, problems persist into emerging adulthood.

Puberty and Adolescent Health

What factors contribute to eating disorders at adolescence?

◉ Girls who reach puberty early, who are dissatisfied with their body images, and who grow up in homes in which thinness is important are at risk for developing eating disorders. Twin studies reveal a genetic influence. In addition, **anorexia nervosa** tends to affect girls with perfectionist personalities, overprotective and controlling mothers, and emotionally distant fathers. **Bulimia nervosa,** characterized by compulsive eating and purging, is associated with disengaged parenting. Some bulimics, like anorexics, are perfectionists; others lack self-control both in eating and in other areas of their lives.

Discuss individual, social, and cultural influences on adolescent sexual attitudes and behavior.

◉ Social and cultural factors affect how teenagers manage their sexuality. Compared with attitudes in other parts of the world, North American attitudes toward adolescent sex are relatively restrictive, and the social environment delivers contradictory messages. Sexual attitudes and behavior of adolescents have become more liberal, with a recent slight swing in the other direction.

◉ Early and frequent sexual activity is linked to a variety of factors associated with economic disadvantage. Father absence may contribute uniquely to early sexual activity.

◉ Many sexually active teenagers do not practice contraception regularly. Adolescent cognitive processes and lack of social support for responsible sexual behavior, including access to birth control, underlie the failure of many young people to protect themselves against pregnancy.

Discuss factors involved in the development of homosexuality.

◉ About 3 to 6 percent of young people discover that they are lesbian or gay; an unknown number are bisexual. Biological factors, including heredity and prenatal hormone levels, play an important role in homosexuality. Gay and lesbian teenagers face special challenges in establishing a positive sexual identity.

Discuss factors related to sexually transmitted disease and teenage pregnancy and parenthood, noting prevention and intervention strategies.

◉ Irresponsible sexual activity places teenagers at risk for contracting sexually transmitted diseases (STDs). The most serious of these is AIDS. Drug-abusing and homosexual young people account for most cases, but heterosexual spread has increased. Aside from AIDS, most teenagers have limited knowledge about STDs.

◉ Adolescent pregnancy and parenthood occur at higher rates in the United States than in most industrialized nations. Teenage pregnancy is a problem in Canada as well. Unfavorable life conditions, linked to economic disadvantage, and personal attributes jointly contribute. Adolescent parenthood is associated with high school dropout, reduced chances of marriage, greater likelihood of divorce, and poverty—circumstances that jeopardize the well-being of both adolescent and newborn child.

◉ Improved sex education, access to contraceptives, and programs that build social competence help prevent early pregnancy. Adolescent mothers need school programs that provide job training, instruction in parenting and life-management skills, and child care. They also benefit when family members and other adults offer guidance and support that are sensitive to their developmental needs. When teenage fathers stay involved, their children develop more favorably.

Important Terms and Concepts

androgens (p. 178)
anorexia nervosa (p. 204)
body image (p. 202)
brain plasticity (p. 184)
bulimia nervosa (p. 205)
catch-up growth (p. 189)
cerebellum (p. 186)
cerebral cortex (p. 183)
corpus callosum (p. 188)
distance curve (p. 172)
dominant cerebral hemisphere (p. 185)
epiphyses (p. 174)
estrogens (p. 178)
experience-dependent brain growth
    (p. 188)

experience-expectant brain growth
    (p. 188)
general growth curve (p. 181)
glial cells (p. 183)
growth hormone (GH) (p. 178)
hypothalamus (p. 178)
kwashiorkor (p. 192)
lateralization (p. 184)
marasmus (p. 192)
menarche (p. 197)
myelination (p. 183)
neurons (p. 182)
neurotransmitters (p. 182)
nonorganic failure to thrive (p. 196)
obesity (p. 193)

pituitary gland (p. 178)
primary sexual characteristics (p. 197)
programmed cell death (p. 182)
psychosocial dwarfism (p. 197)
puberty (p. 197)
reticular formation (p. 187)
secondary sexual characteristics (p. 197)
secular trends in physical growth
    (p. 180)
skeletal age (p. 174)
spermarche (p. 198)
synapses (p. 182)
synaptic pruning (p. 183)
thyroxine (p. 178)
velocity curve (p. 173)

"1 Like Flowers"
Ying Yang
Age 7, China

How do children make sense of their extraordinarily complex world? Like the young girl in this painting, eyes wide open and arms outstretched, they eagerly explore, analyze, and integrate the tantalizing stimulation around them. They also benefit from the assistance of more expert partners as they try to meld their observations into new understandings.

Cognitive Development: Piagetian, Core Knowledge, and Vygotskian Perspectives

Leslie, a preschool teacher, paused to look around her class of busy 3- and 4-year-olds and remarked to a visiting parent, "Their minds are such a curious blend of logic, fantasy, and faulty reasoning. Every day, I'm startled by the maturity and originality of what they say and do. Yet at other times, their thinking seems limited and inflexible."

Leslie's comments sum up the puzzling contradictions of young children's thought. Earlier, after hearing a loud thunderclap outside, 3-year-old Sammy exclaimed, "A magic man turned on the thunder!" Leslie patiently responded that people can't turn thunder on or off and that lightning causes thunder. But Sammy persisted. "Then a magic lady did it," he stated with certainty.

In other respects, Sammy's thinking was surprisingly advanced. His favorite picture books were about dinosaurs, and he could name, categorize, and point out similarities and differences among dozens of them. "Anatosaurus and Tyrannosaurus walk on their back legs," he told the class during group time. "Then they can use their front legs to pick up food!" Later, however, at the snack table, Sammy watched Priti pour her milk from a short, wide carton into a tall, thin glass, then looked at his carton, identical to hers, and asked, "How come you got lots of milk, and I got this little bit?" He did not realize that he had just as much as Priti; although his carton was shorter than her glass, it was also wider.

Cognition refers to the inner processes and products of the mind that lead to "knowing." It includes all mental activity—attending, remembering, symbolizing, categorizing, planning, reasoning, problem solving, creating, and fantasizing. Indeed, we could easily expand this list, since mental processes make their way into virtually everything human beings do. Our cognitive powers are crucial for survival. To adapt to changing environmental conditions, other species benefit from camouflage, feathers and fur coats, and remarkable speed. Humans, in contrast, rely on thinking, through which they not only adapt to their environments but also transform them. Among all earthly creatures, we stand out in our extraordinary mental capacities.

This chapter—and the two that follow—address cognitive development: how the intellectual capacities of infants change into the capacities of the child, adolescent, and adult. Researchers of cognitive development address three main issues:

• They chart its *typical course*, identifying transformations that most children undergo from birth to maturity. They ask: Do all aspects of cognition develop uniformly, or do some develop at faster rates than others?

• They examine *individual differences*. At every age, some children think more or less maturely, and differently, than others. Chapters 6 and 7 are largely devoted to the course of cognitive development, whereas Chapter 8 focuses on individual differences. However, we will encounter both concerns in all three chapters.

- They uncover the *mechanisms* of cognitive development—how genetic and environmental factors combine to yield a particular pattern of change. In this chapter, we address three perspectives on cognitive development, each with distinctive ideas about change: (1) *Piaget's cognitive-developmental theory;* (2) the *core knowledge perspective*—an emerging alternative to Piaget's approach; (3) and *Vygotsky's sociocultural theory,* which—in contrast to the biological emphasis of the first two theories—stresses social and cultural contributions to children's thinking.

As we consider each of these views, we will see repeatedly that children move from simpler to more complex cognitive skills, becoming more effective thinkers with age. But we must be careful not to view children's immature capacities as merely incomplete, less effective versions of adults'. Instead, children's focus on a limited amount of information might be adaptive (Bjorklund, 1997). For example, noticing only a few features of an intricate pattern probably protects young babies from overstimulation during a period in which their nervous systems cannot yet handle much complexity. And comparing the amounts of milk in a short, wide carton and a tall, thin glass by attending only to height (not width) may grant preschoolers a thorough grasp of height, in preparation for effectively integrating height with other dimensions.

The adaptiveness of cognitive immaturity has important implications for education. It suggests that hurrying children to higher levels may undermine their progress. Indeed, Piaget was among the first theorists to stress the importance of *readiness* to learn—presenting appropriately challenging tasks while avoiding stimulation that confuses and overwhelms children because it is overly complex. Let's begin with Piaget's theory.

Piaget's Cognitive-Developmental Theory

Swiss cognitive theorist Jean Piaget received his education in zoology, and his theory has a distinct biological flavor. According to Piaget, human infants do not start out as cognitive beings. Instead, out of their perceptual and motor activities, they build and refine psychological structures—organized ways of making sense of experience that permit children to adapt more effectively to the environment. In developing these structures, children are intensely active. They select and interpret experiences using their current structures and modify those structures to take into account more subtle aspects of reality. Because Piaget viewed children as discovering, or *constructing,* virtually all knowledge about their world through their own activity, his theory is described as a **constructivist approach** to cognitive development.

Basic Characteristics of Piaget's Stages

Piaget believed that children move through four stages—sensorimotor, preoperational, concrete operational, and formal operational—during which the exploratory behaviors of infants transform into the abstract, logical intelligence of adolescence and adulthood. Piaget's stage sequence has three important characteristics:

- The stages provide a *general theory* of development, in which all aspects of cognition change in an integrated fashion, following a similar course.
- The stages are *invariant;* they always occur in a fixed order, and no stage can be skipped.
- The stages are *universal;* they are assumed to characterize children everywhere. (Piaget, Inhelder, & Szeminska, 1948/1960)

Piaget regarded the order of development as rooted in the biology of our species—the result of the human brain becoming increasingly adept at analyzing and interpreting experiences common to most children throughout the world. But he emphasized that individual differences in genetic and environmental factors affect the speed with which children move through the stages (Piaget, 1926/1928). To appreciate Piaget's view of how development takes place, let's consider some important concepts.

Piaget's Ideas About Cognitive Change

According to Piaget, specific psychological structures—organized ways of making sense of experience called **schemes**—change with age. At first, schemes are sensorimotor action patterns. Watch a 6-month-old baby catch sight of, grasp, and release objects, and you will see that the "dropping scheme" is fairly rigid—the infant simply lets go of a rattle or teething ring in her hand. By 18 months, the dropping scheme has become deliberate and creative. Given an opportunity, a baby of this age is likely to toss all sorts of objects down the basement stairs, throwing some up in the air, bouncing others off walls, releasing some gently and others forcefully.

⑤ According to Piaget's theory, schemes are at first motor action patterns. As this 1-year-old drops his mechanical toy from a range of heights and onto a range of surfaces, he discovers that his movements have predictable effects.
© Laura Dwight Photography

Soon, instead of just acting on objects, the toddler shows evidence of thinking before she acts. For Piaget, this change marks the transition from a sensorimotor to a cognitive approach to the world—one based on **mental representations,** or internal depictions of information that the mind can manipulate. Our most powerful mental representations are of two kinds: (1) *images,* or mental pictures of objects, people, and spaces, and (2) *concepts,* or categories in which similar objects or events are grouped together. We use a mental image to retrace our steps when we've misplaced something or to imitate another's behavior long after we've observed it. And by thinking in concepts and labeling them (for example, *ball* for all rounded, movable objects used in play), we become more efficient thinkers, organizing our diverse experiences into meaningful, manageable, and memorable units.

In Piaget's theory, two processes account for this change from sensorimotor to representational schemes, and for further changes in representational schemes from childhood to adulthood: *adaptation* and *organization*.

• **ADAPTATION** • The next time you have a chance, notice how infants and children tirelessly repeat actions that lead to interesting effects. They are illustrating a key Piagetian concept. **Adaptation** involves building schemes through direct interaction with the environment. It consists of two complementary activities: *assimilation* and *accommodation*. During **assimilation,** we use our current schemes to interpret the external world. For example, the infant who repeatedly drops objects is assimilating them to his sensorimotor dropping scheme. And the preschooler who sees her first camel at the zoo and calls out, "Horse!" has sifted through her conceptual schemes until she finds one that resembles the strange-looking creature. In **accommodation,** we create new schemes or adjust old ones after noticing that our current way of thinking does not capture the environment completely. The baby who drops objects in different ways is modifying his dropping scheme to take account of the varied properties of objects. And the preschooler who calls a camel a "lumpy horse" has noticed that certain characteristics of camels are not like those of horses and has revised her scheme accordingly.

According to Piaget, the balance between assimilation and accommodation varies over time. When children are not changing much, they assimilate more than they accommodate. Piaget called this a state of cognitive *equilibrium,* implying a steady, comfortable condition. During times of rapid cognitive change, however, children are in a state of *disequilibrium,* or cognitive discomfort. They realize that new information does not match their current schemes, so they shift away from assimilation toward accommodation. Once they have modified their schemes, they move back toward assimilation, exercising their newly changed structures until they are ready to be modified again.

Piaget used the term **equilibration** to sum up this back-and-forth movement between equilibrium and disequilibrium. Each time equilibration occurs, more effective schemes are produced. Because the times of greatest accommodation are the earliest ones, the sensorimotor stage is Piaget's most complex period of development.

• **ORGANIZATION** • Schemes also change through **organization,** a process that takes place internally, apart from direct contact with the environment. Once children form new schemes, they rearrange them, linking them with other schemes to create a strongly interconnected cognitive system. For example, eventually the baby will relate "dropping" to "throwing" and to his developing understanding of "nearness" and "farness." According to Piaget, schemes reach a true state of equilibrium when they become part of a broad network of structures that can be jointly applied to the surrounding world (Piaget, 1936/1952).

In the following sections, first we will consider development as Piaget saw it, noting research that supports his observations. Then, for each stage, we will take up more recent evidence, some inspired by Piaget's theory and some that challenges Piaget's ideas.

The Sensorimotor Stage: Birth to 2 Years

The **sensorimotor stage** spans the first 2 years of life. Its name reflects Piaget's belief that infants and toddlers "think" with their eyes, ears, hands, and other sensorimotor equipment. They cannot yet carry out many activities inside their heads. Yet the advances of the sensorimotor stage are so vast that Piaget divided it into six substages (see Table 6.1 for a summary). Piaget's observations of his own three children served as the basis for this sequence of development. Although this is a very small sample, Piaget watched carefully and also presented his son and two daughters with everyday problems (such as hidden objects) that helped reveal their understanding of the world.

According to Piaget, at birth infants know so little about their world that they cannot purposefully explore it. The **circular reaction** provides a special means of adapting their first schemes. It involves stumbling onto a new experience caused by the baby's own motor activity. The reaction is "circular" because the infant tries to repeat the event again and again. As a result, a sensorimotor response that first occurred by chance becomes strengthened into a new scheme. For example, imagine a 2-month-old who accidentally makes a smacking noise when finishing a feeding. The baby finds the sound intriguing, so she tries to repeat it until she becomes quite expert at smacking her lips.

During the first 2 years, the circular reaction changes in several ways. At first, it centers on the infant's own body. Later, it turns outward, toward manipulation of objects. Finally, it becomes experimental and creative, aimed at producing novel effects in the environment. Infants' difficulty inhibiting new and interesting behaviors may underlie the circular reaction. But this immaturity in inhibition seems to be adaptive, helping to ensure that new skills will not be interrupted before they strengthen (Carey & Markman, 1999). Piaget considered revisions in the circular reaction so important for early development that he named the sensorimotor substages after them (refer again to Table 6.1).

Sensorimotor Development

For Piaget, newborn reflexes are the building blocks of sensorimotor intelligence. At first, in Substage 1, babies suck, grasp, and look in much the same way, no matter what experiences they encounter. In one amusing example, a mother reported to me that her 2-week-old

---

TABLE 6.1 SUMMARY OF PIAGET'S SENSORIMOTOR STAGE

Sensorimotor Substage	Typical Adaptive Behaviors
1. Reflexive schemes (birth–1 month)	Newborn reflexes (see Chapter 4, page 126)
2. Primary circular reactions (1–4 months)	Simple motor habits centered around the infant's own body; limited anticipation of events
3. Secondary circular reactions (4–8 months)	Actions aimed at repeating interesting effects in the surrounding world; imitation of familiar behaviors
4. Coordination of secondary circular reactions (8–12 months)	Intentional, or goal-directed, behavior; ability to find a hidden object in the first location in which it is hidden (object permanence); improved anticipation of events; imitation of behaviors slightly different from those the infant usually performs
5. Tertiary circular reactions (12–18 months)	Exploration of the properties of objects by acting on them in novel ways; imitation of novel behaviors; ability to search in several locations for a hidden object (accurate A–B search)
6. Mental representation (18 months–2 years)	Internal depictions of objects and events, as indicated by sudden solutions to problems; ability to find an object that has been moved while out of sight (invisible displacement); deferred imitation; and make-believe play

daughter lay on the bed next to her sleeping father. Suddenly, he awoke with a start. The baby had latched on and begun to suck on his back!

• **REPEATING CHANCE BEHAVIORS** • Around 1 month, as babies enter Substage 2, they start to gain voluntary control over their actions through the *primary circular reaction,* by repeating chance behaviors largely motivated by basic needs. This leads to some simple motor habits, such as sucking their fists or thumbs. Babies in this substage also begin to vary their behavior in response to environmental demands. For example, they open their mouths differently for a nipple than for a spoon. Young infants also start to anticipate events. A hungry 3-month-old is likely to stop crying as soon as his mother enters the room—an event signaling that feeding time is near.

This 2½-month-old sees her hands touch, open, and close. She tries to repeat these movements, in a primary circular reaction that helps her gain voluntary control over her behavior.
© Michael Newman/PhotoEdit

During Substage 3, which lasts from 4 to 8 months, infants sit up and become skilled at reaching for and manipulating objects. These motor achievements play a major role in turning their attention outward toward the environment. Using the *secondary circular reaction,* they try to repeat interesting events that are caused by their own actions. For example, Piaget (1936/1952) dangled several dolls in front of his 4-month-old son, Laurent. After accidentally knocking them and producing a fascinating swinging motion, Laurent gradually built the sensorimotor scheme of "hitting." Improved control over their own behavior also permits infants to imitate others' behavior more effectively. However, 4- to 8-month-olds cannot adapt flexibly and quickly enough to imitate novel behaviors (Kaye & Marcus, 1981). Therefore, although they enjoy watching an adult demonstrate a game of pat-a-cake, they are not yet able to participate.

At 4 months, this baby accidentally hits a toy hung in front of him. He tries to recapture the interesting effect of the swinging toy. In doing so, he builds a new "hitting scheme" through the secondary circular reaction.
© Laura Dwight Photography

• **INTENTIONAL BEHAVIOR** • In Substage 4, 8- to 12-month-olds combine schemes into new, more complex action sequences. As a result, behaviors that lead to new schemes no longer have a random, hit-or-miss quality—*accidentally* bringing the thumb to the mouth or *happening* to hit the doll. Instead, 8- to 12-month-olds can engage in **intentional, or goal-directed, behavior,** coordinating schemes deliberately to solve simple problems. The clearest example is provided by Piaget's famous object-hiding task, in which he shows the baby an attractive toy and then hides it behind his hand or under a cover. Infants in this substage can find the object. In doing so, they coordinate two schemes: "pushing" aside the obstacle and "grasping" the toy. Piaget regarded these *means–end action sequences* as the foundation for all later problem solving.

Retrieving hidden objects is evidence that infants have begun to master **object permanence,** the understanding that objects continue to exist when they are out of sight. But awareness of object permanence is not yet complete because babies make the **A-not-B search error.** If they reach several times for an object at a first hiding place (A) and see it moved to a second (B), they will still search for it in the first hiding place (A). Consequently, Piaget concluded, they do not have a clear image of the object as persisting when hidden from view.

Substage 4 brings additional advances. First, infants can better anticipate events, so they sometimes use their capacity for intentional behavior to try to change those events. For example, a baby of this age might crawl after

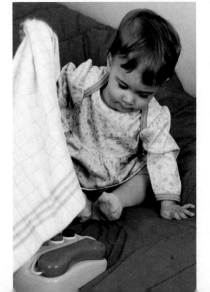

Between 8 and 12 months, babies develop the capacity to find hidden objects, which marks a major advance in cognitive development. In coordinating schemes to uncover and obtain the toy, this infant displays goal-directed behavior—the foundation for all problem solving.
© Laura Dwight Photography

At 14 months, this toddler drops a variety of objects over the edge of a living room table, pushing some gently and others forcefully, in a deliberately experimental approach referred to as a tertiary circular reaction.
© Laura Dwight Photography

At 23 months, this child engages in make-believe play. At first, pretending involves simple schemes that the child has often experienced in everyday life.
© Spencer Grant/PhotoEdit

his mother when she is putting on her coat and whimper to keep her from leaving. Second, babies can imitate behaviors slightly different from those they usually perform. After watching someone else, they try to stir with a spoon, push a toy car, or drop raisins into a cup. Again, they draw on intentional behavior, purposefully modifying schemes to fit an observed action (Piaget, 1945/1951).

In Substage 5, which lasts from 12 to 18 months, the *tertiary circular reaction* emerges. Toddlers repeat behaviors *with variation,* provoking new outcomes. Recall the example on page 221 of the child dropping objects over the basement steps, trying this, then that, then another action. By approaching the world in this deliberately exploratory way, toddlers become better problem solvers. For example, they can figure out how to fit a shape through a hole in a container by turning and twisting it until it falls through, and they can use a stick to obtain a toy that is out of reach. According to Piaget, this capacity to experiment leads to a more advanced understanding of object permanence. Toddlers look in not just one but several locations to find a hidden toy, displaying an accurate A–B search. Their more flexible action patterns also permit them to imitate many more behaviors, such as stacking blocks, scribbling on paper, and making funny faces.

• **MENTAL REPRESENTATION** • In Substage 6, sensorimotor development culminates in mental representation. One sign of this capacity is that 18- to 24-month-olds arrive at solutions to problems suddenly rather than through trial-and-error behavior. In doing so, they seem to experiment with actions inside their heads—evidence that they can mentally represent experiences. Seeing her doll carriage stuck against the wall, Piaget's daughter Lucienne paused for a moment, as if to "think," and then immediately turned the toy in a new direction.

Representation results in several other capacities. First, it enables older toddlers to solve advanced object-permanence problems involving *invisible displacement*—finding a toy moved while out of sight, such as into a small box while under a cover. Second, it permits **deferred imitation**—the ability to remember and copy the behavior of models who are not present. Finally, it makes possible **make-believe play,** in which children act out everyday and imaginary activities. As the sensorimotor period draws to a close, mental symbols are major instruments of thinking.

Follow-Up Research on Infant Cognitive Development

Many studies suggest that infants display a variety of understandings earlier than Piaget believed. For example, recall the operant conditioning research reviewed in Chapter 4, in which newborns sucked vigorously on a nipple to gain access to a variety of interesting sights and sounds. This behavior, which closely resembles Piaget's secondary circular reaction, shows that infants explore and control their external world before 4 to 8 months. In fact, they do so as soon as they are born.

A major method used to find out what infants know about hidden objects and other aspects of physical reality capitalizes on habituation, which we discussed in Chapter 4. In the **violation-of-expectation method,** researchers *habituate* babies to a physical event (expose them to the event until their looking declines). Then they determine whether infants *recover* to (look longer at) an *expected event* (a variation of the first event that follows physical laws) or an *unexpected event* (a variation that violates physical laws). *Recovery to the unexpected event* suggests that the

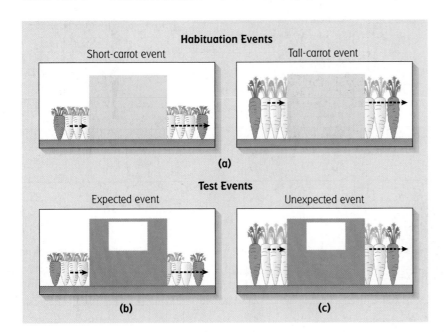

◀ Figure 6.1

Testing young infants for understanding of object permanence using the violation-of-expectation method. (a) First, infants were habituated to two events: a short carrot and a tall carrot moving behind a yellow screen, on alternate trials. Next, the researchers presented two test events. The color of the screen was changed to help infants notice its window. (b) In the *expected event,* the carrot shorter than the window's lower edge moved behind the blue screen and reappeared on the other side. (c) In the *unexpected event,* the carrot taller than the window's lower edge moved behind the screen, did not appear in the window, but then emerged intact on the other side. Infants as young as 2½ to 3½ months recovered to (looked longer at) the *unexpected event,* suggesting that they had some understanding of object permanence. (Adapted from R. Baillargeon & J. DeVos, 1991, "Object Permanence in Young Infants: Further Evidence," *Child Development, 62,* p. 1230. © The Society for Research in Child Development. Reprinted with permission.)

infant is "surprised" by a deviation from physical reality, as indicated by heightened attention and interest, and therefore is aware of that aspect of the physical world.

But the violation-of-expectation method is controversial. Some critics believe that it indicates only limited, implicit (nonconscious) detection of physical events, not the full-blown, conscious understanding that was Piaget's focus in requiring infants to act on their surroundings, as in searching for hidden objects (Bremner & Mareschal, 2004; Hood, 2004). Other critics are convinced that the method reveals only babies' perceptual preference for novelty, not their knowledge of the physical world (Haith, 1999). Let's examine this debate in light of recent research on object permanence.

• **OBJECT PERMANENCE** • In a series of studies using the violation-of-expectation method, Renée Baillargeon and her collaborators claimed evidence for object permanence in the first few months of life. One of Baillargeon's studies is illustrated in Figure 6.1 (Aguiar & Baillargeon, 1999, 2002; Baillargeon & DeVos, 1991). After habituating to a short and a tall carrot moving behind a screen, babies were given two test events: (1) an *expected event,* in which the short carrot moved behind a screen, could not be seen in its window, and reappeared on the other side, and (2) an *unexpected event,* in which the tall carrot moved behind a screen, could not be seen in its window (although it was taller than the window's lower edge), and reappeared. Infants as young as 2½ to 3½ months looked longer at the impossible event, suggesting that they expected an object moved behind a screen to continue to exist.

In additional violation-of-expectation studies, Baillargeon (2004) reported similar results. For example, place a cover over a toy duck, move the cover horizontally along a table, and then lift the cover to reveal no duck. Babies 2½ to 3 months of age look longer at this unexpected event than at an expected event, in which the lifted cover reveals the duck still in place (see Figure 6.2a on page 226) (Wang, Baillargeon, & Paterson, 2005). Or lower an object into a container and then move the container forward and to the side to reveal the object standing in the container's original position. Once again, 2½-month-olds look longer at this *unexpected event* than at an *expected event,* in which the hidden object does not miraculously appear outside its container (see Figure 6.2b on page 226) (Hespos & Baillargeon, 2001).

Nevertheless, several researchers using similar procedures failed to verify some of Baillargeon's findings (Bogartz, Shinskey, & Schilling, 2000; Cashon & Cohen, 2000; Rivera, Wakeley, & Langer, 1999). Baillargeon and others answer that these opposing studies did not include crucial controls. They emphasize that young infants look longer at a wide variety of unexpected events that make it appear as though a hidden object no longer exists (Baillargeon, 2000; Munakata, 2000). Still, critics question what babies' looking preference actually indicates about their knowledge. Also, recall from Chapter 4 (see page 160) that not until age 4 months

▶ **Figure 6.2**

Additional violation-of-expectation events detected by young infants that suggest an understanding of object permanence. Babies 2½ to 3 months of age looked longer at each of these *unexpected events* involving a hidden object than at a corresponding expected event. (a) A hand placed a cover over a toy duck, moved the cover horizontally along a table, and then lifted the cover to reveal no duck. (b) A hand lowered an object into a container and then moved the container forward and to the side, revealing the object standing in the container's original position.

(From R. Baillargeon, 2004, "Infants' Reasoning About Hidden Objects: Evidence for Event-General and Event-Specific Expectations," *Developmental Science, 7,* p. 394. © Blackwell Publishing, Ltd. Reprinted by permission.)

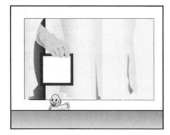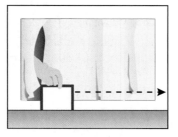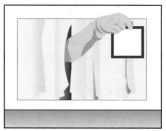

(a)

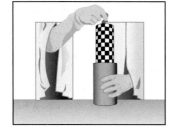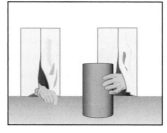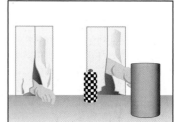

(b)

can infants identify the motion of an object that disappears and reappears from behind a screen as continuous. In other words, younger infants do not appreciate *object identity,* that an object seen previously is the same object—an understanding that, according to some researchers, is necessary for object permanence (Moore & Meltzoff, 1999). These findings suggest that during the first few months, infants' grasp of object permanence is, at best, weak.

If 2- to 3-month-olds do have some notion of object permanence and this understanding strengthens with age, then what explains Piaget's finding that much older babies (who are quite capable of reaching) do not try to search for hidden objects? Consistent with Piaget's theory, research suggests that searching for hidden objects represents a true advance in understanding of object permanence because infants solve some object-hiding tasks before others. Ten-month-olds search for an object placed on a table and covered by a cloth before they search for an object that a hand deposits under a cloth (Moore & Meltzoff, 1999). In the second, more difficult task, infants seem to expect the object to reappear in the hand because that is where the object initially disappeared. When the hand emerges without the object, they conclude that there is no other place the object could be. Not until age 14 months can most babies infer that the hand deposited the object under the cloth (see Figure 6.3).

Around this time, toddlers demonstrate a thorough understanding of hidden objects. Fourteen-month-olds know that objects continue to exist in their hidden locations even after the infants have left the location. After seeing an object hidden in a cupboard, when they returned the next day, they searched correctly, seeking the specific object in its original location. When exposed to a similar cupboard in a new room, infants behaved just as adults do. They saw no reason to search for an object that had been hidden elsewhere (Moore & Meltzoff, 2004).

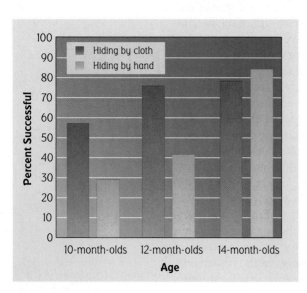

◀ **Figure 6.3**

Performance of 10- to 14-month-olds on two types of object-hiding tasks. In the hiding-by-cloth task, a hand deposited the object on the table, next to a folded cloth. Then the cloth was unfolded over the object. In the hiding-by-hand task, a hand carried the object toward and under the cloth, deposited the object under the cloth on the table, and emerged empty. Ten-month-olds searched for the object hidden by the cloth before they searched for the object hidden by the hand—a task most toddlers performed successfully only at 14 months. (Adapted from Moore & Meltzoff, 1999.)

• **SEARCHING FOR OBJECTS HIDDEN IN MORE THAN ONE LOCATION** • For some years, researchers thought that babies made the A-not-B search error because they had trouble remembering an object's new location after it was hidden in more than one place. But poor memory cannot fully account for infants' unsuccessful performance. For example, between 6 and 12 months, infants increasingly *look* at the correct location, even while *reaching* incorrectly (Ahmed & Ruffman, 1998; Hofstadter & Reznick, 1996).

Perhaps babies search at A (where they found the object on previous reaches) instead of B (its most recent location) because they have trouble inhibiting a previously rewarded motor response (Diamond, Cruttenden, & Neiderman, 1994). In support of this view, the more prior reaches to A, the greater the likelihood that the infant will reach again toward A when the object is hidden at B. Another possibility is that after finding the object several times at A, babies do not attend closely when it is hidden at B (Ruffman & Langman, 2002). A more comprehensive explanation is that a complex, dynamic system of factors—having built a habit of reaching toward A, continuing to look at A, having the hiding place at B look similar to the one at A, and maintaining a constant body posture—increases the chances that the baby will make the A-not-B search error. In a series of studies, disrupting any one of these factors increased 10-month-olds' accurate searching at B (Smith et al., 1999b).

In sum, before 12 months, infants find it difficult to translate what they know about object location into a successful search strategy. The ability to integrate knowledge with action coincides with rapid development of the frontal lobes of the cerebral cortex at the end of the first year (Bell, 1998; Diamond, 1991). Also crucial are a wide variety of experiences perceiving, acting on, and remembering objects.

• **MENTAL REPRESENTATION** • In Piaget's theory, infants lead purely sensorimotor lives; they cannot mentally represent experience until about 18 months of age. Yet 8-month-olds' recall of the location of hidden objects after delays of more than a minute, and 14-month olds' recall after delays of a day or more, indicate that babies construct mental representations of objects and their whereabouts (McDonough, 1999; Moore & Meltzoff, 2004). And studies of deferred imitation, categorization, and problem solving reveal that representational thought is evident even earlier.

▶ *Deferred Imitation.* Piaget studied imitation by noting when his three children demonstrated it in their everyday behavior. Under these conditions, a great deal must be known about the infant's daily life to be sure that deferred imitation—which requires infants to represent a model's past behavior—has occurred.

Laboratory research reveals that deferred imitation is present at 6 weeks of age! Infants who watched an unfamiliar adult's facial expression imitated it when exposed to the same adult the next day (Meltzoff & Moore, 1994). Perhaps young babies use this imitation to identify and communicate with people they have seen before. As motor capacities improve, infants start to copy actions with objects. In one study, 6- and 9-month-olds were shown an "activity" board with twelve novel objects fastened to it—for example, a frog whose legs jump when a cord is pulled. An adult modeled the actions of six of the objects. When tested a day later, infants of both ages were far more likely to produce the actions they had seen than actions associated with objects that had not been demonstrated (Collie & Hayne, 1999). The babies retained and enacted not just one but, on average, three modeled behaviors.

Gains in recall, expressed through deferred imitation, are accompanied by changes in brain-wave activity, as measured by ERPs during memory tasks. This suggests that improvements in memory storage in the cerebral cortex contribute to these advances (Bauer et al., 2003). Between 12 and 18 months, toddlers use deferred imitation skillfully to enrich their range of schemes. They retain modeled behaviors for at least several months, copy the actions of peers as well as adults, and imitate across a change in context—for example, enact at home a behavior learned at child care or on TV (Barr & Hayne, 1999; Hayne, Boniface, & Barr, 2000; Klein & Meltzoff, 1999).

Toddlers even imitate rationally! If they see an adult perform an unusual action for fun (turn on a light with her head, even though her hands are free), they copy the behavior after a week's delay. But if the adult seems to engage in the odd behavior because she must (her

◉ This 3-month-old infant discovered that by kicking, she could shake a mobile made of small blocks, each with a letter A on it. After a delay, the baby continued to kick vigorously only if the mobile she saw was labeled with the same form (the letter A). She did not kick when given a mobile with the number 2. The infant's behavior shows that she groups similar stimuli into categories and can distinguish the category "A" from the category "2."
Courtesy of Carolyn Rovee-Collier

hands are otherwise occupied), 14-month-olds modify their imitative response to a more efficient action (use their hand to turn on the light) (Gergely, Bekkering, & Király, 2003). Around 18 months, toddlers imitate not only an adult's behavior but also the actions he or she *tries* to produce, even if these actions are not fully realized (Meltzoff, 1995). On one occasion, a mother attempted to pour some raisins into a small bag but missed, spilling them onto the counter. A moment later, her 18-month-old son climbed onto a stool and began dropping the raisins into the bag.

These findings reveal that during the second year, toddlers can infer others' intentions and perspectives, which they use to guide their imitative actions. By age 2, children mimic entire social roles—such as Mommy, Daddy, or baby—during make-believe play.

▶ *Categorization.* Even young infants can *categorize,* grouping similar objects and events into a single representation—an ability that is incompatible with a strictly sensorimotor approach to experience. Categorization is especially important for babies: By allowing them to identify regularities in their world, it helps them make sense of experience—to reduce the enormous amount of new information they encounter every day so they can learn and remember (Cohen, 2003; Oakes & Madole, 2003).

Recall the operant conditioning research in which infants kicked to move a mobile attached to their foot by a long cord (see Chapter 4, page 137). Some creative variations of this task have been used to find out about infant categorization. In one series of studies, 3-month-olds kicked a mobile made of a uniform set of stimuli—small blocks, all with the letter A on them. After a delay, kicking returned to a high level only if the babies were given a mobile whose elements were labeled with the same form (the letter A). If the form was changed (from an A to a 2), infants no longer kicked vigorously. While learning to make the mobile move, the babies had mentally grouped together its features, associating the kicking response with the category "A" and, at later testing, distinguishing it from the category "2" (Bhatt et al., 2004; Hayne, Rovee-Collier, & Perris, 1987).

Habituation/recovery has also been used to study infant categorization. Researchers show babies a series of pictures belonging to one category and then see whether the babies recover to (look longer at) a picture that is not a member of the category. Findings reveal that 6- to 12-month-olds structure objects into an impressive array of meaningful categories—food items, furniture, birds, animals, vehicles, kitchen utensils, plants, spatial location ("above," "below," "on," and "in"), and more (Casasola, Cohen, & Chiarello, 2003; Mandler & McDonough, 1998; Oakes, Coppage, & Dingel, 1997; Quinn & Eimas, 1996; Younger, 1985, 1993). Besides organizing the physical world, infants of this age also categorize their emotional and social worlds. Their looking responses reveal that they sort people and their voices by gender and age (Bahrick, Netto, & Hernandez-Reif, 1998; Poulin-DuBois et al., 1994), have begun to distinguish emotional expressions, and can separate people's natural movements from other motions (see Chapter 4, pages 157 and 158).

The baby's earliest categories are *perceptual*—based on similar overall appearance or prominent object part, such as legs for animals and wheels for vehicles. But by the second half of the first year, more categories are *conceptual*—based on com-

◀ **Figure 6.4**

Categorical distinction made by 9- to 11-month-olds. After infants were given an opportunity to examine (by looking or touching) the objects in one category, they were shown a new object from each of the categories. They recovered to (spent more time looking at or touching) the object from the contrasting category, indicating that they distinguished the birds from the airplanes, despite their perceptual similarity. (Adapted from Mandler & McDonough, 1993.)

mon function and behavior (Cohen, 2003; Mandler, 2004). Older infants can make categorical distinctions when the perceptual contrast between two categories—animals and vehicles—is made as minimal as possible (for an illustration, see Figure 6.4). Once infants have formed a variety of object categories, they add event categories, which involve actions, such as a person walking, an animal drinking, or an object bumping another and causing it to move.

In the second year, toddlers become active categorizers. Around 12 months, they touch objects that go together but do not group them. At 16 months, they can group objects into a single category. For example, when given four balls and four boxes, they put all the balls together but not the boxes. Around 18 months, toddlers sort objects into two classes (Gopnik & Meltzoff, 1987a). Compared with habituation/recovery, touching, sorting, and other play behaviors better reveal the meanings that children attach to categories because they are applying those meanings in their everyday behavior. For example, after watching an experimenter give a toy dog a drink from a cup, 14-month-olds, when shown a rabbit and a motorcycle, usually offer the drink only to the rabbit (Mandler & McDonough, 1998). Their behavior reveals that they understand that particular actions are appropriate for some categories of items (animals) but not others (vehicles).

How does the perceptual-to-conceptual change in categorization take place? Although researchers disagree on whether this shift requires a new approach to analyzing experience, most acknowledge that exploration of objects and expanding knowledge of the world contribute to older infants' capacity to move beyond physical features and group objects by their functions and behaviors (Mandler, 2004; Oakes & Madole, 2003). In addition, language both builds on and facilitates categorization. Adult labeling calls infants' attention to commonalities among objects and also promotes vocabulary growth. Toddlers' advancing vocabulary, in turn, fosters categorization (Gopnik & Meltzoff, 1992; Waxman, 2003). And variations among languages lead to cultural differences in conceptual development. Korean toddlers, who learn a language in which object names are often omitted from sentences, develop object-grouping skills later than their English-speaking counterparts (Gopnik & Choi, 1990). At the same time, Korean, but not English, contains a commonly used word *(kkita)*, referring to a tight fit between objects in contact—a ring on a finger, a cap on a pen, or a puzzle piece—and Korean toddlers are advanced in forming the spatial category "tight-fit" (Choi et al., 1999).

▶ *Problem Solving.* As Piaget indicated, around 7 to 8 months, infants develop intentional means–end action sequences and use them to solve simple problems, such as pulling on a cloth to obtain a toy resting on its far end (Willatts, 1999). Soon after, infants' representational skills permit more effective problem solving than Piaget's theory suggests.

By 10 to 12 months, infants can engage in **analogical problem solving**—taking a solution strategy from one problem and applying it to other relevant problems. In one study, babies were given three similar problems, each requiring them to overcome a barrier, grasp a string, and pull it to get an attractive toy. The problems differed in all aspects of their specific features (see Figure 6.5). For the first problem, the parent demonstrated the solution and encouraged the child to imitate. Babies obtained the toy more readily with each additional problem, suggesting that they had formed a flexible mental representation of actions that access an out-of-reach object (Chen, Sanchez, & Campbell, 1997).

With age, children become better at reasoning by analogy, generalizing across increasingly dissimilar situations (Goswami, 1996). But even in the first year, infants have some ability to move beyond trial-and-error experimentation, represent a solution mentally, and use it in new contexts.

▼ **Figure 6.5**

Analogical problem solving by 10- to 12-month-olds. After the parent demonstrated the solution to problem (a), infants solved problems (b) and (c) with increasing efficiency, even though these problems differed from problem (a) in all aspects of their superficial features. (From Z. Chen, R. P. Sanchez, & T. Campbell, 1997, "From Beyond to Within Their Grasp: The Rudiments of Analogical Problem Solving in 10- to 13-Month-Olds," *Developmental Psychology, 33,* p. 792. Copyright © 1997 by the American Psychological Association. Reprinted by permission of the publisher and author.)

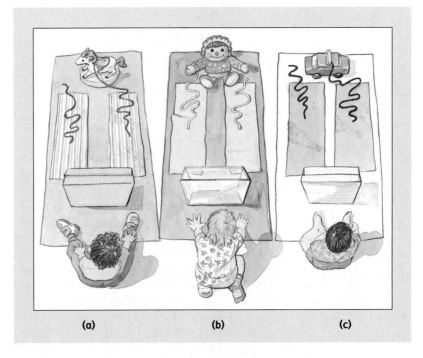

(a)   (b)   (c)

MILESTONES

SOME COGNITIVE ATTAINMENTS OF INFANCY AND TODDLERHOOD

Approximate Age	Cognitive Attainments
Birth–1 month	Exploration using limited motor skills, such as sucking a nipple to gain access to interesting sights and sounds
1–4 months	Awareness of many physical properties, including object permanence, object solidity, and gravity, as suggested by violation-of-expectation findings
	Deferred imitation of an adult's facial expression after a short delay (1 day)
	Categorization of perceptually similar stimuli
4–8 months	Improved physical knowledge and basic numerical knowledge
	Deferred imitation of an adult's novel actions on objects over a short delay (1 day)
	Categorization of many objects and events conceptually—by similar function and behavior
8–12 months	Ability to search for a hidden object after it is covered by a cloth
	Ability to solve simple problems by analogy to a previous problem
12–18 months	Ability to search in several locations for a hidden object (accurate A–B search)
	Awareness that objects continue to exist in their hidden locations even after the toddler has left the location
	Deferred imitation of an adult's novel actions on objects after a long delay (at least several months) and across a change in context
	Active object sorting into a single category
18 months–2 years	Ability to find an object moved while out of sight (invisible displacement)
	Deferred imitation of actions an adult tries to produce, indicating a capacity to infer others' intentions and perspectives
	Deferred imitation of everyday behaviors in make-believe play
	Active object sorting into two categories

Note: These milestones represent overall age trends. Individual differences exist in the precise age at which each milestone is attained.
Which capacities listed in this table indicate that mental representation emerges earlier than predicted by Piaget's sensorimotor substages?

Photos: (top left) © Laura Dwight Photography; (top right) © Laura Dwight/CORBIS; (middle left) © Jennie Woodcock/CORBIS; (middle) © David Young Wolff/PhotoEdit; (bottom left) © Myrleen Ferguson Cate/PhotoEdit; (bottom right) © Laura Dwight Photography

Evaluation of the Sensorimotor Stage

The Milestones table above summarizes the remarkable cognitive attainments we have just considered, along with related milestones that we will take up later in this chapter. Compare this table with the description of Piaget's sensorimotor substages on pages 223–224. You will see that infants anticipate events, actively search for hidden objects, master the A–B object search, flexibly vary their sensorimotor schemes, and engage in make-believe play within Piaget's time frame. Yet other capacities—including secondary circular reactions, first signs of object permanence, deferred imitation, categorization, and analogical problem solving—emerge earlier than Piaget expected.

Notice, also, that the cognitive attainments of infancy do not develop in the neat, stepwise fashion Piaget predicted. Piaget assumed that all representational capacities develop at the same time, at the end of the sensorimotor stage. Yet deferred imitation and the beginnings of analogical problem solving are present long before toddlers can solve Piaget's most advanced object-hiding task. To obtain an object that has been moved while out of sight, infants must go beyond *recall of a past event* to a more complex form of representation: they must *imagine an event they have not seen* (Rast & Meltzoff, 1995). These findings, and others like them, are among an accumulating body of evidence that raises doubts about the accuracy of Piaget's stages.

Disagreements between Piaget's observations and those of recent research also raise controversial questions about how infant development takes place. Consistent with Piaget's ideas, sensorimotor action helps infants construct some forms of knowledge. For example, in Chapter 4, we saw that crawling experience enhances depth perception and ability to find hidden objects. Yet we have also seen evidence that infants comprehend a great deal before they are capable of the motor behaviors that Piaget assumed led to those understandings. How can we account for babies' amazing cognitive accomplishments?

Most researchers believe that young babies have more built-in cognitive equipment for making sense of experience than granted by Piaget, who thought that infants constructed all mental representations out of sensorimotor activity. But intense disagreement exists over how much initial understanding infants have. As we have seen, much evidence on infant cognition rests on the violation-of-expectation method. Researchers who lack confidence in this method argue that babies' cognitive starting point is limited. They believe that newborns begin life with biases for attending to certain information and with general-purpose learning procedures, such as powerful techniques for analyzing complex, perceptual information. Together, these tools enable infants to construct a wide variety of schemes (Bahrick, Lickliter, & Flom, 2004; Huttenlocher, 2002; Kirkham, Slemmer, & Johnson, 2002; Mandler, 2004). Other investigators, convinced by violation-of-expectation findings, argue that infants start life with considerable innate knowledge, which "jump-starts" their cognitive development. We will discuss the strengths and limitations of this *core knowledge perspective*, which has gained ground in the past decade, after considering Piaget's stages of childhood and adolescence.

Are these toddlers able to build a block tower because they had many opportunities to act on objects, as Piaget assumed? Or did they begin life with innate knowledge that enabled them to understand objects and their relationships even though they had little hands-on experience? © Reflections Photolibrary/Corbis

Ask Yourself

REVIEW	Explain how cognition changes according to Piaget's theory, giving examples of assimilation, accommodation, and organization.
REVIEW	Using the text discussion on pages 222–229, construct your own table providing an overview of infant and toddler cognitive development. Which entries in the table are consistent with Piaget's sensorimotor stage? Which ones develop earlier than Piaget anticipated?
APPLY	Mimi's father holds up her favorite teething biscuit, places it under a napkin, and shows Mimi his empty hand. Ten-month-old Mimi, looking puzzled, fails to search for the biscuit. Explain why Mimi finds this object-hiding task difficult.
CONNECT	Recall from Chapter 4 (page 160) that around the middle of the first year, infants become adept at identifying objects by their features (shape, color, and texture) and by their paths of movement, even when they cannot observe the entire path. How might these capacities help infants understand object permanence?

The Preoperational Stage: 2 to 7 Years

As children move from the sensorimotor to the **preoperational stage,** which spans ages 2 to 7, the most obvious change is an extraordinary increase in mental representation. Although infants have some ability to represent their world, this capacity blossoms in early childhood.

Advances in Mental Representation

A visit to a preschool classroom reveals signs of mental representation everywhere—in children's re-creations of experiences in make-believe play, in drawings and paintings that cover the walls, and in their delight at story time. Especially impressive are strides in language.

• LANGUAGE AND THOUGHT • Piaget acknowledged that language is our most flexible means of mental representation. By detaching thought from action, it permits far more efficient thinking than was possible earlier. Thinking in words allows us to overcome the limits of our momentary experiences. We can deal with past, present, and future at once and can combine concepts in unique ways, as when we think about a hungry caterpillar eating bananas or monsters flying through the forest at night.

Despite the power of language, Piaget did not believe that it plays a major role in children's cognitive development. Instead, he claimed that sensorimotor activity leads to internal images of experience, which children then label with words (Piaget, 1936/1952). In support of Piaget's view, children's first words have a strong sensorimotor basis. They usually refer to objects that move or can be acted on, or to familiar actions (see Chapter 9). Also, certain early words seem to depend on nonverbal cognitive achievements. For example, at about the time toddlers master advanced object-permanence problems, they use disappearance words, such as "all gone." When they solve problems suddenly, they use success and failure expressions—"There!" and "Uh-oh!" (Gopnik & Meltzoff, 1987b). In addition, earlier we saw that infants acquire an impressive range of categories long before they use words to label them.

Still, Piaget underestimated the power of language to spur children's cognition. Recall, for example, that toddlers' expanding vocabularies enhance their conceptual skills. Research inspired by Vygotsky's theory, which we take up later, confirms that language is a powerful source of cognitive development, not just an indicator of it.

• **MAKE-BELIEVE PLAY** • Make-believe is another excellent example of the development of representation during early childhood. Piaget believed that through pretending, children practice and strengthen newly acquired representational schemes. Drawing on Piaget's ideas, several investigators have traced changes in make-believe play during the preschool years.

▶ *Development of Make-Believe Play.* Compare an 18-month-old's pretending with that of a 2- to 3-year-old. Three important advances reflect the preschool child's growing symbolic mastery:

- *Over time, play increasingly detaches from the real-life conditions associated with it.* In early pretending, toddlers use only realistic objects—a toy telephone to talk into or a cup to drink from. Most of these earliest pretend acts imitate adults' actions and are not yet flexible. Children younger than age 2, for example, will pretend to drink from a cup but refuse to pretend a cup is a hat (Tomasello, Striano, & Rochat, 1999). They have trouble using an object (cup) as a symbol for another object (hat) when the object (cup) already has an obvious use.

  After age 2, children pretend with less realistic toys, such as a block for a telephone receiver. Gradually, they can flexibly imagine objects and events, without any support from the real world (O'Reilly, 1995; Striano, Tomasello, & Rochat, 2001).

- *Play becomes less self-centered.* At first, make-believe is directed toward the self; for example, children pretend to feed only themselves. A short time later, children direct pretend actions toward other objects, as when the child feeds a doll. And early in the third year, they become detached participants, making a doll feed itself or a parent doll feed a baby doll. Make-believe becomes less self-centered as children realize that agents and recipients of pretend actions can be independent of themselves (McCune, 1993).

- *Play gradually includes more complex combinations of schemes.* An 18-month-old can pretend to drink from a cup but does not yet combine pouring and drinking. Later, children combine pretend schemes with those of peers in **sociodramatic play,** the make-believe with others that is under way by age 2½ and increases rapidly during the next few years (Haight & Miller, 1993). By age 4 to 5, children build on one another's play ideas, create and coordinate several roles, and have a sophisticated understanding of story lines (Göncü, 1993).

With the appearance of sociodramatic play, children not only represent their world but also display *awareness* that make-believe is a representational activity. At age 2 or 3, children distinguish make-believe from real experiences and have begun to grasp that pretending is a deliberate effort to act out imaginary ideas—an understanding that improves steadily over early childhood (Lillard, 1998, 2001; Rakoczy, Tomasello, & Striano, 2004). Listen closely to preschoolers as they jointly create an imaginary scene. You will hear them assign roles and negotiate make-believe plans: "*You pretend to be* the astronaut, *I'll act like* I'm operating the control tower!" "Wait, *I gotta set up* the spaceship." In communicating about pretend, children think about their own and others' fanciful representations—evidence that they have begun to reason about people's mental activities.

▶ *Benefits of Make-Believe Play.* Piaget captured an important aspect of make-believe when he underscored its role in exercising representational schemes. He also noted its emotionally integrative function. Young children often revisit anxiety-provoking events, such as a trip to the doctor's office or discipline by a parent, but with roles reversed so the child is in command and can take charge of the unpleasant experience (Piaget, 1945/1951).

Today, Piaget's view of make-believe as mere practice of representational schemes is regarded as too limited. Play not only reflects but also contributes to children's cognitive and social skills. Sociodramatic play has been studied most thoroughly. In comparison to nonpretend social activities (such as drawing or putting puzzles together), during social pretend preschoolers' interactions last longer, show more involvement, draw larger numbers of children into the activity, and are more cooperative (Creasey, Jarvis, & Berk, 1998).

When we consider these findings, it is not surprising that preschoolers who spend more time in sociodramatic play are seen as more socially competent by their teachers (Connolly & Doyle, 1984). And many studies reveal that make-believe strengthens a wide variety of mental abilities, including sustained attention, memory, logical reasoning, language and literacy, imagination, creativity, understanding of emotions, and the ability to reflect on one's own thinking, inhibit impulses, control one's own behavior, and take another's perspective (Bergen & Mauer, 2000; Berk, 2001a; Elias & Berk, 2002; Kavanaugh & Engel, 1998; Lindsey & Colwell, 2003; Ruff & Capozzoli, 2003).

Between 25 and 45 percent of preschoolers spend much time in solitary make-believe, creating *imaginary companions*—special fantasized friends endowed with humanlike qualities. One preschooler created Nutsy and Nutsy, a pair of boisterous birds living outside her bedroom window. Another child conjured up Maybe, a human of changing gender who could be summoned by shouting out the front door of the family house (Gleason, Sebanc, & Hartup, 2000; Taylor, 1999). In the past, invention of imaginary companions was viewed as a sign of maladjustment, but recent research challenges this assumption. Children with these invisible playmates typically treat their companion with care and affection. And they display more complex pretend play, are advanced in understanding others' viewpoints, and are more sociable with peers (Gleason, 2002; Taylor & Carlson, 1997).

Refer to Applying What We Know below for ways to enhance preschoolers' make-believe. Later we will return to the origins and consequences of make-believe from an alternative perspective—that of Vygotsky.

Ⓖ Make-believe play strengthens a wide variety of mental abilities. Drawing from his rich array of everyday experiences, this child alternates between roles of superhero and chef.

© Ellen Senisi/The Image Works

Applying
What We Know   Enhancing Make-Believe Play in Early Childhood

Strategy	Description
Provide sufficient space and play materials.	A generous amount of space and materials allows for many play options and reduces conflict.
Supervise and encourage children's play without controlling it.	Respond to, guide, and elaborate on preschoolers' play themes when they indicate a need for assistance. Provide open-ended suggestions (for example, "Would the animals like a train ride?"), and talk with the child about the thoughts, motivations, and emotions of play characters. Refrain from directing the child's play; excessive adult control destroys the creativity and joy of make-believe.
Offer a wide variety of both realistic materials and materials without clear functions.	Children use realistic materials, such as trucks, dolls, tea sets, dress-up clothes, and toy scenes (house, farm, garage, airport) to act out everyday roles in their culture. Materials without clear functions (such as blocks, cardboard cylinders, paper bags, and sand) inspire fantastic role play, such as "pirate" and "creature from outer space."
Ensure that children have many rich, real-world experiences to inspire positive fantasy play.	Opportunities to participate in real-world activities with adults and to observe adult roles in the community provide children with rich social knowledge to integrate into make-believe. Restricting television viewing, especially programs with violent content, limits the degree to which violent themes and aggressive behavior become part of children's play. (See Chapter 15, pages 620–621.)
Help children solve social conflicts constructively.	Cooperation is essential for sociodramatic play. Guide children toward positive relationships with agemates by helping them resolve disagreements constructively. For example, ask, "What could you do if you want a turn?" If the child cannot think of possibilities, suggest some options and help the child implement them.

Sources: Berk, 2001a; Frost, Shin, & Jacobs, 1998; Vandenberg, 1998.

• **DRAWINGS** • When given crayon and paper, even toddlers scribble in imitation of others. As preschoolers' ability to mentally represent the world expands, marks on the page take on definite meaning. Cognitive advances—the realization that pictures can serve as symbols, along with improved planning and spatial understanding—influence the development of children's drawings (Golomb, 2004). The emphasis that the child's culture places on artistic expression also contributes.

▶ *From Scribbles to Pictures.* Typically, drawing progresses through the following sequence:

1. *Scribbles.* At first, children's gestures rather than the resulting scribbles contain the intended representation. For example, one 18-month-old took her crayon and hopped it around the page, explaining, as she made a series of dots, "Rabbit goes hop-hop" (Winner, 1986).

2. *First representational forms.* Around age 3, children's scribbles start to become pictures. Often this happens after they make a gesture with the crayon, notice that they have drawn a recognizable shape, and then decide to label it—as with a child who made some random marks on a page and then, noticing a resemblance between his scribbles and noodles, called his creation "chicken pie and noodles" (Winner, 1986).

   Few 3-year-olds spontaneously draw so others can tell what their picture represents. However, in a study in which an adult played a game with children in which pictures stood for objects, more 3-year-olds drew recognizable forms (Callaghan, 1999; Callaghan & Rankin, 2002). When adults draw with children and point out the resemblances between drawings and objects, preschoolers' drawings become more comprehensible and detailed (Braswell & Callanan, 2003).

   A major milestone in drawing occurs when children use lines to represent the boundaries of objects. This enables 3- and 4-year-olds to draw their first picture of a person. Look at the tadpole image—a circular shape with lines attached—on the left in Figure 6.6. It is a universal one in which fine motor and cognitive limitations lead the preschooler to reduce the figure to the simplest form that still looks human. Four-year-olds add features, such as eyes, nose, mouth, hair, fingers, and feet, as the tadpole drawings illustrate.

3. *More realistic drawings.* Greater realism in drawings occurs gradually, as perception, language (ability to describe visual details), memory, and fine motor capacities improve (Toomela, 2002). Five- and 6-year-olds create more complex drawings, like the picture on the right in Figure 6.6, which contains more conventional human and animal figures, in which head and body are differentiated and arms and legs appear.

   Older preschoolers' drawings still contain perceptual distortions because they have just begun to represent depth (Braine et al., 1993). Use of depth cues, such as overlapping objects, smaller size for distant than for near objects, diagonal placement, and converging lines, increases during middle childhood (Nicholls & Kennedy, 1992). And instead of

▶ **Figure 6.6**

Examples of young children's drawings. The universal tadpolelike shape that children use to draw their first picture of a person is shown on the left. The tadpole soon becomes an anchor for greater detail as arms, fingers, toes, and facial features sprout from the basic shape. By the end of the preschool years, children produce more complex, differentiated pictures like the one on the right, drawn by a 6-year-old child.

(Tadpole drawings from H. Gardner, 1980, *Artful Scribbles: The Significance of Children's Drawings,* New York: Basic Books, p. 64. Reprinted by permission of Basic Books, a division of HarperCollins Publishers, Inc. Six-year-old's picture from E. Winner, August 1986, "Where Pelicans Kiss Seals," *Psychology Today, 20* [8], p. 35. Reprinted with permission from *Psychology Today* magazine. Copyright © 1986 Sussex Publishers, Inc.)

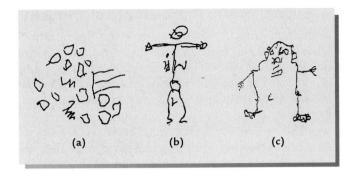

(a)   (b)   (c)

◀ Figure 6.7

Drawings produced by nonschooled 10- to 15-year-old children of the Jimi Valley of Papua New Guinea when they were asked to draw a human figure for the first time. Many produced nonrepresentational scribbles and shapes (a), "stick" figures (b), or "contour" figures (c). Compared with the Western tadpole form, the Jimi "stick" and "contour" figures emphasize the hands and feet. Otherwise, the drawings of these older children resemble those of young preschoolers. (From M. Martlew & K. J. Connolly, 1996, "Human Figure Drawings by Schooled and Unschooled Children in Papua New Guinea," *Child Development, 67,* pp. 2750–2751. © The Society for Research in Child Development, Inc. Adapted by permission.)

depicting objects separately (as in the drawing in Figure 6.6), older school-age children relate them in an organized spatial arrangement (Case & Okamoto, 1996).

▶ *Cultural Variations in Development of Drawing.* In cultures with rich artistic traditions, children's drawings reflect the conventions of their culture and are more elaborate. In cultures with little interest in art, even older children and adolescents produce simple forms. The Jimi Valley is a remote region of Papua New Guinea with no indigenous pictorial art. Many children do not go to school and therefore have little opportunity to develop drawing skills. When a Western researcher asked nonschooled Jimi 10- to 15-year-olds to draw a human figure for the first time, most produced nonrepresentational scribbles and shapes or simple "stick" or "contour" images (see Figure 6.7) (Martlew & Connolly, 1996). These forms, which resemble those of preschoolers, seem to be a universal beginning in drawing. Once children realize that lines must evoke human features, they find solutions to figure drawing that vary somewhat from culture to culture but, overall, follow the sequence of development described earlier.

• **SYMBOL–REAL WORLD RELATIONS** • To make believe and draw—and to understand other forms of representation, such as photographs, models, and maps—preschoolers must realize that each symbol corresponds to a specific state of affairs in everyday life. When do children comprehend symbol–real world relations?

In one study, 2½- and 3-year-olds watched as an adult hid a small toy (Little Snoopy) in a scale model of a room; then children were asked to retrieve it. Next, they had to find a larger toy (Big Snoopy) hidden in the room that the model represented. Not until age 3 could most children use the model as a guide to finding big Snoopy in the real room (DeLoache, 1987). The younger children had trouble with **dual representation**—viewing a symbolic object as both an object in its own right and a symbol. In the study just described, 2½-year-olds did not realize that the model could be *both a toy room and a symbol of another room.* In support of this interpretation, when researchers decreased the prominence of the model room as an object, by placing it behind a window and preventing children from touching it, more 2½ -year-olds succeeded at the search task (DeLoache, 2000, 2002b). Recall a similar limitation in early pretending—that 1½ - to 2-year-olds cannot use an object with an obvious use (cup) to stand for another object (hat).

How do children grasp the dual representation of models, drawings, and other symbols? Adult teaching is helpful. When adults point out similarities between models and real-world spaces, 2½-year-olds perform better on the find-Snoopy task (Peralta de Mendoza & Salsa, 2003). Furthermore, insight into one type of symbol–real world relation helps preschoolers master others. For example, children regard photos and drawings as symbols early, around 1½ to 2 years, because a picture's primary purpose is to stand for something; it is not an interesting object in its own right (Preissler & Carey, 2004). And 3-year-olds who can use a model of a room to locate Big Snoopy readily transfer their understanding to a simple map (Marzolf & DeLoache, 1994).

In sum, exposing young children to diverse symbols—picture books, photos, drawings, make-believe, and maps—helps them appreciate that one object can stand for another (DeLoache, 2002a). With age, children come to understand a wide range of symbols that do not bear a strong physical similarity to what they represent (Liben, 1999)—and doors open to vast realms of knowledge.

◎ Children who experience a variety of symbols come to understand that one object, such as the birdhouse this daughter and her father are making, can stand for another—a full-sized house that people live in. © Ariel Skelley/CORBiS

▲ **Figure 6.8**

Piaget's three-mountains problem. Each mountain is distinguished by its color and by its summit. One has a red cross, another a small house, and the third a snow-capped peak. Children at the preoperational stage respond egocentrically. They cannot select a picture that shows the mountains from the doll's perspective. Instead, they simply choose the photo that reflects their own vantage point.

Limitations of Preoperational Thought

Aside from gains in representation, Piaget described preschool children in terms of what they *cannot*, rather than can, understand (Beilin, 1992). According to Piaget, young children are not capable of **operations**—mental representations of actions that obey logical rules. Instead, their thinking is rigid, limited to one aspect of a situation at a time, and strongly influenced by the way things appear at the moment. As the term *pre*operational suggests, Piaget compared preschoolers to older, more competent children, who are in the concrete operational stage.

• **EGOCENTRIC AND ANIMISTIC THINKING** • For Piaget, the most serious deficiency of preoperational thinking, the one that underlies all others, is **egocentrism**—the failure to distinguish the symbolic viewpoints of others from one's own. He believed that when children first mentally represent the world, they tend to focus on their own viewpoint. Hence, they often assume that others perceive, think, and feel the same way they do.

Piaget's most convincing demonstration of egocentrism involves his *three-mountains problem*, described in Figure 6.8. Egocentrism, he pointed out, is responsible for preoperational children's **animistic thinking**—the belief that inanimate objects have lifelike qualities, such as thoughts, wishes, feelings, and intentions (Piaget, 1926/1930). The 3-year-old who charmingly explains that the sun is angry at the clouds and has chased them away is demonstrating this kind of reasoning. According to Piaget, because young children egocentrically assign human purposes to physical events, magical thinking is common during the preschool years.

Piaget argued that young children's egocentric bias prevents them from *accommodating*, or revising their faulty reasoning in response to their physical and social worlds. To appreciate this shortcoming fully, let's consider some additional tasks that Piaget gave children.

• **INABILITY TO CONSERVE** • Piaget's famous conservation tasks reveal a variety of deficiencies of preoperational thinking. **Conservation** refers to the idea that certain physical characteristics of objects remain the same, even when their outward appearance changes. A typical example is the conservation-of-liquid problem. The child is shown two identical tall glasses of water and asked if they contain equal amounts. Once the child agrees that they do, the water in one glass is poured into a short, wide container, changing the appearance of the water but not its amount, and the child is asked whether the amount of water is the same or has changed. Preoperational children think the quantity has changed. They explain, "There is less now because the water is way down here" (that is, its level is so low) or "There is more because the water is all spread out." In Figure 6.9, you will find other conservation tasks that you can try with children.

Preoperational children's inability to conserve highlights several related aspects of their thinking. First, their understanding is characterized by **centration.** They focus on one aspect of a situation, neglecting other important features. In conservation of liquid, the child *centers* on the height of the water, failing to realize that all changes in height are compensated for by changes in width. Second, children are easily distracted by the *perceptual appearance* of objects. Third, children treat the initial and final *states* of the water as unrelated events, ignoring the *dynamic transformation* (pouring of water) between them.

The most important illogical feature of preoperational thought is *irreversibility*. **Reversibility**—the ability to go through a series of steps in a problem and then mentally reverse direction, returning to the starting point—is part of every logical operation. In the case of conservation of liquid, the preoperational child is unable to imagine the water being poured back into its original container, and so fails to see how the amount must remain the same.

• **LACK OF HIERARCHICAL CLASSIFICATION** • Lacking logical operations, preschoolers have difficulty with **hierarchical classification**—the organization of objects into classes and subclasses on the basis of similarities and differences. Piaget's famous *class inclusion prob-*

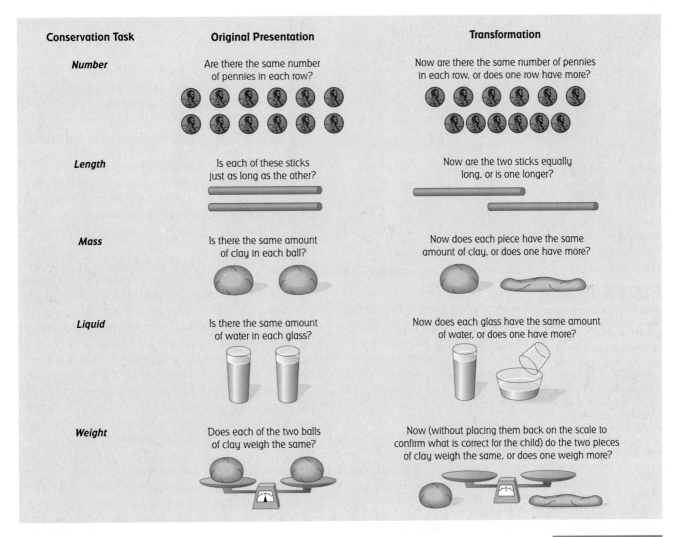

Conservation Task	Original Presentation	Transformation
Number	Are there the same number of pennies in each row?	Now are there the same number of pennies in each row, or does one row have more?
Length	Is each of these sticks just as long as the other?	Now are the two sticks equally long, or is one longer?
Mass	Is there the same amount of clay in each ball?	Now does each piece have the same amount of clay, or does one have more?
Liquid	Is there the same amount of water in each glass?	Now does each glass have the same amount of water, or does one have more?
Weight	Does each of the two balls of clay weigh the same?	Now (without placing them back on the scale to confirm what is correct for the child) do the two pieces of clay weigh the same, or does one weigh more?

▲ **Figure 6.9**

Some Piagetian conservation tasks. Children at the preoperational stage cannot yet conserve. These tasks are mastered gradually over the concrete operational stage. Children in Western nations typically acquire conservation of number, length, mass, and liquid sometime between 6 and 7 years and of weight between 8 and 10 years.

lem, illustrated in Figure 6.10 on page 238, demonstrates this limitation. Preoperational children center on the overriding feature, yellow. They do not think reversibly by moving from the whole class (flowers) to the parts (yellow and blue) and back again.

Follow-Up Research on Preoperational Thought

Over the past three decades, researchers have challenged Piaget's account of a cognitively deficient preschooler. Many Piagetian problems contain unfamiliar elements or too many pieces of information for young children to handle at once. As a result, preschoolers' responses often do not reflect their true abilities. Piaget also missed many naturally occurring instances of effective reasoning by preschoolers. Let's look at some examples.

• **EGOCENTRISM** • Do young children really believe that a person standing elsewhere in a room sees the same thing they see? When researchers change the nature of Piaget's three-mountains problem to include familiar objects and use methods other than picture selection (which is difficult even for 10-year-olds), 4-year-olds show clear awareness of others' vantage points (Borke, 1975; Newcombe & Huttenlocher, 1992).

Nonegocentric responses also appear in young children's conversations. For example, preschoolers adapt their speech to fit the needs of their listeners. Four-year-olds use shorter, simpler expressions when talking to 2-year-olds than to agemates or adults (Gelman & Shatz, 1978). Also, in describing objects, children do not use such words as "big" and "little" in a rigid, egocentric fashion. Instead, they *adjust* their descriptions, taking account of context. By age 3, children judge a 2-inch shoe as small when seen by itself (because it is much smaller than most shoes) but as big for a tiny 5-inch doll (Ebeling & Gelman, 1994).

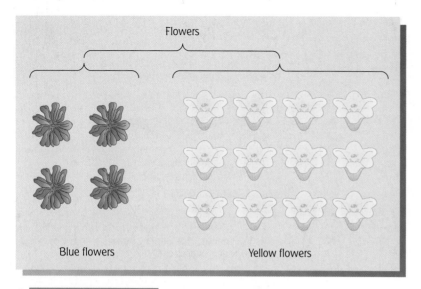

Flowers

Blue flowers   Yellow flowers

▲ **Figure 6.10**

A Piagetian class inclusion problem. Children are shown 16 flowers, 4 of which are blue and 12 of which are yellow. Asked, "Are there more yellow flowers or flowers?" the preoperational child responds, "More yellow flowers," failing to realize that both yellow and blue flowers are included in the category "flowers."

◉ Which of the children in this audience realize that a magician's powers depend on trickery? The younger children look surprised and bewildered. The older children think the magician's antics are funny. Between 4 and 8 years, as familiarity with physical events and principles increases, children's magical beliefs decline.
© J. Sohm/The Image Works

Even toddlers have some appreciation of others' perspectives. In discussing deferred imitation, we saw that they have begun to infer others' intentions (see page 227). And in Chapters 10 and 11, we will encounter evidence that young children have a much greater appreciation of other people's mental states than Piaget's notion of egocentrism implies. In fairness, however, in his later writings Piaget (1945/1951) described preschoolers' egocentrism as a tendency rather than an inability. As we revisit the topic of perspective taking, we will see that it develops gradually throughout childhood and adolescence.

• **ANIMISTIC AND MAGICAL THINKING** •
Piaget overestimated preschoolers' animistic beliefs because he asked children about objects with which they have little direct experience, such as the clouds, sun, and moon. Even infants have begun to distinguish animate from inanimate, as indicated by their remarkable categorical distinctions among living and nonliving things (see pages 228–229). By age 2½, children give psychological explanations—"he likes to" or "she wants to"—for people and occasionally for animals, but rarely for objects (Hickling & Wellman, 2001). They do make errors when questioned about certain vehicles, such as trains and airplanes. But these appear to be self-moving, a basic characteristic of animate beings, and have some lifelike features—for example, headlights that look like eyes (Gelman & Opfer, 2002). Preschoolers' responses result from incomplete knowledge about objects, not from a belief that inanimate objects are alive.

The same is true for other fantastic beliefs of the preschool years. Most 3- and 4-year-olds believe in the supernatural powers of fairies, goblins, and other enchanted creatures. But they deny that magic can alter their everyday experiences—for example, turn a picture into a real object (Subbotsky, 1994). Instead, they think that magic accounts for events they cannot explain, as in 3-year-old Sammy's magical explanation for thunder in the opening to this chapter (Rosengren & Hickling, 2000). Furthermore, older 3-year-olds and 4-year-olds think that violations of physical laws (walking through a wall) and mental laws (turning on the TV just by thinking about it) require magic more than violations of social conventions (taking a bath with shoes on) (Browne & Woolley, 2004). These responses indicate that preschoolers' notions of magic are flexible and appropriate.

Between 4 and 8 years, as familiarity with physical events and principles increases, magical beliefs decline. Children figure out who is really behind the visits of Santa Claus and the Tooth Fairy, and they realize that magicians' feats are due to trickery, not special powers (Subbotsky, 2004; Woolley et al., 1999). Even so, children entertain the possibility that something they imagine might materialize, and they may react with anxiety to scary stories and nightmares. In one study, researchers had 4- to 6-year-olds imagine that a monster was inside one empty box and a puppy inside another. Although almost all the children approached the "puppy" box, many avoided putting their finger in the "monster" box, even though they knew that imagination cannot create reality (Harris et al., 1991).

How quickly children give up certain fantastic ideas varies with religion and culture. For example, Jewish children are more likely than their Christian agemates to express disbelief in Santa Claus and the Tooth Fairy. Having been taught at home that Santa is not real, they seem to generalize this attitude to other magical figures (Woolley, 1997). And cultural myths about wishing—for example, the custom of making a wish before blowing out birthday candles—probably underlie the conviction of most 3- to 6-year-olds that just by wishing, you can sometimes make your desires come true (Woolley, 2000).

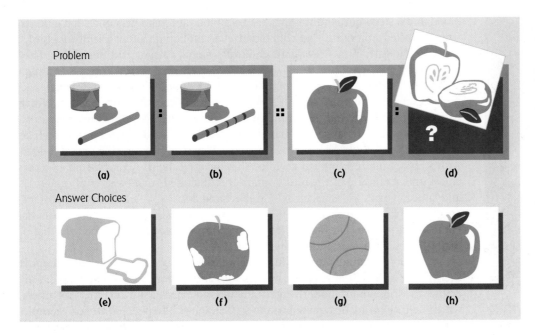

Figure 6.11

Analogical problem about physical transformations. Preschoolers were told they would be playing a picture-matching game. Then the researchers showed each child the first three pictures of a four-picture sequence—in this example, playdough, cut up playdough, and apple—and asked the child to complete the sequence by choosing from five alternatives. Several wrong answers shared features with the right choice—for example, correct physical change but wrong object (e), and correct object but wrong physical change (f). Children as young as 3 years of age could combine the correct physical change with the correct object and solve the problem. (Adapted from Goswami & Brown, 1989.)

• **ILLOGICAL THOUGHT** • Many studies have reexamined the illogical characteristics that Piaget saw in the preoperational stage. Results show that when preschoolers are given tasks that are simplified and made relevant to their everyday lives, they do better than Piaget might have expected.

For example, when a conservation-of-number task is scaled down to include only three items instead of six or seven, 3-year-olds perform well (Gelman, 1972). And when preschoolers are asked carefully worded questions about what happens to substances (such as sugar) after they are dissolved in water, they give accurate explanations. Most 3- to 5-year-olds know that the substance is conserved—that it continues to exist, can be tasted, and makes the liquid heavier, even though it is invisible in the water (Au, Sidle, & Rollins, 1993; Rosen & Rozin, 1993).

Preschoolers' ability to reason about transformations is evident on other problems. For example, they can engage in impressive *reasoning by analogy* about physical changes. As Figure 6.11 shows, when they are presented with the problem, *playdough is to cut-up playdough as apple is to?*, even 3-year-olds choose the correct answer from a set of alternatives, several of which share physical features with the right choice (Goswami, 1996). These findings indicate that in familiar contexts, preschoolers are able to overcome appearances and think logically.

Furthermore, preschoolers have a remarkable understanding of diverse cause-and-effect relationships. For example, they know that the insides of animals differ from the insides of machines. Even though they have little detailed biological or mechanical knowledge, they realize that animal insides are responsible for cause–effect sequences (such as willing oneself to move) that are not possible for nonliving things (Keil & Lockhart, 1999).

Finally, 3- and 4-year-olds use logical, causal expressions, such as *if–then* and *because,* with the same degree of accuracy as adults (McCabe & Peterson, 1988). Illogical reasoning seems to occur only when they grapple with unfamiliar topics, too much information, or contradictory facts that they have trouble reconciling (Ruffman, 1999).

• **CATEGORIZATION** • Although preschoolers have difficulty with Piagetian class inclusion tasks, their everyday knowledge is organized into nested categories at an early age. By the second half of the first year, children have formed a variety of global categories, such as "furniture," "animals," "vehicles," "plants," and "kitchen utensils." Notice that each of these categories includes objects that differ widely in perceptual features. The objects go together because of their common natural kind (animate versus inanimate), function, and behavior, challenging Piaget's assumption that young children's thinking is wholly governed by the way things appear. Indeed, 2- to 5-year-olds readily draw inferences about nonobservable characteristics that category members share (Gopnik & Nazzi, 2003). For example, after being told that a bird has warm

In early childhood, children form categories based on underlying characteristics rather than perceptual features. Guided by knowledge that "dinosaurs have cold blood," this 4-year-old categorizes the pterodactyl (in the foreground) as a dinosaur rather than a bird, even though pterodactyls have wings and can fly.
© Tony Freeman/PhotoEdit

blood and a stegosaurus (dinosaur) has cold blood, preschoolers infer that a ptero-dactyl (labeled a dinosaur) has cold blood, even though it closely resembles a bird.

Over the early preschool years, children's global categories differentiate. They form many *basic-level categories*—ones at an intermediate level of generality, such as "chairs," "tables," "dressers," and "beds." Performance on object-sorting tasks indicates that by the third or fourth year, preschoolers easily move back and forth between basic-level and *superordinate categories*, such as "furniture" (Blewitt, 1994). They also break down basic-level categories into *subcategories*, such as "rocking chairs" and "desk chairs." In fact, a case study of a highly verbal toddler with a strong interest in birds revealed that by age 2, he had constructed a hierar-chical understanding of the bird domain that included such basic-level categories and subcategories as "waterbirds" ("ducks" and "swans"), "landbirds" ("roosters" and "turkeys"), and "other birds" ("bluebirds," "cardinals," and "seagulls") (Mervis, Pani, & Pani, 2003). The boy's category structure was not quite the same as that of many adults, but it was, indeed, hierarchical.

Preschoolers' rapidly expanding vocabularies and general knowledge support their impressive skill at categorizing. As they learn more about their world, they devise theories about underlying characteristics shared by category members, which help them identify new instances (Gelman & Koenig, 2003). For example, they know that animals have an inborn potential for certain physical features and behaviors that determine their identity. And they derive much information from adult explanations. In one study, researchers invented two categories of animals: One had horns, armor, and a spiky tail; the other had wings, large ears, long toes, and a monkeylike tail (see Figure 6.12). Four-year-olds who were given a theory that identified an inner cause for the coexistence of the ani-mals' features—animals in the first category "like to fight," those in the second category "like to hide in trees"—easily classified new examples of animals. Four-year-olds for whom animal features were merely pointed out or who were given a separate function for each feature could not remember the categories (Krascum & Andrews, 1998).

In sum, preschoolers' category systems are not as complex as those of older children and adults. But the capacity to classify on the basis of nonobvious properties and in a hierarchical fashion is present in early childhood.

• **APPEARANCE VERSUS REALITY** • So far, we have seen that preschoolers show remark-ably advanced reasoning when presented with familiar situations and simplified problems. What happens when they encounter objects that have two identities: a real one and an apparent one? Can they distinguish appearance from reality? In a series of studies, John Flavell and his colleagues presented children with objects that were disguised in various ways and questioned them about what each "looks like" and what each "is really and truly." Preschoolers had difficulty. For example, when asked whether a candle that looks like a crayon "is really and truly" a crayon or whether a stone pained to look like an egg "is really and truly" an egg, they often responded "Yes!" Not until age 6 or 7 did children do well on these tasks (Flavell, Green, & Flavell, 1987).

Categories of Animals

"Likes to fight"

"Likes to hide in trees"

New Instances

◀ **Figure 6.12**

Categories of imaginary animals shown to preschoolers. When an adult provided a theory about the coexistence of animals' features—"likes to fight" and "likes to hide in trees"—4-year-olds easily classi-fied new examples of animals with only one or two features. Without the theory, preschoolers could not remember the categories. Theories about underlying characteristics support the formation of many cate-gories in early childhood.
(From R. M. Krascum & S. Andrews, 1998, "The Effects of Theories on Children's Acquisition of Family-Resemblance Categories," *Child Development, 69,* p. 336. © The Society for Research in Child Development, Inc. Reprinted by permission.)

The poor performance of younger children, however, is not entirely due to difficulty in distinguishing appearance from reality, as Piaget suggested. Rather, they have trouble with the *language* of these tasks (Deák, Ray, & Brenneman, 2003). When permitted to solve appearance–reality problems nonverbally, by selecting from an array of objects the one that "really" has a particular identity, most 3-year-olds perform well (Sapp, Lee, & Muir, 2000).

These findings suggest that preschoolers begin to appreciate the appearance–reality distinction sometime during the third year. Note how it involves a capacity we discussed earlier: *dual representation*—the realization that an object can be one thing (a candle) while symbolizing another (a crayon). At first, however, children's understanding is fragile. After putting on a Halloween mask, young preschoolers may be wary and even frightened when they see themselves in a mirror. And not until the school years do children fully appreciate the unreality of much that they see on TV. Performing well on verbal appearance–reality tasks signifies a more secure understanding and is related to further progress in representational ability (Bialystok & Senman, 2004).

Evaluation of the Preoperational Stage

The Milestones table on page 242 provides an overview of these cognitive attainments of early childhood. Compare them with Piaget's description of the preoperational child on pages 236–237. How can we make sense of the contradictions between Piaget's conclusions and the findings of follow-up research? The evidence as a whole indicates that Piaget was partly wrong and partly right about young children's cognitive capacities. When given simplified tasks based on familiar experiences, preschoolers do show the beginnings of logical thinking.

That preschoolers have some logical understanding suggests that they acquire operational reasoning gradually. Over time, children rely on increasingly effective mental approaches to solving problems. For example, children who cannot use counting to compare two sets of items do not conserve number (Sophian, 1995). Once preschoolers learn to count, they apply this skill to conservation-of-number tasks involving only a few items. Then, as counting improves, they extend the strategy to problems with more items. By age 6, they understand that number remains the same after a transformation as long as nothing is added or taken away. Consequently, they no longer need to count to verify their answer (Klahr & MacWhinney, 1998). This sequence indicates that children pass through several phases of understanding, although (as Piaget indicated) they do not fully grasp conservation until the school years.

Evidence that logical operations develop gradually poses yet another challenge to Piaget's stage concept, which assumes abrupt change toward logical reasoning around age 6 or 7. Although the minds of young children still have a great deal of developing to do, research shows that they are considerably more capable than Piaget assumed.

Ask Yourself

REVIEW	Select two of the following features of Piaget's preoperational stage: egocentrism, a focus on perceptual appearances, difficulty reasoning about transformations, and lack of hierarchical classification. Cite findings that led Piaget to conclude that preschoolers are deficient in those ways. Then present evidence that Piaget underestimated preschoolers' cognitive capacities.
APPLY	At home, 4-year-old Will understands that his tricycle isn't alive and can't move by itself. Yet when Will went fishing with his family and his father asked, "Why do you think the river is flowing along?" Will responded, "Because it's alive and wants to." What explains this contradiction in Will's reasoning?
CONNECT	When do children realize that a scale model of a room represents a real room? When do they first grasp the real and apparent identities of disguised objects (such as a stone painted to look like an egg)? What cognitive capacity underlies both attainments?
REFLECT	Did you have an imaginary companion as a young child? If so, what was your companion like, and why did you create it? Were your parents aware of your companion? What was their attitude toward it?

MILESTONES

SOME COGNITIVE ATTAINMENTS OF EARLY CHILDHOOD

Approximate Age	Cognitive Attainments
2–4 years 	Shows a dramatic increase in representational activity, as reflected in the development of language, make-believe play, drawing, and understanding of dual representation
	Takes the perspective of others in simplified, familiar situations and in everyday, face-to-face communication
	Distinguishes animate beings from inanimate objects; denies that magic can alter everyday experiences
	Grasps conservation, notices transformations, reverses thinking, and understands many cause-and-effect relationships in familiar contexts
	Categorizes objects on the basis of common natural kind, function, and behavior and devises ideas about underlying characteristics that category members share
	Sorts familiar objects into hierarchically organized categories
	Distinguishes appearance from reality
4–7 years	Becomes increasingly aware that make-believe (and other thought processes) are representational activities
	Replaces magical beliefs about fairies, goblins, and events that violate expectations with plausible explanations
	Solves verbal appearance–reality problems, signifying a more secure understanding

Note: These milestones represent overall age trends. Individual differences exist in the precise age at which each milestone is attained.

Photos: (top) © Ellen B. Senisi/The Image Works; (bottom) © Peter Hvizdak/The Image Works

The Concrete Operational Stage: 7 to 11 Years

According to Piaget, the **concrete operational stage**, which extends from about 7 to 11 years, marks a major turning point in cognitive development. Thought is far more logical, flexible, and organized than it was earlier, more closely resembling the reasoning of adults than that of younger children.

Concrete Operational Thought

Concrete operations are evident in the school-age child's performance on a wide variety of Piagetian tasks. Let's look closely at these diverse accomplishments.

• **CONSERVATION** • The ability to pass *conservation tasks* provides clear evidence of *operations*. In conservation of liquid, for example, children state that the amount of liquid has not changed, and they are likely to offer an explanation something like this: "The water's shorter but it's also wider. Pour it back; you'll see it's the same amount." Notice how, in this response, the child coordinates several aspects of the task rather than centering on only one. The older child engages in *decentration*, recognizing that a change in one aspect of the water (its height) is compensated for by a change in another aspect (its width). This explanation also illustrates *reversibility*—the capacity to imagine the water being returned to the original container as proof of conservation.

• **CLASSIFICATION** • Between ages 7 and 10, children pass Piaget's *class inclusion problem*. This indicates that they are more aware of classification hierarchies and can focus on relations between a general and two specific categories at the same time—that is, on three relations at once (Hodges & French, 1988; Ni, 1998). Collections—stamps, coins, rocks, bottle caps, and more—become common in middle childhood. At age 10, one boy I know spent hours sorting and resorting

⑥ In Piaget's concrete operational stage, school-age children think in an organized and logical fashion about concrete objects. This 8-year-old boy understands that the hamster on one side of the balance scale is just as heavy as the metal weights on the other, even though the two types of objects look and feel quite different from each other.
© Tim Davis/Photo Researchers, Inc.

his large box of baseball cards. At times he grouped them by league and team membership, at other times by playing position and batting average. He could separate the players into a variety of classes and subclasses and easily rearrange them.

• **SERIATION** • The ability to order items along a quantitative dimension, such as length or weight, is called **seriation.** To test for it, Piaget asked children to arrange sticks of different lengths from shortest to longest. Older preschoolers can create the series, but they do so haphazardly. They put the sticks in a row but make many errors and take a long time to correct them. In contrast, 6- to 7-year-olds are guided by an orderly plan. They create the series efficiently by beginning with the smallest stick, then moving to the next largest, and so on, until the ordering is complete.

The concrete operational child can also seriate mentally, an ability called **transitive inference.** In a well-known transitive inference problem, Piaget (1967) showed children pairings of differently colored sticks. From observing that stick A is longer than stick B and that B is longer than stick C, children must infer that A is longer than C. Notice how this task, like Piaget's class inclusion task, requires children to integrate three relations at once—A–B, B–C, A–C. When researchers take steps to ensure that children remember the premises (A–B and B–C), 7- to 8-year-olds can grasp transitive inference (Andrews & Halford, 1998; Wright & Dowker, 2002).

• **SPATIAL REASONING** • Piaget found that school-age children's understanding of space is more accurate than that of preschoolers. Let's take two examples—understanding of directions and maps.

▶ *Directions.* When asked to name an object to the left or right of another person, 5- and 6-year-olds answer incorrectly; they apply their own frame of reference. Between 7 and 8 years, children start to perform *mental rotations,* in which they align the self's frame to match that of a person in a different orientation. As a result, they can identify left and right for positions they do not occupy (Roberts & Aman, 1993). Around 8 to 10 years, children can give clear, well-organized directions for how to get from one place to another by using a "mental walk" strategy in which they imagine another person's movements along a route (Gauvain & Rogoff, 1989). Six-year-olds give more organized directions after they walk the route themselves or are specially prompted. Otherwise, they focus on the end point without describing exactly how to get there (Plumert et al., 1994).

▶ *Cognitive Maps.* Children's mental representations of familiar large-scale spaces, such as their neighborhood or school, are called **cognitive maps.** Drawing a map of a large-scale space requires considerable perspective-taking skill because the entire space cannot be seen at once (Piaget & Inhelder, 1948/1956). Instead, children must infer its overall layout by relating its separate parts.

Preschoolers and young school-age children include *landmarks* on the maps they draw, but their placement is fragmented. When asked to place stickers showing the location of desks and people on a map of their classroom, they perform better. But if the map is rotated to a position other than the orientation of the classroom, they have difficulty placing the stickers (Liben & Downs, 1993). Their use of a rotated map to find objects hidden in a room improves when the locations form a meaningful pattern, such as the outline of a dog (see Figure 6.13 on page 244). Showing children the pattern on the map helps them *reason by analogy* from the rotated map to corresponding locations in the room (Uttal et al., 2001).

In the early school grades, children's maps become more coherent. They draw landmarks along an *organized route of travel*—an attainment that resembles their improved direction giving. By the end of middle childhood, children form an *overall configuration of a large-scale space* in which landmarks and routes are interrelated (Newcombe, 1982). And they readily draw and read maps when the orientation of the map and the space it represents do not match (Liben, 1999).

Besides cognitive development, cultural frameworks influence children's map making. In many non-Western communities, people rarely use maps for way-finding. Instead, neighbors, street vendors, and shopkeepers are prime sources of

◉ An improved ability to categorize underlies children's interest in collecting objects during middle childhood. These older school-age children sort baseball cards into an elaborate structure of classes and subclasses.
© Bob Daemmrich/The Image Works

◉ This fourth grader, who is constructing a map that depicts the overall layout of her neighborhood, represents landmarks and routes of travel as interrelated.
© David Young-Wolff/PhotoEdit

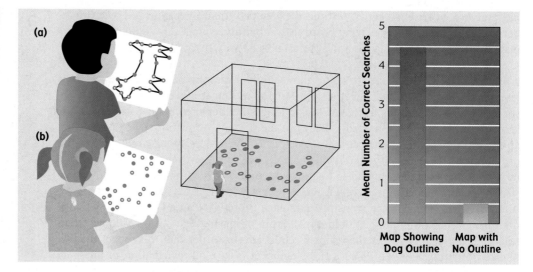

► Figure 6.13

Five-year-olds' use of a rotated map to find objects hidden in a room. In one condition (a), locations on the map were connected to form a meaningful pattern—outline of a dog. In a second condition (b), the locations on the map were not connected. The map showing the dog outline resulted in more correct searches than did the map with no outline. The meaningful pattern seemed to help children reason by analogy from the rotated map to locations in the room. (Adapted from Uttal et al., 2001.)

information. Also, compared to their Western counterparts, non-Western children less often ride in cars and more often walk, which results in intimate neighborhood knowledge. When a researcher had 12-year-olds in small cities in India and the United States draw maps of their neighborhoods, the Indian children represented a rich array of landmarks and aspects of social life, such as people and vehicles, in a small area surrounding their home. The American children, in contrast, drew a more formal, extended space, highlighted main streets and key directions (north–south, east–west), but included few landmarks and features (see Figure 6.14) (Parameswaran, 2003). Although the American children's maps scored higher in cognitive maturity, the cultural meanings that children attached to the task accounted for this difference. When asked to create a map to "help people find their way," the Indian children drew spaces as far-reaching and organized as the American children's.

Limitations of Concrete Operational Thought

As suggested by the name of this stage, concrete operational thinking suffers from one important limitation: Children think in an organized, logical fashion only when dealing with concrete information they can perceive directly. Their mental operations work poorly with abstract ideas—ones not apparent in the real world. Children's solutions to transitive inference problems provide a good illustration. When shown pairs of sticks of unequal length, 8-year-olds readily figure out that if stick A is longer than stick B and stick B is longer than stick C, then stick A is longer than stick C. But they have great difficulty with a hypothetical version of this task, such as "Susan is taller than Sally and Sally is taller than Mary. Who is the tallest?" Not until age 11 or 12 can children solve this problem.

That logical thought is at first tied to immediate situations helps account for a special feature of concrete operational reasoning. You may have noticed that school-age children master Piaget's concrete operational tasks step by step, not all at once. For example, they usually grasp conservation of number, followed by length, liquid, and mass, followed by weight. Piaget used the term **horizontal décalage** (meaning development within a stage) to describe this gradual mastery of logical concepts. Horizontal décalage also illustrates the concrete operational child's difficulty with abstractions. School-age children do not come up with general logical principles and then apply them to all relevant situations. Rather, they seem to work out the logic of each problem separately.

Follow-Up Research on Concrete Operational Thought

According to Piaget, brain development combined with experience in a rich and varied external world should lead children everywhere to reach the concrete operational stage. Yet already we have seen that culture profoundly affects children's task performance, and schooling is influential as well (Rogoff, 2003; Rogoff & Chavajay, 1995).

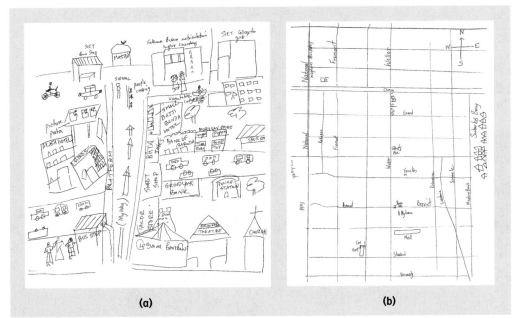

(a)　　　　　　　　　　(b)

◀ **Figure 6.14**

Maps drawn by 12-year-olds from India and the United States. (a) The Indian child depicted many landmarks and features of social life in a small area near her home. (b) The American child drew a more extended space, highlighted main streets and key directions, but included few landmarks and people.
(From G. Parameswaran, 2003, "Experimenter Instructions as a Mediator in the Effects of Culture on Mapping One's Neighborhood," *Journal of Environmental Psychology, 23,* pp. 415–416. © 2003 Elsevier Ltd. Reprinted by permission.)

In tribal and village societies, conservation is often delayed. For example, among the Hausa of Nigeria, who live in small agricultural settlements and rarely send their children to school, even the most basic conservation tasks—number, length, and liquid—are not understood until age 11 or later (Fahrmeier, 1978). This suggests that taking part in relevant everyday activities helps children master conservation and other Piagetian problems (Light & Perret-Clermont, 1989). Many children in Western nations, for example, have learned to think of "fairness" in terms of equal distribution—a value emphasized by their culture. They have many opportunities to divide materials, such as crayons, Halloween treats, and lemonade, equally among their friends. Because they often see the same quantity arranged in different ways, they grasp conservation early.

The very experience of going to school seems to promote mastery of Piagetian tasks. When children of the same age are tested, those who have been in school longer do better on transitive inference problems (Artman & Cahan, 1993). Opportunities to seriate objects, to learn about order relations, and to remember the parts of a complex problem are probably responsible. Yet certain nonschool, informal experiences can also foster operational thought. Brazilian 6- to 9-year-old street vendors, who seldom attend school, do poorly on Piaget's class inclusion tasks. But they perform much better than schoolchildren on versions relevant to street vending—for example, "If you have 4 units of mint chewing gum and 2 units of grape chewing gum, is it better to sell me the mint gum or [all] the gum?" (Ceci & Roazzi, 1994). Similarly, around age 7 to 8, Zinacanteco Indian girls of southern Mexico, who learn to weave elaborately designed fabrics as an alternative to schooling, engage in mental transformations to figure out how a warp strung on a loom will turn out as woven cloth— reasoning expected at the concrete operational stage. North American children of the same age, who do much better than Zinacanteco children on Piaget's tasks, have great difficulty with these weaving problems (Maynard & Greenfield, 2003).

On the basis of findings like these, some investigators have concluded that the forms of logic required by Piagetian tasks do not emerge spontaneously but are heavily influenced by training, context, and cultural conditions. The Milestones table on page 246 summarizes the cognitive attainments of middle childhood discussed in the preceding sections, along with those that will follow in adolescence.

⑥ This Zinacanteco Indian girl of southern Mexico learns the centuries-old practice of backstrap weaving. Although North American children perform better on Piaget's tasks, Zinacanteco children are far more adept at the complex mental transformations required to figure out how warp strung on a loom will turn out as woven cloth.
© Lauren Grenfield/VII

MILESTONES

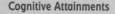

SOME COGNITIVE ATTAINMENTS OF MIDDLE CHILDHOOD AND ADOLESCENCE

Approximate Age		Cognitive Attainments
Middle childhood 7–11 years		Thinks in a more organized, logical fashion about concrete information, as indicated by gradual mastery of Piagetian conservation, class inclusion, and seriation problems, including transitive inference
		Displays more effective spatial reasoning, as indicated by ability to give clear directions and construct well-organized cognitive maps
Adolescence 11–18 years		Reasons abstractly in situations that offer many opportunities for hypothetico-deductive reasoning and propositional thought
		Grasps the logical necessity of propositional thought, permitting reasoning about premises that contradict reality
		Displays imaginary audience and personal fable, which gradually decline
		Improves in decision-making strategies

Note: These milestones represent overall age trends. Individual differences exist in the precise age at which each milestone is attained.

Photos: (top) © Cindy Charles/PhotoEdit; (bottom) © Ariel Skelley/CORBIS

Ask Yourself

REVIEW	Mastery of conservation provides one illustration of Piaget's horizontal décalage. Review the preceding sections and list additional examples that show that operational reasoning develops gradually.
APPLY	Nine-year-old Adrienne spends many hours helping her father build furniture in his woodworking shop. How might this experience facilitate Adrienne's performance on Piagetian seriation problems?
CONNECT	Explain how advances in perspective taking contribute to school-age children's improved capacity to give directions and construct cognitive maps.

The Formal Operational Stage: 11 Years and Older

According to Piaget, around age 11 young people enter the **formal operational stage,** in which they develop the capacity for abstract, scientific thinking. Whereas concrete operational children can "operate on reality," formal operational adolescents can "operate on operations" (Inhelder & Piaget, 1955/1958). In other words, they no longer require concrete things and events as objects of thought but can come up with new, more general logical rules through internal reflection.

Hypothetico-Deductive Reasoning

At adolescence, young people become capable of **hypothetico-deductive reasoning.** When faced with a problem, they start with a *general theory* of all possible factors that might affect an outcome and *deduce* from it specific *hypotheses* (or predictions) about what might happen. Then they test these hypotheses in an orderly fashion to see which ones work in the real world. Notice how this form of problem solving begins with possibility and proceeds to reality. In contrast, concrete operational children start with reality—with the most obvious predictions about a situation. When these are not confirmed, they cannot think of alternatives and fail to solve the problem.

Adolescents' performance on Piaget's famous *pendulum problem* illustrates this new approach. Suppose we present several school-age children and adolescents with strings of different lengths, objects of different weights to attach to the strings, and a bar from which to hang the strings (see Figure 6.15). Then we ask each of them to figure out what influences the speed with which a pendulum swings through its arc.

Formal operational adolescents come up with four hypotheses: (1) the length of the string, (2) the weight of the object hung on it, (3) the height to which the object is raised before it is released, and (4) the force with which the object is pushed. Then, by varying one factor at a time while holding all others constant, they try out each possibility. Eventually they discover that only string length makes a difference.

In contrast, concrete operational children experiment unsystematically. They cannot separate the effects of each variable. They may test for the effect of string length without holding weight constant, comparing, for example, a short, light pendulum with a long, heavy one. Also, school-age children fail to notice variables that are not immediately suggested by the concrete materials of the task—the height and the force with which the pendulum is released.

Propositional Thought

A second important characteristic of the formal operational stage is **propositional thought.** Adolescents can evaluate the logic of propositions (verbal statements) without referring to real-world circumstances. In contrast, children can evaluate the logic of statements only by considering them against concrete evidence in the real world.

In a study of propositional reasoning, a researcher showed children and adolescents a pile of poker chips and asked whether some statements about the chips were true, false, or uncertain. In one condition, the investigator hid a chip in her hand and then presented the following propositions:

"*Either* the chip in my hand is green or it is not green."

"The chip in my hand is green *and* it is not green."

In another condition, the researcher held either a red or a green chip in full view and made the same statements.

School-age children focused on the concrete properties of the poker chips. When the chip was hidden from view, they replied that they were uncertain about both statements. When it was visible, they judged both statements to be true if the chip was green and false if it was red. In contrast, adolescents analyzed the logic of the statements. They understood that the "either–or" statement is always true and the "and" statement is always false, regardless of the poker chip's color (Osherson & Markman, 1975).

Although Piaget did not view language as playing a central role in children's cognitive development, he acknowledged its importance during adolescence. Abstract thought requires language-based and other symbolic systems that do not stand for real things—for example, those of higher mathematics. Secondary school students use such systems in algebra and geometry. Formal operational thought also involves verbal reasoning about abstract concepts. Adolescents show that they can think in this way when they ponder the relations among time, space, and matter in physics or wonder about justice and freedom in philosophy and social studies.

Consequences of Abstract Thought

The development of formal operations leads to dramatic revisions in the way adolescents see themselves, others, and the world in general. But just as adolescents are occasionally awkward in the use of their larger, transformed bodies, so they are initially faltering in their abstract thinking. Although teenagers' self-concern, idealism, criticism, and indecisiveness often perplex and worry adults, they usually are beneficial in the long run.

▲ **Figure 6.15**

Piaget's pendulum problem. Adolescents who engage in hypothetico-deductive reasoning think of all possibilities. Then they vary one factor at a time while holding all others constant. Soon they discover that the weight of the object, the height from which it is released, and how forcefully it is pushed have no effect on the speed with which the pendulum swings through its arc. Only string length makes a difference.

In Piaget's formal operational stage, adolescents engage in propositional thought. As these students discuss problems in a precalculus class, they show that they can reason with symbols that do not necessarily represent objects in the real world. © Will Hart

Applying

What We Know   Handling Teenagers' New Capacity for Abstract Thought

Abstract Thought Expressed as . . .	Suggestion
Sensitivity to public criticism	Refrain from finding fault with the adolescent in front of others. If the matter is important, wait until you can speak to the teenager alone.
Exaggerated sense of personal uniqueness	Acknowledge the adolescent's unique characteristics. At opportune times, point out how you felt similarly as a young teenager, encouraging a more balanced perspective.
Idealism and criticism	Respond patiently to the adolescent's grand expectations and critical remarks. Point out positive features of targets, helping the teenager see that all worlds and people are blends of virtues and imperfections.
Difficulty making everyday decisions	Refrain from deciding for the adolescent. Model effective decision making, and offer diplomatic suggestions about the pros and cons of alternatives, the likelihood of various outcomes, and learning from poor choices.

Applying What We Know above suggests ways to handle the everyday consequences of teenagers' newfound capacity for abstraction.

• **SELF-CONSCIOUSNESS AND SELF-FOCUSING** • Adolescents' capacity to reflect on their own thoughts means that they think more about themselves. Piaget believed that a new form of egocentrism accompanies this stage: the inability to distinguish the abstract perspectives of self and others (Inhelder & Piaget, 1955/1958). Followers of Piaget suggested that as a result, two distorted images of the relation between self and others appear.

The first is the **imaginary audience,** adolescents' belief that they are the focus of everyone else's attention and concern (Elkind & Bowen, 1979). As a result, they become extremely self-conscious, often going to great lengths to avoid embarrassment. The imaginary audience helps us understand the long hours adolescents spend inspecting every detail of their appearance. It also accounts for their sensitivity to public criticism. To teenagers, who believe that everyone is monitoring their performance, a critical remark from a parent or teacher can be mortifying.

A second cognitive distortion is the **personal fable.** Because teenagers are sure that others are observing and thinking about them, they develop an inflated opinion of their own importance. They feel that they are special and unique. Many adolescents view themselves as reaching great heights of glory and also as sinking to unusual depths of despair—experiences that others could not possibly understand (Elkind, 1994). As one teenager wrote in her diary, "My parents' lives are so ordinary, so stuck in a rut. Mine will be different. I'll realize my hopes and ambitions." When combined with a sensation-seeking personality, the personal fable seems to contribute to adolescent risk taking by convincing teenagers of their invulnerability. In one study, young people with both high personal-fable and high sensation-seeking scores took more sexual risks, more often used drugs, and committed more delinquent acts than their agemates (Greene et al., 2000).

The imaginary audience and the personal fable are strongest during the transition from concrete to formal operations, after which they gradually decline (Enright, Lapsley, & Shukla, 1979; Lapsley et al., 1988). Yet these visions of the self probably do not result from egocentrism, as Piaget suggested. Instead, they are partly an outgrowth of advances in perspective taking, which cause young teenagers to be more concerned with what others think (Vartanian & Powlishta, 1996). In addition, when adolescents were asked why they worry about the opinions of others, they responded that they do so because others' evaluations have important *real* consequences— for self-esteem, peer acceptance, and social support (Bell & Bromnick, 2003). Finally, teenagers have emotional reasons for clinging to the idea that others are concerned with their appearance and behavior. Doing so helps them maintain a hold on important relationships as they struggle to separate from parents and establish an independent sense of self (Vartanian, 1997).

• **IDEALISM AND CRITICISM** • Because abstract thinking permits adolescents to go beyond the real to the possible, it opens up the world of the ideal and of perfection. Teenagers can imagine alternative family, religious, political, and moral systems, and they want to explore them. As a result, they often construct grand visions of a perfect world, with no injustice, discrimination, or tasteless behavior. The disparity between teenagers' idealistic view and adults' more realistic one creates tension between parent and child. Aware of the perfect family against which their parents and siblings fall short, adolescents become faultfinding critics.

Overall, however, teenage idealism and criticism are advantageous. Once adolescents come to see other people as having both strengths and weaknesses, they have a much greater capacity to work constructively for social change and to form positive and lasting relationships (Elkind, 1994).

• **DECISION MAKING** • Although adolescents handle many cognitive tasks more effectively than they did when younger, when it comes to decision making in everyday life, they often do not engage in a rational process: (1) identifying the pros and cons of each alternative, (2) assessing the likelihood of various possible outcomes, (3) evaluating their choice to see whether their goals were met and, if not, (4) learning from the mistake and making a better future decision. To study decision making, researchers gave adolescents hypothetical dilemmas, such as whether to have cosmetic surgery or which parent to live with after divorce, and asked them to explain how they would decide. Adults outperformed adolescents, especially the younger ones, on diverse decision-making elements. They more often considered alternatives, weighed the benefits and risks of each, and suggested advice-seeking (Halpern-Felsher & Cauffman, 2001). Other evidence shows that adolescents are less likely than adults to learn from feedback by revising their decision-making strategies (Byrnes, 2002).

Why do teenagers have difficult with decision making? As "first-timers," they do not have enough knowledge to consider the pros and cons of many experiences and to predict how they might react to them. At the same time, they encounter many more complex situations involving competing goals—for example, how to maintain status within the peer group while avoiding getting drunk at a party. Furthermore, teenagers often feel overwhelmed by their expanding range of options—abundant school courses, extracurricular activities, social events, and material goods to choose from. As a result, their efforts to choose frequently break down, and they resort to habit, act on impulse, or postpone decision making. And recall from Chapter 5 that heightened responsiveness to excitatory neurotransmitters in the brain contributes to adolescents' emotional reactivity. High emotional arousal interferes with good decision making.

Over time, young people learn from their successes and failures, gather information from others about factors that affect decision making, and reflect on the decision-making process (Byrnes, 2003; Jacobs & Klaczynski, 2002). Consequently, their confidence and performance in decision making improve.

Follow-Up Research on Formal Operational Thought

Research on formal operational thought poses questions similar to those we discussed with respect to Piaget's earlier stages: Does abstract reasoning appear earlier than Piaget expected? And do all individuals reach formal operations during their teenage years?

• **ARE CHILDREN CAPABLE OF ABSTRACT THINKING?** • School-age children show the glimmerings of hypothetico-deductive reasoning, but they are not as competent at it as adolescents and adults. For example, in simplified situations, 6-year-olds understand that hypotheses must be confirmed by appropriate evidence. They also realize that once it is supported, a hypothesis shapes predictions about what might happen in the future (Ruffman et al., 1993). But school-age children cannot sort out evidence that bears on three or more variables at once. And as we will see when we take up information-processing research on scientific reasoning in Chapter 7, children have difficulty explaining why a pattern of observations supports a hypothesis, even when they recognize the connection between the two.

School-age children's capacity for propositional thought is also limited. For example, they have great difficulty reasoning from premises that contradict reality or their own beliefs. Consider the following set of statements: "If dogs are bigger than elephants and elephants are bigger than mice, then dogs are bigger than mice." Children younger than age 10 judge this reasoning to be false, because some of the relations specified do not occur in real life (Moshman & Franks, 1986). In thinking about the problem, they automatically access well-learned knowledge from long-term memory—for example, "elephants are larger than dogs"—that casts doubt on the truthfulness of the premises. Children find it more difficult than adolescents to inhibit activation of such knowledge (Simoneau & Markovits, 2003; Klaczynski, Schuneman, & Daniel, 2004). Partly for this reason, they often fail to grasp the **logical necessity** of propositional reasoning—that the accuracy of conclusions drawn from premises rests on the rules of logic, not on real-world confirmation.

Furthermore, in reasoning with propositions, school-age children do not think carefully about the major premise and, therefore, violate the most basic rules of logic (Markovits, Schleifer, & Fortier, 1989). For example, when given the following problem, they almost always draw an incorrect conclusion:

Major premise: If Susan hits a tambourine, then she will make a noise.

Second premise: Suppose that Susan does not hit a tambourine.

Question: Did Susan make a noise?

Wrong Conclusion: No, Susan did not make a noise.

Notice that the major premise did *not* state that Susan can make a noise *if, and only if,* she hits a tambourine. Adolescents generally detect that Susan could make noise in other ways, partly because they are better at searching their knowledge for examples that contradict wrong conclusions (Klaczynski & Narasimham, 1998b; Markovits et al., 1998).

As Piaget's theory indicates, around age 11, young people can analyze the logic of propositions regardless of their content. As they get older, they handle problems requiring increasingly complex inferences. In justifying their reasoning, they move from giving a concrete example ("She could have hit a drum instead of a tambourine") to mentioning a logical rule ("We can be certain that Susan did not hit a tambourine. But we cannot be certain that Susan did not make a noise; she might have done so in many other ways") (Müller, Overton, & Reese, 2001; Venet & Markovits, 2001).

• DO ALL INDIVIDUALS REACH THE FORMAL OPERATIONAL STAGE? •

Try giving one or two of the formal operational tasks just described to some of your friends and see how well they do. You are likely to find that some well-educated adults have difficulty! About 40 to 60 percent of college students fail Piaget's formal operational problems (Keating, 1979).

Why are so many college students, and adults in general, not fully formal operational? One reason is that people are most likely to think abstractly in situations in which they have had extensive experience. This conclusion is supported by evidence that taking college courses leads to improvements in formal reasoning related to course content. For example, math and science prompt gains in propositional thought, social science in methodological and statistical reasoning (Lehman & Nisbett, 1990). Consider these findings, and you will see that formal operations, like the concrete reasoning that preceded it, is often specific to situation and task (Keating, 1990).

Another reason adolescents and adults do not always engage in formal operational thinking is that they often fall back on less demanding, intuitive judgments (Jacobs & Klaczynski, 2002). In one study, researchers gave adolescents a hypothetical problem in which they had to choose, on the basis of two arguments, between taking a traditional lecture class and taking a computer-based class. One argument contained large-sample information: course evaluations from 150 students, 85 percent of whom liked the computer-based class. The other argument involved small-sample, personalized evidence: complaints of two honor-roll students, who hated the computer-based class and enjoyed the traditional class. Many adolescents acknowledged that relying on the large-sample argument was "more intelligent." But despite this logical understanding, most based their choice on the small-sample argument, lapsing into a "seeing is believing" way of thinking that they often use in everyday life (Klaczynski, 2001).

In many tribal and village societies, formal operational tasks are not mastered at all (Cole, 1990). For example, when asked to engage in propositional thought, people in nonliterate societies often refuse. Take this hypothetical proposition: "In the North, where there is snow, all bears are white. Novaya Zemlya is in the North, and it always has snow. What color are the bears there?" In response, a Central Asian peasant explains that he must see the event to discern its logical implications. The peasant insists on firsthand knowledge, whereas the interviewer states

Ⓢ These adolescents of Irian Jaya province in Indonesia live in highland rainforests and have little contact with the outside world. Although the boys would probably have difficulty with Piaget's formal operational tasks, they deftly build a tree house, mentally coordinating multiple variables to ensure that the structure is stable and sturdy. Clearly they are capable of highly complex reasoning in familiar situations.
© Anders Ryman/CORBIS

that truth can be based on ideas alone. Yet the peasant uses propositions to defend his point of view: "*If* a man . . . had seen a white bear and had told about it, [*then*] he could be believed, *but* I've never seen one and *hence* I can't say" (Luria, 1976, pp. 108–109). Although he rarely displays it in everyday life, the peasant clearly is capable of formal operational thought!

Piaget acknowledged that without the opportunity to solve hypothetical problems, people in some societies might not display formal operations. Still, researchers ask, Does the formal operational stage result largely from children's and adolescents' independent efforts to make sense of their world, as Piaget claimed? Or is it a culturally transmitted way of thinking that is specific to literate societies and is taught in school? This question remains unresolved.

Ask Yourself

REVIEW	Using the concepts of hypothetico-deductive reasoning and propositional thought, illustrate the difference between school-age children's cognition and that of adolescents.
APPLY	Thirteen-year-old Rosie had a crush on a boy who failed to return her affections. After her mother assured her that there would be other boys, Rosie snapped, "Mom! You don't know what it's like to be in love!" Does Rosie's thinking illustrate the imaginary audience or the personal fable? Explain.
CONNECT	What questions raised about Piaget's formal operational stage are similar to those raised about the concrete operational stage?
REFLECT	Can you recall engaging in idealistic thinking or poor decision making when you were a young teenager? Cite examples. How has your thinking changed?

Piaget and Education

Piaget has had a major impact on education, especially during early and middle childhood. Three educational principles derived from his theory continue to have a widespread influence on teacher training and classroom practices:

- *Discovery learning.* In a Piagetian classroom, children are encouraged to discover for themselves through spontaneous interaction with the environment. Instead of presenting ready-made knowledge verbally, teachers provide a rich variety of activities designed to promote exploration—art, puzzles, table games, dress-up clothing, building blocks, books, measuring tools, musical instruments, and more.

- *Sensitivity to children's readiness to learn.* A Piagetian classroom does not try to speed up development. Piaget believed that appropriate learning experiences build on children's current thinking. Teachers watch and listen to their students, introducing experiences that permit them to practice newly discovered schemes and that are likely to challenge their incorrect ways of viewing the world. But teachers do not impose new skills before children indicate that they are interested or ready, because this leads to superficial acceptance of adult formulas rather than true understanding.

- *Acceptance of individual differences.* Piaget's theory assumes that all children go through the same sequence of development, but at different rates. Therefore, teachers must plan activities for individuals and small groups rather than just for the class as a whole. In addition, teachers evaluate educational progress by comparing each child to his or her own previous development. They are less interested in how children measure up to normative standards, or the average performance of same-age peers.

Like his stages, educational applications of Piaget's theory have met with criticism. Perhaps the greatest challenge has to do with his insistence that young children learn mainly through acting on the environment and his neglect of other important avenues, such as verbal teaching and corrective feedback (Brainerd, 2003). Nevertheless, Piaget's influence on education has been powerful. He gave teachers new ways to observe, understand, and enhance young children's development and offered strong theoretical justification for child-oriented approaches to teaching and learning.

⊚ Overall Evaluation of Piaget's Theory

Piaget's contributions to the field of child development are greater than those of any other theorist. He awakened psychologists and educators to a view of children as curious knowledge seekers who contribute actively to their own development. Furthermore, Piaget was among the first to both describe and explain development. His pioneering efforts inspired the current focus on *mechanisms of cognitive change*—precise accounts of biological, psychological, and environmental factors that lead children to modify their thinking, which we will encounter in Chapter 7 (McClelland & Siegler, 2001). Finally, Piaget's theory offers a useful "road map" of cognitive development—one that is accurate in many respects, though wrong in others. His milestones of preoperational, concrete operational, and formal operational thought remain powerful aids to understanding emotional, social, and moral development.

Nevertheless, the wealth of research that Piaget's theory inspired has uncovered weaknesses in his theory. Let's consider two major challenges posed by his critics.

Is Piaget's Account of Cognitive Change Clear and Accurate?

Think for a moment about Piaget's explanation of cognitive change—in particular, equilibration and its attendant processes of adaptation and organization. Because Piaget focused on broad transformations in thinking, exactly what the child does to equilibrate is vague (Siegler & Ellis, 1996). As an example, recall our description of organization—that the structures of each stage form a coherent whole. Piaget was not explicit about how the diverse achievements of each stage are bound together by a single, underlying form of thought. Indeed, efforts to confirm this coherence have not succeeded. On a variety of tasks, infants and young children appear more competent, and adolescents and adults less competent, than Piaget assumed. Today, researchers agree that the child's efforts to assimilate, accommodate, and reorganize structures cannot adequately explain these patterns of change.

Furthermore, Piaget's belief that infants and young children must act on the environment to revise their thinking is too narrow a notion of how learning takes place. Cognitive development is not always self-generating. Left to their own devices, children may not notice aspects of a situation necessary for an improved understanding. Because Piaget's theory places so much emphasis on the child's initiative, it has been of limited practical usefulness in devising teaching strategies that foster children's optimum learning.

Does Cognitive Development Take Place in Stages?

We have seen that many cognitive changes proceed slowly and gradually. Few abilities are absent during one period and suddenly present in another. Also, few periods of cognitive equilibrium exist. Instead, children constantly modify structures and acquire new skills. Today, virtually all experts agree that children's cognition is not as broadly stagelike as Piaget believed (Bjorklund, 2004; Flavell, Miller, & Miller, 2002). At the same time, contemporary researchers disagree on how general or specific cognitive development actually is.

Some theorists agree with Piaget that development is a *general process*—that it follows a similar course across the diverse cognitive domains of physical, numerical, and social knowledge. But they reject the existence of stages. Instead, they believe that thought processes are alike at all ages—just present to a greater or lesser extent—and that variations in children's knowledge and experience largely account for uneven performance across domains. These assumptions form the basis of the *information-processing perspective,* discussed in Chapter 7.

Other researchers think that the stage notion is valid but that it must be modified. They point to strong evidence for certain stagelike changes, such as the flourishing of representation around age 2 and the move toward abstraction in adolescence. Yet they recognize many smaller develop-

⊚ Although Piaget insisted that young children learn mainly by acting on the environment, verbal teaching, corrective feedback, and other methods also play important roles. In this hands-on science lesson using microscopes and pond water, children learn in different ways—some looking to the teacher for guidance, some exploring on their own, some writing in journals.
© Ellen Senisi/The Image Works.

ments that lead up to these transformations. In Chapter 7, we will consider a *neo-Piagetian perspective* that combines Piaget's stage approach with information-processing ideas (Case, 1996, 1998; Halford, 2002). In this view, Piaget's strict definition of stage needs to be modified into a less tightly knit concept, one in which related competencies develop over an extended period, depending on brain development and specific experiences.

Still others deny not only Piaget's stages but also his belief that the human mind is made up of general reasoning abilities that can be applied to any cognitive task. They argue that the remarkable competencies of infants and young children indicate that cognitive development begins with far more than sensorimotor reflexes; rather, infants come into the world with several basic, built-in types of knowledge, each of which jump-starts vital aspects of cognition. We will take up this *core knowledge* perspective in the next section.

Piaget's Legacy

Although Piaget's description of development is no longer fully accepted, researchers are far from consensus on how to modify or replace it. Some have begun to search for points of contact among the alternative perspectives just mentioned. Others blend Piaget's emphasis on the child as an active agent with a stronger role for context—the objects, events, and people in children's lives. For example, followers of Vygotsky's theory are intensively studying social and cultural influences on children's thinking, largely neglected by Piaget.

Diverse theories and lines of investigation leave research into children's thinking far more fragmented today than several decades ago, when Piaget's theory held sway. Nevertheless, researchers continue to draw inspiration from Piaget's lifelong quest to understand how children acquire new capacities. His findings have served as the starting point for virtually every major contemporary line of research on cognitive development.

Ask Yourself

REVIEW	Cite examples of findings that have led contemporary researchers to challenge Piaget's account of cognitive change.
CONNECT	How are educational principles derived from Piaget's theory consistent with his emphasis on an active child who takes responsibility for her own learning?
REFLECT	Which aspects of Piaget's theory do you accept? Which do you doubt? Explain, citing research evidence.

The Core Knowledge Perspective

According to the **core knowledge perspective,** infants begin life with innate, special-purpose knowledge systems referred to as *core domains of thought.* Each of these prewired understandings permits a ready grasp of new, related information and therefore supports early, rapid development of certain aspects of cognition. Core knowledge theorists claim that infants could not make sense of the multifaceted stimulation around them without being genetically "set up" to comprehend crucial aspects of it. Each core domain has a long evolutionary history and is essential for survival (Carey & Markman, 1999; Spelke & Newport, 1998).

Two domains have been studied extensively in infancy. The first is *physical knowledge*—in particular, understanding of objects and their effects on one another. The second is *numerical knowledge*—the capacity to keep track of multiple objects and to add and subtract small quantities. Physical and numerical knowledge permitted our ancestors to secure food and other resources from the environment.

The core knowledge perspective asserts that an inherited foundation makes possible remarkably advanced knowledge systems in early childhood. In Chapter 9, we will consider a nativist (or inborn) view of preschoolers' amazing language skill that regards *linguistic knowledge* as etched into the structure of the human brain. Furthermore, infants' early orientation toward people (see Chapter 4) provides the foundation for rapid development of *psychological knowledge*—in particular, understanding of mental states (such as emotions, desires, beliefs, and perspectives), which is vital for surviving in human groups. And children demonstrate

How much does this 5-month-old baby already know about the physical properties of the three plastic toys in front of her? According to core knowledge researchers, already she has some basic number concepts, in that she can discriminate quantities up to three.

Courtesy of Liz Napolitano

impressive *biological knowledge,* including ideas about inheritance of characteristics and understanding of bodily processes, such as birth, growth, illness, and death.

The core knowledge perspective assumes that each core domain develops independently. Rather than regarding development as a general process, core knowledge theorists see it as *domain-specific* and uneven. And although initial knowledge is assumed to be innate, that knowledge becomes more elaborate as children explore, play, and interact with others (Geary & Bjorklund, 2000; Leslie, 2004). Children are viewed as *naïve theorists,* building on core knowledge concepts to explain their everyday experiences in the physical, psychological, and biological realms. Let's examine a sampling of findings that shed light on the existence of core domains of thought.

Infancy: Physical and Numerical Knowledge

Do infants display impressive physical and numerical understandings so early that some knowledge must be innate? Once again, the violation-of-expectation method has been used to answer this question. Besides research on early awareness of object permanence (see pages 225–226), core knowledge theorists point to evidence indicating that young infants are aware of basic object properties and build on this knowledge quickly, acquiring more detailed understandings (Baillargeon, 2004).

For example, 2½-month-olds seem to recognize that one solid object cannot move through another solid object. In one study, some infants saw an object lowered into a container with an opening, whereas others saw an object lowered into a container with no opening (see Figure 6.16). Babies in the closed-container condition looked longer, suggesting that

Expected Event: Open-Container Condition

Unexpected Event: Closed-Container Condition

▲ **Figure 6.16**

Testing infants for understanding of object solidity using the violation-of-expectation method. Infants in the *expected event: open-container condition* saw a tall object and a tall container standing a short distance apart. An adult's right hand grasped a knob attached to the top of the object, while her left hand rotated the container forward so infants could see its opening. After a few seconds, the container was returned to its original position. Then the right hand lifted the object and lowered it into the container. Finally, the hand lifted the object out of the container and set it down. Infants in the *unexpected event: closed-container condition* saw the same event, with one exception: The container's top was closed so it should have been impossible for the object to be lowered into the container. (In actuality, the container had a false, magnetic top that adhered to the bottom of the object, which could be lowered into it.) Five-month-olds looked longer at the unexpected, closed-container event, suggesting awareness of object solidity. (From S. J. Hespos & R. Baillargeon, 2001, "Reasoning About Containment Events in Very Young Infants," *Cognition, 78,* p. 213. © 2001 Elsevier Science. Reprinted by permission.)

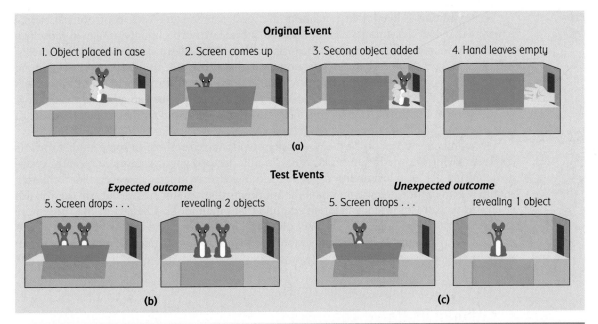

▲ **Figure 6.17**

Testing infants for basic number concepts. (a) First, infants saw a screen raised in front of a toy animal. Then an identical toy was added behind the screen. Next, the researchers presented two outcomes. (b) In the *expected outcome,* the screen dropped to reveal two toy animals. (c) In the *unexpected outcome,* the screen dropped to reveal one toy animal. Five-month-olds shown the unexpected outcome looked longer than 5-month-olds shown the expected outcome. The researchers concluded that infants can discriminate the quantities "one" and "two" and use that knowledge to perform simple addition: 1 + 1 = 2. A variation of this procedure suggested that 5-month-olds could also do simple subtraction: 2 − 1 = 1. (From K. Wynn, 1992, "Addition and Subtraction by Human Infants," *Nature, 358,* p. 749. Reprinted by permission.)

this impossible event violated their notions of physical reality (Hespos & Baillargeon, 2001). Within the next few months, infants extend this understanding. By 5 to 6 months, they look longer when an object much wider than an opening appears to pass through that opening than they do at an appropriately sized object passing through (Sitskoorn & Smitsman, 1995). And around 7½ months, they spend more time looking at an object too tall to fit inside a container that disappears into the container than they do at an object that is the right height to fit inside (Hespos & Baillargeon, 2001).

Furthermore, in the first half-year, infants are sensitive to the effects of gravity. They stare intently when a moving object stops in midair without support (Spelke et al., 1992). This understanding advances quickly. Six- and 7-month-olds have some notion of object support. Their attention increases when an object is placed on top of another object yet most of its bottom surface does not contact the lower object. Under these conditions, infants appear to realize that the object on top should fall (Baillargeon, 1994).

Research also suggests that young infants have basic number concepts (Spelke, 2000). In the best known of these studies, 5-month-olds saw a screen raised to hide a single toy animal. Then the infants saw a hand placing a second, identical toy behind the screen. Finally, the screen was removed to reveal either one or two toys. If infants kept track of and represented the two objects (which would require them to add one object to another), then they should look longer at the impossible, one-toy display—which is what they did (see Figure 6.17). In additional experiments, 5-month-olds given this task looked longer at three objects than two. Overall, these results, and those of similar studies, suggest that infants discriminate quantities up to three and use that knowledge to perform simple arithmetic—both addition and subtraction (in which two objects are covered by a screen and one object is removed) (Kobayashi et al., 2004; Wynn, 1992, 1998).

Other research shows that 6-month-olds can distinguish among large sets of items, as long as the difference between those sets is very great. For example, they can tell the difference between 8 and 16 dots, but not between 6 and 12 (Lipton & Spelke, 2003; Xu & Spelke, 2000). As a result, some researchers believe that infants can represent approximate large-number values, in addition to the small-number discriminations evident in Figure 6.17.

These findings—like other violation-of-expectation results—are controversial. Some researchers report that infants cannot add and subtract. In experiments similar to those just described, looking preferences were inconsistent (Langer, Gillette, & Arriaga, 2003; Wakeley, Rivera, & Langer, 2000). These investigators note that claims for number concepts in young infants are surprising, given other research indicating that before 14 to 16 months, toddlers have difficulty with less-than and greater-than relationships between small sets. In Chapter 7, we will see that not until the preschool years do children add and subtract small numbers of objects correctly.

Overall, then, studies on early knowledge provide mixed results. In some studies, infants display amazing knowledge; in others, they do not. Perhaps young infants' knowledge is evident only under certain conditions. If such knowledge is innate, however, older children should reason in the same way as infants about events that tap this knowledge, yet they do not always do so. Core knowledge theorists respond that infant looking behaviors may be a more reliable indicator of understanding than older children's verbal and motor behaviors, which may not always display their true competencies (Wynn, 2002). Critics argue that, rather than being built in, physical and numerical knowledge must be constructed over an extended time period (Haith & Bensen, 1998).

Children as Naïve Theorists

Do children form naïve theories, or explanations of events, that differ between core domains? A growing number of researchers believe they do. According to this **theory theory** (meaning *theory of children as theorists*), after observing an event, children explain, or theorize about, its cause by drawing on innate concepts. Then they test their naïve theory against experience, revising it when it cannot adequately account for new information (Gelman, 2003; Gopnik & Nazzi, 2003; Wellman & Gelman, 1998). These revisions often lead to stagelike changes—dramatic, qualitative shifts in the complexity of concepts and explanations. Notice that this account of cognitive change is similar to Piaget's. But theory theorists claim that because children start with innate knowledge, their reasoning advances quickly, with sophisticated cause-and-effect explanations evident much earlier than Piaget proposed.

The most extensively investigated naïve theory is children's *theory of mind*—the psychological knowledge of self and others that forms rapidly during the preschool years, which we will consider in Chapters 7 and 11. Preschoolers also have naïve physical and biological theories. In one study, researchers asked 3- and 4-year-olds to explain events that had either a psychological, a physical, or a biological cause. Children reasoned about each event in ways consistent with its core domain. For example, a child who pours orange juice instead of milk on his cereal received mostly psychological explanations ("He *thought* it was milk"), a boy who tries to float in the air by jumping off a stool but falls received mostly physical explanations ("He's too *heavy* to float"), and a girl who tries to hang from a tree branch forever but lets go tended to receive biological explanations ("Her arms got *hurting*"). Also, most of the explanations preschoolers offer in everyday conversation are psychological, physical, or biological and are linked appropriately to the behaviors of humans, animals, and objects (Hickling & Wellman, 2001; Wellman, Hickling, & Schultz, 1997).

Although young children are impressive theorists, their explanations in different domains develop at different rates. Physical and psychological explanations are prevalent at age 2, probably because these understandings originate in infancy. Biological explanations increase with age. Because grasping biological processes is difficult, young preschoolers frequently explain biological events with psychological concepts (Carey, 1995, 1999; Inagaki & Hantano, 2002). For example, when asked whether they can tell a pain to go away or a heartbeat to stop, many 3-year-olds say yes! In contrast, 4-year-olds know that they cannot control biological processes (Inagaki, 1997). Still, psychological accounts of biological events persist into the early school years, as research on children's understanding of death reveals (see the Biology and Environment box on the following page).

The later emergence of biological knowledge characterizes children in widely varying cultures, suggesting that unlike other core domains, it may have only a weak innate foundation, or may not be innately specified but, instead, may depend entirely on a lengthy process of construction based on experience. Consider children's knowledge of biological inheritance. When

Children's Understanding of Death

Five-year-old Miriam arrived at preschool the day after her dog Pepper died. Instead of joining other children, she stayed close to her teacher Leslie, who noticed Miriam's discomfort. "What's wrong?" Leslie asked.

"Daddy said Pepper was so sick the vet had to put him to sleep." For a moment, Miriam looked hopeful: "When I get home, Pepper might wake up."

Leslie answered directly: "No, Pepper won't get up again. He's not asleep. He's dead, and that means he can't sleep, eat, run, or play anymore."

Miriam wandered off. Later, she returned to Leslie and, tears streaming from her eyes, confessed, "I chased Pepper too hard."

Leslie put her arm around Miriam. "Pepper didn't die because you chased him. He was very old and sick," she explained.

Over the next few days, Miriam asked many more questions: "When I go to sleep, will I die?" "Can a tummy ache make you die?" "Does Pepper feel better now?" "Will Mommy and Daddy die?"

Development of the Death Concept

An accurate understanding of death is based on five ideas:

1. *Permanence:* Once a living thing dies, it cannot be brought back to life.
2. *Inevitability:* All living things eventually die.
3. *Cessation:* All living functions, including thought, feeling, movement, and body processes, cease at death.
4. *Applicability:* Death applies only to living things.
5. *Causation:* Death is caused by a breakdown of bodily functioning.

To understand death, children must acquire some basic notions of biology—that animals and plants are living things containing certain body parts that are essential for maintaining life. They must also break down their global category of "not alive" into *dead, inanimate, unreal,* and *nonexistent* (Carey, 1999). Until children grasp these ideas, they interpret death in terms of familiar experiences—as a change in

behavior. Consequently, they may believe, as Miriam did, that they caused a relative's or pet's death, that having a stomachache can cause someone to die, and that death is like sleep. When researchers asked 4- to 6-year-olds whether dead people need food, air, and water; whether they go to the bathroom; whether they sleep and dream; and whether a cut on their body would heal, more than half of those who had not yet started to acquire biological understandings answered yes (Slaughter, Jaakkola, & Carey, 1999).

Most children master the components of the death concept by age 7. *Permanence* is the first and most easily understood idea. When Leslie explained that Pepper would not get up again, Miriam accepted this fact quickly, perhaps because she had seen it in other situations—in the dead butterflies and beetles she picked up and inspected while playing outside. Appreciation of *inevitability* and *cessation* follow soon after. At first, children think that certain people do not die—themselves, people like themselves (other children), and people with whom they have close emotional ties. Also, many preschoolers view dead things as retaining living capacities (Kenyon, 2001; Speece & Brent, 1996). *Applicability* and *causation,* the most difficult components to master, require a firm grasp of the biological concepts just noted.

Cultural Influences

A mature appreciation of death is usually reached by middle childhood and ethnic variations suggest that religious teachings affect children's understanding. A comparison of four ethnic groups in Israel revealed that Druze and Moslem children's death concepts differed from those of Christian and Jewish children (Florian & Kravetz, 1985). The Druze emphasis on reincarnation and the greater religiosity of both Druze and Moslem groups may have led more of their children to deny permanence and nonfunctionality. Similarly, children of Southern Baptist families, who believe in an afterlife, are less likely to endorse permanence than are children from Unitarian families, who focus on achieving peace and justice in today's world (Candy-Gibbs, Sharp, & Petrun, 1985).

Experiences with death also influence understanding. Children growing up on Israeli kibbutzim (agricultural settlements) who have witnessed

terrorist attacks, family members' departure on army tours, and parental anxiety about safety express a full grasp of the death concept by age 5 (Mahon, Goldberg, & Washington, 1999). Actually experiencing the death of a close relative or friend greatly accelerates appreciation of permanence and inevitability, even among children as young as age 3 (Reilly, Hasazi, & Bond, 1983).

Enhancing Children's Understanding

Parents often worry needlessly that discussing death candidly with children fuels their fears. But children with a good grasp of the facts of death have an easier time accepting it. Direct explanations, like Leslie's, that match the child's capacity to understand, work best. When adults use clichés or make misleading statements, children may take these literally and react with confusion. For example, after a parent told her 5-year-old daughter, "Grandpa went on a long trip," the child wondered, "Why didn't he take me?" (Wolfelt, 1997). Sometimes children ask difficult questions: "Will I die?" "Will you die?" Parents can be both truthful and comforting by taking advantage of children's sense of time. "Not for many, many years," they can say. "First I'm going to enjoy you as a grown-up and be a grandparent."

Another way to foster an accurate appreciation of death is to teach preschoolers about the biology of the human body. Three- to 5-year-olds given lessons in the role of the heart, kidneys, lungs, brain, digestion, bones, and muscles in sustaining life have more advanced death concepts than children not given such lessons (Slaughter & Lyons, 2003).

Adult–child discussions should also be culturally sensitive. Rather than presenting scientific evidence as negating religious beliefs, parents and teachers can help children blend the two sources of knowledge. As children get older, they often combine their appreciation of the death concept with religious and philosophical views, which offer solace during times of bereavement. Indeed, mystical explanations, such as being called by God and existing in a nonmaterial state, increase during adolescence as young people think more deeply about the nature of existence and grapple with spiritual ideas (Cuddy-Casey & Orvaschel, 1997). Open, honest, and respectful communication about death contributes to both cognitive development and emotional well-being.

◄ As long as parents provide candid, age-appropriate explanations, their children can gain an accurate appreciation of what happens when living things die. These parents comfort their children after the death of the family's dog by talking and reading about the experience. © Michael Newman/PhotoEdit

told stories about a child born to one parent and raised by another, not until ages 5 to 7 do North American and European children consistently predict that an adopted child will resemble her birth parents in physical characteristics (such as hair type and skin color) but resemble her adoptive parents in beliefs and skills (Solomon et al., 1996; Weissman & Kalish, 1999; Gimenez & Harris, 2002).

In some non-Western village societies, this distinction between the influence of biology and that of social learning on human traits is not attained until adolescence or adulthood (Bloch, Solomon, & Carey, 2001; Mahalingham, 1999). The Vezo of Madagascar, for example, hold certain folk beliefs that make it harder for their children to grasp biological inheritance. The Vezo say that a pregnant mother who spends much time thinking about another person can cause her baby to look like that person! Because Vezo children do not go to school, they are not exposed to biology lessons that contradict such folk beliefs (Astutj, Solomon, & Carey, 2004). They must, instead, notice and gradually make sense of the fact that children and their biological parents resemble each other physically—a challenging task that is not mastered until ages 14 to 20.

Nevertheless, controversy persists over whether biology is a core domain of thought (Hirschfeld, 1996; Slaughter & Lyons, 2003). Most claim that more evidence is needed to answer this question with certainty.

Evaluation of the Core Knowledge Perspective

Core knowledge theorists offer a fascinating evolutionary account of why certain cognitive skills emerge early and develop rapidly. And more seriously than other perspectives, they have addressed the question, What allows learning to get off the ground? As a result, they have enriched our understanding of infants' and young children's thinking.

Nevertheless, critics take issue with the core knowledge assumption that infants are endowed with *knowledge.* As we have already noted, infant looking in violation-of-expectation studies may indicate only a perceptual preference, not the existence of concepts or reasoning. And some skeptics claim that human evolution may not have equipped infants with ready-made knowledge, which might limit their ability to adapt to environmental changes (Haith, 1999). At present, just what babies start out with—domain-specific understandings or minimal perceptual biases that combine with powerful, general learning strategies to permit rapid discovery of various types of knowledge—continues to be hotly debated.

Although the core knowledge perspective emphasizes native endowment, it acknowledges that experience is essential for children to elaborate this initial knowledge. So far, however, it has not offered greater clarity than Piaget's theory concerning how biology and environment jointly produce cognitive change. For example, it does not tell us just what children do to revise their innate structures. And it says little about which experiences are most important in each domain and how those experiences advance children's thinking. Finally, the core knowledge perspective shares with Piaget's theory a view of children as independently building more adequate structures. It pays little attention to children's learning in interaction with others— the unique strength of Vygotsky's theory, which we take up next. Despite these limitations, the ingenious studies and provocative findings of core knowledge research have sharpened the field's focus on specifying the starting point for human cognition and carefully tracking the changes that build on it.

Ask Yourself

REVIEW	What are core domains of thought? Cite an example of infants' innate knowledge in the physical domain and the numerical domain. Why do some researchers question whether infants actually have such knowledge?
REVIEW	Why do core knowledge researchers characterize young children as naïve theorists? Cite findings that support the theory theory. Cite evidence that challenges the existence of an innately based biological theory.
CONNECT	Describe similarities and differences between Piaget's theory and the core knowledge perspective.

Vygotsky's Sociocultural Theory

Piaget's theory and the core knowledge perspective emphasize the biological side of cognitive development. In both, the most important source of cognition is the child himself—a busy, self-motivated explorer who forms ideas and tests them against the world. Lev Vygotsky also believed that children are active seekers of knowledge, but he emphasized that rich social and cultural contexts profoundly affect their thinking.

Early events in Vygotsky's life contributed to his vision of human cognition as inherently social and language-based. As a university student, he was interested primarily in a verbal field—literature. After graduating, he first became a teacher and only later turned to psychology. Because Vygotsky died of tuberculosis at age 37, his theory is not as complete as Piaget's. Nevertheless, the field of child development has experienced a burst of interest in Vygotsky's sociocultural perspective. The major reason for his appeal lies in his rejection of an individualistic view of the developing child in favor of a socially formed mind (Rogoff, 2003; Tudge & Scrimsher, 2003).

According to Vygotsky, infants are endowed with basic perceptual, attention, and memory capacities that they share with other animals. These develop during the first 2 years through direct contact with the environment. Then rapid growth of language leads to a profound change in thinking. It broadens preschoolers' participation in social dialogues with more knowledgeable individuals, who encourage them to master culturally important tasks. Soon young children start to communicate with themselves in much the same way they converse with others. As a result, basic mental capacities are transformed into uniquely human, higher cognitive processes. Let's see how this happens.

Children's Private Speech

Watch preschoolers going about their daily activities, and you will see that they frequently talk out loud to themselves as they play and explore the environment. For example, as a 4-year-old worked a puzzle at preschool one day, I heard him say, "Where's the red piece? I need the red one. Now a blue one. No, it doesn't fit. Try it here."

Piaget (1923/1926) called these utterances *egocentric speech*, reflecting his belief that young children have difficulty taking the perspectives of others. For this reason, he said, their talk is often "talk for self" in which they run off thoughts in whatever form they happen to occur, regardless of whether a listener can understand. Piaget believed that cognitive development and certain social experiences—specifically, disagreements with peers—eventually bring an end to egocentric speech. Through arguments with agemates, children repeatedly see that others hold viewpoints different from their own. As a result, egocentric speech declines and is replaced by social speech, in which children adapt what they say to their listeners.

Vygotsky (1934/1986) objected strongly to Piaget's conclusions. He reasoned that children speak to themselves for self-guidance. Because language helps children think about mental activities and behavior and select courses of action, Vygotsky regarded it as the foundation for all higher cognitive processes, including controlled attention, deliberate memorization and recall, categorization, planning, problem solving, abstract reasoning, and self-reflection. As children get older and find tasks easier, their self-directed speech is internalized as silent, inner speech—the verbal dialogues we carry on with ourselves while thinking and acting in everyday situations.

Over the past three decades, almost all studies have supported Vygotsky's perspective (Berk, 2003). As a result, children's self-directed speech is now called **private speech** instead of egocentric speech. Research shows that children use more of it when tasks are difficult, after they make errors, and when they are confused about how to proceed. For example, Figure 6.18 shows how 4- and 5-year-olds' private speech increased as researchers made a color-sequencing task more difficult. Also, just as Vygotsky predicted, private speech goes underground with age, changing into whispers and silent lip movements (Patrick & Abravanel, 2000; Winsler & Naglieri, 2003). Furthermore, children who freely use private speech during a challenging activity are more attentive and involved and show greater improvement in performance (Berk & Spuhl, 1995; Winsler, Diaz, & Montero, 1997).

▼ **Figure 6.18**

Relationship of private speech to task difficulty among 4- and 5-year-olds. Researchers increased the difficulty of a color-sequencing task, in which children listened to a list of colors and then placed colored stickers on a page to match the list. The longer the color list, the more private speech children used. (From E. Patrick and E. Abravanel, 2000, "The Self-Regulatory Nature of Preschool Children's Private Speech in a Naturalistic Setting," *Applied Psycholinguistics, 21,* p. 55. Reprinted by permission.)

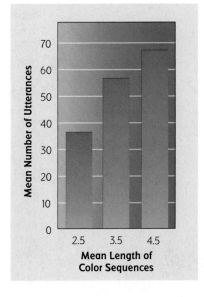

⊚ This 3-year-old makes a sculpture from playdough and plastic sticks with the aid of private speech. As Vygotsky theorized, preschool children often guide their thinking by talking to themselves while they play and tackle other challenging tasks.

© Laura Dwight Photography

Finally, compared with their normally achieving agemates, children with learning and behavior problems engage in higher rates of private speech over a longer period of development (Berk, 2001b; Paladino & Berk, 2005). They seem to call on private speech to help compensate for the impairments in cognitive processing and attention that make academic tasks more difficult for them.

Social Origins of Cognitive Development

Where does private speech come from? Vygotsky (1930–1935/1978) believed that children's learning takes place within the **zone of proximal development**—a range of tasks too difficult for the child to do alone but possible with the help of adults and more skilled peers. Consider the joint activity of 3-year-old Sammy and his mother, who helps him put together a difficult puzzle:

Sammy: I can't get this one in. *[Tries to insert a piece in the wrong place.]*

Mother: Which piece might go down here? *[Points to the bottom of the puzzle.]*

Sammy: His shoes. *[Looks for a piece resembling the clown's shoes but tries the wrong one.]*

Mother: Well, what piece looks like this shape? *[Points again to the bottom of the puzzle.]*

Sammy: The brown one. *[Tries it, and it fits; then attempts another piece and looks at his mother.]*

Mother: "Try turning it just a little." *[Gestures to show him.]*

Sammy: "There!" *[Puts in several more pieces while his mother watches.]*

Sammy's mother keeps the puzzle within his zone of proximal development, at a manageable level of difficulty, by questioning, prompting, and suggesting strategies.

To promote cognitive development, social interaction must have certain features. The first is **intersubjectivity,** the process whereby two participants who begin a task with different understandings arrive at a shared understanding (Newson & Newson, 1975). Intersubjectivity creates a common ground for communication, as each partner adjusts to the perspective of the other. Adults try to promote it when they translate their own insights in ways that are within the child's grasp. As the child stretches to understand the adult, she is drawn into a more mature approach to the situation (Rogoff, 1998).

The capacity for intersubjectivity is present early, in parent–infant mutual gaze, exchange of emotional signals, and imitation. Later, language facilitates it. As conversational skills improve, preschoolers increasingly seek others' help and direct that assistance to ensure that it is beneficial (Whitington & Ward, 1999). Between ages 3 and 5, children strive for intersubjectivity in dialogues with peers, as when they affirm a playmate's message, add new ideas, and contribute to ongoing play to sustain it. They can also be heard saying, "I think [this way]. What do you think?"—evidence for a willingness to share viewpoints (Berk, 2001a). In these ways, children begin to create zones of proximal development for one another.

A second important feature of social interaction is **scaffolding**—adjusting the support offered during a teaching session to fit the child's current level of performance. When the child has little notion of how to proceed, the adult uses direct instruction, breaking the task down into manageable units, suggesting strategies, and offering rationales for using them. As the child's competence increases, effective scaffolders—such as Sammy's mother—gradually and sensitively withdraw support, turning over responsibility to the child. Then children take the language of these dialogues, make it part of their private speech, and use this speech to organize their independent efforts.

Scaffolding captures the form of teaching interaction that occurs as children work on school or school-like tasks, such as puzzles, model building, picture matching, and (later) academic assignments. It may not apply to other contexts that are just as vital for cognitive development—for example, play or everyday activities, during which adults usually support children's efforts without deliberately instructing. To account for children's diverse opportunities to learn through involvement with others, Barbara Rogoff (1998, 2003) suggests the term **guided participation,** a broader concept than scaffolding that refers to shared endeavors between more expert and less expert participants, without specifying the precise features of communication. Consequently, it allows for variations across situations and cultures.

What evidence supports Vygotsky's ideas on the social origins of cognitive development? A wealth of research indicates that when adults establish intersubjectivity by being stimulating, responsive, and supportive, they foster many competencies—attention, language, complex play, and understanding of others' perspectives (Bornstein et al., 1992b; Charman et al., 2001; Morales et al., 2000). Furthermore, children of effective scaffolders use more private speech and are more successful when attempting difficult tasks on their own (Berk & Spuhl,

By using gestures and simple words, this father helps his child figure out how to fit the dolls into their spaces on the toy bus. By presenting a task within the child's zone of proximal development and fine-tuning his support to the child's needs, he promotes his child's cognitive development.
© Laura Dwight/PhotoEdit

1995; Conner & Cross, 2003). Adult cognitive support—teaching in small steps and offering strategies—predicts children's mature thinking. And adult emotional support—offering encouragement and transferring responsibility to the child—predicts children's effort (Neitzel & Stright, 2003). The result is a winning combination for successful learning.

Vygotsky's View of Make-Believe Play

In accord with his emphasis on social experience and language as vital forces in cognitive development, Vygotsky (1933/1978) regarded make-believe play as a unique, broadly influential zone of proximal development in which *children advance themselves* as they try out a wide variety of challenging skills. In Vygotsky's theory, make-believe is the central source of development during the preschool years, leading development forward in two ways. First, as children create imaginary situations, they learn to act in accord with internal ideas, not just in response to external stimuli. Children's object substitutions are crucial in this process. While pretending, children continually use one object to stand for another. By making a stick represent a horse or a folded blanket represent a sleeping baby, they change an object's usual meaning. Gradually they realize that thinking (or the meaning of words) is separate from objects and that ideas can be used to guide behavior.

A second feature of make-believe—its rule-based nature—also strengthens children's capacity to think before they act. Pretend play, Vygotsky pointed out, constantly demands that children act against their impulses because they must follow the rules of the play scene (Duncan & Tarulli, 2003). For example, a child pretending to go to sleep obeys the rules of bedtime behavior. Another child imagining himself to be a father and a doll to be a child conforms to the rules of parental behavior. As children enact rules in make-believe, they come to better understand social norms and expectations and strive to follow them.

Much evidence fits with Vygotsky's conclusion that make-believe play serves as a zone of proximal development, supporting the emergence and refinement of many competencies. Turn back to pages 232–233 to review evidence that make-believe enhances a diverse array of cognitive and social skills. Pretend play is also rich in private speech—a finding that supports its role in helping children bring action under the control of thought (Krafft & Berk, 1998). In a recent study, preschoolers who engaged in more complex sociodramatic play showed greater gains in following classroom rules over a 4-month period (Elias & Berk, 2002).

Finally, Vygotsky took issue with Piaget's view that make-believe arises spontaneously in the second year of life. Vygotsky argued that, like other higher cognitive processes, the elaborate pretending of the preschool years has social origins. Research reviewed in the From Research to Practice box on page 262 supports the view that children learn to pretend under the supportive guidance of experts.

Social Origins of Make-Believe Play

One of the activities my husband, Ken, used to do with our two sons when they were young was to bake pineapple upside-down cake, a favorite treat. One Sunday afternoon when a cake was in the making, 21-month-old Peter stood on a chair at the kitchen sink, busily pouring water from one cup to another.

"He's in the way, Dad!" complained 4-year-old David, trying to pull Peter away from the sink.

"Maybe if we let him help, he'll give us some room," Ken suggested. As David stirred the batter, Ken poured some into a small bowl for Peter, moved his chair to the side of the sink, and handed him a spoon.

"Here's how you do it, Petey," instructed David, with an air of superiority. Peter watched as David stirred, then tried to copy his motion. When it was time to pour the batter, Ken helped Peter hold and tip the small bowl.

"Time to bake it," said Ken.

"Bake it, bake it," repeated Peter, as he watched Ken slip the pan into the oven.

Several hours later, we observed one of Peter's earliest instances of make-believe play. He got his pail from the sandbox and, after filling it with a handful of sand, carried it into the kitchen and put it down on the floor in front of the oven. "Bake it, bake it," Peter called to Ken. Together, father and son placed the pretend cake inside the oven.

Until recently, most researchers studied make-believe play apart from the social environment in which it occurs, by observing children as they played alone. Probably for this reason, Piaget and his followers concluded that toddlers discover make-believe independently, once they are capable of representational schemes. Vygotsky's theory has challenged this view. He believed that society provides children with opportunities to represent culturally meaningful activities in play. Make-believe, like other complex mental activities, is first learned under the guidance of experts (Berk, 2001a). In the example just described, Peter extended his capacity to represent daily events when Ken drew him into the baking task and helped him act it out in play.

Current evidence supports the idea that early make-believe is the combined result of children's readiness to engage in it and social experiences that promote it. In one observational study of middle-SES toddlers, 75 to 80 percent of make-believe involved mother–child interaction (Haight & Miller, 1993). At 12 months, make-believe was fairly one-sided; almost all play episodes were initiated by mothers. By the end of the second year, mothers and children displayed mutual interest in getting make-believe started; half of pretend episodes were initiated by each.

When adults participate, toddlers' make-believe is more elaborate (O'Reilly & Bornstein, 1993). For example, play themes are more varied. And toddlers are more likely to combine schemes into complex sequences, as Peter did when he put the sand in the bucket ("making the batter"), carried it into the kitchen, and (with Ken's help) put it in the oven ("baking the cake"). The more parents pretend with their toddlers, the more time their children devote to make-believe. And in certain collectivist societies, such as Argentina and Japan, mother–toddler other-directed pretending, as in feeding or putting a doll to sleep, is particularly rich in maternal expressions of affection and praise (Bornstein et al., 1999a).

In some cultures, older siblings are toddlers' first play partners. For example, in Indonesia and Mexico, where extended-family households and sibling caregiving are common, make-believe is more frequent and complex with older siblings than with mothers. As early as 3 to 4 years of age, children provide rich, challenging stimulation and support to their younger brothers and sisters, take these teaching responsibilities seriously, and, with age, become better at them (Zukow-Goldring, 2002). In a study of Zinacanteco Indian children of southern Mexico, by age 8, sibling teachers were highly skilled at showing 2-year-olds how to play at everyday tasks, such as washing and cooking. They often combined verbal descriptions with demonstrations, explained, provided feedback, and guided toddlers physically through the task (Maynard, 2002).

Although older siblings in Western middle-SES families less often deliberately teach, they nevertheless serve as influential

▲ In Mexico, where sibling caregiving is common, younger children engage in more frequent and complex make-believe play with their older siblings than with their mothers. This 5-year-old uses a simple box to devise a rich, challenging pretend scene for her little sister.
© Karen Halverson/Omni-Photo Communication

models of playful behavior. In a study of New Zealand families of Western European descent, when both a parent and an older sibling were available, toddlers more often imitated the actions of the sibling. Toddlers were especially interested in imitating when siblings engaged in make-believe or in routines (such as answering the phone or raking leaves) that could inspire pretending. Furthermore, toddlers' imitations included many actions with cultural significance (Barr & Hayne, 2003). For example, some enacted behaviors unique to the New Zealand Maori culture, such as swinging a *poi* (an object used in a ceremonial dance). Imitating Western customs, such as shaking hands and clinking two glasses together in a "cheers" gesture, was also common.

Make-believe play is a major means through which children extend their cognitive skills and learn about important activities in their culture. Vygotsky's theory, and the findings that support it, tell us that providing a stimulating environment is not enough to promote early cognitive development. In addition, toddlers must be invited and encouraged by more skilled members of their culture to participate in the social world around them. Parents and teachers can enhance early make-believe by playing often with toddlers and guiding and elaborating on their make-believe themes.

Vygotsky and Education

Vygotsky's theory offers new visions of teaching and learning—ones that emphasize the importance of social context and collaboration. Today, educators are eager to use his ideas. Like Piagetian classrooms, Vygotskian classrooms accept individual differences and provide opportunities for children's active participation. Yet a Vygotskian classroom goes beyond independent discovery: It promotes *assisted discovery.* Teachers guide children's learning, tailoring their interventions to each child's zone of proximal development. Assisted discovery is also fostered by *peer collaboration.* Children with varying abilities work in groups, teaching and helping one another.

Vygotsky's educational message for the preschool years is to provide socially rich, meaningful activities in children's zones of proximal development and a wealth of opportunities for make-believe play—the ultimate means of fostering the self-discipline required for later academic learning. Once formal schooling begins, Vygotsky emphasized literacy activities (John-Steiner & Mahn, 1996; Scrimsher & Tudge, 2003). As children talk about literature, mathematics, science, and social studies, their teachers inform, correct, and ask them to explain. As a result, children reflect on their own thought processes and shift to a higher level of cognitive activity in which they think about how to symbolize ideas in socially useful ways. Gradually they become proficient in manipulating and controlling the symbol systems of their culture.

Let's look at two Vygotsky-based educational innovations, each of which incorporates assisted discovery and peer collaboration.

Reciprocal Teaching

Originally designed to improve reading comprehension in students achieving poorly, this teaching method has been extended to other subjects and all schoolchildren. In **reciprocal teaching,** a teacher and two to four students form a collaborative group and take turns leading dialogues on the content of a text passage. Within the dialogues, group members apply four cognitive strategies: questioning, summarizing, clarifying, and predicting.

The dialogue leader (at first the teacher, later a student) begins by *asking questions* about the content of the text passage. Students offer answers, raise additional questions, and, in case of disagreement, reread the original text. Next, the leader *summarizes* the passage, and children discuss the summary and *clarify* unfamiliar ideas. Finally, the leader encourages students to *predict* upcoming content based on clues in the passage (Palincsar & Klenk, 1992).

Elementary and junior high school students exposed to reciprocal teaching show impressive gains in reading comprehension compared with controls taught in other ways (Lederer, 2000; Rosenshine & Meister, 1994). Notice how reciprocal teaching creates a zone of proximal development in which children gradually assume more responsibility for comprehending text passages. Also, by collaborating with others, children forge group expectations for high-level thinking and acquire skills vital for learning and success in everyday life.

Reciprocal teaching is a Vygotsky-inspired educational innovation in which a teacher and two to four pupils form a cooperative learning group and engage in dialogue about a text passage. Elementary and junior high school pupils who participate in reciprocal teaching show impressive gains in reading comprehension.
© Bob Daemmrich/PhotoEdit

Cooperative Learning

Although reciprocal teaching uses peer collaboration, a teacher is present to guide it, helping to ensure its success. According to Vygotsky, more expert peers can also spur children's development, as long as they adjust the help they provide to fit the less mature child's zone of proximal development. Recall that Piaget, too, thought that peer interaction could contribute to cognitive change. In fact, he regarded discussion with agemates as more valuable than discussion with adults because a child might superficially accept an adult authority's perspective without critically examining it. Piaget also asserted that clashing viewpoints—arguments jarring the child into noticing a peer's point of view—were necessary for peer interaction to foster logical thought (Tudge & Winterhoff, 1993).

Today, peer collaboration is used in many classrooms, but evidence is mounting that it promotes development only under certain conditions. A crucial factor is **cooperative learning,** in which small groups of classmates work toward common goals. Conflict and disagreement seem less important than the extent to which peers achieve intersubjectivity—by resolving differences of opinion, sharing responsibility, and providing one another with sufficiently elaborate explanations to correct misunderstandings (Webb, Troper, & Fall, 1995). And in line with Vygotsky's theory, children's planning and problem solving improve more when their peer partner is an "expert"—especially capable at the task (Azmitia, 1988).

Cultural variations exist in students' ability to learn cooperatively. Working in groups comes more easily to children reared in collectivist than in individualistic cultures. For example, Navajo children do so more readily than Caucasian-American children (Ellis & Gauvain, 1992). Japanese classroom practices, in which children solve problems by building on one another's ideas, are situated in a larger culture that values interdependence (Hatano, 1994). In contrast, North American cultural-majority children typically consider competition and independent work to be natural—a perspective that interferes with their ability to attain intersubjectivity in groups.

For cooperative learning to succeed, Western children usually require extensive guidance in how to work together. In several studies, groups of three to four students trained in collaborative processes displayed more cooperative behavior, gave higher-level explanations, and enjoyed learning more than did untrained groups (Gillies, 2000, 2003; Terwel et al., 2001). In other research, the quality of children's collaborative discussions predicted gains in diverse cognitive skills that persisted for weeks beyond the cooperative learning experience (Fleming & Alexander, 2001). Teaching through cooperative learning broadens Vygotsky's concept of the zone of proximal development, from a single child in collaboration with an expert partner (adult or peer) to multiple partners with diverse forms of expertise stimulating and encouraging one another.

Evaluation of Vygotsky's Theory

In granting social experience a fundamental role in cognitive development, Vygotsky's theory helps us understand the wide cultural variation in cognitive skills. Unlike Piaget, who emphasized universal cognitive change, Vygotsky's theory leads us to expect highly diverse paths of development. For example, the reading, writing, and mathematical activities of children who go to school in literate societies generate cognitive capacities that differ from those in tribal and village cultures, where children receive little formal schooling. But the elaborate spatial skills of Australian Aborigines, whose food-gathering missions require that they find their way through barren desert regions, and the proportional reasoning of Brazilian fishermen, promoted by their navigational experiences, are just as advanced (Carraher, Schliemann, & Carraher, 1988; Kearins, 1981). Each is a unique form of symbolic thinking required by activities that make up that culture's way of life.

At the same, Vygotsky's theory underscores the vital role of teaching in cognitive development. According to Vygotsky (1934/1986), from communicating with more expert partners, children engage in "verbalized self-observation"; they start to reflect on, revise, and control their own thought processes. In this way, parents' and teachers' engagement with children prompts profound advances in the complexity of children's thinking.

Vygotsky's theory has not gone unchallenged. Although he acknowledged the role of diverse symbol systems (such as pictures, maps, and mathematical expressions) in the development of higher cognitive processes, he elevated language to highest importance. In some cultures, however, verbal dialogues are not the only means, or even the most important means, through which children learn. When Western parents help children with challenging tasks, they assume a great deal of responsibility for children's motivation by frequently giving verbal instructions and conversing with the child. Their communication resembles the teaching that takes place in school, where their children will spend years preparing for adult life. In cultures that place less emphasis on schooling and literacy, parents often expect children to take greater responsibility for acquiring new skills through keen observation and participation in community activities (Rogoff, 2003). Turn to the Cultural Influences box on the following page for research that illustrates this difference.

Finally, in focusing on social and cultural influences, Vygotsky said little about biological contributions to children's cognition. For example, his theory does not address how elementary

CULTURAL INFLUENCES

Children in Village and Tribal Cultures Observe and Participate in Adult Work

In Western societies, children are largely excluded from participating in adult work, which generally takes place in settings beyond the home. The role of equipping children with the skills they need to become competent workers is assigned to school. In early childhood, middle-class parents' interactions with children dwell on preparing the children to succeed in school through child-focused activities—especially adult–child conversations and play that enhance language, literacy, and other school-related knowledge. In village and tribal cultures, children receive little or no schooling, spend their days in contact with or participating in adult work, and start to assume mature responsibilities in early childhood (Rogoff et al., 2003). Consequently, parents have little need to rely on conversation and play to teach children.

A study comparing 2- and 3-year-olds' daily lives in four cultures—two U.S. middle-class suburbs, the Efe hunters and gatherers of the Republic of Congo, and a Mayan agricultural town in Guatemala—documented these differences (Morelli, Rogoff, & Angelillo, 2003). In the U.S. communities, young children had little access to adult work and spent much time involved in adult–child conversations and play that catered to children's interests and provided academic lessons. In contrast, the Efe and Mayan children rarely engaged in these child-focused activities. Instead, they spent their day in close proximity to adult work, which often took place in or near the Efe campsite or the Mayan family home. Compared to their American counterparts, Mayan and Efe children spent far more time observing adult work.

An ethnography of a remote Mayan village in Yucatán, Mexico, shows that

when young children are legitimate onlookers and participants in a daily life structured around adult work, their competencies differ sharply from those of Western preschoolers (Gaskins, 1999). Yucatec Mayan adults are subsistence farmers. Men tend cornfields, aided by sons age 8 and older. Women oversee the household and yard; they prepare meals, wash clothes, and care for the livestock and garden, assisted by daughters and by sons not yet old enough to work in the fields. To the extent they can, children join in these activities from the second year on. When not participating with adults, they are expected to be self-sufficient. Young children make many nonwork decisions for themselves—how much to sleep and eat, what to wear, when to bathe (as long as they do so every afternoon), and even when to start school. As a result, Yucatec Mayan preschoolers are highly competent at self-care. In contrast, their make-believe play is limited; when it occurs, they usually enact adult work. Otherwise, they watch others—for hours each day.

Yucatec Mayan parents rarely converse or play with preschoolers or scaffold their learning. Rather, when children imitate adult tasks, parents conclude that they are ready for more responsibility. Then they assign chores, selecting tasks the child can do with little help so that adult work is not disturbed. If a child cannot do a task, the

▲ In Yucatec Mayan culture, adults rarely converse with children or scaffold their learning. And rather than engaging in make-believe, children join in the work of their community from an early age, spending many hours observing adults. This Mayan preschooler watches intently as her grandmother washes dishes. When the child begins to imitate adult tasks, she will be given additional responsibilities.
© Beryl Goldberg

adult takes over and the child observes, reengaging when able to contribute.

Expected to be autonomous and helpful, Yucatec Mayan children seldom display attention-getting behaviors or ask others for something interesting to do. From an early age, they can sit quietly for long periods with little fussing—through a lengthy religious service or a 3-hour truck ride. And when an adult interrupts their activity and directs them to do a chore, they respond eagerly to the type of command that Western children frequently avoid or resent. By age 5, Yucatec Mayan children spontaneously take responsibility for tasks beyond those assigned.

motor, perceptual, memory, and problem-solving capacities spark changes in children's social experiences, from which more advanced cognition springs. Nor does it tell us just how children internalize social experiences to advance their mental functioning (Berk & Winsler, 1995; Moll, 1994). Consequently, like the other perspectives addressed in this chapter, Vygotsky's theory is vague in its explanation of cognitive change. It is intriguing to speculate about the broader theory that might exist today had Piaget and Vygotsky—the two twentieth-century giants of cognitive development—had a chance to meet and weave together their extraordinary accomplishments.

Ask Yourself

REVIEW	Describe characteristics of social interaction that support children's cognitive development. How does such interaction create a zone of proximal development?
REVIEW	How, according to Vygotsky, is make-believe play the ideal social context for cognitive development in early childhood?
APPLY	Tanisha sees her 5-year-old son, Toby, talking aloud to himself while he plays. She wonders whether she should discourage this behavior. Using Vygotsky's theory and related research, explain why Toby talks to himself. How would you advise Tanisha?
CONNECT	Explain how Piaget's and Vygotsky's theories complement one another. How would classroom practices inspired by these theories be similar? How would they be different?

⊚ Summary

Piaget's Cognitive-Developmental Theory

According to Piaget, how does cognition develop?

⊚ Influenced by his background in biology, Piaget viewed cognitive development as an adaptive process in which thinking gradually achieves a better fit with external reality. Piaget's **constructivist approach** assumes that by acting on the environment, children move through four invariant and universal stages, in which all aspects of cognition undergo similar changes. According to Piaget, infants begin life with little in the way of built-in structures; only at the end of the second year are they capable of a cognitive approach to the world through **mental representations.**

⊚ In Piaget's theory, psychological structures, or **schemes,** change in two ways. The first is through **adaptation,** which consists of two complementary activities: **assimilation** and **accommodation.** The second is through **organization,** the internal

rearrangement of schemes to form a strongly interconnected cognitive system. **Equilibration** sums up the changing balance of assimilation and accommodation that gradually leads to more effective schemes.

The Sensorimotor Stage: Birth to 2 Years

Describe the major cognitive attainments of the sensorimotor stage.

⊚ Piaget's **sensorimotor stage** is divided into six substages. Through the **circular reaction,** the newborn baby's reflexes gradually transform into the more flexible action patterns of the older infant. During Substage 4, infants develop **intentional,** or **goal-directed, behavior** and begin to understand **object permanence.** Substage 5 brings a more flexible, exploratory approach, and infants no longer make the **A-not-B search error.** In Substage 6, sensorimotor development culminates with mental representation, as shown by sudden solutions to sensorimotor problems, mastery of object

permanence problems involving invisible displacement, **deferred imitation,** and **make-believe play.**

What does follow-up research say about the accuracy of Piaget's sensorimotor stage?

⊚ Many studies suggest that infants display a variety of understandings earlier than Piaget believed. Some awareness of object permanence, as revealed by the **violation-of-expectation method,** may be evident in the first few months. In addition, young infants display deferred imitation, categorization, and **analogical problem solving,** suggesting that mental representation develops concurrently with sensorimotor schemes during the first 2 years.

⊚ Today, investigators believe that newborns have more built-in equipment for making sense of their world than Piaget assumed, although they disagree on how much initial understanding infants have. Furthermore, the cognitive attainments of infancy do not develop in the neat, stepwise fashion predicted by Piaget's substages.

The Preoperational Stage: 2 to 7 Years

Describe advances in mental representation and limitations of thinking during the preoperational stage.

Ⓢ Rapid advances in mental representation, including language, make-believe play, and drawing, occur during the **preoperational stage.** With age, make-believe becomes increasingly complex, evolving into **sociodramatic play.** Preschoolers' make-believe not only reflects but also contributes to cognitive and social development. During the preschool years, drawings progress from scribbles to increasingly detailed and realistic-looking representational forms.

Ⓢ **Dual representation** improves rapidly during the third year of life. Children realize that photographs, drawings, models, and simple maps correspond to circumstances in the real world. Insight into one type of symbol–real-world relation helps preschoolers understand others.

Ⓢ According to Piaget, preschoolers are not yet capable of **operations** because they are **egocentric**; they often fail to take into account the perspectives of others. Because egocentrism prevents children from accommodating, it contributes to **animistic thinking, centration,** a focus on superficial perceptual appearances, and lack of **reversibility** in problem solving. These difficulties cause preschoolers to fail **conservation** and **hierarchical classification** tasks.

What does follow-up research say about the accuracy of Piaget's preoperational stage?

Ⓢ When preschoolers are given simplified problems relevant to their everyday lives, their performance appears more mature than Piaget assumed. They recognize differing perspectives, distinguish animate from inanimate objects, and reason by analogy about transformations. Furthermore, their language reflects accurate causal reasoning and hierarchical classification, and they form many categories based on nonobservable characteristics. They also notice distinctions between appearance and reality, an understanding that improves with age.

Ⓢ These findings pose yet another challenge to Piaget's stage concept. Rather than being absent, logical thinking develops gradually during early childhood.

The Concrete Operational Stage: 7 to 11 Years

What are the major characteristics of the concrete operational stage?

Ⓢ During the **concrete operational stage,** thought is far more logical and organized than it was earlier. The ability to conserve indicates that children can decenter and reverse their thinking. In addition, they are better at hierarchical classification and **seriation,** including **transitive inference.**

Ⓢ School-age children's spatial reasoning improves, as their ability to give directions reveals. In addition, **cognitive maps** become more organized and accurate during middle childhood.

Ⓢ Concrete operational thought is limited in that children have difficulty reasoning about abstract ideas. Piaget used the term **horizontal décalage** to describe the school-age child's gradual mastery of logical concepts.

What does follow-up research say about the accuracy of Piaget's concrete operational stage?

Ⓢ Cultural practices and schooling profoundly affect children's mastery of Piagetian tasks. Concrete operations seem to be greatly influenced by training, context, and cultural conditions.

The Formal Operational Stage: 11 Years and Older

Describe major characteristics of the formal operational stage and their consequences for adolescents' typical reactions.

Ⓢ In Piaget's **formal operational stage,** abstract thinking develops. Adolescents engage in **hypothetico-deductive reasoning.** When faced with a problem, they think of all possibilities, including ones that are not obvious, and test them systematically. **Propositional thought** also develops. Young people can evaluate the logic of verbal statements apart from real-world circumstances.

Ⓢ Early in this stage, two distorted images of the relation between self and other appear: the **imaginary audience** and the **personal fable.** Research suggests that these visions of the self result from advances in perspective taking and the realization that others' opinions have real consequences.

Ⓢ Because abstract thinking fosters idealism, teenagers become faultfinding critics. Despite advances in cognition, adolescents are less competent than adults at diverse aspects of decision making.

What does follow-up research say about the accuracy of Piaget's formal operational stage?

Ⓢ School-age children display the beginnings of abstraction, but they are not as competent as adolescents. They cannot sort out evidence that bears on three or more variables at once, and they do not grasp the **logical necessity** of propositional reasoning. Also, because they do not think carefully about the major premise, they violate the most basic rules of logic.

Ⓢ Adolescents and adults are most likely to think abstractly in situations in which they have had extensive experience. Also, they often fall back on less demanding, intuitive judgments instead of using formal operational reasoning. Furthermore, in many tribal and village societies, formal operational tasks are not mastered at all. These findings suggest that Piaget's highest stage is promoted by specific learning opportunities made available in school.

Piaget and Education

Describe educational implications of Piaget's theory.

Ⓢ Piaget's theory has had a major impact on educational programs in early and middle childhood. A Piagetian classroom promotes discovery learning, sensitivity to children's readiness to learn, and acceptance of individual differences.

© ARIEL SKELLEY/CORBIS

Overall Evaluation of Piaget's Theory

Summarize contributions and shortcomings of Piaget's theory.

◉ Piaget awakened psychologists and educators to children's active contributions to their own development and inspired the contemporary focus on mechanisms of cognitive change. His stages provide a useful "road map" of cognitive development.

◉ At the same time, Piaget's notions of adaptation, organization, and equilibration offer only a vague account of how children's cognition develops. Also, children's cognitive attainments are less coherent and more gradual than Piaget's stages indicate.

◉ Consequently, some researchers reject Piaget's stages while retaining his view of cognitive development as an active, constructive process. Others support a less tightly knit stage concept. Still others deny both Piaget's stages and his belief that the human mind is made up of general reasoning abilities.

The Core Knowledge Perspective

Explain the core knowledge perspective on cognitive development, noting research that supports its assumptions.

◉ According to the **core knowledge perspective,** infants begin life with innate, core domains of thought that support early, rapid cognitive development. Each core domain has a long evolutionary history, is essential for survival, and develops independently, resulting in uneven, domain-specific changes. Some violation-of-expectation research suggests that young infants have impressive physical and numerical knowledge. Overall, however, findings on early, ready-made knowledge are mixed.

◉ The **theory theory** regards children as naïve theorists who draw on innate concepts to explain their everyday experiences, often in remarkably advanced ways. Then children test their naïve theory against experience, revising it when it cannot adequately account for new information.

◉ In support of this view, children reason about everyday events in ways consistent with the event's core domain. Physical and psychological explanations emerge early, but young

children often use psychological concepts to theorize about biological events. The late emergence of biological knowledge suggests that it may have only a weak innate foundation or may not be innately specified.

Summarize the strengths and limitations of the core knowledge perspective.

◉ Core knowledge researchers are testing intriguing ideas about why certain cognitive skills emerge early and develop rapidly. Critics, however, believe that results of violation-of-expectation studies are not strong enough to show that infants are endowed with knowledge. So far, the core knowledge perspective has not offered greater clarity than Piaget's theory on how cognition changes.

Vygotsky's Sociocultural Theory

Explain Vygotsky's view of cognitive development, noting the importance of social experience and language.

◉ In Vygotsky's sociocultural theory, language development broadens preschoolers' participation in dialogues with more knowledgeable individuals, who encourage them to master culturally important tasks. These social experiences transform basic mental capacities into uniquely human, higher cognitive processes. According to Vygotsky, as experts assist children with tasks within their **zone of proximal development,** children integrate the language of these dialogues into their **private speech** and use it to organize their independent efforts. As children get older and find tasks easier, they internalize private speech as silent, inner speech, which they call on for self-guidance and self-direction.

© RAYMOND GEHMAN/CORBIS

Describe features of social interaction that promote transfer of culturally adaptive ways of thinking to children, and discuss Vygotsky's view of the role of make-believe play in development.

◉ **Intersubjectivity,** which creates a common ground for communication, and **scaffolding,** involving adult assistance that

adjusts to the child's current level of performance, promote cognitive development. The term **guided participation** recognizes cultural and situational variations in the ways that adults support children's efforts.

◉ According to Vygotsky, make-believe play is a unique, broadly influential zone of proximal development. As children create imaginary situations and follow the rules of the make-believe scene, they learn to act in accord with internal ideas rather than on impulse. In Vygotsky's theory, make-believe play, like other higher cognitive processes, is the product of social collaboration.

Vygotsky and Education

Describe educational implications of Vygotsky's theory.

◉ A Vygotskian classroom emphasizes assisted discovery through teachers' guidance and peer collaboration. When formal schooling begins, literacy activities prompt children to shift to a higher level of cognitive activity, in which they proficiently manipulate and control the symbol systems of their culture.

◉ Educational practices inspired by Vygotsky's theory include **reciprocal teaching** and **cooperative learning,** in which peers resolve differences of opinion and work toward common goals. Western children usually require extensive training for cooperative learning to succeed.

Evaluation of Vygotsky's Theory

Cite strengths and limitations of Vygotsky's theory.

◉ Vygotsky's theory helps us understand wide cultural variation in cognitive skills and underscores the vital role of teaching in cognitive development. In some cultures, however, verbal dialogues are not the only means, or even the most important means, through which children learn.

◉ In focusing on social and cultural influences, Vygotsky said little about biological contributions to children's cognition. Also, exactly how children internalize social experiences to advance their thinking remains unclear.

Important Terms and Concepts

A-not-B search error (p. 223)
accommodation (p. 221)
adaptation (p. 221)
analogical problem solving (p. 229)
animistic thinking (p. 236)
assimilation (p. 221)
centration (p. 236)
circular reaction (p. 222)
cognitive maps (p. 243)
concrete operational stage (p. 242)
conservation (p. 236)
constructivist approach (p. 220)
cooperative learning (p. 264)
core knowledge perspective (p. 253)
deferred imitation (p. 224)
dual representation (p. 235)
egocentrism (p. 236)

equilibration (p. 221)
formal operational stage (p. 246)
guided participation (p. 261)
hierarchical classification (p. 236)
horizontal décalage (p. 244)
hypothetico-deductive reasoning (p. 246)
imaginary audience (p. 248)
intentional, or goal-directed, behavior (p. 223)
intersubjectivity (p. 260)
logical necessity (p. 250)
make-believe play (p. 224)
mental representation (p. 221)
object permanence (p. 223)
operations (p. 236)
organization (p. 221)
personal fable (p. 248)

preoperational stage (p. 231)
private speech (p. 259)
propositional thought (p. 247)
reciprocal teaching (p. 263)
reversibility (p. 236)
scaffolding (p. 260)
scheme (p. 221)
sensorimotor stage (p. 222)
seriation (p. 243)
sociodramatic play (p. 232)
theory theory (p. 256)
transitive inference (p. 243)
violation-of-expectation method (p. 224)
zone of proximal development (p. 260)

"Jurong Bird Park"
Chen Yie
Age 10, Singapore

How do these inquisitive nature lovers, on a school field trip to a bird park, process information? During the school years, their capacity to attend to, remember, transform, store, retrieve, and use information to solve problems expands greatly.

Cognitive Development: An Information-Processing Perspective

On Fridays in Mr. Sharp's fourth-grade class, the children often played memory games. One day, Mr. Sharp announced, "I'm going to put 12 words on the board and leave them up for 1 minute. Let's see how many you can recall."

Milk, shoe, jug, soup, hand, plate, foot, cake, gloves, sock, head, bowl, Mr. Sharp wrote quickly. He left the words up for a few moments, then erased them.

Victor's hand shot up. "I've got 'em!" he exclaimed, and recited the words perfectly.

"Let's find out how Victor did that," said Mr. Sharp.

"I put all the food together, the kitchen stuff together, and the clothes together," Victor explained. "Then I repeated the words in each group over and over."

Now consider a different scene—a researcher interviewing Kpelle farmers of Liberia about how they would sort familiar objects to remember them (Glick, 1975). Adults in this nonliterate culture arranged the objects in pairs—a knife with an orange, a hoe with a potato—rather than putting all the tools in one pile and the food items in another. Puzzled that the Kpelle adults failed to use the more effective memorizing techniques typical of Western schoolchildren like Victor, the researcher asked why. Many Kpelle replied that a wise person would learn the Kpelle way. In exasperation, the researcher blurted out, "Then how would a fool do it?" Immediately, he got the kinds of object groupings he had first expected!

Information processing is not a unified theory of cognitive development but, rather, an approach followed by researchers who engage in thorough study of one or a few aspects of cognition. A central goal is to uncover *mechanisms of change*—to find out how children and adults operate on different kinds of information, detecting, transforming, storing, accessing, and modifying it further as it makes its way through the cognitive system.

This chapter provides an overview of the information-processing perspective. First, we review models of the human cognitive system that are major forces in child development research. Next, we turn to two basic processes that enter into all human thinking: attention and memory. We also consider how children's expanding knowledge of the world and awareness of their own mental activities affect these processes.

As we examine these topics, we will return to a familiar theme: the impact of task demands and cultural context on children's thinking. A comparison of Victor's memorizing techniques with those of the Kpelle suggests that culture can greatly influence information processing. We pay special attention to how schooling, with its emphasis on literacy, mathematics, scientific reasoning, and retention of discrete pieces of information, channels cognitive development in culturally specific ways. Although information-processing theorists are especially interested in internal, self-generated cognitive changes, they also want to find out how external influences—teaching techniques, the design of learning environments and tasks, and cultural values and practices—affect children's thinking. Our discussion concludes with an evaluation of information processing as a framework for understanding cognitive development.

The Information-Processing Approach

Most information-processing theorists view the mind as a complex symbol-manipulating system through which information flows, much as in a computer. Information from the environment is *encoded*—taken in by the system and retained in symbolic form. Then a variety of internal processes operate on it, *recoding* it, or revising its symbolic structure into a more effective representation, and then *decoding* it, or interpreting its meaning by comparing and combining it with other information in the system. When these cognitive operations are complete, individuals use the information to make sense of their experiences and to solve problems.

Notice the clarity and precision of the computer analogy of human mental functioning. Using computer-like diagrams and flowcharts, researchers can map the exact series of steps children and adults follow when faced with a task or problem. Some researchers do this in such detail that the same mental operations can be programmed into a computer. Then the researcher conducts *simulations* to see if the computer responds as children and adults do on certain tasks. Other investigators intensively study children's and adults' thinking by tracking eye movements, analyzing error patterns, and examining self-reports of mental activity. Regardless of approach, all share a strong commitment to explicit models of thinking and thorough testing of each component.

General Models of Information Processing

Most information-processing researchers adopt, either directly or indirectly, a computer-like view of the cognitive system that emerged in the late 1960s and early 1970s. Called the *store model*, it focuses on general units of cognitive functioning, such as sensation and memory (Klahr & MacWhinney, 1998). A second, more recent model, *connectionism*—also computer based—is part and parcel of cognitive neuroscientists' quest to understand what happens in the brain as cognition changes (de Haan & Johnson, 2003a).

The Store Model

The **store model** of the information-processing system assumes that we hold, or store, information in three parts of the mental system for processing: the *sensory register; working*, or *short-term, memory;* and *long-term memory* (see Figure 7.1) (Atkinson & Shiffrin, 1968). As information flows through each, we can use **mental strategies** to operate on and transform it, increasing the chances that we will retain information, use it efficiently, and think flexibly, adapting the information to changing circumstances. To understand this more clearly, let's look at each component of the mental system.

• **COMPONENTS OF THE STORE MODEL** • First, information enters the **sensory register.** Here, sights and sounds are represented directly and stored briefly. Look around you, and then close your eyes. An image of what you saw persists for a few seconds, but then it decays, or disappears, unless you use mental strategies to preserve it. For example, you can *attend to* some information more carefully, increasing the chances that it will transfer to the next step of the information-processing system.

The second part of the mind is **working,** or **short-term, memory,** where we actively apply mental strategies as we "work" on a limited amount of information. For example, if you are studying this book effectively, you are taking notes, repeating information to yourself, or grouping pieces of information together. Why do you apply these strategies? The sensory register, though limited, can take in a wide panorama of information. The capacity of working memory is more restricted. By meaningfully connecting pieces of information into a single

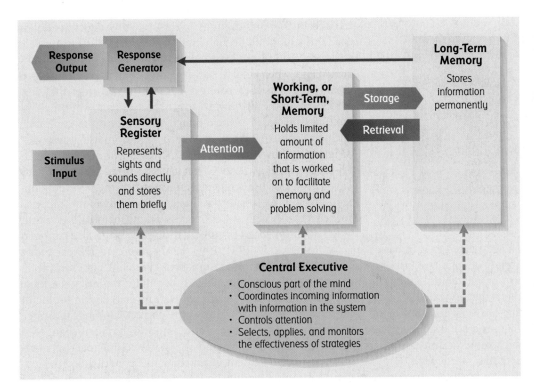

Store model of the human information-processing system. Information flows through three parts of the mental system: the *sensory register; working,* or *short-term, memory;* and *long-term memory.* In each, mental strategies can be used to manipulate information, increasing the efficiency of thinking and the chances that information will be retained. Strategies also permit us to think flexibly, adapting information to changing circumstances. The *central executive* is the conscious, reflective part of working memory. It coordinates incoming information already in the system, decides what to attend to, and oversees the use of strategies.

representation, we reduce the number of separate pieces we must attend to, thereby making room in working memory for more. Also, the more thoroughly we learn information, the more *automatically* we use it. Automatic processing expands working memory by permitting us to focus on more than one piece of information simultaneously.

To manage its complex activities, a special part of working memory—called the **central executive**—directs the flow of information. It decides what to attend to, coordinates incoming information with information already in the system, and selects, applies, and monitors strategies (Baddeley, 1993, 2000). The central executive is the conscious, reflective part of our mental system. As we will see later, it is sometimes referred to as *metacognition,* which means awareness and understanding of thought.

The longer we hold information in working memory, the greater the likelihood that it will transfer to the third, and largest, storage area—**long-term memory,** our permanent knowledge base, which is limitless. In fact, we store so much in long-term memory that we sometimes have problems with *retrieval,* or getting information back from the system. To aid retrieval, we apply strategies, just as we do in working memory. Information in long-term memory is *categorized* according to a master plan based on contents, much like a library shelving system. As a result, we can retrieve it easily by following the same network of associations used to store it in the first place.

• **IMPLICATIONS FOR DEVELOPMENT** • When applied to development, the store model suggests that two broad aspects of the cognitive system increase with age: (1) the *basic capacity* of its stores, especially working memory, and (2) the extent and effectiveness of *strategy use.* Research we will consider throughout this chapter indicates that, with age, children gradually acquire more effective strategies for retaining information. Does basic capacity—the amount of information that can be held in mind *without* applying strategies—also expand?

In a study aimed at answering this question, researchers presented first- and fourth-grade children and adults with two sets of lists of spoken digits to remember. Such lists are often used to assess **memory span**—the longest sequence of items a person can recall, a measure of working memory capacity. Typically, scores improve from about 2 digits

◎ While conducting a complex science experiment, this girl relies on her central executive, a part of working memory that allocates attention, oversees the use of strategies, and coordinates incoming information with information already in the system.
© Gabe Palmer/CORBIS

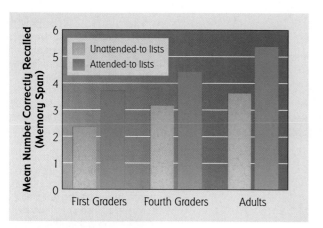

▲ **Figure 7.2**

Digits recalled from attended-to lists and unattended-to lists by first and fourth graders and adults. Memory span increased with age under both conditions, indicating that development involves expansion of basic capacity (unattended-to list performance) and more effective strategy use (attended-to list performance).

(Adapted from Cowan et al., 1999.)

at 2½ years, to 4 or 5 digits at 7 years, to 6 or 7 digits in adolescence and adulthood. In the *attended-to lists,* no distracters were introduced to prevent participants from using strategies; they listened and, when cued by a display on a computer screen, typed as many digits as they could remember, in the order they had heard them. In the *unattended-to lists,* participants, while they listened, also played a picture-matching game on the computer, which, by distracting them, prevented them from using strategies. As Figure 7.2 shows, memory span increased with age on both sets of lists (Cowan et al., 1999). That gains occurred even when participants did not use strategies indicates that memory development involves expansion of basic working-memory capacity. More effective strategy use enhances working memory even more.

Research on speed of information processing also supports an age-related gain in basic capacity. Robert Kail (1991, 1993, 1997) gave 7- to 22-year-olds a variety of cognitive tasks in which they had to respond as quickly as possible. For example, in a visual search task, they were shown a single digit and asked to signal if it was among a set of digits that appeared on a screen. In a mental addition task, they were given addition problems and answers, and they had to indicate whether the solutions were correct. Findings indicated that processing time decreased with age on all tasks. Even more important, rate of change—a fairly rapid decline in processing time that trailed off around age 12—was similar across many activities (see Figure 7.3). This pattern was also evident when participants performed perceptual–motor tasks, such as releasing a button or tapping as fast as possible—activities that do not rely on strategies (Kail, 1991).

The changes in processing speed shown in Figure 7.3 have been found in Canada, Korea, and the United States (Fry & Hale, 1996; Kail & Park, 1992). Similarity in development across diverse tasks in several cultures implies a fundamental change in the information-processing system, perhaps due to myelination or synaptic pruning in the brain (see Chapter 5) (Kail, 2003). Increased speed of processing enhances working-memory capacity (Luna et al., 2004). It permits older children and adults to scan information more quickly, to transform it more rapidly with strategies, and therefore to hold more information in their cognitive systems at once.

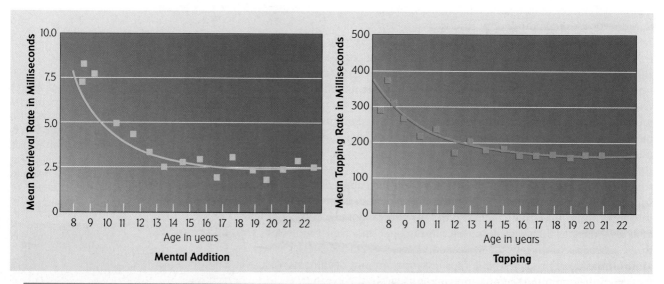

▲ **Figure 7.3**

Age-related decline in processing time, illustrated for mental addition and tapping. Processing speed improves similarly across many tasks, even perceptual–motor activities such as tapping as fast as possible, which do not rely on mental strategies. This common trend implies an age-related gain in basic processing capacity. (From R. Kail, 1988, "Developmental Functions for Speeds of Cognitive Processes," *Journal of Experimental Child Psychology, 45,* p. 361. Copyright © 1988 by Academic Press. Reprinted by permission of the publisher and author; and R. Kail, 1991, "Processing Time Declines Exponentially During Childhood and Adolescence," *Developmental Psychology, 27,* p. 265. Copyright © 1991 by the American Psychological Association. Adapted by permission of the publisher and author.)

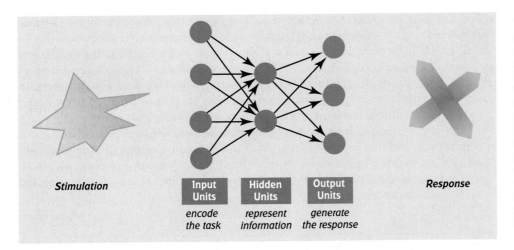

Stimulation   Input Units   Hidden Units   Output Units   *Response*

encode the task   represent information   generate the response

◀ **Figure 7.4**
A simplified example of an artificial neural network. Processing units in the computer are organized into layers, much like the brain's neurological structure. Stimulation turns on input units, which encode the task. Hidden units represent information, and output units generate a response. Researchers program connections between units to change with experience, granting the network the capacity to learn. Connections that lead to correct responses strengthen; those that lead to incorrect responses weaken.

Connectionism

Researchers in the field of developmental cognitive neuroscience (see Chapter 5, page 189) want to know exactly what happens in the brain as children master new skills. To find out, they are using computers to devise **connectionist,** or **artificial neural network, models,** which simulate the workings of the most basic information-processing units: neurons and their connections.

An artificial neural network consists of thousands of simple processing units organized into layers, much like the brain's neurological structure. A typical network includes an *input layer,* which encodes the task; one or more *hidden layers,* which represent information needed to perform the task; and an *output layer,* which generates a response (see Figure 7.4). Like neurons, the units send signals when the stimulation they receive from other units reaches a certain strength. Because information is distributed throughout the system—over all the units, acting in parallel (simultaneously)—artificial neural networks are sometimes called *parallel distributed processing systems.*

Because the connections between units are programmed to change with experience, the network has an impressive capacity to learn. After being given a task, it receives feedback about the accuracy of its responses. If a response is correct, the connections that produced the response strengthen; if a response is incorrect, the connections weaken. Researchers compare the network's responses with those of people, including children of different ages. If the two are alike, the researchers conclude that the network is a good model of human learning.

Connectionists have succeeded in depicting changes in children's performance on a variety of tasks. These include object permanence, early vocabulary growth, mastery of basic grammatical rules, formation of certain concepts, and problem solving (Jones, Ritter, & Wood, 2000; Mareschal, 2003; Plunkett et al., 1997). Findings reveal that a great deal of inner change in the strength of connections generally occurs before a network—and therefore a child behaving similarly—consistently displays a correct response (Plunkett, 1998). Consequently, networks show that gradual, internal learning often precedes changes in behavior that appear abrupt, or stage-like, when viewed from outside the system. For example, recall from Chapter 6 that infants' knowledge of object permanence, assessed through looking preferences in violation-of-expectation studies, precedes knowledge based on reaching. Connectionist models suggest that neural networks are initially weak, sufficient only to support looking. Reaching requires stronger connections—ones that integrate information across regions of the cerebral cortex (Johnson & Mareschal, 2001; Munakata & McClelland, 2003).

In connectionist models, just a few built-in procedures get learning started. Consequently, connectionists claim that their findings present a powerful argument against the core knowledge perspective, which assumes that infants begin life with innate, special-purpose knowledge systems (see Chapter 6, page 253). Instead, connectionists believe that the human cognitive system is a general processing device that gradually attains domain-specific competencies as a result of relevant learning opportunities (Karmiloff-Smith, 1999; Thelen & Bates, 2003).

Nevertheless, artificial neural networks remain some distance from their goal of duplicating the operation of the human brain. Perhaps because their internal representations are limited to connection strengths, networks learn slowly, usually requiring many more exposures to a task than children and adults. Networks do not consciously focus on important information, nor do they construct plans, hypotheses, and propositions, which foster complex, highly efficient human learning (Cowan, 2003; Plunkett, 1998). Finally, we will see when we address strategy choice, a developmental model of information processing, children are great experimenters. To arrive at the most efficient means of solving a problem, they change their strategies not just after they make errors (as artificial neural networks do) but even after they succeed!

Still, connectionist models help us understand the cognitive consequences of changes in neural connections, and they remind us that a full understanding of cognitive development must take into account the operation of its most basic units (Johnson & Mareschal, 2001). Currently, connectionists are trying to devise more complete models of brain functioning and the contexts in which children learn.

Developmental Theories of Information Processing

Although both store and connectionist models have implications for development, neither began with the aim of explaining how children's thinking changes. However, several *developmental* approaches to information processing have attracted widespread attention. We will consider two of these views. The first, Case's *neo-Piagetian perspective,* is the most influential of several approaches that use Piaget's theory as a starting point for constructing an overall vision of cognitive development (Halford, 2002). The second, Siegler's *model of strategy choice,* draws on evolutionary concepts of variation and selection to explain the diversity and ever-changing nature of children's cognition.

Case's Neo-Piagetian Theory

Robbie Case's (1992, 1998) **neo-Piagetian theory** accepts Piaget's stages but attributes change within each, as well as movement from one stage to the next, to increases in working-memory capacity. Each major stage involves a distinct type of cognitive structure—in infancy, sensory input and physical actions; in early childhood, internal representations of events and actions; in middle childhood, simple transformations of representations; and in adolescence, complex transformations of representations. As children become more efficient cognitive processors, the amount of information they can hold and combine in working memory expands, making this sequence possible.

Three factors are responsible for gains in working-memory capacity:

- *Brain development.* Recall our discussion of synaptic growth, synaptic pruning, and myelination in Chapter 5. These neurological changes improve the efficiency of thought, leading to readiness for each stage. According to Case, biology imposes a system-wide ceiling on cognitive development. At any given time, the child cannot exceed a certain upper limit of processing capacity.

- *Practice with schemes and automization.* In Case's theory, Piagetian schemes are the child's mental strategies. As the child repeatedly uses schemes, they become more automatic. This frees working memory for combining existing schemes and generating new ones. Notice how Case's mechanisms of change offer a clarified view of Piaget's concepts of assimilation and accommodation. *Practicing schemes* (assimilation) leads to *automization,* which *releases working memory* for other activities, permitting *scheme combination and construction* (accommodation).

- *Formation of central conceptual structures.* Once the schemes of a Piagetian stage become sufficiently automatic, enough working-memory capacity is available to consolidate them into an improved representational form. As a result, children generate **central conceptual structures,** networks of concepts and relations that permit them to think about a wide range of situations in more advanced ways. Consequently, processing capacity expands further (Case, 1996, 1998). When children form new central conceptual structures, they move to the next stage of development.

Let's take a familiar set of tasks—conservation—to illustrate Case's ideas. Imagine a 5-year-old who cannot yet conserve liquid but who has some isolated schemes—for example, (1) after water is poured from a tall glass into a short glass, the height of the water level is reduced; and (2) after water is poured from a thin into a wide glass, the width of the water increases. As the child gains experience in transferring liquids from one container to another, these schemes become automatic, and she combines them into a conserving response. A similar sequence occurs in other conservation situations, such as those involving length, mass, and weight. Eventually the child coordinates several task-specific conserving responses into a new, broadly applicable principle—a central conceptual structure. When this happens, cognition moves from simple to complex transformations of representations, or from concrete to formal operational thought.

Case and his colleagues have applied his theory to many tasks, including solving arithmetic word problems, understanding stories, drawing pictures, sight-reading music, handling money, and interpreting social situations (Case, 1992, 1998; Case & Okamoto, 1996). In each task, preschoolers' central conceptual structures focus on one dimension. In understanding stories, for example, they grasp only a single story line. By the early school years, central conceptual structures coordinate two dimensions. Children combine two story lines into a single plot. Around 9 to 11 years, central conceptual structures integrate multiple dimensions. Children tell coherent stories with a main plot and several subplots. Figure 7.5 shows similar changes in children's drawings.

Case's theory offers an information-processing account of the *horizontal décalage*—that many understandings appear in specific situations at different times rather than being mastered all at once. First, different forms of the same logical insight, such the various conservation tasks, vary in their processing demands. Those acquired later require more working-memory capacity. Second, children's experiences vary widely. A child who often listens to and tells stories but rarely draws pictures displays more advanced central conceptual structures in storytelling. Compared with Piaget's, Case's theory is better able to account for unevenness in cognitive development.

Children who do not show central conceptual structures expected for their age can usually be trained to attain them, and their improved understanding readily transfers to academic tasks (Case, Griffin, & Kelly, 2001). Consequently, the application of Case's theory to teaching is helping children who are behind in academic performance learn more effectively. Although

⊚ As these children pour water from one container to another, their understanding of what happens to the height and width of the liquid becomes better coordinated, and conservation of liquid is achieved. Once this idea becomes automatic, enough working-memory capacity is available to form a central conceptual structure—a general representation of conservation that can be applied in many situations.
© Lawrence Migdale/Stock Boston, LLC.

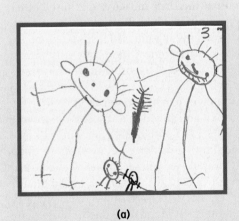

(a) (b) (c)

▲ **Figure 7.5**

Development of central conceptual structures in Case's neo-Piagetian theory. Case identified the same general sequence in children's performance on many tasks. Here, it is shown for drawings. Children were asked to "draw a picture of a mother and a father holding hands in a park, with their little baby on the grass in front of them, and a tree far off behind." (a) Preschoolers focused on one dimension. They depicted objects separately, ignoring their spatial arrangement. (b) During the early school years, children coordinated two dimensions. Their drawings showed both the features of objects and their relationship to one another. (c) Nine- to 11-year-olds integrated multiple dimensions. They used perspective to represent several points of reference, such as near, midway, and far.

(From R. Case & Y. Okamoto, 1996, "The Role of Central Conceptual Structures in the Development of Children's Thought," *Monographs of the Society for Research in Child Development, 61* [1–2, Serial No. 246] p. 106. © The Society for Research in Child Development, Inc. Adapted by permission. Courtesy of Robbie Case.)

it must be tested with many more tasks, Case's theory is unique in offering an integrated picture of how children's basic capacity, practice with strategies, and constructive efforts to reorganize their thinking interact to produce development.

Siegler's Model of Strategy Choice

Robert Siegler's (1996) **model of strategy choice** is one of several current efforts to apply an evolutionary perspective to children's cognition. When given challenging problems, children generate a *variety* of strategies. With experience, some strategies are *selected*; they become more frequent and "survive." Others become less frequent and "die off." As with physical characteristics, *variation* and *selection* characterize children's mental strategies, yielding adaptive problem-solving techniques.

To study children's strategy use, Siegler used the microgenetic research design (see Chapter 2, page 63), presenting children with many problems over an extended time period. He found that children experiment with diverse strategies on many types of problems—basic math facts, numerical estimation, conservation, memory for lists of items, reading first words, telling time, spelling, even tic-tac-toe. Consider 5-year-old Darryl, who was adding marbles tucked into pairs of small bags that his kindergarten teacher had set out on a table. As Darryl dealt with each pair, his strategies varied. Sometimes he guessed, without applying any strategy. At other times, he counted from 1 on his fingers. For example, for bags containing 2 + 4 marbles, his fingers popped up one by one as he exclaimed, "1, 2, 3, 4, 5, 6!" Occasionally he started with the lower digit, 2, and "counted on" ("2, 3, 4, 5, 6"). Or he began with the higher digit, 4, and counted on ("4, 5, 6"), a strategy called *min* because it minimizes the work. Sometimes he retrieved the answer from memory.

Siegler found that strategy use for basic math facts—and other types of problems—follows an *overlapping-waves pattern* (see Figure 7.6). Even 2-year-olds solving simple problems, such as how to use a tool to obtain an out-of-reach toy, display it (Chen & Siegler, 2000). While trying strategies, children observe which work best, which work less well, and which are ineffective. Gradually they select strategies on the basis of two adaptive criteria: *accuracy* and *speed*—in the case of basic addition, the *min* strategy. As children home in on effective strategies, they learn more about the problems at hand. As a result, correct solutions become more strongly associated with problems, and children display the most efficient strategy—automatic retrieval of the answer.

How do children move from less to more efficient strategies? Often they discover a faster procedure by using a more time-consuming technique. For example, by repeatedly counting on his fingers, Darryl began to recognize the number of fingers he held up (Siegler & Jenkins, 1989). Also, certain problems dramatize the need for a better strategy. When Darryl opened a pair of bags with 10 marbles in one and 2 in the other, he realized that *min* would be best. Reasoning about concepts relevant to the problems at hand also helps (Canobi, Reeve, & Pattison, 1998). First graders more often use *min* after they realize that regardless of the order in which two sets are combined, they yield the same results (2 + 4 = 6 and 4 + 2 = 6). Finally, when children are taught an effective strategy, they usually adopt it and abandon less successful techniques (Alibali, 1999; Siegler & Booth, 2004). Sometimes, however, children do not take advantage of new, more adaptive strategies right away. As we will see in later sections, using a new strategy requires considerable effort, taxing the capacity of working memory. Children may resist giving up a well-established strategy for a new one because gains in speed of thinking are small at first.

Siegler's model reveals that no child thinks in just one way, even on the same task. A child given the same problem on two occasions often uses different approaches. Even on a single item, children may generate varying procedures, as indicated by occasions in which their words and gestures differ (see the From Research to Practice box on the following page for the significance of these mismatches). Strategy variability is vital

▼ **Figure 7.6**

Overlapping-waves pattern of strategy use in problem solving. When given challenging problems, a child generates a variety of strategies, each represented by a wave. The waves overlap because the child tries several strategies at the same time. Use of each strategy, depicted by the height of the wave, is constantly changing. As the child observes which strategies work best, which work less well, and which are ineffective, the one that results in the most rapid, accurate solutions wins out. (Adapted from R. S. Siegler, *Emerging Minds: The Process of Change in Children's Thinking*, copyright © 1996 by Oxford University Press, Inc. Used by permission of Oxford University Press, Inc.)

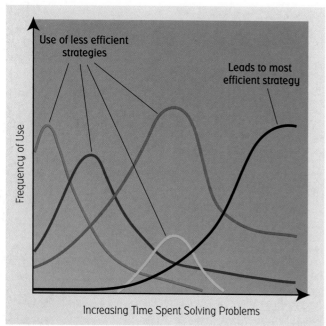

FROM RESEARCH TO PRACTICE

Speech-Gesture Mismatches: Using the Hand to Read the Mind

Mr. Beal introduced his fourth-grade class to the concept of equivalence—that the quantity on one side of an equals sign is the same as the quantity on the other side. Then he watched as several children stepped up to the blackboard to work the following problem: $5 + 3 + 4 = \underline{\quad} + 4$.

Kerry tried first. "I added $5 + 3 + 4 + 4$ equals 16," she said, pointing at each number as she mentioned it and then at the blank as she gave her answer, ignoring the placement of the equals sign. Kerry's speech and gestures were consistent; both revealed an incorrect strategy.

Noel went next. Although she gave the same incorrect explanation, her gestures sent a different message. As she spoke, she pointed to each number on the left, next touched the equals sign, then moved to the 4 on the right, and finally rested her finger on the blank. Noel showed a *speech-gesture mismatch*. Her hand movements suggested she knew more than she could say. Over the next few weeks, Noel mastered equivalence problems more rapidly than Kerry. How can we account for Noel's faster progress?

According to Susan Goldin-Meadow and her colleagues, children who produce speech-gesture mismatches are in a transitional state. Their behavior indicates that they are considering two contradictory strategies at once, a sign of readiness to learn. In a microgenetic study, the researchers identified two groups of children who did not have a full understanding of addition-based equivalence problems:

speech-gesture matched and speech-gesture mismatched. Then, as the children worked more problems, some in each group received feedback on the accuracy of their answers along with instruction that explained the equivalence principle, whereas others received no intervention. Finally, children's learning was assessed as they worked problems on their own (Alibali & Goldin-Meadow, 1993).

Speech-gesture mismatch children who received instruction were more likely than others to move out of that state to a correct answer, based on a speech-gesture match. They also more often generalized their new knowledge to multiplication-based equivalence problems ($5 \times 3 \times 4 = 5 \times \underline{\quad}$). Interestingly, the few speech-gesture match children who improved with instruction generalized what they learned only if they first passed through a speech-gesture mismatch phase. Correct strategies appeared first in gesture and only later in speech.

Children on the verge of learning appear to have strategies that are accessible to gesture but not to speech (Goldin-Meadow, 2002). Perhaps expressing a strategy in gesture that differs from one in speech facilitates awareness of conflicting ideas, encouraging the child to resolve the discrepancy in favor of the more effective strategy. Children in a mismatch state are particularly open to teaching. Speech-gesture mismatches also may indicate that the neural pathways of interest to connectionists are growing stronger and are about to reach a critical juncture.

▲ A 7-year-old works to understand a homework assignment. If her hand gestures indicate that she understands more than she can articulate—known as a speech-gesture mismatch—this may be an opportune moment for instruction.
© Elizabeth Crews/The Image Works

Parents and teachers can use children's gestures to provide instruction at the most opportune moment. Indeed, many adults are attuned to children's speech-gesture mismatches, and others can be taught to notice them (Kelly et al., 2002). In one study, adults were more likely to teach a variety of problem-solving strategies to children who displayed mismatches than to children who did not (Goldin-Meadow & Singer, 2003). In doing so, they encouraged the "mismatchers" to try out many strategies, which—as Siegler's model of strategy choice makes clear—facilitates learning.

for devising new, more adaptive ways of thinking, which "evolve" through extensive experience solving problems.

We have a better understanding of the mechanisms that lead children to choose among strategies than of those that produce strategy variation. Nevertheless, the model of strategy choice offers a powerful image of development that overcomes deficiencies of the stage approach in accounting for both diversity and constant change in children's thinking.

Attention

The central sections of this chapter address children's processing in the major parts of the cognitive system—how children encode information, operate on it in working memory so it will transfer to long-term memory, and retrieve it so they can think and solve problems. We begin with research on the development of attention. Attention is fundamental to human thinking because it determines the information that will be considered in any task. Parents and teachers notice that young children spend only a short time involved in a task, have difficulty focusing on details, and are easily distracted. During early and middle childhood, attention improves greatly, becoming more selective, adaptable, and planful.

Sustained, Selective, and Adaptable Attention

During the first year, infants attend to novel and eye-catching events, orienting to them more quickly and tracking their movements more effectively (Richards & Holley, 1999). With the transition to toddlerhood, children become increasingly capable of intentional, or goal-directed, be-havior (see Chapter 6, page 223). Consequently, attraction to novelty declines (but does not disappear), and *sustained attention* improves, especially when children play with toys. When toddlers engage in goal-directed behavior even in a limited way, such as stacking blocks or putting them in a container, they must sustain attention to reach the goal. In a study of toddlers and young preschoolers engaged in play

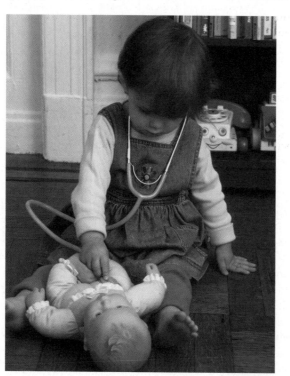

Toddlers and young preschoolers make great strides in sustained attention, especially as they play in goal-directed ways with toys. In turn, they generate more complex play goals, as illustrated by this 4-year-old who, in playing doctor, checks the heartbeat of her doll.
© Laura Dwight/PhotoEdit

with toys, sustained attention increased sharply between 2 and 3½ years of age (Ruff & Capozzoli, 2003).

Rapid growth of the frontal lobes of the cerebral cortex (see Chapter 5), the capacity to generate increasingly complex play goals (children must concentrate to attain them), and adult scaffolding of attention are jointly responsible for this gain in sustained attention. Parents who help their toddlers and young preschoolers maintain a focus of attention—by offering suggestions, questions, and comments about the child's current interest—have children who are more mature, cognitively and socially, when reassessed a year or two later (Bono & Stifter, 2003; Landry et al., 2000). Many skills, including language, exploration, problem solving, social interaction, and cooperation, benefit from an improved ability to concentrate.

As sustained attention increases, children become better at focusing on just those aspects of a situation that are relevant to their goals. Researchers study this increasing selectivity of attention by introducing irrelevant stimuli into a task and seeing how well children respond to its central elements. For example, they might present a stream of numbers on a computer screen and ask children to press a button whenever a particular sequence of two digits (such as "1" and then "9") appears. Findings with this task, and others, show that selective attention improves sharply between ages 6 and 10, with gains continuing into adulthood (Goldberg, Maurer, & Lewis, 2001; Lin, Hsiao, & Chen, 1999; Smith et al., 1998).

Older children also flexibly adapt their attention to task requirements. For example, when asked to sort cards with pictures that vary in both color and shape, children age 5 and older can switch their basis of sorting from color to shape when asked to do so; younger children persist in sorting in just one way (Brooks et al., 2003; Zelazo, Frye, & Rapus, 1996). Furthermore, with age, children adapt their attention to changes in their own learning. When given lists of items to learn and allowed to select half for further study, first graders do not choose systematically. But by third grade, children select those they had previously missed (Masur, McIntyre, & Flavell, 1973). In the study of complex information, such as prose passages, the ability to allocate attention based on previous performance continues to improve into the college years (Brown, Smiley, & Lawton, 1978).

How do children acquire selective, adaptable attentional strategies? Gains in two factors—cognitive inhibition and attentional strategies—are important.

• **COGNITIVE INHIBITION** • Selective attention depends on **cognitive inhibition**—the ability to control internal and external distracting stimuli. Individuals who are skilled at cognitive inhibition can prevent the mind from straying to alternative attractive thoughts and can keep stimuli that are unrelated to a current goal from capturing their attention (Dempster & Corkill, 1999). By ensuring that working memory is not cluttered with irrelevant stimuli, cognitive inhibition supports many information-processing skills (Bjorklund & Harnishfeger, 1995; Handley et al., 2004; Klenberg, Korkman, & Lahti-Nuuttila, 2001). Besides helping children remember, reason, and solve problems, it helps them control behavior in social situations. In later chapters, we will see that to get along with others, children must learn to restrain impulses, keep negative emotions in check, and resist temptation.

The ability to inhibit thoughts and behavior improves from infancy on. Between 3 and 4 years of age, for example, preschoolers perform considerably better in situations in which they must follow some commands but not others, as in the game, "Simon Says." Among younger children, a verbal directive ("Touch your nose") almost always triggers a response (Jones, Rothbart, & Posner, 2003). On more complex tasks that involve ignoring distracting stimuli, marked gains in inhibition occur from early to middle childhood and continue into adolescence (Johnson, Im-Bolter, & Pascual-Leone, 2003). Improved inhibition is linked to development of the cerebral cortex. ERP and fMRI measures reveal a steady, age-related increase in activation of diverse cortical regions, especially the frontal lobes, while children and adolescents engage in activities that require suppression of inappropriate responses (Bartgis, Lilly, & Thomas, 2003; Luna et al., 2001). When the frontal lobes are damaged, children and adults usually cannot ignore irrelevant information (Dempster, 1995).

In sum, by clearing unnecessary stimuli from working memory, cognitive inhibition enhances processing capacity. Greater capacity, in turn, opens the door to effective strategy use, which increases capacity further.

• **ATTENTIONAL STRATEGIES** • Patricia Miller and her colleagues found that development of a selective attentional strategy follows a predictable sequence. They showed 3- to 9-year-olds a large box with rows of doors that could be opened. On half the doors were pictures of cages, indicating that behind each was an animal. On the other half were pictures of houses, indicating that they contained household objects. Children were told to remember the location of each object in one group and that, during a study period, they could open any doors they wished. Memory was tested by showing children pictures of each relevant object, one at a time, and asking them to point to where that object was located (DeMarie-Dreblow & Miller, 1988; Miller et al., 1986; Woody-Ramsey & Miller, 1988). The researchers found that the emergence and refinement of the most efficient attentional strategy—opening only doors with relevant pictures on them—tended to occur in the following four phases:

1. **Production deficiency.** Preschoolers rarely engage in attentional strategies. In other words, they fail to *produce* strategies when they could be helpful. On the task just described, they simply opened all the doors.

2. **Control deficiency.** Slightly older children sometimes produce strategies, but not consistently. They fail to *control*, or execute, strategies effectively. For example, 5-year-olds began to apply a selective attentional strategy—opening only relevant doors—but did not always use it. At times, they reverted to opening irrelevant doors.

3. **Utilization deficiency.** Young elementary school children execute strategies consistently, but their performance either does not improve or improves less than that of older children. For many 6- and 7-year-olds, opening only the relevant doors did not increase memory for locations of objects after the pictures were removed from the doors.

4. **Effective strategy use.** By the mid-elementary school years, children use strategies consistently, and performance improves. (Miller, 2000)

As we will soon see, these phases also characterize children's use of memory strategies. Why, when children first use a strategy, does it sometimes not work well? Recall from our discussion of Siegler's model of strategy choice that initially, applying a strategy requires so much effort and attention that little working memory capacity remains to perform other parts of the task well (Woody-Dorning & Miller, 2001). Consistent with this interpretation, reducing the demands of the task by having an adult perform the strategy for the child (by opening relevant doors) led to substantial gains in memory for object locations (DeMarie-Dreblow & Miller, 1988).

Yet another reason a new strategy may not lead to performance gains is that young children are not good at monitoring their task performance (Schneider & Bjorklund, 1998). Because they fail to keep track of how well a strategy is working, they do not apply it consistently or refine it in other ways.

Planning

With age, children's attention changes in another way: It becomes more planful. **Planning** involves thinking out a sequence of acts ahead of time and allocating attention accordingly to reach a goal (Scholnick, 1995). The seeds of effective planning are present in infancy. When researchers showed 2- and 3-month-olds a series of pictures that alternated in a predictable left–right sequence, the babies quickly learned to shift their focus to the location of the next stimulus before it appeared (Wentworth & Haith, 1998). Even the attention of very young infants seems to be "future oriented," as indicated by their ability to anticipate routine events.

For tasks that are familiar and not too complex, preschoolers sometimes generate and follow a plan. For example, by age 4, they search for a lost object in a play yard systematically, looking only in locations between where they last saw the object and where they discovered it missing (Wellman, Somerville, & Haake, 1979).

Still, planning has a long way to go. When asked to compare detailed pictures, school-age children are more systematic in their visual search than preschoolers (Vurpillot, 1968). And on complex tasks, they make decisions about what to do first and what to do next in a more orderly fashion. In one study, 5- to 9-year-olds were given lists of items to obtain from a play grocery store. Older children more often took time to scan the store before shopping. They also paused more often to look for each item before moving to get it. Consequently, they followed shorter routes through the aisles (Gauvain & Rogoff, 1989; Szepkouski, Gauvain, & Carberry, 1994).

The development of planning illustrates how attention becomes coordinated with other cognitive processes. To solve problems involving multiple steps, children must postpone action in favor of weighing alternatives, organizing task materials (such as items on a grocery list), and remembering the steps of their plan so they can attend to each one in sequence. Along the way, they must monitor how well the plan works and revise it if necessary. Clearly, planning places heavy demands on working-memory capacity. Not surprisingly, even when young children do plan, they often forget important steps.

Children learn much from cultural tools that support planning, including directions for making objects and playing games, recipes for cooking, and patterns for sewing and construction—especially when they collaborate with more expert planners. When 4- to 7-year-olds were observed jointly constructing a toy with their mothers using a step-by-step plan, the mothers tailored their support to children's understanding. They gave preschoolers more introductory information about the usefulness of plans and how to implement specific steps—for example, "Do you want to look at the picture and see what goes where? What piece do you need for number one?" Older children received more information about the features of plans, as in, "This part of the picture is blown up, so you can see how to put these small parts together." After working with their mothers, younger children referred to the plan more often when building on their own (Gauvain, 2004; Gauvain, Ossa, & Hurtado-Ortiz, 2001). Having many opportunities to practice planning helps children understand its components and use that knowledge. Parents can foster planning by encouraging it in everyday activities, from homework assignments to loading the dishwasher. The demands of school tasks—and teachers' explanations for how to plan—also contribute to improved planning.

The attentional strategies we have considered are crucial for success in school. Unfortunately, some school-age children have great difficulty paying attention. See the Biology and Environment box on pages 284–285 for a discussion of the serious learning and behavior problems of children with attention-deficit hyperactivity disorder.

◎ This boy participates in traditional Viking boat building under the guidance of an expert in Newfoundland, Canada. By engaging in this complex, multi-stepped project, the child learns important lessons about planning—what to do first and what to do next in an orderly fashion.
© Richard T. Nowitz/CORBIS

Ask Yourself

REVIEW	What aspect of brain development supports gains in cognitive inhibition? How does cognitive inhibition increase processing capacity?
REVIEW	Cite advances in information processing that contribute to improved planning in middle childhood. What can adults do to promote children's planning skills?
APPLY	At age 7, Jonah played his piano pieces from beginning to end instead of spending extra time on the hard sections. Around age 8, he devoted more time to sections he knew least well, but his performance did not improve for several months. What explains Jonah's gradual strategy development and improvement in performance?
REFLECT	Describe an instance in which you applied a strategy for the first time but experienced a utilization deficiency. Why do you think the deficiency occurred, and how did you overcome it?

BIOLOGY AND ENVIRONMENT

Children with Attention-Deficit Hyperactivity Disorder

While the other fifth graders worked quietly at their desks, Calvin squirmed, dropped his pencil, looked out the window, fiddled with his shoelaces, and talked aloud. "Hey Joey," he yelled over the heads of several classmates, "wanna play ball after school?" But Joey and the other children weren't eager to play with Calvin. On the playground, Calvin was physically awkward and failed to follow the rules of the game. He had trouble taking turns at bat; in the outfield, he tossed his mitt up in the air and always seemed to be looking elsewhere when the ball came his way. Calvin's desk was a chaotic mess. He often lost pencils, books, and other materials he needed to complete his work, and he had difficulty remembering assignments and when they were due.

Symptoms of ADHD

Calvin is one of 3 to 5 percent of school-age children with **attention-deficit hyperactivity disorder (ADHD),** which involves inattention, impulsivity, and excessive motor activity resulting in academic and social problems (American Psychiatric Association, 1994). Boys are diagnosed three to nine times more often than girls. However, many girls with ADHD may be overlooked because their symptoms usually are not as flagrant (Abikoff et al., 2002).

Children with ADHD cannot stay focused on a task that requires mental effort for more than a few minutes. In addition, they often act impulsively, ignoring social rules and lashing out with hostility when frustrated. Many (but not all) are *hyperactive.* They charge through their days with excessive motor activity, exhausting parents and teachers and so irritating other children that they are quickly rejected. For a child to be diagnosed with ADHD, these symptoms must have appeared before age 7 as a persistent problem.

Because of their difficulty concentrating, children with ADHD score 7 to 15 points lower than other children on intelligence tests (Barkley, 2002a). According to one view that has amassed substantial research support, two related deficits underlie ADHD symptoms: (1) an impairment in executive processing (refer to the central executive in Figure 7.1 on page 273), which interferes with the child's ability to use thought to guide behavior, and (2) an impairment in inhibition, which makes it difficult to delay action in favor of thought (Barkley, 2003b). Consequently, such children do poorly on tasks requiring sustained attention, find it hard to ignore irrelevant information, and have difficulty with memory, planning, reasoning, and

problem solving in academic and social situations (Barkley, 2003b).

Origins of ADHD

ADHD runs in families and is highly heritable: Identical twins share it much more often than fraternal twins do (Rasmussen et al., 2004; Rietvelt et al., 2004). Children with ADHD also show abnormal brain functioning, including reduced electrical and blood-flow activity and structural abnormalities in the *frontal lobes* of the cerebral cortex and in other areas involved in attention, inhibition of behavior, and additional aspects of motor control. These include the *caudate nucleus,* a cortical structure that translates commands from the frontal cortex into motor behavior, and the *cerebellum,* a structure at the rear and base of the brain that supports both motor control and executive processing (see page 186 in Chapter 5) (Castellanos et al., 2003; Sowell et al., 2003). Also, the brains of children with ADHD grow more slowly and are about 3 percent smaller in overall volume than those of those unaffected agemates (Castellanos et al., 2002; Durston et al., 2004). Several genes that affect neurotransmitter and hormone levels have been implicated in the disorder (Biederman & Spencer, 2000; Quist & Kennedy, 2001).

Memory

As attention improves, so do memory strategies, deliberate mental activities we use to increase the likelihood of holding information in working memory and transferring it to our long-term knowledge base. Although memory strategies emerge during the preschool years, at first they are not very successful. In middle childhood, these techniques take a giant leap forward (Schneider, 2002).

Strategies for Storing Information

Researchers have studied the development of three strategies that enhance memory for new information: rehearsal, organization, and elaboration.

At the same time, ADHD is associated with environmental factors. Prenatal teratogens—particularly those involving long-term exposure, such as illegal drugs, alcohol, and cigarettes—are linked to inattention and hyperactivity (Milberger et al., 1997). Furthermore, children with ADHD are more likely to come from homes in which marriages are unhappy and family stress is high (Bernier & Siegel, 1994). But a stressful home life rarely causes ADHD. Instead, the behaviors of these children can contribute to family problems, which intensify the child's preexisting difficulties.

Treating ADHD

Calvin's doctor eventually prescribed stimulant medication, the most common treatment for ADHD. As long as dosage is carefully regulated, these drugs reduce activity level and improve attention, academic performance, and peer relations for about 70 percent of children who take them (Greenhill, Halperin, & Abikoff, 1999). Stimulant medication seems to increase activity in the frontal lobes, thereby improving the child's capacity to sustain attention and to inhibit off-task and self-stimulating behavior.

Although stimulant medication is relatively safe, its impact is short-term. Drugs cannot teach children to compensate for inattention and impulsivity. The most effective treatment approach combines medication with interventions that model and reinforce appropriate academic and social behavior (Arnold et al., 2003). Family inter-

vention is also important. Inattentive, overactive children strain the patience of parents, who are likely to react punitively and inconsistently—a child-rearing style that strengthens inappropriate behavior. Breaking this cycle through training parents in effective child-rearing skills is as important for children with ADHD as it is for the defiant, aggressive youngsters discussed in Chapter 12. In fact, in 45 to 65 percent of cases, these two sets of behavior problems occur together (Barkley, 2002b).

Although some media reports suggest that the number of North American children diagnosed with ADHD has increased greatly, two large surveys yielded similar overall prevalence rates 20 years ago and today. Nevertheless, the incidence of ADHD is much higher in some communities than others. At times, children are overdiagnosed and unnecessarily medicated because of their parents' and teachers' impatience with inattentive, active behavior that is actually within normal range. At other times, children are underdiagnosed and do not receive the treatment they need. In Great Britain, for example, doctors' hesitancy to label children as ADHD and to prescribe medication leaves many highly inattentive and hyperactive children undiagnosed. In Hong Kong, where academic success is particularly important, children are diagnosed at

▲ This girl frequently engages in disruptive behavior at school. Children with ADHD have great difficulty staying on task and often act impulsively, ignoring social rules.
© Christina Kennedy/PhotoEdit

more than twice the rate seen in North America (Taylor, 2004).

ADHD is a lifelong disorder, with affected individuals at risk for persistent antisocial behavior, depression, and other problems (Barkley, 2003a; Fisher et al., 2002). In adulthood, people with ADHD continue to need help structuring their environments, regulating negative emotion, selecting appropriate careers, and understanding their condition as a biological deficit rather than a character flaw.

• **REHEARSAL AND ORGANIZATION** • The next time you have a list of things to learn, such as major cities in your state or country, or items to buy at the grocery store, take note of your behavior. You are likely to repeat the information to yourself, a memory strategy called **rehearsal.** And you will probably group related items (for example, all the cities in the same part of the country), a strategy called **organization.**

Why are young children not adept at rehearsal and organization? Memory strategies require sufficient working-memory capacity and time and effort to perfect. Even when school-age children begin to use these strategies more often—around age 7 for rehearsal and age 8 for organization—many show *control* and *utilization deficiencies* (Bjorklund & Coyle, 1995). For example, 7- to 8-year-olds often rehearse in a piecemeal fashion. After being given

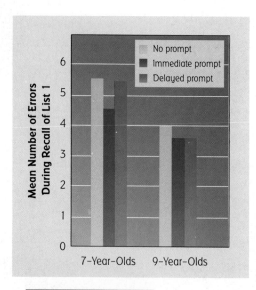

▲ Figure 7.7

Influence of 7- and 9-year-olds' use of organization as a memory strategy on retroactive interference. When given two lists of toys to memorize, 9-year-olds experienced less retroactive interference (made fewer errors in recall of list 1) than 7-year-olds overall. The younger children profited from an immediate prompt to reorganize list 2 into vehicles. The older children benefited from both an immediate prompt and a delayed prompt, given one day later just prior to a test for retention. They could switch their basis of categorization after a day's delay. (Adapted from Howe, 2004.)

the word *cat* in a list of items, they say, "Cat, cat, cat." In contrast, older children combine previous words with each new item, saying "Desk, man, yard, cat, cat," an approach that results in much better memory (Kunzinger, 1985). Similarly, younger children usually organize items by their association in everyday life: "hat–head," "carrot–rabbit." Older children group such items into clothing, body parts, food, and animals. These more abstract, *taxonomic categories* (based on common properties) permit children to organize more efficiently by placing a greater number of items in a few categories. Consequently, recall improves dramatically (Bjorklund et al., 1994).

Experience with materials that form clear categories helps children use organization and apply the strategy to less clearly related materials. In longitudinal research, many young schoolchildren organized inconsistently (a *control deficiency*) and, when they did organize, showed little or no gain in performance (a *utilization deficiency*). In contrast, between ages 8 and 10, after realizing how effective organization is, most children suddenly began using it regularly, and their recall improved immediately (Schlagmüller & Schneider, 2002; Weinert & Schneider, 1999).

Skillful use of organization helps reduce *retroactive interference*, a common memory problem in which newly acquired information impairs memory for previously learned, similar information. In one study, 7- and 9-year-olds learned two lists of toys. Then some children were exposed to a memory prompt, either immediately or one day later, just before a test for retention: An adult pointed out that the items in list 2 could also be categorized as vehicles, to differentiate them from list 1. As Figure 7.7 shows, the younger children displayed less retroactive interference (fewer errors on list 1) only when prompted to reorganize list 2 immediately after learning. The older children, in contrast, profited from both immediate and delayed prompting (Howe, 2004). As more effective organizers, they could switch their basis of categorization to aid their memories, even after a day's delay.

Furthermore, older children are more likely to apply several memory strategies at once, rehearsing, organizing, and stating category names. The more strategies they use simultaneously, the better they remember (Coyle & Bjorklund, 1997). Although younger children's use of multiple memory strategies has little impact on performance, their tendency to experiment is adaptive, allowing them to discover which strategies work best on different tasks and how to combine them effectively. For example, second to fourth graders know that a good way to study lists is to organize the items first, next rehearse category names, and then rehearse individual items (Hock, Park, & Bjorklund, 1998). Recall from Siegler's model of strategy choice that children experiment with strategies when faced with many cognitive challenges.

• **ELABORATION** • By the end of middle childhood, children start to use a third memory strategy, **elaboration**. It involves creating a relationship, or shared meaning, between two or more pieces of information that are not members of the same category. For example, if two of the words you must learn are *fish* and *pipe*, you might generate the verbal statement or mental image, "The fish is smoking a pipe." Elaboration is a highly effective memory technique, which becomes more common during adolescence as young people improve at holding two or more items in mind while generating meaningful associations. Elaboration develops late because it requires considerable effort and working-memory capacity (Schneider & Pressley, 1997).

CULTURE, SCHOOLING, AND MEMORY STRATEGIES • Rehearsal, organization, and elaboration are techniques that people usually employ when they need to remember information for its own sake. On many other occasions, memory occurs as a natural by-product of participation in daily activities (Rogoff, 2003). In a study illustrating this idea, 4- and 5-year-olds were told either to *play with* a set of toys or to *remember* them. The play condition produced far better recall. Rather than just naming or touching objects, the children engaged in many spontaneous organizations that helped them recall. These included common uses of objects (putting a shoe on a doll's foot) and narrating their activities: "I'm squeezing this lemon," or "Fly away in this helicopter, doggie" (Newman, 1990).

These findings help explain why the Kpelle farmers described at the beginning of this chapter viewed grouping by everyday use as "the wise way" to organize familiar objects. People in non-Western cultures who have no formal schooling rarely use or benefit from instruction in memory strategies because they see no practical reason to use these techniques (Rogoff & Mistry, 1985).

Tasks that require children to remember isolated bits of information, which are common in school, provide a great deal of motivation to use memory strategies. In fact, Western children get so much practice with this type of learning that they do not refine techniques that rely on spatial location and arrangement of objects—cues that are readily available in everyday life (Mistry, 1997). For example, Guatemalan Mayan 9-year-olds do slightly better than their North American agemates when told to remember the placement of 40 familiar objects in a play scene. North American children often rehearse object names when it would be more effective to keep track of spatial relations (Rogoff & Waddell, 1982). Viewed in this way, the development of memory strategies is not just a matter of a more competent information-processing system. It is also a product of task demands and cultural circumstances.

Retrieving Information

Once information enters our long-term knowledge base, we must *retrieve* (or recover) it to use it again. Information can be retrieved from memory in three ways: through recognition, recall, and reconstruction. As we discuss the development of these approaches to remembering, we will consider how children's expanding knowledge base affects their memory performance. We will also delve into the accuracy of a special type of memory—children's eyewitness accounts in legal proceedings—that can seriously affect their own and others' welfare.

• **RECOGNITION AND RECALL** • Try showing a young child a set of 10 pictures or toys. Then mix them up with some unfamiliar items and ask the child to point to the ones in the original set. Noticing that a stimulus is identical or similar to one previously experienced is called **recognition.** It is the simplest form of retrieval, since the material to be remembered is fully present during testing to serve as its own retrieval cue.

As habituation research discussed in Chapters 4 and 6 shows, even young infants are good at recognition. The ability to recognize a larger number of stimuli over longer delays improves steadily with age, reaching a near-adult level during the preschool years. For example, after viewing a series of 80 pictures, 4-year-olds correctly discriminated 90 percent from pictures not in the original set (Brown & Campione, 1972). Because recognition appears early and develops rapidly, it is probably a fairly automatic process that does not depend on a deliberate search of long-term memory. Nevertheless, the ability of older children to apply strategies during storage, such as rehearsal and organization, increases the number of items recognized later (Mandler & Robinson, 1978).

Now give the child a more challenging task. While keeping the items out of view, ask the child to name the ones she saw. This requires **recall**—generating a mental representation of an absent stimulus. The beginnings of recall appear before 1 year of age as long as memories are strongly cued. Think back to our discussion of deferred imitation in Chapter 6. Its presence in infancy is good evidence for recall. Nevertheless, one of the most obvious features of young children's memories is that their recall in tasks that require retention of pieces of information is much poorer than their recognition. At age 2 they can recall no more than one or two items, at age 4 only about 3 or 4 (Perlmutter, 1984).

Of course, recognition is much easier than recall for adults as well. Still, in comparison to older children and adults, young children's recall is quite deficient. Better recall in early childhood is strongly associated with language development, which greatly enhances long-lasting representations of past experiences (Simcock & Hayne, 2003). But even when asked to recall an event that happened weeks earlier, young children report only part of what could be remembered. In one longitudinal study, sixth graders were asked to tell what happened when they went to an archeological museum in kindergarten. They said less about the experience than when they had been asked the same question as kindergartners, 6 weeks after the

⊚ A father in Kabul, Afghanistan, draws water from a well, and his son distributes it among ceramic pitchers. As the boy engages in this meaningful work, he demonstrates keen memory for relevant information—how to pour without spilling, how much water each pitcher can hold. Yet on a list-memory task of the kind often given in school, he may not perform well.
© Richard Lord/The Image Works

museum trip. But in response to specific retrieval cues, including photos of the event, sixth graders remembered a great deal. And in some respects, their recall was more accurate. For example, they inferred that adults had hidden artifacts in a sandbox for them to find, whereas in kindergarten they simply recalled digging for objects (Hudson & Fivush, 1991).

Compared with recognition, recall shows far greater improvement because older children make use of a wider range of retrieval cues. With age, the long-term knowledge base grows larger and becomes organized into increasingly elaborate, hierarchically structured networks (Schneider, 2002). When representations of experiences are interconnected in long-term memory, many internal retrieval cues can be used to recall them later.

• **RECONSTRUCTION** • Read the following passage about George, an escaped convict. Then close your book and try to write the story down or tell it to a friend:

> George was alone. He knew they would soon be here. They were not far behind him when he left the village, hungry and cold. He dared not stop for food or shelter for fear of falling into the hands of his pursuers. There were many of them; they were strong and he was weak. George could hear the noise as the uniformed band beat its way through the trees not far behind him. The sense of their presence was everywhere. His spine tingled with fear. Eagerly he awaited the darkness. In darkness he would find safety. (Brown et al., 1977, p. 1456)

Now compare your version with the original. Is it a faithful reproduction? Or did you add to, condense, or distort information?

When we must remember complex, meaningful material, we do not merely copy material into the system at storage and faithfully reproduce it at retrieval. Instead, we select and interpret information we encounter in our everyday lives in terms of our existing knowledge. Once we have transformed the material, we often have difficulty distinguishing it from the original (Bartlett, 1932). Notice how this *constructivist* approach to information processing is consistent with Piaget's theory, especially his notion of assimilating new information to existing schemes (Schneider & Bjorklund, 1998).

Constructive processing can take place during any phase of information processing. It can occur during storage. In fact, the memory strategies of organization and elaboration are within the province of constructive memory because both involve generating relationships between stimuli. Constructive processing can also involve **reconstruction** of information, or recoding it while it is in the system or being retrieved.

Do children reconstruct stored information? The answer is clearly yes. Children's reconstructive processing has been studied by asking them to recall stories. When children retell a story, like adults, they condense, integrate, and add information. By age 5 or 6, children recall the important features of a story and forget the unimportant ones, combine information into more tightly knit units, reorder the sequence of events to make it more logical, and even include new information that fits with the meaning of a passage (Bischofshausen, 1985). For example, after elementary school students listened to the story of George, the escaped convict, their reconstructions included the following statements: "All the prison guards were chasing him." "He was running so the police would be so far away that their dogs would not catch his trail" (Brown et al., 1977, p. 1459).

Furthermore, when children receive new information related to a story they previously recalled, they reconstruct the story further. In one study, before telling each of three stories, an adult gave kindergartners information about a main character that was positive ("a nice" child), negative ("not a nice" child), or neutral. Children reconstructed the main character's behaviors to fit with prior information (Greenhoot, 2000). Those in the positive condition offered a more positive account and those in the negative condition a more negative account than did those in the neutral condition. Seven to 10 days later, a fourth story provided children with additional information about the main character.

◉ On the Kanawake Mohawk reservation in Montreal, Canada, a girl tells a story to her friends. In doing so, she selects and interprets events and details, engaging in the memory process called reconstruction.

© Martha Cooper/Peter Arnold, Inc.

In some conditions, the new information was consistent with the original information, whereas in others, it conflicted—for example, the "nice child" was described as a "mean child." Children again revised their recollections of the main character's behavior accordingly. And in a further recall session, the children's reconstructions were even more biased in that direction.

In revising information in meaningful ways, children provide themselves with a wealth of helpful retrieval cues that they can use during recall. Over time, as originally provided information decays, children make more inferences about actors and actions, adding events and interpretations that help make sense of a story. This process increases the coherence of reconstructed information and, therefore, its memorableness. At the same time, as these findings reveal, much of the information children and adults recall can be inaccurate.

• **ANOTHER VIEW OF RECONSTRUCTION: FUZZY-TRACE THEORY** • So far, we have emphasized deliberate reconstruction of meaningful material, using new information and the long-term knowledge base to interpret it. According to C. J. Brainerd and Valerie Reyna's (1993, 2001) **fuzzy-trace theory,** when we first encode information, we reconstruct it automatically, creating a vague, fuzzy version called a **gist,** which preserves essential content without details and is especially useful for reasoning. Although we can retain a literal, verbatim version as well, we have a bias toward gist because it requires less working-memory capacity, freeing attention for the steps involved in thinking. For example, consider a person choosing among several recipes to prepare a dish for dinner. To decide, he relies on gist representations, noting which recipes are easier and have low-cost ingredients. But once he has selected a recipe, he needs verbatim information to prepare it. Because he is unlikely to have remembered those details, he consults the cookbook.

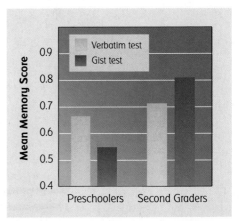

▲ **Figure 7.8**

Preschoolers' and second graders' performance on verbatim and gist memory questions. Preschoolers did better on the verbatim than the gist memory test, whereas the reverse was true for second graders. (Adapted from Brainerd & Gordon, 1994.)

Fuzzy-trace theorists take issue with the assumption that all reconstructions are transformations of verbatim memory. Instead, they believe that both verbatim and gist memories are present and are stored separately so they can be used for different purposes. In support of this idea, shortly after being read a brief story, children can discriminate between sentences they actually heard and ones they did not hear but that are consistent with the story's gist. Only over time, as the complete, verbatim memory decays more quickly than the efficiently represented gist, do children begin to say that statements consistent with but not actually in the story were ones they heard (Reyna & Kiernan, 1994). Fuzzy-trace theory also helps us understand why children (and adults) often reason effectively without recalling specifics.

With age, children rely less on verbatim memory and more on fuzzy, reconstructed gists. To illustrate this change, researchers presented children with the following problem: "Farmer Brown owns many animals. He has 3 dogs, 5 sheep, 7 chickens, 9 horses, and 11 cows." Then the researchers asked two types of questions: (1) questions requiring verbatim knowledge ("How many cows does Farmer Brown own, 11 or 9?") and (2) questions requiring only gist information ("Does Farmer Brown have more cows or more horses?"). As Figure 7.8 shows, preschoolers were better at answering verbatim- than gist-dependent questions, whereas the reverse was true for second graders (Brainerd & Gordon, 1994).

Fuzzy-trace theory adds to our understanding of reconstruction by indicating that it can occur immediately, as soon as information is encoded, without distorting verbatim memories. The extent to which gist and verbatim representations undergo further reconstruction depends on the type of task (telling an entire story versus answering a single question) and the passage of time. Fuzzy-trace research reveals that although memory is vital for reasoning, getting bogged down in details (as young children tend to do) can interfere with effective problem solving. And because fuzzy traces are less likely than verbatim memories to be forgotten, gists can serve as enduring retrieval cues, contributing to improved recall with age (Brainerd & Reyna, 1995).

The Knowledge Base and Memory Performance

We have suggested that children's expanding knowledge promotes improved memory by making new, related information more meaningful so that it is easier to store and retrieve. To test this idea, Michelene Chi (1978) looked at how well third- through eighth-grade chess experts could remember complex chessboard arrangements. The children recalled the configurations

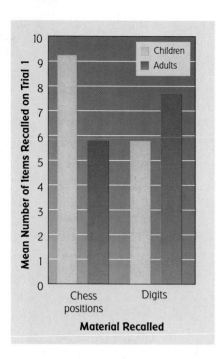

◄ Figure 7.9

Performance of skilled child chess players and adults on two tasks: memory for complex chessboard arrangements and memory for numerical digits. The child chess experts recalled more on the chess task, the adults on the digit task. These findings show that size of the knowledge base contributes to memory performance. (Adapted from Chi, 1978.)

considerably better than adults who knew how to play chess but were not especially knowledgeable—findings that cannot be explained by the selection of very bright youngsters with exceptional memories. When the same participants recalled a list of numbers, the adults did better (see Figure 7.9).

In Chi's study of chess-playing children, better memory was credited to a larger knowledge base. Experts also have more elaborately structured knowledge. In another study, researchers classified elementary school children as either experts or novices in knowledge of soccer. Then they gave both groups lists of soccer and nonsoccer items to learn. As in Chi's study, experts remembered far more items on the soccer list (but not on the nonsoccer list) than nonexperts (Schneider & Bjorklund, 1992). And during recall, the experts' listing of items was better organized, as indicated by clustering of items into categories. This greater organization at retrieval suggests that highly knowledgeable children apply memory strategies in their area of expertise with little or no effort—by rapidly associating new items with the large number they already know. Because their recall *is automatized*, experts can devote more working-memory capacity to using recalled information to reason and solve problems (Bjorklund & Douglas, 1997).

Though powerfully influential, knowledge is not the only important factor in children's strategic memory processing. Children who are expert in an area are usually highly motivated as well. Faced with new information, they ask themselves, "What can I do to learn this more effectively?" As a result, they not only acquire knowledge more quickly but also *actively use what they know* to add more. In contrast, academically unsuccessful children fail to ask how previously stored information can clarify new material. This, in turn, interferes with the development of a broad knowledge base (Schneider & Bjorklund, 1998). In sum, extensive knowledge and use of memory strategies support one another.

Scripts

Our vast, taxonomically organized and hierarchically structured general knowledge system, often called **semantic memory,** must grow out of the young child's **episodic memory,** or memory for many personally experienced events. How semantic memory emerges from specific, real-world experiences is one of the most puzzling questions about memory development.

Like adults, preschoolers remember familiar events—what you do when you go to child care or get ready for bed—in terms of **scripts,** general descriptions of what occurs and when it occurs in a particular situation. Young children's scripts begin as a structure of main acts. For example, when asked to tell what happens at a restaurant, a 3-year-old might say, "You go in, get the food, eat, and then pay." Although children's first scripts contain only a few acts, they are almost always recalled in correct sequence. This is true even for 1- and 2-year-olds, who cannot yet verbally describe events but can act them out with toys. Still, adults must work hard to obtain young children's scripted reports, asking questions and prompting (Bauer, 1997, 2002). With age, scripts become more spontaneous and elaborate, as in the following restaurant account given by a 5-year-old child: "You go in. You can sit in the booths or at a table. Then you tell the waitress what you want. You eat. If you want dessert, you can have some. Then you pay and go home" (Hudson, Fivush, & Kuebli, 1992).

Scripts are a special form of reconstructive memory. When we experience repeated events, we fuse them into the same script representation. Then any specific instance of a scripted experience becomes hard to recall. For example, unless it was out of the ordinary, you probably cannot remember exactly what you had for dinner two days ago. The same is true for young children. In this way, scripts prevent long-term memory from being cluttered with unimportant information.

Ⓢ As this athletic girl expands her knowledge of the intricacies of soccer, she will be increasingly able to commit new soccer information to memory and recall it automatically by rapidly associating new information with what she already knows.

© Peter Hvizdak/The Image Works

Scripts are a basic means through which children (and adults) organize and interpret everyday experiences. Once formed, they can be used to predict what will happen on similar occasions in the future. Young children rely on scripts in make-believe play and when listening to and telling stories. Scripts also support children's earliest efforts at planning by helping them represent sequences of actions that lead to desired goals (Hudson, Sosa, & Shapiro, 1997).

Some researchers believe that scripts are the developmental link between early episodic memory and a semantic memory store (Lucariello, 1998). In several studies, preschoolers remembered script-related items (such as peanut butter, bologna, cheese—lunch foods) in clustered form and recalled them more easily than a list of items belonging to the same taxonomic category (toast, cheese, ice cream—foods) (Lucariello, Kyratzis, & Nelson, 1992; Yu & Nelson, 1993). As children develop an array of script sequences, they may merge objects that share the same function but occur in different scripts (eating toast for breakfast, peanut butter for lunch) into a typical taxonomic category (food).

Although scripts may support children's taxonomic categorization, they are not the exclusive means through which children build their semantic memories. Recall from Chapter 6 that even preschoolers can sort objects into categories at different levels of generality (basic, superordinate, and subordinate) and move back and forth between those levels (see page 240). In a series of studies, 3- to 7-year-olds could categorize food items into both script and taxonomic categories. Although the children categorized more accurately with age, they did not shift from script to taxonomic categorization (Nguyen & Murphy, 2003). Nevertheless, when given a choice between matching a food item (bologna) with a script associate (cheese) or a taxonomic associate (ice cream), 3-year-olds showed no preference (both types of categories were just forming), 4-year-olds preferred the script category, and 7-year-olds preferred the taxonomic category.

By age 7, children clearly use script and taxonomic categories for different purposes—the former to group items on the basis of shared everyday situations, the latter to group items on the basis of common properties (Nguyen & Murphy, 2003). Just how children build and structure their semantic memory remains largely unknown. As we saw in Chapter 6, vocabulary development and adult explanations of category memberships are helpful.

Ⓖ Over time, this child is unlikely to remember the details of this particular breakfast. Instead, she will fuse the event with other similar events and recall it in script form—in terms of what typically occurs when she gets up in the morning.
© Michelle D. Bridwell/PhotoEdit

Autobiographical Memory

Scripts are not the only type of episodic memory. Another is **autobiographical memory,** representations of one-time events that are long-lasting because they are imbued with personal meaning. Perhaps you recall the day a sibling was born, the first time you took an airplane, or a birthday celebration. How does memory for autobiographical events develop and persist for a lifetime?

Research indicates that at least two developments are important for children to form an autobiographical memory. First, they must have a sufficiently clear self-image to serve as an anchor for personally significant events. That is, they must be able to encode events as "something that happened to me"—a milestone reached around 2 years of age (see Chapter 11) (Howe, 2003). Second, children must integrate their experiences into a meaningful, time-organized life story. They learn to structure personally significant memories in narrative form by conversing about them with adults, who expand on their fragmented recollections (Nelson, 1993). As early as 1½ to 2 years, children start to talk about the past, and their capacity to participate in memory-related conversations increases greatly during early childhood. In this short excerpt, a mother is talking with her nearly 3-year-old daughter about a recent Halloween celebration:

Child: Once on Halloween the kids was over and I had a princess dress on me.

Mother: You had a princess dress on? Did you get any candy? Did you go door to door? What happened?

Child: We went treating.

Mother: You went treating! And who took you?

Child: Andrea's mother took us ... and we brought a pumpkin too.

Mother: What did you do with the pumpkin?

Child: We lighted it.

Mother: What did it look like? Was it scary?

Child: Uh-huh. Dad made cuts in it with a razor. He made a face too. That was funny.

(Fivush & Hamond, 1990, p. 223)

⑨ Parents who talk about the past help their children build an autobiographical narrative of personally meaningful experiences. As this boy discusses photos in the family album with his father, he recalls significant events and integrates them into his life story.
© Jeff Greenberg/Index Stock

Parents' conversations about the past become more complex as preschoolers' language skills expand. As children participate in these dialogues, they adopt the narrative thinking that the dialogues generate. Notice how this process is consistent with Vygotsky's theory that social interaction with more expert partners leads to new cognitive skills (see Chapter 6).

Adults use two styles to elicit children's autobiographical narratives. Parents who use the *elaborative style* ask many and varied questions, add information to children's statements, and volunteer their own recollections and evaluations of events, as the mother did in the conversation just given. In contrast, parents who use the *repetitive style* provide little information and ask the same short-answer questions over and over: "Do you remember the zoo?" "What did we do at the zoo?" "What did we do there?" These differences depend, in part, on the emotional quality of the parent–child relationship. Parents and preschoolers with secure attachment bonds engage in more elaborate reminiscing, whereas those with insecure bonds generally limit themselves to the repetitive style (Fivush & Reese, 2002). Preschoolers who experience elaborative dialogues produce more coherent and detailed personal stories when followed up 1 to 2 years later (Farrant & Reese, 2000; Reese, Haden, & Fivush, 1993).

Between 2 and 6 years, children's descriptions of special, one-time occurrences become better organized, detailed, and evaluative (and therefore imbued with personal meaning). Older children also add more background information, placing events in the larger context of their lives (Fivush, Haden, & Adam, 1995; Haden, Haine, & Fivush, 1997). Girls are more advanced than boys in this sequence. And Western children produce narratives with more talk about thoughts, emotions, and preferences than do Asian children. These differences fit with variations in parent–child conversations. Parents reminisce in more detail with daughters (Bruce, Dolan, & Phillips-Grant, 2000; Reese, Haden, & Fivush, 1996). And collectivist cultural values lead Asian parents to discourage their children from talking about themselves (Han, Leichtman, & Wang, 1998). Perhaps because women's early experiences were integrated into more coherent narratives, they report an earlier age of first memory and more vivid early memories than men report. Similarly, first memories of Western adults are, on the average, 6 months earlier than those of Asians (Wang, 2003).

Nevertheless, practically none of us can retrieve events that happened to us before age 3. Yet much evidence shows that we both learned and remembered during our early years. Why do we experience this *infantile amnesia?* Refer to the Biology and Environment box on the following page for research aimed at answering this question.

Eyewitness Memory

Until recently, children younger than age 5 were rarely asked to testify, and not until age 10 were they assumed fully competent to do so. As a result of societal reactions to rising rates of child abuse and the difficulty of prosecuting perpetrators, legal requirements for child testimony have been relaxed in the United States and Canada. Children as young as age 3 frequently serve as witnesses (Ceci & Bruck, 1998).

Compared with preschoolers, school-age children are better at giving accurate, detailed descriptions of past experiences and correctly inferring others' motives and intentions. Older children are also more resistant to misleading questions of the sort attorneys ask when they probe for more information or, in cross-examination, try to influence the content of the child's

Infantile Amnesia

If infants and toddlers remember many aspects of their everyday lives, how do we explain **infantile amnesia**—that most of us cannot retrieve events that happened to us before age 3? The reason for this forgetting cannot be merely the passage of time, because we can recall many events that happened long ago (Eacott, 1999). At present, several complementary explanations of infantile amnesia exist.

One theory credits brain development. Vital changes in the frontal lobes of the cerebral cortex may pave the way for an *explicit* memory system—one in which children remember deliberately rather than *implicitly*, without conscious awareness (Boyer & Diamond, 1992; Rovee-Collier & Barr, 2001). In support of this idea, 9- and 10-year-olds shown pictures of their preschool classmates react physiologically in ways consistent with remembering, even when they do not consciously recall the child (Newcombe & Fox, 1994).

A related conjecture is that older children and adults often use verbal means for storing information, whereas infants' and toddlers' memory processing is largely nonverbal—an incompatibility that may prevent long-term retention of their experiences. To test this idea, researchers sent two adults to the homes of 2- to 4-year-olds with a highly unusual toy that the children were likely to remember: The Magic Shrinking Machine, depicted in Figure 7.10. One of the adults showed the child how, after inserting an object in an opening on top of the machine and turning a crank that activated flashing lights and musical sounds, the child could retrieve a smaller, identical object from behind a door on the front of the machine. (The second adult discreetly dropped the smaller object down a chute leading to the door.) The child was encouraged to participate as the machine "shrunk" additional objects.

A day later, the researchers tested the children to see how well they recalled the event. Results revealed that their nonverbal memory—based on acting out the "shrinking" event and recognizing the "shrunken" objects in photos—was excellent. But even when they had the vocabulary, children younger than age 3 had trouble describing features of the "shrinking" experience. Verbal recall increased sharply between ages 3 and 4—the period during which children "scramble over the amnesia barrier" (Simcock & Hayne, 2003, p. 813). A second study showed that preschoolers could not translate their nonverbal memory for the game into language after 6 months to 1 year had elapsed and their language had improved dramatically. Their verbal reports were "frozen in time," reflecting their limited language skill at the time they played the game (Simcock & Hayne, 2002).

These findings help us reconcile infants' and toddlers' remarkable memory skills with infantile amnesia. During the first few years, children rely heavily on nonverbal techniques, such as visual images and motor actions, to remember. As language develops, children first use words to talk about the here and now. Only after age 3 do they often represent events verbally and participate in elaborate conversations with adults about them. As children encode one-time events in verbal form, they increase the accessibility of those memories at later ages because they can use language-based cues to retrieve them (Hayne, 2004).

At the same time, other findings suggest that the advent of a clear self-image contributes to the end of infantile amnesia. In longitudinal research, toddlers who were advanced in development of a sense of self demonstrated better verbal memories a year later while conversing about past events with their mothers (Harley & Reese, 1999). Very likely, the decline of infantile amnesia is a change to which both biology and social experience contribute. Brain development and adult–child interaction may jointly foster self-awareness and language, which permit children to talk with adults about significant past experiences (Nelson & Fivush, 2004). As a result, preschoolers begin to construct a long-lasting autobiographical narrative of their lives and enter into the history of their family and community.

▼ **Figure 7.10**

The Magic Shrinking Machine, used to test young children's verbal and nonverbal memory of an unusual event. After being shown how the machine worked, the child participated in selecting objects from a polka-dot bag, dropping them into the top of the machine (a), and turning a crank, which produced a "shrunken" object (b). When tested the next day, 2 to 4-year-olds' nonverbal memory for the event was excellent. But below 36 months, verbal recall was poor, based on the number of features recalled about the game during an open-ended interview (c). Recall improved between 36 and 48 months, the period during which infantile amnesia subsides. (From G. Simcock & H. Hayne, 2003, "Age-Related Changes in Verbal and Nonverbal Memory During Early Childhood," *Developmental Psychology, 39,* pp. 806, 808. Copyright © by the American Psychological Association. Reprinted by permission.) Photos: Ross Coombes/Courtesy of Harlene Hayne.

(a)

(b)

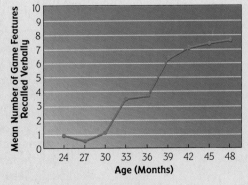

(c)

response (Roebers & Schneider, 2001). What makes younger children more prone to memory errors? Several factors are involved:

- Responding to interview questions is challenging for children whose language competence is not well developed. Preschoolers often are unaware when they do not understand, and they answer the question anyway.

- When an adult asks a yes-or-no question ("Was he holding a screwdriver?"), younger children are more likely to agree, perhaps out of a desire to please.

- Preschoolers are especially poor at *source-monitoring*—identifying where they got their knowledge, even minutes after they acquired it. They often confuse what they heard or saw on TV with what actually occurred.

- Preschoolers' bias toward verbatim representations (encoding specifics) leads them to forget more easily than older children, whose gist memories persist over time and serve as retrieval cues for details.

- Because younger children are less competent at using narratives to report their autobiographical memories systematically and completely, they may omit information that they actually remember (Brainerd, Reyna, & Poole, 2000; Gordon, Baker-Ward, & Ornstein, 2001; Poole & Lindsay, 2001).

ⓖ This 11-year-old testifies in court, pointing to the location on a map where he witnessed an event. Older children are better at giving detailed accounts of past experiences and resisting attempts to bias their responses.

© AP/Wide World Photos

Nevertheless, when properly questioned, even 3-year-olds can recall personally relevant events accurately—including highly stressful ones. In one study, children at least 26 months old at the time of an accidental injury and visit to the emergency room reported their experiences accurately two years later (Peterson & Rideout, 1998).

• **SUGGESTIBILITY** • Court testimony often involves repeated questioning by adults who have a vested interest in the child's responses. When a biased adult repeatedly asks specific questions, some of which suggest incorrect facts or reinforce the child for giving desired answers, they increase inaccurate reporting by preschool and school-age children alike (Bruck & Ceci, 2004). In one study, 4- to 5-year-olds and 6- to 7-year-olds were asked to recall details about a visitor who had come to their classroom a week earlier. Half the children received a low-pressure interview containing leading questions that implied abuse ("He took your clothes off, didn't he?"). The other half received a high-pressure interview in which an adult told the child that her friends had said "yes" to the leading questions, praised the child for agreeing ("You're doing great"), and, if the child did not agree, repeated the question. As Figure 7.11 shows, children were far more likely to give false information in the high-pressure condition—a difference that was consistent across the two age groups (Finnilä et al., 2003). As these findings illustrate, events that children fabricate can be quite fantastic. Moreover, once a child constructs a false memory, it can persist. When later questioned by an impartial interviewer, many children continue to give false reports (Garven, Wood, & Malpass, 2000).

By the time children appear in court, weeks, months, or even years have passed since the target events. When a long delay is combined with biased interviewing procedures and with stereotyping of the accused ("He's in jail because he's been bad"), children can easily be misled into giving false information (Ceci, Fitneva, & Gilstrap, 2003). As the specifics of what actually occurred fade, children may substitute a script reflecting what typically happens. As a result, they may report features consistent with the original situation (for example, checking the stomach in a physical exam) that were not really part of it (Ornstein et al., 1997). The more *distinctive*—different from its background context—an event is, the more likely children are to recall it accurately after the passage of time. For example, two years later, children recall more details about an injury than about medical treatment, which tends to be similar across many injuries (Peterson, 1999).

To ease the task of providing testimony, special interviewing methods have been devised for children. In many child sexual abuse cases, anatomically correct dolls are used to prompt chil-

▶ **Figure 7.11**

Influence of biased interviewing procedures on preschool and school-age children's suggested responses. Children of both age groups—4- to 5-year-olds and 6- to 7-year-olds—responded similarly. In both conditions, children gave suggested responses to leading questions, but in the high-pressure condition, which combined leading questions with social pressure to agree with the interviewer's bias (statements that the child's friends had agreed and praise for agreeing), suggested responses increased threefold. (Adapted from Finnilä et al., 2003.)

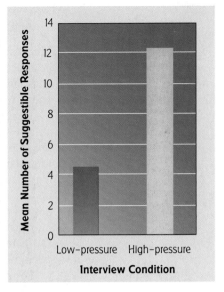

dren's recall. Although this method helps older children provide more detail about experienced events, it increases the suggestibility of preschoolers, prompting them to report physical and sexual contact that never happened (Goodman et al., 1999).

• **INTERVENTIONS** • Adults must prepare child witnesses so they understand the courtroom process and know what to expect. In some places, "court schools" take children through the setting and give them an opportunity to role-play court activities. As part of this process, children can be encouraged to admit not knowing an answer rather than guessing or going along with what an adult expects. Practice interviews about unrelated events, in which children learn to provide the most accurate, detailed information possible on four categories of information—setting, participants, actions, and conversations—are helpful (Saywitz, Goodman, & Lyon, 2002). For example, when 3- and 4-year-olds are trained to monitor the source of their memories (recall whether an event occurred in real life or on TV) and to reject misleading source information, they responded more accurately to questions about new events (Thierry & Spence, 2002).

In addition, legal professionals must use interviewing procedures that increase children's accurate reporting. Unbiased, open-ended questions or statements that prompt children to disclose details—"Tell me what happened" or "You said there was a man; tell me about the man"—reduce the risk of suggestibility (Holliday, 2003). Also, a warm, supportive interview tone fosters accurate recall, perhaps by easing children's fears. Under these conditions, children feel freer to counter an interviewer's false suggestions (Ceci, Bruck, & Battin, 2000).

If children are likely to experience emotional trauma or later punishment (as in a family dispute) for answering questions, courtroom procedures can be adapted to protect them. For example, children can testify over closed-circuit TV so they do not have to face an abuser. When it is not wise for a child to participate directly, expert witnesses can provide testimony that reports on the child's psychological condition and includes important elements of the child's story. For such testimony to be worthwhile, however, witnesses must be impartial and trained in how to question children to minimize false reporting (Bruck, Ceci, & Hembrooke, 1998).

Ask Yourself

REVIEW	According to fuzzy-trace theory, why do we encode information in gist form? Describe the development of gist and verbatim representations, and explain how gist representations contribute to improved reasoning and recall with age.
APPLY	When asked what happens at kindergarten, 5-year-old Ali replies, "First, you have center time and circle time. Sometimes you listen to a story. Next you eat your snack and go outdoors." But Ali can't remember what she did during center time two days ago. Explain Ali's memory performance. Why is this type of memory useful?
CONNECT	Using what you have learned about development of gist and autobiographical memory, explain why preschoolers' eyewitness testimony usually is less accurate than that of older children. What situational factors make children's reporting more inaccurate?
REFLECT	Describe your earliest autobiographical memory. How old were you when the event occurred? Do your responses fit with research on infantile amnesia?

Metacognition

Throughout this chapter, we have mentioned many ways in which cognitive processing becomes more reflective and deliberate with age. These trends suggest that another form of knowledge may influence how well children remember and solve problems: **Metacognition** refers to awareness and understanding of various aspects of thought.

During early and middle childhood, metacognition expands greatly as children construct a naïve **theory of mind,** a coherent understanding of people as mental beings, which they revise as they encounter new evidence. Most investigations into theory of mind address children's "mind reading"— their ability to detect their own and other people's perceptions, feelings, desires, and beliefs. We will take up this aspect when we consider emotional and social understanding in Chapters 10 and 11. A second facet of metacognitive research concerns children's knowledge of mental activity, or *what it means to think*. To work most effectively, the information-processing system must be aware of itself. It must arrive at such realizations as "I'd better write that phone number down or I'll forget it" and "This paragraph is complicated; I'll have to read it again to grasp the author's point."

For metacognitive knowledge to be helpful, children must monitor what they do, calling on what they know about thinking to overcome difficulties. In the following sections, we consider these higher-level, "executive" aspects of information processing.

Metacognitive Knowledge

With age, knowledge of mental activities expands in three ways. Children become increasingly conscious of cognitive capacities, strategies for processing information, and task variables that aid or impede performance.

• **KNOWLEDGE OF COGNITIVE CAPACITIES** • Listen closely to young children's conversations, and you will find early awareness of mental activities. Such words as *think, remember,* and *pretend* are among the first verbs in children's vocabularies. After age 2½, they use these words appropriately to refer to internal states, as when they say, "I thought the socks were in the drawer, 'cept they weren't" (Wellman, 1990). By age 3, children realize that thinking takes place inside their heads and that a person can think about something without seeing it, talking about it, or touching it (Flavell, Green, & Flavell, 1995).

But preschoolers' understanding of the workings of the mind is still limited. Three- and 4-year-olds are unaware that people continue to think while they wait, look at pictures, listen to stories, or read books. They conclude that mental activity stops when there are no obvious cues to indicate a person is thinking. When told to try to have no thoughts at all and to indicate whether they had some thoughts anyway, most 8-year-olds said they had, but only a few 5-year-olds did (see Figure 7.12) (Flavell, Green, & Flavell, 1993, 1995, 2000). Furthermore, children younger than 6 pay little attention to the *process* of thinking but, instead, focus on outcomes of thought. When questioned about subtle distinctions between mental states, such as *know* and *forget,* they express confusion (Lyon & Flavell, 1994). They often insist that they have always known information they just learned (Taylor, Esbensen, & Bennett, 1994).

In contrast, school-age children have a more complete grasp of cognitive processes. Six- and 7-year-olds realize, for example, that doing well on a task depends on paying attention—concentrating and exerting effort (Miller & Bigi, 1979). Around this time, children's understanding of sources of knowledge expands. They realize that people can extend their knowledge not just by directly observing events and talking to others but also by making *mental inferences* (Carpendale & Chandler, 1996; Miller, Hardin, & Montgomery, 2003). By age 10, children distinguish mental activities on the basis of *certainty of knowledge.* They are aware that if you "remember," "know," or "understand," you are more certain than if you "guess," "estimate," or "compare." By late elementary school, children also grasp the interrelatedness of memory and understanding—that remembering is crucial for understanding and that understanding strengthens memory (Schwanenflugel, Fabricius, & Noyes, 1996; Schwanenflugel, Henderson, & Fabricius, 1998).

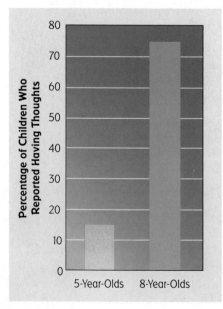

▼ **Figure 7.12**

Children ages 5 and 8 told to have no thoughts or ideas who responded that they had some anyway. Far fewer 5-year-olds than 8-year-olds indicated that they had any thoughts. Preschoolers greatly underestimate the amount of mental activity people experience. (Adapted from Flavell, Green, & Flavell, 2000.)

How, then, should we describe the difference between the young child's understanding of cognitive capacities and that of the older child? Preschoolers know that people have an internal mental life, but they view the mind as a passive container of information. Consequently, they greatly underestimate the amount of mental activity that goes on in people and are not good at inferring what people know or are thinking about. In view of their limited awareness of how knowledge is acquired, it is not surprising that preschoolers rarely engage in planning or use memory strategies. In contrast, older children regard the mind as an active, constructive agent that selects and transforms information (Flavell, 2000; Kuhn, 2000).

School-age children's capacity for more complex thinking contributes greatly to their more reflective, process-oriented view of the mind. Relevant experiences are also involved. In a study of rural children of Cameroon, Africa, those who attended school had a more advanced awareness of mental activities than those who did not (Vinden, 2002). In school, teachers often call attention to the workings of the mind when they remind children to pay attention, remember mental steps, and evaluate their reasoning. And as children engage in reading, writing, and math, they often use *private speech*, at first speaking aloud and later silently to themselves. As they "hear themselves think," they probably detect many aspects of mental life (Astington, 1995).

School-age children have an improved ability to reflect on their own mental life. This child is aware that external aids to memory are often necessary to ensure that information will be retained.
© Laura Dwight Photography

• **KNOWLEDGE OF STRATEGIES** • Consistent with their more active view of the mind, school-age children are far more conscious of mental strategies than preschoolers are. For example, when shown video clips depicting two children using different recall strategies and asked which one is likely to produce better memory, kindergarten and young elementary school children knew that rehearsing or categorizing is better than looking or naming. Older children were aware of more subtle differences—for example, that organizing is better than rehearsing (Justice, 1986; Schneider, 1986). And between third and fifth grade, children develop a much better understanding of how and why strategies work (Alexander et al., 2003).

Once children become conscious of the many factors that influence mental activity, they combine them into an integrated understanding. By the end of middle childhood, children take account of *interactions* among variables—how age and motivation of the learner, effective use of strategies, and nature and difficulty of the task work together to affect cognitive performance (Wellman, 1990). In this way, metacognition truly becomes a comprehensive theory.

Cognitive Self-Regulation

Although metacognitive knowledge expands, school-age children often have difficulty putting what they know about thinking into action. They are not yet good at **cognitive self-regulation,** the process of continually monitoring progress toward a goal, checking outcomes, and redirecting unsuccessful efforts. For example, most third to sixth graders know that they should group items when memorizing, reread a complicated paragraph to make sure they understand it, and relate new information to what they already know. But they do not always engage in these activities.

To study cognitive self-regulation, researchers sometimes look at the impact children's awareness of memory strategies has on how well they remember. By second grade, the more children know about memory strategies, the more they recall—a relationship that strengthens over middle childhood (Pierce & Lange, 2000). Furthermore, children who can explain why a memory strategy works use it more effectively, which results in better memory performance (Justice et al., 1997). And when children apply a useful strategy consistently, their knowledge of strategies strengthens, resulting in a bidirectional relationship between metacognition and strategic processing that enhances self-regulation (Schlagmüller & Schneider, 2002).

Children's difficulties with self-regulation on complex tasks are evident in their *comprehension monitoring*—their sensitivity to how well they understand a spoken or written message. Compared with younger students, 12- and 13-year-olds more often notice when a passage does not make sense. Rather than moving ahead, they slow down and look back to see if

◉ The extent of this boy's cognitive self-regulatory capacities becomes evident during his piano lesson. For example, does he ignore his mistakes, or does he isolate difficult passages for further practice? His teacher can foster his self-regulatory skills by pointing out special demands of a piece, showing him strategies for mastering it, and encouraging him to monitor his progress.

© Gideon Mendel/CORBIS

they missed important information. Their greater sensitivity to text errors means that they are more likely to revise their written work (Beal, 1990).

What explains the gradual development of cognitive self-regulation? Monitoring learning outcomes is cognitively demanding, requiring constant evaluation of effort and progress. At first, children's efforts suffer from control and utilization deficiencies (see page 285). By adolescence, cognitive self-regulation is a strong predictor of academic success (Joyner & Kurtz-Costes, 1997). Students who do well in school know when their learning is going well and when it is not. If they run up against obstacles, such as poor study conditions, a confusing text passage, or an unclear class presentation, they take steps to organize the learning environment, review the material, or seek other sources of support. This active, purposeful approach contrasts sharply with the passive orientation of students who achieve poorly (Zimmerman & Risemberg, 1997).

Parents and teachers can foster self-regulation. In one study, researchers observed parents instructing their children in problem solving during the summer before third grade. Parents who patiently pointed out important features of the task and suggested strategies had children who, in the classroom, more often discussed ways to approach problems and monitored their own performance (Stright et al., 2002). Explaining the effectiveness of strategies is particularly helpful (Pressley, 1995). When adults tell children not just what to do but why to do it, they provide a rationale for future action.

Consult Applying What We Know below for ways to foster children's cognitive self-regulation. Children who acquire effective self-regulatory skills succeed at challenging academic tasks. As a result, they develop a sense of *academic self-efficacy*—confidence in their own ability, which supports the use of self-regulation in the future (Schunk & Zimmerman, 2003). As we turn now to development within academic skill areas, the importance of self-regulation will be ever-present. But first, turn to the Milestones table on the following page, which summarizes the diverse changes in information processing we have considered.

Applying
What We Know   Promoting Children's Cognitive Self-Regulation

Strategy	Description
Stress the importance of planful learning.	Encourage children to analyze the learning task and to plan—by considering a variety of ways to approach the task and by setting appropriate learning goals, including how much time and practice they will need to complete the task.
Suggest effective learning strategies.	Show children how to use effective learning strategies, and explain why those strategies are effective, so children know when and why to use those strategies in the future.
Emphasize monitoring of progress.	Encourage children to monitor themselves to ensure that they are making progress toward their learning goals, by asking themselves questions, such as, "Am I staying focused?" "Am I using the strategy, as planned?" "Is the strategy working, or do I need to adjust it?"
Provide for evaluation of strategy effectiveness.	Have children evaluate their performance to improve learning, by answering self-posed questions, such as, "How well did I perform?" "Were my learning strategies effective?" "What strategy might work better?" "What other tasks might benefit from these strategies?"

Source: Schunk & Zimmerman, 2003.

MILESTONES

DEVELOPMENT OF INFORMATION PROCESSING

Age	Basic Capacities	Strategies	Knowledge	Metacognition
2–5 years 	Many processing skills are evident, including attention, recognition, recall, and reconstruction. Overall capacity of the system increases.	Attention becomes more focused and sustained. Beginnings of memory strategies are present, but they are seldom used spontaneously and have little impact on performance. Variability and adaptive selection among strategies are evident.	Knowledge expands and becomes better organized. Familiar events are remembered in scripts, which become more elaborate. Autobiographical memory emerges, takes on narrative organization, and becomes more detailed.	Awareness of mental activities is present, but preschoolers view the mind as a passive container of information.
6–10 years	Overall capacity of the system continues to increase.	Attention becomes more selective, adaptable, and planful. Cognitive inhibition improves. Memory strategies of rehearsal and taxonomic organization are used spontaneously and more effectively. Ability to combine strategies increases. Ability to draw inferences in reconstructive processing improves. Reliance on gist memory for reasoning increases. 	Knowledge continues to expand and become better organized.	View of the mind as an active, constructive agent develops. Knowledge of cognitive processes and their relationships grows. Knowledge of the impact of strategies on performance increases. Knowledge of interaction among cognitive processes, strategies, and type of task increases. Cognitive self-regulation improves gradually.
11 years–adulthood	Overall capacity of the system continues to increase, but at a slower pace.	Memory strategy of elaboration appears.	Knowledge expands further and becomes more intricately organized.	Metacognitive knowledge and cognitive self-regulation continue to improve.

Note: These milestones represent overall age trends. Individual differences exist in the precise age at which each milestone is attained.

Photos: (top) © Laura Dwight Photography; (middle) © Robert Brenner/PhotoEdit; (bottom) © Myrleen Ferguson Cate/PhotoEdit

Ask Yourself

REVIEW	What evidence indicates that preschoolers view the mind as a passive container of information, whereas school-age children view it as an active, constructive agent?
APPLY	Although 9-year-old Melody knows she should look over her homework, she nevertheless often turns in assignments with careless mistakes. What might account for the gap between what Melody knows and what she does?
CONNECT	How are the suggestions for fostering cognitive self-regulation on page 298 consistent with Vygotsky's emphasis on the social origins of higher cognitive processes?

Applications of Information Processing to Academic Learning

Over the past two decades, fundamental discoveries about the development of information processing have been applied to children's mastery of academic skills. In various subject matters, researchers are identifying the cognitive ingredients of skilled performance, tracing their development, and distinguishing good from poor learners by pinpointing differences in cognitive skills. They hope, as a result, to design teaching methods that will improve children's learning. In the following sections, we discuss a sampling of these efforts in reading, mathematics, and scientific reasoning.

Reading

When we read, we use many skills at once, taxing all aspects of our information-processing systems. We must perceive single letters and letter combinations, translate them into speech sounds, recognize the visual appearance of many common words, hold chunks of text in working memory while interpreting their meaning, and combine the meanings of various parts of a text passage into an understandable whole. In fact, reading is so demanding that most or all of these skills must be done automatically. If one or more are poorly developed, they will compete for space in our limited working memories, and reading performance will decline. Becoming a proficient reader is a complex process that begins in the preschool years.

• **EARLY CHILDHOOD** • Preschoolers understand a great deal about written language long before they begin to read and write in conventional ways. This is not surprising when we consider that children in industrialized nations live in a world filled with written symbols. Each day, they observe and participate in activities involving storybooks, calendars, lists, and signs. As part of these experiences, they try to figure out how written symbols convey meaning. Children's active efforts to construct literacy knowledge through informal experiences are called **emergent literacy.**

Young preschoolers search for units of written language as they "read" memorized versions of stories and recognize familiar signs, such as "PIZZA" at their favorite fast-food counter. But they do not yet understand the symbolic function of the elements of print (Bialystock & Martin, 2003). Many preschoolers think that a single letter stands for a whole word or that each letter in a person's signature represents a separate name. In fact, initially preschoolers do not distinguish drawing from writing. Around age 4, their writing shows some distinctive features of print, such as separate forms arranged in a line. But they often include picturelike devices, such as writing "sun" by using a yellow marker or a circular shape (Levin & Bus, 2003). Using their understanding of the symbolic function of drawings, they make a "drawing of print."

Preschoolers revise these ideas as their cognitive capacities improve, as they encounter print in many contexts, and as adults help them with written communication. Gradually, they notice more features of written language and depict writing that varies in function, as in the "story" and "grocery list" in Figure 7.13. Eventually children figure out that letters are parts of words and are linked to sounds in systematic ways, as you can see in the invented spellings that are typical between ages 5 and 7. At first, children rely on sounds in the names of letters: "ADE LAFWTS KRMD NTU A LAVATR" ("eighty elephants crammed into a[n] elevator"). Over time, they grasp sound–letter correspondences. They also learn that some letters have more than one common sound and that context affects their use (*a* is pronounced differently in *cat* than in *table*) (McGee & Richgels, 2004).

Literacy development builds on a broad foundation of spoken language and knowledge about the world. Over time, children's language and literacy progress facilitate one another (Dickinson et al., 2003). **Phonological awareness—** the ability to reflect on and manipulate the sound structure of spoken language, as indicated by sensitivity to changes in

▼ **Figure 7.13**

A story (a) and a grocery list (b) written by a 4-year-old child. This child's writing has many features of real print. It also reveals an awareness of different kinds of written expression. (From L. M. McGee & D. J. Richgels, 2004, *Literacy's Beginnings* (4th ed.), Boston: Allyn and Bacon, p. 76. Reprinted by permission.)

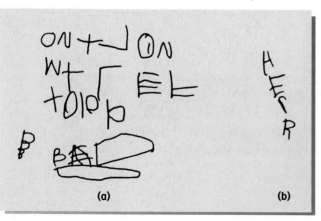

(a)   (b)

sounds within words, to rhyming, and to incorrect pronunciation—is a strong predictor of emergent literacy knowledge (Foy & Mann, 2003). Vocabulary and grammatical development are also influential. And adult–child narrative conversations enhance diverse language skills essential for literacy progress.

The more informal literacy experiences preschoolers have, the better their language and emergent literacy development (Dickinson & McCabe, 2001). Pointing out letter–sound correspondences and playing language-sound games foster phonological awareness (Foy & Mann, 2003). *Interactive* storybook reading, in which adults discuss story content with preschoolers, promotes many aspects of language and literacy development. Adult-supported writing activities that focus on narrative, such as preparing a letter or a story, also have wide-ranging benefits (Purcell-Gates, 1996; Wasik & Bond, 2001). In longitudinal research, each of these literacy experiences predicted improved reading achievement in middle childhood (Senechal & LeFevre, 2002; Storch & Whitehurst, 2001).

Compared with their economically advantaged agemates, preschoolers from low-income families have fewer home and preschool language and literacy learning opportunities—a major reason that they are behind in reading achievement throughout the school years (Serpell et al., 2002). In a program that "flooded" child-care centers with children's books and provided caregivers with training on how to get 3- and 4-year-olds to spend time with books, children showed much greater gains in emergent literacy knowledge than a control group not experiencing the intervention. These differences were still evident after the children entered kindergarten (Neuman, 1999). For ways to support early childhood literacy development, refer to Applying What We Know below.

Ⓖ Preschoolers acquire a great deal of literacy knowledge informally as they participate in everyday activities involving written symbols. This 4-year-old tries to write his name while a classmate helps by holding up his name card so he can easily see the letters.

© Laura Dwight Photography

Applying What We Know
Supporting Emergent Literacy in Early Childhood

Strategy	Explanation
Provide literacy-rich home and preschool environments.	Homes and preschools with abundant reading and writing materials—including a wide variety of children's storybooks, some relevant to children's ethnic backgrounds—open the door to a wealth of language and literacy experiences.
Engage in interactive book reading.	When adults discuss story content, ask open-ended questions about story events, explain the meaning of words, and point out features of print, they promote language development, comprehension of story content, knowledge of story structure, and awareness of units of written language.
Provide outings to libraries, museums, parks, zoos, and other community settings.	Visits to child-oriented community settings enhance children's general knowledge and offer many opportunities to see how written language is used in everyday life. They also provide personally meaningful topics for narrative conversation, which enhance many language skills essential for literacy development.
Point out letter–sound correspondences, play rhyming and other language-sound games, and read rhyming poems and stories.	Experiences that help children isolate the sounds in words foster phonological awareness—a powerful predictor of early childhood literacy knowledge and later reading and spelling achievement.
Support children's efforts at writing, especially narrative products.	Assisting children in their efforts to write—especially letters, stories, and other narratives—fosters many language and literacy skills.
Model literacy activities.	When children see adults engaged in reading and writing activities, they better understand the diverse, everyday functions of literacy skills and the knowledge and pleasure that literacy brings. As a result, children's motivation to become literate is strengthened.

Sources: Dickinson & McCabe, 2001; McGee & Righels, 2004.

ⓖ Effective reading instruction involves a complex mix of elements—among them, balancing basic-skills and whole-language teaching. This first-grade teacher works with a small group, embedding phonics in exposure to interesting stories and challenging writing tasks.

© Syracuse Newspapers/The Image Works

• **MIDDLE CHILDHOOD** • As children make the transition from emergent to conventional literacy, phonological awareness continues to predict reading (and spelling) progress. It enables children to isolate speech segments and link them with their written symbols, in languages as different as English and Chinese. Other information-processing activities also contribute. Recall that processing speed increases dramatically during middle childhood. It fosters the ability to rapidly convert visual symbols into sounds, which also distinguishes good from poor readers (Kail, Hall, & Caskey, 1999; McBride-Chang & Kail, 2002). In addition, visual scanning and discrimination are important and improve with reading experience (Rayner, Pollatsek, & Starr, 2003). Performing all these skills efficiently releases working memory for higher-level activities involved in comprehending the text's meaning.

Until recently, researchers were embroiled in an intense debate over how to teach children to read. On one side were those who took a **whole-language approach.** They argued that reading should be taught in a way that parallels natural language learning. From the very beginning, children should be exposed to text in its complete form—stories, poems, letters, posters, and lists—so that they can appreciate the communicative function of written language. According to these experts, as long as reading is kept meaningful, children will be motivated to discover the specific skills they need (Watson, 1989). On the other side were those who advocated a **phonics approach.** In their view, children should be given simplified reading materials and, at first, should be coached on *phonics*—the basic rules for translating written symbols into sounds. Only later, after they have mastered these skills, should they get complex reading material (Rayner & Pollatsek, 1989).

Many studies have resolved this debate by showing that children learn best with a mixture of both approaches. In kindergarten, first, and second grades, teaching that includes phonics boosts reading achievement scores, especially for children who are behind in reading progress (Berninger et al., 2003; Xue & Meisels, 2004). And when teachers combine real reading and writing with teaching of phonics and engage in other excellent teaching practices—encouraging children to tackle reading challenges and integrating reading into all school subjects—first graders show far greater literacy progress (Pressley et al., 2002).

Why might combining phonics with whole language work best? Learning relations between letters and sounds enables children to *decode,* or decipher, words they have never seen before. Yet if practice in basic skills is overemphasized, children may lose sight of the goal of reading: understanding. Children who read aloud fluently without registering meaning know little about effective reading strategies—for example, that they must read more carefully if they will be tested than if they are reading for pleasure, or that explaining a passage in their own words is a good way to monitor comprehension. Providing instruction aimed at increasing children's knowledge and use of reading strategies readily enhances reading performance of children from third grade on (Van Keer, 2004; Dickson et al., 1998).

Around age 7 to 8, a major shift occurs from "learning to read" to "reading to learn" (Ely, 2005). As decoding and comprehension skills reach a high level of efficiency, adolescent readers can become actively engaged with the text. They adjust the way they read to fit their current purpose—at times seeking new facts and ideas, at other times questioning or agreeing or disagreeing with the writer's viewpoint.

Mathematics

Mathematical reasoning, like reading, builds on informally acquired knowledge. Recall from Chapter 6 that some evidence suggests that infants have basic numerical knowledge (see page 255). Between 14 and 16 months, toddlers display a beginning grasp of **ordinality,** or order relationships between quantities—for example, that *three* is more than *two* and *two* is more than *one*—an attainment that serves as the basis for more complex understandings (Starkey, 1992).

• **EARLY CHILDHOOD** • In the early preschool years, children start to attach verbal labels (such as *lots, little, big,* and *small*) to amounts and sizes. And sometime in the third year, they begin to count. At first, counting may be little more than a memorized routine—"Onetwothreefourfivesix!" But by the time preschoolers turn 3, most can count rows of about five objects, saying the correct number words, although they do not know exactly what the words mean. For example, when asked for *one,* they give 1 item, but when asked for *two, three, four,* or *five,* they usually give a larger, but incorrect, amount. Nevertheless, 2½- to 3½-year-olds realize that when a number label changes—for example, from *five* to *six*—the number of items should change (Sarnecka & Gelman, 2004). They understand that a number word refers to a unique quantity.

By age 3½ to 4, most children have mastered the meaning of numbers up to *ten,* count correctly, and grasp the vital principle of **cardinality**—that the last word in a counting sequence indicates the quantity of items in a set (Bermejo, 1996; Zur & Gelman, 2004). Mastery of cardinality increases the efficiency of children's counting. By age 4, children use counting to solve arithmetic problems. At first, their strategies are tied to the order of numbers as presented; when given 2 + 4, they count on from 2 (Bryant & Nunes, 2002). But soon they experiment with various other strategies. As a result, they master the *min* strategy, a more efficient approach (refer back to Siegler's model of strategy choice, page 278). Around this time, children realize that subtraction cancels out addition. Knowing, for example, that 4 + 3 = 7, they infer without counting that 7 − 3 = 4 (Rasmussen, Ho, & Bisanz, 2003). Grasping this principle, along with other basic rules of addition and subtraction, greatly facilitates rapid computation.

The arithmetic knowledge just described emerges universally around the world. But in homes and preschools where adults provide many occasions for counting, comparing quantities, and adding and subtracting in meaningful situations, children acquire these understandings sooner. In a math intervention program for low-income 4-year-olds, teachers included math activities in almost all classroom routines. For example, children counted the number of steps needed to get from various locations in the classroom to the play yard and identified a partner who held a card with a certain number of dots on it. Compared with children in other classrooms, children in the intervention program scored higher in math concepts and enjoyed math activities more (Arnold et al., 2002). Solid, secure early childhood math knowledge is essential for the wide variety of mathematical skills children will be taught once they enter school.

Ⓢ It's time for this shopper to count and pay for her items at a preschool play grocery store. When children are exposed to rich, informal mathematical activities, they acquire a solid foundation of math concepts and skills. They also learn that math is interesting, enjoyable, and useful.
© Bob Daemmrich/The Image Works

• **MIDDLE CHILDHOOD** • Mathematics teaching in elementary school builds on and greatly enriches children's informal knowledge of number concepts and counting. Written notation systems and formal computational techniques enhance children's ability to represent numbers and compute. Over the early elementary school years, children acquire basic math facts through a combination of frequent practice, reasoning about number concepts, and teaching that conveys effective strategies. (Return to page 276 for research supporting the importance of both extended practice and a grasp of concepts.) Eventually, children retrieve answers automatically and apply this knowledge to more complex problems.

Arguments about how to teach mathematics resemble those about reading. Extensive speeded practice is pitted against "number sense," or understanding. Again, a blend of these two approaches is most beneficial. In learning basic math, poorly performing students use cumbersome techniques (such as counting all items in an addition problem) or try to retrieve answers from memory too soon. Their responses are often sluggish and wrong because they have not sufficiently experimented with strategies to test which ones are most effective. And on tasks that reveal their understanding of math concepts, their performance is weak (Canobi, 2004; Canobi, Reeve, & Pattison, 2003). This suggests that encouraging students to apply strategies and making sure they understand why certain ones work well are vital for solid mastery of basic math.

A similar picture emerges for more complex skills, such as carrying in addition, borrowing in subtraction, and operating with decimals and fractions. When taught by rote, children cannot apply the procedure to new problems. Instead, they persistently make mistakes, using a "math rule" that they recall incorrectly because they do not understand it (Carpenter et al., 1999). Look at the following subtraction errors:

$$
\begin{array}{r}
427 \\
-138 \\
\hline
311
\end{array}
\qquad
\begin{array}{r}
7{,}002 \\
-5{,}445 \\
\hline
1{,}447
\end{array}
$$

In the first problem, the child consistently subtracts a smaller from a larger digit, regardless of which is on top. In the second, columns with zeros are skipped in a borrowing operation, and the bottom digit is written as the answer.

In contrast, when provided with rich opportunities to experiment with problem solving, to grasp the reasons behind strategies, and to evaluate solution techniques, children seldom make these errors. In one study, second graders who were taught in these ways not only mastered correct procedures but even invented their own successful strategies, some of which were superior to standard, school-taught methods! Consider this solution:

$$
\begin{array}{r}
{}^{3}\cancel{4}\,{}^{15}\cancel{6}\,{}^{14}\cancel{5}\,{}^{12}\cancel{2} \\
-1\quad 9\quad 6\quad 8 \\
\hline
2\quad 6\quad 8\quad 4
\end{array}
$$

In subtracting, the child performed all trades first, flexibly moving either from right to left or from left to right, and then subtracted all four columns—a highly efficient, accurate approach (Fuson & Burghard, 2003). In a German study, the more teachers emphasized conceptual knowledge, by having children actively construct meanings in word problems before practicing computation and memorizing math facts, the more children gained in math achievement from second to third grade (Staub & Stern, 2002).

Current evidence suggests that many schools in the United States place too much emphasis on computational drill (Woodward, 2004). We will see in Chapter 15 that in cross-cultural comparisons of math achievement, students in Asian nations typically score at the top. Furthermore, in high school, Canadian students—and students in many other Western nations—outperform U.S. students. As the Cultural Influences box on the following page illustrates, Asian students receive a variety of supports for acquiring mathematical knowledge. The result is deeper processing—formation of secure numerical concepts that provide a firm foundation for mastery of new skills.

Scientific Reasoning

During a free moment in physical education class, 13-year-old Heidi wondered why more of her tennis serves and returns passed the net and dropped in her opponent's court when she used a particular brand of balls. "Is it something about their color or size?" she asked herself. "Hmm . . . or could it be their surface texture—that might affect their bounce."

The heart of scientific reasoning is coordinating theories with evidence. A scientist can clearly describe the theory he or she favors, knows what evidence is needed to support it and what would refute it, and can explain how pitting evidence against theories has led to the acceptance of one theory as opposed to others. What evidence would Heidi need to confirm her theory about the tennis balls?

Deanna Kuhn (2002) has conducted extensive research into the development of scientific reasoning, using problems that resemble Piaget's tasks, in that several variables might affect an outcome. In one series of studies, third, sixth, and ninth graders and adults were provided with evidence, sometimes consistent and sometimes conflicting with theories. Then they were questioned about the accuracy of each theory.

For example, participants were given a problem much like the one Heidi posed. They were asked to theorize about which of several features of sports balls—size (large or small), color (light or dark), surface texture (rough or

These teenagers test a theory about the physical capacities and behavior of a dinosaur species by collecting data on the size and shape of its tracks. As they coordinate theory with evidence and reflect on and revise their thinking strategies, they make gains in scientific reasoning.
© Michelle Bridwell/PhotoEdit

CULTURAL INFLUENCES

Asian Children's Understanding of Multidigit Addition and Subtraction

Many North American students have difficulty with multidigit addition and subtraction problems requiring trades between columns. Often they try to solve these problems by rote, without grasping crucial aspects of the procedure. They seem to have a single-digit conception of multidigit numbers. For example, they tend to view the 3 in 5,386 as just 3 rather than as 300. As a result, when they carry to or borrow from this column, they are likely to compute the value incorrectly.

Chinese, Japanese, and Korean children, by contrast, are highly accurate at multidigit addition and subtraction. What accounts for their superior performance? To find out, Karen Fuson and Youngshim Kwon (1992) observed Korean second and third graders solving two- and three-digit problems and asked them to explain how they arrived at their answers. The children's performance was excellent, even when they had not yet had formal instruction on the topic, and accurate understanding of multidigit numbers was clearly responsible. No Korean child viewed a "1" mark signaling trading to the tens column as *one*, as North American children often do. Instead, they clearly identified it as *ten* if it came from the ones column (addition) and as *one hundred* if it came from the hundreds column (subtraction).

Especially remarkable were third graders' clear explanations of how to perform complex, multistep trading operations that stump their North American agemates. In fact, most Korean third graders no longer wrote extra marks when solving these problems. They handled intricate trading procedures mentally.

Several language and cultural factors contribute to the sharp skill advantage of Asian over North American children. First, English words for two-digit numbers (such as *twelve* and *thirteen*) are irregular and do not convey the idea of tens and ones.

Asian-language number words (*ten-two, ten-three*) make this composition obvious. Chinese-, Japanese-, and Korean-speaking 5-year-olds know that numbers in the teens are composed of a tens-value and a ones-value, whereas their North American agemates show no evidence of this understanding (Miura & Okamoto, 2003). Asian number words also are shorter and more quickly pronounced. This facilitates counting strategies and increases the speed with which children can retrieve math facts from long-term memory (Geary et al., 1996). Finally, although use of the abacus is no longer regularly taught in Asian schools, many Chinese, Japanese, and Korean children take abacus lessons. Abacus operations chunk numbers into fives and tens, which fosters highly efficient multidigit calculation (Murata, 2004).

Asian teaching practices support rapid mastery of multidigit problems as well. For example, teachers frequently use phrases that explicitly describe the trading operation. Instead of carrying, they say "raise up"; instead of borrowing, "bring down." Finally, multidigit problems are introduced earlier in Asian schools, and teachers more often explain how and when to use effective strategies (Naito & Miura, 2001; Perry, 2000). Taken together, these findings highlight several ways in which North American adults might ease children's mastery of fundamental numerical concepts.

▲ Cultural and language-based factors contribute to Asian children's skill at manipulating multidigit numbers. The abacus supports these Japanese students' understanding of place value. Ones, tens, hundreds, and thousands are each represented by a different column of beads, and calculations are performed by moving the beads to different positions. As children become skilled at using the abacus, they generate mental images that assist them in solving complex arithmetic problems. © Fiji Foto/The Image Works

▶ **Figure 7.14**

Which features of these sports balls—size, color, surface texture, or presence or absence of ridges—influence the quality of a player's serve? This set of evidence suggests that color might be important, since light-colored balls are largely in the good-serve basket and dark-colored balls in the bad-serve basket. But the same is true for texture! The good-serve basket has mostly smooth balls; the bad-serve basket, rough balls. Since all light-colored balls are smooth and all dark-colored balls are rough, we cannot tell whether color or texture makes a difference. But we can conclude that size and presence or absence of ridges are not important, since these features are equally represented in the good-serve and bad-serve baskets. (Adapted from Kuhn, Amsel, & O'Loughlin, 1988.)

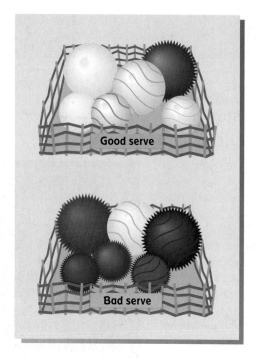

smooth), or presence or absence of ridges on the surface—influences the quality of a player's serve. Next, they were told about the theory of Mr. (or Ms.) S, who believes that the ball's size is important, and the theory of Mr. (or Ms.) C, who thinks color makes a difference. Finally, the interviewer presented evidence by placing balls with certain characteristics into two baskets, one labeled "good serve" and the other "bad serve" (see Figure 7.14).

• **AGE-RELATED CHANGE** • Kuhn and her collaborators (1988) found that the capacity to reason like a scientist improved with age. The youngest participants often ignored conflicting evidence or distorted it in ways consistent with their theory. When one third grader, who judged that size was causal (with large balls producing good serves and small balls producing bad serves), was shown incomplete evidence (a single, large, light-colored ball in the good-serve basket and no balls in the bad-serve basket), he still insisted on the accuracy of Mr. S's theory (which was also his own). Asked to explain, he stated flatly, "Because this ball is big . . . the color doesn't really matter" (Kuhn, 1989, p. 677).

These findings, and others like them, reveal that instead of viewing evidence as separate from and bearing on a theory, children often blend the two into a single representation of "the way things are." The ability to distinguish theory from evidence and use logical rules to examine their relationship in complex, multivariable situations improves from childhood into adolescence and adulthood (Kuhn & Dean, 2004; Kuhn & Pearsall, 2000).

• **HOW SCIENTIFIC REASONING DEVELOPS** • What factors support skill at coordinating theory with evidence? Greater working-memory capacity, permitting a theory and the effects of several variables to be compared at once, is vital. In addition, adolescents benefit from exposure to increasingly complex problems and instruction that highlights critical features of tasks and effective strategies. Consequently, scientific reasoning is strongly influenced by years of schooling, whether individuals grapple with traditional scientific tasks (like the sports ball problem) or engage in informal reasoning—for example, justifying a theory about what causes children to fail in school (Kuhn, 1993).

Many researchers believe that sophisticated *metacognitive understanding* is at the heart of scientific reasoning (Kuhn, 1999; Moshman, 1999). Microgenetic research (see page 63 in Chapter 2) shows that when children regularly pit theory against evidence over many weeks, they experiment with various strategies, reflect on and revise them, and become aware of the nature of logic. Then they apply their abstract appreciation of logic to a wide variety of situations. The ability to *think about* theories, *deliberately isolate* variables, and *actively seek* disconfirming evidence is rarely present before adolescence (Kuhn, 2000; Moshman, 1998).

Although they are far more competent than children, adolescents and adults vary widely in scientific reasoning skills. Many continue to show a self-serving bias, in that they apply logic more effectively to ideas they doubt than to ideas they favor (Klaczynski, 1997; Klaczynski & Narasimham, 1998a). Reasoning scientifically requires the metacognitive capacity to evaluate one's objectivity—a disposition to be fair-minded rather than self-serving (Moshman, 1999). As we will see in Chapter 11, this flexible, open-minded approach is not just a cognitive attainment but a personality trait—one that assists teenagers greatly in forming an identity and developing morally.

Adolescents develop scientific reasoning skills in a similar step-by-step fashion on different kinds of tasks. In a series of studies, 10- to 20-year-olds were given sets of problems graded in difficulty. For example, one set consisted of causal-experimental tasks like the sports ball problem in Figure 7.14. Another set contained quantitative-relational tasks like Piaget's pendulum problem. And still another set was made up of verbal propositional tasks (see page 247 in Chapter 6). In each type of task, adolescents mastered component skills in sequential order by expanding their metacognitive awareness (Demetriou et al., 1993, 1996, 2002). For example, on causal-experimental tasks, they first became aware of the many variables—separately and in combination—that could influence an outcome. This enabled them to formulate and test hypotheses. Over time, adolescents combined separate skills into a smoothly functioning system, constructing a general model that they could apply to many instances of a given type of problem.

Return to page 276 and review Robbie Case's information-processing view of Piaget's stages. Does Case's concept of *central conceptual structures* remind you of the metacognitive advances just described? Piaget also underscored the role of metacognition in formal operational thought when he spoke of "operating on operations" (see Chapter 6, page 246). However, information-processing findings reveal that scientific reasoning does not result from an abrupt, stagewise change, as Piaget believed. Instead, it develops gradually out of many specific experiences that require children and adolescents to match theory against evidence and reflect on their thinking.

Evaluation of the Information-Processing Approach

A major strength of the information-processing approach is its explicitness and precision in breaking down complex cognitive activities into their components. Information processing has provided a wealth of detailed evidence on how younger versus older and more-skilled versus less-skilled individuals attend, remember, reason, and solve problems. It also offers precise mechanisms of cognitive development; Table 7.1 summarizes the most important of these. As you review them, think back to theories and findings that illustrate the role of each. Finally, because of its precision, information-processing research has contributed greatly to the design of teaching techniques that advance many aspects of children's thinking.

Nevertheless, the information-processing perspective has several limitations. The first, ironically, stems from its central strength: By analyzing cognition into its components, information processing has had difficulty reassembling them into a broad, comprehensive theory of development. We have seen that the neo-Piagetian perspective is one effort to build a general theory by retaining Piaget's stages while drawing on information-processing mechanisms to explain cognitive change.

Furthermore, the computer metaphor, although it brings precision to research on the human mind, has drawbacks. Computer models of cognitive processing, though complex in

TABLE 7.1 MECHANISMS OF COGNITIVE DEVELOPMENT FROM THE INFORMATION-PROCESSING PERSPECTIVE

Mechanism	Description
Basic processing capacity	Capacity of the mental system increases as a result of brain development.
Processing efficiency	Speed of basic operations increases, freeing up working memory for additional mental activities.
Encoding of information	Encoding, in the form of attention, becomes more thorough and better adapted to task demands.
Cognitive inhibition	Ability to prevent internal and external distracting stimuli from capturing attention improves, freeing up working memory for remembering, reasoning, and solving problems.
Strategy execution	Strategies become more effective, improving storage, retrieval, and use of information for reasoning and problem solving.
Knowledge	Amount and structure of the knowledge base increase, making new, related information more meaningful so it is easier to store and retrieve.
Metacognition	Awareness and understanding of cognitive processes expand and self-regulation improves, leading strategies to be applied more effectively in a wider range of situations.

their own right, do not reflect the richness of real-life learning experiences. For example, they overlook aspects of cognition that are not linear and logical, such as imagination and creativity. In addition, computers do not have desires, interests, and intentions. Nor can they engage in interaction with others, as children do when they learn from parents, teachers, and peers. Perhaps because of the narrowness of the computer metaphor, information processing has not yet told us much about the links between cognition and other areas of development. Investigators have applied information-processing assumptions to children's thinking about certain aspects of their social world, and we will see some examples in later chapters. But extensions of Piaget's theory still prevail when it comes to research on children's social and moral understanding.

Finally, information-processing research has been slow to respond to the growing interest in the biological bases of cognitive development. Connectionist theories have begun to fill this gap by creating computer simulations that model human information processing at a neural level. Evolutionary ideas, as well, have started to appear in information-processing theories, as Siegler's model of strategy choice illustrates. And the work of developmental cognitive neuroscientists is enlarging our appreciation of how changes in the brain are related to children's processing skills.

Despite its shortcomings, the information-processing approach holds great promise. The near future is likely to bring new breakthroughs in understanding mechanisms of cognitive development and neurological changes that underlie various mental activities, and in identifying teaching techniques that support children's learning.

Ask Yourself

REVIEW	Why are gains in processing capacity and metacognition important for the development of scientific reasoning? What can teachers do to promote the development of scientific reasoning?
APPLY	Review Heidi's reasoning about the impact of several variables on the bounce of tennis balls on page 304. What features of her thinking suggest that she is beginning to reason scientifically?
CONNECT	Using mechanisms of cognitive development discussed in this chapter, explain why teaching both basic skills and understanding of concepts and strategies is vital for children's progress in reading and mathematics.
REFLECT	Describe early, informal experiences important for literacy and math development that you experienced while growing up. How do you think those experiences contributed to your academic progress after you started school?

Summary

The Information-Processing Approach

What unique features characterize the information-processing approach to cognitive development?

◎ The information-processing approach views the mind as a complex, symbol-manipulating system through which information flows, much like a computer. The computer analogy helps researchers analyze thinking into its components, each of which can be studied thoroughly to yield a detailed understanding of what children and adults do when faced with a task or problem.

General Models of Information Processing

Describe the store and connectionist models, noting implications for cognitive development.

◎ The **store model** assumes that we hold, or store, information in three parts of the system, where **mental strategies** operate on it so that it can be retained and used efficiently and flexibly. The **sensory register** and **working,** or **short-term, memory** are limited in capacity. Within working memory, the **central executive** directs the flow of information and the use of strategies, influencing the extent to which information is transferred to **long-term memory,** our limitless, permanent knowledge base.

◎ The store model suggests that two broad aspects of the cognitive system increase with age: (1) the basic capacity of its stores, especially working memory, and (2) the extent and effectiveness of strategy use. Research on **memory span** supports both of these trends. Speed of processing increases rapidly in middle childhood, contributing to improved processing capacity.

◎ **Connectionist,** or **artificial neural network, models** use computer simulations to model the workings of neurons in the brain. Thousands of simple processing units, organized into layers, are programmed to change with experience. Researchers compare the network's responses with those of children and adults. Findings reveal that gradual, internal learning often precedes changes in behavior that appear stagelike when viewed from outside the system. Because just a few built-in procedures get learning started, connectionists claim that the human cognitive system is a general processing device. However, artificial neural networks learn far more slowly than children and adults.

Developmental Theories of Information Processing

Describe and evaluate Case's neo-Piagetian theory and Siegler's model of strategy choice.

◎ According to Case's **neo-Piagetian theory,** cognitive development results from gains in working-memory capacity. Brain development and automization of strategies due to practice release working memory for combining old schemes and generating new ones. When schemes consolidate into **central conceptual structures,** working memory expands further, and the child moves up to a new Piagetian stage. Case's theory accounts for the horizontal décalage through variations in the complexity of tasks and children's experiences. His powerful ideas must be tested with many more tasks.

◎ Siegler's **model of strategy choice** applies an evolutionary perspective to children's cognition. Strategy development follows an overlapping-waves pattern. Faced with challenging problems, children try a variety of strategies, gradually selecting from them on the basis of accuracy and speed. Siegler's findings reveal that no child thinks in just one way, even on the same task. So far, mechanisms that lead children to choose among strategies are clearer than those that produce strategy variation.

Attention

Describe the development of attention, including selective, adaptable, and planful strategies.

◎ Attention becomes more sustained as children generate increasingly complex play goals. As sustained attention increases, children become more selective—better at focusing on relevant aspects of a task. Older children are also better at adapting attention to task requirements. Gains in **cognitive inhibition** are particularly marked in middle childhood and are linked to development of the cerebral cortex, especially the frontal lobes. Improved inhibition underlies children's greater selectivity of attention.

◎ Development of attentional (and memory) strategies tends to occur in the following four phases: (1) **production deficiency** (failure to use the strategy); (2) **control deficiency** (failure to execute the strategy consistently); (3) **utilization deficiency** (consistent use of the strategy, but little or no improvement in performance); and (4) **effective strategy use.**

◎ During middle childhood, children become better at **planning.** On tasks that require systematic visual search or the coordination of many acts, school-age children are more likely than preschoolers to proceed in an orderly fashion. Children learn much about planning through use of cultural tools that support it, adult guidance and encouragement, and many opportunities to practice.

◎ Deficits in executive processing and inhibition may underlie the serious attentional and impulse-control difficulties of children with **attention-deficit hyperactivity disorder (ADHD).** Children with ADHD have serious academic and social problems.

Memory

Describe the development of memory strategies of rehearsal, organization, and elaboration, noting the influence of task demands and culture.

◎ Although the beginnings of memory strategies can be seen during the preschool years, young children seldom engage in

rehearsal or **organization.** As use of these strategies improves, children combine them; the more strategies children use simultaneously, the better they remember. Because it requires considerable working-memory capacity, **elaboration** is a late-developing strategy that appears at the end of middle childhood and becomes more common during adolescence.

◎ Like young children, people in non-Western cultures who have had no formal schooling rarely use or benefit from instruction in memory strategies. Tasks requiring children to memorize isolated bits of information in school promote deliberate memorization in middle childhood.

Describe the development of three approaches to memory retrieval: recognition, recall, and reconstruction.

◎ **Recognition,** the simplest form of retrieval, is a fairly automatic process that is highly accurate by the preschool years. In contrast, **recall,** or generating a mental representation of an absent stimulus, is more difficult and shows much greater improvement with age, as older children make use of a wider range of retrieval cues.

◎ Even young children engage in **reconstruction** when remembering complex, meaningful material. Over time, as originally provided information decays and new information is presented, children make more inferences about actors and actions. This increases the coherence of reconstructed information and, therefore, its memorableness. However, reconstruction shows that much recalled information can be inaccurate.

◎ According to **fuzzy-trace theory,** information is reconstructed automatically at encoding into a vague, fuzzy version called a **gist,** which is stored separately from the verbatim version and is especially useful for reasoning. With age, children rely less on verbatim memory and more on gist memory, which contributes to improved reasoning and recall.

How do gains in knowledge enhance memory performance?

◉ Gains in size and structure of the knowledge base enhance memory performance by making new, related information easier to store and retrieve. More-knowledgeable children show greater organization at retrieval, which suggests that they apply memory strategies in their area of expertise with little or no effort. Children differ not only in what they know but also in how motivated they are to use their knowledge to acquire new information. Extensive knowledge and use of memory strategies support one another.

Describe the development and function of scripts and autobiographical memory.

◉ Like adults, young children remember familiar experiences in terms of **scripts**—general descriptions of what occurs and when it occurs in a particular situation. Scripts become more elaborate with age and permit children to predict what might happen on future similar occasions. Scripts may support the transition from **episodic memory** to **semantic memory.**

◉ Research suggests that changes in the frontal lobes of the cerebral cortex, the advent of a clear self-image, and the development of verbal means for storing information contribute to the end of **infantile amnesia** after age 3. As preschoolers talk with adults about personally significant past events, they adopt the narrative thinking generated in these dialogues, forming an **autobiographical memory.** Children whose parents use an elaborative rather than a repetitive conversational style will produce more coherent and detailed personal stories.

How does eyewitness memory change with age, and what factors influence the accuracy of children's reports?

◉ Compared with preschoolers, school-age children are better at giving accurate, detailed, and complete eyewitness accounts and at resisting adults' misleading questions. When properly questioned, however, preschoolers can recall personally relevant events accurately.

◉ When a biased adult repeatedly asks leading questions, children are far more likely to give false information. Stereotyping of the accused as "bad" and a long delay between the events and the child's eyewitness report

further contribute to inaccurate reporting. Interventions that increase the likelihood of children's accurate recall include practice interviews, open-ended questioning that prompts children to disclose details, and a warm interview tone.

Metacognition

Describe the development of metacognitive knowledge and cognitive self-regulation, and explain why cognitive self-regulation is vital for success on complex tasks.

◉ **Metacognition** expands greatly as children construct a naïve **theory of mind,** a coherent understanding of people as mental beings. From early to middle childhood, children's awareness of cognitive capacities, strategies, and task variables becomes more accurate and complete. In addition, their view of the mind changes from a passive to an active, process-oriented approach to mental functioning. Once children become conscious of the many factors that influence mental activity, they take account of interactions among variables, and metacognition becomes a comprehensive theory.

◉ **Cognitive self-regulation**—continually monitoring progress toward a goal, checking outcomes, and redirecting unsuccessful efforts—develops slowly. The relationship between knowledge of memory strategies and recall strengthens over middle childhood. Gains in comprehension monitoring also reflect improved cognitive self-regulation. By adolescence, cognitive self-regulation is a strong predictor of academic success. Parents and teachers who suggest self-regulatory strategies and explain why they are effective help children apply those strategies in new situations.

Applications of Information Processing to Academic Learning

Discuss the development of reading, mathematics, and scientific reasoning, noting the implications of research findings for teaching.

◉ **Emergent literacy** reveals that young children understand a great deal about written language before they read and write in conventional ways. Preschoolers gradually revise incorrect ideas about the meaning of written symbols as their cognitive capacities improve, as they encounter writing in many contexts, and as adults help them with written communication.

© WILL HART/PHOTOEDIT

◉ **Phonological awareness** is a strong predictor of emergent literacy knowledge and of later reading and spelling achievement. Adult–child narrative conversations and many informal literacy-related experiences also contribute to literacy development.

◉ As children make the transition to conventional literacy, phonological awareness, processing speed, and visual scanning and discrimination contribute to reading progress. Research shows that a combination of **whole-language** and **phonics approaches** is most effective for teaching beginning reading.

◉ Like reading, mathematical reasoning builds on informally acquired knowledge. Toddlers display a beginning grasp of **ordinality,** which serves as the basis for more complex understandings. As preschoolers gain experience with counting, they grasp **cardinality** and begin to solve simple addition and subtraction problems. When adults provide many occasions for counting and comparing quantities, children acquire basic numerical understandings sooner.

◉ During the early school years, children acquire basic math facts through a combination of frequent practice and reasoning about number concepts. Children's mistakes in solving more complex problems reveal that they sometimes apply strategies incorrectly because they do not understand the basis for them. Mathematics instruction that combines practice in experimenting with strategies and conceptual understanding is best.

◉ Research on scientific reasoning reveals that the ability to coordinate theory with evidence improves from childhood to adolescence. Greater working-memory capacity and exposure to increasingly complex problems in school contribute to the metacognitive understanding necessary for reasoning scientifically—thinking about theories, isolating variables, and seeking disconfirming evidence.

Evaluation of the Information-Processing Approach

Summarize the strengths and limitations of the information-processing approach.

⊚ A major strength of the information-processing approach is its precision in breaking down cognition into its components so that each can be studied thoroughly. As a result, information processing has uncovered a variety of mechanisms of cognitive change and has contributed to the design of teaching techniques that advance children's thinking.

⊚ Nevertheless, information processing has not yet led to a comprehensive theory or told us much about the links between cognition and other areas of development. Although information-processing researchers have been slow to address the biological bases of cognitive development, they are making strides in this area.

⊚ Important Terms and Concepts
⊚

attention-deficit hyperactivity disorder (ADHD) (p. 284)
autobiographical memory (p. 291)
cardinality (p. 303)
central conceptual structures (p. 276)
central executive (p. 273)
cognitive inhibition (p. 281)
cognitive self-regulation (p. 297)
connectionist, or artificial neural network, models (p. 275)
control deficiency (p. 282)
effective strategy use (p. 282)
elaboration (p. 286)
emergent literacy (p. 300)

episodic memory (p. 290)
fuzzy-trace theory (p. 289)
gist (p. 289)
infantile amnesia (p. 293)
long-term memory (p. 273)
memory span (p. 273)
mental strategies (p. 272)
metacognition (p. 296)
model of strategy choice (p. 278)
neo-Piagetian theory (p. 276)
ordinality (p. 302)
organization (p. 285)
phonics approach (p. 302)
phonological awareness (p. 300)

planning (p. 282)
production deficiency (p. 282)
recall (p. 287)
recognition (p. 287)
reconstruction (p. 288)
rehearsal (p. 285)
scripts (p. 290)
semantic memory (p. 290)
sensory register (p. 272)
store model (p. 272)
theory of mind (p. 296)
utilization deficiency (p. 282)
whole-language approach (p. 302)
working, or short-term, memory (p. 272)

"Untitled"
Mahdi Saheb Mohammed
Age 8, Kuwait

This young artist understands much about small business life—how merchants categorize, display, and measure goods, and how customers vigorously express their desires. Although intelligence tests predict children's success at school tasks, they are far less effective at assessing the practical know-how and visually expressive talent evident in this work of art.

Intelligence

Five-year-old Eric sat in a small, unfamiliar testing room while Mrs. Thomas, an adult he had met only moments before, prepared to give him an intelligence test. Eric had been eager to accompany Mrs. Thomas when she arrived at his kindergarten classroom, but once the testing session began, he looked bewildered.

Mrs. Thomas started with some word definitions. "Eric," she asked, "how are wood and coal alike? How are they the same?"

Eric shrugged his shoulders. "Well, they're both hard," he said.

Mrs. Thomas continued: "And an apple and a peach?"

"They taste good," responded Eric, scanning Mrs. Thomas's face for any sign that he was doing all right.

Mrs. Thomas looked back pleasantly but moved along. "A ship and an automobile?"

Eric paused, unsure of what Mrs. Thomas meant. Finally, he returned to his first response: "They're hard," he replied.

"Iron and silver?"

"They're hard," Eric repeated, still trying to figure out what Mrs. Thomas's questions were all about.

The **psychometric approach** to cognitive development is the basis for the wide variety of intelligence tests available for assessing children's mental abilities. As we see from Mrs. Thomas's approach to testing Eric, the psychometric perspective, unlike the Piagetian, Vygotskian, and information-processing views, is far more product oriented than process oriented. It is largely concerned with outcomes and results—how many and what kinds of questions children of different ages answer correctly. Psychometric researchers ask questions like these:

• What factors, or dimensions, make up intelligence, and how do they change with age?

• How can intelligence be measured so that scores predict future academic achievement, career attainment, and other aspects of intellectual success?

• To what extent do children of the same age differ in intelligence, and what explains those differences?

As we examine these questions, we will quickly become immersed in the long-standing debate over the contribution of nature (heredity) and nurture (environment) to intelligence, along with the related controversy over whether intelligence tests are biased, or inaccurate, measures of the mental abilities of members of certain ethnic minority groups. We will see that the cognitive perspectives considered in previous chapters, as well as research on environmental contexts, have added much to our understanding of children's test performance. We conclude with the development of giftedness, in the form of talent and creativity.

🌀 Definitions of Intelligence

Jot down a list of behaviors that you regard as typical of highly intelligent people. Does your list contain just one or two items or a great many? In a study in which laypeople and experts completed a similar exercise, both groups viewed intelligence as made up of at least three broad attributes: verbal ability, practical problem solving, and social competence (Sternberg & Detterman, 1986). But respondents differed in their descriptions of these attributes. And contemporary experts showed much less agreement about the makeup of intelligence than did experts in a similar study conducted a half-century earlier! Clearly, most people think of intelligence as a complex combination of attributes, and there is little consensus among experts on its ingredients.

Defining children's intelligence is especially challenging because behaviors that reflect intelligent behavior change with age. To illustrate, researchers asked students in an introductory psychology course to list five traits of intelligent 6-month-olds, 2-year-olds, 10-year-olds, and adults. Refer to Table 8.1 for the students' responses. Notice how sensorimotor responsiveness becomes less important with age, whereas verbal ability, problem solving, and reasoning become more important. Furthermore, when the students estimated correlations between various abilities, they predicted some close connections, but they thought others would correlate weakly (Siegler & Richards, 1980). This tension between intelligence as a single ability versus a collection of loosely related skills is ever present in historical and current theories on which mental tests are based.

Alfred Binet: A Holistic View

The social and educational climate of the late nineteenth and early twentieth centuries led to the development of the first intelligence tests. The most important influence was the beginning of universal public education in Europe and North America. When all children—not just society's privileged—could enroll in school, educators called for methods to identify students who could not profit from regular classroom instruction. The first successful intelligence test, constructed by French psychologist Alfred Binet and his colleague Theodore Simon in 1905, responded to this need.

The French Ministry of Instruction asked Binet to devise an objective method for assigning pupils to special classes—one based on mental ability, not classroom disruptiveness. Other researchers had tried to assess intelligence using simple measures of sensory responsiveness and reaction time (Cattell, 1890; Galton, 1883). In contrast, Binet believed that test items should tap complex mental activities involved in intelligent behavior, such as memory and reasoning. Consequently, Binet and Simon (1908) devised a test of general ability that included a variety of verbal and nonverbal items, each of which required thought and judgment. Their

🌀 Behaviors that reflect intelligence change with age. As this older sister carefully considers the layout and proportions of her painting, her younger brother observes and learns from her.
© Dex Images, Inc./CORBIS

TABLE 8.1 FIVE TRAITS MOST OFTEN MENTIONED BY COLLEGE STUDENTS AS CHARACTERIZING INTELLIGENCE AT DIFFERENT AGES

6-Month-Olds	2-Year-Olds	10-Year-Olds	Adults
1. Recognition of people and objects	1. Verbal ability	1. Verbal ability	1. Reasoning
2. Motor coordination	2. Learning ability	2, 3, 4. Learning ability; problem solving; reasoning (all three tied)	2. Verbal ability
3. Alertness	3. Awareness of people and environment		3. Problem solving
4. Awareness of environment	4. Motor coordination	5. Creativity	4. Learning ability
5. Verbalization	5. Curiosity		5. Creativity

Source: R. S. Siegler & D. D. Richards, 1980, "College Students' Prototypes of Children's Intelligence." Paper presented at the annual meeting of the American Psychological Association, New York. Adapted by permission of the author.

test was also the first to associate items of increasing difficult with chronological age (Sternberg & Jarvin, 2003). This enabled Binet and Simon to estimate how much a child was behind or ahead of her agemates in intellectual development.

The Binet test was so successful in predicting school performance that it became the basis for new intelligence tests. In 1916, Lewis Terman at Stanford University adapted it for use with English-speaking schoolchildren. Since then, the English version has been known as the *Stanford-Binet Intelligence Scale.* As we will see later, the Stanford-Binet has changed greatly; it no longer provides just a single, holistic measure of intelligence.

The Factor Analysts: A Multifaceted View

To find out whether intelligence is a single trait or an assortment of abilities, researchers used a complicated correlational procedure called **factor analysis,** which identifies sets of test items that cluster together, meaning that test-takers who do well on one item in a cluster tend to do well on the others. Distinct clusters are called *factors.* For example, if vocabulary, verbal comprehension, and verbal analogy items all correlate highly, they form a factor that the investigator might label "verbal ability." Using factor analysis, many researchers tried to identify the mental abilities that contribute to successful intelligence test performance.

• **EARLY FACTOR ANALYSTS** • British psychologist Charles Spearman (1927) was the first influential factor analyst. He found that all test items he examined correlated with one another. As a result, he proposed that a common underlying **general intelligence,** called **"g,"** influenced each of them. At the same time, noticing that the test items were not perfectly correlated, Spearman concluded that they varied in the extent to which "g" contributed to them and suggested that each item, or a set of similar items, also measured a **specific intelligence** that was unique to the task.

Spearman downplayed the significance of specific intelligences. He regarded "g" as central and supreme, and was especially interested in understanding it. With further study, he inferred that "g" represents abstract reasoning capacity because test items that involved forming relationships and applying general principles clustered together especially strongly. They also were the best predictors of cognitive performance outside the testing situation.

American psychologist Louis Thurstone (1938) soon took issue with the importance of "g." His factor analysis of college students' scores on more than 50 intelligence tests indicated that separate, unrelated factors exist. Declaring the supremacy of these factors, Thurstone called them *primary mental abilities.*

• **CONTEMPORARY EXTENSIONS** • Spearman and Thurstone eventually resolved their differences, as each acknowledged findings that supported the other's perspective (Brody, 2000). Current theorists and test designers combine both approaches by proposing *hierarchical models* of mental abilities. At the highest level is "g," assumed to be present to a greater or lesser degree in all separate factors. These factors, in turn, are measured by *subtests,* groups of related items. Subtest scores provide information about a child's strengths and weaknesses. They also can be combined into a total score representing general intelligence.

Contemporary theorists have extended factor-analytic research. The two most influential are R. B. Cattell and John Carroll. Each offers a unique, multifaceted perspective on intelligence.

▶ *Crystallized versus Fluid Intelligence.* According to Raymond B. Cattell (1971, 1987), in addition to "g," intelligence consists of two broad factors: **Crystallized intelligence** refers to skills that depend on accumulated knowledge and experience, good judgment, and mastery of social customs—abilities acquired because they are valued by the individual's culture. On intelligence tests, vocabulary, general information, and arithmetic problems are examples of items that emphasize crystallized intelligence. In contrast, **fluid intelligence** depends more heavily on basic information-processing skills—the ability to detect relationships among stimuli, the speed with which the individual can analyze information, and the capacity of working memory. Fluid intelligence is assumed to be influenced more by conditions in the brain and less by culture. It often works with crystallized intelligence to support effective reasoning, abstraction, and problem solving (Horn & Noll, 1997).

Among children who are similar in cultural and educational background, crystallized and fluid intelligence are highly correlated and difficult to distinguish in factor analyses, probably

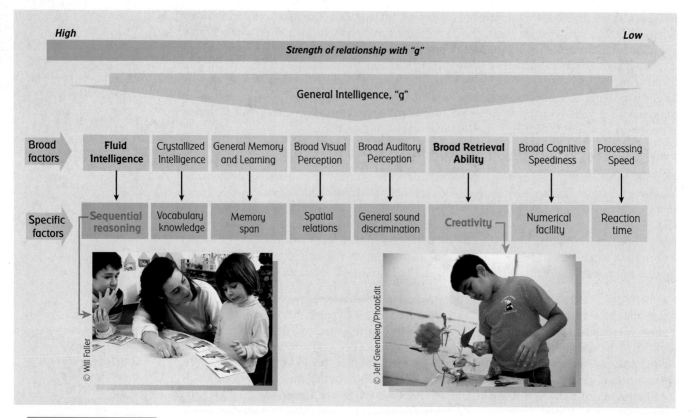

Figure 8.1

Carroll's hierarchical model of intelligence. At the top is general intelligence, or "g." The second tier shows eight broad abilities, or factors, arranged from left to right in terms of decreasing strength of relationship with "g." In the third tier are examples of narrow factors, specific behaviors through which people display the broad abilities. The child on the left is completing a sequential-reasoning task in which she arranges pictures to tell a story—a type of fluid intelligence. The child on the right is applying his broad retrieval ability as he uses art materials creatively. Carroll's model reflects the wide array of abilities tapped by mental tests, but no single test includes all of his factors. (Adapted from Carroll, 1993.)

because children high in fluid intelligence acquire information more easily. But when children differ greatly in cultural and educational experiences, the two abilities show little relationship; children with the same fluid capacity may perform quite differently on crystallized tasks (Horn, 1994). As these findings suggest, Cattell's theory has important implications for the issue of *cultural bias* in intelligence testing. Tests aimed at reducing culturally specific content usually emphasize fluid over crystallized items.

▶ *The Three-Stratum Theory of Intelligence.* Using improved factor-analytic methods, John Carroll (1993, 1997) reanalyzed relationships between items in hundreds of studies. His findings yielded a **three-stratum theory of intelligence** that elaborates the models proposed by Spearman, Thurstone, and Cattell. Carroll represented the structure of intelligence as having three tiers. As Figure 8.1 shows, "g" presides at the top. In the second tier are an array of *broad abilities,* which Carroll considered to be the basic biological components of intelligence; they are arranged from left to right in terms of decreasing relationship with "g." In the third tier are *narrow abilities*—specific behaviors through which people display the second-tier factors.

Carroll's model is the most comprehensive factor-analytic classification of mental abilities to date. As we will see in the next section, it provides a useful framework for researchers seeking to understand mental-test performance in cognitive-processing terms. It also reminds us of the great diversity of intellectual factors. Currently, no test measures all of Carroll's factors.

Recent Advances in Defining Intelligence

Many researchers believe that factors on intelligence tests have limited usefulness unless we can identify the cognitive processes responsible for those factors. Once we discover exactly what separates individuals who can solve certain mental test items from those who cannot, we will know more about why a particular child does well or poorly and what skills must be worked on to improve performance.

Combining Psychometric and Information-Processing Approaches

To overcome the limitations of factor analysis, some investigators combine psychometric and information-processing approaches. They conduct **componential analyses** of children's test scores. This means that they look for relationships between aspects (or components) of information processing and children's intelligence test performance.

Many studies reveal that speed of processing, measured in terms of reaction time on diverse cognitive tasks, is modestly related to general intelligence and to gains in mental test performance over time (Deary, 2001). As early as age 3 months, reaction time to visual stimuli predicts preschool intelligence (Dougherty & Haith, 1997). These findings suggest that individuals whose central nervous systems function more efficiently, permitting them to take in and manipulate information quickly, have an edge in intellectual skills. In support of this interpretation, fast, strong ERPs (event-related potentials, or EEG brain waves in response to stimulation) predict both speedy cognitive processing and higher mental test scores (Rijsdijk & Boomsma, 1997; Schmid, Tirsch, & Scherb, 2002). Furthermore, fMRI research reveals that the metabolic rate of the cerebral cortex during complex tasks is lower for high-scoring individuals, suggesting that they require less mental energy for intricate thinking (Vernon et al., 2001).

But efficient thinking is not the only aspect of cognition linked to better intelligence test scores. Flexible attention, memory, and reasoning strategies are just as important, and they explain some of the relationship between response speed and good test performance (Lohman, 2000; Miller & Vernon, 1992). Children who focus on relevant information and who memorize and reason adeptly acquire more knowledge and can retrieve it rapidly. When faced with challenging test items, they use that knowledge to think more effectively. Componential research has also highlighted cognitive processes that are unrelated to test scores but that greatly aid children's thinking in everyday life. Certain aspects of metacognition—awareness of problem-solving strategies and planning skills—are not good predictors of mental test performance (Alexander & Schwanenflugel, 1996; Bishop et al., 2001).

As the research just reviewed illustrates, identifying relationships between cognitive processing and mental test scores brings us closer to isolating the cognitive skills that contribute to high intelligence. But notice how these efforts regard mental ability as entirely due to causes within the child. Recall from previous chapters that cultural and situational factors profoundly affect children's thinking. Robert Sternberg has expanded the componential approach into a comprehensive theory that views intelligence as a product of inner and outer forces.

Sternberg's Triarchic Theory

As Figure 8.2 shows, Sternberg's (1997, 2001, 2002) **triarchic theory of successful intelligence** identifies three broad, interacting intelligences: (1) *analytical intelligence,* or information-processing skills; (2) *creative intelligence,* the capacity to solve novel problems; and (3) *practical intelligence,* application of intellectual skills in everyday

These first graders solve math problems with a special set of small blocks and help from each other. Children who apply strategies effectively acquire more knowledge and can retrieve it rapidly. As a result, they score higher on intelligence tests.
© Richard Hutchings/PhotoEdit

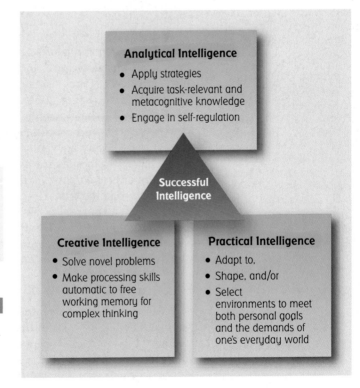

Analytical Intelligence
- Apply strategies
- Acquire task-relevant and metacognitive knowledge
- Engage in self-regulation

Successful Intelligence

Creative Intelligence
- Solve novel problems
- Make processing skills automatic to free working memory for complex thinking

Practical Intelligence
- Adapt to,
- Shape, and/or
- Select environments to meet both personal goals and the demands of one's everyday world

▶ **Figure 8.2**

Sternberg's triarchic theory of successful intelligence.
People who behave intelligently balance three interrelated intelligences—analytical, creative, and practical—to achieve success in life, defined by their personal goals and the requirements of their cultural communities.

situations. Intelligent behavior involves balancing all three intelligences to achieve success in life, according to one's personal goals and the requirements of one's cultural community.

• **ANALYTICAL INTELLIGENCE** • The first intelligence, *analytical,* consists of the information-processing components that underlie all intelligent acts: applying strategies, acquiring task-relevant and metacognitive knowledge, and engaging in self-regulation. On mental tests, however, processing skills are used in only a few of their potential ways, resulting in far too narrow a view of intelligent behavior. We have seen many examples of how children in tribal and village societies do not invest in or perform well on measures of "school" knowledge. Yet these children thrive when processing information in out-of-school situations that most Westerners would find highly challenging.

• **CREATIVE INTELLIGENCE** • In any context, success depends not only on processing familiar information but also on generating useful solutions to new problems. People who are *creative* think more skillfully than others when faced with novelty. Given a new task, they apply their information-processing skills in exceptionally effective ways, rapidly making those skills automatic so that working memory is freed for more complex aspects of the situation. Consequently, they quickly move to high-level performance. Although all of us are capable of creativity to some degree, only a few individuals excel at generating novel solutions. We will address the ingredients of creativity in greater detail at the end of this chapter.

• **PRACTICAL INTELLIGENCE** • Finally, intelligence is a *practical,* goal-oriented activity aimed at one or more of the following purposes: *adapting to, shaping,* and *selecting an environment.* Intelligent people skillfully *adapt* their thinking to fit with both their desires and the demands of their everyday worlds. When they cannot adapt to a situation, they try to *shape,* or change, it to meet their needs. If they cannot shape it, they *select* new contexts that better match their skills, values, or goals. Practical intelligence reminds us that intelligent behavior is never culture-free. Because of their backgrounds, some children do well at the behaviors required for success on intelligence tests, and they easily adapt to the tasks and testing conditions. Others, with different life histories, misinterpret the testing context or reject it because it does not suit their needs. Yet such children often display sophisticated abilities in daily life—for example, telling stories, engaging in complex artistic activities, or interacting skillfully with other people.

To examine the validity of the triarchic theory, Sternberg and his collaborators gave thousands of children and adolescents in Finland, Spain, Russia, and the United States test items that tap analytical, creative, and practical skills. Factor analyses repeatedly indicated that the three intelligences are relatively distinct (Sternberg, 2003a; Sternberg et al., 1999, 2001; Grigorenko & Sternberg, 2001).

The triarchic theory highlights the complexity of intelligent behavior and the limitations of current intelligence tests in assessing that complexity. For example, out-of-school, practical forms of intelligence are vital for life success, and they help explain why cultures vary widely in the behaviors they regard as intelligent (Sternberg et al., 2000). When researchers asked ethnically diverse parents for their idea of an intelligent first grader, Caucasian Americans mentioned cognitive traits. In contrast, ethnic minorities (Cambodian, Filipino, Vietnamese, and Mexican immigrants) saw noncognitive capacities—motivation, self-management, and social skills—as particularly important (Okagaki & Sternberg, 1993). According to Sternberg, mental tests can easily underestimate, and even overlook, the intellectual strengths of some children, especially ethnic minorities.

Gardner's Theory of Multiple Intelligences

In yet another view of how information-processing skills underlie intelligent behavior, Howard Gardner's (1983, 1993, 2000) **theory of multiple intelligences** defines intelligence in terms of distinct sets of processing operations that permit individuals to solve problems, create products, and discover new knowledge in a wide range of culturally valued activities. Dismissing the idea of general intelligence, Gardner proposes at least eight independent intelligences (see Table 8.2).

TABLE 8.2 GARDNER'S MULTIPLE INTELLIGENCES

Intelligence	Processing Operations	End-State Performance Possibilities
Linguistic	Sensitivity to the sounds, rhythms, and meaning of words and the functions of language	Poet, journalist
Logico-mathematical	Sensitivity to, and capacity to detect, logical or numerical patterns; ability to handle long chains of logical reasoning	Mathematician
Musical	Ability to produce and appreciate pitch, rhythm (or melody), and aesthetic quality of the forms of musical expressiveness	Instrumentalist, composer
Spatial	Ability to perceive the visual-spatial world accurately, to perform transformations on those perceptions, and to re-create aspects of visual experience in the absence of relevant stimuli	Sculptor, navigator
Bodily-kinesthetic	Ability to use the body skillfully for expressive as well as goal-directed purposes; ability to handle objects skillfully	Dancer, athlete
Naturalist	Ability to recognize and classify all varieties of animals, minerals, and plants	Biologist
Interpersonal	Ability to detect and respond appropriately to the moods, temperaments, motivations, and intentions of others	Therapist, salesperson
Intrapersonal	Ability to discriminate complex inner feelings and to use them to guide one's own behavior; knowledge of one's own strengths, weaknesses, desires, and intelligences	Person with detailed, accurate self-knowledge

Sources: Gardner, 1993, 1998a, 2000.

Gardner believes that each intelligence has a unique biological basis, a distinct course of development, and different expert, or "end-state," performances. At the same time, he emphasizes that a lengthy process of education is required to transform any raw potential into a mature social role (Torff & Gardner, 1999). This means that cultural values and learning opportunities have a great deal to do with the extent to which a child's strengths are realized and the ways they are expressed.

Gardner acknowledges that if tests were available to assess all these abilities, they should show little relationship to one another. But he regards neurological support for their separateness as particularly compelling. Research indicating that damage to a certain part of the adult brain influences only one ability (such as linguistic or spatial), while sparing others, suggests that the affected ability is independent. The existence of people with unusual profiles of intelligence also fits with Gardner's belief in distinct abilities. Individuals with *savant syndrome,* who display one area of outstanding strength alongside deficits in many others, provide an illustration. Children with *autism* occasionally show this pattern. Though severely impaired in language and communication, a few autistic individuals have remarkable abilities, always featuring dazzling memory (Treffert & Wallace, 2002). These usually involve numerical and spatial skills—such as effortless calculation, detailed drawing, or performance of long piano pieces after hearing them only once—that are primarily housed in the right hemisphere of the cerebral cortex. Savant syndrome often is associated with damage to the left cerebral hemisphere, which may have caused the right hemisphere to compensate, yielding an "island of strength" (Miller et al., 1998).

Does Gardner's view remind you of the *core knowledge perspective,* discussed in Chapter 6? Indeed, he accepts the existence of innately specified, core domains of thought, present at birth or emerging early in life. Then, as children respond to the demands of their culture, they transform those intelligences to fit the activities they are called on to perform. Gardner's work has been especially helpful in efforts to understand and nurture children's special talents, a topic we will take up at the end of this chapter.

⑥ According to Gardner, children are capable of at least eight distinct intelligences. As this girl classifies a fern that grows along a nature trail, she enriches her naturalist intelligence.

© Cathy Melloan/PhotoEdit

FROM RESEARCH TO PRACTICE

Social and Emotional Intelligence

During recess, Muriel handed a birthday party invitation to every fifth-grade girl except Claire, who looked on sadly as her classmates chattered about the party. But one of Muriel's friends, Jessica, looked troubled. Pulling Muriel aside, she exclaimed, "Why'd you do that? You hurt Claire's feelings and embarrassed her! If you bring invitations to school, you've got to give

everybody one!" And after school, Jessica offered these comforting words to Claire: "If you aren't invited, I'm not going, either!"

Jessica's IQ is only slightly above average, but she excels at acting wisely in social situations. Although early theorists of mental abilities recognized the existence of *social intelligence*, they gave it scant attention. Only in the 1960s did researchers

construct the first tests of social aptitude (Hendricks, Guilford, & Hoepfner, 1969; O'Sullivan, Guilford, & deMille, 1965). Test items assessed the capacity of adolescents and adults to detect others' thoughts and feelings and to come up with effective solutions to social problems. Although studies reported positive correlations between social scores and IQ, these were modest. And factor analyses revealed that social intelligence, like nonsocial intelligence, is made up of diverse abilities (Kihlstrom & Cantor, 2000). Jessica, for example, takes Claire's perspective, communicates sensitively, displays mature morality, and expresses herself confidently.

Today, abilities formerly called social intelligence are labeled *emotional intelligence* — a term that has captured public attention because of popular books suggesting that it is an overlooked set of skills that can greatly improve life success (Goleman, 1995, 1998). Defined in diverse ways, **emotional intelligence** includes perceiving emotions accurately, expressing emotion appropriately, understanding the causes and consequences of emotions, and managing one's own and others' feelings to facilitate thinking and social interaction (Salovey & Pizzaro, 2003).

In one test of emotional intelligence, researchers devised items requiring people to exhibit diverse emotional skills—for example, to rate the strength of emotion

▲ The child on the left displays high emotional intelligence as he establishes eye contact, reads his friend's sadness accurately, and offers comfort. Researchers hope to devise tests of emotional intelligence that can identify children who might profit from interventions aimed at fostering social and emotional skills. © Don Smetzer/PhotoEdit

Critics of Gardner's theory, however, question the independence of his intelligences. They point out that the unusual skills of people with savant syndrome are mechanical and inflexible because those skills are not aided by other abilities. In contrast, excellence in most fields requires a combination of intelligences. A talented musician, for example, uses logico-mathematical intelligence to interpret the score, linguistic intelligence to respond to teaching, spatial intelligence to orient to the keyboard, interpersonal intelligence to react to the audience, and intrapersonal intelligence to play expressively. Furthermore, some exceptionally gifted individ-

TABLE 8.3 SAMPLE ITEMS FROM THE MULTIFACTOR EMOTIONAL INTELLIGENCE SCALE

Factor	Test Item
Perceiving emotions	Eight photos of faces are shown, each followed by six emotion labels: happiness, anger, fear, sadness, disgust, and surprise. The test-taker answers on a 5-point scale whether a given emotion is "definitely not present" (1) or "definitely present" (5).
Assimilating emotions into cognitive processes	"Imagine that Jonathan is one of your relatives. He is a tall, muscular person. Jonathan said something to you that made you feel both guilty and afraid. Feeling both guilty and afraid about Jonathan, how does he seem?" Ability to assimilate present mood into judgments is assessed by having the test-taker rate the following emotions on a 5-point scale, from "definitely does not describe" (1) to "definitely does describe" (5): sad, trusting, tense, cynical, aggressive, controlling, and hasty.
Understanding emotion	"Optimism most closely combines which of two emotions? (a) pleasure and anticipation, (b) acceptance and joy, (c) surprise and joy, (d) pleasure and joy."
Managing (regulating) emotion	"You have been dating the same person for several months and feel very comfortable. Lately, you are thinking that this relationship may be the one. . . . The last thing you expected was the phone call you received saying that the relationship is over. . . ." The test-taker rates emotion-management responses from "extremely ineffective" (1) to "extremely effective" (5). One such response is "block it out and . . . throw yourself into your work."

From J. D. Mayer, D. R. Caruso, & P. Salovey, 1999, "Emotional Intelligence Meets Traditional Standards for an Intelligence," *Intelligence, 27,* 267–298. Adapted by permission.

expressed in photographs of faces, to identify how a change in emotion might bring about a change in judgment of another person, and to rate responses for their effectiveness in controlling a negative emotion (see Table 8.3). Factor analyses of the scores of hundreds of adolescents and young adults identified several emotional abilities (perceiving, expressing, understanding, and managing emotion) as well as a higher-order general factor (Mayer, Salovey, & Caruso, 2003). Like social intelligence, emotional intelligence—especially understanding emotion—is modestly related to IQ. It also is positively associated with self-esteem, sociability, and current life satisfaction and negatively related to

aggressive behavior (Bohnert, Crnic, & Lim, 2003; Law, Wong, & Song, 2004; Mayer, Salovey, & Caruso, 2000).

At present, only a few assessments of emotional intelligence are available for children. These require careful training of teachers in observing and recording children's emotional skills during everyday activities, gathering information from parents, and taking into account children's ethnic backgrounds (Denham, 2005; Denham & Burton, 2003). As more and better measures are devised, they may help identify children with weak social and emotional competencies who would profit from intervention. Some researchers worry that emotional ability scores will lead psy-

chologists and educators to make simplistic comparisons among children and to lose sight of the fact that the adaptiveness of emotional and social behavior often varies across situations (Saarni, 2000).

Although much work remains, the concepts of social and emotional intelligence have increased teachers' awareness that providing experiences that meet students' social and emotional needs can improve their adjustment (Graczyk et al., 2000). Lessons that teach respect and caring for others, communication skills, cooperation, and resistance to unfavorable peer pressure—using active learning techniques that provide skill practice both in and out of the classroom—are becoming more common.

uals have abilities that are broad rather than limited to a particular domain (Goldsmith, 2000). Finally, current mental tests do tap several of Gardner's intelligences (linguistic, logico-mathematical, and spatial), and evidence for "g" suggests that they have common features.

Nevertheless, Gardner calls attention to several abilities not measured by intelligence tests. For example, his interpersonal and intrapersonal intelligences include a set of capacities for dealing with people and understanding oneself. As the From Research to Practice box above indicates, researchers are attempting to define and measure these vital abilities.

Ask Yourself

REVIEW	Using Sternberg's triarchic theory, explain the limitations of current mental tests in assessing the complexity of human intelligence.
APPLY	Eight-year-old Charya, an immigrant from Cambodia, had difficulty responding to test items asking for word definitions and general information. But she solved puzzles easily, and she quickly figured out which number comes next in a complex series. How does Charya score in crystallized and fluid intelligence? What might explain the difference?
CONNECT	Describe similarities between Gardner's theory of multiple intelligences and the core knowledge perspective on cognitive development (see Chapter 6, pages 253–254). What questions raised about this view also apply to Gardner's theory?
REFLECT	Select one of your intellectual strengths from Gardner's multiple intelligences, listed in Table 8.2. How do you display that intelligence? What other intelligences contribute to your strong performance?

Measuring Intelligence

Although intelligence tests sample only a narrow range of human cognitive capacities, psychologists and educators give them to school-age children because the scores, as we will see shortly, are modest to good predictors of future success—in school, on the job, and in other aspects of life. The *group-administered tests* given every so often in classrooms permit large numbers of students to be tested at once and are useful for instructional planning and for identifying students who require more extensive evaluation with *individually administered tests*. Unlike group tests, which teachers can give with minimal training, individual tests require considerable training and experience to give well. The examiner not only considers the child's answers but also carefully observes the child's behavior, noting such reactions as attention to and interest in the tasks and wariness of the adult. These observations provide insights into whether the test score accurately reflects the child's ability.

Some Commonly Used Intelligence Tests

Two individual tests—the Stanford-Binet and the Wechsler—are most often used to identify highly intelligent children and diagnose those with learning problems. Figure 8.3 provides examples of items that typically appear on intelligence tests for children.

• **THE STANFORD-BINET INTELLIGENCE SCALES** • The modern descendant of Alfred Binet's first successful intelligence test is the **Stanford-Binet Intelligence Scales, Fifth Edition,** for individuals from age 2 to adulthood. This latest edition measures general intelligence and five intellectual factors: fluid reasoning, quantitative reasoning, knowledge, visual-spatial processing, and working memory (Roid, 2003). In addition, each factor includes both a verbal mode and a nonverbal mode of testing, yielding 10 subtests in all. The nonverbal subtests, which do not require spoken language, are especially useful when assessing individuals with limited English, with hearing impairments, or with communication disorders. The quantitative reasoning and knowledge factors emphasize crystallized intelligence (culturally loaded, fact-oriented information), such as vocabulary and arithmetic problems. In contrast, the fluid reasoning, visual-spatial processing, and working-memory factors tap fluid intelligence and therefore are assumed to be less culturally biased.

A special edition of the test, the *Stanford-Binet Intelligence Scales for Early Childhood*, consists of a reduced number of items, tailored for assessing children between 2 years of age and 7 years 3 months. This makes the current Stanford-Binet more useful than its previous edition for diagnosing intellectual difficulties in early childhood.

• **THE WECHSLER INTELLIGENCE SCALE FOR CHILDREN** • The **Wechsler Intelligence Scale for Children–IV (WISC–IV)** is the fourth edition of a widely used test for 6- through 16-year-olds. A downward extension of it, the *Wechsler Preschool and Primary Scale of*

Intelligence–III (WPPSI–III), is appropriate for children 2 years 6 months through 7 years 3 months (Wechsler, 2002, 2003). The Wechsler tests offered both a measure of general intelligence and a variety of factor scores long before the Stanford-Binet. As a result, many psychologists and educators came to prefer them.

The WISC-IV includes four broad intellectual factors: verbal reasoning, perceptual reasoning, working memory, and processing speed. Each factor is made up of two or three subtests, yielding 10 separate scores in all. The WISC-IV was designed to downplay crystallized, culture-dependent intelligence, which is emphasized on only one of its four factors (verbal reasoning). The remaining three factors focus on fluid, information-processing skills. According to the test designers, the result is the most theoretically current and "culture-fair" intelligence test available (Williams, Weis, & Rolfhus, 2003).

The Wechsler tests were the first to use samples representing the total population of the United States, including ethnic minorities, to devise standards for interpreting test scores. Previous editions of the WISC have been adapted for children in Canada, where both English and French versions are available (Sarrazin, 1999; Wechsler, 1996).

Aptitude and Achievement Tests

Two other types of tests are closely related to intelligence tests. **Aptitude tests** assess an individual's potential to learn a specialized activity. For example, mechanical aptitude is the capacity to acquire mechanical skills, musical aptitude is the capacity to acquire musical skills, and scholastic aptitude is the capacity to master school tasks. The well-known Scholastic Assessment Test (SAT) and American College Testing Assessment (ACT), which you may have submitted as part of your college application, yield measures of scholastic aptitude. **Achievement tests** differ from aptitude tests in that they aim to assess not potential to learn, but actual knowledge and skill attainment. When a school district assesses fourth-grade reading comprehension or a college professor gives a final exam, an achievement test has been used.

Note, however, that differences among intelligence, aptitude, and achievement tests are not clear-cut. On each, certain items, especially those assessing verbal and math skills, are similar. As this overlap suggests, most tests tap both aptitude and achievement, though in different balances. The three test types do differ in breadth of content. Intelligence tests assess the widest array of skills. Aptitude tests are narrower, in that they focus on particular skill areas. And achievement tests cover the narrowest range because they are aimed at measuring recent learning, usually in particular school subjects.

Tests for Infants

Accurately measuring the intelligence of infants is especially challenging because babies cannot answer questions or follow directions. All we can do is present them with stimuli, coax them to respond, and observe their behavior. In addition, infants are not necessarily cooperative. They are likely to become distracted, fatigued, or bored during testing. Some tests depend heavily on information supplied by parents to compensate for the uncertain behaviors of these young test-takers.

TYPICAL VERBAL ITEMS

Vocabulary	Tell me what *carpet* means.
General Information	What day of the week comes right after Thursday?
Verbal Comprehension	Why are police officers needed?
Similarities	How are a ship and a train alike?
Arithmetic	If a $60 jacket is 25% off, how much does it cost?

TYPICAL PERCEPTUAL- AND SPATIAL-REASONING ITEMS

Block Design	Make these blocks look just like the picture.
Picture Concepts	Choose one object from each row to make a group of objects that goes together.
Spatial Visualization	Which of the boxes on the right can be made from the pattern on the left?

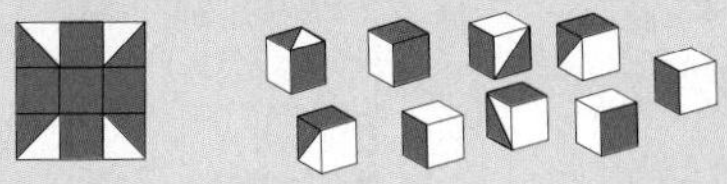

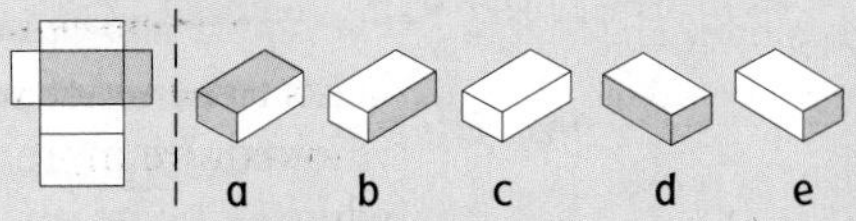

TYPICAL WORKING-MEMORY ITEMS

Digit Span	Repeat these digits in the same order. Now repeat these digits (a similar series) backward. 2, 6, 4, 7, 1, 8
Letter - Number Sequencing	Repeat these numbers and letters, first giving the numbers, then the letters, each in correct sequence. 8 G 4 B 5 N 2

TYPICAL PROCESSING-SPEED ITEM

Symbol Search	If the shape on the left is the same as any of those on the right, mark YES. If the shape is not the same, mark NO. Work as quickly as you can without making mistakes.

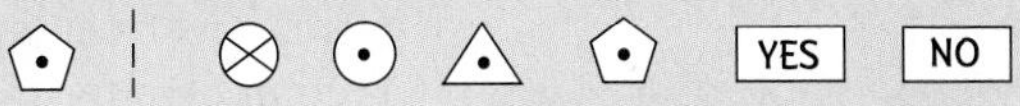

▲ **Figure 8.3**

Test items like those on commonly used intelligence tests for children. The verbal items emphasize culturally loaded, fact-oriented information. The perceptual- and spatial-reasoning, working-memory, and processing-speed items emphasize aspects of information processing and are assumed to assess more biologically based skills.

A trained examiner tests a baby with the Bayley Scales of Infant Development while her mother looks on. Although this item taps problem solving, most infant tests emphasize perceptual and motor responses, which predict later intelligence poorly.
© Laura Dwight Photography

Most infant measures consist largely of perceptual and motor responses, along with a few items that tap early language and cognition. For example, the *Bayley Scales of Infant Development,* a commonly used test for children between 1 month and 3½ years, consists of two parts: (1) the Mental Scale, which includes such items as turning to a sound, looking for a fallen object, building a tower of cubes, and naming pictures, and (2) the Motor Scale, which assesses fine and gross motor skills, such as grasping, sitting, drinking from a cup, and jumping (Bayley, 1993).

Despite careful construction, infant tests that emphasize these types of items are poor predictors of mental ability during childhood because infant perceptual and motor behaviors do not reflect the same aspects of intelligence assessed at older ages. To increase its predictive validity, the most recent version of the Bayley test includes a few items that emphasize infant memory, problem solving, categorization, and other complex cognitive skills, which are more likely to correlate with later mental test scores. Nevertheless, traditional infant tests are somewhat better at making long-term predictions for very low-scoring babies (Kopp, 1994). As a result, they are largely used for *screening*—helping to identify for further observation and intervention infants who are likely to have developmental problems.

Recall from Chapter 4 that speed of habituation and recovery to visual stimuli is among the best infant correlates of later intelligence because it assesses speed and flexibility of thinking (see page 138). Consequently, a test made up entirely of habituation/recovery items, the *Fagan Test of Infant Intelligence,* has been constructed. To take it, the infant sits on the mother's lap and views a series of pictures. After exposure to each one, the examiner records looking time toward a novel picture that is paired with the familiar one. Outside of highly controlled laboratory conditions, however, measurements of babies' looking behavior are unreliable, or inconsistent from one occasion to the next. Because of its low test–retest reliability (see Chapter 2, page 51), the Fagan test is less successful than researchers' assessments of infant habituation/recovery in predicting childhood mental test scores. And contradictory findings exist concerning whether Fagan test scores are useful for identifying infants at risk for delays in mental development (Andersson, 1996; Fagan & Detterman, 1992; Tasbihsazan, Nettelbeck, & Kirby, 2003).

Computation and Distribution of IQ Scores

Scores on intelligence tests for infants, children, and adults are arrived at in the same way—by computing an **intelligence quotient (IQ),** which indicates the extent to which the raw score (number of items passed) deviates from the typical performance of same-age individuals. To make this comparison possible, test designers engage in **standardization** of the test. When a test is constructed, it is given to a large, representative sample of individuals, which serves as the *standard* for interpreting individual scores.

Within the standardization sample, scores at each age level form a **normal distribution** in which most scores cluster around the mean, or average (see Figure 8.4). As we move away

▶ **Figure 8.4**

Normal distribution of intelligence test scores. To determine what percentage of same-age individuals in the population a person with a certain IQ outperformed, add the figures to the left of that IQ score. For example, an 8-year-old child with an IQ of 115 scored better than 84 percent of the population of 8-year-olds.

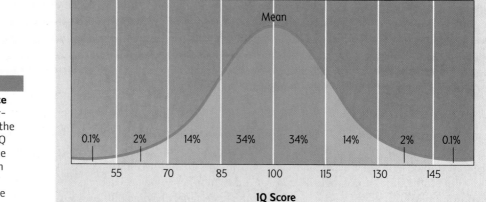

Mean

| 0.1% | 2% | 14% | 34% | 34% | 14% | 2% | 0.1% |

55   70   85   100   115   130   145

IQ Score

from the mean, toward either extreme, we find fewer individuals. This distribution, which resembles a *bell shape,* results whenever researchers measure individual differences in large samples. When an intelligence test is standardized, the mean IQ is set at 100. An individual's IQ is higher or lower than 100 by an amount that depends on how much the person's test performance deviates from the standardization-sample mean.

Because we know the percentage of people who fall within each unit of the normal curve, we can figure out exactly what any IQ score means. For example, a child with an IQ of 100 performed better than 50 percent of same-age children. A child with an IQ of 85 did better than only 16 percent, whereas a child with an IQ of 130 outperformed 98 percent. The IQs of the great majority of people (96 percent) fall between 70 and 130; only a few achieve higher or lower scores.

Ask Yourself

REVIEW	Why are aptitude and achievement tests closely related to intelligence tests, and to each other?
APPLY	Assia's score on the Stanford-Binet Intelligence Scales is 115; Leila's score is 145. Using Figure 8.4, explain how well each child performed in relation to other children her age.
CONNECT	Both the Stanford-Binet and the Wechsler tests provide a measure of general intelligence and an array of subtest scores. What evidence presented earlier in this chapter supports the use of these hierarchical models of intelligence?

What Do Intelligence Tests Predict, and How Well?

Psychologists and educators who use test scores to make decisions about children's educational placement assume that the scores are good indicators of future intelligence and scholastic performance. How well does IQ actually fare as a predictive measure?

Stability of IQ Scores

Stability refers to how effectively IQ at one age predicts itself at the next. Do children who obtain a particular IQ score at 3 or 4 years of age perform about the same during elementary school and again when tested in high school? To answer this question, researchers rely on longitudinal studies in which the same children are tested repeatedly.

• **CORRELATIONAL STABILITY** • One way of examining the stability of IQ is to correlate scores obtained at different ages. This tells us whether children who score low or high in comparison to their agemates at one age continue to do so later. Examining these correlations, researchers have identified two generalizations about the stability of IQ:

- *The older the child at time of first testing, the better the prediction of later IQ.* Preschool IQs do not predict school-age scores well; correlations are typically no better than in the .30s. But after age 6, stability improves, with many correlations in the .70s and .80s. Relationships between two testings in adolescence are as high as the .80s and .90s (Hayslip, 1994; Kaufman & Lichtenberger, 2002).

- *The closer in time two testings are, the stronger the relationship between the scores.* For example, in one long-term study, 4-year-old IQ correlated with 5-year-old IQ at .52, but prediction dropped to .46 by age 9 and to .42 by age 12 (Schneider et al., 1999).

Why do preschool scores predict less well than later scores? One reason is that the nature of test items changes with age, from concrete knowledge to abstract reasoning and problem solving. Success on the first type of item may require different skills than success on the second. Another explanation is that during periods of rapid development, children frequently change places in a distribution. One child may spurt ahead and reach a plateau, whereas a second child, moving along slowly and steadily, may catch up and eventually overtake the first. Finally, IQ may become more stable after schooling is under way because daily classroom activities and test items become increasingly similar. Then, variations among children in quality of school experiences and in mastery of those experiences may help sustain individual differences in IQ.

A wealth of research indicates that IQ predicts academic achievement. However, other factors, such as motivation and personality characteristics, are also important in accounting for children's learning in school.
© Laura Dwight Photography

• **STABILITY OF ABSOLUTE SCORES** • So far, we have looked at IQ stability in terms of how well children maintain their relative standing among agemates. Stability can also be viewed in *absolute* terms—by examining each child's profile of IQ scores over repeated testings. Longitudinal research reveals that the majority of children show substantial IQ fluctuations during childhood and adolescence—10 to 20 points in most cases, and sometimes much more (McCall, 1993; Weinert & Hany, 2003).

Children who change the most tend to have orderly profiles in which scores either increase or decrease with age. A close look at personality traits and life experiences associated with these profiles reveals that gainers tended to be more independent and competitive about doing well in school. In addition, their parents were more likely to use warm, rational discipline and to pressure them to succeed. In contrast, decliners often had parents who used either very severe or very lax discipline and who offered little intellectual stimulation (Honzik, Macfarlane, & Allen, 1948; McCall, Appelbaum, & Hogarty, 1973; Sontag, Baker, & Nelson, 1958).

When children who live in poverty are selected for special study, many show mental test score declines. According to the **environmental cumulative deficit hypothesis,** the negative effects of underprivileged rearing conditions increase the longer children remain in them. As a result, early cognitive deficits lead to more deficits, which become harder to overcome (Klineberg, 1963). In support of this idea, many studies show that children from economically disadvantaged families fall further and further behind their agemates in both IQ and achievement as they get older, and that children who suffer from a greater number of stressors (such as parental divorce, job loss, or illness, or deaths in the family) experience greater declines (Gutman, Sameroff, & Eccles, 2002; Gutman, Sameroff, & Cole, 2003). The downward trend is clearly environmental: In an investigation of African-American children growing up under conditions of severe economic deprivation in the rural South, older siblings consistently obtained lower IQ scores than their younger brothers and sisters. No sibling differences emerged among children living in California whose families were better off economically (Jensen, 1974).

In sum, many children show substantial changes in the absolute value of IQ that are the combined result of personal characteristics, child-rearing practices, and living conditions. Nevertheless, once IQ becomes reasonably stable in a correlational sense, it predicts a variety of important outcomes.

IQ as a Predictor of Academic Achievement

In thousands of studies, correlations between IQ and achievement test scores range from .40 to .70 and are typically between .50 and .60 (Brody, 1997). Students with higher IQs also get better grades and stay in school longer. Beginning at age 7, IQ is moderately correlated with adult educational attainment (McCall, 1977).

Why does IQ predict scholastic performance? Researchers differ in their answers to this question. Some believe that both IQ and achievement depend on the same abstract reasoning processes that underlie "g." Consistent with this interpretation, IQ correlates best with achievement in the more abstract school subjects, such as English, mathematics, and science (Jensen, 1998).

Other researchers argue that both IQ and achievement tests draw on the same pool of culturally specific information. From this perspective, an intelligence test is, in fact, partly an achievement test, and a child's past experiences affect performance on both measures. Support for this view comes from evidence that crystallized intelligence (which reflects acquired knowledge) is a better predictor of academic achievement than is its fluid counterpart (Kaufman, Kamphaus, & Kaufman, 1985).

As you can imagine, researchers who believe that heredity contributes greatly to individual differences in IQ prefer the first of these explanations. Those who favor the power of environment prefer the second. We will delve into this nature–nurture debate shortly, but for now let's note that although IQ predicts achievement better than any other tested measure, the correlation is far from perfect. Other factors, such as motivation and personality characteristics that lead some children to try hard in school, are at least as important as IQ in accounting for individual differences in school performance (Neisser et al., 1996).

IQ as a Predictor of Occupational Attainment

If IQ scores were unrelated to long-term life success, psychologists and educators would probably be less concerned with them. But research indicates that childhood IQ predicts adult occupational attainment just about as well as it correlates with academic achievement. By second grade, children with the highest IQs are more likely, when they grow up, to enter prestigious professions, such as engineering, law, medicine, and science (McCall, 1977).

Again, the relationship between IQ and occupational attainment is far from perfect. Factors related to family background, such as parental encouragement, modeling of career success, and connections in the world of work, also predict occupational choice and attainment (Bell et al., 1996). Furthermore, one reason that IQ is associated with occupational status is that IQ-like tests (the SAT and ACT) affect access to higher education. Educational attainment is a stronger predictor of occupational success and income than is IQ (Ceci & Williams, 1997).

Personality is also a prominent factor in occupational achievement. In 1923, Lewis Terman initiated a longitudinal study of more than 1,500 children with IQs above 135, who were followed throughout their lives. By middle age, more than 86 percent of men in the sample had entered high-status professional and business occupations (Terman & Oden, 1959). But not all were professionally successful. Looking closely at those who fared best compared to those who fared worst, Terman found that their IQs were similar, averaging around 150. But the highly successful group appeared to have "a special drive to succeed, a need to achieve" from elementary school onward (Goleman, 1980, p. 31).

Finally, once a person enters an occupation, **practical intelligence**—mental abilities apparent in the real world but not in testing situations—predict on-the-job performance as well as, and sometimes better than, IQ. Yet mental test performance and practical intelligence require distinctly different capacities. Whereas test items are formulated by others, are complete in the information they provide, are often detached from real life, and have only one solution, practical problems are not clearly defined, are embedded in everyday experiences, and generally have several appropriate solutions, each with strengths and limitations (Sternberg et al., 2000). Practical intelligence can be seen in the assembly line worker who discovers the fewest moves needed to complete a product or the business manager who increases productivity by making her subordinates feel valued. Unlike IQ, practical intelligence does not vary with ethnicity. And the two types of intelligence are unrelated and make independent contributions to job success (Sternberg, 2003; Wagner, 2000).

In sum, occupational outcomes are a complex function of traditionally measured intelligence, education, family influences, motivation, and practical know-how. Current evidence indicates that IQ, though influential, is not more important than these other factors.

◉ Practical intelligence is unrelated to IQ. Yet in the adult work world, practical intelligence predicts job performance as well as or better than IQ. As this boy consults a recipe so that he can prepare a meal for his family, he demonstrates his considerable practical know-how.
© Laura Dwight Photography

IQ as a Predictor of Psychological Adjustment

IQ is moderately correlated with emotional and social adjustment. For example, higher-IQ children and adolescents tend to be better liked by their agemates. But the reasons for this association are not clear. Besides IQ, good peer relations are associated with patient but firm child-rearing practices and an even-tempered, sociable personality, both of which are positively correlated with IQ (Hogan, Harkness, & Lubinski, 2000; Scarr, 1997).

Another way of exploring the relationship of IQ to psychological adjustment is to look at the mental test performance of aggressive young people who frequently engage in lawbreaking acts. On average, juvenile delinquents score about 8 points lower in IQ than do nondelinquents

(Coie & Dodge, 1998). A lower IQ increases the risk of school failure, which is associated with delinquency. Another possible interpretation is that a history of adjustment difficulties, including unruly behavior, prevents children from taking advantage of home and school experiences that promote both IQ and academic learning. In support of this view, research in China and the United States reveals that although early aggression predicts later academic difficulties, early academic difficulties do not predict later aggression (Chen, Rubin, & Li, 1997; Masten et al., 1995). And a longitudinal study reported that low IQ at age 3 was associated with antisocial behavior at age 10 only when young children also scored high in emotional and behavior problems and when their poor intellectual functioning persisted (Leech et al., 2003).

Finally, many psychological disorders, such as high anxiety, social withdrawal, and depression, are unrelated to mental test scores. IQ's imperfect prediction of all life success indicators provides strong justification for refusing to rely on IQ alone when forecasting a child's future or making important educational placement decisions.

Ask Yourself

REVIEW	Provide two competing explanations for the correlation between IQ and academic achievement.
APPLY	When 5-year-old Paul had difficulty adjusting to kindergarten, his teacher arranged for special testing. Paul's IQ turned out to be below average, at 95. When discussing Paul's score with his parents and teacher, what should the psychologist say about the stability of IQ?
CONNECT	Describe evidence from previous chapters that non-Western children with little or no formal schooling display considerable practical intelligence, despite poor performance on tasks commonly used to assess Western children's cognitive skills. (*Hint:* See Chapter 6, page 265, and Chapter 7, page 287.)

Ethnic and Socioeconomic Variations in IQ

People in industrialized nations are stratified on the basis of what they do at work and how much they earn for doing it—factors that determine their social position and economic well-being. Researchers assess a family's standing on this continuum through an index called **socioeconomic status (SES),** which combines three interrelated—but not completely overlapping—variables: (1) years of education and (2) the prestige of one's job and the skill it requires, both of which measure social status; and (3) income, which measures economic status.

© In this group of young Canadian students, differences in IQ scores may correlate with their ethnicities and socioeconomic status. Research aimed at uncovering the reasons for these differences has generated heated controversy.
© Will Hart/PhotoEdit

In searching for the roots of socioeconomic disparities, researchers have compared the IQ scores of SES and ethnic groups because certain ethnicities (for example, African American and Hispanic) are heavily represented at lower SES levels and others (for example, Caucasian and Asian American) at middle and upper SES levels. These findings are responsible for the IQ nature–nurture debate. If group differences in IQ exist, then either heredity varies with SES and ethnicity, or certain groups must have fewer opportunities to acquire the skills needed for successful test performance.

In the 1970s, the IQ nature–nurture controversy escalated after psychologist Arthur Jensen (1969) published a controversial monograph in the *Harvard Educational Review,* entitled "How Much Can We Boost IQ and Scholastic Achievement?" Jensen's answer to this question was "not much." He argued that heredity is largely responsible for individual, ethnic, and SES differences in IQ, a position he still maintains (Jensen, 1998, 2001). Jensen's work sparked an outpouring of responses and research studies. Scientists also posed ethical challenges because they were deeply concerned that his conclusions would fuel social prejudices. The controversy was rekindled by Richard Herrnstein and Charles Murray in *The Bell Curve* (1994). Like Jensen, these authors argued that the contribution of heredity to individual and SES differences in IQ is substantial. And although they did not arrive at a firm conclusion, they implied that heredity plays a sizable role in the black–white IQ gap.

As with Jensen's monograph, some researchers praised Herrnstein and Murray's book; others, underscoring its damaging social consequences, deplored it. But before we consider relevant research, let's look closely at group differences in IQ, which lie at the heart of the controversy.

Differences in General Intelligence

American black children score, on average, 15 points below American white children on measures of general intelligence, although the difference has been shrinking (Hedges & Nowell, 1998; Loehlin, 2000). Research comparing adolescents who had emigrated from Zimbabwe to Canada revealed a black–white IQ gap of similar magnitude (Rushton & Jensen, 2003). Hispanic-American children fall midway between African-American and white children, and Asian Americans score slightly higher than their white counterparts—about 3 points (Ceci, Rosenblum, & Kumpf, 1998).

The IQ gap between middle- and low-SES children is about 9 points (Jensen & Figueroa, 1975). Because 34 percent of African-American children and 45 percent of African-immigrant children in Canada live in poverty, compared to 16 percent of all North American children, a reasonable question is whether SES fully accounts for the black–white IQ difference. It accounts for some, but not all, of it. When researchers control for parental education and income, the black–white IQ gap is reduced by one-third to one-half (Brooks-Gunn et al., 2003; Jensen & Reynolds, 1982; Smith, Duncan, & Lee, 2003).

No ethnic differences exist on infant measures of habituation/recovery to visual stimuli, which are good predictors of later IQ (Fagan & Singer, 1983). But before age 3, African-American children lag behind their white peers on other mental tests, a difference that persists into adulthood (Peoples, Fagan, & Drotar, 1995). Still, IQ varies greatly *within* each ethnic and SES group. For example, as Figure 8.5 shows, the IQ distributions of blacks and whites overlap substantially. About 16 percent of blacks score above the white mean, and the same percentage of whites score below the black mean. In fact, ethnicity and SES account for only about one-fourth of the total variation in IQ. Nevertheless, these group differences are large enough and their consequences serious enough that they cannot be ignored.

Differences in Specific Mental Abilities

Are ethnic and SES differences limited to certain kinds of mental abilities? Arthur Jensen believes so. He distinguishes two types of intelligence: (1) *associative,* which emphasizes rote memory and is measured by such items as digit span and recall of basic arithmetic facts, and (2) *conceptual,* which emphasizes abstract reasoning and problem solving and is measured by items

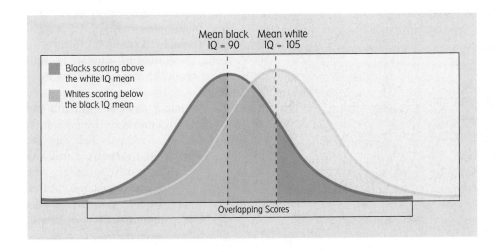

◀ **Figure 8.5**

IQ score distributions for black and for white children. The means represent approximate values obtained in studies of children reared by their biological parents.

strongly correlated with "g," such as vocabulary, verbal comprehension, block design, and spatial visualization. (Turn back to Figure 8.3 on page 323 to review examples of these items.)

According to Jensen, black–white and (to a lesser extent) SES differences in IQ are due to conceptual abilities; the groups are similar in associative intelligence (Jensen, 1998, 2002). Furthermore, Jensen indicated that among the various conceptual abilities, black children do worst on the least culturally loaded, most fluid items (such as block design and spatial visualization) and best on crystallized tasks (such as vocabulary). Therefore, he argued, black–white IQ differences are not caused by cultural bias in the tests. Jensen's conclusion—that blacks are less well endowed than whites with higher-order, abstract forms of intelligence—intensified public outcries over the racist implications of his work.

Is there support for Jensen's theory? In a series of studies, Jensen (2001) found that specific mental abilities strongly correlated with "g" show large black–white gaps, whereas abilities weakly correlated with "g" show little or no black–white difference. But other researchers report contrary findings. In a Dutch investigation, IQ differences between cultural-majority children and African-, Caribbean-, and Turkish-immigrant children were better explained by culturally specific knowledge than by "g" (Helms-Lorenz et al., 2003). And in a study of U.S. preschoolers, the black–white gap was far larger on a test of vocabulary than on a test of general intelligence (Smith, Duncan, & Lee, 2003).

These findings suggest that "g" contributes to, but is not the only basis for, ethnic and SES differences in IQ. At present, findings on specific mental abilities are not consistent enough to favor either a genetic or a cultural-bias explanation. To account for individual and group differences in IQ, we must turn to other evidence.

Explaining Individual and Group Differences in IQ

Over the past three decades, researchers have carried out hundreds of studies aimed at explaining individual, ethnic, and SES differences in mental abilities. The research is of three broad types: (1) investigations addressing the importance of heredity; (2) those that look at whether IQ scores are biased measures of the abilities of low-SES and minority children; and (3) those that examine the influence of children's home environments on their mental test performance.

Genetic Influences

Recall from Chapter 3 that behavioral geneticists examine the relative contributions of heredity and environment to complex traits by conducting *kinship studies,* which compare the characteristics of family members. Let's look closely at what they have discovered about IQ.

• **HERITABILITY OF INTELLIGENCE** • In Chapter 3, we introduced the *heritability estimate.* To review briefly, researchers correlate the IQs of family members who vary in the extent to which they share genes. Then, using a complicated statistical procedure to compare the correlations, they arrive at an index of heritability, ranging from 0 to 1, which indicates the proportion of variation in a specific population due to genetic factors.

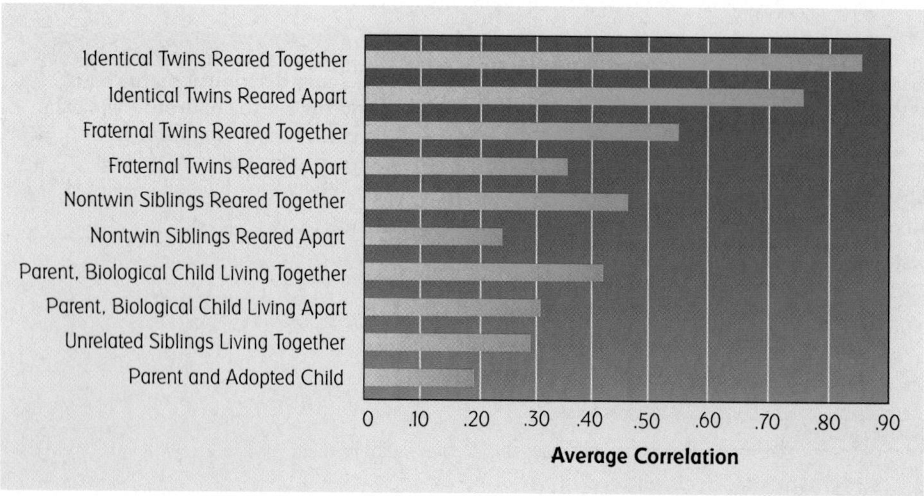

Figure 8.6 summarizes findings on IQ correlations from more than 100 studies on approximately 50,000 pairs of twins and other relatives (Bouchard & McGue, 1981). Notice that the greater the genetic similarity between family members, the more they resemble one another in IQ. In fact, two correlations reveal that heredity is, without question, partially responsible

▼ **Figure 8.6**

Worldwide summary of IQ correlations between twins and other relatives. The correlations show that the greater the genetic similarity between family members, the more similar their IQ scores. But the same correlations also show that greater environmental similarity yields more similar IQ scores.
(Adapted from Bouchard & McGue, 1981; Scarr, 1997.)

Identical Twins Reared Together
Identical Twins Reared Apart
Fraternal Twins Reared Together
Fraternal Twins Reared Apart
Nontwin Siblings Reared Together
Nontwin Siblings Reared Apart
Parent, Biological Child Living Together
Parent, Biological Child Living Apart
Unrelated Siblings Living Together
Parent and Adopted Child

0   .10   .20   .30   .40   .50   .60   .70   .80   .90
Average Correlation

for individual differences in mental test perform-ance. The correlation for identical twins reared apart (.76) is much higher than for fraternal twins reared together (.55).

Age-related changes in these twin correlations provide additional support for the contribution of heredity. As Figure 8.7 shows, correlations for iden-tical twins increase modestly into adulthood, whereas those for fraternal twins drop sharply at adolescence. Do these trends remind you of the *niche-picking* idea, discussed in Chapter 3? Com-mon rearing experiences support the similarity of fraternal twins during childhood. But as they get older and are released from the influence of their families, each fraternal twin follows a path of devel-opment, or finds a niche, that fits with his or her unique genetic makeup. As a result, their IQ scores diverge. In contrast, the genetic likeness of identical twins causes them to seek out similar niches in ado-lescence and adulthood. Consequently, their IQ

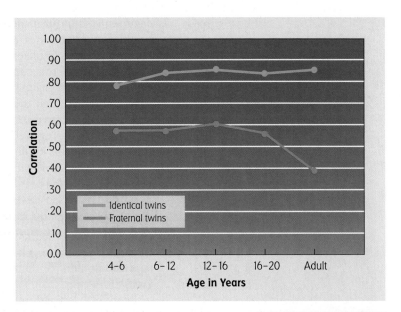

resemblance strengthens (Loehlin, Horn, & Willerman, 1997; McGue et al., 1993).

Although kinship research underscores the importance of heredity, the correlations in Figure 8.6 reveal that environment is clearly involved. Correlations for twin, nontwin sibling, and parent–child pairs living together are stronger than for those living apart. And parents and adopted children, as well as unrelated siblings living together, show low positive correla-tions, again supporting the influence of environment.

As indicated in Chapter 3, heritability estimates usually are derived from comparisons of identical and fraternal twins. In Western industrialized nations, the typical value is about .50, which means that half the variation in IQ is due to individual differences in heredity. But the values vary greatly from study to study, ranging from the .40s to the .80s (Plomin, 2003).

Furthermore, recall from Chapter 3 that this moderate heritability estimate might be too high because twins reared together often experience very similar overall environments. Even when reared apart, twins often have been placed in homes that are advantaged and similar in many ways. When the range of environments to which twins are exposed is restricted, heri-tabilities underestimate the role of environment and overestimate the role of heredity.

In sum, although heritability research offers convincing evidence that genes contribute to IQ, disagreement persists over how large the role of heredity really is. And heritability esti-mates do not reveal the complex processes through which genes and experiences influence intelligence as children develop.

• **DO HERITABILITY ESTIMATES EXPLAIN ETHNIC AND SES VARIATIONS IN IQ?** • Despite the limitations of the heritability estimate, Jensen (1969, 1998) relied on it to support the argument that ethnic and SES differences in IQ have a strong genetic basis. This line of rea-soning is widely regarded as inappropriate. Although heritability estimates computed *within* black and white populations are similar, they provide no direct evidence on what accounts for between-group differences (Plomin et al., 2001; Suzuki & Valencia, 1997). Furthermore, recall from Chapter 3 that the heritability of IQ is *higher* under advantaged (higher-SES) than dis-advantaged (lower-SES) rearing conditions (Bronfenbrenner & Morris, 1998; Turkheimer, 2003). Factors associated with low income and poverty, including weak or absent prenatal care, family stress, low-quality schools, and lack of community supports for effective child rearing, prevent children from attaining their genetic potential.

In a well-known example, geneticist Richard Lewontin (1976, 1995) showed that using within-group heritabilities to account for between-group differences is like comparing differ-ent seeds in different soil. Imagine planting a handful of flower seeds in a pot of soil generously enriched with fertilizer and another handful in a pot with very little fertilizer. The plants in each pot vary in height, but those in the first pot grow much taller than those in the second. *Within each group,* individual differences in plant height are largely due to heredity because the growth

▲ **Figure 8.7**

Cross-sectional age-related changes in IQ correlations for identical and fraternal twins. Correlations for identi-cal twins increase modestly into adulthood, whereas those for fraternal twins drop sharply at adolescence. Similar trends appear when twins are followed longitudinally. The findings are derived from studies including thousands of twin pairs.

(From M. McGue, T. J. Bouchard, Jr., W. G. Iacono, & D. T. Lykken, 1993, "Behavioral Genetics of Cognitive Ability: A Life-Span Perspective," in R. Plomin & G. E. McClearn, Eds., *Nature, Nurture, and Psychology,* p. 63. Washington, DC: American Psychological Association. Copyright © 1993 by the American Psychological Association. Adapted by permission.)

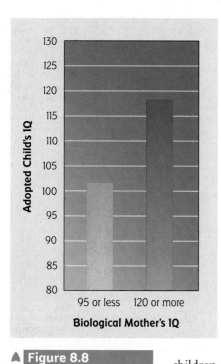

IQs of adopted children as a function of biological mothers' IQ in the Texas Adoption Project. Children of both low-IQ and high-IQ biological mothers scored above average in IQ, but those of the high-IQ mothers did better. (Adapted from Loehlin, Horn, & Willerman, 1997.)

environments of all plants were about the same. But the average difference in height *between the two groups* is probably environmental because the second group got far less fertilizer.

To be sure of this conclusion, we could design a second study in which we expose the second group of seeds to a full supply of fertilizer and see if they reach an average height that equals that of the first group. Then we would have powerful evidence that environment is responsible for the group difference. As we turn now to adoption research, we will see that researchers have conducted natural experiments of this kind.

Adoption Studies: Joint Influence of Heredity and Environment

In adoption studies, researchers gather two types of information: (1) correlations of the IQs of adopted children with those of their biological and adoptive parents' for insight into genetic and environmental influences, and (2) changes in the absolute value of the IQ as a result of growing up in an advantaged adoptive family, for evidence on the power of the environment.

In one investigation, called the Texas Adoption Project, children of two extreme groups of biological mothers—those with IQs below 95 and those with IQs above 120—were compared. All the children were adopted at birth by parents well above average in income and education. During the school years, the children of the low-IQ biological mothers scored above average in IQ, indicating that an advantaged environment can greatly improve test performance At the same time, they did not do as well as children of high-IQ biological mothers placed in similar adoptive families (see Figure 8.8). Furthermore, parent–child correlations revealed that as the children grew older, they became more similar in IQ to their biological mothers and less similar to their adoptive parents (Loehlin, Horn, & Willerman, 1997). Adoption research confirms that both environment and heredity contribute significantly to IQ.

When children of biological mothers low in IQ, education, and income are adopted into affectionate, stimulating homes in the first 6 months of life, the children consistently score above average in IQ. This suggests that the role of environment in SES differences in mental test scores is substantial. But concluding that SES differences are entirely environmental may be too extreme. Although children of low-SES biological mothers adopted into higher-SES families attain above-average IQs, they score somewhat lower than their adoptive parents' biological children. This difference could be due to heredity, to environmental influences prior to adoption (such as prenatal conditions), to parents' tendency to treat their biological and adopted children differently, or to a combination of these factors. In addition, adoption studies repeatedly reveal stronger correlations between the IQ scores of biological relatives than between those of adoptive relatives (Bouchard, 1997; Plomin et al., 2001; Scarr, 1997). Consequently, some researchers believe that the SES–IQ relationship is partly genetic.

Adoption research also sheds light on ethnic differences in IQ. When African-American children were placed in economically well-off white homes during the first year of life, they scored high on intelligence tests. In two such studies, adopted black children attained mean IQs of 110 and 117 by middle childhood, well above average and 20 to 30 points higher than the typical scores of children growing up in low-income black communities (Moore, 1986; Scarr & Weinberg, 1983).

But because adoptees' IQs declined in adolescence in one investigation, some researchers claim that adoptive rearing environments influence IQ only temporarily, in childhood. However, the IQ drop may have resulted from the use of different tests at the two ages. It also might have been caused by the challenges faced by minority adolescents in forming an ethnic identity that blends their birth and adoptive backgrounds. When this process is filled with emotional turmoil, it can affect motivation on intelligence tests (DeBerry, Scarr, & Weinberg, 1996; Waldman, Weinberg, & Scarr, 1994).

Adoption findings do not completely resolve questions about ethnic differences in IQ. Nevertheless, the IQ gains of black children reared in the culture of the tests and schools are consistent with a wealth of evidence indicating that poverty severely depresses the scores of many ethnic minority children (Nisbett, 1998). Dramatic gains in IQ from one generation to the next further support the notion that, given new experiences and opportunities, members of oppressed groups can move far beyond their current test performance. See the Cultural Influences box on page 334 to find out about the *Flynn effect.*

Race and Ethnicity: Genetic or Cultural Groupings?

DNA analyses reveal wide genetic variation *within* races (identified by physical features, such as skin color) and minimal genetic variation *between* them (Lewontin, 2003; Templeton, 2002). Members of ethnic groups that have been the focus of the IQ nature–nurture controversy are far more similar in cultural values, experiences, and opportunities than in genetic makeup.

Nevertheless, many people incorrectly assume that genetic, racial differences underlie ethnic group differences in psychological traits. Yet racial labels themselves are often arbitrary. In the United States, "black" designates people with dark skin. In Brazil and Peru, where "black" refers to hair texture, eye color, and stature, many African Americans would be called "white." Asians and the !Kung of Botswana, Africa, could be regarded as one race because they have similarly shaped eyes. Alternatively, Asians, Native Americans, and Swedes might be grouped together because of their similarly shaped teeth (Begley, 1995; Renzetti & Curran, 1998).

Differences in racial designations over time and across nations underscore their unclear boundaries. On the U.S. Census form, ten racial categories appeared in 1930, only five in 1990, and six in 2000, with respondents permitted to check more than one race—all six, if they chose! In Canada, the 1996 census form was the first to require a declaration of race; in both 1996 and 2001, it listed thirteen categories and asked respondents to mark as many as appropriate. In research as in census surveys, people self-identify, expressing their cultural heritage and sense of group belonging. Finally, ethnic mixing is extensive in countries as culturally diverse as the United States and Canada. Consider this Hawaiian native's description of his ethnicity: "I'm Asian on my birth certificate and the census form, but I'm really multiracial. My mother's parents were Japanese, my father's mother was Filipino, and my father's father was Irish."

As one scholar of race relations recently summed up, "Classification of human beings into races is in the end a futile exercise" (Payne, 1998, p. 32). And perpetuating the belief that some ethnic groups are genetically inferior in IQ promotes an ever-present danger: unfair allocation of resources, making an unfounded assumption seem true.

Cultural Bias in Testing

Reread Eric's responses to Mrs. Thomas's mental test questions at the beginning of this chapter. Can we conclude that he has a weak grasp of similarities between objects? Or are the testing conditions and the content of the test items ill suited to revealing his abilities? A controversial question raised about ethnic differences in IQ has to do with whether they result from *test bias.* If a test samples knowledge and skills that not all groups of children have had equal opportunity to learn, or if the testing situation impairs the performance of some groups but not others, then the resulting score is a biased, or unfair, measure.

Some experts reject the idea that intelligence tests are biased, claiming that they are intended to represent success in the common culture. According to this view, because IQ predicts academic achievement equally well for majority and minority children, IQ tests are fair to both groups (Brown, Reynolds, & Whitaker, 1999; Jensen, 1980, 2002). Others take a broader view of test bias. They believe that lack of exposure to certain communication styles and knowledge, and negative stereotypes about the test-taker's ethnic group, can undermine children's performance (Ceci & Williams, 1997; Sternberg 2002). Let's look at the evidence.

• **COMMUNICATION STYLES** • Ethnic minority families often foster unique language skills that do not match the expectations of most classrooms and testing situations. Shirley Brice Heath (1982, 1989), an anthropologist who spent many hours observing in low-SES black homes in a southeastern U.S. city, found that black adults asked their children questions unlike those asked in white middle-SES families. From an early age, white parents ask knowledge-training

These boys are brothers who are growing up in the same stimulating, advantaged home. Adoption research supports the view that rearing environment is responsible for the black–white IQ gap. African-American children placed in economically well-off white homes early in life score high on intelligence tests because they are "reared in the culture of the tests and schools." © Ken Chernus/ Getty Images/Taxi

CULTURAL INFLUENCES

The Flynn Effect: Massive Generational Gains in IQ

After gathering IQ scores from 20 industrialized nations that had either military mental testing or frequent testing of other large, representative samples, James Flynn (1994, 1999) reported a finding so consistent and intriguing that it became known as the **Flynn effect:** IQs have increased steadily from one generation to the next. The largest increases have occurred on tests of spatial reasoning—tasks often assumed to be "culture-fair" and, therefore, largely genetically based. Figure 8.9 shows these gains for one such test, administered to military samples consisting of almost all young men in Belgium, Israel, the Netherlands, and Norway. IQ rose, on average, 18 points per generation (30 years).

Consistent with this *secular trend* (see page 180 in Chapter 5 to review this concept), when intelligence tests are revised, the new standardization sample almost always performs better than the previous one. After locating every study in which the same individuals had taken two or more versions of Stanford-Binet or Wechsler tests (a total of 73 samples, with more than 7,500 participants), Flynn used the data to estimate the rate of IQ change between 1932 and 1978. On average, IQ increased about 1/3 point per year, steadily over time and similarly across all ages, for a total of 14 points over the 46-year period. When subtest scores were examined, gains were (again) largest for spatial tasks and for tasks that require quick problem solving, such as verbal similarities (for example, "How are dawn and dusk alike?").

The Flynn effect is environmental: Improved nutrition and education, technological innovations (including TV and computers), more time devoted to cognitively demanding leisure activities (from chess to video games), a generally more stimulating world, and greater test-taking motivation may have contributed to the better reasoning ability of each successive generation (Flynn, 2003; Williams, 1998). Furthermore, the Flynn effect is spreading to the developing world. The IQs of rural schoolchildren in Kenya underwent a large increase from 1984 to 1998. During this period, children's diets improved, TV sets appeared in some households, parental education and literacy increased, and family size declined, permitting parents to devote more time and resources to each child (Daley et al., 2003).

Notice that the generational gain in intelligence (18 points) is larger than the black–white IQ gap (about 15 points), indicating that environmental explanations for ethnic differences in IQ are highly plausible. Flynn argues that large, environmentally induced IQ increases over time present a major challenge to the assumption that black–white and other ethnic variations in IQ are mostly genetic (Dickens & Flynn, 2001).

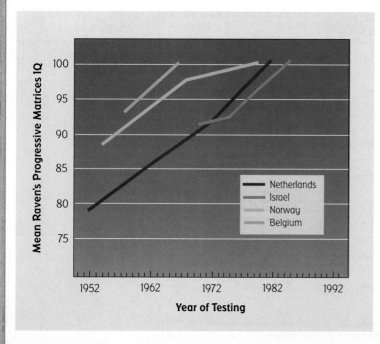

◀ **Figure 8.9**

The Flynn effect: Generational gains in performance on a test of spatial reasoning in four nations. Findings are based on military testing that includes nearly all young adults in each country. (From J. R. Flynn, 1999, "Searching for Justice: The Discovery of IQ Gains over Time," *American Psychologist, 54,* p. 7. Copyright © by the American Psychological Association. Adapted by permission.)

questions—"What color is it?" "What's this story about?"—that resemble the questioning style of tests and classrooms. In contrast, the black parents asked only "real" questions—ones they themselves could not answer. Often these were analogy questions ("What's that like?") or story-starter questions ("Didja hear Miss Sally this morning?") that called for elaborate responses about personal experiences and had no "right answer."

Heath and other researchers report that these experiences lead low-SES black children to develop complex verbal skills at home, such as storytelling and exchanging quick-witted remarks. But their language emphasizes emotional and social concerns rather than facts about the world. Not surprisingly, black children may be confused by the "objective" questions they encounter on tests and in classrooms.

Also, African-American children often take a unique approach to storytelling that reflects a culturally specific form of narrative (also see page 291 in Chapter 7 and page 385 in Chapter 9). Rather than using the *topic-focused style* of most school-age children, who describe an experience from beginning to end, they use a *topic-associating* style in which they blend several similar experiences. One African-American 9-year-old, for example, related having a tooth pulled, then described seeing her sister's tooth being pulled, next told how she had removed one of her baby teeth, and concluded, "I'm a pullin' teeth expert . . . call me, and I'll be over'" (McCabe, 1997, p. 164). Yet many teachers criticize this culturally distinctive narrative form as "disorganized," and it is not included in verbal test items. In contrast, mental tests often ask children to rearrange events in consecutive order.

Furthermore, many ethnic minority parents without extensive schooling prefer a collaborative style of communication when completing tasks with children. They work together in a coordinated, fluid way, each focused on the same aspect of the problem. This pattern of adult–child engagement has been observed in Native American, Canadian Inuit, Hispanic, and Guatemalan Mayan cultures (Chavajay & Rogoff, 2002; Crago, Annahatak, & Ningiuruvik, 1993; Delgado-Gaitan, 1994). With increasing education, parents establish a hierarchical style of communication, like that of classrooms and tests. The parent directs each child to carry out an aspect of the task, and children work independently. The sharp discontinuity between home and school communication practices may contribute to low-SES minority children's lower IQ and school performance (Greenfield, Quiroz, & Raeff, 2000).

Indeed, intelligence testing is an extreme of this directive approach. Tasks can be presented in only one way, and those taking the test cannot get feedback. When an adult refuses to reveal whether the child is on the right track, minority children may react with "disruptive apprehension"—giving any answer that comes to mind and rejecting the personal relevance of the testing situation (Ferguson, 1998). Notice how, in the chapter introduction, Eric repeated his first answer, perhaps because he could not figure out the task's meaning. Had Mrs. Thomas prompted him to look at the questions in a different way, his performance might have been better.

◉ Many ethnic minority parents without extensive schooling prefer collaborative communication when completing tasks with children. This mother, of the Yakut people of Siberia, prepares food collaboratively with her daughter. If the child is not accustomed to the hierarchical style of communication typical of classrooms, she may do poorly on tests and assignments. © Bryan & Cherry Alexander Photography

TEST CONTENT • Many researchers argue that IQ scores are affected by specific information acquired as part of majority-culture upbringing. In one study, low-SES African-American preschoolers were given a vocabulary test widely used to estimate general intelligence. Most children scored below average, often missing words that adults in their cultural community identified as having alternative meanings—for example, *frame*, which refers to "physique"; *digging*, which signifies "liking someone"; and *wrapping*, which can be interpreted as "rapping," a popular style of music (Champion, 2003a). The children might not have had an opportunity to learn the standard meanings of these words.

Unfortunately, attempts to change tests, by eliminating verbal, fact-oriented (crystallized) items and relying only on spatial reasoning (fluid) tasks, have not raised the scores of ethnic minority children very much (Reynolds & Kaiser, 1990) Yet performance even on fluid test items depends on learning opportunities. In one study, children's Block Design scores (see the sample item in Figure 8.3) were related to how often they had played a popular but expensive game that (like the test) required them to arrange blocks to duplicate a design as quickly as possible (Dirks, 1982). Playing video games that require fast responding and mental rotation of visual images also increases success on spatial test items (Subrahmanyam & Greenfield, 1996).

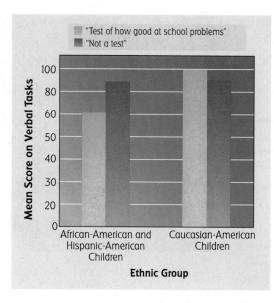

Legend:
"Test of how good at school problems"
"Not a test"

Y-axis: Mean Score on Verbal Tasks (0, 20, 30, 40, 50, 60, 80, 100)

X-axis (Ethnic Group):
African-American and Hispanic-American Children
Caucasian-American Children

◀ **Figure 8.10**

Effect of stereotype threat on test performance. Among African-American and Hispanic-American children who were aware of ethnic stereotypes, being told that verbal tasks were a "test of how good children are at school problems" led to far worse performance than being told the tasks "were not a test." These statements had little impact on the performance of Caucasian-American children. (Adapted from McKown & Weinstein, 2003.)

Low-income minority children, who often grow up in more "people-oriented" than "object-oriented" homes, may lack opportunities to use games and objects that promote certain intellectual skills.

Furthermore, the sheer amount of time a child spends in school is a strong predictor of IQ. When children of the same age enrolled in different grades are compared, those who have been in school longer score higher on intelligence tests. Similarly, dropping out of school causes IQ to decline. The earlier young people leave school, the greater their loss of IQ points (Ceci, 1991, 1999). Taken together, these findings indicate that children's exposure to the factual knowledge and ways of thinking valued in classrooms has a sizable impact on their intelligence test performance.

Ⓖ As minority children become increasingly aware of stereotypes during middle childhood, a teacher's remark, such as "This is a test," or "This will tell me how good you are at schoolwork," is enough to induce stereotype threat, which undermines academic performance in African-American and Hispanic children.
© Will McIntyre/Corbis

STEREOTYPES • Imagine trying to succeed at an activity when the prevailing attitude is that members of your group are incompetent. The fear of being judged on the basis of a negative stereotype, called **stereotype threat,** can trigger anxiety that interferes with performance (Steele, 1997; Steele & Aronson, 1995). Stereotype threat undermines the test-taking of college students, and recent evidence shows that it does the same to elementary school children. In one study, researchers gave African-American, Hispanic-American, and Caucasian 6- to 10-year-olds verbal tasks. Some children were told that the tasks "were not a test," whereas others were informed that they were "a test of how good children are at school problems"—a statement designed to induce stereotype threat in the ethnic minority children. Among children who were aware of ethnic stereotypes (such as "black people aren't smart"), African Americans and Hispanics performed far worse in the "test" condition than in the "not a test" condition. Caucasian children, in contrast, performed similarly in both conditions. The researchers concluded that only under the "not a test" instructions did the minority children do as well as would have been expected on the basis of a prior measure of their verbal ability (see Figure 8.10) (McKown & Weinstein, 2003).

Over middle childhood, children become increasingly conscious of ethnic stereotypes, and those from stigmatized groups are especially mindful of them. By junior high school, many low-SES, minority students start to devalue doing well in school—to say it is not important to them (Major et al., 1998; Osborne, 1994). Self-protective disengagement, sparked by stereotype threat, may be responsible. Notice how stereotype threat and disengagement create a vicious cycle. As stereotyped group members underperform and opt out of academic activities, their behavior provides the dominant group with further justification for the negative stereotype.

Reducing Cultural Bias in Testing

Although not all experts agree, many acknowledge that IQ scores can underestimate the intelligence of culturally different children. A special concern exists about incorrectly labeling minority children as slow learners and assigning them to remedial classes, which are far less stimulating than regular school experiences. Because of this danger, test scores need to be combined with assessments of children's adaptive behavior—their ability to cope with the demands of their everyday environments. The child who does poorly on an IQ test yet plays a complex game on the playground, figures out how to rewire a broken TV, or cares for younger siblings responsibly is unlikely to be mentally deficient.

In addition, culturally relevant testing procedures enhance minority children's performance. In an approach called **dynamic assessment,** an innovation consistent with Vygotsky's *zone of proximal development,* the adult introduces purposeful teaching into the testing situation to find out what the child can attain with social support (Lidz, 2001). Three factors distinguish dynamic assessment from traditional, static approaches:

- The focus is on the *processes* involved in learning and development (rather than on intellectual products).
- *Feedback* is provided after each task (rather than no feedback).
- The *adult–child relationship* is based on teaching and help individualized for each child (rather than a neutral relationship that is identical for all children). (Grigorenko & Sternberg, 1998)

Dynamic assessment often follows a pretest–intervene–retest procedure. While intervening, the adult seeks the teaching style best suited to the child and conveys strategies that the child can generalize to new situations.

Research consistently shows that "static assessments," such as IQ scores, frequently underestimate how well children do on test items after receiving adult assistance. Children's receptivity to teaching and their capacity to transfer what they have learned to novel problems add considerably to the prediction of future performance (Sternberg & Grigorenko, 2002; Tzuriel, 2001). In one study, Ethiopian 6- and 7-year-olds who had recently immigrated to Israel scored well below their Israeli-born agemates on spatial reasoning tests. The Ethiopian children had little experience with this type of thinking. But after several dynamic assessment sessions in which the adult suggested effective strategies, the Ethiopian children's scores rose sharply, nearly equaling those of Israeli-born children (see Figure 8.11). They also transferred their learning to new test items (Tzuriel & Kaufman, 1999).

Dynamic assessment is time consuming and requires extensive knowledge of cultural values and practices to work well with minority children. As yet, the approach is not more effective than traditional tests in predicting academic achievement. Better correspondence may emerge in classrooms where teaching interactions resemble the dynamic testing approach—namely, individualized assistance on tasks carefully selected to help the child move beyond her current level of development (Grigorenko & Sternberg, 1998).

But rather than adapting testing to support high-quality classroom learning experiences, North American education is placing greater emphasis on traditional test scores. To upgrade the academic achievement of poorly performing students, a *high-stakes testing* movement has arisen, which makes progress through the school system contingent on test performance. As the Social Issues box on page 338 indicates, this stepped-up emphasis on passing standardized tests has narrowed the focus of instruction in many classrooms to preparing for the tests, and it may widen SES and ethnic group differences in educational attainment.

◉ This teacher uses dynamic assessment in a classroom of Inuit children in Nunavik, Canada. The approach, which tailors instruction to the child's individual needs, reveals what a child can attain with social support and improves the performance of ethnic minority students. © JANE GEORGE/ AFP/Getty Images

▶ **Figure 8.11**

Influence of dynamic assessment on mental test scores of Ethiopian-immigrant and Israeli-born 6- and 7-year-olds. Each child completed test items in a preteaching phase, a postteaching phase, and a transfer phase, in which they had to generalize their learning to new problems. After dynamic assessment, Ethiopian and Israeli children's scores were nearly equal. Ethiopian children also transferred their learning to new test items, performing much better in the transfer phase than in the preteaching phase. (Adapted from Tzuriel & Kaufman, 1999.)

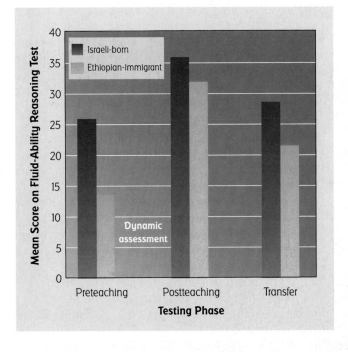

High-Stakes Testing

To better hold schools accountable for educating students, during the past two decades many U.S. states and Canadian provinces mandated that students pass exams for high school graduation. As these high-stakes achievement tests spread, schools stepped up their testing programs, extending them downward to elementary school. Some U.S. states and school districts also made grade promotion (in New York City, as early as the third grade) and secondary-school academic course credits contingent on test scores (Gootman, 2005).

The U.S. No Child Left Behind Act, authorized by Congress in 2002, broadens high-stakes testing to the identification of "passing" and "failing" schools. The law mandates that each state evaluate every public school's performance through annual achievement testing and publicize the results. Schools that consistently perform poorly (have a high percentage of failing students) must give parents options for upgrading their children's education, such as transfers to nearby, higher-performing schools or enrollment in remedial classes. When they lose students, such schools also lose state and federal funds. In some states, school-wide rewards for high scores and penalties for low scores are already in place. These include, on the positive side, official praise and financial bonuses to school staff and, on the negative side, withdrawal of accreditation, state takeover, and closure.

Proponents of high-stakes testing believe that it will introduce greater rigor into classroom teaching, improve student motivation and achievement, and either turn around poor-performing schools or protect students from being trapped in them. In some places, increasing numbers of students have reached U.S state and Canadian provincial standards after being given educational resources, such as special tutoring (Grissmer et al., 2000). But accumulating evidence indicates that high-stakes testing often undermines, rather than upgrades, the quality of education.

For example, in a Canadian study, researchers examined the impact of requiring students to pass British Columbia's high school exit exam on 8th-, 10th-, and 12th-grade science teaching. Observing classes and interviewing teachers, they found that 12th-grade teachers narrowed the scope of what they taught to strings of facts to be memorized for the test. As a result, 8th and 10th graders, in some respects, were doing more advanced work than 12th graders—conducting more experiments, exploring topics in greater depth, and engaging in more critical thinking. Indeed, teachers stated that by 12th grade, students had little patience for thinking deeply. If class time was being spent on something that wouldn't be tested, they simply "tuned out" (Wideen et al., 1997).

An additional concern is that high-stakes testing promotes fear—a poor motivator for upgrading teaching and learning. Principals and teachers worry about losing funding and their jobs if students do poorly. And many students who pass courses, and even do well in them, fail exams because a time-limited test with several dozen multiple-choice questions can tap only a small sampling of skills covered in the classroom. As experts in assessment point out, tests measuring achievement at the school or district level are imprecise instruments for making decisions about individuals (Sacks, 1999). The students most likely to score poorly are minority youths living in poverty. When they are punished with course failure and grade retention, their self-esteem and motivation drop sharply, and they are likely to drop out (Kornhaber, Orfield, & Kurlaender, 2001). A Massachusetts study demonstrated that relying solely on test scores and ignoring teacher-assigned grades (which take into account effort and a broad range of skills) amplify achievement gaps between white and black students, and between boys and girls in math and science (Brennan et al., 2001).

The trend toward "teaching to tests" induced by high-stakes testing contrasts sharply with the emphasis on teaching for deeper understanding in countries that

▲ The current high-stakes testing movement emphasizes standardized tests as the means of assessing and improving student performance. In response, many classrooms have narrowed the focus of instruction to preparing children for these tests. © Bob Daemmrich/PhotoEdit

rank at the top in cross-cultural comparisons of academic achievement (see Chapter 15). Even after hundreds of hours of class time devoted to test preparation, tens of thousands of Canadian and U.S. students in high schools with diploma-driven exams fail and do not graduate. To cite just one example, in the Canadian province of Ontario, more than 60,000 high school seniors—most of them low-SES minorities, recent immigrants not yet proficient in English, or young people with learning problems—were in danger of not graduating in 2005 because they had failed the grade 10 literacy exam (OSSTF, 2005). Most try these tests again, but some fail repeatedly, with potentially dire consequences for the course of their lives. Clearly, many issues remain for lawmakers and educators to resolve about the use of high-stakes tests, including their ethnic and gender fairness and their questionable power to spark school reforms that make students better learners.

In view of its many problems, should intelligence testing in schools be suspended? Most experts regard this solution as unacceptable. Without testing, important educational decisions would be based only on subjective impressions—a policy that could increase the discriminatory placement of minority children. Intelligence tests are useful as long as they are interpreted carefully by psychologists and educators who are sensitive to cultural influences on test performance. And despite their limitations, IQ scores continue to be valid measures of school learning potential for the majority of Western children.

Home Environment and Mental Development

As noted earlier, children of the *same* ethnic and SES background vary greatly in mental test scores. Many studies support the conclusion that factors in the home environment contribute to these differences.

Researchers divide home influences into two broad types. The first type, **shared environmental influences,** pervade the general atmosphere of the home and, therefore, *similarly* affect siblings living in it. Examples include the availability of stimulating toys and books and parental modeling of cognitively challenging activities. The second type, **nonshared environmental influences,** make siblings different from one another. Unique treatment by parents, birth order and spacing, and special events that affect one sibling more than the other (such as moving to a new neighborhood) are examples.

• **SHARED ENVIRONMENTAL INFLUENCES** • Two types of research shed light on the role of shared environmental influences: (1) studies in which researchers observe home environmental qualities and relate them to IQ; and (2) studies examining the impact of family beliefs about intellectual success on student performance.

▶ *Observations of Home Environmental Qualities.* The **Home Observation for Measurement of the Environment (HOME)** is a checklist for gathering information about the quality of children's home lives through observation and parental interview (Caldwell & Bradley, 1994). Refer to Applying What We Know below for factors that HOME measures in infancy and toddlerhood, early childhood, and middle childhood.

Applying
What We Know — Features of a High-Quality Home Life in Infancy and Toddlerhood, Early Childhood, and Middle Childhood: The HOME Subscales

Infancy and Toddlerhood	Early Childhood	Middle Childhood
1. Emotional and verbal responsiveness of the parent	1. Parental pride, affection, and warmth	1. Emotional and verbal responsiveness of the parent
2. Parental acceptance of the child	2. Avoidance of physical punishment	2. Emotional climate of the parent–child relationship
3. Parental involvement with the child	3. Language stimulation	3. Parental encouragement of social maturity
4. Organization of the physical environment	4. Stimulation of academic behavior	4. Provision for active stimulation
5. Provision of appropriate play materials	5. Stimulation through toys, games, and reading material	5. Growth-fostering materials and experiences
6. Variety in daily stimulation	6. Parental modeling and encouragement of social maturity	6. Family participation in developmentally stimulating experiences
	7. Variety in daily stimulation	7. Parental involvement in child rearing
	8. Physical environment: safe, clean, and conducive to development	8. Physical environment: safe, clean, and conducive to development

Sources: Bradley, 1994; Bradley et al., 2001.

Evidence on HOME confirms the findings of decades of research—that stimulation provided by parents is moderately linked to mental development. Regardless of SES and ethnicity, an organized, stimulating physical setting and parental encouragement, involvement, and affection repeatedly predict better language and IQ scores in toddlerhood and early childhood (Espy, Molfese, & DiLalla, 2001; Klebanov et al., 1998; Roberts, Burchinal, & Durham, 1999). In a study in which researchers controlled for both SES and home environmental quality, the black–white disparity in preschoolers' IQ diminished to just a few points (Smith, Duncan, & Lee, 2003).

The extent to which parents talk to infants and toddlers is particularly important. It contributes strongly to early language progress, which, in turn, predicts intelligence and academic achievement in elementary school (Hart & Risley, 1995). Recall from Chapter 7 that knowledge of the sound structure of language (phonological awareness), vocabulary and grammatical development, and wide-ranging general knowledge are vital for learning to read.

The HOME–IQ relationship declines in middle childhood, perhaps because older children spend increasing amounts of time in school and other out-of-home settings (Luster & Dubow, 1992). Nevertheless, two middle-childhood HOME scales are especially strong predictors of academic achievement: provision for active stimulation (for example, encouraging hobbies and organizational memberships) and family participation in developmentally stimulating experiences (visiting friends, attending theater performances) (Bradley, Caldwell, & Rock, 1988).

Yet we must interpret these correlational findings with caution. In all the studies, children were reared by their biological parents, with whom they share not just a common environment but also a common heredity. Parents who are genetically more intelligent might provide better experiences as well as give birth to genetically brighter children, who evoke more stimulation from their parents. Note that this hypothesis refers to *genetic–environmental correlation* (see Chapter 3, page 117), and research supports it. The HOME–IQ correlation is stronger for biological children than for adopted children, suggesting that parent–child genetic similarity elevates the relationship (Saudino & Plomin, 1997).

But heredity does not account for all the association between home environment and mental development. In several studies, family living conditions—both HOME scores and affluence of the surrounding neighborhood—continued to predict children's IQ beyond the effect of maternal intelligence and education (Chase-Lansdale et al., 1997; Klebanov et al., 1998; Sameroff et al., 1993). These findings highlight the vital importance of environmental quality.

▶ *Family Beliefs About Intellectual Success.* Regardless of SES, newly arrived parents from Asia and Latin America emphasize the importance of intellectual success, and their children do remarkably well in school. (Return to the Cultural Influences box on page 50 of Chapter 2 to review these findings.) Parental support for achievement is greater in higher-SES families in which both parent and child IQs are higher, making it difficult to isolate the impact of family beliefs on children's performance. Is IQ responsible for immigrant families' high valuing of intellectual endeavors and their children's superior academic performance? Probably not; recent arrivals are unlikely to be more intelligent than North American–born children whose parents arrived a decade or two earlier. Rather, immigrant parents' belief that education is the surest way to improve life chances seems to play a profound role (Kao, 2000).

Parental beliefs are also linked to academic performance among nonimmigrant children. For example, in a study of low-SES African-American families, parental expectations for children's edu-

© An elementary school teacher discusses a Mexican-immigrant student's school-work with the child and her mother. When parents place a high value on educational endeavors, their children are more successful in school—a relationship that cannot be explained by SES or IQ.
© Mary Kate Denny/PhotoEdit

cational attainment were positively correlated with 8- to 10-year-olds' reading and math achievement (Halle, Kurtz-Costes, & Mahoney, 1997). Similarly, an investigation of Asian-American, Hispanic, and Caucasian-American families revealed that within each group, the more education parents expected their fourth and fifth graders to attain, the higher the children's school grades (Okagaki, 2001; Okagaki & Frensch, 1998). Parental expectations were not merely responsive to their child's prior achievements. Rather, regardless of children's grades the previous year, parental beliefs predicted school performance. Warm, appropriately demanding child rearing may be the means through which parents convey their beliefs to their children (Okagaki, 2001). We will consider parenting and achievement further in Chapters 11 and 14.

• **NONSHARED ENVIRONMENTAL INFLUENCES** • The experiences of children growing up in the same family, while similar in some ways, differ in others. Parents may favor one child, for example. Each child also experiences sibling relationships differently. And children may be assigned special roles—for example, one expected to achieve in school, a second to get along well with others.

Kinship research suggests that nonshared environmental factors are more powerful than shared influences. Turn back to Figure 8.6 on page 330. Notice the relatively low correlations between unrelated siblings living together—a direct estimate of the effect of shared environment on IQ. Recall, also, that in adolescence the IQ resemblance between fraternal twins declines (see page 331). This trend also characterizes nontwin siblings, and it is particularly marked for unrelated siblings, whose IQs at adolescence are no longer correlated. These findings indicate that the impact of the shared environment on IQ is greatest in childhood (Finkel & Pedersen, 2001; Loehlin, Horn, & Willerman, 1997). Thereafter, it gives way to nonshared influences, as young people spend more time outside the home, encounter experiences unlike those of their siblings, and seek environments consistent with their genetic makeup.

Nevertheless, very few studies have examined nonshared environmental influences on IQ. The most extensively studied factors are sibling birth order and spacing. For years, researchers thought that earlier birth order and wider spacing might grant children more parental attention and stimulation and, therefore, result in higher IQs. But recent evidence indicates that birth order and spacing are unrelated to IQ (Rodgers, 2001; Rodgers et al., 2000). Why is this so? Parents' differential treatment of siblings appears to be far more responsive to siblings' personalities, interests, and behaviors than it is to these family-structure variables.

Finally, some researchers believe that the most potent nonshared environmental influences are unpredictable one-time events—an inspiring English teacher, a summer at a special camp, or perhaps a period of intense sibling rivalry (McCall, 1993). To understand the role of these nonshared factors in mental development, we need more intensive case studies of children growing up in the same family than have been accomplished to date.

Ask Yourself

REVIEW	Why can't heritability estimates explain ethnic differences in IQ? Using research findings, describe environmental factors that contribute to these differences.
APPLY	Kelsey and Sammi have parents who encourage their daughters to do well in school. One summer, Kelsey assisted her uncle in his biology research lab, while Sammi went to dance camp. The following year, Kelsey took extra high school math and science classes, while Sammi enrolled in theater classes. Identify shared and nonshared environmental influences on Kelsey's and Sammi's mental development.
CONNECT	Explain how dynamic testing is consistent with Vygotsky's zone of proximal development and with scaffolding (see Chapter 6, page 260).
REFLECT	Do you think that intelligence tests are culturally biased? What evidence and observations influenced your conclusions?

Early Intervention and Intellectual Development

In the 1960s, when the United States launched a "war on poverty," many early intervention programs for economically disadvantaged preschoolers were initiated. Their underlying assumptions were that learning problems are best treated early, before formal schooling begins, and that early enrichment could offset the declines in IQ and achievement common among low-SES children. **Project Head Start,** begun by the U.S. federal government in 1965, is the most extensive of these programs. A typical Head Start center provides children with a year or two of preschool, along with nutritional and health services. Parent involvement is central to the Head Start philosophy. Parents serve on policy councils and contribute to program planning. They also work directly with children in classrooms, attend special programs on parenting and child development, and receive services directed at their own emotional, social, and vocational needs. Currently, more than 19,000 U.S. Head Start centers serve about 910,000 children (Head Start Bureau, 2004).

In 1995, Canada initiated **Aboriginal Head Start** for First Nations, Inuit, and Métis children younger than age 6, 60 percent of whom live in poverty. Like Project Head Start, the program provides children with preschool education and nutritional and health services and encourages parent involvement. It also builds on the children's knowledge of Aboriginal languages and cultures. Currently, Aboriginal Head Start has about 120 sites and serves more than 3,900 children (Health Canada, 2004a).

Benefits of Early Intervention

More than two decades of research establishing the long-term benefits of early intervention helped Head Start survive. The most comprehensive of these studies was coordinated by the Consortium for Longitudinal Studies, which combined data from seven interventions implemented by universities or research foundations. Results showed that poverty-stricken children who attended programs had higher IQ and achievement test scores than controls during the first 2 to 3 years of elementary school. After that time, differences in test scores evaporated (Lazar & Darlington, 1982). Nevertheless, children and adolescents who received intervention remained ahead on real-life measures of school adjustment. They were less likely to be placed in special education or retained in grade, and a greater number graduated from high school. They also showed lasting benefits in attitudes and motivation: They were more likely to give achievement-related reasons (such as school or job accomplishments) for being proud of themselves.

A separate report on one program—the High/Scope Perry Preschool Project—revealed benefits lasting well into adulthood. More than one hundred African-American 3- and 4-year-olds were randomly assigned either to a cognitively enriching two-year preschool program or to no intervention. During weekly visits to the homes of the intervention group, teachers showed parents how to teach and read to their children. Besides improved school adjustment, preschool intervention was associated with increased employment and reduced pregnancy and delinquency rates in adolescence. At age 27, those who had gone to preschool were more likely to have graduated from high school and college, have higher earnings, be married, and own their own home. And they were less likely than their no-preschool counterparts to have been arrested, to have spent time in prison, and to have ever been on welfare (see Figure 8.12) (Weikart, 1998). The most recent follow-up, at age 40, revealed that the intervention group sustained its advantage on all measures of life success, including education, income, law-abiding behavior, and family life (Schweinhart et al., 2004).

Do the effects of these well-designed and well-delivered interventions generalize to Head Start

These 4-year-olds benefit from Project Head Start, a comprehensive early intervention program that provides poverty-stricken preschoolers with rich, stimulating educational experiences and nutritional and health services.
CP Photo/Aaron Harris

and other community-based preschool programs? Gains in school adjustment are similar, though not as strong. Head Start preschoolers are more economically disadvantaged than children in other programs and hence have more severe learning and behavior problems. And quality of services is more variable across community programs (NICHD Early Child Care Research Network, 2001; Ramey, 1999). But when interventions are of documented excellence, favorable outcomes are broader and longer lasting and include higher rates of high school graduation and college enrollment and a reduction in adolescent drug use and delinquency (Reynolds et al., 2001).

Nevertheless, a consistent finding is that gains in IQ and achievement test scores from attending Head Start and other interventions quickly dissolve. One reason is that these children typically enter inferior public schools in poverty-stricken neighborhoods, an experience that undermines the benefits of preschool education (Brooks-Gunn, 2003). In contrast, in a program that began at age 4 and continued through third grade, achievement score gains were still evident in junior high school (Reynolds & Temple, 1998). And when intensive intervention starts in infancy and persists through early childhood, IQ gains endure into adulthood (see the Social Issues box on page 344).

The gains in school adjustment that result from attending a one- or two-year Head Start program are still impressive. They may be due in part to program effects on parents. The more involved parents are in Head Start, the better their child-rearing practices and the more stimulating their home learning environments. These factors are positively related to preschoolers' independence and task persistence in the classroom and to their year-end academic, language, and social skills (Marcon 1999b; Parker et al., 1999).

The Future of Early Intervention

A typical parent component of early intervention focuses on teaching parenting skills and encouraging parents to act as supplementary interveners for their children. Emphasizing developmental goals for *both* parents and children may extend the program's benefits (Zigler & Styfco, 2001). A parent who is helped to move out of poverty through education, vocational training, and other social services is likely to gain in psychological well-being, planning for the future, and beliefs and behaviors that foster children's motivation in school. When combined with child-centered intervention, these gains should translate into exceptionally strong benefits for children.

At present, this *two-generation approach* is too new to have yielded much research. But one pioneering effort, New Chance, a program delivered at 16 sites across the United States, is cause for optimism. It provides teenage mothers with services for themselves and their babies, including education, employment, family planning, life management, parent training, and child health care. A follow-up when children were 5 years old revealed that parent participants were more likely to have earned a high school diploma, were less likely to be on welfare, and had higher family earnings than controls who received less intensive intervention. In addition, program children experienced warmer and more stimulating home environments, were more likely to have attended Head Start, and had higher verbal IQs (Granger & Cytron, 1999; Quint, Box, & Polit, 1997).

Head Start and other similar interventions are highly cost-effective. Program expenses are far less than the funds required to provide special education, treat criminal behavior, and support unemployed adults. Economists estimate that the lifetime return to society is more than $250,000 on an investment of $15,000 per preschool child—a total savings of many billions of dollars were every poverty-stricken preschooler in the United States and Canada to be enrolled (Heckman & Masterov, 2004). Because of funding shortages, however, many eligible children do not receive services.

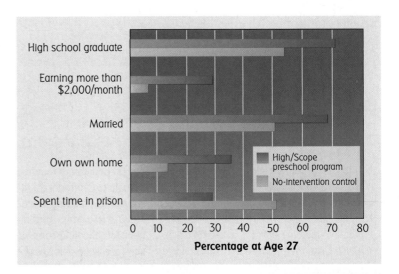

Percentage at Age 27

▲ **Figure 8.12**

Some outcomes of the High/Scope Perry Preschool Project on follow-up at age 27. Although two years of a cognitively enriching preschool program did not eradicate the effects of growing up in poverty, children who received intervention were advantaged over no-intervention controls on all measures of life success when they reached adulthood. (Adapted from Schweinhart et al., 2004.)

SOCIAL ISSUES

The Carolina Abecedarian Project: A Model of Early Intervention

In the 1970s, an experiment was begun to find out if educational enrichment starting at a very early age could prevent the declines in mental development that affect children born into extreme poverty. In the Carolina Abecedarian Project, more than one hundred 3-week- to 3-month-old infants from poverty-stricken families were randomly assigned to either a treatment or a control group. Treatment infants were enrolled in full-time, year-round child care through the preschool years. There they received stimulation aimed at promoting motor, cognitive, language, and social skills and, after age 3, literacy and math concepts. At all ages, special emphasis was placed on rich, responsive adult–child verbal communication. All children received nutrition and health services; the primary difference between treatment and controls was the child-care experience.

As Figure 8.13 shows, by 12 months of age, the IQs of the two groups diverged, and the treatment group sustained its IQ advantage until last tested—at 21 years of

age. In addition, throughout their years of schooling, treatment youths achieved considerably better than controls in reading and math. These gains translated into more years of schooling completed and higher rates of college enrollment and employment in skilled jobs (Campbell et al., 2001, 2002; Ramey & Ramey, 1999).

While the children were in elementary school, the researchers conducted a second experiment to compare the impact of early and later intervention. From kindergarten through second grade, half the treatment group and half the control group were provided a resource teacher, who introduced into the home educational activities address-

ing the child's specific learning needs. School-age intervention had no impact on IQ. And although it enhanced children's academic achievement, the effects were weaker than the impact of very early intervention (Campbell & Ramey, 1995).

The Carolina Abecedarian Project shows that providing continuous, high-quality enrichment from infancy through the preschool years reduces the negative impact of poverty on children's mental development. It confirms the conclusions of a recent review of many programs: The greater the "dose" of educational intervention, the more powerful its effects (Nelson, Westhues, & MacLeod, 2003).

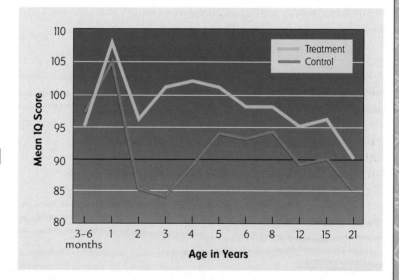

▶

IQ scores of treatment and control children from infancy to 21 years in the Carolina Abecedarian Project. At 1 year, treatment children outperformed controls, an advantage consistently maintained through 21 years of age. The IQ scores of both groups declined gradually during childhood and adolescence—a trend probably due to the damaging impact of poverty on mental development. (Adapted from Campbell et al., 2001.)

Giftedness: Creativity and Talent

Throughout this chapter, we have seen that intelligence includes much more than mental abilities that predict success in school. Today, educators recognize that **gifted** children—those who display exceptional intellectual strengths—have diverse characteristics. Some have IQ scores above 130, the standard definition of giftedness based on intelligence test performance

(Gardner, 1998b). High-IQ children, as we have seen, are particularly quick at academic work. They have keen memories and an exceptional capacity to solve challenging academic problems. Yet recognition that intelligence tests do not sample the entire range of human mental skills has led to an expanded conception of giftedness, which includes creativity.

Creativity is the ability to produce work that is *original* yet *appropriate*—something that others have not thought of but that is useful in some way (Lubart, 2003; Sternberg, 2003). In addition to the product's quality, the process of arriving at it affects judgments of creativity. Rather than following established rules, a creative work pulls together previously disparate ideas. Typically, it also involves hard work and the need to overcome obstacles on the way to the final product (Weisberg, 1993).

In addition to its value on the job and in daily life, creativity is vital for societal progress. Without it, there would be no new inventions, scientific findings, movements in art, or social programs. Therefore, understanding its ingredients and nurturing them from childhood are of paramount importance. As we will see in the following sections, ideas about creativity have changed radically during the past two decades.

The Psychometric View

Until recently, a purely cognitive perspective dominated research on creativity. Commonly used tests tapped **divergent thinking**—the generation of multiple and unusual possibilities when faced with a task or problem. Divergent thinking contrasts with **convergent thinking,** emphasized on intelligence tests, which involves arriving at a single correct answer (Guilford, 1985).

Because highly creative children (like high-IQ children) are often better at some types of tasks than others, a variety of tests of divergent thinking are available (Runco, 1992a, 1993; Torrance, 1988). A verbal measure might ask children to name uses for common objects (such as a newspaper). A figural measure might ask them to come up with drawings based on a circular motif (see Figure 8.14). A "real-world problem" measure requires students to suggest solutions to everyday problems. Responses to all these tests can be scored for the number of ideas generated and their originality. For example, on a verbal test, saying that a newspaper can be used "as handgrips for a bicycle" would be more original than saying it can be used "to clean things."

Tests of divergent thinking are referred to as the *psychometric approach to creativity* because they permit scores to be compared to the performance of standardization samples. Yet critics of these measures point out that they are poor predictors of creative accomplishment in everyday life because they tap only one of the complex cognitive contributions to creativity. And they say nothing about personality traits, motivation, and environmental circumstances that foster creative potential. Still, divergent-thinking tests do tap relevant skills, have been the major focus of research on creativity in children, and (as we will see shortly) have enhanced our understanding of the development of creativity.

A Multifaceted View

Recent theories agree that many elements must converge for creativity to occur (Csikszentmihalyi, 1999; Simonton, 1999; Weisberg, 1993). One influential multifaceted approach is Robert Sternberg and Todd Lubart's (1991,

▼ **Figure 8.14**

Responses of an 8-year-old who scored high on a figural measure of divergent thinking. This child was asked to make as many pictures as she could from the circles on the page. The titles she gave her drawings, from left to right, are as follows: "Dracula," "one-eyed monster," "pumpkin," "Hula-Hoop," "poster," "wheelchair," "earth," "moon," "planet," "movie camera," "sad face," "picture," "stoplight," "beach ball," "the letter O," "car," "glasses." Tests of divergent thinking tap only one of the complex cognitive contributions to creativity. (Reprinted by permission of Laura Berk.)

TABLE 8.4 RESOURCES NECESSARY FOR CREATIVITY

Cognitive	Personality	Motivational and Environmental
Problem finding	Innovative style of thinking	Settings rich in stimulation
Divergent thinking	Curiosity	Emphasis on intellectual curiosity
Convergent thinking: evaluating competing ideas	Willingness to take intellectual risks	Systematic teaching that builds talent
Insight	Tolerance of ambiguity	Availability of time to reflect on ideas
Knowledge	Courage of one's convictions	Encouragement of original ideas and evaluation of those ideas
		Emphasis on intrinsic motivation

1996) **investment theory of creativity.** According to Sternberg and Lubart, pursuing a novel project (one not being tackled by others) increases the chances of arriving at a creative, highly valued product. But whether a person invests in novelty—initiates an original project and brings it to fruition—depends on that person's cognitive, personality, motivational, and environmental resources, summarized in Table 8.4. Each must be present to catalyze creativity, although strength in one (such as perseverance) can compensate for weakness in another (an environment that is lukewarm toward novel ideas).

Contrary to popular belief, creativity is neither determined at birth nor the prized possession of an elite few. Many people can develop it to varying degrees, and it is likely to reach greater heights when nurtured from an early age. Let's look at the components of creativity and how to strengthen them in children.

• **COGNITIVE RESOURCES** • Creative work brings together a variety of high-level cognitive skills. It requires *problem finding*—detecting a gap in current knowledge, a need for a new product, or a deficiency in existing procedures. Once a problem is found, *the ability to define it*—to move it from a vague to a clearly specified state—becomes important. In both children and adults, the more effort devoted to defining the problem, the more original the final product (Runco & Okuda, 1988; Sternberg, 2003b).

Divergent thinking is essential for generating novel solutions to problems. At the same time, the successful creator must also set aside fruitless options in favor of the best responses. Therefore, creativity involves *alternating between divergent and convergent thinking.* In narrowing the range of possibilities, creative individuals rely on *insight processes*—combining and restructuring elements in sudden but useful ways. For example, the use of analogies and metaphors to identify unique connections is common among people who have made outstanding creative contributions (Barron, 1988). At an early age, children engage in this kind of thinking (see Chapter 6, page 239, and Chapter 9, page 374). Furthermore, *evaluating competing ideas* to select the most promising one is vital. School-age children's evaluative ability can be enhanced by instructions to critically assess the originality of ideas (Runco, 1992b).

Finally, extensive *knowledge* is necessary to make a creative contribution to any field. Without it, people cannot recognize or understand new ideas. Consider this cognitive ingredient, and you will see why high creativity is usually manifested as **talent**—outstanding performance in one or a few related fields. Case studies reveal that talent has roots in specialized interests and skills that appear in childhood. And research supports the *10-year-rule* in development of master-level creativity—a decade between initial exposure to a field and sufficient expertise to produce a creative work (Simonton, 2000; Winner, 2003). Furthermore, IQ and creativity correlate only

How can we nurture creativity? One approach is to challenge children to design and implement original solutions to problems. These 11-year-olds won a science award by figuring out how to construct a tower of straws that conformed to a given set of specifications.
© Ellen Senisi/The Image Works

modestly, typically around .20 to .40 (Lubart, 2003). Beyond an above-average general intelligence, other factors are necessary for creative giftedness.

• **PERSONALITY RESOURCES** • Personality characteristics foster the cognitive components of creativity, ensuring that they will be applied and will reach fruition (Sternberg & Lubart, 1996). The following traits are crucial:

- *Innovative style of thinking.* Creative individuals not only see things in new ways, but also enjoy doing so. They prefer loosely structured activities involving innovative problem finding rather than already defined tasks.

- *Tolerance of ambiguity and perseverance.* Working toward creative goals brings periods when pieces of the problem do not fit together. At those times, children and adults may give up or pursue the first (but not the best) solution. Creativity requires patience and persistence in the face of obstacles.

- *Willingness to take risks.* Creativity requires a willingness to deviate from the crowd, to undertake challenges when outcomes are uncertain.

- *The courage of one's convictions.* Because their ideas are novel, creators may at times doubt them, especially when skeptical teachers or peers criticize them. People who think creatively often encounter resistance, ranging from puzzlement to hostility. Independence of judgment and high self-esteem are necessary for creative endeavors.

• **MOTIVATIONAL RESOURCES** • Motivation for creativity must be *task focused* rather than *goal focused*. Task-focusing motivators, such as the desire to meet a high standard, energize work and keep attention on the problem. Goal-focusing motivators, often extrinsic rewards such as grades and prizes, divert attention from the task to these other goals, thereby impairing performance. In one study, 7- to 11-year-old girls worked on collages, some competing for prizes and others expecting that the prizes would be raffled off. The products of those in the first group were much less creative (Amabile, 1982).

Extrinsic rewards are not always detrimental to creativity. Teaching children how to engage in divergent thinking on a task and rewarding them for original responses increases the frequency of those responses (Collins & Amabile, 1999). And an occasional reward for a creative product can underscore the social value of creativity and encourage children to embark on innovative projects. But when rewards are overemphasized, children see only "the carrot at the end of the stick," and creativity suffers.

• **ENVIRONMENTAL RESOURCES** • Studies of the backgrounds of talented children and highly accomplished adults often reveal a family life focused on the child's needs—parents who are warm and sensitive, who provide a stimulating home life, who are devoted to developing their child's abilities, and who provide models of hard work and high achievement. But rather than being driving and overambitious, these parents are reasonably demanding (Winner, 1996, 2000). They arrange for caring teachers while the child is young and for more rigorous master teachers as the talent develops.

Extreme giftedness often results in social isolation. Many gifted children and adolescents spend much time alone, partly because their highly driven, nonconforming, and independent styles leave them out of step with peers and partly because they enjoy solitude, which is necessary to develop their talents. Still, gifted children desire gratifying peer relationships, and some—more often girls than boys—try to hide their abilities in hopes of being better liked. Compared with their ordinary agemates, gifted youths, especially girls, report more emotional and social difficulties, including low self-esteem and depression (Gross, 1993; Winner, 2000).

Classrooms in which gifted youths can interact with like-minded peers, choose topics for extended projects, take intellectual

Classrooms that stress original uses of knowledge over knowledge acquisition and correct answers foster creativity. When talented students are not sufficiently challenged, they can lose their drive to excel.

© Peter M. Fisher/Corbis

risks, and reflect on ideas without being rushed to the next assignment foster creativity. Unfortunately, in many classrooms, knowledge acquisition is usually stressed over using knowledge originally, leading children's thinking to become *entrenched,* or limited to commonplace associations that produce correct answers. When talented students are not sufficiently challenged, they sometimes lose their drive to excel. And when pushed too hard by parents and teachers, by adolescence these students are likely to ask, "Why am I doing this?" If the answer is not "Because it interests me," they may decide not to pursue their gift anymore (Winner, 1997, 2000, p. 166).

Refer to Applying What We Know below for ways that parents and teachers can promote children's creativity. Although many schools offer programs for the gifted, debate about their effectiveness typically focuses on factors irrelevant to creativity—for example, whether to offer enrichment in regular classrooms, pull children out for special instruction (the most common practice), or advance brighter pupils to a higher grade. Overall, gifted children fare well academically and socially within each of these models (Moon & Feldhusen, 1994). At the same time, interventions aimed at protecting students' self-esteem are crucial in selective educational settings. In a study of more than 100,000 students in 26 countries, the more selective the high school, the lower the students' academic self-esteem (Marsh & Hau, 2003). A successful student in elementary school who enters a selective secondary school may suddenly find herself average or below average, with potentially detrimental effects on motivation.

Some societies can be so narrowly focused on high academic achievement as an index of success that they dampen the development of creativity. The high value placed on collectivism in Asian cultures often leads teachers to emphasize mastery of knowledge and analytical skills over generating new ideas, which requires students to stand out from the crowd. In one study, Chinese college students' artwork was judged less creative than that of U.S. students, by experts from both countries (Niu & Sternberg, 2001). In interventions aimed at promoting creative expression in high school art classes in Beijing, students were asked to make collages. One group received a general instruction to be creative, a second group specific instructions in how to be creative ("fold or tear materials so their shapes and sizes do not limit creative expres-

Applying
What We Know   Promoting Children's Creativity

Suggestion	Description
Encourage idea generation and evaluation.	Offer opportunities for divergent thinking and praise it, even when some ideas are silly or irrelevant. Then engage children in constructive criticism: When an idea has little value, suggest new approaches that include aspects of the child's idea, thereby demonstrating that most ideas must be refined to be useful.
Encourage sensible risk-taking.	Provide assignments and activities that include choices and that have more than one acceptable answer. Too often, perfect tests scores and papers based on one right answer receive praise, causing children to avoid new ways of thinking.
Encourage tolerance of ambiguity.	Point out that creative individuals often feel unsure of whether they are on the right track. Ask children to accept these feelings and to spend time working through uncertainty, emphasizing that doing so will result in better ideas.
Help children believe in their ability to be creative.	Remind children that the value of a creative idea does not depend on teachers' or classmates' approval but, rather, on the idea's originality and usefulness.
Help children find what they love to do.	Encourage children to explore new fields rather than just accepting interests that you value. To help them uncover their true interests, ask them to demonstrate an ability or talent for their class, and point out the diversity of worthwhile interests.
Model creative thinking.	Balance teaching knowledge with teaching how to think about that knowledge. Help children reason across subjects, pointing out that creative insights often result from integrating material across fields, not from memorizing information.

Source: Sternberg, 2003b.

sion"), and a control group no creativity instructions. Students in the two creative conditions generated products that were more creative than those produced by students in the control group, with the specific-instruction group performing best (Niu & Sternberg, 2003). A brief prompt—especially, guidance in how to be creative—readily enhanced artistic originality.

Gardner's theory of multiple intelligences has inspired several model school programs that provide enrichment to all students in diverse disciplines, so any child capable of high-level, creative performance can manifest it. Meaningful activities, each tapping a specific intelligence or set of intelligences, serve as contexts for assessing strengths and weaknesses and, on that basis, teaching new knowledge and original thinking (Gardner, 1993, 2000). For example, linguistic intelligence might be fostered through storytelling or playwriting; spatial intelligence through drawing, sculpting, or taking apart and reassembling objects; and kinesthetic intelligence through dance or pantomime.

Evidence is still needed on how effectively such programs nurture children's talent and creativity. But they have already succeeded in one way—by highlighting the strengths of some students who previously had been considered unexceptional or even at risk for school failure. Consequently, they may be especially useful in identifying talented low-SES, ethnic minority children, who are often underrepresented in school programs for the gifted (Suzuki & Valencia, 1997). How best to maximize the creative resources of the coming generation—the future poet and scientist as well as the everyday citizen—is a challenge for future research.

Ask Yourself

REVIEW	Summarize the benefits of early intervention programs, such as Head Start, for poverty-stricken children. What program characteristics might contribute to and strengthen those benefits?
CONNECT	Using what you learned about brain development in Chapter 5 (see pages 182–188), explain why intensive intervention for poverty-stricken children starting in infancy and continuing through early childhood has a greater impact on IQ than intervention starting later.
CONNECT	How is high-stakes testing likely to affect encouragement of creativity in North American classrooms? Explain.
REFLECT	Describe several childhood experiences that you believe enhanced your creativity, along with ones that might have discouraged it. In the latter instances, what would you do differently to foster children's creative potential? Use research to justify your recommendations.

◎ Summary

Definitions of Intelligence

Describe changing definitions of intelligence, from Binet's first successful test to the modern factor analysts.

◎ The **psychometric approach** to cognitive development is the basis for the variety of intelligence tests used to assess individual differences in children's mental abilities. In the early 1900s, Alfred Binet developed the first successful test, which provided a single, holistic measure of intelligence.

◎ **Factor analysis** emerged as a major means for determining whether intelligence is a single trait or a collection of many abilities. The research of Spearman and Thurstone led to two schools of thought. The first, sup-

porting Spearman, regarded test items as reflecting **general intelligence**, or "**g**," but acknowledged the existence of various types of **specific intelligence.** The second, supporting Thurstone, viewed intelligence as a set of distinct primary mental abilities.

◎ Contemporary theorists and test designers combine Spearman's and Thurstone's approaches into hierarchical models of mental abilities. Cattell's distinction between **crystallized** and **fluid intelligence** has influenced attempts to reduce cultural bias in intelligence testing. Carroll's **three-stratum theory of intelligence** is the most comprehensive classification of mental abilities to be confirmed by factor-analytic research.

Recent Advances in Defining Intelligence

Why have researchers conducted componential analyses of intelligence test scores, and how have Sternberg's triarchic theory and Gardner's theory of multiple intelligences expanded contemporary definitions of intelligence?

◎ To provide process-oriented explanations of mental test performance, some researchers conduct **componential analyses** of children's scores by correlating them with laboratory measures of information processing. Findings reveal that basic efficiency of thinking and effective strategy use are related to measures of general intelligence. Sternberg's **triarchic theory of successful intelligence** extends these efforts. It views intelligence as a complex interaction of analytical intelligence (information-processing skills), creative intelligence (ability to solve novel problems), and practical intelligence (adapting, shaping, and selecting environments to fit with one's desires and the demands of one's everyday world).

© DAVID GROSSMAN/THE IMAGE WORKS

⊚ According to Gardner's **theory of multiple intelligences,** at least eight distinct intelligences exist, each of which has a unique biological basis and a distinct course of development. Gardner's theory has been influential in efforts to understand and nurture children's special talents.

⊚ The capacity to detect others' thoughts and feelings and to deal effectively with social problems, formerly known as social intelligence, today is labeled **emotional intelligence**.

Measuring Intelligence

Cite commonly used intelligence tests for children, and discuss prediction of later IQ from infant tests.

⊚ The **Stanford-Binet Intelligence Scales, Fifth Edition,** and the **Wechsler Intelligence Scale for Children–IV (WISC–IV)** are most often used to identify highly intelligent children and diagnose those with learning problems. Each provides a measure of general intelligence as well as a profile of subtest scores, and each has a downward extension, appropriate for assessing the intelligence of preschoolers.

⊚ Closely related to intelligence tests are **aptitude tests,** which assess potential to learn a specialized activity, and **achievement tests,** which assess actual knowledge and skill attainment. Yet distinctions among the three types of tests are not clear-cut; similar items can be found on each.

⊚ Most infant tests consist largely of perceptual and motor responses. They predict childhood mental ability poorly because they do not represent the same aspects of intelligence assessed at older ages. Because of low test–retest reliability, the Fagan Test of Infant Intelligence, made up entirely of items assessing habituation/recovery to visual stimuli, is less successful than laboratory measures in predicting childhood mental test scores.

How are IQ scores computed and distributed?

⊚ Scores on intelligence tests are arrived at by computing an **intelligence quotient (IQ).** It compares the test-taker's raw score to the scores of a **standardization** sample of same-age individuals, which form a **normal,** or bell-shaped, **distribution,** with mean IQ set at 100. IQ is higher or lower, depending on how much test performance deviates from the mean of the standardization sample.

What Do Intelligence Tests Predict, and How Well?

Discuss the stability of IQ and its prediction of academic achievement, occupational attainment, and psychological adjustment.

⊚ IQs obtained after age 6 show substantial correlational stability. The older the child at time of first testing and the closer in time the testings are, the stronger the relationship between the scores. Nevertheless, most children display considerable age-related change in the absolute value of IQ. Children who live in poverty often experience declines due to an **environmental cumulative deficit,** or the compounding effects of underprivileged rearing conditions.

⊚ IQ is an effective predictor of academic achievement, occupational attainment, and certain aspects of psychological adjustment. However, the underlying causes of these correlational findings are complex. IQ is far from a perfect predictor of life success; family background, personality, motivation, education, and **practical intelligence** also contribute substantially.

Ethnic and Socioeconomic Variations in IQ

Describe ethnic and socioeconomic variations in IQ.

⊚ Black children and children of low **socioeconomic status (SES)** score lower on intelligence tests than white and middle-SES children, respectively, findings responsible for kindling the IQ nature–nurture debate. Jensen attributes the poorer scores of these children largely to a genetic deficiency in conceptual abilities, tapped by items strongly correlated with "g." However, the theory has been challenged by subsequent research.

© MICHAEL NEWMAN/ PHOTOEDIT

Explaining Individual and Group Differences in IQ

Describe and evaluate the contributions of heredity and environment to individual and group differences in IQ.

⊚ Heritability estimates support a moderate role for heredity in IQ individual differences. Kinship studies comparing IQ correlations of identical and fraternal twins indicate that the contribution of heredity strengthens with development. However, heritabilities cannot be used to explain ethnic and SES differences in test scores.

⊚ Adoption studies indicate that advantaged rearing conditions can raise the absolute value of children's IQs substantially. At the same time, adopted children's scores correlate more strongly with those of their biological than those of their adoptive relatives, providing support for the influence of heredity.

⊚ Black children reared in economically well-off white homes attain IQs substantially above average by middle childhood. No evidence supports the assumption that heredity underlies the ethnic differences that have been the focus of the IQ nature–nurture debate.

⊚ Consistent gains in IQ from one generation to the next, known as the **Flynn effect,** are the result of environmental factors. The Flynn effect challenges the assumption that black–white and other ethnic variations in IQ are mostly genetic.

Evaluate evidence on whether IQ is a biased measure of the intelligence of ethnic minority children, and discuss efforts to reduce test bias.

⊚ Experts disagree on whether intelligence tests yield biased measures of the mental abilities of low-income minority children. IQ predicts academic achievement equally well for majority and minority children. However, culturally specific communication styles, lack of familiarity with test content, and **stereotype threat** can lead to test scores that underestimate minority children's intelligence.

⊚ Assessments of children's adaptive behavior can serve as a safeguard against inaccurate mental test scores. By introducing purposeful teaching into the testing situation to find out what the child can attain with social support, **dynamic assessment** narrows the gap between a child's actual and potential performance.

Summarize the impact of shared and nonshared environmental influences on IQ.

🌀 **Shared** and **nonshared environmental influences** contribute to individual differences in mental development. Research with the **Home Observation for Measurement of the Environment (HOME)** indicates that overall quality of the home—a shared environmental influence—consistently predicts language progress and IQ. Although the HOME–IQ relationship results in part from parent–child genetic similarity, a warm, stimulating family environment does promote mental ability. Family beliefs about the

© MYRLEEN FERGUSON CATE/PHOTOEDIT

importance of intellectual success have a powerful impact on academic performance.

🌀 Kinship research suggests that nonshared environmental factors are more powerful than shared influences and strengthen in adolescence and adulthood. Birth order and spacing, once thought to be influential, are unrelated to IQ. The most potent nonshared factors may be unpredictable, one-time events. Understanding the role of nonshared factors requires intensive case studies of children growing up in the same family.

Early Intervention and Intellectual Development

Discuss the impact of early intervention on intellectual development.

🌀 **Project Head Start** is the most extensive federally funded preschool program for low-income children in the United States. In Canada, **Aboriginal Head Start** serves First Nations, Inuit, and Métis preschoolers living in poverty.

🌀 Research on high-quality early interventions implemented by universities or research foundations shows that immediate IQ and achievement score gains evaporate within a few years. However, lasting benefits occur in school adjustment. Participants are less likely to be placed in special education classes or retained in grade and are more likely to graduate from high school. And one program yielded advantages for preschool intervention children, over no-intervention controls, on adulthood indicators of life success, including education, income, and law-abiding behavior.

🌀 The earlier intervention starts, the longer it lasts, and the more intensive the program, the broader and more enduring the benefits. To induce lasting mental test score gains, early intervention must be followed by high-quality public school education. Two-generation programs, with developmental goals for both parents and children, may result in more powerful long-term outcomes. Early intervention programs are highly cost-effective; they result in great savings in funds otherwise required to deal with learning problems, lawbreaking behavior, and unemployment.

Giftedness: Creativity and Talent

Describe and evaluate evidence on the development of creativity, including the

psychometric view and the multifaceted approach of investment theory.

🌀 Recognition that intelligence tests do not sample the full range of human mental skills has expanded conceptions of **giftedness** to include **creativity.** The psychometric approach to creativity, which emphasizes the distinction between **divergent** and **convergent thinking,** is too narrow to predict real-world creative accomplishment. Consequently, it has given way to new, multifaceted approaches. Because people usually demonstrate creativity in one or a few related areas, it is usually manifested as **talent.**

🌀 According to Sternberg and Lubart's **investment theory of creativity,** a wide variety of intellectual, personality, motivational, and environmental resources are necessary to initiate creative projects and bring them to fruition. Highly talented children have parents and teachers who nurture their exceptional abilities. However, extreme giftedness may result in social isolation, and gifted youths often report emotional and social difficulties.

🌀 Gifted children are best served by educational programs that grant them opportunities to interact with like-minded peers, take intellectual risks, reflect on ideas, and acquire skills relevant to their talents. Asian cultures' collectivism often leads teachers to emphasize mastery of knowledge and analytical skills over generating new ideas. Instructions to be creative can enhance students' originality.

🌀 Important Terms and Concepts

"Three Women Sell Pigs"
Hong Anh
Age 11, Vietnam

While offering pigs for sale, these women appear engrossed in animated conversation—chatting about passersby in the market, relating stories of their families, and sharing the concerns of their lives. Language is an awesome human achievement. How does it develop so rapidly and easily in childhood?

Language Development

"Done!" exclaimed 1-year-old Erin, wriggling in her high chair.

Oscar and Marilyn looked at each other and exclaimed in unison, "Did she say, 'Done'?" Lifting Erin down, Marilyn responded, "Yes! You're done," to her daughter's first clear word. In the next few weeks, more words appeared—among them "Mama," "Dada," "please," "thanks," and "sure."

Marilyn spoke to Erin and her 11-year-old brother, Amos, in English. But Oscar, determined that his second child would become bilingual, used only Spanish, his native tongue. As Erin reached the 18-month mark, her vocabulary grew rapidly, and she mixed words from the two languages. "Book!" she called out, thrusting her favorite picture book toward Oscar in a gesture that meant, "Read this!" As father and daughter "read" together, Erin labeled: "*Nariz*" ("nose"). "*Boca*" ("mouth"). "Head." "*Ojos*" ("eyes"). "Hippo." "*Grande!*" (referring to the size of the hippo). On reaching the last page, she exclaimed, "*Gracias!*" and slipped off Oscar's lap.

By her second birthday, Erin had a vocabulary of several hundred words and often combined them: "So big!" "*Muy grande*" ("very big"), "More cracker." "*Dame galleta*" ("Give me cracker"), and "*No quiero*" ("I don't want to"). Amused by Erin's willingness to imitate almost anything, Amos taught her a bit of slang. During mealtime discussions, Erin would interject, "Geta picture" ("Get the picture"). And when asked a question, she sometimes casually answered, "Whatever."

At age 2½, Erin conversed easily. After the family returned from an excursion to the aquarium, Marilyn asked, "What did you see?"

"A big turtle put his head in the shell," Erin replied.

"Why did he do that?" Marilyn inquired.

"He goed away. He's sleepy."

If Amos interrupted, Erin would cleverly recapture her mother's attention. On one occasion, she commanded in a parental tone of voice, "Amos, go do your homework!"

Language—the most awesome of universal human achievements—develops with extraordinary speed in early childhood. At age 1, Erin used single words to name familiar objects and convey her desires. A brief year and a half later, she had a diverse vocabulary and combined words into grammatically correct sentences. Even her mistakes ("goed") revealed an active, rule-oriented approach to language. Before her third birthday, Erin creatively used language to satisfy her desires, converse with others, and experiment with social roles. And she easily moved between her two native tongues, speaking English with her mother and brother and Spanish with her father.

Children's amazing linguistic accomplishments raise puzzling questions about development. How are a vast vocabulary and intricate grammatical system acquired in such a short time? Is language a separate capacity, with its own prewired, special-purpose neural system in the brain? Or is it governed by powerful general cognitive abilities that humans also apply to other aspects of their physical and social worlds? Do all children acquire language in the same way, or do individual and cultural differences exist?

Our discussion opens with the fiery theoretical debate of the 1950s between behaviorist B. F. Skinner and linguist Noam Chomsky, which inspired a burst of research into language development. Next we turn to infant preparatory skills that set the stage for the child's first words. Then, to fully appreciate the diverse linguistic skills children master, we follow the common practice of dividing language into four components. For each, we consider, first, what develops, then the more controversial question of how children acquire so much in so little time. We conclude with a discussion of the challenges and benefits of bilingualism—mastering two languages—in childhood.

⊚ To engage in effective verbal communication, these preschoolers must manage principles of sound, meaning, structure, and everyday use. How they accomplish this feat so rapidly raises some of the most puzzling questions about development.
© Steven Rubin/The Image Works

Components of Language

Language consists of several subsystems that have to do with sound, meaning, overall structure, and everyday use. Knowing language entails mastering each of these aspects and combining them into a flexible communication system.

The first component, **phonology,** refers to the rules governing the structure and sequence of speech sounds. If you have ever visited a foreign country in which you did not know the language, you probably wondered how anyone could analyze the rapid flow of speech into organized strings of words. Yet in English, you easily apply an intricate set of rules to comprehend and produce complicated sound patterns. How you acquired this ability is the story of phonological development.

Semantics, the second component, involves vocabulary—the way underlying concepts are expressed in words and word combinations. When young children first use a word, it often does not mean the same thing as it does to an adult. To build a versatile vocabulary, preschoolers must refine the meanings of thousands of words and connect them into elaborate networks of related terms.

Once mastery of vocabulary is under way, children combine words and modify them in meaningful ways. **Grammar,** the third component of language, consists of two main parts: **syntax,** the rules by which words are arranged into sentences, and **morphology,** the use of grammatical markers that indicate number, tense, case, person, gender, active or passive voice, and other meanings (the -s and -ed endings are examples in English).

Finally, **pragmatics** refers to the rules for engaging in appropriate and effective communication. To converse successfully, children must take turns, stay on the same topic, and state their meaning clearly. They also must figure out how gestures, tone of voice, and context clarify meaning. Furthermore, because society dictates how language should be spoken, pragmatics involves *sociolinguistic knowledge.* Children must acquire certain interaction rituals, such as verbal greetings and leave-takings. They must adjust their speech to mark important social relationships, such as differences in age and status. Finally, they must master their culture's narrative mode of sharing personally meaningful experiences with others.

As we take up the four components of language, you will see that they are interdependent. Acquisition of each facilitates mastery of the others.

Theories of Language Development

During the first half of this century, research on language development identified milestones that applied to children around the globe: All babbled around 6 months, said their first words at about 1 year, combined words at the end of the second year, and had mastered a vast vocabulary and most grammatical constructions by 4 to 5 years of age. The regularity of these achievements suggested a process largely governed by maturation. At the same time, language seemed to be learned: Without exposure to language, children born deaf or severely neglected did not acquire verbal communication. This apparent contradiction set the stage for an intense nature–nurture debate. By the end of the 1950s, two major figures had taken opposing sides.

The Behaviorist Perspective

Behaviorist B. F. Skinner (1957) proposed that language, just like other behavior, is acquired through *operant conditioning*. As the baby makes sounds, parents reinforce those that are most like words with smiles, hugs, and speech in return. For example, at 12 months, my older son, David, often babbled like this: "book-a-book-a-dook-a-dook-a-book-a-nook-a-book-aaa." One day while he babbled away, I held up his picture book and said, "Book!" Very soon, David was saying "book-aaa" in the presence of books.

Some behaviorists say children rely on *imitation* to rapidly acquire complex utterances, such as whole phrases and sentences (Moerk, 1992). Imitation can combine with reinforcement to promote language, as when a parent coaxes, "Say 'I want a cookie,'" and delivers praise and a treat after the child responds, "Wanna cookie!"

Although reinforcement and imitation contribute to early language development, few researchers cling to the behaviorist perspective today. Think about the process of language development just described. Adults would have to engage in intensive language tutoring—continuously modeling and reinforcing—to yield the extensive vocabulary and complex sentences of a typical 6-year-old. Even for the most conscientious parents, this seems like a physically impossible task. Furthermore, children create novel utterances that are not reinforced by or copied from others, such as Erin's use of "goed" at the beginning of this chapter. And when children do imitate language structures, they do so selectively, mostly focusing on building their vocabularies (as David did in repeating the word "book") and on refining aspects of language that they are working on at the moment (Owens, 2005).

In sum, the kind of learning described by Skinner and other behaviorists cannot account for language development. Rather than learning specific sentences, young children develop a working knowledge of language rules. Nevertheless, as we will see, adults do influence children's language by interacting with them in particular ways.

The Nativist Perspective

Linguist Noam Chomsky (1957) first convinced the scientific community that children assume much responsibility for their own language learning. In contrast to the behaviorist view, he proposed a *nativist* account that regards language as a uniquely human accomplishment, etched into the structure of the brain.

Focusing on grammar, Chomsky reasoned that the rules for sentence organization are too complex to be directly taught to or discovered by even a cognitively sophisticated young child. Children and adults alike readily produce and understand an unlimited range of sentences—often ones that they have never said or heard before. To account for this extraordinary facility with language, Chomsky proposed that all children have a **language acquisition device (LAD),** an innate system that permits them, as soon as they have acquired sufficient vocabulary, to combine words into grammatically consistent, novel utterances and to understand the meaning of sentences they hear.

How can a single LAD account for children's mastery of diverse languages around the world? According to Chomsky (1976, 1997), within the LAD is a **universal grammar,** a built-in storehouse of rules that apply to all human languages. Young children use this knowledge to decipher grammatical categories and relationships in any language to which they are exposed. Because the LAD is specifically suited for language processing, children master the structure of language spontaneously, with only limited language exposure. Therefore, in sharp contrast to the behaviorist view, the nativist perspective regards deliberate training by parents as unnecessary for language development (Pinker, 1994). Instead, the LAD ensures that language, despite its complexity, will be acquired early and swiftly.

BIOLOGY AND ENVIRONMENT

Deaf Children Invent Language

Can children develop complex, rule-based language systems with only minimal language input, or with input so inconsistent that the rules of grammar are not readily apparent? If so, this evidence would serve as strong support for Chomsky's idea that humans are born with a biological program for language development. Research reveals that deaf children can generate an intricate natural language, even when reared in linguistically deficient environments.

Minimal Language Input

In a series of studies, Susan Goldin-Meadow (2003) and her colleagues followed deaf preschoolers whose parents discouraged manual signing and addressed them verbally. None of the children made progress in acquiring spoken language or used even the most common gestures of their nation's sign language. Nevertheless, they spontaneously produced a gestural communication system, called *homesign,* strikingly similar in basic structure to hearing children's verbal language.

The deaf children developed gestural vocabularies with distinct forms for nouns and verbs that they combined into novel sentences conforming to grammatical rules that were not necessarily those of their parents' spoken language (Goldin-Meadow, Mylander, & Butcher, 1995; Goldin-Meadow et al., 1994). For example, to describe a large bubble he had just blown, one child first pointed at a bubble jar and then used

two open palms with fingers spread to denote the act of "blowing up big." Furthermore, by age 4, children produced gestural sentences that were more complex than those of their mothers (Goldin-Meadow & Mylander, 1998). Children seemed to be taking the lead in creating these gesture systems.

Language becomes a flexible means of communicating when it is used to talk about nonpresent objects and events. In referring to the nonpresent, the deaf children followed the same sequence of development as hearing children—first denoting objects and events in the recent past or anticipated but immediate future, next the more remote past and future, and finally hypothetical and fantasized events (Goldin-Meadow, 1999; Morford & Goldin-Meadow, 1997). Homesigning children conversed in the nonpresent far more often than their parents did. One homesigning child pointed over his shoulder to signify the past, then pointed to a picture of a poodle, and finally pointed to the floor in front of him, saying, "I used to have a poodle!"

Hearing children reach language milestones earlier than children acquiring homesign, indicating that a rich language environment fosters the attainments just mentioned. But without access to conventional language, deaf children generate their own language system. In Nicaragua,

▲ In Nicaragua, educators brought deaf children and adolescents together to form a community; within two decades, they developed a language—Nicaraguan Sign Language.
© Nicaraguan Sign Language Projects, Inc.

educators brought deaf children and adolescents, each with a unique homesign, together to form a community. Although they had no shared language, in less than 2 decades they developed one—Nicaraguan Sign Language—that matched other human languages in structural complexity (Senghas & Coppola, 2001).

Inconsistent Language Input

An unusual study of a rare child whose language environment was not the typical rich form—offering examples of all linguistic structures—also illustrates children's remarkable capacity to invent language. Simon, a

• **SUPPORT FOR THE NATIVIST PERSPECTIVE** • Are children biologically primed to acquire language? Research reviewed in the Biology and Environment box above, which suggests that children have a remarkable ability to invent new language systems, provides some of the most powerful support for this perspective. Three additional sets of evidence—efforts to teach language to animals, localization of language functions in the human brain, and investigations into whether a sensitive period for language development exists—are consistent with Chomsky's view. Let's look at each in turn.

deaf child, was born to deaf parents who did not start to learn American Sign Language (ASL), which is as elaborate as any spoken language, until they were adolescents. (As with the deaf youngsters just described, their hearing parents exposed them only to oral language in childhood.) Simon's parents communicated with him in ASL from infancy. But because they were late ASL learners, they had not attained the grammatical complexity of native signers, and their use of many ASL structures was inconsistent. (See the section on a sensitive period for language development on page 359.) Simon has a hearing younger sibling and goes to a school with hearing teachers and children; his only ASL input comes from his parents.

When Simon reached age 7, Jenny Singleton and Alyssa Newport (2004) gave him a challenging ASL grammatical task, which assessed his knowledge of the verb *to move*. In ASL, accurately expressing motion requires up to seven grammatical markers, which indicate (1) the object's path, (2) the object's orientation, (3) the manner in which the object moves (for example, bouncing or rolling), (4) the object's location relative to a secondary object, (5) the position of the secondary object with respect to the path, (6) the features of the moving object (category, size, or shape), and (7) the features of the secondary object. The researchers compared Simon's performance to that of several reference groups: his parents, deaf school-age children of deaf native-signing parents, and deaf native-signing adults.

Findings confirmed that Simon's parents' use of ASL grammar was much weaker than that of native-signing adults.

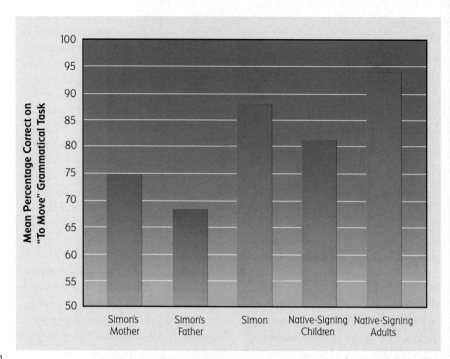

▲ **Figure 9.1**

Simon's performance on a challenging ASL grammatical task, compared with the performance of his parents and native-signing children and adults. Despite inconsistent input from his late-ASL-learning parents, 7-year-old Simon showed excellent mastery of ASL grammar, exceeding the average performance of native-signing deaf children and approaching the performance of native-signing deaf adults. (Adapted from Singleton & Newport, 2004.)

Yet Simon's language did not mirror his parents' error-ridden input. Instead, he introduced a level of regularity into his language that surpassed his parents' usage. As Figure 9.1 shows, his score on the "to move" task exceeded the average score of native-signing deaf children and approached the performance of native-signing deaf adults. Simon managed to extract the regularities that did exist in his parents' language and to magnify them,

ending up with a highly systematic grammar that differed substantially from the language to which he was exposed.

Deaf children's remarkable capacity to invent language, despite minimal or inconsistent input, is compatible with the existence of a biologically based language acquisition device. As we will see, however, other theorists claim that nonlinguistic cognitive capacities applied to the task of communicating are responsible.

▶ *Can Animals Acquire Language?* Is the ability to master a grammatically complex language system unique to humans? To find out, many attempts have been made to teach language to animals, including dolphins, parrots, gorillas, orangutans, and chimpanzees. With extensive training, these animals can acquire a vocabulary ranging from several dozen to several hundred symbols and can produce and respond to short, novel sentences, although they do so less consistently than a preschool child (Herman & Uyeyama, 1999; Pepperberg, 2000; Savage-Rumbaugh & Shanker, 1998).

Bonobo chimp Kanzi uses an artificial language in which he expresses meaning by pressing keys on a symbol board to communicate with Dr. Sue Savage-Rumbaugh, who is tracking his language development.

© FRANS LANTING/Minden Pictures

Chimpanzees are closest to humans in the evolutionary hierarchy. Common chimps, the species studied most often, have been taught artificial languages (in which a computer keyboard generates visual symbols) and American Sign Language. Yet even after years of training, common chimps are unable produce strings of three or more symbols that conform to a rule-based structure. Their language limitations may be due in part to a narrow understanding of others' mental states. Common chimps can accurately predict others' goals if those goals are readily apparent in their behavior—for example, whether or not someone is willing to share food with them. But they may be unaware of less obvious intentions, including ones that motivate use of language—namely, that others want to exchange knowledge and ideas (Tomasello, Call, & Hare, 2003).

Bonobo chimps are more intelligent and social than common chimps. The linguistic attainments of a Bonobo named Kanzi are especially impressive (Savage-Rumbaugh, 2001). While young, Kanzi picked up his mother's artificial language by observing trainers interact with her. Then Kanzi's caregivers encouraged his language by communicating both in the artificial language and in English. Kanzi rarely combined words because he preferred to join a word to a gesture, such as "*carry* + [gesture to person]," meaning "you carry Kanzi." But through listening to fluent speech, he acquired remarkable comprehension of English, including the ability to discriminate hundreds of English words and to act out unusual sentences he had not heard before, such as "Put the money in the mushroom." Most of the time, Kanzi also could detect the difference between novel, reversed sentences, such as "Take the potato outdoors" and "Go outdoors and get the potato" (Savage-Rumbaugh et al., 1993; Shanker, Savage-Rumbaugh, & Taylor, 1999).

Still, researchers disagree on Kanzi's linguistic achievements. Some argue that he is a remarkable conversationalist who wants to share information (Greenspan & Shanker, 2004). Others claim that he uses language only to get what he wants (a strawberry to eat) rather than to share information (talk about strawberries) (Seidenberg & Petitto, 1987). And Kanzi's comprehension of grammar does not exceed that of a human 2-year-old, who (as we will see) is not far along in grammatical development. Overall, Chomsky's assumption of a uniquely human capacity for an elaborate grammar receives support. No evidence exists that even the brightest animals can comprehend and produce sentences that are both complex *and* novel.

▶ *Language Areas in the Brain.* Recall from Chapter 5 that for most individuals, language is housed largely in the left hemisphere of the cerebral cortex. Within it are two important language-related structures (see Figure 9.2). To clarify their functions, researchers have, for several decades, studied adults who experienced damage to these structures and display *aphasias,* or communication disorders. The patients' linguistic deficits suggested that **Broca's area,** located in the frontal lobe, supports grammatical processing and language production, whereas **Wernicke's area,** located in the temporal lobe, plays a role in comprehending word meaning.

But recent brain-imaging research suggests more complicated relationships between language functions and brain structures. The impaired pronunciation and grammar of patients with Broca's aphasia and the meaningless speech streams of patients with Wernicke's aphasia involve the spread of injury to nearby cortical areas and widespread abnormal activity in the left cerebral hemisphere, triggered by the brain damage (Bates et al., 2003). Contrary to what has long been believed, Broca's and Wernicke's areas are not solely or even mainly responsible for specific language functions. Nevertheless, depending on the site of injury to the left hemisphere, language deficits do vary predictably. Damage to the frontal lobe usually yields language production problems, damage to the other lobes comprehension problems—patterns that are highly consistent across individuals (Dick et al., 2004),

The broad association of language functions with left-hemispheric regions is consistent with Chomsky's notion of a brain prepared to process language. However, we must be cautious about this conclusion. Recall from Chapter 5 that at birth, the brain is not fully lateralized; it is highly plastic. Language areas in the cerebral cortex *develop* as children acquire language (Bates, 1999;

Mills, Coffey-Corina, & Neville, 1997). Although the left hemisphere is biased for language processing, if it is injured in the first few years, other regions take over language functions, and most such children attain normal language competence (see page 186 in Chapter 5). Thus, left-hemispheric localization is not necessary for effective language processing. Indeed, as noted in Chapter 5, deaf adults who as children learned sign language depend more on the right hemisphere. Additional research reveals that many parts of the brain participate in language activities to differing degrees, depending on the language skill and the individual's mastery of that skill (Huttenlocher, 2002; Neville & Bavelier, 1998).

Once grammatical competence develops, it may depend more on specific brain structures than the other components of language. In studies of adults who had their left hemispheres removed because of disease or abnormalities that caused severe seizures, grammatical abilities suffered much more than semantic or pragmatic abilities, which seem to draw more on right-hemispheric regions (Baynes & Gazzaniga, 1988). Similarly, in older children with left-hemispheric brain damage, grammar is more impaired than other language functions (Stromswold, 2000). Finally, when the young brain allocates language to the right hemisphere after injury, it localizes it in roughly the same regions that typically support language in the left hemisphere (Mueller et al., 1998). This suggests that those regions are uniquely disposed for language processing.

▶ *A Sensitive Period for Language Development.* Erik Lenneberg (1967) first proposed that children must acquire language during the age span of brain lateralization, which he believed to be complete by puberty. Evidence for a sensitive period that coincides with brain lateralization would support the nativist position that language development has unique biological properties.

To test this idea, researchers tracked the recovery of severely abused children who experienced little human contact in childhood. The most thoroughly studied is Genie, a normally developing child who said her first words just before she was isolated in the back room of her parents' house at 1½ years of age. After that, until she was found at 13½, no one talked to her, and she was beaten when she made any noise. With several years of training by dedicated teachers, Genie acquired a large vocabulary and good comprehension of conversation, but her grammar and communication skills remained limited (Curtiss, 1977, 1989). Genie's case and others like it fit with the existence of a sensitive period, but the findings are inconclusive. As we will see in Chapter 14, persistent child abuse disrupts brain growth and functioning; this, rather than deprivation of language input, might have caused Genie's deficits.

More conclusive evidence comes from studies of deaf adults who acquired their first language—American Sign Language (ASL)—at different ages. The later learners, whose parents chose to educate them through the oral method, which relies on speech and lip-reading and discourages signing, did not acquire spoken language because of their profound deafness. Consistent with Lenneberg's prediction, those who learned ASL in adolescence or adulthood never became as proficient as those who learned in childhood (recall Simon's parents, in Figure 9.1, who scored lower on a test of complex grammar than he did because they did not acquire ASL until adolescence) (Mayberry, 1994; Newport, 1991). Furthermore, the typical right-hemispheric localization of ASL functions, which require visual–spatial processing of hand, arm, and facial movements, is greatly reduced in individuals who learned ASL after puberty (Newman et al., 2001). However, a precise age cutoff for a decline in first-language competence has not been established.

What about acquiring a second language? Is this task harder after a sensitive period for language development has passed? In one study, researchers examined U.S. census data, selecting immigrants from Spanish- and Chinese-speaking countries who had resided in the United States for at least 10 years. The census form had asked the immigrants to rate how competently they spoke English, from "not at all" to "very well"—self-reports that correlate strongly with objective language measures. As age of immigration increased from infancy and early childhood into adulthood, English proficiency declined, regardless of respondents' level of education

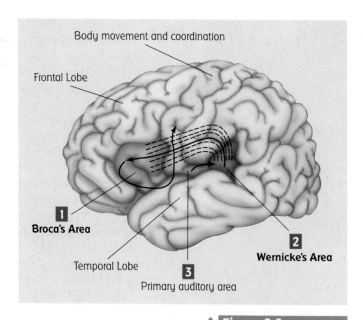

▲ **Figure 9.2**

Broca's and Wernicke's areas, in the left hemisphere of the cerebral cortex. **(1)** Broca's area, located in the frontal lobe, supports grammatical processing and language production. **(2)** Wernicke's area, located in the temporal lobe, is involved in comprehending word meaning. Contrary to what was once believed, however, neither area is solely or even mainly responsible for these functions. Instead, each cooperates with many other regions of the left hemisphere. Wernicke's area and Broca's area communicate through a bundle of nerve fibers represented by dashed lines in the figure. Among the regions from which Wernicke's area receives impulses is **(3)** the primary auditory area, where sensations from the ears are sent. Broca's area communicates with motor areas involved in speaking.

⊚ Acquiring a second language becomes more difficult with age, but these children in an ethnically diverse preschool in Toronto are well within the sensitive period. Those who are learning English as a second language will probably attain the competence of native speakers.
CP Photo/Frank Gunn

(see Figure 9.3) (Hakuta, Bialystok, & Wiley, 2003). Furthermore, ERP and fMRI measures of brain activity indicate that second-language processing is less lateralized in older than in younger learners (Neville & Bruer, 2001). But second-language competence does not drop sharply at adolescence, as Lenneberg predicted. Rather, a continuous, age-related decrease occurs.

• **LIMITATIONS OF THE NATIVIST PERSPECTIVE** • Chomsky's theory has had a major impact on current views of language development. It is now widely accepted that humans have a unique, biologically based capacity to acquire language. Still, Chomsky's account of development has been challenged on several grounds.

First, researchers have had great difficulty specifying the universal grammar that Chomsky believes underlies the widely varying grammatical systems of human languages. A persistent source of dissatisfaction is the absence of a complete description of these abstract grammatical structures, or even an agreed-on list of how many exist, or the best examples of them. Critics of Chomsky's theory doubt that one set of rules can account for all grammatical forms (Maratsos, 1998; Tomasello, 2003). How children manage to link such rules with the strings of words they hear is also unclear (Bowerman, 1997).

Second, Chomsky's assumption that grammatical knowledge is innately determined does not fit with certain observations of language development. Once children begin to use an innate grammatical structure, we would expect them to apply it across the board, to all relevant instances in their language. But although children make extraordinary strides in grammatical development in the preschool years, their mastery of many forms is not immediate, but continuous and gradual. Complete mastery of some forms (such as the passive voice) is not achieved until well into middle childhood (Tager-Flusberg, 2005). This suggests that more learning and discovery are involved than Chomsky assumed.

Dissatisfaction with Chomsky's theory has also arisen from its lack of comprehensiveness. For example, it cannot explain how children weave statements together into connected discourse and sustain meaningful conversations. Perhaps because Chomsky did not dwell on the pragmatic side of language, his theory grants little attention to the quality of language input or to social experience in supporting language progress. Furthermore, the nativist perspective does not regard children's cognitive capacities as important. Yet in Chapter 6, we saw that cognitive development is involved in children's early vocabulary growth. And studies of children with mental retardation (see the Biology and Environment box on the following page) show that cognitive competence also influences children's grammatical mastery.

▶ **Figure 9.3**

Relationship between age of immigration to the United States and self-rated English proficiency, illustrated for native Spanish speakers. As age of immigration increased, English proficiency decreased for individuals at all levels of education, from a few years of elementary school to a college education. Findings for native Chinese speakers were similar.
(From K. Hakuta, E. Bialystok, & E. Wiley, 2003, "Critical Evidence: A Test of the Critical Period Hypothesis for Second-Language Acquisition," *Psychological Science, 14,* p. 37. © American Psychological Society. Reprinted by permission.)

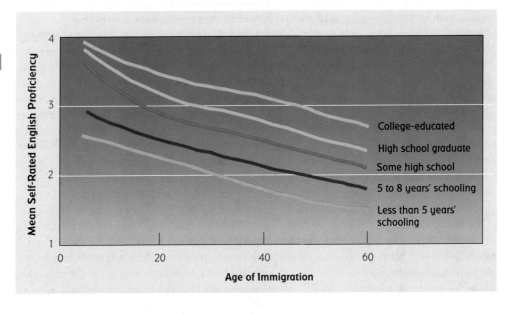

Language Development in Children with Williams Syndrome

Williams syndrome is a rare disorder caused by deletion of genetic material on the seventh chromosome. Affected individuals have facial, heart, and kidney abnormalities and mild to serious mental retardation. With IQ scores typically ranging from 50 to 70, they are just as mentally impaired as individuals with Down syndrome. Yet compared to children with Down syndrome, children with Williams syndrome are far more advanced in language skills (Bellugi et al., 2000). For many years, researchers took this apparent "decoupling" of cognition and language as evidence that language is controlled by an innate LAD. To see why this conclusion is no longer warranted, let's look at the language attainments associated with this disorder.

Infants with Williams syndrome are strongly oriented toward the social world—extremely gregarious and fascinated by faces and voices (Jones et al., 2000). Although their language development is delayed, it is impressive. During the preschool years, children with Williams syndrome have larger vocabularies and produce grammatically more complex sentences than children with Down syndrome (Mervis & Robinson, 2000). For example, the longest sentence of one 3-year-old with Williams syndrome was "Please have some grapes in my cup right now." Her counterpart with Down syndrome said, "Here-ya-go" and "Hold me" (Jarrold, Baddeley, & Hewes, 1998, p. 361). By adolescence, the vocabularies of individuals with Williams syndrome contain many unusual words. When asked to name as many animals as possible, one teenager said, "weasel, newt, salamander, Chihuahua, ibex, yak" (Bellugi et al., 1992, p. 11).

Yet affected individuals have trouble with highly challenging grammatical rules. For example, French-speaking adolescents with Williams syndrome do poorly on grammatical gender assignment—matching masculine and feminine articles (such as *un* versus *une*) with nouns by attending to word endings and noting exceptions. Normally developing French children master this gender system by age 4 (Karmiloff-Smith et al., 1997). In a study of English-speaking adults, difficulties with subtle verb forms ("He struggle the dog" rather than "He struggled with the dog") appeared (Karmiloff-Smith et al., 1998).

Why does Williams syndrome lead to an uneven language profile—areas of both strength and weakness? Growing evidence indicates that the cognitive deficits of Williams syndrome profoundly alter the course of language development. Children with the disorder are relatively good at memorizing but poor at rule learning (Bates, 2004; Karmiloff-Smith et al., 2003). To compensate for this weakness, they capitalize on their social strengths, attending closely to faces and voices and acquiring as much language by rote as they can.

In support of this rote approach, toddlers with Williams syndrome do not build their early vocabularies on intentional gestures (such as pointing) and advances in categorization, as normally developing children do (Laing et al., 2002). Instead, they more often mimic others, so much so that their parents report that they frequently speak without fully comprehending what they are saying. Working-memory capacity (as measured by digit span) is more strongly correlated with grammatical development in children with Williams syn-

▲ The impish smile and facial features of this child, who has Williams syndrome, suggest that she is strongly oriented toward the social world. In keeping with their sociability, children with Williams syndrome display impressive language skills given their mild to serious mental retardation. Yet the cognitive deficits of Williams syndrome impair children's ability to master the most complex rules of language.
Courtesy of the Williams Syndrome Foundation

drome than in typically developing children (Robinson, Mervis, & Robinson, 2003). This suggests, again, a heavy reliance on memory to learn language.

In sum, although the language of individuals with Williams syndrome is impressive in view of their cognitive limitations, it is impaired in significant ways. These findings indicate that language is not as separate from other human mental abilities as Chomsky's concept of the LAD assumes.

The Interactionist Perspective

In recent years, new theories of language development have arisen, replacing the dichotomy of the Skinner–Chomsky debate with an emphasis on *interactions* between inner predispositions and environmental influences. One type of interactionist theory applies the information-processing perspective to language development; a second type emphasizes social interaction.

• **INFORMATION-PROCESSING THEORIES** • The most influential information-processing accounts are derived from research with connectionist, or artificial neural network, models (see Chapter 7, page 275, to review). Researchers program computers to simulate the multilayered networks of neural connections in the brain and then expose them to various types of language input. Tests with language sounds, words, and basic grammatical forms show that over time, these networks detect adult linguistic patterns: Neural connections that represent adult usage strengthen, while those that are primitive or incorrect weaken. The system is not biased to learn language. Instead, connectionist theorists assume that children make sense of their complex language environments by applying powerful, analytic cognitive capacities of a general kind rather than capacities especially tuned to language (Bates, 1999; Elman, 2001; MacWhinney, 1999).

Other theorists blend Chomsky's nativist perspective with the information-processing proposal that the human brain is extraordinarily skilled at detecting patterns. Recall the research presented in Chapter 4 (see page 151), which showed that 8-month-old babies are extraordinary *statistical analyzers* of the sound stream, capable of detecting which adjacent sounds often occur together and which do not—a pattern analysis that helps them discriminate words in fluent speech. According to *statistical learning theory,* infants identify basic patterns of language with the same strategies that they use to make sense of their nonlinguistic experiences. At the same time, researchers recognize that such statistical computations are not sufficient to account for mastery of higher-level aspects of language—for example, intricate grammatical structures that require a grasp of distant relationships between words and phrases (Newport & Aslin, 2000). Currently, statistical learning theorists are investigating how sensitivity to statistical regularities might combine with other general-cognitive and language-specific processing abilities to explain children's acquisition of increasingly complex language structures.

Proponents of information-processing approaches draw on biological evidence, pointing out that regions of the brain housing language also govern other similar perceptual, motor, and cognitive abilities. For example, ERP and fMRI studies reveal that damage to the left hemisphere, including Wernicke's area, results in difficulty comprehending both language and other patterned stimuli, such as music and series of moving lights that depict familiar shapes (Bates et al., 2003; Koelsch et al., 2002; Saygin et al., 2004). Indeed, Wernicke's area—once thought to be language-specific—is actually more strongly associated with comprehension of nonverbal than of verbal sound (Dick et al., 2004).

Information-processing theorists have tested their ideas mostly with simplified language stimuli, presented to artificial neural networks and to children in laboratories. In many instances, they cannot be certain that the learning strategies identified generalize to children's language acquisition in everyday social contexts. Other interactionist theorists believe that children's social skills and language experiences are centrally involved in language development.

• **SOCIAL INTERACTIONIST THEORIES** • According to the social interactionist perspective, native capacity, a strong desire to understand others and to be understood by them, and a rich language environment combine to help children discover the functions and regularities of language. An active child, well endowed for making sense of language, strives to communicate. In doing so, she cues her caregivers to provide appropriate language experiences, which in turn help her relate the content and structure of language to its social meanings (Bohannon & Bonvillian, 2005; Chapman, 2000).

Among social interactionist theorists, disagreement continues over whether children make sense of their complex language environments by applying general cognitive capacities or capacities specially tuned to language (Bloom, 1999; Tomasello, 2003). Nevertheless, as we chart the course of language development, we will encounter much support for their central premise—that children's social competencies and language experiences greatly affect language development. At the same time, these ideas have not escaped the critical eye of contemporary researchers. Social interactionists assume that language grows out of communication, yet some children show large disparities between pragmatics and others aspects of language. For example, the conversational skills of children with mental retardation often lag behind other language achievements (Levy, 1996).

In reality, native endowment, cognitive-processing strategies, and social experience may operate in different balances with respect to each component of language. Today, we still know much more about the course of language development than about precisely how it takes place.

www

Ask Yourself

REVIEW	Summarize outcomes of attempts to teach language to animals. Are results consistent with the nativist assumption that human children are uniquely endowed with an LAD? Explain.
REVIEW	How do the two types of interactionist theories of language development differ from behaviorist and nativist views, and from each other?
APPLY	Describe evidence supporting the existence of a sensitive period for second-language learning. What are the practical implications of these findings for teaching children a second language?
CONNECT	Cite research in this chapter and in Chapter 5 indicating that with age, areas of the cortex become increasingly specialized for language. Relate these findings to the concept of brain plasticity.

Prelinguistic Development: Getting Ready to Talk

From the very beginning, infants are prepared to acquire language. During the first year of life, sensitivity to language, cognitive and social milestones, and environmental supports pave the way for the onset of verbal communication.

Receptivity to Language

Recall from Chapter 4 that newborns are especially sensitive to the pitch range of the human voice and prefer speech—especially their mother's voice and their native tongue—to other sounds, perhaps because of repeated exposure to their mother speaking during pregnancy. In addition, newborns have an astonishing ability to make fine-grained distinctions between the sounds of virtually any human language. Because this skill may help them crack the phonological code of their native tongue, let's look at it more closely.

• LEARNING NATIVE-LANGUAGE SOUND CATEGORIES AND PATTERNS • As adults, we analyze the speech stream into **phonemes,** the smallest sound units that signal a change in meaning, such as the difference between the consonant sounds in "pa" and "ba." Phonemes are not the same across all languages. For example, "ra" and "la" are distinct sounds to English speakers, but Japanese individuals hear them as the same. Similarly, English speakers have trouble perceiving the difference between two "p" sounds—a soft "p" and a sharp "p" with a burst of air—used to distinguish meaning in the Thai language. This tendency to perceive as identical a range of sounds that belong to the same phonemic class is called **categorical speech perception.** Like adults, newborns are capable of it. But they are sensitive to a much wider range of categories than exists in their own language (Jusczyk, 2003).

As infants listen actively to the talk of people around them, they focus on meaningful sound variations. Between 6 and 8 months, they start to organize speech into the phonemic categories of their own language—that is, they stop attending to sounds that will not be useful in mastering their native tongue (Kuhl et al., 1992; Polka & Werker, 1994). Soon after, they recognize familiar words in spoken passages, listen longer to speech with clear clause and phrase boundaries, and divide the speech stream into wordlike segments (see Chapter 4, page 151, to review).

Infants also extend their rhythmic sensitivity to individual words. Using phoneme sequences and stress patterns, 7-month-olds can distinguish sounds that typically begin words from those that do not (Jusczyk, Houston, & Newsome, 1999). For example, English and Dutch infant learners often rely on the onset of a strong syllable to indicate a new word, as in "animal" and "pudding." By 10 months, they can detect words that start with weak syllables, such as "surprise" (Jusczyk, 2001). Interestingly, the reverse pattern—earlier detection of words starting with weak syllables—characterizes infants acquiring Canadian French, in which words more often have a weak–strong stress pattern (Polka & Sundara, 2003).

Taken together, these findings reveal that in the second half of the first year, infants have begun to detect the internal structure of sentences and words—information that will be vital for linking speech units with their meanings (Werker & Tees, 1999). How do babies accomplish these feats? We have seen that 8-month-olds are vigilant *statistical analyzers* of sound patterns; they can distinguish adjacent syllables that frequently occur together (signaling that they belong to the same word) from those that seldom occur together (signaling a word boundary) (Saffran, Aslin, & Newport, 1996). Research suggests that infants first use these statistical learning abilities to locate words in speech. Then they focus on the words, detecting regular patterns of syllable stress in their language (Thiessen & Saffran, 2003). Furthermore, babies of this age are budding *rule learners*. At 7 months, they can distinguish an ABA from an ABB pattern in the structure of short, nonsense-word sequences—a capacity that may eventually help them grasp basic syntax (Marcus et al., 1999) (see page 152 in Chapter 4).

Do infants actually apply these analytic skills—discovered by presenting them with artificial sound sequences in laboratories—to the language they hear in everyday life? Recent analyses of maternal speech to English- and Dutch-learning babies indicates that real words can easily be extracted by attending to frequent, co-occurring syllables and to stress patterns (Swingley, 2005). Clearly, infants acquire a greatly deal of language-specific knowledge before they start to talk around 12 months of age. As we will see, certain features of adult speech greatly assist them in detecting meaningful speech units.

• **ADULT SPEECH TO YOUNG LANGUAGE LEARNERS** • Adults in many countries speak to infants and toddlers in **child-directed speech (CDS),** a form of communication made up of short sentences with high-pitched, exaggerated expression, clear pronunciation, distinct pauses between speech segments, and repetition of new words in a variety of contexts ("See the *ball*." "The *ball* bounced!" "I love that *ball!*") (Fernald et al., 1989; Kuhl, 2000). Deaf parents use a similar style of communicating when signing to their babies (Masataka, 1996).

Parents do not seem to be deliberately trying to teach infants to talk when they use CDS; many of the same speech qualities appear when adults communicate with foreigners. Rather, CDS probably arises from adults' desire to hold young children's attention and ease their task of understanding, and it works effectively in these ways. From birth on, infants prefer to listen to CDS over other kinds of adult talk (Aslin, Jusczyk, & Pisoni, 1998). By 5 months, they are more emotionally responsive to it and can discriminate the tone quality of CDS with different meanings—for example, approving versus soothing utterances (Moore, Spence, & Katz, 1997; Werker, Pegg, & McLeod, 1994).

Parents continually fine-tune CDS, adjusting the length and content of their utterances to fit children's needs. In a study carried out in four cultures, American, Argentinean, French, and Japanese mothers tended to speak to 5-month-olds in emotion-laden ways, emphasizing greetings, repeated sounds, and affectionate names. At 13 months, when toddlers understood much more, a greater percentage of maternal speech was information laden—concerned with giving directions,

◎ This mother speaks to her baby in short, clearly pronounced sentences with high-pitched, exaggerated intonation. Adults in many countries use this form of language, called child-directed speech, which eases language learning for infants and toddlers.
© Esbin-Anderson/Omni-Photo Communications

asking questions, and describing what was happening at the moment (Bornstein et al., 1992a). Furthermore, in Chapter 4 we saw that parents combine speech with messages in other modalities (for example, naming an object while moving it), thereby enabling infants to use their capacity for intermodal matching to make sense of language (see page 152).

The more effectively parents modify their verbal input to suit their babies' learning needs, the better toddlers' language comprehension at age 18 months (Murray, Johnson, & Peters, 1990). In addition, many of the first words and phrases that toddlers produce occur often in the child-directed speech to which they are exposed (Cameron-Faulkner, Lieven, & Tomasello, 2003).

First Speech Sounds

Around 2 months, babies begin to make vowel-like noises, called **cooing** because of their pleasant "oo" quality. Gradually, consonants are added, and around 4 months **babbling** appears, in which infants repeat consonant–vowel combinations in long strings, such as "babababababa" and "nanananana."

The timing of early babbling seems to be due to maturation: Babies everywhere (even those who are deaf) start babbling at about the same age and produce a similar range of early sounds. But for babbling to develop further, infants must hear human speech. If a baby is hearing impaired, these speechlike sounds are greatly delayed or, in the case of deaf infants, are totally absent (Oller, 2000).

Babies initially produce a limited number of sounds, then expand to a much broader range (Oller et al., 1997). Around 7 months, babbling includes consonant–vowel syllables common in spoken languages. By 10 months, it reflects the sound and intonation patterns of the child's language community, some of which are transferred to their first words (Boysson-Bardies & Vihman, 1991).

Deaf infants exposed to sign language from birth babble with their hands in much the same way hearing infants do through speech (Petitto & Marentette, 1991). Furthermore, hearing babies who have deaf, signing parents produce babble-like hand motions with the rhythmic pattern of natural sign languages (Petitto et al., 2001, 2004). This sensitivity to language rhythm—evident not just in perception of speech but also in the babbles babies produce, whether in manual or spoken mode—supports both discovery and production of meaningful language units.

Listen to an older baby babble, and notice that certain sounds appear in particular contexts—for example, when exploring objects, looking at books, and walking upright (Blake & Boysson-Bardies, 1992). Infants seem to be experimenting with the sound system and meaning of language before they speak in conventional ways. Babbling continues for 4 or 5 months after infants say their first words.

Becoming a Communicator

At birth, infants are already prepared for some aspects of conversational behavior. For example, newborns can initiate interaction by making eye contact and terminate it by looking away. Around 4 months, infants start to gaze in the same direction adults are looking, a skill that becomes more accurate between 9 and 15 months of age (Tomasello, 1999). Adults also follow the baby's line of vision and comment on what the infant sees. In this way, they label the baby's environment. This **joint attention,** in which the child attends to the same object or event as the caregiver, who offers verbal information, contributes greatly to early language development. Infants and toddlers who often experience it sustain attention longer, comprehend more language, produce meaningful gestures and words earlier, and show faster vocabulary development (Carpenter, Nagell, & Tomasello, 1998b; Flom & Pick, 2003; Silvén, 2001).

By 3 months, the beginnings of conversation can be seen. At first, the mother vocalizes at the same time as the baby—an event that may help infants realize that others attend to their speech sounds (Elias & Broerse, 1996). Between 4 and 6 months, interaction between parent and baby begins to include give-and-take, as in turn-taking games such as pat-a-cake and peekaboo. At first, the parent starts the game, with the baby as an amused observer. But 4-month-olds are sensitive to the structure and timing of these interactions, smiling more to an organized than a disorganized peekaboo exchange (Rochat, Querido, & Striano, 1999). By 12 months, babies participate actively, trading roles with the caregiver. As they do so, they practice the turn-taking pattern of human conversation, a vital context for acquiring language and communication skills. Infants' play maturity and vocalizations during games predict advanced language progress between 1 and 2 years of age (Rome-Flanders & Cronk, 1995).

Between 9 and 12 months, as infants become capable of intentional behavior, they use two types of preverbal gestures to influence the behavior of others. The first is the **protodeclarative,** in which the baby touches an object, holds it up, or points to it while looking at others to make sure they notice. In the second, the **protoimperative,** the infant gets another person to do something by reaching, pointing, and often making sounds at the same time (Carpenter, Nagell, & Tomasello, 1998a; Fenson et al., 1994). Over time, some of these gestures become explicitly symbolic—much like those in children's early make-believe play (see Chapter 6). For example, a 1- to 2-year-old might flap her arms to indicate "butterfly" or raise her palms to signal "all gone" (Goldin-Meadow, 1999).

Early in the second year, turn-taking and gestural communication come together, especially in situations in which children's messages do not communicate clearly. When adults label toddlers' reaching and pointing gestures ("Oh, you want a cookie!"), toddlers learn that using language quickly leads to desired results. Soon they integrate words with gestures, using the gesture to expand their

This 14-month-old uses the protodeclarative to direct her mother's attention to a fascinating sight. As the mother provides labels that show she understands, she promotes the toddler's transition to verbal language.
© Laura Dwight Photography

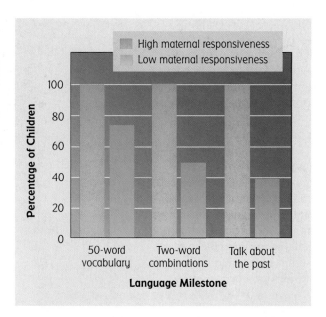

▲ **Figure 9.4**

Relationship of maternal responsiveness at 13 months to attainment of language milestones at 21 months. Mothers high in responsiveness fell in the top 10 percent in responding to their toddler's vocalizations with verbal prompts, imitations, and expansions. Mothers low in maternal responsiveness fell in the bottom 10 percent. Toddlers of highly responsive mothers were advanced in attaining major language milestones. (Adapted from Tamis-LeMonda, Bornstein, & Baumwell, 2001.)

verbal message, as in pointing to a toy while saying "give." Gradually, gestures recede, and words become the dominant symbolic form (Iverson, Capirci, & Caselli, 1994; Namy & Waxman, 1998). Nevertheless, these word–gesture combinations forecast the transition to two-word utterances. The earlier toddlers produce them, the sooner they combine words at the end of the second year (Goldin-Meadow & Butcher, 2003).

We have stressed that caregivers who respond sensitively and involve infants in dialogue-like exchanges encourage early language progress. Yet in some cultures, such as the Kaluli of Papua New Guinea, the people of Western Samoa, and the Maya of southern Mexico, adults rarely communicate with young children and never play social games with them. Not until infants crawl and walk do siblings take charge, talk to toddlers, and respond to their vocalizations. Yet Kaluli, Samoan, and Mayan children acquire language within the normal time frame (de León, 2000; Ochs, 1988).

These findings suggest that adult molding of communication during the first year is not essential. But by the second year, caregiver–child interaction contributes greatly to the transition to language. In observations of mother–child play at 9 and 13 months, the frequency with which mothers joined in the child's activity, offered verbal prompts, and imitated and expanded on the child's vocalizations predicted how early children attained major language milestones, including first words, a 50-word vocabulary, two-word combinations, and use of language to talk about the past. The relationship of maternal responsiveness to language progress was particularly strong at 13 months (see Figure 9.4) (Tamis-LeMonda, Bornstein, & Baumwell, 2001).

As the From Research to Practice box on the following page illustrates, when a child's disability makes it difficult for parents to engage in responsive communication, children show profound delays in both language and cognitive development. For ways that caregivers can support early language learning, see Applying What We Know below.

Applying

What We Know — Supporting Early Language Learning

Strategy	Consequence
Respond to infants' coos and babbles with speech sounds and words.	Encourages experimentation with sounds that can later be blended into first words. Provides experience with the turn-taking pattern of human conversation.
Establish joint attention and comment on what the child sees.	Promotes sustained attention, earlier onset of language, and faster vocabulary development.
Play social games, such as pat-a-cake and peekaboo, with infants and toddlers.	Promotes all aspects of conversational dialogue.
Engage children in frequent conversations.	Promotes faster language development and academic competence during the school years.
Expand slightly on what the child just said, adding new information.	Saying something like, "You want juice? I have some juice. It's apple juice!" to a toddler models use of language just ahead of the child's current level, thereby promoting language progress.
Read to children often, engaging them in dialogues about picture books.	Provides exposure to many aspects of language, including vocabulary, grammar, communication skills, and information about written symbols and story structures important for literacy progress.

Parent-Child Interaction:
Impact on Language and Cognitive Development of Deaf Children

About 1 in every 1,000 North American infants is born profoundly or fully deaf (Deafness Research Foundation, 2003). When a deaf child cannot participate fully in communication with parents and other caregivers, development is severely compromised. Yet the consequences of deafness for children's language and cognition vary with social context, as comparisons of deaf children of hearing parents with deaf children of deaf parents reveal.

Over 90 percent of deaf children have hearing parents who are not fluent in sign language. In toddlerhood and early childhood, these children often are delayed in language and complex make-believe play. In middle childhood, many achieve poorly in school and are deficient in social skills. Yet deaf children of deaf parents escape these difficulties! Their language (use of sign) and play maturity are on a par with hearing children's. After school entry, deaf children of deaf parents learn easily and get along well with adults and peers (Bornstein et al., 1999b; Spencer & Lederberg, 1997).

These differences can be traced to early parent–child communication. Beginning in infancy, hearing parents of deaf children are less positive, less responsive to the child's efforts to communicate, less effective at achieving joint attention and turn-taking, less involved in play, and more directive and intrusive (Spencer, 2000; Spencer & Meadow-Orlans, 1996). In contrast, the quality of interaction between deaf children and deaf parents is similar to that of hearing children and hearing parents.

Children with limited and less sensitive parental communication lag behind their agemates in achieving verbal control over their behavior—in thinking before they act and in planning. Deaf children of hearing parents frequently display impulse-control problems (Arnold, 1999).

Hearing parents are not at fault for their deaf child's problems. Instead, they lack experience with visual communication, which enables deaf parents to respond readily to a deaf child's needs. Deaf parents know they must wait for the child to turn toward them before interacting (Loots & Devise, 2003). Hearing parents tend to speak or gesture while the child's attention is directed elsewhere—a strategy that works with a hearing but not with a deaf partner. When the child is confused or unresponsive, hearing parents often feel overwhelmed and become overly controlling (Jamieson, 1995).

The impact of deafness on language and cognitive development can best be understood by considering its effects on parents and other significant people in the child's life. Deaf children need access to language models—deaf adults and peers—to experience a natural language-learning situation. And their hearing parents benefit from social support along with training in how to interact sensitively with a nonhearing partner. On

▲ Hearing parents of deaf children can help their children develop language skills by making sure that from an early age they have many opportunities to interact with adults and peers fluent in sign language. Because this boy has had access to rich, natural language-learning experiences, he will be protected from serious developmental problems.
© Spencer Grant/PhotoEdit

average, deafness is not diagnosed until 2½ years of age. Yet available screening techniques can identify deaf babies soon after birth, permitting immediate enrollment in programs aimed at fostering effective parent–child interaction. When children with profound hearing loss are identified and start to receive intervention within the first year of life, they show much better language, cognitive, and social development (Yoshinaga-Itano, 2003).

Ask Yourself

REVIEW	Cite findings indicating that both infant capacities and caregiver communication contribute to prelinguistic development.
APPLY	Fran frequently corrects her 17-month-old son Jeremy's attempts to talk and—fearing that he won't use words—refuses to respond to his gestures. How might Fran be contributing to Jeremy's slow language progress?
CONNECT	Explain how parents' use of child-directed speech illustrates Vygotsky's zone of proximal development (see Chapter 6, page 260).
REFLECT	Find an opportunity to speak to an infant or toddler. Next, direct some similar utterances to one of your friends. What features distinguish the way you spoke to the baby from the way you spoke to the adult? How might those features promote early language progress?

Phonological Development

If you listened in on a 1- or 2-year-old trying out her first handful of words, you probably would hear an assortment of interesting pronunciations— "nana" for "banana," "oap" for "soap," and "weddy" for "ready," as well as some wordlike utterances that do not resemble adult forms. For "translations" of these, you must ask the child's parent. Phonological development is a complex process that depends on the child's ability to attend to sound sequences, produce sounds, and combine them into understandable words and phrases. Between 1 and 4 years of age, children make great progress at this task. In trying to talk like people around them, young children draw on their impressive capacity to distinguish the phonemic categories of their native language, which is well developed by the end of the first year. They also adopt temporary strategies for producing sounds that bring adult words within their current range of physical and cognitive capabilities (Menn & Stoel-Gammon, 2005). Let's see how they do so.

The Early Phase

Children's first words are influenced in part by the small number of sounds they can pronounce (Hura & Echols, 1996; Vihman, 1996). The easiest sound sequences start with consonants, end with vowels, and include repeated syllables, as in "Mama," "Dada," "bye-bye," and "nigh-nigh" (for "night-night"). Sometimes young speakers use the same sound to represent a variety of words, a feature that makes their speech hard to understand (Ingram, 1999). For example, one toddler substituted "bat" for as many as 12 different words, including "bad," "bark," "bent," and "bite."

These observations reveal that early phonological and semantic development are related. Languages cater to young children's phonological limitations. Throughout the world, sounds resembling "Mama," "Dada," and "Papa" refer to parents, so it is not surprising that these are among the first words children everywhere produce. Also, in child-directed speech, adults often use simplified words to talk about things of interest to toddlers. For example, rabbit becomes "bunny" and train becomes "choo-choo." These word forms support the child's first attempts to talk.

One-year-olds first learning to talk know how familiar words—such as *dog, baby,* and *ball*—are supposed to sound, even when they mispronounce them. Researchers showed 14-month-olds pairs of objects (such as a baby and a dog), accompanied by a voice speaking the word for one of the objects, with either correct pronunciation ("baby"), slight mispronunciation ("vaby"), or considerable mispronunciation ("raby") (Swingley & Aslin, 2002). The toddlers easily detected the correct pronunciation of words they had heard many times: They looked longer at the appropriate object when a word was pronounced correctly than when it was either mildly or extremely mispronounced (see Figure 9.5).

Nevertheless, when learning a new word, toddlers often do not pick up the fine details of its sounds—a failure that contributes to their pronunciation errors. In several studies, 14-month-olds were unable to associate two similar-sounding nonsense words ("bih" and "dih") with different objects, even though they easily detect the "b"–"d" contrast in sound discrimination tasks (Fennell & Werker, 2003; Stager & Werker, 1997). Why don't toddlers apply their impressive sensitivity to speech sounds when acquiring new words? Associating words with their referents places extra demands on toddlers' limited working memories. Intent on communicating, they focus on the word–referent pairing while sacrificing the word's sounds, which they encode imprecisely.

As toddlers' vocabularies increase, they become better at using their perceptual abilities to distinguish similar-sounding new words. Once they acquire several sets of words that sound alike, they may be motivated to attend more closely to fine-grained distinctions between others.

Appearance of Phonological Strategies

By the middle of the second year, children move from trying to pronounce whole syllables and words to trying to pronounce each individual sound within a word. As a result, they can be

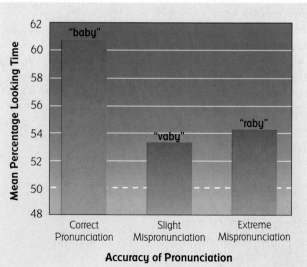

▼ **Figure 9.5**

One-year-olds know the correct pronunciation of familiar words. Fourteen-month-olds were shown pairs of familiar objects (such as a baby and a dog) accompanied by a voice speaking the word for one of the objects with either correct pronunciation ("baby"), slight mispronunciation ("vaby"), or considerable mispronunciation ("raby"). Babies looked longest at the appropriate object when a word was pronounced correctly. Notice that in each condition, time spent looking at the correct object exceeded 50 percent, indicating that babies could recognize the words whether or not they were pronounced correctly. (Adapted from Swingley & Aslin, 2002.)

TABLE 9.1 COMMON PHONOLOGICAL STRATEGIES USED BY YOUNG CHILDREN TO SIMPLIFY PRONUNCIATION OF ADULT WORDS

Strategy	Example
Repeating the first consonant-vowel in a multisyllable word	"TV" becomes "didi," "cookie" becomes "gege."
Deleting unstressed syllables in a multisyllable word	"Banana" becomes "nana," "giraffe" becomes "raffe."
Replacing fricatives (hissing sounds) with stop consonant sounds	"Sea" becomes "tea," "say" becomes "tay."
Replacing consonant sounds produced in the rear and palate area of the vocal tract with ones produced in the frontal area	"Kid" becomes "tid," "goose" becomes "doose."
Replacing liquid sounds ("l" or "r") with glides ("y" or "w")	"Lap" becomes "yap," "ready" becomes "weddy."
Deleting the final consonant of a word	"Bike" becomes "bai," "more" becomes "muh," "bottom" becomes "bada."
Reducing a consonant cluster to a single consonant	"Clown" becomes "cown," "play" becomes "pay."

Source: Ingram, 1986.

heard experimenting with phoneme patterns. One 21-month-old pronounced "juice" as "du," "ju," "dus," "jus," "sus," "zus," "fus," "tfus," "jusi," and "tfusi" within a single hour (Fee, 1997). This marks an intermediate phase of development in which pronunciation is partly right and partly wrong. Because young children get more practice perceiving and producing phoneme patterns that occur frequently in their language, they pronounce words that contain those patterns more accurately and rapidly. Words that are unique in how they sound are generally difficult to pronounce (Munson, 2001). A close look reveals that children apply systematic strategies to challenging words so that these words fit with their pronunciation capacities yet resemble adult utterances. Although individual differences exist in the precise strategies that children adopt (see Table 9.1 for examples), they follow a general developmental pattern (Vihman, 1996).

At first, children produce *minimal words,* in which they focus on the stressed syllable and try to pronounce its consonant–vowel combination ("du" or "ju" for "juice"). Soon they add ending consonants ("jus"), adjust vowel length ("beee" for "please"), and add unstressed syllables ("mae-do" for "tomato"). Finally, they produce the full word with a correct stress pattern, although they may still need to refine its sounds ("timemba" for "remember," "pagetti" for "spaghetti") (Demuth, 1996; Salidis & Johnson, 1997).

The errors children make are similar across a range of languages, including Cantonese, Czech, English, French, Italian, Quiché (a Guatemalan Mayan language), Spanish, and Swedish. But differences in rate of phonological progress exist, depending on the complexity of a language's sound system and the importance of certain sounds for conveying meaning. Cantonese-speaking children, for example, develop more quickly than English-speaking children. In Cantonese, many words are single syllables, but a change in tone of a syllable can lead to a change in meaning. Chinese children master this tone system by age 2 (So & Dodd, 1995). Among children acquiring English, "v" is a late-appearing sound, whereas Swedish children master it early. In English, "v" is relatively infrequent; in Swedish, it is common and vital for distinguishing words (Ingram, 1999).

Over the preschool years, children's pronunciation improves greatly. Maturation of the vocal tract and the child's active problem-solving efforts are largely responsible, since children's phonological errors are very resistant to adult correction. One father tried repeatedly to get his 2½-year-old daughter to pronounce the word "music," but each time she persisted with "ju-jic." When her father made one last effort, she replied, "Wait 'til I big. Then I say ju-jic, Daddy!"

Ⓢ The phonological strategies young children apply to challenging words to bring them within their pronunciation capacities are similar across a range of languages. The systematic pronunciation errors this Spanish-speaking child makes are probably much like those of French or Swedish youngsters.
© Omni Photo Communications Inc./Index Stock

Later Phonological Development

Although phonological development is largely complete by age 5, a few syllable stress patterns that signal subtle differences in meaning are acquired in middle childhood and adolescence. For example, when shown pairs of pictures and asked to identify which is the "greenhouse" and which is the "green house," most children recognized the correct label by third grade and produced it between fourth and sixth grade (Atkinson-King, 1973). Changes in syllabic stress after certain abstract words take on endings— "humid" to "humidity," "method" to "method-ical"—are not mastered until adolescence (Camarata & Leonard, 1986).

These late attainments are probably affected by the semantic complexity of the words, in that hard-to-understand words are more difficult to pronounce. Even at later ages, working simultaneously on the sounds and meaning of a new word may overload the cognitive system, causing children to sacrifice pronunciation temporarily until they better grasp the word's meaning.

Ask Yourself

REVIEW	Why do toddlers often fail to pick up the fine details of a new word's sounds, even though they can perceive those sounds?
APPLY	As his father placed a bowl of pasta on the dinner table, 2-year-old Luke exclaimed, "So 'licious!" Explain Luke's phonological strategy.
REFLECT	Keep a week-long log of words that you mispronounce or do not pronounce fluently (you slow down to say them). Are they words that convey complex concepts or words with sounds that are relatively infrequent in English or in your native tongue? Research indicates that these factors, which affect children's pronunciation, also affect the pronunciation of adults.

Semantic Development

Word comprehension begins in the middle of the first year. When 6-month-olds listened to the words "Mommy" and "Daddy" while looking at side-by-side videos of their parents, they looked longer at the video of the named parent (Tincoff & Jusczyk, 1999). At 9 months, after hearing a word paired with an object, babies looked longer at other objects in the same category than at those in a different category (Balaban & Waxman, 1997). On average, children say their first word around 12 months. By age 6, they have a vocabulary of about 10,000 words (Bloom, 1998). To accomplish this feat, children learn about 5 new words each day.

As these achievements reveal, children's **comprehension,** the language they understand, develops ahead of **production,** the language they use. For example, toddlers follow many simple directions, such as "Bring me your book" or "Don't touch the lamp," even though they cannot yet express all these words in their own speech. A 5-month lag exists between children's comprehension of 50 words (at about 13 months) and production of 50 words (around 18 months) (Menyuk, Liebergott, & Schultz, 1995).

Why is comprehension ahead of production? Think back to the distinction made in Chapter 7 between two types of memory—recognition and recall. Comprehension requires only that children recognize the meaning of a word, whereas production demands that they recall, or actively retrieve from their memories, both the word and the concept for which it stands. Failure to say a word does not mean that toddlers do not understand it. If we rely only on what children say, we will underestimate their language progress.

The Early Phase

To learn words, children must identify which concept each label picks out in their language community. Ask several parents to list their toddlers' first words. Notice how the words build on the sensorimotor foundations Piaget described and on categories children form during their first 2 years (see Chapter 6). First words refer to important people ("Mama," "Dada"), animals ("dog," "cat"), objects that move ("ball," "car," "shoe"), foods ("milk," "apple"), familiar actions ("bye-bye," "more," "up"), or outcomes of familiar actions ("dirty," "hot," "wet") (Hart, 2004; Nelson, 1973). As Table 9.2 reveals, in their first 50 words, toddlers rarely name things that just sit there, like "table" or "vase."

In Chapter 6, we noted that certain early words are linked to specific cognitive achievements. Recall that about the time children master advanced object permanence problems, they use disappearance terms, like "all gone." Success and failure expressions such as "There!" and "Uh-oh!" appear when toddlers can solve problems suddenly. According to one pair of

TABLE 9.2 TYPES OF WORDS APPEARING IN TODDLERS' 50-WORD VOCABULARIES

Word Type	Description	Typical Examples	Percentage of Total Words[a]
Object words	Words used to refer to the "thing world"	*Apple, ball, bird, boat, book, car, cookie, Dada, doggie, kitty, milk, Mama, shoe, snow, truck*	66
Action words	Words that describe, demand, or accompany action or that express attention or demand attention	*Bye-bye, go, hi, look, more, out, up*	13
State words (modifiers)	Words that refer to properties or qualities of things or events	*All gone, big, dirty, hot, mine, pretty, outside, red, uh-oh, wet*	9
Personal/social words	Words that express emotional states and social relationships	*No, ouch, please, want, yes, thank you*	8
Function words	Words that fill a solely grammatical function	*For, is, to, what, where*	4

[a]Average percentages are given, based on a sample of 18 American toddlers.
Source: Nelson, 1973.

researchers, "Children seem motivated to acquire words that are relevant to the particular cognitive problems they are working on at the moment" (Gopnik & Meltzoff, 1986, p. 1057).

Besides cognition, emotion influences early word learning. At first, when acquiring a new word for an object, person, or event, 1½-year-olds say it neutrally; they need to listen carefully to learn, and expressing strong emotion diverts their attention. As words become better learned, toddlers integrate talking and expressing feelings (Bloom, 1998). "Shoe!" said one enthusiastic 22-month-old as her mother tied her shoelaces before an outing. At the end of the second year, toddlers label their emotions with words like "happy," "mad," and "sad"—a development we will consider in Chapter 10.

Young toddlers add to their vocabularies slowly, at a pace of 1 to 3 words per week. Gradually, the number of words learned accelerates. The increase is much more rapid in comprehension than in production, as illustrated by English and Italian learners' vocabulary growth between 8 and 16 months, shown in Figure 9.6 (Caselli et al., 1995). Because rate of word learning between

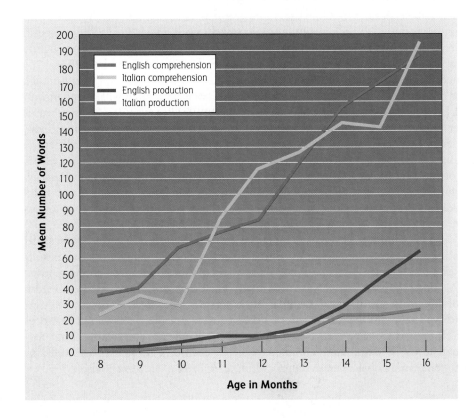

◀ Figure 9.6

English and Italian learners' vocabulary growth between 18 and 24 months. The increase in vocabulary size is far more rapid in comprehension than in production. Rate of word learning gradually accelerates.

(From Caselli, M. C., et al., 1995, "A Cross-Linguistic Study of Early Lexical Development," *Cognitive Development, 10,* p. 172. Reprinted by permission of Elsevier Science.)

18 and 24 months is so impressive (1 or 2 words per day), many researchers concluded that toddlers undergo a *spurt in vocabulary*—a transition between a slow and a faster learning phase once the number of words produced reaches 50 to 100. Recent evidence, however, indicates that a vocabulary spurt characterizes only a minority of young children (Ganger & Brent, 2004). Most show a steady, continuous increase in rate of word learning that persists through the preschool years, when children add as many as 9 new words per day.

How do young children build their vocabularies so quickly? An improved ability to categorize experience (see Chapter 6), retrieve words from memory, and pronounce new words is involved (Dapretto & Bjork, 2000; Gershoff-Stowe & Smith, 1997). In addition, a better grasp of others' intentions, evident in toddlers' imitation around 18 months (see page 228), supports rapid vocabulary growth because it helps toddlers figure out what others are talking about (Bloom, 2000; Tomasello, 2003). Furthermore, as toddlers' experiences broaden, they have a wider range of interesting objects and events to label. For example, children approaching age 2 more often mention places to go ("park," "store") and vehicles ("truck," "fire engine," "bike"). And as they construct a clearer self-image, they add more words that refer to themselves ("me," "mine," "Katy") and to their own and other's bodies and clothing ("eyes," "mouth," "jacket") (Hart, 2004).

Researchers have discovered that children can connect a new word with an underlying concept after only a brief encounter, a process called **fast-mapping.** When an adult labeled an oddly shaped plastic ring with the nonsense word "koob" during a game, children as young as 2 picked up the word's meaning (Dollaghan, 1985). Even 15- to 18-month-olds comprehend new labels remarkably quickly. But they need more repetitions of the word's use across several situations than preschoolers, who better remember and categorize speech-based information (Akhtar & Montague, 1999). During the preschool years, children become increasingly adept at fast-mapping two or more new words encountered in the same situation (Rice, 1990; Wilkinson, Ross, & Diamond, 2003).

• **INDIVIDUAL AND CULTURAL DIFFERENCES** • Although the average age at which children produce their first word is 12 months, the range is large, from 8 to 18 months—variation that results from a complex blend of genetic and environmental influences. Many studies show that girls are slightly ahead of boys in vocabulary growth until 2 years of age, when boys gradually catch up (Reznick & Goldfield, 1992). The most common biological explanation is girls' faster rate of physical maturation, believed to promote earlier development of the left cerebral hemisphere. Besides the child's sex, temperament makes a difference. Toddlers who are reserved and cautious often wait until they understand a great deal before trying to speak. When they finally do speak, their vocabularies increase rapidly, although they remain slightly behind their agemates in language skills during the preschool years (Spere et al., 2004).

The surrounding language environment, too, contributes to these differences. Mothers talk much more to toddler-age girls than to boys, and parents converse less often with shy than with sociable children (Leaper, Anderson, & Sanders, 1998; Patterson & Fisher, 2002). The more words caregivers use, the greater the number integrated into the child's vocabulary (Weizman & Snow, 2001). Because low-SES children experience less verbal stimulation in their homes than higher-SES children, their vocabularies tend to be smaller, regardless of sex and ethnicity. In an observational study of mothers interacting with their 2-year-olds, amount and quality of maternal conversation fully accounted for SES differences in children's vocabularies. Limited parent–child storybook reading—an activity conducive to vocabulary growth—probably contributed to persisting, smaller vocabularies in the low-SES preschoolers at age 4½ (Hoff, 2003a, 2004).

Children also have unique styles of early language learning. Most toddlers use a **referential style;** their vocabularies consist mainly of words that refer to objects. A smaller number of toddlers use an **expressive style;** compared with referential children, they produce many more social formulas and pronouns, such as "stop it," "thank you," "done," and "I want it." Recall, from the opening of this chapter, Erin's early use of largely expressive-style words. Toddlers' language styles reflect early ideas about the functions of language. Referential-style children think words are for naming things, whereas expressive-style children believe words are for talking about people's feelings and needs. The vocabularies of referential-style children grow faster because all languages contain many more object labels than social phrases (Bates et al., 1994; Nelson, 1973).

What accounts for a toddler's choice of a particular language style? Rapidly developing, referential-style children often have an especially active interest in exploring objects. They also eagerly imitate their parents' frequent naming of objects, and their parents imitate back—a strategy that supports swift vocabulary growth by helping children remember new labels (Masur & Rodemaker, 1999). Expressive-style children tend to be highly sociable, and their parents more often use verbal routines ("How are you?" "It's no trouble") that support social relationships (Goldfield, 1987).

The two language styles are also linked to culture. Whereas object words are particularly common in the vocabularies of English-speaking toddlers, social routines are more numerous among Chinese, Japanese, and Korean toddlers. When mothers' speech is examined, it reflects this difference. Perhaps because their culture emphasizes the importance of group membership, Asian mothers teach social routines as soon as their children begin to speak (Choi & Gopnik, 1995; Fernald & Morikawa, 1993; Tardif, Gelman, & Xu, 1999). When we consider the findings as a whole, early vocabulary development supports the social interactionist emphasis on the combined impact of children's inner dispositions and their linguistic and social worlds.

In Western societies, many mothers stress object labels to young language learners. In contrast, these African mothers of Botswana respond verbally to their toddlers' glances and vocalizations to other people, not to exploration of objects.
© Devore/Anthro-Photo File

• **TYPES OF WORDS** • Three types of words—object, action, and state—are most common in young children's vocabularies. Careful study of each provides important information about the course of semantic development.

▶ *Object and Action Words.* Many young language learners have more object than action words in their beginning vocabularies (Au, Dapretto, & Song, 1994; Caselli et al., 1995). If actions are an especially important means through which infants find out about their world, then why this early emphasis on naming objects?

One reason is that nouns refer to concepts (such as *table, bird,* or *dog)* that are easy to perceive. When adults label an object, they frequently help the child discern the word's meaning by showing and repeating the label. As a result, toddlers readily match objects with their appropriate labels. In contrast, verbs require more complex understandings—of relationships between objects and actions. For example, *go* involves a person going somewhere, *fix* a person fixing something. In addition, when adults use verbs, the actions to which they refer usually are not taking place (Gleitman & Gleitman, 1992). When a parent says the word *move,* most likely nothing present is moving. Instead, she is referring to a past event ("Someone *moved* the bowl") or a future event ("Let's *move* the bowl").

Nevertheless, the linguistic environment affects toddlers' relative use of object and action words. As noted in our discussion of early language-learning styles, English-speaking mothers often name objects for their children. In one study, they rarely prompted 20-month-olds to produce verbs. Instead they often used verbs to get toddlers to perform actions ("Can you *spin* that wheel?"). Consequently, the toddlers comprehended more verbs than they produced (Goldfield, 2000). In Chinese, Japanese, and Korean, nouns are often omitted entirely from adult sentences, and verbs are stressed. As a result, Asian toddlers typically produce action words first and use them more often than their English-speaking counterparts (Kim, McGregor, & Thompson, 2000; Tardif, Gelman, & Xu, 1999).

▶ *State Words.* Between 2 and 2½ years, children's use of *state* (or modifier) words expands to include labels for attributes of objects, such as size and color ("big," "red") as well as possession ("my toy," "Mommy purse"). Words referring to the functions of objects ("dump truck," "pickup truck") appear soon after (Nelson, 1976).

When state words are related in meaning, general distinctions (which are easier) appear before more specific ones. Thus, among words referring to the size of objects, children first acquire *big–small,* then *tall–short, high–low,* and *long–short,* and finally *wide–narrow* and *deep–shallow.* The same is true for temporal terms. Between ages 3 and 5, children first

© Cognitive development influences young children's mastery of state (or modifier) words. This child is likely to say "on" the spoon and "in" the cup before she says "under" the sand. Adult labeling of object locations will help her master these terms.
© Dennis MacDonald/PhotoEdit

master *now* versus *then* and *before* versus *after,* followed by *today* versus *yesterday* and *tomorrow* (Stevenson & Pollitt, 1987).

State words referring to the location of objects provide additional examples of how cognition influences vocabulary development. Before age 2, children can easily imitate an adult's action in putting an object *in* or *on* another object, but they have trouble imitating the placement of one object *under* another. These terms appear in children's vocabularies in just this order, with all three achieved around 2½ years of age (Clark, 1983).

Because state words refer to qualities of objects and actions, children can use them to express a wide variety of concepts. As preschoolers master these words, their language becomes increasingly flexible.

• **UNDEREXTENSIONS AND OVEREXTENSIONS** • When young children first learn words, they often do not use them just as adults do. They may apply words too narrowly, an error called **underextension.** For example, at 16 months, my younger son used the word "bear" to refer only to a special teddy bear to which he had become attached. A more common error between 1 and 2½ years is **overextension**—applying a word to a broader collection of objects and events than is appropriate. For example, a toddler might use the word "car" for buses, trains, trucks, and fire engines.

Toddlers' overextensions reflect their remarkable sensitivity to categorical relations. They apply a new word to a group of similar experiences, such as "dog" for any furry, four-legged animal or "open" to mean opening a door, peeling fruit, and untying shoe laces. Furthermore, the toddler who refers to trucks, trains, and bikes as "cars" is likely to point to these objects correctly when given their names in comprehension tasks (Naigles & Gelman, 1995). This suggests that children often overextend deliberately because they have difficulty recalling or have not acquired a suitable word. In addition, when a word is hard to pronounce, toddlers frequently substitute a related one they can say (Bloom, 2000; Elsen, 1994). As vocabulary and pronunciation improve, overextensions disappear.

• **WORD COINAGES AND METAPHORS** • To fill in for words they have not yet learned, children as young as age 2 coin new words based on ones they already know. At first, children use the technique of compounding. For example, a child might say "plant-man" for a gardener. Later they convert verbs into nouns and nouns into verbs, as in one child's use of "needle it" for mending something. Soon after, children discover more specialized word coinage techniques, such as adding *-er* to identify the doer of an action—for example, "crayoner" for a child using crayons. Children give up coined words as soon as they acquire conventional labels for their intended meanings (Clark, 1995). Still, these expressions reveal a remarkable, rule-governed approach to language.

Preschoolers also extend language meanings through metaphor. For example, one 3-year-old described a stomachache as a "fire engine in my tummy" (Winner, 1988). The metaphors young preschoolers use and understand are based largely on concrete, sensory comparisons: "clouds are pillows," "leaves are dancers." Once their vocabulary and knowledge of the world expand, they make non-sensory comparisons, such as "Friends are like magnets" (Karadsheh, 1991; Keil, 1986). Metaphors permit children to communicate in especially vivid and memorable ways.

Later Semantic Development

Between the start and end of elementary school, vocabulary increases fourfold, eventually exceeding 40,000 words. On average, school-age children learn about 20 new words each day, a rate of growth exceeding that of early childhood (see Figure 9.7). In addition to fast-mapping, school-age children enlarge their vocabularies by analyzing the structure of complex words. From *happy* and *decide,* they quickly derive the meanings of *happiness* and *decision* (Anglin, 1993). They also figure out many more word meanings from context (Nagy & Scott, 2000).

As at earlier ages, children benefit from engaging in conversation with more expert speakers, especially when their partners use complex words and explain them (Weizman & Snow, 2001). But because written language contains a far more diverse and complex vocabulary than spoken language, reading contributes enormously to vocabulary growth in middle childhood and adolescence. Children who engage in as little as 21 minutes of independent reading per day are exposed to nearly 2 million words per year (Cunningham & Stanovich, 1998).

As their knowledge expands and becomes better organized (see Chapter 7), school-age children think about and use words more precisely. Word definitions offer examples of this change. Five- and 6-year-olds give concrete descriptions that refer to functions or appearance—for example, *knife:* "when you're cutting carrots"; *bicycle:* "it's got wheels, a chain, and handlebars." By the end of elementary school, synonyms and explanations of categorical relationships appear—for example, *knife:* "Something you could cut with. A saw is like a knife. It could also be a weapon" (Wehren, De Lisi, & Arnold, 1981). This advance reflects older children's ability to deal with word meanings on an entirely verbal plane. They can add new words to their vocabulary simply by being given a definition.

School-age children's more reflective and analytical approach to language permits them to appreciate the multiple meanings of words. For example, they recognize that many words, such as *cool* or *neat,* have psychological as well as physical meanings: "What a cool shirt!" or "That movie was really neat!" This grasp of double meanings permits 8- to 10-year-olds to comprehend subtle mental metaphors, such as "sharp as a tack" and "spilling the beans" (Nippold, Taylor, & Baker, 1996; Wellman & Hickling, 1994). It also leads to a change in children's humor. By the mid–elementary school years, riddles and puns that go back and forth between different meanings of a key word are common, such as: "Hey, did you take a bath?" "Why, is one missing?" (Ely & McCabe, 1994).

The capacity for abstract thinking permits adolescents to add such words as *counterintuitive* and *philosophy* to their vocabularies. They also become masters of sarcasm and irony (Winner, 1988). When his mother fixes a dish for dinner that he dislikes, a 16-year-old might quip, "Oh boy, my favorite!" School-age children sometimes realize that a sarcastic remark is insincere if it is said in an exaggerated, mocking tone of voice. But adolescents and adults need only notice the discrepancy between a statement and its context to grasp the intended meaning (Capelli, Nakagawa, & Madden, 1990).

In addition, adolescents can better grasp figurative language. Proverbs—especially those that express subtle attitudes—are among the most challenging. They can be used to comment ("Blood is thicker than water"), interpret ("His bark is worse than his bite"), advise ("Humility often gains more than pride"), warn ("Of idleness comes no goodness"), and encourage ("Every cloud has a silver lining"). And they make sense only in certain situations. "Too many cooks spoil the broth" is good advice when someone offers to help balance a checkbook but bad advice when that person offers to assist with cleaning up a classroom (Nippold, 2000). Reading proficiency fosters understanding of proverbs, which improves greatly during adolescence (Nippold, Allen, & Kirsch, 2001). And a better grasp of the meaning of figurative language enables teenagers to appreciate adult literary works.

Ideas About How Semantic Development Takes Place

Research shows that adult feedback facilitates semantic development. When adults go beyond correcting and explain ("That's not a car. It's a truck. See, it has a place to put things in"), toddlers are more likely to move toward conventional word meanings (Chapman, Leonard, & Mervis, 1986). Still, adults cannot tell children exactly what concept each new word picks out. For example, if an adult points to a dog and calls it a "doggie," the word may refer to four-legged animals, the dog's shaggy ears, or its barking sound. Therefore, the child's cognitive processing must play a major role.

• **THE INFLUENCE OF MEMORY** • Young children's fast-mapping is supported by a special part of working memory, a **phonological store** that permits us to retain speech-based information. The more rapidly 4-year-olds can recall a just-presented sequence of nonsense words (a measure of phonological memory skill), the larger their current vocabulary and the greater their vocabulary growth over the following year (Gathercole, 1995; Gathercole et al., 1999). This suggests that a child with good phonological memory has a better chance of transferring new words to long-term memory and linking them with relevant concepts.

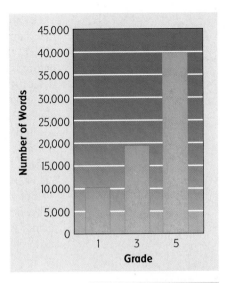

▲ **Figure 9.7**

Estimated vocabulary from grades 1 to 5. Rate of vocabulary growth during the school years exceeds that of early childhood. (Adapted from Anglin, 1993.)

By the end of the second year, phonological memory is so good that toddlers can recognize familiar words on the basis of their initial sounds. On hearing the name of a familiar object, 18- to 24-month-olds shifted their gaze to the correct member of a pair of objects before the word was completely spoken (Fernald et al., 1998). And when given only the first two or three phonemes of familiar word ("ba" for "baby," "daw" for "doggie), toddlers of this age looked at the correct object, responding as accurately and quickly as they did to the whole word. Furthermore, toddlers with better verbal recognition scores had larger productive vocabularies (Fernald, Swingley, & Pinto, 2001). Early in development, phonological memory is linked to advanced vocabulary development. Being able to identify a word rapidly on the basis of initial sounds has clear advantages. It frees working memory for other language tasks, such as comprehending longer and more complex strings of words.

But phonological memory does not provide a full account of word learning. After age 5, semantic knowledge influences the speed with which children form phonological traces, and both factors affect vocabulary growth (Gathercole et al., 1997). Even at younger ages (as we will see next), children rely heavily on words they already know to detect the meanings of new ones.

• **STRATEGIES FOR WORD LEARNING** • To explain semantic development, Eve Clark (1990, 1993, 1995) proposed **lexical contrast theory.** It assumes that two principles govern vocabulary growth: *conventionality,* children's natural desire to acquire the words and word meanings of their language community; and *contrast,* which explains how new word meanings are added. According to Clark, children assume that the meaning of each word they hear is unique. Therefore, when they hear a new label, they try to figure out its meaning by contrasting it with words they know and assigning it to a gap in their vocabulary.

Many researchers have criticized lexical contrast theory for not being specific about the hypotheses young children use to determine new word meanings. One speculation is that in the early phases of vocabulary growth, children adopt a **mutual exclusivity bias;** that is, they assume that words refer to entirely separate (nonoverlapping) categories (Markman, 1992). Toddlers seem to rely on mutual exclusivity when the objects named are perceptually distinct. For example, after hearing the names of two very different novel objects (a clip and a horn), 2-year-olds assigned each word correctly, to the whole object and not to a part of it (Waxman & Senghas, 1992). Mutual exclusivity is especially useful when speakers provide few or no cues about a new word's meaning. In one study, 15- and 19-month-olds were presented with a familiar object and a bucket they knew contained some objects. On hearing a new word, they searched the bucket. When the bucket was removed, they looked around the room, as if to see whether it contained a better referent for the new word than the familiar object (Markman, Wasow, & Hansen, 2003).

But mutual exclusivity cannot account for what young children do when objects have more than one name. By age 3, preschoolers' memory, categorization, and language skills have expanded, and they readily assign multiple labels to many objects (Déak, Yen, & Pettit, 2001). For example, they refer to a sticker of a gray goose as "sticker," "goose," and "gray." Children often call on other components of language for help in these instances. According to one hypothesis, called **syntactic bootstrapping,** children discover many word meanings by observing how words are used in *syntax,* or the structure of sentences (Gleitman, 1990; Hoff & Naigles, 2002). Consider an adult who says, "This is a *citron* one," while showing a child a yellow car. As early as 21 months, children interpret a new word used as an adjective as referring to a property of the object (Hall & Graham, 1999; Waxman & Markow, 1998).

Young children also take advantage of the rich social information that adults frequently provide when they introduce new words. For example, they often draw on their expanding ability to infer others' intentions and perspectives (Akhtar & Tomasello, 2000). In one study, an adult performed an action on an object and then used a new label while looking back and forth between the child and the object, as if to invite the child to play. Two-year-olds capitalized on this social information to conclude that the label referred to the action, not the object (Tomasello & Akhtar, 1995). And when an adult first designates the whole object ("See

© Young children rely on any useful information available to figure out the meanings of new words. For example, this boy might be attending to how his mother uses the word *apple* in the structure of sentences. Or he might be noticing social cues, such as his mother's eye movements and actions on the object.
© Michael Newman/PhotoEdit

the bird") and then points to a part of it ("That's a beak"), 3-year-olds realize that *beak* is a certain part, not the whole bird (Saylor, Sabbagh, & Baldwin, 2002).

Adults also inform children directly about word meanings. Consider an adult who says, "That soap is *made of* lye." Relying on the phrase *made of,* preschoolers interpret *lye* to refer to the soap's material qualities rather than the dish on which the soap rests (Deák, 2000). When no social cues or direct information is available, children as young as age 2 demonstrate remarkable flexibility in their word-learning strategies. They treat a new word applied to an already-labeled object as a second name for the object (Deák & Maratsos, 1998).

Children acquire vocabulary so efficiently and accurately that some theorists believe that they are innately biased to induce word meanings using certain principles, such as mutual exclusivity (Woodward & Markman, 1998). Critics point out that a small set of built-in, fixed principles are not sufficient to account for the varied, flexible manner in which children draw on any useful information available to master vocabulary (Deák, 2000). And many word-learning strategies cannot be innate, since children acquiring different languages use different approaches to mastering the same meanings. For example, English-speaking children rely on syntactic bootstrapping to tell the difference between one object ("This is *a dax*"), multiple objects of the same category ("Those are *daxes*"), and a proper name ("This is *Dax*") (Hall, Lee, & Belanger, 2001). In Japanese, all nouns are treated the same syntactically ("This is *dax*"). Nevertheless, Japanese preschoolers find ways to compensate for the missing syntactic cues, learning just as quickly as their English-speaking agemates (Imai & Haryu, 2001).

An alternative perspective is that word learning is governed by the same cognitive strategies that children apply to nonlinguistic stimuli. These strategies become more effective as children's knowledge of categories, vocabulary size, and sensitivity to social cues improve (Hollich, Hirsh-Pasek, & Golinkoff, 2000; Markson & Bloom, 1997). Preschoolers are most successful at figuring out new word meanings when several kinds of information are available. Researchers have just begun to study the multiple cues children use for different types of words, and how their combined strategies change with development (Saylor, Baldwin, & Sabbagh, 2005; Saylor & Sabbagh, 2004). We still have much to discover about how children's inner capacities join with diverse patterns of information in the environment to yield the phenomenal pace of semantic development.

Ask Yourself

REVIEW	Using your knowledge of phonological and semantic development, explain why "Mama" and "Dada" are usually among children's first words.
APPLY	Katy's first words included "see," "give," and "thank you," and her vocabulary grew slowly during the second year. What style of language learning did she display, and what factors might have contributed to it?
APPLY	At age 20 months, Nathan says "candy" when he sees buttons, pebbles, marbles, cough drops, and chocolate kisses. Are Nathan's naming errors random or systematic? Why are they an adaptive way of communicating?
CONNECT	Explain how children's strategies for word learning support an interactionist perspective on language development.

Grammatical Development

Studying children's grammar requires that they use more than one word in an utterance. Researchers have puzzled over the following questions about grammatical development: Do children build a consistent grammar resembling that of adults relatively easily and quickly, or do they acquire more complex forms little by little? Are language-specific strategies, general cognitive strategies, or both involved in children's progress? What is the role of adult teaching—in particular, corrective feedback for grammatical errors? As we chart the course of grammatical development, we will consider evidence on these issues.

TABLE 9.3 COMMON MEANINGS EXPRESSED BY CHILDREN'S TWO-WORD UTTERANCES

Meaning	Example
Agent–action	"Tommy hit"
Action–object	"Give cookie"
Agent–object	"Mommy truck" (meaning "Mommy, push the truck")
Action–location	"Put table" (meaning "Put X on the table")
Entity–location	"Daddy outside"
Possessor–possession	"My truck"
Attribution–entity	"Big ball"
Demonstrative–entity	"That doggie"
Notice–noticed object	"Hi mommy," "Hi truck"
Recurrence	"More milk"
Nonexistence–nonexistent or disappeared object	"No shirt," "No more milk"

Source: Brown, 1973

First Word Combinations

Sometime between 1½ and 2½ years, as productive vocabulary approaches 200 words, children combine two words, such as "Mommy shoe," "go car," and "more cookie." These two-word utterances are called **telegraphic speech** because, like a telegram, they focus on high-content words and leave out smaller, less important ones, such as *can, the,* and *to.* For children learning languages that emphasize word order, such as English and French, endings like *-s* and *-ed* are not yet present. In languages in which word order is flexible and small grammatical markers are stressed, children's first sentences include them from the start (de Villiers & de Villiers, 1999).

Children the world over use two-word utterances to express a wide variety of meanings (see Table 9.3). Are they applying a consistent grammar? According to one view, a more complete, and perhaps adultlike, grammar lies behind these two-word sentences (Gleitman et al., 1988; Pinker, 1994; Valian, 1991). Consistent with this idea, children often use the same construction to express different propositions. For example, a child might say, "Mommy cookie" when he sees his mother eating a cookie and also when he wants his mother to give him a cookie. Perhaps the more elaborate structures are present in the child's mind, but he cannot yet produce the longer word string.

Other researchers argue that two-word sentences are largely made up of simple formulas, such as "more + X" and "eat + X," with many different words inserted in the X position. Toddlers rarely make gross word-order errors, such as saying "chair my" instead of "my chair." But their word-order regularities are usually copies of adult word pairings, as when an adult says, "How about *more sandwich?*" or "Let's see if you can *eat the berries?*" (Tomasello & Brooks, 1999). When children entering the two-word phase were taught several noun and verb nonsense words (for example, *meek* for a doll and *gop* for a snapping action), they easily combined the new nouns with words they knew well, as in "more meek." But as Figure 9.8 shows, they seldom formed word combinations with the new verbs (Tomasello et al., 1997). This suggests that they did not yet grasp subject–verb and verb–object relations, which are the foundation of grammar.

In sum, as they begin to combine words, children are absorbed in figuring out word meanings and using their limited vocabularies in whatever way possible to get their thoughts across (Maratsos, 1998). Soon, however, children grasp the basic structure of their language.

From Simple Sentences to Complex Grammar

In the third year, three-word sentences appear in which English-speaking children follow a subject–verb–object word order. Children learning other languages adopt the word orders of the adult speech to which they are exposed. For example, for "It is broken," a German child says, "Kaputt is der" (literally translated as "Broken is it"). Between ages 2½ and 3, children create sentences in which adjectives, articles, nouns, verbs, and prepositional phrases start to conform to an adult structure, indicating that they have begun to master the grammatical categories of their language.

Nevertheless, studies of children acquiring diverse languages, including Dutch, English, Hebrew, Inuktitut (spoken by the Inuit of Arctic Canada), Italian, Portuguese, and Russian, reveal that their first use of grammatical rules is piecemeal—applied to only one or a few verbs, not across the board. As children listen for familiar verbs in adult discourse, they expand their own utterances containing those verbs, drawing on adult usage as their model (Allen, 1996; Gathercole, Sebastián, & Soto, 1999; Lieven, Pine & Baldwin, 1997; Stoll, 1998). One child, for example, added the preposition *with* to the verb *open* ("You open with scissors") but not to the word *hit* ("He hit me stick").

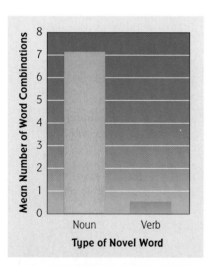

▲ **Figure 9.8**

Number of word combinations with novel nouns and verbs produced by 18- to 23-month-olds. After learning the meaning of several noun and verb nonsense words, toddlers often combined the new nouns with other words they knew well. However, they seldom formed word combinations with the new verbs, suggesting that their two-word utterances were not based on subject–verb and verb–object structures, which are the foundation of grammar. (Adapted from Tomasello et al., 1997.)

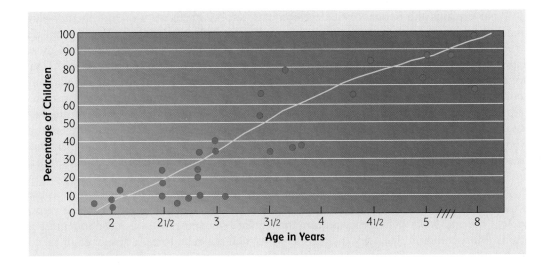

Figure 9.9
Percentage of children in different studies who could use a new verb in the subject–verb–object form after hearing it in another construction. Each dot in the graph represents the findings of one study. The ability to use the new verb—an indicator of the child's capacity to apply the subject–verb–object structure broadly—rose steadily with age. Children mastered this fundamental grammatical construction gradually. (From M. Tomasello, 2000, "Do Young Children Have Adult Syntactic Competence?" *Cognition, 74,* p. 223. Reprinted by permission of Elsevier Science.)

Preschoolers refine and generalize their early grammatical forms gradually. In a number of investigations, English-learning children were tested for their ability to generate novel sentences that conformed to basic English syntax. They had to use a new verb in the subject–verb–object form after hearing it in a different construction, such as passive ("Ernie is getting *gorped* by the dog"). The percentage of children who performed well (when asked what the dog was doing, they could respond, "He's gorping Ernie") rose steadily with age. But as Figure 9.9 shows, not until 3½ to 4 could the majority of children apply the fundamental subject–verb–object structure broadly, to newly acquired verbs (Tomasello, 2000, 2003).

• **DEVELOPMENT OF GRAMMATICAL MORPHEMES** • As the examples just cited suggest, once children form three-word sentences, they add **grammatical morphemes**[1]—small markers that change the meaning of sentences, as in "John's dog" and "he *is* eating." English-speaking 2- and 3-year-olds acquire these morphemes in a regular sequence, shown in Table 9.4 (Brown, 1973; de Villiers & de Villiers, 1973). Given the difficulty of the task, however, their errors are surprisingly few (Maratsos, 1998).

TABLE 9.4 ORDER OF ACQUISITION OF ENGLISH GRAMMATICAL MORPHEMES

Morpheme	Example
1. Verb present progressive ending ("-ing")	"He singing."
2. Preposition "on"	"On horsie."
3. Preposition "in"	"In wagon."
4. Noun plural ("-s")	"Cats."
5. Verb irregular past tense	"He ran." "It broke."
6. Noun possessive	"Daddy's hat."
7. Verb uncontractible "be" form used with adjective, preposition, or noun phrase	"Are kitties sleepy?"
8. Articles "a" and "the"	"A cookie." "The bunny."
9. Verb regular past tense ending ("-ed")	"He kicked it."
10. Verb present tense, third person singular regular ending	"He likes it."
11. Verb present tense, third person singular irregular ending	"She has [from *have*] a cookie." "He does [from *do*] a good job."
12. Auxiliary verb uncontractible "be" forms	"Are you eating?"
13. Verb contractible "be" forms used with adjective, preposition, or noun phrase	"He's inside." "They're sleepy."
14. Auxiliary verb contractible "be" forms	"He's coming." "Doggie's eating."

Source: Brown, 1973.

[1]A *morpheme* is the smallest unit of meaning in speech; any further division violates the meaning or produces meaningless units. Both "dog" and "-s" are morphemes; "-s" is a *grammatical morpheme.*

What explains this sequence of development? Two characteristics of morphemes play important roles. The first is *structural complexity*. For example, adding the ending *-ing* or *-s* is structurally less complex than using forms of the verb *to be*. In the latter, the child must express correct tense and also make the subject and verb agree ("I am coming" versus "They are coming"). And children learning English express location (the prepositions *in* and *on*) sooner than children learning Serbo-Croatian, in which structures for location are more complex (Johnston & Slobin, 1979). Second, grammatical morphemes differ in *semantic complexity*, or the number and difficulty of the meanings they express. For example, adding *-s* to a word requires only one semantic distinction—the difference between one and more than one. In contrast, using *to be* involves many more, including an understanding of person, number, and time of occurrence (Brown, 1973; Slobin, 1982).

Look again at Table 9.4, and you will see that some morphemes with irregular forms are acquired before those with regular forms. For example, children use past-tense irregular verbs, such as *ran* and *broke*, before they acquire the regular *-ed* ending. But once children grasp a regular morphological rule, they extend it to words that are exceptions, a type of error called **overregularization.** "My toy car *breaked*" and "We each have two *foots*" are expressions that start to appear between 2 and 3 years of age and persist into middle childhood (Marcus et al., 1992). The extent to which children overregularize varies greatly across words. They less often make the error on frequently used verbs. One 2½-year-old nearly always produced the irregular past tenses of *go* and *say*—"I *went* there," "I *said* that." For rarely used verbs, however, the error rate can be higher than 50 percent (Maratsos, 2000). This child frequently overregularized *grow* ("I *growed* tall") and *sing* ""("She *singed* Jingle Bells").

Why do children show this inconsistent pattern? Because they hear frequently used irregular forms often in adult speech, they probably learn those by rote memory. For less common irregulars, children alternate between correct and overregularized forms for many months or even several years. According to one view, the two forms compete with one another, and as children hear more instances in others' speech, the irregular form eventually wins out (Maratsos, 2000). A second view is that overregularization reveals an early, rule-governed approach to language (Pinker & Ullman, 2002). At times, preschoolers overregularize well-learned exceptions—for example, when they say "ated," "felled," or "feets" (Bybee & Slobin, 1982). In these instances, perhaps their memory for irregular morphemes fails, so they call on the rule, and overregularization results.

Development of Complex Grammatical Forms

Once children master the auxiliary verb *to be*, the door is open to a variety of new expressions. Negatives and questions are examples.

• **NEGATIVES** • Three types of negation appear in the following order in 2½- to 3-year-olds learning languages as different as Cantonese, English, and Tamil (spoken in India): (1) *nonexistence,* in which the child remarks on the absence of something ("No cookie" or "All gone crackers"); (2) *rejection,* in which the child expresses opposition to something ("No take bath"); and (3) *denial,* in which the child denies the truthfulness of something ("That not my kitty") (Bloom, 1970; Clancy, 1985; Vaidyanathan, 1991; Tam & Stokes, 2001).

These early constructions probably result from imitating parental speech. When parents express nonexistence or rejection, they often put *no* at the beginning of the sentence: "No more cookies" or "No, you can't have another cracker." Around 3 to 3½ years, children add auxiliary verbs and become sensitive to the way they combine with negatives. As a result, correct negative forms appear: "There aren't any more cookies" (nonexistence), "I don't want a bath" (rejection), and "That isn't my kitty" (denial) (Tager-Flusberg, 2005).

• **QUESTIONS** • Like negatives, questions first appear during the early preschool years and develop in an orderly sequence. English-speaking children, as well as those who speak many other languages, can use rising intonation to convert an utterance into a yes/no question: "Mommy baking cookies?" As a result, they produce such expressions quite early.

Correct question form in English requires that children invert the subject and auxiliary verb. In *wh-* questions—ones that begin with *what, where, which, who, when, why,* and *how*—

the *wh-* word must also be placed at the beginning of the sentence. When first creating questions, 2-year-olds use many formulas: "Where's *X*?" "What's *X*?" "Can I *X*?" (Dabrowska, 2000; Tomasello, 1992). Preschoolers' question asking remains quite variable for the next couple of years. An analysis of one child's questions revealed that he inverted the subject and verb when asking certain questions but not when asking others. As a result, he produced some incorrect constructions ("What she will do?" "Why he can go?") while also using correct forms ("How do you like it?" "What do you want?") The correct expressions were ones he heard most often in his mother's speech (Rowland & Pine, 2000). As with other aspects of grammar, children seem to master the question form piecemeal and gradually.

Among English-, Korean-, and Tamil-speaking preschoolers, correct question form appears first for yes/no questions and later for *wh-* questions (Clancy, 1989; Vaidyanathan, 1988). The latter are semantically and structurally more difficult. Among *wh-* questions, *what, where,* and *who* tend to be asked before *how, why,* and *when,* which are harder to understand and answer (de Villiers, 2000).

• **OTHER COMPLEX CONSTRUCTIONS** • Between ages 3½ and 6, children produce more complex constructions, and their usage increasingly conforms to the rules of their language. First, connectives appear that join whole sentences ("Mom picked me up, *and* we went to the park") and verb phrases ("I got up *and* ate breakfast"). The most general connective, *and,* is used first, followed by connectives expressing more specific meanings, such as *then* and *when* for temporal relations, *because* and *so* for causal relations, *if* for conditionals, and *but* for opposition (Bloom et al., 1980).

Later, children produce embedded sentences ("I think *he will come*"), tag questions ("Dad's going to be home soon, *isn't he?*"), indirect object–direct object structures ("He showed *his friend* the present"), and passive sentences ("The dog *was patted by* the girl"). As the preschool years draw to a close, children use most of the grammatical structures of their native language competently (Tager-Flusberg, 2005).

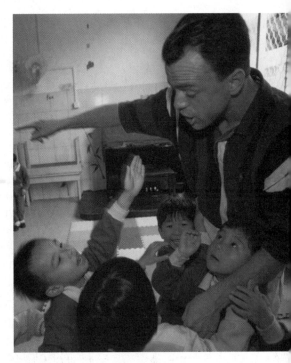

Ⓖ "Can I be with you?" this young boy seems to ask, with all the passion he can muster. Both Korean- and English-speaking preschoolers master yes/no questions before *wh-* questions, which are semantically and structurally more difficult.
© Michael S. Yamashita/CORBIS

Later Grammatical Development

During the school years, children's mastery of complex constructions improves. The passive voice is an example. At all ages, children produce more abbreviated passive statements ("It got broken" or "They got lost") than full passives ("The glass was broken by Mary"). During middle childhood and early adolescence, children use the passive voice—including full passive statements—more often (Horgan, 1978).

Older children also apply the passive voice to a wider range of nouns and verbs. Preschoolers comprehend the passive best when the subject of the sentence is an animate being and the verb is an action word ("The *boy is kissed* by the girl"). Over the school years, children extend the passive form to inanimate subjects, such as *hat* ("The *hat* was worn by the man"), and experiential verbs, such as *see* or *know* ("The dog *was seen* by the cat") (Lempert, 1990; Pinker, Lebeaux, & Frost, 1987).

What accounts for this developmental trend? Recall that action is salient to young children in mastering vocabulary, a bias that may affect their mastery of complex grammar as well. But language input is also influential. English-speaking adults rarely use full and experiential passives in everyday conversation. In languages in which adults use these forms often, such as Inuktitut (spoken by the Inuit people), children produce them earlier (Allen & Crago, 1996). Furthermore, with training, English-speaking preschoolers readily produce full passives. But children younger than age 3½ do not use the passive construction flexibly (Brooks & Tomasello, 1999).

Another grammatical achievement of middle childhood is advanced understanding of infinitive phrases, such as the difference between "John is eager to please" and "John is easy to please" (Chomsky, 1969). Like gains in vocabulary, appreciation of these subtle grammatical distinctions is supported by children's improved capacity to analyze and reflect on language and to attend to multiple linguistic and situational cues.

Ideas About How Grammatical Development Takes Place

Preschoolers' mastery of most of the grammar of their language is truly astounding. How to explain this feat is perhaps the most disputed issue in the study of language development.

• **STRATEGIES FOR ACQUIRING GRAMMAR** • Evidence that grammatical development is an extended rather than a sudden process has raised questions about Chomsky's nativist account. Some experts have concluded that grammar is a product of general cognitive development—children's tendency to search the environment for consistencies and patterns of all sorts (Bates & MacWhinney, 1987; Bloom, 1991; Budwig, 1995; Maratsos, 1998; Tomasello, 2003). Yet among these theorists, debate continues over just how children master grammar.

According to one view, young children rely on other properties of language to detect basic grammatical regularities. In **semantic bootstrapping,** for example, they use word meanings to figure out sentence structure. Children might begin by grouping together words with "agent qualities" (entities that cause actions) as subjects and words with "action qualities" as verbs and then merge these semantic categories with observations of how words are used in sentences (Bates & MacWhinney, 1987; Braine, 1994). In this way, children lay down a basic grammatical framework, which they modify over time to take exceptions into account. A major problem for semantic bootstrapping is that in some languages, semantic categories (such as "agent") and basic grammatical structures (such as "subject") do not match up. In Tagalog, a language spoken in the Philippines, certain agents can be subjects, but others cannot! Yet Tagalog-speaking children acquire the main grammar of their language within a typical time frame (Maratsos, 1998).

Other theorists believe that children master grammar through direct observation of the structure of language. That is, they notice which words appear in the same positions in sentences, take the same morphological endings, and are similarly combined with other words. Over time, they group words into grammatical categories and use them appropriately in sentences (Bloom, 1999; Maratsos & Chalkley, 1980; Tomasello, 2003). Connectionist models (see page 275) have tested this idea by seeing whether artificial neural networks exposed to language input resembling the input children receive show a similar course of grammatical development. So far, neural-network mastery of some grammatical morphemes and aspects of syntax comes close to children's patterns of learning (Elman, 2001; Klahr & MacWhinney, 1998). But the correspondence is not perfect, and no current neural-network system offers a comprehensive account of grammatical development.

Still other theorists, while also focusing on processing mechanisms, agree with the essence of Chomsky's position that children are specially tuned for language learning. One idea accepts semantic bootstrapping but proposes that the grammatical categories into which children group word meanings are innate—present at the outset (Pinker, 1989, 1999). Critics, however, point out that children's early word combinations do not show a grasp of grammar.

According to another theory, although children do not start with innate knowledge, they have a special *language-making capacity*—special built-in procedures for analyzing language—that supports the discovery of grammatical regularities. Research on children learning more than 40 different languages reveals common patterns, consistent with a basic set of strategies (Slobin, 1985, 1997). Yet controversy persists over whether there is a universal language-processing device or whether children who hear different languages devise unique strategies (de Villiers & de Villiers, 1999; Marchman & Thal, 2005).

• **ENVIRONMENTAL SUPPORT FOR GRAMMATICAL DEVELOPMENT** • Besides investigating the child's capacities, researchers have been interested in aspects of the language environment that might ease the task of mastering grammar. Previous research reported that although adults frequently correct children's mistaken inferences about word meaning ("That's not a bird, it's a butterfly"), they rarely provide direct feedback about grammar (Brown & Hanlon, 1970). Consequently, some researchers have argued that adult instruction about how to correct grammatical errors is so minimal that children must have an innate language acquisition device that guides their acquisition of grammatical rules.

Yet parents often correct their child's grammatical errors *indirectly*—in ways that inform the child about conventional usage while keeping the conversation going. In a study in which three English-learning and two French-learning children were followed from age 2 to 4, researchers coded thousands of utterances for errors in pronunciation, word choice, and grammar, along with parents' immediate responses and children's reactions to those responses (Chouinard & Clark, 2003). Findings revealed that parents reformulated as many as two-thirds of children's erroneous expressions—a rate that was similar across the error types and the five children. As the children grew older and used language more competently, parental corrections declined. But overall, parents gave extensive feedback, and the children seemed to use it. They repeated the parental reformulation, acknowledged it, or provided additional information about 40 percent of the time.

Many adult reformulations briefly ask children to clarify what they mean so interaction can continue. For example, when one 2½-year-old said, "I like to hug *him*" (meaning his sister), his mother queried, "Hug Ava?" Other reformulations inform children about grammar through two techniques, often in combination: **recasts**—restructuring inaccurate speech into correct form; and **expansions**—elaborating on children's speech, increasing its complexity (Bohannon & Stanowicz, 1988). For example, if a child says, "I gotted new red shoes," the parent might respond, "Yes, you got a pair of new red shoes," *recasting* the incorrect features of the child's statement as well as *expanding* its complexity. Parents and nonparents alike respond in these ways after children make errors. When sentences are well formed, adults usually continue the topic of conversation or (less often) repeat exactly what the child just said (Bohannon & Stanowicz, 1988).

Nevertheless, the impact of such feedback has been challenged. In some cultures, parents and other adults rarely converse with young children and recast or expand their utterances (Valian, 1999). But in these cases, older siblings may take over this task, and parents may provide feedback in other, culturally prescribed ways. For example, on certain occasions, New Guinean Kaluli and Western Samoan adults tell children what to say by facing the child toward her listener, speaking for the child, and commanding, *"Elema,"* which means, "Say like that" (Ochs, 1988). Western, low-SES parents engage in similar practices (Hart & Risley, 1995).

Other researchers raise a more serious objection about parental reformulations: Whereas some studies report that they have a corrective effect on children's grammar, others show no impact (Strapp & Federico, 2000; Valian, 1999). Rather than eliminating specific errors, recasts and expansions may serve a broader purpose, modeling conventional alternatives and encouraging children to experiment with them.

In sum, virtually all investigators agree that young children are amazing processors of linguistic structure. But the extent to which factors in the language environment help them correct errors and take the next grammatical step forward remains a hotly contested issue in child language research.

◉ As this preschooler tells her father what she is cooking, he might expand her short sentences and recast them into grammatically correct form. Although researchers differ on the impact of this feedback, it does demonstrate good grammar and may encourage children to experiment with new forms.

© Laura Dwight Photography

Ask Yourself

REVIEW	To what extent do children use a consistent grammar in their early two- and three-word utterances? Explain, using research evidence.
APPLY	Three-year-old Jason's mother told him that the family would take a vacation in Miami. The next morning, Jason announced, "I gotted my bags packed. When are we going to Your-ami?" How do language researchers explain Jason's errors?
CONNECT	Provide several examples of how children's cognitive development influences their mastery of grammar.
REFLECT	Do you favor a nativist, an information-processing, or a social interactionist account of grammatical development, or some combination? Use research evidence to support your position.

Pragmatic Development

In addition to mastering phonology, vocabulary, and grammar, children must learn to use language effectively in social contexts. For a conversation to go well, participants must take turns, stay on the same topic, state their messages clearly, and conform to cultural rules that govern how individuals are supposed to interact. During the preschool years, children make considerable headway in mastering the pragmatics of language.

Acquiring Conversational Skills

Young children are already skilled conversationalists. In face-to-face interaction, they initiate verbal exchanges, make eye contact, respond appropriately to their partner's remarks, and take turns (Bloom et al., 1996; Pan & Snow, 1999). The number of turns over which children can sustain interaction and their ability to maintain a topic over time increases with age, but even 2-year-olds are capable of effective conversation (Snow et al., 1996).

Additional conversational strategies are added in early childhood. One of these is the **turnabout,** in which the speaker not only comments on what has just been said but also adds a request to get the partner to respond again. Because 2-year-olds cannot generate many words in each turn, they seldom use turnabouts, but children do so increasingly over the next few years (Goelman, 1986). Between ages 5 and 9, more advanced conversational strategies appear, such as **shading,** in which a change of topic is initiated gradually by modifying the focus of discussion (Wanska & Bedrosian, 1985).

Effective conversation also depends on understanding **illocutionary intent**—that is, what a speaker means to say, even if the form of the utterance is not perfectly consistent with it. By age 3, children comprehend a variety of requests for action not directly expressed as requests, such as "I need a pencil" or "Why don't you tickle me?" (Garvey, 1974). During middle childhood, illocutionary knowledge develops further. For example, after forgetting to do his chores, an 8-year-old understands that when his mother says, "The garbage is beginning to smell," she really means, "Take that garbage out!" Appreciating form–intention pairings like this one requires children to make subtle inferences that are beyond preschoolers' cognitive capacities (Ackerman, 1978).

Still, surprisingly advanced conversational abilities are present at a very early age, and adults' patient, sensitive interactions with young children encourage and sustain them. Throughout this chapter, we have seen examples of how adult–child conversation fosters language development. Whether observed at home or in preschool, it is consistently related to general measures of language progress (Hart & Risley, 1995; NICHD Early Child Care Research Network, 2000a). Dialogues about storybooks are particularly effective. They expose children to great breadth of language knowledge, including how to communicate in a clear, coherent narrative style—a skill that undoubtedly contributes to the association between joint storybook reading and literacy development (see Chapter 7, page 301).

Low-SES preschoolers benefit especially. Those who experience daily reading at home or in child care, compared with those who do not, are greatly advanced in language comprehension and production (Whitehurst et al., 1994). Shared reading with parents is particularly powerful, perhaps because parents are better able than teachers to read to the child often and to tailor their conversations to the child's interests and abilities (Lonigan & Whitehurst, 1998).

Finally, the presence of a sibling enhances young children's conversational skills. Toddlers closely monitor interactions between their twin or older sibling and parent, and they often try to join in. When they do, the conversations last longer, with each participant taking more turns (Barton & Strosberg, 1997; Barton & Tomasello, 1991). As they listen to conversations, younger siblings pick up important skills, such as use of personal pronouns ("I" versus "you"), which are more common in the early vocabularies of later-born than of first-born siblings (Oshima-Takane, Goodz, & Derevensky, 1996). Finally, when interacting with two young children as opposed to just one, middle-SES English-speaking mothers made more statements aimed at regulating social exchanges, including ones that sustained the conversation. And older siblings' remarks to their younger

Low-SES preschoolers benefit greatly from participating in dialogues about storybooks. By providing this experience, this teacher shows these children how to communicate in a clear narrative style, thereby promoting both language and literacy development.

© Laura Dwight Photography

brother or sister overwhelmingly focused on regulating interaction: "Do you like Kermit?" "OK, your turn" (Oshima-Takane & Robbins, 2003). This emphasis probably contributes to younger siblings' skill at conversing with others.

Communicating Clearly

To communicate effectively, we must produce clear verbal messages and must recognize when messages we receive are unclear so we can ask for more information. These aspects of language are called **referential communication skills.**

Typically, laboratory tasks designed to assess children's ability to communicate clearly present them with challenging situations in which they must describe to a listener one object among a group of similar objects. For example, in one study, 3- to 10-year-olds were shown several eight-object arrays. In each, the objects were similar in size, shape, and color. Most 3-year-olds gave ambiguous descriptions. When asked for clarification, they relied heavily on gestures, such as pointing. The ability to send clear messages improved steadily with age (Deutsch & Pechmann, 1982).

When preschoolers are given simpler tasks or engage in face-to-face interaction with familiar people, they adjust their speech to their listener's perspective quite well. But consider what happens when young children talk on the phone. Here is an excerpt of one 4-year-old's phone conversation with his grandfather:

> *Grandfather:* How old will you be?
>
> *John:* Dis many. *[Holding up four fingers.]*
>
> *Grandfather:* Huh?
>
> *John:* Dis many. *[Again holding up four fingers.]* (Warren & Tate, 1992, pp. 259–260)

Preschoolers' referential communication is less mature in highly demanding situations in which they cannot see their listeners' reactions or rely on typical conversational aids, such as gestures and objects to talk about. But when asked to tell a listener how to solve a simple puzzle, 3- to 6-year-olds give more specific directions over the phone than in person, indicating that they realize the need for more verbal description on the phone (Cameron & Lee, 1997). Between ages 4 and 8, both conversing and giving directions over the phone improve greatly. Telephone talk provides an excellent example of how preschoolers' communication skills depend on the demands of the situation.

Children's ability to evaluate the adequacy of messages they receive also improves with age. Around age 3, preschoolers start to ask others to clarify ambiguous messages. At first, children recognize when a message provides a poor description of a concrete object (Ackerman, 1993). Only later can they tell when a message contains inconsistencies. For example, when researchers showed 4- and 5-year-olds the scene in Figure 9.10 and instructed, "Put the frog on the book in the box," preschoolers could not resolve the ambiguity. Most put a frog on the empty book rather than in the box, even though they used similar embedded phrases in their own speech ("The frog *on the book* went to Mrs. Squid's house") (Hurewitz et al., 2000). This task requires the listener to attend to and integrate two competing representations. Yet recall from Chapter 6 that preschoolers tend to focus on only one aspect of a situation (here, the first prepositional phrase). Furthermore, to succeed, children must engage in *comprehension monitoring* (see Chapter 7)—a skill that improves during middle childhood and adolescence.

Narratives

Conversations with adults about past experiences contribute to dramatic gains in children's ability to produce well-organized, detailed, expressive narratives (see page 292 in Chapter 7). When asked to relate a personally important event, 4-year-olds typically produce brief renditions called *leapfrog narratives* because they jump from one event to another in a disorganized fashion. Between 4½ and 5, children start to produce *chronological narratives,* in which

Ⓖ Parent–toddler–sibling dialogues seem to offer a unique context for acquiring the pragmatics of language. The toddler in this family may become especially skilled at joining in conversations and adapting her speech to the needs of her listeners.

© Myrleen Ferguson Cate/PhotoEdit

▼ **Figure 9.10**

Scene used to test for referential communication skills. When an adult instructed, "Put the frog on the book in the box," 4- and 5-year-olds could not resolve the ambiguity between the phrases "on the book" and "in the box." They stuck to their first inference and put one of the frogs on the empty book. Not until middle childhood can children integrate the two competing representations by selecting the frog on the book and placing it in the box. (Adapted from Hurewitz et al., 2000.)

ⓢ Family mealtimes provide rich experiences in listening to and telling personal stories. Perhaps because of their mastery of narrative, children who regularly eat meals with their parents are advanced in language and literacy development.
© Laura Dwight Photography

they place events in temporal sequence and build to a high point: "We went to the lake. Then we fished and waited. Paul waited, and he got a huge catfish." Around age 6, chronological narratives extend into *classic narratives*, in which children add a resolution: "After Dad cleaned the catfish, we cooked it and ate it all up!" (Peterson & McCabe, 1983).

Preschoolers' limited working memories are partly responsible for their restricted narratives. In addition, young children often presume more shared knowledge than their listener has, so they offer little orienting information about events, such as time, place, and participants. Preschoolers' narratives also contain few *evaluations*—comments about how and why events took place and about their own and others' thoughts, feelings, and intentions. During middle childhood, orienting information, detailed descriptions, and connectives that lend coherence to the story ("next," "then," "so," "finally") increase. And evaluative comments rise dramatically, becoming common by age 8 to 9 (Bliss, McCabe, & Miranda, 1998; Ely, 2005). When parents use the elaborative strategy discussed in Chapter 7 to help young children construct narratives, preschoolers produce more organized, detailed, and evaluative personal stories (see page 292).

Because children pick up the narrative styles of parents and other significant adults in their lives, their narrative forms vary widely across cultures. As noted in Chapter 8, instead of relating a single experience from beginning to end, African-American children often use a *topic-associating style*, blending several similar anecdotes. As a result, their narratives are usually longer and more complex than those of North American white children (Champion, 2003b). Japanese children also connect events with a common theme, using a structure that resembles *haiku*, a culturally valued poetic form (Minami, 1996).

The ability to generate clear oral narratives contributes to literacy development, enhancing reading comprehension and preparing children for producing longer, more explicit written narratives. Families who regularly eat meals together have children who are advanced in language and literacy development, perhaps because mealtimes offer many opportunities to listen to and relate personal stories (Beals, 2001).

Sociolinguistic Understanding

Language adaptations to social expectations are called **speech registers.** As early as the preschool years, children are sensitive to them. In one study, 4- to 7-year-olds were asked to act out roles with hand puppets. Even the youngest children showed that they understood the stereotypic features of different social positions. They used more commands when playing socially dominant and male roles, such as teacher, doctor, and father. When playing less dominant and feminine roles, such as pupil, patient, and mother, they spoke more politely and used more indirect requests (Andersen, 1992, 2000).

The importance of register adjustments is reflected in how often parents teach social routines, such as politeness. Infants are encouraged to wave "bye-bye" before they can grasp the gesture's meaning. By age 2, when children fail to say "please" and "thank you," or "hi" and "good-bye," parents usually model and demand an appropriate response (Becker, 1990).

Some cultures have elaborate systems of polite language. In Japan, for example, politeness affects many aspects of verbal and nonverbal communication, which vary with gender, age, social status, and familiarity of speaker and listener. Japanese mothers and preschool teachers constantly model and teach these expressions, so children acquire a large repertoire of polite forms early in the preschool years (Nakamura, 2001). For example, when greeting customers in a make-believe store, even 1-year-olds use the polite greeting "*Irasshaimase!*" ("Welcome!"). Two- and 3-year-olds use more complicated polite speech, such as "*Mata oide-kudasai*" ("Please come again"). And 3- and 4-year-olds make considerable headway in acquiring the complex honorific/humble language of Japanese society.

Although cultures vary in their emphasis on polite language, parents everywhere seem to realize that a child can get by without perfectly correct pronunciation, grammar, and a large vocabulary. But failing to use socially acceptable speech can lead to scorn and rejection, causing a child's message not to be received at all.

Ask Yourself

REVIEW	Summarize findings indicating that adult–child conversations promote preschoolers' pragmatic skills as well as general language progress.
APPLY	What pragmatic skills are evident in Erin's utterances, presented in the introduction to this chapter? How did Erin's parents and brother encourage her pragmatic development?
CONNECT	What cognitive advances contribute to the development of referential communication?
REFLECT	List examples of speech registers that you use in daily life. What childhood experiences might have influenced your mastery of these registers?

Development of Metalinguistic Awareness

Older children's linguistic achievements reflect their more analytical approach to language. This ability to think about language as a system is called **metalinguistic awareness.** Researchers have been especially interested in when it emerges and the role it plays in a variety of language-related accomplishments.

Consider the following exchange between a mother and her 4-year-old child:

Child: What's that?

Mother: It's a typewriter.

Child: [frowning] No, you're the typewriter, that's a typewrite. (Karmiloff-Smith et al., 1996)

As the child's remark illustrates, metalinguistic awareness begins in early childhood. This preschooler, conscious of word endings, expected *-er* to signify an animate agent, like *baker* or *dancer.*

Around age 4, children know that word labels are arbitrary and not part of the objects to which they refer. When asked if an object could be called by a different name in a new language, they say "yes." They also can make some basic syntactic judgments—for example, that a puppet who says, "Nose your touch" or "Dog the pat," is saying his sentences backwards (Chaney, 1992). And by age 5, children have a good sense of the concept of "word." When an adult reading a story stops to ask, "What was the last word I said?" they almost always answer correctly for all parts of speech. They do not say "on-the-floor" instead of "floor" or "is-a" instead of "a" (Karmiloff-Smith et al., 1996). These early metalinguistic understandings are good predictors of vocabulary and grammatical development (Smith & Tager-Flusberg, 1982).

Nevertheless, full flowering of metalinguistic skills does not occur until middle childhood, as cognition advances and teachers point out features of language in reading and writing activities. Between ages 4 and 8, children make great strides in *phonological awareness.* Whereas preschoolers are sensitive to rhyme and other changes in word sounds, third graders can identify all the phonemes in a word (Ehri et al., 2001). Around age 8, children also can judge the grammatical correctness of a sentence even if its meaning is false or senseless (Bialystok, 1986). In addition, metalinguistic knowledge is evident in elementary school children's improved ability to define words and appreciate their multiple meanings in puns, riddles, and metaphors—skills that continue to improve into adolescence.

Metalinguistic awareness strengthens as language use becomes more automatic, freeing children from the immediate linguistic context so they can think about how messages are communicated. Recall from Chapter 7 that phonological awareness predicts success at reading and spelling. Training children in phonological awareness is a promising technique for encouraging early literacy development.

As we will see next, bilingual children are advanced in metalinguistic awareness, as well as other cognitive skills. But before we conclude with this topic, refer to the Milestones table on page 388, which provides an overview of language development.

LANGUAGE DEVELOPMENT

Age	Phonology	Semantics	Grammar	Pragmatics
Birth–1 year	Has categorical speech perception Coos, then babbles Organizes speech sounds into phonemic categories of native language Babbles reflect sound and intonation patterns of native language.	Prefers to listen to mother's voice and to native language Analyzes speech stream for words and syllable stress patterns Recognizes familiar words Uses preverbal gestures	Notices the structure of word sequences, distinguishing ABA from ABB patterns Develops sensitivity to clause and phrase boundaries	Establishes joint attention Engages in vocal exchanges and turn-taking games
1–2 years	Recognizes correct pronunciation of familiar words Uses systematic strategies to simplify word pronunciation	Says first words Vocabulary grows to several hundred words. Sometimes underextends and overextends word meanings	Combines two words in telegraphic speech As three-word sentences appear, gradually adds grammatical morphemes	Engages in conversational turn-taking and topic maintenance
3–5 years	Phonological awareness increases. Pronunciation improves greatly.	Coins words to fill in for words not yet mastered Understands metaphors based on concrete, sensory comparisons	Gradually generalizes grammatical forms Continues to add grammatical morphemes in a regular order Gradually produces complex grammatical structures	Masters additional conversational strategies, such as the turnabout Begins to grasp illocutionary intent Adjusts speech to listener's perspective and to social expectations Asks for clarification of ambiguous messages Produces chronological narratives
6–10 years	Phonological awareness extends to all phonemes in a word. Masters syllable stress patterns signaling subtle differences in meaning	At school entry, has a vocabulary of about 10,000 words Grasps meanings of words on the basis of definitions Appreciates the multiple meanings of words, as indicated by metaphors and humor	Refines complex grammatical structures, such as the passive voice and infinitive phrases	Uses advanced conversational strategies, such as shading Continues to refine understanding of illocutionary intent Communicates clearly in demanding situations, such as on the telephone Produces classic narratives rich in orienting information and evaluations
11 years–adulthood	Masters syllable stress patterns of abstract words	Has a vocabulary of over 40,000 words that includes many abstract terms Understands subtle, nonliteral word meanings, as in sarcasm, irony, and proverbs	Continues to refine complex grammatical structures	Ability to communicate clearly and in accordance with social expectations in diverse situations improves.

Note: These milestones represent overall age trends. Individual differences exist in the precise age at which each milestone is attained.

Bilingualism: Learning Two Languages in Childhood

Throughout the world, many children grow up *bilingual,* learning two languages, and sometimes more than two. Recall from Chapter 2 that both the United States and Canada have large immigrant populations. An estimated 15 percent of American children—6 million in all—speak a language other than English at home (U.S. Census Bureau, 2004b). Similarly, the native languages of 12 percent of Canadian children—nearly 700,000—are neither English nor French, the country's two official languages. In the French-speaking province of Quebec, 41 percent of the population are French–English bilinguals. In the remaining English-speaking provinces, the French–English bilingualism rate is about 10 percent (Statistics Canada, 2002c).

Children can become bilingual in two ways: (1) by acquiring both languages at the same time in early childhood, as Erin did, or (2) by learning a second language after mastering the first. Children of bilingual parents who teach them both languages in early childhood show no special problems with language development. From the start, they separate the language systems, distinguishing their sounds, mastering equivalent words in each, and attaining early language milestones according to a typical timetable (Bosch & Sebastian-Galles, 2001; Holowka, Brosseau-Lapré, & Petitto, 2002). Preschoolers acquire normal native ability in the language of their surrounding community and good-to-native ability in the second language, depending on their exposure to it (Genesee, 2001). But when school-age children acquire a second language after they already speak a first, it generally takes them 3 to 5 years to become as competent in the second language as native-speaking agemates (Hakuta, 1999).

Until recently, a widespread belief in the United States was that childhood bilingualism led to cognitive and linguistic deficits and a sense of personal rootlessness because the bilingual child was thought to identify only weakly with mainstream culture. This negative attitude has been fueled by ethnic prejudices, since bilingualism in the United States is strongly associated with low-SES minority status. A large body of research now shows that children who become fluent in two languages are advanced in cognitive development. They do better than others on tests of selective attention, analytical reasoning, concept formation, and cognitive flexibility (Bialystok, 1999, 2001). Also, their metalinguistic skills are particularly well developed. They are more aware that words are arbitrary symbols, more conscious of some aspects of language sounds, and better at noticing errors of grammar and meaning—capacities that enhance reading achievement (Bialystok & Herman, 1999; Campbell & Sais, 1995).

The advantages of bilingualism provide strong justification for bilingual education programs in schools. The Social Issues box on page 390 describes the vastly differing approaches to bilingual education in the United States and Canada. In both countries, however, many immigrant children do not receive support for their native language in classrooms. Yet bilingualism provides one of the best examples of how language, once learned, becomes an important tool of the mind and fosters cognitive development. Currently, some schools are trying a new form of bilingual education. In these *two-way bilingual programs,* children with limited proficiency in English who speak a common native language and those with fluency in English are assigned in equal numbers to the same classroom. Instruction is directed at helping all children become fluent in both languages and appreciate the cultures associated with them (Calderón & Minaya-Rowe, 2003; Perez, 2004). The goal is to foster the linguistic, cognitive, and cultural enrichment of the entire nation.

About 15 percent of American children speak a language other than English, and 12 percent of Canadian children speak a language other than English or French at home. Here children and their parents gather to watch a parade celebrating the Chinese New Year. Most are probably bilingual—a capacity that enhances cognitive development and metalinguistic skills.
© A. Ramey/Stock Boston, LLC

Two Approaches to Bilingual Education: Canada and the United States

Canadian national education policies actively promote bilingual education. Children with an official minority-language background (French in the English-speaking provinces and English in French-speaking Quebec) have the right to elementary and secondary education in their respective languages. In addition, schools are encouraged to provide programs that maintain the languages and cultures of immigrants to Canada, and also to promote First Nations languages. Although such programs are in short supply, funding for them is increasing. Overall, Canada places a high value on bilingual education directed at enhancing minority children's native-language competence.

Nationally, English–French bilingualism is on the rise, having increased by 8 percent since the mid-1990s (Statistics Canada, 2002c). A major reason is Canada's *language immersion programs*, in which English-speaking elementary school children are taught entirely in French for several years. Currently, about 7 percent of Canadian elementary school children are enrolled. The immersion strategy succeeds in developing children who are proficient in both languages, and who, by grade 6, achieve as well in reading, writing, and math as their counterparts in the regular English program (Harley & Jean, 1999; Holobow, Genesee, & Lambert, 1991; Turnbull, Hart, & Lapkin, 2003). The Canadian government is taking steps to expand language immersion opportunities for children and youths, in hopes of increasing the percentage of 15- to 19-year-olds who speak both English and French from one-fourth to one-half in the coming decade (Government of Canada, 2004a).

In the United States, fierce disagreement exists over how to educate minority children with limited English proficiency. Some believe that time spent communicating in the child's native tongue detracts from English-language achievement, which is crucial for success in the worlds of school and work. Other educators, committed to developing minority children's native language while fostering mastery of English, note that providing instruction in the native

tongue lets minority children know that their heritage is respected. In addition, it prevents *semilingualism* — inadequate proficiency in both languages. Minority children who gradually lose their first language as a result of being taught the second end up limited in both languages for a time, a circumstance that leads to serious academic difficulties (Ovando & Collier, 1998). Semilingualism is believed to contribute to the high rates of school failure and dropout among low-SES Hispanic young people, who make up 50 percent of the American language-minority population.

At present, public opinion and educational practice favor English-only instruction. Many U.S. states have passed laws declaring English to be their official language, creating conditions in which schools have no obligation to teach minority students in languages other than English. Yet in classrooms where both languages are integrated into the curriculum, minority children are more involved in learning, participate more actively in class discussions, and acquire the second language more easily. In contrast, when teachers speak only in a language that U.S. minority children can barely understand, the children display frustration, boredom, and withdrawal (Crawford, 1995, 1997).

▲ In this English–Spanish bilingual classroom serving low–SES third graders who have recently immigrated to the United States, children's first and second languages are both integrated into the curriculum. As a result, the children are more involved in learning, participate more actively in class discussions, and acquire the second language more easily.
© Jonathan Nourok/PhotoEdit

Supporters of U.S. English-only education often point to the success of Canadian language immersion programs, in which classroom lessons are conducted in the second language. Yet Canadian parents enroll their children in immersion classrooms voluntarily, and their children's first and second languages are both majority languages—equally valued by their nation. Furthermore, teaching in the child's native language is merely delayed, not ruled out. For U.S. non-English-speaking minority children, whose native languages are not valued by the larger society, a different strategy seems necessary: one that promotes children's native-language skills while they learn English (Cloud, Genesee, & Hamayan, 2000).

Ask Yourself

REVIEW	Explain why metalinguistic awareness expands greatly in middle childhood. What might account for bilingual children's advanced metalinguistic skills?
APPLY	Reread the examples of Erin's language at the beginning of this chapter. Were Marilyn and Oscar wise to teach Erin both English and Spanish? Does Erin's mixing of the two languages indicate confusion? Justify your answers with research findings.
REFLECT	Did you acquire a second language at home or study one in school? When did you begin, and how proficient are you in the second language? Considering what you now know about bilingual development and education, what changes would you make in your second-language learning, and why?

Summary

Components of Language

What are the four components of language?

Language consists of four subsystems that children combine into a flexible communication system: (1) **phonology,** the rules governing the structure and sequence of speech sounds; (2) **semantics,** the way underlying concepts are expressed in words; (3) **grammar,** consisting of **syntax,** the rules by which words are arranged in sentences, and **morphology,** markers that vary word meaning; and (4) **pragmatics,** the rules for engaging in appropriate and effective conversation.

Theories of Language Development

Describe and evaluate three major theories of language development.

According to the *behaviorist* perspective, language is learned through operant conditioning and imitation. Behaviorism has difficulty accounting for the speed of language progress and for children's novel, rule-based utterances.

Chomsky's *nativist* perspective proposes a **language acquisition device (LAD)** containing a **universal grammar,** or storehouse of rules that apply to all languages. The LAD permits children, as soon as they have sufficient vocabulary, to speak grammatically and comprehend sentences in any language to which they are exposed.

Consistent with Chomsky's ideas, chimpanzees' comprehension of grammar is limited to that of a human 2-year-old; a complex language system is unique to humans. The roles of **Broca's area** in grammatical processing and language production and **Wernicke's area** in comprehending word meaning are more complicated than previously assumed. But the broad association of language functions, especially grammatical competence, with left-hemispheric regions of the cerebral cortex is consistent with Chomsky's notion of a brain prepared to process language. Evidence for a sensitive period for language development also supports the nativist view that language has unique biological properties.

Difficulty specifying a universal grammar that underlies the vast diversity among the world's languages challenges the nativist perspective. Children's continuous and gradual mastery of many constructions is also inconsistent with the notion of innately determined grammatical knowledge.

According to the *interactionist* perspective, language development results from exchanges between inner predispositions and environmental influences. The most influential information-processing accounts are connectionist, or artificial neural network, models, which show that powerful, general cognitive capacities are sufficient to detect certain linguistic patterns. Other evidence confirms that babies are extraordinary statistical analyzers of the sound stream who identify basic patterns of language with the same strategies they use to make sense of nonlinguistic experiences.

Social interactionist theorists believe that children's social skills and language experiences combine with native capacity to profoundly affect language development. But debate continues over the whether children make sense of their complex language environments by applying general cognitive capacities or capacities specially tuned to language.

Prelinguistic Development: Getting Ready to Talk

Describe receptivity to language, development of speech sounds, and conversational skills during infancy.

Infants are prepared for language learning. Newborns are capable of **categorical speech perception** and sensitive to a wider range of **phonemes** than children and adults. Between 6 and 8 months, infants start to organize speech into the phonemic categories of their own language. In the second half of the first year, they have begun to analyze the internal structure of sentences and words. **Child-directed speech (CDS)** eases the young child's task of making sense of language.

Infants begin **cooing** around 2 months, **babbling** around 4 months. Over the first year, the range of babbled sounds expands. Then, as infants get ready to talk, sound and intonation patterns start to resemble those of the child's native language. Certain patterns of babbles appear in particular contexts, suggesting that infants are experimenting with the semantic function of language.

© ROBERT BRENNER/PHOTOEDIT

⦿ Conversational behavior emerges in the first few months, as infants and caregivers establish **joint attention** and the adult comments on what the baby sees. Turn-taking is present in early vocal exchanges. By the end of the first year, babies become active participants in turn-taking games and use two preverbal gestures, the **protodeclarative** and the **protoimperative,** to influence others' behavior. Soon, words are uttered and gestures diminish as children make the transition to verbal communication. By the second year, caregiver–child interaction contributes greatly to language progress.

Phonological Development

Describe the course of phonological development.

⦿ First words are influenced partly by what children can pronounce. When learning to talk, children experiment with sounds, sound patterns, and speech rhythms. Because associating new words with their referents taxes toddlers' working memories, they often do not pick up the fine details of a new word's sounds, which contributes to early pronunciation errors.

⦿ Young children apply systematic phonological strategies to simplify challenging pronunciations. Gradually, minimal words are refined into full words with correct stress patterns. Variations in rate of phonological progress exist, depending on the complexity of a language's sound system and the importance of certain sounds for conveying meaning.

⦿ Pronunciation improves greatly as the vocal tract matures and preschoolers engage in active problem solving. Accent patterns signaling subtle differences in meaning are not mastered until middle childhood and adolescence.

Semantic Development

Describe the course of semantic development, noting individual differences.

⦿ Vocabulary increases rapidly in early childhood; language **comprehension** develops ahead of **production.** First words build on early cognitive and emotional foundations. For most children, the pace of vocabulary development increases steadily and continuously from toddlerhood through the preschool years. To build vocabulary quickly, children engage in **fast-mapping.**

⦿ Girls show faster early vocabulary growth than boys, and reserved, cautious toddlers may wait for a while before beginning to speak. Because lower-SES children experience less verbal stimulation, their vocabularies tend to be smaller. Most toddlers use a **referential style** of language learning, in which early words consist largely of names for objects. Some use an **expressive style,** in which social formulas are common and vocabularies grow more slowly.

⦿ Early vocabularies typically emphasize object words; action and state words appear soon after, an order influenced by cognitive development and adult speech to children. When first learning new words, children make errors of **underextension** and **overextension.** Word coinages and metaphors permit children to expand the range of meanings they can express.

⦿ Vocabulary growth in middle childhood exceeds that of the preschool years, with reading contributing enormously. School-age children can grasp word meanings from definitions, and comprehension of metaphor and humor expands. Adolescents' ability to reason abstractly leads to an enlarged vocabulary and to appreciation of subtle meanings, as in irony, sarcasm, and the figurative language of proverbs.

Discuss ideas about how semantic development takes place, including the influence of memory and strategies for word learning.

⦿ A special part of working memory, a **phonological store** that permits us to retain speech-based information, supports vocabulary growth in early childhood. After age 5, semantic knowledge influences how quickly children form phonological traces, and both factors affect word learning.

⦿ According to **lexical contrast theory,** children figure out the meaning of a new word by contrasting it with words they already know and assigning it to a gap in their vocabulary. The **mutual exclusivity bias** explains children's acquisition of some, but not all, early words. In addition, preschoolers engage in **syntactic bootstrapping,** observing how words are used in the structure of sentences to figure out word meanings. They also make use of adults' social cues and directly provided information. Intense disagreement exists over whether children are innately biased to detect word meanings or whether they use the same cognitive strategies they apply to nonlinguistic stimuli.

Grammatical Development

Describe the course of grammatical development.

⦿ Between 1½ and 2½ years, children combine two words to express a variety of meanings. These first sentences are called **telegraphic speech** because they leave out smaller, less important words. Early two-word combinations probably do not reflect adult grammatical rules.

⦿ As children generate three-word sentences, their first use of grammatical rules is piecemeal, applied to only one or a few verbs. They refine and generalize structures gradually. English-speaking children add **grammatical morphemes** in a consistent order that is a product of both structural and semantic complexity. Once children acquire a regular morphological rule, they **overregularize,** or extend it to words that are exceptions, more often for rarely used irregular words. Over time, expressions based on auxiliary verbs, such as negatives and questions, are mastered.

⦿ Between ages 3½ and 6, a variety of complex constructions are added. Certain forms, such as the passive voice and infinitive phrases, continue to be refined in middle childhood.

Discuss ideas about how grammatical development takes place, including strategies and environmental supports for mastering new structures.

⦿ Some experts believe that grammar is a product of general cognitive development. According to one view, children rely on other properties of language to figure out basic grammatical regularities. In **semantic**

bootstrapping, they use word meanings to figure out sentence structure.

⑨ Others believe that children master grammar through direct observation of language structure. Connectionist models have tested this idea, but no current artificial neural-network system fully accounts for grammatical development.

⑨ Still others agree with the essence of Chomsky's theory that children are specially tuned for language learning. One idea accepts semantic bootstrapping but proposes that grammatical categories are innate. Another speculation is that children have a built-in set of procedures for analyzing language, which supports the discovery of grammatical regularities.

⑨ While conversing with children, adults often provide indirect feedback about grammatical errors by asking for brief clarifications and by restructuring their speech, using **recasts** and **expansions.** However, the impact of such feedback on grammatical development has been challenged.

Pragmatic Development

Describe the course of pragmatic development, including social influences.

⑨ Even 2-year-olds are effective conversationalists—early skills that are fostered by caregiver–child interaction. Conversations with adults consistently predict general measures of language progress.

⑨ Strategies that help sustain interaction, such as **turnabout** and **shading,** are added in early and middle childhood. During this time, children's understanding of **illocutionary intent** improves, and they also acquire more effective **referential communication skills.**

© OSCAR BURRIEL/SCIENCE PHOTO LIBRARY/PHOTO RESEARCHERS, INC.

⑨ From the preschool to school years, children produce more organized, detailed, and evaluative narratives, which vary widely in form across cultures. The ability to generate clear oral narratives contributes to literacy development.

⑨ Preschoolers are sensitive to **speech registers.** From an early age, parents tutor children in politeness routines, emphasizing the importance of adapting language to social expectations.

Development of Metalinguistic Awareness

Describe the development of metalinguistic awareness, noting its influence on language and literacy skills.

⑨ Preschoolers show the beginnings of **metalinguistic awareness,** and their understandings are good predictors of vocabulary and grammatical development and, in the case of phonological awareness, literacy development. Major advances in metalinguistic skills take place in middle childhood.

Bilingualism: Learning Two Languages in Childhood

What are the advantages of bilingualism in childhood?

⑨ Children who learn two languages in early childhood separate the language systems from the start and acquire each according to a typical timetable. When school-age children acquire a second language after mastering the first, they take 3 to 5 years to attain the competence of native-speaking agemates. Bilingual children are advanced in cognitive development and metalinguistic awareness. The advantages of bilingualism provide strong justification for bilingual education programs in schools.

---

⑨ Important Terms and Concepts

babbling (p. 364)
Broca's area (p. 358)
categorical speech perception (p. 363)
child-directed speech (CDS) (p. 364)
comprehension (p. 370)
cooing (p. 364)
expansions (p. 383)
expressive style (p. 372)
fast-mapping (p. 372)
grammar (p. 354)
grammatical morphemes (p. 379)
illocutionary intent (p. 384)
joint attention (p. 365)
language acquisition device (LAD) (p. 355)

lexical contrast theory (p. 376)
metalinguistic awareness (p. 387)
morphology (p. 354)
mutual exclusivity bias (p. 376)
overextension (p. 374)
overregularization (p. 380)
phoneme (p. 363)
phonological store (p. 375)
phonology (p. 354)
pragmatics (p. 354)
production (p. 370)
protodeclarative (p. 365)
protoimperative (p. 365)
recasts (p. 383)

referential communication skills (p. 385)
referential style (p. 372)
semantic bootstrapping (p. 382)
semantics (p. 354)
shading (p. 384)
speech registers (p. 386)
syntactic bootstrapping (p. 376)
syntax (p. 354)
telegraphic speech (p. 378)
turnabout (p. 384)
underextension (p. 374)
universal grammar (p. 355)
Wernicke's area (p. 358)

"Tenderness"
Veronica Beatriz Rebella
Age 14, Uruguay

In the calm harmony of this image, the mother and her clothing become a soft, safe nest of emotional closeness for the child. When parents care for infants and toddlers with love and sensitivity, the baby's feelings of security and competence build quickly.

Reprinted with permission from the International Museum of Children's Art, Oslo, Norway.

CHAPTER 10

Emotional Development

On a spring day, 4-month-old Zach, cradled in the arms of his father, arrived at the door of my classroom, which had been transformed into a playroom for the morning. Behind him came 13-month-old Emily and 23-month-old Brenda, led by their mothers. My students and I spent the next hour watching the three children closely. Especially captivating were the children's emotional reactions to people and objects. As Zach's dad lifted him in the air, Zach responded with a gleeful grin. A tickle followed by a lively kiss on the tummy produced an excited giggle. When I offered Zach a rattle, his brows knit, his face sobered, and he eyed it intently as he mobilized all his energies to reach for it.

Transferred to my arms and then to the laps of several students, Zach remained at ease (although he reserved a particularly broad smile for his father). In contrast, Emily and Brenda were wary of this roomful of strangers. I held out a toy and coaxed Emily toward it. She pulled back and glanced at her mother, as if to check whether the new adult and tantalizing object were safe to explore. When her mother encouraged her, Emily approached cautiously and accepted the toy. A greater capacity to understand the situation, along with her mother's explanations, helped Brenda adjust, and soon she was engrossed in play. During the hour, Brenda displayed a wide range of emotions, including embarrassment at seeing chocolate on her chin in a mirror and pride as I remarked on the tall block tower she had built.

Emotional development—formerly overshadowed by cognition—today is an exciting, rapidly expanding area of research. Our discussion opens with the functions of emotions in all aspects of human activity. Next, we chart age-related gains in children's emotional expression and understanding. As we do so, we will account for Zach, Emily, and Brenda's expanding emotional capacities. Our attention then turns to individual differences in temperament and personality. We will examine biological and environmental contributions to these differences and their consequences for future development. Finally, we take up attachment to the caregiver, the infant's first affectionate tie. We will see how the feelings of security that grow out of this bond support the child's exploration, sense of independence, and expanding social relationships.

◎ The Functions of Emotions

In the past day or so, you may have felt happy, sad, fearful, or angry in response to a grade on a test or a conversation with a friend. These events engender emotion because you care about their outcomes. Your **emotion** is a rapid appraisal of the personal significance of the situation, which prepares you for action. For example, happiness leads you to approach a situation, sadness to passively withdraw, fear to actively move away, and anger to overcome obstacles. An emotion, then, expresses your readiness to establish, maintain, or change your relation to the environment on a matter of importance to you (Saarni, Mumme, & Campos, 1998).

Recent theories, gathered under the **functionalist approach to emotion,** emphasize that the broad function of emotions is to energize behavior aimed at attaining personal goals (Barrett & Campos, 1987; Campos, Frankel, & Camras, 2004; Frijda, 2000; Saarni, Mumme, & Campos, 1998). Events can become personally relevant in several ways. First, you may already have a goal in mind, such as doing well on a test, so the testing situation prompts strong emotion. Second, others' social behavior may alter a situation's significance for you, as when a friend visits and you respond warmly to her friendly greeting. Third, a sensation or a state of mind— any sight, sound, taste, smell, touch, memory, or imagining—can become personally relevant and evoke either positive or negative emotion. Your emotional reaction, in turn, affects your desire to repeat the experience.

Notice how emotions arise from ongoing exchanges between the person and the environment, flexibly serving different functions as the individual's circumstances change. According to functionalist theorists, emotions are central in all our endeavors—cognitive processing, social behavior, and even physical health (Halle, 2003). Let's see how emotions organize and regulate experiences in each domain.

Emotions and Cognitive Processing

Emotional reactions can lead to learning that is essential for survival. For example, a caregiver's highly charged "No!" is sufficient to keep most newly walking toddlers from touching an electric outlet or careening down a staircase. The toddler need not experience a shock or a fall to avoid these dangers.

The emotion–cognition relationship is evident in the impact of anxiety on performance. Among children and adults, very high or very low anxiety impairs thinking, but moderate anxiety can be facilitating (Sarason, 1980). Emotions also powerfully affect memory. For example, children highly upset by an inoculation at the doctor's office tend to remember the event more clearly than do less stressed children (Goodman et al., 1991). At the same time, agitated children usually are so attentive to the fear-arousing event that they do not notice what is happening in their broader surroundings (Bugental et al., 1992).

The relationship between emotion and cognition is bidirectional—a dynamic interplay already under way in early infancy (Lewis, 1999). In one study, researchers taught 2- to 8-month-olds to pull a string to activate pleasurable sights and sounds. As the infants learned the task, they responded with interest, happiness, and surprise. Then, for a short period, pulling the string no longer turned on the attractive stimuli. The babies' emotional reactions quickly changed—mostly to anger but occasionally to sadness. Once the contingency was restored, the infants who had reacted angrily showed renewed interest and enjoyment, whereas the sad babies turned away (Lewis, Sullivan, & Ramsay, 1992). Emotions were interwoven with cognitive processing, serving as outcomes of mastery and as the energizing force for continued involvement and learning.

Emotions and Social Behavior

Children's emotional signals, such as smiling, crying, and attentive interest, powerfully affect the behavior of others. Similarly, the emotional reactions of others regulate children's social behavior.

Careful analyses of caregiver–infant interaction reveal that by 3 months, a complex communication system is in place in which each partner responds in

◎ This 6-month-old breaks into a broad grin after seeing the surprising effect of pressing his feet against the paper. Infants express great delight in motor and cognitive mastery, and their happiness encourages caregivers to be all the more affectionate and stimulating.

Photo Courtesy of Sarah Hyman and Elizabeth Napolitano

an appropriate and carefully timed fashion to the other's cues (Weinberg et al., 1999). In several studies, researchers disrupted this exchange of emotional signals by having the parent assume either a still-faced, unreactive pose or a depressed emotional state. Infants tried facial expressions, vocalizations, and body movements to get the parent to respond again. When these efforts failed, they turned away, frowned, and cried (Hernandez & Carter, 1996; Moore, Cohn, & Campbell, 2001). The still-face reaction is identical in American, Canadian, and Chinese babies, suggesting that it might be a built-in withdrawal response to caregivers' lack of communication (Kisilevsky et al., 1998). Clearly, when engaged in face-to-face interaction, even young infants expect their partners to be emotionally responsive. To learn more about the impact of maternal depression on children's emotional and social adjustment, consult the From Research to Practice box on page 398.

With age, emotional expressions become deliberate means through which infants communicate, and babies monitor the emotional expressions of others to assess their intentions and perspectives. For example, mothers initiate nearly all positive emotional exchanges with young babies. By 9 months, infants become initiators, smiling before their mother smiles (Cohn & Tronick, 1987). Furthermore, recall from Chapter 9 that by the end of the first year, babies become increasingly skilled at *joint attention*—following the caregiver's line of regard (see page 365). In these joint attentional episodes, infants and toddlers pick up not only verbal information but also emotional information. Later in this chapter, we will see that when faced with unfamiliar people, objects, or events, older infants pay close attention to their caregiver's affect, using it as a guide for how to respond. Through this checking of others' emotions, called *social referencing*, young children learn how to behave in a great many everyday situations. One 18-month-old, on first witnessing his newborn baby sister cry, monitored his mother's reaction. On subsequent occasions, he patted the baby and comforted, "No, no, Peach [her nickname], no tears."

Emotions and Health

Much research indicates that emotions influence children's physical well-being. In Chapter 5, we discussed two childhood growth disorders—*nonorganic failure to thrive* and *psychosocial dwarfism*—that result from emotional deprivation. Many other studies indicate that persistent psychological stress, manifested in anxiety, depressed mood, anger, and irritability, is associated with a variety of health difficulties from infancy to adulthood. For example, stress elevates heart rate and blood pressure and depresses the immune response—reactions that may explain its relationship with cardiovascular disease, infectious illness, and several forms of cancer. Stress also reduces digestive activity, as blood flows to the brain, heart, and extremities to mobilize the body for action. Consequently, it can cause gastrointestinal difficulties, including constipation, diarrhea, colitis, and ulcers (Kemeny, 2003; Ray, 2004).

In a dramatic demonstration of the emotion–health relationship, researchers followed children adopted into Canadian homes who had been exposed to chronic stress as a result of at least 8 months of early rearing in extremely deprived Romanian orphanages. Compared with agemates who had been adopted shortly after birth, the children showed extreme reactivity to stress, as indicated by high concentrations of the stress hormone *cortisol* in their saliva—a physiological response linked to illness, retarded physical growth, and learning and behavior problems, including deficits in concentration and control of anger and other impulses. The longer the children spent in orphanage care, the higher their cortisol levels, even 6½ years after adoption (Gunnar et al., 2001; Gunnar & Cheatham, 2003). Furthermore, despite placement in advantaged adoptive homes, some orphanage children displayed persisting, anxious food-related behaviors, including hoarding, difficulty responding to physical cues of fullness, and extreme distress when their access to food was temporarily threatened (Gunnar, Bruce, & Grotevant, 2000; Johnson, 2000).

Fortunately, sensitive adult care reduces stress reactivity in emotionally traumatized children. In one study, researchers devised a special intervention for difficult-to-manage preschoolers with disrupted home lives. Over several months, a therapist worked with the children in a weekly playgroup, and their foster parents received extensive social support and coaching in parenting skills. After 5 weeks, the children's cortisol levels and behavior problems declined (Fisher et al., 2000). In contrast, children in regular foster care who received no intervention showed a rise in both cortisol production and difficult behaviors.

Maternal Depression and Child Development

Approximately 8 to 10 percent of women experience chronic depression—mild to severe feelings of sadness, distress, and withdrawal that continue for months or years. Often, the beginnings of this emotional state cannot be pinpointed; it simply becomes a part of the person's daily life. In other instances, depression emerges or strengthens after childbirth but fails to follow the usual pattern of subsiding as the new mother adjusts to hormonal changes in her body and gains confidence in caring for her baby. Julia experienced this type—called *postpartum depression*. Although genetic makeup increases the risk of depressive illness, Julia's case shows that social and cultural factors are also involved (Swendsen & Mazure, 2000).

During Julia's pregnancy, her husband, Kyle, showed so little interest in the baby that Julia began to worry that having a child might be a mistake. Then, shortly after Lucy's birth, Julia's mood plunged. She became anxious and weepy, overwhelmed by Lucy's needs, and angry that she no longer had control over her own schedule. When Julia approached Kyle about her own fatigue and his unwillingness to help with the baby, he snapped that she was overreacting to every move he made. Julia's childless friends stopped by just once to see Lucy but did not call again.

Julia's depressed mood quickly affected her baby. In the weeks after birth, infants of depressed mothers sleep poorly, are less attentive and responsive to their surroundings, and have elevated levels of stress hormones. The more extreme the depression and the greater the number of stressors in a mother's life (such as marital discord, little or no social support, and poverty), the more the parent–child relationship suffers (Simpson et al., 2003). Julia, for example, rarely smiled at, comforted, or talked to Lucy, who responded to her mother's sad, vacant gaze by turning away, crying, and often looking sad or angry herself (Herrera, Reissland, & Shepherd, 2004; Stanley, Murray, & Stein, 2004). By 6 months of age, Lucy displayed mental and emotional symptoms— delays in development, a negative, irritable

mood, and attachment difficulties (Martins & Gaffan, 2000).

When maternal depression persists, the parent–child relationship worsens. Depressed mothers view their infants and children more negatively than do independent observers (Hart, Field, & Roitfarb, 1999). And they use inconsistent discipline—sometimes lax, at other times too forceful. As we will see in later chapters, children who experience these maladaptive parenting practices often have serious adjustment problems. To avoid their parent's insensitivity, they sometimes withdraw into a depressed mood themselves. Or they may mimic their parent's anger and become impulsive and antisocial (Hay et al., 2003). In several studies, infants and preschoolers of depressed mothers showed atypical EEG brain-wave patterns—reduced activation of the left hemisphere (which governs positive emotion) and increased activation of the right hemisphere (which governs negative emotion) (see page 183 in Chapter 5). These alterations, a sign of difficulty controlling negative emotional arousal, are associated with increased behavior problems (Dawson et al., 1999, 2003; Jones, Field, & Davalos, 2000).

Over time, the parenting and adjustment difficulties just described lead children to develop a pessimistic world view—one in which they lack confidence in themselves and perceive their parents and other people as threatening. Children who constantly feel in danger are especially likely to become overly aroused in stressful situations, easily losing control in the face of cognitive and social challenges (Cummings & Davies, 1994). Although children of depressed parents may inherit a tendency to develop emotional and behavior problems, quality of parenting is a major factor in their adjustment.

Early treatment of maternal depression is vital to prevent the disorder from interfering with the parent–child relationship and harming children. Often, family members must assist the mother in seeking help, as she may not have the emotional energy to do so. Antidepressant medication may be prescribed. In most cases, short-term treat-

▲ Depression disrupts parents' capacity to engage with children. This infant tries hard to get his despondent mother to react. If her unresponsiveness continues, the baby is likely to turn away, cry, and become negative and irritable. Over time, this disruption in the parent–child relationship leads to serious emotional and behavior problems. © Laura Dwight/PhotoEdit

ment is successful; as the mother's depression lifts, her young children's altered brain activity and other symptoms fade (Dawson et al., 2003; Steinberg & Bellavance, 1999).

In Julia's case, a counselor worked with the family for several months, helping Julia and Kyle with their marital problems and encouraging them to be more sensitive and patient with Lucy. Therapy that encourages depressed mothers to revise their negative views of their babies and that teaches them to engage in emotionally positive, patient, and responsive caregiving reduces young children's attachment and developmental problems (Cicchetti, Toth, & Rogosch, 2004). When depressed mothers do not respond to intervention, a warm relationship with the father or another caregiver can safeguard their children's well-being (Crockenberg & Leerkes, 2003b).

Other Features of the Functionalist Approach

In addition to the vital role of emotions in cognitive, social, and physical development, functionalist theorists point out that emotions contribute to the emergence of self-awareness. For example, the interest and excitement that babies display when acting on novel objects help them forge a *sense of self-efficacy*—confidence at being able to control events in their surroundings (Harter, 1998). By the middle of the second year, when self-awareness is sufficiently developed, children begin to experience a new array of emotions. Recall Brenda's expressions of pride and embarrassment—two feeling states that have to do with evaluations of the self's goodness or badness (Saarni, Mumme, & Campos, 1998).

Finally, the functionalist approach emphasizes that to adapt to their physical and social worlds, children must gain control over their emotions, just as they do their motor, cognitive, and social behavior. As part of this increasing *emotional self-regulation*, children must master their culture's rules for when and how to convey emotion. As a result, by late childhood, few emotions are expressed as openly and freely as they were in the early years of life. With these ideas in mind, let's chart the course of emotional development.

Ask Yourself

REVIEW	Using research findings, provide an example of the impact of emotions on children's (1) cognitive processing, (2) social behavior, and (3) physical health.
APPLY	Recently divorced, Jeannine—mother of 3-month-old Jacob—feels lonely, depressed, and anxious about finances. How might Jeannine's emotional state affect Jacob's emotional and social adjustment? What can be done to help Jeannine and Jacob?
REFLECT	Using one of your own experiences, illustrate the bidirectional relationship between emotion and cognition.

Development of Emotional Expression

Because infants cannot describe their feelings, determining exactly which emotions they are experiencing is a challenge. Although vocalizations and body movements provide some information, facial expressions offer the most reliable cues. Cross-cultural evidence reveals that people around the world associate photographs of different facial expressions with emotions in the same way (Ekman, 2003; Ekman & Friesen, 1972). These findings, which suggest that emotional expressions are built-in social signals, inspired researchers to analyze infants' facial patterns carefully to determine the range of emotions they display at different ages. A commonly used method for doing so, the MAX System, is illustrated in Figure 10.1.

Basic emotions—happiness, interest, surprise, fear, anger, sadness, disgust—are universal in humans and other primates, have a long evolutionary history of promoting survival, and can be directly inferred from facial expressions. Do infants come into the world with the ability to

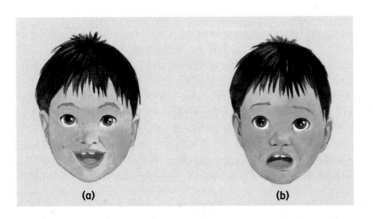

(a)   **(b)**

◀ **Figure 10.1**

Which emotions are these babies displaying? The MAX (Maximally Discriminative Facial Movement) System is a widely used method for classifying infants' emotional expressions. Facial muscle movements are carefully rated to determine their correspondence with basic feeling states, since people around the world associate different facial gestures with emotions in the same way. For example, cheeks raised and corners of the mouth pulled back and up signal happiness (a). Eyebrows raised, eyes widened, and mouth opened with corners pulled straight back denote fear (b). (From Izard, 1979)

Ⓢ Basic emotions have a long evolutionary history, as can be seen in the blissful state of this mother chimpanzee cuddling her 8-day-old infant. Like human infants, baby chimps respond positively to their mother's happy emotional messages, which foster a warm, supportive parent-infant bond. © AP/Wide World Photos

express these basic emotions? Although signs of some emotions are present, babies' earliest emotional life consists of little more than two global arousal states: attraction to pleasant stimulation and withdrawal from unpleasant stimulation (Camras et al., 2003; Fox, 1991; Sroufe, 1979). Caregivers must draw on other information, especially context—how much the baby has eaten, slept, or been comforted or stimulated—to interpret the infant's emotion. Only gradually do emotions become clear, well-organized signals.

The *dynamic systems perspective* helps us understand how this happens. According to this view, children coordinate separate skills into more effective systems as the central nervous system develops and the child's goals and experiences change (see Chapter 4). Videotaping the facial expressions of her daughter from 6 to 14 weeks, Linda Camras (1992) found that in the early weeks, the infant displayed a fleeting angry face as she was about to cry and a sad face as her crying waned. These expressions first appeared on the way toward or away from full-blown distress and were not clearly linked to the baby's experiences and desires. With age, she was better able to sustain an angry signal when she encountered a blocked goal and a sad signal when she could not overcome an obstacle.

According to one view, sensitive, contingent caregiver communication, in which parents selectively mirror aspects of the baby's diffuse emotional behavior, helps infants construct discrete emotional expressions that more closely resemble those of adults (Gergely & Watson, 1999). Around 6 months, face, gaze, voice, and posture form distinct, organized patterns that vary meaningfully with environmental events. For example, babies typically respond to their parent's playful interaction with a joyful face, positive vocalizations, and a relaxed posture, as if to say, "This is fun!" In contrast, an unresponsive parent often evokes a sad face, fussy vocalizations, and a drooping body (sending the message, "I'm despondent") or an angry face, crying, and "pick me up" gestures (as if to say, "Change this unpleasant event!"). By the middle of the first year, emotional expressions are well organized and specific, and therefore they can tell us a great deal about the infant's internal state (Weinberg & Tronick, 1994; Yale et al., 1999).

Four emotions—happiness, anger, sadness, and fear—have received the most research attention. Let's see how they develop.

Happiness

Happiness—first expressed in blissful smiles and later through exuberant laughter—contributes to many aspects of development. Infants smile and laugh when they conquer new skills, displaying their delight in motor and cognitive mastery. As the smile encourages caregivers to be affectionate and stimulating, the baby smiles even more. Happiness binds parent and child into a warm, supportive relationship that fosters the infant's developing competence.

Ⓢ Babies' first laughs appear around 3 to 4 months, as their ability to process information speeds up. By the middle of the first year, infants laugh and smile more with familiar people, as this boy does in a joyous moment with his mother. © VCL/Spencer Rowell/Getty Images/Taxi

During the early weeks, newborn babies smile when full, during REM sleep, and in response to gentle touches and sounds, such as stroking of the skin, rocking, and the mother's soft, high-pitched voice. By the end of the first month, infants smile at interesting sights, but these must be dynamic and eye-catching, such as a bright object jumping suddenly across the baby's field of vision. Between 6 and 10 weeks, the human face evokes a broad grin called the **social smile** (Sroufe & Waters, 1976). By 3 months, infants smile most often when interacting with familiar people (Ellsworth, Muir, & Hains, 1993). These changes parallel the development of infant perceptual capacities—in particular, babies' sensitivity to visual patterns, including the human face (see Chapter 4).

Laughter, which appears around 3 to 4 months, reflects faster processing of information than does smiling. As with smiling, the first laughs occur in response to very active stimuli, such as the parent saying playfully, "I'm gonna get you!" and kissing the baby's tummy. As infants understand more about their world, they laugh at events that contain subtler elements of surprise, such as a silent game of peekaboo (Sroufe & Wunsch, 1972).

Around the middle of the first year, infants smile and laugh more when interacting with familiar people, a preference that strengthens the parent–child bond. Like adults, 10- to 12-month-olds have several smiles, which vary with context. They show a broad, cheek-raised smile to a parent's greeting; a reserved, muted smile to a friendly stranger; and a mouth-open smile during stimulating play (Dickson, Fogel, & Messinger, 1998). During the second year, the smile becomes a deliberate social signal. Toddlers break their play with an interesting toy to communicate their delight to an attentive adult (Jones & Raag, 1989).

Anger and Sadness

Newborn babies respond with generalized distress to a variety of unpleasant experiences, including hunger, painful medical procedures, changes in body temperature, and too much or too little stimulation (see Chapter 4). From 4 to 6 months into the second year, angry expressions increase in frequency and intensity. Older infants react with anger in a wider range of situations—when an interesting object or event is removed, their arms are restrained, the caregiver leaves for a brief time, they are put down for a nap, or they cannot control an expected outcome—for example, pulling a string that previously produced interesting sights and sounds but no longer does so (Camras et al., 1992; Stenberg & Campos, 1990; Sullivan & Lewis, 2003).

Why do angry reactions increase with age? Cognitive and motor development are intimately involved. As infants acquire the capacity for intentional behavior (see Chapter 6), they value control over their own actions and the effects they produce (Alessandri, Sullivan, & Lewis, 1990). Older infants can also better identify the agent of a painful stimulus or a blocked goal. Consequently, their anger is particularly intense when a caregiver from whom they have come to expect warm behavior causes discomfort (Stenberg, Campos, & Emde, 1983). The rise in anger is also adaptive. New motor capacities permit babies to use the energy mobilized by anger to defend themselves or overcome obstacles (Izard & Ackerman, 2000). At the same time, anger motivates caregivers to ease a baby's distress and, in the case of separation, may discourage them from leaving again soon.

Expressions of sadness also occur in response to pain, removal of an object, and brief separations, but they are less frequent than anger (Alessandri, Sullivan, & Lewis, 1990; Izard, Hembree, & Huebner, 1987; Shiller, Izard, & Hembree, 1986). In contrast, sadness is common when infants are deprived of a familiar, loving caregiver or when caregiver–infant communication is seriously disrupted (refer again to the From Research to Practice box on page 398).

Fear

Like anger, fear rises during the second half of the first year. Older infants hesitate before playing with a new toy, and newly crawling infants soon show fear of heights (see Chapter 4). But the most frequent expression of fear is to unfamiliar adults, a reaction called **stranger anxiety**. Many infants and toddlers are quite wary of strangers, although the reaction does not always occur. It depends on several factors: temperament (some babies are generally more fearful), past experiences with strangers, and the current situation (Thompson & Limber, 1991). When an unfamiliar adult picks up the infant in a new setting, stranger anxiety is likely. But if the adult sits still while the baby moves around and a parent remains nearby, infants often show positive and curious behavior (Horner, 1980). The stranger's style of interaction—expressing warmth, holding out an attractive toy, playing a familiar game, and approaching slowly rather than abruptly—reduces the baby's fear.

Infant-rearing practices can modify stranger anxiety, as cross-cultural research reveals. The maternal death rate is high among the Efe hunters and gatherers of the Congo, West Africa. To ensure infant survival, a collective caregiving system exists in which, beginning at birth, Efe babies are passed from one adult to another. Consequently, Efe infants show little stranger anxiety (Tronick, Morelli, & Ivey, 1992). In contrast, in Israeli kibbutzim (cooperative agricultural settlements), living in an isolated community vulnerable to terrorist attacks has led to widespread wariness of strangers. By the end of the first year, when infants look to others for cues about how to respond emotionally, kibbutz babies display far greater stranger anxiety than their city-reared counterparts (Saarni, Mumme, & Campos, 1998).

The rise in fear after 6 months of age keeps newly crawling and walking babies' enthusiasm for exploration in check. Once wariness develops, babies use the familiar caregiver as a **secure base**, or point from which to explore, venturing into the environment and then returning for emotional support. As part of this adaptive system, encounters with strangers lead to

This 1-year-old ventures off confidently, as long as her mother remains near as a secure base to which she can return should she become uneasy or frightened. The rise in fear after 6 months of age restrains infants' compelling urge to set out on their own.
© David Young-Wolff/PhotoEdit

two conflicting tendencies in the baby: approach (indicated by interest and friendliness) and avoidance (indicated by fear). The infant's behavior is a balance between the two.

Eventually, as cognitive development permits toddlers to discriminate more effectively between threatening and nonthreatening people and situations, stranger anxiety and other fears decline. This change is adaptive, because adults other than caregivers will soon be important in children's development. Fear also wanes as children acquire a wider array of strategies for coping with it, as you will see shortly when we discuss emotional self-regulation.

Self-Conscious Emotions

Besides basic emotions, humans are capable of a second, higher-order set of feelings, including shame, embarrassment, guilt, envy, and pride. These are called **self-conscious emotions** because each involves injury to or enhancement of our sense of self. For example, when we are ashamed or embarrassed, we have negative feelings about our behavior or accomplishments, and we want to retreat so others will no longer notice our failings. We feel guilt when we know that we have harmed someone and we want to correct the wrongdoing and repair the relationship. In contrast, pride reflects delight in the self's achievements, and we are inclined to tell others what we have accomplished and to take on further challenges (Saarni, Mumme, & Campos, 1998).

Self-conscious emotions appear at the end of the second year, as toddlers become firmly aware of the self as a separate, unique individual. Shame and embarrassment can be seen as 18- to 24-month-olds lower their eyes, hang their heads, and hide their faces with their hands. Guiltlike reactions are also evident; one 22-month-old returned a toy she had grabbed and patted her upset playmate. Pride, as well, emerges around this time, and envy is present by age 3 (Barrett, 1998; Garner, 2003; Lewis et al., 1989).

Besides self-awareness, self-conscious emotions require an additional ingredient: adult instruction in when to feel proud, ashamed, or guilty. The situations in which adults encourage these feelings vary from culture to culture. In Western individualistic nations, most children are taught to feel pride over personal achievement—throwing a ball the farthest, winning a game, or getting good grades. In collectivist cultures, such as China and Japan, calling attention to purely personal success evokes embarrassment and self-effacement. And violating cultural standards by failing to show concern for others—a parent, a teacher, or an employer—sparks intense shame (Akimoto & Sanbonmatsu, 1999; Lewis, 1992).

As their self-concepts develop, children become increasingly sensitive to praise and blame or to the possibility of such feedback. By age 3, self-conscious emotions are clearly linked to self-evaluation (Lewis, 1995; Stipek, 1995). Preschoolers show much more pride when they succeed on difficult rather than easy tasks and much more shame when they fail simple rather than hard tasks (Lewis, Alessandri, & Sullivan, 1992). Parenting behavior influences these early self-evaluative reactions. Parents who repeatedly give feedback about the worth of the child and her performance ("That's a bad job! I thought you were a good girl") have children who experience self-conscious emotions intensely—more shame after failure, more pride after success. In contrast, parents who focus on how to improve performance ("You did it this way; now try doing it that way") induce moderate, more adaptive levels of shame and pride and greater persistence on difficult tasks (Kelley, Brownell, & Campbell, 2000; Lewis, 1998).

Among Western children, intense shame is associated with feelings of personal inadequacy ("I'm stupid," "I'm a terrible person") and is linked to maladjustment—withdrawal and depression as well as intense anger and aggression at others who participated in the shame-evoking situation (Lindsay-Hartz, de Rivera, & Mascolo, 1995; Mills, 2005). In contrast, guilt—as long as it occurs in appropriate circumstances and is not accompanied by shame—is related to good adjustment, perhaps because it helps children resist harmful impulses. Guilt also motivates a misbehaving child to repair the damage and behave more considerately (Ferguson et al., 1999; Tangney, 2001).

The consequences of shame for children's adjustment, however, may vary across cultures. In Asian collectivist societies, where people define themselves in relation to their social group, shame is viewed as an adaptive reminder of the importance of others' judgments (Bedford, 2004). Chinese parents, for example, believe that it is important for a misbehaving child to feel ashamed.

© Self-conscious emotions appear at the end of the second year. This Guatemalan 2-year-old undoubtedly feels a sense of pride as she helps care for her elderly grandmother—an activity highly valued in her culture.

© Celia Roberts/Earth Images

As early as age 2½, they frequently use shame to teach right from wrong, while mindful that excessive shaming could harm the child's self-esteem (Fung, 1999). Not surprisingly, Chinese children add the word *shame* to their vocabularies by age 3, much earlier than their North American counterparts do (Shaver, Wu, & Schwartz, 1992).

As children develop inner standards of excellence and good behavior and a sense of personal responsibility, the circumstances under which they experience self-conscious emotions change. Unlike preschoolers, school-age children experience pride and guilt without adult monitoring and encouragement. An adult need not be present for an accomplishment to spark pride and a transgression to arouse guilt (Harter & Whitesell, 1989). Also, school-age children do not report guilt for any mishap, as they did at younger ages, but only for intentional wrongdoing, such as ignoring responsibilities, cheating, or lying (Ferguson, Stegge, & Damhuis, 1991). These changes reflect the older child's more mature sense of morality, a topic we will take up in Chapter 12.

Emotional Self-Regulation

Besides expressing a wider range of emotions, children learn to manage their emotional experiences. **Emotional self-regulation** refers to the strategies we use to adjust our emotional state to a comfortable level of intensity so we can accomplish our goals. It requires several cognitive capacities that we discussed in Chapter 7—attention focusing and shifting, the ability to inhibit thoughts and behavior, and planning, or actively taking steps to relieve a stressful situation (Eisenberg et al., 1995b; Eisenberg & Spinrad, 2004). When you remind yourself that an anxiety-provoking event will be over soon, suppress your anger at a friend's behavior, or decide not to see a horror movie because it might frighten you, you are engaging in emotional self-regulation.

Notice that emotional self-regulation requires voluntary, effortful management of emotions. This voluntary control improves gradually, due to development of the frontal lobes of the cerebral cortex and the assistance of caregivers, who help children manage their emotions and teach them strategies for doing so (Eisenberg & Morris, 2002; Fox & Calkins, 2003). Individual differences in voluntary control of emotion are evident in infancy and, by early childhood, contribute so vitally to children's adjustment that—as we will see in a later section—*effortful control* is regarded as a major dimension of temperament. Let's turn now to changes in emotional self-regulation from infancy to adolescence.

• **INFANCY** • In the early months of life, infants have only a limited capacity to regulate their emotional states. Although they can turn away from unpleasant stimulation and can mouth and suck when their feelings get too intense, they are easily overwhelmed by internal and external stimuli. As a result, they depend on the soothing interventions of caregivers—lifting the distressed infant to the shoulder, rocking, and talking softly.

Rapid development of the cerebral cortex increases the baby's tolerance for stimulation. Between 2 and 4 months, caregivers build on this capacity by initiating face-to-face play and attention to objects. In these interactions, parents arouse pleasure in the baby while adjusting the pace of their behavior so the infant does not become overwhelmed and distressed. As a result, the baby's tolerance for stimulation increases (Kopp & Neufeld, 2003). By 4 months, the ability to shift attention helps infants control emotion. Babies who more readily turn away from unpleasant events are less prone to distress (Axia, Bonichini, & Benini, 1999). At the end of the first year, crawling and walking enable infants to regulate feelings by approaching or retreating from various stimuli.

Parents who "read" and respond contingently and sympathetically to the baby's emotional cues have infants who are less fussy, more easily soothed, and more interested in exploration. In contrast, parents who wait to intervene until the infant has become extremely agitated reinforce the baby's rapid rise to intense distress (Eisenberg, Cumberland, & Spinrad, 1998). This makes it harder for parents to soothe the baby in the future—and for the baby to learn to calm herself. When caregivers do not regulate stressful experiences for infants, brain structures that buffer stress may fail to develop properly, resulting in an anxious, emotionally reactive child with a reduced capacity for regulating emotion (Nelson & Bosquet, 2000). In one study, 5-month-olds who readily cried intensely when their arms were restrained were more likely to become 10-month-olds who had difficulty regulating emotion after a toy was removed from their hands (Braungart & Stifter, 1996).

By the end of the second year, gains in representation and language lead to new ways of regulating emotion. Although 2-year-olds often redirect their attention for short periods when they are distressed, they are better able to do so in the presence of a supportive adult (Grolnick, Bridges, & Connell, 1996). And they are not yet good at using language to manage their emotions. But once children start to describe their internal states, they can guide caregivers to help them. For example, while listening to a story about monsters, one 22-month-old whimpered, "Mommy, scary." Her mother put down the book and gave her a consoling hug.

• **EARLY CHILDHOOD** • After age 2, children frequently talk about their feelings and actively try to control them. By age 3 to 4, they verbalize a variety of emotional self-regulation strategies. For example, they know they can blunt emotions by restricting sensory input (covering their eyes or ears to block out an unpleasant sight or sound), talking to themselves ("Mommy said she'll be back soon"), or changing their goals (deciding that they don't want to play anyway after being excluded from a game). Children's use of these strategies means fewer emotional outbursts over the preschool years (Thompson, 1990a). As the examples suggest, shifting attention away from sources of frustration continues to be an effective strategy for preschoolers to use in managing emotion. Three-year-olds who can distract themselves when frustrated tend to become school-age children whom teachers rate as high in cooperation and low in problem behaviors (Gilliom et al., 2002).

By watching adults handle their own feelings, preschoolers pick up strategies for regulating emotion. Warm, patient parents who use verbal guidance to help children understand and control their feelings, including suggesting and explaining strategies, strengthen the child's capacity to handle stress (Gottman, Katz, & Hooven, 1997). In contrast, when parents rarely express positive emotion, dismiss their child's feelings as unimportant, and have difficulty controlling their own anger and hostility, children have continuing problems managing emotion that seriously interfere with psychological adjustment (Calkins & Johnson, 1998; Eisenberg et al., 2001; Gilliom et al., 2002; Katz & Windecker-Nelson, 2004).

As with infants, preschoolers who experience negative emotion intensely have greater difficulty inhibiting their feelings and shifting their attention away from disturbing events. Young children with poor emotion-regulation skills are more likely to respond with irritation to others' distress, to react angrily or aggressively when frustrated, to get along poorly with teachers and peers, and to have difficulty adjusting to classroom routines (Chang et al., 2003; Denham et al., 2002; Shields et al., 2001). Because these emotionally reactive children become increasingly difficult to rear, they often are targets of ineffective parenting, which compounds their poor emotional self-regulation.

Of course, even children with good emotion-regulation skills sometimes find it hard to manage their feelings. Preschoolers' vivid imaginations, combined with their incomplete grasp of the distinction between appearance and reality, make fears common in early childhood. Consult Applying What We Know on the following page for ways adults can help children manage fears.

• **MIDDLE CHILDHOOD AND ADOLESCENCE** • Rapid gains in emotional self-regulation occur after school entry. As children compare their accomplishments with their classmates' and care more about peer approval, they must learn to manage negative emotion that threatens their sense of self-worth.

Common fears of the school years include poor academic performance and rejection by classmates. And as children begin to understand the realities of the wider world, the possibility of personal harm (being robbed or shot) and media events (wars and disasters) often trouble them (Gullone, 2000). School-age children's fears are shaped in part by their culture. For example, in China, where self-restraint and compliance with social standards are highly valued, more children mention failure and adult criticism as salient fears than in Australia or North America.

◉ After the terrorist attacks of September 11, 2001, parents and teachers helped children regulate their fears by discussing the events and reassuring them of their safety. Some, such as teachers at the school these children attend, suggested ways to give support—in this case, by making a flag for families of the victims and attaching messages of sympathy.
© AP/Wide World Photos

Applying What We Know — Helping Children Manage Common Fears of Early Childhood

Fear	Suggestion
Monsters, ghosts, and darkness	Reduce exposure to frightening stories in books and on TV until the child is better able to sort out appearance from reality. Make a thorough "search" of the child's room for monsters, showing him that none are there. Leave a night-light burning, sit by the child's bed until he falls asleep, and tuck in a favorite toy for protection.
Preschool or child care	If the child resists going to preschool but seems content once there, then the fear is probably separation. Provide a sense of warmth and caring while gently encouraging independence. If the child fears being at preschool, find out what is frightening—the teacher, the children, or perhaps a crowded, noisy environment. Provide extra support by accompanying the child and gradually lessening the amount of time you are present.
Animals	Do not force the child to approach a dog, cat, or other animal that arouses fear. Let the child move at her own pace. Demonstrate how to hold and pet the animal, showing the child that when treated gently, the animal is friendly. If the child is larger than the animal, emphasize this: "You're so big. That kitty is probably afraid of *you!*"
Intense fears	If a child's fear is intense, persists for a long time, interferes with daily activities, and cannot be reduced in any of the ways just suggested, it has reached the level of a *phobia*. Sometimes phobias are linked to family problems, and counseling is needed to reduce them. At other times, phobias diminish without treatment as the child's capacity for emotional self-regulation improves.

Chinese children, however, are not more fearful overall. The number and intensity of fears they report resemble those of Western children (Ollendick et al., 1996).

By age 10, most children shift adaptively between two general strategies for managing emotion. In **problem-centered coping,** they appraise the situation as changeable, identify the difficulty, and decide what to do about it. If problem solving does not work, they engage in **emotion-centered coping,** which is internal, private, and aimed at controlling distress when little can be done about an outcome (Kliewer, Fearnow, & Miller, 1996; Lazarus & Lazarus, 1994). For example, when faced with an anxiety-provoking test or a friend who is angry at them, older school-age children view problem solving and seeking social support as the best strategies. But when outcomes are beyond their control—for example, after having received a bad grade—they opt for distraction or try to redefine the situation in ways that help them accept current conditions: "Things could be worse. There'll be another test." Compared with preschoolers, school-age children more often use these internal strategies to regulate emotion, a change due to their improved ability to appraise situations and reflect on thoughts and feelings (Brenner & Salovey, 1997). Consequently, fears gradually decline (Gullone, 2000).

Cognitive development and a wider range of social experiences permit children to flexibly vary their coping strategies. When the development of emotional self-regulation has gone well, young people acquire a sense of *emotional self-efficacy*—a feeling of being in control of their emotional experience (Saarni, 2000). This fosters a favorable self-image and an optimistic outlook, which assist them further in the face of emotional challenges.

Acquiring Emotional Display Rules

In addition to regulating internal emotional states, children must learn to control what they communicate to others. Young preschoolers have some ability to modify their expressive behavior. For example, when denied a cookie before dinnertime, one 2-year-old paused, picked up her blanket, and walked from the hard kitchen floor to the soft family-room carpet where she could comfortably throw herself down and howl loudly!

At first, children modify emotional expressions to serve personal needs, and they exaggerate their true feelings (as this child did to get attention and a cookie). Soon, they learn to damp down their expressive behavior and substitute other reactions, such as smiling when feeling anxious or disappointed. All societies have **emotional display rules** that specify when, where, and how it is appropriate to express emotions.

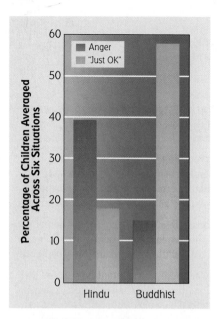

▲ **Figure 10.2**

Hindu and Buddhist children's reports of feeling anger and "just OK" in response to emotionally charged situations. Hindu children reported that they would feel more anger. Buddhist children, whose religion values a calm, peaceful disposition, more often stated that they would feel "just OK." The children sometimes selected other emotions, such as "happy," "sad," or "scared," but these did not differ between the two subcultures and are not shown. (Adapted from Cole & Tamang, 1998.)

As early as the first few months, parents encourage infants to suppress negative emotion by imitating their expressions of interest, happiness, and surprise more often than their expressions of anger and sadness. Boys get more of this training than girls, in part because boys have a harder time regulating negative emotion (Malatesta et al., 1986; Weinberg et al., 1999). As a result, the well-known sex difference—females as emotionally expressive and males as emotionally controlled—is promoted at a tender age.

Although caregiver shaping of emotional behavior begins early, children only gradually gain the ability to conform to display rules. Not until age 3 can they pose an expression they do not feel. These emotional "masks" are largely limited to positive feelings of happiness and surprise. Children of all ages (and adults as well) find it harder to act angry, sad, or disgusted than pleased (Lewis, Sullivan, & Vasen, 1987). Social pressures are responsible for these trends. To foster harmonious relationships, most cultures teach children to communicate positive feelings and inhibit unpleasant emotional displays.

From interacting with parents, teachers, and peers, children increase their knowledge of how to express negative emotion in ways likely to evoke a desired response from others. School-age children increasingly prefer verbal strategies to crying, sulking, or aggression (Shipman et al., 2003). As these findings suggest, children gradually become consciously aware of display rules. Kindergartners typically say they obey the rules to avoid punishment and gain approval from others. By third grade, children understand the value of display rules for ensuring social harmony (Jones, Abbey, & Cumberland, 1998). School-age children who justify emotional display rules by referring to concern for others' feelings are rated as especially helpful, cooperative, and socially responsive by teachers and as better liked by peers (Garner, 1996; McDowell & Parke, 2000).

Cultures that stress collectivism place particular emphasis on emotional display rules, although they vary in how they teach children to inhibit negative displays. In a striking illustration, researchers studied children in two collectivist subcultures in rural Nepal. In response to stories about emotionally charged situations (such as peer aggression or an unjust parental punishment), Hindu children more often said they would feel angry and would try to mask their feelings. Buddhist children, in contrast, interpreted the situation so they did not experience anger; saying they would feel "just OK," they explained, "Why be angry? The event already happened" (see Figure 10.2). In line with this difference, Hindu mothers reported that they often instruct their children in how to control their emotional behavior. Buddhist mothers, in contrast, pointed to the value their religion places on a calm, peaceful disposition (Cole & Tamang, 1998). In comparison to both Nepalese groups, U.S. children preferred conveying their anger. To an unjust punishment, they answered, "If I say I'm angry, he'll stop hurting me!" (Cole, Bruschi, & Tamang, 2002). Notice how this response fits with the Western individualistic emphasis on personal rights and self-expression.

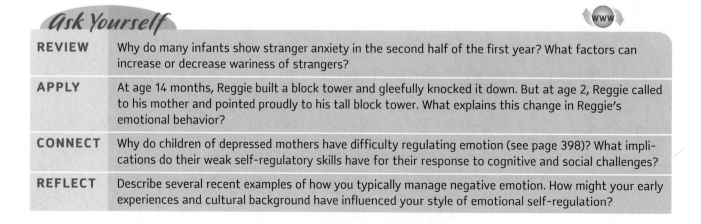

Ask Yourself

REVIEW	Why do many infants show stranger anxiety in the second half of the first year? What factors can increase or decrease wariness of strangers?
APPLY	At age 14 months, Reggie built a block tower and gleefully knocked it down. But at age 2, Reggie called to his mother and pointed proudly to his tall block tower. What explains this change in Reggie's emotional behavior?
CONNECT	Why do children of depressed mothers have difficulty regulating emotion (see page 398)? What implications do their weak self-regulatory skills have for their response to cognitive and social challenges?
REFLECT	Describe several recent examples of how you typically manage negative emotion. How might your early experiences and cultural background have influenced your style of emotional self-regulation?

Understanding and Responding to the Emotions of Others

Children's emotional expressiveness is intimately tied to their ability to interpret the emotional cues of others. We have seen that in the first few months, infants match the feeling tone of the caregiver in face-to-face communication. Early on, babies detect others' emotions through a fairly automatic process of *emotional contagion,* just as we tend to feel happy or sad when we sense these emotions in others. Around 4 months, infants become sensitive to the structure and timing of face-to-face interactions (see Chapter 9, page 365). When they gaze, smile, or vocalize, they now expect their social partner to respond in kind (Rochat, Striano, & Blatt, 2002). Within these exchanges, babies become increasingly aware of the range of emotional expressions (Montague & Walker-Andrews, 2001).

Around 5 months, infants perceive facial expressions as organized patterns, and they can match the emotion in a voice with the appropriate face of a speaking person (see Chapter 4). Babies' responses to emotional expressions as organized wholes indicate that these signals have become meaningful to them. As skill at establishing joint attention improves, infants realize that an emotional expression not only has meaning but also is a meaningful reaction to a specific object or event (Moses et al., 2001; Walker-Andrews, 1997). Once these understandings are in place, infants actively seek emotional information from trusted caregivers.

As this mother reads to her infant, her expressions of pleasure are contagious. Once the baby realizes that emotional expressions are meaningful reactions to specific objects and events, he will actively seek emotional information from his mother.
© Felicia Martinez/PhotoEdit

Social Referencing

Social referencing involves relying on another person's emotional reaction to appraise an uncertain situation. Beginning at 8 to 10 months, when infants start to evaluate objects and events in terms of their own safety and security, social referencing occurs often. Many studies show that a caregiver's emotional expression (happy, angry, or fearful) influences whether a 1-year-old will be wary of strangers, play with an unfamiliar toy, or cross the deep side of the visual cliff (see Chapter 4, page 154) (Repacholi, 1998; Stenberg, 2003; Striano & Rochat, 2000). The parent's voice alone, or the voice in combination with a facial expression, is more effective in guiding infants' behavior than the parents' facial expression alone (Mumme, Fernald, & Herrera, 1996; Vaish & Striano, 2004). When babies hear emotion in an adult's voice, they more readily approach or avoid an uncertain situation, perhaps because they do not need to turn toward the adult but can focus on evaluating the novel event. In addition, the voice offers more information—not just emotional cues, but also verbal instructions about what to do.

Parents can capitalize on social referencing to teach their youngster how to react to everyday events. Social referencing also permits toddlers to compare their own assessments of events with those of others. By the middle of the second year, they appreciate that others' emotional reactions may differ from their own. In one study, an adult showed 14- and 18-month-olds broccoli and crackers. In one condition, she acted delighted with the taste of broccoli but disgusted with the taste of crackers. In the other condition, she showed the reverse preference. When asked to share the food, 14-month-olds offered only the type of food they themselves preferred—usually crackers. In contrast, 18-month-olds gave the adult whichever food she appeared to like, regardless of their own preferences (Repacholi & Gopnik, 1997).

In sum, social referencing helps young children move beyond simply reacting to others' emotional messages. They use those signals to guide their own actions and to find out about others' internal states and preferences (Saarni, Mumme, & Campos, 1998).

Emotional Understanding in Childhood

During the preschool years, children's emotional understanding expands rapidly, as their everyday talk about emotions reveals:

Two-year-old: [After father shouted at child, she became angry, shouting back] "I'm mad at you, Daddy. I'm going away. Good-bye."

Two-year-old: [Commenting on another child who refused to take a nap and cried] "Mom, Annie cry. Annie sad."

Six-year-old: [In response to mother's comment, "It's hard to hear the baby crying"] "Well, it's not as hard for me as it is for you." *[When mother asked why]* "Well, you like Johnny better than I do! I like him a little, and you like him a lot, so I think it's harder for you to hear him cry."

Six-year-old: [Comforting a small boy in church whose mother had gone up to communion]
"She'll be right back. Don't be afraid. I'm here." (Bretherton et al., 1986, pp. 536, 540, 541)

• **COGNITIVE DEVELOPMENT AND EMOTIONAL UNDERSTANDING** • As these examples show, early in the preschool years, children refer to causes, consequences, and behavioral signs of emotion, and over time their understanding becomes more accurate and complex (Stein & Levine, 1999). By age 4 to 5, they correctly judge the causes of many basic emotions ("He's happy because he's swinging very high"; "He's sad because he misses his mother"). Preschoolers' explanations tend to emphasize external factors over internal states, a balance that changes with age (Levine, 1995). In Chapter 11, we will see that after age 4, children appreciate that both desires and beliefs motivate behavior. As a result, their grasp of how internal factors can trigger emotion expands.

Preschoolers can also predict what a playmate expressing a certain emotion might do next. Four-year-olds know that an angry child might hit someone and that a happy child is more likely to share (Russell, 1990). And they realize that thinking and feeling are interconnected—that a person reminded of a previous sad experience is likely to feel sad (Lagattuta, Wellman, & Flavell, 1997). Furthermore, they come up with effective ways to relieve others' negative feelings, such as hugging to reduce sadness (Fabes et al., 1988).

In middle childhood, ability to consider conflicting cues when explaining others' emotions improves. When asked what might be happening in a picture showing a happy-faced child with a broken bicycle, 4- and 5-year-olds tended to rely only on the emotional expression: "He's happy because he likes to ride his bike." By age 8 to 9, children

⊚ A preschooler stops playing when she notices a classmate's distress. An early, impressive understanding of the causes and consequences of emotions may enable her to appreciate why the boy is unhappy and to predict what he might do next.
© Laura Dwight Photography

more often reconciled the two cues: "He's happy because his father promised to help fix his broken bike" (Gnepp, 1983; Hoffner & Badzinski, 1989). Similarly, older children recognize that people can experience more than one emotion at a time, that the emotions may differ in intensity, and that each may be either positive or negative (Pons et al., 2003). Preschoolers, by contrast, staunchly deny that two emotions can occur at once, much as they do not integrate two variables (height and width) in a Piagetian conservation-of-liquid task (see Chapter 6, page 236).

An appreciation of mixed emotions helps school-age children realize that people's expressions may not reflect their true feelings (Saarni, 1999). It also fosters awareness of self-conscious emotions. For example, 8- and 9-year-olds understand that shame combines two feelings: anger at ourselves for a personal inadequacy and sadness at having disappointed another (Harter, 1999). As with the development of *metacognition* (thinking about thought), discussed in Chapter 7, striking gains in thinking about emotion occur in middle childhood.

• **SOCIAL EXPERIENCE AND EMOTIONAL UNDERSTANDING** • The more mothers label emotions and explain them in conversing with preschoolers, the more "emotion words" children use. Maternal prompting of emotional thoughts ("What makes him afraid?") is a good predictor of 2-year-olds' emotion language. For older preschoolers, explanations ("He's sad because his dog ran away") are more important (Cervantes & Callanan, 1998). Does this remind you of the concept of *scaffolding*, discussed in Chapter 6—that to be effective, adult teaching must adjust to children's increasing competence?

Preschoolers whose parents frequently acknowledge their emotional reactions and explicitly teach them about diverse emotions are better able to judge others' emotions when tested at later ages (Denham & Kochanoff, 2002). Discussions in which family members disagree are particularly helpful. In one study, mothers who explained feelings and who negotiated and compromised during conflicts with their 2-1/2-year-olds had children who, at age 3, were advanced in understanding emotion and used similar strategies to resolve disagreements (Laible & Thompson, 2002). Such dialogues seem to help children reflect on the causes and consequences of emotion while modeling mature communication skills. Furthermore, 3- to 5-year-olds who have a warm, relaxed relationship with their mothers (a secure attachment bond) better understand emotion, perhaps because secure attachment is related to richer mother–child conversations about feelings (Laible & Thompson, 1998, 2000).

As preschoolers learn more about emotion from conversing with adults, they transfer this knowledge to other contexts, engaging in more emotion talk with siblings and friends, especially during sociodramatic play (Brown, Donelan-McCall, & Dunn, 1996; Hughes & Dunn, 1998). Make-believe, in turn, contributes to emotional understanding, especially when children play with siblings (Youngblade & Dunn, 1995). The intense nature of the sibling relationship, combined with frequent acting out of feelings, makes pretending an excellent context for early learning about emotions. And when parents intervene in sibling disputes by reasoning and negotiating, preschoolers gain in sensitivity to their siblings' feelings (Perlman & Ross, 1997). They more often refer to their siblings' emotional perspective ("You get mad when I don't share") and engage in less fighting.

Knowledge about emotions helps children greatly in their efforts to get along with others. As early as 3 to 5 years of age, it is related to friendly, considerate behavior and willingness to make amends after harming another (Brown & Dunn, 1996; Dunn, Brown, & Maguire, 1995). Also, the more preschoolers refer to feelings when interacting with playmates, the better liked they are by their peers (Fabes et al., 2001). Children seem to recognize that acknowledging others' emotions and explaining their own enhance the quality of relationships.

Empathy and Sympathy

In empathy, understanding and expression of emotions are interwoven, since both awareness of the emotions of another and the vicarious experience of those emotions are required for an empathic response. Current theorists agree that **empathy** involves a complex interaction of cognition and affect: the ability to detect different emotions, to take another's emotional perspective, and to *feel with* that person, or respond emotionally in a similar way. Beginning in the preschool years, empathy is an important motivator of **prosocial**, or **altruistic, behavior**—actions that benefit another person without any expected reward for the self (Eisenberg & Fabes, 1998). Yet empathy does not always yield acts of kindness and helpfulness. In some children, empathizing with an upset adult or peer escalates into *personal distress*. In trying to reduce these feelings, the child focuses on his own anxiety rather than on the person in need. Consequently, empathy does not give way to **sympathy**—feelings of concern or sorrow for another's plight.

• **DEVELOPMENT OF EMPATHY** • Empathy has roots early in development. Newborn babies tend to cry in response to the cry of another baby, a reaction that may be the primitive beginnings of an empathic response (Dondi, Simion, & Caltran, 1999). In sensitive, face-to-face communication, infants "connect" emotionally with their caregivers—experiences believed to be the foundation for empathy and concern for others (Zahn-Waxler, 1991).

Like self-conscious emotions, true empathy requires children to understand that the self is distinct from other people. As self-awareness develops, children nearing 2 years of age begin to empathize. They not only sense another's unhappiness but often try to relieve it. For example, one 21-month-old reacted to his mother's simulated sadness by offering comforting words, giving her a hug, trying to distract her with a hand puppet, and asking the researcher to help (Zahn-Waxler & Radke-Yarrow, 1990). As language develops, children rely more on words to console others, a change that indicates a more reflective level of empathy. When a 6-year-old noticed that his mother was distressed at not being able to find a motel after a long day's travel, he said, "You're pretty upset, aren't you, Mom? You're pretty sad. Well, I think it's going to be all right. I think we'll find a nice place and it'll be all right" (Bretherton et al., 1986, p. 540).

Empathy increases over the elementary school years as children understand a wider range of emotions and take multiple cues into account in assessing others' feelings (Ricard & Kamberk-Kilicci, 1995). During late childhood and adolescence, advances in perspective taking permit an empathic response not just to people's immediate distress but also to their general life condition (Hoffman, 2000). The ability to empathize with the poor, oppressed, and sick requires an advanced form of perspective taking in which the young person understands that people lead continuous emotional lives beyond the current situation.

Ⓢ Outside the playhouse at preschool, a young boy offers comfort to his friend. As children's language skills expand and their ability to take the perspective of others improves, empathy also increases, motivating prosocial, or altruistic, behavior.
© Lawrence Migdale/Pix

• **INDIVIDUAL DIFFERENCES** • Temperament plays a role in whether empathy occurs and whether it prompts sympathetic, prosocial behavior or a personally distressed, self-focused response. Twin studies reveal that empathy is moderately heritable (Zahn-Waxler et al., 2001). Children who are sociable, assertive, and good at regulating emotion are most likely to help, share, and comfort others in distress. In contrast, poor emotion regulators less often display sympathetic concern and prosocial behavior (Eisenberg et al., 1996, 1998). Aggressive children's high hostility, weakened capacity to take another's perspective, and impulsive acting out of negative feelings blunt their capacity for empathy and sympathy. Many show a decline—rather than the typical rise—in concern for others during middle childhood (Hastings et al., 2000). And shy children may not display sympathetic concern because they are easily overwhelmed by anxiety when others are distressed (Eisenberg et al., 1996).

Individual differences in empathy and sympathy are evident in children's facial and psychophysiological responses. In a series of studies, children watched videotapes of people in need, such as two children lying on the ground crying. Children who reacted with facial or physiological markers of concern—an interested, caring expression or a decrease in heart rate, suggesting orienting and attention—usually behaved prosocially when offered a chance to help. Children who showed facial and physiological evidence of distress—frowning, lip biting, and a rise in heart rate—were less prosocial (Fabes et al., 1994; Miller et al., 1996). Similarly, empathy is related to EEG brain-wave activity—a mild increase in the left hemisphere (which houses positive emotion) among children showing facial signs of empathy, and a sharp increase in the right hemisphere (which houses negative emotion) among children who lack empathy with another's emotional needs (Jones, Field, & Davalos, 2000; Pickens, Field, & Nawrocki, 2001).

Parenting profoundly influences empathy and sympathy. Parents who are warm, who encourage their child's emotional expressiveness, and who show a sensitive, empathic concern for their youngster's feelings have children who are likely to react in a concerned way to the distress of others—relationships that persist into adolescence and emerging adulthood (Eisenberg & McNally, 1993; Koestner, Franz, & Weinberger, 1990; Strayer & Roberts, 2004). Besides modeling sympathy, parents can teach the importance of kindness and can intervene when a child displays inappropriate emotion—parenting behaviors that predict high levels of sympathetic responding in children (Eisenberg, 2003). And parents can provide opportunities for children to show sympathetic concern through charitable giving and community service activities.

In contrast, angry, punitive parenting disrupts empathy and sympathy at an early age. In one study, researchers observed physically abused toddlers at a child-care center. Compared with nonabused agemates, they rarely expressed concern at a peer's unhappiness. Instead, they responded with fear, anger, and physical attacks (Klimes-Dougan & Kistner, 1990). The children's reactions resembled the behavior of their parents, who also responded insensitively to the suffering of others.

These findings, like others discussed so far, reveal wide variations in children's emotional dispositions. As we turn now to the topic of temperament, we will encounter additional evidence for the joint contribution of heredity and environment to these differences. But first, consult the Milestones table on the following page for an overview of the emotional attainments just considered.

Ask Yourself

REVIEW	What do preschoolers understand about emotion, and how do cognition and social experience contribute to their understanding?
REVIEW	Why is good emotional self-regulation vital for empathy to result in sympathy and prosocial behavior?
APPLY	When 15-month-old Ellen fell down while running, her mother smiled and exclaimed, "Oh, wasn't that a funny tumble!" How is Ellen likely to respond emotionally, and why?
CONNECT	Cite ways in which parenting contributes to emotional understanding, self-conscious emotions, empathy, and sympathy. Do you see any patterns? Explain.

MILESTONES

EMOTIONAL DEVELOPMENT

Age	Emotional Expressiveness	Emotional Understanding	
Birth–6 months	Social smile emerges. Laughter appears. Expressions of happiness increase when interacting with familiar people. Emotional expressions gradually become well-organized patterns that are meaningfully related to environmental events.	Detects emotions by matching the caregiver's feeling tone in face-to-face communication	
7–12 months	Anger and fear increase in frequency and intensity. Uses caregiver as a secure base Regulates emotion by approaching and retreating from stimulation	Detects the meaning of others' emotional signals Engages in social referencing	
1–2 years	Self-conscious emotions emerge but depend on the monitoring and encouragement of adults. Begins to use language to assist with emotional self-regulation	Begins to appreciate that others' emotional reactions may differ from one's own Acquires a vocabulary of emotional terms Displays empathy	
3–6 years	Self-conscious emotions are clearly linked to self-evaluation. As representation and language improve, uses active strategies for regulating emotion Begins to conform to emotional display rules; can pose a positive emotion he or she does not feel	Understanding of causes, consequences, and behavioral signs of emotion improves in accuracy and complexity. As language develops, empathy becomes more reflective.	
7–11 years	Self-conscious emotions become integrated with inner standards of excellence and good behavior. Uses internal strategies for engaging in emotional self-regulation; shifts adaptively between problem-centered and emotion-centered coping Conformity to and conscious awareness of emotional display rules improve.	Can consider conflicting cues when explaining others' emotions Is aware that people can have mixed feelings and that their expressions may not reflect their true feelings Empathy increases as emotional understanding improves.	

Note: These milestones represent overall age trends. Individual differences exist in the precise age at which each milestone is attained.

Photos: (left and top right) © Laura Dwight Photography; (lower right) © David Young-Wolff/PhotoEdit

Temperament and Development

When we describe one person as cheerful and upbeat, another as active and energetic, and still others as calm, cautious, persistent, or prone to angry outbursts, we are referring to **temperament**—early-appearing, stable individual differences in reactivity and self-regulation. *Reactivity* refers to variations in quickness and intensity of emotional arousal, attention, and motor action. *Self-regulation,* as we have seen, refers to strategies that modify reactivity (Rothbart, 2004; Rothbart & Bates, 1998). Researchers have become increasingly interested in temperamental variations among children because the psychological traits that make up temperament are believed to form the cornerstone of the adult personality.

In 1956, Alexander Thomas and Stella Chess initiated the New York Longitudinal Study, a groundbreaking investigation of the development of temperament that followed 141 children from early infancy well into adulthood. Results showed that temperament can increase a child's chances of experiencing psychological problems or, alternatively, protect a child from the negative effects of a highly stressful home life. At the same time, Thomas and Chess (1977) discovered that parenting practices can modify children's temperaments considerably.

These findings stimulated a growing body of research on temperament, including its stability, biological roots, and interaction with child-rearing experiences. Let's begin to explore these issues by looking at the structure, or makeup, of temperament and how it is measured.

The Structure of Temperament

Thomas and Chess's nine dimensions, listed in Table 10.1, served as the first influential model of temperament, inspiring all others that followed. When detailed descriptions of infants' and children's behavior obtained from parent interviews were rated on these dimensions, certain characteristics clustered together, yielding three types of children:

- The **easy child** (40 percent of the sample). This child quickly establishes regular routines in infancy, is generally cheerful, and adapts easily to new experiences.
- The **difficult child** (10 percent of the sample). This child has irregular daily routines, is slow to accept new experiences, and tends to react negatively and intensely.
- The **slow-to-warm-up child** (15 percent of the sample). This child is inactive, shows mild, low-key reactions to environmental stimuli, is negative in mood, and adjusts slowly to new experiences.

Note that 35 percent of the children did not fit any of these categories. Instead, they showed unique blends of temperamental characteristics.

Of the three types, the difficult pattern has sparked the most interest because it places children at high risk for adjustment problems—both anxious withdrawal and aggressive behavior in early and middle childhood (Bates, Wachs, & Emde, 1994; Thomas, Chess, & Birch, 1968). Compared with difficult children, slow-to-warm-up children present fewer problems in the early

TABLE 10.1 TWO MODELS OF TEMPERAMENT

Thomas and Chess		Rothbart	
Dimension	**Description**	**Dimension**	**Description**
Activity level	Ratio of active periods to inactive ones	***Reactivity***	
Rhythmicity	Regularity of body functions, such as sleep, wakefulness, hunger, and excretion	Activity level	Level of gross motor activity
Distractibility	Degree to which stimulation from the environment alters behavior—for example, whether crying stops when a toy is offered	Attention span/ persistence	Duration of orienting or interest
		Fearful distress	Wariness and distress in response to intense or novel stimuli, including time to adjust to new situations
Approach/ withdrawal	Response to a new object, food, or person		
Adaptability	Ease with which child adapts to changes in the environment, such as sleeping or eating in a new place	Irritable distress	Extent of fussing, crying, and distress when desires are frustrated
		Positive affect	Frequency of expression of happiness and pleasure
Attention span and persistence	Amount of time devoted to an activity, such as watching a mobile or playing with a toy	***Self-Regulation***	
Intensity of reaction	Energy level of response, such as laughing, crying, talking, or gross motor activity	Effortful control	Capacity to voluntarily suppress a dominant, reactive response in order to plan and execute a more adaptive response
Threshold of responsiveness	Intensity of stimulation required to evoke a response		
Quality of mood	Amount of friendly, joyful behavior as opposed to unpleasant, unfriendly behavior		

Sources: Left: Thomas & Chess, 1977. Right: Rothbart, Ahadi, & Evans, 2000; Rothbart & Mauro, 1990.

years. However, they tend to show excessive fearfulness and slow, constricted behavior in the late preschool and school years, when they are expected to respond actively and quickly in classrooms and peer groups (Chess & Thomas, 1984; Schmitz et al., 1999).

A second model of temperament, devised by Mary Rothbart, is also shown in Table 10.1. It combines overlapping dimensions of Thomas and Chess and other researchers. For example, "distractibility" and "attention span and persistence" are considered opposite ends of the same dimension, which is called "attention span/persistence." This model also includes a dimension not identified by Thomas and Chess, "irritable distress," which permits reactivity triggered by frustration to be distinguished from reactivity due to fear. And it deletes overly broad dimensions, such as "rhythmicity," "intensity of reaction," and "threshold of responsiveness" (Rothbart, Ahadi, & Evans, 2000; Rothbart & Mauro, 1990). A child who is rhythmic in sleeping is not necessarily rhythmic in eating or bowel habits. And a child who smiles and laughs intensely is not necessarily intense in fear, irritability, or motor activity.

Rothbart's dimensions are supported by factor analyses of many measures of children's temperament (see page 315 in Chapter 8 to review the concept of factor analysis). Notice how her dimensions represent the three underlying components included in the definition of temperament: (1) *emotion* ("fearful distress," "irritable distress," and "positive affect"), (2) *attention* ("attention span/persistence"), and (3) *action* ("activity level"). According to Rothbart, individuals differ not only in their reactivity on each dimension, but also in their effortful capacity to manage that reactivity. **Effortful control** is the self-regulatory dimension of temperament; it involves voluntarily suppressing a dominant response in order to plan and execute a more adaptive response (Rothbart, 2003; Rothbart & Bates, 1998). Variations in effortful control are evident in how effectively a child can focus and shift attention, inhibit impulses, and engage in problem solving to manage negative emotion.

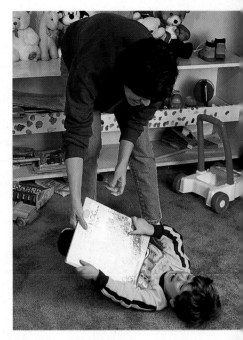

Ⓖ This mother wants her 3-year-old to put his toys away and turn to another activity—perhaps lunchtime or an errand. Transitions seem like crises for this difficult child, who reacts negatively and intensely to disruptions and new experiences.
© B. Daemmrich/The Image Works

Measuring Temperament

Temperament is often assessed through interviews or questionnaires given to parents. Behavior ratings by pediatricians, teachers, and others familiar with the child, as well as laboratory observations by researchers, have also been used. Parental reports are convenient and take advantage of parents' depth of knowledge of the child across many situations (Gartstein & Rothbart, 2003). At the same time, information from parents has been criticized as being biased. For example, parents' prebirth expectations for their infant's temperament affect their later reports (Diener, Goldstein, & Mangelsdorf, 1995). And mothers who are anxious or depressed tend to view their babies as more difficult (Mebert, 1991). Nevertheless, parental reports are moderately related to researchers' observations of children's behavior (Mangelsdorf, Schoppe, & Buur, 2000). And parent perceptions are useful for understanding the way parents view and respond to their child.

Although observations by researchers in the home or laboratory avoid the subjectivity of parental reports, they can lead to other inaccuracies. In homes, observers find it hard to capture all relevant information, especially rare but important events, such as infants' response to frustration. And in the unfamiliar lab setting, distress-prone children who calmly avoid certain experiences at home may become too upset to complete the session if the lab does not permit avoidance (Wachs & Bates, 2001). Still, researchers can better control children's experiences in the lab. And they can conveniently combine observations of behavior with psychophysiological measures to gain insight into the biological bases of temperament.

In a recent series of studies, investigators found that a spatial-conflict task, similar to tasks given to adults, can be used to measure effortful control as early as 2½ to 3 years of age. As Figure 10.3 on page 414 shows, the child watched a computer screen showing a house on the left and a house on the right, each of which contained a cartoon character. On each trial, a picture of one of the characters appeared, sometimes directly above the correct house (a spatially compatible trial) and at other times directly above the incorrect house (a spatially incompatible trial). The child had to help the character find its home by touching the matching house—a response that, on incompatible trials, required suppression of the strong impulse to reach to the same side as the stimulus picture. Children's performance was positively related to other measures of effortful control, including waiting to eat a tasty snack and parent-rated skill at

▲ Figure 10.3

Spatial-conflict task used to measure effortful control in preschoolers. On *spatially compatible trials,* a matching cartoon character appears directly above the correct house, and the child must help it find its home by touching the house on the same side of the screen—a relatively easy task for young preschoolers. On *spatially incompatible trials,* such as the example shown above, the matching character appears above the incorrect house. The child must suppress the strong impulse to reach toward the same side of the screen, substituting a reach to the opposite side. Reconciling such competing tendencies is central to effortful control. (Adapted from Rothbart et al., 2003.)

inhibiting impulses and coping with frustration (Gerardi-Caulton, 2000; Rothbart et al., 2003). fMRI research indicates that in adults, such conflict tasks activate specific areas of the frontal lobes involved in resolving opposing tendencies between many parts of the brain (Botvinick et al., 2001). Investigators speculate that reconciling competing tendencies is central to effortful control. Gains in performance on spatial-conflict tasks in the third year of life may mark the early development of these neural networks.

Most psychophysiological research has focused on two types of children, who fall at opposite extremes of the positive-affect and fearful-distress dimensions of temperament (refer again to Table 10.1): **inhibited, or shy, children,** who react negatively to and withdraw from novel stimuli, and **uninhibited, or sociable, children,** who display positive emotion to and approach novel stimuli. As the Biology and Environment box on the following page reveals, biologically based reactivity, evident in heart rate, hormone levels, and EEG brain waves in the frontal region of the cerebral cortex, differentiate children with inhibited and uninhibited temperaments. Nevertheless, parenting practices are crucially important in whether an inhibited style is sustained over time.

Stability of Temperament

Many studies indicate that young children who score low or high on attention span, irritability, sociability, shyness, or effortful control tend to respond similarly when assessed again several months to a few years later and, occasionally, even into the adult years (Caspi et al., 2003; Kochanska & Knack, 2003; Pedlow et al., 1993; Rothbart, Ahadi, & Evans, 2000; Ruff & Rothbart, 1996). However, the overall stability of temperament is low to moderate (Putnam, Samson, & Rothbart, 2000). Although some children remain the same, many others change.

A major reason is that temperament itself develops with age. To illustrate, let's look at irritability and activity level. Recall from Chapter 4 that the early months are a period of fussing and crying for most babies. As infants better regulate their attention and emotions, many who seemed irritable become calm and content. In the case of activity level, the meaning of the behavior changes. At first, an active, wriggling infant tends to be highly aroused and uncomfortable, whereas an inactive baby is often alert and attentive. But as infants move on their own, the reverse is so! An active crawler is usually alert and interested in exploration, whereas a very inactive baby may be fearful and withdrawn.

These inconsistencies help us understand why long-term predictions about early temperament are most accurately made after the second year of life, when biologically based styles of responding are better established (Caspi, 1998; Lemery et al., 1999). In line with this idea, earlier we discussed evidence indicating that neurological supports for effortful control strengthen between ages 2½ and 3. Longitudinal research reveals that during the third year, children show increasing consistency in performance across a wide variety of effortful-control tasks—for example, waiting to open a present, selectively attending to a stimulus while ignoring competing stimuli, and lowering their voice to a whisper. Furthermore, preschoolers who were high in fearful reactivity as 2-year-olds tended to score slightly better than their agemates in effortful control as 4-year-olds. In contrast, angry, irritable 2-year-olds were less effective at effortful control at later ages (Kochanska, Murray, & Harlan, 2000; Kochanska & Knaack, 2003). The efficiency of children's attempts to manage their emotionality, and thereby alter their reactivity in early childhood, depend on the type and strength of the reactive emotion involved.

In sum, many factors affect the extent to which a child's temperament remains stable, including development of the biological systems on which temperament is based, the child's capacity for effortful control, and the success of her efforts, which depend on the quality and intensity of her emotional reactivity. When we consider the evidence as a whole, the low to moderate stability of temperament makes sense. It also confirms that experience can modify biologically based temperamental traits substantially, although children rarely change from one extreme to another—that is, a shy preschooler practically never becomes highly sociable. With these ideas in mind, let's turn to genetic and environmental contributions to temperament and personality.

Development of Shyness and Sociability

Two 4-month-old babies, Larry and Mitch, visited the laboratory of Jerome Kagan, who observed their reactions to various unfamiliar experiences. When exposed to new sights and sounds, such as a moving mobile decorated with colorful toys, Larry tensed his muscles, moved his arms and legs with agitation, and began to cry. In contrast, Mitch remained relaxed and quiet, smiling and cooing with apparent pleasure.

As toddlers, Larry and Mitch returned to the laboratory, where they experienced procedures designed to induce uncertainty. Electrodes were placed on their bodies and blood pressure cuffs on their arms to measure heart rate; toy robots, animals, and puppets moved before their eyes; and unfamiliar people behaved in atypical ways or wore novel costumes. While Larry whimpered and quickly withdrew, Mitch watched with interest, laughed, and approached the toys and strangers.

On a third visit, at age 4 1/2, Larry barely talked or smiled during an interview with an unfamiliar adult, whereas Mitch asked questions and communicated his pleasure. In a playroom with two unfamiliar peers, Larry pulled back and watched, while Mitch made friends quickly.

In longitudinal research on several hundred Caucasian children, Kagan (1998) found that about 20 percent of 4-month-old babies were (like Larry) easily upset by novelty; 40 percent (like Mitch) were comfortable, even delighted, with new experiences. In about 20 to 30 percent of these extreme groups, temperamental style persisted: Those resembling Larry tended to become fearful, inhibited toddlers and preschoolers; those resembling Mitch developed into outgoing, uninhibited youngsters (Kagan, 2003; Kagan & Saudino, 2001). But most children modified their dispositions, becoming less extreme over time. Biological makeup and child-rearing experiences jointly influenced both stability and change in temperamental style.

Physiological Correlates of Shyness and Sociability

Kagan believes that individual differences in arousal of the *amygdala,* an inner brain structure that controls avoidance reactions, contribute to these contrasting temperaments. In shy, inhibited children, novel stimuli easily excite the amygdala and its connections to the cerebral cortex and the sympathetic nerv-

ous system, which prepares the body to act in the face of threat. In sociable, uninhibited children, the same level of stimulation evokes minimal neural excitation. In support of this theory, while viewing photos of unfamiliar faces, adults who had been classified as inhibited in the second year of life showed greater fMRI activity in the amygdala than adults who had been uninhibited as toddlers (Schwartz et al., 2003). And the two emotional styles are distinguished by additional physiological responses, mediated by the amygdala:

- *Heart rate.* From the first few weeks of life, the heart rates of shy children are consistently higher than those of sociable children, and they speed up further in response to unfamiliar events (Snidman et al., 1995).
- *Cortisol.* Saliva concentration of the stress hormone cortisol tends to be higher in shy than in sociable children (Gunnar & Nelson, 1994; Kagan & Snidman, 1991).
- *Pupil dilation, blood pressure, and skin surface temperature.* Compared with sociable children, shy children show greater pupil dilation, rise in blood pressure, and cooling of the fingertips when faced with novelty (Kagan et al., 1999).

Another physiological correlate of approach–withdrawal to people and objects is the pattern of brain waves in the right and left frontal lobes of the cerebral cortex. Shy infants and preschoolers show greater EEG activity in the right frontal lobe, which is associated with negative emotional reactivity; sociable children show the opposite pattern (Calkins, Fox, & Marshall, 1996). Neural activity in the amygdala is transmitted to the cerebral cortex and probably contributes to these differences. Inhibited children also show greater, generalized activation of the cerebral cortex, an indicator of high emotional arousal and close monitoring of new situations for potential threats (Henderson et al., 2004).

Child-Rearing Practices

According to Kagan (1998), extremely shy and extremely sociable children inherit a physiology that biases them toward a particular temperamental style. Yet heritability research indicates that genes contribute only modestly to shyness and sociability. Experience, too, has a powerful impact.

Child-rearing practices affect the chances that an emotionally reactive baby will become a fearful child. Warm, supportive parenting reduces shy infants' and preschoolers' intense physiological reaction to novelty; cold, intrusive parenting heightens anxiety and social reserve (Rubin, Burgess, & Hastings, 2002). When parents protect infants and toddlers who dislike novelty from minor stresses, they make it harder for the child to overcome an urge to retreat from unfamiliar events. Parents who make appropriate demands for their baby to approach new experiences help the child overcome fear (Rubin et al., 1997).

When early inhibition persists, it leads to excessive cautiousness, social withdrawal, low self-esteem, and loneliness (Fordham & Stevenson-Hinde, 1999; Rubin, Stewart, & Coplan, 1995). Persistent shyness increases the risk of severe anxiety problems in adolescence, especially social phobia—intense fear of being humiliated in social situations (Prior et al., 2000; Schwartz, Snidman, & Kagan, 1999). For inhibited children to gain control over their reticence and develop effective social skills and rewarding relationships, parenting must be tailored to their temperament—a theme we will encounter again in this and later chapters.

▶ A strong physiological response to uncertain situations prompts this child to cling to her father. His patient but insistent encouragement can modify her physiological reactivity and help her overcome her urge to retreat from unfamiliar events.
© Laura Dwight Photography

Genetic and Environmental Influences

The word *temperament* implies a genetic foundation for individual differences in personality. Research indicates that identical twins are more similar then fraternal twins across a wide range of temperamental traits (activity level, shyness/sociability, irritability, attention span, and persistence) and personality measures (introversion/extroversion, anxiety, agreeableness, and impulsivity) (Caspi, 1998; DiLalla, Kagan, & Reznick, 1994; Emde et al., 1992; Goldsmith et al., 1999; Saudino & Cherny, 2001). In Chapter 3, we noted that heritability estimates derived from kinship studies suggest a moderate role for genetic factors in temperament and personality: On average, about half of individual differences have been attributed to differences in genetic makeup (Rothbart & Bates, 1998).

Nevertheless, genetic influences vary with the temperamental trait and the age of the individual being studied. For example, heritability estimates are much higher for expressions of negative emotion than for positive emotion. And the role of heredity is considerably less in infancy than in childhood and later years, when temperament becomes more stable (Wachs & Bates, 2001).

Although genetic influences on temperament are clear, environment is also powerful. For example, persistent nutritional and emotional deprivation profoundly alters temperament, resulting in maladaptive emotional reactivity (Wachs & Bates, 2001). Recall from Chapter 5 that even after dietary improvement, children exposed to severe malnutrition in infancy remain more distractible and fearful than their agemates. And earlier in this chapter, we noted that children who spent their infancy in deprived orphanages are easily overwhelmed by stress. Their poor regulation of emotion results in inattention and weak impulse control, including frequent expressions of anger (see page 397).

Other research shows that child rearing has much to do with whether or not infants and young children maintain their temperamental traits. In fact, heredity and environment often jointly contribute to temperament, since a child's approach to the world affects the experiences to which she is exposed. To see how this works, let's look closely at ethnic differences in temperament.

• **CULTURAL VARIATIONS** • Compared with North American Caucasian infants, Chinese and Japanese babies tend to be less active, irritable, and vocal, more easily soothed when upset, and better at quieting themselves (Kagan et al., 1994; Lewis, Ramsay, & Kawakami, 1993). And some Asian infants are more emotionally restrained. Chinese 1-year-olds, for example, smile and cry less than Caucasian-American babies (Camras et al., 1998).

These variations may have genetic roots, but they are supported by cultural beliefs and practices. Japanese mothers usually say that babies come into the world as independent beings who must learn to rely on their mothers through close physical contact. North American mothers typically believe just the opposite—that they must wean the baby away from dependency into autonomy. Consistent with these beliefs, Asian mothers interact gently and soothingly, relying heavily on gestures, whereas Caucasian mothers use a more active, stimulating, verbal approach (Rothbaum et al., 2000b). Also, recall from our discussion of emotional self-regulation that Chinese and Japanese adults discourage babies from expressing strong emotion, which contributes further to their infants' tranquility. These differences in child rearing enhance early ethnic variations in temperament.

⊚ At birth, Chinese infants are calmer, more easily soothed when upset, and better at quieting themselves than are Caucasian infants. Although these differences may have biological roots, cultural variations in child rearing support them.
© George F. Mobley/National Geographic Image Collection

• **NONSHARED ENVIRONMENT** • In families with several children, an additional influence on temperament is at work. Recall from Chapter 8 that *nonshared environmental influences*—those that make siblings different from one another—play an important role in intelligence. They are influential in personality development as well. Listen to the comments parents make, and you will see that they often look for personality differences: "She's a lot more active." "He's more sociable." "She's far more persistent." As a result, parents often regard siblings as more distinct than other observers do. In a large study of 1- to 3-year-old twin pairs, parents rated identical twins as resembling each other less in temperament than indicated by researchers' ratings. And whereas researchers rated fraternal twins as moderately similar, parents viewed them as somewhat opposing in temperamental style (see Figure 10.4) (Saudino, 2003).

Parents' tendency to emphasize each child's unique qualities affects their child-rearing practices. In a study of 3-year-old identical twins, mothers treated each pair member differently, and this differential treatment predicted twin differences in psychological adjustment. The twin who received more warmth and less punitive parenting was more positive in mood and prosocial behavior and lower in behavior problems (Deater-Deckard et al., 2001). Each child, in turn, evokes responses from caregivers that are consistent with parental beliefs and the child's developing temperament.

Besides different experiences within the family, siblings have distinct experiences with peers, teachers, and others in their community that affect personality development (Caspi, 1998). And as they get older, siblings often actively seek ways to differ from one another. For all these reasons, both identical and fraternal twins tend to become increasingly dissimilar in personality with age (McCartney, Harris, & Bernieri, 1990). The less contact twins have with one another, the stronger this effect.

Are nonshared factors more important in personality development than *shared environmental influences*—those that affect all siblings similarly? In Chapter 14, we will see that shared factors, such as family stress and child-rearing styles, also affect children's personalities. In sum, we must think of temperament and personality as affected by a complex mix of environmental conditions, some child-specific and others stemming from shared family conditions.

Temperament as a Predictor of Children's Behavior

Research on temperament provides a powerful illustration of the child's contribution to his or her own development. Children's temperamental traits consistently predict their cognitive and social functioning.

Almost as soon as it can be measured, children's attention span forecasts their learning and cognitive development. For example, persistence during the first year correlates with infant mental test scores and preschool IQ (Matheny, 1989). During early and middle childhood, persistence continues to predict IQ, along with literacy and mathematical progress and grades in school. In contrast, distractibility, high activity level, and difficult temperament are linked to poor school performance (Coplan, Barber, & Lagacé-Séguin, 1999; Martin, Olejnik, & Gaddis, 1994; Strelau, Zawadzki, & Piotrowska, 2001).

Temperament is also related to social behavior. Highly active preschoolers are very sociable with peers, but they also become involved in more conflict than their less active agemates. Shy, inhibited children often watch classmates and engage in anxious behaviors that discourage interaction, such as hovering around play activities and rarely speaking (Henderson et al., 2004). And as we will see in Chapter 12, inhibited children's high anxiety leads to more discomfort after wrongdoing and a greater sense of responsibility to others. As a result, early fearfulness protects children against the development of aggression. In contrast, irritable, impulsive children are at risk for aggressive and antisocial conduct (Sanson, Hemphill, & Smart, 2004).

In some cases, as with shy children, social behavior seems to be a direct result of temperament. In other instances, it is due to the way people respond to the child's emotional style (Seifer, 2000). For example, active and impulsive children often are targets of negative interaction, which leads to conflict. As Chapter 12 will make clear, the link between early impulsivity and later lawbreaking and aggressive acts has much to do with the inept parenting that distractible, headstrong children often evoke.

Finally, children's capacity for effortful control—their ability to restrain negative emotion and impulsive action—is linked to diverse aspects of competence. These include cooperation, moral maturity (such as concern about wrongdoing and willingness to apologize), empathy, sympathy, and prosocial behaviors of sharing and helpfulness (Eisenberg et al., 2004; Kochanska & Knaack, 2003). As we will see next, parenting practices can impede or promote children's effortful control, thereby profoundly altering the link between early temperament and development.

Temperament and Child Rearing: The Goodness-of-Fit Model

Thomas and Chess (1977) proposed a **goodness-of-fit model** to describe how temperament and environmental pressures can together produce favorable outcomes. Goodness of fit involves creating child-rearing environments that recognize each child's temperament while encouraging more adaptive functioning. If a child's disposition interferes with learning or getting along with others, adults must gently but consistently counteract the child's maladaptive style.

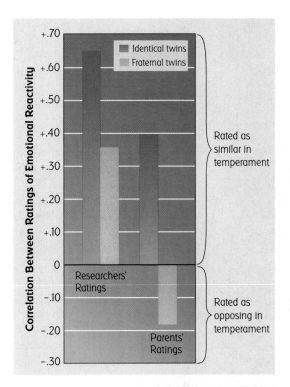

▲ **Figure 10.4**

Temperament correlations for identical and fraternal twin pairs, as rated by researchers and parents. In a study of over two hundred 1- to 3-year-old twin pairs, parents rated identical twins as resembling each other less in temperament than indicated by researchers' ratings. And whereas researchers rated fraternal twins as moderately similar, parents rated them as somewhat opposing in temperament, yielding the negative correlation shown above. The correlations depicted here are for emotional reactivity. Activity level, shyness, and attention span/persistence yielded a similar pattern of correlations, confirming that parents often emphasize personality differences between their children. (Adapted from Saudino, 2003.)

This mother's soothing presence helps her child regulate intense emotional reactions. The good fit that exists between parenting and child temperament will gradually result in more adaptive child behavior and prevent adjustment problems.

© David Young-Wolff/PhotoEdit

Goodness of fit helps explain why difficult children (who withdraw from new experiences and react negatively and intensely) are at high risk for later adjustment problems. These children frequently experience parenting that fits poorly with their dispositions. As infants, they are less likely to receive sensitive caregiving (van den Boom & Hoeksma, 1994). By the second year, parents of difficult children often resort to angry, punitive discipline, which undermines the development of effortful control. As the child reacts with defiance and disobedience, parents become increasingly stressed (Coplan, Bowker, & Cooper, 2003). As a result, they continue their coercive tactics and also discipline inconsistently, at times rewarding the child's noncompliance by giving in to it (Calkins, 2002). A bidirectional relationship emerges between child difficultness and negative parenting that sustains and even promotes the child's irritable, conflict-ridden style. When parents manage to break this cycle by being positive and involved and engaging in sensitive, face-to-face play that helps babies regulate emotion, difficultness declines by age 2 (Feldman, Greenbaum, & Yirmiya, 1999).

Effective parenting, however, depends on life conditions. In a comparison of the temperaments of Russian and American babies, Russian infants were more emotionally negative, fearful, and upset when frustrated (Gartstein, Slobodskaya, & Kinsht, 2003). Faced with a depressed national economy, which resulted in longer work hours and increased stress, Russian parents may have lacked time and energy to engage in the sensitive, coordinated interaction with their babies that protects against difficultness.

Cultural values also affect the fit between parenting and child temperament. Previous research revealed that a collectivist orientation, which discourages self-assertion, led Chinese adults to evaluate shy, withdrawn children positively, as advanced in social maturity. Consistent with this view, several studies reported that compared with North American parents, Chinese parents were more accepting and encouraging and less punitive toward inhibited children. Consequently, shy Chinese youngsters of a decade or two ago appeared well adjusted, academically and socially (Chen, Rubin, & Li, 1995; Chen et al., 1998).

But rapid expansion of a competitive market economy in China, in which success depends on self-assertion and sociability, may be responsible for a recent change in Chinese parents' and teachers' attitudes toward childhood shyness (Xu & Peng, 2001; Yu, 2002). In an investigation of fourth graders in Shanghai, the direction of the association between shyness and adjustment changed over time. Whereas shyness was positively correlated with teacher-rated competence, peer acceptance, leadership, and academic achievement in 1990, these relationships weakened in 1998 and reversed in 2002, when they mirrored findings of Western research (see Figure 10.5) (Chen et al., 2005). Thus, cultural context makes a difference in whether shy children receive support or disapproval, and whether they adjust well or display emotional and social problems.

An effective match between rearing conditions and child temperament is best accomplished early, before unfavorable temperament–environment relationships produce maladjustment. Both difficult and shy children benefit from warm, accepting parenting that makes firm but reasonable demands for mastering new experiences. In the case of reserved, inactive toddlers, highly stimulating maternal behavior (questioning, instructing, and pointing out objects) fosters exploration. Yet these same parental behaviors have a negative impact on active babies, dampening their curiosity (Gandour, 1989; Miceli et al., 1998).

The goodness-of-fit model reminds us that infants come into the world with unique dispositions that adults have to accept. Parents can neither take full credit for their children's virtues nor

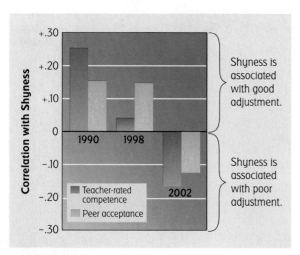

◀ **Figure 10.5**

Changes over time in correlations between shyness and adjustment among Chinese fourth graders. Shy Chinese children of a decade or two ago appeared competent and well adjusted. But as China's market economy expanded and valuing of self-assertion and sociability increased, the direction of the correlations shifted. In 2002, shyness was negatively associated with adjustment, mirroring findings of Western research. The correlations depicted here are for teacher-rated competence and peer acceptance. Those for leadership (holding offices in student organizations) and academic achievement underwent a similar pattern of change. (Adapted from Chen et al., 2005.)

be blamed for all their faults. But parents can transform an environment that exaggerates a child's problems into one that builds on the youngster's strengths. In the following sections, we will see that goodness of fit is also at the heart of infant–caregiver attachment. This first intimate relationship grows out of interaction between parent and baby, to which the emotional styles of both partners contribute.

Ask Yourself

REVIEW	How do genetic and environmental factors work together to influence a child's temperament? Cite examples from research on nonshared environmental influences, cultural variations in temperament, and goodness of fit.
APPLY	Mandy and Jeff are parents of 2-year-old inhibited Sam and 3-year-old difficult Maria. Explain the importance of effortful control to Mandy and Jeff, and suggest ways they can strengthen it in each of their children.
CONNECT	Compared with their agemates, shy, inhibited 2-year-olds are less likely to respond with sympathetic, prosocial behavior to an unfamiliar peer in distress (Young, Fox, & Zahn-Waxler, 1999). Using the distinction between empathy and sympathy on page 409, explain why.
REFLECT	How would you describe your temperament as a young child? What type of parenting fits well with that temperament?

Development of Attachment

Attachment is the strong, affectionate tie we have with special people in our lives that leads us to feel pleasure when we interact with them and to be comforted by their nearness during times of stress. By the second half of the first year, infants have become attached to familiar people who have responded to their needs. Watch how babies of this age single out their parents for special attention. When the mother enters the room, the baby breaks into a broad, friendly smile. When she picks him up, he pats her face, explores her hair, and snuggles against her body. When he feels anxious, he crawls into her lap and clings closely.

Freud first suggested that the infant's emotional tie to the mother provides the foundation for all later relationships. Although Freud was correct that the quality of the infant–parent bond is vitally important, contemporary research indicates that his ideas merit revision: The contribution of attachment to long-term development depends not just on the infant's early experiences but also on the ongoing parent–child relationship.

Attachment has also been the subject of intense theoretical debate. Recall from Chapter 1 how the *psychoanalytic perspective* regards feeding as the central context in which caregivers and babies build this close emotional bond. *Behaviorism*, too, emphasizes the importance of feeding, but for different reasons. According to a well-known behaviorist explanation, as the caregiver satisfies the baby's hunger (primary drive), the infant learns to prefer her soft caresses, warm smiles, and tender words of comfort (secondary drive) because these events have been paired with tension relief.

Although feeding is an important context in which mothers and babies build a close relationship, attachment does not depend on hunger satisfaction. In the 1950s, a famous experiment showed that rhesus monkeys reared with terry-cloth and wire-mesh "surrogate mothers" clung to the soft terry-cloth substitute, even though the wire-mesh "mother" held the bottle and infants had to climb on it to be fed (Harlow & Zimmerman, 1959). Similarly, human infants become attached to family members who seldom feed them, including fathers, siblings, and grandparents. And you may have noticed that toddlers in Western cultures who sleep alone and experience frequent daytime separations from their parents sometimes develop strong emotional ties to cuddly objects, such as blankets or teddy bears. Yet such objects have never played a role in infant feeding!

Another problem with psychoanalytic and behaviorist accounts of attachment is that the emphasis is mainly on the caregiver's contribution to the attachment relationship. Little attention is given to the importance of the infant's characteristics.

Baby monkeys reared with "surrogate mothers" from birth preferred to cling to a soft terry-cloth "mother" instead of a wire-mesh "mother" that held a bottle. These findings reveal that the drive-reduction explanation of attachment, which assumes that the mother–infant relationship is based on feeding, is incorrect.
© Martin Rogers/Stock Boston, LLC

Bowlby's Ethological Theory

Today, **ethological theory of attachment,** which recognizes the infant's emotional tie to the caregiver as an evolved response that promotes survival, is the most widely accepted view.

John Bowlby (1969), who first applied this idea to the infant–caregiver bond, was originally a psychoanalyst. In his theory, he retained the psychoanalytic idea that quality of attachment to the caregiver has profound implications for the child's feelings of security and capacity to form trusting relationships.

At the same time, Bowlby was inspired by Konrad Lorenz's studies of imprinting (see Chapter 1). He believed that the human infant, like the young of other animal species, is endowed with a set of built-in behaviors that keep the parent nearby to protect the infant from danger and to provide support for exploring and mastering the environment (Waters & Cummings, 2000). Contact with the parent also ensures that the baby will be fed, but Bowlby pointed out that feeding is not the basis for attachment. Rather, the attachment bond has strong biological roots. It can best be understood in an evolutionary context in which survival of the species—through guaranteeing both safety and competence—is of utmost importance.

According to Bowlby, the infant's relationship with the parent begins as a set of innate signals that call the adult to the baby's side. Over time, a true affectionate bond develops, supported by new emotional and cognitive capacities as well as by a history of warm, sensitive care. Attachment develops in four phases:

ⓢ Although separation anxiety increases between 6 and 15 months of age, its occurrence depends on infant temperament, context, and adult behavior. This child shows distress as his mother says good-bye, but because his caregiver is supportive and sensitive, his anxiety will probably be short-lived.
© David Young-Wolff/PhotoEdit

1. *Preattachment phase* (birth to 6 weeks). Built-in signals—grasping, smiling, crying, and gazing into the adult's eyes—help bring newborn babies into close contact with other humans. Once an adult responds, infants encourage her to remain nearby because closeness comforts them. Babies of this age recognize their own mother's smell and voice, and they will soon recognize her face (see Chapter 4). However, they are not yet attached to her, since they do not mind being left with an unfamiliar adult.

2. *"Attachment-in-the-making" phase* (6 weeks to 6–8 months). During this phase, infants respond differently to a familiar caregiver than to a stranger. For example, the baby smiles, laughs, and babbles more freely with the mother and quiets more quickly when she picks him up. As infants interact with the parent and experience relief from distress, they learn that their own actions affect the behavior of those around them. Babies now begin to develop a *sense of trust*—the expectation that the caregiver will respond when signaled—but they still do not protest when separated from her.

3. *"Clear-cut" attachment phase* (6–8 months to 18 months–2 years). Now attachment to the familiar caregiver is evident. Babies display **separation anxiety**—they become upset when the adult on whom they have come to rely leaves. Separation anxiety does not always occur; like stranger anxiety (see page 401), it depends on infant temperament and on the current situation. But in many cultures, it increases between 6 and 15 months (see Figure 10.6). Its appearance suggests that infants have a clear understanding that the caregiver continues to exist when not in view. Consistent with this idea, babies who have not yet mastered Piagetian object permanence (see Chapter 6) usually do not become anxious when separated from their mothers (Lester et al., 1974).

    Besides protesting the parent's departure, older infants and toddlers try hard to maintain her presence. They approach, follow, and climb on her in preference to others. And, as indicated earlier in this chapter, they use her as a *secure base* from which to explore.

4. *Formation of a reciprocal relationship* (18 months–2 years and on). By the end of the second year, rapid growth in representation and language permits toddlers to understand some of the factors that influence the parent's coming and going and to predict her return. As a result, separation protest declines. Now children start to negotiate with the caregiver, using requests and persuasion to alter her goals. For example, one 2-year-old asked her parents to read a story before leaving her with a baby-sitter. The extra time with her parents, along with a better understanding of where they were going ("to have dinner with Uncle Charlie") and when they would be back ("right after you go to sleep"), helped this child withstand her parents' absence.

With age, children depend less on the physical proximity of caregivers and more on a sense of confidence that they will be accessible and responsive in times of need. According to Bowlby

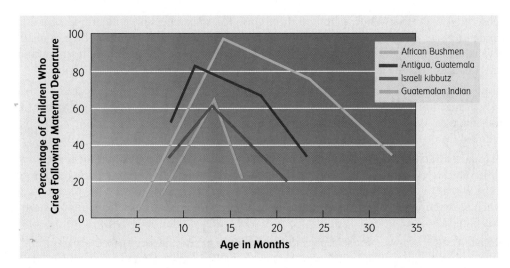

◀ **Figure 10.6**

Development of separation anxiety. In cultures around the world, separation anxiety emerges in the second half of the first year, increases until about 15 months, and then declines. (From J. Kagan, R. B. Kearsley, & P. R. Zelazo, 1978, *Infancy: Its Place in Human Development*, Cambridge, MA: Harvard University Press, p. 107. Copyright 1978 by the President and Fellows of Harvard College. All rights reserved. Reprinted by permission.)

(1980), out of their experiences during these four phases, children construct an enduring affectionate tie that they use as a secure base in the parents' absence. This image serves as an **internal working model,** or set of expectations about the availability of attachment figures, their likelihood of providing support during times of stress, and the self's interaction with those figures. The internal working model becomes a vital part of personality, serving as a guide for all future close relationships (Bretherton & Munholland, 1999). With age, children constantly "update"—or revise and expand—the internal working model as their cognitive, emotional, and social capacities increase, as they interact further with parents, and as they form other close bonds with adults, siblings, and friends.

Measuring the Security of Attachment

Although virtually all family-reared babies become attached to a familiar caregiver by the second year, the quality of this relationship differs from child to child. Some infants appear secure in the presence of the caregiver; they know they can count on her for protection and support. Others seem anxious and uncertain.

A widely used laboratory technique for measuring the quality of attachment between 1 and 2 years of age is the **Strange Situation.** In designing it, Mary Ainsworth and her colleagues (1978) reasoned that if the development of attachment has gone well, infants and toddlers should use the parent as a secure base from which to explore an unfamiliar playroom. In addition, when the parent leaves, an unfamiliar adult should be less comforting than the parent. The Strange Situation takes the baby through eight short episodes in which brief separations from and reunions with the parent occur (see Table 10.2).

TABLE 10.2 EPISODES IN THE STRANGE SITUATION

Episode	Events	Attachment Behavior Observed
1	Experimenter introduces parent and baby to playroom and then leaves.	
2	Parent is seated while baby plays with toys.	Parent as a secure base
3	Stranger enters, is seated, and talks to parent.	Reaction to unfamiliar adult
4	Parent leaves room. Stranger responds to baby and offers comfort if baby is upset.	Separation anxiety
5	Parent returns, greets baby, and offers comfort if necessary. Stranger leaves room.	Reaction to reunion
6	Parent leaves room.	Separation anxiety
7	Stranger enters room and offers comfort.	Ability to be soothed by stranger
8	Parent returns, greets baby, offers comfort if necessary, and tries to reinterest baby in toys.	Reaction to reunion

Note: Episode 1 lasts about 30 seconds; each of the remaining episodes lasts about 3 minutes. Separation episodes are cut short if the baby becomes very upset. Reunion episodes are extended if the baby needs more time to calm down and return to play.

Source: Ainsworth et al., 1978.

Observing the responses of infants to these episodes, researchers have identified a secure attachment pattern and three patterns of insecurity; a few babies cannot be classified (Ainsworth et al., 1978; Barnett & Vondra, 1999; Main & Solomon, 1990). Although separation anxiety varies among the groups, the baby's reunion responses define attachment quality.

- **Secure attachment.** These infants use the parent as a secure base. When separated, they may or may not cry, but if they do, it is because the parent is absent and they prefer her to the stranger. When the parent returns, they actively seek contact, and their crying is reduced immediately. About 65 percent of North American infants show this pattern.

- **Avoidant attachment.** These infants seem unresponsive to the parent when she is present. When she leaves, they usually are not distressed, and they react to the stranger in much the same way as to the parent. During reunion, they avoid or are slow to greet the parent, and when picked up, they often fail to cling. About 20 percent of North American infants show this pattern.

- **Resistant attachment.** Before separation, these infants seek closeness to the parent and often fail to explore. When she leaves, they are usually distressed, and on her return, they mix clinginess with angry, resistive behavior, struggling when held and sometimes hitting and pushing. In addition, many continue to cry and cling after being picked up and cannot be comforted easily. About 10 to 15 percent of North American infants show this pattern.

- **Disorganized/disoriented attachment.** This pattern reflects the greatest insecurity. At reunion, these infants show confused, contradictory behaviors. They might look away while being held by the parent or approach her with flat, depressed emotion. Most communicate their disorientation with a dazed facial expression. A few cry out after having calmed down or display odd, frozen postures. About 5 to 10 percent of North American infants show this pattern.

Infants' reactions in the Strange Situation closely resemble their use of the parent as a secure base and their response to separation and reunion at home (Blanchard & Main, 1979; Pederson & Moran, 1996). For this reason, the procedure is a powerful tool for assessing attachment security.

The **Attachment Q-Sort** is an alternative method, suitable for children between 1 and 4 years of age, that permits attachment to be assessed through observations in the home (Waters et al., 1995). An observer (the parent or a highly trained informant) sorts a set of 90 descriptors of child behavior—such as "Child greets mother with a big smile when she enters the room," "If mother moves very far, child follows along," and "Child uses mother's facial expressions as a good source of information"—into nine categories, ranging from highly descriptive to not at all descriptive of the child. Then a score is computed that indicates where the child falls along a continuum ranging from high to low security. Because the Q-Sort taps a wider array of attachment-related behaviors than the Strange Situation, it may better reflect the parent–infant relationship in everyday life.

The Q-sort method is time consuming, requiring a nonparent informant to spend several hours observing the child before sorting the descriptors, and it does not differentiate between types of insecurity. But the Q-Sort responses of expert observers correspond well with infants' secure-base behavior in the Strange Situation. Parents' Q-Sort judgments, however, show little relationship with Strange Situation assessments (van IJzendoorn et al., 2004). Parents of insecure children, especially, may lack skills for accurately reporting their child's attachment behaviors.

Stability of Attachment

Research on the stability of attachment patterns between 1 and 2 years of age yields a wide range of findings. In some studies, as many as 70 to 90 percent of babies remain the same in their reactions to parents; in others, only 30 to 40 percent do (Thompson, 1998, 2000). A close look at which babies stay the same and which ones change yields a more consistent picture. Quality of attachment is usually secure and stable for middle-SES babies experiencing favorable life conditions. And infants who move from insecurity to security typically have well-adjusted mothers with positive family and friendship ties. Perhaps many became parents before they were psychologically ready but, with social support, grew into the role. In contrast, in low-SES families with many daily stresses, little social support, and parental psychological problems, attachment status generally moves away from security or changes from one insecure pattern to another (Belsky et al., 1996; Vondra, Hommerding, & Shaw, 1999; Vondra et al., 2001).

These findings indicate that securely attached babies more often maintain their attachment status than insecure babies, whose relationship with the caregiver is, by definition, fragile and uncertain. The exception to this trend is disorganized/disoriented attachment—an insecure pattern that is as stable as attachment security, with nearly 70 percent retaining this classification over the second year (Barnett, Ganiban, & Cicchetti, 1999; Hesse & Main, 2000). As you will see, many disorganized/disoriented infants experience extremely negative caregiving, which may disrupt emotional self-regulation so severely that the baby's confused behavior persists.

Overall, many children show short-term instability in attachment quality. A few studies reveal high long-term stability from infancy to middle childhood and—on the basis of interviews about relationships with parents—into adolescence and emerging adulthood (Hamilton, 2000; Waters et al., 2000). But once again, participants came from middle-SES homes, and most probably had stable family lives. In one poverty-stricken sample, many participants moved from secure attachment in infancy to insecure attachment in emerging adulthood. Child maltreatment, maternal depression, and poor family functioning in early adolescence distinguished these young people from the few who stayed securely attached. Disorganized/disoriented participants, however, typically remained insecure over the long term, expressing confused, ambivalent feelings toward their parents, many of whom had been abusive (Weinfield, Whaley, & Egeland, 2004; Weinfield, Sroufe, & Egeland, 2000).

Cultural Variations

Cross-cultural evidence indicates that attachment patterns may have to be interpreted differently in certain cultures. For example, as Figure 10.7 reveals, German infants show considerably more avoidant attachment than American babies do. But German parents encourage their infants to be nonclingy and independent, so the baby's behavior may be an intended outcome of cultural beliefs and practices (Grossmann et al., 1985). In contrast, a study of infants of the Dogon people of Mali, Africa, revealed that none showed avoidant attachment to their mothers (True, Pisani, & Oumar, 2001). Even when grandmothers are primary caregivers (as is the case with first-born sons), Dogon mothers remain available to their babies, holding them close and nursing them promptly in response to hunger and distress.

Japanese infants, as well, rarely show avoidant attachment (refer again to Figure 10.7). An unusually high number are resistantly attached, but this reaction may not represent true insecurity. Japanese mothers rarely leave their babies in others' care, so the Strange Situation probably creates greater stress for them than for infants who frequently experience maternal separations (Takahashi, 1990). Also, Japanese parents value the infant clinginess and attention seeking that are part of resistant attachment, considering them to be normal indicators of infant closeness and dependency (Rothbaum et al., 2000a). Despite these cultural variations and others, the secure pattern is still the most common attachment classification in all societies studied to date (van IJzendoorn & Sagi, 1999).

Factors Affecting Attachment Security

What factors might influence attachment security? Researchers have looked closely at four important influences: (1) opportunity to establish a close relationship; (2) quality of caregiving; (3) the baby's characteristics; and (4) family context, including parents' internal working models.

• **OPPORTUNITY FOR ATTACHMENT** • What happens when a baby does not have the opportunity to establish a close tie to a caregiver? In a series of studies, René Spitz (1946) observed institutionalized infants who had been given up by their mothers between 3 and 12 months of age. The babies were placed in a large ward where each shared a nurse with at least seven other babies. In contrast to the happy, outgoing behavior they had shown before separation, they wept, withdrew from their surroundings, lost weight, and had difficulty sleeping. If a consistent caregiver did not replace the mother, the depression deepened rapidly.

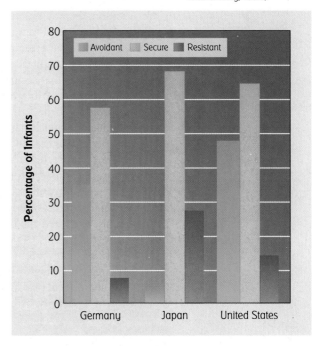

▼ **Figure 10.7**

A cross-cultural comparison of infants' reactions in the Strange Situation. A high percentage of German babies seem avoidantly attached, whereas a substantial number of Japanese infants appear resistantly attached. Note that these responses may not reflect true insecurity. Instead, they are probably due to cultural differences in child-rearing practices.

(Adapted from van IJzendoorn & Kroonenberg, 1988.)

These institutionalized infants experienced emotional difficulties because they were prevented from forming a bond with one or a few adults (Rutter, 1996). In another study, which supports this conclusion, researchers followed the development of infants in an institution that offered a good caregiver–child ratio and a rich selection of books and toys. Nevertheless, staff turnover was so rapid that the average child had a total of 50 caregivers by the age of 4½! Many of these children became "late adoptees" who were placed in homes after age 4. Most developed deep ties with their adoptive parents, indicating that a first attachment bond can develop as late as 4 to 6 years of age (Tizard & Rees, 1975).

But these children were also more likely to display attachment difficulties, including an excessive desire for adult attention, "overfriendliness" to unfamiliar adults and peers, failure to check back with the parent in new situations, and few friendships. Adopted children who spent their first 6 months or more in deprived Romanian institutions frequently have similar relationship problems (Hodges & Tizard, 1989; O'Connor et al., 2003). Although follow-ups into adulthood are necessary to be sure, these results leave open the possibility that fully normal development depends on establishing close ties with caregivers early in life.

• **QUALITY OF CAREGIVING** • Dozens of studies report that **sensitive caregiving**—responding promptly, consistently, and appropriately to infants and holding them tenderly and carefully—is moderately related to attachment security in both biological and adoptive mother–infant pairs and in diverse cultures and SES groups (DeWolff & van IJzendoorn, 1997; Posada et al., 2002, 2004; Stams, Juffer, & van IJzendoorn, 2002; van IJzendoorn et al., 2004). In contrast, insecurely attached infants tend to have mothers who engage in less physical contact, handle them awkwardly, behave in a "routine" manner, and are sometimes negative, resentful, and rejecting (Ainsworth et al., 1978; Isabella, 1993; Pederson & Moran, 1996).

Also, in several studies of North American babies, a special form of communication called **interactional synchrony** separated the experiences of secure from insecure babies. It is best described as a sensitively tuned "emotional dance," in which the caregiver responds to infant signals in a well-timed, rhythmic, appropriate fashion. In addition, both partners match emotional states, especially the positive ones (Isabella & Belsky, 1991; Kochanska, 1998). Earlier we saw that sensitive face-to-face play, in which interactional synchrony occurs, helps infants regulate emotion. But moderate adult–infant coordination is a better predictor of attachment security than "tight" coordination, in which the adult responds to most infant cues (Jaffe et al., 2001). Perhaps warm, sensitive caregivers use a relaxed, flexible style of communication in which they comfortably accept and repair emotional mismatches, returning to a synchronous state.

In addition, the way different cultures view maternal sensitivity depends on their values and goals for children's development. Among the Gusii people of Kenya, mothers rarely cuddle, hug, or interact playfully with their babies, although they are very responsive to their infants' needs. Yet most Gusii infants appear securely attached, using the mother as a secure base (LeVine et al., 1994). This suggests that security depends on attentive caregiving, not necessarily on moment-by-moment contingent interaction. Puerto Rican mothers, who highly value obedience and socially appropriate behavior, often physically direct and limit their babies' actions—a style of caregiving linked to attachment security in Puerto Rican culture. Yet such physical control predicts insecurity in Western cultures, where it is regarded as intrusive (Carlson & Horwood, 2003).

Compared with securely attached infants, avoidant babies tend to receive overstimulating care. Their mothers might, for example, talk energetically to them while they are looking away or falling asleep. By avoiding the mother, these infants try to escape from overwhelming interaction. Resistant infants often experience inconsistent care: Their mothers are unresponsive to infant signals, but when the baby begins to explore, they interfere, shifting the infant's attention back to themselves. As a result, the baby is overly dependent as well as angry at the mother's lack of involvement (Cassidy & Berlin, 1994; Isabella & Belsky, 1991).

When caregiving is highly inadequate, it is a powerful predictor of disruptions in attachment. Child abuse and neglect (topics we will consider in Chapter 14) are associated with all three forms of attachment insecurity. Among maltreated infants, disorganized/disoriented attachment is

◎ Attachment patterns vary with cultural beliefs and practices. Among the Dogon people, who live in small farming villages in Mali, Africa, maternal care consists of constant nearness to babies and prompt, gentle responsiveness to distress. In that culture, none of the infants were avoidantly attached to their mothers.
© Wolfgang Kaehler/Corbis

especially high (Barnett, Ganiban, & Cicchetti, 1999; van IJzendoorn, Schuengel, & Bakermans; Kranenburg, 1999). Depressed mothers and parents suffering from a traumatic event, such as loss of a loved one, also tend to promote the uncertain behaviors of this pattern (Teti et al., 1995; van IJzendoorn, 1995). Observations reveal that some of these mothers display frightening, contradictory, and unpleasant behaviors, such as looking scared, mocking or teasing the baby, holding the baby stiffly at a distance, roughly pulling the baby by the arm, or seeking reassurance from the upset child (Goldberg et al., 2003; Lyons-Ruth, Bronfman, & Parsons, 1999; Schuengel, Bakermans-Kranenburg, & van IJzendoorn, 1999). The baby's disorganized behavior seems to reflect a conflicted reaction to the parent, who sometimes comforts but at other times arouses fear.

◎ This mother and baby engage in a sensitively tuned form of communication called interactional synchrony, in which they match emotional states, especially the positive ones. © Jeff Greenberg/PhotoEdit

• **INFANT CHARACTERISTICS** • Because attachment is the result of a *relationship* that builds between two partners, infant characteristics should affect how easily it is established. In Chapter 3, we saw that prematurity, birth complications, and newborn illness make caregiving more taxing. In stressed, poverty-stricken families, these difficulties are linked to attachment insecurity (Wille, 1991). But when parents have the time and patience to care for a baby with special needs and view their infants positively, at-risk newborns fare quite well in attachment security (Cox, Hopkins, & Hans, 2000; Pederson & Moran, 1995).

Infants also vary considerably in temperament, but its role in attachment security has been intensely debated. Some researchers believe that infants who are irritable and fearful may simply react to brief separations with intense anxiety, regardless of the parent's sensitivity to the baby (Kagan, 1998). Consistent with this view, emotionally reactive, difficult babies are more likely to develop later insecure attachments (van IJzendoorn et al., 2004; Vaughn & Bost, 1999).

But other evidence suggests that caregiving is involved in the relationship between infant difficultness and attachment insecurity. In a study extending from birth to age 2, difficult infants more often had highly anxious mothers, a combination that often resulted in a "disharmonious relationship" in the second year—characterized by both maternal insensitivity and attachment insecurity (see Figure 10.8) (Symons, 2001). Infant difficultness and maternal anxiety seemed to perpetuate one another, impairing caregiving and the security of the parent–infant bond. In another investigation that focused on disorganized/disoriented

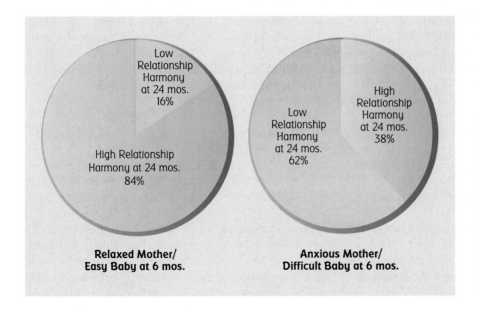

**Relaxed Mother/
Easy Baby at 6 mos.**

Low Relationship Harmony at 24 mos. 16%

High Relationship Harmony at 24 mos. 84%

**Anxious Mother/
Difficult Baby at 6 mos.**

Low Relationship Harmony at 24 mos. 62%

High Relationship Harmony at 24 mos. 38%

◀ **Figure 10.8**

Influence of mother–infant distress at 6 months on relationship harmony at 24 months. In a study extending over the first 2 years, the combination of high maternal anxiety and high infant difficultness frequently impaired caregiving, resulting in many mothers and babies with low relationship harmony—characterized by maternal insensitivity and attachment insecurity—in the second year. (Adapted from Symons, 2001.)

babies, negative emotional reactivity increased sharply between 12 and 18 months. Attachment disorganization was not caused by a difficult temperament; instead, it preceded difficultness and seemed to promote it (Barnett, Ganiban, & Cicchetti, 1999).

Indeed, extensive research confirms that caregiving can override the impact of infant characteristics on attachment security. When researchers combined data from more than a thousand mother–infant pairs, they found that maternal problems—such as mental illness, teenage parenthood, and child abuse—were associated with a sharp rise in attachment insecurity. In contrast, child problems—ranging from prematurity and developmental delays to serious physical disabilities and psychological disorders—had little impact on attachment quality (van IJzendoorn et al., 1992).

Finally, if children's traits determined security of attachment, we would expect attachment to be at least moderately heritable, just as temperament is. Yet twin comparisons reveal that the heritability of attachment is virtually nil (O'Connor & Croft, 2001). Identical twins are not more alike than fraternal twins (or other siblings) in attachment security. About two-thirds of siblings—whether identical twins, fraternal twins, nontwin siblings, unrelated siblings, or foster infants—establish similar attachment patterns with their parent. Yet these siblings often differ in temperament (Dozier et al., 2001; van IJzendoorn, 1995). This suggests that the strongest environmental influences on attachment security are *nonshared* experiences, reflecting most parents' efforts to adjust their caregiving to each child's individual needs.

A major reason that children's characteristics do not show strong relationships with attachment quality is that their influence depends on goodness of fit. From this perspective, *many* child attributes can lead to secure attachment as long as the caregiver sensitively adjusts her behavior to fit the baby's needs (Seifer & Schiller, 1995; Sroufe, 1985). Interventions that teach parents to interact sensitively with difficult-to-care-for infants are highly successful in enhancing both quality of caregiving and attachment security (Bakermans-Kranenburg et al., 2003). But when parents' capacity is strained—by their own personality or by stressful living conditions—then infants with illnesses, disabilities, and difficult temperaments are at risk for attachment problems.

• **FAMILY CIRCUMSTANCES** • As we have indicated in this and previous chapters, quality of caregiving can be fully understood only in terms of the larger context of the parent–child relationship. Job loss, a failing marriage, financial difficulties, and other stressors can undermine attachment by interfering with the sensitivity of parental care. Or these stressors can affect babies' sense of security directly, by exposing them to angry adult interactions or unfavorable child-care arrangements (Thompson & Raikes, 2003).

The arrival of a new sibling illustrates how family circumstances can affect attachment quality. In one study, first-born preschoolers who declined in attachment security after the birth of a baby had mothers who were depressed, anxious, or hostile before the birth. These symptoms were associated with marital friction (which the first-borns probably sensed) as well as with unfavorable mother–first-born interaction. When mothers had cooperative marriages, coped well with the second birth, and stayed involved with their older child, preschoolers maintained a secure attachment bond (Teti et al., 1996). The availability of social supports, especially a good mother–father relationship and mutual assistance with caregiving, reduces family stress and predicts greater attachment security (Owen & Cox, 1997).

• **PARENTS' INTERNAL WORKING MODELS** • Parents bring to the family context a long history of attachment experiences, out of which they construct internal working models that they apply to the bonds established with their babies. To assess parents' "state of mind" with respect to attachment, Mary Main and her colleagues devised the *Adult Attachment Interview,* which asks adults to recall and evaluate childhood attachment experiences (Main & Goldwyn, 1998).

As Table 10.3 shows, quality of mothers' working models is clearly related to their children's attachment security in infancy and early childhood—results replicated in Canada, Germany, Great Britain, the Netherlands, and the United States. Parents who show objectivity and balance in discussing their childhoods tend to have securely attached infants. In contrast, parents who dismiss the importance of early relationships or describe them in angry, confused ways usually have

TABLE 10.3 RELATIONSHIP OF MOTHERS' INTERNAL WORKING MODELS TO INFANT ATTACHMENT SECURITY

Type of Maternal Working Model	Description	Infant Attachment Classification[a]
Autonomous/ secure	These mothers show objectivity and balance in discussing their childhood experiences, whether these were positive or negative. They neither idealize their parents nor feel angry about the past. Their explanations are coherent and believable.	Secure
Dismissing	These mothers devalue the importance of their attachment relationships. They tend to idealize their parents without being able to recall specific experiences. What they do recall is discussed intellectually, with little emotion.	Avoidant
Overinvolved	These mothers talk about their childhood experiences with highly charged emotion, sometimes expressing anger toward their parents. They appear overwhelmed and confused about their early attachments and cannot discuss them coherently.	Resistant
Unresolved	These mothers show characteristics of any of the three other patterns. At the same time, they reason in a disorganized and confused way when loss of a loved one or experiences of physical or sexual abuse are discussed.	Disorganized/ disoriented

[a]Correspondences between type of maternal working model and infant attachment classification hold for 60 to 70 percent of mother–infant pairs.

Sources: Benoit & Parker, 1994; Main & Goldwyn, 1994; Pederson et al., 1998.

insecurely attached babies (Steele, Steele, & Fonagy, 1996; van IJzendoorn, 1995). Caregiving behavior helps explain these associations. Mothers with autonomous/secure representations are warmer and more sensitive with their babies. They are also more likely to be supportive and to encourage learning and mastery in their older children, who, in turn, are more affectionate and comfortably interactive with them (Pederson et al., 1998; Slade et al., 1999).

But we must be careful not to assume any direct transfer of parents' childhood experiences to quality of attachment with their own children. Internal working models are *reconstructed memories* affected by many factors, including relationship experiences over the life course, personality, and current life satisfaction. According to longitudinal research, certain negative life events can weaken the link between an individual's own attachment security in infancy and a secure internal working model in adulthood. And insecurely attached babies who become adults with insecure internal working models often have lives that, based on adulthood self-reports, are fraught with family crises (Waters et al., 2000; Weinfield, Sroufe, & Egeland, 2000).

In sum, our early rearing experiences do not destine us to become sensitive or insensitive parents. Rather, the way we *view* our childhoods—our ability to come to terms with negative

◎ How might the internal working model of the 2-year-old girl seated in her mother's lap (left) have influenced the relationship she forged more than three decades later with her own baby (right)? Research indicates that early attachment pattern is one among many factors that can affect later intimate ties. Relationship experiences over the life course, personality, and current life satisfaction are also influential.

Courtesy of Elizabeth Napolitano

events, to integrate new information into our working models, and to look back on our own parents in an understanding, forgiving way—is much more influential in how we rear our children than the actual history of care we received (Main, 2000).

Multiple Attachments: The Father's Special Role

We have already indicated that babies develop attachments to a variety of familiar people—not just mothers but also fathers, siblings, grandparents, and professional caregivers. The quality of these attachments can vary, depending on infants' experiences with each person. Although Bowlby (1969) made room for multiple attachments in his theory, he believed that infants are predisposed to direct their attachment behaviors to a single special person, especially when they are distressed. Consistent with this view, when anxious or unhappy, most babies prefer to be comforted by their mother. But this preference declines over the second year. And when babies are not distressed, they approach, ask to be held by, vocalize to, and smile at both parents equally (Lamb, 1997).

Like that of mothers, fathers' sensitive caregiving predicts secure attachment—an effect that becomes stronger the more time they spend with their babies (van IJzendoorn & De Wolff, 1997). And fathers of 1- to 5-year-olds enrolled in full-time child care report feeling just as much anxiety as mothers about separating from their child and just as much concern about the impact of these daily separations on the child's well-being (Deater-Deckard et al., 1994).

But as infancy progresses, mothers and fathers in many cultures—Australia, India, Israel, Italy, Japan, and the United States—relate to babies in different ways. Mothers devote more time to physical care and expressing affection. Fathers spend more time in playful interaction—a vital context in which they build secure attachments with their babies (Lamb, 1987; Roopnarine et al., 1990). Mothers and fathers also play differently. Mothers more often provide toys, talk to infants, and engage in conventional games, such as pat-a-cake and peekaboo. In contrast, fathers tend to engage in more exciting, highly physical bouncing and lifting games that provide bursts of stimulation, especially with their infant sons (Yogman, 1981).

In some families, this picture of "mother as caregiver" and "father as playmate" has changed in response to women's increased workforce participation. Employed mothers tend to engage in more playful stimulation of their babies than unemployed mothers, and their husbands are somewhat more involved in caregiving (Cox et al., 1992). When fathers are the primary caregivers, they retain their arousing play style (Lamb & Oppenheim, 1989). Such highly involved fathers are less gender stereotyped in their beliefs, have sympathetic, friendly personalities, often had fathers who were more involved in rearing them, and regard parenthood as an especially enriching experience (Cabrera et al., 2000; Levy-Shiff & Israelashvili, 1988).

Fathers' involvement with babies takes place within a complex system of family attitudes and relationships. When pregnancies were intended rather than accidental and when both parents believe that men can nurture infants, fathers devote more time to caregiving (Beitel & Parke, 1998; Brown & Eisenberg, 1995). A warm, gratifying marital bond supports both parents' involvement, but it is particularly important for fathers (Braungart-Rieker, Courtney, & Garwood, 1999; Frosch, Mangelsdorf, & McHale, 2000). See the Cultural Influences box on the following page for cross-cultural evidence that documents this conclusion—and that also shows the powerful role of paternal warmth in children's development.

Attachment and Later Development

According to psychoanalytic and ethological theories, the inner feelings of affection and security that result from a healthy attachment relationship support all aspects of psychological development. In an extensive longitudinal study consistent with this view, Alan Sroufe and his collaborators found that preschoolers who were securely attached as babies showed more elaborate make-believe play and greater enthusiasm, flexibility, and persistence in problem solving by 2 years of age. At age 4, these children were rated by preschool teachers as high in self-esteem, social competence, and empathy. In contrast, the teachers viewed avoidantly attached agemates as isolated and disconnected, and resistantly attached agemates as disruptive and difficult. Studied again at age 11 in summer camp, children who had been secure infants had more favorable relationships with peers, closer friendships, and better social skills, as judged by camp counselors (Elicker, Englund, & Sroufe, 1992; Matas, Arend, & Sroufe, 1978; Shulman, Elicker, & Sroufe, 1994).

CULTURAL INFLUENCES

The Powerful Role of Paternal Warmth in Development

Research in diverse cultures demonstrates that fathers' warmth contributes greatly to children's long-term favorable development. In studies of many societies and ethnic groups around the world, researchers coded paternal expressions of love and nurturance—evident in such behaviors as cuddling, hugging, comforting, playing, verbally expressing love, and praising the child's behavior. Fathers' sustained affectionate involvement predicted later cognitive, emotional, and social competence as strongly, and occasionally more strongly, than did mothers' warmth (Rohner & Veneziano, 2001; Veneziano, 2003). And in Western cultures, paternal warmth protected children against a wide range of difficulties, including childhood emotional and behavior problems and adolescent substance abuse and delinquency (Grant et al., 2000; Rohner & Brothers, 1999; Tacon & Caldera, 2001).

In families where fathers devote little time to physical caregiving, they express warmth through play. In a German study, fathers' play sensitivity—accepting toddlers' play initiatives, adapting play behaviors to toddlers' capacities, and responding appropriately to toddlers' expressions of emotion— predicted children's secure internal working models of attachment during middle childhood and adolescence (Grossmann et al., 2002). Through stimulating play, fathers seemed to transfer to young children a

sense of confidence in exploration and in the parental relationship, which may strengthen their capacity to master many later challenges.

What factors promote paternal warmth? Cross-cultural research reveals a consistent relationship between the amount of time fathers spend near infants and toddlers and their expressions of caring and affection (Rohner & Veneziano, 2001). Consider the Aka hunters and gatherers of Central Africa, where fathers spend more time in physical proximity to their babies than in any other known society. Observations reveal that Aka fathers are within arm's reach of infants more than half the day. They pick up, cuddle, and play with their babies at least five times as often as fathers in other hunting-and-gathering societies. Why are Aka fathers so involved? The bond between Aka husband and wife is unusually cooperative and intimate. Throughout the day, couples share hunting, food preparation, and social and leisure activities. The more time Aka parents spend together, the greater the father's loving interaction with his baby (Hewlett, 1992).

In Western cultures as well, mothers' and fathers' warm interactions with babies are closely linked (Rohner & Veneziano, 2001). At the same time, paternal warmth promotes long-term favorable development, beyond the influence of maternal warmth. Evidence for the power of fathers' affection,

▲ This Japanese father engages in the exciting, active play that characterizes fathers in many cultures. In both Western and non-Western nations, fathers' warmth predicts long-term favorable development. And in Western societies, it protects against a range of adjustment problems in childhood and adolescence.
© Ronnie Kaufman/Corbis

reported in virtually every culture and ethnic group studied, may help motivate more men to engage in nurturing care of young children.

These findings have been taken by some researchers to mean that secure attachment in infancy causes improved cognitive, emotional, and social competence in later years. Yet contrary evidence exists. In other longitudinal research, secure infants sometimes developed more favorably than insecure infants, and sometimes did not (Lewis, 1997; Schneider, Atkinson, & Tardif, 2001; Stams, Juffer, & van IJzendoorn, 2002). Disorganized/disoriented attachment, however, is an exception. It is consistently related to high hostility and aggression during the preschool and school years (Lyons-Ruth, 1996; Lyons-Ruth, Easterbrooks, & Cibelli, 1997).

What accounts for the inconsistency in research findings on the consequences of early attachment quality? Mounting evidence indicates that *continuity of caregiving* determines whether attachment security is linked to later development (Lamb et al., 1985; Thompson,

2000). When parents respond sensitively not just in infancy but also during later years, children are likely to develop favorably. In contrast, parents who react insensitively for a long time have children who establish lasting patterns of avoidant, resistant, or disorganized behavior and are at greater risk for developmental difficulties.

A close look at the relationship between parenting and children's adjustment in the first few years supports this interpretation. Recall that many mothers of disorganized/disoriented infants have serious psychological difficulties and engage in highly maladaptive caregiving—conditions that usually persist and are strongly linked to children's poor adjustment (Lyons-Ruth, Bronfman, & Parsons, 1999). Furthermore, when more than a thousand children were tracked from 1 to 3 years of age, those with histories of secure attachment followed by sensitive mothering scored highest in cognitive, emotional, and social outcomes. Those with histories of insecure attachment followed by insensitive mothering scored lowest. And those with mixed histories of attachment and maternal sensitivity scored in between (Belsky & Fearon, 2002). Specifically, insecurely attached infants whose mothers became more positive and supportive in early childhood showed signs of developmental recovery.

Does this trend remind you of our discussion of *resilience* in Chapter 1? A child whose parental caregiving improves or who has other compensating affectionate ties outside the immediate family can bounce back from adversity. In contrast, a child who experiences tender care in infancy but lacks sympathetic ties later is at risk for problems.

Nevertheless, a secure attachment in infancy is important because it launches the parent–child relationship on a positive path, increasing the likelihood of—though not guaranteeing—continued parental sensitivity. Much research shows that an early warm, positive parent–child tie, sustained over time, promotes many aspects of children's development—a more confident and complex self-concept, more advanced emotional understanding, more favorable and supportive relationships with teachers and peers, more effective social skills, a stronger sense of moral responsibility, and higher motivation to achieve in school (Thompson, Easterbrooks, & Padilla-Walker, 2003). But the effects of early attachment security are *conditional*—dependent on the quality of the infant's future relationships. Finally, as our discussion has already revealed and as you will see again in future chapters, attachment is but one of the complex influences on children's psychological development.

Ask Yourself

REVIEW What factors explain stability in attachment pattern for some children and change for others? Are these factors also involved in the link between attachment in infancy and later development? Explain.

APPLY In evaluating her childhood attachment experiences, Monica recalls her mother as tense and distant. Is Monica's newborn daughter likely to develop an insecure infant–mother attachment? Explain, using research on adults' internal working models.

CONNECT Review research on emotional self-regulation on pages 403–405. How do the caregiving experiences of securely attached infants promote development of emotional self-regulation?

REFLECT How would you characterize your internal working model? What factors, in addition to your early relationship with your parents, might have influenced it?

Attachment, Parental Employment, and Child Care

Over the past three decades, women have entered the labor force in record numbers. Today, more than 60 percent of North American mothers with a child under age 2 are employed (Statistics Canada, 2002b; U.S. Census Bureau, 2004b). In response to this trend, researchers and laypeople alike have raised questions about the impact of child care and daily separations of infant from parent on the attachment bond.

The Social Issues box on the following page reviews the current controversy over whether child care threatens the development of young children. As you will see, the weight of evidence suggests that *quality of care* is crucially important. Infants and young children exposed to long

Does Child Care in Infancy Threaten Attachment Security and Later Adjustment?

Research suggests that infants placed in full-time child care are more likely than home-reared babies to display insecure attachment—especially avoidance—in the Strange Situation (Belsky, 1992, 2001). Does this mean that babies who experience daily separations from their employed parents and placement in child care are at risk for developmental problems? Let's look closely at the evidence.

Attachment Quality

In studies reporting an association between child care and attachment quality, the rate of insecurity among child-care infants is somewhat higher than among non-child-care infants—about 36 versus 29 percent (Lamb, Sternberg, & Prodromidis, 1992). But not all investigations report that babies in child care differ in attachment quality from those cared for solely by parents (NICHD Early Child Care Research Network, 1997; Roggman et al., 1994). The relationship between child care and emotional well-being depends on both family and child-care experiences.

Family Circumstances

We have seen that family conditions affect attachment security. Many employed women find the pressures of handling two full-time jobs—work and motherhood—stressful. Some mothers, fatigued and harried because they receive little caregiving assistance from the child's father, may respond less sensitively to their babies, thereby risking the infant's security (Stifter, Coulehan, & Fish, 1993). Other employed mothers probably value and encourage their infant's independence, or their babies may be unfazed by brief separations because they are used to separating from their parents. In these cases, avoidance in the Strange Situation may represent healthy autonomy rather than insecurity (Clarke-Stewart, Allhusen, & Goosens, 2001).

Quality and Extent of Child Care

Long periods spent in poor-quality child care may contribute to a higher rate of insecure attachment. In the U.S. National Institute of Child Health and Development (NICHD) Study of Early Child Care—the largest longitudinal study to date, including more than 1,300 infants and their families residing in ten U.S. communities—child care alone did not contribute to attachment insecurity.

But when babies were exposed to combined home and child-care risk factors—insensitive caregiving at home along with insensitive caregiving in child care, long hours in child care, or more than one child-care arrangement—the rate of insecurity increased. Overall, mother–child interaction was more favorable when children received better-quality child care and spent fewer hours in child care (NICHD Early Child Care Research Network, 1997, 1999).

Furthermore, when children in the NICHD sample reached 3 years of age, a history of higher-quality child care predicted better social skills (NICHD Early Child Care Research Network, 2002b). At the same time, at age 4½ to 5, children averaging more than 30 child-care hours per week displayed more behavior problems, especially defiance, disobedience, and aggression (NICHD Early Child Care Research Network, 2003a). This does not necessarily mean that child care causes behavior problems. Rather, heavy exposure to substandard care, which is widespread in the United States, may promote these difficulties. In Australia, infants enrolled full-time in government-funded, high-quality child care have a higher rate of secure attachment than infants informally cared for by relatives, friends, or baby-sitters. And amount of time in child care is unrelated to Australian preschoolers' behavior problems (Love et al., 2003).

Still, some children might be particularly stressed by long child-care hours. Many infants, toddlers, and preschoolers attending child-care centers for full days show a mild increase in saliva concentrations of the stress hormone cortisol across the day—a pattern that does not occur on days they spend at home. In one study, children rated as highly fearful by their caregivers experienced an especially sharp increase in cortisol levels (Watamura et al., 2003). Inhibited children may find the social context of child care—constantly being in the company of large numbers of peers—particularly stressful.

Conclusions

Taken together, research results suggest that some infants may be at risk for attachment insecurity and adjustment problems due to inadequate child care, long hours in child care, and the joint pressures their mothers experience from full-time employment and

▲ At the end of her day in child care, a toddler eagerly greets her mother. High-quality child care and fewer hours in child care are associated with favorable mother–child interaction, which contributes to attachment security. © Elizabeth Crews

parenthood. But it is inappropriate to use these findings to justify a reduction in infant child-care services. When family incomes are limited or mothers who want to work are forced to stay at home, children's emotional security is not promoted.

Instead, it makes sense to increase the availability of high-quality child care, to provide paid employment leave so parents can limit the hours their children spend in child care (see pages 112–113), and to educate parents about the vital role of sensitive caregiving and child-care quality in early emotional development. For child care to foster attachment security, the professional caregiver's relationship with the baby is vital. When caregiver–child ratios are generous, group sizes are small, and caregivers are educated about child development and child rearing, caregivers' interactions are more positive and children develop more favorably (NICHD Early Child Care Research Network, 2000a, 2002a). Child care with these characteristics can become part of an ecological system that relieves rather than intensifies parental and child stress, thereby promoting healthy attachment and development.

hours of mediocre to poor nonparental care, regardless of whether they come from middle- or low-SES homes, score lower on measures of cognitive and social skills (Hausfather et al., 1997; Kohen et al., 2000; NICHD Early Child Care Research Network, 2000b, 2001, 2003b).

In contrast, good child care can reduce the negative impact of a stressed, poverty-stricken home life, and it sustains the benefits of growing up in an economically advantaged family (Lamb, 1998; NICHD Early Child Care Research Network, 2003b). In Swedish longitudinal research, entering high-quality child care in infancy and toddlerhood was associated with cognitive, emotional, and social competence in middle childhood and adolescence (Andersson, 1989, 1992; Broberg et al., 1997).

Visit some child-care settings and take notes on what you see. In contrast to most European countries and to Australia and New Zealand, where child care is nationally regulated and funded to ensure its quality, reports on child care in the United States and Canada are cause for concern. Neither country has devised a national child-care strategy that protects and supports all young children. Instead, child-care standards are set by the states and provinces and vary widely. In studies of child-care quality in each nation, only 20 to 25 percent of child-care centers and family child-care settings (in which a caregiver cares for children in her home) provided infants and toddlers with sufficiently positive, stimulating experiences to promote healthy psychological development; most settings offered substandard care (Doherty et al., 2000; Goelman et al., 2000; NICHD Early Child Care Research Network, 2000a). Unfortunately, children from low-income and poverty-stricken families are especially likely to have inadequate child care (Pungello & Kurtz-Costes, 1999). As a result, these children receive a double dose of vulnerability—at home and in the child-care environment.

Refer to Applying What We Know below for signs of high-quality child care for infants and toddlers, based on standards for **developmentally appropriate practice.** These standards,

Applying
What We Know — Signs of Developmentally Appropriate Infant and Toddler Child Care

Program Characteristic	Signs of Quality
Physical setting	Indoor environment is clean, in good repair, well lighted, and well ventilated. Fenced outdoor play space is available. Setting does not appear overcrowded when children are present.
Toys and equipment	Play materials are appropriate for infants and toddlers and are stored on low shelves within easy reach. Cribs, highchairs, infant seats, and child-sized tables and chairs are available. Outdoor equipment includes small riding toys, swings, slide, and sandbox.
Caregiver–child ratio	In child-care centers, caregiver–child ratio is no greater than 1 to 3 for infants and 1 to 6 for toddlers. Group size (number of children in one room) is no greater than 6 infants with 2 caregivers and 12 toddlers with 2 caregivers. In family child care, caregiver is responsible for no more than 6 children; within this group, no more than 2 are infants and toddlers. Staffing is consistent, so infants and toddlers can form relationships with particular caregivers.
Daily activities	Daily schedule includes times for active play, quiet play, naps, snacks, and meals. It is flexible rather than rigid, to meet the needs of individual children. Atmosphere is warm and supportive, and children are never left unsupervised.
Interactions among adults and children	Caregivers respond promptly to infants' and toddlers' distress; hold, talk to, sing to, and read to them; and interact with them in a manner that respects the individual child's interests and tolerance for stimulation.
Caregiver qualifications	Caregiver has some training in child development, first aid, and safety.
Relationships with parents	Parents are welcome anytime. Caregivers talk frequently with parents about children's behavior and development.
Licensing and accreditation	Child-care setting, whether a center or a home, is licensed by the state or province. In the United States, voluntary accreditation by the National Academy of Early Childhood Programs, *www.naeyc.org/accreditation,* or the National Association for Family Child Care, *www.nafcc.org,* is evidence of an especially high-quality program. Canada is working on a voluntary accreditation system, under the leadership of the Canadian Child Care Federation, *www.cccf-fcsge.ca.* The province of Alberta has already begun to test an accreditation model.

Sources: Bredekamp & Copple, 1997; National Association for the Education of Young Children, 1998.

devised by the U.S. National Association for the Education of Young Children, specify program characteristics that meet the developmental and individual needs of young children, based on both current research and consensus among experts. When child care meets standards for developmentally appropriate practice, children's learning opportunities and the warmth, sensitivity, and stability of their caregivers are especially high (Helburn, 1995).

Child care in the United States and Canada is affected by a macrosystem of individualistic values and weak government regulation and funding. Furthermore, many parents think that their children's child-care experiences are higher in quality than they really are (Helburn, 1995). Inability to identify good care means that many parents do not demand it. Recognizing that child care is in a state of crisis, in recent years the U.S. and Canadian federal governments, and some states and provinces, have allocated additional funds to subsidize its cost, especially for low-income families. Though far from meeting the need, this increase in resources has had a positive impact on child-care quality and accessibility (Canada Campaign 2000, 2003a; Children's Defense Fund, 2004). In Canada, the province of Québec leads the nation with universal child care for infants and preschoolers. Every Québec family pays the same minimal daily fee for government-supported services.

These developments are hopeful signs because good child care is a cost-effective means for supporting the development of all children, and it can serve as effective early intervention for children whose development is at risk, much like the programs we discussed in Chapter 8. We will revisit the topics of parental employment and child care in Chapter 14, when we consider their consequences for development during childhood and adolescence in greater detail.

Ask Yourself

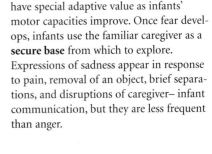

REVIEW	Cite evidence that high-quality infant and toddler child care supports development, whereas poor-quality care undermines it.
APPLY	Randi and Mike are worried that placing their 6-month-old baby, Lucinda, in child care may disrupt Lucinda's sense of security. List steps that Randi and Mike can take to ensure that Lucinda's experiences—at home and in child care—support her emotional and social development.

Summary

The Functions of Emotions

Describe the functionalist approach to emotional development.

According to the **functionalist approach,** the broad function of **emotions** is to energize behavior aimed at attaining personal goals. Functionalist theorists regard emotions as central, adaptive forces in all aspects of human activity, including cognitive processing, social behavior, and physical health. In addition, emotions contribute to the emergence of self-awareness, which makes possible new, self-evaluative emotions. Furthermore, to adapt to their physical and social worlds, children must gradually gain voluntary control over their emotions.

Development of Emotional Expression

How does the expression of happiness, anger, sadness, and fear change during infancy?

During the first half-year, **basic emotions** are gradually coordinated into more effective systems. By the middle of the first year, they are well-organized signals that vary meaningfully with environmental events.

Happiness strengthens the parent–child bond and reflects as well as supports cognitive and physical mastery. As infants' sensitivity to visual patterns improves between 6 and 10 weeks, the **social smile** appears. By 3 months, infants smile most often when interacting with familiar people. Soon laughter, associated with faster information processing, emerges.

Anger and fear, especially in the form of **stranger anxiety,** increase in the second half of the first year, as infants become better able to evaluate objects and events. These emotions

© CHRIS LOWE/INDEX STOCK IMAGERY

have special adaptive value as infants' motor capacities improve. Once fear develops, infants use the familiar caregiver as a **secure base** from which to explore. Expressions of sadness appear in response to pain, removal of an object, brief separations, and disruptions of caregiver– infant communication, but they are less frequent than anger.

Describe the development of self-conscious emotions, emotional self-regulation, and conformity to emotional display rules.

At the end of the second year, self-awareness and adult instruction provide the foundation for **self-conscious emotions,** such as shame, embarrassment, guilt, envy, and pride. With age, self-conscious emotions become more internally governed. Among Western children, guilt is often related to good adjustment, whereas intense shame is associated with feelings of personal inadequacy. Parents who repeatedly give feedback about the worth of the child and her performance have children who experience overly high, maladaptive levels of shame and pride.

© LAURA DWIGHT PHOTOGRAPHY

⊚ **Emotional self-regulation** emerges as the frontal lobes of the cerebral cortex develop and caregivers sensitively assist infants in adjusting their emotional reactions. As motor, cognitive, and language development proceed, children gradually acquire more effective self-regulatory strategies. Warm, patient parenting, including guidance in understanding and controlling feelings, fosters emotional self-regulation. Children who experience negative emotion intensely find it harder to inhibit their feelings and shift their attention away from disturbing events.

⊚ By the end of middle childhood, most children have an adaptive set of techniques for regulating emotion. They shift between **problem-centered coping** and **emotion-centered coping,** depending on the situation. Emotionally well-regulated children are optimistic and cooperative and have favorable relationships with teachers and peers.

⊚ During the preschool years, children start to conform to the **emotional display rules** of their culture, but only gradually do they become adept at doing so. In middle childhood, they grow consciously aware of these rules and come to understand their value for ensuring social harmony.

Understanding and Responding to the Emotions of Others

Describe the development of emotional understanding from infancy into adolescence.

⊚ As infants develop the capacity to meaningfully interpret emotional expressions, they actively seek emotional information from trusted caregivers. **Social referencing** appears at the end of the first year. By the middle of the second year, toddlers begin to appreciate that others' emotional reactions may differ from their own.

⊚ Preschoolers have an impressive understanding of the causes, consequences, and behavioral signs of emotion. The capacity to consider conflicting cues when explaining others' feelings develops during middle childhood. Older children also realize that people can experience mixed emotions.

⊚ Parents who establish a warm relationship with their children, acknowledge their emotional reactions, and converse with and teach them about emotions have children who are advanced in emotional understanding. Interactions with peers, especially sociodramatic play, are excellent contexts for learning about emotions.

Distinguish empathy and sympathy, and describe the development of empathy from infancy into adolescence, noting individual differences.

⊚ The development of **empathy** involves a complex interaction of cognition and affect. Empathy is an important motivator of **prosocial, or altruistic, behavior.** Yet if empathic emotion escalates into personal distress, empathy is unlikely to prompt **sympathy** and resulting acts of kindness and helpfulness.

⊚ As self-awareness emerges, toddlers begin to empathize. Gains in language, emotional understanding, and perspective taking support an increase in empathic responding during childhood and adolescence. Eventually, empathy is evoked not just by people's immediate distress but by their general life condition.

⊚ Temperament affects whether empathy gives way to sympathy. Children who are sociable, assertive, and good at regulating emotion are more likely to behave prosocially than children who often display negative emotion.

⊚ Parents who are nurturant, display empathic concern, and set clear limits on children's display of inappropriate emotion foster the development of empathy and sympathy. In contrast, angry, punitive parenting disrupts these capacities at an early age.

Temperament and Development

What is temperament, and how is it measured?

⊚ Children differ greatly in **temperament,** or early-appearing, stable individual differences in emotional, attentional, and behavioral reactivity and in self-regulation. Three  © NANCY SHEEHAN/PHOTOEDIT patterns of temperament—the **easy child,** the **difficult child,** and the **slow-to-warm-up child**—were identified in the New York Longitudinal Study. Rothbart's dimensions of temperament represent three underlying components: emotion, attention, and

action. Individuals differ not only in their reactivity on each dimension but also in **effortful control,** or their ability to regulate that reactivity.

⊚ Temperament is often assessed through parental reports. Although laboratory observations avoid the subjectivity of parental reports, the unfamiliar setting introduces other biases. Still, researchers can better control children's experiences in the lab.

⊚ Researchers have begun to combine laboratory observations with psychophysiological measures to distinguish temperamental styles, For example, a spatial-conflict task that activates frontal lobe areas involved in reconciling competing tendencies can be used to measure effortful control as early as 2½ to 3 years of age. A combination of laboratory and psychophysiological measures has been used to distinguish **inhibited, or shy, children** from **uninhibited,** or **sociable, children.**

Discuss the role of heredity and environment in the stability of temperament, the relationship of temperament to cognitive and social functioning, and the goodness-of-fit model.

⊚ Because temperament itself develops with age, stability from one age period to the next is generally low to moderate. Long-term prediction from early temperament is most accurately made after the second year of life, when styles of responding are better established.

⊚ Kinship studies indicate that temperament is moderately heritable. At the same time, environment powerfully affects the development of temperament. Nonshared influences, evident in parents' tendency to emphasize each child's unique qualities, are influential, and shared experiences, such as family stress and child-rearing styles, also contribute. Ethnic differences in temperament may have biological roots but are supported by cultural beliefs and practices.

⊚ Temperament is consistently related to cognitive performance and social behavior. The **goodness-of-fit model** describes how temperament and environmental pressures work together to affect later development. Parenting practices that create a good fit with the child's temperament help difficult, shy, and highly active children achieve more adaptive functioning. Cultural values affect goodness of fit, as illustrated by the recent change in attitudes toward childhood shyness in China.

Development of Attachment

What are the unique features of ethological theory of attachment?

The development of **attachment,** the strong affectionate tie we feel for special people in our lives, has been the subject of intense theoretical debate. Although psychoanalytic and drive-reduction (behaviorist) explanations exist, the most widely accepted perspective is **ethological theory of attachment.** It views babies as biologically prepared to contribute to ties established with their caregivers, which promote survival by ensuring both safety and competence.

In early infancy, a set of built-in behaviors encourages the parent to remain close to the baby. Around 6 to 8 months, **separation anxiety** and use of the parent as a secure base indicate that a true attachment bond has formed. As representation and language develop, preschoolers better understand the parent's coming and going, and separation anxiety declines. Out of early caregiving experiences, children construct an **internal working model** that serves as a guide for all future close relationships.

Cite the four attachment patterns assessed by the Strange Situation and the Attachment Q-Sort, and discuss factors that affect the development of attachment.

The **Strange Situation** is a widely used laboratory technique for measuring the quality of attachment between 1 and 2 years of age. Using it, researchers have identified four attachment patterns: **secure, avoidant, resistant,** and **disorganized/disoriented.** An alternative method, based on home observations, is the **Attachment Q-Sort,** which is suitable for children between 1 and 4 years of age. Rather than identifying quality of attachment, it yields a score ranging from low to high security.

Attachment is usually secure and stable for infants reared in middle-SES families with favorable life conditions. For infants in low-SES families with many daily stresses and for children who encounter serious family problems, quality of attachment often changes. Cultural conditions must be considered in interpreting the meaning of attachment patterns.

© LAURA DWIGHT PHOTOGRAPHY

A variety of factors affect attachment security. Infants deprived of affectionate ties with one or a few adults show lasting emotional and social problems. **Sensitive caregiving** is moderately related to secure attachment. **Interactional synchrony** also separates the experiences of secure from insecure babies. However, cultures differ in how they view sensitivity, and the importance of interactional synchrony is probably limited to certain cultures.

Attachment is not heritable but, instead, results from nonshared experiences in which parents adjust their caregiving to their child's individual needs. Even ill and emotionally reactive, difficult infants are likely to become securely attached if parents adapt their caregiving to suit the baby's needs.

Family circumstances influence caregiving behavior and attachment security. Parents' internal working models show substantial correspondence with their own children's attachment status. However, internal working models are reconstructed memories; transfer of parents' childhood experiences to quality of attachment with their own children is indirect and affected by many factors.

Discuss fathers' attachment relationships with their infants and the role of early attachment quality in later development.

Infants develop strong affectionate ties to fathers, whose sensitive caregiving predicts secure attachment. Fathers in a variety of cultures devote more time than mothers to stimulating, playful interaction, through which they build secure attachments with their babies.

Continuity of parental care is the crucial factor that determines whether attachment security is linked to later development. Children can recover from an insecure attachment history if caregiving improves. Nevertheless, a secure attachment in infancy is important because it launches the parent–child relationship on a positive path, increasing the likelihood of continued parental sensitivity.

Attachment, Parental Employment, and Child Care

Discuss the effects of parental employment and child care on attachment security and early psychological development.

The majority of North American mothers with children under age 2 are employed. Spending many hours in mediocre to poor-quality child care contributes to insecure attachment and less favorable cognitive, emotional, and social development.

When child-care settings meet professionally accepted standards for **developmentally appropriate practice,** children's learning opportunities and the warmth, sensitivity, and stability of their caregivers are especially high. Good child care can also serve as effective early intervention for children whose development is at risk.

Important Terms and Concepts

"Untitled"
May Linn Clement
Age 13, Norway

As young people construct their identities, they search for what is true and real about themselves. This dreamlike painting portrays a multifaceted self—a girl who is part of the natural world but also distinct from it because of her uniquely human abilities.

Self and Social Understanding

"Grandpa, look at my new shirt!" exclaimed 4-year-old Ellen at her family's annual reunion. "See, it's got Barney and Baby Bop on it and . . ."

Ellen's voice trailed off as she realized that all eyes were turned toward her 1-year-old cousin, who was about to take his first steps. As little David tottered forward, the grownups laughed and cheered. No one, not even Grandpa, who was usually so attentive and playful, took note of Ellen and her new shirt.

Ellen retreated to the bedroom, where she threw a blanket over her head. Arms outstretched, she peered through the blanket's loose weave and made her way back to the living room, where she saw Grandpa leading David about the room. "Here I come, the scary ghost," announced Ellen as she purposefully bumped into David, who toppled over and burst into tears.

Pulling off the blanket, Ellen quickly caught her mother's disapproving expression. "I couldn't see him, Mom! The blanket was over my face," Ellen explained sheepishly.

Ellen's mother insisted that Ellen help David up and apologize at once. At the same time, she marveled at Ellen's skillful capacity for trickery.

This chapter addresses the development of **social cognition,** or how children come to understand their multifaceted social world. Like our discussion of cognitive development in Chapters 6 and 7, this chapter is concerned with thinking about and interpreting experience. But the experience of interest is no longer the child's physical surroundings. Instead, it is the characteristics of the self and other people.

Researchers interested in social cognition seek answers to questions like these: When do infants discover that they are separate beings, distinct from other people and objects? How does children's understanding of their own and others' mental lives change with age? For example, what new realizations underlie Ellen's creative act of deception? When children and adolescents are asked to describe their own and others' characteristics, what do they say?

As we answer these and other questions, you will see that the following trends, which we identified for cognitive development, also apply to children's understanding of their social world:

- Social-cognitive development proceeds *from concrete to abstract.* Children start by noticing observable characteristics—their own and others' appearance and behavior. Soon after, they become aware of internal processes—the existence of desires, beliefs, intentions, abilities, and attitudes.

- Social cognition becomes *better organized* with age as children integrate separate behaviors into an appreciation of their own and others' personalities and identities.

- Children revise their ideas about the causes of behavior—from *simple, one-sided explanations* to *complex, interacting relationships* that take into account both person and situation.

- Social cognition moves toward *metacognitive understanding*. As children get older, their thinking is no longer limited to social reality. They also think about their own and other people's social thoughts.

Although nonsocial and social cognition share many features, they also differ. Consider how much easier it is to predict the motion of a physical object, such as a rolling ball, than the actions of people. Movements of things can be fully understood from the physical forces that act on them. In contrast, a person's behavior is affected not only by others' actions, but also by inner states that cannot be observed directly.

In view of this complexity, we might expect social cognition to develop more slowly than nonsocial cognition. Surprisingly, it does not. Unique features of social experience probably help children make sense of its complexity early in life. First, because people are animated beings and objects of deep emotional investment, they are especially interesting to think about. Second, social experience constantly presents children with discrepancies between the behaviors they expect and those that occur, prompting them to revise their social cognitions. Finally, children and the people with whom they interact are all human beings, with the same basic nervous system and a background of similar experiences. This means that interpreting behavior from the self's point of view often helps us understand others' actions. When it does not, humans are equipped with a powerful capacity—*perspective taking*—that enables us to imagine what another's thoughts and feelings might be.

Our discussion is organized around three aspects of development: thinking about the self, thinking about other people, and thinking about relationships between people. Already, we have considered some social–cognitive topics in previous chapters—for example, referential communication skills in Chapter 9 and emotional understanding in Chapter 10. Children's sense of morality is another important social–cognitive topic, but research on it is so extensive that it merits a chapter of its own. We will consider the development of moral reasoning in Chapter 12.

Emergence of Self and Development of Self-Concept

Virtually all investigators agree that the self has two distinct aspects, identified by philosopher William James (1890/1963) more than a century ago:

- The **I-self,** a sense of self as *knower* and *actor,* includes the following realizations: *self-awareness,* that the self is separate from the surrounding world and has a private, inner life not accessible to others; *self-continuity,* that the self remains the same person over time; *self-coherence,* that the self is a single, consistent, bounded entity; and *self-agency,* that the self controls its own thoughts and actions.

- The **me-self** is a sense of self as *object of knowledge and evaluation.* It consists of all qualities that make the self unique: *material characteristics,* such as physical appearance and possessions; *psychological characteristics,* including desires, attitudes, beliefs, thought processes, and personality traits; and *social characteristics,* such as roles and relationships with others.

The I-self and the me-self are complementary. The I-self can be thought of as the *active observer;* it emerges first, followed by the me-self, which is made up of the *cognitive representations* that arise from the observing process (see Figure 11.1) (Harter, 1999; Lewis, 1994). In sum, self-development begins with the dawning of self-awareness in infancy and gradually evolves into a rich, multifaceted, organized view of the self's characteristics and capacities during childhood and adolescence.

Self-Awareness

As early as the first few months of life, infants smile and return friendly behaviors to their reflection in a mirror. When do they realize that the charming baby gazing and grinning back is the self?

• **BEGINNINGS OF THE I-SELF** • At birth, infants sense that they are physically distinct from their surroundings. For example, newborns display a stronger rooting reflex in response to external stimulation (an adult's finger touching their cheek) than to self-stimulation (their own hand contacting their cheek) (Rochat & Hespos, 1997). Newborns' remarkable capacity for

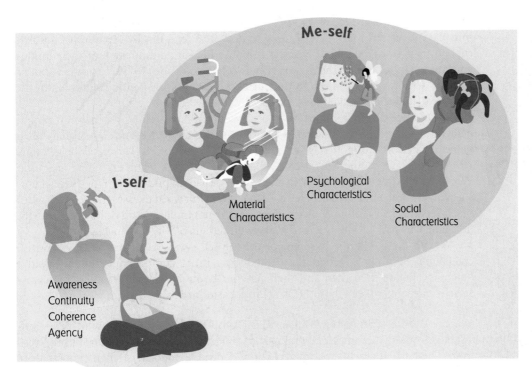

◀ **Figure 11.1**

The I-self and the me-self. The I-self is a sense of self as knower and actor. It is the active observer. The me-self is a sense of self as object of knowledge and evaluation. It is made up of the cognitive representations that arise from the observing process.

intermodal perception (see page 160 in Chapter 4) supports the beginnings of the I-self (Rochat, 2003). As they feel their own touch, feel and watch their limbs move, and feel and hear themselves cry, babies experience intermodal matches that differentiate their own body from surrounding bodies and objects.

Over the first few months, infants distinguish their own visual image from other stimuli, although self-awareness is still limited—expressed only in perception and action. When shown two side-by-side video images of their kicking legs, one from their own perspective (camera behind the baby) and one from an observer's perspective (camera in front of the baby), 3-month-olds looked longer at the observer's view (see Figure 11.2a). In another video-image comparison, they looked longer at a reversal of their leg positions than at a normal view (see Figure 11.2b) (Rochat, 1998). By 4 months, infants look and smile more at video images of others than at video images of themselves, indicating that they treat another person (as opposed to the self) as a potential social partner (Rochat & Striano, 2002).

According to many theorists, the I-self develops as infants increasingly realize that their own actions cause objects and people to react in predictable ways (Harter, 1998). In support of this idea, when parents encourage exploration and respond sensitively to infant signals (indications of a secure attachment bond), their children tend to be advanced in constructing a sense of self as agent (see Figure 11.3a on page 440). For example, between 1 and 2 years of age, babies with such parents display more complex, self-related actions during pretend play, such as making a doll labeled as the self take a drink or kiss a teddy bear (Pipp, Easterbrooks, & Harmon, 1992).

As infants act on the environment, they notice effects that help them sort out self, other people, and objects (Rochat, 2001). For example, batting a mobile and seeing it swing in a pattern different from the infant's own actions informs the baby about the relation between self and physical world. Smiling and vocalizing at a caregiver who smiles and vocalizes back helps clarify the relation between self and social world. The contrast between these experiences helps infants build an image of self as separate from, but vitally connected to, external reality.

• **BEGINNINGS OF THE ME-SELF** • During the second year, as toddlers start to construct the me-self, they become consciously aware of the self's physical features. In one study, 9- to 24-month-olds were placed in front of a mirror. Then, under the pretext of wiping the baby's face,

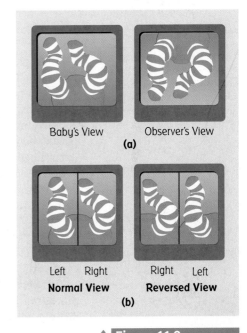

Baby's View   Observer's View
(a)

Left   Right   Right   Left
Normal View   **Reversed View**
(b)

▲ **Figure 11.2**

Three-month-olds' emerging self-awareness, as indicated by reactions to video images. (a) When shown two side-by-side views of their kicking legs, babies looked longer at the novel, observer's view than at their own view. (b) When shown a normal view of their leg positions alongside a reversed view, infants looked longer at the novel, reversed view. (Adapted from Rochat, 1998.)

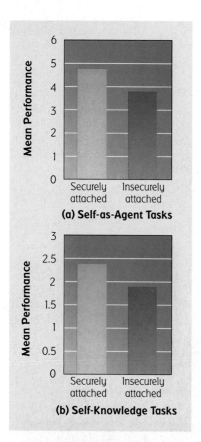

▲ **Figure 11.3**

Relationship of attachment quality to toddlers' performance on self-as-agent and self-knowledge tasks. Compared with insecure toddlers, securely attached toddlers displayed (a) more complex, self-related actions during pretend play and (b) more complex knowledge of the self's features. (Adapted from Pipp, Easterbrooks, & Harmon, 1992.)

each mother was asked to rub red dye on her child's nose. Younger infants touched the mirror as if the red mark had nothing to do with them. But by 15 months, toddlers rubbed their strange-looking noses, a response indicating awareness of their unique appearance—the "me" in the mirror (Lewis & Brooks-Gunn, 1979). In addition, some toddlers act silly or coy in front of the mirror, playfully experimenting with the way the self looks (Bullock & Lutkenhaus, 1990).

Around age 2, **self-recognition**—identification of the self as a physically unique being—is well under way. Children point to themselves in photos, and almost all use their name or a personal pronoun ("I" or "me") to refer to themselves (Lewis & Brooks-Gunn, 1979). It will take another year before children grasp the me-self as extending over time. When shown a live video of themselves, 2- and 3-year-olds quickly reach for a Post-it note stuck on top of their head as they see it on the screen. But when they see the note in a video that is replayed a few minutes after being recorded, not until age 4 do children remove the note and, when asked who was on TV, say with certainty, "Me" (Povinelli, 2001).

As with the I-self, development of the me-self seems to be fostered by sensitive caregiving. Securely attached toddlers display more complex featural knowledge (such as labeling their own and their parents' body parts) than do their insecurely attached agemates (see Figure 11.3b) (Pipp, Easterbrooks, & Brown, 1993).

• **SELF-AWARENESS AND EARLY EMOTIONAL AND SOCIAL DEVELOPMENT** • Self-awareness quickly becomes a central part of children's emotional and social lives. Recall from Chapter 10 that self-conscious emotions depend on toddlers' strengthening sense of self. Self-awareness also leads to initial efforts to appreciate another's perspective. For example, it is associated with the beginnings of empathy (see page 409) and self-conscious behavior: bashfulness and embarrassment. Furthermore, mirror self-awareness precedes the appearance of sustained, mutual peer imitation—a partner banging an object, the toddler copying the behavior, the partner imitating back, and the toddler copying again (Asendorpf, Warkentin, & Baudonniere, 1996). These exchanges indicate that the toddler not only is interested in the playmate but also realizes that the playmate is interested in him or her.

Two-year-olds' self-recognition leads to a sense of ownership. The stronger 2-year-olds' self-definitions, the more possessive they tend to be, claiming objects as "Mine!" (Levine, 1983; Fasig, 2000). A firmer sense of self also enables children to cooperate in resolving disputes over objects, playing games, and solving simple problems (Brownell & Carriger, 1990; Caplan et al., 1991). Accordingly, when trying to promote friendly peer interaction, parents and teachers can accept young children's possessiveness as a sign of self-assertion ("Yes, that's your toy") and then encourage compromise ("but in a little while, would you give someone else a turn?"), rather than insisting on sharing.

The Categorical and Remembered Selves

Language is a powerful tool in self-development. Because it permits children to represent and express the me-self more clearly, it greatly enhances young preschoolers' self-awareness.

Between 18 and 30 months, a **categorical self** develops as children classify themselves and others on the basis of age ("baby," "boy," or "man"), sex ("boy" versus "girl," "woman" versus "man"), physical characteristics ("big," "strong"), and even goodness and badness ("I good girl." "Tommy mean!"). They also start to refer to the self's competencies ("Did it!" "I can't") (Stipek, Gralinski, & Kopp, 1990).

Recall from Chapter 7 that adult–child conversations about the past lead to an autobiographical memory. This life-story narrative grants the child a **remembered self**—a more coherent and enduring portrait than is offered by the isolated, episodic memories of the first few years.

⊚ Even wearing a firefighter's hat, this 2-year-old recognizes himself in the mirror as a separate being, distinct from other people and objects. His consciousness of his own physical features indicates that he has begun to construct the me-self. © Laura Dwight/CORBIS

Cultural Variations in Personal Storytelling: Implications for Early Self-Concept

Preschoolers of many cultural backgrounds participate in personal storytelling with their parents. Striking cultural differences exist in parents' selection and interpretation of events in these early narratives, affecting the way children come to view themselves.

In one study, researchers spent hundreds of hours over a 2-year period studying the storytelling practices of six middle-SES Irish-American families in Chicago and six middle-SES Chinese families in Taiwan. From extensive videotapes of adults' conversations with 2½-year-olds, the investigators identified personal stories and coded them for content, quality of their endings, and evaluation of the child (Miller, Fung, & Mintz, 1996; Miller et al., 1997).

Parents in both cultures discussed pleasurable holidays and family excursions in similar ways and with similar frequency. Chinese parents, however, more often told long stories about the child's misdeeds, such as using impolite language, writing on the wall, or playing in an overly rowdy way. These narratives were conveyed with warmth and caring, stressed the impact of misbehavior on others ("You made Mama lose face"), and often ended with direct teaching of proper behavior ("Saying dirty words is not good"). By contrast, in the few instances in which Irish-American stories

referred to transgressions, parents downplayed their seriousness, attributing them to the child's spunk and assertiveness.

Early narratives about the child seem to launch preschoolers' self-concepts on culturally distinct paths. Influenced by Confucian traditions of strict discipline and social obligations, Chinese parents integrated these values into their personal stories, affirming the importance of not disgracing the family and explicitly conveying expectations in the story's conclusion. Although Irish-American parents disciplined their children, they rarely dwelt on misdeeds in storytelling. Rather, they cast the child's shortcomings in a positive light, perhaps to promote self-esteem. Whereas most North Americans believe that favorable self-esteem is crucial for healthy development, Chinese adults generally regard it as unimportant or even negative—as impeding the child's willing-

ness to listen and be corrected (Miller et al., 2002). Consistent with this view, the Chinese parents did little to cultivate their child's individuality. Instead, they used storytelling to guide the child toward socially responsible behavior. Hence, the Chinese child's self-image emphasizes obligations to others, whereas the North American child's is more autonomous.

▶ This Chinese child listens as his mother speaks gently to him about proper behavior. Chinese parents often tell preschoolers stories about the child's misdeeds, stressing the negative impact of misbehavior on others. The Chinese child's self-concept, in turn, emphasizes social obligations. © Peter Turnley/Corbis

By participating in personal storytelling, children come to view the self as a unique, continuously existing individual embedded in a world of others. As early as age 2, parents use these discussions to impart rules, standards, and evaluative information about the child, as when they say, "You added the milk when we made mashed potatoes. That's a very important job!" (Burger & Miller, 1999; Nelson, 2003). As the Cultural Influences box above reveals, these narratives are a major means through which caregivers imbue the young child's me-self with cultural values.

The Inner Self: Young Children's Theory of Mind

As children think more about themselves and others, they form a naive *theory of mind*—a coherent understanding of their own and others' rich mental lives. Recall from Chapter 7 that after age 2½, children refer to mental states frequently and appropriately in everyday language. Although they confuse certain mental terms (see page 296), young preschoolers are clearly aware of an **inner self** of private thoughts and imaginings.

How does the young child view this inner self, and how does this view change with age? Investigators are interested in this question because ideas about the mind are powerful tools in predicting and explaining our own and others' everyday behavior.

• **EARLY UNDERSTANDINGS OF MENTAL STATES** • Over the first year of life, infants build an implicit appreciation of people as animate beings whose behavior is governed by intentions, desires, and feelings. This sets the stage for the verbalized mental understandings that blossom in early childhood.

As early as 2 months, infants distinguish animate beings from inanimate objects; they imitate people's actions but not objects' simulations of those actions (Legerstee, 1991). In Chapter 10, we saw that 3-month-olds smile more at people than at objects and become upset when people pose a still face and fail to communicate. By 6 months, when infants see people talk, they expect the talk to be directed at other people and not at inanimate objects (Legerstee, Barna, & DiAdamo, 2000). At the end of the first year, babies view people as intentional beings who can share and influence one another's mental states, a milestone that opens the door to new forms of communication—joint attention, social referencing, preverbal gestures, and language. These interactive skills, in turn, enhance toddlers' mental understandings (Tomasello & Rakoczy, 2003). As they approach age 2, toddlers display a clearer grasp of people's emotions and desires, evident in their budding capacity to empathize and their realization that others' perspectives can differ from their own ("Daddy like carrots. I no like carrots.").

As language for talking about the mind expands in the third year, children appreciate the connections among perceiving, feeling, and desiring. For example, seeing that a person peeking inside a box is *happy*, 2½ -year-olds predict that the box contains a *desirable* rather than an *undesirable* snack. In addition, they often talk about links between perception and desire ("I *want see* beaver") and emotion and desire ("I *like* celery, so I *want* celery"). Occasionally, they link all three ("You *want* to *see* how he *cried*") (Wellman, Phillips, & Rodriguez, 2000). But although 2-year-olds have started to integrate mental states, their understanding is limited to a simplistic **desire theory of mind**. They think that people always act in ways consistent with their desires and do not understand that less obvious, more interpretive mental states, such as beliefs, also affect behavior (Bartsch & Wellman, 1995).

• **DEVELOPMENT OF BELIEF–DESIRE REASONING** • Between ages 3 and 4, children use such words as *think* and *know* to refer to their own and others' thoughts and beliefs (Wellman, 2002). And from age 4 on, they exhibit a **belief–desire theory of mind,** a more sophisticated view in which both *beliefs* and *desires* determine *actions*, and they understand the relationship between these inner states (Gopnik & Wellman, 1994; Ziv & Frye, 2003). Turn back to the beginning of this chapter, and notice how 4-year-old Ellen deliberately tries to alter her mother's *belief* about the motive behind her pretending, in hopes of warding off any *desire* on her mother's part to punish her. From early to middle childhood, efforts to alter others' beliefs increase, suggesting that children more firmly realize the power of belief to influence action.

Dramatic evidence for preschoolers' belief–desire reasoning comes from games that test whether they realize that *false beliefs*—ones that do not represent reality accurately—can guide people's behavior. For example: Show a child two small closed boxes, one a familiar Band-Aid box and the other a plain, unmarked box (see Figure 11.4). Then say, "Pick the box you think has the Band-Aids in it." Almost always, children pick the marked container. Next, open the boxes and show that child that, contrary to her own belief, the marked one is empty and the unmarked one contains the Band-Aids. Finally, introduce the child to a hand puppet and explain, "Here's Pam. She has a cut, see? Where do you think she'll look for Band-Aids? Why would she look in there? Before you looked inside, did you think that the plain box contained Band-Aids? Why?" (Bartsch & Wellman, 1995; Gopnik & Wellman, 1994). Only a handful of 3-year-olds—but many 4-year-olds—can explain Pam's and their own false beliefs.

Children's understanding of false belief strengthens over the preschool years, becoming more secure by age 6 (Wellman, Cross, & Watson, 2001). Mastery of false belief signals a change in representation—the ability to view beliefs as *interpretations,* not just reflections, of reality. Does this remind you of school-age children's more active view of the mind, discussed in Chapter 7? Belief–desire reasoning may mark the beginnings of this overall change.

School-age children's realization that people can increase their knowledge by making *mental inferences* (see page 296 in Chapter 7) enables false-belief understanding to extend further. In several studies, researchers told children complex stories involving one character's belief about a second character's belief. Then the children answered questions about what the first character thought the second character would do (see Figure 11.5).

▼ **Figure 11.4**

Example of a false-belief task. (a) An adult shows a child the contents of a Band-Aid box and of an unmarked box. The Band-Aids are in the unmarked container. (b) The adult introduces the child to a hand puppet named Pam and asks the child to predict where Pam would look for the Band-Aids and to explain Pam's behavior. The task reveals whether children understand that without having seen that the Band-Aids are in the unmarked container, Pam will hold a false belief.

(a)

(b)

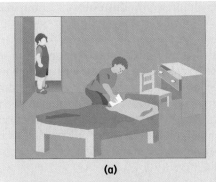

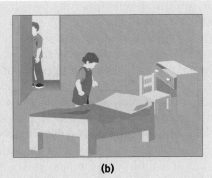

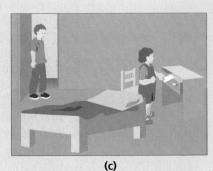

(a)

Jason has a letter from a friend. Lisa wants to read the letter, but Jason doesn't want her to. Jason puts the letter under his pillow.

(b)

Jason leaves the room to help his mother.

(c)

While Jason is gone, Lisa takes the letter and reads it. Jason returns and watches Lisa, but Lisa doesn't see Jason. Then Lisa puts the letter in Jason's desk.

▲ **Figure 11.5**

Example of a second-order false-belief task. To study the understanding of second-order false belief (that people's beliefs about other people's beliefs can be wrong), researchers tell children complex stories. After relating the story depicted in the sequence of pictures shown here, the researcher asks the child a second-order false-belief question: "Where does Lisa think Jason will look for the letter? Why?" Around age 7, children answer correctly—that Lisa thinks Jason will look under his pillow because Lisa doesn't know that Jason saw her put the letter in the desk. (Adapted from Astington, Pelletier, & Homer, 2002.)

By age 7, children were aware that people form beliefs about other people's beliefs and that these *second-order beliefs* can be wrong! Once children appreciate *second-order false belief,* they can better pinpoint the reasons that another person arrived at a certain belief (Astington, Pelletier, & Homer, 2002). This assists them greatly in understanding others' perspectives.

• **CONSEQUENCES OF BELIEF–DESIRE REASONING** • As soon as it emerges, the capacity to use both beliefs and desires to predict people's behavior helps children interact more favorably with others. The better 3- to 6-year-olds perform on false-belief tasks, the more advanced they are in social skills, as rated by teachers (Watson et al., 1999). False-belief understanding also predicts gains in 3- and 4-year-olds' sociodramatic play—specifically, the capacity to engage in joint planning, to negotiate pretend roles, and to imagine verbally, without the support of real objects (Jenkins & Astington, 2000).

Once children grasp the relation between beliefs and behavior, they refine their understanding, applying it to a wider range of situations. For example, children who pass false-belief tasks have more accurate eyewitness memories (Templeton & Wilcox, 2000). They realize that one person can present misinformation to another, which can affect the second individual's beliefs. Consequently, in reporting observed events, such children are more likely to resist attempts to mislead them. Development of a belief–desire theory may be a major reason that children's eyewitness memories become more dependable after age 6, when appreciation of the belief–reality distinction is more secure (see Chapter 7, page 292).

School-age children soon use their grasp of the relation between beliefs and behavior to persuade others. Third graders are more adept than kindergartners and first graders in considering people's beliefs when trying to convince them to do something. They know, for example, that a boy who wants a kitten but whose mother believes that cats scratch furniture should focus on telling his mother that the cat is declawed, rather than that it is litter trained (Bartsch & London, 2000).

In sum, the development of a belief–desire theory strengthens children's sensitivity to people's beliefs and promotes their reasoned attempts to change those beliefs. As a result, it contributes to many social competencies.

• **FACTORS CONTRIBUTING TO YOUNG CHILDREN'S THEORY OF MIND** • How do children develop a theory of mind at such a young age? Although great controversy surrounds this question, research suggests that language, cognitive abilities, make-believe play, and social experiences all contribute.

▶ *Language.* Understanding the mind requires the ability to reflect on thoughts, which is made possible by language. A grasp of false belief is related to language ability equivalent at least to that of an average 4-year-old (Jenkins & Astington, 1996). And children who spontaneously use, or who are trained to use, complex sentences with mental-state words are more likely to pass false-belief tasks (de Villiers & de Villiers, 2000; Hale & Tager-Flusberg, 2003). Among the Quechua village people of the Peruvian highlands, adults refer to mental states such as "think" and "believe" indirectly, because their language lacks mental-state terms. Quechuan children have difficulty with false-belief tasks for years after children in industrialized nations have mastered them (Vinden, 1996).

▶ *Cognitive Abilities.* The ability of 3- and 4-year-olds to inhibit inappropriate responses, think flexibly, and plan predicts current performance on false-belief tasks as well as improvements over time (Carlson & Moses, 2001; Hughes, 1998). Like language, these cognitive skills enhance children's capacity to reflect on their experiences and mental states. Gains in cognitive inhibition, considered in Chapter 7, predict false-belief understanding particularly strongly, perhaps because to do well on false-belief tasks, children must suppress an irrelevant response—namely, the tendency to assume that others' knowledge and beliefs are the same as their own (Birch & Bloom, 2003; Carlson, Moses, & Claxton, 2004).

▶ *Security of Attachment and Maternal "Mind-Mindedness."* In longitudinal research, mothers of securely attached babies were more likely to comment appropriately on their infants' mental states: "Do you *remember* Gramma?" "Do you *want* that toy?" "You really *like* that swing?" This maternal "mind-mindedness" was positively associated with later performance on false-belief and other theory-of-mind tasks (Meins et al., 1998, 2002). Furthermore, securely attached babies more often had mothers who continued to describe their children, when they reached preschool age, in terms of mental characteristics: "She's got a mind of her own!" or "He shows respect for other people" (Meins et al., 2003).

Parental commentary about mental states exposes infants and young children to concepts and language that help them think about their own and others' mental lives. During the preschool years, children seem to integrate this information into their understanding of the relations among desires, beliefs, and behavior. Some researchers suggest that children's reflections on inner states are among the representations that make up their internal working models of close relationships (see page 421 in Chapter 10) (Symons, 2004; Thompson & Raikes, 2003). This mental-state knowledge emerges earlier—and seems to be more objective and richer—among securely attached children, whose parents frequently refer to and converse with them about desires, intentions, beliefs, and emotions.

▶ *Make-Believe Play.* Earlier we noted that theory of mind fosters children's sociodramatic play. But make-believe also offers a rich context for thinking about the mind. As children act out roles, they often create situations they know to be untrue in the real world and reason about their implications (Harris & Leevers, 2000). These experiences may increase children's awareness that belief influences behavior. In support of this idea, preschoolers who engage in extensive fantasy play are more advanced than agemates in their understanding of false belief and other aspects of the mind (Astington & Jenkins, 1995). And the better 3- and 4-year-olds can reason about situations that contradict a real-world state of affairs, the more likely they are to pass false-belief tasks (Riggs & Peterson, 2000).

ⓒ Having older siblings fosters an understanding of false belief, probably because sibling interactions often highlight the influence of beliefs on behavior—through teasing, trickery, make-believe play, and discussing feelings.
© Tony Freeman/PhotoEdit

▶ *Social Interaction.* Preschoolers with siblings tend to be more aware of false belief, and those with older siblings especially so. Having older siblings is associated with exposure to more family talk about thoughts and beliefs, and with younger siblings' participation in such discussions (Jenkins et al., 2003; Peterson, 2001). Similarly, preschool friends who often engage in mental-state talk are ahead in false-belief understanding (Hughes & Dunn, 1998). Interacting with more mature members of society also contributes. In a study of Greek preschoolers, daily contact with many adults and older children predicted mastery of false belief (Lewis et al., 1996). These encounters offer extra opportunities to observe different viewpoints and talk about inner states.

Core knowledge theorists (see Chapter 6, page 253) believe that to profit from the social experiences just described, children must be biologically prepared to develop a theory of mind. They claim that children with *autism,* for whom mastery of false belief is either greatly delayed or absent, are deficient in the brain mechanism that enables humans to detect mental states. See the Biology and Environment box on the following page to find out more about the biological basis of reasoning about the mind.

"Mindblindness" and Autism

Sidney stood at the water table in Leslie's classroom, repeatedly filling a plastic cup and dumping out its contents. Dip-splash, dip-splash, dip-splash he went, until Leslie came over and redirected his actions. Without looking at Leslie's face, Sidney moved to a new repetitive pursuit: pouring water from one cup into another and back again. As other children entered the play space and conversed, Sidney hardly noticed. He rarely spoke, and when he did, he usually used words to get things he wanted, not to exchange ideas.

Sidney has *autism,* the most severe behavior disorder of childhood. The term *autism,* which means "absorbed in the self," is an apt description of Sidney. Like other children with the disorder, by age 3 he displayed deficits in three core areas of functioning: First, he had only limited ability to engage in nonverbal behaviors required for successful social interaction, such as eye gaze, facial expressions, gestures, and give-and-take. Most of the time, he seemed aloof and uninterested in other people. Second, his language was delayed and stereotyped. He used words to echo what others said and to get things he wanted, not to exchange ideas. Third, he engaged in much less make-believe play than children who were developing normally or who had other developmental problems (Frith, 2003). And Sidney showed another typical feature of autism: his interests, which focused on the physical world, were narrow and overly intense. For example, one day he sat for more than an hour spinning a toy Ferris wheel.

Researchers agree that autism stems from abnormal brain functioning, usually due to genetic or prenatal environmental causes. From the first year on, children with the disorder have larger than average brains, perhaps due to massive overgrowth of synapses and lack of synaptic pruning, which accompanies normal development of cognitive, language, and communication skills (Courchesne, Carper, & Akshoomoff, 2003). Furthermore, fMRI studies reveal that autism is associated with reduced activity in brain regions known to mediate emotional and social responsiveness and thinking about mental activities (Castelli et al., 2002;

Mundy, 2003). Other brain structures may also be involved.

Growing evidence reveals that children with autism have a deficient theory of mind. Long after they reach the intellectual level of an average 4-year-old, they have great difficulty with false-belief tasks. Most find it hard to attribute mental states to others or themselves (Steele, Joseph, & Tager-Flusberg, 2003). Such words as *believe, think, know, feel,* and *pretend* are rarely part of their vocabularies (Yirmiya, Solomonica-Levi, & Shulman, 1996).

As early as the second year, autistic children show deficits in social capacities that may contribute to awareness of others' mental states. Compared with other children, they less often establish joint attention, engage in social referencing, or imitate an adult's novel behaviors (Mundy & Stella, 2000). Furthermore, they are relatively insensitive to a speaker's gaze as a cue to what he or she is talking about. Instead, children with autism often assume that another person's language refers to what they themselves are looking at—a possible reason for their frequent use of nonsensical expressions (Baron-Cohen, Baldwin, & Crowson, 1997).

Do these findings indicate that autism is due to a specific cognitive deficit that leaves the child "mindblind" and therefore unable to engage in human sociability? Some researchers think so (Baron-Cohen, 2001; Scholl & Leslie, 2000). But others point out that individuals with autism are not alone in poor performance on tasks assessing mental understanding; nonautistic, mentally retarded individuals also do poorly (Yirmiya et al., 1998). This suggests that some kind of general intellectual impairment may be involved.

One conjecture is that children with autism are impaired in *executive processing* (refer to the central executive in the information-processing model on page 273 in Chapter 7). This leaves them deficient in a variety of cognitive abilities that underlie flexible, goal-oriented thinking, including shifting attention to address relevant

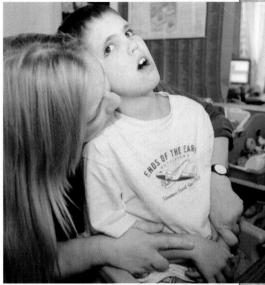

▲ This child, who has autism, is hardly aware of his mother's voice or touch as she tries to direct his attention to the computer. Researchers disagree on whether autistic children's "mindblindness" is due to a specific deficit in social understanding or to a general intellectual impairment involving executive processing.
© Jan Sonnenmair/Aurora & Quanta Productions, Inc.

aspects of a situation, inhibiting irrelevant responses, applying strategies to hold information in working memory, and generating plans (Geurts et al., 2004; Joseph & Tager-Flusberg, 2004). These cognitive weaknesses may account for the difficulty autistic children have with problems, such as conservation, that require them to integrate several contexts at once (before, during, and after the transformation of a substance) (Yirmiya & Shulman, 1996). An inability to think flexibly would also interfere with understanding the social world, since social interaction requires quick integration of information from various sources and evaluation of alternative possibilities.

It is not clear which of these hypotheses is correct. In fact, some research suggests that impairments in social awareness, integrative thinking, and verbal ability contribute independently to autism (Morgan, Maybery, & Durkin, 2003). Perhaps several biologically based deficits underlie the tragic social isolation of children like Sidney.

Self-Concept

As children develop an appreciation of their inner mental world, they think more intently about themselves. During early childhood, the me-self—knowledge and evaluation of the self's characteristics—expands (Harter, 2003). Children begin to construct a **self-concept,** the set of attributes, abilities, attitudes, and values that an individual believes defines who he or she is.

◎ Preschoolers' self-concepts emphasize observable characteristics. If asked to tell about himself, this 5-year-old might say, "I can make a huge snow shield!" In a few years, he will begin to mention personality traits, such as "I'm friendly and determined."
© Steve Mason/Getty Images/ PhotoDisc Green

• **EARLY CHILDHOOD** • Ask a 3- to 5-year-old to tell you about himself, and you are likely to hear something like this: "I'm Tommy. See, I got this new red T-shirt. I'm 4 years old. I can brush my teeth, and I can wash my hair all by myself. I have a new Tinker Toy set, and I made this big, big tower." As these statements indicate, preschoolers have self-concepts that are very concrete. Usually they mention observable characteristics—name, physical appearance, possessions, and everyday behaviors (Harter, 1996; Watson, 1990).

By age 3½, children also describe themselves in terms of typical emotions and attitudes, as in "I'm happy when I play with my friends" or "I don't like being with grownups." This suggests a beginning understanding of their unique psychological characteristics (Eder & Mangelsdorf, 1997). As further support for this budding grasp of personality, when given a trait label, such as "shy" or "mean," 4-year-olds infer appropriate motives and feelings. For example, they know that a shy person doesn't like to be with unfamiliar people (Heyman & Gelman, 1999). But preschoolers do not refer directly to traits; they don't say, "I'm helpful" or "I'm shy." This capacity must wait for greater cognitive maturity.

• **MIDDLE CHILDHOOD** • Over time, children organize their observations of typical behaviors and internal states into general dispositions. A major shift takes place between ages 8 and 11, as reflected in this response from an 11-year-old:

My name is A. I'm a human being. I'm a girl. I'm a truthful person. I'm not pretty. I do so-so in my studies. I'm a very good cellist. I'm a very good pianist. I'm a little bit tall for my age. I like several boys. I like several girls. I'm old-fashioned. I play tennis. I am a very good swimmer. I try to be helpful. I'm always ready to be friends with anybody. Mostly I'm good, but I lose my temper. I'm not well liked by some girls and boys. I don't know if I'm liked by boys or not. (Montemayor & Eisen, 1977, pp. 317–318)

Notice that instead of specific behaviors, this child emphasizes competencies: "I'm a very good cellist" (Damon & Hart, 1988). Also, she clearly describes her personality and mentions both positive and negative traits—"truthful" but "not pretty," a "good cellist [and] pianist" but only "so-so in my studies." Older school-age children are far less likely to describe themselves in unrealistically positive, all-or-none ways (Harter, 2003).

A major reason for these qualified self-descriptions is that school-age children often make **social comparisons,** judging their appearance, abilities, and behavior in relation to those of others. Although 4- to 6-year-olds can compare their own performance to that of a single peer, older children can compare multiple individuals, including themselves. Consequently, they conclude that they are "very good" at some things, "so-so" at others, and "not good" at still others (Butler, 1998).

• **ADOLESCENCE** • In early adolescence, young people unify separate traits ("smart" and "talented") into more abstract descriptors ("intelligent"). But these generalizations about the self are not interconnected and often are contradictory. For example, 12- to 14-year-olds might mention such opposing traits as "intelligent" and "airhead" or "shy" and "outgoing." These disparities result from social pressures to display different selves in different relationships—with parents, classmates, close friends, and romantic partners. As adolescents' social world expands, contradictory self-descriptions become more common, and teenagers frequently agonize over "which is the real me" (Harter, 1999, 2003).

By middle to late adolescence, teenagers combine their traits into an organized system. Their use of qualifiers ("I have a *fairly* quick temper," "I'm not *thoroughly* honest") reveals their awareness that psychological qualities often change from one situation to the next. Older adolescents also add integrating principles, which make sense of formerly troublesome contradictions. For example, one young person remarked, "I'm very adaptable. When I'm around my friends, who think that what I say is important, I'm very talkative, but around my family I'm quiet because they're never interested enough to really listen to me" (Damon, 1990, p. 88).

Compared with school-age children, teenagers place more emphasis on social virtues, such as being friendly, considerate, kind, and cooperative. Adolescents' statements about themselves reflect their preoccupation with being viewed positively by others. In addition, personal and moral values appear as key themes in older adolescents' self-concepts. For example, here is how 16-year-old Ben described himself in terms of honesty to himself and others:

> I like being honest like with yourself and with everyone.... [A person] could be, in the eyes of everyone else the best person in the world, but if I knew they were lying or cheating, in my eyes they wouldn't be.... When I'm friendly, it's more to tell people that it's all right to be yourself. Not necessarily don't conform, but just whatever you are, you know, be happy with that.... So I'm not an overly bubbly person that goes around, "Hi, how are you?" ... But if someone wants to talk to me, you know, sure. I wouldn't, like, not talk to someone. (Damon & Hart, 1988, pp. 120–121)

Ben offers a well-integrated account of his personal traits and values that is very different from the fragmented, listlike self-descriptions of children. As adolescents revise their views of themselves to include enduring beliefs and plans, they move toward the kind of unity of self that is central to identity development.

Cognitive, Social, and Cultural Influences on Self-Concept

What factors are responsible for these revisions in self-concept? Cognitive development certainly affects the changing *structure* of the self. School-age children, as we saw in Chapter 6, can better coordinate several aspects of a situation in reasoning about their physical world. Similarly, in the social realm, they combine typical experiences and behaviors into stable psychological dispositions, blend positive and negative characteristics, and compare their own characteristics with those of many other peers (Harter, 1999, 2003). In middle childhood, children also gain a clearer understanding of traits as linked to specific desires (a "generous" person *wants* to share) and, therefore, as causes of behavior (Yuill & Pearson, 1998). For this reason, they may mention traits more often. And formal operational thought transforms the adolescent's vision of the self into a complex, well-organized, internally consistent picture (Harter, 1999, 2003).

The changing *content* of the self is a product of both cognitive capacities and feedback from others. Sociologist George Herbert Mead (1934) described the self as a **generalized other**—a blend of what we imagine important people in our lives think of us. He proposed that a psychological self emerges when the child's I-self adopts a view of the me-self that resembles others' attitudes toward the child. Mead's ideas indicate that *perspective-taking skills*—in particular, an improved ability to infer what other people are thinking—are crucial for developing a self-concept based on personality traits. During middle childhood and adolescence, young people become better at "reading" messages they receive from others and incorporating these into their self-definitions. As school-age children internalize others' expectations, they form an *ideal self* that they use to evaluate their *real self*. As we will see shortly, a large discrepancy between the two can greatly undermine self-esteem, leading to sadness, hopelessness, and depression.

During middle childhood, as children enter a wider range of settings in school and community, they look to more people for information about themselves. Children's frequent reference to social groups in their self-descriptions reflects this shift. "I'm a Boy Scout, a paper boy, and a Prairie City soccer player," remarked one 10-year-old. Gradually, as children move into adolescence, their sources of self-definition become more selective. Although parents remain influential, self-concept becomes increasingly vested in feedback from close friends (Oosterwegel & Oppenheimer, 1993).

Keep in mind that the content of self-concept varies from culture to culture. In earlier chapters, we noted that Asian parents stress harmonious interdependence, whereas Western parents emphasize separateness and self-assertion. Consequently, in China and Japan, the self is defined in relation to the social group. In the United States, the self usually becomes the "property" of a self-contained individual (Markus & Kitayama, 1991). Turn back to the Cultural Influences box on page 441, and notice this difference in mothers' personal storytelling with their young children.

◉ During the school years, children's self-concepts expand to include feedback from a wider range of people as they spend more time in settings beyond the home. As part of a school activity, these children assemble baskets for donation to the Salvation Army. Helpfulness and kindness are probably important aspects of their self-definitions.
© Journal Courier/Steve Warmowski/The Image Works

MILESTONES

EMERGENCE OF SELF AND DEVELOPMENT OF SELF-CONCEPT

Age	Milestones
1–2 years	Aware of self as physically distinct and as causing people and objects to react in predictable ways
	Recognizes image of self in mirrors and photos and on videotape
	Uses own name or personal pronoun to label image of self
3–5 years	Forms a categorical self by classifying the self and others on the basis of age, gender, physical characteristics, goodness and badness, and competencies
	Constructs a remembered self, in the form of a life-story narrative
	Desire theory of mind expands into a belief–desire theory, as indicated by mastery of false-belief tasks
	Forms a self-concept consisting of observable characteristics and typical emotions and attitudes
6–10 years	Emphasizes personality traits and both positive and negative attributes in self-concept
	Makes social comparisons among multiple individuals
11 years and older	Unifies separate traits, such as "smart" and "talented," into more abstract descriptors, such as "intelligent," in self-concept
	Combines traits making up self-concept into an organized system

Note: These milestones represent overall age trends. Individual differences exist in the precise age at which each milestone is attained.

Photos: (top) © Laura Dwight Photography; (middle) © Tony Freeman/PhotoEdit; © Syracuse Newspapers/John Berry/The Image Works

Strong collectivist values also exist in many subcultures within Western nations. In one study, researchers gathered children's self-descriptions in a Puerto Rican fishing village and a small town in the United States. The Puerto Rican children often described themselves as "polite," "respectful," and "obedient" and justified these social traits by noting others' positive reactions to them. In contrast, the small-town American children typically mentioned individualistic traits, such as interests, preferences, and skills (Damon, 1988). In characterizing themselves, children from individualistic cultures seem to be more egoistic and competitive, those from collectivist cultures more concerned with the welfare of others—a finding that underscores the powerful impact of the social environment on self-concept.

The Milestones table above summarizes the vast changes in the self from infancy through adolescence.

Ask Yourself

REVIEW	What factors contribute to development of a belief–desire theory of mind, and why is each factor influential?
REVIEW	Describe major changes in self-concept from early childhood to adolescence. What factors lead self-descriptions to change in these ways?
APPLY	List indicators of healthy self-development in the first 2 years, and suggest ways that parents can promote a sturdy sense of self in infants and toddlers.
CONNECT	Recall from Chapter 6 (page 238) that between ages 4 and 8, children figure out who is really behind the activities of Santa Claus and the Tooth Fairy, and they realize that magicians use trickery. How might these understandings be related to their developing theory of mind?

Self-Esteem: The Evaluative Side of Self-Concept

So far, we have focused on how the general structure and content of self-concept change with age. Another component of self-concept is **self-esteem,** the judgments we make about our own worth and the feelings associated with those judgments. High self-esteem implies a realistic evaluation of the self's characteristics and competencies, coupled with an attitude of self-acceptance and self-respect.

Self-esteem ranks among the most important aspects of self-development because evaluations of our own competencies affect emotional experiences, future behavior, and long-term psychological adjustment. As soon as a categorical self with features that can be judged positively or negatively is in place, children become self-evaluative beings. Around age 2, they call a parent's attention to an achievement, such as completing a puzzle, by pointing and saying something like "Look, Mom!" In addition, 2-year-olds are likely to smile when they succeed at a task set for them by an adult and to look away or frown when they fail (Stipek, Recchia, & McClintic, 1992). Self-esteem originates early, and its structure becomes increasingly elaborate with age.

The Structure of Self-Esteem

Take a moment to think about your own self-esteem. Besides a global appraisal of your worth as a person, you make a variety of separate self-judgments concerning how well you perform at different activities.

Researchers have studied the multifaceted nature of self-esteem by applying *factor analysis* (see page 315 in Chapter 8) to children's ratings of the extent to which statements like these are true: "I am good at homework." "I'm usually the one chosen for games." "Most kids like me." By age 4, preschoolers have several self-judgments—for example, about learning things in school, making friends, getting along with parents, and feeling physically attractive (Marsh, Ellis, & Craven, 2002). Compared with that of older children, however, their understanding is limited.

The structure of self-esteem depends on evaluative information available to children and the ability to process that information. Around age 7 to 8, children in diverse Western cultures have formed at least four broad self-evaluations: academic competence, social competence, physical/athletic competence, and physical appearance. Within these are more refined categories that become increasingly distinct with age (Marsh, 1990; Marsh & Ayotte, 2003; Van den Bergh & De Rycke, 2003). For example, academic self-worth divides into performance in language arts, math, and other subjects, social self-worth into peer and parental relationships, and physical/athletic competence into skill at various sports.

Furthermore, school-age children's newfound ability to view themselves in terms of stable dispositions permits them to combine their separate self-evaluations into a general psychological image of themselves—an overall sense of self-esteem (Harter, 1999, 2003). Consequently, self-esteem takes on the hierarchical structure shown in Figure 11.6. Separate self-evaluations,

▼ **Figure 11.6**

Hierarchical structure of self-esteem in the mid-elementary school years. From their experiences in different settings, children form at least four separate self-esteems: academic competence, social competence, physical/athletic competence, and physical appearance. These differentiate into additional self-evaluations and combine to form a general sense of self-esteem. (Photo credits: *Far left:* © Laura Dwight Photography; *Middle left:* © George Disario/CORBIS; *Middle right:* © Mitch Wojnarowicz/ The Image Works; *Far right:* Charles Gupton/Stock Boston, LLC)

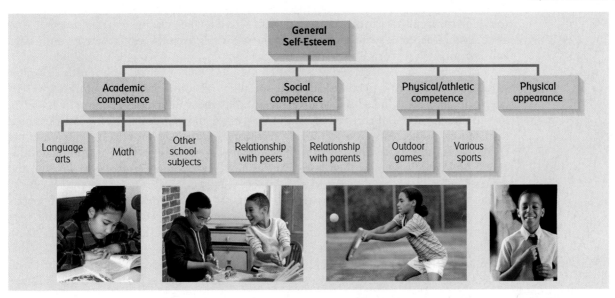

however, do not contribute equally to general self-esteem. Instead, children come to attach greater importance to certain self-judgments and to weight these more heavily in the total picture. Although individual differences exist, during childhood and adolescence perceived physical appearance correlates more strongly with global self-worth than any other self-esteem factor (Hymel et al., 1999). The emphasis that society and the media place on appearance has major implications for young people's overall satisfaction with themselves.

The arrival of adolescence adds several new dimensions of self-esteem—close friendship, romantic appeal, and job competence—that reflect important concerns of this period (Harter, 1999, 2003). Furthermore, adolescents become more discriminating in the people to whom they look for validation of their self-esteem. Some rely more on parents, others on teachers, and still others on peers—differences that reflect the extent to which teenagers believe that people in each context are interested in and respect them as individuals (Harter, Waters, & Whitesell, 1998).

Changes in Level of Self-Esteem: The Role of Social Comparisons

Because preschoolers have trouble distinguishing between their desired and their actual competence, when asked how well they can do something, they usually rate their own ability as extremely high and often underestimate the difficulty of tasks. Over the first few years of elementary school, self-esteem declines (Marsh, Craven, & Debus, 1998; Wigfield et al., 1997). As children increasingly engage in social comparison, they adjust their self-esteem to a more realistic level that matches the opinions of others, as well as objective performance.

To protect their self-worth, most children eventually balance social comparison information with personal achievement goals (Ruble & Flett, 1988). Perhaps for this reason, the drop in self-esteem in the early school years is usually not harmful. Then, from fourth grade on, self-esteem rises and remains high for the majority of young people, who report feeling especially good about their peer relationships and athletic capabilities (Cole et al., 2001; Twenge & Campbell, 2001). The main exception to this trend is a decline in self-worth for some adolescents after transition to junior high and high school. Entry into a new school, accompanied by new teacher and peer expectations, may temporarily interfere with the ability to make realistic judgments about behavior and performance. In Chapter 15, we will take up these school transition effects. For most young people, however, becoming an adolescent leads to feelings of pride and self-confidence.

Influences on Self-Esteem

From middle childhood to adolescence, individual differences in self-esteem become increasingly stable (Trzesniewski, Donnellan, & Robins, 2003). At the same time, positive relationships emerge among self-esteem, valuing of various activities, and success at those activities—relationships that strengthen with age. For example, academic self-esteem predicts how important, useful, and enjoyable children judge school subjects to be, their willingness to try hard, and their achievement in those subjects (Jacobs et al., 2002; Valentine, DuBois, & Cooper, 2004). In a Canadian study, academic self-worth in elementary school was associated with educational attainment 10 years later, in emerging adulthood (Guay, La Rose, & Boivin, 2004). Children with high social self-esteem are consistently better liked by their classmates (Harter, 1999). And as we saw in Chapter 5, sense of athletic competence is positively associated with investment in and performance at sports.

Furthermore, across age, sex, SES, and ethnic groups, individuals with mostly favorable self-esteem profiles tend to be well adjusted, sociable, and conscientious. In contrast, low self-esteem in all areas is linked to a wide array of adjustment difficulties (DuBois et al., 1999; Robins et al., 2001). But certain self-esteem factors are more strongly related to adjustment than others. Adolescents who feel highly dissatisfied with parental relationships often are aggressive and antisocial. Those with poor academic self-esteem tend to be anxious and unfocused. And those who view their peer relationships negatively are likely to be anxious and depressed (Leadbeater et al., 1999; Marsh, Parada, & Ayotte, 2004). And although virtually all teenagers become increasingly concerned about others' opinions, those who are overly dependent on social approval place their self-worth continually "on the line." As a result, they report frequent self-esteem shifts—on average, about once a week (Harter & Whitesell, 2003).

From age 5 on, children are aware that self-esteem has important consequences. They say that individuals who like themselves would do better at a challenging task and cope more easily with a peer's rebuff (Daniels, 1998). Because self-esteem is related to individual differences in children's

◉ At an annual youth summit, this young teen speaks confidently about her commitment to Drug-Free Youth (DFY), a U.S. national substance-abuse prevention organization. Self-esteem typically rises during adolescence, as do optimism and pride in new competencies.
© Jeff Greenberg/The Image Works

behavior, researchers have been intensely interested in identifying factors that cause it to be high for some children and low for others.

◉ Children from collectivist cultures rarely engage in social comparison to enhance their self-esteem. In a masquerade dance at their annual village carnival, these Caribbean children of St. Kitts display a strong sense of connection with their social group. Compared with children in individualistic societies, they are likely to be less concerned with whether another child is better at a skill than they are.
© Catherine Karnow/Woodfin Camp & Associates

• **CULTURE** • As with self-concept, cultural forces profoundly affect self-esteem. An especially strong emphasis on social comparison in school may underlie the finding that despite their higher academic achievement, Chinese and Japanese children score lower than American children in self-esteem—a difference that widens with age (Hawkins, 1994; Twenge & Crocker, 2002). In Asian classrooms, competition is tough and achievement pressure is high. At the same time, Asian children less often call on social comparisons to promote their own self-esteem. Because Asian cultures value social harmony, they tend to be reserved about judging themselves positively but generous in their praise of others (Falbo et al., 1997).

Gender-stereotyped expectations for physical attractiveness, athletic prowess, and achievement have a detrimental effect on the self-esteem of many girls. In adolescence, girls score slightly lower than boys in overall sense of self-worth, partly because they feel less confident about their physical appearance, academic competence, and athletic abilities. Despite a widely held assumption that boys' overall self-esteem is much higher than girls', in fact the gender difference is only slight (Cole et al., 2001; Marsh & Ayotte, 2003; Young & Mroczek, 2003). Girls may think less well of themselves because they internalize this negative cultural message.

Compared with their Caucasian agemates, African-American children tend to have slightly higher self-esteem, perhaps because of warm, extended families and a stronger sense of ethnic pride (Gray-Little & Hafdahl, 2000). Also, African-American girls, who are more satisfied with their physical appearance and peer relations, are less likely than Caucasian girls to decline in self-esteem in early adolescence (Eccles et al., 1999). Finally, children and adolescents who attend schools or live in neighborhoods where their SES and ethnic groups are well represented feel a stronger sense of belonging and have fewer self-esteem problems (Gray-Little & Carels, 1997).

• **CHILD-REARING PRACTICES** • Children and adolescents whose parents are warm and accepting and who provide reasonable expectations for mature behavior feel especially good about themselves (Carlson, Uppal, & Prosser, 2000; Feiring & Taska, 1996). Warm, positive parenting lets young people know that they are accepted as competent and worthwhile. And firm but appropriate expectations, backed up with explanations, help them make sensible choices and evaluate themselves against reasonable standards.

When parents too often help or make decisions for their child, children and adolescents suffer from low self-esteem. These controlling parents communicate a sense of inadequacy to children. Having parents who are repeatedly disapproving and insulting is also linked to low self-esteem (Kernis, 2002; Pomerantz & Eaton, 2000). Adolescents subjected to such experiences need constant reassurance, and their self-worth fluctuates with every evaluative remark by an adult or peer. Many rely heavily on peers rather than adults to affirm their self-esteem—a risk factor for adjustment difficulties (DuBois et al., 1999, 2002).

In contrast, overly tolerant, indulgent parenting is linked to unrealistically high self-esteem, which also undermines development. Children who feel superior to others tend to lash out at challenges to their overblown self-images and to have adjustment problems, including meanness and aggression (Hughes, Cavell, & Grossman, 1997).

Of special concern is that North American cultural values have increasingly emphasized a focus on the self, perhaps leading parents to indulge children and boost their self-esteem too much. As Figure 11.7 illustrates, the self-esteem of U.S children and adolescents has risen sharply over the past few decades—a period in which much popular literature for parents advised promoting children's self-esteem (Twenge &

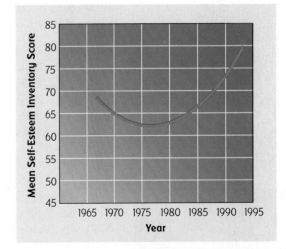

▲ **Figure 11.7**

Generational change in U.S. junior high school students' self-esteem from 1965 to 1995. Self-esteem dropped slightly during the late 1960s and 1970s as the divorce rate skyrocketed, schools became larger and more impersonal, and poverty increased. From 1980 on, a period of considerable public focus on boosting children's self-esteem, average self-esteem rose sharply. Self-esteem scores for younger and older students showed a similar rise.
(From J. M. Twenge & W. K. Campbell, 2001, "Age and Birth Cohort Differences in Self-Esteem: A Cross-Temporal Meta-Analysis," *Personality and Social Psychology Review, 5,* p. 336. Adapted by permission.)

451

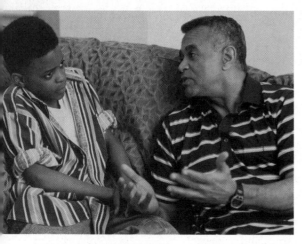

🔘 Although this child is uncomfortable with his father's direct approach, the father shows his concern and commitment by sitting close and leveling with his son about his expectations. As a result, the boy is likely to build a realistic, credible sense of self-esteem.
© David Harry Stewart/Getty Images Stone

Campbell, 2001). Yet compared with previous generations, American youths are achieving less well and displaying more antisocial behavior and other adjustment problems (Berk, 2005). Research confirms that children do not benefit from compliments, such as "You're terrific," that have no basis in real attainment. Instead, the best way to foster a positive, secure self-image is to encourage children to strive for worthwhile goals. Indeed, when school-age children are followed over time, a bidirectional relationship emerges between achievement and self-esteem: Good performance fosters self-esteem, and self-esteem fosters good performance (Guay, Marsh, & Boivin, 2003).

What can adults do to promote this mutually supportive relationship between motivation and self-esteem, and how can they avoid undermining it? Research on the precise content of adults' messages to children in achievement situations provides some answers.

Achievement-Related Attributions

Attributions are our common, everyday explanations for the causes of behavior—the answers we provide to the question "Why did I or another person do that?" We group the causes of our own and others' behavior into two broad categories: external, environmental causes and internal, psychological causes. Then we further divide the category of psychological causes into two types: *ability* and *effort*. In assigning a cause, we use certain rules: If a behavior occurs for many people but only in a single situation (for example, the whole class gets A's on Mrs. Apple's French test), we conclude that it is externally caused (the test was easy). In contrast, if an individual displays a behavior in many situations (Sally always gets A's on French tests), we judge the behavior to be internally caused—by ability, effort, or both.

In Chapter 8, we showed that although intelligence predicts school achievement, the relationship is far from perfect. Differences among children in **achievement motivation**—the tendency to persist at challenging tasks—explain why some less intelligent students do better in school than their more intelligent classmates. Today, researchers regard achievement-related attributions as the main reason some children are competent learners who display initiative when faced with obstacles to success, whereas others give up easily.

🔘 Most preschoolers are "learning optimists" who believe they can succeed if they keep on trying. Their attributions support initiative in the face of challenging tasks.
© Owen Franken/Corbis

• **EMERGENCE OF ACHIEVEMENT-RELATED ATTRIBUTIONS** • By the end of the second year, children turn to adults for evaluations of their accomplishments (Stipek, Recchia, & McClintic, 1992). And around age 3, they begin making attributions about their successes and failures. These attributions affect their *expectancies of success,* which influence their willingness to try hard in the future.

Many studies show that preschoolers are "learning optimists" who rate their own ability very high, often underestimate task difficulty, and hold positive expectancies of success. When asked to react to a situation in which one person does worse on a task than another, young children indicate that the lower-scoring person can still succeed if she keeps on trying (Schuster, Ruble, & Weinert, 1998). Cognitively, preschoolers cannot yet distinguish the precise causes of their successes and failures. Instead, they view all good things as going together: A person who tries hard is also a smart person who is going to succeed.

Nevertheless, by age 3, some children give up easily when faced with a challenge, such as working a hard puzzle. They conclude that they cannot do the task and express shame and despondency after failing. These nonpersisters have a history of critical maternal feedback about their worth and performance. In contrast, their enthusiastic, highly motivated agemates have mothers who patiently encourage while offering information about how to succeed (Kelley, Brownell, & Campbell, 2000). When preschool nonpersisters use dolls to act out an adult's reaction to failure, they expect disapproval. For example, they say, "He's punished because he can't do the puzzle," whereas persisters say, "He worked hard but just couldn't finish. He wants to try again" (Burhans & Dweck, 1995).

Preschoolers readily internalize adult evaluations. Whereas persisters view themselves as "good," nonpersisters see themselves as "bad" and deserving of negative feedback (Heyman, Dweck, & Cain, 1992). Already, nonpersisters seem to base their self-worth entirely on others' judgments, not on inner standards. Consequently, they show early signs of maladaptive achievement behaviors that become more common during middle childhood.

• MASTERY-ORIENTED VERSUS LEARNED-HELPLESS CHILDREN

• As a result of improved reasoning skills and frequent evaluative feedback, school-age children gradually become able to distinguish ability, effort, and external factors in explaining their performance (Dweck, 2002). Those who are high in achievement motivation make **mastery-oriented attributions,** crediting their successes to ability—a characteristic they can improve through trying hard and can count on when faced with new challenges. This **incremental view of ability**—that it can be altered through effort—influences the way mastery-oriented children interpret negative events. They attribute failure to factors that can be changed or controlled, such as insufficient effort or a difficult task (Heyman & Dweck, 1998). So whether these children succeed or fail, they take an industrious, persistent approach to learning.

Unfortunately, children who develop **learned helplessness** attribute their failures, not their successes, to ability. When they succeed, they are likely to conclude that external events, such as luck, are responsible. Furthermore, unlike their mastery-oriented counterparts, they hold an **entity view of ability**—that it cannot be changed. They do not think that competence can be improved by trying hard (Cain & Dweck, 1995). So when a task is difficult, these children experience an anxious loss of control. They give up, saying, "I can't do this," before they have really tried.

Children's attributions affect their goals. Mastery-oriented children focus on *learning goals*—increasing their ability through effort and seeking information on how to do so. In contrast, learned-helpless children focus on *performance goals*—obtaining positive and avoiding negative evaluations of their fragile sense of ability. Over time, the ability of learned-helpless children no longer predicts how well they do. In one study, the more fourth to sixth graders held self-critical attributions, the lower they rated their competence, the less they knew about effective study strategies, the more they avoided challenge, and the poorer their academic performance. These outcomes strengthened their entity view of ability (Pomerantz & Saxon, 2001). Because learned-helpless children fail to connect effort with success, they do not develop the metacognitive and self-regulatory skills necessary for high achievement (see Chapter 7). Lack of effective learning strategies, reduced persistence, and a sense of loss of control sustain one another in a vicious cycle (Heyman & Dweck, 1998).

In adolescence, young people attain a fully differentiated understanding of the relationship between ability and effort. They realize that people who vary in ability can achieve the same outcome with different degrees of effort (Butler, 1999). When adolescents view their own ability as fixed and low, they conclude that mastering a challenging task is not worth the cost—extremely high effort. To protect themselves from painful feelings of failure, these learned-helpless young people select less demanding courses and careers. As Figure 11.8 shows, learned helplessness prevents children from realizing their potential.

◎ Repeated negative evaluations can cause children to develop learned helplessness. While his classmate is focused intensely on the lesson, this boy has become completely derailed by his sense of defeat.
© Stephanie Maze/CORBIS

▼ **Figure 11.8**

Consequences of mastery-oriented and learned-helpless attributional styles.

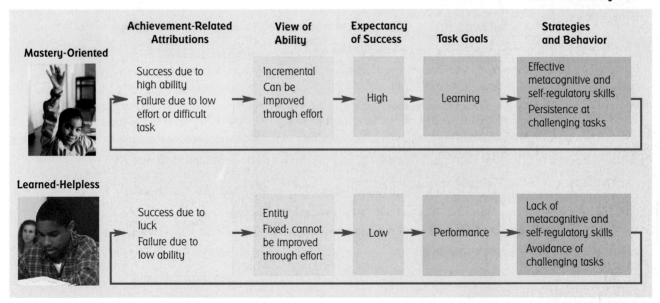

• **INFLUENCES ON ACHIEVEMENT-RELATED ATTRIBUTIONS** • What accounts for the different attributions of mastery-oriented and learned-helpless children? As with pre-schoolers, adult communication plays a key role. Children with a learned-helpless style tend to have parents who set unusually high standards while believing that their child is not very capable and must work harder than others to succeed. When these children fail, the adult might say, "You can't do that, can you? It's OK if you quit" (Hokoda & Fincham, 1995). After the child succeeds, the adult might respond, "Gee, I'm surprised you got that A," or give feedback evaluating the child's traits—for example, "You're so smart." Trait statements promote an entity view of ability, which leads children to question their competence in the face of setbacks and to retreat from challenge (Mueller & Dweck, 1998).

Teachers' messages also affect children's attributions. When teachers are caring and helpful and emphasize learning over performance goals, they tend to have mastery-oriented students (Anderman et al., 2001; Daniels, Kalkman, & McCombs, 2001). In a study of 1,600 third to eighth graders, students who viewed their teachers as providing positive, supportive learning conditions worked harder and participated more in class—factors that predicted high achievement, which sustained children's belief in the role of effort. In contrast, students with unsupportive teachers regarded their performance as externally controlled (by their teachers or by luck). This attitude predicted withdrawal from learning activities and declining achievement—outcomes that led children to doubt their ability (Skinner, Zimmer-Gembeck, & Connell, 1998).

Some children are especially likely to have their performance undermined by adult feedback. Despite their higher achievement, girls more often than boys blame their ability for poor performance. Girls also tend to receive messages from teachers and parents that their ability is at fault when they do not do well (Cole et al., 1999; Ruble & Martin, 1998). And in several studies, African-American and Mexican-American children received less favorable feedback from teachers (Irvine, 1986; Losey, 1995). Furthermore, when ethnic minority children observe that adults in their own family are not rewarded by society for their achievement efforts, they may try less hard themselves (Ogbu, 1997).

Applying

What We Know   Fostering a Mastery-Oriented Approach to Learning

Provision of tasks	Select tasks that are meaningful, responsive to a diversity of pupil interests, and appropriately matched to current competence so the child is challenged but not overwhelmed.
Parent and teacher encouragement	Communicate warmth, confidence in the child's abilities, the value of achievement, and the importance of effort in success.
	Model high effort in overcoming failure.
	(For teachers) Communicate often with parents, suggesting ways to foster children's effort and progress.
	(For parents) Monitor schoolwork; provide scaffolded assistance that promotes knowledge of effective strategies and self-regulation.
Performance evaluations	Make evaluations private; avoid publicizing success or failure through wall posters, stars, privileges to "smart" children, and prizes for "best" performance.
	Stress individual progress and self-improvement.
School environment	Offer small classes, which permit teachers to provide individualized support for mastery.
	Provide for cooperative learning and peer tutoring, in which children assist each other; avoid ability grouping, which makes evaluations of children's progress public.
	Accommodate individual and cultural differences in styles of learning.
	Create an atmosphere that values academics and sends a clear message that all pupils can learn.

Sources: Ames, 1992; Eccles, Wigfield, & Schiefele, 1998.

MILESTONES

DEVELOPMENT OF SELF-ESTEEM

Age	Milestones
1–2 years	Expressions of pleasure in mastery are evident.
	Sensitivity to adults' evaluations appears.
3–5 years	Self-esteem is typically high and consists of several separate self-evaluations.
	Achievement-related attributions appear but are undifferentiated; for example, a person who tries hard is smart and will succeed.
6–10 years	Self-esteem becomes hierarchically organized; separate self-evaluations (academic, social, and physical/athletic competence, physical appearance) are integrated into an overall self-image.
	Self-esteem declines as children make social comparisons, then rises.
	Achievement-related attributions differentiate into ability, effort, and external factors.
11 years–adulthood	New dimensions of self-esteem are added (close friendship, romantic appeal, job competence).
	Self-esteem continues to rise.
	Achievement-related attributions reflect full differentiation of ability and effort.

Note: These milestones represent overall age trends. Individual differences exist in the precise age at which each milestone is attained.

Photos: (top) © Nancy Richmond/The Image Works; (middle) © Laura Dwight/PhotoEdit; (bottom) © Barbara Stitzer/PhotoEdit

Finally, cultural values affect the likelihood that children will develop learned helplessness. Compared with North Americans, Asian parents and teachers believe that success depends much more on effort than on ability and that trying hard is a moral responsibility—messages they transmit to children (Grant & Dweck, 2001; Tuss, Zimmer, & Ho, 1995). And Israeli children growing up on *kibbutzim* (cooperative agricultural settlements) are shielded from learned helplessness by classrooms that emphasize mastery and interpersonal harmony rather than ability and competition (Butler & Ruzany, 1993).

• **FOSTERING A MASTERY-ORIENTED APPROACH** • Attribution research suggests that at times, well-intended messages from adults undermine children's competence. **Attribution retraining** is an intervention that encourages learned-helpless children to believe that they can overcome failure by exerting more effort. Most often, children are first given tasks that are hard enough that they will experience some failure. Then they get repeated feedback that helps them revise their attributions, such as "You can do it if you try harder." Children are also given additional feedback after they succeed, such as "You're really good at this" or "You really tried hard on that one," so that they view their success as due to both ability and effort rather than to chance.

Another approach is to encourage low-effort students to focus less on grades and more on mastery for its own sake. A large-scale study showed that classrooms emphasizing the intrinsic value of acquiring new knowledge led to impressive gains in academic self-esteem and motivation of failing students (Ames, 1992). Instruction in metacognition and self-regulation is also helpful, to make up for development lost in this area and to ensure that renewed effort will pay off (Borkowski & Muthukrisna, 1995).

To work well, attribution retraining is best begun early, before children's views of themselves become hard to change (Eccles, Wigfield, & Schiefele, 1998). An even better approach is to prevent learned helplessness, using the strategies summarized in Applying What We Know on the previous page. Consult the Milestones table above for an overview of the development of self-esteem.

Ask Yourself

REVIEW	Describe and explain changes in the structure and level of self-esteem from early childhood to adolescence.
APPLY	Should parents try to promote children's self-esteem by telling them they're "smart" and "wonderful"? Is it harmful if children do not feel good about everything they do? Why or why not?
CONNECT	What cognitive changes support the transition to a self-concept emphasizing competencies, personality traits, and social comparisons? (*Hint:* See pages 276–277 in Chapter 7.)
REFLECT	Describe your attributions for academic successes and failures during childhood. What are those attributions like now? What experiences do you think contributed to your attributions?

Constructing an Identity: Who Should I Become?

Adolescents' well-organized self-descriptions and differentiated sense of self-esteem provide the cognitive foundation for forming an **identity,** first recognized by psychoanalyst Erik Erikson (1950, 1968) as a major personality achievement and a crucial step toward becoming a productive, content adult. Constructing an identity involves defining who you are, what you value, and the directions you choose to pursue in life. One expert described it as an explicit theory of oneself as a rational agent—one who acts on the basis of reason, takes responsibility for those actions, and can explain them (Moshman, 1999). This search for what is true and real about the self drives many choices—vocation, interpersonal relationships, community involvement, ethnic-group membership, and expression of one's sexual orientation, as well as moral, political, and religious ideals.

Erikson believed that successful psychosocial outcomes of infancy and childhood pave the way toward a coherent, positive identity. (Return to Chapter 1, page 18, to review Erikson's stages.) Although the seeds of identity formation are planted early, not until late adolescence and emerging adulthood do young people become absorbed in this task. According to Erikson, in complex societies, teenagers experience an *identity crisis*—a temporary period of distress as they experiment with alternatives before settling on values and goals. Those who go through a process of inner soul-searching eventually arrive at a mature identity. They sift through characteristics that defined the self in childhood and combine them with new commitments. Then they mold these into a solid inner core that provides a sense of sameness as they move through different roles in daily life. Once formed, identity continues to be refined throughout life as people reevaluate earlier commitments and choices.

Current theorists agree with Erikson that questioning of values, plans, and priorities is necessary for a mature identity, but they no longer refer to this process as a "crisis" (Grotevant, 1998). Although identity development is traumatic and disturbing for some young people, for most it is not. *Exploration* followed by *commitment* better describes the typical experience. Young people gradually try out life possibilities, gathering important information about themselves and their environment and sorting through that information for the purpose of making enduring decisions. In the process, they forge an organized self-structure (Arnett, 2000a; Moshman, 1999).

Erikson described the negative outcome of adolescence as *identity confusion*. Some young people appear shallow and directionless, either because earlier conflicts have been resolved negatively or because society restricts their choices to ones that do not match their abilities and desires. As a result, they are unprepared for the psychological challenges of adulthood.

Does research support Erikson's ideas about identity development? In the following sections, we will see that young people go about the task of defining the self in ways that closely match Erikson's description.

Paths to Identity

Using a clinical interviewing procedure devised by James Marcia (1966, 1980), researchers evaluate progress in identity development on two key criteria derived from Erikson's theory: exploration and commitment. Their various combinations yield four *identity statuses:*

As these adolescents exchange opinions about a recent news event, they explore diverse values and priorities. Constructing an identity involves experimenting with alternatives before settling on personally meaningful life choices.
© Tony Freeman/PhotoEdit

TABLE 11.1 THE FOUR IDENTITY STATUSES

Identity Status	Description	Example
Identity achievement	Having already explored alternatives, identity-achieved individuals are committed to a clearly formulated set of self-chosen values and goals. They feel a sense of psychological well-being, of sameness through time, and of knowing where they are going.	When asked how willing she would be to give up going into her chosen occupation if something better came along, Darla responded, "Well, I might, but I doubt it. I've thought long and hard about law as a career. I'm pretty certain it's for me."
Identity moratorium	*Identity moratorium* means "delay or holding pattern." These individuals have not yet made definite commitments. They are in the process of exploring—gathering information and trying out activities, with the desire to find values and goals to guide their lives.	When asked whether he had ever had doubts about his religious beliefs, Ramon said, "Yes, I guess I'm going through that right now. I just don't see how there can be a God and yet so much evil in the world."
Identity foreclosure	Identity-foreclosed individuals have committed themselves to values and goals without exploring alternatives. They accept a ready-made identity that authority figures (usually parents but sometimes teachers, religious leaders, or romantic partners) have chosen for them.	When asked if she had ever reconsidered her political beliefs, Hillary answered, "No, not really, our family is pretty much in agreement on these things."
Identity diffusion	Identity-diffused individuals lack clear direction. They are neither committed to values and goals nor actively trying to reach them. They may never have explored alternatives or may have found the task too threatening and overwhelming.	When asked about his attitude toward nontraditional gender roles, Joel responded, "Oh, I don't know. It doesn't make much difference to me. I can take it or leave it."

identity achievement, commitment to values, beliefs, and goals following a period of exploration; **identity moratorium,** exploration without having reached commitment; **identity foreclosure,** commitment in the absence of exploration; and **identity diffusion,** an apathetic state characterized by lack of both exploration and commitment. Table 11.1 summarizes these identity statuses.

Identity development follows many paths. Some young people remain in one status, whereas others experience many status transitions. And the pattern often varies across *identity domains,* such as sexual orientation, vocation, and religious, political, and other world views. Most young people change from "lower" statuses (foreclosure or diffusion) to "higher" statuses (moratorium or achievement) between their mid-teens and mid-twenties, but some move in the reverse direction (Kroger, 2001; Meeus, 1996). The number of domains explored and the intensity with which they are examined vary widely, depending on the contexts young people want to enter and the importance they attach to them. Almost all grapple with work, close relationships, and family. Others add political, religious, community, and leisure-time commitments, some of which are more central to their identity than others.

Because attending college gives young people many opportunities to explore career options and lifestyles, they make more progress toward formulating an identity than they did in high school (Meeus et al., 1999). In the years after college, emerging adults often sample a broad range of life experiences before choosing a life course. Some, for example, take short-term volunteer jobs in such programs as the U.S. Peace Corps or the Canada Corps; others travel extensively on their own. Young people who go to work immediately after high school graduation often settle on a self-definition earlier than college-educated youths. But those who find it difficult to realize their occupational goals because they lack training or vocational choices are at risk for long-term identity foreclosure or diffusion (Cohen et al., 2003; Eccles et al., 2003).

At one time, researchers thought that adolescent girls postponed the task of establishing an identity and, instead, focused on Erikson's next stage, intimacy development. Some girls do show more sophisticated reasoning in identity domains related to intimacy, such as sexuality and family versus career priorities. Otherwise, adolescents of both sexes typically make progress on identity concerns before experiencing genuine intimacy in relationships (Kroger, 2000; Meeus et al., 1999).

Identity Status and Psychological Well-Being

According to identity theorists, individuals who move away from foreclosure and diffusion toward moratorium and achievement build a well-structured identity that integrates various

Adolescent Suicide: Annihilation of the Self

The suicide rate increases over the lifespan. It is lowest in childhood and highest in old age, but it jumps sharply at adolescence. Currently, suicide is the third-leading cause of death among American youths (after motor vehicle collisions and homicides) and the second-leading cause among Canadian youths (after motor vehicle collisions). Perhaps because North American teenagers experience more stresses and fewer supports than they did in the past, the rate of adolescent suicide tripled in both the United States and Canada between the mid-1960s and the mid-1990s, followed by a slight decline. At the same time, adolescent suicide rates vary widely among industrialized nations. Denmark, Greece, Italy, and Spain have low rates; Australia, Canada, Japan, and the United States have intermediate rates; and Finland, New Zealand, and Singapore have high rates (Lester, 2003). Although many theories exist, international differences remain unexplained.

Factors Related to Adolescent Suicide

Striking sex differences in suicidal behavior exist. The number of boys who kill themselves exceeds the number of girls by 4 or 5 to 1. This may seem surprising, given that girls show higher rates of depression. Yet the findings are not inconsistent. Girls make more unsuccessful suicide attempts and use methods from which they are more likely to be revived, such as a sleeping pill overdose. In contrast, boys tend to select more active techniques that lead to instant death, such as firearms or hanging. Gender-role expectations may be responsible; less tolerance exists for feelings of helplessness and failed efforts in males than in females (Canetto & Sakinofsky, 1998).

African Americans and Hispanics have slightly lower suicide rates than Caucasian Americans. Higher levels of support through extended families may be responsible. However, suicide among African-American adolescent males has recently risen; currently, the rate approaches that of Caucasian-American males. And Native-American and Canadian Aboriginal youths commit suicide at rates two to seven times national averages (Health Canada, 2003a; Joe & Marcus, 2003). High rates of profound family poverty, school failure, alcohol and drug use, and depression probably underlie these trends. Gay, lesbian, and bisexual youths also are at high risk for suicide, making attempts at a rate three times higher than other adolescents. Those who have tried to kill themselves report more family conflict, inner turmoil about their sexuality, problems in romantic relationships, and peer rejection due to their sexual orientation (Savin-Williams & Ream, 2003b).

Suicidal adolescents often show signs of extreme despondency during the period before the suicidal act. Many verbalize the wish to die, lose interest in school and friends, neglect their personal appearance, and give away treasured possessions. These warning signs appear in two types of young people. In the first group are highly intelligent teenagers who are solitary, withdrawn, and unable to meet their own standards or those of important people in their lives. Members of a second, larger group show antisocial tendencies. These young people express their unhappiness through bullying, fighting, stealing, increased risk taking, and drug abuse (Fergusson, Woodward, & Horwood, 2000). Besides being hostile and destructive, they turn their anger and disappointment inward.

Heredity and environment jointly contribute to suicidal behavior. As we have just seen, personality traits—either high introversion or high impulsivity and recklessness—are predisposing factors. A family history of emotional and antisocial disorders and suicide is often present, and frequently the teenager has been diagnosed with a mental disorder. In addition, suicidal young people are more likely to have experienced high

domains. As a result, they experience a gratifying sense of personal continuity and social connection—of being the same person across time and contexts and of becoming a competent member of the adult community (Snarey & Bell, 2003; van Hoof & Raaijmakers, 2003).

A wealth of research supports the conclusion that identity achievement and moratorium are psychologically healthy routes to a mature self-definition, whereas long-term foreclosure and diffusion are maladaptive. Young people who are identity achieved or actively exploring have a higher sense of self-esteem, are more likely to engage in abstract and critical thinking, report greater similarity between their ideal self and their real self, and are more advanced in moral reasoning (Josselson, 1994; Marcia et al., 1993). Although adolescents in moratorium are often anxious about the challenges that lie before them, they join with identity-achieved individuals in using an autonomous, information-gathering style when making decisions and solving problems (Berzonsky & Kuk, 2000; Kroger, 1995).

Adolescents who get stuck in either foreclosure or diffusion have adjustment difficulties. Foreclosed individuals tend to be dogmatic, inflexible, and intolerant. Some regard any difference of opinion as a threat (Kroger, 1995). Most fear rejection by people on whom they depend for

rates of stressful life events, including economic disadvantage, parental separation and divorce, low level of family warmth, frequent parent–child conflict, and abuse and neglect. Stressors typically increase during the period preceding a suicide attempt or completion (Beautrais, 2003; Wagner, Silverman, & Martin, 2003). Triggering events include parental blaming of the teenager for family problems, the breakup of an important peer relationship, or the humiliation of having been caught engaging in irresponsible, antisocial acts.

Why does suicide increase in adolescence? Teenagers' improved ability to plan ahead seems to be involved. Although some act impulsively, many young people at risk take purposeful steps toward killing themselves (McKeown et al., 1998). Other cognitive changes also contribute. Belief in the personal fable (see Chapter 6) leads many depressed young people to conclude that no one could possibly understand the intense pain they feel. As a result, their despair, hopelessness, and isolation deepen.

Prevention and Treatment

Picking up on the signals that a troubled teenager sends is a crucial first step in suicide prevention. Parents and teachers must be trained to recognize warning signs. Schools and community settings, such as recreational and religious organizations, can help by providing knowledgeable, approachable, and sympathetic adults, peer support groups, and information about telephone

hot lines (Spirito et al., 2003). Once a teenager takes steps toward suicide, staying with the young person, listening, and expressing compassion and concern until professional help can be obtained are essential.

Intervention with depressed and suicidal adolescents takes many forms, from antidepressant medication to individual, family, and group therapy. Sometimes hospitalization is necessary to ensure the teenager's safety. Until the adolescent improves, removing weapons, knives, razors, scissors, and drugs from the home is vital. On a broader scale, gun-control legislation that limits adolescents' access to the most frequent and deadly suicide method in the United States would greatly reduce both the number of suicides and the high teenage homicide rate. In Canada and other industrialized nations with strict gun-control policies, teenage deaths due to firearms are, on average, only one-sixteenth as likely to occur as in the United States (Fingerhut & Christoffel, 2002).

After a suicide, family and peer survivors need support to help them cope with grief, anger, and guilt over not having been able to help the victim. Teenage suicides often take place in clusters. When one occurs, it increases the likelihood of other suicides among depressed peers

▲ A tendency to react to stressful events passively and dependently contributes to girls' higher rate of depression. Because adolescent depression can lead to long-term emotional problems, it deserves to be taken seriously. © Lawrence Manning/Corbis

who knew the young person or heard about the death through the media (Bearman & Moody, 2004; Gould, Jamieson, & Romer, 2003). In view of this trend, an especially watchful eye must be kept on vulnerable adolescents after a suicide happens. Restraint by journalists in reporting teenage suicides on television and in newspapers also aids prevention.

affection and self-esteem. A few foreclosed teenagers who are alienated from their families and society may join cults or other extremist groups, uncritically adopting a way of life that is different from their past. Persistently diffused teenagers are the least mature in identity development. They typically entrust themselves to luck or fate, have an "I don't care" attitude, and tend to go along with whatever the "crowd" is doing. As a result, they often experience time management and academic difficulties (Berzonsky & Kuk, 2000). And they are the most likely of all young people to use and abuse drugs. Often at the heart of their apathy and impulsiveness is a sense of hopelessness about the future (Archer & Waterman, 1990). Many are at risk for serious depression and suicide—problems that rise sharply during adolescence (see the Social Issues box above).

Influences on Identity Development

Adolescent identity formation begins a lifelong, dynamic process that blends personality and context. A change in either the individual or the context opens up the possibility of reformulating identity (Kunnen & Bosma, 2003). A wide variety of factors influence identity development.

• **PERSONALITY** • Identity status, as we saw in the previous section, is both cause and consequence of personality characteristics. Adolescents who assume that absolute truth is always attainable tend to be foreclosed, whereas those who lack confidence in the prospect of ever knowing anything with certainty are more often in a state of identity diffusion. Adolescents who appreciate that they can use rational criteria to choose among alternatives are more likely to be in a state of moratorium or identity achievement (Berzonsky & Kuk, 2000; Boyes & Chandler, 1992). This flexible, open-minded approach helps them greatly in identifying and pursuing educational, vocational, and other life goals.

• **FAMILY** • Recall that parents who provide both emotional support and freedom to explore have infants and toddlers who develop a healthy sense of agency. A similar link between parenting and identity exists at adolescence. When the family serves as a "secure base" from which teenagers can confidently move out into the wider world, identity development is enhanced. Adolescents who feel attached to their parents and say they provide effective guidance, but who also feel free to voice their own opinions, tend to be identity achieved or in a state of moratorium (Berzonsky, 2004; Grotevant & Cooper, 1998). Foreclosed teenagers usually have close bonds with parents, but they lack opportunities for healthy separation. Finally, diffused young people devalue the importance of their attachments to parents and report low levels of parental support and of warm, open communication (Reis & Youniss, 2004; Zimmerman & Becker-Stoll, 2002).

• **PEERS** • As adolescents interact with a diversity of peers, their exposure to ideas and values expands. Close friends help young people explore options by providing emotional support, assistance, and role models of identity development (Josselson, 1992). Within friendships, adolescents learn much about themselves. In one study, 15-year-olds with warm, trusting peer ties were more involved in exploring relationship issues—for example, thinking about what they valued in close friends and in a life partner (Meeus, Oosterwegel, & Vollebergh, 2002). In another study, college students' attachment to friends predicted exploration of careers and progress in choosing one (Felsman & Blustein, 1999). In sum, friends—like parents—can serve as a "secure base" as adolescents grapple with possibilities.

• **SCHOOL AND COMMUNITY** • Identity development also depends on schools and communities that offer rich and varied opportunities for exploration. Schools can foster identity development in many ways—through classrooms that promote high-level thinking, extracurricular and community activities that enable teenagers to take on responsible roles, teachers and counselors who encourage low-SES and ethnic minority students to go to college, and vocational training programs that immerse adolescents in the real world of adult work (Cooper, 1998).

Regional variations in opportunity can lead to differences in identity development. For example, between ages 13 and 17, exploration increases among Australian adolescents living in urban environments, whereas it decreases among youths in rural areas. Lack of educational and vocational options in Australian rural regions is probably responsible (Nurmi, Poole, & Kalakoski, 1996). Regardless of where they live, young people benefit from a chance to talk with adults and older peers who have worked through identity questions.

• **THE LARGER SOCIETY** • The larger cultural context and historical time period affect identity development. Among contemporary young people, exploration and commitment tend to occur earlier in the identity domains of gender-role preference and vocational choice than in religious and political values (Flanagan et al., 1999; Kerestes & Youniss, 2003). Yet a generation ago, when the Vietnam War divided Americans and disrupted the lives of thousands of young people, the political beliefs of American youths took shape sooner (Archer, 1989). Societal forces are also responsible for the special problems that gay, lesbian, and bisexual youths (see Chapter 5) and ethnic minority adolescents face in forming a secure identity, as the Cultural Influences box on the following page describes.

Identity Development Among Ethnic Minority Adolescents

Most adolescents are aware of their cultural ancestry, and it is not a matter of intense concern for them. But for teenagers who are members of minority groups, **ethnic identity**—a sense of ethnic group membership and attitudes and feelings associated with that membership—is central to the quest for identity, and it presents complex challenges. As they develop cognitively and become more sensitive to feedback from the broader social environment, minority youths become painfully aware that they are targets of prejudice and discrimination. This discovery complicates their efforts to develop a sense of cultural belonging and a set of personally meaningful goals.

Minority youths often feel caught between the standards of the larger society and the traditions of their culture of origin. In many immigrant families from collectivist cultures, adolescents' commitment to obeying their parents and fulfilling family obligations lessens the longer the family has been in the immigrant-receiving country (Phinney, Ong, & Madden, 2000). Some immigrant parents are overly restrictive of their teenagers out of fear that assimilation into the larger society will undermine their cultural traditions, and their youngsters rebel, rejecting aspects of their ethnic background.

Other minority teenagers react to years of shattered self-esteem, school failure, and barriers to success in the mainstream culture by defining themselves in contrast to majority values. A Mexican-American teenager who had given up on school commented, "Mexicans don't have a chance to go on to college and make something of themselves" (Matute-Bianche, 1986, pp. 250–251). At

the same time, discrimination can interfere with the formation of a positive ethnic identity. In one study, Mexican-American youths who had experienced more discrimination were less likely to explore their ethnicity and to report feeling good about it. Those with low ethnic pride showed a sharp drop in self-esteem in the face of discrimination (Romero & Roberts, 2003).

Because it is painful and confusing, minority adolescents often dodge the task of forming an ethnic identity. Many are diffused or foreclosed on ethnic identity issues (Markstrom-Adams & Adams, 1995). Young people with parents of different ethnicities face extra challenges. In a large survey of high school students, part-black biracial teenagers reported as much discrimination as their monoracial black counterparts, yet they felt less positively about their ethnicity. And compared with monoracial minorities, many biracials—including black–white, black–Asian, white–Asian, black–Hispanic, and white–Hispanic—regarded ethnicity as less central to their identities (Herman, 2004). Perhaps because these adolescents did not feel as if they belonged to any ethnic group, they discounted the significance of ethnic identity and (in the case of part-black biracials) viewed their minority background somewhat negatively.

When family members encourage adolescents to behave proactively, by disproving ethnic stereotypes of low achievement or antisocial behavior, young people typically surmount the threat that discrimination poses to a favorable ethnic identity (Phinney & Chavira, 1995). In addition, adolescents whose families have taught them the history, traditions, values, and language of their ethnic group and who frequently interact with same-ethnicity peers are more likely

to forge a favorable ethnic identity (Phinney et al., 2001b).

How can society help minority adolescents resolve identity conflicts constructively? Here are some relevant approaches:

● Promote effective parenting, in which children and adolescents benefit from family ethnic pride, yet are encouraged to explore the meaning of ethnicity in their own lives.

● Ensure that schools respect minority youths' native languages, unique learning styles, and right to a high-quality education.

● Foster contact with peers of the same ethnicity, along with respect between ethnic groups (Garcia Coll & Magnuson, 1997).

A strong, secure ethnic identity is associated with higher self-esteem, optimism, and sense of mastery over the environment (Smith et al., 1999a). For these reasons, adolescents with a positive connection to their ethnic group are better adjusted. They cope more effectively with stress, achieve more favorably in school, and have fewer emotional and behavior problems than agemates who identify only weakly with their ethnicity (Chavous et al., 2003; Wong, Eccles, & Sameroff, 2003). For teenagers faced with adversity, ethnic identity is a powerful source of resilience.

Forming a **bicultural identity**—by exploring and adopting values from both the adolescent's subculture and the dominant culture—offers added benefits. Biculturally identified adolescents tend to be achieved in other areas of identity as well. And their relations with members of other ethnic groups are especially favorable (Phinney et al., 2001a; Phinney & Kohatsu, 1997). In sum, achievement of ethnic identity enhances many aspects of emotional and social development.

◀ These girls from the Mohawk Reserve in Kahnawake, outside Montréal, Québec, wear traditional costumes. When minority youths encounter respect for their cultural heritage in schools and communities, they are most likely to retain ethnic values and customs as an important part of their identities. © Martha Cooper/Peter Arnold, Inc.

Applying
What We Know   Supporting Healthy Identity Development

Strategy	Explanation
Engage in warm, open communication.	Provides both emotional support and freedom to explore values and goals
Initiate discussions that promote high-level thinking at home and at school.	Encourages rational and deliberate selection among competing beliefs and values
Provide opportunities to participate in extracurricular activities and vocational training programs.	Permits young people to explore the real world of adult work
Provide opportunities to talk with adults and peers who have worked through identity questions.	Offers models of identity achievement and advice on how to resolve identity concerns
Provide opportunities to explore ethnic heritage and learn about other cultures in an atmosphere of respect.	Fosters identity achievement in all areas and ethnic tolerance, which supports the identity explorations of others

The identity explorations of young people make the late teens and early twenties an especially full, intense time of life. Experiences are not always agreeable; many youths encounter disappointments, are forced to revise their goals, and are disturbed by conditions in their society and the world (Arnett, 2000b; Cohen et al., 2003). Nevertheless, almost all are optimistic about the future (Harris Poll, 2001). For ways in which adults can support healthy identity development in adolescence, consult Applying What We Know above.

Ask Yourself

REVIEW	Explain how the four identity statuses are linked to psychological adjustment.
APPLY	Eighteen-year-old Brad's parents worry that he will waste time at college because he is unsure about his major and career goals. Explain why Brad's uncertainty might actually be advantageous for his identity development.
CONNECT	Return to pages 446–447 and 450 to review changes in self-concept and self-esteem in adolescence. How do these changes pave the way for identity development?
REFLECT	How would you characterize your identity status? Is it the same or different across domains of sexuality, close relationships, vocation, religious beliefs, and political values? Describe your path of identity development in important domains, along with factors that may have influenced it.

Thinking About Other People

Children's understanding of other people—the inferences they make about others' personality traits and viewpoints—has much in common with their developing understanding of themselves. These facets of social cognition also become increasingly differentiated and well organized with age.

Person Perception

Person perception refers to the way we size up the attributes of people with whom we are familiar. Researchers study person perception by asking children to describe people they know, using methods similar to those that focus on children's self-concepts. For example, the researcher might ask, "Can you tell me what kind of person _____ is?"

• **UNDERSTANDING PEOPLE AS PERSONALITIES** • Like their self-descriptions, before age 8, children's descriptions of others focus on commonly experienced emotions and attitudes, concrete activities, and behaviors. Over time, children discover consistencies in the actions of people they know, and they mention personality traits.

At first, these references are closely tied to behavior and consist of implied dispositions: "He's always fighting with people" or "She steals and lies" (Rholes, Newman, & Ruble, 1990). Later, children mention traits directly, but they use vague, stereotyped language, such as "good," "nice," or "acts smart." Gradually, sharper trait descriptions appear—for example, "honest," "trustworthy," "generous," "polite," and "selfish"—and children become more convinced of the stability of such dispositions (Droege & Stipek, 1993; Ruble & Dweck, 1995).

During adolescence, as abstract thinking becomes better established, inferences about others' personalities are drawn together into organized character sketches (O'Mahoney, 1989). As a result, between ages 14 and 16, teenagers present rich accounts of people they know that integrate physical traits, typical behaviors, and inner dispositions.

• **UNDERSTANDING ETHNICITY AND SOCIAL CLASS** • Person perception also includes making sense of diversity and inequality among people. Most 3- and 4-year-olds have formed basic concepts of race and ethnicity, in that they can apply labels of "black" and "white" to pictures, dolls, and people (Aboud, 2003; Katz & Kofkin, 1997). Indicators of social class—education and occupational prestige—are not accessible to young children. Nevertheless, they can distinguish rich from poor on the basis of physical characteristics, such as clothing, residence, and possessions (Ramsey, 1991).

By the early school years, children absorb prevailing societal attitudes toward social groups. Because race, ethnicity, and social class are closely related in Western nations, children connect power and privilege with white people and poverty and inferior status with people of color (Ramsey, 1995). How do children acquire these attitudes? They do not necessarily do so by directly adopting the attitudes of parents and friends. In one study, although white school-age children assumed that parents' and friends' racial attitudes would resemble their own, no similarities in attitudes were found (Aboud & Doyle, 1996). Perhaps white parents are reluctant to discuss their racial and ethnic views with children, and children's friends say little as well. Faced with limited or ambiguous information, children may fill in the gaps using information they encounter in the media and elsewhere in their environments, and then rely on their own attitudes as the basis for inferring others'.

Consistent with this idea, research indicates that children pick up much information about group status from implicit messages in their surroundings. In a recent experiment, 7- to 12-year-olds attending a summer school program were randomly assigned to social groups, denoted by colored T-shirts (yellow or blue) that the children wore. The researchers hung posters in the classroom that depicted unfamiliar yellow-group members as having higher status—for example, as having won more athletic and spelling competitions. When teachers recognized the social groups by using them as the basis for seating arrangements, task assignments, and bulletin-board displays, children in the high-status group evaluated their own group more favorably than the other group, and children in the low-status group appeared to view their own group less favorably. When teachers ignored the social groupings, however, no prejudice emerged (Bigler, Brown, & Markell, 2001). These findings indicate that children do not necessarily form stereotypes when some basis for them exists—in this instance, information on wall posters. But when an authority figure validates a status hierarchy, children do form biased attitudes.

▶ *In-Group and Out-Group Biases: Development of Prejudice.* In their everyday worlds, children readily use skin color as the basis for judging likability—an evaluation that can override obvious desirable characteristics of minority group members. In an Australian study, white 5- to 7-year-olds drew pictures for an art competition and were told that, on the basis of the quality of their drawing ("excellent" or "OK"), they had been assigned to a team "of drawers just like you." The children pinned their picture to a board with photos of their team—two other white children. Then they viewed photos of members of the other team, who were either ethnically similar to themselves (white) or ethnically different (Asian Pacific Islanders). The children rated their own team as more likable than the other team, and the

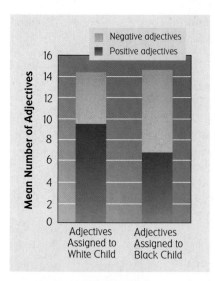

▲ Figure 11.9

White Canadian 5-year-olds' expressions of in-group favoritism and out-group prejudice. When asked to sort positive and negative adjectives into boxes labeled as belonging to a white child and a black child, white Canadian 5-year-olds assigned a greater number of positive adjectives (such as *clean, nice, smart*) to the white child than to the black child—evidence for in-group favoritism. In addition to viewing the black child less positively, the white Canadian 5-year-olds also assigned a greater number of negative adjectives (such as *dirty, naughty, cruel*) to the black child—evidence for *out-group prejudice.* (Adapted from Aboud, 2003.)

same-ethnicity other team as more likable than the different-ethnicity team, even when the ethnically different children were better at drawing (Nesdale et al., 2004).

As these findings indicate, white children generally evaluate their ethnic in-group favorably and ethnic out-groups less favorably or negatively—biases that also characterize adults. *In-group favoritism* emerges first, during the preschool years, and strengthens until ages 7 to 8. That is, children initially simply prefer their own group, generalizing from the self to similar others (Cameron et al., 2001; Bennett et al., 2004). *Out-group prejudice* requires a more challenging social comparison between in-group and out-group.

Nevertheless, it does not take long for white children to acquire negative attitudes toward ethnic minority out-groups, especially when they have little direct experience with them. When white Canadian 4- to 7-year-olds living in a white community and attending nearly all-white schools were asked to sort positive and negative adjectives into boxes labeled as belonging to a white child and a black child, out-group prejudice emerged at age 5 (see Figure 11.9). Furthermore, the more favorably the white children viewed their in-group, the more unfavorably they regarded the out-group (Aboud, 2003). Children with a stronger in-group bias seemed to use it as the basis for judging out-groups more negatively.

Unfortunately, many ethnic minority children show a reverse pattern: *out-group favoritism.* Having absorbed their culture's ethnic stereotypes, they tend to assign positive characteristics to the privileged ethnic majority and negative characteristics to their own group. In a study demonstrating this bias, researchers asked African-American 5- to 7-year-olds to recall information in stories either consistent or inconsistent with stereotypes of blacks. The children recalled more stereotypic traits—a trend that was stronger among those who agreed with negative cultural views of African Americans or who rated their own skin tone as lighter and, therefore, may have identified themselves with the white majority (Averhart & Bigler, 1997). Similarly, a Canadian investigation revealed that Native second to fourth graders recalled more positive attributes about white Canadians and more negative attributes about Native Canadians (Corenblum, 2003). And like their white Canadian agemates, Native Canadian children attributed a white Canadian child's successful task performance to ability or effort but attributed a Native Canadian child's similar success to luck or an easy task (Corenblum et al., 1996). A societal context that devalues people of color makes minority children vulnerable to internalizing those beliefs.

Recall that with age, children pay more attention to dispositions and make finer distinctions between people. The capacity to classify the social world in multiple ways permits school-age children to understand that people can be both "the same" and "different"—that those who look different need not think, feel, or act differently (Aboud & Amato, 2001). Consequently, prejudice—negative attitudes toward minorities—declines. After age 7 to 8, both majority and minority children express in-group favoritism, and white children's out-group derogation often weakens (Ruble et al., 2004). Most school-age children and adolescents are also quick to verbalize the wrongness of excluding others from peer-group and learning activities on the basis of skin color, evaluating such discrimination as unfair (Killen et al., 2002).

Nevertheless, children vary in the extent to which they hold ethnic and social-class biases. The following personal and situational factors are influential:

● *A fixed view of personality traits.* Children who come to believe that personality is fixed tend to judge people rigidly as either good or bad and to ignore the motives behind their behavior. These trait-stability endorsers, compared with children who see personality as changeable, readily form extreme impressions of individuals or groups on the basis of limited information. For example, they are likely to infer that "a new girl at school who makes up a lie to try to get other kids to like her" is a bad kid, or that "a kid who told a classmate her art work is ugly" goes to a school full of mean kids (Heyman & Dweck, 1998; Levy & Dweck, 1999).

● *High self-esteem.* A surprising finding is that children (and adults) with very high self-esteem are more likely to hold unfair ethnic biases (Baumeister et al., 2003; Bigler, Brown, & Markell, 2001). Individuals who think extremely well of themselves seem to belittle disadvantaged individuals or groups as a way of confirming their favorable self-evaluation. Researchers are not yet sure what motivates people to use this means of maintaining a positive self-image.

© These children perform a Polynesian song on the playground of their culturally diverse school. Collaboration with members of other ethnic groups and traditions can reduce the tendency to classify the social world on the basis of race and ethnicity and to view one's own group positively and other groups negatively.
© Michael J. Doolittle/The Image Works

- *A social world in which people are sorted into groups.* The more adults highlight group distinctions for children, the greater the chances that white children will display in-group favoritism and out-group prejudice (Bigler, Brown, & Markell, 2001; Kowalski & Lo, 1999).

▶ *Reducing Prejudice in Children.* A wealth of research shows that an effective way to reduce prejudice—in children and adults alike—is through intergroup contact, in which ethnically different individuals have equal status, work toward common goals, and become personally acquainted, while authority figures (such as parents and teachers) expect them to engage in such interaction. Children assigned to cooperative learning groups, in which they work toward joint goals with peers of diverse backgrounds and characteristics, show low levels of prejudice in their expressions of likability and in their behavior (Pettigrew, 1998). Still, once ethnic biases form, they are hard to undo. Although children who experience cooperative learning relate to their ethnic minority peers more positively, many continue to harbor negative stereotypes (Hewstone, 1996).

Long-term contact and collaboration among neighborhood, school, and community groups may be the best ways to reduce ethnic prejudices (Ramsey, 1995). In accordance with this view, white 5- and 6-year-olds attending an ethnically mixed school relied on their everyday experiences to construct generally positive out-group attitudes (Aboud, 2003). Classrooms that expose children to ethnic diversity and that encourage them to understand and value those differences prevent children from forming early negative biases toward ethnic minorities that are difficult to overcome.

Finally, inducing children to view others' traits as malleable is a promising approach to reducing prejudice. The more school-age children and adolescents believe that people can change their personalities, the more they report liking, wanting to spend time with, and perceiving themselves as similar to members of disadvantaged out-groups. Furthermore, young people who believe in the malleability of human attributes spend more time volunteering to help the needy—for example, by serving meals to the homeless or reading to poverty-stricken preschoolers (Karafantis & Levy, 2004). Volunteering may, in turn, promote a malleable view of others because it induces young people to imagine themselves in the place of the underprivileged, and thus helps them appreciate the social conditions that lead to disadvantage. In the next section, we will see that children's developing capacity to take the perspective of others contributes greatly to interpersonal understanding and positive social behavior.

Perspective Taking

In this and previous chapters, we have emphasized that **perspective taking**—the capacity to imagine what other people may be thinking and feeling—is important for a wide variety of social–cognitive achievements: understanding others' emotions (Chapter 10); appreciating false belief; developing referential communication skills (Chapter 9), self-concept, self-esteem, and person perception; and inferring intentions.

© As these children participate in an animated debate,
they engage in self-reflective
perspective taking—viewing
their own attitudes toward an
issue from another person's
perspective.

© James Shaffer/PhotoEdit

Recall that Piaget regarded *egocentrism*—preschoolers' inability to take the viewpoint of another—as the major feature responsible for the immaturity of their thought, in both the physical and social domains. Yet we have seen that toddlers have some capacity for perspective taking as soon as they become consciously self-aware in the second year of life. Nevertheless, Piaget's ideas inspired a wealth of research on children's capacity to take another's perspective, which improves steadily over childhood and adolescence.

• **SELMAN'S STAGES OF PERSPECTIVE TAKING** • Robert Selman developed a five-stage sequence of perspective-taking skill, based on children's and adolescents' responses to social dilemmas in which characters have differing information and opinions about an event. As Table 11.2 indicates, longitudinal and cross-sectional findings reveal that at first, children have only a limited idea of what other people might be thinking and feeling. Over time, they become more aware that people can interpret the same event quite differently. Soon, they can "step into another person's shoes" and reflect on how that person might regard their own thoughts, feelings, and behavior. (Note that this level of perspective taking is similar to second-order false belief, described on page 443.) Finally, older children and adolescents can evaluate two people's perspectives simultaneously, at first from the vantage point of a disinterested spectator and later by making reference to societal values (Gurucharri & Selman, 1982; Selman, 1980).

Cognitive development contributes to advances in perspective taking. Children who fail Piaget's concrete operational tasks tend to be at Selman's Level 0; those who pass concrete but not formal operational tasks tend to be at Levels 1 and 2; and young people who are increasingly formal operational tend to be at Levels 3 and 4 (Keating & Clark, 1980; Krebs & Gillmore, 1982). Furthermore, each set of Piagetian tasks tends to be mastered somewhat earlier than its related perspective-taking level (Walker, 1980). This suggests that additional cognitive and social capacities contribute to gains in perspective taking.

• **OTHER ASSESSMENTS OF PERSPECTIVE TAKING** • According to several theorists, preschoolers' limited capacity to take another's perspective is largely due to their passive view of the mind—their assumption that what a person knows results from observing rather than actively interpreting experience (Chandler & Carpendale, 1998). To explore this idea,

TABLE 11.2 SELMAN'S STAGES OF PERSPECTIVE TAKING

Stage	Approximate Age Range	Description
Level 0: Undifferentiated perspective taking	3–6	Children recognize that self and other can have different thoughts and feelings, but they frequently confuse the two.
Level 1: Social-informational perspective taking	4–9	Children understand that different perspectives may result because people have access to different information.
Level 2: Self-reflective perspective taking	7–12	Children can "step in another person's shoes" and view their own thoughts, feelings, and behavior from the other person's perspective. They also recognize that others can do the same.
Level 3: Third-party perspective taking	10–15	Children can step outside a two-person situation and imagine how the self and other are viewed from the point of view of a third, impartial party.
Level 4: Societal perspective taking	14–adult	Individuals understand that third-party perspective taking can be influenced by one or more systems of larger societal values.

Sources: Selman, 1976; Selman & Byrne, 1974.

researchers have devised gamelike tasks that assess children's realization that people's preexisting knowledge and beliefs affect their viewpoints.

One approach is to see whether children realize that younger, and therefore less knowledgeable, individuals view new information differently than older individuals do. In one study, 4- to 8-year-olds were asked whether a baby and an adult would know the location of an object after seeing where it had been placed or, alternatively, being told where it had been placed (Montgomery, 1993). Children of all ages judged correctly that both the baby and the adult would know through directly perceiving. But 4-year-olds—even though they said that babies don't know what most words mean—incorrectly thought that the baby could learn from the verbal message. Performance improved between ages 6 and 8 (see Figure 11.10).

Other research confirms that not until age 6 do children understand that a person's *prior knowledge* affects their ability to understand new information. Between 6 and 8 years, children also realize that people's *preexisting beliefs* can affect their viewpoints. And around this time, they understand that two people can interpret the same ambiguous information differently (Miller, 2000).

Perspective-taking tasks for older children and adolescents have focused on **recursive thought,** the form of perspective taking that involves thinking about what another person is thinking. Selman's stages suggest that thinking recursively (Levels 3 and 4) improves from middle childhood to adolescence, a trend that is supported by research. When first through sixth graders were asked to describe cartoons like those in Figure 11.11, only 50 percent of sixth graders succeeded on one-loop recursions, and few could handle two-loop recursions (Miller, Kessel, & Flavell, 1970). Not until midadolescence do young people grasp complex recursive understanding.

Recursive thought makes human interaction truly reciprocal. People often call on it to clear up misunderstandings, as when they say, "*I thought you would think* I was just kidding when I said that." Recursive thinking is also involved in clever attempts to disguise our real thoughts and feelings: "He'll think I'm jealous if I tell him I don't like his new car, so I'll act like I do" (Perner, 1988). Finally, the capacity to think recursively contributes to the intense self-focusing and concern with the imaginary audience typical of early adolescence (see Chapter 6). "Often to their pain, adolescents are much more gifted at this sort of wondering than first graders are" (Miller, Kessel, & Flavell, 1970, p. 623).

Perspective taking varies greatly among children of the same age. Experiences in which adults and peers explain their own viewpoints and encourage children to consider others' perspectives contribute to these individual differences (Dixon & Moore, 1990). Consistent with these findings, children in collectivist cultures, which emphasize cooperation and group harmony, do better on perspective-taking tasks than children in individualistic cultures (Keats & Fang, 1992).

• **PERSPECTIVE TAKING AND SOCIAL BEHAVIOR** •
Perspective-taking skills help children get along with others. When we anticipate people's points of view, we can also respond to their needs more effectively. Good perspective takers are more likely to display empathy and sympathy, and they are better at thinking of effective ways to handle difficult social situations (Eisenberg, Murphy, & Shepard, 1997; Marsh, Serafica, & Barenboim, 1981). For these reasons, they tend to be better liked by peers (FitzGerald & White, 2003).

Although good perspective taking is crucial for mature social behavior, situational and personal factors determine whether it will lead to prosocial acts. In a competitive task, skilled perspective takers are often as good at defending their own viewpoint as they are at cooperating. Also, even when children appreciate another person's thoughts and feelings, temperament influences their behavior. Recall from Chapter

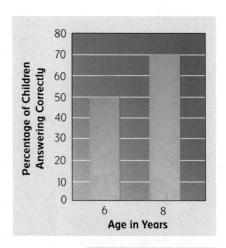

▲ **Figure 11.10**

Development of children's understanding that a person's prior knowledge affects understanding of new information. When asked whether a baby and an adult would know the location of an object after being told where it had been placed, 4-year-olds did not realize that a baby could not learn from a verbal message. Performance on this perspective-taking task improved between ages 6 and 8. (Adapted from Montgomery, 1993.)

One-loop recursion
"The boy is thinking that he is thinking about himself."

Two-loop recursion
"The boy is thinking that the girl is thinking of the father thinking of the mother."

▲ **Figure 11.11**

Cartoon drawings depicting recursive thought. Not until midadolescence do young people master the complexities of this self-embedded form of perspective taking. (From P. H. Miller, F. S. Kessel, & J. H. Flavell, 1970, "Thinking About People Thinking About People Thinking About . . . : A Study of Social Cognitive Development," *Child Development, 41,* p. 616. © The Society for Research in Child Development, Inc. Reprinted by permission.)

10 that children who are skilled at emotional self-regulation are more likely to help others in distress and to handle social conflicts constructively.

Finally, children and adolescents with poor social skills—in particular, those with the angry, aggressive styles we will take up in Chapter 12—have great difficulty imagining the thoughts and feelings of others. They often mistreat both adults and peers without experiencing the guilt and remorse prompted by awareness of another's point of view. Interventions that provide coaching and practice in perspective taking help reduce antisocial behavior and increase prosocial responding (Chalmers & Townsend, 1990; Chandler, 1973).

Ask Yourself

REVIEW	Describe changes in children's understanding of intention over the preschool years.
REVIEW	How does perspective taking contribute to effective social skills?
APPLY	Ten-year-old Marla is convinced that her classmate Bernadette, who gets poor grades, is lazy. In contrast, Jane thinks that Bernadette tries hard but can't concentrate because her parents are getting a divorce. Why is Marla more likely than Jane to harbor social prejudices?
CONNECT	What features of concrete operational thought might explain its association with Selman's self-reflective perspective taking? Why is formal operational thought important for third-party and societal perspective taking?

Thinking About Relations Between People: Understanding Conflict

As children develop, they apply their insights about themselves and others to an understanding of relations between people. Most research on this aspect of social cognition has to do with friendship and conflicts. We will take up friendship in Chapter 15. Here we focus on how children think about and resolve situations in which their goals and the goals of agemates are at odds.

Social Problem Solving

Children, even when they are good friends, sometimes come into conflict. Yet even preschoolers seem to handle most quarrels constructively; only rarely do their disagreements result in hostile encounters. Overall, conflicts are not very frequent when compared with children's friendly, cooperative interactions.

Nevertheless, peer conflicts are important. Watch children engage in disputes over play objects ("That's mine!" "I had it first!"), entry into and control over play activities ("I'm on your team, Jerry." "No, you're not!"), and disagreements over facts, ideas, and beliefs ("I'm taller than he is." "No, you aren't!"). As you can see, they take these matters quite seriously. Over time, preschoolers' conflicts shift from material concerns to mental and social issues (Chen et al., 2001). In Chapter 6, we noted that resolution of conflict, rather than conflict per se, promotes development. Social conflicts offer children invaluable learning opportunities for **social problem solving**—the generation and application of strategies that prevent or resolve disagreements, resulting in outcomes that are acceptable to others while also being beneficial to the self. To engage in social problem solving, children must bring together diverse social understandings.

Nicki Crick and Kenneth Dodge (1994) organize the steps of social problem solving into the circular model shown in Figure 11.12. Notice how this flowchart takes an *information-processing approach*, clarifying exactly what a child must do to grapple with and solve a social problem. Once this is known, processing deficits can be identified and intervention can be tailored to children's individual needs.

Social problem solving profoundly affects peer relations. Children who get along well with agemates interpret social cues accurately, formulate goals that enhance relationships (such as being helpful to peers), and have a repertoire of effective problem-solving strategies. In contrast, children with peer difficulties often hold biased social expectations. Consequently, they

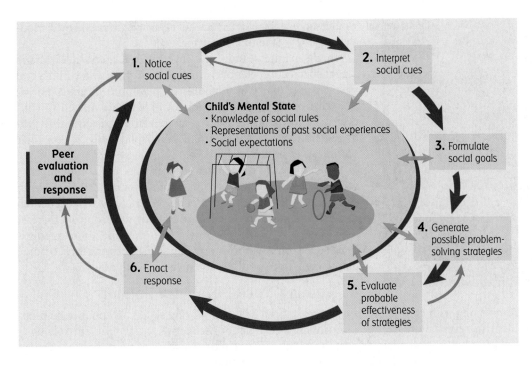

◄ **Figure 11.12**

An information-processing model of social problem solving. The model is circular because children often engage in several information-processing activities at once—for example, interpreting information as they notice it and continuing to consider the meaning of another's behavior while they generate and evaluate problem-solving strategies. The model also takes into account the impact of mental state on social information processing—in particular, children's knowledge of social rules, their representations of past social experiences, and their expectations for future experiences. Peer evaluations and responses to enacted strategies are also important factors in social problem solving.

(Adapted from N. R. Crick & K. A. Dodge, 1994, "A Review and Reformulation of Social Information-Processing Mechanisms in Children's Social Adjustment," *Psychological Bulletin, 115,* 74–101, Figure 2 (adapted), p. 76. Copyright © 1994 by the American Psychological Association. Adapted by permission.)

attend selectively to social cues (such as hostile acts) and misinterpret others' behavior (interpreting an unintentional jostle as hostile). Their social goals (satisfying an impulse, getting even with or avoiding a peer) often lead to strategies that damage relationships (Erdly & Asher, 1999; Youngstrom et al., 2000).

Development of Social Problem Solving

Most research on social problem solving focuses on strategy generation—by asking young children to think of ways to deal with hypothetical conflicts, such as wanting to play with a toy someone else has. Findings reveal that the quantity and quality of children's strategies improve with age. Younger children, as well as children with poor peer relations, describe strategies that impulsively meet their needs, such as grabbing, hitting, or ordering another child to obey. By age 5 to 7, children more often assert their needs in ways that take into account the needs of others. They tend to rely on friendly persuasion and compromise, to think of alternative strategies when an initial one does not work, and to resolve disagreements without adult intervention (Chen et al., 2001; Mayeiux & Cillessen, 2003). And sometimes they suggest creating new, mutual goals. In doing so, they recognize that solutions to current problems have an important bearing on the future of the relationship (Yeates, Schultz, & Selman, 1991).

Other researchers have expanded the study of social problem solving to find out at what points, besides strategy generation, socially competent children differ from less competent children. Dodge and his collaborators (1986) assessed school-age children's skillfulness at five of the problem-solving steps shown in Figure 11.12. A videotape dramatized a problem involving entry into a play group. In the first scene, two children played a board game, and the researchers measured each participant's ability to *encode and interpret social cues* about the video characters' willingness to let a third child join the game. Then children *generated strategies* for joining the game, and their responses were coded as follows:

- *Competent:* polite requests to play and other friendly comments
- *Aggressive:* threats, physical force, and barging in without asking
- *Self-centered:* statements about the self, such as "Hey, I know how to play that!"
- *Passive:* shy, hovering responses, such as waiting and "hanging around"
- *Appeals to authority:* for example, "The teacher said I could play."

Next, participants viewed five more scenes in which a child tried to enter the game using each of these strategies, and they engaged in *strategy evaluation* by indicating whether or not the technique

Ⓢ Children differ in their social competence—that is, their ability to generate strategies for successful social interactions, such as entering a play group. Intervening with children who have weak social problem-solving skills can enhance development.
© Mary Kate Denny/PhotoEdit

would succeed. Finally, participants *enacted a response* by demonstrating a way of joining the game.

In a separate session, the investigators assessed children's actual social competence by having them gain entry into a real peer-group activity in a laboratory playroom. Results showed that all five social problem-solving skills were related to children's performance. Each social-cognitive measure also predicted how effectively children joined play activities on their school playground.

Over the early elementary school years, the components of social problem solving become more strongly associated with socially competent behavior (Dodge & Price, 1994). As children move through the first few years of school, they confront increasingly complex social situations, which demand more sophisticated social information-processing skills. These, in turn, become increasingly important for getting along with others.

Training Social Problem Solving

Intervening with children who have weak social problem-solving skills can enhance development in several ways. Besides improving peer relations, effective social problem solving is linked to better academic performance. It also gives children a sense of mastery in the face of stressful life events, and it reduces the risk of adjustment difficulties in children from low-income and troubled families (Dubow et al., 1991; Goodman, Gravitt, & Kaslow, 1995).

In one widely applied social problem-solving training program, preschoolers and kindergartners discuss how to resolve social problems acted out with puppets in daily sessions over several months. In addition, teachers intervene as conflicts arise in the classroom, point out consequences of children's behavior ("How do you think Johnny feels when you hit him?"), and help children think of alternative strategies ("Can you think of a different way to solve this problem so you both won't be mad?"). In several studies, trained children, in contrast to untrained controls, improved in their ability to think about social problems and in teacher-rated adjustment—gains still evident months after the program ended (Shure, 2001). School-age children benefit from similar interventions (Gettinger, Doll, & Salmon, 1994).

Practice in enacting responses may strengthen these positive outcomes. Often children know how to solve a social problem effectively but do not apply their knowledge (Rudolph & Heller, 1997). Also, children who have enacted maladaptive responses repeatedly may need to rehearse alternatives to overcome their habitual behaviors and to spark more adaptive social information processing.

On a final note, social-cognitive training is not the only means for helping children with social difficulties. Because their parents often model poor social problem-solving skills and use ineffective child-rearing practices, family intervention may be necessary—a topic we will return to several times in later chapters.

Ask Yourself   🌐 www

REVIEW	Describe the skills of a 6-year-old who is an effective social problem solver.
APPLY	Illustrate the influence of temperament on social problem solving by explaining how an impulsive child and a shy, inhibited child, respectively, might respond at each social problem-solving step in Figure 11.12 on page 469.
CONNECT	How might improved perspective taking contribute to gains in social problem solving from early to middle childhood?
REFLECT	What were your in-group and out-group biases like as an elementary school child? Cite personal and situational factors that might have influenced those biases. What are your attitudes like today? Have they been affected by intergroup contact and volunteer experiences? Explain.

◎ Summary

What is social cognition, and how does it differ from nonsocial cognition?

◎ Researchers interested in the development of **social cognition** study how children's understanding of themselves, other people, and relationships between people changes with age. Compared with nonsocial cognition, social cognition involves the challenge of comprehending how both inner states and external forces affect people's behavior.

Emergence of Self and Development of Self-Concept

Describe the development of self-awareness in infancy and toddlerhood and its consequences for young children's emotional and social capacities.

◎ The earliest aspect of the self to emerge is the **I-self**, a sense of self as knower and actor, first evident in newborns' experience of intermodal matches that differentiate their own body from their surroundings. The I-self develops as infants increasingly realize that their own actions cause objects and people to react in predictable ways. Infants and toddlers whose parents encourage exploration and respond to their signals sensitively (indicators of secure attachment) are advanced in constructing an I-self.

◎ During the second year, toddlers start to construct the **me-self**, a reflective observer who treats the self as an object of knowledge and evaluation. By the end of the second year, **self-recognition** is well under way, as revealed by toddlers' reactions to their own image in mirrors and photos and their use of language to refer to themselves. Around age 4, children grasp the me-self as extending over time.

◎ Toddlers' increasing self-awareness underlies the emergence of self-conscious emotions, perspective taking, empathy, sustained imitative play, peer competition for objects, and cooperation.

Describe the development of the categorical, remembered, and inner selves, and cite consequences of and contributors to preschoolers' belief–desire theory of mind.

◎ Language development permits young preschoolers to construct a **categorical self** as they classify themselves and others on the basis of age, sex, physical characteristics, and goodness and badness. Conversations with adults about the past lead to an autobiographical memory—a life-story narrative that grants the child a **remembered self** imbued with cultural values.

◎ Infants' implicit appreciation of people as animate beings whose behavior is governed by intentions, desires, and feelings and who can share inner states sets the stage for an **inner self** of private thoughts and imaginings. As 2-year-olds talk about mental states, they form a **desire theory of mind**, in which they integrate desire with perception and emotion.

◎ Around age 4, children develop a **belief–desire theory of mind;** mastery of false-belief tasks reveals that they understand that both beliefs and desires determine actions. As school-age children come to realize that people can increase their knowledge by making mental inferences, they grasp second-order false belief—that one person's belief about another's belief can be wrong.

◎ Belief–desire reasoning is related to advances in social skills. Among children who pass false-belief tasks, sociodramatic play is more mature and eyewitness memories more accurate. School-age children apply their expanding understanding of the relation between beliefs and behavior to their efforts to persuade others.

◎ Many factors contribute to the development of belief–desire reasoning, including language development; cognitive skills of inhibition, flexible thinking, and planning; parent–child conversations about mental states; make-believe play; and social interaction with siblings, friends, and adults.

◎ Some researchers believe that the human brain is biologically prepared to develop a belief–desire theory. Others think that belief–desire understanding is supported by general cognitive development.

Discuss the development of self-concept from early childhood through adolescence, noting cognitive, social, and cultural influences.

◎ The me-self expands as preschoolers construct a **self-concept,** or set of beliefs about their own characteristics. In middle childhood, self-concept changes from a focus on observable characteristics and typical emotions and attitudes to an emphasis on personality traits, positive and negative characteristics, and **social comparisons.** In adolescence, self-descriptions become more abstract and form an organized system that places greater emphasis on social virtues and personal and moral values.

◎ Changes in self-concept are supported by cognitive development, perspective-taking skills (as suggested by Mead's concept of the **generalized other**), and feedback from others. In describing themselves, children tend to be more egoistic and competitive in individualistic cultures, more concerned with the welfare of others in collectivist cultures.

Self-Esteem: The Evaluative Side of Self-Concept

Discuss development of and influences on self-esteem from early childhood through adolescence.

◎ **Self-esteem,** the judgments we make about our own worth, differentiates, becomes hierarchically organized, and declines over the first few years of elementary school as children start to make social comparisons. Except for a temporary drop associated with school transition, self-esteem rises from fourth grade on, and new dimensions are added in adolescence. For most young people, becoming an adolescent leads to feelings of pride and self-confidence.

◎ From middle childhood to adolescence, individual differences in self-esteem become increasingly stable and correlated with everyday behaviors. Generally positive self-esteem profiles are associated with positive adjustment, and low self-regard in all areas is associated with a wide array of adjustment difficulties.

⑨ Cultural forces affect self-esteem, as illustrated by Asian children's lower self-esteem in comparison to American children's and by the slight self-esteem advantage of African-American over Caucasian-American children and adolescents.

⑨ Children of parents who are warm and accepting and who provide reasonable expectations for mature behavior have comparatively high self-esteem. In contrast, excessive parental control is linked to low self-esteem, and indulgent parenting to unrealistically high self-esteem.

Discuss the development of achievement-related attributions, noting the influence of cognitive development and adults' messages to children, and suggest ways to foster a mastery-oriented style.

⑨ Research on achievement-related **attributions** has identified adult messages that affect children's self-esteem and **achievement motivation.** During middle childhood, children begin to distinguish ability, effort, and external factors in attributions for success and failure.

⑨ Children with **mastery-oriented attributions** credit their successes to high ability and their failures to insufficient effort. They hold an **incremental view of ability**—that it can be improved by trying hard. In contrast, children with **learned helplessness** attribute their successes to external factors, such as luck, and their failures to low ability. They hold an **entity view of ability**—a belief that ability cannot be changed. Mastery-oriented children focus on learning goals, learned-helpless children on performance goals.

⑨ Adolescents have a fully differentiated understanding of the relationship between ability and effort. Those with learned helplessness quickly conclude that mastering a challenging task is not worth the cost—extremely high effort. As a result, they fail to realize their potential.

⑨ Children who experience negative feedback about their ability, messages that evaluate their traits, pressure to focus on performance goals, and lack of support from teachers are likely to develop learned helplessness. Teachers who are caring and

helpful, who emphasize learning over performance goals, and who stress effort and interpersonal harmony in their classrooms foster a mastery orientation.

⑨ **Attribution retraining,** which encourages learned-helpless children to believe that they can overcome failure if only they exert more effort, has improved the self-evaluations and task performance of learned-helpless children. Teaching children to focus less on grades and more on mastering tasks for their own sake is an effective approach, as is providing instruction in metacognition and self-regulation.

Constructing an Identity: Who Should I Become?

Describe the quest for identity, the four identity statuses, and factors that influence identity development.

⑨ Erikson first recognized **identity**—the construction of a solid self-definition consisting of self-chosen values and goals—as the major personality achievement of adolescence. In complex societies, a period of exploration followed by commitment is necessary to form a personally meaningful identity.

⑨ **Identity achievement** (exploration followed by commitment) and **identity moratorium** (exploration without having reached commitment) are psychologically healthy identity statuses. Long-term **identity foreclosure** (commitment without exploration) and **identity diffusion** (lack of both exploration and commitment) are related to adjustment difficulties. Because college offers students many opportunities to explore career options and lifestyles, young people make more progress toward achieving an identity in college than they did in high school.

⑨ Adolescents who take a flexible, open-minded approach to grappling with competing beliefs and values and who feel attached to parents but free to voice their own opinions are likely to be advanced in identity development. Close friends support young people as they explore options. Schools and communities that provide young people of all backgrounds with rich and varied options for exploration also foster identity achievement. Ethnic minority youths who construct a strong, secure **ethnic identity** or a **bicultural identity** are advantaged in many aspects of emotional and social development.

Thinking About Other People

Discuss gains in children's appreciation of others' personalities and their understanding of ethnicity and social class, including factors that contribute to ethnic prejudices.

⑨ **Person perception** concerns how we size up the attributes of people with whom we are familiar. Like their self-concepts, children's descriptions of other people place greater emphasis on personality traits and become more differentiated and organized with age.

⑨ Basic concepts of race and ethnicity emerge in the preschool years, and children distinguish rich from poor on the basis of physical characteristics. By the early school years, children absorb prevailing attitudes toward social groups. But they do not necessarily directly adopt the attitudes of parents and friends; rather, they seem to pick up information about group status from implicit messages in their surroundings.

⑨ White children who have had little direct experience with ethnic minorities show in-group favoritism and out-group prejudice by age 5. Having absorbed their culture's ethnic stereotypes, many ethnic minority children show the reverse bias: out-group favoritism.

⑨ The capacity to classify the social world in multiple ways leads to a decline in prejudice in middle childhood. Children who view personality as fixed, have high self-esteem, and experience a social world in which people are sorted into groups are more likely to harbor ethnic prejudices.

⑨ Prejudice can be reduced through long-term intergroup contact and collaboration. Inducing children to view others' traits as malleable—a perspective that volunteer activities may encourage—may also be helpful.

Cite major changes in perspective taking from early childhood into adolescence, and explain the role of perspective-taking skill in children's social behavior.

⑨ **Perspective taking** improves greatly from childhood to adolescence, as Selman's five-stage sequence indicates. Mastery of Piagetian tasks and a view of the mind as an active interpreter of experience are related to advances in perspective taking. Around age 6, children understand that prior knowledge affects people's ability to understand new information. Between 6 and 8 years, they realize that people's preexisting beliefs can affect their viewpoints. During adolescence, **recursive thought** is mastered.

◉ The ability to understand the viewpoints of others contributes to many social skills and is associated with peer acceptance.

Angry, aggressive young people have great difficulty imagining the thoughts and feelings of others. Interventions that teach perspective-taking skills help reduce antisocial behavior and increase prosocial responding.

Thinking About Relations Between People: Understanding Conflict

Describe the components of social problem solving, the development of social problem-solving skills, and ways to help children who are poor social problem solvers.

◉ With age, children become better at resolving conflict through **social problem solving.** Components of the social problem-solving process—encoding and interpreting social cues, clarifying social goals, generating and evaluating strategies, and enacting responses—become more strongly linked to socially competent behavior in middle childhood. Training in social problem solving leads to improved peer relations and academic performance.

◉ Important Terms and Concepts

achievement motivation (p. 452)
attribution retraining (p. 455)
attributions (p. 452)
belief–desire theory of mind (p. 442)
bicultural identity (p. 461)
categorical self (p. 440)
desire theory of mind (p. 442)
entity view of ability (p. 453)
ethnic identity (p. 461)
generalized other (p. 447)
I-self (p. 438)

identity (p. 456)
identity achievement (p. 457)
identity diffusion (p. 457)
identity foreclosure (p. 457)
identity moratorium (p. 457)
incremental view of ability (p. 453)
inner self (p. 441)
learned helplessness (p. 453)
mastery-oriented attributions (p. 453)
me-self (p. 438)
person perception (p. 462)

perspective taking (p. 465)
recursive thought (p. 467)
remembered self (p. 440)
self-concept (p. 446)
self-esteem (p. 449)
self-recognition (p. 440)
social cognition (p. 437)
social comparisons (p. 446)
social problem solving (p. 468)

"My Dream"
Valeriya Galimovna
Age 7, Russia

In this benevolent vision, a gentle protector hovers over the world. What accounts for the development of this artist's keen moral sensibilities? Human nature, family, peer, school, and culture all contribute to the cognitive, emotional, and behavioral ingredients of morality.

Moral Development

Three-year-old Leisl grabbed a toy from Ava, a neighbor girl who had come to play. "Give it back," Ava cried. "It's mine!"

Leisl's mother bent down. "Look!" she explained. "Ava's about to cry. She was playing with the teddy bear, and when you took it, you made her sad. Let's give back the bear to Ava." Gently, she freed the toy from Leisl's hands and returned it to Ava. For a moment, Leisl looked hurt, but she soon busied herself with her blocks. A few moments later, Leisl turned to Ava. "Want some of these blocks?" she offered generously, making a pile of blocks for Ava. "We can share!"

Now consider Leisl at age 11, reacting to a newspaper article about an elderly woman, soon to be evicted from her crumbling home because city inspectors have judged it a fire and health hazard. "Look at what they're trying to do to this poor lady!" exclaimed Leisl. "They wanna throw her out of her house. You don't just knock someone's home down! Where're her friends and neighbors? Why aren't they over there fixing up that house?"

Eleven-year-old Leisl has come a long way from the preschool child just beginning to appreciate the rights and feelings of others. That beginning, however, is an important one. Preschooler Leisl's prosocial invitation to her visiting playmate is not unique—it is part of an emerging picture. Accompanying the emergence of self-awareness and improved representational capacities at the end of the second year is another crowning achievement: The child becomes a moral being. Recall that around this time, empathy and sympathetic concern emerge (see Chapter 10), and children soon begin to evaluate their own and others' behavior as "good" or "bad" (see Chapter 11). As children's cognition and language develop and their social experiences broaden, they express increasingly elaborate moral thoughts accompanied by intense emotion that—as with 11-year-old Leisl—sometimes escalates to moral outrage.

What accounts for children's expanding appreciation of standards of conduct and the increasing depth of their moral sensibilities? Philosophers have pondered this question for centuries, and contemporary investigators have addressed it with such intensity that research on moral development exceeds that on all other aspects of social development.

The determinants of morality can be found at both societal and individual levels. In all cultures, morality is promoted by an overarching social organization that specifies rules for good conduct. At the same time, morality has roots in each major aspect of our psychological makeup:

● Morality has an *emotional component,* since powerful feelings cause us to empathize with another's distress or feel guilty when we are the cause of that distress.

● Morality also has an important *cognitive component.* Children's developing social understanding permits them to make more profound judgments about actions they believe to be right or wrong.

- Morality has a vital *behavioral component,* since experiencing morally relevant thoughts and feelings only increases the likelihood, but does not guarantee, that people will act in accord with them.

Traditionally, these three facets of morality have been studied separately: Biological and psychoanalytic theories focus on emotions, cognitive-developmental theory on moral thought, and social learning theory on moral behavior. Today, a growing body of research reveals that all three facets are interrelated. Still, major theories disagree on which is primary. And as we will see, the aspect a theory emphasizes has major implications for how it conceptualizes the basic trend of moral development: the shift from superficial, or externally controlled, responses to behavior that is based on inner standards, or moral understanding. Truly moral individuals do not just do the right thing for the sake of social conformity or the expectations of authority figures. Instead, they have developed compassionate concerns and ideals of good conduct, which they follow in a wide variety of situations.

Our discussion of moral development begins by highlighting the strengths and limitations of the theories just mentioned on the basis of recent research. Next we consider the important related topic of self-control. The development of a personal resolve to keep the self from doing anything it feels like doing is crucial for translating moral commitments into action. We conclude with a discussion of the other side of self-control—the development of aggression.

⑤⑤ Morality as Rooted in Human Nature
⑥

In the 1970s, biological theories of human social behavior suggested that many morally relevant behaviors and emotions have roots in our evolutionary history (Wilson, 1975). This view was supported by the work of ethologists, who observed animals aiding other members of their species, often at great personal risk. For example, ants, bees, and termites show extremes of self-sacrifice. Large numbers will sting or bite an animal that threatens the hive, a warlike response that often results in their own death. Dogs who breach a master's prohibition by damaging furniture or defecating indoors sometimes display intense regret, in the form of distress and submission (Lorenz, 1983).

Among primates, chimpanzees (who are genetically closest to humans) conform to moral-like rules, which group members enforce in one another. For example, when males attack females, they avoid using their sharp canine teeth. If a male does harm a female, the entire colony responds with a chorus of indignant barks, sometimes followed by a band of females chasing off the aggressor (de Waal, 1996). Chimps also reciprocate favors; they generously groom and share food with those who have done the same for them. And they engage in kind and comforting acts. Juveniles sometimes soothe frightened or injured peers, and adult females practice adoption when a baby loses its mother (Goodall, 1990). Furthermore, shortly after a physical fight, the former combatants may embrace, hold hands, and groom, intensifying friendly behaviors in an apparent effort to restore their long-term relationship (de Waal, 2001). On the basis of this evidence, researchers reasoned that evolution must have made similar biologically based provisions for moral acts in human beings.

⑤ According to sociobiologists, morally relevant behaviors such as sharing and cooperating are rooted in the genetic heritage of our species. These chimpanzees gather to share food while enjoying one another's company.

© Steve Bloom Images/Alamy

How might genes influence behaviors that support the social group and, thereby, the survival of the species? Many researchers believe that prewired emotional reactions are involved (Haidt, 2001; Hoffman, 2000; Trivers, 1971). In Chapter 10, we noted that newborns cry when they hear another baby cry, a possible precursor of empathy. As toddlers approach age 2, they show empathic concern, and they react with distress to behaviors that threaten not just their own well-being but also that of others. Perhaps these emotions underlie human prosocial acts.

Furthermore, researchers have identified an area within the frontal region of the cerebral cortex (the ventromedial area, located just behind the bridge of the nose) that is vital for emotional responsiveness to the suffering of others and to one's own misdeeds. Adults with damage to this area do not react negatively to images of extreme human harm, although they know they should feel something. And they show less concern than others about conforming to social norms (Barrash, Tranel, & Anderson, 2000; Damasio, 1994). When ventromedial damage occurs early, it severely disrupts social learning, resulting in extreme antisocial behavior (Anderson et al., 1999). Furthermore, EEG and fMRI research reveals that psychopaths, who inflict harm on others without any trace of empathy or guilt, show reduced activity in this brain region (Raine, 1997).

But like most other human behaviors, morality cannot be fully explained by its biological foundations. Recall from Chapter 10 that morally relevant emotions, such as pride, guilt, empathy, and sympathy, require strong caregiving supports in order to develop. And their mature expression depends on cognitive development. Furthermore, although emotion is one basis for moral action, it is not a complete account, since following our empathic feelings is not always moral. For example, most of us would question the behavior of a parent who decides not to take a sick child to the doctor out of empathy with the child's fear and anxiety over doctor visits.

Still, the biological perspective reminds us of morality's adaptive value. Because the capacity to serve the self's needs is present early, humans, along with other highly social species, have evolved a brain-based moral substrate that counteracts self-centered motives and promotes concern for others.

Morality as the Adoption of Societal Norms

The two perspectives we are about to discuss—psychoanalytic theory and social learning theory—offer different accounts of how children become moral beings. Yet both regard moral development as a matter of **internalization**: adopting societal standards for right action as one's own. In other words, both focus on how morality moves from society to individual—how children acquire norms, or prescriptions for good conduct, widely held by members of their social group.

Our examination of these theories will reveal that several factors jointly affect the child's willingness to adopt societal standards:

● Parental style of discipline, which varies with the type of misdeed

● The child's characteristics, including age and temperament

● The parent's characteristics

● The child's view of both the misdeed and the reasonableness of parental demands

As this list indicates, internalization results from a combination of influences within the child and the rearing environment. When the process goes well, external forces foster the child's positive inclinations and counteract the child's negative inclinations (Turiel, 1998). In the following sections, we will see many examples of this idea.

Psychoanalytic Theory

According to Sigmund Freud, morality emerges between ages 3 and 6, the period when the well-known Oedipus and Electra conflicts arise. Young children desire to possess the parent of the other sex, but they give up this wish because they fear punishment and loss of parental love. To maintain the affection of their parents, children form a *superego*, or conscience, by *identifying* with the same-sex parent, whose moral standards they take into their own personality. Finally, children are thought to internalize—along with moral standards—intense emotion. They turn the hostility previously aimed at the same-sex parent toward themselves, and that internalized hostility leads to painful feelings of guilt each time they disobey the superego (Freud, 1925/1961). According to Freud, moral development is largely complete by age 5 or 6, with some strengthening of the superego in middle childhood.

Today, most researchers disagree with Freud's account of conscience development. First, Freud's view of guilt as a hostile impulse redirected toward the self is no longer accepted. As we will see, high levels of self-blame are not associated with moral internalization. Instead, school-age children experience guilt when they intentionally engage in an unacceptable act and feel personally responsible for the outcome (see Chapter 10). Second, notice how fear of punishment and loss of parental love are assumed to motivate conscience formation and moral behavior (Tellings, 1999). Yet children whose parents frequently use threats, commands, or physical force tend to violate standards often and feel little guilt (Kochanska et al., 2002). And if a parent withdraws love—for example, refuses to speak to a child or states a dislike for

⊚ This teacher uses inductive discipline to explain to a child the impact of her transgression on others. Induction supports conscience development by indicating how the child should behave, encouraging empathy and sympathetic concern, and clarifying the reasons behind adult expectations.
© Laura Dwight Photography

the child—children often respond with high levels of self-blame after misbehaving. They might think, "I'm no good," or "Nobody loves me." Eventually, these children may protect themselves from overwhelming feelings of guilt by denying the emotion. So they, too, develop a weak conscience (Kochanska, 1991; Zahn-Waxler et al., 1990).

• **THE POWER OF INDUCTIVE DISCIPLINE** • In contrast, a special type of discipline supports conscience development. In **induction,** an adult helps the child notice others' feelings by pointing out the effects of the child's misbehavior on others, noting especially their distress and making clear that the child caused it. For example, to a young preschool child, the parent might say, "She's crying because you won't give back her doll." Notice how Leisl's mother did something similar in the introduction to this chapter. Later in the preschool years, parents can explain why the child's action was inappropriate, perhaps by referring to the other person's intentions: "Don't yell at him. That makes him feel sad. He was trying to help you!" And with further cognitive advances, more subtle psychological explanations can be given: "He felt proud of his tower, and you hurt his feelings by knocking it down" (Hoffman, 2000).

As long as generally warm parents provide explanations that match the child's ability to understand while firmly insisting that the child listen and comply, induction is effective as early as 2 years of age. In one study, preschoolers whose mothers used inductive reasoning were more likely to make up for their misdeeds, as Leisl did when she invited Ava to play with her blocks. Children exposed to induction also showed more prosocial behavior, in that they spontaneously gave hugs, toys, and verbal sympathy to others in distress (Zahn-Waxler, Radke-Yarrow, & King, 1979). In another investigation, the combination of parental warmth and induction predicted 3-year-old boys' capacity to refrain from wrongdoing and to confess and repair damages after misbehavior. These indicators of moral self-control, in turn, were linked to fewer behavior problems involving inattention and aggression (Kerr et al., 2004).

The success of induction may lie in its power to cultivate children's active commitment to moral norms, in the following ways:

- Induction tells children how to behave so they can call on this information in future situations.
- By pointing out the impact of the child's actions on others, parents encourage empathy and sympathetic concern, which motivate use of the inductive information in prosocial behavior (Krevans & Gibbs, 1996).
- Providing children with reasons for changing their behavior invites them to judge the appropriateness of parental expectations, which in turn encourages the child to adopt standards because they make sense.
- When children experience induction consistently, they may form a script for the negative emotional consequences of harming others—child harms, inductive message points out harm, child feels empathy for victim, child makes amends—that deters future transgressions (Hoffman, 2000).

In contrast, discipline that relies too heavily on threats of punishment or withdrawal of love produces such high levels of fear and anxiety that children cannot think clearly enough to figure out what they should do. In the long run, these practices do not get children to internalize moral norms. However, warnings, disapproval, and commands are sometimes necessary to get an unruly child to listen to an inductive message (Hoffman, 2000).

• **THE CHILD'S CONTRIBUTION** • Notice how Freud's theory places a heavy burden on parents, who must ensure through their disciplinary practices that children develop an internalized conscience. Although good discipline is crucial, children's characteristics also affect the success of parenting techniques. For example, in Chapter 10 we noted that empathy is moderately heritable. A more empathic child requires less power assertion and is more responsive to induction.

Temperament is also influential. Mild, patient tactics—requests, suggestions, and explanations—are sufficient to prompt guilt reactions and conscience development in anxious, fearful preschoolers (Kochanska et al., 2002). In contrast, gentle discipline has little impact on fearless, impulsive children. And power assertion also works poorly, undermining the child's emerging capacity for impulse control and, thereby, impairing moral internalization (Kochanska & Knaack, 2003). Instead, parents of impulsive youngsters can foster conscience development by ensuring a secure attachment relationship and combining firm correction of misbehavior with induction (Fowles & Kochanska, 2000; Kochanska, 1997a).

Why is this so? When children are so low in anxiety that parental interventions do not cause them enough discomfort to promote development of a strong conscience, a close bond with the parent provides an alternative foundation for morality. It motivates children to listen to parents' inductions and follow their rules as a means of preserving an affectionate, supportive relationship.

In sum, to foster early moral development, parents must tailor their disciplinary strategies to their child's personality. Does this remind you of goodness of fit, discussed in Chapter 10? Return to page 417 to review this idea.

• **THE ROLE OF GUILT** • Although little support exists for Freudian ideas about conscience development, Freud was correct that guilt is an important motivator of moral action. Inducing *empathy-based guilt* (expressions of personal responsibility and regret, such as "I'm sorry I hurt him") by explaining that the child's behavior is causing pain or distress to a victim and has disappointed the parent is a means of influencing children without using coercion. Empathy-based guilt reactions are associated with stopping harmful actions, repairing damage caused by misdeeds, and engaging in future prosocial behavior (Baumeister, 1998). At the same time, parents must help children deal with guilt feelings constructively—by guiding them to make up for immoral behavior rather than minimizing or excusing it (Bybee, Merisca, & Velasco, 1998).

Finally, contrary to what Freud believed, guilt is not the only force that compels us to act morally. And moral development is not an abrupt event that is virtually complete by the end of early childhood. Rather, it is a gradual process, beginning in the preschool years and extending into adulthood.

• **RECENT PSYCHOANALYTIC IDEAS** • Responding to the limitations of Freud's theory, recent psychoanalytic research underscores the importance of a positive parent–child relationship, emphasizing attachment as a vital foundation for acquiring moral standards (Emde et al., 1991). Earlier we noted the importance of combining warmth with induction to promote conscience development, and the strong role of attachment in impulsive children's moral internalization. And our discussion in Chapter 10 highlighted warmth and low punitiveness as vital for promoting *effortful control,* the self-regulatory dimension of temperament that (as we will see later) contributes to moral maturity. In one longitudinal study, attachment security at 14 months predicted children's eagerness to cooperate with parental demands. Children's cooperative spirit, in turn, increased the likelihood of patient, supportive parenting, which was positively associated with an internalized conscience at age 4½ (Kochanska et al., 2004).

Furthermore, current psychoanalytic theorists believe that the superego children build from parental teachings consists not just of prohibitions, or "don'ts" (as Freud emphasized), but also of positive guidelines for behavior, or "do's." After formulating a punitive superego, Freud acknowledged that conscience includes a set of ideals based on love rather than on threats of punishment, but he said little about this aspect. Erik Erikson, in his psychosocial theory, placed greater emphasis on the superego as a positive, constructive force that leads to *initiative,* a sense of ambition and purpose (see Chapter 1, page 18). The positive side of conscience probably emerges first, out of toddlers' participation in morally relevant activities with caregivers, such as helping to wipe up spilled milk or move a delicate object from one place to another. In these situations, parents offer generous praise, and the young child smiles broadly with pride—an early sign of internalization of parental moral standards.

A short time later, parents' warnings and disapproval of forbidden acts evoke "hurt feelings," which may be the forerunners of guilt. Soon, toddlers use their capacity for social referencing to

For fearless, impulsive children, a secure attachment relationship motivates the child to respond to parental discipline. If this mother is generally warm and patient, her 5-year-old is more likely to obey her command not to run into the street.
© Michelle D. Bridwell/PhotoEdit

check back with the parent, searching for emotional information to guide their behavior. With a disapproving glance or shake of the head, parents offer subtle but powerful messages about the moral meaning of the child's actions (see Chapter 10) (Emde & Oppenheim, 1995). Notice how recent psychoanalytic formulations retain continuity with Freud's theory in regarding emotion as the basis for moral development—as the platform on which mature commitment to moral norms is built.

Social Learning Theory

The social learning perspective does not regard morality as a special human activity with a unique course of development. Rather, moral behavior is acquired just like any other set of responses: through reinforcement and modeling.

• **THE IMPORTANCE OF MODELING** • Operant conditioning—following up children's "good behavior" with reinforcement in the form of approval, affection, and other rewards—is not enough to enable children to acquire moral responses. For a behavior to be reinforced, it must first occur spontaneously. Yet many prosocial acts, such as sharing, helping, or comforting an unhappy playmate, do not occur often enough at first for reinforcement to explain their rapid development in early childhood. Instead, social learning theorists believe that children learn to behave morally largely through *modeling*—observing and imitating adults who demonstrate appropriate behavior (Bandura, 1977; Grusec, 1988). Once children acquire a moral response, such as sharing or telling the truth, reinforcement in the form of praising the act ("That was a nice thing to do") and the child's character ("You're a very kind and considerate boy") increases its frequency (Mills & Grusec, 1989).

Many studies show that having helpful or generous models increases young children's prosocial responses. And certain characteristics of the model affect children's willingness to imitate:

● *Warmth and responsiveness.* Preschoolers are more likely to copy the prosocial actions of an adult who is warm and responsive rather than one who is cold and distant (Yarrow, Scott, & Waxler, 1973). Warmth seems to make children more attentive and receptive to the model, and is itself a model of a prosocial response.

● *Competence and power.* Children admire and therefore tend to select competent, powerful models to imitate—the reason they are especially willing to copy the behavior of older peers and adults (Bandura, 1977).

● *Consistency between assertions and behavior.* When models say one thing and do another— for example, announce that "it's important to help others" but rarely engage in helpful acts—children generally choose the most lenient standard of behavior that adults demonstrate (Mischel & Liebert, 1966).

Models are most influential during the preschool years. At the end of early childhood, children with a history of consistent exposure to caring adults tend to behave prosocially whether or not a model is present. By that time, they have internalized prosocial and other good-conduct rules from repeated observations of and encouragement by others (Mussen & Eisenberg-Berg, 1977).

• **THE EFFECTS OF PUNISHMENT** • Many parents are aware that yelling at, slapping, or spanking children for misbehavior are ineffective disciplinary tactics. A sharp reprimand or use of physical force to restrain or move a child is justified when immediate obedience is necessary—for example, when a 3-year-old is about to run into the street. In fact, parents are most likely to use forceful methods under these conditions. When they wish to foster long-term goals, such as acting kindly toward others, they tend to rely on warmth and reasoning (Kuczynski, 1984). Furthermore, parents often combine power assertion with reasoning in response to very serious transgressions, such as lying and stealing (Grusec & Goodnow, 1994).

When used frequently, however, punishment promotes only momentary compliance, not lasting changes in children's behavior. Children who are repeatedly criticized, shouted at, or hit are likely to display the unacceptable response again as soon as adults are out of sight and they can get away with it. Many studies confirm that the more harsh threats, angry physical control (yanking an object from the child, handling the child roughly), and physical punishment children experience, the more likely they are to develop serious, lasting mental health problems. These include weak internalization of moral rules; depression, aggression, antisocial behavior, and poor academic performance during childhood and adolescence; and criminality, depressive and alcoholic symptoms, and partner and child abuse in adulthood (Brezina, 1999; Gershoff, 2002a; Kochanska, Aksan, & Nichols, 2003).

Harsh punishment has several undesirable side effects:

- When parents insult and spank, they often do so in response to children's aggression (Holden, Coleman, & Schmidt, 1995). Yet the punishment itself models aggression!

- Harshly treated children react with anger, resentment, and a chronic sense of being personally threatened, which prompts a focus on the self's distress rather than a sympathetic orientation to others' needs (see Chapter 10, page 409).

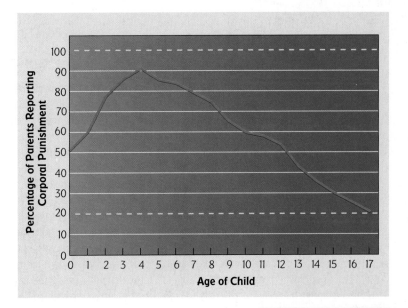

▲ **Figure 12.1**

Prevalence of corporal punishment by child's age. Estimates are based on the percentage of American parents in a nationally representative sample of nearly 1,000 reporting one or more instances of spanking, slapping, pinching, shaking, or hitting with a hard object in the past year. Physical punishment increases sharply during early childhood and then declines, but it is high at all ages. (From M. A. Straus & J. H. Stewart, 1999, "Corporal Punishment by American Parents: National Data on Prevalence, Chronicity, Severity, and Duration in Relation to Child and Family Characteristics," *Clinical Child and Family Psychology Review, 2,* p. 59. Adapted by permission of Kluwer Academic/Plenum Publishers and the author.)

- Children who are frequently punished soon learn to avoid the punishing adult. As a result, those adults have little opportunity to teach desirable behaviors.

- As harsh punishment "works" to stop children's misbehavior temporarily, it offers immediate relief to adults, who thus are reinforced for using coercive discipline. As a result, a punitive adult is likely to punish with greater frequency over time, a course of action that can spiral into serious abuse. Indeed, corporal punishment—the use of physical force to inflict pain but not injury—and physical abuse of children are closely linked (Gershoff, 2002a).

- School-age children, adolescents, and adults whose parents used corporal punishment are more accepting of such discipline: The more they were physically punished, the more strongly they endorse the practice (Bower-Russa, Knutson, & Winebarger, 2001; Deater-Deckard et al., 2003; Holden & Zambarano, 1992). In this way, use of corporal punishment may transfer to the next generation.

Parents with mental health problems—who are emotionally reactive, depressed, or aggressive—are more likely to be punitive as well as to have hard-to-manage children, whose disobedience evokes more parental harshness (Belsky & Hsieh, 1998; Clark, Kochanska, & Ready, 2000; Kochanska, Aksan, & Nichols, 2003). These findings suggest that heredity contributes to the link between punitive discipline and children's adjustment difficulties. But heredity is not a complete explanation. Return to page 119 in Chapter 3 to review findings indicating that good parenting can prevent children with a family background of antisocial behavior from becoming antisocial themselves. Other research indicates that parental harshness predicts emotional and behavior problems in children of diverse temperaments (O'Connor et al., 1998).

In view of these findings, the widespread use of corporal punishment by North American parents is cause for concern. A survey of a nationally representative sample of U.S. households revealed that although corporal punishment increases from infancy to age 5 and then declines, it is high at all ages (see Figure 12.1). Overall, more than 90 percent of American parents and 70 percent of Canadian parents admit to having hit or spanked their children (Durrant, Broberg, & Rose-Krasnor, 2000; Straus & Stewart, 1999). An alarming 35 to 50 percent of infants—who are not yet capable of complying with adult directives—get spanked or hit. Parents are most likely to physically punish toddlers and preschoolers repeatedly. And many do not limit themselves to a slap or a spank. More than one-fourth of physically punishing parents report having used a hard object, such as a brush or a belt, to hit their children (Gershoff, 2002b; Straus & Stewart, 1999).

A prevailing North American belief is that corporal punishment, if implemented by caring parents, is harmless, perhaps even beneficial. But as the Cultural Influences box on page 482 reveals, this assumption is valid only under conditions of limited use in certain social contexts. Consistent negative outcomes for most children indicate that parents are wise to refrain from harsh physical discipline.

Ethnic Differences in the Consequences of Physical Punishment

In an African-American community, six elders, all of whom had volunteered to as serve mentors for parents facing child-rearing challenges, met to discuss parenting issues at a social service agency. It quickly became clear that their attitudes toward discipline were strikingly different from those of the white social workers who had brought them together. Each of the African-American elders argued that successful child rearing required the use of appropriate physical tactics. They also voiced strong disapproval of screaming or cursing at children, calling such out-of-control parental behavior "abusive." Ruth, the oldest and most respected member of the group, characterized good parenting as a complex combination of warmth, teaching, talking nicely, and disciplining physically. She related how an older neighbor advised her to handle her own children when she was a young parent:

> She said to me says, don't scream at . . . your children . . . you talk to them real nice and sweet and when they do something ugly and you don't like it . . . she say you get a nice little switch and you won't have any trouble with them and from that day I raised my children that's the way I raised 'em. (Mosby et al., 1999, pp. 511–512)

The others chimed in, emphasizing the importance of *mild* punishment. "Just tap 'em a little bit." Touch 'em with it [the switch]." "When you do things like [get too harsh] you're wronging yourself" (p. 512).

Parents are especially likely to discipline physically when their own lives are stressful and their children are subject to dangerous neighborhood and peer influences. Use of physical punishment is highest among low-SES ethnic minority parents, who are more likely than middle-SES white

parents to advocate slaps and spankings (Pinderhughes et al., 2000; Straus & Stewart, 1999). Although corporal punishment is linked to a wide array of negative child outcomes, exceptions do exist.

In one longitudinal study, researchers followed several hundred families for 12 years, collecting information from mothers on disciplinary strategies in early and middle childhood, and from both mothers and their children on youth problem behaviors in adolescence. Even after many child and family characteristics had been controlled, the findings were striking: In Caucasian-American families, physical punishment was positively associated with adolescent aggression and antisocial behavior. In African-American families, by contrast, the more mothers had disciplined physically in childhood, the less their teenagers displayed angry, acting-out behavior and got in trouble at school and with the police (Lansford et al., 2004).

African-American and Caucasian-American parents seem to mete out physical punishment differently. In black families, such discipline is culturally approved and generally mild, delivered in a context of parental warmth, and aimed at helping children become responsible adults. White parents, in contrast, typically consider physical punishment to be wrong, so when they resort to it, they are usually highly agitated and rejecting of the child (Graziano & Hamblen, 1996). As a result, black youths may come to view spanking as a practice carried out with their best interests in mind, whereas white youths may regard it as an "act of personal aggression" (Gunnoe & Mariner, 1997, p. 768).

Whether a child perceives the parent as accepting or rejecting may make a difference in the long-term consequences of

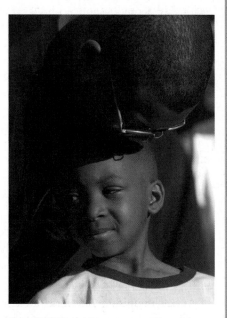

▲To discipline children, many African-American parents use mild physical punishment. Because the practice is culturally approved and delivered in an overall context of parental warmth, African-American youths may come to view it as a well-meaning effort to encourage maturity and to prevent them from engaging in risky behaviors.
© Sean Cayton/The Image Works

physical punishment. In support of this view, when several thousand ethnically diverse children were followed from the preschool through the early school years, spanking was associated with a rise in behavior problems if parents were cold and rejecting, but not if they were warm and supportive (McLoyd & Smith, 2002).

These findings are not an endorsement of physical punishment. Other forms of discipline, including time out, withdrawal of privileges, and the positive strategies listed on page 484, are far more effective. But it is noteworthy that the meaning and impact of physical discipline vary dramatically with cultural context.

• **ALTERNATIVES TO HARSH PUNISHMENT** • Alternatives to criticism, slaps, and spankings can reduce the side effects of punishment. A technique called **time out** involves removing children from the immediate setting—for example, by sending them to their rooms—until they are ready to act appropriately. Time out is useful when a child is out of control (Betz, 1994). It usually requires only a few minutes to change children's behavior, and it also

▶ **Figure 12.2**

How does inconsistent punishment affect children's behavior? To find out, researchers conducted an experiment in which they had mothers talk on the telephone while their toddlers played. Mothers in the "reprimand/give in" condition (who reprimanded half of their child's inappropriate demands and gave in to the other half) had toddlers with far higher rates of negative emotion and unruly behavior than did mothers in the "reprimand" condition (who reprimanded all inappropriate demands) and mothers in the "reprimand/ignore" condition (who reprimanded half of the inappropriate demands and ignored the other half). (Adapted from Acker & O'Leary, 1996.)

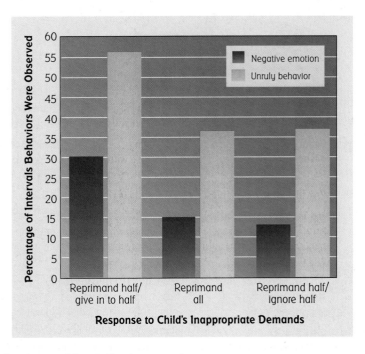

offers a "cooling off" period for angry parents. Another approach is *withdrawal of privileges*, such as getting an allowance or watching a favorite TV program. Removing privileges may generate some resentment in children, but it allows parents to avoid harsh techniques that could easily intensify into violence.

Although its usefulness is limited, punishment can play a valuable role in moral development. Earlier we noted that mild warnings and disapproval are occasionally necessary to get the child to attend to the parent's inductive teaching. When parents do decide to use punishment, they can increase its effectiveness in several ways:

- *Consistency.* Permitting children to act inappropriately on some occasions but scolding them on others leaves them confused about how to behave, and the unacceptable act persists. In a study in which researchers had mothers carry on a telephone conversation while their toddlers played, reprimanding half the children's inappropriate demands for attention ("Please don't interrupt") and giving in to the other half led to a dramatic increase in children's negative emotion and unruly behavior (see Figure 12.2) (Acker & O'Leary, 1996). As our consideration of the development of aggression at the end of this chapter will make clear, giving in to children's misbehavior contributes to a rise in aggressive behavior.

- *A warm parent–child relationship.* Children of involved, caring parents find the interruption in parental affection that accompanies punishment to be especially unpleasant. As a result, they want to regain parental warmth and approval as quickly as possible.

- *Explanations.* Explanations help children recall the misdeed and relate it to expectations for future behavior. Consequently, providing reasons for mild punishment (such as time out) leads to a far greater reduction in misbehavior than using punishment alone (Larzelere et al., 1996).

• **POSITIVE RELATIONSHIPS, POSITIVE DISCIPLINE** • The most effective forms of discipline encourage good conduct—by building a mutually respectful bond with the child, letting the child know ahead of time how to act, and praising mature behavior (Zahn-Waxler & Robinson, 1995). When sensitivity, cooperation, and shared positive emotion are evident in joint activities between mothers and their toddlers or preschoolers, children show firmer conscience development—expressing empathy after transgressions, behaving responsibly, playing fairly in games, and considering others' welfare (Kochanska, 1997b; Kochanska, Forman, & Coy, 1999). An early, mutually responsive, pleasurable mother–child tie continues to predict a firmer conscience into the early school years (Kochanska & Murray, 2000). Parent–child closeness leads children to heed parental demands because children feel a sense of commitment to the relationship. Note that this social-learning emphasis on positive emotion as a foundation for moral development is also consistent with psychoanalytic ideas.

Ⓢ Sensitivity, cooperation, and shared positive affect between parent and child support conscience development. Building on this girl's commitment to the relationship, her mother can encourage competent behavior.
© Michael Newman/PhotoEdit

Applying
What We Know   Using Positive Discipline

Strategy	Explanation
Use transgressions as opportunities to teach.	When a child engages in harmful or unsafe behavior, use induction, which motivates children to make amends and behave prosocially.
Reduce opportunities for misbehavior.	On a long car trip, bring back-seat activities that relieve children's restlessness. At the supermarket, converse with children and permit them to assist with shopping. As a result, children learn to occupy themselves constructively when options are limited.
Provide reasons for rules.	When children appreciate that rules are fair to all concerned, not arbitrary, they strive to follow the rules because these are reasonable and rational.
Arrange for children to participate in family routines and duties.	By joining with adults in preparing a meal, washing dishes, or raking leaves, children develop a sense of responsible participation in family and community life and acquire many practical skills.
When children are obstinate, try compromising and problem solving.	When a child refuses to obey, express understanding of the child's feelings ("I know it's not fun to clean up"), suggest a compromise ("You put those away, I'll take care of these"), and help the child think of ways to avoid the problem in the future. Responding firmly but kindly and respectfully increases the likelihood of willing cooperation.
Encourage mature behavior.	Express confidence in children's capacity to learn and appreciation for effort and cooperation, as in "You gave that your best!" "Thanks for helping!" Adult encouragement fosters pride and satisfaction in succeeding, thereby inspiring children to improve further.
Be sensitive to children's physical and emotional resources.	When children are tired, ill, or bored, they are likely to engage in attention-getting, disorganized, or otherwise improper behavior as a reaction to discomfort. In these instances, meeting the child's needs makes more sense than disciplining.

Consult Applying What We Know above for ways to discipline positively. Parents who use these strategies focus on long-term social and life skills—cooperation, problem solving, and consideration for others. As a result, they greatly reduce the need for punishment.

Limitations of "Morality as the Adoption of Societal Norms" Perspective

As previously noted, both psychoanalytic and social learning theories view moral development as a process of adopting societal norms. Personal commitment to societal norms is, without question, an essential aspect of moral development. Without an internalized, shared moral code and the cultivation of empathy through inductive discipline, people would disregard one another's rights whenever their desires conflicted and would transgress as soon as others could not observe their behavior.

Nevertheless, theories that regard morality as entirely a matter of internalizing norms have been criticized because prevailing standards may be at odds with important ethical principles and social goals. Under these conditions, deliberate violation of norms is not immoral but justifiable and courageous. Think, for a moment, about historical figures who rose to greatness because they refused to accept certain societal norms. Abraham Lincoln's opposition to slavery, Susan B. Anthony's leadership in the crusade for women's suffrage, and Martin Luther King, Jr.'s campaign to end racial prejudice are examples.

With respect to children, parental concern about internalization is often accompanied by other goals. At times, parents regard noncompliance as acceptable if the child provides a reasonable justification (Kuczynski & Hildebrandt, 1997). Consider a boy who violates a parental prohibition by cutting a cake reserved for a family celebration and giving a piece to a hungry playmate. As the parent begins to reprimand, the boy explains that the playmate had not eaten all day and

◉ Parents who engage in positive discipline encourage good conduct by building a cooperative relationship with their children, letting them know ahead of time how to act, and reducing opportunities for misbehavior. These parents brought along plenty of activities to keep their children occupied during a long plane trip.
© Myrleen Cate/Index Stock

that the refrigerator was nearly empty, leaving no alternative. In this instance, many parents would value the morality of the boy's claims along with his reasoning and negotiation skills.

Cognitive-developmental theorists believe that neither identification with parents nor teaching, modeling, and reinforcement are the major means through which children become moral. The cognitive-developmental approach assumes that individuals, instead of internalizing existing rules and expectations, develop morally through **construction**—actively attending to and interrelating multiple perspectives on situations in which social conflicts arise and thereby deriving new moral understandings. In other words, children make moral judgments on the basis of concepts they construct about justice and fairness. As these concepts become increasingly adequate with age, children experience them as having a rational basis and arrive at a deeper understanding of morality—as something that *must be true* in the social world, just as conservation *must be true* in the physical world (Gibbs, 1991, 2003).

In sum, the cognitive-developmental position on morality is unique in its view of the child as a thinking moral being who wonders about right and wrong and searches for moral truth. These theorists regard changes in children's reasoning as the heart of moral development.

Ask Yourself

REVIEW	Describe evidence indicating that many morally relevant behaviors have roots in our evolutionary history.
REVIEW	Summarize the main features of the psychoanalytic and social learning perspectives on moral development. Why has each been criticized?
APPLY	Alice and Wayne want their two young children to become morally mature, caring individuals. List parenting practices that would foster these goals, and explain why each is effective.
REFLECT	Did you display a strong, internalized conscience as a child? How do you think temperament, parenting practices, family living conditions, and cultural background affected your childhood moral maturity?

Morality as Social Understanding

According to the cognitive-developmental perspective, cognitive maturity and social experience lead to advances in moral understanding, from a superficial orientation to physical power and external consequences toward a more profound appreciation of interpersonal relationships, societal institutions, and lawmaking systems (Gibbs, 1995, 2003). As their grasp of social cooperation expands, children's ideas about what ought to be done when the needs and desires of people conflict also change, toward increasingly just, fair, and balanced solutions to moral problems.

Piaget's Theory of Moral Development

Piaget's (1932/1965) early work on children's moral judgments was the original inspiration for the cognitive-developmental perspective. To study children's ideas about morality, Piaget relied on open-ended clinical interviews: He questioned 5- to 13-year-old Swiss children about their understanding of rules in the game of marbles. In addition, he gave children stories in which characters' intentions to engage in right or wrong action and the consequences of their behavior varied. In the best known of these stories, children were asked which of two boys—well-intentioned John, who breaks 15 cups while on his way to dinner, or ill-intentioned Henry, who breaks 1 cup while stealing some jam—is naughtier, and why. From children's responses, Piaget identified two broad stages of moral understanding.

• **HETERONOMOUS MORALITY (ABOUT 5 TO 10 YEARS)** • *Heteronomous* means under the authority of another. As the term **heteronomous morality** suggests, children in this first stage view rules as handed down by authorities (God, parents, and teachers), as having a permanent existence, as unchangeable, and as requiring strict obedience. For example, young children state that the rules of the game of marbles cannot be changed, explaining that "God didn't teach [the new rules]," "you couldn't play any other way," or "it would be cheating. . . . A fair rule is one that is in the game" (Piaget, 1932/1965, pp. 58, 59, 63).

According to Piaget, two factors limit children's moral understanding: (1) the power of adults to insist that children comply, which promotes unquestioning respect for rules and those who enforce them; and (2) cognitive immaturity, especially children's limited capacity to imagine other perspectives. Because young children think that all people view rules the same way, their moral understanding is characterized by **realism**—that is, children regard rules as external features of reality rather than as cooperative principles that can be modified at will.

Together, adult power, egocentrism, and realism result in superficial moral understandings. In judging an act's wrongness, younger children focus on outcomes rather than on intent to do harm. For example, in the story about John and Henry mentioned earlier, they regard John as naughtier, despite his innocent intentions, because he broke more cups.

• **AUTONOMOUS MORALITY, OR THE MORALITY OF COOPERATION (ABOUT 10 YEARS AND OLDER)** • Cognitive development, gradual release from adult control, and peer interaction lead children to make the transition to the second stage, **autonomous morality,** in which they no longer view rules as fixed but see them as flexible, socially agreed-on principles that can be revised to suit the will of the majority. Piaget regarded peer disagreements as especially facilitating (see Chapter 6). Through them, children realize that people's perspectives on moral action can differ and that intentions, not concrete consequences, should serve as the basis for judging behavior.

Furthermore, as children interact as equals with peers, they learn to settle conflicts in mutually beneficial ways. Gradually, they start to use a standard of fairness called *reciprocity*, in which they express the same concern for the welfare of others as they do for themselves. Piaget found that at first, children's grasp of reciprocity is a "crude," tit-for-tat understanding: "You scratch my back and I'll scratch yours." This defines the beginning of the morality of cooperation. Older children and adolescents move beyond this payback morality to an advanced understanding of reciprocity as mutuality of expectations, called **ideal reciprocity.** Most of us are familiar with it in the form of the Golden Rule: "Do unto others as you would have them do unto you." Ideal reciprocity helps young people realize that rules can be reinterpreted and revised to take into account individual circumstances, thereby ensuring just outcomes for all.

Evaluation of Piaget's Theory

Follow-up research indicates that Piaget's theory accurately describes the general direction of change in moral judgment. In many studies, as children get older, outer features, such as physical damage or getting punished, give way to subtler considerations, such as the actor's intentions or the needs and desires of others. Also, much evidence confirms Piaget's conclusion that moral understanding is supported by cognitive maturity, gradual release from adult control, and peer interaction. We will consider these findings when we turn to extensions of Piaget's work by Lawrence Kohlberg and his followers. Nevertheless, several aspects of Piaget's theory have been questioned because they underestimate the moral capacities of young children.

• **INTENTIONS AND MORAL JUDGMENTS** • Look again at the story about John and Henry on page 485. Because bad intentions are paired with little damage and good intentions with a great deal of damage, Piaget's method yields a conservative picture of young children's ability to appreciate intentions. When questioned about moral issues in a way that makes a person's intent stand out as strongly as the harm that person does, preschool and early school-age children are quite capable of judging ill-intentioned people as naughtier and more deserving of punishment than well-intentioned ones (Helwig, Zelazo, & Wilson, 2001; Jones & Thomson, 2001).

As further evidence, by age 4, children clearly recognize the difference between two morally relevant intentional behaviors: truthfulness and lying. They approve of telling the truth and disapprove of lying, even when a lie remains undetected (Bussey, 1992). And by age 7 to 8—earlier than one might expect from Piaget's findings—children integrate their judgments of lying and truth telling with prosocial and antisocial intentions. For example, they give a very negative rating to telling the truth in certain social situations—for example, bluntly saying to a friend that you don't like her drawing (Bussey, 1999). Influenced by collectivist values of social harmony and self-effacement, Chinese children are more likely than Canadian children to rate lying favorably when an intention involves modesty, as when a student who has thoughtfully picked up the garbage in the school yard says, "I didn't do it." In contrast, both Chinese and Canadian children rate lying about antisocial acts as "very naughty" (Lee et al., 1997).

Nevertheless, an advanced understanding of the morality of intentions does await autonomous morality. Younger children are more likely to *center,* or focus on, salient features and consequences in their judgments, while neglecting other important information. For example, preschoolers more often than older children evaluate lies as always wrong (Peterson, Peterson, & Seeto, 1983). And although they disapprove of undetected lies, they also judge lies that lead to punishment more negatively than lies that do not (Bussey, 1992).

Furthermore, through the early school years, children generally interpret statements of intention in a rigid, heteronomous fashion. They believe that once you say you will do something, you are obligated to follow through, even if uncontrollable circumstances (such as an accident) make it difficult or impossible to do so. By age 9 or 10, children realize that not keeping your word is much worse in some situations than in others—namely, when you are able to do so and have permitted another person to count on your actions (Mant & Perner, 1988). In sum, Piaget was partly right and partly wrong about this aspect of moral reasoning.

• **REASONING ABOUT AUTHORITY** • Research on young children's understanding of authority reveals that they do not regard adults with the unquestioning respect Piaget assumed. Even preschoolers judge certain acts, such as hitting and stealing, to be wrong regardless of the opinions of authorities. When asked to explain, 3- and 4-year-olds express concerns about harming other people rather than obeying adult dictates (Smetana, 1981, 1985).

By age 4, children have differentiated notions about the legitimacy of authority figures that they refine during the school years. In several studies, kindergartners through sixth graders were asked questions designed to assess their view of how broad an adult's authority should be. Almost all denied that adults have general authority. For example, they rejected a principal's right to set rules and issue directives in settings other than his own school (Laupa, 1995).

With respect to nonmoral concerns, such as the rules to be followed in a game, children usually base the legitimacy of authority on a person's knowledge of the situation, not on social position. And when a directive is fair and caring (for example, telling children to stop fighting or to share candy), children view it as right, regardless of who states it—a principal, a teacher, a class president, or another child. This is even true for Korean children, whose culture places a high value on respect for and deference to adults. Korean 7- to 11-year-olds evaluate negatively a teacher's or principal's order to keep fighting, to steal, or to refuse to share—a response that strengthens with age (Kim, 1998; Kim & Turiel, 1996).

As these findings reveal, adult status is not required for preschool and school-age children to view someone as an authority. Peers who are knowledgeable or who act to protect others' rights are regarded as just as legitimate. But in reasoning about authority, preschool and young elementary school children do tend to center on the superficial: They place somewhat greater weight than older children on power, status, and impressive consequences for not obeying the authority. Nevertheless, younger children can coordinate several factors—the attributes of the individual, the type of behavior to be controlled, and the context in which it occurs—at a much earlier age than Piaget anticipated.

• **STAGEWISE PROGRESSION** • An additional point about Piaget's theory is that many children display both heteronomous and autonomous reasoning, which raises doubts about whether each stage represents a general, unifying organization of moral judgment responses. But in fairness, Piaget (1932/1965) also observed this mixture in children and, therefore, regarded the two moralities as fluid, overlapping phases rather than tightly knit stages.

Finally, moral development is currently viewed as a more extended process than Piaget believed. In fact, Kohlberg's six-stage sequence, to which we turn next, identifies three stages beyond the first appearance of autonomous morality. Nevertheless, Kohlberg's theory is a direct continuation of the research that Piaget began.

◉ These Korean first graders have been reared in a culture that places a high value on deference to adults. Still, if their teacher directed them to cheat or steal, they would say that her immoral order should not be obeyed.
© Jack Stein Grove/PhotoEdit

Kohlberg's Extension of Piaget's Theory

Like Piaget, Kohlberg used a clinical interviewing procedure to study moral development. But whereas Piaget asked children to judge and explain which of two children in a pair of stories was naughtier, Kohlberg used a more open-ended approach: He presented people with hypothetical moral dilemmas and asked what the main actor should do and why.

• THE CLINICAL INTERVIEW • In Kohlberg's **Moral Judgment Interview,** individuals resolve dilemmas that present conflicts between two moral values and justify their decisions. The best known of these is the "Heinz dilemma," which pits the value of obeying the law (not stealing) against the value of human life (saving a dying person):

> In Europe, a woman was near death from cancer. There was one drug the doctors thought might save her. A druggist in the same town had discovered it, but he was charging ten times what the drug cost him to make. The sick woman's husband, Heinz, went to everyone he knew to borrow the money, but he could only get together half of what it cost. The druggist refused to sell the drug for less or let Heinz pay later. So Heinz got desperate and broke into the man's store to steal the drug for his wife. Should Heinz have done that? Why or why not? (paraphrased from Colby et al., 1983, p. 77)

In addition to explaining their answer, participants are asked to evaluate the conflicting moral values on which the dilemma is based. Scoring of responses is intricate and demanding—perhaps the most complex of any interview scoring system (Gibbs, Basinger, & Grime, 2003; Miller, 1998).

Moral maturity is determined by the *way an individual reasons about the dilemma,* not the *content of the response* (whether or not to steal). Individuals who believe that Heinz should steal the drug and those who think he should not can be found at each of Kohlberg's first four stages. At the highest two stages, moral reasoning and content come together. Individuals do not just agree on why certain actions are justified; they also agree on what people ought to do when faced with a moral dilemma. Given a choice between obeying the law and preserving individual rights, the most advanced moral thinkers support individual rights (in the Heinz dilemma, stealing the drug to save a life). As we look at development in Kohlberg's scheme, we will see that moral reasoning and content are independent at first, but eventually they are integrated into a coherent ethical system (Kohlberg, Levine, & Hewer, 1983).

• A QUESTIONNAIRE APPROACH • For more efficient gathering and scoring of moral reasoning, researchers have devised short-answer questionnaires. The most recent is the **Sociomoral Reflection Measure–Short Form (SRM–SF).** Like Kohlberg's clinical interview, the SRM–SF asks individuals to evaluate the importance of moral values and produce moral reasoning. Here are 4 of its 11 questions:

- Let's say a friend of yours needs help and may even die, and you're the only person who can save him or her. How important is it for a person (without losing his or her own life) to save the life of a friend?

- What about saving the life of anyone? How important is it for a person (without losing his or her own life) to save the life of a stranger?

- How important is it for people not to take things that belong to other people?

- How important is it for people to obey the law? (Gibbs, Basinger, & Fuller, 1992, pp. 151–152)

After reading each question, participants rate the importance of the value it addresses (as "very important," "important," or "not important") and write a brief explanation of their rating. The explanations are coded according to a revised rendition of Kohlberg's stages.

The SRM–SF is far less time consuming than the Moral Judgment Interview because it does not require people to read and think about lengthy descriptions of moral dilemmas. Instead, participants merely evaluate moral values and justify their evaluations. Nevertheless, scores on the SRM–SF correlate well with those obtained from the Moral Judgment Interview and show similar age trends (Basinger, Gibbs, & Fuller, 1995; Gibbs, Basinger, & Grime, 2003). Apparently, moral reasoning can be measured without using dilemmas—a discovery that is likely to ease the task of conducting moral development research.

• **KOHLBERG'S STAGES OF MORAL UNDERSTANDING** • In his initial investigation, Kohlberg (1958) extended the age range Piaget studied, including participants who were well into adolescence by administering the Moral Judgment Interview to 10-, 13-, and 16-year-old boys. Then he followed the participants longitudinally, reinterviewing them at 3- to 4-year intervals over the next 20 years (Colby et al., 1983). Analyzing age-related changes in the boys' moral judgments, Kohlberg generated his six-stage sequence. As with Piaget's progression of development, Kohlberg's first three stages characterize children as moving from a morality focused on outcomes to a morality based on ideal reciprocity. Inclusion of older adolescents yielded the fourth stage, in which young people expand their notion of ideal reciprocity to encompass societal rules and laws as vital for ensuring that people treat one another justly. On the basis of the moral judgment responses of a small minority of adolescents, Kohlberg extended his sequence further, positing the fifth and sixth stages. As we will see, these stages have remained infrequent in subsequent research.

Kohlberg organized his six stages into three general levels and made stronger claims than Piaget about a fixed order of moral change. In doing so, however, Kohlberg drew on characteristics that Piaget used to describe his cognitive stage sequence:

- Kohlberg regarded his moral stages as invariant and universal—a sequence of steps that people everywhere move through in a fixed order.
- He viewed each new stage as building on reasoning of the preceding stage, resulting in a more logically consistent and morally adequate concept of justice.
- Kohlberg saw each stage as an organized whole—a qualitatively distinct structure of moral thought that a person applies across a wide range of situations (Colby & Kohlberg, 1987).

Recall from Chapter 6 that those theorists who continue to adhere to a stagewise view of cognitive development accept a flexible notion of stage. Similarly, we will see that Kohlberg's claims about a tightly organized sequence of moral stages have been challenged.

Furthermore, Kohlberg believed that moral understanding is promoted by the same factors that Piaget considered important for cognitive development: (1) disequilibrium, or actively grappling with moral issues and noticing weaknesses in one's current thinking, and (2) gains in perspective taking, which permit individuals to resolve moral conflicts in increasingly complex and effective ways. As we examine Kohlberg's developmental sequence and illustrate it with responses to the Heinz dilemma, look for changes in cognition and perspective taking that each stage assumes.

▶ *The Preconventional Level.* At the **preconventional level,** morality is externally controlled. As in Piaget's heteronomous stage, children accept the rules of authority figures, and actions are judged by their consequences. Behaviors that result in punishment are viewed as bad, and those that lead to rewards are seen as good.

- *Stage 1: The punishment and obedience orientation.* Children at this stage find it difficult to consider two points of view in a moral dilemma. As a result, they ignore people's intentions and instead focus on fear of authority and avoidance of punishment as reasons for behaving morally.

Prostealing: "If you let your wife die, you will get in trouble. You'll be blamed for not spending the money to help her, and there'll be an investigation of you and the druggist for your wife's death." (Kohlberg, 1969, p. 381)

Antistealing: "You shouldn't steal the drug because you'll be caught and sent to jail if you do. If you do get away, [you'd be scared that] the police would catch up with you any minute." (Kohlberg, 1969, p. 381)

- *Stage 2: The instrumental purpose orientation.* Children become aware that people can have different perspectives in a moral dilemma, but at first this understanding is very concrete. They view right action as flowing from self-interest. Reciprocity is understood as equal exchange of favors: "You do this for me and I'll do that for you."

How does this boy explain his decision to help a classmate pick up her books and papers? If he expects her to do a favor for him in return, his reasoning falls at Kohlberg's preconventional level. If his actions are governed by the Golden Rule, "Do unto others as you would have others do unto you," then he has advanced to Kohlberg's conventional level.
© Michael Newman/PhotoEdit

Prostealing: "The druggist can do what he wants and Heinz can do what he wants to do.... But if Heinz decides to risk jail to save his wife, it's his life he's risking; he can do what he wants with it. And the same goes for the druggist; it's up to him to decide what he wants to do." (Rest, 1979, p. 26)

Antistealing: "[Heinz] is running more risk than it's worth [to save a wife who is near death]." (Rest, 1979, p. 27)

▶ *The Conventional Level.* At the **conventional level,** individuals continue to regard conformity to social rules as important, but not for reasons of self-interest. Rather, they believe that actively maintaining the current social system ensures positive human relationships and societal order.

- *Stage 3: The "good boy–good girl" orientation, or the morality of interpersonal cooperation.* The desire to obey rules because they promote social harmony first appears in the context of close personal ties. Stage 3 individuals want to maintain the affection and approval of friends and relatives by being a "good person"—trustworthy, loyal, respectful, helpful, and nice. The capacity to view a two-person relationship from the vantage point of an impartial, outside observer supports this new approach to morality. At this stage, the individual understands *ideal reciprocity,* as expressed in the Golden Rule.

Prostealing: "No one will think you're bad if you steal the drug, but your family will think you're an inhuman husband if you don't. If you let your wife die, you'll never be able to look anyone in the face again." (Kohlberg, 1969, p. 381)

Antistealing: "It isn't just the druggist who will think you're a criminal, everyone else will too. After you steal it, you'll feel bad thinking how you brought dishonor on your family and yourself." (Kohlberg, 1969, p. 381)

- *Stage 4: The social-order-maintaining orientation.* At this stage, the individual takes into account a larger perspective—that of societal laws. Moral choices no longer depend on close ties to others. Instead, rules must be enforced in the same evenhanded fashion for everyone, and each member of society has a personal duty to uphold them. The Stage 4 individual believes that laws cannot be disobeyed under any circumstances because they are vital for ensuring societal order and cooperative relations between individuals.

Prostealing: "He should steal it. Heinz has a duty to protect his wife's life; it's a vow he took in marriage. But it's wrong to steal, so he would have to take the drug with the idea of paying the druggist for it and accepting the penalty for breaking the law later."

Antistealing: "It's a natural thing for Heinz to want to save his wife but.... Even if his wife is dying, it's still his duty as a citizen to obey the law. No one else is allowed to steal, why should he be? If everyone starts breaking the law in a jam, there'd be no civilization, just crime and violence." (Rest, 1979, p. 30)

▶ *The Postconventional or Principled Level.* Individuals at the **postconventional level** move beyond unquestioning support for the rules and laws of their own society. They define morality in terms of abstract principles and values that apply to all situations and societies.

◉ Rallying against tobacco use, these young people evaluate the rules and laws of their society on the basis of how well they serve the interests of the majority. They express a principled level of morality.
© Bob Daemmrich/PhotoEdit

- *Stage 5: The social-contract orientation.* At Stage 5, individuals regard laws and rules as flexible instruments for furthering human purposes. They can imagine alternatives to their own social order, and they emphasize fair procedures for interpreting and changing the law. When laws are consistent with individual rights and the interests of the majority, each person follows them because of a *social-contract orientation*—free and willing participation in the system because it brings about more good for people than if it did not exist.

Prostealing: "Although there is a law against stealing, the law wasn't meant to violate a person's right to life. Taking the drug does violate the law, but Heinz is justified in stealing in this instance. If Heinz is prosecuted for stealing, the law needs to be reinterpreted to take into account situations in which it goes against people's natural right to keep on living."

- *Stage 6: The universal ethical principle orientation.* At this highest stage, right action is defined by self-chosen ethical principles of conscience that are valid for all humanity, regardless of law and social agreement. These values are abstract, not concrete moral rules like the Ten Commandments. Stage 6 individuals typically mention such principles as equal consideration of the claims of all human beings and respect for the worth and dignity of each person.

Prostealing: "If Heinz does not do everything he can to save his wife, then he is putting some value higher than the value of life. It doesn't make sense to put respect for property above respect for life itself. [People] could live together without private property at all. Respect for human life and personality is absolute, and accordingly [people] have a mutual duty to save one another from dying." (Rest, 1979, p. 37)

Research on Kohlberg's Stages

Is there support for Kohlberg's developmental sequence? If so, movement through the stages should be related to age, cognitive development, and gains in perspective taking. Also, moral reasoning should conform to the strict stage properties that Kohlberg assumed.

• **AGE-RELATED CHANGE** • A wealth of research reveals that progress through Kohlberg's stages is consistently related to age. The most convincing evidence comes from Kohlberg's 20-year longitudinal continuation of his first study (Colby et al., 1983). The correlation between age and moral judgment maturity was strong, at +.78. In addition, on the basis of responses to Kohlberg's hypothetical dilemmas, almost all participants moved through the stages in the predicted order, without skipping steps or returning to less mature reasoning once a stage had been attained. Other longitudinal studies using hypothetical dilemmas confirm these findings (Rest, 1986; Walker, 1989; Walker & Taylor, 1991b). However, as will become clear in the next section, when researchers use real-life dilemmas, age-related change is less tidy and more variable.

A striking finding is that development of moral reasoning is slow and gradual. Figure 12.3 shows the extent to which individuals used each stage of moral reasoning between ages 10 and 36 in Kohlberg's longitudinal study. Notice how Stages 1 and 2 decrease in early adolescence, whereas Stage 3 increases through mid-adolescence and then declines. Stage 4 rises over the teenage years until, by early adulthood, it is the typical response. Few people move beyond it to Stage 5. As noted earlier, postconventional morality is so rare that no clear evidence exists that Kohlberg's Stage 6 actually follows Stage 5. The highest stage of moral development is a matter of speculation.

• **ARE KOHLBERG'S STAGES ORGANIZED WHOLES?** • If each of Kohlberg's stages forms an organized whole, then individuals should use the same level of moral reasoning across many tasks and situations—not just for hypothetical dilemmas but for everyday moral problems as well. In focusing on hypothetical dilemmas, Kohlberg emphasized the rational weighing of alternatives but neglected other influences on moral judgment. When researchers asked adolescents and adults to recall and discuss a real-life moral dilemma, they focused most often on relationships—whether to continue helping a friend who is taking advantage of you, whether to live with your mother or with your father after their separation. Although participants mentioned reasoning as the most frequent strategy for resolving these dilemmas, they

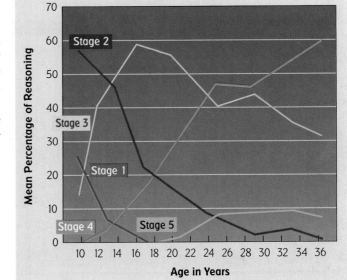

▶ **Figure 12.3**

Longitudinal trends in moral reasoning at each stage in Kohlberg's 20-year study of adolescent boys. Note that as the lower stages decline, Stage 4 reasoning increases slowly and gradually with age, eventually becoming the typical response.

(From A. Colby, L. Kohlberg, J. C. Gibbs, & M. Lieberman, 1983, "A Longitudinal Study of Moral Judgment," *Monographs of the Society for Research in Child Development, 48* [1–2, Serial No. 200], p. 46. © The Society for Research in Child Development, Inc. Reprinted by permission.)

also posed other strategies, such as talking through issues with others, relying on intuition that their decision was right, and calling on notions of religion and spirituality. Especially striking were expressions of anguish in working through everyday dilemmas. People mentioned feeling drained, confused, and torn by temptation—a motivational and emotional side of moral judgment not tapped by hypothetical situations (Walker, 2004; Walker et al., 1995, 1999).

Although everyday moral reasoning corresponds to Kohlberg's scheme, it typically falls at a lower stage than responses to hypothetical dilemmas (Walker & Moran, 1991). Real-life problems seem to elicit reasoning below a person's actual capacity because they bring out many practical considerations. Hypothetical situations, in contrast, evoke the upper limits of adolescents' and adults' moral thought because they allow reflection without the interference of personal risks. As one participant in a study involving both types of dilemmas observed, "It's a lot easier to be moral when you have nothing to lose" (Walker et al., 1995, pp. 381–382).

◎ Will the 14-year-old girls on the left accept a peer's offer of a cigarette? Real-life moral dilemmas, involving on-the-spot decision making, bring out the motivational and emotional sides of moral judgment along with practical considerations involved in resolving conflicts.
© Elizabeth Zuckerman/PhotoEdit

The influence of situational factors on moral reasoning indicates that like Piaget's cognitive stages, Kohlberg's moral stages are loosely organized. Rather than developing in a neat, stepwise fashion, people draw on a range of moral responses that vary with context. With age, this range shifts upward as less mature moral reasoning is gradually replaced by more advanced moral thought (Fischer & Bidell, 1998; Siegler, 1996).

• **COGNITIVE PREREQUISITES FOR MORAL REASONING** • Moral maturity, whether based on Piaget's theory or that of Kohlberg, is positively correlated with IQ, performance on Piagetian cognitive tasks, and perspective-taking skill (Lickona, 1976; Walker & Hennig, 1997). Kohlberg (1976) argued that each moral stage requires certain cognitive and perspective-taking capacities, but that these are not enough to ensure moral advances. In addition, reorganization of thought unique to the moral domain is necessary. In other words, Kohlberg hypothesized that cognitive and perspective-taking attainments are *necessary but not sufficient conditions* for each moral stage.

Research indicates that, consistent with Kohlberg's predictions, children and adolescents at each moral stage score at either a higher stage or the matching stage of cognition and perspective taking, shown in Table 12.1 (Krebs & Gillmore, 1982; Selman, 1976; Walker, 1980). Still, the domain in which the cognitive ingredients required for more mature moral judgment first emerge—cognitive, social, or moral—remains unclear. In Chapters 6 and 7, we encountered a wealth of evidence indicating that children display more advanced reasoning on tasks with

TABLE 12.1 RELATIONSHIPS AMONG KOHLBERG'S MORAL, PIAGET'S COGNITIVE, AND SELMAN'S PERSPECTIVE-TAKING STAGES

Kohlberg's Moral Stage	Description	Piaget's Cognitive Stage	Selman's Perspective-Taking Stage[a]
Punishment and obedience orientation	Fear of authority and avoidance of punishment	Preoperational, early concrete operational	Social-informational
Instrumental purpose orientation	Satisfying personal needs	Concrete operational	Self-reflective
"Good boy–good girl" orientation	Maintaining the affection and approval of friends and relatives	Early formal operational	Third-party
Social-order-maintaining orientation	A duty to uphold laws and rules for their own sake	Formal operational	Societal
Social contract orientation	Fair procedures for changing laws to protect individual rights and the needs of the majority		
Universal ethical principle orientation	Abstract universal principles that are valid for all humanity		

[a]To review these stages, return to Table 11.2 on page 466.

which they have more extensive experience. Young people who frequently grapple with social and moral issues may actually construct the cognitive supports for more development directly—while reasoning about social or moral concerns (Damon, 1977; Gibbs, 2003).

Finally, Kohlberg's stage order makes sense to adolescents and adults who have not studied his theory. When Russian high school and Dutch university students were asked to sort statements typical of Kohlberg's stages, they tended to rank reasoning at each consecutive stage as more sophisticated. However, the higher the stage, the more participants disagreed in their rankings because they had difficulty ordering statements beyond their own current stage (Boom, Brugman, & van der Heijden, 2001).

Are There Sex Differences in Moral Reasoning?

As we have seen, real-life moral dilemmas highlight the contribution of emotion to moral judgment. Return to Leisl's moral reasoning in the opening to this chapter and notice how her argument focuses on caring and commitment to others. Carol Gilligan (1982) is the best-known figure among those who have argued that Kohlberg's theory—originally formulated on the basis of interviews with males—does not adequately represent the morality of girls and women. Gilligan believes that feminine morality emphasizes an "ethic of care" that is devalued in Kohlberg's system. Leisl's reasoning falls at Kohlberg's Stage 3 because it is based on interpersonal obligations. In contrast, Stages 4 to 6 stress justice—an abstract, rational commitment to moral ideals. According to Gilligan, a concern for others is a *different*, not less valid, basis for moral judgment than a focus on impersonal rights.

Many studies have tested Gilligan's hypothesis that Kohlberg's approach underestimates the moral maturity of females, and most do not support it (Turiel, 1998). On hypothetical dilemmas as well as everyday moral problems, adolescent and adult females display reasoning at the same stage as their male counterparts, and sometimes at a higher stage. Also, themes of justice and caring appear in the responses of both sexes, and when girls do raise interpersonal concerns, they are not downgraded in Kohlberg's system (Jadack et al., 1995; Kahn, 1992; Walker, 1995). These findings suggest that although Kohlberg emphasized justice rather than caring as the highest of moral ideals, his theory includes both sets of values.

Still, Gilligan makes a powerful claim that research on moral development has been limited by too much attention to rights and justice (a "masculine" ideal) and too little attention to care and responsiveness (a "feminine" ideal). Some evidence shows that although the morality of males and females taps both orientations, females do tend to stress care, or empathic perspective taking, whereas males either stress justice or focus equally on justice and care (Jaffe & Hyde, 2000; Wark & Krebs, 1996; Weisz & Black, 2002).

The difference in emphasis appears most often in real-life rather than hypothetical dilemmas. Consequently, it may be largely a function of women's greater involvement in daily activities involving care and concern for others. In one study, American and Canadian 17- to 26-year-old females showed more complex reasoning about care issues than their male counterparts. But as Figure 12.4 shows, Norwegian males were just as advanced as Norwegian females in care-based understanding (Skoe, 1998). Perhaps Norwegian culture, which endorses gender equality at home, at school, and in the workplace, induces boys and men to think deeply about interpersonal obligations.

Collectivist values of Asian cultures explicitly emphasize care and concern for others as a societal norm. In one study, Japanese adolescents almost always integrated care and justice reasoning. At the same time, both males and females stressed caring, which they regarded as a communal responsibility. As one boy remarked, *yasashii* (kindness/gentleness) and *omoiyari* (empathy) are "something 'normal' that everyone shows" (Shimizu, 2001).

Ⓢ Kristopher Knowles, age 14, accompanied by supporters, completes his cross-Canada walk to raise awareness for organ donation, having visited over 200 cities and towns and generated over 800 media stories. Kristopher has been waiting for a liver since birth. After surviving twenty operations, he decided to take action, not just for himself but for thousands of people worldwide who also await a life-saving transplant. Kristopher's feat exemplifies complex, care-based moral understanding.
© CP Photo/Adrian Wyld

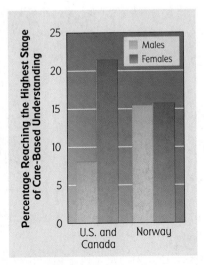

▶ **Figure 12.4**

Complex reasoning about care issues among U.S. and Canadian versus Norwegian males and females. In this study of 17- to 26-year-olds, North American females scored much higher than males in complex care-based understanding. In contrast, Norwegian males and females displayed equally advanced care-based understanding. (Adapted from Skoe, 1998.)

Although current evidence indicates that justice and caring are not gender-specific morali-ties, Gilligan's work has expanded our conception of the highly moral person. In several inves-tigations, researchers examined the development of care-based reasoning using dilemmas that ask adolescents and adults to reason about relationships—for example, a lonely parent wanting to move in with an adult child. Findings revealed gradual change from an egocentric focus on the self's needs, to a self-sacrificing focus on others' needs, to balanced consideration of the needs of both self and other, generally paralleling age-related change in justice-based reasoning (Pratt, Skoe, & Arnold, 2004; Skoe & Diessner, 1994). Perhaps Piaget (1932/1965) himself said it best: "Between the more refined forms of justice . . . and love properly so called, there is no longer any real conflict" (p. 324).

Influences on Moral Reasoning

Earlier we mentioned Kohlberg's belief that actively grappling with moral issues is vital for moral change. As we will see in the following sections, many factors are related to moral understanding, including the young person's personality and a wide range of social experiences—peer interaction, child-rearing practices, schooling, and aspects of culture. Growing evidence suggests that these experiences work in at least two ways: (1) They encourage young people to take the perspective of others, and (2) they induce cognitive disequilibrium by presenting young people with cognitive challenges, which stimulate them to think about moral problems in more complex ways.

• **PERSONALITY** • A flexible, open-minded approach to new information and experiences is linked to gains in moral reasoning, just as it is to identity development (Hart et al., 1998; Matsuba & Walker, 1998). Because open-minded young people are more socially skilled, they have more opportunities for social participation (Block & Block, 1980). A richer social life enhances exposure to others' perspectives, and open-mindedness helps adolescents derive moral insights from the exposure. In contrast, adolescents who have difficulty adapting to new experiences are less likely to be interested in others' moral ideas and justifications.

• **CHILD-REARING PRACTICES** • Child-rearing practices associated with mature moral reasoning combine warmth with exchange of ideas. Children and adolescents who gain most in moral understanding in succeeding years have parents who tell stories with moral implications, engage in moral discussions, encourage prosocial behavior, and create a supportive atmosphere by listening sensitively, asking clarifying questions, and presenting higher-level reasoning (Pratt, Skoe, & Arnold, 2004; Wyatt & Carlo, 2002).). In contrast, children whose parents lecture, use threats, or make sarcastic remarks show little or no change (Walker & Taylor, 1991a).

In sum, the kind of parent who facilitates moral understanding is verbal, rational, and affec-tionate and promotes a cooperative style of family life. Notice that these are the very charac-teristics, discussed earlier in this chapter, that foster moral internalization in young children.

• **SCHOOLING** • Years of schooling completed is one of the most powerful predictors of moral understanding. Moral reasoning advances in late adolescence and emerging adulthood only as long as a person remains in school (Dawson, 2002; Speicher, 1994). Perhaps higher edu-cation has a strong impact on moral development because it introduces young people to social issues that extend beyond personal relationships to entire political or cultural groups. Indeed, college students who report more academic perspective-taking opportuni-ties (for example, classes that emphasize open discussion of opin-ions) and who indicate that they have become more aware of social diversity tend to be advanced in moral reasoning (Mason & Gibbs, 1993a, 1993b).

• **PEER INTERACTION** • Research supports Piaget's belief that interaction with agemates can promote moral understand-ing. Adolescents who report more close friendships, who more often participate in conversations with their friends, and whom classmates view as leaders score higher in moral reasoning (Schonert-Reichl, 1999). Studies conducted in Africa underline the importance of exposure to diverse peer value systems for stimulating moral thought. Kenyan and Nigerian students enrolled in ethnically mixed high schools and colleges were

◉ Discussions about moral issues in which peers con-front, critique, and attempt to clarify one another's statements lead to gains in moral understanding.
© Bob Daemmrich/Stock Boston, LLC

advanced in moral development compared with those enrolled in homogeneous settings (Edwards, 1978; Maqsud, 1977).

As Piaget suggested, peer conflict probably contributes to gains in moral reasoning by making children aware of others' perspectives. But as noted in Chapter 6, conflict resolution, rather than conflict per se, may be the feature of peer disagreements that stimulates cognitive development—nonmoral and moral alike. When children engage in negotiation and compromise, they realize that social life can be based on cooperation between equals rather than on authority relations (Damon, 1988; Killen & Nucci, 1995). Within children's friendships, conflicts often arise but are worked out collaboratively. The mutuality and intimacy of friendship, which foster decisions based on consensual agreement, may contribute to moral development.

Peer experiences involving discussion and role-playing of moral problems have provided the framework for interventions aimed at improving high school and college students' moral understanding. Findings reveal that for these interventions to be effective, young people must exchange and try to comprehend different viewpoints. Observations of college students discussing moral dilemmas revealed that those who confronted, critiqued, and attempted to clarify one another's statements gained in moral maturity. Nongainers, in contrast, made assertions, told personal anecdotes, or expressed confusion about the task (Berkowitz & Gibbs, 1983). However, because moral development is a gradual process, many peer interaction sessions over weeks or months typically are necessary to produce moral change.

• **CULTURE** • Individuals in industrialized nations move through Kohlberg's stages more rapidly and advance to a higher level than individuals in village societies, who rarely move beyond Stage 3. One explanation of these cultural differences focuses on the importance of larger social structures in advanced moral understanding. In village societies, moral cooperation is based on direct relations between people. Yet reasoning at Stage 4 and beyond depends on appreciating the role of laws and government institutions in resolving moral conflict (Gibbs, Basinger, & Grime, 2005; Snarey, 1995).

In support of this view, in cultures where young people participate in the institutions of their society at early ages, moral reasoning is advanced. For example, on *kibbutzim,* small but technologically complex agricultural settlements in Israel, children receive training in the governance of their community in middle childhood. By third grade, they mention more concerns about societal laws and rules when discussing moral conflicts than do Israeli city-reared or U.S. children (Fuchs et al., 1986). During adolescence and adulthood, a greater percentage of kibbutz than American individuals reach Kohlberg's Stages 4 and 5 (Snarey, Reimer, & Kohlberg, 1985).

A second possible reason for cultural variation is that responses to dilemmas in some cultures cannot be scored in Kohlberg's scheme. Recall from Chapter 11 that self-concepts in collectivist cultures (including village societies) are more other-directed than in Western Europe and North America. This difference also characterizes moral reasoning (Miller, 1997). In village societies, moral statements that portray the individual as vitally connected to the social group are common. For example, one New Guinea village leader placed the blame for the Heinz dilemma on the entire community, stating, "If I were the judge, I would give him only light punishment because he asked everybody for help but nobody helped him" (Tietjen & Walker, 1985, p. 990).

Similarly, members of Asian nations place more weight on obligations to others than do people in Western societies. East Indians, for example, less often hold individuals accountable for moral transgressions. In their view, the self and social surroundings are inseparable (Miller & Bersoff, 1995). This perspective is evident even among well-educated adults in India, who would be expected to be at Kohlberg's higher stages. In discussing the Heinz dilemma, they resist choosing a course of action, explaining that a moral solution should be the burden of the entire society. As one woman put it,

⑥ Growing up on an Israeli kibbutz, these boys receive training in the governance of their society at an early age. As a result, they probably understand the role of societal laws and rules in resolving conflicts and are advanced in moral reasoning.
© ASAP/Sarit Uzieli/ Photo Researchers, Inc.

> The problems that Heinz is up against are not individual problems that are affecting one or two Heinzes of the world. These are social problems. Forget Heinz in Europe, just come to India.... Heinz's story is being repeated all around us all the time with wives dying, with children dying, and there is no money to save them.... So Heinz in his individual capacity—yes, okay, steal the drug, but it's not going to make any difference on a large scale.... I don't think in the final analysis a solution can be worked out on an individual basis.... It will probably have to be tackled on a macro level. (Vasudev & Hummel, 1987, p. 110)

These findings raise the question of whether Kohlberg's highest stages represent a culturally specific way of thinking—one limited to Western societies that emphasize individual rights and an appeal to an inner, private conscience. At the same time, a common justice morality is clearly evident in the dilemma responses of people from vastly different cultures.

Moral Reasoning and Behavior

A central assumption of the cognitive-developmental perspective is that moral understanding should affect moral motivation. As young people grasp the moral "logic" of human social cooperation, they are upset when this logic is violated. As a result, they realize that behaving in line with the way one thinks is vital for creating and maintaining a just social world (Gibbs, 2003). On the basis of this idea, Kohlberg predicted that moral thought and behavior should come together at the higher levels of moral understanding (Blasi, 1994). Consistent with this idea, higher-stage adolescents more often act prosocially by helping, sharing, and defending victims of injustice (Carlo et al., 1996; Comunian & Gielan, 2000). They also less often engage in cheating, aggression, and other antisocial behaviors (Gregg, Gibbs, & Fuller, 1994; Taylor & Walker, 1997).

Yet even though a clear connection between moral thought and action exists, it is only modest. We have already seen that moral behavior is influenced by a great many factors besides cognition, including the emotions of empathy, sympathy, and guilt; individual differences in temperament; and a long history of experiences that affect moral choice and decision making.

Moral self-relevance—the degree to which morality is central to self-concept—also affects moral behavior. When moral goals are personally important, individuals are more likely to feel obligated to act on their moral judgments (Blasi, 1994; Walker, 2004). In a study of low-SES African-American and Hispanic teenagers, those who emphasized moral traits and goals in their self-descriptions displayed exceptional levels of community service. These highly prosocial young people, however, did not differ from their agemates in moral reasoning (Hart & Fegley, 1995). That a synthesis of moral concern with sense of self can motivate moral action is also supported by a study of people who have made outstanding contributions to moral causes, such as civil rights, the fight against poverty, medical ethics, and religious freedom. Interviews with these moral exemplars revealed that their most distinguishing characteristic is "seamless integration" of moral vision with personal identity (Colby & Damon, 1992, p. 309).

Research has yet to identify the origins of a sense of personal responsibility for moral action. But several theorists believe that relationships with significant others—such as parents, teachers, and friends—play vital roles, perhaps by modeling prosocial behavior and by fostering emotional processes of empathy and guilt, which combine with moral cognition to powerfully motivate moral behavior (Blasi, 1995; Kohlberg & Diessner, 1991). Another conjecture is that certain school-based experiences can energize moral commitment. These include *just educational environments*—ones in which teachers guide students in democratic decision making and rule-setting, resolving disputes civilly, and taking responsibility for others' welfare (Atkins, Hart, & Donnelly, 2004). A compassionate and just school climate may be particularly important for poverty-stricken, ethnic minority children and youths. For many such youths, meaningful participation in the school community may be the crucial factor that prevents them from pessimistically concluding that prejudice and diminished opportunity are pervasive in society and, therefore, insurmountable (Hart & Atkins, 2002)

Schools can also expand students' opportunities to experience and explore moral emotions, thoughts, and actions by promoting civic engagement. As the From Research to Practice box on the following page reveals, providing young people with opportunities to volunteer in their communities can help them see the connection between their personal interests and the public interest—an insight that may foster all aspects of morality.

Religious Involvement and Moral Development

Recall that in resolving real-life moral dilemmas, many people voice notions of religion and spirituality. For these individuals, morality and spirituality are inseparable; their moral values, judgments, and behaviors are deeply embedded in their faith. Yet only recently have researchers begun to examine the influence of religion and spirituality on moral development.

Religion is especially important in North American family life. In recent national polls, nearly two-thirds of Americans and about one-half of Canadians reported being religious, compared with one-third of people in Great Britain and Italy, and even fewer elsewhere in Western

Development of Civic Responsibility

On Thanksgiving day, Jill, Todd, and Brett joined their parents at a soup kitchen to serve holiday dinners to poverty-stricken people. Throughout the year, Jill and Brett volunteered on Saturday mornings at a nursing home, where they conversed with bedridden elders. In the months before a congressional election, the three teenagers attended special youth meetings with candidates and raised concerns. "What's your view on preserving our environment?" Todd asked. "How would you prevent the proposed tax cut from mostly benefiting the rich?" Jill chimed in. At school, Brett and his girlfriend formed an organization devoted to promoting ethnic and racial tolerance.

Already, these young people have a strong sense of civic responsibility—a complex capacity that combines cognition, emotion, and behavior. Civic responsibility has the following components:

- *Knowledge* of political issues and of the means through which citizens can resolve differing views fairly
- *Feelings* of attachment to the community, of wanting to make a difference in its welfare
- *Skills* for achieving civic goals, such as how to contact and question public officials and conduct meetings so that all participants have a voice (Flanagan & Faison, 2001)

When young people engage in community service that exposes them to people in need or to public issues, they are especially likely to express a commitment to future service and to working toward important societal goals, such as eradicating poverty or ethnic prejudice (Metz, McLellan, & Youniss, 2003). New research reveals that family, school, and community experiences contribute to adolescents' civic responsibility.

Family Influences

Teenagers whose parents encourage their children to form opinions about controversial issues are more knowledgeable and interested in civic issues and better able to see them from more than one perspective (Santoloupo & Pratt, 1994). Also, adolescents who report that their parents engage

in community service and stress compassion for the less fortunate tend to hold socially responsible values. When asked what causes such social ills as unemployment, poverty, and homelessness, these teenagers more often mention situational and societal factors (lack of education, government policies, or the state of the economy) than individual factors (low intelligence or personal problems). Youths who endorse situational and societal causes, in turn, have more altruistic life goals, such as working to eradicate poverty or to preserve the earth for future generations (Flanagan & Tucker, 1999).

School and Community Influences

A democratic climate at school—one in which teachers hold high academic and moral standards for all students, promote discussion of controversial issues, and insist that students listen to and respect one another's ideas—fosters a sense of civic responsibility. Teenagers who say their teachers engage in these practices are more aware of political issues, better able to analyze them critically, and more committed to social causes (Flanagan & Faison, 2001).

Participation in extracurricular activities at school and in youth organizations is also associated with civic commitment that persists into adulthood (see Chapter 15, page 628). Two aspects of these involvements seem to account for their lasting impact. First, they introduce adolescents to the vision and skills required for mature civic engagement. Within student government, clubs, teams, and other groups, young people see how their actions affect the wider school and community. They realize that collectively, they can achieve results greater than any one person can achieve alone. And they learn to work together, balancing strong convictions with compromise (Atkins, Hart, & Donnelly, 2004; Youniss, McLellan, & Yates, 1997). Second, while producing a weekly newspaper, participating in a dramatic produc-

▲ These teenage volunteers gather food donations for the needy outside a grocery store on "Make a Difference Day." Family, school, and community experiences contribute to their sense of civic responsibility.
© Nancy Richmond/The Image Works

tion, or implementing a service project, young people explore political and moral ideals. Often they redefine their identities to include a responsibility to combat others' misfortunes (Wheeler, 2002).

The power of family, school, and community to promote civic responsibility may lie in discussions, educational practices, and activities that jointly foster moral thought, emotion, and behavior. In a comparison of nationally representative samples of 14-year-olds in 28 nations, North American young people excelled at community service, with 50 percent of students reporting membership in organizations devoted to volunteering (Torney-Purta, 2002). But low-SES, inner-city youths score substantially lower than higher-SES youths in civic knowledge and participation, although they express high interest in social justice and contributing to society (Hart & Atkins, 2002). A broad, societal commitment to fostering civic character must pay special attention to providing supportive school and community experiences for these young people, so their eagerness to make a difference can be realized.

ⓢ Although formal religious involvement declines for many adolescents, those who remain part of a religious community are advantaged in moral values and behavior. For example, they are more likely to engage in community service. These young people participate in an outdoor cleanup project with their church youth group.
© Jeff Greenberg/PhotoEdit

Europe (Adams, 2003; Jones, 2003). Among individuals affiliated with a church, synagogue, or mosque and regularly attending religious services, many are parents with children. By middle childhood, children have begun to formulate religious and spiritual ideas that are remarkably complex and that serve as moral forces in their lives (see the Cultural Influences box on the following page).

During adolescence, formal religious involvement declines—among American youths, from 55 percent at ages 13 to 15 to 40 percent at ages 17 to 18 (Donahue & Benson, 1995; Kerestes & Youniss, 2003). The drop coincides with increased autonomy and efforts to construct a personally meaningful religious identity—a task usually not complete until the late teens or twenties (Hunsberger, Pratt, & Pancer, 2001).

Adolescents who remain part of a religious community are advantaged in moral values and behavior. Compared with nonaffiliated youths, they are more involved in community service activities aimed at helping the less fortunate (Kerestes, Youniss, & Metz, 2004; Youniss, McLellan, & Yates, 1999). And religious involvement promotes responsible academic and social behavior and discourages misconduct (Dowling et al., 2004). It is a powerful preventive of teenage drug and alcohol use and, to a lesser extent, of early sexual activity. It is also associated with a lower incidence of delinquency, although its impact is not as strong as positive parent–child and peer ties (Regnerus, Smith, & Fritsch, 2003).

A variety of factors probably contribute to these favorable outcomes:

● Religious involvement provides young people with expanded networks of caring adults and peers—conditions that foster moral maturity. In a study of a large sample of inner-city high school students, religiously involved adolescents were more likely to report trusting relationships with parents, adults, and friends who share similar worldviews. The more shared activities and conversations young people reported with members of this network, the higher they scored in empathic concern and prosocial behavior (King & Furrow, 2004).

● Religious education and youth activities directly teach concern for others, offer opportunities to engage in moral discussions, and promote civic engagement.

● Adolescents who feel a sense of connection to a higher being may develop certain inner strengths—including moral self-relevance and prosocial values—that help them cope with life's difficulties, resolve real-life moral dilemmas maturely, and translate their thinking into action (Furrow, King, & White, 2004; Spencer, Fegley, & Harpalani, 2003).

Because most teenagers identify with a religious denomination and say they believe in a higher being, religious institutions may be uniquely suited to foster moral and prosocial commitments (Bridges & Moore, 2002). Some evidence suggests that youths in inner-city neighborhoods with few alternative sources of social support benefit most from religious involvement (Jang & Johnson, 2001). Religious institutions that reach out to these young people may alter the course of their lives. An exception is seen in religious cults, where rigid indoctrination into the group's beliefs, suppression of individuality, and estrangement from society all work against moral maturity (Richmond, 2004).

Further Challenges to Kohlberg's Theory

Although there is much support for Kohlberg's theory, it continues to face challenges. The most important of these concern Kohlberg's conception of moral maturity and the appropriateness of his stages for characterizing the moral reasoning of young children.

A key controversy has to do with Kohlberg's belief that moral maturity is not achieved until the postconventional level. Yet if people had to reach Stages 5 and 6 to be considered truly morally mature, few individuals anywhere would measure up! John Gibbs (1991, 2003) argues that "postconventional morality" should not be viewed as the standard against which other levels are judged immature. Gibbs finds maturity in a revised understanding of Stages 3 and 4. These stages are not "conventional," or based on social conformity, as Kohlberg assumed. Instead, they require profound moral constructions—an understanding of ideal reciprocity as

Children's Understanding of God

When asked, "What is God?" here is how several 6- to 9-year-olds responded:

- "You can pray anytime you feel like it, and they [Jesus and God] are sure to hear you because they got it worked out so one of them is on duty at all times."

- "God hears everything, not just prayers, so there must be an awful lot of noise in His ears, unless He has thought of a way to turn it off."

- "God is a spirit who can go anywhere." *What is a spirit?* "It's a ghost, like in the movies." (From Briggs, 2000; Gandy, 2004.)

Ideas about God differ radically from ideas about ordinary experiences because they violate real-world assumptions. Recall from Chapter 6 that between ages 4 and 8, children distinguish magical beings (such as Santa Claus and the Tooth Fairy) from reality (see page 238). At the same time, they embrace other beliefs that are part of their culturally transmitted religion. To avoid confusion, they must isolate their concepts of God from their grasp of human agents, placing God in a separate religious realm governed by superhuman rules (Woolley, 2000). This is a challenging task for preschool and school-age children.

Previous research, strongly influenced by Piaget's theory, led to a uniform conclusion: Children assign *anthropomorphic* (human) characteristics to God, whom they view as a parentlike figure residing in the sky. Not until adolescence does this concrete image of God as "big person" give way to an abstract, mystical view of God as formless, all-knowing (omniscient), all-powerful (omnipotent), and transcending the limits of time (Hyde, 1990).

Consider the responses of children just given, which contain a variety of concrete images—God as being "on duty in the sky" and as overwhelmed by the "noise in His ears." But along with these humanlike references, children included a variety of superhuman properties. Recent evidence reveals that even preschoolers are not limited to human, parental images of God. The procedures typically used to investigate children's religious knowledge—asking them to

respond to open-ended questions—are so cognitively demanding that children often fall back on their highly detailed notions of humans to fill in for their sketchier thoughts about God.

Research reveals that when adults are given similarly demanding tasks (asked to comprehend and retell short stories about God), they, too, give many anthropomorphic responses (Barrett, 1998). In contrast, when researchers make tasks less demanding, children say that God has supernatural powers not available to humans, such as seeing and hearing everything. For example, in research in the United States and in a Mexican Mayan village, most 5- to 6-year-olds year-olds given a typical false-belief task (see page 442 in Chapter 11) indicated that their parents might hold a false belief, but God would not (Knight et al., 2004). Children of this age also say that God, but not a humanlike puppet, can see an object in a darkened box (Barrett, Richert, & Driesenga, 2001). And with respect to God's omnipotence, even preschoolers state with certainty that God, but not humans, gives life to all natural things (animals, plants, and trees) (Petrovich, 1997).

Indeed, the most striking feature of children's concepts of God is their mix of tangible and intangible features. In this respect, their religious thinking is far more similar to

adults' than was previously thought. That children's representations of God are not restricted to a "big person" image suggests that their thinking is strongly influenced by religious education. Indeed, wide cultural variation in children's and adults' ideas exists (Barrett, 2002; Barrett & Van Orman, 1996). In several studies, school-age children drew pictures of God. In line with theological teachings of their denomination, Mormons, Lutherans, Mennonites, and Catholics more often represented God as humanlike (Pitts, 1976; Tamminen, 1991). Further, children sometimes say things about God that seem strange or amusing because their culturally relevant knowledge is often incomplete. During the school years, they frequently ask thoughtful questions about God aimed at broadening their understanding, such as: "Does God have parents?" and "Why doesn't God stop bad things from happening?"

Finally, some children are aware of the emotional comfort and guidance that visions of God can provide, as these comments indicate: "He comes down and helps you when you're sad or lonely or can't get to sleep at night." "In case you forget, He reminds you to act nice" (Berk, 2004). By adolescence and perhaps before, religiosity is linked to psychological well-being and to prosocial attitudes and behavior.

▲ A 7-year-old and his family greet the priest after a Catholic Mass. When questioned properly, most children this age indicate that God has both humanlike and supernatural powers—concepts that resemble those of adults. © Myrleen FergusonCate/PhotoEdit

the basis for relationships between people (Stage 3) and for widely accepted moral standards, set forth in rules and laws (Stage 4).

Gibbs (2003) regards "postconventional" moral reasoning as a highly reflective, metacognitive endeavor in which people grapple with existential issues, such as Why go on living? Why be moral? Most people who contemplate such questions have attained advanced education, usually in philosophy—which sheds light on why Stages 5 and 6 are so rare. Occasionally, however, as a result of soul-searching life crises, life-threatening events, or spiritual awakenings, individuals without formal training in philosophy generate ethical insights into the meaning of existence—transformations that may heighten their resolve to lead a moral life. As a result, Gibbs notes, "postconventional" moral judgment occasionally can be seen as early as adolescence, when young people first become capable of the formal operational and perspective-taking capacities needed to engage in it.

Finally, Kohlberg's stages largely describe changes in moral reasoning during adolescence and adulthood. They tell us much less about moral understanding in early and middle childhood. Indeed, Kohlberg's moral dilemmas are remote from the experiences of most children and may not be clearly understood by them. When children are given moral dilemmas relevant to their everyday lives, their responses indicate that Kohlberg's preconventional level, much like Piaget's heteronomous morality, underestimates their moral reasoning. Nancy Eisenberg created dilemmas that do not make reference to laws but instead pit satisfying one's own desires against acting prosocially—for example, going to a birthday party versus taking time to help an injured peer and missing the party as a result (Eisenberg, 1986; Eisenberg et al., 1991, 1995a). Children and adolescents' *prosocial moral reasoning* about such dilemmas is clearly advanced when compared with Kohlberg's stages. Furthermore, research suggests that empathic perspective taking strengthens prosocial moral thought and its realization in everyday behavior (Eisenberg, Zhoe, & Koller, 2001; Lasoya & Eisenberg, 2001).

In sum, Kohlberg's belief in an early, externally governed morality meant that he failed to uncover young children's internally based judgments of right and wrong. In the following sections, we consider additional evidence on children's moral reasoning.

Ask Yourself

REVIEW	What features of Kohlberg's theory extend Piaget's theory of moral development?
REVIEW	How does an understanding of ideal reciprocity contribute to moral development? Why might Kohlberg's Stages 3 and 4 be morally mature constructions? At which stage is Leisl's reasoning about the elderly woman who is to be evicted from her home, presented in the introduction to this chapter? Explain.
APPLY	Tam grew up in a small village culture, Lydia in a large industrial city. At age 15, Tam reasons at Kohlberg's Stage 2, Lydia at Stage 4. What factors probably account for the difference? Is Lydia's reasoning morally mature? Explain.
CONNECT	What experiences that promote mature moral reasoning are also likely to foster identity development? Explain. (See Chapter 11, pages 459–460.)

Moral Reasoning of Young Children

Researchers focusing on children's moral understanding have addressed (1) their ability to distinguish moral obligations from social conventions and matters of personal choice, and (2) their ideas about fair distribution of rewards. Findings reveal more advanced reasoning than Kohlberg's preconventional, externally controlled vision of early morality assumes.

Distinguishing Moral, Social-Conventional, and Personal Domains

As early as age 3, children have a rudimentary grasp of justice. Many studies reveal that preschool and young elementary school children distinguish **moral imperatives,** which protect people's rights and welfare, from two other domains of action: **social conventions,** customs determined solely by consensus, such as table manners, dress styles, and rituals of social inter-action; and **matters of personal choice,** which do not violate rights or harm others, are not socially regulated, and therefore are up to the individual (Ardila-Rey & Killen, 2001; Nucci, 1996; Yan & Smetana, 2003).

• **MORAL VERSUS SOCIAL-CONVENTIONAL DISTINCTIONS** • Interviews with 3- and 4-year-olds reveal that they judge moral violations (such as stealing an apple) as more wrong than violations of social conventions (eating ice cream with your fingers). They also say that a moral violation is more generalizably wrong—not OK regardless of the setting in which it is committed, such as another country or school. And they indicate that a moral (but not a social-conventional) transgression would still be wrong if an authority figure (parent or teacher) did not see them commit it and no rules existed to prohibit it (Smetana, 1995; Tisak, 1995).

How do young children arrive at these distinctions? According to Elliott Turiel (1998), they do so by actively making sense of their experiences. They observe that after a moral offense, peers respond with strong negative emotion, describe their own injury or loss, tell another child to stop, or retaliate. And an adult who intervenes is likely to call attention to the rights and feelings of the victim. In contrast, peers do not react as intensely to violations of social convention. And in these situations, adults usually demand obedience without expla-nation or point to the importance of keeping order (Turiel, Smetana, & Killen, 1991).

But despite their realization that moral transgressions are worse than social-conventional violations, preschool and young school-age children (as Piaget pointed out) tend to reason rigidly *within* the moral domain—claiming that, for example, stealing and lying are always wrong, even when a person has a morally sound reason for engaging in these acts (Lourenco, 2003). As they construct a flexible appreciation of moral rules, children clarify and link moral imperatives and social conventions. Gradually their understanding becomes more complex, taking into account an increasing number of variables, including the purpose of the rule; peo-ple's intentions, knowledge, and beliefs; and the context of people's behavior.

During the school years, for example, children distinguish social conventions with a clear *purpose* (not running in school hallways to prevent injuries) from ones with no obvious jus-tification (crossing a "forbidden" line on the playground). They regard violations of purpose-ful conventions as closer to moral transgressions (Buchanan-Barrow & Barrett, 1998). With age, they also realize that people's *intentions* and the *context* of their actions affect the moral implications of violating a social convention. In a Canadian study, many 6-year-olds always disapproved of flag-burning, citing its physical consequences. By contrast, 8- to 10-year-olds' judgments reflected subtle discriminations: They stated that because of a flag's symbolic value, burning it to express disapproval of a country or to start a cooking fire is worse than burning it accidentally. They also stated that public flag-burning is worse than private flag-burning because of the emotional harm inflicted on others. At the same time, they recognized that burning a flag is a form of freedom of expression. Most acknowledged that in a country that treated its citizens unfairly, it would be acceptable (Helwig & Prencipe, 1999).

In middle childhood, children also realize that people whose *knowledge* differs may not be equally responsible for moral transgressions. Many 7-year-olds are tolerant of a teacher's decision to give more snack to girls than to boys because she thinks (incorrectly) that girls need more food. But when a teacher gives girls more snack because she holds an *immoral belief* ("It's all right to be nicer to girls than boys"), almost all children judge her actions negatively (Wainryb & Ford, 1998).

• **RELATION OF PERSONAL AND MORAL DOMAINS** • As children's grasp of moral imperatives and social conventions strengthens, so does their conviction that certain choices, such as hairstyle, friends, and leisure activities, are up to the individual (Nucci, 1996; Nucci, Camino, & Sapiro, 1996). Early on, children learn that parents and teachers are willing to com-promise on personal issues and, at times, on social-conventional matters, but not on moral concerns. Likewise, when children and adolescents challenge adult authority, they typically do so within the personal domain (Nucci & Weber, 1995). At adolescence, as insistence that par-ents not intrude on the personal arena increases, disputes over personal issues occur more often. Disagreements are sharpest on matters that are both personal and social-conventional and therefore subject to interpretation—for example, a messy bedroom, which can be viewed as both individual and communal space (Smetana & Asquith, 1994).

⊚ This girl is in frequent conflict with her parents over issues of personal freedom versus communal obligations. In her view, her messy bedroom is a matter of personal choice. In her parents' view, it is a social-conventional matter that affects the entire family.
© Laura Dwight Photography

Notions of personal choice, in turn, enhance children's moral understanding. As early as age 6, children view freedom of speech and religion as individual rights, even if laws exist that deny those rights (Helwig & Turiel, 2002). And they regard laws that discriminate against individuals—for example, laws that deny certain people access to medical care or education—as wrong and worthy of violating (Helwig & Jasiobedzka, 2001). In justifying their responses, children appeal to personal privileges and, by the end of middle childhood, to democratic ideals, such as the importance of individual rights for maintaining a fair society.

At the same time, older school-age children place limits on individual choice, depending on circumstances. While regarding nonacademic matters (such as where to go on field trips) as best decided democratically, they believe that the academic curriculum is the province of teachers, based on teachers' superior ability to make such choices (Helwig & Kim, 1999). And when issues of fairness are brought to their attention, fourth graders faced with conflicting moral and personal concerns—such as whether or not to be friends with a classmate of a different ethnicity or gender—typically decide in favor of fairness (Killen et al., 2002). By adolescence, young people think more intently about conflicts between personal freedom and community obligation—for example, whether, and under what conditions, it is permissible for governments to restrict speech, religion, marriage, childbearing, and other individual rights (Helwig, 1995; Wainryb, 1997).

• CULTURE AND MORAL, SOCIAL-CONVENTIONAL, AND PERSONAL DISTINCTIONS •
Children and adolescents in diverse Western and non-Western cultures use similar criteria to reason about moral, social-conventional, and personal concerns (Neff & Helwig, 2002; Nucci, 2002). For example, Chinese young people, whose culture places a high value on respect for authority, nevertheless say that adults have no right to interfere in children's personal matters, such as how they spend their free time (Helwig et al., 2003). A Colombian child illustrated this vehement defense of the right to personal control when asked about the legitimacy of a teacher telling a student where to sit during circle time. In the absence of a moral reason from the teacher, the child emphatically declared, "She should be able to sit wherever she wants" (Ardila-Rey & Killen, 2001, p. 249).

Still, certain behaviors are classified differently across cultures. For example, East Indian Hindu children believe that eating chicken the day after a father's death is morally wrong because Hindu religious teachings specify that it prevents the father's soul from reaching salvation. North American children, in contrast, regard this practice as an arbitrary convention (Shweder, Mahapatra, & Miller, 1990). But when children are asked about acts that obviously lead to harm or violate rights—such as breaking promises, destroying another's property, or kicking harmless animals—cross-cultural similarity prevails (Turiel, 1998). We are reminded, once again, that justice considerations are a universal feature of moral thought.

Distributive Justice

⊚ These fourth-grade boys are figuring out how to divide a handful of penny candy fairly among themselves. Already, they have a well-developed sense of distributive justice.
© Jeff Greenberg/PhotoEdit

In everyday life, children frequently experience situations that involve **distributive justice—** beliefs about how to divide material goods fairly. Heated discussions take place over how much weekly allowance is to be given to siblings of different ages, who has to sit where in the family car on a long trip, and how six hungry playmates can share an eight-slice pizza. William Damon (1977, 1988) has traced children's changing concepts of distributive justice over early and middle childhood.

Even 4-year-olds recognize the importance of sharing, but their reasons often seem self-serving: "I shared because if I didn't, she wouldn't play with me" or "I let her have some, but most are for me because I'm older." These explanations are consistent with Selman's "undifferentiated perspective-taking" level (see Chapter 11, page 466). As children enter middle childhood, they express more mature notions of distributive justice. Their basis of reasoning follows an age-related, three-step sequence:

INTERNALIZATION OF MORAL NORMS AND DEVELOPMENT OF MORAL UNDERSTANDING

Age	Internalization of Moral Norms	Moral Understanding
2–5 years	Models many morally relevant behaviors Responds with empathy-based guilt to transgressions	Tends to focus on salient features and consequences in moral judgment, such as physical damage, getting punished, or an adult's power or status Begins to show sensitivity to others' intentions in moral judgment At the end of this period, has a differentiated understanding of authority figures' legitimacy Distinguishes moral imperatives, social conventions, and matters of personal choice At the end of this period, bases distributive justice on equality
6–11 years	Internalizes many norms of good conduct, including prosocial standards 	Continues to emphasize superficial factors, including physical consequences and self-interest, in moral judgment (Piaget's "heteronomous" and Kohlberg's preconventional Stages 1 and 2 morality) Gradually understands ideal reciprocity and emphasizes people's intentions and expectations in moral judgment (Piaget's autonomous and Kohlberg's "conventional" Stage 3 morality) Clarifies and links moral imperatives, social conventions, and matters of personal choice and, in judging violations, considers more variables—the purpose of the rule, people's intentions, and the context Includes merit and, eventually, equity and benevolence in distributive justice reasoning
12 years–adulthood		Increasingly emphasizes ideal reciprocity as the basis for interpersonal relationships and societal laws (Kohlberg's "conventional" Stages 3 and 4 morality) Highly reflective moral judgments that grapple with existential issues appear among a few individuals, usually with advanced education (Kohlberg's "postconventional" Stages 5 and 6). The relationship between moral reasoning and behavior strengthens.

Note: These milestones represent overall age trends. Individual differences exist in the precise age at which each milestone is attained.

Photos: (top) © BananaStock/Alamy Royalty Free; (middle) © Mary Kate Denny/PhotoEdit; (bottom) © Steve Skjold/Alamy Images

1. *Strict equality* (5–6 years). Children in the early school grades are intent on making sure that each person gets the same amount of a treasured resource, such as money, turns in a game, or a delicious treat.

2. *Merit* (6–7 years). A short time later, children say extra rewards should go to someone who has worked especially hard or otherwise performed in an exceptional way.

3. *Equity and benevolence* (around 8 years). Finally, children recognize that special consideration should be given to those at a disadvantage—for example, that an extra amount might be given to a child who cannot produce as much or who does not get any allowance. Older children also adapt their basis of fairness to fit the situation, relying more on equality when interacting with strangers and more on benevolence when interacting with friends (McGillicuddy-De Lisi, Watkins, & Vinchur, 1994).

According to Damon (1988), parental advice and encouragement support these developing standards of justice, but the give-and-take of peer interaction is especially important (Kruger, 1993). Advanced distributive justice reasoning, in turn, is associated with more effective social problem solving and with a greater willingness to help and share with others (Blotner & Bearison, 1984; McNamee & Peterson, 1986).

The research reviewed in the preceding sections reveals that moral understanding in childhood is a rich, diverse phenomenon. To represent fully the development of moral thought, researchers must examine children's responses to a wide range of problems. Consult the Milestones table above to review changes in moral internalization and construction during childhood and adolescence.

Development of Morally Relevant Self-Control

The study of moral judgment tells us what people think they should do, and why, when faced with a moral problem. But people's good intentions often fall short. Whether children and adults act in accord with their beliefs depends in part on characteristics we call willpower, firm resolve, or, more simply, self-control. In Chapter 10, we considered individual differences in the broad temperamental dimension of *effortful control*—the extent to which children can manage their reactivity. Here we focus specifically on self-control in the moral domain: inhibiting urges to act in ways that violate moral standards, sometimes called *resistance to temptation*. In the first part of this chapter, we noted that inductive discipline and modeling promote self-controlled behavior in children. But these practices become effective only when children have the ability to resist temptation. When and how does this capacity develop?

Toddlerhood

The beginnings of self-control are supported by achievements of the second year, discussed in earlier chapters. To behave in a self-controlled fashion, children must have some ability to think of themselves as separate, autonomous beings who can direct their own actions. And they must have the representational and memory skills to recall a caregiver's directive and apply it to their own behavior. Cognitive inhibition (see Chapter 7) and emotional self-regulation (see Chapter 10) are also essential (Rothbart & Bates, 1998).

As these capacities emerge between 12 and 18 months, the first glimmerings of self-control appear in the form of **compliance.** Toddlers start to show clear awareness of caregivers' wishes and expectations and can obey simple requests and commands. Parents are usually delighted at toddlers' newfound ability to comply because it indicates that they are ready to learn the rules of social life. Nevertheless, control of the child's actions during the second year depends heavily on caregiver support. According to Vygotsky (1934/1986), children cannot guide their own behavior until they have integrated standards represented in adult–child dialogues into their own self-directed speech (see Chapter 6). Compliance quickly leads to toddlers' first consciencelike verbalizations—for example, correcting the self by saying, "No, can't" before touching a delicate object or jumping on the sofa (Kochanska, 1993).

Researchers typically study self-control by creating situations in the laboratory much like the ones just mentioned. Each calls for **delay of gratification**—waiting for a more appropriate time and place to engage in a tempting act. In one study, toddlers were given three delay-of-gratification tasks. In the first, they were asked not to touch an interesting toy telephone that was within arm's reach. In the second, raisins were hidden under cups, and the toddlers were instructed to wait until an adult said it was all right to pick up a cup and eat a raisin. In the third, they were told not to open a gift until the adult had finished her work. On all problems, the ability to wait increased between 18 and 30 months. Children who were especially self-controlled were also advanced in language development (Vaughn, Kopp, & Krakow, 1984).

As with effortful control in general, biologically based temperamental factors and quality of caregiving combine to influence young children's capacity to delay gratification (Calkins & Fox, 2002; Kochanska & Knaack, 2003). Inhibited children find it easier to wait, whereas angry, irritable children find it harder. But regardless of temperament, toddlers who experience parental warmth and gentle encouragement are more likely to comply with an eager, willing spirit and to resist temptation (Kochanska, Murray, & Harlan, 2000; Lehamn et al., 2002). Such parenting seems to encourage as well as model patient, nonimpulsive behavior. As self-control improves, parents gradually increase the range of rules they expect toddlers to follow, from safety and respect for property and people to family routines, manners, and responsibility for simple chores (Gralinski & Kopp, 1993).

How will this 5-year-old resist temptation? If she focuses on the taste of the cookies, she will likely give in quickly. She will be able to wait longer if she diverts her attention by covering her eyes, engaging in another activity, or imagining the cookies to be wheels or Frisbees. © Laura Dwight Photography

Childhood and Adolescence

Although the capacity for self-control is in place by the third year, it is not complete. Cognitive development—in particular, gains in attention and mental representation—enables children to use a variety of effective self-instructional strategies. As a result, resistance to temptation improves during childhood and adolescence.

• **STRATEGIES FOR RESISTING TEMPTATION** • Walter Mischel has studied what children think and say to themselves that promotes resistance to temptation. In several studies, preschoolers were shown two rewards: a highly desirable one that they would have to wait for and a less desirable one that they could have anytime (Mischel, 1996; Mischel & Ayduck, 2004). The most self-controlled preschoolers used any technique they could to divert their attention from the desired objects: covering their eyes, singing, even trying to sleep!

In everyday situations, preschoolers find it difficult to keep their minds off tempting activities and objects for long. When their thoughts do turn to an enticing but prohibited goal, the way they mentally represent it has much to do with their success at self-control. Mischel found that teaching preschoolers to transform the stimulus in ways that de-emphasize its arousing qualities—an approach that helps children shift attention and inhibit emotional reactivity—promotes delay of gratification. In one study, some preschoolers were told to think about marshmallows imaginatively as "white and puffy clouds." Others were asked to focus on their realistic "sweet and chewy properties." Children in the stimulus-transforming, imaginative condition waited much longer before eating the marshmallow reward (Mischel & Baker, 1975).

Having something interesting to do while waiting can also help preschoolers resist temptation. In a modified delay-of-gratification task in which preschoolers could engage in enjoyable work (feeding marbles to a colorfully decorated, "hungry" Baby Bird), the amount of time children waited for a nearby, attractive reward more than doubled over simply waiting passively (see Figure 12.5). Pleasurable work helped divert children's attention from the rewards. But when the work was unappealing (sorting marbles), preschoolers were less successful at delaying gratification. They often looked up from the boring work, which increased the likelihood that the enticing reward would capture their attention (Peake, Hebl, & Mischel, 2002).

During the school years, children become better at thinking up their own strategies for resisting temptation. By this time, self-control has been transformed into a flexible capacity for **moral self-regulation**—the ability to monitor one's own conduct, constantly adjusting it as circumstances present opportunities to violate inner standards (Bandura, 1991).

• **KNOWLEDGE OF STRATEGIES** • Recall from Chapter 7 that metacognitive knowledge, or awareness of strategies, contributes to the development of self-regulation. When interviewed about situational conditions and self-instructions likely to help delay gratification, over middle childhood, children suggested a broader array of arousal-reducing strategies. But not until the late elementary school years did they mention techniques involving transformations of rewards or their own arousal states. For example, one 11-year-old recommended saying, "The marshmallows are filled with an evil spell." Another said he would tell himself, "I hate marshmallows; I can't stand them. But when the grown-up gets back, I'll tell myself 'I love marshmallows' and eat it" (Mischel & Mischel, 1983, p. 609).

Perhaps awareness of transforming ideation appears late in development because it requires the abstract, hypothetical reasoning powers of formal operational thought. But once this advanced metacognitive understanding emerges, it greatly facilitates moral self-regulation (Rodriguez, Mischel, & Shoda, 1989).

Individual Differences

Mischel and his collaborators found that toddlers who could divert their attention and wait patiently during a short separation from their mother tended to perform better during a delay-of-gratification task at age 5 (Sethi et al., 2000). And in a series of studies, 4-year-olds better at delaying

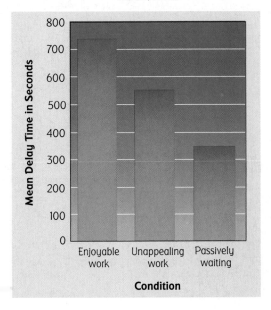

▼ **Figure 12.5**

Influence of engaging in a work task on preschoolers' delay of gratification.
Availability of enjoyable work (feeding a "hungry" Baby Bird marbles) greatly increased children's capacity to wait. When the work was unappealing (sorting marbles), preschoolers' attention often strayed to the enticing reward; hence, they were not as successful at waiting. Children in both work conditions delayed longer than agemates who simply waited passively.

(Adapted from Peake, Hebl, & Mischel, 2002.)

TABLE 12.2 CHARACTERISTICS OF "HOT" AND "COOL" PROCESSING SYSTEMS IN THE DEVELOPMENT OF SELF-CONTROL

Hot System	Cool System
Emotional	Cognitive
"Go"	"Know"
Simple	Complex
Reflexive	Reflective
Fast	Slow
Develops early	Develops later
Accentuated by stress	Attenuated by stress
Stimulus control	Self-control

Source: J. Metcalfe & W. Mischel, 1999, "A Hot/Cool-System Analysis of Delay of Gratification: Dynamics of Willpower," *Psychological Review, 106,* p. 4. Copyright © by the American Psychological Association. Reprinted by permission of the publisher and author.

gratification were especially adept as adolescents in applying metacognitive skills to their behavior. Their parents saw them as more responsive to reason, as better at concentrating and planning ahead, and as coping with stress more maturely. When applying to college, those who had been self-controlled preschoolers scored somewhat higher on the Scholastic Assess-ment Test (SAT), although they were no more intelligent than other individuals (Mischel, Shoda, & Peake, 1988; Shoda, Mischel, & Peake, 1990). Furthermore, children who are better at delaying gratification can wait long enough to interpret social cues accurately, which supports effective social problem solving and positive peer relations (Gronau & Waas, 1997).

Mischel proposes that the interaction of two processing systems—*hot* and *cool*—governs the development of self-control and accounts for individual differences (Metcalfe & Mischel, 1999; Mischel & Ayduk, 2004). Table 12.2 displays the characteristics of each. With age, the emotional, reactive hot system becomes interconnected with the cognitive, reflective cool system. When an arousing experience occurs, interconnections between the systems permit individuals to divert energy away from hot processing to cool thinking, as indicated by the delay-of-gratification strategies and the metacognitive awareness of the strategies just considered.

Throughout childhood and adolescence, temperament and parenting continue to jointly influence the extent to which cool-system representations gain control over hot-system reactivity. When temperamentally vulnerable children are exposed to highly power-assertive, inconsistent discipline, the cool system develops poorly or fails to function, permitting the hot system to prevail. Such children display hostile, unruly behavior and serious deficits in moral conduct. Refer to the Milestones table below for a summary of changes in self-control and aggression—our next topic.

MILESTONES

DEVELOPMENT OF MORALLY RELEVANT SELF-CONTROL AND AGGRESSION

Age	Self-Control	Aggression
1½–5 years	Compliance and delay of gratification emerge and improve. Benefits from adult-provided strategies for delaying gratification	Instrumental aggression declines, while hostile aggression increases. Physical aggression declines, while verbal aggression increases. Relational aggression appears.
6–11 years	Generates an increasing variety of strategies for delaying gratification Displays a flexible capacity for moral self-regulation	Hostile aggression—largely verbal and relational—continues to increase. Girls' relational aggression becomes increasingly indirect.
12–20 years	Continues to gain in moral self-regulation	Teacher- and peer-reported aggression declines. Delinquency rises, then declines.

Note: These milestones represent overall age trends. Individual differences exist in the precise age at which each milestone is attained.

Photos: (left) © 2004 Laura Dwight Photography; (right) © David Young-Wolff/PhotoEdit

Ask Yourself

REVIEW	What experiences help children differentiate moral imperatives, social conventions, and matters of personal choice? How does children's understanding change from early to middle childhood?
APPLY	Parker Elementary School is offering a cash award to the classroom that sells the most raffle tickets for the school fund-raiser. Children in the winning classroom will decide how to divide the award fairly. How are first through third graders likely to differ in their decision making?
CONNECT	Explain how school-age children's understanding of moral imperatives and distributive justice takes into account an increasing number of variables. What cognitive and social-cognitive changes, discussed in Chapters 6 and 11, probably support these advances?
REFLECT	Describe a recent instance in which your cool processing system dominated your hot-system reactivity, resulting in resistance to temptation. What did your cool processing system do to gain control? Using research evidence, explain why those strategies were effective.

The Other Side of Self-Control: Development of Aggression

Beginning in late infancy, all children display aggression from time to time. As interactions with siblings and peers increase, aggressive outbursts occur more often (Coie & Dodge, 1998; Tremblay, 2002). Although at times aggression serves prosocial ends (for example, stopping a victimizer from harming others), the large majority of human aggressive acts are clearly antisocial.

As early as the preschool years, some children show abnormally high rates of hostility. They verbally and physically assault others with little or no provocation. If allowed to continue, their belligerent behavior can lead to lasting delays in moral development and deficits in self-control, resulting in an antisocial lifestyle. To understand this process, let's see how aggression develops during childhood and adolescence.

Emergence of Aggression

During the second half of the first year, infants develop the cognitive capacity to identify sources of anger and frustration and the motor skills to lash out at them (see Chapter 10). By the early preschool years, two general types of aggression emerge. The most common is **instrumental aggression,** in which children want an object, privilege, or space and, in trying to get it, push, shout at, or otherwise attack a person who is in the way. The other type, **hostile aggression,** is meant to hurt another person.

Hostile aggression comes in at least three varieties:

- **Physical aggression** harms others through physical injury—for example, pushing, hitting, kicking, or punching others, or destroying another's property.
- **Verbal aggression** harms others through threats of physical aggression, name-calling, or hostile teasing.
- **Relational aggression** damages another's peer relationships through social exclusion, malicious gossip, or friendship manipulation.

Although verbal aggression is always direct, physical and relational aggression can be either *direct* or *indirect.* For example, hitting injures a person directly, whereas destroying property indirectly inflicts physical harm. Similarly, saying, "Do what I say, or I won't be your friend," directly conveys relational aggression. In contrast, spreading rumors, refusing to talk to a peer, or manipulating friendships by remarking behind someone's back, "Don't play with her; she's a nerd" are indirect ways of harming another's relationships.

These preschoolers display instrumental aggression as they struggle over an attractive toy. Instrumental aggression declines with age, as preschoolers' improved ability to delay gratification helps them avoid grabbing others' possessions.
© Laura Dwight Photography

Aggression in Early and Middle Childhood

Both the form of aggression and the way it is expressed change during the preschool years. Between 2 and 6 years, physical aggression tends to decline, whereas verbal aggression increases (Tremblay et al. 1999). Rapid language development contributes to this change, but it is also due to adults' and peers' strong negative reactions to physical attacks. Furthermore, instrumental aggression declines as preschoolers' improved capacity to delay gratification enables them to avoid grabbing others' possessions. In contrast, hostile aggression increases over early and middle childhood (Tremblay, 2000). Older children are better able to recognize malicious intentions and, as a result, more often retaliate in hostile ways.

By the late preschool years, boys are the more physically aggressive of the two sexes, more often attacking to block the dominance goals that are typical of boys—a difference evident in many cultures (Coie & Dodge, 1998). In Chapter 13, when we take up sex differences in aggression in greater detail, we will see that biological factors—in particular, male sex hormones, or androgens—are influential. At the same time, the development of gender roles is important. As soon as preschoolers become aware of gender stereotypes—that males and females are expected to behave differently—physical aggression drops off more sharply in girls than in boys (Fagot & Leinbach, 1989).

Although girls have a reputation for being both more verbally and relationally aggressive than boys, Chapter 13 will reveal that sex differences in these two types of hostility are actually minimal. As we will see, beginning in the preschool years girls concentrate most of their aggressive acts in the relational category, whereas boys inflict harm in more variable ways and, therefore, display overall rates of aggression that are considerably higher than girls'. At the same time, girls more often select indirect relational tactics that—in disrupting intimate bonds especially important to girls—can be particularly mean. And whereas physical attacks are usually brief, acts of indirect relational aggression may extend for hours, weeks, or even months (Nelson, Robinson, & Hart, 2005; Underwood, 2003). In one instance, a second-grade girl formed a "pretty-girls club" at school and convinced its members to avoid several classmates by saying that the excluded girls were "ugly and smelly"— harassment that persisted for nearly an entire school year. In view of such hostilities on the part of girls, in childhood, at least, it may not be meaningful to describe one sex as more aggressive than the other.

Aggression and Delinquency in Adolescence

Although most young people decline in teacher- and peer-reported aggression in adolescence, the teenage years are accompanied by a rise in delinquent acts. Although North American youth crime has declined over the past decade, young people under age 18 continue to account for a large proportion of police arrests—about 17 percent in the United States and 23 percent in Canada (Statistics Canada, 2003a; U.S. Department of Justice, 2004). When teenagers are asked directly, and confidentially, about lawbreaking, almost all admit that they have been guilty of an offense of one sort or another (Farrington, 1987). Most of the time, these crimes are minor: petty stealing, disorderly conduct, and acts that are illegal only for minors, such as underage drinking, violating curfews, and running away from home.

Both police arrests and self-reports show that delinquency rises over the early teenage years, remains high during middle adolescence, and then declines into emerging adulthood. What accounts for this trend? Among young teenagers, antisocial behavior increases as a result of the desire for peer approval. Over time, peers become less influential, moral reasoning improves, and young people enter social contexts (such as marriage, work, and career) that are less conducive to lawbreaking.

For most adolescents, a brush with the law does not forecast long-term antisocial behavior. But repeated

Ⓖ Delinquency rises during the early teenage years and remains high during middle adolescence. Although most of the time it involves petty stealing and disorderly conduct, a small percentage of young people engage in repeated, serious offenses and are at risk for a life of crime. © Barbara Burnes/Photo Researchers, Inc.

arrests are cause for concern. Teenagers are responsible for 16 percent of violent crimes in the United States and for 8 percent in Canada (Statistics Canada, 2003a; U.S. Department of Justice, 2004). A small percentage develop into recurrent offenders, who commit most of these crimes. Some enter a life of crime.

In adolescence, the gender gap in physical aggression widens (Chesney-Lind, 2001). Depending on the estimate, about three to eight times as many boys as girls commit major crimes. Compared to a decade ago, girls account for a larger proportion of adolescent violence—about 18 percent. Girls' offenses, however, are largely limited to simple assault, the least serious category, encompassing such behaviors as pushing or spitting. Violent crime continues to be overwhelmingly the domain of boys (National Center for Juvenile Justice, 2004; Sprott & Doob, 2003). Although SES and ethnicity are strong predictors of arrests, they are only mildly related to teenagers' self-reports of antisocial acts. The difference is due to the tendency to arrest, charge, and punish low-SES, ethnic minority youths more often than their higher-SES white and Asian counterparts (U.S. Department of Justice, 2004).

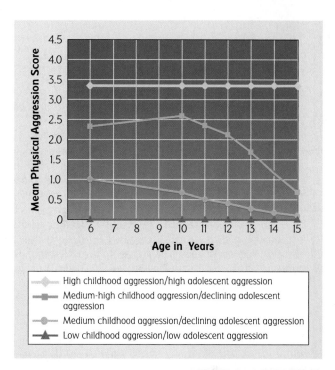

Stability of Aggression

Children high in either physical or relational aggression relative to their agemates tend to remain so over time (Vaillancourt et al., 2003). Following more than 1,000 Canadian, New Zealand, and American boys from ages 6 to 15, researchers identified four main patterns of change shown in Figure 12.6. Kindergarten boys high in physical aggression (4 percent of the sample) were especially likely to move to high-level adolescent aggression, becoming involved in violent delinquency. In contrast, kindergarten boys who were moderately physically aggressive usually declined in aggression over time. And boys who rarely physically aggressed in early childhood typically remained nonaggressive. However, a small number of boys high in oppositional behavior (such as disobedience and inconsiderateness) but not in physical aggression were prone to less violent forms of adolescent delinquency (such as theft) (Brame, Nagin, & Tremblay, 2001; Nagin & Tremblay, 1999).

Girls who consistently engage in disruptive behavior in childhood are also more likely to have continuing conduct problems (Coté et al., 2001). Like high physical aggression, high relational aggression often persists and is linked to rising rates of antisocial behavior during childhood and adolescence (Crick et al., 1999).

As the Biology and Environment box on page 510 confirms, aggressive behavior that emerges in childhood is far more likely to translate into long-term adjustment difficulties than aggression that first appears in adolescence. In recent years, researchers have made considerable progress in identifying personal and environmental factors that sustain aggression. Although some children—especially those who are impulsive and overactive—are at risk for aggression, whether or not they become aggressive depends on child-rearing conditions. Strife-ridden families, poor parenting practices, aggressive peers, and televised violence are strongly linked to antisocial acts. In this chapter, we focus on family and peer influences, reserving TV influences for Chapter 15. We will also see that community and cultural influences can heighten or reduce children's risk of sustaining a hostile interpersonal style.

The Family as Training Ground for Aggressive Behavior

The same child-rearing practices that undermine moral internalization and self-control are related to physical and relational aggression. Love withdrawal, power assertion, negative comments and emotions, physical punishment, and inconsistent discipline are linked to antisocial behavior from early childhood through adolescence, in children of both sexes and in many cultures (Bradford et al., 2003; Capaldi et al., 2002; Chen et al., 2001; Rubin et al., 2003; Yang et al., 2004).

▲ **Figure 12.6**

Longitudinal trends in boys' physical aggression from 6 to 15 years of age. The patterns are based on a sample of more than 1,000 boys from Canada, New Zealand, and the United States. Boys with high-level childhood physical aggression were especially likely to sustain their aggressive style. In contrast, boys with medium-high and medium levels of aggression usually declined in aggressive responding. And boys who rarely displayed aggression in childhood typically remained nonaggressive. (From R. E. Tremblay, 2000, "The Development of Aggressive Behaviour During Childhood: What Have We Learned in the Past Century? *International Journal of Behavioral Development, 24,* p. 136. Reprinted by permission.)

Two Routes to Adolescent Delinquency

Persistent adolescent delinquency follows two paths of development, the first with an onset of conduct problems in childhood, the second with an onset in adolescence. The early-onset type is far more likely to lead to a life-course pattern of aggression and criminality. The late-onset type usually does not persist beyond the transition to emerging adulthood (Farrington & Loeber, 2000).

Both childhood-onset and adolescent-onset youths engage in serious offenses; associate with deviant peers; participate in substance abuse, unsafe sex, and dangerous driving; and spend time in correctional facilities. Why does antisocial activity more often persist and escalate into violence in the first group than in the second? Longitudinal studies yield similar answers to this question. So far, the findings are clearest for boys, who are the focus of most research. But several investigations report that girls who were physically aggressive in childhood are also at risk for later problems—occasionally violent delinquency, but more often other norm-violating behaviors and psychological disorders (Broidy et al., 2003; Chamberlain, 2003). And early relational aggression is linked to adolescent conduct problems as well.

Early-Onset Type

Early-onset youngsters seem to inherit traits that predispose them to aggressiveness (Pettit, 2004). Difficult and fearless temperamental styles characterize physically aggressive boys; they are emotionally negative, restless, willful, and impulsive as early as age 2. In addition, they show subtle deficits in cognitive functioning that seem to contribute to disruptions in the development of language, memory, and cognitive and emotional self-regulation (Loeber et al., 1999; Shaw et al., 2003). Some have attention-deficit hyperactivity disorder (ADHD), which compounds their learning and self-control problems (see Chapter 7, pages 284–285).

Yet these biological risks are not sufficient to sustain antisocial behavior. Most early-onset boys do not display serious delinquency followed by adult criminality. Among those who follow the life-course path, inept parenting transforms their undercontrolled style into hostility, defiance, and persistent aggression— a strong predictor of violent delinquency in adolescence (Broidy et al, 2003; Brame, Nagin, & Tremblay, 2001). As physically aggressive children fail academically and are rejected by peers, they are deprived of opportunities for learning vital social skills. Soon they befriend other deviant youths, who facilitate one another's violent behavior while relieving loneliness (see Figure 12.7) (Lacourse et al., 2003). Early-onset teenagers' limited cognitive and social skills result in high rates of school dropout and unemployment, contributing further to their antisocial involvements. Often these boys experience their first arrest before age 14—a good indicator that they will be chronic offenders by age 18 (Patterson & Yoerger, 2002).

Although the evidence is less strong than for physical aggression, preschoolers high in relational aggression also tend to be hyperactive and frequently in conflict with peers and adults (Willoughby, Kupersmidt, & Bryant, 2001). As these behaviors trigger peer rejection, relationally aggressive girls befriend other girls high in relational hostility, and their relational aggression rises (Werner & Crick, 2004). Adolescents high in relational aggression are often angry, vengeful, and defiant of adult rules. Among teenagers who combine physical and relational hostility, these oppositional reactions intensify, increasing the likelihood of serious antisocial activity (Prinstein, Boergers, & Vernberg, 2001).

Late-Onset Type

Other youths first display antisocial behavior around the time of puberty, gradually increasing their involvement. Their conduct problems arise from the peer context of early adolescence, not from biological deficits and a history of unfavorable development. For some, quality of parenting may decline for a time, perhaps as a result of family stresses or the challenges of disciplining an unruly teenager (Moffitt et al., 1996). But when age brings gratifying adult privileges, these youths draw on prosocial skills mastered before adolescence and give up their antisocial ways.

A few late-onset youths, however, continue to engage in antisocial acts. The seriousness of their adolescent offenses seems to trap them in situations that close off opportunities for responsible behavior. In one study, finding a satisfying job and forming positive, close relationships coincided with an end to criminal offending by age 20 (Clingempeel & Henggeler, 2003).

These findings suggest a need for a fresh look at policies aimed at stopping youth crime. Keeping youth offenders locked up for many years disrupts their vocational lives and access to social support during a crucial period of development, condemning them to a bleak future.

▼ Figure 12.7

Path to chronic delinquency for adolescents with childhood-onset antisocial behavior. Difficult temperament and cognitive deficits characterize many of these youths in early childhood; some have attention-deficit hyperactivity disorder. Inept parenting transforms biologically based self-control difficulties into hostility and defiance. (Adapted from Patterson, DeBaryshe, & Ramsey, 1989.)

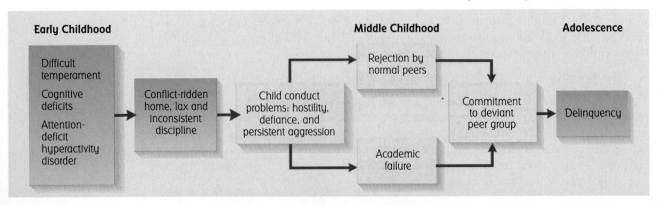

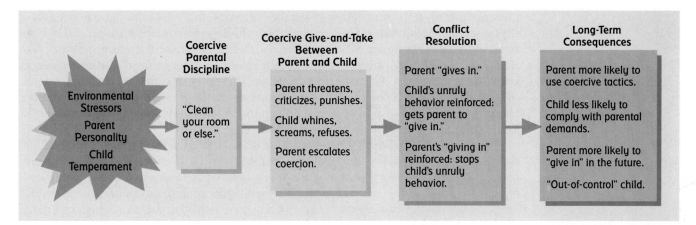

▲ Figure 12.8

Coercive interaction pattern that promotes and sustains aggression between family members.

Home observations of aggressive children reveal that anger and punitiveness quickly create a conflict-ridden family atmosphere and an "out-of-control" child. As Figure 12.8 shows, the pattern begins with forceful discipline, which occurs more often with stressful life experiences (such as economic hardship or an unhappy marriage), a parent with an unstable personality, or a difficult child (Coie & Dodge, 1998). Typically, the parent threatens, criticizes, and punishes, and the child whines, yells, and refuses until the parent "gives in." The sequence is likely to be repeated, since at the end of each exchange, both parent and child get relief from stopping the unpleasant behavior of the other, so the behaviors repeat and escalate (Patterson, 1995, 1997).

These cycles soon generate anxiety and irritability among other family members, who join in the hostile interactions. Compared with siblings in typical families, preschool siblings who have critical, punitive parents are more verbally and physically aggressive toward one another. Destructive sibling conflict, in turn, contributes to poor impulse control and antisocial behavior by the early school years (Garcia et al., 2000).

Boys are more likely than girls to be targets of harsh physical discipline and parental inconsistency because they are more active and impulsive, and therefore harder to control. When children with these characteristics are exposed to emotionally negative, inept parenting, their capacity for emotional self-regulation is disrupted, and they lash out when disappointed or frustrated (Chang et al., 2003; NICHD Early Child Care Research Network, 2004b). As a result, aggression persists (refer again to the Biology and Environment box).

Besides fostering aggression directly, parents can encourage it indirectly, through poor supervision of children (Vitaro, Brendgen, & Tremblay, 2000). Unfortunately, children from conflict-ridden homes who already display serious antisocial tendencies are most likely to experience inadequate parental monitoring. As a result, few if any limits are placed on out-of-home activities and association with antisocial friends, who encourage their hostile style of responding.

Social-Cognitive Deficits and Distortions

Children who are products of the family processes just described soon acquire a violent and callous view of the social world. They see hostile intent where it does not exist—in situations where a peer's intentions are unclear, where harm is accidental, and even where a peer is trying to be helpful (Lochman & Dodge, 1998; Orbio de Castro et al., 2002). When aggressive children feel threatened (a researcher tells them that a peer they will work with is in a bad mood and might pick a fight), they are especially likely to interpret accidental mishaps as hostile (Williams et al., 2003). As a result, they make many unprovoked attacks, which trigger aggressive retaliations.

Furthermore, compared with their nonaggressive agemates, aggressive children are convinced that there are more benefits and fewer costs for engaging in hostile acts. They are more likely to think that aggression "works" to produce tangible rewards and to reduce teasing, taunting, and other unpleasant behaviors by others (Perry, Perry, & Rasmussen, 1986). And when tempted to aggress, they are more concerned about achieving control and less concerned about a victim's suffering or being disliked by peers (Boldizar, Perry, & Perry, 1989).

Yet another biased feature of many aggressive children's social cognition is overly high self-esteem. Despite their academic and social failings, chronic aggressors commonly believe that they are superior, competent beings. When their arrogant, cocky behavior inevitably results in challenges to their inflated and hence vulnerable self-image, they react with anger and lash out at others (Baumeister, Smart, & Boden, 1996). Furthermore, antisocial young people may neutralize their basic biological capacity for empathy by using such cognitive distortion techniques as blaming their victims. As a result, they retain a positive self-evaluation after behaving aggressively (Liau, Barriga, & Gibbs, 1998). Looking back on his burglaries, one delinquent reflected, "If I started feeling bad, I'd say to myself, 'Tough rocks for him. He should have had his house locked better and the alarm on'" (Samenow, 1984, p. 115).

Recall, also, that antisocial young people are delayed in maturity of moral judgment. And they are low in moral self-relevance as well. In a study of 16- to 19-year-old college students, those with immature moral reasoning and low moral self-relevance were prone to self-serving cognitive distortions (such as blaming the victim and minimizing the harm done), which predicted high levels of acting-out behavior. Compared with boys, girls scored higher in moral self-relevance and lower in self-serving cognitive distortions—likely contributors to their lower rates of antisocial activity (Barriga et al., 2001).

Finally, although we have seen that aggressive children are typically impaired in social cognition and social skills, some—called *bistrategic controllers*—combine aggressive and positive social tactics to access highly desirable resources, such as the best role in a school activity or the attentions of peers. Bistrategic controllers view themselves as both aggressive and socially skilled, and their classmates agree. They are also adept at perspective taking and social problem solving and are knowledgeable about moral norms—social-cognitive strengths that they use to manipulate others to get what they want while concealing their aggression from adults (Hawley, 2003a, 2003b). Because of their success at maneuvering themselves into positions of influence, bistrategic controllers attract considerable peer admiration. However, little is known about the long-term development of these children, who meld selfish motives with impressive social savvy. Although they appear well adjusted, their morality may be limited to helping others only when motivated by self-interest.

Community and Cultural Influences

Children's tendency to engage in destructive, injurious behavior increases under certain environmental conditions. When the peer-group atmosphere is tense and competitive, hostility is more likely (DeRosier et al., 1994). These group characteristics are more common in poverty-stricken neighborhoods with a wide range of stressors, including poor-quality schools, limited recreational and employment opportunities, and adult criminal subcultures (Pagani et al., 1999).

Such neighborhoods predict aggression beyond family influences (Farrington & Loeber, 2000). Children and adolescents have easy access to deviant peers, drugs, and (in the United States) firearms, all of which are linked to violence. And youths are especially likely to be recruited into antisocial gangs, whose members commit the vast majority of violent delinquent acts (Thornberry & Krohn, 2001). Furthermore, schools in these locales typically fail to meet students' developmental needs. Large classes, weak instruction, and rigid rules are associated with higher rates of lawbreaking, even after other influences are controlled (Hawkins & Lam, 1987).

Ethnic and political prejudices further magnify the risk of angry, combative responses. In inner-city ghettos and in war-torn areas of the world, large numbers of children live in the midst of constant danger, chaos, and deprivation. As the Cultural Influences box on the following page reveals, these youngsters are at risk for severe emotional stress, deficits in moral reasoning, and behavior problems.

Helping Children and Parents Control Aggression

Treatment for aggressive children must break the cycle of hostilities between family members and promote effective ways of relating to others. Interventions with preschool and school-age children have been most successful. Once antisocial patterns persist into adolescence, so many factors act to sustain them that treatment is far more difficult.

• **COACHING, MODELING, AND REINFORCING ALTERNATIVE BEHAVIORS** • Procedures based on social learning theory have been devised to interrupt destructive family interaction. Parent training programs exist in which a therapist observes inept practices, models alternatives, and has parents practice them. Parents learn not to give in to an acting-out child

Impact of Ethnic and Political Violence on Children

Violence stemming from ethnic and political tensions is increasingly being felt around the world. Children's experiences under armed conflict are diverse. Some may participate in the fighting, either because they are forced to or because they want to please adults. Others are kidnapped, terrorized, or tortured. Those who are bystanders often come under direct fire and may be killed or physically maimed for life. And many watch in horror as family members, friends, and neighbors flee, are wounded, or die. During the past decade, wars have left 4 to 5 million children physically disabled, 20 million homeless, and more than 1 million separated from their parents (UNICEF, 2005). Half of all casualties of worldwide conflict are children.

When war and social crises are temporary, most children can be comforted and do not show long-term emotional difficulties. But chronic danger requires children to make substantial adjustments, and their psychological functioning can be seriously impaired. Many children of war lose their sense of safety, become desensitized to violence, are haunted by terrifying memories, and build a pessimistic view of the future. Anxiety and depression, as well as aggression and antisocial behavior, generally increase (Garbarino, Andreas, & Vorrasi, 2002; McIntyre & Ventura, 2003). These outcomes seem to be culturally universal, appearing among children from every war zone studied—from Bosnia, Angola, Rwanda, and the Sudan to the West Bank, Afghanistan, and Iraq (Barenbaum, Ruchkin, & Schwab-Stone, 2004).

Parental affection and reassurance are the best protection against lasting problems. When parents offer security and serve as role models of calm emotional strength, most children can withstand even extreme war-related violence (Smith et al., 2001). Children who are separated from parents must rely on help from their communities. Preschool and school-age orphans in Eritrea who were placed in residential settings where they could form close emotional ties with at least one adult showed less emotional stress 5 years later than orphans placed in impersonal settings (Wolff & Fesseha, 1999). Education and recreation programs are powerful safeguards, too, providing children with a sense of consistency in their lives along with teacher and peer supports.

The September 11, 2001, terrorist attack on the World Trade Center caused some American children to experience extreme wartime violence firsthand. Children in Public School 31 in Brooklyn, New York, for example, stared out classroom windows as planes rushed toward the towers and engulfed them in flames, and as the towers crumbled. Many worried about the safety of family members, and some lost them. In the aftermath, most expressed intense fears—for example, that terrorists were infiltrating their neighborhoods and that planes flying overhead might smash into nearby buildings.

Unlike many war-traumatized children in the developing world, P.S. 31 students received immediate intervention—a "trauma curriculum" in which they grappled with their emotions through writing, drawing, and discussion and participated in experiences aimed at restoring trust and tolerance (Lagnado, 2001). Older children learned about the feelings of their Muslim classmates, the dire condition of children in Afghanistan, and ways to help victims as a means of overcoming a sense of helplessness.

When wartime drains families and communities of resources, international organizations must step in and help children. Efforts to preserve children's physical, psychological, and educational well-being may be the best way to stop transmission of violence to the next generation.

▼ These young victims of air raids in Kabul, Afghanistan, witnessed the destruction of their neighborhoods and the maiming and deaths of family members and friends. In a therapy session at a mental health hospital, they draw pictures. One, by a 7-year-old, portrays his schoolmates who died. © AP/Wide World Photos

and not to escalate forceful attempts to control misbehavior. In addition, they are taught to pair commands with reasons and to replace verbal insults and harsh physical punishment with more effective strategies, such as time out and withdrawal of privileges. After several weeks of such training, children's antisocial behavior declines, and parents view their youngsters more positively—benefits still evident 1 to 4 years later in comparisons with families not receiving intervention (McMahon, 1999; Patterson & Fisher, 2002). When parents also receive help in coping with stressors in their own lives, parent training is even more effective (Kazdin & Whitley, 2003).

On the child's side, interventions that teach nonaggressive ways of resolving conflict are helpful. Sessions in which children model and role-play cooperation and sharing and see that these behaviors lead to rewarding social outcomes reduce aggression and increase positive social behavior. Many aggressive children also need help with language delays and deficits that interfere with the development of self-control. Encouraging parents to converse with their young children, especially about how to regulate strong negative emotion, helps children develop internalized controls. Once aggressive children begin to change, parents must be reminded to give them attention and approval for prosocial acts (Kazdin, 2000). The coercive cycles of parents and aggressive children are so pervasive that these children often are punished even when they do behave appropriately.

• **SOCIAL-COGNITIVE INTERVENTIONS** • The social-cognitive deficits and distortions of aggressive children prevent them from sympathizing with another person's pain and suffering—an important inhibitor of aggressive behavior. Furthermore, since aggressive children have few opportunities to witness family members acting in sensitive, caring ways, they miss early experiences that are vital for promoting empathy and sympathy (see Chapter 10). In such children, these responses may have to be directly taught.

Social-cognitive treatments focus on improving social information processing in antisocial youths. In one, adolescents were taught to attend to relevant, nonhostile social cues, to seek additional information before acting, and to evaluate potential responses in terms of their effectiveness. These interventions increase skill in solving social problems, decrease endorsement of beliefs supporting aggression, reduce hostile behaviors, and improve relationships with teachers and peers (Guerra & Slaby, 1990; Webster-Stratton, Reid, & Hammond, 2001). Training in perspective taking is also helpful (see Chapter 11) because it promotes more accurate interpretation of social cues, empathy, and sympathetic concern for others.

• **COMPREHENSIVE APPROACHES** • According to some researchers, effective treatment for antisocial youths must be multifaceted, encompassing parent training, social understanding, relating to others, and self-control. In a program called EQUIP, *positive peer culture*—an adult-guided but adolescent-conducted small-group approach aimed at creating a climate in which prosocial acts replace antisocial behavior—served as the basis for treatment. By themselves, peer-culture groups do not reduce antisocial behavior, and they sometimes increase it (Dishion, Poulin, & Burraston, 2001; Guerra, Attar, & Weissberg, 1997). But in EQUIP, the approach is supplemented with training in social skills, anger management, correction of cognitive distortions, and moral reasoning (Gibbs, 2004; DiBiase, Gibbs, & Potter, 2005; Potter, Gibbs, & Goldstein, 2001). Delinquents who participated in EQUIP displayed improved social skills and conduct during the following year relative to controls receiving no intervention. Also, the more advanced moral reasoning that emerged during group meetings seemed to have a long-term impact on antisocial youths' ability to inhibit lawbreaking behavior (Leeman, Gibbs, & Fuller, 1993).

Yet even multidimensional treatments can fall short if young people remain embedded in hostile home lives, poor-quality schools, antisocial peer groups, and violent neighborhoods. In another program, called Multisystemic Therapy, therapists trained parents in communication, monitoring, and discipline skills; integrated violent youths into positive school, work, and leisure activities; and disengaged them from violent peers. Compared with conventional services or individual therapy, the intervention led to improved parent–child relations, a dramatic drop in number of arrests over a four-year period, and—when participants did commit crimes—a reduction in their severity (Huey & Henggeler, 2001). Efforts to create nonaggressive environments—at the family, community, and cultural levels—are needed to help delinquent youths and to foster healthy development of all young people. We will return to this theme in later chapters.

Ask Yourself

REVIEW	Cite factors that contribute to an improved ability to delay gratification from early to middle childhood, and explain why each makes a difference.
REVIEW	Explain how heredity and environment jointly contribute to persistent aggression.
APPLY	Zeke had been a well-behaved child in elementary school, but around age 13, he started spending time with the "wrong crowd." At age 16, he was arrested for property damage. Is Zeke likely to become a long-term offender? Why or why not?
CONNECT	Reread the section on adolescent parenthood in Chapter 5 (pages 211–213) and the section on adolescent suicide in Chapter 11 (pages 458–459). What factors do these problems have in common with chronic delinquency?

Summary

Morality as Rooted in Human Nature

Describe and evaluate the biological perspective on morality.

◉ The biological perspective on moral development assumes that morality is grounded in the genetic heritage of our species, perhaps through prewired emotional reactions. Humans share many morally relevant behaviors with other species, and the ventromedial area of the frontal region of the cerebral cortex is vital for emotional responsiveness to others' suffering. Nevertheless, human morality cannot be fully explained by its biological foundations. Morally relevant emotions require strong caregiving supports and cognitive attainments for their mature expression.

Morality as the Adoption of Societal Norms

Describe and evaluate the psychoanalytic perspective on moral development.

◉ Both psychoanalytic and social learning theories regard moral development as a matter of **internalization:** the adoption of societal standards for right action as one's own. Internalization is not just a straightforward process of taking over externally imposed prescriptions. Instead, it is the combined result of factors within the child and the rearing environment.

◉ According to Freud, morality emerges with the resolution of the

© MYRLEEN FERGUSON CATE/ PHOTOEDIT

Oedipus and Electra conflicts during the preschool years. Fear of punishment and loss of parental love lead children to form a superego through identification with the same-sex parent and to redirect hostile impulses toward the self in the form of guilt.

◉ Although guilt is an important motivator of moral action, Freud's interpretation of it is no longer widely accepted. In contrast to Freudian predictions, power assertion and love withdrawal do not foster conscience development. Instead, **induction** is far more effective and seems to cultivate children's active commitment to moral norms.

◉ Temperament affects children's responsiveness to parenting techniques. Mild, patient tactics are sufficient to promote conscience development in anxious, fearful preschoolers. For fearless, impulsive children, a secure attachment relationship motivates children to respond to firm parental correction of misbehavior and to listen to parental inductions.

◉ Recent psychoanalytic ideas place greater emphasis on the early formation of a positive parent–child relationship as important for conscience formation. However, they retain continuity with Freud's theory in regarding emotion as the basis for moral development.

Describe and evaluate the social learning perspective on moral development, including the importance of modeling, the effects of punishment, and alternatives to harsh discipline.

◉ Social learning theory views moral behavior as acquired in the same way as other responses: through modeling and reinforcement. Effective models are warm and powerful and display consistency between what they say and what they do. By middle childhood, children have internalized many prosocial and other rules for good conduct.

◉ Harsh punishment does not promote moral internalization and socially desirable behavior. Instead, it provides children with aggressive models, leads them to avoid the punishing adult, can spiral into serious abuse, and results in children's acceptance of such discipline and, consequently, potential use of similar methods when they themselves become parents. Alternatives, such as **time out** and withdrawal of privileges, can reduce these undesirable side effects, as long as parents apply them consistently, maintain a warm relationship with the child, and offer explanations that fit the transgression.

◉ The most effective forms of discipline encourage good conduct. Parents who build a positive relationship with the child have children who want to adopt parental standards because they feel a sense of commitment to the relationship.

Morality as Social Understanding

Describe Piaget's theory of moral development, and evaluate its accuracy.

◉ Piaget's cognitive-developmental perspective assumes that morality develops through **construction**—actively thinking about multiple aspects of situations in which social conflicts arise and deriving new moral understandings.

⊚ Piaget's work was the original inspiration for the cognitive-developmental perspective. He identified two stages of moral understanding: **heteronomous morality,** in which children view moral rules in terms of **realism** and as fixed dictates of authority figures; and **autonomous morality,** in which children base fairness on **ideal reciprocity** and regard rules as flexible, socially agreed-on principles.

⊚ Piaget's theory describes the general direction of moral development, but it underestimates the moral capacities of young children. Preschool and early school-age children take intentions into account in making moral judgments, although they interpret intentions in a rigid fashion. Furthermore, they have differentiated notions about the legitimacy of authority figures. With respect to nonmoral issues, they base authority on knowledge, not social position. When a directive is morally valid, they view it as important, regardless of whether an authority figure endorses it.

Describe Kohlberg's extension of Piaget's theory, methods for assessing moral reasoning, and evidence on the accuracy of his stages.

⊚ According to Kohlberg, moral development is a gradual process that extends beyond childhood into adolescence and adulthood. Examining **Moral Judgment Interview** responses of adolescent boys who were followed longitudinally, Kohlberg constructed his three-level, six-stage sequence. Besides Kohlberg's clinical interview, efficient questionnaires for assessing moral understanding exist. The most recently devised is the **Sociomoral Reflection Measure–Short Form (SRM–SF).**

⊚ Kohlberg concluded that moral reasoning advances through three levels, each of which contains two stages: (1) the **preconventional level,** in which morality is viewed as controlled by rewards, punishments, and the power of authority figures; (2) the **conventional level,** in which conformity to laws and rules is regarded as necessary to preserve positive human relationships and societal order; and (3) the **postconventional level,** in which individuals define morality in terms of abstract, universal principles of justice.

⊚ Kohlberg's stages are strongly related to age, and people move through them slowly, in the predicted order. In focusing on hypothetical moral dilemmas, however, Kohlberg's theory assesses only the rational weighing of alternatives and overlooks other strategies involved in moral judgment. Because situational factors affect moral reasoning, Kohlberg's stages are best viewed in terms of a loose rather than a strict concept of stage.

⊚ Piaget's cognitive and Selman's perspective-taking stages are related to advances in moral reasoning. However, the domain in which the cognitive prerequisites for mature moral reasoning first emerge—cognitive, social, or moral—remains unclear.

⊚ Contrary to Gilligan's claim, Kohlberg's theory does not underestimate the moral maturity of females. Instead, justice and caring moralities coexist but vary in prominence between males and females, from one situation to the next, and across cultures.

Describe influences on moral reasoning, its relationship to moral behavior, and continuing challenges to Kohlberg's theory.

⊚ A flexible, open-minded approach to new information and experiences is linked to gains in moral reasoning. Among experiences that contribute are warm, rational child-rearing practices, years of schooling, and peer interactions that resolve conflict through negotiation and compromise.

⊚ Cross-cultural research indicates that a certain level of societal complexity is required for the development of Kohlberg's higher stages. Although his theory does not encompass aspects of moral reasoning prominent in non-Western societies, a common justice morality is evident in individuals from vastly different cultures.

⊚ Maturity of moral reasoning is moderately related to a wide variety of moral behaviors. Many other factors also influence moral action, including emotions, temperament, personality, history of morally relevant experiences, and **moral self-relevance**— the degree to which morality is central to self-concept.

⊚ By middle childhood, children have begun to formulate religious and spiritual ideas that serve as moral forces in their lives. Although formal religious involvement declines in adolescence, young people who remain part of a religious community are

advantaged in moral values and behavior. Religious affiliation is linked to community service, responsible academic and social behavior, and avoidance of misconduct.

⊚ A revised conception of moral development regards maturity of moral judgment as achieved at Kohlberg's Stages 3 and 4, when young people grasp ideal reciprocity—attainments that are not "conventional" but, rather, require profound moral constructions. Because Kohlberg's dilemmas are remote from the experiences of children and not clearly understood by them, his theory overlooks moral-reasoning capacities that develop in early and middle childhood.

Moral Reasoning of Young Children

Explain how children distinguish moral imperatives from social conventions and matters of personal choice, and trace changes in their understanding from childhood into adolescence.

⊚ Even preschoolers have a rudimentary grasp of justice in that they distinguish **moral imperatives** from **social conventions** and **matters of personal choice.** Through actively making sense of people's everyday social experiences and emotional reactions, young children conclude that moral transgressions (but not social conventions) are wrong in any context, regardless of whether rules or authorities prohibit them. School-age children gradually clarify and link moral imperatives and social conventions, taking into account more variables, including the purpose of the rule; people's intentions, knowledge, and beliefs; and the context of their behavior.

⊚ As children clarify and interrelate moral imperatives and social conventions, their conviction that certain matters are up to the individual strengthens. Notions of personal choice support the development of moral concepts of individual rights and freedom, which evolve from appeals to personal privileges to appreciation of democratic ideals over middle childhood.

Describe the development of distributive justice reasoning, noting factors that foster mature understanding.

⊚ Children's concepts of **distributive justice** change over middle childhood, from equality to merit to equity and benevolence. Peer disagreements, along with efforts to resolve them, make children more sensitive to others' perspectives, which fosters their developing ideas of fair distribution.

Development of Morally Relevant Self-Control

Trace the development of morally relevant self-control from early childhood into adolescence, noting implications of individual differences for cognitive and social competencies.

⊚ The emergence of self-control is supported by self-awareness and by the representational and memory capacities of the second year. The first glimmerings of self-control appear in the form of **compliance.** The capacity for **delay of gratification** increases steadily over the third year. Language development and sensitive, supportive parenting foster self-control.

⊚ During the preschool years, children profit from adult-provided delay-of-gratification strategies and from having something interesting to do while waiting. Over middle childhood, children produce an increasing variety of strategies themselves and become consciously aware of which ones work well and why, leading to a flexible capacity for **moral self-regulation.**

⊚ Individual differences in delay of gratification predict diverse cognitive and social competencies, including responsible behavior

and social problem solving. Development of self-control appears to be governed by two processing systems: an emotional, reactive "hot system" that eventually is dominated by a cognitive, reflective "cool system."

The Other Side of Self-Control: Development of Aggression

Discuss the development of aggression from infancy into adolescence, noting individual, family, community, and cultural influences, and describe successful interventions.

⊚ Aggression first appears in late infancy. Whereas **instrumental aggression** declines, **hostile aggression** increases over early and middle childhood. At least three types of hostile aggression are evident: **physical aggression** (more common among boys), **verbal aggression,** and **relational aggression.** Physical and relational aggression can be either direct or indirect.

© MATY KATE DENNY/PHOTOEDIT

⊚ During early childhood, physical aggression tends to decline while verbal aggression increases. By the late preschool years, boys are more physically aggressive than girls. Sex differences in verbal and relational aggression are minimal, although girls' relational hostility can be particularly mean.

⊚ Although teacher- and peer-reported aggression declines in adolescence, delin-

quent acts increase, especially for boys. However, a few youths sustain a high level of physical aggression from childhood to adolescence, committing violent crimes. Young children high in relational aggression also tend to sustain their relational hostility and display continuing conduct problems.

⊚ Impulsive, overactive children are at risk for high aggression, but whether or not they remain aggressive depends on child-rearing conditions. Strife-ridden family environments and power-assertive, inconsistent discipline promote self-perpetuating cycles of aggressive behavior.

⊚ Children who are products of these family processes develop social-cognitive deficits and distortions that add to the long-term maintenance of aggression. Widespread poverty, harsh living conditions, and schools that fail to meet students' developmental needs increase antisocial acts among children and adolescents.

⊚ Among interventions designed to reduce aggression, training parents in child discipline and teaching children alternative ways of resolving conflict are helpful. Social-cognitive interventions that focus on improving social information processing and perspective taking have yielded benefits as well. However, the most effective treatments are comprehensive, addressing the multiple factors that sustain antisocial behavior.

⊚ Important Terms and Concepts

autonomous morality (p. 486)
compliance (p. 504)
construction (p. 485)
conventional level (p. 490)
delay of gratification (p. 504)
distributive justice (p. 502)
heteronomous morality (p. 485)
hostile aggression (p. 507)
ideal reciprocity (p. 486)

induction (p. 478)
instrumental aggression (p. 507)
internalization (p. 477)
matters of personal choice (p. 501)
moral imperatives (p. 500)
Moral Judgment Interview (p. 488)
moral self-regulation (p. 505)
moral self-relevance (p. 496)
physical aggression (p. 507)

postconventional level (p. 490)
preconventional level (p. 489)
realism (p. 486)
relational aggression (p. 507)
social conventions (p. 500)
Sociomoral Reflection Measure–Short Form (SRM–SF) (p. 488)
time out (p. 482)
verbal aggression (p. 507)

"I, My Mother, and Sister Went for a Walk"
Marija Zukovskaja
Age 7, Lithuania

Every detail of air and sky is distinct and alive as a mother and her daughters take a stroll on a bright summer day. Biology and environment jointly contribute to this artist's dazzling, firmly "feminine" frame of mind.

Development of Sex Differences and Gender Roles

On a typical morning, in our university laboratory preschool, 4-year-old Jenny eagerly entered the housekeeping corner and put on a frilly long dress and high heels. Karen, setting the table nearby, produced whimpering sound effects for the baby doll in the crib. Jenny lifted the doll, sat down in the rocking chair, gently cradled the baby in her arms, and whispered, "You're hungry, aren't you?" A moment later, Jenny announced, "This baby won't eat. I think she's sick. Ask Rachel if she'll be the nurse." Karen ran off to find Rachel, who was coloring at the art table.

Meanwhile, Nathan called to Tommy, "Wanna play traffic?" Both boys dashed energetically toward the cars and trucks in the block corner. Soon David joined them. "I'll be policeman first!" announced Nathan, climbing onto a chair. "Green light, go!" shouted the young police officer. With this signal, Tommy and David scurried on all fours around the chair, each pushing a large wooden truck. "Red light!" exclaimed Nathan, and the trucks screeched to a halt.

"My truck beat yours," Tommy informed David.

"Only 'cause I need gas," David responded.

"Let's build a runway for the trucks," suggested Nathan. The three construction engineers began gathering large blocks for the task.

At an early age, children adopt many gender-linked standards of their culture. Jenny, Karen, and Rachel use dresses, dolls, and household props to act out a stereotypically feminine scene of nurturance. In contrast, Nathan, Tommy, and David's play is active, competitive, and masculine in theme. And both boys and girls interact more with agemates of their own sex.

What causes young children's play and social preferences to become so strongly gender typed, and how do these attitudes and behaviors change with age? Do societal expectations affect the way children think about themselves as masculine and feminine beings, thereby limiting their potential? To what extent do widely held beliefs about the characteristics of males and females reflect reality? Is it true that the average boy is aggressive, competitive, and good at spatial and mathematical skills, whereas the average girl is passive, nurturant, and good at verbal skills? How large are differences between the sexes, and in what ways do heredity and environment contribute to them? These are the central questions asked by researchers who study gender typing. In this chapter, we will answer each of them.

Perhaps more than any other area of child development, the study of gender typing has responded to societal change. Until the early 1970s, psychologists regarded the adoption of gender-typed beliefs and behaviors as essential for healthy adjustment. Since then, progress in women's rights has led to major shifts in how they view sex differences. Today, many people recognize that some gender-typed characteristics, such as extreme aggressiveness and competitiveness on the part of males and passivity and conformity on the part of females, are serious threats to mental health.

Consistent with this realization, theoretical revision marks the study of gender typing. Social learning theory, with its emphasis on modeling and reinforcement, and cognitive-developmental theory, with its focus on children as active thinkers about their social world, are major current approaches to gender typing. However, neither is sufficient by itself. We will see that an information-processing view, *gender schema theory,* combines elements of both theories to explain how children acquire gender-typed knowledge.

New theories have contributed new terms. Considerable controversy surrounds the labels *sex* and *gender.* Some researchers use these words interchangeably. Others use *sex* for biologically based differences, *gender* for socially influenced differences. Still others object to this convention because our understanding of many differences is still evolving. Also, it perpetuates too strong a dichotomy between nature and nurture (Halpern, 2000). In this book, I use the term *sex* when simply referring to a difference between males and females, without inferring the source of the difference. In contrast, I use *gender* when discussing genetic or environmental influences, or both (Deaux, 1993).

Central to our discussion is a set of special terms. Two involve the public face of gender in society. **Gender stereotypes** are widely held beliefs about characteristics deemed appropriate for males and females. **Gender roles** are the reflection of these stereotypes in everyday behavior. **Gender identity** is the private face of gender. It refers to perception of the self as relatively masculine or feminine in characteristics. Finally, **gender typing** is a broadly applied term which refers to any association of objects, activities, roles, or traits with biological sex in ways that conform to cultural stereotypes of gender and, therefore, encompasses all the gender-linked responses just mentioned (Liben & Bigler, 2002). As we explore each facet of gender typing in children and adolescents, you will see that biological, cognitive, and social factors are involved.

Gender Stereotypes and Gender Roles

Gender stereotypes have appeared in religious, philosophical, and literary works for centuries. Consider the following literary excerpts, from ancient times to the present:

- "Woman is more compassionate than man and has a greater propensity to tears. . . . But the male . . . is more disposed to give assistance in danger, and is more courageous than the female." (Aristotle, cited in Miles, 1935)
- "A man will say what he knows, a woman says what will please." (Jean Jacques Rousseau, *Emile,* 1762/1955)
- "Man with the head and woman with the heart;
  Man to command and woman to obey;
  All else confusion." (Alfred, Lord Tennyson, *Home They Brought Her Warrior,* 1842)
- "Love is a mood—no more—to a man,
  And love to a woman is life or death." (Ella Wheeler Wilcox, *Blind,* 1882)
- "Women ask: How do you get a man to open up? Men ask: Why does she always want to talk about the relationship?" (Gray, *Mars and Venus on a Date,* 1997)

Although the past three decades have brought a new level of awareness about the wide range of roles possible for each gender, strong beliefs about sex differences remain. In the 1960s, researchers began asking people what personality characteristics they consider typical of men and women. Widespread agreement emerged in many studies. As Table 13.1 illustrates, **instrumental traits,** reflecting competence, rationality, and assertiveness, were regarded as masculine; **expressive traits,** emphasizing warmth, caring, and sensitivity, were viewed as feminine. Despite intense political activism promoting gender equality in the 1970s and 1980s, these stereotypes have remained essentially unchanged (Lueptow, Garovich, & Lueptow, 2001; Lutz & Ruble, 1995; Vonk & Ashmore, 2003). Furthermore, cross-cultural research conducted in 30 nations reveals that the instrumental–expressive dichotomy is a widely held stereotype around the world (Williams & Best, 1990).

Besides personality traits, other gender stereotypes exist. These include physical characteristics (tall, strong, and sturdy for men; soft, dainty, and graceful for women), occupations (truck driver, insurance agent, and chemist for men; elementary school teacher, secretary, and nurse for women), and activities or behaviors (good at fixing things and leader in groups for men; good at child care and decorating the home for women) (Biernat, 1991; Powlishta et al., 2001).

The variety of attributes consistently identified as masculine or feminine, their broad acceptance, and their stability over time suggest that gender stereotypes are deeply ingrained patterns of thinking. What's more, they cast men in a generally positive light and women in a negative light. The traits, activities, and roles associated with the male gender are more numerous, diverse, and desirable than those associated with the female gender. For example, in Western cultures, stereotypically masculine occupations are far more numerous than feminine occupations (Liben & Bigler, 2002). And only a few masculine attributes, such as "aggressive" and "criminal," are negative; the overwhelming majority are advantageous and high-status. Feminine attributes, in contrast, are mostly unfavorable and low-status.

Adults apply gender stereotypes to children with a special intensity. In a study in which 20- to 40-year-olds were shown photos of children and adults and asked to rate each on "masculine," "feminine," and "neutral" personality traits, adults differentiated boys from girls more sharply than they did men from women (see Figure 13.1) (Powlishta, 2000). Given that many adults view children through a gender-biased lens, perhaps it is not surprising that by the second year, children have begun to absorb these messages.

Gender Stereotyping in Early Childhood

Recall from Chapter 11 that between 18 months and 3 years, children label their own and others' sex, using such words as "boy" and "girl" and "woman" and "man." Once these categories are in place, children sort out what they mean in terms of activities and behaviors. Consequently, gender stereotypes appear and expand rapidly. Before age 2, children have begun to acquire subtle associations with gender that most of us hold—men as rough and sharp, women as soft and round. In one study, 18-month-olds linked such items as fir trees and hammers with males, although they had not yet learned comparable feminine associations (Eichstedt et al., 2002). Preschoolers associate toys, articles of clothing, tools, household items, games, occupations, and colors (pink and blue) with one sex or the other (Poulin-Dubois et al., 2002; Ruble & Martin, 1998). They have even acquired gender-stereotyped metaphors, such as "bears are for boys" and "butterflies are for girls" (Leinbach, Hort, & Fagot, 1997).

During early childhood, gender-stereotyped beliefs strengthen—so much so that many children apply them as blanket rules rather than flexible guidelines. When children were asked whether gender stereotypes could be violated, half or more of 3- and 4-year-olds answered "no" to clothing, hairstyle, and play with certain toys (such as Barbie Dolls and G.I. Joes). Although they were less insistent about other types of play and occupations, many still said a girl can't play roughly or be a doctor (Blakemore, 2003). Already, children view their world in a strongly gender-stereotyped fashion. In several studies, researchers labeled a target child as a boy or a girl and then provided either gender-typical or gender-atypical information about the target's characteristics. Next, children rated the target on additional gender-stereotypic attributes. Preschoolers usually relied on only the gender label in making judgments, while ignoring the specific information. For example, when told, "Tommy is a boy. Tommy's best friend is a girl, and Tommy

TABLE 13.1 PERSONALITY TRAITS REGARDED AS STEREOTYPICALLY MASCULINE OR FEMININE

Masculine Traits	Feminine Traits
Active	Aware of others' feelings
Acts as a leader	Considerate
Adventurous	Cries easily
Aggressive	Devotes self to others
Ambitious	Emotional
Competitive	Excitable in a major crisis
Doesn't give up easily	Feelings hurt easily
Dominant	Gentle
Feels superior	Home oriented
Holds up well under pressure	Kind
Independent	Likes children
Makes decisions easily	Neat
Not easily influenced	Needs approval
Outspoken	Passive
Rough	Tactful
Self-confident	Understanding of others
Takes a stand	Warm in relations with others

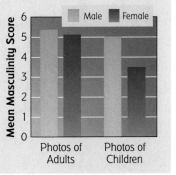

▲ **Figure 13.1**

Adults' ratings of photos of adults and children for "masculine" personality traits. Adults perceived little difference in the adult photos but a sharp difference in the child photos, rating boys as far more "masculine" in personality traits than girls. Ratings for "feminine" personality traits were similar: Adults reported a much greater difference between boys and girls than between men and women.

(Adapted from Powlishta, 2000.)

By age 1½, children make gender-stereotyped choices about games and toys, a tendency that increases with age. These children's toys and style of play are already highly gender stereotyped.
© Michael Siluk/The Image Works and © Laura Dwight Photography

likes to play house," children under age 6 nevertheless said that Tommy would much rather play with cars and train engines than with sewing machines and dolls (Biernat, 1991; Martin, 1989).

The rigidity of preschoolers' gender stereotypes helps us understand some commonly observed everyday behaviors. Shown a picture of a Scottish bagpiper wearing a kilt, a 4-year-old is likely to say, "Men don't wear skirts!" At preschool, children exclaim that girls can't be police officers and boys can't take care of babies. These one-sided judgments are a joint product of gender stereotyping in the environment and young children's cognitive limitations—in particular, their difficulty coordinating conflicting sources of information. Most preschoolers do not yet realize that characteristics *associated with* one's sex—activities, toys, occupations, hairstyle, and clothing—do not *determine* whether a person is male or female. They have trouble understanding that males and females can be different in terms of their bodies but similar in many other ways.

Gender Stereotyping in Middle Childhood and Adolescence

By age 5, gender stereotyping of activities and occupations is well established. During middle childhood and adolescence, knowledge of stereotypes increases in the less obvious areas of personality traits and achievement (Signorella, Bigler, & Liben, 1993). At the same time, older children realize that gender-stereotypic attributes are associated, not defining, features of gender. Consequently, beliefs about characteristics and capacities possible for males and females become more flexible (Martin, Ruble, & Szkrybalo, 2002).

• **PERSONALITY TRAITS** • To assess stereotyping of personality traits, researchers ask children to assign "masculine" adjectives ("tough," "rational," "cruel") and "feminine" adjectives ("gentle," "affectionate," "dependent") to either a male or a female stimulus figure. Recall from Chapter 11 that not until middle childhood are children good at sizing up people's dispositions. This same finding carries over to awareness of gender stereotypes.

Research in many countries reveals that stereotyping of personality traits increases steadily in middle childhood, becoming adultlike around age 11 (Best, 2001; Heyman & Legare, 2004). A large Canadian study examined the pattern of children's trait learning and found that the stereotypes acquired first reflected *in-group favoritism*. Kindergartners through second graders had greatest knowledge of trait stereotypes that portrayed their own gender in a positive light. Once trait stereotyping was well under way, elementary school students were most familiar with "positive feminine" traits and "negative masculine" traits (Serbin, Powlishta, & Gulko, 1993). In addition to learning specific traits, children of both sexes seemed to pick up a widely held general impression—that of girls as "sugar and spice and everything nice" and of boys as "snakes and snails and puppy dog tails."

• **ACHIEVEMENT AREAS** • Shortly after entering elementary school, children figure out which academic subjects and skill areas are "masculine" and which are "feminine." They often regard reading, spelling, art, and music as more for girls and view mathematics, athletics, and mechanical skills as more for boys (Eccles, Jacobs, & Harold, 1990; Jacobs & Weisz, 1994). These stereotypes influence children's preferences for and sense of competence at certain subjects. For example, in both Asian and Western nations, boys tend to feel more competent than girls at math and science, whereas girls tend to feel more competent than boys at language arts—even when children of equal skill level are compared (Andre et al., 1999; Freedman-Doan et al., 2000; Hong, Veach, & Lawrenz, 2003).

Furthermore, girls frequently seem to adopt a more general stereotype of males as smarter than females, and apply this to themselves. In a study of more than 2,000 second to sixth graders from diverse cultures—Eastern and Western Europe, Japan, Russia, and the United States—girls consistently had higher school grades than boys. Yet although they were aware of their performance standing, they did not report stronger beliefs in their own ability. Compared with boys, girls discounted their talent (Stetsenko et al., 2000). Recall from Chapter 11 that when girls have difficulty with school tasks, parents and teachers are likely to attribute their difficulties to lack of ability. Apparently, gender stereotyping of academic talent occurs in many parts of the world.

An encouraging sign is that some children's gender-stereotyped beliefs about achievement areas may be changing. In a recent investigation, U.S. elementary school girls from economically advantaged homes regarded children of each gender as equally good at math. But when the girls were asked about adults, their judgments reverted to the stereotype—that men were better than women (see Figure 13.2). Boys, in contrast, held stereotyped views of math ability for both children and adults (Steele, 2003).

• **TOWARD GREATER FLEXIBILITY** • Clearly, school-age children are knowledgeable about a wide variety of gender stereotypes. At the same time, they develop a more open-minded view of what males and females *can do,* a trend that continues into adolescence.

In studying gender stereotyping, researchers usually ask children whether or not both genders can display a personality trait or activity—a response that measures **gender-stereotype flexibility,** or overlap in the characteristics of males and females. In the Canadian study mentioned on page 522, stereotype knowledge and flexibility were assessed; as Figure 13.3 reveals, both increased from kindergarten to sixth grade (Serbin, Powlishta, & Gulko, 1993).

Gender stereotypes become more flexible as children develop the cognitive capacity to integrate conflicting social cues. As they realize that a person's sex is not a certain predictor of his or

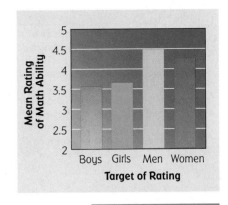

▲ **Figure 13.2**

School-age girls' ratings of the math ability of children and adults. The girls regarded children of each gender as equally good at math. Their ratings of adults, however, reverted to the stereotype of men being better at math than women. (Adapted from Steele, 2003.)

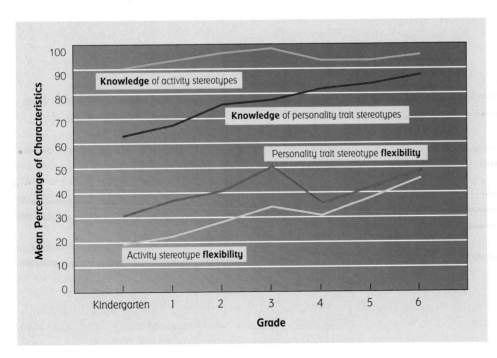

◄ **Figure 13.3**

Changes in gender-stereotype knowledge and flexibility from kindergarten to sixth grade. Canadian schoolchildren responded to a questionnaire assessing their gender-stereotype knowledge and the flexibility of their gender-stereotyped beliefs (whether they thought both genders could display a personality trait or activity). Both stereotype knowledge and flexibility increased from kindergarten to sixth grade. (From L. A. Serbin, K. K. Powlishta, & J. Gulko, 1993, "The Development of Sex Typing in Middle Childhood," *Monographs of the Society for Research in Child Development, 38*(2, Serial No. 232), p. 35. © The Society for Research in Child Development, Inc. Adapted by permission.)

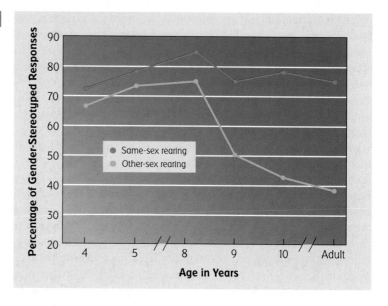

► Figure 13.4

Gender-stereotyped responses of 4- to 10-year-olds and adults to stories about boy and girl babies reared on island by members of their own sex or of the other sex. Younger children thought that gender-stereotyped characteristics would emerge regardless of rearing environment. By the end of middle childhood, children viewed gender typing as socially rather than biologically influenced. They thought that other-sex rearing would produce far less stereotyped children than would same-sex rearing. (Adapted from Taylor, 1996.)

her personality traits, activities, and behavior, they no longer rely on a gender label alone to predict what a person will be like—they also consider the individual's unique characteristics.

Accompanying this change is a greater tendency to view gender differences as socially rather than biologically influenced. In one study, 4- to 10-year-olds and adults were told stories about hypothetical boy and girl babies reared on an island by members either of their own sex or of the other sex. Then they were asked what "masculine" and "feminine" properties each child would develop. As Figure 13.4 shows, preschool and younger school-age children believed that gender-stereotyped characteristics would emerge, regardless of rearing environment. But by the end of middle childhood, children thought that a child reared by the other sex would be nonstereotyped in many ways (Taylor, 1996).

Nevertheless, acknowledging that boys and girls *can* cross gender lines does not mean that children always *approve* of doing so. They take a harsh view of certain violations—boys playing with dolls and wearing girls' clothing and girls acting noisily and roughly. They are especially intolerant when boys engage in these "cross-gender" acts, which children regard as nearly as bad as moral transgressions (Blakemore, 2003; Levy, Taylor, & Gelman, 1995). Clearly, evaluations of certain male deviations from gender roles are negative at all ages, a finding that reflects greater social pressure on boys and men to conform to gender stereotypes. As we will see later when we take up gender identity, children's disapproval of gender-role violations can seriously affect the psychological adjustment of peers who are targets of their criticism.

Individual and Group Differences in Gender Stereotyping

By middle childhood, almost all children have acquired extensive knowledge of gender stereotypes. But they vary widely in the makeup of their understanding. The various components of gender stereotyping—activities, behaviors, occupations, and personality traits—do not correlate highly. A child who is very knowledgeable in one area may not be very knowledgeable in the others (Serbin, Powlishta, & Gulko, 1993). This suggests that gender typing is like "an intricate puzzle that the child pieces together in a rather idiosyncratic way" (Hort, Leinbach, & Fagot, 1991, p. 196). To build a coherent notion of gender, children must assemble many elements. The precise pattern in which they acquire the pieces, the rate at which they do so, and the flexibility of their beliefs vary greatly from child to child.

Group differences in gender stereotyping also exist. The strongest of these is sex related: Boys hold more rigid gender-stereotyped views than girls throughout childhood and adolescence (Steele, 2003; Turner, Gervai, & Hinde, 1993). A few studies, however, report no sex differences (Serbin, Powlishta, & Gulko, 1993; Taylor, 1996). And in one study, adolescents of both sexes responded to vignettes about hypothetical high-achieving peers with greater liking for the high-achieving girls (Quatman, Sokolik, & Smith, 2000). One heartening possibility is that older boys, at least, are beginning to view gender roles as encompassing more varied possibilities.

The limited evidence available on ethnic minorities suggests that African-American children hold less stereotyped views of females than do Caucasian-American children (Bardwell, Cochran, & Walker, 1986). Perhaps this is a response to the less traditional gender roles seen in African-American families; for example, more black than white mothers are employed (U.S. Census Bureau, 2004b).

Finally, in adolescence and adulthood, higher-SES individuals tend to hold more flexible gender-stereotyped views than their lower-SES counterparts (Lackey, 1989; Serbin, Powlishta, & Gulko, 1993). Years of schooling and a wider array of life options may contribute to this difference.

Gender Stereotyping and Gender-Role Adoption

Do children's gender-stereotyped patterns of thinking influence gender-role adoption, thereby restricting their experiences and potential? The evidence is mixed. Gender-typed preferences and behaviors increase sharply over the preschool years—the same period in which children rapidly acquire stereotypes. And boys—the more stereotyped of the two sexes—show greater conformity to their gender role (Bussey & Bandura, 1992; Ruble & Martin, 1998).

But these parallel patterns do not tell us definitively that gender stereotyping shapes children's behavior. In fact, in some cases, influence may operate in the reverse direction, since certain gender-role preferences are acquired long before children know much about stereotypes. For example, by the middle of the second year, boys and girls favor different toys. When researchers showed toddlers paired photos of vehicles and dolls, 18-month-old boys looked longer than girls at the vehicles, whereas 18-month-old girls looked longer than boys at the dolls (see Figure 13.5) (Serbin et al., 2001).

Furthermore, children who are well versed in gender-related expectations are sometimes highly gender typed, and sometimes not, in their everyday activities (Downs & Langlois, 1988; Serbin, Powlishta, & Gulko, 1993; Weinraub et al., 1984). Why might this be so? First, we have seen that children master the separate components of gender-stereotyped knowledge in diverse ways, each of which may have different implications for their behavior. Second, by middle childhood, virtually all children know a great deal about gender stereotypes—knowledge so universal that it cannot predict variations in their behavior.

Rather than stereotype knowledge, stereotype flexibility is a good predictor of children's gender-role adoption in middle childhood. Children who believe that many stereotyped characteristics are appropriate for both sexes (for example, that playing with trucks is OK for girls) are more likely to cross gender lines in their own choices of activities, playmates, and occupational roles (Liben, Bigler, & Krogh, 2002; Serbin, Powlishta, & Gulko, 1993; Signorella, Bigler, & Liben, 1993). This suggests that gender stereotypes affect behavior only when children incorporate those beliefs into their own gender identities—self-perceptions of what they can and should do at play, in school, and as future participants in society. Now let's turn to various influences that promote children's gender-typed beliefs and behaviors.

▼ **Figure 13.5**

Eighteen-month-old girls' and boys' looking times at vehicles and dolls. Already, gender-role preferences are evident: Boys looked longer at the vehicles, whereas girls looked longer at the dolls. (Adapted from Serbin et al., 2001.)

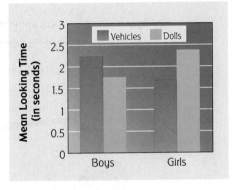

◎ Children who are well versed in gender stereotypes do not always behave in ways consistent with their knowledge. Perhaps because this African-American boy has observed family members engaged in nonstereotyped activities, he enacts similar roles in his preschool classroom.
© Laura Dwight Photography

Ask Yourself

REVIEW	Explain how preschoolers' cognitive limitations combine with their experiences to contribute to rigid gender stereotyping in early childhood.
REVIEW	What factors allow for flexibility in gender stereotyping in middle childhood and adolescence? How is gender-stereotype flexibility related to gender-typed preferences and behavior?
APPLY	Dennis is the top student in his seventh-grade cooking class. His friends Tom and Bill tease him relentlessly. Cite evidence that explains this negative reaction to Dennis's "cross-gender" behavior.
CONNECT	Describe parallels between the development of gender and ethnic attitudes (see Chapter 11, pages 460–461).

Influences on Gender Stereotyping and Gender-Role Adoption

According to social learning theorists, gender-stereotyped knowledge and behaviors are transmitted to children through direct teaching. As we will see shortly, much research is consistent with this view. Others argue, however, that biological makeup leads each sex to be uniquely suited to particular roles and that most societies do little more than encourage gender differences that are genetically based. Is there evidence to support this idea?

The Case for Biology

Although practically no contemporary theorist would argue that "biology is destiny," serious questions about biological influences on gender typing remain. According to an evolutionary perspective, the adult life of our male ancestors was largely oriented toward competing for mates, that of our female ancestors toward rearing children. Therefore, males became genetically primed for dominance and females for intimacy, responsiveness, and cooperativeness. These sex differences in behavior exist in 97 percent of mammalian species, including chimpanzees, our closest evolutionary relative (de Waal, 1993). Evolutionary theorists claim that family and cultural forces can influence the intensity of biologically based sex differences, leading some individuals to be much more gender typed than others. But experience cannot eradicate those aspects of gender typing etched into our biological makeup because these differences served adaptive functions in human history (Geary, 1999; Maccoby, 2002).

Ⓒ A Bangladeshi girl breaks bricks with her mother after the capital city, Dhaka, was ravaged by floods. Current conditions may alter the extent to which a culture promotes instrumental traits in boys and expressive traits in girls.
© RAFIQUR RAHMAN\Reuters/Corbis

Two sources of evidence have been used to support the role of biology: (1) cross-cultural similarities in gender stereotypes and gender-role adoption and (2) the influence of hormones on gender-role behavior. Let's examine each in turn.

• **HOW MUCH CROSS-CULTURAL SIMILARITY EXISTS IN GENDER TYPING?** • Earlier in this chapter, we noted that the instrumental–expressive dichotomy is reflected in the gender stereotyping of many national groups. Although this finding fits with the idea that social influences simply build on genetic differences between the sexes, we must be cautious in drawing this conclusion.

A close look at cross-cultural findings reveals that most societies promote instrumental traits in males and expressive traits in females, although great diversity exists in the magnitude of this difference (Whiting & Edwards, 1988b). For example, in Nyansongo, a small agricultural settlement in Kenya, mothers work 4 to 5 hours a day in the gardens. They assign the care of young children, the tending of the cooking fire, and the washing of dishes to older siblings. Because children of both sexes perform these duties, girls do not have total responsibility for "feminine" tasks and have more time to interact with agemates. Their greater freedom and independence lead

CULTURAL INFLUENCES

Sweden's Commitment to Gender Equality

Among all nations in the world, Sweden is unique in the value it places on gender equality. More than a century ago, Sweden's ruling political party adopted equality as a central goal. One social class was not to exploit another, nor one gender another. In the 1960s, Sweden's expanding economy attracted women into the labor force in large numbers, raising the question of who would help sustain family life. Calling on the principle of equality, the Swedish people responded: Fathers, just like mothers (Plantin, Mansson, & Kearney, 2003).

The Swedish "equal roles family model" maintains that husband and wife should have the same opportunity to pursue a career and should be equally responsible for housework and child care. To support this goal, Swedish fathers have had the right to paid parental employment leave longer than fathers in any other nation—since 1974. In addition, Sweden made child-care centers available, so toddlers and preschoolers could be cared for outside the home. Otherwise, a class of less privileged women might be exploited for caregiving and domestic work—an outcome that would contradict the principle of equality. And because full-time employment for both parents often strains a family with young children, Sweden mandated that mothers and fathers with children younger than age 8 could reduce the length of their working day to 6 hours, with a corresponding reduction in pay but not in benefits (Sandqvist, 1992).

According to several indicators, Sweden's family model is very successful. Maternal employment is extremely high; over 80 percent of mothers of infants and preschoolers are employed. Child-care centers are numerous, of high quality, and heavily subsidized by the government (Kallós & Broman, 1997). Although Swedish fathers do not yet share housework and child care equally with mothers, they are more involved than fathers in North America and in other Western European nations. Today, 70 percent of Swedish fathers take at least some parental employment leave—on average, nearly 2 months, more than fathers take in any other nation in the world (Haas, 2003).

Has Sweden's progressive family policy affected the gender beliefs and behaviors of its population? A study of Swedish and American adolescents found that valuing the "masculine" over the "feminine" role was less pronounced in Sweden than in the United States. Swedish young people regarded each gender as a blend of instrumental and expressive traits, and they more often viewed gender roles as a matter of learned tasks and domains of expertise than as inborn traits or rights and duties (Intons-Peterson, 1988). Similarly, large, nationally representative surveys in Western European countries revealed that Swedish adults held more favorable attitudes toward maternal employment. For example, more Swedish than British and Norwegian respondents agreed that "a working mother could estab-

▲ Sweden places a high value on gender equality. Compared with fathers in North America and other Western European nations, Swedish fathers are more involved in housework and child care. This father enjoys a paid paternity leave during the first 15 months of his child's life (see Chapter 3, page 113).
© Mikael Svensson/Alamy

lish just as warm and secure a relationship with her children as a mother who does not work" (Knudsen & Waerness, 2003).

Traditional gender typing has not been eradicated in Sweden. But great progress has been made as a result of steadfastly pursuing a program of gender equality for several decades.

them to score higher than girls of other tribal and village cultures in dominance, assertiveness, and playful roughhousing. In contrast, boys' caregiving responsibilities mean that they often display help-giving and emotional support (Whiting & Edwards, 1988a). Among industrialized nations, Sweden is widely recognized as a society in which traditional gender-linked beliefs and behaviors are considerably reduced (see the Cultural Influences box above).

These examples indicate that experience can profoundly influence gender typing. Nevertheless, reversals of traditional gender roles are rare (Daly & Wilson, 1988). Because cross-cultural findings are inconclusive, scientists have turned to a more direct test of the importance of biology: the impact of sex hormones on gender typing.

• SEX HORMONES AND GENDER TYPING • In Chapters 3 and 5, we discussed how genetic makeup, mediated by hormones, regulates sexual development and body growth. Sex hormones also affect brain development and neural activity in many animal species, and they do so in humans as well (Hines & Green, 1991). Are hormones, which so pervasively affect body structures, also important in gender-role adoption?

▶ *Play Styles and Preference for Same-Sex Peers.* Experiments with animals reveal that prenatally administered androgens (male sex hormones) increase active play in both male and female mammals. Androgens also promote male-typical sexual behavior and aggression and suppress maternal caregiving in a wide variety of species (Beatty, 1992).

Eleanor Maccoby (1998) argues that at least some of these hormonal effects extend to humans. Recall from the introduction to this chapter that as early as the preschool years, children seek out playmates of their own sex—a preference observed in many mammalian species and cultures (Beatty, 1992; Whiting & Edwards, 1988a). At age 4, children already spend three times as much time with same-sex as with other-sex playmates. By age 6, this ratio has climbed to 11 to 1 (Maccoby & Jacklin, 1987; Martin & Fabes, 2001). Throughout the school years, children continue to show a strong preference for same-sex peers.

Why is gender segregation so widespread and persistent? According to Maccoby, early on, hormones affect play styles, leading to rough, noisy movements among boys and to calm, gentle actions among girls. Then, as children interact with peers, they choose partners whose interests and behaviors are compatible with their own. By age 2, girls already appear overwhelmed by boys' rambunctious behavior. When a girl and a boy are paired in a laboratory play session, the girl is likely to stand idly by while the boy explores the toys (Benenson, Apostoleris, & Parnass, 1997; Maccoby & Jacklin, 1987). Nonhuman primates react similarly. When a male juvenile initiates rough, physical play, male peers join in, whereas females withdraw (Beatty, 1992).

During the preschool years, girls increasingly seek out other girls and like to play in pairs because of a common preference for quieter activities involving cooperative roles. Boys come to prefer larger-group play with other boys, who share a desire to run, climb, play-fight, compete, and build up and knock down (Fabes, Martin, & Hanish, 2003). Social pressures for "gender-appropriate" play and cognitive factors—in particular, gender stereotyping, the tendency to evaluate members of one's own sex more positively, and expectations of negative reactions from others for play with other-sex children—also contribute to gender segregation. But sex hormones are involved, a conclusion supported by studies of exceptional sexual development in humans.

◎ Sex hormones are believed to influence children's play styles—calm, gentle actions in girls and rough, noisy movements in boys. Then, preschoolers choose same-sex partners who share their interests and behavior. Social pressures for "gender-appropriate" play may also promote gender segregation.
© Ellen Sinisi/The Image Works and
© Tom Prettyman/PhotoEdit

▶ *Exceptional Sexual Development.* For ethical reasons, we cannot experimentally manipulate hormones to see how they affect human behavior. But cases exist in which hormone levels varied naturally or were modified for medical reasons.

Congenital adrenal hyperplasia (CAH) is a disorder in which a genetic defect causes the adrenal system to produce unusually high levels of androgens from the prenatal period onward. Although the physical development of boys remains unaffected, girls with CAH are usually born with masculinized external genitals. Most undergo surgical correction in infancy and receive continuous drug therapy to overcome the hormone imbalance.

Interview and observational studies support the conclusion that prenatal androgen exposure supports certain aspects of "masculine" gender-role behavior. Compared with other girls, girls with CAH tend to be higher in activity level; to like cars, trucks, and blocks better than dolls; to prefer boys as playmates; and to be more interested in "masculine" careers, such as truck driver, soldier, or pilot (Hines, 2004; Meyer-Bahlburg et al., 2004). Furthermore, when women with CAH look back on their childhoods, they recall preferring "masculine play" and feeling dissatisfied with their female identity (Hines, Brook, & Conway, 2004). The greater CAH girls' exposure to prenatal androgens, the more "masculine" their play and career interests (Hall et al., 2004; Servin et al., 2003). Even normal variation in prenatal androgen exposure is linked to gender-typed play behavior in girls (Hines, 2003).

Other research on individuals reared as members of the other sex because they had ambiguous genitals indicates that sexual identity (comfort with being male or female) usually is consistent with gender of rearing, regardless of genetic sex (Zucker, 2001). But in those cases, children's biological sex and prenatal hormone exposure (which caused the ambiguous genitals) are discrepant—circumstances that might permit successful assignment to either gender. What about children whose genetic sex and prenatal hormone exposure match but whose genitals are ambiguous as a result of injury? Refer to the Biology and Environment box on page 530 for a case study of David, a boy who experienced serious sexual-identity and adjustment problems because his biological makeup and sex of rearing were at odds.

Taken together, research indicates that sex hormones influence gender typing, with the most consistent findings involving activity level and associated preferences for "gender-appropriate" play, toys, and careers. But we must be careful not to minimize the role of experience. As we will see next, environmental forces build on genetic influences to promote children's awareness of and conformity to gender roles.

The Case for Environment

A wealth of evidence reveals that environmental factors provide powerful support for gender-role development. As we will see, adults view boys and girls differently—and treat them differently. In addition, children's social contexts—home, school, and community—offer many opportunities to observe males and females behaving in gender-stereotypical ways. And as soon as children enter the world of the peer group, their agemates promote vigorous gender typing.

• **PERCEPTIONS AND EXPECTATIONS OF ADULTS** • When adults are asked to observe neutrally dressed infants who are labeled as either boy or girl, they "see" qualities that fit with the baby's artificially assigned sex. In research of this kind, adults tend to rate infants' physical features and (to a lesser extent) their personality traits in a gender-stereotyped fashion (Stern & Karraker, 1989; Vogel et al., 1991). Boys, for example, are viewed as firmer, larger, better coordinated, and hardier, girls as softer, finer featured, more delicate, and less alert.

During childhood and adolescence, parents continue to hold different perceptions and expectations of their sons and daughters. They want their preschoolers to play with "gender-appropriate" toys and, with respect to child-rearing values, describe achievement, competition, and control of emotion as important for sons and warmth, "ladylike" behavior, and closely supervised activities as important for daughters (Brody, 1999; Turner & Gervai, 1995). Furthermore, when asked about attitudes toward "cross-gender" behavior, parents of preschoolers responded more negatively to the idea of boys than of girls crossing gender lines. And they predicted that "cross-gender" children of both sexes would grow up to be slightly less well adjusted than "typical" children (Sandnabba & Ahlberg, 1999).

David: A Boy Who Was Reared as a Girl

A married man and father in his mid-thirties, David Reimer talked freely about his interest in auto mechanics, his problems at work, and the challenges of child rearing. But when asked about his first 15 years of life, he distanced himself, speaking as if the child of his early life were another person. In essence, she was.

David—named Bruce at birth—underwent the first infant sex reassignment ever reported on a genetically and hormonally normal child. To find out about David's development, researchers interviewed him intensively and studied his medical and psychotherapy records (Diamond & Sigmundson, 1999; Colapinto, 2001).

When Bruce was 8 months old, his penis was accidentally severed during circumcision. Soon afterward, his desperate parents heard about psychologist John Money's success in assigning a sex to children born with ambiguous genitals. They traveled from their home in Canada to Johns Hopkins University in Baltimore, where, under Money's oversight, 22-month-old Bruce had surgery to remove his testicles and sculpt his genitals to look like those of a girl. The operation complete, Bruce's parents named their daughter Brenda.

Brenda's upbringing was tragic. From the outset, she resisted her parents' efforts to steer her in a "feminine" direction. Brian (Brenda's identical twin brother) recalled that Brenda looked like a delicate, pretty girl—until she moved or spoke: "She walked like a guy. Sat with her legs apart. She talked about guy things. . . . She played with my toys: TinkerToys, dump trucks" (Colapinto, 2001, p. 57). Brian was quiet and gentle in personality. Brenda, in contrast, was a dominant, rough-and-tumble child who picked fights with other children and usually won. Former teachers and classmates agreed that Brenda was the more traditionally masculine of the two children.

At school, Brenda's boyish behavior led classmates to taunt and tease her. When she played with girls, she tried organizing large-group, active games, but they weren't interested. Friendless and uncomfortable as a girl, Brenda increasingly displayed behavior problems. During periodic medical follow-ups, she drew pictures of herself as a boy and refused additional surgery to create a vagina. Reflecting on Brenda's elementary school years, David explained that she realized she was not a girl and never would be.

As adolescence approached, Brenda's parents moved her from school to school and from therapist to therapist in an effort to help her fit in socially and accept a female identity. But Brenda reacted with anxiety and insecurity, and conflict with her parents increased. At puberty, when Brenda's shoulders broadened and her body added muscle, her parents insisted that she begin estrogen therapy to feminize her appearance. Soon she grew breasts and added fat around her waist and hips. Repelled by her own feminizing shape, Brenda began overeating to hide it. Her classmates reacted to her confused appearance with stepped-up brutality.

At last, Brenda was transferred to a therapist who recognized her despair and encouraged her parents to tell her about her infancy. When Brenda was 14, her father explained the circumcision accident. David recalled reacting with relief. Deciding to return to his biological sex immediately, he chose for himself the name David, after the biblical lad who slew a giant and overcame adversity. David soon started injections of the androgen hormone testosterone to masculinize his body, and he underwent surgery to remove his breasts and to construct a penis. Although his adolescence continued to be troubled, in his twenties he fell in love with Jane, a single mother of three children, and married her.

David's case confirms the impact of genetic sex and prenatal hormones on a person's sense of self as male or female. At the same time, his childhood highlights the importance of experience. David expressed outrage at adult encouragement of dependency in girls—after all, he had experi-

▲ Because of a medical accident when he was a baby, David Reimer underwent the first sex reassignment on a genetically and hormonally normal baby: He was reared as a girl. His case shows the overwhelming impact of biology on gender identity. He is pictured here at age 36, a married man and father. Two years later, the troubled life that sprang from David's childhood ended tragically, in suicide. Courtesy of David Reimer

enced it firsthand. In adulthood, David worked in a slaughterhouse with all male employees, who were extreme in their gender stereotyping. At one point he wondered, if he had had a typical childhood, would he have become like them? He can never know the answer to that question, of course, but his case does clarify one issue: His gender reassignment failed because his male biology overwhelmingly demanded a consistent sexual identity.

Although David tried to surmount his tragic childhood, the troubled life that sprang from it persisted. When he was in his mid-thirties, his twin brother, Brian, committed suicide. Then, after David had lost his job and had been swindled out of his life savings in a shady investment deal, his wife left him, taking the children with her. Grief-stricken, David sank into a deep depression. On May 4, 2004, at age 38, he shot himself.

• **TREATMENT BY PARENTS** • Do adults actually treat children in accord with stereotypical beliefs? A combined analysis of many studies reported that on the whole, differences in the way parents socialize boys and girls are small (Lytton & Romney, 1991). This does not mean that parental treatment is unimportant: It simply indicates that if we generalize across age periods, contexts, and behaviors, we find only a few clear trends. When the evidence is examined closely, however, consistent effects emerge. Younger children receive more direct training in gender roles than older children—a finding that is not surprising, since gender typing occurs especially rapidly during early childhood (Fagot & Hagan, 1991). And wide variation from study to study suggests that some parents practice differential treatment far more intensely than others.

▶ *Infancy and Early Childhood.* In infancy and early childhood, parents encourage a diverse array of gender-specific play activities and behaviors. As early as the first few months of life— before children can express their own preferences—parents create different environments for boys and girls. Bedrooms are decorated with distinct colors and themes. Parents give their sons toys that stress action and competition (such as guns, cars, tools, and footballs), while giving their daughters toys that emphasize nurturance, cooperation, and physical attractiveness (dolls, tea sets, jump ropes, and jewelry) (Leaper, 1994).

Parents also actively reinforce independence in boys and closeness and dependency in girls. For example, parents react more positively when a son plays with cars and trucks, demands attention, runs and climbs, or tries to take toys from others. In contrast, when interacting with daughters, they more often direct play activities, provide help, encourage participation in household tasks, engage in conversation, make supportive statements (approval, praise, and agreement), and refer to emotions (Fagot & Hagan, 1991; Kuebli, Butler, & Fivush, 1995). Furthermore, mothers more often *label emotions* when talking to girls. In doing so, they seem to teach daughters to "tune in" to others' feelings. In contrast, when talking to boys, mothers more often *explain emotions*, noting causes and consequences—an approach that emphasizes why it is important to control the expression of emotion (Cervantes & Callanan, 1998; Fivush, 1989). Gender-typed play contexts amplify this differential communication. For example, when playing housekeeping, mothers engage in high rates of supportive, emotional talk with girls (Leaper, 2000).

As these findings suggest, language is a powerful *indirect* means for teaching children about gender stereotypes and gender roles. Earlier in this chapter, we saw that most young children hold rigid beliefs about gender. Although their strict views are due in part to cognitive limitations, children also draw on relevant social experiences to construct these views. Like ethnic biases discussed in Chapter 11 (see page 463), young children's gender biases often bear little resemblance to those of their parents (Tenenbaum & Leaper, 2002). But as seen in the From Research to Practice box on pages 532–533, even parents who believe strongly in gender equality—without being consciously aware of what they are doing—use language that highlights gender distinctions and informs children about traditional gender roles.

Early in development, then, parents provide a rich array of experiences—through play materials and social interaction—that encourage assertiveness, exploration, engagement with the physical world, and emotional control in boys and imitation, reliance on others, and emotional sensitivity in girls. At the same time, these experiences provide young children with a rich array of cues for constructing a view of the world that emphasizes stereotypical gender distinctions.

▶ *Middle Childhood and Adolescence.* As children's skills expand during the school years, issues of achievement become more salient to parents. Observations of mothers and fathers interacting with their youngsters in teaching situations reveal that parents continue to demand greater independence from boys. For example, when a child requests help, parents are more likely to ignore or refuse to respond to a son but to help a daughter right away. The way parents provide help to children of each sex differs, too. With sons, they usually behave in a more mastery-oriented fashion, setting higher standards and pointing out important features of the task—particularly during gender-typed activities. When researchers observed parents teaching their 11- and 13-year-olds a physics task, fathers tended to use

◎ This Laotian father helps his son with homework while siblings look on. Although the father has had only two years of schooling, he adopts a mastery orientation, pointing out specific features of the task. In teaching situations, parents often hold higher expectations for boys and encourage more complex thinking in boys than in girls.
© Jorgen Schytte/Peter Arnold, Inc.

Children Learn About Gender Through Mother-Child Conversations

In an investigation of the potential for language to shape children's beliefs and expectations about gender, mothers were asked to converse with their 2- to 6-year-olds about picture books containing images depicting male and female children and adults engaged in various activities, half of which were consistent with, and half inconsistent with, gender stereotypes. Each picture was accompanied by the question, "Who can X?" where X was the activity on the page.

One mother, who believed in gender equality, turned to a picture of a boy driving a boat and asked, "Who's driving the boat?"

Her 4-year-old son replied, "A sail-man."

The mother affirmed, "A sail-man. Yup, a sailor," and then asked, "Who can be a sailor? Boys and girls?"

"Boys," the child replied.

"Boys . . . OK," the mother again affirmed.

The child stated more decisively, "Only boys."

Again the mother agreed, "Only boys," and turned the page (Gelman, Taylor, & Nguyen, 2004, p. 104).

A detailed analysis of picture-book conversations revealed that mothers' directly expressed attitudes about gender stereotypes were neutral, largely because they typically posed questions to their children, as the mother above did about the driver of the boat. But by age 4, children often voiced stereotypes, and mothers commonly affirmed them—nearly one-third of the time! When not affirming, mothers generally either moved on with the conversation or repeated the question, as in the conversation above. They explicitly countered a child's stereotype only rarely—just 2 percent of the time—and typically only when prompted by book pages with stereotype-inconsistent pictures.

Although the researchers did not ask mothers to discuss gender, the mothers called attention to it even when they did not have to do so. In the English language, many nouns referring to people convey age-related information (*kid, baby, 2-year-old, preschooler, teenager, grownup, senior*), whereas only a few encode gender (*male, female, sister, brother, aunt, uncle*). Yet when mothers used a noun to refer to a person, more than half the time they explicitly called attention to gender, even though the people shown in the books varied as much in age (children versus adults) as in gender. Mothers labeled gender, either with nouns or with pronouns (which in English always refer to gender), especially often when conversing with 2-year-olds: "Is that a he or a she?" "That's a boy." "There's a girl." Such statements encourage toddlers to sort their social world into gender categories, even

▶ While reading, this mother may unknowingly teach her child to view the world in gender-linked terms—by referring to gender when she does not need to and by making generic gender statements, such as "Most girls prefer X" or "Boys usually don't like X."

© Tony Freeman/PhotoEdit

more cognitively demanding speech—explanations, high-level questions, and scientific vocabulary—with sons than with daughters (Tenenbaum & Leaper, 2003). And while their child explored interactive science exhibits at a children's museum, both mothers and fathers offered many more scientific explanations to boys than to girls (see Figure 13.7 on page 534) (Crowley et al., 2001).

Consistent with their interaction patterns, parents hold gender-differentiated perceptions of and expectations for children's competencies in various school subjects. In longitudinal research on sixth graders, Janis Jacobs and Jacqueline Eccles (1992) found that mothers rated sons as more competent than daughters at math, regardless of their child's actual performance. Mothers' gender-typed judgments, in turn, influenced children's self-perceptions of math ability, the effort children devoted to math, and their later math performance (Eccles et al., 2000). When the participants were followed up two years after high school graduation and again at age 24 to 25, mothers' early perceptions no longer predicted sons' outcomes. But they continued to predict daughters' self-perceptions and also their career choices. Young women whose mothers had regarded them as highly capable at math were far more likely to choose a physical science career (Bleeker & Jacobs, 2004). Yet mothers rarely made such optimistic

Mothers' and children's use of generic references to gender during storybook conversations. Generic utterances were broad in scope, in that they referred to many, or nearly all, males and females. Therefore, they encouraged children to view individuals of the same gender as alike and to ignore individual differences. Mothers' and children's use of generics increased dramatically between ages 2 and 6. At age 2, mothers produced more generics than children. By age 6, children produced more generics than mothers. (From S. A. Gelman, M. G. Taylor, & S. P. Nguyen, 2004, "Mother–Child Conversations About Gender," *Monographs of the Society for Research in Child Development, 69*(1, Serial No. 275), p. 46. © The Society for Research in Child Development, Inc. Adapted by permission.)

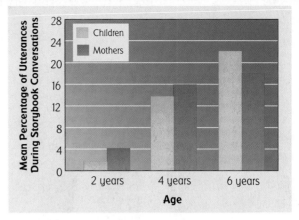

when the statements themselves do not explicitly convey stereotypes.

Furthermore, both mothers and children frequently expressed *generic utterances*—ones that were broad in scope in that they referred to many, or nearly all, males and females, such as "Boys can be sailors." "Most girls don't like trucks." Even when generics were gender-neutral ("Lots of girls in this book") or denied a stereotype ("Boys can be ballet dancers, too."), they prompted children to view individuals of the same gender as alike and to ignore exceptions. Other research indicates that generics promote gender-role conformity. Later in this chapter, we will see that statements such as "This toy is for girls" induce children to prefer the toy labeled for their own sex and to avoid the toy labeled for the other sex.

As Figure 13.6 shows, mothers' and children's use of generics increased sharply between ages 2 and 6, a period in which gender stereotyping and gender-role conformity rise dramatically. Initially, the mothers led the way in generic talk; at age 2, they introduced these category-wide generalizations nearly three times as often as children. By age 6, however, children were producing generics more often than mothers. In addition, mother–child pairs produced more generics about males than about females, and generics were especially common in speech to and from boys, who are the more gender typed of the two sexes.

As these findings reveal, without directly teaching stereotypes, parents—through language—provide a wealth of implicit cues about them that enable children to readily construct them. Even though the mothers in the study overwhelmingly believed in gender equality, they did little to instill those ideas in their children. On the contrary, their most common response to their children's stereotypical comments was to affirm them! Concerted efforts to avoid gendered language might be a powerful means of combating stereotypical thinking in children. Adults can

- refrain from labeling gender when it is unnecessary to do so, by using *child, friend, adult,* or *person* instead of *boy, girl, man,* or *woman.*

- avoid using generic expressions, by substituting references to individuals ("That person wants to be a firefighter") or by using qualifiers ("Some boys and some girls want to be firefighters").

- monitor their own inclination to affirm children's stereotypical claims, countering these as often as possible.

- discuss gender biases in language with children, pointing out how words can shape inappropriate beliefs and expectations and asking children to avoid the use of gender labels and generics in their own conversations.

judgments, with long-term negative implications for girls' achievement. Indeed, women's progress in entering such fields as engineering, mathematics, and physics has been slow. In the United States, only 11 percent of engineers and 10 percent of physicists are women. Women's representation is somewhat better in Canada, at 23 and 30 percent (Statistics Canada, 2003d; U.S. Census Bureau, 2004b).

Parents' differential treatment of boys and girls extends to the freedom granted children in their everyday lives. Parents use more directive speech (imperatives and specific suggestions) with girls than with boys (Leaper, Anderson, & Sanders, 1998). Furthermore, when insisting that children meet their daily responsibilities, mothers of sons more often pair control with autonomy granting. That is, they tend to ask boys to make decisions ("When do you think would be a good time for you to do your music practice?"), whereas for girls, they tend to decide ("Do your practicing right after dinner") (Pomerantz & Ruble, 1998b). Although school-age children interpret parental control without autonomy granting as well-intentioned guidance, they also say it makes them feel incompetent (Pomerantz & Ruble, 1998a).

Other signs of boys' greater freedom are evident in parental willingness to let them range farther from home without supervision and in assignment of chores. In many cultures, girls

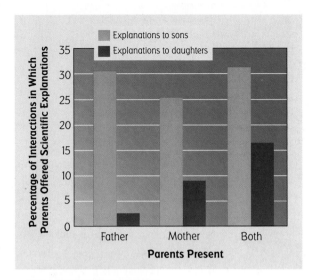

▲ Figure 13.7

Parents' scientific explanations while their son or daughter explored interactive science exhibits at a children's museum. Regardless of whether the father, the mother, or both parents were present, parents offered many more explanations to sons than to daughters.

(From K. Crowley, M. A. Callanan, H. R. Tenenbaum, & E. Allen, 2001, "Parents Explain More Often to Boys Than to Girls During Shared Scientific Thinking," *Psychological Science, 12,* p. 260. © Copyright American Psychological Society. Reprinted by permission.)

are given tasks such as food preparation, cleaning, and baby-sitting that keep them close to home, whereas boys are given responsibilities that take them into the surrounding world, such as yard work and errands (Whiting & Edwards, 1988a). As noted earlier, when cultural circumstances require children to perform "cross-gender" chores (as in Nyansongo), the range of behaviors practiced expands.

Do these findings suggest that children in Western cultures should be assigned more "cross-gender" tasks? The consequences of doing so are not straightforward. Research shows that when fathers hold stereotypical views yet their sons engage in "feminine" housework, boys experience strain in the father–child relationship, feel stressed by their responsibilities, and judge themselves as less competent (McHale et al., 1990).

In contrast, a match between parental values and nontraditional child-rearing practices leads to benefits for children. In one study, 6-year-olds growing up in countercultural families that were committed to gender equality were compared with agemates living in conventional homes or experiencing other countercultural alternatives, such as communes emphasizing spiritual and pronature values. Children in gender-countercultural homes were less likely to classify objects and occupations in stereotypical ways, and girls more often aspired to nontraditional careers (Weisner & Wilson-Mitchell, 1990). Other research indicates that in nontraditional homes where fathers devote as much or more time to child care as mothers, children tend to be less gender-typed in emotional expression—sons more emotionally sensitive, daughters more self-confident (Brody, 1997).

▶ *Mothers versus Fathers.* In most aspects of differential treatment of boys and girls, fathers discriminate the most. For example, in Chapter 10 we saw that fathers tend to engage in more physically stimulating play with their infant sons than daughters, whereas mothers tend to play in a quieter way with babies of both sexes. In childhood, fathers more than mothers encourage "gender-appropriate" behavior, and they place more pressure to achieve on sons than on daughters (Gervai, Turner, & Hinde, 1995; Wood, Desmarais, & Gugula, 2002).

Parents also seem especially committed to ensuring the gender typing of children of their own sex. While mothers go on shopping trips and bake cookies with their daughters, fathers play catch, help coach the Saturday morning soccer game, and go fishing with their sons. Parents not only spend more time with children of their own sex but also are more vigilant about monitoring the activities of same-sex children while the children are away from home (Leaper, 2002; Tucker, McHale, & Crouter, 2003). This pattern of greater involvement with same-sex children is another aspect of gender-role training that is more pronounced for fathers (Parke, 1996).

• TREATMENT BY TEACHERS • In some ways, preschool and elementary school teachers reinforce children of both sexes for "feminine" rather than "masculine" behavior. In classrooms, men and women teachers alike usually value obedience and discourage assertiveness (Fagot, 1985a). This "feminine bias" is believed to promote discomfort for boys in school, but it may be as harmful, or even more so, for girls, who willingly conform, with possible long-term negative consequences for their sense of independence and self-esteem.

Teachers also act in ways that maintain and even extend gender roles taught at home. They often emphasize gender distinctions, as when they say, "Will the girls line up on one side and the boys on the other?" or "Boys, I wish you'd quiet down like the girls!"—labeling that promotes gender stereotyping, in-group favoritism, and out-group prejudice in children (Bigler, 1995). At the same time, teachers interrupt girls more than boys during conversation, thereby promoting boys' social dominance and girls' passivity. By age 4, children respond in kind: Boys interrupt their female teachers more than girls do (Hendrick & Stange, 1991).

At older ages, teachers praise boys for their knowledge, girls for their obedience. And although they discourage unruliness in all children, teachers do so more frequently and forcefully with boys. When girls misbehave, teachers are more likely to negotiate, coming up with a joint plan to improve their conduct (Erden & Wolfgang, 2004). Teachers' more frequent use of disapproval and controlling discipline with boys seems to result from an expectation that boys will misbehave more often than girls—a belief based partly on boys' actual behavior and partly on gender stereotypes. When teachers reprimand girls, it is usually for giving a wrong answer (Good & Brophy, 2003).

Just as teachers can promote gender typing, they can counteract it by modifying the way they communicate with children. For example, when teachers introduce new materials in a non-gender-biased fashion, praise all students for independence and persistence, and ignore attention seeking and dependency, children's activity choices and behaviors change accordingly (Serbin, Connor, & Citron, 1978; Serbin, Connor, & Iler, 1979). But most of the time, such changes are short lived. As soon as the usual interaction patterns resume

in the classroom, children return to their former ways of responding. Like nontraditional families, schools that are successful in modifying gender typing have clearly articulated philosophies about gender equality that pervade all aspects of classroom life (Gash & Morgan, 1993).

◉ Teachers may reinforce gender roles learned at home—for example, by praising boys for their knowledge and girls for their obedience.
© Michael Newman/PhotoEdit

• **OBSERVATIONAL LEARNING** • In addition to direct pressures from adults, numerous gender-typed models are available in children's environments. Despite societal changes, children continue to encounter many real people who conform to traditional gender roles. In schools, for example, women are more likely to be teachers, especially in the early grades, whereas men more often hold administrative positions. In their communities, too, children more often see male police officers and female nurses than the reverse.

Reflections of gender in the media are also stereotyped. As we will see in Chapter 15, portrayal of gender roles in television programs has changed very little in recent years. And gender stereotypes are rampant in video games (Calvert et al., 2003; Dietz, 1998). In addition, despite an increase in gender-equitable storybooks and textbooks, many children read older titles in which males are main characters, take center stage in exciting plot activities, and display assertiveness and creativity, while females are submissive, dependent, and passive (Tepper & Cassidy, 1999; Turner-Bowker, 1996).

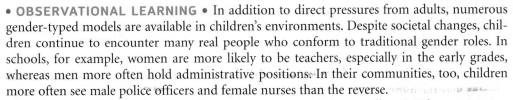

When children are exposed to nonstereotyped models, they are less traditional in their beliefs and behaviors. Children who often see their parents cross traditional gender lines—mothers who are employed or who engage in "masculine" household tasks (repairing appliances, washing the car), fathers who engage in "feminine" household tasks (ironing, cooking, child care)—less often endorse gender stereotypes (Turner & Gervai, 1995; Updegraff, McHale, & Crouter, 1996). Girls with career-oriented mothers show special benefits. They are more likely to engage in typically masculine activities (such as physically active play), have higher educational aspirations, and hold nontraditional career goals (Hoffman, 2000).

Furthermore, among children of divorced parents, boys in father-absent homes and girls in mother-absent homes are less gender typed, perhaps because they have fewer opportunities to observe traditional gender roles than in a two-parent household (Brenes, Eisenberg, & Helmstadter, 1985; Williams, Radin, & Allegro, 1992). And compared with agemates in two-parent families, children from single-parent homes are more likely to have at least one other-sex friend (Kovacs, Parker, & Hoffman, 1996).

• **PEERS** • The extent to which children associate almost exclusively with peers of their own sex makes the peer context an especially potent source of gender-role learning. In a study in which researchers followed preschoolers and kindergartners over the school year, children who spent more time playing with same-sex partners in the fall showed greater gains in gender typing—in terms of toy choices, activity level, aggression, and extent of play near adults—in the spring (Martin & Fabes, 2001).

▶ *Gender-Role Learning in Gender-Segregated Peer Groups.* By age 3, same-sex peers positively reinforce one another for "gender-appropriate" play by praising, imitating, or joining in. In contrast, when preschoolers engage in "cross-gender" activities—for example, when boys play with dolls or girls with cars and trucks—peers criticize them. Boys are especially intolerant of "cross-gender" play in their male companions (Fagot, 1984). A boy who frequently crosses gender lines is likely to be ignored by other boys, even when he does engage in "masculine" activities!

Children also develop different styles of social influence in gender-segregated peer groups. To get their way in large-group play, boys often rely on commands, threats, and physical force. Girls' preference for playing in pairs leads to greater concern with a partner's needs, evident in girls' use of polite requests, persuasion, and acceptance. Girls soon find that these gentle tactics succeed with other girls but not with boys, who ignore their courteous overtures (Leaper, 1994; Leaper, Tenenbaum, & Shaffer, 1999). Consequently, an additional reason that girls may stop interacting with boys is that they do not find it very rewarding to communicate with an unresponsive social partner.

Over time, children form beliefs about the acceptability of gender-segregated play, and those beliefs strengthen gender segregation and the stereotyped activities associated with it. In one study, 3- to 6-year-olds believed that peers would be more likely to approve of their behavior when they played with same-sex agemates—a conviction that predicted children's association with same-sex peers (Martin et al., 1999). As boys and girls separate, in-group favoritism becomes another factor that sustains the separate social worlds of boys and girls, resulting in "two distinct subcultures" of shared knowledge, beliefs, interests, and behaviors (Maccoby, 2002).

Some educators believe that forming mixed-sex activity groups in classroom and recreational settings is a vital means for reducing gender stereotyping and broadening developmental possibilities for both sexes. To be successful, however, interventions may have to modify the styles of social influence typically learned in same-sex peer relations. Otherwise, boys are likely to dominate and girls to react passively, thereby strengthening traditional gender roles and the stereotypes each sex holds of the other.

The majority of North American children and adolescents regard excluding an agemate from a peer-group activity (such as a music club) on the basis of the individual's gender as unfair. But between fourth and seventh grade, more young people—especially boys—say it is OK to exclude on the basis of gender than on ethnicity (see Figure 13.8). When asked to explain, they point to concerns about group functioning that often are based on sex differences in interests and communication styles. As two 14-year-olds noted, "But boys, they talk about stuff, that you know, girls just don't like." "They [boys and girls] probably wouldn't relate on very many things" (Killen et al., 2002, p. 56).

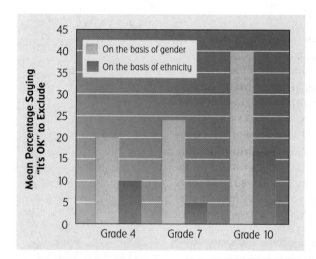

▲ Figure 13.8

Percentage of children and adolescents saying "It's OK" to exclude an agemate from a peer-group activity on the basis of gender and ethnicity. When asked about excluding an other-sex or other-ethnicity peer from a peer-group activity (a music club in which members trade CDs), many more young people said that it is OK to do so on the basis of gender than on the basis of ethnicity. Willingness to exclude on the basis of gender increased with age, with many participants justifying their decision by pointing to sex differences in interests and communication styles. (Adapted from Killen et al., 2002.)

▶ *Cultural Variations.* Although gender segregation is pervasive, cultures and subcultures differ in the extent of gender-typed communication within those groups. African-American and Hispanic-American lower-SES girls, for example, are generally more assertive and independent in their interactions with one another and with boys than are Caucasian-American girls (Goodwin, 1998). A comparison of Chinese and American preschoolers' play revealed similar differences. Chinese 5-year-old girls, for example, used more direct commands, complaints, and critical statements when interacting with both same- and other-sex peers than their American counterparts did. And Chinese boys frequently combined commands with warning, appeasing, and justifying statements, which reduced dominance relations in boys' playgroups ("Better not open that. You'll spill it." "I'll do it. I'm here to help you !") (Kyratzis & Guo, 2001).

In collectivist societies where group cohesion is highly valued, children may not feel a need to work as hard at maintaining same-sex peer relations through traditional interaction patterns. In addition to reducing children's ethnic prejudices (see Chapter 11), ethnically integrated classrooms might reduce gender-typed peer communication as the "cross-gender" influence attempts of some children "rub off" on others.

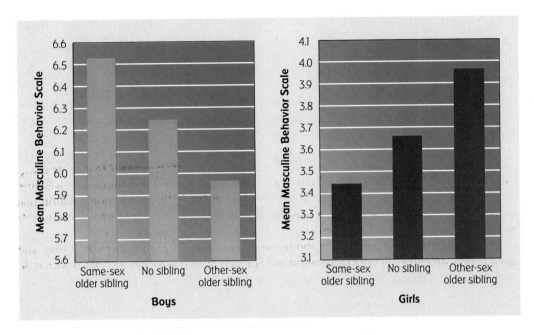

◀ **Figure 13.9**

"Masculine" behavior scores for preschool boys and girls with same-sex older siblings, other-sex older siblings, and no siblings. In this British study in which mothers reported on the play and other behaviors of their 3-year-olds, children with same-sex older siblings were more gender typed than children with no siblings, who were more gender typed than children with other-sex older siblings. Notice how boys with the lowest masculine behavior scores have older sisters, whereas girls with the highest masculine behavior scores have older brothers. (Adapted from Rust et al., 2000.)

• **SIBLINGS** • Growing up with siblings of the same or the other sex also affects gender typing. But compared with peer influences, sibling effects are more complex because their impact depends on birth order and family size (McHale, Crouter, & Whiteman, 2003).

Whereas younger siblings have little impact on older siblings' gender typing, older siblings serve as powerful models for younger siblings. In a British study, more than 5,000 mothers provided information on the play and other behaviors of their 3-year-old children, each of whom had either one older sibling or no siblings. As Figure 13.9 shows, children with same-sex siblings were more gender typed than children with no siblings, who in turn were more gender typed than children with other-sex older siblings (Rust et al., 2000). Older siblings' influence expands during the school years, affecting younger siblings' sex-stereotyped attitudes, personality traits, and leisure pursuits (McHale et al., 2001).

Curiously, however, other research contradicts these findings, indicating that children with same-sex siblings are less stereotyped in their interests and personality traits than those from mixed-sex families (Grotevant, 1978; Tauber, 1979). How can these conflicting results be explained? Recall from Chapter 10 that siblings often strive to be different from one another. This effect is strongest when children are of the same sex and come from large families, in which they may feel a greater need to stand out. A close look reveals that studies reporting a *modeling and reinforcement effect* (an increase in gender typing among same-sex siblings) focus on children from two-child families. In contrast, those reporting a *differentiation effect* often include children from larger families.

In addition, parents may sometimes relax pressures toward gender typing when their children are all of the same sex. Consistent with this idea, mothers are more willing to give their child a gender-atypical toy as a gift if the child has an older, same-sex sibling (Stoneman, Brody, & MacKinnon, 1986). Also, in all-girl and all-boy families, children are more likely to be assigned "cross-gender" chores because no "gender-appropriate" child is available to do the job. Therefore, families in which siblings are all of the same sex may provide some special opportunities to step out of traditional gender roles.

In sum, older siblings are influential models in the gender typing of young siblings. But aspects of the family context, including family size and parental pressures, can alter this modeling effect.

◎ When siblings are the same sex, they are more likely to be assigned "cross-gender" chores. These sisters help by carrying out the recycling bin—a responsibility typically reserved for boys.
© David Young-Wolff/PhotoEdit

Ask Yourself

REVIEW	Summarize parent, peer, and sibling influences on gender-role adoption. Why are sibling influences more complex than parent and peer influences?
APPLY	List findings indicating that language and communication—between parents and children, between teachers and children, and between peers—powerfully affect children's gender stereotyping and gender-role learning. What recommendations would you make to counteract these influences?.
CONNECT	Girls are more susceptible than boys to learned helplessness in achievement situations. Explain why this is so, using research in this chapter (see pages 531–533) and in Chapter 11 (see page 454).
REFLECT	Think back to your peer associations in early and middle childhood. Did you play primarily with peers of your own sex? What gender-linked attitudes and behaviors were emphasized in your peer associations? How did you view members of the other sex?

Gender Identity

Besides biological and environmental influences, another factor eventually affects gender stereotyping and gender-role behavior: *gender identity*, a person's perception of the self as relatively masculine or feminine in characteristics. In middle childhood, researchers can measure gender identity by asking children to rate themselves on personality traits because at that time, self-concepts start to emphasize psychological dispositions over concrete behaviors (see Chapter 11). A child or adult with a "masculine" identity scores high on traditionally masculine items (such as *ambitious, competitive,* and *self-sufficient*) and low on traditionally feminine items (such as *affectionate, cheerful,* and *soft-spoken*). Someone with a "feminine" identity does just the reverse. Although most people view themselves in gender-typed terms, a substantial minority (especially females) have a gender identity called **androgyny**, scoring high on *both* masculine and feminine personality characteristics.

Gender identity is a good predictor of psychological adjustment. "Masculine" and androgynous children and adults have a higher sense of self-esteem, whereas feminine individuals often think poorly of themselves (Alpert-Gillis & Connell, 1989; Boldizar, 1991). In line with their flexible self-definitions, androgynous individuals are more adaptable—for example, able to show masculine independence or feminine sensitivity, depending on the situation (Taylor & Hall, 1982). They also show greater maturity of moral judgment than individuals with other gender-role orientations (Bem, 1977).

A close look at these findings, however, reveals that the masculine component of androgyny is largely responsible for the superior psychological health of androgynous women over those with traditional identities (Taylor & Hall, 1982; Whitley, 1983). Feminine women seem to have adjustment difficulties because many of their attributes are not valued highly by society. Nevertheless, the existence of an androgynous identity demonstrates that children can acquire a mixture of positive qualities traditionally associated with each gender—an orientation that may best help them realize their potential. In a future society in which feminine traits are socially rewarded to the same extent as masculine traits, androgyny may very well represent the ideal personality.

Emergence of Gender Identity

How do children develop a gender identity? According to *social learning theory*, behavior comes before self-perceptions. Preschoolers first acquire gender-typed responses through modeling and reinforcement; only later do they organize these behaviors into gender-linked ideas about themselves. In contrast, *cognitive-developmental theory* maintains that self-perceptions come before behavior. Over the preschool years, children acquire a cognitive appreciation of the permanence of their sex. They develop **gender constancy**—a full understanding of the biologically based permanence of their gender, which combines three understandings: gender labeling, gender stability, and gender consistency. Then they use this knowledge to guide their behavior. Let's trace the development of gender constancy during the preschool years.

• **DEVELOPMENT OF GENDER CONSTANCY** • Lawrence Kohlberg (1966) proposed that before age 6 or 7, children cannot maintain the constancy of their gender, just as they cannot pass Piagetian conservation problems. They attain this understanding only gradually, by moving through the following stages of development:

1. **Gender labeling.** During the early preschool years, children can label their own sex and that of others correctly. But when asked such questions as "When you [a girl] grow up, could you ever be a daddy?" or "Could you be a boy if you wanted to?" young children freely answer yes (Slaby & Frey, 1975). In addition, when shown a doll whose hairstyle and clothing are transformed before their eyes, children indicate that the doll's sex is no longer the same (McConaghy, 1979).

2. **Gender stability.** At this stage, children have a partial understanding of the permanence of sex, in that they grasp its stability over time. But even though they know that male and female babies will eventually become boys and girls, and then men and women, they continue to insist that changing hairstyle, clothing, or "gender-appropriate" activities will change a person's sex as well (Fagot, 1985b; Slaby & Frey, 1975).

3. **Gender consistency.** During the late preschool and early school years, children understand that sex is biologically based and remains the same even if a person decides to dress in "cross-gender" clothes or engage in nontraditional activities (Emmerich, 1981; McConaghy, 1979).

Many studies confirm that the development of gender constancy follows this sequence. As Kohlberg assumed, mastery of gender constancy is associated with attainment of conservation (De Lisi & Gallagher, 1991). It is also strongly related to the ability to distinguish appearance from reality—to appreciate that an object can look one way (like a crayon) but really be something else (a candle) (see page 240 in Chapter 6). Indeed, gender consistency tasks can be considered a type of appearance–reality problem, in that children must distinguish what a person looks like from who he or she really is (Trautner, Gervai, & Nemeth, 2003).

In many cultures, young children do not have access to basic biological knowledge about gender because they rarely see members of the other sex naked. Therefore, they distinguish males and females using the only information they do have: hairstyle, clothing, and behavior. Still, providing preschoolers with information about genital differences does not result in gender constancy. Preschoolers who have such knowledge usually say that changing their clothing or hairstyle will not change their sex, but when asked to justify their responses, they do not refer to sex as an innate and unchanging quality of people (Szkrybalo & Ruble, 1999). This suggests that cognitive immaturity, not social experience, is largely responsible for young children's difficulty grasping the permanence of sex.

• **HOW WELL DOES GENDER CONSTANCY PREDICT GENDER-ROLE ADOPTION?** • Is cognitive-developmental theory correct that gender constancy is responsible for children's gender-typed behavior? Perhaps you have already concluded that evidence for this assumption is weak. "Gender-appropriate" behavior appears so early in the preschool years that modeling and reinforcement must contribute to its initial appearance, as social learning theory suggests.

Although gender constancy does not initiate gender-role conformity, the cognitive changes that lead up to it do seem to facilitate gender typing. Preschoolers who reach the stage of gender labeling early show especially rapid development of "gender-appropriate" play preferences and are more knowledgeable about gender stereotypes than their late-labeling peers (Fagot, Leinbach, & O'Boyle, 1992). Similarly, understanding of gender stability is related to gender stereotyping, preference for same-sex playmates, and choice of "gender-appropriate" toys (Martin & Little, 1990). These findings suggest that as soon as children form basic gender categories, they use them to acquire gender-relevant information and to modify their own behavior.

At present, researchers are not sure how full development of gender constancy contributes to gender typing. One speculation is that reaching the stage of gender consistency strengthens children's gender-role conformity in the late preschool and early school years (Martin & Ruble, 2004). But research indicates that overall, the impact of gender consistency on gender typing is not great. As we will see next, gender-role adoption is more powerfully affected by children's beliefs about how tight the connection must be between their own gender and their behavior.

© This 4-year-old girl of rural Azerbaijan in southwestern Asia, who wears a colorful headscarf that is part of her culture's traditional feminine dress, draws a picture in her child-care center. Because most children her age have not yet attained gender consistency (the understanding that sex is biologically based and permanent), were a boy to put on a head scarf, she might insist that his changed appearance indicates that he has actually become a girl.
SHEZAD NOORANI/Peter Arnold, Inc.

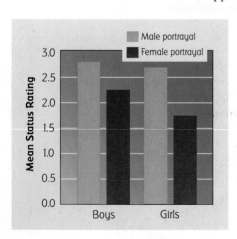

© During middle childhood, girls feel freer than boys to engage in "cross-gender" activities. This 10-year-old girl participates in a fishing derby with her father.
© Syracuse Newspapers/John Berry/The Image Works

Gender Identity in Middle Childhood

During middle childhood, boys' and girls' gender identities follow different paths. Self-ratings on personality traits reveal that from third to sixth grade, boys strengthen their identification with the "masculine" role, while girls' identification with "feminine" characteristics declines. Although girls still lean toward the "feminine" side, they are the more androgynous of the sexes—more likely than boys to describe themselves as having "other-gender" characteristics (Serbin, Powlishta, & Gulko, 1993). This difference is also evident in children's activities. Whereas boys usually stick to "masculine" pursuits, girls experiment with a wider range of options. Besides cooking, sewing, and baby-sitting, they join organized sports teams, work on science projects, and build forts in the backyard. And more often than boys, girls consider taking on work roles stereotyped for the other gender, such as firefighter and astronomer (Liben & Bigler, 2002).

These changes are due to a mixture of cognitive and social forces. School-age children of both sexes are aware that society attaches greater prestige to "masculine" characteristics. For example, they rate "masculine" occupations as having higher status than "feminine" occupations. And by age 11, they regard a novel job (such as *clipster*, "a person who tests batteries") portrayed with a male worker as having higher status than the identical job portrayed a with female worker (see Figure 13.10) (Liben, Bigler, & Krogh, 2001). In view of the strong association of males' activities with high status, it is not surprising that girls start to identify with "masculine" traits and are attracted to some typically masculine activities.

Messages from adults and agemates are also influential. Parents (especially fathers) are far less tolerant when sons, as opposed to daughters, cross gender lines. Similarly, a tomboyish girl can make her way into boys' activities without losing the approval of her female peers, but a boy who hangs out with girls is likely to be ridiculed and rejected.

As school-age children make social comparisons and characterize themselves in terms of stable dispositions, their gender identity expands to include the following self-evaluations, which have crucial implications for children's adjustment:

- *gender typicality*—the degree to which the child feels similar to others of the same gender, based on his or her own personal evaluation. Children can feel gender-typical for different reasons. For example, one boy might derive this feeling from excelling at math, another from being a good athlete. Although children need not be highly gender typed to judge themselves as gender-typical, psychological well-being depends on feeling—at least to some degree—that they "fit in" with their same-sex peers (Egan & Perry, 2001).

- *gender contentedness*—the degree to which the child feels satisfied with his or her gender assignment. Like gender typicality, gender contentedness promotes happiness and satisfaction with oneself.

- *felt pressure to conform to gender roles*—the degree to which the child feels parents and peers disapprove of his or her gender-related traits. Because such pressure reduces the likelihood that children will explore options related to their interests and talents, children who feel strong gender-typed pressures are likely to be distressed and dissatisfied.

In a longitudinal study of third through seventh graders, *gender-typical* and *gender-contented* children gained in self-esteem over the following year. In contrast, children who were *gender-atypical* and *gender-discontented* declined in self-worth. Furthermore, gender-atypical children who reported *intense pressure to conform to gender roles* experienced serious difficulties, in the form of

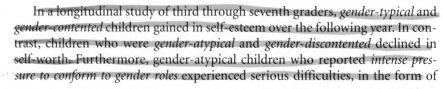

◀ **Figure 13.10**

Eleven-year-olds' status ratings of novel jobs portrayed with male and female workers. Although children had no prior knowledge of these jobs and therefore had not previously stereotyped them as "masculine" or "feminine," simply portraying the job with a male worker resulted in higher status ratings. (Adapted from Liben, Bigler, & Krogh, 2001.)

withdrawal, sadness, disappointment, and anxiety (Yunger, Carver, & Perry, 2004). Clearly, how children feel about themselves in relation to their gender group becomes vitally important in middle childhood, and those who experience rejection because of their gender-atypical traits suffer profoundly. (Return to the Biology and Environment box on page 530, and note how David's dissatisfaction with his gender assignment joined with vicious peer condemnation to severely impair his adjustment.)

© Early adolescence is a period of gender intensification. Puberty magnifies gender differences in appearance, causing teenagers to think about themselves in gender-linked ways. © Spencer Grant/PhotoEdit

Gender Identity in Adolescence

The arrival of adolescence is typically accompanied by **gender intensification**—increased gender stereotyping of attitudes and behavior, and movement toward a more traditional gender identity (Basow & Rubin, 1999; Galambos, Almeida, & Petersen, 1990). Although gender intensification occurs in both sexes, it is stronger for early-adolescent girls, who were more androgynous during middle childhood. Overall, girls continue to be less gender typed than boys, but they now feel less free to experiment with "other-gender" activities and behaviors than they did earlier (Huston & Alvarez, 1990).

What accounts for gender intensification? Biological, social, and cognitive factors are involved. Puberty magnifies sex differences in appearance, causing adolescents to spend more time thinking about themselves in gender-linked ways. Pubertal changes also prompt gender-typed pressures from others. Parents—especially those with traditional gender-role beliefs—may encourage "gender-appropriate" activities and behavior to a greater extent than they did in middle childhood (Crouter, Manke, & McHale, 1995). And when adolescents start to date, they often become more gender typed as a way of increasing their attractiveness (Maccoby, 1998). For example, in encounters with boys, girls frequently use disclaimers, such as "I may be wrong" and "sort of"—a tentative speech style their male partners prefer (Carli, 1995). Finally, cognitive changes—in particular, greater concern with what others think—make young teenagers more responsive to gender-role expectations.

As young people move toward a mature personal identity, they become less concerned with others' opinions of them and more involved in finding meaningful values to include in their self-definitions (see Chapter 11). As a result, highly stereotypical self-perceptions decline, especially when parents and teachers encourage adolescents to question the value of gender stereotypes for themselves and their society. Thus, the social environment is a major force in promoting gender-role flexibility in adolescence, just as it was at earlier ages.

Gender Schema Theory

Currently, researchers recognize that children's gender identities arise from their experiences, as social learning theory assumes. Then, in line with cognitive-developmental theory, these self-perceptions guide behavior. **Gender schema theory** is an information-processing approach to gender typing that combines social learning and cognitive-developmental features. It also integrates the various elements of gender typing—gender stereotyping, gender identity, and gender-role adoption—into a unified picture of how masculine and feminine orientations emerge and are often strongly maintained (Martin, Ruble, & Szkrybalo, 2002; Martin & Halverson, 1987).

At an early age, children pick up gender-typed preferences and behaviors from others. At the same time, they organize their experiences into *gender schemas,* or masculine and feminine categories, that they use to interpret their world. A young child who says, "Only boys can be doctors" or "Cooking is a girl's job" already has some well-formed gender schemas. As soon as preschoolers can label their own gender, they select gender schemas consistent with it and apply those categories to themselves. Their self-perceptions then become gender typed and serve as additional gender schemas that children use to process information and guide their own behavior.

We have seen that some children endorse gender-typed views more strongly than others, so individual differences exist in the extent to which children build networks of gender

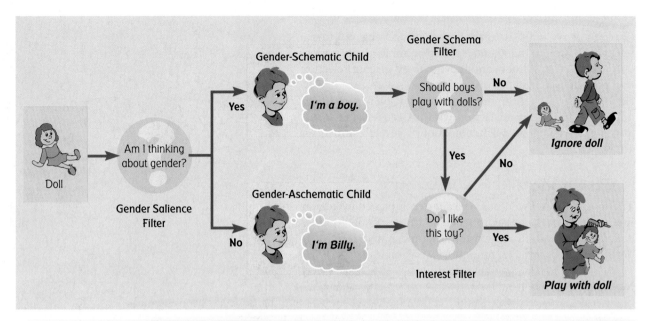

▲ **Figure 13.11**

Cognitive pathways for gender-schematic and gender-aschematic children. In *gender-schematic children,* the gender-salience filter immediately makes gender highly relevant: Billy sees a doll and thinks, "I'm a boy. Should boys play with dolls?" Drawing on his experiences, he answers "yes" or "no." If he answers "yes" and the doll interests him, he plays with the doll. If he answers "no," he avoids the "gender-inappropriate" toy. *Gender-aschematic children* rarely view the world in gender-linked terms: Billy simply asks, "Do I like this toy?" and responds on the basis of his interests. (Reprinted by permission of Rebecca Bigler, University of Texas, Austin.)

schemas like the ones just described. Figure 13.11 shows different cognitive pathways for children who often apply gender schemas to their experiences and children who rarely do (Liben & Bigler, 2002). Consider Billy, who encounters a doll. If Billy is a *gender-schematic child,* his *gender-salience filter* immediately makes gender highly relevant. Then, drawing on his prior learning, he asks himself, "Should boys play with dolls?" If he answers "yes" and the toy interests him, he will approach it, explore it, and learn more about it. If he answers "no," he will respond by avoiding the "gender-inappropriate" toy. Alternatively, suppose Billy is a *gender-aschematic child* who seldom views the world in gender-linked terms. On encountering the doll, he simply asks himself, "Do I like this toy?" and responds on the basis of his interests.

To examine the consequences of gender-schematic processing, researchers showed 4- and 5-year-olds toys that were "gender-neutral" and that varied in attractiveness. An adult labeled some as boys' toys and others as girls' toys and left a third group unlabeled. Most children engaged in gender-schematic reasoning, preferring toys labeled for their gender and predicting that same-sex peers would also like those toys. Highly attractive toys, especially, lost their appeal when they were labeled as for the other gender (Martin, Eisenbud, & Rose, 1995). Indeed, because gender-schematic preschoolers typically conclude, "What I like, children of my own sex will also like," they often use their own preferences to add to their gender biases! For example, a girl who dislikes oysters may declare, "Only boys like oysters!" even though she has never actually been exposed to information related to such a stereotype (Liben & Bigler, 2002).

Gender-schematic thinking is so powerful that when children see others behaving in "gender-inconsistent" ways, they often cannot remember the behavior or distort their memory to make it "gender consistent"—for example, when shown a picture of a male nurse, remember him as a doctor (Liben & Signorella, 1993). Over time, children increase their knowledge of people, objects, and events that fit with their gender schemas, and they learn much less about "cross-gender" activities and behaviors.

Researchers are experimenting with ways to reduce children's tendency to view the world in gender-schematic terms. Training children in cognitive skills that counteract gender-biased social messages has produced some impressive results. When researchers taught 5- to 10-year-

◉ Would these children continue playing if an adult labeled cards as a boys' game or a girls' game? Powerful gender schemas lead children to like a toy or game less if they believe it is for the other gender. © Image Source/Alamy

MILESTONES

GENDER TYPING

Age	Gender Stereotyping and Gender-Role Adoption	Gender Identity
1–5 years	"Gender-appropriate" toy preferences emerge and strengthen. Gender stereotyping of activities, occupations, and behaviors expands. Gender segregation in peer interaction emerges and strengthens. Girls' preference for play in pairs, boys' for play in larger groups, appears.	Gender constancy develops in a three-stage sequence: gender labeling, gender stability, and gender consistency.
6–11 years	Gender-stereotyped knowledge expands, especially for personality traits and achievement areas. Gender stereotyping becomes more flexible.	"Masculine" gender identity strengthens among boys; girls' gender identity becomes more androgynous.
12–18 years	Gender-role conformity increases in early adolescence and then declines. Gender segregation becomes less pronounced.	Gender identity becomes more traditional in early adolescence, after which highly stereotypical self-perceptions decline.

Note: These milestones represent overall age trends. Individual differences exist in the precise age at which each milestone is attained and in the extent of gender typing.

Photos: (top) © Laura Dwight Photography; (middle) © Esbin/Anderson/The Image Works; (bottom) © Bob Daemmrich/PhotoEdit

olds that ability and interest, not gender, determine whether a person can perform an activity well, children gained in stereotype flexibility and memory for "gender-inconsistent" information (story characters engaged in "cross-gender" tasks). Interestingly, classification training with gender-neutral stimuli that required children to sort objects into two categories at once (by shape and color) had the same effect (Bigler & Liben, 1992). As these findings reveal, interventions that promote multidimensional thinking about gender and other aspects of the world can help children develop more gender-equitable beliefs. Nevertheless, gender-schematic thinking could not operate so forcefully to restrict knowledge and learning opportunities if society did not teach children a wide variety of gender-linked associations.

The Milestones table above provides an overview of the changes in gender stereotyping, gender identity, and gender-role adoption we have considered.

Ask Yourself

REVIEW	Describe the general path of gender identity development, from early childhood through adolescence, noting differences between boys and girls
APPLY	While looking at a book, 4-year-old Roger saw a picture of a boy cooking at a stove. Later, he recalled the person in the picture as a girl rather than a boy. Using gender schema theory, explain Roger's memory error.
CONNECT	What gains in perspective taking lead young teenagers to be very concerned with what others think and, therefore, probably contribute to gender intensification. (See page 467 in Chapter 11.)
REFLECT	Is your gender identity "masculine," "feminine," or androgynous? What biological and social factors might have influenced your gender identity?

To What Extent Do Boys and Girls *Really* Differ in Gender-Stereotyped Attributes?

So far, we have examined the relationship of biological, social, and cognitive factors to children's gender-typed preferences and behavior. But we have said little about the extent to which boys and girls actually differ in mental abilities and personality traits. Over the past several decades, thousands of studies have measured sex differences in these characteristics. At the heart of these efforts is the age-old nature–nurture debate. Researchers have looked for stable differences between males and females and, from there, have searched for the biological and environmental roots of each variation.

To avoid basing conclusions on single studies and small, potentially biased samples, researchers often use a technique called *meta-analysis,* in which they reanalyze the data of many investigations together. Besides telling us whether a sex difference exists, this method provides an estimate of its size. Table 13.2 summarizes differences between boys and girls in mental abilities and personality traits, based on current evidence. The majority of findings listed in the table are small to moderate. Furthermore, as Figure 13.12 shows, the distributions for males and females usually overlap greatly. Sex differences usually account for no more than 5 to 10 percent of individual differences, leaving most to be explained by other factors.

TABLE 13.2 SEX DIFFERENCES IN MENTAL ABILITIES AND PERSONALITY TRAITS

Characteristic	Sex Difference
Verbal abilities	Girls are advantaged in early language development and in reading and writing achievement during the school years.
Spatial abilities	Beginning in early childhood, boys outperform girls in certain spatial skills, a difference that persists throughout the lifespan.
Mathematical abilities	In the early school grades, girls do better than boys in math computation. As young people progress through school, boys do better than girls on complex problems involving abstract reasoning and geometry. The difference is greatest among high-achieving students.
School achievement	Girls get better grades than boys in all academic subjects in elementary school, after which the difference declines. In junior high school, boys start to show an advantage in mathematics and physical sciences.
Achievement motivation	Sex differences in achievement motivation are linked to type of task. Boys perceive themselves as more competent and have higher expectancies of success in "masculine" achievement areas, such as mathematics, sports, and mechanical skills. Girls have higher expectancies and set higher standards for themselves in "feminine" areas, such as reading, writing, literature, and art.
Emotional sensitivity	Girls score higher than boys in emotional understanding and on self-report measures of empathy and sympathy. Girls' advantage in prosocial behavior is greatest for kindness and considerateness, less apparent for helping behavior.
Fear, timidity, and anxiety	Girls are more fearful and timid than boys, a difference that is present in the first year of life. In school, girls are more anxious about failure and try harder to avoid it. In contrast, boys are greater risk takers, a difference reflected in their higher injury rates throughout childhood and adolescence.
Compliance and dependency	Girls more readily comply with directives from adults and peers. They also seek help from adults more often and score higher in dependency on personality tests.
Activity level	Boys are more active than girls.
Depression	Adolescent girls are more likely than boys to report depressive symptoms.
Aggression	By the late preschool years, boys are more physically aggressive than girls. Adolescent boys are far more likely than girls to become involved in antisocial behavior and violent crime. The sex difference favoring girls in relational aggression is small and, in some studies, nonexistent.
Developmental problems	Problems more common among boys than girls include speech and language disorders, reading disabilities, and behavior problems such as hyperactivity, hostile acting-out behavior, and emotional and social immaturity. More boys are born with genetic disorders, physical disabilities, and mental retardation.

Consequently, males and females are actually more alike than different in developmental potential. Nevertheless, as we will see shortly, a few sex differences are considerable.

Keep in mind that sex differences can change over time. For example, over the past several decades, the gender gap has narrowed in all areas of mental ability for which differences have been identified (Halpern, 2000). This trend is a reminder that sex differences are not fixed; the general picture of how boys and girls differ may not be the same in a few decades as it is today.

Mental Abilities

Sex differences in mental abilities have sparked almost as much controversy as the ethnic and SES differences in IQ considered in Chapter 8. Although boys and girls do not differ in general intelligence, they do vary in specific mental abilities. Many researchers believe that heredity is involved in the disparities, and they have attempted to identify the biological processes responsible. But no biological factor operates in a social and cultural vacuum. For each ability we will consider, experience plays a major role.

• **VERBAL ABILITIES** • Early in development, girls are ahead of boys in language progress. They begin to talk earlier and show faster vocabulary growth during the second year, after which boys catch up (see Chapter 9). Throughout the school years, girls attain higher scores in reading and writing achievement and account for a lower percentage of children referred for remedial reading instruction (Halpern, 2000, 2004). Girls continue to score slightly higher on tests of verbal ability in adolescence (Statistics Canada, 2003b; U.S. Department of Education, 2003b).

Recall from Chapter 9 that girls show a biological advantage in earlier development of the left hemisphere of the cerebral cortex, where language is usually localized. At the same time, mothers talk considerably more to girls than to boys. From the preschool years through adolescence, mother–daughter narratives about past experiences are more organized and elaborative than mother–son narratives, and girls' and boys' independently generated narratives differ similarly (Peterson & Roberts, 2003). Furthermore, we have seen that children tend to think of language arts as a "feminine" subject, that parents rate daughters as more competent at it, and that elementary school classrooms are feminine-biased settings in which boys' higher activity level and greater tendency toward noncompliance elicit more teacher disapproval.

• **MATHEMATICAL ABILITIES** • Sex differences in mathematical abilities are apparent by first grade. Girls more often depend on concrete manipulatives to solve basic math problems, whereas boys more often mentally represent numbers and rapidly retrieve answers from memory (Carr & Jessup, 1997; Fennema et al., 1998). Girls' better verbal skills and more methodical approach to problem solving contribute to an advantage in arithmetic computation in the early grades. But as students progress in school and the math curriculum becomes increasingly challenging, boys start to outperform girls, especially on complex problems involving abstract reasoning and geometry (Bielinski & Davison, 1998; Hedges & Nowell, 1995).

When all students are considered, the size of this male advantage is small. But among the most capable, the gender gap is greater. In widely publicized research on more than 100,000 bright seventh and eighth graders who, since the early 1980s, have been invited to take the Scholastic Assessment Test (SAT) long before they needed to do so for college admission, boys outscored girls on the mathematics subtest year after year. Yet even this disparity has been shrinking. A quarter-century ago, 13 times as many boys as girls scored over 700 out of a possible 800 on the math portion of the SAT; today, the ratio is just 2.8 to 1 (Benbow & Stanley, 1983; Lubinski & Benbow, 1994; Monastersky, 2005).

Some researchers believe that heredity contributes substantially to the gender gap in math, especially to the tendency for more boys to be extremely talented. Accumulating evidence indicates that boys' superior reasoning ability originates in two skill areas. First, boys' more rapid numerical memory permits them to devote more energy to complex mental operations. Second, boys' superior spatial reasoning greatly enhances their mathematical problem solving (Geary et al., 2000). See the Biology and Environment box on page 546 for further discussion of this issue.

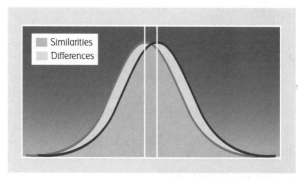

Similarities
Differences

▲ **Figure 13.12**

Typical distributions of scores in studies comparing males and females on mental abilities and personality traits. For most characteristics, the distributions overlap greatly. This means that males and females are actually much more alike than different.

Sex Differences in Spatial Abilities

Spatial skills are a key focus in researchers' efforts to explain sex differences in mathematical reasoning. The gender gap favoring males is large for *mental rotation tasks,* in which individuals must rotate a three-dimensional figure rapidly and accurately inside their heads (see Figure 13.13). Males also do considerably better on *spatial perception tasks,* in which people must determine spatial relationships by considering the orientation of the surrounding environment. Sex differences on *spatial visualization tasks,* involving analysis of complex visual forms, are weak or nonexistent, perhaps because many different strategies can be used to solve them. Both males and females may come up with effective procedures (Linn & Petersen, 1985; Voyer, Voyer, & Bryden, 1995).

Sex differences in spatial abilities emerge in early childhood and persist throughout the lifespan (Levine et al., 1999). The pattern is consistent enough to suggest a biological explanation. One hypothesis is that heredity, through exposure to androgen hormones, enhances right hemispheric functioning, giving males a spatial advantage. (Recall that for most people, spatial skills are housed in the right hemisphere of the cerebral cortex.) In support of this idea, girls and women whose prenatal androgen levels were abnormally high show superior performance on spatial

rotation tasks (Berenbaum, 2001). And in some studies, spatial performance varies systematically with daily and annual androgen levels in men and women (Van Goozen et al., 1995; Temple & Carney, 1995).

Why might a biologically based sex difference in spatial abilities exist? Evolutionary theorists point out that spatial skills predict rapid, accurate map drawing and interpretation, areas in which boys and men do better than girls and women. During human evolution, the cognitive abilities of males became adapted for hunting, which required generating mental representations of large-scale spaces to find one's way (Choi & Silverman, 2003; Jones, Braithwaite, & Healy, 2003).

Although biology is involved in males' superior spatial performance, experience also makes a difference. Children who engage in manipulative activities, such as block play, model building, and carpentry, do better on spatial tasks (Baenninger & Newcombe, 1995). Playing video games that require rapid mental rotation of visual images also enhances spatial scores (Subrahmanyam & Greenfield, 1996). Boys spend far more time than girls at these pursuits.

Research confirms that superior spatial skills contribute to the greater ease with which boys solve complex math problems. In studies of junior high and high school students, *both*

This seventh-grade girl is the gold medal winner in her age category in the Canada-Wide Science Fair. In her project, which examines the hazards of cell phone use while driving, she used advanced mathematical skills, data analysis, and graphing. An excellent math curriculum, including emphasis on spatial strategies and confidence-building experiences, may have contributed to her outstanding performance. © CP Photo/Calgary Herald-Colleen Kidd

spatial ability and self-confidence at doing math were related to performance on complex math problems, with spatial skills being the stronger predictor (Casey, Nuttall, & Pezaris, 1997, 2001). Boys are advantaged in both spatial abilities and math self-confidence. In sum, biology and environment *jointly* explain variations in spatial and math performance—both within and between the sexes.

Mental Rotation
Choose the responses that show the standard in a different orientation.

Spatial Perception
Pick the tilted bottle that has a horizontal water line.

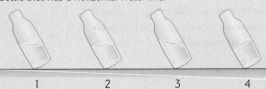

Spatial Visualization
Find the figure embedded in this complex shape.

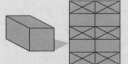

◄ **Figure 13.13**

Types of spatial tasks. Large sex differences favoring males appear on mental rotation, and males do considerably better than females on spatial perception. In contrast, sex differences on spatial visualization are weak or nonexistent.

(From M. C. Linn & A. C. Petersen, 1985, "Emergence and Characterization of Sex Differences in Spatial Ability: A Meta-Analysis," *Child Development, 56,* pp. 1482, 1483, 1485. © The Society for Research in Child Development, Inc. Reprinted by permission.)

Although heredity is involved, social pressures are also influential. We have seen that children often view math as a "masculine" subject. Also, many parents think boys are better at it—an attitude that encourages girls to view themselves as having to work harder at math to do well, to blame their errors on lack of ability, and to regard math as less useful for their future lives. These beliefs, in turn, reduce girls' interest in math and their willingness to consider math- or science-related careers (Bleeker & Jacobs, 2004; Catsambis, 1994). Furthermore, *stereotype threat*—the fear of being judged on the basis of a negative stereotype (see page 336 in Chapter 8)—causes females to do worse than their abilities allow on difficult math problems (Steele, 1997). The result of all these influences is that girls—even those who are highly talented—are less likely to develop effective math reasoning skills.

In nations where more women are in the labor force and their professional opportunities are similar to those of men, sex differences in secondary school math achievement are smaller (Baker & Jones, 1993; Riegle-Crumb, 2000). Under these conditions, girls sense that excelling at math is meaningful and attainable, and they express more positive math attitudes. Paralleling the decline in sex differences in math achievement is an increase in girls' enrollment in advanced math and science courses. Today, North American boys and girls reach advanced levels of high school math and science study in nearly equal proportions—a crucial factor in reducing sex differences in knowledge and skill (Statistics Canada, 2003b; U.S. Department of Education, 2003a).

Still, extra steps must be taken to promote girls' interest in and confidence at math and science. When parents hold nonstereotyped beliefs, adolescent daughters are less likely to avoid math and science and more likely to achieve well. In schools, teachers must better demonstrate the relevance of math and science to everyday life. Girls, especially, respond positively toward math and science taught from an applied, hands-on perspective (Eccles, 1994). Exposure to successful women scientists as role models is also likely to improve girls' belief in their own capacity to succeed.

Finally, far too little attention has been paid to enhancing girls' spatial skills, which (as the Biology and Environment box on the previous page indicates) contribute substantially to their weaker mathematical reasoning. A math curriculum that teaches children how to apply effective spatial strategies—drawing diagrams, mentally manipulating visual images, searching for numerical patterns, and graphing—is vital beginning in kindergarten (National Council of Teachers of Mathematics, 2000). Because girls are biased toward verbal processing, they may not realize their math and science potential unless they are specifically taught how to think spatially. Waiting until secondary school to intervene may be too late. By then, students' math problem-solving skills are well practiced and, therefore, difficult to change.

◎ Children respond eagerly to a question from John Mighton, the Canadian mathematician who developed Junior Undiscovered Math Prodigies (JUMP)—a program based on the assumption that every child can think with numbers and succeed mathematically.
© Toronto Star 2003

Personality Traits

Sex differences in personality are in line with gender stereotypes. The traits most often studied include emotional sensitivity, compliance and dependency, depression, and aggression.

• **EMOTIONAL SENSITIVITY** • Females are more emotionally sensitive than males, a difference that appears quite early. Beginning in the preschool years, girls perform slightly better when asked to infer others' emotional states and the causes of those states. Relative to boys, girls are especially adept at understanding the more complex, self-conscious emotions—an advantage that extends into adulthood (Brown & Dunn, 1996; Bosacki & Moore, 2004; Bybee, 1998). Except for anger, girls also express their feelings more freely and intensely in everyday interaction (Geary, 1998).

It would be reasonable to expect these differences to extend to empathy, sympathy, and prosocial behavior, but the evidence is mixed. On self-report measures, girls and women score higher than boys and men. When they are observed for behavioral signs, however, the gender difference is less consistent. Girls show a slight advantage in prosocial responding that is mostly evident in

Ⓢ Girls' greater emotional sensitivity is probably environmentally determined, since boys are just as caring and affectionate in certain situations—for example, when interacting with a cherished pet. © Tony Freeman/PhotoEdit

kindness and considerateness, less apparent in helping behavior (Eisenberg & Fabes, 1998). When asked to describe the prosocial acts of their peers, adolescents reported many as-yet-unstudied examples that require self-confidence and assertiveness and, therefore, might be especially common among boys (Bergin, Talley, & Hamer, 2003). These include helping others develop skills (giving tips on how to play basketball), providing physical assistance (volunteering to mow the neighbor's lawn), and confronting others for harmful or otherwise inappropriate behavior.

As with other attributes, both biological and environmental explanations for sex differences in emotional sensitivity exist. According to one evolutionary account, females are genetically primed to be more emotionally sensitive as a way of ensuring their effectiveness as caregivers. Yet research suggests that girls are not naturally more nurturant. Before age 5, boys and girls spend equal amounts of time talking to and playing with babies (Fogel et al., 1987). In middle childhood, Caucasian boys' willingness to relate to infants declines. Yet African-American school-age boys, who endorse fewer gender stereotypes, smile, touch, and look at babies just as much as girls do (Reid & Trotter, 1993). Furthermore, sex differences in emotional sensitivity are not evident in mothers' and fathers' interactions with their babies. In Chapter 10, we saw that fathers are just as affectionate and competent at caregiving as mothers. And in Chapter 4, we noted that men and women react similarly to the sound of a crying baby.

Cultural expectations that girls be warm and expressive and boys be distant and self-controlled seem largely responsible for the gender gap in emotional sensitivity. In infancy, mothers respond more often to a girl's happiness and distress than to a boy's (Malatesta et al., 1986). During childhood, parents are more likely to use inductive discipline (which promotes sympathetic concern) and to pressure girls to be thoughtful and caring (Zahn-Waxler, Cole, & Barrett, 1991). In addition, recall that parents spend more time talking about emotions when conversing with daughters. Taken together, these findings suggest that girls receive far more encouragement to express and reflect on feelings than boys do.

● **COMPLIANCE AND DEPENDENCY** ● Beginning in the preschool years, girls are more compliant than boys, to both adult and peer demands. Girls also seek help and information from adults more often and score higher in dependency on personality tests (Feingold, 1994). These patterns of behavior are learned, and they have much to do with the activity environments in which boys and girls spend their time.

From an early age, girls are encouraged into adult-structured activities both at home and at school. Consequently, they spend more time near adults. In contrast, boys are attracted to activities in which adults are minimally involved or entirely absent (Carpenter, 1983; Powlishta, Serbin, & Moller, 1993). Compliance and bids for help and attention appear more often in adult-structured contexts, whereas assertiveness, leadership, and creative use of materials occur more often in unstructured pursuits.

Ideally, boys and girls should experience a balance of adult-structured and unstructured activities, in order to develop both the capacity to be assertive and the ability to comply with others' directives. In one study, assigning preschool boys and girls to classroom activities differing in adult structure easily modified their assertive and compliant tendencies (Carpenter, Huston, & Holt, 1986).

● **DEPRESSION** ● Depression—feeling sad, frustrated, and hopeless about life, accompanied by loss of pleasure in most activities and disturbances in sleep, appetite, concentration, and energy— is the most common psychological problem of adolescence. About 15 to 20 percent of teenagers have had one or more major depressive episodes, a rate comparable to that of adults. From 2 to 8 percent are chronically depressed—gloomy and self-critical for many months and sometimes years (Rushton, Forcier, & Schectman, 2002). Even in childhood, depression is not absent: Serious depression afflicts about 1 to 2 percent of children, most of whom continue to display severe depression in adolescence. Yet depressive symptoms increase sharply between ages 13 and 15, when sex differences emerge—as Figure 13.14 illustrates for a large Norwegian sample. Similar trends have been documented in Canada, Great Britain, New Zealand, and the United States (Galambos, Leadbeater, & Barker, 2004; Hankin et al., 1998; Angold & Rutter, 1992). Adolescent girls are twice as likely as boys to report persistent depressive symptoms—a difference sustained throughout the lifespan. If allowed to persist, depression seriously impairs social, academic, and vocational functioning (Nolen-Hoeksema, 2002).

Combinations of biological and social factors lead to depression; the precise blend differs from one individual to the next. Kinship studies reveal that heredity plays an important role (Glowinski et al., 2003). Genes can promote depression by affecting the balance of neurotransmitters in the brain, the development of brain regions involved in inhibiting negative emotion, or the body's hormonal response to stress (Kaufman & Charney, 2003).

But experience can also activate depression, promoting any of the biological changes just described. Parents of depressed children and adolescents have a high incidence of depression and other psychological disorders. Although a genetic risk may be passed from parent to child, in earlier chapters we also saw that depressed or otherwise stressed parents often engage in maladaptive parenting. As a result, their child's emotional self-regulation, attachment, and self-esteem may be impaired, with serious consequences for many cognitive and social skills (Cicchetti & Toth, 1998). Depressed youths usually display a learned-helpless attributional style, in which they view positive academic and social outcomes as beyond their control. Consequently, numerous events can spark depression in a vulnerable young person—for example, failing at something important, parental divorce, or the end of a close friendship or romantic partnership.

Why are girls more prone to depression? We know that biological changes associated with puberty are not responsible, because the gender difference is limited to industrialized nations. In developing countries, rates of depression are similar for males and females and are occasionally higher in males (Culbertson, 1997). Even when females do exceed males in depression, the size of the difference varies. For example, it is smaller in China than in North America, perhaps because of decades of efforts by the Chinese government to eliminate gender inequalities (Greenberger et al., 2000).

Instead, stressful life events and gender-typed coping styles seem to be responsible. Early maturing girls are especially prone to depression, particularly when they also face other stressful life events (Ge, Conger, & Elder, 2001a). And the gender intensification of early adolescence often strengthens passivity and dependency—maladaptive approaches to the tasks expected of teenagers in complex cultures. Consistent with this explanation, adolescents who identify strongly with "feminine" traits are more depressed, regardless of their sex (Wichstrøm, 1999). Girls who repeatedly feel overwhelmed develop an overly reactive physiological stress response and cope more poorly with challenges in the future (Nolen-Hoeksema, 2002). In this way, stressful experiences and stress-reactivity feed on one another, sustaining depression. In contrast, girls with either an androgynous or a "masculine" gender identity show a low rate of depressive symptoms, no different from that of masculine-identified boys (Wilson & Cairns, 1988).

Unfortunately, teachers and parents tend to minimize the seriousness of adolescents' depressive symptoms. Because of the popular stereotype of adolescence as a period of "storm and stress," many adults interpret depression as just a passing phase. Yet without intervention that improves coping strategies and reduces hyperreactivity to stress, adolescent depression is likely to evolve into a lifelong pattern.

• AGGRESSION • Aggression has attracted more research attention than any other sex difference. In Chapter 12, we noted that by the late preschool years, boys are more *physically aggressive* than girls. But sex differences in *verbal aggression* (threats of physical harm, name-calling, and hostile teasing) and *relational aggression* (aimed at damaging another's social relationships)—are much less clear.

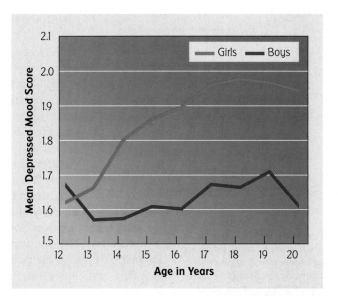

▲ **Figure 13.14**

Change in depressive symptoms from age 12 to age 20 in a cross-sectional study of over 12,000 Norwegian adolescents. Girls showed a more rapid rise in depression around the time of puberty than boys. Similar trends occur in other industrialized nations. (From L. Wichstrøm, 1999, "The Emergence of Gender Difference in Depressed Mood During Adolescence: The Role of Intensified Gender Socialization," *Developmental Psychology, 35,* p. 237. Copyright © 1999 by the American Psychological Association. Reprinted by permission of the publisher and author.)

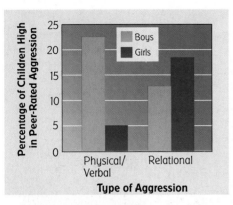

▲ **Figure 13.15**

Percentage of third through sixth graders rated by peers as highly physically/verbally aggressive and highly relationally aggressive. More than 1,100 children identified classmates who often engage in physical/verbal aggression (hitting, kicking, punching, or insulting) and relational aggression (spreading rumors, gossiping, telling friends they will stop liking them unless the friends obey). Findings showed that many more boys than girls were named as high in physical/verbal aggression (largely due to physical attacks among boys). The sex difference favoring girls in relational aggression was much smaller. (Adapted from Crick, 1996.)

Although many people assume that girls more often harm one another with words, the evidence is inconsistent: Some studies indicate that boys are more verbally aggressive, whereas others show no sex difference (Kashani & Shepperd, 1990; Salmivalli, Kaukiainen, & Lagerspetz, 2000). Similarly, a common assumption is that girls are more likely to engage in the rumor spreading, social exclusion, and other types of relationship manipulation that make up relational aggression. But once again, a growing number of studies reveal that the sex difference favoring girls is generally small (as Figure 13.15 illustrates) and sometimes nonexistent (Crick, Casas, & Mosher, 1997; Underwood, Galen, & Paquette, 2001; Willoughby, Kupersmidt, & Bryant, 2001). Girls often *appear* much more relationally aggressive than boys because many girls use relational tactics nearly exclusively. Boys, by contrast, draw on a diversity of means to inflict harm—whatever works at the moment.

Although children of both sexes report that relational aggression is very hurtful, girls find it especially so, reporting more distress when they are targets (Galen & Underwood, 1997). Because girls place a high value on close relationships, harming a friendship is a powerful way to hurt a peer. There are other reasons, too, that relational aggression may account for the large majority of girls' hostile acts. First, girls spend more time in close proximity to adults and are more sensitive to adult approval. They may emphasize relational aggression because it is hard for adults to detect and, therefore, to punish. Second, as Chapter 15 will make clear, dominance relations are less clear in girls' than in boys' peer groups. As a result, girls may jockey for social position frequently, engaging in relationship manipulation to protect their own status (Underwood, 2003).

Our discussion of the origins of sex differences in aggression focuses largely on physical aggression. At present, much less is known about factors that contribute to relational aggression.

▶ **Biological Influences.** Because males' greater physical aggression is evident early in life, generalizes across cultures, and is found in many animal species, most researchers believe that biology is involved. Earlier we mentioned that androgen hormones are related to aggression in animals; they are also believed to play a role in humans. But recall that although children with CAH were exposed prenatally to abnormally high androgen levels, they were not more aggressive. This suggests that in humans, androgen exposure results in only a tendency to aggress. That is, androgens may promote certain behaviors that, in some circumstances, increase the likelihood of aggressive outcomes.

One possibility is that prenatal androgens promote physical activity—behaviors likely to change into aggression in certain situations. For example, an active, competitive child who often participates in large-group activities might become more aggressive than a child who prefers small-group pursuits. To explore this idea, researchers brought kindergartners and first graders to a laboratory, where some played a game in same-sex pairs and others in same-sex tetrads (groups of four). In the game, children rolled a die, which indicated how many beads they could take from either a common pile (a noncompetitive move) or another player (a competitive move). Whereas group size had no impact on girls' competitive moves, boys displayed nearly twice as many competitive moves in tetrads as in dyads (Benenson et al., 2001). Recall that compared with girls, boys spend more time playing in large groups—an attraction, according to evolutionary theorists, adapted to preparing them for the competitive adult life of their male ancestors. Large groups, in turn, serve as contexts in which competition may promote aggression.

Another hypothesis is that sex hormones influence brain functioning in ways that affect emotional reactions. According to this view, hormone levels induce more frequent displays of excitement, anger, or anxiety, which make aggression more likely under certain conditions. Consistent with this prediction, adolescent boys with high androgen levels are more dominant and, therefore, more likely to respond with aggression when provoked by peers (Olweus et al., 1988; Tremblay et al., 1997). In one study, higher estrogen and androgen levels were related to adolescent girls' expressions of anger in a discussion session with their parents (Inoff-Germain et al., 1988).

Although more research is needed, current evidence indicates that multiple pathways exist between sex hormones and physical aggression. Clearly, too, environmental conditions have much to do with whether or not hormonally induced emotions and behaviors are channeled into aggressive acts.

▶ *Environmental Influences.* In Chapter 12, we showed how coercive child-rearing practices and strife-ridden families promote aggressive behavior. For several reasons, boys are more likely than girls to be affected. Parents more often use physical punishment with boys, which encourages them to adopt the same tactics in their own relationships. Also, arguing between husband and wife, though stimulating aggression among all family members, more often triggers hostility in boys. In a study in which 2-year-olds overheard angry verbal exchanges between adults while playing with a familiar peer in a laboratory, girls tended to show fearful, withdrawing reactions, such as freezing in place and covering or hiding their faces. In contrast, boys engaged in more aggression, lashing out at their playmates (Cummings, Iannotti, & Zahn-Waxler, 1985). After observing adults' angry exchanges, boys report feeling more hostile than girls (Hennessy, Rabideau, & Cicchetti, 1994).

At the same time, parents and teachers respond differently to boys' and girls' physical aggression. They often give boys positive attention or relax rules, coaxing, begging, or ignoring rather than using clear, firm prohibitions. In contrast, they usually respond negatively to girls' assertive and aggressive acts (Arnold, McWilliams, & Harvey-Arnold, 1998; Kerig, Cowan, & Cowan, 1993; Radke-Yarrow & Kochanska, 1990). The stereotype reflected in the saying "Boys will be boys" may lead many adults to overlook or tolerate boys' hostility unless it is extreme. This sets up conditions in which boys receive tacit approval for physical aggression, whereas girls suppress it. In view of these findings, it is not surprising that school-age boys expect less parental disapproval and report feeling less guilty for aggression than girls (Perry, Perry, & Weiss, 1989).

Gender-segregated peer groups extend adults' lessons about expressing aggression, with boys often engaging in high rates of bossy, rough, aggressive acts and girls encouraging one another to refrain from physical fighting. In one study, emotionally reactive preschool and kindergarten boys who mostly played with other boys increased in teacher-reported problem behaviors (such as "starts fights" or "is defiant to adults") in the course of the school year. In contrast, problem behaviors decreased among emotionally reactive girls who often played with others girls (Fabes et al., 1997). Perhaps, instead, these girls begin to vent their anger indirectly. By middle childhood, girls' relational aggression is more malicious than boys', and girls are more likely to direct it against close friends (Simmons, 2002).

In sum, early experiences tend to promote physical aggression in boys but to dampen it in girls and, instead, encourage them to substitute covert, relational outlets for their hostility. Overall, biological predispositions and social encouragement jointly contribute to sex differences in aggression.

◉ During the school years, boys report feeling more hostile than girls after observing adults' angry exchanges. This boy attempts to minimize the effect by blocking out his parents' argument.
© David Young-Wolff/PhotoEdit

◉ Developing Non-Gender-Stereotyped Children

We have seen that children's developmental possibilities can be seriously limited by persistent gender stereotypes in their culture. Although many researchers and laypeople alike recognize the importance of rearing children who feel free to express their human qualities without fear of violating gender-role expectations, no easy recipe exists for accomplishing this difficult task. It must be tackled on many fronts—at home, at school, and in the wider society.

Biology clearly affects children's gender typing, channeling boys toward active, competitive play and girls toward quieter, more intimate interaction—a difference that leads each sex, on average, to seek out activities and social experiences consistent with those predispositions. But substantial revisions in gender roles and in relationships between males and females—along with wide individual, family, and cultural variations—reveal that most aspects of gender typing are not built into human nature (Maccoby, 2000b). Furthermore, a long human childhood ensures that experiences can greatly influence biologically based sex differences (Geary & Bjorklund, 2000).

Applying

What We Know   Reducing Children's Gender Stereotyping and Gender-Role Conformity

Strategy	Explanation
Offer children a diversity of toy and activity choices.	Encouraging children to select toys and activities on the basis of their interests, not "gender-appropriateness," counters gender stereotypes while providing children with a broader array of experiences.
Avoid transmitting gender stereotypes of achievement areas.	Conveying gender stereotypes about what boys and girls are "good at" reduces children's sense of competence at, interest in, and motivation to achieve in areas stereotyped for the other gender, thereby preventing children from realizing their academic potential. Point out that high effort improves competence in all achievement areas.
Teach children to appreciate differences among individuals.	Informing children about individual differences reduces the pressure they feel to be just like members of their own group, thereby discouraging adoption of stereotypical attitudes and behaviors. For example, adults can say, "She's so interesting because she's different from me!"
Avoid unnecessary references to gender and gender stereotypes in your language.	Avoiding gender labels and generic utterances ("The boys aren't paying attention." "Most girls like art.") by referring, instead, to individuals ("Mark, Sam, and Jenny aren't paying attention." "Susie likes art.") prevents children from viewing same-sex individuals as alike and from accepting gender stereotypes.
Provide non-gender-stereotyped models.	Exposing children to adults engaged in nonstereotyped activities and occupations promotes children's awareness of multiple choices for themselves, not just gender-stereotyped choices.
Stress the complexity of gender groups.	Saying, for example, "Some boys are good at math and some girls are good at math," or "Some boys like sports, and some boys don't like sports," teaches children that ability and interest, not gender, determine how well a person performs an activity.
Arrange for mixed-sex interaction.	Children who have opportunities to engage in joint endeavors with other-sex peers are less likely to form stereotyped and prejudicial attitudes toward the other gender.
Discuss gender biases with children.	Discussing why certain social roles (such as the president or prime minister) are linked to only one gender helps children to appreciate environmental causes of bias and to reject explanations based on innate sex differences.

Throughout our discussion, we have mentioned strategies for reducing gender stereotyping and gender-role conformity. Refer to Applying What We Know above for a summary. But even children who are fortunate enough to grow up in homes and schools that minimize stereotyping will eventually encounter it in the media and in what men and women typically do in their communities. Consequently, children need early experiences that repeatedly counteract their readiness to absorb our culture's extensive network of gender-linked associations.

Sandra Bem (1993, 1998) suggests that parents and teachers make a concerted effort to delay young children's learning of gender-stereotyped messages because preschoolers' cognitive limitations lead them to assume that cultural practices determine gender. Adults can begin by eliminating traditional gender roles from their own behavior and from the alternatives they provide for children. For example, mothers and fathers can take turns making dinner, bathing children, and driving the family car and can provide sons and daughters with both trucks and dolls, both pink and blue clothing. Teachers can make sure that all children spend some time each day in adult-structured and unstructured activities. Adults can also avoid language that conveys gender stereotypes, and they can shield children from media presentations that do the same.

Once children notice the wide array of gender stereotypes in their society, parents and teachers can point out exceptions. For example, they can arrange for children to see men and women pursuing nontraditional careers. And they can reason with children, explaining that interests and skills, not sex, should determine a person's occupation. Adults can also discuss with older children the historical roots and current consequences of gender inequalities—why, for example, there have been few female presidents and prime ministers, why fathers rarely stay home with their children, and why stereotyped views of men and women are hard to change. Research shows that school-age children who hold flexible beliefs about what boys and girls can do are more likely to notice instances of gender discrimination (Brown & Bigler, 2004). As children build concepts of themselves and their social world that are not limited by a masculine–feminine dichotomy, they contribute to the transformation of societal values. And they bring us closer to a time when people will be released from the constraints of traditional gender roles.

Ask Yourself

REVIEW	Cite evidence indicating that both biological and environmental factors contribute to girls' advantage in verbal abilities and to boys' advantage in mathematical reasoning.
REVIEW	Explain the *indirect* link between androgen hormones and boys' greater overt aggression, noting the influence of both family and peer-group experiences.
APPLY	Thirteen-year-old Donna reached puberty early and feels negatively about her physical appearance. She also has a "feminine" gender identity. Explain why Donna is at risk for depression.
CONNECT	Using Bronfenbrenner's ecological systems theory (see Chapter 1, page 28), describe steps that can be taken at each level of the environment to reduce gender stereotyping in children.

Summary

Explain how the study of gender typing has responded to societal change.

Largely because of progress in women's rights, **gender typing** is no longer regarded as essential for healthy psychological development. Researchers are more interested in how children might be released from gender-based definitions of appropriate behavior.

Gender Stereotypes and Gender Roles

Cite examples of gender stereotypes, and describe the development of gender stereotyping from early childhood into adolescence.

Despite recent progress in women's rights, gender stereotypes have remained essentially unchanged. **Instrumental traits** continue to be regarded as masculine, **expressive traits** as feminine—a dichotomy that is widely held around the world. Stereotyping of physical characteristics, occupations, and activities is also common.

Children begin to acquire **gender stereotypes** and **gender roles** early in the preschool years. As gender categories form, gender-stereotyped beliefs and behaviors increase rapidly. By middle childhood, children are aware of many stereotypes, including those that focus on activities, occupations, personality traits, and achievement areas.

Because of cognitive limitations, preschoolers hold rigid gender-stereotypic beliefs. Gains in **gender-stereotype flexibility** occur in middle childhood and adolescence; children develop a more open-minded view of what males and females can do, although they often do not approve of males who violate gender-role expectations.

© BILL AARON/PHOTOEDIT

Cite individual and group differences in gender stereotyping, and discuss the relationship of gender stereotyping to gender-role adoption.

Children acquire the components of gender stereotyping—activities, behaviors, occupations, and personality traits—in different patterns and to different degrees. Boys hold more rigid gender-stereotyped views than girls, white children more than black children. Also, middle-SES adolescents and adults hold more flexible views than their lower-SES counterparts.

Awareness of gender stereotypes is only weakly related to gender-role adoption.

Stereotype flexibility, however, is a moderately good predictor of children's willingness to cross gender lines during the school years.

Influences on Gender Stereotyping and Gender-Role Adoption

Discuss the role of biology in gender stereotyping and gender-role adoption, including cross-cultural evidence and the influence of hormones.

According to an evolutionary perspective, males are genetically primed for dominance and females for intimacy, responsiveness, and cooperation. Cross-cultural similarities in gender typing have been used to support the role of biology. However, great diversity exists in the extent to which cultures endorse the instrumental–expressive dichotomy and encourage gender-role conformity.

Prenatal androgen levels contribute to sex differences in play styles and to children's preference for same-sex peers. Research on children with congenital adrenal hyperplasia (CAH) supports the role of androgens in certain aspects of "masculine" gender-role adoption. CAH girls show a preference for vehicle and building toys and for boys as playmates. In instances in which children are reared as members of the other sex because of ambiguous genitals caused by a prenatal hormone imbalance, gender typing is usually consistent with sex of rearing, regardless of genetic sex. However, when biological makeup and sex of rearing are at odds, children experience serious sexual-identity and adjustment problems.

Discuss environmental influences on gender stereotyping and gender-role adoption, including expectations and treatment by parents, teachers, and peers; observational learning; and the impact of siblings.

◎ Beginning in infancy, adults hold gender-stereotyped perceptions and expectations of boys and girls and create different environments for them. By the preschool years, parents reinforce their children for many "gender-appropriate" play activities and behaviors. They also frequently use language in ways that highlight gender distinctions and inform children about traditional gender roles.

◎ During middle childhood, parents demand more from boys in achievement situations and hold gender-stereotyped beliefs about children's abilities in various school subjects, with consequences for children's self-confidence, motivation, achievement, and later career choices. Fathers differentiate between boys and girls more than mothers do. Also, each parent takes special responsibility for the gender typing of the same-sex child.

◎ Teachers reinforce children of both sexes for "feminine" behavior and also act in ways that promote traditional gender roles. Besides direct pressure from adults, children have many opportunities to observe gender-typed models in the surrounding environment. When children are exposed to nonstereo-typed models, such as parents who cross traditional gender lines in household tasks or career choice, they are less traditional in their beliefs and behaviors.

◎ When interacting with children of their own sex, boys and girls receive further rein-forcement for "gender-appropriate" play, come to believe in the appropriateness of having same-sex playmates, and develop different styles of social influence. Boys more often rely on commands, threats, and physical force, girls on polite requests and persuasion—differences that strengthen gender segregation.

◎ The impact of siblings on gender typing varies with birth order and family size. In small, two-child families, younger children tend to imitate the gender-role behavior of their older sibling. In larger families, same-sex siblings often strive to be different from one another. Consequently, they are likely to be less stereotyped in their interests and personality traits.

© ALAN CAREY/THE IMAGE WORKS

Gender Identity

Explain the meaning of androgyny, and describe and evaluate the accuracy of social learning and cognitive-developmental views of the development of gender identity in early childhood.

◎ Researchers measure **gender identity** by asking children and adults to rate themselves on "masculine" and "feminine" personality traits. Although most people have traditional identities, some are androgynous, scoring high on both masculine and feminine char-acteristics. At present, the masculine com-ponent of **androgyny** is largely responsible for its association with superior psychologi-cal adjustment.

◎ According to social learning theory, preschoolers first acquire gender-typed responses through modeling and reinforce-ment and only later organize them into cognitions about themselves. Cognitive-developmental theory suggests that **gender constancy** must be achieved before children can develop gender-typed behavior.

◎ Children master gender constancy by moving through three stages: **gender label-ing, gender stability,** and **gender consistency.** Understanding of gender constancy is asso-ciated with attainment of conservation and the appearance–reality distinction. In con-trast to cognitive-developmental predictions, "gender-appropriate" behavior is acquired long before gender constancy. However, other cognitive attainments—gender labeling and gender stability—strengthen preschoolers' gender-role adoption.

What changes in gender identity occur in middle childhood and adolescence?

◎ In middle childhood, boys strengthen their identification with the "masculine" role, whereas girls become more androgy-nous. The greater prestige of "masculine" characteristics makes them attractive to girls. At the same time, parents and peers are more tolerant of girls crossing gender lines than of boys doing so. School-age children's gender identities also expand to include self-evaluations of gender typicality, gender contentedness, and felt pressure to conform to gender roles—each of which affects psychological well-being.

◎ Early adolescence is a period of **gender intensification:** The gender identities of both sexes become more traditional. Physical and cognitive changes prompt young teenagers to spend more time thinking about them-selves in gender-linked ways, and gender-typed pressures from parents and peers increase. As young people move toward a mature personal identity, highly stereotypical self-perceptions decline.

Explain how gender schema theory accounts for the persistence of gender stereotypes and gender-role preferences.

◎ **Gender schema theory** is an information-processing approach to gender typing that combines social learning and cognitive-developmental features. As children learn gender-typed preferences and behaviors, they form masculine and feminine categories, or gender schemas, that they apply to themselves and use to interpret their world.

© MICHAEL NEWMAN/ PHOTOEDIT

◎ Children differ in the extent to which they build networks of gender schemas: Highly gender-schematic children attend to and approach schema-consistent informa-tion and avoid or misinterpret schema-inconsistent information. As a result, they learn much more about "gender-appropriate" than "gender-inappropriate" activities and behaviors.

To What Extent Do Boys and Girls Really Differ in Gender-Stereotyped Attributes?

Describe sex differences in mental abilities and personality attributes, noting factors that contribute to those differences.

◎ Most sex differences in mental abilities and personality traits are small to moderate.

Girls are ahead in early language development, score better in reading and writing achievement and math computation, are advantaged in emotional understanding, and are more prone to depression. Boys are better at certain spatial skills and at complex mathematical reasoning. Although boys display more physical aggression, sex differences in relational aggression are minimal.

◎ Biological factors contribute to differences between boys and girls in language development and spatial and math performance. At the same time, adult encouragement and learning opportunities play strong roles. Girls' greater emotional sensitivity, compliance, and dependency are largely due to gender-stereotyped expectations and child-rearing practices.

◎ Depression is the most common psychological problem of the teenage years. The higher rate of depression in adolescent girls is the combined result of the challenges of adolescence and gender-typed coping styles. Gender intensification in early adolescence often strengthens passivity, dependency, and selflessness in girls, which interfere with their mastery of developmental tasks and ability to handle stressful life events.

◎ Androgen hormones contribute to greater physical aggression in males. However, hormones exert their effects indirectly, by influencing activity level, emotional reactions, or dominance, all of which increase the likelihood of aggression under certain conditions. Compared with girls, boys react with greater hostility to parental arguments. Parents and teachers are more likely to encourage physical aggression in boys while suppressing it in girls. Gender-segregated peer groups extend these adult lessons.

Developing Non-Gender-Stereotyped Children

Cite ways to reduce gender stereotyping in children.

◎ Most aspects of gender typing are not built into human nature. And a long human childhood ensures that experience can greatly modify biologically based sex differences. Parents and teachers can counteract young children's readiness to absorb gender-linked associations by eliminating traditional gender roles from their own behavior and from the alternatives they provide for children. They can also avoid language that conveys gender stereotypes and can shield children from gender-biased media messages. Once children notice gender stereotypes, adults can point out exceptions and discuss the arbitrariness of many gender inequalities.

◎ Important Terms and Concepts

androgyny (p. 538)
expressive traits (p. 520)
gender consistency (p. 539)
gender constancy (p. 538)
gender identity (p. 520)

gender intensification (p. 541)
gender labeling (p. 539)
gender roles (p. 520)
gender schema theory (p. 541)
gender stability (p. 539)

gender-stereotype flexibility (p. 523)
gender stereotypes (p. 520)
gender typing (p. 520)
instrumental traits (p. 520)

"My Family"
Also Pablo Fernandez
Age 5, Mexico

Under a glorious wash of earth and sky, mother, father, and children enjoy a family outing. Although other contexts also mold the child, none equals the family in power and breadth of influence.

Reprinted with permission from the International Museum of Children's Art, Oslo, Norway.

CHAPTER 14

The Family

"I don't remember much family togetherness when I was a kid," 19-year-old Hannah reflected over dinner with Aunt Eva and Uncle Charlie. "Our parents couldn't talk things out with each other, and they weren't very open with us, either. We almost never sat down to a meal or went anywhere together. I went to Girl Scouts and to summer camp. I liked the activities, and I made good friends, but they couldn't make up for the lack of warm family time."

When Hannah was 9, her parents divorced, and she moved across the country with her mother. At first, her father arranged visits every few months; he would take Hannah out to eat, to the movies, and to the amusement park and would buy her whatever she wanted. Back home, when Hannah objected to her mother's rules and demands, her mother would rail at her father, calling him a "Disneyland Dad" who focused on fun and took no responsibility for Hannah's upbringing. As these arguments flared repeatedly, the visits trailed off, and eventually Hannah's father seldom made contact.

To make ends meet, Hannah's mother, an accountant, extended her work hours to evenings and weekends. Hannah would make herself a box of macaroni and cheese for dinner, eat by herself, and then—neglecting her homework—spend hours watching TV or just daydreaming. She found it hard to concentrate, and her grades suffered. In high school, stormy relationships with boyfriends left Hannah feeling depressed and rejected. Aimless and "at sea," she was convinced she couldn't do anything.

At 16, Hannah got her driver's license and began visiting Aunt Eva and Uncle Charlie, who lived in a neighboring city. They took the time to listen to Hannah, encourage her, and help her with her time management, academic, and relationship problems. Hungering for a sense of family togetherness, Hannah responded, spending more and more time with her aunt and uncle. Two years later, when Hannah graduated from high school with plans to enter a university, she attributed her turn-about in motivation and self-confidence to her aunt and uncle's steady warmth, involvement, and guidance.

The family is the child's first, and longest-lasting, context for development. Compared with other species, human children develop slowly, requiring years of support and teaching before they master the complexities of their physical and social environment and are ready to be independent. This gradual journey to maturity has left an imprint on human social organization everywhere: Families are pervasive, and parenting is universally important in children's lives. Children who lack a satisfying, supportive family life are likely to crave it, and some, like Hannah, find what they seek in extended family or another special adult.

Of course, other contexts also mold children's development, but in power and breadth of influence, none equals the family. The attachments children form with parents and siblings usually last a lifetime, and they serve as models for relationships in the wider world of neighborhood and school. Within the family, children experience their first social conflicts. Discipline by parents and arguments with siblings provide important lessons in compliance and cooperation and opportunities to learn how to influence the behavior of others. Finally, within the family, children learn the language, skills, and social and moral values of their culture.

We begin our discussion of the family by examining the reasons that this social unit came into being and has survived for thousands of years. Then we describe the current view of the family as a *social system* with many interacting influences on the child. Next, we look closely at the family as the core socializing agency of society by considering child-rearing styles, the many factors that influence them, and their consequences for children's development. We also take up recent social changes that have led to great diversity in family lifestyles. Finally, recognizing that the contemporary family is especially vulnerable to a breakdown in protective, emotionally supportive parent–child relationships, we conclude by considering the origins and consequences of child maltreatment.

Evolutionary Origins

The family in its most common form—a lifelong commitment between a man and woman who feed, shelter, and nurture their children until they reach maturity—arose tens of thousands of years ago among our hunting-and-gathering ancestors. Many other species live in social groups, but rarely do they organize into family-like units. Only 3 percent of birds and mammals, for example, form families (Emlen, 1995). Even among monkeys and apes, our closest evolutionary ancestors, families are almost nonexistent.

Anthropologists believe that bipedalism—the ability to walk upright on two legs—was an important evolutionary step that led to the development of the human family unit. Once arms were freed to carry things, our ancestors found it easier to cooperate and share, especially in providing for the young. Men usually traveled in search of game, while women gathered fruit and vegetables as a temporary food supply when hunting was unsuccessful. The human family pattern in which a man and a woman assumed special responsibility for their own children emerged because it enhanced survival. It ensured a relatively even balance of male hunters and female gatherers within a social group, thereby creating the greatest possible protection against starvation during times when game was scarce (Lancaster & Whitten, 1980).

An extended relationship between a man and a woman also increased male certainty that a newborn baby was actually *his* offspring—confidence necessary for him to provide mother and child with food and shelter and to invest in child rearing (Bjorklund, Yunger, & Pellegrini, 2002). And the long period of dependency of human offspring meant that adult reproductive success—children's survival to sexual maturity and the birth of grandchildren—required parental investment over many years. Thus, to increase the odds of child survival and to make possible the rearing of multiple offspring, fathers helped with child rearing (Geary, 2000). Human fathers devote more time to parenting than the vast majority of other male mammals (Clutton-Brock, 1991).

Kinship groups expanded to include ties with other relatives, most often grandparents but also aunts, uncles, and cousins. These larger kin networks, or clans, offered greater chances for

The family structure in which a man and woman make a lifelong commitment to each other and care for their young until they reach maturity arose tens of thousands of years ago because it enhanced survival. The couple on the left, who have four children, own and operate a children's bookshop in Kansas City, Missouri. The couple on the right, who live in Bali, Indonesia, have five children. The father fishes with a line and a tiny boat; his wife sells whatever he catches at the market. © Uwe Ommer/ Families/ Taschen edition

successful competition with other humans for food and other resources, and also for the protection and rearing of offspring. Within the clan, elders helped their children and other younger relatives reproduce by assisting with mate selection and child care, thereby increasing the likelihood that their own genetic heritage would continue (Geary & Flinn, 2001). And because economic and social obligations among family members were so important for survival, strong emotional bonds evolved to foster long-term commitment among parents, children, and other relatives (Nesse, 1990; Williams, 1997).

Functions of the Family

Besides promoting survival of its members, the family unit of our evolutionary ancestors performed the following vital services for society:

- *Reproduction.* Replacing dying members.
- *Economic services.* Producing and distributing goods and services.
- *Social order.* Devising procedures for reducing conflict and maintaining order.
- *Socialization.* Training the young to become competent, participating members of society.
- *Emotional support.* Helping others surmount emotional crises and fostering in each person a sense of commitment and purpose.

In the early history of our species, families probably served all or most of these functions. But as societies became more complex, the demands placed on the family became too much for it to sustain alone. Consequently, other institutions developed to assist with certain functions, and families became linked to larger social structures. For example, political and legal institutions assumed responsibility for ensuring societal order, and schools built on the family's socialization function. Religious institutions supplemented both child-rearing and emotional support functions by offering family members educational services and beliefs that enhanced their sense of purpose (Parke & Kellam, 1994).

Although some family members still carry out economic tasks together (as in family-run farms and businesses), this function has largely been taken over by institutions that make up the world of work. The contemporary family consumes far more goods and services than it produces. Consequently, whereas children used to contribute to families' economic well-being, today they are economic liabilities. According to a conservative estimate, today's new parents will spend about $185,000 in the United States and $168,000 in Canada to rear a child from birth to age 18, and many will incur substantial additional expense for higher education and financial dependency during emerging adulthood—a reality that has contributed to the declining birth rate in industrialized nations (Child Care Advocacy Association of Canada, 2004; U.S. Department of Agriculture, 2004a).

Although some functions are shared with other institutions, three important ones especially concerned with children—reproduction, socialization, and emotional support—remain primarily the province of the family. Researchers interested in finding out how families fulfill these functions take a **social systems perspective,** viewing the family as a complex set of interacting relationships influenced by the larger social context.

The Family as a Social System

The social systems perspective on family functioning grew out of researchers' efforts to describe and explain the complex patterns of interaction between family members. As you will see, it has much in common with Bronfenbrenner's *ecological systems theory,* discussed in Chapter 1. Family systems theorists recognize that parents do not mechanically shape their children. Rather, as you already know from earlier chapters, *bidirectional influences* exist, whereby family members mutually influence one another. The very term *family system* implies a network of interdependent relationships (Parke & Buriel, 1998; Lerner et al., 2002). These system influences operate both directly and indirectly.

Direct Influences

Recently, as I passed through the checkout counter at the supermarket, I witnessed the following two episodes, in which parents and children directly influenced each other:

- Five-year-old Danny looked longingly at the tempting rows of candy as his mother lifted groceries from her cart onto the counter. "Pleeeease, can I have it, Mom?" Danny begged, holding up a large package of bubble gum. "Do you have a dollar? Just one?"

    "No, not today," his mother answered. "Remember, we picked out your special cereal. That's what I need the dollar for." Gently taking the bubble gum from his hand, Danny's mother handed him the box of cereal. "Here, let's pay," she said, lifting Danny so he could see the checkout counter.

- Three-year-old Meg was sitting in the shopping cart while her mother transferred groceries to the counter. Suddenly Meg turned around, grabbed a bunch of bananas, and started to pull them apart.

    "Stop it, Meg!" shouted her mother, snatching the bananas from Meg's hand. But as she turned her attention to paying with her debit card, Meg reached for a chocolate bar from a nearby shelf. "Meg, how many times have I told you, *don't touch!*" Loosening the candy from Meg's tight little fist, Meg's mother slapped her hand. Meg's face turned red with anger as she began to wail.

These observations fit with a wealth of research on the family system. Studies of families of diverse ethnicities show that when parents are firm but warm (like Danny's mom), children tend to comply with their requests. And when children cooperate, their parents are likely to be warm and gentle in the future. In contrast, parents who discipline with harshness and impatience (like Meg's mother) tend to have children who resist and rebel. And because children's misbehavior is stressful for parents, they may increase their use of punishment, leading to more unruliness by the child (Stormshak et al., 2000; Whiteside-Mansell et al., 2003). In these examples, the behavior of one family member helps sustain a form of interaction in another that either promotes or undermines children's well-being.

Indirect Influences

The impact of family relationships on child development becomes even more complicated when we consider that interaction between any two family members is affected by others present in the setting. Recall from Chapter 1 that Bronfenbrenner called these indirect influences the effect of *third parties*. Researchers have become intensely interested in how a range of relationships—mother with father, parent with sibling, grandparent with parent—modify the child's direct experiences in the family. In fact, as the From Research to Practice box on the following page reveals, a child's birth can have a third-party impact on parents' interaction that may affect the child's development and well-being.

Third parties can serve as supports for development, or they can undermine it. For example, when parents' marital relationship is warm and considerate, mothers and fathers praise and stimulate their children more and nag and scold them less. In contrast, when a marriage is tense and hostile, parents tend to be less responsive to their children's needs and to criticize, express anger, and punish (Cox, Paley, & Harter, 2001; McHale et al., 2002). Children chronically exposed to angry, unresolved parental conflict show myriad problems related to disrupted emotional security and emotional self-regulation (Harold et al., 2004). These include both *internalizing difficulties* (especially among girls), such as blaming themselves, feeling worried and fearful, and trying to repair their parents' relationship; and *externalizing difficulties* (especially among boys), including feeling threatened and displaying more overt and relational aggression (Davies & Lindsay, 2004; Hart et al., 1998). Furthermore, in research carried out in nations as diverse as Bangladesh, China, Bosnia, and the United States, parental conflict consistently undermined good parenting by increasing criticism and belittling of adolescents and decreasing monitoring of their whereabouts and activities. These parenting practices, in turn, heightened youth behavior problems (Bradford et al., 2003).

Yet even when parental arguments strain children's adjustment, other family members may help restore effective interaction. Grandparents are a case in point. As we will see, they can promote children's development in many ways—both directly, by responding warmly and assisting with caregiving, and indirectly, by providing parents with child-rearing advice, models

The Transition to Parenthood

The early weeks after a baby enters the family are full of profound changes—constant caregiving, less time for couples to devote to each other, and added financial responsibilities. These demands usually cause the roles of husband and wife to become more traditional, even for couples who are strongly committed to gender equality and are accustomed to sharing household tasks. Typically, mothers spend more time at home with the baby, whereas fathers focus more on their provider role (Cowan & Cowan, 2000; Salmela-Aro et al., 2000).

For most new parents, the arrival of a baby does not cause significant marital strain. Marriages that are gratifying and supportive tend to remain so and resemble childless marriages in overall happiness (Feeney et al., 2001; Miller, 2000). But troubled marriages usually become more distressed after a baby is born. In a study of newlyweds who were interviewed annually for 6 years, the husband's affection, expression of "we-ness" (values and goals similar to his wife's), and awareness of his wife's daily life predicted mothers' stable or increasing marital satisfaction after childbirth. In contrast, the husband's negativity and the couple's out-of-control conflict predicted a drop in mothers' satisfaction (Shapiro, Gottman, & Carrere, 2000).

Also, violated expectations about division of labor in the home affect new parents' well-being. For most dual-earner couples, the larger the difference in men's and women's caregiving responsibilities, the greater the decline in marital satisfaction after childbirth, especially for women—with negative consequences for parent–infant interaction. In contrast, sharing caregiving tasks predicts greater sensitivity by both parents to their baby (Feldman, 2002). An exception exists, however, for employed lower-SES women who endorse traditional gender roles. When their husbands take on considerable child-care responsibilities, these mothers report more distress, perhaps because they feel disappointed at being unable to fulfill their desire to do most of the caregiving (Goldberg & Perry-Jenkins, 2003).

Postponing childbearing until the late twenties or thirties eases the transition to parenthood. Waiting permits couples to pursue occupational goals, gain life experience, and plan to become parents when they feel psychologically ready (Taniguchi, 1999). Under these circumstances, men are more enthusiastic about becoming fathers and therefore more willing to participate. And women whose careers are well under way are more likely to encourage their husbands to share housework and child care (Coltrane, 1990).

A second birth typically requires that fathers take an even more active role in parenting—by caring for the first-born while the mother is recuperating and by sharing in the high demands of tending to both a baby and a young child. Consequently, well-functioning families with a newborn second child typically show a pulling back from the traditional division of responsibilities that occurred after the first birth. In a study that tracked parents from the end of pregnancy through the first year after their second child's birth, fathers became increasingly aware of their vital role in fostering favorable day-to-day family functioning. As one father commented, "It took only one child to make my wife a mother, but two to make me a father" (Stewart, 1990, p. 142). Fathers' willingness to place greater emphasis on the parenting role is strongly linked to mothers' adjustment after the arrival of a second baby. And the support and encouragement of family, friends, and spouse are crucial for fathers' well-being.

Special interventions exist to ease the transition to parenthood. For those who are not at high risk for problems, couples' groups led by counselors are highly effective (Cowan & Cowan, 1995). In one program, first-time expectant couples gathered once a week for 6 months to discuss their dreams for the family and changes in relationships sparked by the baby's arrival. Eighteen months after the program ended, participating fathers described themselves as more involved with their child than did fathers in a no-intervention condition. Perhaps because of fathers' caregiving assistance, participating mothers maintained their prebirth satisfaction with family and work roles. Three years after the birth, the marriages of all participating

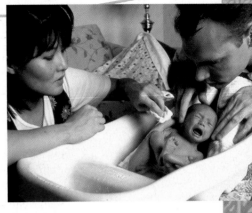

▲ After arriving home from the hospital, these first-time parents comfort their baby during a bath. In a warm, gratifying marriage, sharing caregiving tasks enhances marital satisfaction and is related to parents' sensitivity toward the baby. © Michael Newman/PhotoEdit

couples were still intact and just as happy as they had been before parenthood. In contrast, 15 percent of couples receiving no intervention had divorced (Cowan & Cowan, 1997).

For high-risk parents struggling with poverty or the birth of a child with disabilities, interventions must be more intensive. Programs in which a trained intervener visits the home and enhances both social support and the parent–child relationship have resulted in improved parent–infant interaction and benefits for children's cognitive and social development up to 5 years after the intervention (Meisels, Dichtelmiller, & Liaw, 1993).

Generous, paid employment leave—widely available in industrialized nations, but not in the United States—is crucial for easing the transition to parenthood (see Chapter 3, page 112). Because of financial pressures, many new mothers who are eligible for unpaid work leave take far less than they are guaranteed by U.S. federal law, and new fathers take little or none at all (Han & Waldfogel, 2003). Flexible work hours are also helpful. When favorable workplace policies exist and couples try to support each other's needs, the stress caused by the birth of a baby stays at manageable levels. Family relationships are worked out after a few months, and most infants flourish, bringing great satisfaction to their parents and making the sacrifices of this period worthwhile.

of child-rearing skill, and even financial assistance (Drew, Richard, & Smith, 1998). Of course, as with any indirect influence, grandparents can sometimes be harmful. When quarrelsome relations exist between grandparents and parents, children may suffer.

Adapting to Change

Think back to the *chronosystem* in Bronfenbrenner's theory (see page 29 in Chapter 1). The interplay of forces within the family is dynamic and ever changing, as each member adapts to the development of other members.

For example, as children acquire new skills, parents adjust the way they treat their more competent youngsters. To cite just one example, turn back to Chapter 4, page 142, and review how babies' mastery of crawling leads parents to engage in more game playing and expressions of affection, as well as restriction of the child's activities. These changes in child rearing pave the way for new achievements and further revisions in family relationships. Can you think of other illustrations of this idea, discussed in earlier chapters?

Parents' development affects children as well. Later we will see that the mild increase in parent–child conflict that often occurs in early adolescence is not solely due to teenagers' striving for independence. This is a time when most parents have reached middle age and—conscious that their children will soon leave home and establish their own lives—are reconsidering their own commitments (Steinberg & Silk, 2002). Consequently, while the adolescent presses for greater autonomy, the parent presses for more togetherness. This imbalance promotes friction, which parent and teenager gradually resolve by accommodating to changes in each another (Collins, 1997). Indeed, no social unit other than the family is required to adjust to such vast changes in its members.

The Family System in Context

The social systems perspective, as we noted earlier, views the family as affected by surrounding social contexts. As the *mesosystem* and *exosystem* in Bronfenbrenner's model make clear, connections to the neighborhood and the larger community—both *formal organizations,* such as school, workplace, recreation center, child-care center, and religious institution, and *informal social networks* of relatives, friends, and neighbors—influence parent–child relationships.

In several studies, low-SES families were randomly assigned vouchers to move out of public housing into neighborhoods varying widely in affluence. Compared with their peers who remained in poverty-stricken areas, children and youths who moved into low-poverty neighborhoods showed substantially better physical and mental health and school achievement (Goering, 2003; Leventhal & Brooks-Gunn, 2003).

Unstable, inner-city neighborhoods with dilapidated housing; schools, parks, and playgrounds in disarray; and lack of community centers introduce stressors that undermine parental warmth, involvement, and monitoring and increase parental harshness and inconsistency. When a run-down, impoverished neighborhood combines with poor parenting, rates of problem behaviors in children and antisocial activity among youths are especially high (Brody et al., 2003; Kohen et al., 2002). In contrast, strong family ties to the surrounding social context—as indicated by contact with friends and relatives, organized youth activities, and regular church, synagogue, or mosque attendance—reduce youth adjustment problems (Garbarino & Kostelny, 1993; Magnuson & Duncan, 2002).

How do links between family and community reduce stress and promote child development? One answer lies in their provision of social support, which leads to the following benefits:

- *Parental interpersonal acceptance.* A neighbor or relative who listens and tries to relieve a parent's concern enhances her self-esteem. The parent, in turn, is likely to behave in a more sensitive and involved manner toward her children.

- *Parental access to valuable information and services.* A friend who suggests where a job or housing might be found or who looks after children while the parent attends to other pressing needs helps make the multiple roles of spouse, provider, and caregiver easier to fulfill.

⑥ According to the social systems perspective, ties to the community are essential for families to function at their best. As these parents and their children participate in a fund-raising event for breast cancer, they also form networks of social support.
© Jeff Greenberg/The Image Works

- *Child-rearing controls and role models.* Friends, relatives, and other community members may encourage and demonstrate effective ways of interacting with children and discourage ineffective practices.

- *Direct assistance with child rearing.* As children and adolescents participate in their parents' social networks and in youth-oriented community activities, other adults can influence children directly through warmth, stimulation, and exposure to a wider array of competent models. In this way, family–neighborhood ties can reduce the impact of ineffective parenting (Silk et al., 2004). Nearby adults can also intervene when they see young people skipping school or behaving antisocially.

The Better Beginnings, Better Futures Project of Ontario, Canada, is a government-sponsored set of pilot programs aimed at preventing the dire consequences of neighborhood poverty. The most successful of these efforts used a local elementary school as its base, providing children with in-class, before- and after-school, and summer enrichment activities, as well as programs during school breaks and holidays. Workers also visited each child's parents regularly, informed them about community resources, and encouraged their involvement in the child's school and neighborhood life (Peters, Petrunka, & Arnold, 2003). An evaluation after four years revealed wide-ranging benefits—gains in neighborhood satisfaction, family functioning, effective parenting, and children's reading skills, together with a reduction in emotional and behavior problems.

No researcher could possibly study all aspects of the social systems perspective on the family at once. But throughout this chapter, we will continually see examples of how its interlocking parts combine to influence development.

Ask Yourself

REVIEW	Why, in our evolutionary history, was the family adaptive?
APPLY	On a trip to a shopping center, you see a father getting angry with his young son. Using the social systems perspective, list as many factors as you can that might account for the father's behavior.
CONNECT	How does the goodness-of-fit model, discussed in Chapter 10 (see page 417), illustrate central features of the social systems perspective on family functioning?
REFLECT	Provide examples of links between your family and the surrounding community during your own childhood. How did those ties promote your development and well-being?

Socialization Within the Family

Among the family's functions, socialization centers on children's development. Parents start to socialize their children in earnest during the second year, when toddlers are first able to comply with their directives (see Chapter 12). As children get older, parents gradually step up socialization pressures, but they vary greatly in how they go about the task. In previous chapters, we have seen how parents can foster children's competence—by building a parent–child relationship based on affection and cooperation, by serving as models and reinforcers of mature behavior, by using reasoning and inductive discipline, and by guiding and encouraging children's mastery of new skills. Now let's put these elements together into an overall view of effective parenting.

Styles of Child Rearing

Child-rearing styles are combinations of parenting behaviors that occur over a wide range of situations, creating an enduring child-rearing climate. In a landmark series of studies, Diana Baumrind gathered information on child rearing by watching parents interact with their preschoolers (Baumrind, 1971; Baumrind & Black, 1967). Her findings, and those of others who have extended her work, reveal three features that consistently differentiate an effective style from less effective ones:

TABLE 14.1 FEATURES OF CHILD-REARING STYLES

Child-Rearing Style	Acceptance and Involvement	Control	Autonomy Granting
Authoritative	Is warm, responsive, attentive, patient, and sensitive to the child's needs	Makes reasonable demands for maturity, and consistently enforces and explains them	Permits the child to make decisions in accord with readiness Encourages the child to express thoughts, feelings, and desires When parent and child disagree, engages in joint decision making when possible
Authoritarian	Is cold and rejecting and frequently degrades the child	Makes many demands coercively, using force and punishment. Often engages in psychological control, withdrawing love and robbing the child of his or her individuality.	Makes decisions for the child Rarely listens to the child's point of view
Permissive	Is warm but overindulgent or inattentive	Makes few or no demands	Permits the child to make many decisions before the child is ready
Uninvolved	Is emotionally detached and withdrawn	Makes few or no demands	Is indifferent to the child's decision making and point of view

- *Acceptance* of the child and *involvement* in the child's life to establish an emotional connection with the child.
- *Control* of the child to promote more mature behavior.
- *Autonomy granting* to encourage self-reliance (Barber & Olsen, 1997; Gray & Steinberg, 1999; Hart, Newell, & Olsen, 2002).

Table 14.1 shows how child-rearing styles differ in these features. Let's discuss each style in turn.

This father uses an authoritative style as he allows his son to assemble the outfit he will wear on a family outing. He engages in appropriate autonomy granting, encouraging the child to express his thoughts and opinions.
© Myrleen Ferguson Cate/PhotoEdit

• **AUTHORITATIVE CHILD REARING** • The **authoritative child-rearing style**—the most successful approach to child rearing—involves high acceptance and involvement, adaptive control techniques, and appropriate autonomy granting. Authoritative parents are warm, attentive, and sensitive to their child's needs. They establish an enjoyable, emotionally fulfilling parent–child relationship that draws the child into close connection. At the same time, authoritative parents exercise firm, reasonable control of their child's behavior: They insist on appropriate maturity, give reasons for their expectations, use disciplinary encounters as "teaching moments" to promote the child's self-regulation, and monitor their child's whereabouts and activities. Finally, authoritative parents engage in gradual, appropriate *autonomy granting,* allowing the child to make decisions in areas where he is ready to make choices. They also place a premium on communication, encouraging the child to express her thoughts, feelings, and desires. And when parent and child disagree, authoritative parents engage in joint decision making when possible. Their willingness to accommodate to the child's perspective increases the likelihood that the child will listen to their perspective in situations where compliance is vital (Kuczynski & Lollis, 2002; Russell, Mize, & Bissaker, 2004).

Throughout childhood and adolescence, authoritative parenting is linked to many aspects of competence. These include an upbeat mood, self-control, task persistence, and cooperativeness during the preschool years and, at older ages, high self-esteem, responsiveness to parents' views, social and moral maturity, and favorable school performance (Amato & Fowler, 2002; Herman et al., 1997; Aunola, Stattin, & Nurmi, 2000; Luster & McAdoo, 1996; Mackey, Arnold, & Pratt, 2001; Steinberg, Darling, & Fletcher, 1995).

• **AUTHORITARIAN CHILD REARING** • Parents who use an **authoritarian child-rearing style** are low in acceptance and involvement, high in coercive control, and low in autonomy granting. Authoritarian parents appear cold and rejecting; they frequently degrade their child by mocking and putting her down. To exert control, they yell, command, criticize, and threaten. "Do it because I said so!" is their attitude. If the child disobeys, authoritarian parents resort to force and punishment. They also make decisions for their child and expect the child to accept their word unquestioningly. If the child does not, authoritarian parents resort to force and punishment.

Children of authoritarian parents are anxious and unhappy, are low in self-esteem and self-reliance, and tend to react with hostility when frustrated. Like their parents, they resort to force when they do not get their way. Boys, especially, show high rates of anger and defiance. Although girls also engage in acting-out behavior, they are more likely to be dependent, lacking interest in exploration, and overwhelmed by challenging tasks (Hart et al., 2004; Nix et al., 1999; Thompson, Hollis, & Richards, 2003). Children and adolescents exposed to the authoritarian style typically do poorly in school. However, because of their parents' concern with controlling their behavior, they tend to achieve better and to commit fewer antisocial acts than peers with undemanding parents—that is, those whose parents use the two styles we will consider next.

Notice how the authoritarian style is biased in favor of parents' needs; it suppresses children's self-expression and independence. Growing evidence indicates that authoritarian parents' form of control contributes greatly to their children's adjustment problems. In addition to unwarranted direct control ("Do what I say!"), authoritarian parents engage in a more subtle type called **psychological control**—behaviors that intrude on and manipulate children's verbal expressions, individuality, and attachments to parents. (Barber, 1996). These parents—out of a desire to decide virtually everything for the child—frequently interrupt or put down the child's ideas, decisions, or choice of friends. When they are dissatisfied, they withdraw love, making their affection or attention contingent on the child's compliance with their wishes. And they harbor excessively high expectations, insisting that the child meet an absolute standard rather than a standard that fits the child's developing capacities. Children subjected to psychological control are robbed of their individuality. They exhibit both the anxious, withdrawn response and the defiant, aggressive behaviors that are linked to parental authoritarianism (Barber & Harmon, 2002; Silk et al., 2003).

In addition to coercive tactics, authoritarian parents often engage in psychological control, in which they infringe on the child's individuality and attachments by putting down the child's ideas and decisions and withdrawing love if the child does not comply. In response, children become anxious and withdrawn or defiant and aggressive, as well as low in self-esteem and self-reliance.
© David Young-Wolff/PhotoEdit

• **PERMISSIVE CHILD REARING** • The **permissive child-rearing style** is warm and accepting. Rather than being involved, however, permissive parents are either overindulgent or inattentive. Permissive parents engage in little *control* of their children's behavior. Instead of gradually granting autonomy, they allow children to make many decisions for themselves at an age when they are not yet capable of doing so. Their children can eat meals and go to bed whenever they wish and can watch as much television as they want. They do not have to learn good manners or do household chores. Although some permissive parents truly believe that this approach is best, many others simply lack confidence in their ability to influence their child's behavior.

Children of permissive parents are impulsive, disobedient, and rebellious. Compared with children whose parents exert more control, they are also overly demanding and dependent on adults, and they show less persistence on tasks and poorer school achievement—behaviors that are especially evident among boys. In adolescence, parental indulgence continues to be related to poor self-control. Permissively reared teenagers do less well academically, are more defiant of authority figures, and display more antisocial behavior than teenagers whose parents communicate clear expectations (Barber & Olsen, 1997; Baumrind, 1991, 1997; Kurdek & Fine, 1994; Lamborn et al., 1991).

• **UNINVOLVED CHILD REARING** • The **uninvolved child-rearing style** combines low acceptance and involvement with little control and general indifference to issues of autonomy. Uninvolved parents may be emotionally detached and depressed, so overwhelmed by the many stresses in their lives that they have no time and energy for children (Maccoby & Martin, 1983). As a result, they may respond to the child's immediate demands for easily accessible objects. But any parenting strategies that involve long-term goals, such as establishing and enforcing rules about homework and social behavior, listening to the child's point of view, providing guidance about appropriate choices, and monitoring the child's whereabouts and activities, are weak and fleeting.

At its extreme, uninvolved parenting is a form of child maltreatment called *neglect.* It is likely to characterize depressed parents with many stresses in their lives, such as marital conflict, little or no social support, and poverty. Especially when it begins early, neglect disrupts virtually all aspects of development, including attachment, cognition, play, and emotional and social skills (see Chapter 10, page 397). Even when parental disengagement is less extreme, children and adolescents display many problems—poor emotional self-regulation, school achievement difficulties, and frequent antisocial behavior (Aunola, Stattin, & Nurmi, 2000; Baumrind, 1991; Kurdek & Fine, 1994; Lamborn et al., 1991).

What Makes the Authoritative Style Effective?

Table 14.2 summarizes outcomes associated with each child-rearing style just considered. As with other correlational findings, the relationship between the authoritative style and children's competence is open to interpretation. Perhaps parents of well-adjusted children use demanding tactics because their youngsters have cooperative, obedient dispositions, not because firm control is an essential ingredient of effective parenting.

Children's characteristics do contribute to the ease with which parents can apply the authoritative style. Recall from earlier chapters that temperamentally fearless, impulsive children and emotionally negative, difficult children are more likely to evoke coercive, inconsistent discipline. At the same time, extra warmth and firm control succeed in modifying these children's maladaptive styles (Hart et al., 1998; Olson et al., 2000). In the case of fearful, inhibited children, parents must suppress their tendency to overprotect and take over solving the child's social problems—practices that, as we saw in Chapter 10, worsen the shy child's difficulties. Instead, inhibited children benefit from extra encouragement to be assertive and to express their autonomy (Rubin, Burgess, & Coplan, 2002).

Longitudinal research indicates that authoritative child rearing promotes maturity and adjustment in children of diverse temperaments. As the findings just mentioned illustrate, some children, because of their dispositions, require "heavier doses" of certain authoritative features than others (Hart, Newell, & Olson, 2004, p. 764). Over time, the relationship between parenting and children's attributes becomes increasingly bidirectional as each participant modifies the actions of the other and forms expectancies for the other's behavior based on past interactions (Kuczynski, 2003).

Consider a longitudinal investigation of consequences of parental monitoring of adolescents' activities that extended from ages 14 to 18. The more parents knew about their child's whereabouts and activities, the greater the decline in teenagers' delinquent acts over time. And the greater the decline in delinquency, the greater the increase in parents' knowledge of their youngsters' daily life (Laird et al., 2003).

What explains these bidirectional associations, in which parental monitoring promotes responsible youth behavior, which in turn leads to gains in parental knowledge? Parents who exert appropriate oversight over their adolescents' lives are likely to parent effectively in other

TABLE 14.2 RELATIONSHIP OF CHILD-REARING STYLES TO DEVELOPMENT AND ADJUSTMENT

Child-Rearing Style	Outcomes	
	Childhood	**Adolescence**
Authoritative	Upbeat mood; high self-esteem, self-control, task persistence, and cooperativeness	High self-esteem, social and moral maturity, and academic achievement
Authoritarian	Anxious, withdrawn, and unhappy mood; hostile when frustrated; poor school performance	Less well adjusted than agemates reared with the authoritative style, but somewhat better school performance and less antisocial behavior than agemates reared with permissive or uninvolved styles
Permissive	Impulsive, disobedient, and rebellious; demanding and dependent on adults; poor persistence at tasks and school performance	Poor self-control and school performance; defiance and antisocial behavior
Uninvolved	Deficits in attachment, cognition, play, and emotional and social skills	Poor emotional self-regulation, low academic self-esteem and school performance; antisocial behavior

ways, giving teenagers both less opportunity and less reason to engage in delinquency. And when parents take proactive steps to intervene in their child's antisocial behavior, they set the stage for a more positive parent–child relationship, in which teenagers are more willing to provide them with information. In contrast, when monitoring is lax and delinquency rises, parent–child interaction may become increasingly negative. As a result, parents may further disengage from parenting, both to avoid unpleasant parent–child exchanges and to reduce contact with a child whom they have come to dislike.

Most children and adolescents seem to regard the affection, appropriate control, and respect for self-determination that make up authoritative child rearing as a well-intentioned parental effort to increase their competence. As a result, even hard-to-rear youngsters gradually respond to authoritativeness with increased cooperation and maturity, which increases parents' pleasure and approval of the child, parents' sense of self-efficacy at child rearing, and their likelihood of continuing to be authoritative. In sum, authoritative child rearing seems to create a *positive emotional context* for parental influence in the following ways:

- Children are far more likely to comply with and internalize control that appears fair and reasonable, not arbitrary, to them (see Chapter 12).

- Warm, involved parents who are secure in the standards they hold for their children provide models of caring concern as well as confident, self-controlled behavior. Perhaps for this reason, children of such parents are advanced in emotional self-regulation and emotional and social understanding—factors linked to social competence (Lindsey & Mize, 2000).

- Parents who combine warmth with rational and reasonable control are likely to be more effective reinforcing agents, praising children for striving to meet their expectations and making good use of disapproval, which works best when applied by an adult who has been warm and caring (see Chapter 12).

- Authoritative parents make demands and engage in autonomy granting that fits with children's ability to take responsibility for their own behavior. By letting children know that they are competent individuals who can do things successfully for themselves, these parents foster favorable self-esteem and cognitive and social maturity (see Chapter 11).

- Supportive aspects of the authoritative style, including parental acceptance, involvement, and rational control, help protect children from the negative effects of family stress and poverty (Beyers et al., 2003; Pettit, Bates, & Dodge, 1997).

Still, a few theorists remain convinced that parenting has little impact on children's development. They claim that because parents and children share genes, parents will provide children with genetically influenced child rearing that does little more than enhance children's built-in propensities. As the Biology and Environment box on page 568 reveals, this conclusion has been rebutted with a host of findings demonstrating that parenting contributes vitally to children's competence.

Adapting Child Rearing to Children's Development

Because authoritative parents continually adapt to children's increasing competence, their practices change with children's age. A gradual lessening of control over the child's behavior and an increase in autonomy granting support development.

• **PARENTING IN MIDDLE CHILDHOOD: COREGULATION** • In middle childhood, the amount of time children spend with parents declines dramatically. The child's growing independence means that parents must deal with new issues. As one mother commented, "I've struggled with how many chores to assign, how much allowance to give, whether their friends are good influences, and what to do about problems at school. And then there's the challenge of how to keep track of them when they're out of the house or even when they're home and I'm not there to see what's going on."

Although parents face new concerns, child rearing becomes easier for those who established an authoritative style during the early years. Reasoning works more effectively with school-age children because of their greater capacity for logical thinking and their increased respect for parents' expert knowledge (Collins, Madsen, & Susman-Stillman, 2002). As children demonstrate that they can manage daily activities and responsibilities, effective parents

Does Parenting Really Matter?

Several highly publicized reviews of research have concluded that parents are only minor players in children's development—that their impact is overshadowed by the effects of children's genetic makeup and the peer culture (Harris, 1998, 2002). These claims are largely based on evidence that siblings reared in the same family show little resemblance in temperament and personality (see Chapter 10, page 416, to review), a finding interpreted to mean that parenting is merely a reaction to children's genetic dispositions and does not change children in any appreciable way. No wonder, then, say proponents of the parents-matter-little position, that many studies report only a weak to moderate parenting effect on children's development. A related contention is that children and adolescents resemble their friends more strongly than their siblings. Therefore, peers must be far more powerful than parents in influencing children's behavior.

These assertions have been refuted by a host of researchers, who offer evidence that parents—though not the sole influence—exert a profound impact (Berk, 2005; Collins et al., 2000; Hart, Newell, & Olsen, 2003; Maccoby, 2000a; Steinberg, 2001). Let's examine their findings more closely:

● *Recent, well-designed research reveals that the relation between parenting and children's development is sometimes substantial.* For example, in one large-scale study, the correlation between authoritative parenting and adolescents' social responsibility was .76 for mothers, .49 for fathers (Hetherington et al., 1999). Similarly, when parents engage in joint problem solving with their adolescent youngsters, establish firm, consistent control, and monitor the adolescent's whereabouts, research shows strong negative relationships with antisocial behavior (Patterson & Forgatch, 1995).

● *Parenting often has different effects on different children.* When weak associations between parenting and children's development are found, they are not necessarily due to the feeble impact of parenting. Rather, some child-rearing practices affect different children in different ways. Much evidence indicates that parents respond differently to children with different temperaments. But the relationship is not just a reactive one. In this and previous chapters, we have seen that parents can modify the behavior of impulsive, difficult, and shy, inhibited children. As Eleanor Maccoby (2000a) concluded, "The idea that in a long-standing relation such as one between parent and child, the child would be influencing the parent but the parent would not be influencing the child is absurd" (p. 18).

● *Longitudinal research suggests that parenting affects children's development.* Many longitudinal studies indicate that the influence of parenting on diverse aspects of children's development holds even after controlling for children's earlier characteristics (see, for example, Bornstein et al., 1996; Carlson, 1998; Laird et al., 2003; Pettit, Bates, & Dodge, 1997). These findings suggest that the influence of parents is profound and lasting.

● *Parenting interventions show that when child rearing improves, children's development changes accordingly.* The most powerful evidence that parents matter comes from intervention experiments. In one study, recently divorced single mothers of school-age sons were randomly assigned to a year of parent training and support. Compared to no-intervention controls, the mothers reduced their use of coercive discipline over time; at the conclusion of the intervention, their sons showed fewer behavior problems (Forgatch & DeGarmo, 1999). In another, similar program, school-age children whose divorcing mothers attended an 11-week parenting skills class not only showed better immediate adjustment than youths whose parents did not attend, but the children were still functioning more favorably at a six-year follow-up (Wolchick et al., 2003). Furthermore, recall from Chapter 12 that training programs targeting parenting skills can break cycles of parent–child hostility, thereby reducing children's aggressive behavior (see page 512).

● *Parents influence children's peer relations.* Children and adolescents resemble their friends because young people choose friends who are similar to themselves. But beginning in the preschool years, parents propel children toward certain peers by managing their social activities. And as we will see in Chapter 15, authoritative child rearing affects the values and inclinations children and adolescents bring to the peer situation and, therefore, their choice of friends and their peer interactions and activities (Furman et al., 2002; Laird et al., 2003; Pettit et al., 2001; Zhou et al., 2002).

● *Some parenting influences cannot be measured easily.* Many people report memorable moments with parents that made a lasting impression. In contrast, a parent's broken promise or discovered deception can destroy parent–child trust and change the impact of future parenting (Maccoby, 2000a).

In sum, parenting effects combine in complex ways with many other factors, including heredity and peers. Indeed, the contribution of each factor cannot be partitioned neatly from the others, just as nature and nurture are interwoven throughout development.

In view of current evidence, what can parents do to ensure the best outcomes for children? Craig Hart (1999) offers four recommendations:

● Teach moral values, to help children make wise choices in the face of their genetic inclinations and pressures from peers.

● Adapt parenting to help children overcome unfavorable dispositions. Using coercive control instead of rational firmness with an impulsive child, or overprotection instead of encouragement with an inhibited youngster, worsens maladaptive behavior.

● Foster children's positive capacities through rich, varied experiences—academic, social, athletic, artistic, musical, and spiritual.

● Engage in authoritative child rearing, a style that consistently predicts positive outcomes for children and adolescents.

▼ A wealth of research confirms that parents profoundly affect children's development. This mother and her children visit a nature museum where together they examine fascinating sea creatures. When warm parents provide rich, varied experiences, they foster children's positive capacities.
© Michael Newman/PhotoEdit

gradually shift responsibilities from adult to child. This does not mean that they let go entirely. Instead, they engage in **coregulation,** a form of supervision in which parents exercise general oversight while permitting children to be in charge of moment-by-moment decision making. Coregulation grows out of a cooperative relationship between parent and child—one based on give-and-take and mutual respect. Parents must guide and monitor from a distance and effectively communicate expectations when they are with their children. And children must inform parents of their whereabouts, activities, and problems so parents can intervene when necessary (Maccoby, 1984). Coregulation supports and protects children while preparing them for adolescence, when they will make many important decisions themselves.

Although school-age children often press for greater independence, they know how much they need their parents' support. In one study, fifth and sixth graders described parents as the most influential people in their lives (Furman & Buhrmester, 1992). They often turned to their parents for affection, advice, enhancement of self-worth, and assistance with everyday problems.

• **PARENTING IN ADOLESCENCE: FOSTERING AUTONOMY** • During adolescence, striving for **autonomy**—a sense of oneself as a separate, self-governing individual—becomes a salient task. Autonomy has two vital aspects: (1) an *emotional component*—relying more on oneself and less on parents for support and guidance, and (2) a *behavioral component*—making decisions independently by carefully weighing one's own judgment and the suggestions of others to arrive at a well-reasoned course of action (Steinberg & Silverberg, 1986). Autonomy is closely related to adolescents' quest for identity. Young people who successfully construct personally meaningful values and life goals are autonomous. They have given up childish dependency on parents for a more mature, responsible relationship.

Autonomy receives support from a variety of changes within the adolescent. In Chapter 5, we saw that puberty triggers psychological distancing from parents. In addition, as young people look more mature, parents give them more independence and responsibility. Cognitive development also paves the way toward autonomy. Abstract thinking permits teenagers to solve problems and to foresee the consequences of their actions more effectively. And an improved ability to reason about social relationships leads adolescents to *deidealize* their parents, viewing them as "just people." Consequently, they no longer bend as easily to parental authority as they did at earlier ages.

Warm, supportive parent–adolescent ties that permit young people to explore ideas and social roles foster adolescent autonomy, predicting high self-reliance, work orientation, academic competence, and favorable self-esteem (Slicker & Thornberry, 2002; Vazsonyi, Hibbert, & Snider, 2003). Conversely, parents who are coercive or psychologically controlling interfere with the development of autonomy. These tactics breed intense, emotionally negative exchanges between parent and teenager (Kim et al., 2001). And they are linked to low self-esteem, depression, and antisocial behavior—consequences that persist into emerging adulthood (Aquilino & Supple, 2001; Barber & Harmon, 2002).

Nevertheless, sustaining effective parenting is challenging, and parents often report that living with teenagers is stressful. In Chapter 12, we noted that interest in making choices about personal matters strengthens in adolescence. Yet parents and teenagers—especially young teenagers—differ sharply on the appropriate age for young people to receive certain responsibilities and privileges, such as control over clothing, school courses, and going out with friends (Smetana, 2002). Parents typically say that the young person is not yet ready for these signs of independence at a point when the teenager thinks they should have been granted long ago! Although adolescents often resist, firm (but not overly restrictive) parental monitoring of the young person's daily life consistently predicts favorable adjustment. Besides preventing delinquency, parental monitoring is linked to other positive outcomes—a reduction in sexual activity, improved school performance, and positive psychological well-being (Crouter & Head, 2002; Jacobson & Crockett, 2000).

Recall, also, that the family is a system that must adapt to changes in its members. Most parents of adolescents have reached middle age and are also changing. While teenagers face a boundless future and a wide array of choices, their parents must come to terms with the fact that their own possibilities are narrowing. The pressures experienced by each generation act in opposition to one another (Holmbeck, 1996). Parents often can't understand why the adolescent wants to skip family activities to be with peers. And teenagers fail to appreciate that parents want the family to be together as often as possible because an important period in adult life—parenthood—will soon be over.

© As this mother and son together pack his lunch for school, they engage in coregulation. She exercises general oversight but permits him to take charge of specific decisions. During middle childhood, this transitional form of supervision helps prepare children for adolescence.
© Bill Aron/PhotoEdit

Ⓢ Adolescent autonomy is best achieved in the context of warm parenting. As her mother takes a pre-prom portrait, the daughter smiles warmly, and her demeanor suggests a healthy balance of togetherness and independence.
© Ronnie Kaufman/Corbis

Throughout adolescence, the quality of the parent–child relationship is the single most consistent predictor of mental health (Steinberg & Silk, 2002). In well-functioning families, young people remain attached to parents and seek their advice, but they do so in a context of greater freedom (Steinberg, 2001). The mild conflict that typically occurs along the way facilitates adolescent identity and autonomy by helping family members learn to express and tolerate disagreement. Conflicts also inform parents of adolescents' changing needs and expectations, signaling that adjustments in the parent–child relationship are necessary.

By late adolescence, most parents and children achieve this mature, mutual relationship, and positive parent–child interaction is on the rise. The diminishing time that Western teenagers spend with their families—for youths in the United States, from 33 percent of waking hours in fifth grade to 14 percent in twelfth grade—has little to do with conflict (Larson et al., 1996). Mostly, it results from the large quantity of unstructured time available to teenagers in North America and Western Europe—on average, nearly half of their waking hours (Larson, 2001). Young people tend to fill these free hours with activities that take them away from home, including part-time jobs, an increasing array of leisure and volunteer pursuits, and time with friends. However, this drop in family time is not universal. In one study, urban low- and middle-SES African-American youths showed no decline from childhood to adolescence in hours spent at home with family, a pattern typical in cultures with collectivist values (Larson et al., 2001).

Socioeconomic and Ethnic Variations in Child Rearing

Study after study confirms that the authoritative style predicts favorable development in children and adolescents of diverse SES levels, ethnicities, nationalities, and family structures, including single-parent, two-parent, and stepparent families (Crouter & Head, 2002; Slicker & Thornberry, 2002; Vazaonyi, Hibbert, & Snider, 2003). At the same time, SES and ethnic variations in parenting exist.

• **SOCIOECONOMIC STATUS** • Recall that SES is an index that combines years of education, prestige and skill required by one's job, and income—factors that are interrelated because educational attainment influences career opportunities and earnings. As SES rises and falls, parents and children face changing circumstances that affect family functioning, with each component of SES contributing. Researchers have yet to unravel these specific influences. Parental education and earnings exert substantial influence, with occupation playing a lesser but nevertheless important role (Duncan & Magnusson, 2003).

SES is linked to child-rearing values and expectations. When asked about personal qualities they desire for their children, lower-SES parents tend to emphasize external characteristics, such as obedience, politeness, neatness, and cleanliness. In contrast, higher-SES parents emphasize psychological traits, such as curiosity, happiness, self-direction, and cognitive and social maturity (Duncan & Magnusson, 2003; Hoff, Laursen, & Tardiff, 2002; Tudge et al., 2000). In addition, fathers in higher-SES families tend to be more involved in child rearing and household responsibilities. Lower-SES fathers, partly because of gender-stereotyped beliefs and partly through economic necessity, focus more on the provider role (Rank, 2000).

These differences are reflected in family interaction. Parents higher in SES talk to, read to, and otherwise stimulate their babies and preschoolers more (see Chapter 9, page 372). When their children are older, higher-SES parents use more warmth, explanations, inductive discipline, and verbal praise and set higher developmental goals for their children. Commands ("You do that because I told you to"), criticism, and physical punishment all occur more often in low-SES households (Bradley & Corwyn, 2003).

Education contributes substantially to these variations in child rearing. Higher-SES parents' interest in providing verbal stimulation and nurturing inner traits is supported by years of schooling, during which they learned to think about abstract, subjective ideas (Uribe, LeVine, & LeVine, 1994). Also, the greater economic security of higher-SES parents permits them to devote more time, energy, and material resources to nurturing their children's psychological characteristics. High levels of stress sparked by economic insecurity, along with a stronger belief in the value of physical punishment, contribute to low-SES parents' greater use of coercive discipline (Pinderhughes et al., 2000).

Furthermore, many lower-SES parents feel a sense of powerlessness and lack of influence in their relationships beyond the home. At work, for example, they have to obey the rules of others in positions of power and authority. When they get home, their parent–child interaction seems to duplicate these experiences—but now they are in the authority role. Higher-SES parents, in contrast, have more control over their own lives. At work, they are used to making independent decisions and convincing others of their point of view. At home, they are more likely to teach these skills to their children (Greenberger, O'Neil, & Nagel, 1994).

• **AFFLUENCE** • Despite advanced education and material wealth, affluent parents—who are widely assumed to give their youngsters every advantage—too often fail to engage in parenting that promotes healthy development. In several studies, researchers followed youths growing up in high-SES suburbs through the adolescent years (Luthar & Latendresse, 2005a). By seventh grade, many showed serious problems that worsened in high school. For example, they were more likely to engage in substance use and to report high levels of anxiety and depression than inner-city, low-SES youths (Luthar & Becker, 2002). Furthermore, among affluent (but not inner-city) teenagers, use of cigarettes, alcohol, hard drugs, and marijuana was correlated with anxiety and depression, suggesting that these wealthy young people took drugs to self-medicate—a practice that predicts persistent abuse. By eleventh grade, 20 percent had coexisting substance abuse, emotional, academic, and behavior problems (Luthar & Sexton, 2004).

Why are so many affluent youths troubled? Research indicates that they often experience two adverse parenting conditions:

- *Excessive achievement pressures.* Adolescents whose parents value their accomplishments more than their character are more likely to display anxiety, depression, and substance use. These young people often view achievement failures as personal failures.

- *Isolation from adults.* Poorly adjusted youths report both less parental after-school supervision and less parental emotional closeness than their better-adjusted counterparts. And like their professionally and socially occupied parents, many of these teenagers lead overscheduled lives, in which an excessive number of activities keep them busy but disconnected from their families (Luthar & Becker, 2002). Overall, wealthy parents are nearly as physically and emotionally unavailable to their youngsters as inner-city parents coping with serious financial strain.

Interestingly, for both affluent and inner-city youths, a simple routine—eating dinner with parents—is associated with a reduction in adjustment difficulties, even after many other aspects of parenting are controlled (see Figure 14.1) (Luthar & Latendresse, 2005b). Interventions that make wealthy parents aware of the high costs of a competitive, overscheduled lifestyle and minimal involvement with their children are badly needed.

• **POVERTY** • When families slip into poverty, effective parenting and children's development are profoundly threatened. Consider the case of Zinnia Mae, who grew up in Trackton, a close-knit black community located in a small southeastern American city (Heath, 1990). As unemployment struck Trackton and citizens moved away, 16-year-old Zinnia Mae caught a ride to Atlanta. Two years later, Zinnia Mae was the mother of a daughter and twin boys, and she had moved into a high-rise in public housing.

Each of Zinnia Mae's days was much the same. She watched TV and talked with friends on the phone. The children had only one set meal (breakfast) and otherwise ate whenever they were hungry or bored. Their play space was limited to the living-room sofa and a mattress on the floor. Toys consisted of scraps of a blanket, spoons and food cartons, a small rubber ball, a few plastic cars, and a roller skate abandoned in the building. Zinnia Mae's most frequent words were "I'm so tired." She worried about where to find a baby-sitter so she could go to the laundry or grocery, and about what she would do if she located the twins' father, who had stopped sending money.

At the researcher's request, Zinnia Mae agreed to tape record her family interactions. Cut off from family and community ties and overwhelmed by financial strain and feelings of helplessness,

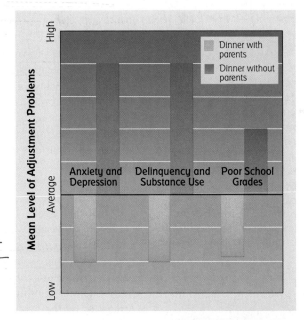

▲ **Figure 14.1**

Relationship of regularly eating dinner with parents to affluent youths' adjustment problems. Compared with sixth graders who often ate dinner with their parents, those who rarely did so were far more likely to display anxiety and depression, delinquency and substance use, and poor school grades, even after many other aspects of parenting were controlled. In this study, frequent family mealtimes also protected inner-city youths from delinquency and substance use, and from classroom learning problems. (Adapted from Luthar & Latendresse, 2005b.)

ⓒ This family, struggling to make ends meet, is forced to live in their car. For many poor families, pulling themselves out of poverty is a distant goal with numerous obstacles, often including health problems, depression, and exhaustion.
© Michael Newman/PhotoEdit

ⓒ Chinese parents tend to be highly controlling of their children, out of a belief in strict discipline, respect for elders, and socially desirable behavior. They are also more likely than North American parents to shame a misbehaving child, to withdraw love, and to use physical punishment. But Chinese children whose parents use coercive and psychologically controlling strategies excessively are usually anxious, depressed, and aggressive.
© Jeff Greenberg/The Image Works

she found herself unable to join in activities with her children. In 500 hours of tape, she started a conversation with her children only 18 times.

The constant stressors that accompany poverty gradually weaken the family system. Poor families have many daily hassles—bills to pay, the car breaking down, loss of welfare and unemployment payments, something stolen from the house, to name just a few. When daily crises arise, parents become depressed, irritable, and distracted, hostile interactions increase, and children's development suffers (Evans, 2004). Negative outcomes are especially severe in single-parent families, in families that must live in poor housing and dangerous neighborhoods, and in homeless families—conditions that make everyday existence even more difficult, while reducing social supports that assist in coping with economic hardship (Leventhal & Brooks-Gunn, 2003).

Besides stress and conflict, reduced parental involvement and depleted home learning environments (like that of Zinnia Mae) profoundly affect poor children's cognitive and emotional well-being (Duncan & Brooks-Gunn, 2000). As noted in earlier chapters, poverty that begins early and persists has devastating effects on children's physical and mental health, intelligence, and school achievement.

• ETHNICITY • Although authoritative parenting is broadly advantageous, ethnic minority parents often have distinct child-rearing beliefs and practices that respond to cultural values and family context. Let's take some examples.

Compared with Western parents, Chinese parents describe their parenting as less warm and more controlling. Chinese parents withhold praise, believing that it causes children to feel self-satisfied and disrupts their achievement motivation (Chen, 2001; Chao, 1994). High control reflects the Confucian belief in strict discipline, respect for elders, and socially desirable behavior, taught by deeply involved parents. Although Chinese parents report using induction and other reasoning-oriented discipline as much as North American parents do, they are more likely to shame a misbehaving child (see Chapter 10), to withdraw love, and to use physical punishment (Wu et al., 2002). When these practices become excessive, resulting in an authoritarian style high in psychological or coercive control, Chinese children display the same negative outcomes that North American children do: anxiety, depression, and aggressive behavior (Bradford et al., 2003; Olsen et al., 2002; Nelson et al., 2005; Yang et al., 2003).

In Hispanic and Asian Pacific Island families, firm insistence on respect for parental authority is paired with high parental warmth—a combination suited to promoting competence and strong feelings of family loyalty (Harrison et al., 1994). In one study, Mexican-American mothers living in poverty who adhered strongly to their cultural traditions were more likely to combine warmth with strict, even somewhat harsh, control than Mexican-American mothers who had assimilated to U.S. culture. This warmth–control combination served a protective function: It was associated with a reduction in child and adolescent conduct problems (Hill, Bush, & Roosa, 2003). Consistent with the high value they place on parental commitment, Hispanic-American fathers are more likely than their Caucasian-American counterparts to spend time with and monitor their school-age and adolescent youngsters. And although at one time regarded as coercive, contemporary Hispanic fathers are more nurturant than the stern authority figure of the past (Jambunathan, Burts, & Pierce, 2000; Toth & Xu, 1999).

Although wide variation exists in African-American families, black mothers—especially those who are young, single, and less educated—often expect immediate obedience (Kelley, Power, & Wimbush, 1992). But consistent with findings just reported for Mexican Americans, when African-American families live in depleted, crime-ridden neighborhoods and have few social supports, strict control may prevent antisocial involvements. Other research suggests that black parents use firm control for broader reasons—to promote self-reliance, self-regulation, and a watchful attitude in risky surroundings, which protects children from becoming victims of crime (Brody & Flor, 1998).

Consistent with this view, low-SES African-American parents who use more controlling strategies tend to have more cognitively and socially competent children (Brody, Stoneman, & Flor, 1995, 1996). Recall, also, that a childhood history of physi-

The African-American Extended Family

The African-American extended family can be traced to the African heritage of most black Americans. In many African societies, newly married couples do not start their own households. Instead, they live with a large extended family, which assists its members with all aspects of daily life. This tradition of maintaining a broad network of kinship ties traveled to North America during the period of slavery. Since then, it has served as a protective shield against the destructive impact of poverty and racial prejudice on African-American family life. Today, more black than white adults have relatives other than their own children living in the same household. African-American parents also live closer to kin, often establish familylike relationships with friends and neighbors, see more relatives during the week, and perceive relatives as more important in their lives (Kane, 2000).

By providing emotional support and sharing income and essential resources, the African-American extended family helps reduce the stress of poverty and single parenthood. Extended-family members often help with child rearing, and adolescent mothers living in extended families are more likely to complete high school and get a job and less likely to be on welfare than mothers living on their own—factors that benefit children's well-being (Gordon, Chase-Lansdale, & Brooks-Gunn, 2004; Trent & Harlan, 1994).

For single mothers who were very young at the time of their child's birth, extended-family living continues to be associated with more positive mother–child interaction during the preschool years. Otherwise, establishing an independent household with the help of nearby relatives is related to improved child rearing. Perhaps this arrangement permits the more mature teenage mother who has developed effective parenting skills to implement them (Chase-Lansdale, Brooks-Gunn, & Zamsky, 1994). In families rearing adolescents, kinship support increases the likelihood of effective parenting, which is related to adolescents' self-reliance, emotional well-being, and reduced delinquency (Taylor & Roberts, 1995).

Finally, the extended family plays an important role in transmitting African-American culture. Compared with nuclear family households, extended-family arrangements place more emphasis on cooperation and moral and religious values. And older black adults, such as grandparents and great-grandparents, regard educating children about their African heritage as especially important (Mosley-Howard & Evans, 2000; Taylor, 2000). These influences strengthen family bonds, protect children's development, and increase the chances that the extended-family lifestyle will carry over to the next generation.

▼ Strong bonds with extended-family members have helped protect many African-American children growing up under conditions of poverty and single parenthood. This extended family gathers to celebrate the eighty–fifth birthday of their oldest member. © Michael Schwartz/The Image Works

cal punishment is associated with a reduction in antisocial behavior among African-American adolescents, but with an increase in such behavior among Caucasian-American adolescents (see page 482 in Chapter 12). Most African-American parents who use strict, "no-nonsense" discipline use physical punishment sparingly. And they typically combine it with warmth and reasoning—parenting practices that predict favorable adjustment, regardless of ethnicity (Bluestone & Tamis-LeMonda, 1999).

The family structure and child-rearing customs of many minorities buffer the stress and disorganization caused by poverty. As the Cultural Influences box above illustrates, the **extended-family household,** in which one or more adult relatives live with the parent–child **nuclear family unit,** is a vital feature of ethnic minority family life that has enabled many families to rear children successfully, despite severe economic deprivation and prejudice. Extended family ties provide yet another example of the remarkable capacity of families to mobilize cultural traditions to safeguard children's development under conditions of high life stress.

Ask Yourself

REVIEW	Explain why authoritative parenting is linked to favorable academic and social outcomes among children and adolescents. Is the concept of authoritative parenting useful for understanding effective parenting across cultures? Explain
APPLY	Prepare a short talk for a parent–teacher organization, maintaining that parents matter greatly in children's lives. Support each of your points with research evidence.
CONNECT	Explain how factors that promote autonomy in adolescence also foster identity development. (To review the influence of parenting on identity, see pages 460–462 in Chapter 11.)
REFLECT	How would you classify your parents' child-rearing styles? What factors might have influenced their approach to child rearing?

Family Lifestyles and Transitions

Families in industrialized nations have become more diverse. Today, there are fewer births per family unit, more adults who want to adopt, more lesbian and gay parents who are open about their sexual orientation, and more never-married parents. In addition, transitions in family life over the past several decades—a dramatic rise in marital breakup, remarried parents, and employed mothers—have reshaped the family system.

In the following sections, we discuss these changes in the family, emphasizing how each affects family relationships and children's development. As you consider this array of family forms, think back to the social systems perspective. Note how children's well-being continues to depend on the quality of family interaction, which is sustained by supportive ties to kin and community and favorable policies in the larger culture.

From Large to Small Families

In 1960, the average number of children per North American couple was 3.1. Currently, it is 1.8 in the United States and 1.6 in Canada, compared with 1.7 in Australia and Great Britain, 1.6 in Sweden, 1.4 in Japan, and 1.3 in Germany (U.S. Census Bureau, 2004b; United Nations, 2004b). A major reason for this decline, in addition to more effective birth control, is that many women are reaping the economic and personal rewards of a career. A family size of one or two children is more compatible with a woman's decision to divide her energies between family and work. Also, more couples are delaying having children until they are well established professionally and secure economically (see Chapter 3). Adults who postpone parenthood are likely to have fewer children. Finally, marital instability has resulted in smaller families: More couples today get divorced before their childbearing plans are complete.

• FAMILY SIZE AND CHILD DEVELOPMENT • Popular advice to prospective parents often recommends limiting family size in the interests of "child quality." Many such counselors contend that parental affection, attention, and material resources are diluted with each additional birth, resulting in children who are intellectually less able—especially those who are later born. Do large families make low-IQ children, as prevailing attitudes suggest? Or do parents with lower IQs—as a result of heredity, environment, or both—tend to have larger families? For decades, researchers could not resolve this issue because they had access only to samples of unrelated children growing up in different homes, in which comparisons of first-born and later-born children were confounded with other family characteristics, such as SES (which declines as family size increases).

Starting in 1972, the U.S. National Longitudinal Survey of Youth (NLSY) followed a representative sample of more than 3,000 U.S. 14- to 22-year-olds; in 1986 the children of the original participants were added to the investigation. Because both cohorts took IQ tests, researchers could examine the relationship of IQ to sibling birth order within families to determine whether having more children depresses children's intellectual functioning. They also could correlate maternal IQ with family size, for insight into whether lower-IQ parents are prone to have larger families.

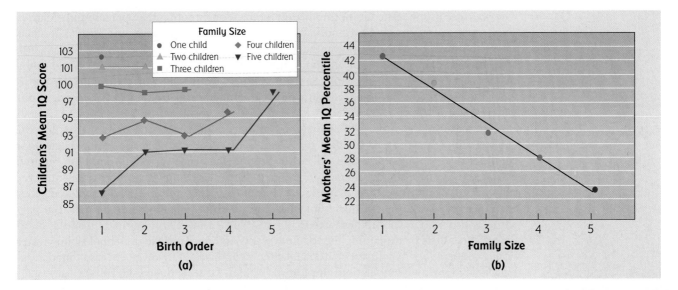

As the horizontal lines in Figure 14.2a reveal, children's IQs did not decline with later birth order—a finding that contradicts the assumption that large families make low-IQ children. At the same time, the differences among the lines show that the larger the family, the lower the IQs of all siblings. And as Figure 14.2b indicates, the link between family size and children's IQ can be explained by the strong trend for mothers with poorer mental test scores to give birth to more children (Rodgers et al., 2000). In other NLSY research, among children of bright, economically advantaged mothers, the family size–IQ correlation disappeared (Guo & VanWey, 1999).

Although many good reasons exist for limiting family size, the concern that additional births will reduce children's intelligence and life chances is not warranted. Instead, young people with lower IQs—many of whom dropped out of school, live in poverty, lack hope for their future, and fail to engage in family planning—are most likely to have large families. For adolescents with these risk factors, educational and family planning interventions are crucial (see Chapter 5, page 213).

• **GROWING UP WITH SIBLINGS** • Despite a declining family size, 80 percent of North American and European children still grow up with at least one sibling (Dunn, 2004b). Siblings exert important influences on development, both directly, through relationships with one another, and indirectly, through the impact an additional child has on the behavior of parents. In previous chapters, we examined some consequences of having brothers and sisters, including effects on early language development, personality, self and social understanding, and gender typing. Now let's look closely at the quality of the sibling relationship.

▶ *Emergence of Sibling Relationships.* The arrival of a baby brother or sister is a difficult experience for most preschoolers, who quickly realize that now they must share their parents' attention and affection. They often become demanding and clingy, engage in deliberate naughtiness, and display other immature behaviors. Security of attachment also declines, more so if they are over age 2 (old enough to feel threatened and displaced) and the mother is under stress due to marital or psychological problems (Baydar, Greek, & Brooks-Gunn, 1997; Teti et al., 1996).

Yet resentment is only one feature of a rich emotional relationship that starts to build between siblings after the baby's birth. The older child can also be seen kissing, patting, and calling out, "Mom, he needs you" when the baby cries—signs of affection and sympathetic concern. By the end of the baby's first year, siblings typically spend much time together, with the preschooler helping, sharing toys, imitating, and expressing friendliness in addition to anger and ambivalence (Dunn & Kendrick, 1982). Infants of this age are comforted by the presence of their preschool-age brother or sister during the mother's short absences. And during the second year, toddlers often imitate and join in play with the older child (Dunn, 1989).

Because of their frequency and emotional intensity, sibling interactions become unique contexts in which social competence expands. Between their second and fourth birthdays, younger siblings take a more active role in play. As a result, sibling conversations increase. And siblings

▲ **Figure 14.2**

Do large families make low-IQ children? Findings of the U.S. National Longitudinal Survey of Youth answer this question with certainty: No. (a) Horizontal lines show that children's IQs did not decline with later birth order, as would be predicted if large families diluted the quality of children's experiences. To the contrary, in the largest families, the youngest children tended to score higher than their siblings. But notice the differences among the lines, which indicate that the larger the family, the lower the IQs of all siblings. (b) The link between family size and children's IQ can be explained by the strong trend for mothers with lower IQs to have larger families.

(From J. L. Rodgers, H. H. Cleveland, E. van den Oord, & D. C. Rowe, 2000, "Resolving the Debate Over Birth Order, Family Size, and Intelligence," *American Psychologist, 55,* pp. 607, 609. Copyright © by the American Psychological Association. Reprinted by permission.)

who are close in age relate to one another on a more equal footing than parents and children. They often engage in joint pretend, talk about feelings, tease, deceive, and—when conflicts arise—call attention to their own wants and needs. The skills acquired during sibling interaction contribute to understanding of emotions and other mental states, perspective taking, moral maturity, and competence in relating to other children. Consistent with these outcomes, positive sibling ties predict favorable adjustment, even among hostile children at risk for social difficulties (Stormshak et al., 1996).

Nevertheless, individual differences in sibling relationships appear shortly after the younger sibling's arrival. In Chapter 10, we noted that temperament affects how positive or conflict-ridden sibling interaction will be. In addition, maternal warmth toward both children is related to positive sibling interaction and to preschoolers' support of a distressed younger sibling (Volling, 2001; Volling & Belsky, 1992). Of course, a child's temperament and other attributes might account for quality of interaction with both siblings and parents. But parenting is also influential: Mothers who frequently play with their young children and head off potential conflicts by explaining the toddler's wants and needs to the preschool sibling foster sibling cooperation. In contrast, maternal harshness and lack of involvement result in increasingly antagonistic sibling relationships (Howe, Aquan-Assee, & Bukowski, 2001).

Also, a good marriage is linked to preschool siblings' capacity to cope adaptively with jealousy and conflict (Volling, McElwain, & Miller, 2002). Perhaps good communication between parents serves as a model of effective problem solving. It may also foster a happy family environment, which results in less reason for siblings to feel jealous.

▶ *Sibling Relationships in Middle Childhood and Adolescence.* Sibling rivalry tends to increase in middle childhood. As children participate in a wider range of activities, parents often compare siblings' traits and accomplishments. The child who gets less parental affection, more disapproval, or fewer material resources is likely to be resentful and to show poorer adjustment over time (Brody, 2004; Dunn, 2004b).

For same-sex siblings who are close in age, parental comparisons are more frequent, resulting in more quarreling and antagonism and poorer adjustment. This effect is particularly strong when parenting is cold or harsh (Feinberg & Hetherington, 2001). A survey of a nationally representative sample of nearly 23,000 Canadian children revealed that differential treatment of siblings increased when parents were under stress as a result of financial worries, marital conflict, the pressures of caring for several children, or single parenthood (Jenkins, Rasbash, & O'Connor, 2003). Parents whose energies are drained become less careful about being fair. Children react especially intensely when fathers prefer one child. Perhaps because fathers spend less time with children, their favoritism is more noticeable and triggers greater anger (Brody, Stoneman, & McCoy, 1992; Brody et al., 1992).

Although conflict rises during the school years, siblings continue to rely on one another for companionship, emotional support, and assistance with everyday tasks. In a study in which siblings reported on their shared daily activities in evening telephone interviews, participants mentioned that older children often assisted younger siblings with academic and peer challenges. And both members of sibling pairs offered each other assistance with family issues (Tucker, McHale, & Crouter, 2001). When parents are distant and uninvolved, siblings sometimes fill in and become more supportive of one another (Bank, Patterson, & Reid, 1996).

Like parent–child relationships, sibling interactions adapt to development at adolescence. As younger siblings become more self-sufficient, they accept less direction from their older brothers and sisters. Consequently, sibling influence declines during the teenage years. Furthermore, as adolescents become more involved in friendships and romantic relationships, they invest less time and energy in their siblings, who are part of the family from which they are trying to establish autonomy. As a result, sibling relationships often become less intense, in both positive and negative feelings (Hetherington, Henderson, & Reiss, 1999; Stocker & Dunn, 1994).

Despite a drop in companionship, attachment between siblings, like closeness to parents, remains strong for most young people. Teenage brothers and sisters who established a positive bond in early childhood and whose parents continue to be warm and involved are more likely to express affection and caring (Dunn, Slomkowski, & Beardsall, 1994). Also, mild sibling differences in perceived parental affection no longer trigger jealousy

◉ Although sibling rivalry tends to increase in middle childhood, siblings also provide one another with emotional support and help with difficult tasks. © Erika Stone

but, instead, predict increasing sibling warmth (Feinberg et al., 2003). In Chapter 10, we noted that siblings often strive to be different from one another (see page 417). Perhaps adolescents interpret a unique parental relationship—as long as it is generally accepting—as a gratifying sign of their own individuality.

Older siblings frequently offer useful advice as their younger teenage brothers and sisters face challenges in peer relationships, schoolwork, and decisions about the future. A positive sibling bond during early adolescence is linked to future, more gratifying friendships (Yeh & Lempers, 2004). And young people who have difficulty making friends sometimes turn to siblings for compensating support (Seginer, 1998).

One-Child Families

Although sibling relationships bring many benefits, they are not essential for healthy development. Contrary to popular belief, only children are not spoiled. Rather, they are advantaged in some respects. North American children growing up in one-child families are higher in self-esteem and achievement motivation. Consequently, they do better in school and attain higher levels of education (Falbo, 1992). One reason may be that only children have somewhat closer relationships with parents, who may exert more pressure for mastery and accomplishment. Furthermore, only children have just as many close, high-quality friendships as children with siblings. However, they tend to be less well accepted in the peer group, perhaps because they have not had opportunities to learn effective conflict-resolution strategies through sibling interactions (Kitzmann, Cohen, & Lockwood, 2002).

Favorable development also characterizes only children in China, where a one-child family policy has been strictly enforced in urban areas for more than two decades to control overpopulation. Compared with agemates who have siblings, Chinese only children are advanced in cognitive development and academic achievement (Falbo & Poston, 1993; Jiao, Ji, & Jing, 1996). They also feel more emotionally secure, perhaps because government disapproval promotes tension in families with more than one child (Yang et al., 1995). Chinese mothers go out of their way to ensure that their children have regular contact with first cousins (who are considered siblings). Perhaps as a result, Chinese only children do not differ from agemates with siblings in social skills and peer acceptance (Chen, Rubin, & Li, 1995; Hart et al., 1998). The next generation of Chinese only children, however, will have no first cousins.

Adoptive Families

Adults who are infertile, who are likely to pass along a genetic disorder, or who are older and single but want a family are turning to adoption in increasing numbers. Others who have children by birth may choose to expand their families through adoption. Adoption agencies try to ensure a good fit by seeking parents of the same ethnic and religious background as the child and, where possible, trying to choose parents who are the same age as most biological parents. Because the availability of healthy babies has declined (fewer young unwed mothers give up their babies than in the past), more people are adopting from other countries or taking children who are older or who have developmental problems.

Still, adopted children and adolescents—whether or not they are born in their adoptive parents' country—have more learning and emotional difficulties than other children, a difference that increases with the child's age at time of adoption (Levy-Shiff, 2001; Miller et al., 2000). There are many possible reasons for adoptees' more problematic childhoods. The biological mother may have been unable to care for the child because of problems believed to be partly genetic, such as alcoholism or severe depression. If so, she may have passed this tendency to her offspring. Or perhaps she experienced stress, poor diet, or inadequate medical care during pregnancy. Furthermore, children adopted after infancy are more likely than their nonadopted peers to have a preadoptive history of conflict-ridden family relationships, lack of parental affection, and neglect and abuse. Finally, adoptive parents and children, who are genetically unrelated, are less alike in intelligence and personality than are biological relatives—differences that may threaten family harmony.

Despite these risks, most adopted children fare well, and those with preexisting problems usually make rapid progress (Johnson, 2002; Kim, 2002). In a Swedish longitudinal study, researchers followed more than 600 infant

© Limiting family size is a basic national policy in the People's Republic of China. In urban areas, the majority of couples have no more than one child.
© Paul Conklin/PhotoEdit

© This adopted African-American baby plays with her Caucasian older sisters. Will she develop an identity that is a healthy blend of her birth and rearing backgrounds? The answer depends on the extent to which her adoptive parents expose her to her African-American heritage.
© Jim Pickerell/Stock Boston, LLC

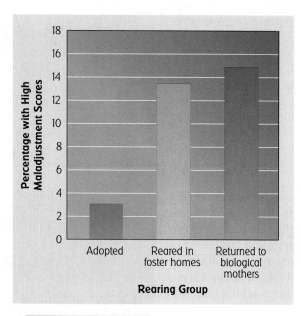

▲ **Figure 14.3**

Relationship of type of rearing to maladjustment among a sample of Swedish adolescents who had been candidates for adoption at birth. Compared with the other two groups, adopted youths were rated by teachers as having far fewer problems, including anxiety, withdrawal, aggression, inability to concentrate, peer difficulties, and poor school motivation. (Adapted from Bohman & Sigvardsson, 1990.)

⊚ Research suggests that homosexual parents are as committed to and effective at child rearing as heterosexual parents. Their children seem to be well adjusted, and the large majority develop a heterosexual orientation. © Marilyn Humphries/The Image Works

adoption candidates into adolescence. Some were adopted shortly after birth; some were reared in foster homes; and some were reared by their biological mothers, who initially gave up their babies and then changed their minds and took them back. As Figure 14.3 shows, adoptees developed much more favorably than children growing up in foster families or returned to their birth mothers (Bohman & Sigvardsson, 1990). And in a study of internationally adopted children in the Netherlands, sensitive maternal care and secure attachment in infancy predicted cognitive and social competence at age 7 (Stams, Juffer, & van IJzendoorn, 2002). So even when children are not genetically related to their parents, an early warm, trusting parent–child relationship fosters development. Children with troubled family histories who are adopted at older ages also develop feelings of trust and affection for their adoptive parents as they come to feel loved and supported in their new families (Sherrill & Pinderhughes, 1999).

By adolescence, however, adoptees' lives are often complicated by unresolved curiosity about their roots. Some have difficulty accepting the possibility that they may never know their birth parents. Others worry about what they would do if their birth parents suddenly reappeared (Grotevant & Kohler, 1999). Despite concerns about their origins, most adoptees appear optimistic and well adjusted as adults. And as long as their parents took steps to help them learn about their heritage in childhood, young people adopted into a different ethnic group or culture generally develop identities that are healthy blends of their birth and rearing backgrounds (Brooks & Barth, 1999).

Clearly, adoption is a satisfying family alternative for most parents and children who experience it. Good outcomes can be promoted by careful pairing of children with parents and provision of guidance to adoptive families by well-trained social service professionals.

Gay and Lesbian Families

Several million American and tens of thousands of Canadian gay men and lesbians are parents, most through previous heterosexual marriages, some through adoption, and a growing number through reproductive technologies (Ambert, 2003; Patterson, 2002). In the past, laws assuming that homosexuals could not be adequate parents led those who divorced a heterosexual partner to lose custody of their children. Today, some U.S. states and the nation of Canada hold that sexual orientation by itself is irrelevant to custody. A few U.S. states, however, ban gay and lesbian adoptions (Laird, 2003).

Most research on homosexual families is limited to volunteer samples. Findings of these investigations indicate that gay and lesbian parents are as committed to and effective at child rearing as heterosexual parents. Also, whether born to or adopted by their parents or conceived through donor insemination, the children of homosexuals did not differ from the children of heterosexuals in mental health, peer relations, and gender identity (Allen & Burrell, 1996; Flaks et al., 1995; Golombok & Tasker, 1996). Two additional studies, which surmounted the potential bias associated with a volunteer sample by including all lesbian-mother families who had conceived children at a fertility clinic, also reported that children were developing favorably (Brewaeys et al., 1997; Chan, Raboy, & Patterson, 1998). And among participants drawn from a representative sample of British mothers and their 7-year-olds, once again, children reared in lesbian-mother families did not differ from children reared in heterosexual families in adjustment and gender-role preferences, even after SES, children's age, and number of children in the family were controlled (Golombok et al., 2003).

Nevertheless, research on homosexual families is restricted to small samples, and critics argue that those whom researchers fail to locate or who decline to participate might differ from those in existing studies. Furthermore, many children of gay and lesbian parents experience peer teasing and shunning by the heterosexual parents of some of their peers (Morris, Balsam, & Rothbaum, 2001). Still, the children studied to date fare well emotionally and socially and—with the support of parents and teachers—might even develop certain character strengths, such as high empathy and tolerance (Ambert, 2003; Patterson, 2001).

Virtually all studies have concluded that children of homosexual parents do not differ from other children in sexual orientation; the large majority are heterosexual (Patterson, 2002). But some evidence suggests that more youths from homosexual families experiment for a time with partners of both sexes, perhaps as a result of being reared in families and communities highly tolerant of nonconformity and difference (Bos, van Balen, & van den Boom, 2004; Stacey & Biblarz, 2001).

Never-Married Single-Parent Families

About 10 percent of American children and 5 percent of Canadian children live with a single parent who has never married and does not have a partner. Of these parents, about 90 percent are mothers, 10 percent fathers (U.S. Census Bureau, 2004b; Vanier Institute of the Family, 2004). More single women over age 30 in high-status occupations have become parents in recent years. However, they are still few in number, and little is known about how their children fare.

In the United States, the largest group of never-married parents is African-American young women. Over 60 percent of births to black mothers in their twenties are to women without a partner, compared with 13 percent of births to white women (U.S. Census Bureau, 2004b). African-American women postpone marriage more and childbirth less than women in other U.S. ethnic groups. Job loss, persistent unemployment, and consequent inability of many black men to support a family have contributed to the postponement of marriage.

Never-married black mothers tap the extended family, especially their own mothers and sometimes male relatives, for help in rearing their children (Gasden, 1999; Jayakody & Kalil, 2002). For about one-third, marriage occurs within nine years after birth of the first child, not necessarily to the child's biological father (Wu, Bumpass, & Musick, 2001). These couples generally function like other first-marriage parents. Their children are often unaware that the father is a stepfather, and parents do not report the child-rearing difficulties usually associated with remarriage that we will discuss shortly (Ganong & Coleman, 1994).

Still, single mothers find it harder to overcome poverty. About 47 percent of white mothers and 59 percent of black mothers have a second child while unmarried. And they are far less likely than divorced mothers to receive paternal child support payments. Consequently, many children in single-mother homes display adjustment problems associated with economic hardship (Lipman et al., 2002). Furthermore, children of never-married mothers who lack a father's warmth and involvement achieve less well in school and engage in more antisocial behavior than children in low-SES, first-married families (Coley, 1998). But marriage to the child's biological father benefits children only when the father is a reliable source of economic and emotional support. For example, when a mother pairs up with an antisocial father, her child is at far greater risk for conduct problems than if she had reared the child alone (Jaffee et al., 2003). Overall, strengthening social support, education, and employment opportunities for low-income parents would greatly enhance the well-being of unmarried mothers and their children.

Divorce

Between 1960 and 1985, divorce rates in industrialized nations rose dramatically and then, in most countries, stabilized. The United States has the highest divorce rate in the world, Canada the sixth highest (see Figure 14.4). Of the 45 percent of American and 30 percent of Canadian marriages that end in divorce, half involve children. At any given time, one-fourth of American and one-fifth of Canadian children live in single-parent households. Although most reside with their mothers, the percentage in father-headed households has increased steadily, to about 12 percent in both nations (Hetherington & Stanley-Hagan, 2002; Statistics Canada, 2004b).

Children of divorce spend an average of 5 years in a single-parent home. For many, divorce leads to new family relationships. About

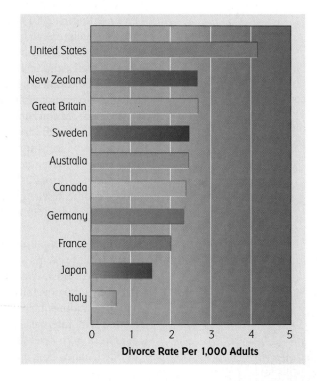

▼ **Figure 14.4**

Divorce rates in ten industrialized nations. The U.S. divorce rate is the highest in the industrialized world, far exceeding divorce rates in other countries. The Canadian divorce rate is the sixth highest. (Adapted from Australian Bureau of Statistics, 2004; U.S. Census Bureau, 2004b; United Nations, 2001.)

Divorce Rate Per 1,000 Adults

two-thirds of divorced parents marry a second time. Half of their children eventually experience a third major change: the end of their parents' second marriage (Hetherington & Kelly, 2002).

These figures reveal that divorce is not a single event in the lives of parents and children. Instead, it is a transition that leads to a variety of new living arrangements, accompanied by changes in housing, income, and family roles and responsibilities. Since the 1960s, many studies have reported that marital breakup is quite stressful for children. But research also reveals great individual differences (Amato & Booth, 2000; Hetherington, 2003). How well children fare depends on many factors: the custodial parent's psychological health, the child's characteristics, and social supports within the family and surrounding community.

• **IMMEDIATE CONSEQUENCES** • Family conflict often rises around the time of divorce as parents try to settle disputes over children and possessions. Once one parent moves out, additional events threaten supportive interactions between parents and children. Mother-headed households typically experience a sharp drop in income. In the United States and Canada, the majority of divorced mothers with young children live in poverty, getting less than the full amount of child support from the absent father or none at all (Children's Defense Fund, 2005; Statistics Canada, 2004b). They often have to move to new housing for economic reasons, reducing supportive ties to neighbors and friends.

The transition from marriage to divorce often leads to high maternal stress, depression, and anxiety and to a disorganized family situation (Hope, Power, & Rodgers, 1999; Marks & Lambert, 1998). Predictable events and routines—meals and bedtimes, household chores, and joint parent–child activities—usually disintegrate. As children react with distress and anger to their less secure home lives, discipline may become harsh and inconsistent. Contact with noncustodial fathers decreases over time (Hetherington & Kelly, 2002). Fathers who see their children only occasionally are inclined to be permissive and indulgent. This often conflicts with the mother's style of parenting and makes her task of managing the child on a day-to-day basis even more difficult.

The more parents argue and fail to provide children with warmth, involvement, and consistent guidance, the poorer children's adjustment. About 20 to 25 percent of children in divorced families display severe problems, compared with about 10 percent in nondivorced families (Greene et al., 2003; Martinez & Forgatch, 2002; Pruett et al., 2003). At the same time, reactions vary with children's age, temperament, and sex.

▶ *Children's Age.* The cognitive immaturity of preschool and early school-age children makes it difficult for them to grasp the reasons behind their parents' separation. Younger children often blame themselves and take the marital breakup as a sign that both parents may abandon them (Pryor & Rogers, 2001). They may whine and cling, displaying intense separation anxiety.

Older children can better understand that strong differences of opinion, incompatible personalities, and lack of caring for each other caused their parents' divorce—insights that may reduce some of their pain. Still, many school-age and adolescent youngsters react strongly, particularly when family conflict is high and supervision of children is low. Escaping into undesirable peer activities—such as running away, truancy, early sexual activity, and delinquency—and poor school achievement are common (Hetherington & Stanley-Hagan, 1999; Simons & Chao, 1996).

Not all older children react this way. For some—especially the oldest child in the family—divorce can trigger more mature behavior. These youngsters may willingly take on extra burdens, such as household tasks, care and protection of younger siblings, and emotional support of a depressed, anxious mother. But if these demands are too great, older children may eventually become resentful and withdraw into some of the destructive behavior patterns just described (Hetherington, 1995, 1999).

▶ *Children's Temperament and Sex.* When temperamentally difficult children are exposed to stressful life events and inadequate parenting, their problems are magnified (Lengua et al., 2000). In contrast, easy children are less often targets of parental anger and also cope more effectively with adversity.

These findings help us understand sex differences in response to divorce. Girls sometimes respond with internalizing reactions, such as crying, self-criticism, and withdrawal. More often, children of both sexes show demanding, attention-getting, acting-out behavior. But in mother-custody families, boys are at slightly greater risk for academic, emotional, and behavior problems

(Amato, 2001). Recall from Chapter 13 that boys are more active and noncompliant—behaviors that increase with exposure to parental conflict and inconsistent discipline. Research reveals that long before the marital breakup, some children (mostly sons) of divorcing couples were impulsive and defiant—behaviors that may have contributed to—as well as been caused by—their parents' marital problems (Chase-Lansdale, Cherlin, & Kiernen, 1995; Hetherington, 1999). As a result, these children enter the period of turmoil surrounding divorce with reduced capacity to cope with stress.

Perhaps because their behavior is so unruly, many boys of divorcing parents receive less emotional support from mothers, teachers, and peers. Furthermore, the coercive interaction cycles between angry, defiant sons and their divorced mothers soon spread to sibling relations (Hetherington & Kelly, 2002). These outcomes compound adjustment difficulties. After divorce, children with preexisting behavior problems often get worse (Hanson, 1999).

© After parents divorce, children in mother-custody homes who stay involved with their fathers fare better in development. Boys often adjust more favorably when the father is the custodial parent. © Paul Barton/Corbis

• **LONG-TERM CONSEQUENCES** • The majority of children show improved adjustment by 2 years after divorce. Yet overall, children and adolescents of divorced parents continue to score slightly lower than children of continuously married parents in academic achievement, self-esteem, social competence, and emotional and behavior problems (Amato, 2001). For a few, persistent difficulties translate into poor adjustment in adulthood. Children with difficult temperaments who were entrenched in family conflict are more likely to drop out of school, to be depressed, and to engage in antisocial behavior in adolescence. And divorce is linked to problems with sexuality and development of intimate ties. Young people who experienced parental divorce, especially more than once, display higher rates of early sexual activity, adolescent parenthood, and divorce in their adult lives (Wolfinger, 2000).

The overriding factor in positive adjustment following divorce is effective parenting—in particular, how well the custodial parent handles stress and shields the child from family conflict, and the extent to which each parent uses authoritative child rearing (Leon, 2003; Wolchik et al., 2000). Where the custodial parent is the mother, contact with fathers is also important. The more paternal contact and the warmer the father–child relationship, the less children of divorce react with defiance and aggression (Dunn et al., 2004). Also, for girls, a good father–child relationship protects against early sexual activity and unhappy romantic involvements (Clarke-Stewart & Hayward, 1996; McLanahan, 1999). High father–child contact, however, is more likely in families where the mother–child relationship is positive and divorced parents communicate and support one another in their parenting roles (Dunn, 2004a).

Furthermore, several studies report that outcomes for sons tend to be better when the father is the custodial parent (Clarke-Stewart & Hayward, 1996; McLanahan, 1999). Fathers' greater economic security and image of authority seem to help them engage in effective parenting with sons. And boys in father–custody families may benefit from greater involvement of both parents because noncustodial mothers participate more than noncustodial fathers in their children's lives.

Although divorce is painful for children, remaining in an intact but high-conflict family is worse than making the transition to a low-conflict, single-parent household (Green et al., 2003). However, more parents today are divorcing because they are moderately (rather than extremely) dissatisfied with their relationship. Research suggests that children in these low-discord homes are especially puzzled and upset. Perhaps these youngsters' inability to understand the marital breakup and grief over the loss of a seemingly happy home life explain why the adjustment problems of children of divorce have intensified over time (Amato, 2001; Reifman et al., 2001).

Regardless of the extent of parents' friction, those who set aside their disagreements and support one another in their child-rearing roles greatly increase the chances that their children will grow up competent, stable, and happy. As Figure 14.5 shows, in a study of 8- to 15-year-olds, young people who

▼ **Figure 14.5**

Relationship of child-rearing styles to children's adjustment following divorce. High parental acceptance and consistency in discipline are associated with a low level of behavior problems. As child rearing diminished in quality, behavior problems increased. When both parental acceptance and consistency in discipline were low, behavior problems were severe. All 8- to 15-year-olds in this study had experienced a highly stressful divorce. (Adapted from Wolchik et al., 2000.)

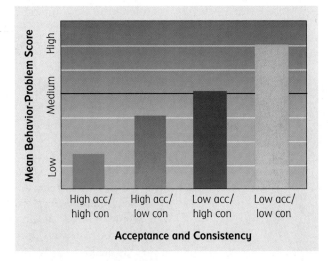

experienced both high parental acceptance and high consistency of discipline had the lowest levels of adjustment problems (Wolchik et al., 2000). Caring extended-family members, teachers, siblings, and friends also reduce the likelihood that divorce will result in long-term difficulties (Hetherington, 2003; Lussier et al., 2002).

• **DIVORCE MEDIATION, JOINT CUSTODY, AND CHILD SUPPORT** • Awareness that divorce is highly stressful for parents and children has led to community-based services aimed at helping them through this difficult time. One such service is **divorce mediation,** a series of meetings between divorcing couples and a trained professional aimed at reducing family conflict, including legal battles over property division and child custody. Where child custody is in dispute, some U.S. states require mediation. Canadian divorce law mandates that lawyers inform divorcing couples about mediation and encourage it. Research reveals that mediation increases out-of-court settlements, cooperation and involvement of both parents in child rearing, and parents' and children's feelings of well-being (Emery, 2001). In one study, parents who had resolved disputes through mediation remained more involved in their children's lives 12 years later (Emery et al., 2001).

To further encourage parents to resolve their disputes, parent education programs are becoming increasingly common. During several sessions, professionals teach parents about the impact of conflict on children and emphasize the importance of constructive conflict resolution and of mutual support in child rearing. Because of its demonstrated impact on parental cooperation, parent education prior to filing for divorce is increasingly becoming mandatory across Canada (Department of Justice Canada, 2003, 2004). In many U.S. states, the court may require parents to attend a program.

An increasingly common child custody option is **joint custody,** which grants divorced parents equal say in important decisions about the child's upbringing, as a means of encouraging both to remain involved in their children's lives. In most instances, children reside with one parent and see the other on a fixed schedule, much like the typical sole-custody situation. But in other cases, parents share physical custody, and children move between homes and sometimes schools and peer groups. These transitions can be especially hard on some children. Joint-custody parents report little conflict—fortunately so, since the success of the arrangement depends on parental cooperation. And their children—regardless of living arrangements—tend to be better adjusted than their counterparts in sole maternal-custody homes (Bauserman, 2002).

Finally, many single-parent families depend on child support from the absent parent to relieve financial strain. All U.S. states and Canadian provinces have procedures for withholding wages from parents who fail to make these court-ordered payments. Although child support is usually not enough to lift a single-parent family out of poverty, it can ease the burden substantially. An added benefit is that noncustodial fathers are more likely to maintain contact with children if they pay child support (Garfinkel & McLanahan, 1995). Applying What We Know on the following page summarizes ways to help children adjust to their parents' divorce.

Blended Families

Life in a single-parent family often is temporary. About 60 percent of divorced parents remarry within a few years. Others *cohabit,* or share a sexual relationship and a residence with a partner outside of marriage. Parent, stepparent, and children form a new family structure called the **blended,** or **reconstituted, family.** For some children, this expanded family network is positive and brings greater adult attention. But most have more problems than children in stable, first-marriage families. Stepparents often introduce new child-rearing practices, and having to switch to new rules and expectations can be stressful. In addition, children often regard steprelatives as intruders. But how well they adapt is, once again, related to the overall quality of family functioning (Hetherington & Kelly, 2002). This depends on which parent forms a new relationship, the child's age and sex, and the complexity of blended-family relationships. As we will see, older children and girls seem to have the hardest time.

◉ The older boys in this blended family may view their new stepmother as a threat to their freedom as well as to the bond they have with their father. Family life education and counseling can help parents and children adapt to these complex new circumstances. © Kayte M. Deioma/ PhotoEdit

Applying
What We Know   Helping Children Adjust to Their Parents' Divorce

Suggestion	Explanation
Shield children from conflict.	Witnessing intense parental conflict is very damaging to children. If one parent insists on expressing hostility, children fare better if the other parent does not respond in kind.
Provide children with as much continuity, familiarity, and predictability as possible.	Children adjust better during the period surrounding divorce when their lives have some stability—for example, the same school, bedroom, baby-sitter, playmates, and daily schedule.
Explain the divorce and tell children what to expect.	Children are more likely to develop fears of abandonment if they are not prepared for their parents' separation. They should be told that their mother and father will not be living together anymore, which parent will be moving out, and when they will be able to see that parent. If possible, mother and father should explain the divorce together. Parents should provide a reason for the divorce that the child can understand and assure children that they are not to blame.
Emphasize the permanence of the divorce.	Fantasies of parents getting back together can prevent children from accepting the reality of their current life. Children should be told that the divorce is final and that they cannot change this fact.
Respond sympathetically to children's feelings.	Children need a supportive and understanding response to their feelings of sadness, fear, and anger. For children to adjust well, their painful emotions must be acknowledged, not denied or avoided.
Engage in authoritative parenting.	Provide children with affection and acceptance as well as reasonable demands for mature behavior and consistent, rational discipline. Parents who engage in authoritative parenting greatly reduce their children's risk of maladjustment following divorce.
Promote a continuing relationship with both parents.	When parents disentangle their lingering hostility toward the former spouse from the child's need for a continuing relationship with the other parent, children adjust well. Grandparents and other extended-family members can help by not taking sides.

Source: Teyber, 2001.

• **MOTHER–STEPFATHER FAMILIES** • The most common form of blended family is a mother–stepfather arrangement, since mothers generally retain custody of the child. Boys tend to adjust quickly. They welcome a stepfather who is warm, who refrains from exerting his authority too quickly, and who offers relief from the coercive cycles of mother–son interaction. Mothers' friction with sons also declines as a result of greater economic security, the presence of another adult to share household tasks, and an end to loneliness (Visher, Visher, & Pasley, 2003). When stepfathers marry rather than cohabit, they are more involved in parenting. Perhaps men who choose to marry a mother with children are more interested in and skilled at child rearing (Hofferth & Anderson, 2003). Girls, however, often have difficulty with their custodial mother's remarriage. Stepfathers disrupt the close mother–daughter ties that often develop in single-parent families, and girls often react to the new arrangement with sulky, resistant behavior (Bray, 1999).

Note, however, that age affects these findings. Older school-age children and adolescents of both sexes display more irresponsible, acting-out, and antisocial behavior than their peers in non-stepfamilies (Hetherington & Stanley-Hagan, 2000). Parenting in stepfamilies—particularly those with stepsiblings—is highly challenging. Some parents are warmer and more involved with their biological children than with their stepchildren. Older children are more likely to notice and challenge unfair treatment. And adolescents often view the new stepparent as a threat to their freedom, especially if they experienced little parental monitoring in the single-parent family. Still, many teenagers have good relationships with both fathers—a circumstance linked to more favorable development (White & Gilbreth, 2001).

• **FATHER–STEPMOTHER FAMILIES** • Remarriage of noncustodial fathers often leads to reduced contact with their biological children, as these fathers tend to withdraw from their "previous" families (Dunn, 2002). When fathers have custody, however, children typically react negatively to remarriage. One reason is that children living with fathers often start out with more problems. Perhaps the biological mother could no longer handle the unruly child (usually a boy), so the father and his new wife are faced with a youngster who has behavior problems. In other instances, the father is granted custody because of a very close relationship with the child, and his remarriage disrupts this bond (Buchanan, Maccoby, & Dornbusch, 1996). Also, many fathers quickly turn over child-rearing responsibilities to stepmothers, triggering resentment in children.

Girls, especially, have a hard time getting along with their stepmothers. Sometimes (as just mentioned) this occurs because the girl's relationship with her father is threatened by the remarriage. In addition, girls occasionally become entangled in loyalty conflicts between their two mother figures. But the longer girls live in father–stepmother households, the more positive their interaction with stepmothers becomes (Hetherington & Jodl, 1994). With time and patience they do adjust, and eventually most girls benefit from the support of a second mother figure.

• SUPPORT FOR BLENDED FAMILIES • Family life education and counseling can help parents and children in blended families adapt to the complexities of their new circumstances. Effective approaches encourage stepparents to move into their new roles gradually by first building a friendly relationship with the child. Only when a warm bond has formed between stepparents and stepchildren is more active parenting possible (Visher, Visher, & Pasley, 2003). In addition, counselors can offer couples help in forming a "parenting coalition" through which they cooperate and provide consistency in child rearing. By limiting loyalty conflicts, this allows children to benefit from stepparent relationships and from the increased diversity in their lives.

Unfortunately, many children do not have a chance to settle into a happy blended family because the divorce rate for second marriages is even higher than that for first marriages. The more marital transitions children experience, the greater their difficulties (Dunn, 2002). Parents with antisocial tendencies and poor child-rearing skills are particularly likely to have several divorces and remarriages. These families usually require prolonged, intensive therapy.

Maternal Employment and Dual-Earner Families

Today, single and married mothers are in the labor force in nearly equal proportions, and nearly 70 percent of North American mothers are employed. This figure rises from 64 percent during the preschool years to over 78 percent in middle childhood (Statistics Canada, 2003e; U.S. Census Bureau, 2004b). In Chapter 10, we saw that the impact of maternal employment on early development depends on the quality of child care and the continuing parent–child relationship. This same conclusion applies in later years as well. In addition, the mother's work satisfaction, the support she receives from her partner, and the child's sex have a bearing on how children fare.

• MATERNAL EMPLOYMENT AND CHILD DEVELOPMENT • Children of mothers who enjoy their work and remain committed to parenting show especially positive adjustment—higher self-esteem, more positive family and peer relations, less gender-stereotyped beliefs, and better grades in school. Girls, especially, profit from the image of female competence. Regardless of SES, daughters of employed mothers perceive women's roles as involving more freedom of choice and satisfaction and are more achievement and career oriented (Hoffman, 2000).

These benefits result from parenting practices. Employed mothers who value their parenting role are more likely to engage in authoritative child rearing and coregulation (see page 569). Also, children in dual-earner households devote more daily hours to doing homework under parental guidance and participate more in household chores. And maternal employment leads fathers to take on greater child-care responsibility, with a small but increasing number staying home full-time (Gottfried, Gottfried, & Bathurst, 2002; Hoffman & Youngblade, 1999). Paternal contact is associated with higher intelligence and achievement, mature social behavior, and gender-stereotype flexibility (Gottfried, 1991; Radin, 1994).

However, when employment places heavy demands on the mother's schedule or is stressful for other reasons, children are at risk for ineffective parenting. Working many hours or experiencing a negative interpersonal workplace atmosphere is associated with reduced parental sensitivity and poorer cognitive development in children from the preschool through adolescent years (Brooks-Gunn, Han, & Waldfogel, 2002; Costigan, Cox, & Cauce, 2003; Harvey, 1999). Negative consequences for children are magnified when low-SES mothers must spend long days at low-paying, menial, or physically taxing jobs that do little to improve family financial well-being—conditions linked to maternal depression, frustration, and fatigue and to use of harsh, inconsistent discipline (Raver, 2003).

Ⓢ Although balancing work and family responsibilities is challenging, as long as this employed mother enjoys her job, remains committed to parenting, and finds satisfactory child-care arrangements, her child is likely to develop high self-esteem, positive family and peer relations, and flexible beliefs about gender.
© Jonathan Nourok/PhotoEdit

In contrast, part-time employment and flexible work schedules are associated with good adjustment in children and adolescents. These arrangements prevent work–family role conflict, thereby helping parents meet children's needs (Frederiksen-Goldsen & Sharlach, 2000).

• SUPPORT FOR EMPLOYED PARENTS AND THEIR FAMILIES • In dual-earner families, the husband's willingness to share child-care responsibilities helps the mother engage in effective parenting. If the father helps very little or not at all, the mother carries a double load, at home and at work, leading to fatigue, distress, and little time and energy for children.

Employed mothers and dual-earner parents need assistance from work settings and communities in their child-rearing roles. Part-time employment, flexible schedules, job sharing, and paid leave when children are ill help parents juggle the demands of work and child rearing. Equal pay and equal employment opportunities for women also are important. Because these policies enhance financial status and morale, they improve the way mothers feel and behave when they arrive home at the end of the working day.

Child Care

Over the past several decades, the number of North American young children in child care has steadily increased to more than 60 percent in the United States and in some Canadian provinces. As Figure 14.6 shows, most are cared for in child-care centers or family child-care homes or are looked after informally by a relative. With age, children tend to transition from home-based to center care. A great many children, however, experience several types of care at once or frequently switch settings (Federal Interagency Forum on Child and Family Statistics, 2003; NICHD Early Child Care Research Network, 2004c; Statistics Canada, 2005a). Children of higher-income parents and children of very low-income parents are especially likely to be in center care. Many lower-income working parents rely on home care by relatives because they are not eligible for subsidized center-based care (Howes & James, 2002).

• CHILD-CARE QUALITY AND CHILDREN'S DEVELOPMENT • Recall from Chapter 8 that early intervention can enhance the development of economically disadvantaged children. As noted in Chapters 1 and 10, however, much North American child care is of poor quality. Refer to Chapter 10, pages 430–432 for a discussion of the negative consequences of exposing infants and toddlers to substandard child care and to many weekly hours of child care. Preschoolers, as well, suffer when placed in poor-quality child care, scoring lower in cognitive and social skills and higher in behavior problems (Howes & James, 2002; Lamb, 1998; Peiser-Feinberg et al., 2001; NICHD Early Childhood Research Network, 2003b). And when children experience the instability of several child-care settings, their psychological well-being declines. The emotional problems of temperamentally difficult preschoolers worsen considerably (De Schipper, van IJzendoorn, & Tavecchio, 2004; De Schipper et al., 2004).

In contrast, good child care enhances development, especially among low-SES children (NICHD Early Child Care Research Network, 2002b). In one study of more than 200 2- to 4-year-olds from very low-income families, the more time spent in high-quality child-care centers, the less likely children were to display emotional and behavior problems, even after many family characteristics were controlled (Votruba-Drzal, Coley, & Chase-Lansdale, 2004). And in another investigation, which followed 400 very low-income children over the preschool years, center-based care was more strongly associated with cognitive gains than were other child-care arrangements, probably because child-care centers are more likely to provide a systematic educational program. At the same time, better-quality experiences in all types of child care predicted modest improvements in cognitive, emotional, and social development (Loeb et al., 2004).

What are the ingredients of high-quality child care for preschoolers? Large-scale studies of child-care centers and child-care homes reveal that the following factors are important: group size

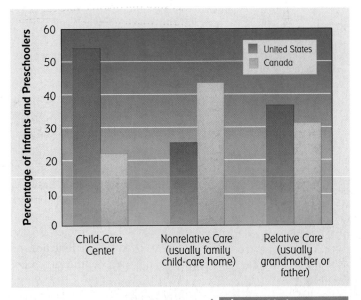

▲ **Figure 14.6**

Who's minding North American young children while their mothers are at work? The percentages refer to settings in which infants and preschoolers spend most time during their mother's working hours. In the United States, more children are in child-care centers than in family child-care homes; Canada shows the reverse trend. A great many children experience more than one type of child care, and with age, they tend to shift from home-based to center care—facts not reflected in the figure.

(Adapted from Statistics Canada, 2005a; Federal Interagency Forum on Child and Family Statistics, 2003.)

Applying

What We Know   Signs of Developmentally Appropriate Early Childhood Programs

Program Characteristic	Signs of Quality
Physical setting	Indoor environment is clean, in good repair, and well ventilated. Classroom space is divided into richly equipped activity areas, including make-believe play, blocks, science, math, games and puzzles, books, art, and music. Fenced outdoor play space is equipped with swings, climbing equipment, tricycles, and sandbox.
Group size	In preschools and child-care centers, group size is no greater than 18 to 20 children with 2 teachers.
Caregiver–child ratio	In child-care centers, teacher is responsible for no more than 8 to 10 children. In child-care homes, caregiver is responsible for no more than 6 children.
Daily activities	Most of the time, children work individually or in small groups. Children select many of their own activities and learn through experiences relevant to their own lives. Teachers facilitate children's involvement, accept individual differences, and adjust expectations to children's developing capacities.
Interactions between adults and children	Teachers move among groups and individuals, asking questions, offering suggestions, and adding more complex ideas. Teachers use positive guidance techniques, such as modeling and encouraging expected behavior and redirecting children to more acceptable activities.
Teacher qualifications	Teachers have college-level specialized preparation in early childhood development, early childhood education, or a related field.
Relationships with parents	Parents are encouraged to observe and participate. Teachers talk frequently with parents about children's behavior and development.
Licensing and accreditation	Child-care setting, whether a center or a home, is licensed by the state or province. In the United States, voluntary accreditation by the National Academy of Early Childhood Programs, *www.naeyc.org/accreditation,* or the National Association for Family Child Care, *www.nafcc.org,* is evidence of an especially high-quality program. Canada is working on a voluntary accreditation system, under the leadership of the Canadian Child Care Federation, *www.cccf-fcsge.ca.*

Sources: Bredekamp & Copple, 1997; National Association for the Education of Young Children, 1998.

(number of children in a single space), caregiver–child ratio, caregivers' educational preparation, and caregivers' personal commitment to learning about and caring for children. When these characteristics are favorable, adults are more verbally stimulating and sensitive to children's needs. Children of diverse ethnicities and SES levels, in turn, develop favorably—effects that persist into the early school years (Burchinal et al., 2000; Burchinal & Cryer, 2003).

Applying What We Know above summarizes the characteristics of high-quality early childhood programs, based on standards devised by the U.S. National Association for the Education of Young Children. Unfortunately, much North American child care is substandard: too often staffed by underpaid adults without specialized educational preparation, overcrowded with children, and (in the case of family child care) unlicensed and therefore not monitored for quality. And in both the United States and Canada, child care is expensive, consuming more than 25 percent of the average earnings of a single parent with two children in most states and provinces (Canada Campaign 2000, 2002; Children's Defense Fund, 2004).

In contrast, in Australia and Western Europe, child care that meets rigorous standards is widely available, and caregivers are paid on the same salary scale as elementary school teachers. Regardless of family income, in Denmark, up to 80 percent of child-care costs are government supported; in Sweden, nearly 90 percent; and in France, 100 percent (Waldfogel, 2001). Because the United States and Canada do not have national child-care policies, they lag behind other industrialized nations in supply, quality, and affordability of child care.

Self-Care

High-quality child care is vital for parents' peace of mind and children's well-being, even during middle childhood. An estimated 2.4 million 5- to 13-year-olds in the United States and several hundred thousand in Canada are **self-care children,** who regularly look after themselves during after-school hours. Self-care rises dramatically with age, from 3 percent of 5- to 7-year-olds to 33 percent of 11- to 13-year-olds. It also increases with SES, perhaps because of the greater safety of higher-income suburban neighborhoods. But when lower-SES parents must use self-care because they lack alternatives, their children spend more hours on their own (Casper & Smith, 2002).

Some studies report that they suffer from low self-esteem, antisocial behavior, poor academic achievement, and fearfulness, whereas others show no such effects. Children's maturity and the way they spend their time seem to explain these contradictions. Among younger school-age children, those who spend more hours alone have more adjustment difficulties (Vandell & Posner, 1999). As children become old enough to look after themselves, those who have a history of authoritative child rearing, are monitored from a distance by parental telephone calls, and have regular after-school chores appear responsible and well adjusted. In contrast, children left to their own devices are more likely to bend to peer pressures and engage in antisocial behavior (Coley, Morris, & Hernandez, 2004; Steinberg, 1986).

Before age 8 or 9, most children need supervision because they are not yet competent to handle emergencies (Galambos & Maggs, 1991). But throughout middle childhood and early adolescence, attending after-school programs with well-trained staffs, generous adult–child ratios, positive adult–child communication, and stimulating activities is linked to better emotional and social adjustment (Pierce, Hamm, & Vandell, 1999). And low-SES children who participate in "after-care" enrichment activities (scouting, music, or art lessons) show special benefits, including better work habits, improved academic performance, and fewer behavior problems (Posner & Vandell, 1994; Vandell, 1999).

Unfortunately, good programs are in especially short supply in low-income neighborhoods. In one survey of inner-city 10- to 14-year-olds, the vast majority did not participate in after-care activities or lessons of any kind. Instead, they watched TV and "hung out" for four or more hours each day (Shann, 2001). A special need exists for well-planned programs in these areas—ones that provide safe environments, enjoyable skill-building activities, and warm relationships with adults.

Ask Yourself

REVIEW	Describe and explain changes in sibling relationships from early childhood to adolescence. How does parenting influence the quality of sibling ties?
APPLY	Steve and Marissa are in the midst of an acrimonious divorce. Their 9-year-old son, Dennis, has become hostile and defiant. How can Steve and Marissa help Dennis adjust?
CONNECT	Review research on resilience in Chapter 1 (see page 10). Are factors that foster resilience similar to those that promote favorable adjustment to divorce and remarriage? Explain.
CONNECT	How does each level in Bronfenbrenner's ecological systems theory—microsystem, mesosystem, exosystem, and macrosystem—contribute to the effects of maternal employment and child care on children's development?

Vulnerable Families: Child Maltreatment

Throughout our discussion of family transitions, we have considered many factors, both within and outside the family, that contribute to parents' capacity to be warm, consistent, and appropriately demanding. As we turn now to the topic of child maltreatment, we will see that when these vital supports for effective child rearing break down, children as well as their parents can suffer terribly.

Incidence and Definitions

Child maltreatment is as old as human history, but only recently has the problem been widely acknowledged and research aimed at understanding it. Perhaps public concern has increased because child maltreatment is especially common in large industrialized nations. In the most recently reported year, 906,000 American children (12 out of every 1,000) and 136,000

Canadian children (10 out of every 1,000) were identified as victims (Trocomé & Wolfe, 2002; U.S. Department of Health and Human Services, 2005). Because most cases go unreported, the true figures are much higher.

Child maltreatment takes the following forms:

- *Physical abuse:* assaults on children, such as kicking, biting, shaking, punching, or stabbing, that inflict physical injury
- *Sexual abuse:* fondling, intercourse, exhibitionism, commercial exploitation through prostitution or production of pornography, and other forms of sexual exploitation
- *Neglect:* failure to provide for a child's basic needs, in terms of food, clothing, medical attention, education, or supervision
- *Emotional abuse:* acts that could cause serious mental or behavioral disorders, including social isolation, repeated unreasonable demands, ridicule, humiliation, intimidation, or terrorizing

Neglect accounts for 40 to 50 percent of reported cases, physical abuse for 30 percent, emotional abuse for 10 to 20 percent, and sexual abuse for 10 percent. But these figures are only approximate, as many children experience more than one form.

Parents commit the vast majority of incidents—more than 80 percent. Other relatives account for about 7 percent. The remainder are perpetrated by parents' unmarried partners, school officials, camp counselors, and other adults. Mothers engage in neglect more often than fathers, whereas fathers engage in sexual abuse more often than mothers. Maternal and paternal rates of physical and emotional abuse are fairly similar. And in an especially heartrending 18 percent of cases, parents jointly commit the abusive acts. Infants and young preschoolers are at greatest risk for neglect; preschool and school-age children are at greatest risk for physical, emotional, and sexual abuse. But each type occurs at every age (Trocomé & Wolfe, 2002; U.S. Department of Health and Human Services, 2005).

Origins of Child Maltreatment

Early findings suggested that child maltreatment was rooted in adult psychological disturbance (Kempe et al., 1962). But although child abuse is more common among disturbed parents, it soon became clear that a single "abusive" personality type does not exist. Sometimes even "normal" parents harm their children! Also, parents who were abused as children do not necessarily become abusers (Buchanan, 1996; Simons et al., 1991).

For help in understanding child maltreatment, researchers turned to the social systems perspective on family functioning. They discovered that many interacting variables—at the family, community, and cultural levels—contribute. Table 14.3 summarizes factors associated with physical and emotional abuse and neglect. For a discussion of child sexual abuse, see the Social Issues box on the following page.

TABLE 14.3 FACTORS RELATED TO CHILD MALTREATMENT

Factor	Description
Parent characteristics	Psychological disturbance; alcohol and drug abuse; history of abuse as a child; belief in harsh, physical discipline; desire to satisfy unmet emotional needs through the child; unreasonable expectations for child behavior; young age (most under 30); low educational level
Child characteristics	Premature or very sick baby; difficult temperament; inattentiveness and overactivity; other developmental problems
Family characteristics	Low income; poverty; homelessness; marital instability; social isolation; physical abuse of mother by husband or boyfriend; frequent moves; large families with closely spaced children; overcrowded living conditions; disorganized household; lack of steady employment; other signs of high life stress
Community	Characterized by violence and social isolation; few parks, child-care centers, preschool programs, recreation centers, or churches to serve as family supports
Culture	Approval of physical force and violence as ways to solve problems

Sources: Cicchetti & Toth, 2000; Wekerle & Wolfe, 2003.

Child Sexual Abuse

Until recently, child sexual abuse was viewed as a rare occurrence. When children came forward to report it, adults did not take their claims seriously. In the 1970s, efforts by professionals along with media attention led to recognition of child sexual abuse as a serious and widespread problem. About 90,000 cases in the United States and 14,000 cases in Canada were confirmed in the most recently reported year (Trocomé & Wolfe, 2002; U.S. Department of Health and Human Services, 2005).

Characteristics of Abusers and Victims

Sexual abuse is committed against children of both sexes but more often against girls. Although most cases are reported in middle childhood, sexual abuse also occurs at younger and older ages. For some victims, the abuse begins early in life and continues for many years (Trickett & Putnam, 1998).

Typically the abuser is a male—a parent or someone the parent knows well. Often it is a father, stepfather, or live-in boyfriend; somewhat less often, an uncle or older brother. In a few instances, mothers are the offenders, more often with sons (Kolvin & Trowell, 1996). Abusers make the child comply in a variety of distasteful ways, including deception, bribery, verbal intimidation, and physical force.

You may wonder how any adult—especially a parent or close relative—could possibly violate a child sexually. Many offenders deny their own responsibility. They blame the abuse on the willing participation of a seductive youngster. Yet children are not capable of making a deliberate, informed decision to enter into a sexual relationship! Even at older ages, they are not free to say yes or no. Instead, the responsibility lies with abusers, who tend to have characteristics that predispose them toward sexual exploitation of children. They have great difficulty controlling their impulses and may suffer from psychological disorders, including alcohol and drug abuse. Often they pick out children who are unlikely to defend themselves or to be believed—those who are physically weak, emotionally deprived, socially isolated, or affected by disabilities, such as blindness, deafness, or mental retardation (Bolen, 2001).

Reported cases of child sexual abuse are linked to poverty, marital instability, and resulting weakening of family ties.

Children who live in homes with a history of constantly changing characters—repeated marriages, separations, and new partners—are especially vulnerable. But children in economically advantaged, stable families are also victims, although their abuse is more likely to escape detection (Putnam, 2003).

Consequences of Sexual Abuse

The adjustment problems of child sexual abuse victims are often severe. Depression, low self-esteem, mistrust of adults, and anger and hostility can persist for years after the abusive episodes. Younger children frequently react with sleep difficulties, loss of appetite, and generalized fearfulness. Adolescents may run away and show suicidal reactions, substance abuse, and delinquency. At all ages, persistent abuse accompanied by force, violence, and a close relationship to the perpetrator (incest) has a more severe impact (Feiring, Taska, & Lewis, 1999; Tricket et al., 2001).

Sexually abused children frequently display sexual knowledge and behavior beyond their years. They have learned from their abusers that sexual overtures are acceptable ways to get attention and rewards. In adolescence, abused young people often become promiscuous and are at risk for early childbearing. In adulthood, child sexual abuse is related to increased arrest rates for sex crimes (mostly against children) and prostitution (Friedrich et al., 2001; Salter et al., 2003). Furthermore, women who were sexually abused are likely to choose partners who abuse them and their children. As mothers, they often engage in irresponsible and coercive parenting, including child abuse and neglect (Pianta, Egeland, & Erickson, 1989). In these ways, the harmful impact of sexual abuse is transmitted to the next generation.

Prevention and Treatment

Treating child sexual abuse is difficult. The reactions of family members—anxiety about harm to the child, anger toward the abuser, and sometimes hostility toward the victim for telling—can increase children's distress. Because sexual abuse typically appears in the midst of other serious family problems,

long-term therapy with children and parents usually is necessary (Olafson & Boat, 2000). The best way to reduce the suffering of victims is to prevent sexual abuse from continuing. Today, courts are prosecuting abusers more vigorously and taking children's testimony more seriously (see Chapter 7). Special efforts are needed to help sexually abused boys, who are less likely than girls to speak about the experience and to receive therapy and court protection (Holmes & Slap, 1998).

Educational programs that teach children to recognize inappropriate sexual advances and whom to turn to for help reduce the risk of abuse. Yet because of controversies over educating children about sexual abuse, few schools offer these interventions. New Zealand is the only country with a national, school-based prevention program targeting sexual abuse. In Keeping Ourselves Safe, children and adolescents learn that abusers are rarely strangers. Parent involvement ensures that home and school work together in teaching children self-protection skills. Evaluations reveal that virtually all New Zealand parents and children support the program and that it has helped many children avoid or report abuse (Briggs, 2002).

▼ In Keeping Ourselves Safe, New Zealand's national school-based child abuse prevention program, teachers and police officers collaborate in teaching children to recognize abusive adult behaviors so children can take steps to protect themselves.
Courtesy of the New Zealand Police

• **THE FAMILY** • Within the family, certain children—those whose characteristics make them more of a challenge to rear—are more likely to become targets of abuse. These include premature or very sick babies and children who are temperamentally difficult, are inattentive or overactive, or have other developmental problems. Child factors, however, only slightly increase the risk of abuse (Sidebotham et al., 2003). Whether such children are maltreated largely depends on parents' characteristics.

Maltreating parents are less skillful than other parents in handling discipline confrontations and getting children to cooperate in working toward common goals. They also suffer from biased thinking about their child. For example, they often evaluate transgressions as worse than they are, attribute their child's misdeeds to a stubborn or bad disposition, and feel powerless in parenting—perspectives that lead them to move quickly toward physical force (Bugental & Happaney, 2004; Haskett et al., 2003).

Once abuse gets started, it quickly becomes part of a self-sustaining relationship. The small irritations to which abusive parents react—a fussy baby, a preschooler who knocks over her milk, or a child who will not mind immediately—soon become bigger ones. Then the harshness increases. By the preschool years, abusive and neglectful parents seldom interact with their children. When they do, they rarely express pleasure and affection; the communication is almost always negative (Wolfe, 1999).

Most parents, however, have enough self-control not to respond to their children's misbehavior or developmental problems with abuse. Other factors combine with these conditions to prompt an extreme response. Unmanageable parental stress is strongly associated with maltreatment. Abusive parents respond to stressful situations with high emotional arousal. And such stressors as low income and education (less than a high-school diploma), unemployment, young maternal age, alcohol and drug use, marital conflict, overcrowded living conditions, frequent moves, and extreme household disorganization are common in abusive homes (Wekerle & Wolfe, 2003). These personal and situational conditions increase the chances that parents will be too overwhelmed to meet basic child-rearing responsibilities or will vent their frustrations by lashing out at their children.

• **THE COMMUNITY** • The majority of abusive and neglectful parents are isolated from both formal and informal social supports. This social isolation has at least two causes. First, because of their own life histories, many of these parents have learned to mistrust and avoid others. They do not have the skills necessary for establishing and maintaining positive relationships. Second, maltreating parents are more likely to live in unstable, run-down neighborhoods that provide few links between family and community, such as parks, child-care centers, preschool programs, recreation centers, and religious institutions (Coulton, Korbin, & Su, 1999). For these reasons, they lack "lifelines" to others and have no one to turn to for help during stressful times.

Furthermore, the stressors associated with living in a violent neighborhood seem to heighten violent responses to conflict in the home. In a study carried out at a summer day camp, school-age children who reported hearing about, experiencing, or witnessing a greater number of neighborhood violent acts (such as shootings, stabbings, and sexual assaults) were more likely to have been physically abused or severely neglected (Lynch & Cicchetti, 1998).

• **THE LARGER CULTURE** • Cultural values, laws, and customs profoundly affect the chances that child maltreatment will occur when parents feel overburdened. Societies that view violence as an appropriate way to solve problems set the stage for child abuse. Although the United States and Canada have laws to protect children from maltreatment, parental use of corporal punishment is widespread, as we saw in Chapter 12.

In addition, the U.S. Supreme Court has twice upheld the right of school officials to use physical discipline. Likewise, the Canadian federal criminal code states that the use of physical means of discipline by parents, teachers, and caregivers is justified, as long as such force is "reasonable under the circumstances." Because this definition is vague, many experts believe that it encourages adults to assault children and provides a ready defense for those who do so (Justice for Children and Youth, 2003). Indeed, Canadian courts have deemed hard spankings, slaps to the head and face, and hitting of the buttocks and legs with belts and sticks to be consistent with the criminal code. Every industrialized nation except the United States and

Canada now prohibits school corporal punishment (Center for Effective Discipline, 2005). Fortunately, some U.S. states and Canadian provinces have passed laws that ban it.

Consequences of Child Maltreatment

The family circumstances of maltreated children impair the development of emotional self-regulation, empathy and sympathy, self-concept, social skills, and academic motivation. Over time, these youngsters show serious learning and adjustment problems, including school failure, severe depression, aggressive behavior, peer difficulties, substance abuse, and delinquency (Bolger & Patterson, 2001; Shonk & Cicchetti, 2001). In a Canadian study, high school students reporting a history of frequent abuse had engaged in more violent crime, including carrying concealed weapons and physically attacking others (Wolfe et al., 2001).

How do these damaging consequences occur? Think back to our discussion in Chapter 12 of the effects of hostile cycles of parent–child interaction, which are especially severe for abused children. Indeed, a family characteristic strongly associated with child abuse is spouse abuse (Cox, Kotch, & Everson, 2003). Clearly, the home lives of abused children overflow with opportunities to learn to use aggression as a way of solving problems.

Furthermore, demeaning parental messages, in which children are ridiculed, humiliated, rejected, or terrorized, result in low self-esteem, high anxiety, self-blame, depression, and efforts to escape from extreme psychological pain—at times severe enough to lead to attempted suicide in adolescence (Wolfe, 1999). At school, maltreated children present serious discipline problems. Their noncompliance, poor motivation, and cognitive immaturity interfere with academic achievement—an outcome that further undermines their chances for life success (Wekerle & Wolfe, 2003).

Finally, the trauma of repeated abuse is associated with central nervous system damage, including abnormal EEG brain-wave activity, fMRI-detected reduced size and impaired functioning of the cerebral cortex and corpus callosum, and heightened production of stress hormones (Cicchetti, 2003; Kaufman & Charney, 2001). These effects increase the chances that cognitive and emotional problems will endure.

Public service announcements, like the one on this billboard, help prevent child abuse by educating people about the problem and informing them where to seek help.

© Rachel Epstein/PhotoEdit

Preventing Child Maltreatment

Because child maltreatment is embedded within families, communities, and society as a whole, efforts to prevent it must be directed at each of these levels. Many approaches have been suggested, including teaching high-risk parents effective child-rearing strategies, providing direct experience with children in high school child development courses, and broad social programs aimed at bettering economic conditions for low-SES families.

We have seen that providing social supports to families is highly effective in easing parental stress. This approach sharply reduces child maltreatment as well (Azar & Wolfe, 1998). A trusting relationship with another person is the most important factor in preventing mothers with childhood histories of abuse from repeating the cycle with their own youngsters (Egeland, Jacobvitz, & Sroufe, 1988). Parents Anonymous, a North American organization that has as its main goal helping child-abusing parents learn constructive parenting practices, does so largely through social supports. Its local chapters offer self-help group meetings, daily phone calls, and regular home visits to relieve social isolation and teach responsible child-rearing skills.

Two-generation approaches to early intervention, aimed at strengthening both child and parent competencies (see Chapter 8, page 343), can reduce child maltreatment substantially (Reynolds & Robertson, 2003). Healthy Families America, a program that began in Hawaii and has since spread to 270 sites around the United States, identifies families at risk for maltreatment during pregnancy or at birth. Each is provided three years of home visitation, in which a trained worker helps parents manage crises, encourages effective child rearing, and puts parents in touch with community services to meet their own and their children's needs. In an evaluation in which several hundred at-risk families were randomly assigned to either an intervention or control group and followed over time, program benefits were clear: By the end of the

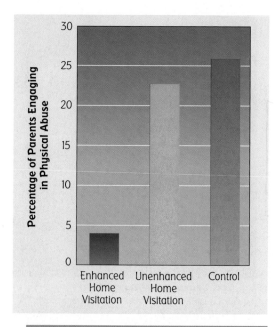

Figure 14.7

Impact of a home visitation program with a cognitive component on preventing physical abuse of young children. In an enhanced home visitation condition, home visitors not only provided social support, encouraged effective child rearing, and connected families with community resources, but also helped at-risk parents change their negative appraisals of their babies and solve child-rearing problems. After one year of intervention, this cognitive component sharply reduced physical abuse of babies (hitting, shaking, beating, kicking, biting) compared with an unenhanced home visitation condition and a no-intervention control. (Adapted from Bugental et al., 2002.)

second year, intervention mothers less often used violent disciplinary tactics and reported more confidence and less stress in parenting (Daro & Harding, 1999).

Adding a *cognitive component* to home visitation dramatically increases its impact. When home visitors helped parents change negative appraisals of their babies—by teaching them to read their child's cues, countering inaccurate interpretations (for example, that the baby is behaving with malicious intent), and working on solving child-rearing problems—physical punishment and abuse dropped sharply by the end of one year of intervention (see Figure 14.7) (Bugental et al., 2002). Positive effects were greatest for parents of difficult-to-care-for babies who had experienced birth complications.

Still, many experts believe that child maltreatment cannot be eliminated as long as violence is widespread and harsh physical punishment is regarded as acceptable. In addition, combating poverty and its diverse correlates—family stress and disorganization, inadequate food and medical care, teenage parenthood, low-birth-weight babies, and parental hopelessness—would protect many children.

Although more cases reach the courts than in decades past, child maltreatment remains a crime that is difficult to prove. Most of the time, the only witnesses are the child victims or other loyal family members. Even in court cases in which the evidence is strong, judges hesitate to impose the ultimate safeguard against further harm: permanently removing the child from the family. There are several reasons for this reluctant attitude. First, in the United States and Canada, government intervention into family life is viewed as a last resort. Second, despite destructive family relationships, maltreated children and their parents are usually attached to one another. Most of the time, neither desires separation. Finally, the U.S. and Canadian legal systems tend to regard children as parental property rather than as human beings in their own right, and this also has stood in the way of court-ordered protection.

Even with intensive treatment, some adults persist in their abusive acts. An estimated 1,500 American children and 100 Canadian children, most of them infants and preschoolers, die from maltreatment each year (Trocomé & Wolfe, 2002; U.S. Department of Health and Human Services, 2005). When parents are unlikely to change their behavior, the drastic step of separating parent from child and legally terminating parental rights is the only justifiable course of action.

Child maltreatment is a distressing and horrifying topic. When we consider how often it occurs in nations that claim to place a high value on the dignity and worth of the individual, it is even more appalling. Yet there is reason to be optimistic. Great strides have been made over the past several decades in understanding and preventing child maltreatment.

Ask Yourself

REVIEW	Explain how personal and situational factors that contribute to child maltreatment illustrate the social systems perspective on family functioning.
APPLY	Claire told her 6-year-old daughter to be careful never to talk to or take candy from strangers. Why is Claire's directive not adequate to protect her daughter from sexual abuse?
CONNECT	After reviewing factors linked to adolescent parenthood (Chapter 5, pages 211–213), explain why it places children at risk for abuse and neglect.
REFLECT	Describe a challenging time for your family during your childhood. What aspects of the experience increased stress? What factors helped you and your parents cope with adversity?

⊚ Summary

Evolutionary Origins

Discuss the evolutionary origins and adaptive value of the family among our hunting-and-gathering ancestors.

⊚ The human family in its most common form can be traced to our hunting-and-gathering ancestors. When bipedalism evolved and arms were freed to carry things, our ancestors found it easier to cooperate and share, especially in providing food for the young. A man and woman assumed special responsibility for their own children because that arrangement enhanced survival. Kinship groups expanded, offering greater success at competing with other humans for resources.

Functions of the Family

Cite the functions modern families perform for society.

⊚ Responsibilities of contemporary families are largely restricted to reproduction, socialization, and emotional support. As societies became more complex, other institutions developed to assist with certain functions, such as educating children and ensuring societal order.

The Family as a Social System

Describe the social systems perspective on family functioning, including its view of family interaction and the influence of surrounding social contexts.

⊚ Contemporary researchers view the family from a **social systems perspective**—as a complex set of interacting relationships affected by the larger social context. Bidirectional influences exist whereby the behaviors of each family member affect those of others—an interplay of forces that must constantly adapt to the development of individual family members. Connections to the community—through formal organizations and informal social networks—grant parents and children social support, thereby promoting effective family interaction and children's development.

Socialization Within the Family

Discuss the features that differentiate major child-rearing styles, and explain how effective parents adapt child rearing to children's growing competence during middle childhood and adolescence.

⊚ Three features differentiate major **child-rearing styles:** (1) acceptance of the child and involvement in the child's life to establish emotional connection; (2) control of the child to promote mature behavior; and (3) autonomy granting to encourage self-reliance. The **authoritative style** is high in acceptance and involvement, emphasizes firm control with explanations, and includes gradual, appropriate autonomy granting. It promotes cognitive, emotional, and social competence from early childhood into adolescence.

© JEFF GREENBERG/PHOTOEDIT

⊚ The **authoritarian style** is low in acceptance and involvement, is high in both coercive and **psychological control,** and restricts instead of grants autonomy. It is associated with anxious, withdrawn, dependent child behavior, especially among girls, and with high rates of anger, defiance, and aggression, especially among boys. The **permissive style** is high in acceptance, low in control, and lax rather than appropriate in autonomy granting. Children who experience it typically show poor self-control and achievement and, in adolescence, are defiant and antisocial. The **uninvolved style** combines low acceptance and involvement with little control or effort to grant autonomy. When it begins early, it disrupts virtually all aspects of development.

⊚ Authoritative child rearing promotes maturity and adjustment in children of diverse temperaments. But because of their dispositions, some children require more emphasis on certain authoritative features. Over time, the relationship between parenting and children's attributes becomes increasingly bidirectional.

⊚ In middle childhood, effective parents engage in **coregulation,** exerting general oversight while permitting children to be in charge of moment-by-moment decision making. During adolescence, mature **autonomy** is fostered by parenting that grants young people independence in accord with their readiness, while maintaining a warm, supportive relationship.

Describe socioeconomic and ethnic variations in child rearing, including the impact of affluence and poverty.

⊚ The authoritative style predicts favorable development irrespective of SES, ethnicity, and family structure. Nevertheless, consistent variations in child rearing exist. Higher-SES parents are more verbal and stimulating and rely more on warmth and explanations; low-SES parents use more commands, criticism, and physical punishment.

⊚ Despite the means to provide their children with every advantage, affluent parents often have youngsters who by adolescence display worsening problems, including substance abuse and emotional, academic, and behavior problems. Excessive achievement pressures and isolation from adults underlie their difficulties.

⊚ When families experience the persistent stressors that accompany poverty, parents become depressed, irritable, and distracted. As a result, parents become less involved in child rearing, hostile family interactions increase, children experience depleted home learning environments, and their cognitive and emotional well-being suffers profoundly.

⊚ Chinese, Hispanic, Asian Pacific Island, and African-American parents tend to be highly controlling. When combined with warmth, high control can be adaptive. Among African-American children, it is associated with cognitive and social competence. But when control becomes excessive, resulting in an authoritarian child-rearing style, it impairs children's adjustment.

⊚ **Extended-family households,** in which one or more adult relatives live with the parent–child **nuclear family unit,** are common among ethnic minorities. Extended-family support helps protect children from the stress and disorganization of poverty.

© BOB DAEMMRICH/THE IMAGE WORKS

Family Lifestyles and Transitions

Describe the influence of family size on child rearing, and explain how sibling relationships change with age and affect development.

⊚ Family size has declined dramatically over the past several decades. But contrary to a widespread assumption, family size and later birth order do not dilute children's experiences, depress their intelligence, or reduce their life chances. Rather, the fact that mothers with low IQs bear more children accounts for the link between family size and children's IQ.

⊚ Most children grow up with at least one sibling. Because of their frequency and emotional intensity, sibling interactions promote many aspects of social competence. Parental warmth fosters cooperative sibling ties; lack of parental involvement, coercive control, and favoritism increase sibling rivalry. Sibling rivalry tends to increase in middle childhood, when parental comparisons become more frequent. In adolescence, sibling relationships become less intense as young people strive for autonomy. Nevertheless, attachment to siblings remains strong for most young people.

⊚ Although sibling relationships bring many benefits, only children are as well adjusted as children with siblings, and they are advantaged in self-esteem, academic achievement, and educational attainment.

How do children fare in adoptive families, gay and lesbian families, and never-married single-parent families?

⊚ Adopted children have more learning and emotional difficulties than other children, and by adolescence, their lives are often complicated by unresolved curiosity about their roots. By adulthood, however, most adoptees are well adjusted. When parents help them learn about their heritage, young people adopted into a different ethnic group or culture typically develop healthy identities that combine their birth and rearing backgrounds.

⊚ Research on gay and lesbian families is largely limited to small, volunteer samples. Findings indicate that children of homosexual parents do not differ from children of heterosexual parents in mental health, peer relations, gender identity, or sexual orientation. During adolescence, more youths from homosexual families experiment with partners of both sexes.

⊚ Many children of never-married mothers display adjustment problems associated with economic hardship. When they lack a father's warmth and involvement, they achieve less well in school and engage in more antisocial behavior than children in low-SES, first-marriage families.

What factors influence children's adjustment to divorce and blended-family arrangements?

⊚ Although all children experience painful emotional reactions during the period surrounding divorce, children with difficult temperaments and boys in general have more academic, emotional, and behavioral difficulties. Over time, children of divorce show improved functioning, but they continue to score slightly lower than children of continuously married parents on a variety of adjustment indicators. Problems with adolescent sexuality, early parenthood, and development of intimate ties surface at later ages.

⊚ The overriding factor in positive adjustment following divorce is effective parenting. Contact with noncustodial fathers is important for children of both sexes, and outcomes for sons tend to be better when fathers have custody.

⊚ Because **divorce mediation** and parent education programs help divorcing parents resolve their disputes and cooperate in child rearing, it can help children adjust. The success of **joint custody** depends on parental cooperation, and children who experience it tend to fare better than children in sole-maternal-custody homes.

⊚ When divorced parents enter new relationships through cohabitation or remarriage, children must adapt to a **blended,** or **reconstituted, family.** How well they fare depends on which parent forms a new relationship, on the age and sex of the child, and on the complexity of blended-family relationships. Girls, older children, and

children in father–stepmother families have more adjustment problems. Stepparents who move into their roles gradually and form a "parenting coalition" with the natural parent help children adjust.

How do maternal employment and life in dual-earner families affect children's development?

⊚ When mothers enjoy their work and remain committed to parenting, maternal employment is associated with favorable consequences for children, including a higher sense of self-esteem, more positive family and peer relations, less gender-stereotyped beliefs, and better grades in school. But when employment is stressful because of time demands or other reasons, children are at risk for ineffective parenting and adjustment difficulties.

⊚ In dual-earner families, the father's willingness to share child rearing is linked to many positive outcomes for children. Workplace supports, such as part-time employment and paid parental leave, help parents meet the demands of work and child rearing.

Discuss the influence of child-care quality on preschoolers' development, the status of child care in the United States and Canada compared with other industrialized nations, and the impact of self-care on school-age children's adjustment.

⊚ North American children experience a diverse array of child-care arrangements while their parents are at work, with home-based care declining and center care increasing as children get older. Preschoolers exposed to poor-quality care score lower in cognitive and social skills and higher in behavior problems. The instability of several child-care settings also impairs young children's adjustment.

⊚ When group size is small, caregiver–child ratios are generous, and caregivers are well educated and personally committed to caring for children, adults communicate in more stimulating and responsive ways. As a result, children develop favorably. Because the United States and Canada do not have national child-care policies, they lag far behind other Western nations in supply, quality, and affordability of child care.

⑨ **Self-care children** who are old enough to look after themselves, are monitored from a distance, and have a history of authoritative parenting appear responsible and well adjusted. In contrast, children left to their own devices are at risk for antisocial behavior. Children in high-quality after-school programs reap academic, emotional, social benefits.

Vulnerable Families: Child Maltreatment

Discuss the multiple origins of child maltreatment, its consequences for development, and prevention strategies.

⑨ Child maltreatment is related to factors within the family, community, and larger culture. Maltreating parents use ineffective discipline, hold a negatively biased view of their child, and feel powerless in parenting. Unmanageable parental stress, social isolation, and neighborhood disintegration and violence greatly increase the chances that abuse and neglect will occur. When a society approves of force and violence as a means for solving problems, child abuse is promoted.

⑨ Maltreated children are impaired in the development of emotional self-regulation, empathy and sympathy, self-concept, social skills, and academic motivation. In addition, the trauma of abuse is associated with abnormal brain-wave activity and a heightened stress response. Over time, children show a wide variety of serious adjustment problems. Successful prevention of child maltreatment requires efforts at the family, community, and cultural levels, including programs that strengthen both child and parent competencies and a reduction in societal violence and poverty.

---

⑨ Important Terms and Concepts

authoritarian child-rearing style (p. 564)
authoritative child-rearing style (p. 564)
autonomy (p. 569)
blended, or reconstituted, family (p. 582)
child-rearing styles (p. 563)

coregulation (p. 569)
divorce mediation (p. 582)
extended-family household (p. 573)
joint custody (p. 582)
nuclear family unit (p. 573)

permissive child-rearing style (p. 565)
psychological control (p. 565)
self-care children (p. 587)
social systems perspective (p. 559)
uninvolved child-rearing style (p. 565)

"Children of a Village"
Maryam Sefait
Age 14, Iran

On a street that seems to have emerged from a storybook—ageless and old but lovingly cared for—children engage in a timeless custom: playing with friends. Peer relationships are vital sources of support for children, contributing greatly to all aspects of development.

Reprinted with permission from the International Museum of Children's Art, Oslo, Norway.

CHAPTER 15

Peers, Media, and Schooling

Stu and Pete became friends in their school's Connections program. By assigning small groups of sixth graders to the same classes and lunch hour, the program aims to smooth the transition to middle school by helping students feel "connected" in their new, large-school environment. During an end-of-year discussion in health class, Mrs. Stevens asked what their new-school experiences had been like.

Stu began, "When we started the year, people were bouncing around, trying to find friends they felt comfortable with, and it wasn't so easy. I wasn't sure I was going to fit in. In the past few weeks, though, Pete and I clicked."

"Same with Katy and me," Jessamyn chimed in. "I used to have another group of friends in fifth grade, but I lost interest. I mean, when they got here, they were trying too hard to be popular."

"Can you explain that a little?" Mrs. Stevens inquired.

"Well, every time they talked to someone, they acted like a different person—kinda two-faced. It was annoying."

"How do you know someone's going to be a good friend? " Mrs. Stevens asked.

"You've gotta have the same interests, and Stu and me, we've kinda got the same personality," replied Pete. "We both like computer stuff like playing games and chatting on *Instant Messenger*. Also, a friend has to be somebody who makes you feel good about yourself. I wouldn't be friends with someone who's always making me feel bad."

"Yeah," Katy agreed. "I know kids who'll say they're a friend but they're real nasty. They don't show any kindness or understanding. Mostly, everyone dislikes them."

Outside the family, what forces strongly influence children and adolescents? The answer is clear: peers, with whom they share countless play, classroom, and extracurricular activities; media—especially television and computers, which consume large amounts of their free time; and school, which assists the family in transmitting culturally valued knowledge to the next generation.

In the first part of this chapter, we look closely at the development of peer sociability, friendship, and peer acceptance, along with their profound significance for psychological adjustment. Next we consider the impact of television and computers on cognitive and social skills. Finally, we turn to the school—how class and school size, educational philosophy, teacher–student interaction, and grouping of students affect educational experiences and learning. We conclude with a look at schooling and achievement in international perspective, with special attention to how well North American schools prepare young people for productive work lives.

The Importance of Peer Relations

Are peer relations crucial for development, and how do they add to children's experiences with caring adults? To find out for sure, we would need to study a group of children reared only by parents and compare them to children growing up under typical conditions. In humans, these circumstances rarely occur naturally and are unethical to arrange experimentally. But such studies with nonhuman primates reveal that peer bonds are vital for social competence. For example, maternally reared rhesus monkeys with no peer contact show immature play, excessive aggression and fearfulness, and less cooperation at maturity (Harlow, 1969).

Parent and peer relations seem to complement one another. Parents provide affection and guidance, which grants children the security and social skills they need to enter the world of peers. Peer interaction, in turn, enables children to expand their social skills. Peers can also stand in, to some extent, for the early parent–child bond. After rearing rhesus monkeys in groups without adults, researchers let them choose between their preferred peer (the one they sought closeness to during rearing), a familiar peer, and an unfamiliar peer. The monkeys spent most time near their preferred peer, who served as a source of security (Higley et al., 1992). Nevertheless, peer-only-reared monkeys do not fare as well as monkeys with typical upbringing. In novel environments, they spend much time anxiously clinging to their preferred agemate. And as they get older, they display behavior problems, including dominance or submission rather than friendly interaction, with unfamiliar peers (Goy & Goldfoot, 1974).

Do these findings generalize to human children? A unique, human parallel to peer-only rearing suggests that in large measure, they do. In the 1940s, Anna Freud and Sophie Dann (1951) studied six young German-Jewish orphans whose parents had been murdered in the Nazi gas chambers shortly after the children's birth. For several years, the children remained together in a concentration camp, without close ties to adults. When World War II ended, they were brought to England and cared for as a group. Observations revealed that they were passionately attached, becoming upset whenever separated. They were also intensely prosocial, freely sharing, comforting, and helping one another. Nevertheless, they displayed many anxious symptoms, including intense thumb sucking, restlessness, immature play, and aggression toward as well as excessive dependency on their caregivers. As they built trusting relationships with adults, the children's play, language, and exploration developed rapidly.

In sum, peers serve as vital sources of support in threatening situations and contribute greatly to development. But they do so more effectively when children also have warm, supportive ties to parents.

 The beginnings of peer sociability emerge in infancy, in the form of touches, smiles, and babbles that gradually develop into coordinated interaction in the second year. Early peer sociability is fostered by a warm, sensitive caregiver–child bond.
© Myrleen Ferguson Cate/PhotoEdit

Development of Peer Sociability

In cultures where agemates have regular contact during the first year of life, peer sociability begins early, gradually evolving into the complex, well-coordinated exchanges of childhood and adolescence. Development of peer sociability is supported by and contributes greatly to cognitive, emotional, and social milestones discussed in previous chapters.

Infant and Toddler Beginnings

When pairs of infants are brought together in a laboratory, looking accompanied by touching is present at 3 to 4 months, peer-directed smiles and babbles by 6 months. These isolated social acts increase until by the end of the first year, an occasional reciprocal exchange occurs in which babies grin, gesture, or otherwise imitate a playmate's behavior (Vandell & Mueller, 1995).

Between 1 and 2 years, coordinated interaction occurs more often, largely in the form of mutual imitation involving jumping, chasing, or banging a toy. These imitative, turn-taking games create joint understandings that aid verbal communication. Around age 2, toddlers use words to talk about and influence a peer's behavior, as when they say "Let's play chase" and, after the game gets going, "Hey, good running!" (Eckerman & Peterman, 2001; Eckerman & Whitehead, 1999). Reciprocal play and positive emotion are especially frequent in toddlers' interactions with familiar agemates, suggesting that they are building true peer relationships (Ross et al., 1992).

Though quite limited, peer sociability is present in the first 2 years, and it is promoted by the early caregiver–child bond. From interacting with sensitive adults, babies learn how to send and interpret emotional signals in their first peer associations (Trevarthen, 2003). Consistent with this idea, toddlers with a warm parental relationship engage in more extended peer exchanges. These children, in turn, display more socially competent behavior as preschoolers (Howes & Matheson, 1992).

The Preschool Years

As children become increasingly self-aware, more effective at communicating, and better at understanding the thoughts and feelings of others, their skill at interacting with peers improves greatly. Mildred Parten (1932), one of the first to study peer sociability among 2- to 5-year-olds, noticed a dramatic increase with age in the ability to engage in joint, interactive play. She concluded that social development proceeds in a three-step sequence. It begins with **nonsocial activity**—unoccupied, onlooker behavior and solitary play. Then it shifts to a limited form of social participation called **parallel play,** in which a child plays near other children with similar materials but does not try to influence their behavior. At the highest level are two forms of true social interaction. One is **associative play,** in which children engage in separate activities, but they exchange toys and comment on one another's behavior. The other is **cooperative play,** a more advanced type of interaction in which children orient toward a common goal, such as acting out a make-believe theme.

Longitudinal evidence indicates that these play forms emerge in the order suggested by Parten, but they do not form a developmental sequence in which later-appearing forms replace earlier ones (Howes & Matheson, 1992). Rather, all types coexist during the preschool years. Watch children move from one play type to another in preschool, and you will see that they often transition from onlooker to parallel to cooperative play and back again (Robinson et al., 2003). Preschoolers seem to use parallel play as a way station—a respite from the high demands of complex social interaction and a crossroad to new activities. Furthermore, although nonsocial activity declines with age, it is still the most frequent form of behavior among 3- to 4-year-olds. Even among kindergartners it continues to take up as about one-third of children's free-play time. And both solitary and parallel play remain fairly stable from 3 to 6 years, accounting for as much of the young child's play as highly social, cooperative interaction (Rubin, Fein, & Vandenberg, 1983).

We now understand that it is the *type*, rather than the amount, of solitary and parallel play that changes during early childhood. In studies of preschoolers' play in Taiwan and the United States, researchers rated the *cognitive maturity* of nonsocial, parallel, and cooperative play by applying the categories shown in Table 15.1. Within each of Parten's play types, older children engaged in more cognitively mature behavior than younger children (Pan, 1994; Rubin, Watson, & Jambor, 1978).

Often parents wonder whether a child who spends large amounts of time playing alone is developing normally. But only *certain types* of nonsocial activity—aimless wandering, hovering near peers, and play involving repetitive motor action—are cause for concern. Children

As these preschool girls combine peanut butter and bird seed to make a bird feeder, they engage in cooperative play—a form of true social interaction in which they act together with a common goal in mind.

© Ellen Senisi/The Image Works

TABLE 15.1 DEVELOPMENTAL SEQUENCE OF COGNITIVE PLAY CATEGORIES

Play Category	Description	Examples
Functional play	Simple, repetitive motor movements with or without objects. Especially common during the first 2 years of life.	Running around a room, rolling a car back and forth, kneading clay with no intent to make something
Constructive play	Creating or constructing something. Especially common between 3 and 6 years.	Making a house out of toy blocks, drawing a picture, putting together a puzzle
Make-believe play	Acting out everyday and imaginary roles. Especially common between 2 and 6 years.	Playing house, school, or police officer; acting out storybook or television characters
Games with rules	Understanding and following rules in play activities.	Playing board games, cards, hopscotch, baseball

Source: Rubin, Fein, & Vandenberg, 1983.

who behave reticently, by watching other children without playing, usually are temperamentally inhibited preschoolers who withdraw because of high social fearfulness (Coplan et al., 2004; Rubin, Burgess, & Hastings, 2002). And children who engage in solitary, repetitive behavior (banging blocks, making a doll jump up and down) tend to be immature, impulsive youngsters who find it difficult to regulate anger and aggression (Coplan et al., 2001). Because of their annoying behavior and hostility, peers usually ostracize them.

But not all preschoolers with low rates of peer interaction are socially anxious or impulsive. To the contrary, most simply like to play by themselves, and their solitary activities are positive and constructive. Teachers encourage such play when they set out art materials, books, puzzles, and building toys. Children who spend much time at these pursuits usually are well-adjusted youngsters who, when they do play with peers, show socially skilled behavior (Coplan et al., 2004; Rubin & Coplan, 1998). A few preschoolers, however, do seem to retreat into solitary activities, such as looking at books or drawing pictures, when they would rather play with others. Their social behavior, for reasons not yet clear, causes classmates to rebuff them. Perhaps because quiet play is less consistent with the "masculine" than the "feminine" gender role, boys who engage in it are at greater risk for negative reactions from both parents and peers and, as a result, may eventually display adjustment problems (Coplan et al., 2001, 2004).

As noted in Chapter 6, *sociodramatic play*—an advanced form of cooperative play—becomes especially common during the preschool years and supports many aspects of cognitive, emotional, and social development. In joint make-believe, preschoolers act out and respond to one another's pretend feelings. They also explore and gain control of fear-arousing experiences when they play doctor or pretend to search for monsters in a magical forest. As a result, they are better able to understand others' feelings and regulate their own (Smith, 2003). Finally, to create and manage complex plots, preschoolers must resolve their disputes through negotiation and compromise.

Middle Childhood and Adolescence

When formal schooling begins, children are exposed to agemates who vary in many ways, including achievement, ethnicity, religion, interests, and personality. Contact with a diversity of peers probably contributes to school-age children's increasing awareness that others have viewpoints different from their own (see Chapter 11). Peer communication, in turn, profits from improved perspective taking. Children of this age can better interpret others' emotions and intentions and take them into account in peer dialogues. They also are aware of the value of emotional display rules in facilitating social interaction (see Chapter 10) (Denham et al., 2004). In addition, school-age children's ability to understand the complementary roles of several players in relation to a set of rules permits the transition to rule-oriented games in middle childhood (refer again to Table 15.1).

School-age children apply their emotional and social knowledge to peer communication. Recall from Chapter 12 that sharing, helping, and other prosocial acts increase in middle childhood. In addition, younger and older children differ in how they help agemates. Kindergartners move right in and give assistance, regardless of whether it is desired. In contrast, school-age children offer to help and wait for a peer to accept before behaving prosocially. In adolescence, agemates work on tasks more cooperatively—staying on task, freely exchanging ideas, asking for opinions, and acknowledging one another's contributions (Azmitia, 1996; Hartup, 1983).

Another form of peer interaction emerges in the preschool years and peaks during middle childhood. Watch children at play in a city park or a schoolyard, and you will see that they sometimes wrestle, roll, hit, and run after one another, alternating roles while smiling and laughing. This friendly chasing and play-fighting is called **rough-and-tumble play.** Research indicates that it is a good-natured, sociable activity that is quite distinct from aggressive fighting. Children in many cultures engage in it with peers whom they like especially well, and they continue interacting after a rough-and-tumble episode rather than separating, as they do after an aggressive encounter (Pellegrini, 2004).

Children's rough-and-tumble play is similar to the social behavior of young mammals of many species. It seems to originate in parents' physical play with babies, especially fathers with sons (see Chapter 10). Childhood

Rough-and-tumble play can be distinguished from aggression by its good-natured quality. In our evolutionary past, it may have been important for the development of fighting skill and dominance relations.
© Laura Dwight Photography

rough-and-tumble is also more common among boys, probably because prenatal exposure to androgens (male sex hormones) predisposes boys toward active play (see Chapter 13). Boys' rough-and-tumble largely consists of playful wrestling, restraining, and hitting, whereas girls tend to engage in running and chasing, with only brief physical contact (Boulton, 1996).

In our evolutionary past, rough-and-tumble play may have been important for the development of fighting skill (Boulton & Smith, 1992). Another possibility is that rough-and-tumble assists children in establishing a **dominance hierarchy**—a stable ordering of group members that predicts who will win when conflict arises. Observations of arguments, threats, and physical attacks between children reveal a consistent lineup of winners and losers that becomes increasingly stable during middle childhood and adolescence, especially among boys. Many children say they can assess their own as well as their peers' strength through rough-and-tumble. They seem to use these encounters to make this judgment in a safe venue before challenging a peer's dominance. Over time, children increasingly choose rough-and-tumble partners who resemble themselves in dominance status (Pellegrini & Smith, 1998).

Like dominance relations among nonhuman animals, those among children serve the adaptive function of limiting aggression. Once a dominance hierarchy is clearly established, hostility is rare. As adolescents reach physical maturity, individual differences in strength become clear, and rough-and-tumble play declines. When it does occur, its meaning changes: It is now a disguise for physical attacks. Adolescent boys' rough-and-tumble is linked to aggression (Pellegrini, 2003). After becoming embroiled in a bout, players "cheat" and hurt their opponent. When asked to explain the episode, boys often respond that they are retaliating, apparently to reestablish dominance among their peers.

Over middle childhood, children interact increasingly often with peers until, by midadolescence, more time is spent with them than with any other social partners. Common interests, novel play activities, and opportunities to interact on an equal footing make peer interaction highly gratifying. As adolescence draws to a close, most young people are proficient in many complex social behaviors.

Influences on Peer Sociability

Children first acquire skills for interacting with peers within the family. Parents' impact on children's peer sociability is both direct, through attempts to influence children's peer relations, and indirect, through their child-rearing practices and play behaviors (Ladd & Pettit, 2002). Situational factors that adults can influence, such as the age mix of children, also make a difference, as do cultural values.

Direct Parental Influences

Outside preschool and child care, young children depend on parents to help them establish rewarding peer associations. Preschoolers whose parents frequently arrange informal peer contact—by scheduling play at home, taking children to community settings such as the library and pool, and enrolling them in organized activities—tend to have larger peer networks and to be more socially skilled (Ladd, LeSieur, & Profilet, 1993). In providing opportunities for peer play, parents show children how to initiate peer contacts and encourage them to be good "hosts" who consider their playmates' needs.

Parents also influence children's social relations by offering guidance on how to act toward others. Their skillful suggestions for managing conflict, discouraging teasing, and entering a play group are associated with preschoolers' social competence and peer acceptance (Parke et al., 2004; Mize & Pettit, 1997). As children get older and acquire effective social skills, parental advice becomes less necessary. In middle childhood, heavy provision of parental guidance is usually aimed at children with peer-relationship problems (McDowell, Parke, & Wang, 2004).

Recall from Chapter 14 that during middle childhood and adolescence, parental monitoring of their child's activities protects school-age children and adolescents from antisocial involvements. Young people's disclosure of information is vital for successful monitoring. The extent to which adolescents tell parents about their whereabouts and companions is an especially strong predictor of adjustment (Stattin & Kerr, 2000). Such

© Parents influence children's peer interaction skills by offering advice, guidance, and examples of how to behave. This father teaches his 3-year-old son how to offer a present as a guest at a birthday party.
© Elizabeth Crews/The Image Works

disclosure, however, depends on a history of consistent monitoring and a well-functioning parent–child relationship, which (as we will see) also promotes positive peer relations.

Indirect Parental Influences

Many child-rearing variables not directly aimed at promoting peer sociability nevertheless spill over into peer relations. For example, inductive discipline and authoritative parenting offer a firm foundation for competence in relating to agemates. In contrast, coercive psychological control and harsh physical punishment engender poor social skills and aggressive behavior (see Chapters 12 and 14).

Furthermore, secure attachments to parents are linked to more responsive, harmonious peer interactions, larger peer networks, and warmer, more supportive friendships during the preschool and school years (Coleman, 2003; Schneider, Atkinson, & Tardif, 2001; Wood, Emmerson, & Cowan, 2004). The emotionally expressive and supportive communication that underlies secure attachment may be responsible for this finding. In one study, researchers observed parent–child conversations and rated them for the strength of the mother–child bond, as indicated by exchange of positive emotion and parental sensitivity to the child's statements and feelings. Kindergartners who were more emotionally "connected" to their mothers displayed more empathy and prosocial behavior toward their classmates. This empathic orientation, in turn, was linked to more positive peer ties (Clark & Ladd, 2000).

Parent–child play seems to be a particularly effective context for promoting peer-interaction skills. During play, parents interact with their child on a "level playing field," much as peers do (Russell, Pettit, & Mize, 1998). Highly involved, emotionally positive, and cooperative play between parents and preschoolers is associated with more positive peer relations. And perhaps because parents play more with children of their own sex, mothers' play is more strongly linked to daughters' competence, fathers' play to sons' competence (Lindsey & Mize, 2000; Pettit et al., 1998).

Finally, the quality of parents' social networks is associated with children's social competence. In one study, parents who reported high-quality friendships had school-age children who interacted more favorably with friends. This relationship was stronger for girls, perhaps because girls spend more time near parents and have more opportunity to observe their parents' friends (Simpkins & Parke, 2001). Furthermore, overlap between parents' and adolescents' social networks—frequent contact among teenagers' friends, their parents, and their friends' parents—is related to better school achievement and low levels of antisocial behavior (Parke et al., 2004). Under these conditions, other adults in parents' networks may promote parents' values and goals and monitor teenagers in their parents' absence.

Age Mix of Children

When observed in age-graded settings, such as child-care centers, schools, and summer camps, children typically interact with others close in age. Yet in cultures where children are not segregated by age for schooling and recreation, cross-age interaction is common.

The theories of Piaget and Vygotsky, discussed in Chapter 6, suggest different benefits from same- versus mixed-age interaction. Piaget emphasized experiences with children equal in status who challenge one another's viewpoints, thereby promoting cognitive, social, and moral development. In contrast, Vygotsky believed that children profit from interacting with older, more capable peers, who model and encourage more advanced skills.

Among preschoolers, the play of younger children is more cognitively and socially mature in mixed-age classrooms than in single-age classrooms. Furthermore, as early as age 3 or 4, children can modify their behavior to fit the needs of a less advanced child, simplifying their rate of communication and assuming more responsibility for a joint activity (Brody, Graziano, & Musser, 1983; Howes & Farver, 1987). Nevertheless, the oldest school-age children in mixed-age settings prefer same-age companions, perhaps because they have more compatible interests and experience more cooperative interaction. Younger children's interaction with same-age partners is also more intense and harmonious, but they often turn to older peers because of their superior knowledge and exciting play ideas.

Children clearly profit from both same-age and mixed-age relationships. From interacting with equals, they learn to cooperate and resolve conflicts, and they develop vital moral under-

© These cousins, who live in central India, play an intricate hand-clapping game called "Chapte." They clap in unison to a jingle with eleven verses that take them through their lifespan and that conclude with their turning into ghosts. The game reflects the value their culture places on group harmony.
© Doranne Jacobson

standings of reciprocity and justice (see Chapters 11 and 12). In mixed-age settings, younger children acquire new competencies from their older companions. And when more mature youngsters help their less mature counterparts, they practice nurturance, guidance, and other prosocial behaviors.

Cultural Values

Peer sociability in collectivist societies, which stress group harmony, differs from that in Western individualistic cultures. For example, children in India generally play in large groups that require high levels of cooperation. Much of their behavior is imitative, occurs in unison, and involves close physical contact. In a game called Atiya Piatiya, children sit in a circle, join hands, and swing while they recite a jingle. In Bhatto Bhatto, they act out a script about a trip to the market, touching each other's elbows and hands as they pretend to cut and share a tasty vegetable (Roopnarine et al., 1994).

Cultural beliefs about the importance of play also affect early peer associations. Adults who view play as mere entertainment are less likely to provide props or to encourage pretend than those who value its cognitive and social benefits (Farver & Wimbarti, 1995a, 1995b). Preschool children of Korean-American parents, who emphasize task persistence as crucial for learning, spend less time than their Caucasian-American counterparts at joint make-believe and more time unoccupied and in parallel play (Farver, Kim, & Lee, 1995).

Return to the description of the daily lives of children growing up in village and tribal cultures on page 265 in Chapter 6. Mayan parents, for example, do not promote children's play. Yet even though they spend little time pretending, Mayan children are socially competent (Gaskins, 2000). Perhaps Western-style sociodramatic play, with its elaborate materials and wide-ranging themes, is particularly important for social development in societies where child and adult worlds are distinct. It may be less crucial when children participate in adult activities from an early age.

In all societies, peer contact rises in adolescence, a trend that is particularly strong in industrialized nations, in which young people spend most of each weekday with agemates in school. Teenagers also spend much out-of-class time together, more in some cultures than in others. For example, adolescents in the United States have about 50 hours of free time per week, those in Western Europe about 45 hours, and those in Asian nations (such as China, Japan, and Korea) about 33 hours (Larson, 2001). As Figure 15.1 reveals, factors that account for this difference include a shorter school year coupled with less demanding academic standards, which lead U.S. youths to spend far less time than Western European and Asian youths on schoolwork (especially homework).

▶ **Figure 15.1**

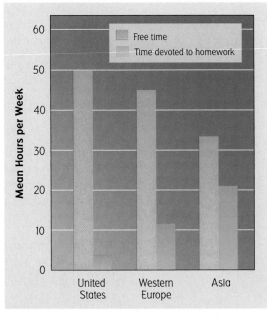

Weekly free time and time devoted to homework by adolescents in the United States, Western European nations, and Asian nations. Figures are averages of those reported in many studies. American teenagers have more free time available to spend with peers than their European and, especially, Asian counterparts, a difference largely explained by American adolescents spending far less time doing homework. (Adapted from Larson, 2001.)

Ask Yourself

REVIEW	Among children who spend much time playing alone, what factors distinguish those who are likely to have adjustment difficulties from those who are well adjusted and socially skilled?
APPLY	Three-year-old Bart lives in the country, with no other preschoolers nearby. His parents wonder whether it is worth driving Bart into town once a week to participate in a peer play group. What advice would you give Bart's parents, and why?
CONNECT	What aspects of parent–child interaction probably account for the relationship between attachment security and children's peer sociability? (*Hint:* See Chapter 10, pages 424, 428–430.)
REFLECT	What did your parents do, directly and indirectly, that might have influenced your peer relationships in childhood and adolescence?

Friendship

Children have encounters and relationships with many peers, but they prefer some peers over others as playmates. Beginning in early childhood, they form **friendships**—close relationships involving companionship in which each partner wants to be with the other. Observations of 1- and 2-year-olds reveal that they initiate play, exchange expressions of positive emotion, and engage in more complex interactions with selected, familiar peers (Howes, 1998). These early mutual relationships may lay the groundwork for deeper, more meaningful friendships in childhood and adolescence.

To study friendship, researchers ask the child or a knowledgeable adult to name friends, then check whether nominated friends return the choice. They also observe friendship interactions, comparing these with other peer relationships (Hartup, 1996). And they interview children about what friendship means. Findings reveal that with age, children's ideas about friendship change, as do certain features of friendships. From the preschool years on, friendship contributes uniquely to children's psychological adjustment.

Thinking About Friendship

To an adult, friendship is a consensual relationship involving companionship, sharing, understanding of thoughts and feelings, and caring for and comforting each other in times of need. In addition, mature friendships endure over time and survive occasional conflicts. But to a child, friendship begins as something far more concrete, based on pleasurable activity. With age, friendship becomes more abstract—a relationship based on mutual consideration and psychological satisfaction (Damon, 1988; Hartup & Abecassis, 2004). Children's changing ideas about friendship follow a three-stage sequence—confirmed by both longitudinal and cross-sectional research.

● **1. FRIENDSHIP AS A HANDY PLAYMATE (ABOUT 4 TO 7 YEARS)** ● Preschoolers understand something about the uniqueness of friendship. They know that a friend is someone "who likes you," with whom you spend a lot of time playing, and with whom you share toys. Because they view friendship concretely, young children regard it as easily begun—for example, by meeting in the neighborhood and saying, "Hi." Friendship does not yet have a long-term, enduring quality. Children at this stage say that a friendship can dissolve when one partner refuses to share, hits, or is not available to play. A 5-year-old's answer to the question "What makes a good friend?" sums up the young child's view of friendship: "Boys play with boys, trucks play with trucks, dogs play with dogs." When the interviewer probed, "Why does that make them good friends?" the child replied, "Because they do the same things" (Selman, 1980, p. 136).

● **2. FRIENDSHIP AS MUTUAL TRUST AND ASSISTANCE (ABOUT 8 TO 10 YEARS)** ● In middle childhood, friendship becomes more complex and psychologically based. Consider the following 8-year-old's ideas:

Why is Shelly your best friend? Because she helps me when I'm sad, and she shares.... What makes Shelly so special? I've known her longer, I sit next to her and got to know her bet-

ter.... *How come you like Shelly better than anyone else?* She's done the most for me. She never disagrees, she never eats in front of me, she never walks away when I'm crying, and she helps me on my homework.... *How do you get someone to like you?* ... If you're nice to [your friends], they'll be nice to you. (Damon, 1988, pp. 80–81)

As these responses show, friendship has become a mutually agreed-on relationship in which children like each other's personal qualities and respond to one another's needs and desires. Because friendship requires that both children want to be together, getting it started takes more time and effort than it did at earlier ages.

Once a friendship forms, *trust* becomes its defining feature. School-age children state that a good friendship is based on acts of kindness signifying that each person can be counted on to support the other. Consequently, older children regard violations of trust, such as not helping when others need help, breaking promises, and gossiping behind the other person's back, as serious breaches of friendship—as Katy did in the chapter introduction. Once a rift occurs, it cannot be patched up as easily as it could at younger ages—by playing nicely after a conflict. Instead, apologies and explanations are necessary (Damon, 1977; Selman, 1980).

© During middle childhood, concepts of friendship become more psychologically based. Although these boys share an interest in basketball, they want to spend time together because they like each other's personal qualities. Mutual trust is central to their friendship: Each counts on the other for support and assistance.
© Tony Freeman/PhotoEdit

• **3. FRIENDSHIP AS INTIMACY, MUTUAL UNDERSTANDING, AND LOYALTY (11 TO 15 YEARS AND OLDER)** • When asked about the meaning of friendship, teenagers stress three characteristics. The most important is *intimacy*, or psychological closeness, which is supported by *mutual understanding* of each other's values, beliefs, and feelings. In addition, more than younger children, teenagers want their friends to be *loyal*—to stick up for them and not to leave them for somebody else (Buhrmester, 1996).

As friendship takes on these deeper features, adolescents regard it as a relationship formed over time by "getting to know someone." In addition, friends are viewed as important in relieving psychological distress, such as loneliness, sadness, and fear. Because true mutual understanding implies forgiveness, only an extreme falling out can terminate a friendship. Here is how one teenager described his best friendship:

Well, you need someone you can tell anything to, all kinds of things that you don't want to spread around. That's why you're someone's friend. *Is that why Jimmy is your friend? Because he can keep a secret?* Yes, and we like the same kinds of things. We speak the same language. My mother says we're two peas in a pod.... *Do you ever get mad at Jimmy?* Not really. *What if he did something that got you really mad?* He'd still be my best friend. I'd tell him what he did wrong and maybe he'd understand. I could be wrong too, it depends. (Damon, 1977, p. 163)

Characteristics of Friendships

Changes in children's thinking about friendships are linked to characteristics of their real friendships. Let's look closely at friendship stability, interaction, and resemblance.

• **FRIENDSHIP SELECTIVITY AND STABILITY** • We would expect greater friendship selectivity and stability as mutual trust and loyalty become more important in children's friendship expectations. Indeed, school-age children grow more selective about their friendships. Preschoolers say they have lots of friends—sometimes, everyone in their class! But by age 8 or 9, children name only a handful of good friends. As teenagers focus on friendship quality, this narrowing continues. Number of best friends declines from four to six in early adolescence to only one or two in emerging adulthood (Hartup & Stevens, 1999). Girls, especially, are more exclusive in their friendships because (as we will see) they typically demand greater closeness than boys (Parker & Asher, 1993).

Although friendship stability increases with age, friendships are remarkably stable at all ages. For younger children, however, stability is largely a function of the constancy of social environments, such as school and neighborhood. From fourth grade through high school, when friendships become psychologically based, about 50 to 70 percent endure over the course of a school year, although they often undergo temporary shifts in the strength of each partner's commitment

(Degirmencioglu et al., 1998). As young people transfer to middle or junior high school, varying rates of pubertal development, encounters with new peers, and romantic interests often lead to a temporary period of greater change in choice of friends (Hardy, Bukowski, & Sippola, 2002).

• **INTERACTION BETWEEN FRIENDS** • At all ages, friends have special ways of interacting. Preschoolers, for example, give twice as much reinforcement, in the form of greetings, praise, and compliance, to children they identify as friends, and they also receive more from them. Friends are more emotionally expressive, talking, laughing, and looking at one another more often than nonfriends do (Hartup, 1996; Vaughn et al., 2001). Spontaneity, intimacy, and sensitivity characterize rewarding friendships very early, although children are not able to express these ideas until much later.

A more mature understanding of friendship seems to spark greater prosocial behavior between friends. When working on a task together, school-age friends help, share, refer to each other's comments, and spend more time focused than preschool friends do (Hartup, 1996; Newcomb & Bagwell, 1995). Cooperation, generosity, mutual affirmation, and self-disclosure (see Figure 15.2) continue to rise into adolescence—trends that may reflect greater effort and skill at preserving the relationship and increased sensitivity to a friend's needs (Phillipsen, 1999). Teenagers are also less possessive of their friends than they were in childhood. They recognize that friends need a certain degree of autonomy—something they also desire for themselves (Rubin, Bukowski, & Parker, 1998).

Friends do not just behave more prosocially. They also disagree and compete with each other more than nonfriends. Because children regard friendship as based on equality, they seem especially concerned about losing a contest to a friend. Also, when children hold differing opinions, friends are more likely than nonfriends to voice them. As early as middle childhood, friends realize that close relationships can survive disagreements if both parties are secure in their liking for one another (Fonzi et al., 1997; Rose & Asher, 1999). Adolescent girls' friendships are more likely to endure when friends are "up front" about tensions in the relationship rather than dismissing them as "no big deal"—a coping strategy that works better for boys (Bowker, 2004). Because girls highly value sharing feelings, passive responses to conflict may restore surface harmony while the underlying discontent lingers. Clearly, friendship provides an important context in which children learn to tolerate criticism and resolve disputes.

The impact that friendships have on children's development depends on the nature of those friends. Children who bring kindness and compassion to their friendships strengthen one another's prosocial tendencies. But when aggressive children make friends, the relationship often magnifies antisocial acts. The friendships of aggressive girls are high in self-disclosure but

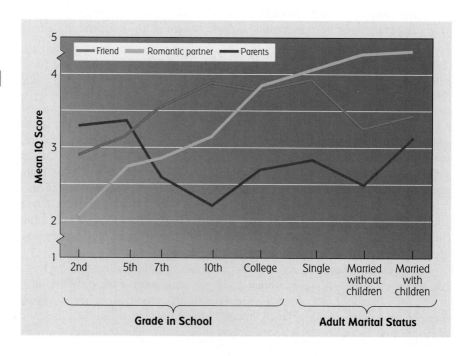

▶ **Figure 15.2**

Age changes in reported self-disclosure to parents and peers, based on data from several studies. Self-disclosure to friends increases steadily during adolescence, reflecting intimacy as a major basis of friendship. Self-disclosure to romantic partners also rises. However, not until the college years does it surpass intimacy with friends. Self-disclosure to parents declines in early adolescence, a time of mild parent–child conflict. As family relationships readjust to the young person's increasing autonomy, self-disclosure to parents rises.

(From D. Buhrmester, 1996, "Need Fulfillment, Interpersonal Competence, and the Developmental Contexts of Early Adolescent Friendship," in W. M. Bukowski, A. F. Newcomb, & W. W. Hartup, Eds., *The Company They Keep: Friendship in Childhood and Adolescence,* New York: Cambridge University Press, p. 168. Reprinted by permission.)

full of relational hostility, including jealousy, conflict, and betrayal. Those of aggressive boys involve frequent expressions of anger, coercive statements, physical attacks, and enticements to rule-breaking behavior (Bagwell & Coie, 2004; Crick & Nelson, 2002; Dishion, Andrews, & Crosby, 1995). These findings indicate that the social problems of aggressive children operate within their closest peer ties.

• **RESEMBLANCE BETWEEN FRIENDS** • The value adolescents attach to feeling "in sync" with their friends suggests that friends will become increasingly similar in attitudes and values with age. Actually, the attributes on which friends are most alike throughout childhood and adolescence are age, sex, ethnicity, and SES. But friends also resemble one another in personality (sociability, aggression, and depression), popularity, academic achievement, prosocial behavior, and judgments (including biased perceptions) of other people (Haselager et al., 1998). In adolescence, they tend to be alike in identity status, educational aspirations, political beliefs, and willingness to try drugs and engage in lawbreaking acts (Akers, Jones, & Coyl, 1998).

Children and adolescents probably choose companions like themselves to increase the supportiveness of friendship. And as we saw in Chapters 11 and 13, school-age children often hold outgroup prejudices, negatively evaluating peers of other ethnicities and the other gender. How do children identify peers who are similar to themselves in other ways? According to some researchers, they go on "shopping expeditions" in their social networks, trying out relationships and sustaining those that "feel right" (Hartup & Abecassis, 2004). As friends spend time more together, they socialize each other, becoming increasingly alike in attitudes, values, school grades, and social behavior (Berndt & Keefe, 1995).

Nevertheless, as teenagers enter a wider range of school and community settings, they choose some friends who differ from themselves. For a time, young teenagers sacrifice similarity in favor of admiration for superficial features—whether a potential friend is popular, physically attractive, or athletically skilled. And early adolescents—both boys and girls—are attracted to high-status, aggressive boys as friends, a trend that contributes to a rise in antisocial behavior and that, for girls, can lead to negative experiences in their first dating relationships (Bukowski, Sippola, & Newcomb, 2000).

The task of forging a personal identity at times leads adolescents to befriend peers with differing attitudes and values, as a means of exploring new perspectives within the security of a compatible relationship. Furthermore, teenagers often judge commonality in certain attributes as more important than in others. For example, compared with Caucasian-American friends, African-American friends place greater emphasis on shared ethnicity and less on similarity in academic performance (Hamm, 2000; Tolson & Urberg, 1993).

Finally, children and adolescents are more likely to form friendships with agemates of other ethnicities when they attend ethnically diverse schools and live in integrated neighborhoods (Quillian & Campbell, 2003). Cross-ethnic friendships in childhood are among the best predictors of reduction in ethnic prejudice—a relationship that persists into adulthood (Ellison & Powers, 1994). As young people form comfortable, lasting close relationships, they come to view ethnically different peers as individuals instead of through the lens of stereotypes (Carlson, Wilson, & Hargrave, 2003).

• **SEX DIFFERENCES IN FRIENDSHIPS** • In middle childhood, children start to report a consistent sex difference in friendships: Emotional closeness is more common between girls than between boys (Markovits, Benenson, & Dolenszky, 2001). Girls frequently get together to "just talk," and their exchanges contain more self-disclosure (sharing of innermost thoughts and feelings) and mutually supportive statements. In contrast, boys more often gather for an activity—usually sports and games that engender control, power, and excitement. When boys talk, their discussions often focus on recognition and mastery issues, such as achievements in sports and school, and involve more competition and conflict (Brendgen et al., 2001; Buhrmester, 1998).

Because of gender-role expectations, girls' friendships typically focus on communal concerns, boys' friendships on achievement and status. This does not mean that boys rarely form close friendship ties. They often do, but the quality of their friendships is more variable. The intimacy of boys' friendships is related to gender identity. Androgynous boys are just as likely as girls to form intimate same-sex ties, whereas boys who identify strongly with the "masculine" role are less likely to do so (Jones & Dembo, 1989).

During adolescence, intimacy and loyalty become defining features of friendship. Yet girls place a higher value than boys on emotional closeness. Girls more often get together to "just talk," and they rate their friendships as higher in self-disclosure and emotional support.
© Cindy Charles/PhotoEdit

Friendship closeness, however, has both benefits and costs. When friends focus on their deeper thoughts and feelings, they tend to *coruminate,* or repeatedly mull over problems and negative emotions. Corumination contributes to high friendship quality, but it also triggers anxiety and depression—symptoms more common among girls than among boys (Rose, 2002). Also, when conflicts arise among intimate friends, more potential exists for one party to harm the other through relational aggression—for example, by divulging sensitive personal information to outsiders. For this reason, girls' closest same-sex friendships tend to be of shorter duration than those of boys (Benenson & Christakos, 2003).

In early adolescence, young people who are either very popular or very unpopular are more likely to have other-sex friends. Teenagers who are not accepted by their own sex sometimes look to the other sex for friendships. Boys have more other-sex friends than do girls, whose desire for closeness leads to a preference for same-sex friendships (Sippola, Bukowski, & Noll, 1997). Among boys without same-sex friends, having an other-sex friend is associated with feelings of competence. Among girls who lack same-sex friends, however, other-sex friendships are linked to less positive well-being (Bukowski, Sippola, & Hoza, 1999). Perhaps these girls are especially likely to befriend boys with negative traits, such as aggression.

Friendship and Adjustment

Warm, gratifying childhood and adolescent friendships are related to many aspects of psychological health and competence into emerging adulthood (Bagwell et al., 2001; Bukowski, 2001), for several reasons:

- *Close friendships provide opportunities to explore the self and develop a deep understanding of another.* Through open, honest communication, friends become sensitive to each other's strengths and weaknesses, needs and desires. They get to know both themselves and their friend especially well, a process that supports the development of self-concept, perspective taking, and identity (Savin-Williams & Berndt, 1990).

- *Close friendships provide a foundation for future intimate relationships.* Look again at Figure 15.2, and you will see that self-disclosure to friends precedes disclosure to romantic partners. Lengthy, often emotionally laden psychological discussions between adolescent friends appear to prepare the young person for love relationships (Sullivan, 1953). Sexuality and romance are common topics of discussion between teenage friends. Such conversations, along with the intimacy of friendship itself, may help adolescents establish and work out problems in romantic partnerships (Connolly & Goldberg, 1999).

- *Close friendships help young people deal with the stresses of everyday life.* Because supportive, prosocial friendships enhance sensitivity to and concern for another, they promote empathy, sympathy, and positive social behavior. As a result, friendships contribute to involvement in constructive youth activities, avoidance of antisocial acts, and psychological well-being (Lansford et al., 2003; Wentzel, Barry, & Caldwell, 2004). Adolescents experiencing family stress who manage to develop close friendships show the same high level of well-being as children from better-functioning families (Gauze et al., 1996).

- *Close friendships can improve attitudes toward and involvement in school.* Close friendship ties promote good school adjustment in both middle- and low-SES students (Berndt & Murphy, 2002). When children and adolescents enjoy interacting with friends at school, perhaps they begin to view all aspects of school life more positively.

Some friendships, however, interfere with well-being. Beginning in the preschool years, the conflict-ridden interactions that occur between physically, verbally, and relationally aggressive friends are associated with poor adjustment (Sebanc, 2003). Longitudinal research reveals that children with aggressive friends increase in antisocial behavior over time (Berndt, 1998; Dishion, Poulin, & Burraston, 2001).

Finally, children who have no friends usually have undesirable personalities: They may be easily angered, shy and anxious, or self-centered (less caring and honest) (Ladd, 1999). Without supportive friendship as a context for acquiring more adaptive social behaviors, the maladaptive behaviors of these children tend to persist.

Ask Yourself

REVIEW	Describe unique qualities of interaction between close friends, and explain how they contribute to development.
REVIEW	Why are aggressive children's friendships likely to magnify their antisocial behavior?
APPLY	In his junior year of high school, Ralph, of Irish Catholic background, befriended Jonathan, a Chinese-American of the Buddhist faith. Both boys are from middle-SES homes and are good students. What might explain Ralph's desire for a friend both similar to and different from himself?
CONNECT	Cite similarities in development of self-concept, described in Chapter 11 (pages 446–447), and ideas about friendship. Explain how the discussion among Stu, Pete, Jessamyn, and Katy in the introduction to this chapter reflects friendship expectations that typically emerge at adolescence.

Peer Acceptance

Peer acceptance refers to likability—the extent to which a child is viewed by a group of age-mates, such as classmates, as a worthy social partner. It differs from friendship in that it is not a mutual relationship but, rather, a one-sided perspective, involving the group's view of an individual. Nevertheless, certain social skills that contribute to friendship also enhance peer acceptance. Consequently, better-accepted children tend to have more friends and more positive relationships with them (Gest, Graham-Bermann, & Hartup, 2001). As with friendship, peer acceptance contributes uniquely to children's adjustment.

Researchers usually assess peer acceptance using self-reports called **sociometric techniques,** which measure *social preferences.* For example, children and adolescents may be asked to nominate several peers in their class whom they especially like or dislike, to indicate for all possible pairs of classmates which one they prefer to spend time with, or to rate each peer on a scale from "like very much" to "like very little" (Hymel et al., 2004). Another approach is to assess **peer reputation**—young people's judgments of whom most of their classmates admire, which identify peers high in *social prominence.* The classmates school-age children and adolescents identify as prominent—looked up to by many others—show only moderate correspondence with the classmates they say they prefer to be with on sociometric measures (Lafontana & Cillessen, 1999; Prinstein & Cillessen, 2003).

Sociometric techniques yield four categories of peer acceptance:

- **Popular children,** who get many positive votes
- **Rejected children,** who are actively disliked
- **Controversial children,** who get a large number of positive and negative votes
- **Neglected children,** who are seldom chosen, either positively or negatively.

About two-thirds of students in a typical elementary school classroom fit one of these categories (Coie, Dodge, & Coppotelli, 1982). The remaining one-third are *average* in peer acceptance; they do not receive extreme scores.

Peer acceptance is a powerful predictor of current and later psychological adjustment. Rejected children, especially, are unhappy, alienated, poorly achieving children with low self-esteem. Both teachers and parents view them as having a wide range of emotional and social problems. Peer rejection in middle childhood is also strongly associated with poor school performance, absenteeism, dropping out, substance use, antisocial behavior, and delinquency in adolescence and with criminality in emerging adulthood (Bagwell, Newcomb, & Bukowski, 1998; Laird et al., 2001; Parker & Asher, 1987).

However, preceding influences—children's characteristics combined with parenting practices—may largely explain the link between peer acceptance and psychological adjustment. School-age children with peer-relationship problems are more likely to have experienced family stress due to low income, parental changes (divorce, remarriage, death), and insensitive child rearing, including coercive discipline (Woodward & Fergusson, 1999). Nevertheless, as we will see, rejected children evoke reactions from peers that contribute to their unfavorable development.

Origins of Acceptance in the Peer Situation

What causes one child to be liked and another to be rejected? A wealth of research reveals that social behavior plays a powerful role.

• **POPULAR CHILDREN** • Although many popular children are kind and considerate, others are admired for their socially sophisticated yet belligerent behavior. Two subtypes of popular children exist:

- **Popular-prosocial children.** The majority of popular children combine academic and social competence. They are good students who communicate with peers in sensitive, friendly, and cooperative ways and who solve social problems constructively. If they disagree with a play partner in a game, they go beyond voicing their displeasure; they suggest what the other child could do instead. When they want to enter an ongoing play group, they adapt their behavior to the flow of the activity (Cillessen & Bellmore, 2004; Newcomb, Bukowski, & Pattee, 1993).

- **Popular-antisocial children.** This smaller subtype, which emerges in late childhood and early adolescence, consists of aggressive youngsters. Some are "tough" boys who are athletically skilled but poor students who get into fights, cause trouble, and defy adult authority. Others are relationally aggressive boys and girls who use ignoring, excluding, and rumor-spreading to manipulate peer relationships in ways that enhance their own status (Cillessen & Mayeux, 2004; Rodkin et al., 2000; Rose, Swenson, & Waller, 2004). Despite their hostility, peers view these youths as "cool," perhaps because of their athletic ability and the sophisticated but devious social skills they use to exploit others. Antisocial youths are especially likely to be popular in classrooms with many aggressive children—conditions that produce a peer culture that highly values aggressive behavior (Stormshak et al., 1999).

Research suggests that popular-antisocial children's peer acceptance offers some protection against lasting adjustment difficulties (Coie et al., 1995; Prinstein & La Greca, 2004). Still, their antisocial acts require intervention. With age, peers like these high-status, aggressive youths less and less, a trend that is stronger for relationally aggressive girls. The more socially prominent and controlling these girls become, the more they engage in relational aggression (Cillessen & Mayeux, 2004). Eventually peers condemn their nasty tactics, and they are likely to be rejected.

• **REJECTED CHILDREN** • Rejected children display a wide range of negative social behaviors. But as with popular children, not all of these disliked children look the same. At least two subtypes exist:

- **Rejected-aggressive children,** the largest subgroup, show severe conduct problems—high rates of conflict, physical and relational aggression, and hyperactive, inattentive, and impulsive behavior. These children also are deficient in social understanding and regulation of negative emotion. For example, they are more likely than others to be poor perspective takers, to misinterpret the innocent behaviors of peers as hostile, to blame others for their social difficulties, and to act on their angry feelings (Coie & Dodge, 1998; Crick, Casas, & Nelson, 2002). Rejected-aggressive children differ from popular-aggressive children in being more extremely belligerent and antagonistic (Prinstein & Cillessen, 2003). Rather than using aggression skillfully to attain status, rejected-aggressive children display blatantly hostile, acting-out behavior, which triggers scorn and avoidance in their peers.

- **Rejected-withdrawn children,** a smaller subgroup, are passive and socially awkward. These timid children are overwhelmed by social anxiety and withdraw in the face of social challenges. As a result, they feel lonely, hold negative expectations for how peers will treat them, and are concerned about being scorned and attacked (Hart et al., 2000; Ladd & Burgess, 1999).

As early as kindergarten, peers exclude rejected children. Soon rejected children's classroom participation declines, their feelings of loneliness rise, their academic achievement falters, and they want to avoid school (Buhs & Ladd, 2001). Rejected children generally befriend other rejected agemates. Most have few friends, and some have none. The combination of persistent rejection and friendlessness is linked to low self-esteem, mistrust of peers, and severe adjustment difficulties (Ladd & Troop-Gordon, 2003).

Bullies and Their Victims

Follow the activities of aggressive children over a school day, and you will see that they reserve their hostilities for certain peers. A particularly destructive form of interaction is **peer victimization,** in which certain children become frequent targets of verbal and physical attacks or other forms of abuse. What sustains these repeated assault–retreat cycles between pairs of children?

Large-scale surveys reveal that about 10 to 20 percent of children are bullies and 15 to 30 percent are repeatedly victimized. Although more bullies are boys who use both physically and relationally aggressive tactics, at times girls bombard a vulnerable classmate with relational hostility (Pepler et al., 2004; Rigby, 2004). A substantial number of bullies are high-status, powerful youngsters. Some are liked for their leadership or athletic abilities, but most are disliked—or eventually become so—because of their cruelty (Vaillancourt, Hymel, & McDougall, 2003). Despite their disapproval of bullies' actions, the majority of peer observers do nothing to help victims. About 20 to 30 percent of onlookers actually encourage bullies, even to the point of joining in (Salmivalli & Voeten, 2004).

Chronic victims are passive when active behavior is expected. On the playground, they hang around chatting or wander on their own. When bullied, they reinforce perpetrators by giving in to their demands, crying, and assuming defensive postures (Boulton, 1999). Most lack defenders in the peer group, so bullies see them as easy prey for flaunting their social dominance. Biologically based traits—an inhibited temperament and a frail physical appearance—contribute to victimization. But victims also have histories of resistant attachment, overly controlling child rearing, and maternal overprotection. These parenting behaviors prompt anxiety, low self-esteem, and dependency, resulting in a fearful demeanor that radiates vulnerability, marking these children for victimization (Snyder et al., 2003). As early as kindergarten, victimization leads to a variety of adjustment difficulties,

including depression, loneliness, low self-esteem, poor school performance, disruptive behavior, and school avoidance (Kochenderfer-Ladd & Wardrop, 2001; Paul & Cillessen, 2003).

Aggression and victimization are not polar opposites. One-third to one-half of victims are also aggressive. Often these children irritate their peers, provoking attacks. Occasionally, they retaliate against powerful bullies, who respond by abusing them again—a cycle that sustains their victim status (Camodeca et al., 2002; Kochenderfer-Ladd, 2003). Among rejected children, bully/victims are the most despised. They often have histories of extremely maladaptive parenting, including child abuse. This combination of highly negative home and peer experiences places them at severe risk for maladjustment (Schwartz, Proctor, & Chien, 2001).

Interventions that change victimized children's negative opinions of themselves, improve their social skills, and teach them to respond in assertive but nonaggressive ways to their attackers are helpful (Gazelle & Ladd, 2002). Another way to assist victimized children is to help them acquire the social skills needed to form and maintain a gratifying friendship. When children have a close friend whom they can turn to for help, bullying episodes typically end quickly. Also, victims and their friends can come up with effective strategies to prevent further attacks. Anxious, withdrawn victims who have a positive friendship show fewer adjustment problems than their counterparts with poor-quality or no friendships (Goldbaum et al., 2003; Hodges et al., 1999).

Nevertheless, victimized children's behavior should not be taken to mean that they are to blame for their abuse. The best way to reduce bullying is to change school and other youth environments (such as sports programs, recreation centers, and neighborhoods), promoting prosocial attitudes and behaviors and enlisting young people's cooperation. Effective approaches include developing school

▲ Children who are physically weak, rejected by their peers, and afraid to defend themselves may be targeted by bullies. Both temperament and child-rearing experiences contribute to their cowering behavior, which reinforces the attacker's abuse. © Michael Newman/PhotoEdit

and community codes against bullying, teaching child bystanders to intervene when bullying occurs, enlisting parents' assistance in changing bullies' behaviors, and (if necessary) moving socially prominent bullies to another class or school (Smith, Ananiadou, & Cowie, 2003).

In Canada, researchers and professionals have devised the Canadian Initiative for the Prevention of Bullying, *www.bullying.org,* a project in which government leaders, national organizations, community groups, and schools are collaborating in the creation of nationwide safe, respectful environments for children and adolescents (Craig, 2005). The U.S. Department of Health and Human Services has launched a nationwide media campaign, Stop Bullying Now, *www.stopbullyingnow. hrsa.gov,* which raises awareness of the harmfulness of bullying through TV and radio public service announcements and provides parents, teachers, and students with information on prevention.

Both rejected-aggressive and rejected-withdrawn children are at risk for peer harassment. But as the Biology and Environment box above reveals, rejected-withdrawn children are especially likely to be targeted by bullies because of their inept, submissive style of interaction (Sandstrom & Cillessen, 2003).

• **CONTROVERSIAL CHILDREN** • Consistent with the mixed peer opinion they engender, controversial children display a blend of positive and negative social behaviors. They are hostile and disruptive, but they also engage in high rates of positive, prosocial acts. Even though some peers dislike them, controversial children have qualities that protect them from exclusion. They have as many friends as popular children and are happy with their peer relationships (Newcomb, Bukowski, & Pattee, 1993). But, like their popular-antisocial counterparts, they often bully agemates to get their way and engage in calculated, relational aggression to sustain their social dominance (DeRosier & Thomas, 2003). The social status of controversial children often changes over time as agemates react to their mixed behavior.

• **NEGLECTED CHILDREN** • Perhaps the most surprising finding on peer acceptance is that neglected children, once thought to be in need of treatment, are usually well adjusted. Although they engage in low rates of interaction and are considered shy by their classmates, they are not less socially skilled than average children. They do not report feeling lonely or unhappy about their social life, and when they want to, they can break away from their usual pattern of playing by themselves (Harrist et al., 1997; Ladd & Burgess, 1999). Perhaps for this reason, neglected status (like controversial status) is usually temporary. Neglected children remind us that an outgoing, gregarious personality style is not the only path to emotional well-being.

Helping Rejected Children

A variety of interventions exist to improve the peer relations and psychological adjustment of rejected children. Most involve coaching, modeling, and reinforcing positive social skills, such as how to initiate interaction with a peer, cooperate in play, and respond to another child with friendly emotion and approval. Several of these programs have produced gains in social competence and peer acceptance still present from several weeks to a year later (Asher & Rose, 1997). Combining social-skills training with other treatments increases their effectiveness. Rejected children often are poor students, and their low academic self-esteem magnifies their negative reactions to teachers and classmates (O'Neil et al., 1997). Intensive academic tutoring improves both school achievement and social acceptance (Coie & Krehbiel, 1984).

Still another approach focuses on training in perspective taking and social problem solving (see Chapter 11). Many rejected-aggressive children are unaware of their own social ineffectiveness and do not take responsibility for their social failures (Coie & Dodge, 1998; Mrug, Hoza, & Gerdes, 2001). Rejected-withdrawn children, in contrast, are likely to develop a *learned-helpless* approach to peer difficulties. They tend to conclude, after repeated rebuffs, that they will never be liked (Wichmann, Coplan, & Daniels, 2004). Both types of rejected children need help attributing their peer difficulties to internal, changeable causes.

Finally, because rejected children's socially incompetent behaviors often originate in a poor fit between the child's temperament and parenting practices, interventions that focus on the child alone may not be sufficient. If the quality of parent–child interaction does not change, rejected children may soon return to their old behavior patterns.

Ask Yourself

REVIEW	Why are rejected children at risk for maladjustment? What experiences with peers probably contribute to their serious, long-term adjustment problems?
REVIEW	What factors make some children susceptible to peer victimization? What consequence does victimization have for adjustment, and how can it be prevented?
CONNECT	Cite parenting influences on children's social skills, and explain why interventions that focus only on the rejected child are unlikely to produce lasting changes in peer acceptance (see pages 601–602). What changes in parent–child relationships are probably necessary?
REFLECT	Name several classmates from your high school days who were high in *social prominence*—admired by many peers. Describe the attributes of these peers. Were they also *socially preferred*—that is, peers whom you and your friends liked personally? Explain.

Peer Groups

Watch children in the schoolyard or neighborhood, and notice how groups of three to a dozen or more often gather. The organization of these collectives changes greatly with age. By the end of middle childhood, children display a strong desire for group belonging. They form **peer groups,** collectives that generate shared values and standards for behavior and a social structure of leaders and followers. Whereas friendships contribute to the development of trust, sensitivity, and intimacy, peer groups provide practice in cooperation, leadership, followership, and loyalty to collective goals. Through these experiences, children experiment with and learn about the functioning of social organizations.

Peer groups first form in middle childhood. These girls have probably established a social structure of leader and followers as they gather for joint activities. Their body language suggests that they feel a strong sense of group belonging. © MM Flash! Light/ Stock Boston, LLC

First Peer Groups

Peer groups organize on the basis of proximity (being in the same classroom) and similarity in sex, ethnicity, and popularity. When these groups are tracked for 3 to 6 weeks, membership changes very little. When they are followed for a year or longer, substantial change can be observed, depending on whether children are reshuffled into different classrooms and loyalties change within the group. When children remain together, 50 to 70 percent of groups consist mostly of the same children from year to year (Cairns, Xie, & Leung, 1998).

The practices of these informal groups lead to a peer culture that typically consists of a specialized vocabulary, dress code, and place to "hang out" during leisure hours. As children develop these exclusive associations, the codes of dress and behavior that grow out of them become more broadly influential. At school, children who deviate are often rebuffed. "Kissing up" to teachers, wearing the wrong kind of shirt or shoes, tattling on classmates, or carrying a strange-looking lunchbox can be grounds for critical glances and comments. These customs bind peers together, creating a sense of group identity.

Most school-age children judge a group's decision to exclude a peer to be wrong, unless the peer threatens group functioning by acting disruptively or lacks interest in or skill at a valued group activity (Killen & Stangor, 2001; Killen et al., 2002). Despite these sophisticated understandings, as we have seen here and in previous chapters, children do exclude, often with hostile tactics. Furthermore, peer groups—at the instigation of their leaders, who can be skillfully aggressive—frequently direct their hostilities toward their own members, ousting no-longer-"respected" children. These cast-outs are profoundly wounded, and many find new group ties hard to establish. Their previous behavior toward the outgroup may reduce their chances of being included elsewhere. As one fifth grader explained, "I think they didn't like me because when I was in the popular group we'd make fun of everyone.... I had been too mean to them in the past" (Adler & Adler, 1998, p. 70). Peer-rejected children often turn to other low-status peers for group belonging. As they associate with children who have poor social skills, they reduce their opportunities to learn socially competent behavior (Bagwell et al., 2001).

The school-age child's desire for group belonging also can be satisfied through formal group ties—scouting, 4-H, religious youth groups, and other associations. Adult involvement holds in check the negative behaviors associated with children's informal peer groups. And as children work on joint projects and help in their communities, they gain in social and moral maturity (Killen & Nucci, 1995; Vandell & Shumow, 1999).

Cliques and Crowds

The peer groups of the early teenage years are more tightly structured than those of middle childhood. They are organized around **cliques,** small groups of about five to seven members who are friends and, therefore, usually resemble one another in family background, attitudes, and values. In early adolescence, cliques are limited to same-sex members. For girls, being in a clique predicts academic and social competence, but not for boys. Clique membership is more important to girls, who often exchange expressions of emotional closeness and support (Henrich et al., 2000). By mid-adolescence, mixed-sex cliques become common.

Often several cliques with similar values form a larger, more loosely organized group called a **crowd.** Unlike the more intimate clique, membership in a crowd is based on reputation and

 These members of a high school swim team form a crowd. To promote team spirit, they paint themselves green before a competition. Unlike the more intimate clique, the larger, more loosely organized crowd grants adolescents an identity within the larger school community.
© David Young-Wolff/PhotoEdit

stereotype. It grants the adolescent an identity within the larger social structure of the school. Prominent crowds in a typical high school are the "brains," or nonathletes who enjoy academics; the "jocks," who are very involved in sports; the "populars," who are class leaders, highly social, and involved in activities; the "partyers," who value socializing but care little about schoolwork; the "nonconformists," who like unconventional clothing and music; the "burnouts," who skip school and get into trouble; and the "normals," average to good students who get along with most other peers (Kinney, 1999; Stone & Brown, 1999).

What influences the sorting of adolescents into cliques and crowds? Teenagers' interests and abilities are involved, since their crowd affiliations are linked to strengths in their self-concepts (Prinstein & La Greca, 2004). In addition, family factors are important. In a study of 8,000 ninth to twelfth graders, adolescents who described their parents as authoritative tended to be members of "brain," "jock," and "popular" groups that accepted both the adult and peer reward systems of the school. In contrast, boys with permissive parents valued interpersonal relationships and aligned themselves with the "partyer" and "burnout" crowds, suggesting a lack of identification with adult reward systems (Durbin et al., 1993).

These findings indicate that many peer group values are extensions of ones acquired at home. Once adolescents join a clique or crowd, it can modify their beliefs and behaviors. In a study of the relationship between crowd affiliation and health-risk behaviors, brains were the lowest risk takers, populars and jocks were intermediate, and nonconformists and burnouts were the highest, often engaging in substance use and unprotected sex and agreeing that they would "do anything on a dare" (LaGreca, Prinstein, & Fetter, 2001). However, the positive impact of having competent, self-controlled peers is greatest for teenagers whose own parents are authoritative. And the negative impact of associating with antisocial, drug-using agemates is strongest for teenagers whose parents use less effective child-rearing styles (Mounts & Steinberg, 1995). In sum, family experiences affect the extent to which adolescents become like their peers over time.

As interest in dating increases, boys' and girls' cliques come together. Mixed-sex cliques provide a supportive context for boys and girls to get to know one another, offering models for how to interact with the other sex and a chance to do so without having to be intimate (Connolly et al., 2004). Gradually, the larger group divides into couples, several of whom spend time together, going to parties and movies. By late adolescence, boys and girls feel comfortable enough about approaching each other directly that the mixed-sex clique disappears (Connolly & Goldberg, 1999).

Crowds also decline in importance. As adolescents settle on personal values and goals, they no longer feel a need to broadcast, through dress, language, and preferred activities, who they are. About half of young people switch crowds from tenth to twelfth grade, mostly in favorable directions. "Brains" and "normal" crowds grow, and deviant crowds lose members as teenagers focus more on their future (Strouse, 1999). Rewarding prosocial friendships and gains in self-esteem are associated with these changes.

Dating

Although sexual interest is affected by the hormonal changes of puberty (see Chapter 14), the beginning of dating is regulated by cultural norms. Asian youths begin dating later and less often have dating partners. Western societies, in contrast, tolerate and even encourage early romantic involvements, which begin in junior high school and increase steadily over the teenage years (see Figure 15.3). During this time, romantic ties last longer. At age 12 to 14, they persist, on average, for only 5 months, but at age 16 and older, they continue for nearly 2 years (Carver, Joyner, & Udry, 2003). The transformation of teenagers' dating goals accounts for this change. Early adolescents date largely for superficial reasons—recreation, peer status, and exploration of sexuality. By late adolescence, young people are ready for greater psychological intimacy, and they look for someone who offers companionship, affection, and social support (Furman, 2002; Shulman & Kipnis, 2001).

Indeed, the achievement of intimacy in adolescent dating relationships lags considerably behind that of friendships. And positive relationships with parents and friends contribute to the development of warm romantic ties (Connolly, Furman, & Konarski, 2000; Hazan & Shaver 1994). Recall from Chapter 10 that according to ethological theory, early attachment bonds lead to construction of an *internal working model,* or set of expectations about attachment figures,

▶ **Figure 15.3**

Increase in romantic relationships during adoles-cence. More than 16,000 American youths responded to an interview in which they indicated whether they had been involved in a romantic relationship during the past 18 months. Romantic involvements increased steadily with age. At 12 years, about one-fourth of young people reported them, a figure that rose to about three-fourths at age 18. (Adapted from Carver, Joyner, & Udry, 2003.)

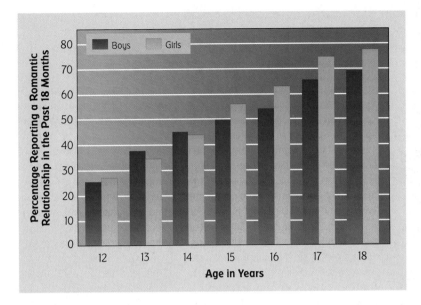

that guides later close relationships. Consistent with this idea, in a study of high school seniors, supportive interactions with parents—and secure models of attachment to parents—predicted adolescents' warm interaction with friends and secure models of friendship. Teenagers' images of friendship security, in turn, were related to their images of security in romantic relationships (Furman et al., 2002). These findings suggest that experiences with parents influence the quality of adolescents' friendships. Then teenagers draw on their friendships to transfer what they have learned to the romantic arena.

Perhaps because early adolescent dating relationships are shallow and stereotyped, early, frequent dating is related to drug use, delinquency, and poor academic achievement (Brown, Feiring, & Furman, 1999; Zimmer-Gembeck, Siebenbruner, & Collins, 2001). These factors, along with a history of aggression in family and peer relationships, increase the likelihood of dating violence (Arriaga & Foshee, 2004). About 10 to 20 percent of adolescents are physically or sexually abused by dating partners, with both boys and girls equally likely to report being victims. Mental health consequences are severe and include increased anxiety, depression, suicide attempts, unhealthy weight control in girls (vomiting and use of laxatives), and risky sexual behaviors (Carver, Joyner, & Udry, 2003; Werkele & Avgoustis, 2003). Furthermore, whereas early-adolescent boys who date gain in status among same-sex peers, girls often experience more conflict as a result of competition and jealousy of other girls. For many reasons, sticking with group activities, such as parties and dances, before becoming involved with a steady boyfriend or girlfriend is best for young teenagers.

Homosexual youths face special challenges in initiating and maintaining visible romances. Their first dating relationships seem to be short-lived and to involve little emotional commitment for different reasons than those of heterosexuals: They fear peer harassment and rejection. Recall from Chapter 5 that because of intense prejudice, homosexual adolescents often retreat into heterosexual dating. In addition, many have difficulty finding a same-sex partner because their homosexual peers have not yet come out. Often their first contacts with other sexual minority youths occur in support groups, where they are free to date publicly and can discuss concerns about coming out (Diamond, 2003).

As long as it does not begin too soon, dating provides lessons in cooperation, etiquette, and dealing with people in a wide range of situations. As older teenagers form close romantic ties, sensitivity, empathy, intimacy, self-esteem, and identity development are enhanced. In addition, teenagers' increasing capacity for interdependence and compromise within dating probably enhances the quality of other peer relationships (Collins, 2003; Furman & Shaffer, 2003).

Still, first romances usually serve as practice for later, more mature bonds. About half of high school romances do not survive graduation, and those that do usually become less satisfying (Shaver, Furman, & Buhrmester, 1985). Because young people are still forming their identities, those who like each other at one time often find that they have little in common later. Nevertheless, warm, caring romantic ties in adolescence can have long-term implications. In a German study, they were positively related to gratifying, committed relationships in emerging adulthood (Seiffge-Krenke, 2003).

◉ First dates usually involve several couples spending time together. As long as dating does not begin too soon, it extends the benefits of adolescent friendship, promoting sensitivity, empathy, intimacy, self-esteem, identity development, and capacity to compromise.

© Mary Kate Denny/PhotoEdit

Adolescent Substance Use and Abuse

In industrialized nations, teenage alcohol and drug use is widespread. By tenth grade, 41 percent of U.S. young people have tried smoking, 64 percent drinking, and 40 percent at least one illegal drug (usually marijuana). At the end of high school, 16 percent smoke cigarettes regularly, 30 percent have engaged in heavy drinking during the past 2 weeks, and over 50 percent have experimented with illegal drugs. About 21 percent have tried at least one highly addictive and toxic substance, such as amphetamines, cocaine, phencyclidine (PCP), Ecstasy (MDMA), inhalants, or heroin. Canadian rates of teenage alcohol and drug use are similar (Statistics Canada, 2003c; U.S. Department of Health and Human Services, 2004e).

These high figures represent an increase during the 1990s, followed by a slight decline, probably resulting from greater parent, school, and media focus on the hazards of drugs. Still, drug use rises steadily over adolescence. Why do so many young people subject themselves to the health risks of these substances? In part, drug taking reflects the sensation seeking of these years. But teenagers also live in drug-dependent cultural contexts. They see adults using caffeine to wake up in the morning, cigarettes

to cope with daily hassles, a drink to calm down in the evening, and other remedies to relieve stress, depression, and physical illness.

In societies where substance use is commonplace, adolescents' involvement with drugs is to be expected. The majority of teenagers who dabble in alcohol, tobacco, and marijuana are not headed for a life of decadence and addiction. Instead, these minimal *experimenters* are psychologically healthy, sociable, curious young people (Shedler & Block, 1990). As Figure 15.4 shows, tobacco and alcohol use is somewhat greater among European than among U.S. adolescents, perhaps because European adults more often smoke and drink. In contrast, illegal drug use is far more prevalent among U.S. teenagers (Hibell, 2001). A greater percentage of American young people live in poverty, which is linked to family and peer contexts that promote illegal drug use. At the same time, use of diverse drugs is lower among African Americans

than among Hispanic and Caucasian Americans. In contrast, Native American and Canadian Aboriginal youths rank highest in drug taking (van der Woerd & Cox, 2001; Wallace et al., 2003). Researchers have yet to explain these variations.

Regardless of type of drug, adolescent drug experimentation should not be taken lightly. Because most drugs impair perception and thought processes, a single heavy dose can lead to permanent injury or death. And a worrisome minority of teenagers move from substance *use* to *abuse*—taking drugs regularly, requiring increasing amounts to achieve the same effect, and using enough to impair their ability to meet school, work, or other responsibilities.

▶ **Figure 15.4**

Tenth-grade students in the United States and Europe who have used various substances. Rates for tobacco and alcohol are based on any use in the past 30 days. Rates for marijuana and other illegal drugs are based on any lifetime use. Tobacco use and alcohol use are greater for European adolescents, whereas illegal drug use is greater for American adolescents. (Adapted from Hibell, 2001.)

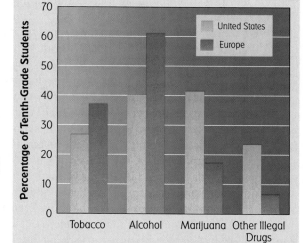

Peer Pressure and Conformity

Conformity to peer pressure is greater in adolescence than in childhood or emerging adulthood—a finding that is not surprising when we consider how much time teenagers spend together. But contrary to popular belief, adolescence is not a period in which young people blindly do what their peers ask. Peer conformity is a complex process that varies with the adolescent's age, current situation, need for social approval, and culture.

A study of several hundred American junior and senior high school students revealed that adolescents felt greatest pressure to conform to the most obvious aspects of the peer culture—dress, grooming, and participation in social activities, such as dating and going to parties. Peer pressure to engage in proadult behavior, such as cooperating with parents and getting good grades, was also strong. Although pressure toward misconduct rose in early adolescence, it was low (Brown, Lohr, & McClenahan, 1986). Many teenagers said that their friends actively discouraged antisocial acts. In similar research conducted in Singapore, a culture that places a high value on family loyalty and

Correlates and Consequences of Adolescent Substance Abuse

In contrast to experimenters, drug abusers are seriously troubled young people who are inclined to express their unhappiness through antisocial acts. Longitudinal evidence reveals that their impulsive, disruptive, hostile styles often are already evident in the preschool years. And compared with other young people, their drug taking starts earlier and may be genetically influenced (Chassin et al., 2003; Silberg et al., 2003). But a wide range of environmental factors also promote it. These include low SES, family mental health problems, parental and older sibling drug abuse, lack of parental warmth and involvement, physical and sexual abuse, and poor school performance. Especially among teenagers with family difficulties, peer encouragement—friends who use and provide access to drugs—increases substance abuse (Prinstein, Boergers, & Spirito, 2001).

Adolescent substance abuse often has lifelong consequences. When teenagers depend on alcohol and hard drugs to deal with daily stresses, they fail to learn responsible decision-making skills and alternative coping techniques. These young people show serious adjustment problems, including chronic anxiety, depression, and antisocial behavior, that are both cause and consequences of heavy drug taking (Simons-Moron & Haynie, 2003). And they often enter into marriage, childbearing, and the work world prematurely and fail at them—painful outcomes that further promote addictive behavior.

Prevention and Treatment

School and community programs that reduce drug experimentation typically combine several components:

- Promoting effective parenting, including monitoring of teenagers' activities
- Teaching adolescents skills for resisting peer pressure
- Reducing the social acceptability of drug taking by emphasizing health and safety risks
- Getting adolescents to commit to not using drugs (Cuijpers, 2002).

But some drug taking seems inevitable. Therefore, interventions that prevent teenagers from harming themselves and others when they do experiment are essential. Many communities offer weekend on-call transportation services that any young person can contact for a safe ride home, with no questions asked. Providing appealing substitute activities, such as drug-free video arcades, dances, and sports activities, is also helpful.

Because drug abuse has different roots than occasional use, different prevention strategies are required. One approach is to work with parents early, reducing family adversity and improving child-rearing skills, before children are old enough to become involved with drugs (Kumpfer & Alvarado, 2003). Programs that teach at-risk teenagers effective strategies for handling life stressors and that build competence through community service reduce alcohol and drug use, just as they reduce teenage pregnancy (see Chapter 5).

When an adolescent becomes a drug abuser, family and individual therapy are generally needed to treat maladaptive parent–child relationships, impulsivity, low-self-esteem, anxiety, and depression.

▲ Many factors contribute to widespread alcohol and drug use among teenagers. Because peer encouragement is one environmental factor that predicts increased substance use, interventions that teach skills for resisting peer pressure reduce experimentation. © Bob Daemmrich/The Image Works

Academic and vocational training to improve life success make a difference as well. But even comprehensive programs have alarmingly high relapse rates (Cornelius et al., 2003).

One recommendation is to usher drug-abusing teenagers into treatment gradually, by starting with support-group sessions that focus on reducing drug taking. Within the group, interveners can focus on teenagers' low motivation to change and resistance to adult referral, which they often view as an infringement on their personal freedom. Such brief interventions lessen drug taking in the short term (Myers et al., 2001). Modest improvement may boost the young person's sense of self-efficacy for behavior change and engender willing entry into intensive treatment—a vital key to its success.

respect for adults, outcomes were much the same, except that peer pressure to meet family and school obligations was highest, exceeding pressure to join in peer-culture pursuits (Sim & Koh, 2003). These findings show that peers and parents often act in concert, toward desirable ends!

Perhaps because of their greater concern with what their friends think of them, early adolescents are more likely than younger or older individuals to give in to peer pressure. Yet when parents and peers disagree, even young teenagers do not consistently rebel against the family. Instead, parents and peers differ in their spheres of greatest influence. Parents have more impact on teenagers' basic life values and educational plans. Peers are more influential in short-term, day-to-day matters, such as dress, music, and choice of friends (Steinberg, 2001). Adolescents' personal characteristics also make a difference. Young people who feel competent and worthwhile are less likely to fall in line behind peers who engage in early sex, delinquency, and frequent drug use (see the From Research to Practice box above).

Finally, authoritative child rearing is related to resistance to peer pressure. Teenagers whose parents are supportive and exert appropriate oversight respect their parents and, therefore,

Peer conformity rises in early adolescence—especially in such matters as dress and grooming. However, with regard to matters of lasting impact, such as values and educational plans, the parents of these girls are probably more influential than their peers. © Spencer Grant/PhotoEdit

usually follow their rules and consider their advice (Sim, 2000). In contrast, adolescents who experience extremes of parental behavior—either too much or too little control—tend to be highly peer oriented. They often rely on friends for advice about their personal lives and future and are willing to break their parents' rules, ignore their schoolwork, and hide their talents to be popular. Under conditions of high life stress, such as poverty or divorce, supportive ties to parents or other caring, involved adults serve as a powerful antidote to unfavorable peer pressures (Masten, 2001).

Before we turn to the impact of media on children and adolescents, you may find it helpful to examine the Milestones table below, which summarizes the development of peer relations.

MILESTONES

DEVELOPMENT OF PEER RELATIONS

Age	Peer Sociability	Friendship	Peer Groups
Birth–2 years	Isolated social acts increase and are gradually replaced by coordinated interaction.	Mutual relationships with familiar peers emerge.	
2½–6 years	Parallel play appears, remains stable, and becomes more cognitively mature. Cooperative play increases, especially sociodramatic play. Rough-and-tumble play emerges.	Friendship is viewed concretely, in terms of play and sharing toys.	
7–11 years	Peer communication skills improve, including interpreting and responding to the emotions and intentions of others. Ability to understand the complementary roles of several players improves, permitting the transition to rule-oriented games. Peer interaction becomes more prosocial. Rough-and-tumble play increases.	Friendship is based on mutual trust and assistance. Interaction between friends becomes more prosocial. Number of close friends declines.	Peer groups emerge.
12–18 years	Peer interaction becomes more cooperative. Rough-and-tumble play declines. More time is spent with peers than any other social partners.	Friendship is based on intimacy, mutual understanding, and loyalty. Friends become more alike in attitudes, values, school grades, and social behavior. Young people choose some friends who differ from themselves. Number of close friends declines further.	Peer groups become more tightly structured, organized around cliques. Cliques with similar values form crowds. As interest in dating increases, mixed-sex cliques form. Romantic relationships begin and gradually last longer. Conformity to peer pressure increases, then declines.

Note: These milestones represent overall age trends. Individual differences exist in the precise age at which each milestone is attained.

Photo credits: (clockwise from top) © Richard Hutchings/PhotoEdit; © Michael Newman/PhotoEdit; © Tom Prettyman/PhotoEdit; © Brand X Pictures/Getty Images

Ask Yourself

REVIEW	What positive functions do peer groups serve in young people's development? What factors lead some peer groups to have harmful consequences?
APPLY	Thirteen-year-old Mattie's parents are warm and consistent in monitoring her activities. At school, Mattie met some girls who want Mattie to tell her parents that she's going to a friend's house but, instead, to meet them at the beach for a party. Is Mattie likely to comply? Explain.
CONNECT	How might gender intensification, discussed on page 541 in Chapter 13, contribute to the shallow quality of early adolescent dating relationships?
REFLECT	How did family experiences influence your crowd membership in high school? How did your crowd membership influence your behavior?

Television

Exposure to television is almost universal in the United States, Canada, and other industrialized countries. Nearly all homes have at least one television set, and most have two or more. Indeed, two-thirds of North American children and adolescents have a TV in their bedroom (Roberts, Foehr & Rideout, 2005). Time spent watching is remarkably similar across developed nations, and young people in the developing world are not far behind (Comstock & Scharrer, 2001; Scharrer & Comstock, 2003).

There is good reason to be concerned about television's impact on children and youths. In an unusual investigation, residents of a small Canadian town were studied just before TV reception became available in their community and again two years later. In those two years, striking changes occurred: In school-age children, a decline in reading ability and creative thinking, a rise in gender-stereotyped beliefs, and an increase in verbal and physical aggression during play; in adolescents, a sharp drop in community participation occurred (Williams, 1986).

But television has as much potential for good as for ill. If the content of TV programming were improved and adults capitalized on it to enhance children's interest in their everyday worlds, television could be a powerful, cost-effective means of strengthening cognitive, emotional, and social development.

How Much Television Do Children View?

Even with the rise of the Internet, TV remains the dominant youth media: The amount of time North American children and adolescents devote to it is extraordinary. Regular TV viewing typically begins between 2 and 3 years. The average North American 2- to 6-year-old watches from 1½ to 2 hours a day. In middle childhood, viewing increases to an average of 3½ hours a day for U.S. children and 2½ hours a day for Canadian children. Then it declines slightly in adolescence, to 2¾ hours in the United States and to just over 2 hours in Canada. These figures reveal that each week, the typical U.S. school-age child devotes 24 hours to TV, the typical Canadian child 17½ hours (Scharrer & Comstock, 2003; Statistics Canada, 2005b). When we add the time the set is on during school holidays and summer vacations, children devote more time to television than to virtually any other waking activity, including interacting with parents and peers, engaging in physical activity, using computers, doing homework, and reading (see Figure 15.5).

▼ Figure 15.5

Time spent watching TV compared with time spent engaged in other pursuits by U.S. 8- to 18-year-olds. In this survey of a nationally representative sample of more than 2,000 U.S. school-age children and adolescents, TV emerged as the dominant activity. Despite the rise of the Internet, TV consumed far more time than recreational computer use. (Adapted from Roberts, Foehr, & Rideout, 2005.)

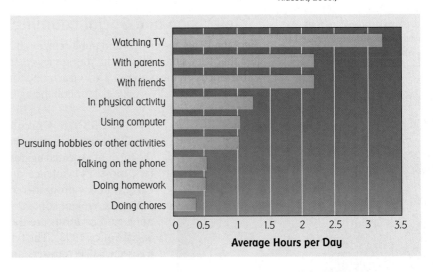

Children vary in their attraction to television. Preschool and school-age boys watch slightly more than girls. Low-SES children also are more frequent viewers, perhaps because their parents are less able to pay for out-of-home entertainment or their neighborhoods provide few alternative activities. Children with a TV in their bedroom spend nearly 1½ hours more per day watching than children without one (Roberts, Foehr, & Rideout, 2005). And if parents tend to watch a lot of TV, their children usually do, too. Extensive TV viewing is associated with family and peer difficulties, perhaps because highly stressed parents and children use it as an escape (Anderson et al., 1996).

Development of Television Literacy

When watching TV programs, children are confronted with a rapid stream of people, objects, places, words, and sounds. Television, or film, has its own specialized code of conveying information. Researchers liken the task of cracking this code to that of learning to read and call it **television literacy.** The symbolic learning involved in understanding television has two interrelated parts: (1) mastering the form of the message, or the meaning of visual and auditory effects such as camera zooms, panoramic views, fade-outs, and split screens, and (2) figuring out the content of the message—integrating scenes, character behavior, and dialogue into an accurate story line (Fitch, Huston, & Wright, 1993).

Young preschoolers have some awareness that a TV image can represent reality. In two studies, 24-month-olds could use a video of an object being hidden to find that object in a real room (Suddendorf, 2003; Schmitt & Anderson, 2002). Nevertheless, their capacity to distinguish televised information from real objects is fragile. In another investigation, 2- and 3-year-olds had difficulty discriminating televised images from actual objects. They said that a bowl of popcorn on TV would spill if the TV were turned upside down and that people could reach into a TV and pick up the objects shown on the screen (Flavell et al., 1990). By age 4, children realize that TV is symbolic, and they work on figuring out what it represents. In judging whether TV images correspond to real-world events, at first they consider all human actors "real" and all cartoon characters "unreal." Around age 5, children make finer discriminations. They say that news and documentaries depict real events and that fictional programs are "just for TV." But not until age 7 do children fully grasp the unreality of TV fiction—that characters do not retain their roles in real life, that their behavior is scripted, and that commercials aim to persuade and, therefore, may not be truthful (Linn, 2005; Wright et al., 1994).

Before age 8, children have difficulty connecting separate TV scenes into a meaningful story line. Consequently, they often fail to detect motives or consequences (Collins, 1983). A character who gets what he wants by punching, shooting, and killing may not be a "bad guy" to a young child, who fails to notice that the character was brought to justice in the end. As a result, children may judge villains and their actions favorably.

In sum, preschool and young elementary school children have an incomplete grasp of TV meanings, assimilate televised information piecemeal, and cannot critically evaluate it. These misunderstandings increase the chances that they will believe and imitate what they see on the screen. Let's look at the impact of TV on children's social learning.

Television and Social Learning

Since the 1950s, researchers and public citizens have been concerned about the attitudes and behaviors that television cultivates in young viewers. Most studies address the impact of TV violence. Others focus on the power of TV to teach undesirable gender and ethnic stereotypes. And growing evidence confirms TV's potential for enhancing children's cognitive and social competence.

• **AGGRESSION** • According to a large-scale survey, 57 percent of American TV programs between 6 A.M. and 11 P.M. contain violent scenes, often in the form of repeated aggressive acts against a victim that go unpunished. In fact, most TV violence does not show victims experiencing any serious harm, and few programs condemn violence or depict other ways of solving problems. Violent content is 9 percent above average in children's programming, and cartoons are the most violent (Center for Communication and Social Policy, 1998). The typical American child finishing elementary school has seen 8,000 murders and more than 100,000 other violent acts on TV

Ⓢ Although television has the potential to support development, too often it teaches negative lessons. Heavy viewers are exposed to violence of all kinds and learn that aggression is an acceptable way to solve problems.
© Peter Byron/PhotoEdit

(Huston et al., 1992). Canadian broadcasters follow a code that sharply restricts televised violence, but Canadians devote two-thirds of their viewing time to American channels (Statistics Canada, 2005b).

Reviewers of thousands of studies have concluded that television violence increases the likelihood of hostile thoughts and emotions and of verbally and physically aggressive behavior (Anderson et al., 2003; Comstock & Scharrer, 1999). The case is strengthened by the fact that investigations using a wide variety of research designs, methods, and participants have yielded similar findings. Although young people of all ages are susceptible, preschool and young school-age children are especially likely to imitate TV violence because of their tendency to accept televised messages.

Violent programming not only creates short-term difficulties in parent and peer relations but also has lasting, negative consequences. In several longitudinal studies, time spent watching TV in childhood and adolescence predicted aggressive behavior in adulthood, after other factors linked to TV viewing (such as child and parent prior aggression, IQ, parent education, family income, and neighborhood crime) were controlled (see Figure 15.6) (Huesmann, 1986; Huesmann, et al., 2003; Johnson et al., 2002). Aggressive children and adolescents have a greater appetite for violent TV. And boys watch more violent programming than girls, in part because violent shows cater to male audiences by using males as lead characters. Nevertheless, violent TV sparks hostile thoughts and behavior even in nonaggressive children; its impact is simply less intense (Bushman & Huesmann, 2001).

Furthermore, television violence "hardens" children to aggression. After just a few exposures, viewers habituate, responding with reduced arousal to real-world instances and tolerating more aggression in others (Anderson et al., 2003). Heavy viewers believe that there is much more violence in society than is actually the case—an effect that is especially strong for children who perceive televised aggression to be relevant to their own lives (Donnerstein, Slaby, & Eron, 1994). As these responses indicate, violent television modifies children's attitudes toward social reality so that they increasingly match what is seen on TV.

The television industry has contested these findings, claiming that they are weak. But the correlation between media violence and aggression is nearly as high as the correlation between smoking and lung cancer. And it is higher than correlations between other widely accepted health factors and outcomes (see Figure 15.7). Because exposure to violent TV is so widespread, its impact can be profound even if only a small percentage of viewers are affected. Laboratory research shows that 15 minutes of mildly violent programming increases aggression in at least one-fourth of viewers (Anderson & Bushman, 2002).

• **ETHNIC AND GENDER STEREOTYPES** • Although educational programming for children is sensitive to issues of equity and diversity, commercial entertainment TV conveys ethnic and gender stereotypes. African Americans and other ethnic minorities are underrepresented. When minorities do appear, they usually are depicted in secondary or lower-status roles, such as domestic workers or unskilled laborers (Berry, 2003; Scharrer & Comstock, 2003). Similarly, women appear less often than men, especially as main characters. Compared with two decades ago, today's female characters are more often involved in careers. But they continue to be portrayed as young, attractive, caring, emotional, victimized, and in romantic and family contexts. In contrast, men are depicted as dominant and powerful

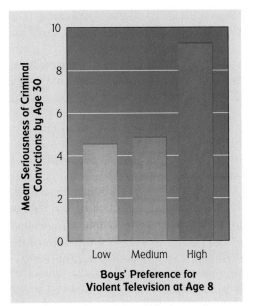

◀ **Figure 15.6**

Relationship between boys' violent television viewing at age 8 and seriousness of criminal convictions by age 30. Longitudinal research showed that boys who watched many violent programs were more likely to commit serious criminal acts in adolescence and early adulthood. (From L. R. Huesmann, 1986, "Psychological Processes Promoting the Relation Between Exposure to Media Violence and Aggressive Behavior by the Viewer," *Journal of Social Issues, 42,* p. 129. Reprinted by permission.)

▼ **Figure 15.7**

Comparison of the consequences of the media violence–aggression relationship with other widely accepted health effects. The correlation between media violence and aggression is almost as strong as the correlation between smoking and lung cancer. It is stronger than the correlation between other health behaviors and outcomes. (Adapted from B. J. Bushman & C. A. Anderson, 2001, "Media Violence and the American Public," *American Psychologist, 56,* p. 481. Copyright © 2001 by the American Psychological Association. Reprinted by permission of the publisher and author.)

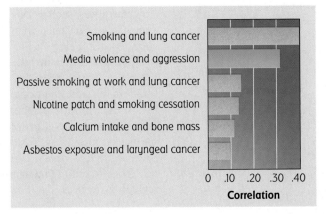

(Signorielli, 2001). Gender stereotypes are especially prevalent in cartoons, music television (MTV), and other entertainment programs for children and youths.

TV viewing is linked to children's gender-stereotyped beliefs (Signorielli, 1993). But non-stereotypic TV images reduce these biases. Positive portrayals of women and ethnic minorities lead to more favorable views and greater willingness to form ethnically diverse friendships (Calvert et al., 2003; Graves, 1993).

• **CONSUMERISM** • The marketing industry aimed at selling products to youths—toys, games, foods, clothing, and a host of other items—has exploded, tripling in corporate expenditures during the past decade, including funds devoted to TV advertising. On average, U.S. children watch 40,000 TV commercials per year, Canadian children 23,000 (Linn, 2004).

By age 3, children can distinguish an obvious TV ad from regular programming by its loudness, fast-paced action, and sound effects. But because many children's shows contain characters and props that are themselves products (dolls, puppets, action figures, and their accessories), the boundary between programs and commercials is blurred, making it impossible for young children to distinguish the two. Furthermore, preschoolers and young elementary school children seldom grasp the selling purpose of TV ads; they think that commercials are meant to help viewers. Around age 8 or 9, most children understand that commercials are meant to sell, and by age 11, they realize that advertisers will resort to clever techniques achieve their goals (Kunkel, 2001; Linn, 2005).

Nevertheless, even older children and adolescents find many commercials alluring. Research suggests that the heavy bombardment of children with advertising contributes to a variety of child and youth problems, including family stress, overweight and obesity, materialism, and substance use. In recent surveys of adults that included many parents, over 90 percent reported that youth-directed ads greatly increase children's nagging of parents to buy items, giving rise to family conflict. In one poll of a nationally representative sample of U.S. parents, almost half agreed that their child would rather go shopping at the mall than hiking with the family (Spencer, 2001). Furthermore, the greater adolescents' exposure to cigarette and alcohol ads—many of which are designed to appeal to them through youthful characters, upbeat music, and party scenes—the more likely they are to smoke and drink (Smith & Atkin, 2003).

Television, Academic and Prosocial Learning, and Imagination

Since the early days of television, educators have been interested in its potential for strengthening academic and social skills, especially among low-SES children. *Sesame Street,* especially, was created to foster children's learning. It uses lively visual and sound effects to stress basic literacy and number concepts and puppet and human characters to teach general knowledge, emotional and social understanding, and social skills. Today, more than two-thirds of North American preschoolers watch *Sesame Street,* and it is broadcast in more than 120 countries (Sesame Workshop, 2005).

The more children watch *Sesame Street,* the higher they score on tests designed to measure the program's learning goals (Fisch, Truglio, & Cole, 1999). One study reported a link between preschool viewing of *Sesame Street* and similar educational programs and getting higher grades, reading more books, placing more value on achievement, and scoring higher on a divergent-thinking test (a measure of creativity) in high school (Anderson et al., 2001). In recent years, *Sesame Street* has reduced its rapid-paced format in favor of more leisurely episodes with a clear story line (Truglio, 2000). Watching children's programs with slow-paced action and easy-to-follow narratives, such as *Mr. Rogers' Neighborhood* and *Barney and Friends,* leads to more elaborate make-believe play than viewing programs that present quick, disconnected bits of information (Singer & Singer, 2005).

Television that includes acts of cooperating, helping, and comforting can increase children's prosocial behavior. In one study, researchers asked more than 500 second to sixth graders to name their favorite educational TV shows and say what they learned from them. The children not only named many prosocial programs but also accurately described the lessons the programs conveyed (Calvert & Kotler, 2003). Much TV, however, mixes prosocial and antisocial messages. Prosocial programs promote children's kind and helpful acts only when they are free of violent content (Hearold, 1986).

Does watching entertainment TV take children away from worthwhile activities? Some evidence suggests that it does. The more preschool and school-age children watch prime-time shows and cartoons, the less time they spend reading and interacting with others and the poorer their performance on tests of academic skills (Huston et al., 1999; Wright et al., 2001). In sum, whereas educational programs can be beneficial, watching entertainment TV—especially heavy viewing—detracts from children's school success and social experiences.

Regulating Children's Television

The ease with which television can manipulate children's beliefs and behavior has resulted in strong public pressures to improve its content. In the United States, the First Amendment right to free speech has hampered these efforts; TV content is only minimally regulated to protect children. Broadcasters are required to provide 3 hours per week of educational and informational programming for children and must limit commercials in certain children's shows to 10½ minutes per hour (Children's Television Act, 1990). All programs must be rated for violent and sexual content, and manufacturers must build the V-Chip (also called the Violence Chip) into new TV sets so parents can block undesired material.

Canada also mandates the V-Chip, along with program ratings. In addition, Canada's broadcasting code bans from children's shows realistic scenes of violence that minimize consequences and cartoons in which violence is the central theme. Further, violent programming intended for adults cannot be shown on Canadian channels before 9 P.M. (Canadian Broadcast Standards, 2003). Still, Canadian children can access violent TV fare on U.S. channels.

At present, it is largely up to parents to regulate their children's media exposure. Until children's television improves, parents must be informed about the dangers of TV viewing and how to control it. See Applying What We Know below for some strategies they can use.

◉ Parents can build on TV programs in constructive ways. For example, by taking her children to a natural history museum after they watched a program about diversity in the animal kingdom, this mother links televised content to other learning experiences.
© Jeff Greenberg/PhotoEdit

Applying What We Know   Regulating TV and Computer Use

Strategy	Explanation
Limit TV viewing and computer use.	Provide clear rules that limit what children and adolescents can view on TV and do on the computer, and stick to the rules. Avoid using the TV or the computer as a baby-sitter for children. Do not place a TV or a computer in a child's bedroom; doing so increases use substantially and makes the child's activity hard to monitor.
Refrain from using TV or computer time to reward or punish children.	When TV or computer access is used to reward or punish, children become increasingly attracted to it.
View TV with children, helping them understand what they see.	When adults express disapproval of on-screen behavior, raise questions about its realism, and encourage children to discuss it, they teach children to evaluate TV content rather than accepting it uncritically.
Link TV content to everyday learning experiences.	Building on TV programs in constructive ways enhances learning by encouraging children into active engagement with their surroundings. For example, a program on animals might spark a trip to the zoo, a visit to the library for books about animals, or new ways of observing and caring for the family pet.
Model good TV and computer practices.	Avoid excess television viewing and computer use and exposure to violent media content yourself. Parental viewing patterns influence children's viewing patterns.
Explain Internet safety rules to school-age children and adolescents.	Point out appropriate online behavior and risks of Internet communication, including bullying, harassment, and exploitation. Emphasize the greatest safety risks: revealing personal information and getting together with people whom the young person has "met" online. For online safety information for teenagers and parents, consult *Teen Safety on the Information Highway*, available at *www.safeteens.com*
Use a warm, involved, rational approach to child rearing.	Children of warm, involved parents who make reasonable demands for mature behavior prefer TV and computer experiences with educational and prosocial content and are unlikely to feel a need to use the TV or computer as an escape.

Computers

Computers are familiar fixtures in the everyday lives of today's children and adolescents, offering a wide range of learning and entertainment tools. Virtually all U.S. and Canadian public schools have integrated computers into their instructional programs and can access the Internet—trends also evident in other industrialized nations (Statistics Canada, 2002a; U.S. Census Bureau, 2004b). About 85 percent of North American children and adolescents live in homes with one or more computers, two-thirds of which have an Internet connection, usually a high-speed link (Roberts, Foehr, & Rideout, 2005; Statistics Canada, 2004c). Although higher-SES homes are more likely to have computers, over 70 percent of lower-SES families now have them.

In a survey of a nationally representative sample of more than 2,000 U.S. 8- to 18-year-olds, the percentage who reported using a computer for recreational activities the previous day rose with age, from 42 percent among 8- to 10-year-olds to 61 percent among 15- to 18-year-olds. Higher SES also predicted increased use. Although boys and girls did not differ in overall computer use, boys spent more time playing games, whereas girls took greater advantage of the computer's social and informational capabilities—instant messaging, e-mailing, and visiting websites (Roberts, Foehr, & Rideout, 2005).

On average, North American school-age children and adolescents use the computer about one hour per day for pleasure, another half-hour for schoolwork. More than half report being "media multitaskers"—that is, engaged in two or more media activities some or most of the time, especially while using the computer. For example, they may have several computer activities going, use the computer while watching TV or listening to music, or do all three at once (Roberts, Foehr, & Rideout, 2005; Media Awareness Network 2001). Media multitasking greatly increases media exposure, although its impact on learning and behavior is not yet known.

Most parents say they purchased a computer to enrich their child's education; about one-third of children and adolescents have a computer in their bedroom. At the same time, parents express great concern about the influence of the Internet and violent computer games, although only a minority of children and youths—30 percent in the United States and 40 percent in Canada—say their parents have rules about computer use and know what sites they visit on the Web (Roberts, Foehr, & Rideout, 2005; Media Awareness Network , 2001). Let's see how computers affect academic and social development.

Computers and Academic Learning

Computers can have rich educational benefits. As early as age 3, children enjoy computer activities and are able to type simple keyboard commands. In classrooms, small groups often gather around computers, and children more often collaborate in computer activities than in other pursuits (Svensson, 2000).

As soon as children begin to read and write, they can use the computer for word processing. It enables them to write freely and experiment with letters and words without having to struggle with handwriting. They can revise their text's meaning and style and also check their spelling. As a result, they worry less about making mistakes, and their written products tend to be longer and of higher quality (Clements, 1995). Often children jointly plan, compose, and revise text, learning from one another (Clements & Sarama, 2003).

Specially designed computer languages introduce children to programming skills. As long as adults support children's efforts, computer programming leads to improved concept formation, problem solving, and creativity (Clements, 1995; Clements & Nastasi, 1992). And because children must detect errors in their programs to get them to work, programming helps them reflect on their thought processes, leading to gains in metacognitive knowledge and self-regulation (Clements, 1990). Furthermore, while programming, children are especially likely to help one another, persist in the face of challenge, and express positive attitudes toward learning (Nastasi & Clements, 1994).

As children get older, they often use the computer for school assignments, largely through word processing and searching the Web for information. But despite their many learning advantages, computers also raise concerns about a "digital divide" between gender and SES groups in certain computer skills. In a Canadian survey of a nationally representative sample of 15- and 16-year-olds, boys more often engaged in writing computer programs, analyzing data, and using spreadsheets and graphics programs. And many more boys than girls expressed interest in computers and rated their computer skills as "excellent" (Looker & Thiessen, 2003). Similarly, confidence in using computers rises with SES (Subrahmanyam et al., 2001).

These findings indicate that schools must ensure that girls and low-SES students have many opportunities to benefit from the cognitively enriching aspects of computer technology. Attaining this goal is not just a matter of equipping classrooms with more technology. Intensive teacher guidance and encouragement are necessary to educate equitably and effectively with computers (Attewell, 2001).

Computers and Social Learning

Children and adolescents spend much time using home computers for entertainment purposes. Games are popular pursuits, especially among boys. Surfing the Web and communicating electronically with friends rise sharply in adolescence. Teenagers prefer the immediacy of instant messaging, which accounts for one-fourth of recreational computer time for boys and nearly one-third for girls (Roberts, Foehr, & Rideout, 2005).

Schools must ensure that all children develop diverse computer skills: writing computer programs, analyzing data, using spreadsheets and graphics, and downloading images from other media, as these girls are doing for a class project. © David Young-Wolff/PhotoEdit

• **COMPUTER GAMES** • Most computer games emphasize speed and action in violent plots in which children advance by shooting at and evading the enemy. Children also play more complex, exploratory, and adventure games, generally with themes of conquest and aggression, and sports games, such as football and soccer. And they greatly enjoy simulation games that involve entering virtual realities and role-playing characters.

Speed-and-action computer games foster selective attention and spatial skills in boys and girls alike (Okagaki & Frensch, 1996; Subrahmanyam & Greenfield, 1996). Yet most game software is unappealing to girls because of its emphasis on violence and male-dominated sports. And an increasing number of studies show that playing violent games, like watching violent TV, increases hostility and aggression (Anderson et al., 2003). Furthermore, video games are full of ethnic and gender stereotypes (Dietz, 1998). Much less is known about the consequences of children's experiences in computerized virtual realities. Researchers speculate that depending on their content, some virtual-reality games may foster complex narrative skills and imagination, whereas others increase uncooperativeness, callousness, and antisocial acts (Singer & Singer, 2005).

Compared with infrequent users, "passionate" game players tend to be withdrawn young people who use games to escape from unpleasant family and school experiences. And a few, who spend several hours a day playing, are addicted; they constantly think about playing when they are not, believe they play too much, but cannot cut back or stop (Salguero & Morán, 2002). Excessive playing of simulation games risks blurring of the distinction between virtual and real life (Turkle, 1995). When such games are violent, they may contribute—along with disengaged parents, antisocial peers, and alienation from school—to commission of heinous acts by at-risk young people. Columbine High School teenage murderers Eric Harris and Dylan Klebold were obsessed with a game called *Doom*, in which players try to rack up the most kills (Subrahmanyam et al., 2001).

• **THE INTERNET AND COMMUNICATION** • Using the computer to communicate is a popular activity among adolescents. Instant messaging—teenagers' preferred means of online interaction—seems to support friendship closeness. Young people's specialized jargon, or "cyber slang," developed to facilitate communication and protect its privacy, has become a familiar part of popular culture—for example, "gg" (gotta go), "mwah" (kiss), "lol" (laugh out loud), "brb" (be right back), "yt" (you there?), "pos" (parents over shoulder). In one study, as amount of instant messaging increased, so did young people's perceptions of intimacy in the relationship (Hu et al., 2004).

Besides communicating with friends they know, adolescents frequently use the Internet to meet new people. As part of their striving for autonomy and identity, they find establishing relationships in cyberspace appealing because it opens up a vast array of alternatives beyond their families, schools, and communities. Although these online ties provide some teens with sources of support, they also pose dangers, as indicated by a growing literature on safety rules for conducting them. In a survey of a nationally representative sample of U.S. 10- to 17-year-old

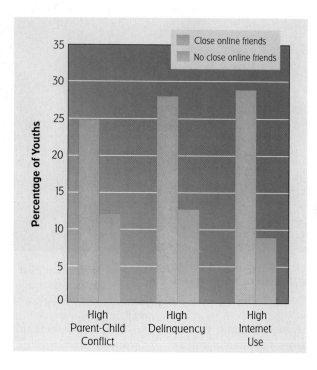

Association of close online friendships with parent–child conflict, delinquency, and high Internet use. In this survey of a nationally representative sample of 1,500 U.S. Internet-using 10- to 17-year-olds, those who reported that they had formed close online friendships or romances were more likely to be troubled youths who spent much time on the Internet. (Adapted from Wolak, Mitchell, & Finkelhor, 2003.)

Internet users, 14 percent of youths reported online close friendships or romances. Although some well-adjusted adolescents formed these bonds, many were youths who reported high levels of conflict with parents, peer victimization, depression, and delinquency, and who spent extensive time on the Internet (see Figure 15.8). They also more often had been asked by online friends for face-to-face meetings and had attended those meetings—without telling their parents (Wolak, Mitchell, & Finkelhor, 2003).

These findings suggest that troubled youths may turn to the Internet to relieve feelings of isolation and rejection—motivations that may make them especially vulnerable to exploitation. Adolescents who lack protective networks—family and friends to talk to about online encounters and appropriate and inappropriate online behaviors—may be overly trusting and may find deceptions and harassment in Internet relationships particularly painful. Under these circumstances, Internet friendships may worsen their problems.

The Internet's potential for increasing disengagement from everyday life and exposing youths to harmful social experiences must be weighed against its value for promoting acquisition of computer skills and information and enabling convenient and satisfying communication. Parents are wise to oversee how much their young people use the home computer—and when they use the Internet, just how they spend their time (refer again to Applying What We Know on page 623).

Ask Yourself

REVIEW	Describe research that supports the academic and social benefits of television and computer use.
APPLY	Thirteen-year-old Tommy spends hours each afternoon surfing the Net, instant messaging with online friends he has never met, and playing computer games. Using research findings, explain why his parents should intervene.
CONNECT	Which of the following children is most likely to be attracted to violent TV: Jane, a popular child; Mack, a rejected child; or Tim, a neglected child? Explain.
REFLECT	How much and what kinds of television viewing and computer use did you engage in as a child and adolescent? Did your parents have rules about watching TV and using the computer, and did they enforce those rules? How do you think your home media environment influenced your development?

Schooling

Unlike the informal world of peer relations, the school is a formal institution designed to transmit the knowledge and skills children need to become productive members of society. Children in the developed world spend many hours in school—on average, about 14,000 by high school graduation. In earlier chapters, we noted that schools are vital forces in children's development, affecting their motivation to learn and modes of remembering, reasoning, problem solving, and social and moral understanding. How do schools exert such a powerful impact? Research looking at schools as complex social systems—class and student body size, educational philosophies, transitions form one school level to the next, teacher–student relationships, and grouping practices—provides important insights.

Class and Student Body Size

The physical plants of all schools tend to be similar: Each has classrooms, hallways, a playground, and a lunchroom. But they also vary widely in the number of students they accommodate in each class and in the school as a whole.

Is there an optimal class size? In a large field experiment, more than 6,000 Tennessee kindergartners were randomly assigned to three class types: "small" (13 to 17 students), "regular" (22 to 25 students) with only a teacher to supervise, and regular with a teacher plus a full-time teacher's aide. These arrangements continued into third grade. Small-class students—especially ethnic minority children—scored higher in reading and math achievement each year and continued to do so after they returned to regular-size classes (Mosteller, 1995). Placing teacher's aides in regular-size classes had no consistent impact. Rather, being in small classes from kindergarten through third grade predicted substantially higher achievement from fourth through ninth grades (Nye, Hedges, & Konstantopoulos, 2001).

Why is small class size beneficial? With fewer children, teachers spend less time disciplining and more time getting to know students and giving individual attention. Also, children who learn in smaller groups show better concentration, higher-quality class participation, and more favorable attitudes toward school (Blatchford et al., 2002, 2003; Finn, Pannozzo, & Achilles, 2003). The impact of small class size on children's social behavior, however, is inconsistent and may depend on the extent to which teachers include social goals in their daily plans (Blatchford, Edmonds, & Martin, 2003; NICHD Early Child Care Research Network, 2004a).

By the time students reach secondary school, they move from class to class and have access to many activities outside classroom instruction. As a result, the relevant physical context is the school as a whole. Student body size profoundly affects school life. Members of smaller schools consistently report more social support and caring. As one teacher at a large high school commented, "A huge problem here is our size. It breeds anonymity. It breeds disconnection.... There is no sense of identification" (Lee et al., 2000, p. 159).

Furthermore, schools with 500 to 700 students or less have fewer people to ensure that clubs, sports events, and social activities will function. As a result, young people enter a greater number and variety of activities and hold more positions of responsibility and leadership. In contrast, plenty of students are available to fill activity slots in large schools, so only an elite few are genuinely active (Barker & Gump, 1964).

In view of these findings, it is not surprising that adolescents in small schools report a greater sense of personal responsibility, competence, and challenge from their extracurricular experiences. This is true even for "marginal" students—those with low IQs, academic difficulties, and poverty-stricken backgrounds (Mahoney & Cairns, 1997). A special advantage of small schools is that potential dropouts are far more likely to join in activities, gain recognition, and remain until graduation. Reorganizations that create "schools within schools"—smaller units within large schools—can have the same effect. Consult the Social Issues box on page 628 for research indicating that extracurricular participation has a lasting, favorable impact on development.

Educational Philosophies

Each teacher brings to the classroom an educational philosophy that plays a major role in children's learning experiences. Two philosophical approaches have received most research attention. They differ in what children are taught, in the way they are believed to learn, and in how their progress is evaluated.

• **TRADITIONAL VERSUS CONSTRUCTIVIST CLASSROOMS** • In a **traditional classroom,** the teacher is the sole authority for knowledge, rules, and decision making and does most of the talking. Students are relatively passive—listening, responding when called on, and completing teacher-assigned tasks. Their progress is evaluated by how well they keep pace with a uniform set of standards for their grade.

A **constructivist classroom,** in contrast, encourages students to *construct* their own knowledge. Although constructivist approaches vary, many are grounded in Piaget's theory, which views children as active agents who reflect on and coordinate their own thoughts, rather than absorbing those of others. A glance inside a constructivist classroom reveals richly equipped learning centers, small groups and individuals solving problems they choose themselves, and a

Extracurricular Activities and Positive Youth Development

The weekend before graduation, Terrell—a senior at an inner-city high school—attended a cast party celebrating the drama club's final performance of the year. That evening, Terrell had played a leading role in a production written and directed by club members. When Mrs. Meyer, the club's adviser, congratulated Terrell, he responded, "I loved this club. When I joined, I wasn't good at English and math and all that stuff, and I thought I couldn't do anything. Working on the sets and acting was so great—finding out that I could do these things well. Before, I wasn't secure with myself. Now I've got this boost of confidence."

Many studies show that high school extracurricular activities that focus on the arts, community service, and vocational development promote diverse academic and social skills and have a lasting positive impact on adjustment. Outcomes include improved academic performance, reduced antisocial behavior, more favorable self-esteem and initiative, greater peer acceptance, and increased concern for others (Mahoney, 2000; Sandstrom & Coie, 1999). The benefits of extracurricular involvement extend into adult life. After many factors were controlled (including SES and academic performance), young people who were more involved in high school clubs and organizations achieved more in their occupations and engaged in more community service in their twenties and thirties (Berk, 1992).

How do extracurricular activities produce such wide-ranging benefits? Not just by giving young people something fun to do during leisure hours. In a Swedish study, adolescents who spent many afternoons and evenings in youth recreation centers that offered such unstructured pastimes as pool, Ping-Pong, video games, and TV showed repeated and persisting antisocial behavior (Mahoney, Stattin, & Magnusson, 2001). In contrast, highly structured, goal-oriented pursuits that require teenagers to take on challenging roles and responsibilities have a positive impact on development. Such activities also include caring and supportive interactions with peers and adults, who impose high expectations, help with problems, and serve as mentors (Roth et al., 1998).

Youths with academic, emotional, and social problems are especially likely to benefit from extracurricular participation. In a study of teenagers experiencing uninvolved parenting, those who engaged in extracurricular pursuits showed far lower levels of depressed mood. This outcome was strongest for adolescents who reported a trusting relationship with an activity adviser who validated their skills and strengthened their motivation to do their best (Mahoney, Schweder, & Stattin, 2002). Furthermore, activity participation sometimes strengthens connectedness between parent and teenager, as family members attend performances and exhibits or otherwise see the fruits of the young person's efforts (Mahoney & Magnuson, 2001).

▲ A group of high school students rehearses for a school play, one of many possible extracurricular activities that build competencies such as improved academic performance, self-esteem, peer acceptance, and concern for others.
© Michael Newman/PhotoEdit

Students seem to recognize the power of their extracurricular experiences to foster a smooth transition to adulthood. They report enjoyment, increased confidence, valuable relationships with adults, new friendships, and gains in setting goals, managing time, and working with others (Dworkin, Larson, & Hansen, 1993). Unfortunately, extracurricular activities are among the first aspects of school life to be eliminated when budgets are cut. Yet a wealth of evidence indicates that, instead, these pursuits should be expanded, with special attempts made to reach academically and socially marginal young people.

teacher who offers guidance and support in response to children's needs. Students are evaluated by considering their progress in relation to their own prior development.

In North America, the pendulum has swung back and forth between these two views. In the 1960s and early 1970s, constructivist classrooms gained in popularity. Then, as concern arose over the academic progress of children and youths, especially in the United States, a "back to basics" movement arose. Classrooms returned to traditional instruction, a style still prevalent today.

The combined results of many studies reveal that older elementary school children in traditional classrooms have a slight edge in academic achievement. But constructivist settings are associated with other benefits—gains in critical thinking, greater valuing of individual differences in classmates, and more positive attitudes toward school (Walberg, 1986).

Despite grave concerns about its appropriateness, many preschool and kindergarten teachers have felt increased pressure to stress teacher-directed, academic training. Yet doing so undermines motivation and emotional well-being. When young children spend much time passively sitting and doing worksheets, as opposed to being actively engaged in learning centers, they display more stress behaviors (such as wiggling and rocking), have less confidence in their abilities, prefer less challenging tasks, and are less advanced in motor, academic, language, and social skills at the end of the school year (Marcon, 1999a; Stipek et al., 1995). Follow-ups reveal lasting effects through elementary school in poorer study habits and achievement (Burts et al., 1992; Hart et al., 1998, 2003). These outcomes are strongest for low-SES children. Yet teachers tend to prefer a traditional approach for economically disadvantaged children—a disturbing trend in view of its negative impact on motivation and learning (Stipek & Byler, 1997).

The heavy emphasis on knowledge absorption as early as kindergarten has contributed to a growing trend among parents to delay their child's school entry. Traditional teaching may also increase the incidence of grade retention. See the From Research to Practice box on page 630 for research on these issues.

• **NEW PHILOSOPHICAL DIRECTIONS** • New approaches to education, grounded in Vygotsky's sociocultural theory, capitalize on the rich social context of the classroom to spur children's learning. In these **social-constructivist classrooms,** children participate in a wide range of challenging activities with teachers and peers, with whom they jointly construct understandings. As children appropriate (take for themselves) the knowledge and strategies generated from working together, they advance in cognitive and social development and become competent, contributing members of their cultural community (Palincsar, 2003). Vygotsky's emphasis on the social origins of complex mental activities has inspired the following educational themes:

- *Teachers and children as partners in learning.* A classroom rich in both teacher–child and child–child collaboration transfers culturally valued ways of thinking to children.

- *Experience with many types of symbolic communication in meaningful activities.* As children master reading, writing, and mathematics, they become aware of their culture's communication systems, reflect on their own thinking, and bring it under voluntary control.

- *Teaching adapted to each child's zone of proximal development.* Assistance that both responds to current understandings and encourages children to take the next step forward helps ensure that each student will make the best progress possible.

In Chapter 6, we considered two Vygotsky-inspired, collaborative practices: reciprocal teaching and cooperative learning (see pages 263–264). Recognizing that collaboration requires a supportive context to be most effective, another Vygotsky-based innovation makes it a school-wide value. Classrooms are transformed into **communities of learners** where teachers guide the overall process of learning, but otherwise, no distinction is made between adult and child contributors: All participate in joint endeavors and have the authority to define and resolve problems. This approach is based on the assumption that different people have different expertises that can benefit the community and that students may become experts to whom others may turn (Engle & Conant, 2002). Classroom activities often consist of long-term projects that address complex, real-world problems. In working toward project goals, children and teachers draw on one another's expertises and those of others within and beyond the school (Strauss, 1998).

◎ In social-constructivist classrooms, which are grounded in Vygotsky's sociocultural theory, children engage in rich literacy activities with teachers and peers. As students jointly construct appropriate understandings, they advance in cognitive and social development.
© Lindfors Photography

School Readiness and Grade Retention

While waiting to pick up their sons from preschool, Susan and Vicky struck up a conversation about kindergarten enrollment. "Freddy will be 5 in August," Susan announced. "He's a month older than the cutoff date."

"But he'll be one of the youngest in the class," Vicky countered. "Better check into what kids have to do in kindergarten these days. Have you asked his teacher what she thinks?"

"Well," Vicky admitted, "she did say Freddy was a bit young."

Since the 1980s, more parents have been delaying their child's kindergarten entry, a trend that recently has accelerated as academic expectations of kindergartners have increased. Aware that boys lag behind girls in development, parents most often hold out sons whose birth dates are close to the cutoff for kindergarten enrollment. Is delaying kindergarten entry beneficial? Although some teachers and principals recommend it, research has not revealed any advantages. Younger children make just as much academic progress as older children in the same grade (Cameron & Wilson, 1990; Graue & DiPerna, 2000). And younger first graders reap academic gains from on-time enrollment; they outperform same-age children a year behind them in school (Stipek & Byler, 2001). Furthermore, delaying kindergarten entry does not seem to prevent or solve emotional and social difficulties. To the contrary, students who are older than the typical age for their grade show high rates of behavior problems—considerably

higher than students who are young for their grade (Stipek, 2002).

A related dilemma concerns whether to retain a student for a second year in kindergarten or in one of the primary grades. A wealth of research reveals no learning benefits but, instead, negative consequences for motivation, self-esteem, peer relations, and school attitudes (Carlton & Winsler, 1999). In a Canadian study, students retained between kindergarten and second grade—regardless of the academic and social characteristics they brought to the situation—showed worsening academic performance, anxiety, and (among boys) disruptiveness throughout elementary school. These unfavorable trends did not characterize nonretained students (Pagani et al., 2001).

As an alternative to kindergarten retention, some school districts place poorly performing children in a "transition" class—a way station between kindergarten and first grade. Transition classes, however, are a form of homogeneous grouping. As with other "low groups," teachers may lower their expectations and teach transition children in a less stimulating fashion than other children.

Each of the options just considered is based on the view that readiness for school largely results from biological maturation. An alternative perspective, based on Vygotsky's sociocultural theory, is that children acquire the knowledge, skills, and attitudes for school success through the assistance of parents and teachers. The U.S. National

▲ Saying good-bye on the first day of school, this father may wonder how ready his son is for classroom learning. Yet delaying kindergarten entry for a year has no demonstrated benefits for academic or social development. © Ariel Skelley/Corbis

Association for the Education of Young Children recommends that all children of legal age start kindergarten and be provided with classroom experiences that foster their individual progress. Research confirms that school readiness is not something to wait for; it can be cultivated.

In one classroom, students studied animal–habitat relationships so they could design an animal of the future, suited to environmental changes. The class formed small research groups, each of which selected a subtopic—for example, defense against predators, protection from the elements, reproduction, or food getting. Each group member assumed responsibility for part of the subtopic, consulting diverse experts and preparing teaching materials. Then group members taught one another, assembled their contributions, and brought them to the community as a whole so the knowledge gathered could be used to solve the problem (Brown, 1997). The result was a deep, multifaceted understanding of the topic that would have been too difficult and time-consuming for any learner to accomplish alone.

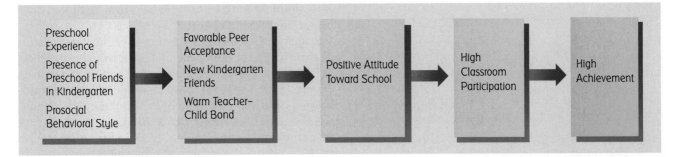

▲ **Figure 15.9**

Factors linked to favorable adaptation to kindergarten.

School Transitions

Besides size and educational philosophy, an additional structural feature of schooling affects students' achievement and psychological adjustment: the timing of transitions from one school level to the next. Entering kindergarten is a major milestone. Children must accommodate to new physical settings, adult authorities, daily schedules, peer companions, and academic challenges.

• **EARLY ADJUSTMENT TO SCHOOL** • In a study of factors that predict effective transition to kindergarten, researchers observed children and interviewed their teachers at the end of preschool and again during their kindergarten year. Children who were cooperative and friendly when interacting with agemates in preschool seemed to transfer these skills to kindergarten. They were better liked by peers and more involved in classroom life. The presence of preschool friends in kindergarten also enhanced adaptation (Ladd & Price, 1987). The continuity of these ties may have provided children with a sense of stability in their otherwise changing school environments.

In further longitudinal research extending over the kindergarten year, children with more preschool experience scored higher on school readiness tests and showed increasingly positive school attitudes. Liking for school predicted greater classroom participation. And participation, in turn, predicted higher achievement. Furthermore, children with friendly, prosocial styles more easily made new friends, gained peer acceptance, and formed a warm bond with their teacher. These favorable relationships also predicted high achievement, perhaps by energizing cooperation and initiative in the classroom (Birch & Ladd, 1997; Ladd, Birch, & Buhs, 1999; Ladd, Buhs, & Seid, 2000; Ladd, Kochenderfer, & Coleman, 1997).

In contrast, kindergartners with antisocial styles (those who are argumentative and aggressive) tend to establish conflict-ridden relationships with teachers and peers, which impair their liking for school, classroom participation, and achievement. And peer-avoidant kindergartners often become overly dependent on teachers, clinging and asking for help when they do not really need it (Birch & Ladd, 1998). These early, poor-quality teacher–child relationships predict academic and behavior problems through elementary school (Hamre & Pianta, 2001).

Figure 15.9 summarizes factors linked to favorable adaptation to kindergarten. A look at these factors suggests that parents can foster good school adjustment by encouraging positive social skills and arranging for their child to attend preschool. In planning the composition of kindergarten classrooms, educators might consider grouping children with their friends. And positive teacher–child ties, while important for all children, are crucial for preventing lasting school difficulties in poorly adjusted kindergartners.

• **SCHOOL TRANSITIONS IN ADOLESCENCE** • Early adolescence is a second important period of school transition: Students typically move from an intimate, self-contained elementary school classroom to a much larger, impersonal secondary school where they must shift from one class to the next. With each school change—from elementary to middle or junior high school and then to high school—adolescents' grades decline. The drop is partly due to tighter academic standards. At the same time, the transition to secondary school often brings less personal attention, more whole-class

Ⓢ Moving from a small, self-contained elementary school classroom to a large, impersonal secondary school is stressful for adolescents. As this cafeteria line suggests, feelings of anonymity increase. Also, school grades and extracurricular participation decline.

© John Maher/Stock Boston, LLC

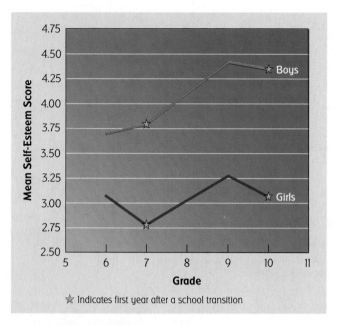

☆ Indicates first year after a school transition

▲ **Figure 15.10**

Self-esteem from sixth to tenth grade in 6–3–3 schools. In this longitudinal study of more than 300 adolescents, boys' self-esteem remained stable after school transition. In contrast, girls' self-esteem dropped sharply in the year after each school change. (Adapted from Simmons & Blyth, 1987.)

instruction, and less chance to participate in classroom decision making (Seidman, Aber, & French, 2004).

In view of these changes, it is not surprising that students rate their middle or junior-high school learning experiences less favorably than their elementary school experiences (Wigfield & Eccles, 1994). They also report that their middle-school teachers care less about them, are less friendly, grade less fairly, and stress competition more and mastery and improvement less. Consequently, many young people feel less academically competent and experience a drop in motivation (Anderman & Midgley, 1997).

Inevitably, each of these transitions requires students to readjust their feelings of self-confidence and self-worth as academic expectations are revised and students enter a more complex social world. A comprehensive study revealed that the timing of school transition is important, especially for girls (Simmons & Blyth, 1987). More than 300 adolescents living in a large Midwestern city were followed from sixth to tenth grade. Some were enrolled in school districts with a 6–3–3 grade organization (a K–6 elementary school, a 3-year junior high, and a 3-year high school). These students made two school changes, one to junior high and one to high school. A comparison group attended schools with an 8–4 grade organization. They made only one school transition, from a K–8 elementary school to high school.

For the sample as a whole, grade point average dropped and feelings of anonymity increased after each transition. Participation in extracurricular activities declined more in the 6–3–3 than in the 8–4 arrangement, the drop being greater for girls. Furthermore, in 8–4 schools, school transition led to gains in self-esteem. In contrast, in 6–3–3 schools, sex differences in self-esteem were striking. Whereas boys remained stable, girls showed a drop with each school change (see Figure 15.10).

These findings show that any school transition is likely to depress adolescents' psychological well-being temporarily, but the earlier it occurs, the more dramatic and long lasting its impact. Girls in 6–3–3 schools fared poorest, the researchers argued, because movement to junior high tended to coincide with other life changes—namely, the onset of puberty and dating. Adolescents who face added strains, such as family disruption, poverty, low levels of involvement and support from parents, or learned helplessness on academic tasks, are at greatest risk for self-esteem and academic difficulties (Rudolph et al., 2001; Seidman et al., 2003).

Distressed young people whose school performance drops sharply often show a persisting pattern of poor self-esteem, motivation, and achievement. In another study, researchers compared "multiple-problem" youths (those having both academic and mental-health problems), youths having difficulties in just one area (either academic or mental health), and well-adjusted youths (those doing well in both areas) across the transition to high school. Although all groups declined in grade point average, well-adjusted students continued to get high marks and multiple-problem youths low marks, with the other groups falling in between. And as Figure 15.11 shows, the multiple-problem youths showed a far greater rise in truancy and out-of-school problem behaviors (Roeser, Eccles, & Freedman-Doan, 1999). For some, school transition initiates a downward spiral in academic performance and school involvement that leads to dropping out.

• **HELPING ADOLESCENTS ADJUST TO SCHOOL TRANSITIONS** • As the findings just reviewed reveal, school transitions often lead to environmental changes that fit poorly with adolescents' developmental needs. They disrupt close relationships with teachers at a time when adolescents need adult support. They emphasize competition during a period of heightened self-focusing. They reduce decision making and choice as the desire for autonomy is increasing. And they interfere with peer networks as young people become more concerned with peer acceptance.

Enhanced support from parents, teachers, and peers eases the strain of school transition. Parental involvement, monitoring, and autonomy granting are associated with better adjustment after entering middle or junior high school (Grolnick et al., 2000). Because most students do better in an 8–4 school arrangement, school districts thinking about reorganization should seriously consider this plan. Also, forming smaller units within large schools permits closer relations with teachers and peers and greater extracurricular involvement (Seidman, Aber, & French, 2004).

Other, less extensive changes are also effective. During the first year after a school transition, homerooms can be provided in which teachers offer academic and personal counseling and work closely with parents to promote favorable school adjustment. Students can also be assigned to classes with several familiar peers or a constant group of new peers—arrangements that promote emotional security and social support. In schools that intervened in these ways, students followed for 3 to 5 years were less likely to decline in academic performance and to display other adjustment problems, including low self-esteem, depression, substance abuse, delinquency, and dropping out of school (Felner et al., 2002).

Finally, teenagers' perceptions of the sensitivity and flexibility of their school learning environments contribute substantially to successful school transitions. When schools minimize competition and differential treatment by ability, middle- and junior-high school students are less likely to feel angry and depressed, to be truant, or to show declines in academic values, self-esteem, and achievement (Roeser, Eccles, & Sameroff, 2000). School rules that strike young people as fair rather than punitive also foster satisfaction with school life (Eccles et al., 1993).

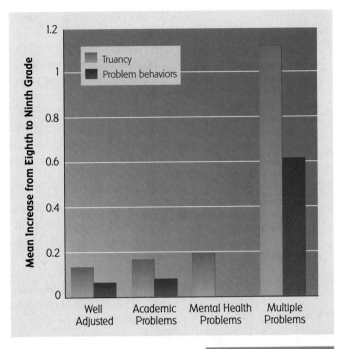

▲ **Figure 15.11**

Increase in truancy and out-of-school problem behaviors across the transition to high school in four groups of students. Well-adjusted students, students with only academic problems, and students with only mental health problems showed little change. (Good students with mental health problems actually declined in problem behaviors, so no blue bar is shown for them.) In contrast, multiple-problem students—with both academic and mental health difficulties—increased sharply in truancy and problem behaviors after changing schools from eighth to ninth grade.

(Adapted from Roeser, Eccles, & Freedman-Doan, 1999.)

Teacher–Student Interaction

The classroom is a complex social system in which teachers engage in as many as 1,000 exchanges with students each day (Jackson, 1968). A vast amount of research exists on teacher–student interaction, most focusing on its significance for academic achievement.

Elementary and secondary school students describe good teachers as caring, helpful, and stimulating—behaviors associated with gains in students' motivation, achievement, and favorable peer relations (Daniels, Kalkman, & McCombs, 2001; Davis, 2003). But with respect to stimulation, a disappointing finding is that too many U.S. teachers emphasize repetitive drill over higher-level thinking, grappling with ideas, and applying knowledge to new situations (Campbell, Hombo, & Mazzeo, 2000). In a longitudinal investigation of more than 5,000 seventh graders, those in more stimulating, academically demanding classrooms showed better attendance and larger gains in math achievement over the following two years (Phillips, 1997).

As we have already seen, teachers do not interact in the same way with all children. Well-behaved, high-achieving students typically get more encouragement and praise, whereas unruly students have more conflicts with teachers and receive more criticism from them (Henricsson & Rydell, 2004). Caring teacher–student relationships have a stronger impact on the achievement and social behavior of low-SES minority young people (Crosno, Kirkpatrick, & Elder, 2004; Meehan, Hughes, & Cavell, 2003). But overall, higher-SES students—who tend to be higher achieving and to have fewer discipline problems—have closer, more sensitive and supportive relationships with teachers (Pianta, Hamre, & Stuhlman, 2003).

Unfortunately, once teachers' attitudes toward students are established, they can become more extreme than is warranted by students' behavior. A special concern is **educational self-fulfilling prophecies**: Children may adopt teachers' positive or negative views and start to live up to them.[1] As early as first grade, teachers' beliefs in children's ability to learn predict students' year-end achievement progress after controlling for students' beginning-of-year performance. This effect is particularly strong when teachers emphasize competition and publicly compare children, regularly favoring the best students (Kuklinski & Weinstein, 2001; Weinstein, 2002).

---

[1]Most research on self-fulfilling prophecies focuses on teacher–student relationships, but the effect can occur in other social contexts, such as parent–child and peer relationships.

Teacher expectations have a greater impact on low achievers than high achievers (Madom, Jussim, & Eccles, 1997). High-achieving students have less room to improve when teachers think well of them, and when a teacher is critical, they can fall back on their long history of success. Low-achieving students' sensitivity to self-fulfilling prophecies can be beneficial when teachers believe in them, but unfortunately, biased teacher judgments are usually slanted in a negative direction. In one study, African-American children were especially responsive to negative teacher expectations in reading, and girls were especially responsive to negative teacher expectations in math (McKown & Weinstein, 2002). Recall our discussion of *stereotype threat* in Chapter 8. A child in the position of confirming a negative stereotype may respond with anxiety and reduced motivation, increasing the likelihood of a negative self-fulfilling prophecy.

Grouping Practices

In many schools, students are grouped by ability or tracked into classes in which students of similar achievement levels are taught together. The practice is designed to reduce the need for teachers to meet a wide range of academic needs.

• **GROUPING IN ELEMENTARY SCHOOL** • *Homogeneous* groups or classes can be a potent source of self-fulfilling prophecies (Smith et al., 1998). Low-group students get more drill on basic facts and skills, engage in less discussion, and progress at a slower learning pace. Gradually, they show a drop in self-esteem and are viewed by themselves and others as "not smart." Not surprisingly, homogeneous grouping widens the gap between high and low achievers (Dornbusch, Glasgow, & Lin, 1996).

Partly because of this finding, some schools have increased the *heterogeneity* of student groups by combining two or three adjacent grades. In *multigrade classrooms,* academic achievement, self-esteem, and attitudes toward school are usually more favorable than in the single-grade arrangement, perhaps because multigrade classrooms often decrease competition and increase harmony (Lloyd, 1999; Ong, Allison, & Haladyna, 2000). Multigrade grouping also affords opportunities for peer tutoring that may contribute to favorable outcomes.

When older or more expert students teach younger or less expert students, both tutors and tutees benefit in self-esteem and achievement (Renninger, 1998).

Finally, recall from our discussion of Vygotsky's theory in Chapter 6 that for expert children to promote learning in less expert children, participants must resolve conflicts, share responsibility, and consider one another's ideas. In North American classrooms, however, small heterogeneous groups of students working together often engage in poorer-quality interaction (less accurate explanations and answers) than homogeneous groups of above-average students (Webb, Nemer, & Chizhik, 1998). In Chapter 6, we noted that for collaboration between heterogeneous peers to succeed, children often need extensive guidance (see page 264). When teachers provide this assistance, heterogeneous classrooms are desirable into middle or junior high school, effectively supporting the motivation and achievement of students who vary widely in academic progress (Gilles, 2003; Gillies & Ashman, 1996).

Ⓢ These second and third graders learn together during a visit to their school library. Compared to children in the typical single-grade arrangement, children in multigrade classrooms are usually advantaged in academic achievement, self-esteem, and attitudes toward school.
© Guy Cali/The Stock Connection

• **GROUPING IN HIGH SCHOOL** • By high school, some homogeneous grouping is unavoidable because certain aspects of education must dovetail with the young person's educational and vocational plans. In the United States and Canada, high school students are counseled into college preparatory, vocational, or general education tracks. Unfortunately, this system perpetuates educational inequalities of earlier years.

Low-SES minority students are assigned in large numbers to noncollege tracks. Longitudinal research following thousands of U.S. students from eighth to twelfth grade reveals that assignment to a college track accelerates academic progress, whereas assignment to a vocational or general education track decelerates it (Hallinan & Kubitschek, 1999). Even in secondary schools that do not have an overarching tracking program, low-SES minority students tend to be assigned to lower course levels in most or all of their academic subjects, resulting in *de facto* (unofficial) *tracking* that sorts students into classes on the basis of their SES and ethnicity (Lucas & Behrends, 2002).

Once a student is assigned to a low track or to lower-level courses, breaking out is difficult. Track or class enrollment is generally based on the student's past performance, which is limited by history of placement. Interviews with black students in one high school revealed that many thought their previous performance did not reflect their ability. Yet teachers and counselors, overburdened with other responsibilities, had little time to reconsider individual cases (Ogbu, 2003). When capable students (as indicated by their achievement test scores) end up in low tracks, they "sink" to the performance level of their trackmates. Furthermore, teachers of noncollege-track classes are less likely to communicate with parents about what they can do to support their adolescent's learning. Many minority parents, in turn, do not understand the tracking system, are unaware of their child's placement, and therefore do not intervene on behalf of their child (Dornbusch & Glasgow, 1997).

High school students are separated into academic and vocational tracks in virtually all industrialized nations. But in China, Japan, and most Western European countries, students take a national exam to determine their track placement in high school. The outcome usually fixes future possibilities for the young person. In North America, educational decisions are more fluid. Students who are not assigned to a college preparatory track or who do poorly in high school can still get a college education. But by the adolescent years, SES differences in quality of education and academic achievement have already sorted students more drastically than is the case in other countries. In the end, many young people do not benefit from this more open system. Compared with other Western nations, the United States and Canada have a higher percentage of young people who regard themselves as educational failures and drop out of high school—about 11 percent in both countries (Statistics Canada, 2004e; U.S. Department of Education, 2004b).

Teaching Students with Special Needs

So far, we have seen that effective teachers flexibly adjust their teaching strategies to accommodate students with a wide range of characteristics. These adjustments, however, are especially challenging when children have learning difficulties.

This boy has disengaged from his high school classroom as well as his classmates. If his inattentiveness is accompanied by other problematic personal, school, and family factors, he may be at risk of dropping out of school.
© Mary Kate Denny/PhotoEdit

• **CHILDREN WITH LEARNING DIFFICULTIES** • U.S. and Canadian legislation mandates that schools place children who require special supports for learning in the "least restrictive" environments that meet their educational needs. In **mainstreaming,** students with learning difficulties are placed in regular classrooms for part of the school day, a practice designed to prepare them better for participation in society. Largely as the result of parental pressures, mainstreaming has been extended to **full inclusion**—placement in regular classrooms full time.

Some mainstreamed students have *mild mental retardation*—their IQs fall between 55 and 70, and they also show problems in adaptive behavior, or skills of everyday living (American Psychiatric Association, 1994). But the largest number—5 to 10 percent of school-age children—have **learning disabilities,** great difficulty with one or more aspects of learning, usually reading. As a result, their achievement is considerably behind what would be expected on the basis of their IQ. The problems of these students cannot be traced to any obvious physical or emotional difficulty or to environmental disadvantage. Instead, subtle deficits in brain functioning are involved. Some disorders run in families, suggesting a genetic influence (Lyon, Fletcher, & Barnes, 2002). In many instances, the cause is unknown.

• **HOW EFFECTIVE ARE MAINSTREAMING AND FULL INCLUSION?** • Does placement of these students in regular classes provide appropriate learning experiences as well as integrated participation in classroom life? Although some mainstreamed and fully included students benefit academically, many do not. Achievement gains depend on both the severity of the disability and the support services available (Klingner et al., 1998). Furthermore, children with disabilities are often rejected by regular-classroom peers. Students with mental retardation are overwhelmed by the social skills of their classmates; they cannot interact adeptly in a conversation or game. And the processing deficits of some students with learning disabilities lead to problems in social awareness and responsiveness (Gresham & MacMillan, 1997; Sridhar & Vaughn, 2001).

Does this mean that children with special needs cannot be served in regular classrooms? Not necessarily. Children with mild to moderate learning difficulties do best under one of two

⊚ The pupil on the left, who has a learning disability, has been fully included in a regular classroom. Because his teacher takes special steps to encourage peer acceptance, individualizes instruction, minimizes comparisons with classmates, and promotes cooperative learning, this boy looks forward to school and is doing well. © Will Hart

conditions: (1) They are fully included but receive consistent support from a special education teacher, who consults with their regular teacher and spends time in their classroom each day, or (2) they receive instruction from a special education teacher in a resource room for part of the day and are mainstreamed for the remainder (Vaughn & Klingner, 1998; Weiner & Tardif, 2004).

In the regular classroom, special steps must be taken to promote peer acceptance. Cooperative learning and peer-tutoring experiences in which teachers guide children with learning difficulties and their classmates in working together lead to friendly interaction, improved peer acceptance, and achievement gains (Fuchs et al., 2002a, 2002b). Teachers can also prepare their class for the arrival of a student with special needs. Under these conditions, mainstreaming and full inclusion may foster emotional sensitivity and prosocial behavior among regular classmates.

Parent–School Partnerships

Regardless of students' abilities, parent involvement in education—keeping tabs on the child's progress, communicating often with teachers, and ensuring that the child is enrolled in challenging, well-taught classes—promotes students' academic motivation and achievement throughout elementary and secondary school (Hill & Taylor, 2004). In a study of a nationally representative sample of more than 15,000 U.S. students, parents' school involvement in eighth grade strongly predicted students' grade point average in tenth grade, beyond the influence of SES and previous academic achievement. This relationship held for each ethnic group included—black, white, Native American, and Asian (Keith et al., 1998). Parents who are in frequent contact with the school send a message to their child about the value of education, model constructive solutions to academic problems, and (as children get older) promote wise educational decisions. Involved parents also learn from other parents about which classes and teachers are the best and how to handle difficult situations. And teachers and parents are more likely to give students consistent messages about academic and behavioral expectations.

Families living in low-income, high-risk neighborhoods face daily stresses that reduce the energy they have for school involvement (Bowen, Bowen, & Ware, 2002). Yet stronger home–school links could relieve some of this stress. Schools can build parent–school partnerships in the following ways:

- Fostering personal relationships between parents and teachers
- Showing parents how to support their child's education at home
- Building bridges between minority home cultures and the culture of the school
- Developing assignments that give parents a meaningful role to play, such as having students find out about their parents' experiences while growing up
- Including parents in basic planning and governance so they remain invested in school goals.

⊚ How Well Educated Are North American Young People?

Our discussion has focused largely on how teachers can support the education of children and adolescents. Yet we have also seen in this and previous chapters that many factors—both within and outside schools—affect children's learning. Societal values, school resources, quality of teaching, and parental encouragement all play important roles. Nowhere are these multiple influences more apparent than when schooling is examined in cross-cultural perspective.

Cross-National Research on Academic Achievement

In international studies of reading, mathematics, and science achievement, young people in Hong Kong, Korea, and Japan are consistently top performers. Canada is among Western nations in the top tier. U.S. students, however, typically perform at the international average, and sometimes below it (Programme for International Student Assessment, 2000, 2003).

▶ **Figure 15.12**

Average mathematics scores of 15-year-olds by country. The Programme for International Student Assessment assessed achievement in many nations around the world. Japan, Korea, and Canada were among the top performers in mathematics, whereas the United States performed below the international average. Similar outcomes occurred in reading and science. (Adapted from Programme for International Student Assessment, 2005.)

	Country	Average Math Achievement Score
High-Performing Nations	Hong Kong	550
	Finland	544
	Korea, Republic of	542
	Netherlands	538
	Japan	534
	Canada	**532**
	Belgium	529
	United Kingdom	529
	Switzerland	527
	Australia	524
	New Zealand	523
Intermediate-Performing Nations	Czech Republic	516
	Iceland	515
	Denmark	514
	France	511
	Sweden	509
	Austria	505
	Germany	503
International Average = 500	Ireland	503
	Norway	495
	Luxembourg	493
	Hungary	490
	Poland	490
	Spain	485
	United States	**483**
Low-Performing Nations	Italy	466
	Portugal	466
	Greece	445
	Mexico	385

Why do U.S. students fall behind in academic accomplishments? According to international comparisons, instruction in the United States is not as challenging and focused as it is in other countries. In the Programme for International Student Assessment, which assessed the academic achievement of 15-year-olds in many countries, students were asked about their study habits. Compared with students in top-achieving nations listed in Figure 15.12, many more U.S. students reported studying by memorizing rather than relating information to previously acquired knowledge. And achievement varies much more among U.S. schools, suggesting that the United States is less equitable in the quality of education it provides (Programme for International Student Assessment, 2005).

Researchers have conducted in-depth research on learning environments in Asian nations, such as Japan, Korea, and Taiwan, to clarify the factors that support high achievement. Except for the influence of language on early counting skills (see Chapter 7, page 305), Asian students do not start school with cognitive advantages. Instead, a variety of social forces combine to foster a strong commitment to learning in Asian families and schools:

- *Cultural valuing of academic achievement.* In Japan, Korea, and Taiwan, natural resources are limited. Progress in science and technology is essential for academic well-being, so mastery of academic skills is vital. Compared to Western countries, these nations invest more in education, including paying higher salaries to teachers (United Nations Development Programme, 2002).

- *Emphasis on effort.* Japanese, Korean, and Taiwanese parents and teachers believe that all children have the potential to master challenging academic tasks if they work hard enough. North American parents and teachers, in contrast, tend to regard native ability as the key to academic success. These differences in attitude contribute to the fact that Asian parents devote many more hours to helping their children with homework (Stevenson, Lee, & Mu, 2000). And Asian youths, influenced by collectivist values, typically strive to achieve because effort is seen as a moral obligation—part of one's responsibility to family and community. In contrast, North American young people view working hard in individualistic terms—as a matter of personal choice (Bempchat & Drago-Severson, 1999).

- *High-quality education for all.* No separate ability groups exist in Japanese, Korean, and Taiwanese elementary schools. Instead, all students receive the same nationally mandated education. Academic lessons are particularly well organized and presented in ways that capture children's attention and encourage high-level thinking (Grow-Maienza, Hahn, & Joo, 2001). And observations in Japanese elementary schools reveal that teachers are three times as likely as U.S. teachers to work outside class with students who need additional help (Woodward & Ono, 2004).

Ⓖ In Japanese schools, a longer school day permits frequent alternation of academic instruction with pleasurable activity, an approach that fosters learning. During one of these breaks, Japanese elementary-school children enjoy a class in the art of calligraphy. © Cameramann/The Image Works

- *More time devoted to instruction.* In Japan, Hong Kong, and Taiwan, the school year is more than 50 days longer than in the United States and about 30 days longer than in Canada (World Education Services, 2005). And on a day-to-day basis, Asian teachers devote much more time to academic pursuits. But Asian schools are not regimented places. An 8-hour school day permits extra recesses, with plenty of time for play, field trips, and extracurricular activities. Frequent breaks may increase Asian children's capacity to learn (Pellegrini & Smith, 1998).

The Asian examples underscore that families, schools, and the larger society must work together to upgrade education. Over the past decade, Canada's international ranking has improved greatly, moving from average to among the world's best. Still, disparities exist: Canada's Atlantic provinces (Nova Scotia, Newfoundland, Prince Edward Island, and New Brunswick) and its territories perform below the Canadian average. Nevertheless, even the Atlantic provinces do far better than the United States (Learning Partnership, 2003). Currently, the United States is investing more tax dollars in elementary and secondary education and strengthening teacher preparation. In addition, many schools are working to increase parent involvement. The results of these efforts can been seen in recent national assessments of educational progress (U.S. Department of Education, 2003a). After two decades of decline, overall academic achievement in the United States has risen, although not enough to enhance its standing internationally.

Effective educational change must take into account the life backgrounds and future goals of students. As we will see next, besides improving academic instruction, special efforts are needed in vocational education to help non-college-bound youths prepare for productive work roles.

Making the Transition from School to Work

Approximately 25 percent of North American young people graduate from high school without plans to go to college. Although they are more likely to find employment than those who drop out, they have fewer work opportunities than high school graduates of several decades ago. About 15 percent of Canadian and 20 percent of U.S. recent high school graduates who do not continue their education are unemployed (Statistics Canada, 2004e; U.S. Department of Education, 2004b). When they do find work, most hold low-paid, unskilled jobs. In addition, they have few alternatives for vocational counseling and job placement as they transition from school to work (Shanahan, Mortimer, & Krüger, 2002).

North American employers regard the recent high school graduate as poorly prepared for a demanding, skilled occupation. Indeed, there is some truth to this conclusion. During high school, almost half of U.S. adolescents are employed—a greater percentage than in any other developed country. But most are middle-SES students in pursuit of spending money rather than vocational exploration and training. Low-income teenagers who need to contribute to family income find it harder to get jobs (U.S. Department of Education, 2004b).

Furthermore, the jobs adolescents hold are largely limited to low-level, repetitive tasks that provide little contact with adult supervisors. Involvement in such jobs is actually harmful. The more hours students work, the poorer their school attendance, the lower their grades, the less likely they are to participate in extracurricular activities, and the more likely they are to drop out (Marsh & Kleitman, 2005). Students working at part-time jobs also feel more distant from their parents and report more drug and alcohol use and delinquent acts (Barling, Rogers, & Kelloway, 1995; Kouvonen & Kivivuori, 2001). And perhaps because of the menial nature of their jobs, employed teenagers tend to be cynical about work life. Many admit to having stolen from their employers (Steinberg, Fegley, & Dornbusch, 1993).

When work experiences are specially designed to meet educational and vocational goals, outcomes are different. Participation in work–study programs is related to positive school and work attitudes and improved academic achievement among low-SES teenagers (Hamilton & Hamilton, 2000). Yet high-quality vocational preparation for non-college-bound North American adolescents is scarce. Unlike some European

Ⓖ Teenagers' employment opportunities are generally limited to menial work. This 16-year-old spends his work hours loading produce in baskets at a farmer's market—a task that does little to extend his knowledge and skills.
© Elena Rooraid/PhotoEdit

nations, the United States and Canada have no widespread training systems to prepare youths for skilled business and industrial occupations and manual trades (Heinz, 1999a).

In Germany, adolescents who do not go to a *Gymnasium* (college-preparatory high school) have access to one of the most successful work–study apprenticeship systems in the world for entering business and industry. About two-thirds of German youths participate. After completing full-time schooling at age 15 or 16, they spend the remaining two years of compulsory education in the *Berufsschule*, which offers part-time vocational courses that they combine with an apprenticeship, which is jointly planned by educators and employers. Students train in work settings for more than 400 blue- and white-collar occupations. Apprentices who complete the program and pass a qualifying examination are certified as skilled workers and earn union-set wages. Businesses provide financial support because they know that the program guarantees a competent, dedicated work force (Heinz, 1999b; Kerckhoff, 2002). Many apprentices are hired into well-paid jobs by the firms that train them.

The success of the German system—and of similar systems in Austria, Denmark, Switzerland, and several East European countries—suggests that a national apprenticeship program would improve the transition from high school to work for North American young people. Nevertheless, implementing an apprenticeship system poses major challenges. Among these are overcoming the reluctance of employers to assume part of the responsibility for vocational training, ensuring cooperation between schools and businesses, and preventing low-SES youths from being concentrated in the lowest-skilled apprenticeship placements, an obstacle that Germany itself has not yet fully overcome (Hamilton & Hamilton, 2000). Currently, small-scale school-to-work projects are under way, in an effort to solve these problems and build bridges between learning and working in the United States and Canada.

A head chef explains food preparation to an apprentice in training. In Germany, high-quality vocational education combined with apprenticeships enable youths who do not go to college to enter well-paid careers. Similar programs in North America could ease the transition from school to work. © Richard Pasley/Stock Boston, LLC

Ask Yourself

REVIEW	List educational practices that promote positive attitudes toward school and academic achievement, and explain why each is effective.
APPLY	Ray is convinced that his 5-year-old son Tripper would learn more in school if only Tripper's kindergarten would provide more teacher-directed lessons and worksheets and reduce the time devoted to learning-center activities. Is Ray correct? Explain.
CONNECT	What common factors contribute to the high academic achievement of students in Asian nations and to the academic success of immigrant youths, discussed on page 50 in Chapter 2?
REFLECT	Describe your experiences in making the transition to middle or junior high school and then to high school. What made these transitions stressful? What helped you adjust?

Summary

The Importance of Peer Relations

Discuss evidence indicating that both parental and peer relationships are vital for children's development.

Research on nonhuman primates suggests that parent and peer relations complement one another. The parent–child bond provides children with the security to enter the world of peers. Peer interaction, in turn, permits children to expand social skills acquired within the family. Studies of peer-only-reared monkeys and human children reveal that peer relations can, to some extent, stand in for the early parent–child bond. However, development is more favorable under typical parental and peer upbringing than under peer-only rearing.

Development of Peer Sociability

Trace the development of peer sociability from infancy into adolescence.

Peer sociability begins in infancy with isolated social acts that are gradually replaced by coordinated exchanges in the second year of life. During the preschool years, interactive play with peers increases.

According to Parten, it moves from **nonsocial activity** to **parallel play** and then to **associative** and **cooperative play.** However, these play forms do not unfold in a straightforward developmental sequence. Despite increases in associative and cooperative play, solitary play and parallel play remain common. Sociodramatic play becomes especially frequent and supports many aspects of cognitive, emotional, and social development.

During middle childhood, peer interaction is more sensitively tuned to others' perspectives, governed by prosocial norms, and focused on rule-oriented games. In addition, **rough-and-tumble play** becomes more common. In our evolutionary past, it may have been important for developing fighting skill and establishing **dominance hierarchies,** which become more stable in middle childhood and adolescence, especially among boys.

Influences on Peer Sociability

How do parental encouragement, age mix of children, and cultural values influence peer sociability?

Parents influence children's peer sociability both directly, through attempts to influence their child's peer relations, and indirectly, through their child-rearing practices and play behaviors. Preschoolers tend to be more socially competent when their parents often arrange informal peer contact and offer guidance on how to act toward others. Secure attachment, authoritative child rearing, inductive discipline, and emotionally positive and cooperative parent–child play foster positive peer relations. And when parents have high-quality social networks, children tend to be more socially skilled.

Although same-age peers engage in more intense and harmonious exchanges, mixed-age interaction has benefits. It provides older children with practice in prosocial behavior and younger children with opportunities to learn from their older companions.

© BILL ARON/PHOTOEDIT

In collectivist societies, large-group, imitative play is common. When caregivers value the cognitive and educational benefits of make-believe and stress individuality and self-expression, sociodramatic play occurs more often. Sociodramatic play may be particularly important for social development in societies where child and adult worlds are distinct.

Friendship

Describe children's developing concepts of friendship, characteristics of friendships in childhood and adolescence, and implications of friendship for psychological adjustment.

Preschool and young school-age children view **friendship** as a concrete relationship based on shared activities and material goods. During middle childhood, children come to understand friendship as a mutual relationship based on trust. Teenagers stress intimacy, mutual understanding, and loyalty as the basis of friendship.

With age, children become more selective about their friendships; number of best friends declines during middle childhood and adolescence. In addition, friendships become more stable and prosocial with age. At the same time, close friends are more likely than nonfriends to disagree and compete, providing contexts in which children learn to tolerate criticism and resolve disputes. However, for aggressive children, friendships often magnify antisocial acts.

Throughout childhood and adolescence, friends tend to be alike in sex, ethnicity, SES, personality, popularity, achievement, and prosocial behavior. By adolescence, they resemble one another in identity status, educational aspirations, political beliefs, and deviance. As adolescents forge a personal identity, they sometimes explore new perspectives by befriending agemates with differing attitudes and values. Young people who attend ethnically diverse schools and live in integrated neighborhoods are more likely to form cross-ethnic friendships.

Girls emphasize emotional closeness in their friendships more than boys do. However, androgynous boys are just as likely as girls to form intimate friendships. In early adolescence, very popular or very unpopular agemates are more likely to have other-sex friends. Compared with girls, boys have more other-sex friends and benefit in terms of feelings of competence.

Warm, gratifying friendships foster self-concept, perspective taking, and identity development, provide a foundation for intimate relationships, offer support in dealing with everyday stresses, and promote positive attitudes toward and involvement in school.

Aggressive friendships, however, seriously undermine development and adjustment.

Peer Acceptance

Describe major categories of peer acceptance, the relationship of physical appearance and social behavior to likability, and ways to help rejected children.

Researchers usually assess **peer acceptance** using **sociometric techniques,** which measure social preferences. Another approach is to assess **peer reputation,** or social prominence—children's judgments of whom their classmates most admire.

Sociometric techniques yield four types of peer acceptance: (1) **popular children,** who are liked by many agemates; (2) **rejected children,** who are actively disliked; (3) **controversial children,** who are both liked and disliked; and (4) **neglected children,** who are seldom chosen, either positively or negatively. As with friendship, peer acceptance contributes uniquely to children's adjustment. Rejected children often experience lasting adjustment problems.

Two subtypes of popular children exist: **popular-prosocial children,** who are academically and socially competent, and **popular-antisocial children,** who are aggressive youngsters whom peers admire, perhaps because of their sophisticated but devious social skills. Rejected children also fall into at least two subtypes: **rejected-aggressive children,** who show high rates of conduct problems, and **rejected-withdrawn children,** who are passive and socially awkward and at risk for **peer victimization.** Controversial children blend positive, prosocial acts with hostile, disruptive behavior. Although neglected children often choose to play by themselves, they are usually socially competent and well adjusted.

© MICHAEL NEWMAN/ PHOTOEDIT

Interventions that lead to gains in rejected children's peer acceptance include coaching in social skills, intensive academic tutoring, and training in perspective taking and social problem solving. Teaching rejected children to attribute peer difficulties to internal, changeable causes motivates them to improve their peer relations. Nevertheless, because socially incompetent behavior often originates in maladaptive parent–child interaction, interventions focusing only on the rejected child are usually not sufficient.

Peer Groups

Describe peer groups in middle childhood and adolescence and their consequences for development.

⑨ By the end of middle childhood, **peer groups** with shared values and standards for behavior and a social structure of leaders and followers emerge. They organize on the basis of proximity (being in the same classroom) and similarity in sex, ethnicity, and popularity. Within peer groups, children practice cooperation, leadership, followership, and loyalty to collective goals.

⑨ Early adolescent peer groups are organized around **cliques,** or small groups of friends with common attitudes and values. Often several cliques form a larger, more loosely organized group called a **crowd** that grants the adolescent an identity within the larger social structure of the school. Although teenagers' interests and abilities affect group membership, parenting practices are also influential. Many peer-group values are extensions of values taught at home.

Dating

⑨ Mixed-sex cliques provide a supportive context for boys and girls to get to know each other. Intimacy in dating relationships, however, lags behind that in friendships, and early, frequent dating is linked to adjustment problems. Positive relationships with parents and friends contribute to the development of warm romantic ties, which enhance emotional and social development. First romances generally dissolve or become less satisfying after graduation from high school.

Peer Pressure and Conformity

What factors influence conformity to peer pressure?

⑨ Peer conformity is greater in adolescence than at younger or older ages, and young teenagers are especially susceptible. However, most peer pressures focus on short-term, day-to-day matters (such as dress and taste in music) and do not conflict with important adult values. Authoritative parenting is related to resistance to peer pressure.

Television

Cite factors that affect how much time children devote to TV viewing, and describe age-related changes in television literacy.

⑨ Children spend more time watching TV than in virtually any other waking activity. Boys and low-SES children tend to be more frequent viewers. Excessive TV watching is linked to family and peer difficulties.

⑨ Cognitive development and experience in watching TV gradually lead to gains in **television literacy.** Before age 8, children do not fully grasp the unreality of TV fiction, assimilate televised information piecemeal, and cannot critically evaluate it.

Discuss the influence of television on children's development, including aggression, ethnic and gender stereotypes, consumerism, academic learning, prosocial behavior, and imagination.

⑨ Studies with a wide variety of research designs indicate that televised violence promotes hostile thoughts and emotions, aggressive behavior, tolerance of aggression in others, and a violent view of the world. TV also conveys stereotypes that affect children's beliefs about ethnicity and gender. Not until age 8 or 9 do they understand the selling purpose of TV commercials. Heavy bombardment of children and youth with advertising contributes to many problems, including family stress, overweight and obesity, and substance use.

⑨ Children pick up many cognitive and academic skills from educational television. Programs with slow-paced action and easy-to-follow story lines foster more elaborate make-believe play, and those with acts of cooperating, helping, and comforting can increase prosocial behavior. Heavy TV viewers of prime-time shows and cartoons, however, spend less time reading and interacting with others and achieve less well in school.

Computers

Discuss computer use of children and adolescents, noting benefits and concerns.

⑨ Computers can have rich educational benefits. In classrooms, students often use computers collaboratively. When children use the computer for word processing, they produce longer, higher-quality written products. Programming promotes improved concept formation, problem solving, and creativity, and as children get older, they often use the computer and the Web for school assign-

ments. However, gender and SES differences exist, with boys and higher-SES young people advantaged in computer skills and confidence in using computers.

⑨ Although boys' extensive use of computers for game play fosters selective attention and spatial skills, violent games promote hostility and aggression. "Passionate" game players tend to be withdrawn young people with family and school problems.

⑨ Using the Internet to communicate seems to support closeness between adolescent friends. But many teenagers meet new people online. Although some online ties are positive, most teenagers who form close friendships or romances on the Internet tend to be troubled young people who seek to relieve feelings of isolation and rejection and who are at risk for exploitation.

Schooling

Discuss the influence of class and student body size and teachers' educational philosophies on academic and social development.

⑨ Schools powerfully influence many aspects of development. Smaller classes in the early elementary grades lead to lasting gains in academic achievement. In small high schools, adolescents are more actively involved in extracurricular activities and develop a sense of responsibility, competence, and challenge from these experiences. Also, "marginal" students are more likely to participate and remain until graduation.

⑨ Teachers' educational philosophies play a major role in children's learning experiences. Older students in **traditional classrooms** have a slight edge in academic achievement over those in **constructivist classrooms,** who are more likely to be critical thinkers, to respect individual differences, and to have positive attitudes toward school. Preschool and kindergarten children in traditional classrooms display more stress behaviors and reduced confidence in their abilities, followed by poorer study habits and achievement that persist through elementary school.

⑨ Students in **social-constructivist classrooms** benefit in both cognitive and social development from working collaboratively with teachers and peers. In classrooms organized as **communities of learners,** collaboration becomes a school-wide value. Teachers and students work on complex, long-term projects with real-world meaning, drawing on one another's expertises and on those of others within and beyond the school.

Cite factors that affect adjustment following school transitions in early childhood and in adolescence.

◉ Factors that predict favorable adjustment in kindergarten include preschool experience, a friendly, prosocial behavioral style, positive school attitudes, supportive ties to peers and teachers, and classroom participation. Kindergartners with antisocial and peer-avoidant styles tend to establish conflict-ridden relationships with teachers, which predict academic and behavior problems.

◉ School transitions in adolescence can be stressful. As school environments become larger and more impersonal, both grades and feelings of competence decline. Girls experience more adjustment difficulties after the transition from elementary to middle or junior high school, since other life changes (puberty and the beginning of dating) tend to occur at the same time. Distressed young people whose school performance drops sharply are at greatest risk for continuing academic difficulties and alienation from school.

Discuss the role of teacher–student interaction and grouping practices in academic achievement.

◉ Patterns of teacher–student interaction affect children's academic progress. Instruction that encourages higher-level thinking is associated with greater student interest and achievement. **Educational self-fulfilling prophecies** are most likely to occur in classrooms that emphasize competition and public evaluation, and they have a greater impact on low achievers.

◉ Homogeneous grouping in elementary school is linked to poorer-quality instruction and a drop in self-esteem and achievement for children in low-ability groups. In contrast, multigrade classrooms promote academic achievement, self-esteem, and positive school attitudes. However, teachers must provide extensive guidance for collaboration between heterogeneous peers to succeed.

◉ By high school, separate educational tracks that dovetail with adolescents' future plans are necessary. Unfortunately, high school tracking in the United States and Canada usually extends the educational inequalities of earlier years. Low-SES students are at risk for unfair placement in noncollege tracks.

Under what conditions is placement of mildly mentally retarded and learning-disabled children in regular classrooms successful, and how can schools increase parent involvement in education?

◉ Some students with mild mental retardation and many with **learning disabilities** are placed in regular classrooms, usually through **mainstreaming** but also through **full inclusion.** The success of regular classroom placement depends on tailoring learning experiences to children's academic needs and promoting positive peer relations.

◉ Schools can increase parent involvement by fostering communication between parents and teachers, building bridges between minority home cultures and the culture of the school, and involving parents in school governance. Reaching out to ethnic minority parents and to parents in poverty-stricken, inner-city areas is especially important.

How Well Educated are North American Young People?

How well are North American young people achieving compared with their counterparts in other industrialized nations, and what prevents North American non-college-bound youths from making an effective school-to-work transition?

◉ In international studies, young people in Asian nations are consistently top performers, and Canada is among Western nations in the top tier. U.S. students, however, typically score at the international average, and sometimes below it. Strong cultural commitment to learning, which pervades homes and schools, is responsible for the academic success of Asian students.

◉ Non-college-bound high school graduates need assistance in making an effective transition from school to work. Unlike their European counterparts, notably Germany, adolescents in the United States and Canada have no widespread vocational training system to assist them in preparing for challenging, well-paid careers in business, industry, and manual trades.

◉ Important Terms and Concepts

associative play (p. 599)
clique (p. 613)
community of learners (p. 629)
constructivist classroom (p. 627)
controversial children (p. 609)
cooperative play (p. 599)
crowd (p. 613)
dominance hierarchy (p. 601)
educational self-fulfilling prophecy
   (p. 633)
friendship (p. 604)

full inclusion (p. 635)
learning disability (p. 635)
mainstreaming (p. 635)
neglected children (p. 609)
nonsocial activity (p. 599)
parallel play (p. 599)
peer acceptance (p. 609)
peer group (p. 613)
peer reputation (p. 609)
peer victimization (p. 611)
popular children (p. 609)

popular-antisocial children (p. 610)
popular-prosocial children (p. 610)
rejected children (p. 609)
rejected-aggressive children (p. 610)
rejected-withdrawn children (p. 610)
rough-and-tumble play (p. 600)
social-constructivist classroom (p. 629)
sociometric techniques (p. 609)
television literacy (p. 620)
traditional classroom (p. 627)

✿ GLOSSARY

A

A-not-B search error The error made by 8- to 12-month-olds after an object is moved from hiding place A to hiding place B. Infants in Piaget's sensorimotor Substage 4 search for it only in the first hiding place. (p. 223)

Aboriginal Head Start A Canadian federal program that provides First Nations, Inuit, and Métis children younger than age 6 with preschool education and nutritional and health services and that encourages parent involvement in program planning and children's learning. It also builds on the children's knowledge of Aboriginal languages and cultures. (p. 342)

accommodation In Piaget's theory, that part of adaptation in which an individual creates new schemes and adjusts old schemes to produce a better fit with the environment. Distinguished from *assimilation*. (p. 221)

achievement motivation The tendency to persist at challenging tasks. (p. 452)

achievement test A test that assesses actual knowledge and skill attainment. Distinguished from *aptitude test*. (p. 323)

adaptation In Piaget's theory, the process of building schemes through direct interaction with the environment. Consists of two complementary activities: *assimilation* and *accommodation*. (p. 221)

affordances The action possibilities a situation offers an organism with certain motor capabilities. Discovery of affordances plays a major role in perceptual differentiation. (p. 163)

age of viability The age at which the fetus can first survive if born early. Occurs sometime between 22 and 26 weeks. (p. 89)

allele Each of two or more forms of a gene located at the same place on the chromosomes. (p. 74)

amnion The inner membrane that forms a protective covering around the prenatal organism and encloses it in amniotic fluid, which helps keep temperature constant and provides a cushion against jolts caused by the mother's movement. (p. 87)

amodal sensory properties Information that is not specific to a single modality but, rather, overlaps two or more sensory systems. Examples include rate, rhythm, duration, intensity, and (for vision and hearing) temporal synchrony. (p. 160)

analogical problem solving Taking a solution strategy from one problem and applying it to other relevant problems. (p. 229)

androgens Hormones released chiefly by the testes, and in smaller amounts by the adrenal glands, that influence the pubertal growth spurt and stimulate muscle growth, body and facial hair, and male sex characteristics. (p. 178)

androgyny A type of gender identity in which the person scores high on both traditionally masculine and feminine personality characteristics. (p. 538)

animistic thinking The belief that inanimate objects have lifelike qualities, such as thoughts, wishes, feelings, and intentions. (p. 236)

anorexia nervosa An eating disorder in which young people (usually females) starve themselves because of a compulsive fear of getting fat and an extremely distorted body image. (p. 204)

Apgar Scale A rating system used to assess the newborn baby's physical condition immediately after birth on the basis of five characteristics: heart rate, respiratory effort, reflex irritability, muscle tone, and color. (p. 105)

aptitude test A test that assesses an individual's potential to learn a specialized activity. Distinguished from *achievement test*. (p. 323)

assimilation In Piaget's theory, that part of adaptation in which an individual uses current schemes to interpret the external world. Distinguished from *accommodation*. (p. 221)

associative play A form of true social participation in which children engage in separate activities but interact by exchanging toys and commenting on one another's behavior. Distinguished from *nonsocial activity, parallel play,* and *cooperative play.* (p. 559)

attachment The strong, affectionate tie that humans have with special people in their lives and that leads them to feel pleasure when interacting with them and to be comforted by their nearness during times of stress. (p. 419)

Attachment Q-Sort An alternative method to the Strange Situation, suitable for children between 1 and 4 years of age, that permits attachment quality to be assessed through observations in the home. Includes a set of 90 descriptors of child behavior that better reflects the parent–infant relationship in everyday life. (p. 422)

attention-deficit hyperactivity disorder (ADHD) A childhood disorder that involves inattention, impulsivity, and excessive motor activity. Often leads to academic and social problems. (p. 284)

attribution retraining An approach to intervention that uses adult feedback to modify the attributions of learned-helpless children, encouraging them to believe that they can overcome failure by exerting more effort. (p. 455)

attributions Common, everyday explanations for the causes of behavior. (p. 452)

authoritarian child-rearing style A child-rearing style that is low in acceptance and involvement, high in coercive and psychological control, and low in autonomy granting. Distinguished from *authoritative, permissive,* and *uninvolved child-rearing styles.* (p. 564)

authoritative child-rearing style A child-rearing style that is high in acceptance and involvement, that emphasizes adaptive control techniques, and that includes appropriate autonomy granting. Distinguished from *authoritarian, permissive,* and *uninvolved child-rearing styles.* (p. 564)

autobiographical memory Representations of special, one-time events that are long-lasting because they are instilled with personal meaning. (p. 291)

autonomous morality Piaget's second stage of moral development, in which children view rules as flexible, socially agreed-on principles that can be revised to suit the will of the majority. (p. 486)

autonomy In adolescence, a sense of oneself as a separate, self-governing individual. Involves relying more on oneself and less on parents for support and guidance and engaging in careful, well-reasoned decision making. (p. 569)

autosomes The 22 matching chromosome pairs in each human cell. (p. 73)

avoidant attachment The quality of insecure attachment characterizing infants who are usually not distressed by parental separation and who avoid the parent when she returns. Distinguished from *secure, resistant,* and *disorganized/disoriented attachment.* (p. 422)

B

babbling Repetition of consonant–vowel combinations in long strings, beginning around 4 months of age. (p. 364)

basic emotions Emotions that are universal in humans and other primates, have a long evolutionary history of promoting survival, and can be directly inferred from facial expressions. Includes happiness, interest, surprise, fear, anger, sadness, and disgust. (p. 399)

behavior modification Procedures that combine conditioning and modeling to eliminate undesirable behaviors and increase desirable responses. (p. 20)

behavioral genetics A field devoted to uncovering the hereditary and environmental origins of individual differences in human traits and abilities. (p. 114)

behaviorism An approach that views directly observable events—stimuli and responses—as the appropriate focus of study and the development of behavior as taking place through classical and operant conditioning. (p. 19)

belief–desire theory of mind The theory of mind that emerges around age 4 in which both beliefs and desires determine behavior. Closely resembles the everyday psychology of adults. (p. 442)

biased sampling Failure to select participants who are representative of the population of interest in a study. (p. 58)

bicultural identity The identity constructed by adolescents who explore and adopt values from both their subculture and the dominant culture. (p. 461)

binocular depth cues Depth cues that rely on each eye receiving a slightly different view of the visual field; the brain blends the two images, creating three-dimensionality. (p. 154)

blended, or reconstituted, family A family structure resulting from cohabitation or remarriage that includes parent, child, and steprelatives. (p. 582)

body image Conception of and attitude toward one's physical appearance. (p. 202)

brain plasticity The ability of other parts of the brain to take over functions of damaged regions. Declines as hemispheres of the cerebral cortex lateralize. (p. 184)

breech position A position of the baby in the uterus that would cause the buttocks or feet to be delivered first. (p. 108)

Broca's area A structure located in the left frontal lobe of the cerebral cortex that supports grammatical processing and language production. (p. 358)

bulimia nervosa An eating disorder in which individuals (mainly females but homosexual and bisexual boys are also vulnerable) engage in strict dieting and excessive exercise accompanied by binge eating, often followed by deliberate vomiting and purging with laxatives. (p. 205)

C

canalization The tendency of heredity to restrict the development of some characteristics to just one or a few outcomes. (p. 117)

cardinality A principle specifying that the last word in a counting sequence indicates the quantity of items in a set. (p. 303)

carrier A heterozygous individual who can pass a recessive trait to his or her offspring. (p. 74)

catch-up growth A return to a genetically influenced growth path once negative conditions improve. (p. 189)

categorical self Early classification of the self according to salient ways in which people differ, such as age, sex, physical characteristics, and goodness and badness. (p. 440)

categorical speech perception The tendency to perceive as identical a range of sounds that belong to the same phonemic class. (p. 363)

central conceptual structures In Case's neo-Piagetian theory, networks of concepts and relations that permit children to think about a wide range of situations in more advanced ways. Generated once the schemes of a Piagetian stage become sufficiently automatic. (p. 276)

central executive In information processing, the conscious, reflective part of working memory that directs the flow of information by deciding what to attend to, coordinating incoming information with information already in the system, and selecting, applying, and monitoring strategies. (p. 273)

centration In Piaget's theory, the tendency to focus on one aspect of a situation and neglect other important features. (p. 236)

cephalocaudal trend An organized pattern of physical growth and motor control that proceeds from head to tail. (p. 143)

cerebellum A brain structure that aids in balance and control of body movements. (p. 186)

cerebral cortex The largest, most complex structure of the human brain, and the one that contains the greatest number of neurons and synapses and that makes possible the unique intelligence of our species. (p. 183)

child development A field devoted to understanding constancy and change from conception through adolescence. (p. 4)

child-directed speech (CDS) A form of language adults use to speak to infants and toddlers that is made up of short sentences with high-pitched, exaggerated expression, clear pronunciation, distinct pauses between speech segments, and repetition of new words in a variety of contexts. (p. 364)

child-rearing styles Combinations of parenting behaviors that occur over a wide range of situations, creating an enduring child-rearing climate. (p. 563)

chorion The outer membrane that forms a protective covering around the prenatal organism. It sends out tiny hair-like villi, from which the placenta begins to emerge. (p. 87)

chromosomes Rod-like structures in the cell nucleus that store and transmit genetic information. (p. 70)

chronosystem In ecological systems theory, temporal changes in children's environments, which produce new conditions that affect development. These changes can be imposed externally or arise from within the child. Distinguished from *microsystem, mesosystem, exosystem,* and *macrosystem.* (p. 29)

circular reaction In Piaget's theory, a means of adapting schemes in which babies try to repeat a chance event caused by their own motor activity. (p. 222)

classical conditioning A form of learning that involves associating a neutral stimulus with a stimulus that leads to a reflexive response. Once the nervous system makes the connections between the two stimuli, the new stimulus will produce the behavior by itself. (p. 135)

clinical interview A method in which the researcher uses a flexible conversational style to probe for the participant's point of view. (p. 46)

clinical, or case study, method A method in which the researcher attempts to obtain as complete a picture as possible of one child's psychological functioning by bringing together a wide range of information, including interviews, observations, test scores, and sometimes psychophysiological measures. (p. 48)

clique A small group of about five to seven members who are friends and, therefore, usually resemble one another in family background, attitudes, and values. (p. 613)

codominance A pattern of inheritance in which both alleles in a heterozygous combination are expressed. (p. 76)

cognitive-developmental theory An approach introduced by Piaget that views children as actively constructing knowledge as they manipulate and explore their world and views cognitive development as taking place in stages. (p. 21)

cognitive inhibition The ability to control internal and external distracting stimuli, thereby ensuring that working memory is not cluttered with irrelevant information. (p. 281)

cognitive maps Mental representations of familiar large-scale spaces, such as neighborhood or school. (p. 243)

cognitive self-regulation The process of continuously monitoring progress toward a goal, checking outcomes, and redirecting unsuccessful efforts. (p. 297)

cohort effects The effects of cultural–historical change on the accuracy of longitudinal and cross-sectional findings. Children developing in the same time period who are influenced by particular cultural and historical conditions make up a cohort. (p. 58)

collectivist societies Societies in which people define themselves as part of a group and stress group goals over individual goals. Distinguished from *individualistic societies.* (p. 34)

community of learners An educational practice inspired by Vygotsky's theory in which teachers guide the overall process of learning, but otherwise no distinction is made between adult and child contributors. All participate in joint endeavors and have the authority to define and resolve problems. (p. 629)

compliance Voluntary obedience to adult requests and commands. (p. 504)

componential analysis A research procedure in which investigators look for relationships between aspects (or components) of information processing and intelligence test performance. Aims to clarify the cognitive processes responsible for test scores. (p. 317)

comprehension In language development, the words children understand. Distinguished from *production.* (p. 370)

concordance rate The percentage of instances in which both members of a twin pair show a trait when it is present in one pair member. Typically used to study the contribution of heredity to emotional and behavior disorders that can be judged as either present or absent. (p. 115)

concrete operational stage Piaget's third stage, during which thought is logical, flexible, and organized in its application to concrete information. Extends from about 7 to 11 years. (p. 242)

conditioned response (CR) In classical conditioning, a response similar to the reflexive response evoked by the unconditioned stimulus (UCS) that, following learning, is produced by a conditioned stimulus (CS). (p. 136)

conditioned stimulus (CS) In classical conditioning, a neutral stimulus that, through pairing with an unconditioned stimulus (UCS), leads to a new, conditioned response (CR). (p. 136)

confounding variables Variables so closely associated that their effects on an outcome cannot be distinguished. (p. 54)

connectionist, or artificial neural network, models Models of mental functioning that focus on the most basic information-processing units, using computer simulations to imitate the workings of neurons and their connections in the brain. If the network's responses resemble those of people, then researchers conclude that it is a good model of human learning. (p. 275)

conservation The understanding that certain physical characteristics of objects remain the same, even when their outward appearance changes. (p. 236)

construction In moral development, actively attending to and interrelating multiple perspectives on situations in which social conflicts arise and thereby deriving new moral understandings. (p. 485)

constructivist approach Piaget's approach to cognitive development, in which children discover virtually all knowledge about their world through their own activity. (p. 220)

constructivist classroom A classroom that is based on the educational philosophy that students create their own knowledge. Often grounded in Piaget's theory. Consists of richly equipped learning centers, small groups and individuals solving problems they choose themselves, and a teacher who guides and supports in response to children's needs. Students are evaluated by considering their progress in relation to their own prior development. Distinguished from *traditional* and *social constructivist classrooms.* (p. 627)

contexts Unique combinations of genetic and environmental circumstances that can result in different paths of development. (p. 8)

continuous development The view that development is a cumulative process of gradually adding more of the same types of skills that were there to begin with. Distinguished from *discontinuous development.* (p. 7)

contrast sensitivity A general principle accounting for early pattern preferences, which states that if babies can detect the contrast in two or more patterns, they prefer the one with more contrast. (p. 155)

control deficiency The inability to execute a mental strategy effectively. Distinguished from *production* and *utilization deficiencies.* (p. 282)

controversial children Children who get a large number of positive and negative votes on sociometric measures of peer acceptance. Distinguished from *popular rejected,* and *neglected children.* (p. 609)

conventional level Kohlberg's second level of moral development, in which moral understanding is based on upholding social rules to ensure positive human relationships and societal order. (p. 490)

convergent thinking Thinking that involves arriving at a single correct answer to a problem. The type of cognition emphasized on intelligence tests. Distinguished from *divergent thinking.* (p. 345)

cooing Pleasant vowel-like noises made by infants, beginning around 2 months of age. (p. 364)

cooperative learning A type of learning in which groups of peers work toward common goals. (p. 264)

cooperative play A form of true social participation, in which children orient toward a common goal, such as acting out a make-believe theme or working on the same project. Distinguished from *nonsocial activity, parallel play,* and *associative play.* (p. 599)

core knowledge perspective A perspective that assumes that infants begin life with innate special-purpose knowledge systems, or core domains of thought, each of which permits a ready grasp of new, related information and therefore supports early, rapid development of certain aspects of cognition. (p. 253)

coregulation A form of supervision in which parents exercise general oversight while permitting children to be in charge of moment-by-moment decision making. (p. 569)

corpus callosum The large bundle of fibers that connects the two hemispheres of the cerebral cortex. (p. 188)

correlation coefficient A number, ranging from +1.00 to −1.00, that describes the strength and direction of the relationship between two variables. (p. 52)

correlational design A research design in which the investigator gathers information on individuals—generally in natural life circumstances—without altering their experiences, and then examines relationships among participants' characteristics and their behavior or development. Does not permit inferences about cause and effect. (p. 52)

creativity The ability to produce work that is original yet appropriate—something that others have not thought of but that is useful in some way. (p. 345)

crossing over During meiosis, the exchange of genes between chromosomes next to each other. (p. 71)

cross-sectional design A research design in which groups of participants of different ages are studied at the same point in time. Distinguished from *longitudinal design*. (p. 58)

crowd A large, loosely organized group consisting of several cliques with similar values. Membership is based on reputation and stereotype. (p. 613)

crystallized intelligence In Cattell's theory, a form of intelligence that refers to skills that depend on accumulated knowledge and experience, good judgment, and mastery of social customs. Distinguished from *fluid intelligence*. (p. 315)

D

debriefing Providing a full account and justification of research activities to participants in a study in which deception was used. (p. 65)

deferred imitation The ability to remember and copy the behavior of models who are not present. (p. 224)

delay of gratification Waiting for a more appropriate time and place to engage in a tempting act. (p. 504)

deoxyribonucleic acid (DNA) Long, double-stranded molecules that make up chromosomes. (p. 70)

dependent variable The variable the researcher expects to be influenced by the independent variable in an experiment. (p. 53)

desire theory of mind The theory of mind of 2- and 3-year-olds, who understand the relationship of desire to perception and emotion but who assume that people's behavior is merely a reflection of their desires. Fails to take account of the influence of interpretive mental states, such as beliefs, on behavior. (p. 442)

developmental psychology A branch of psychology devoted to understanding all changes that human beings experience throughout the lifespan. (p. 4)

developmentally appropriate practice A set of standards devised by the National Association for the Education of Young Children that specifies program characteristics that meet the developmental and individual needs of young children of varying ages, based on current research and the consensus of experts. (p. 432)

differentiation theory The view that perceptual development involves the detection of increasingly fine-grained, invariant features in the environment. (p. 163)

difficult child A child whose temperament is characterized by irregular daily routines, slow acceptance of new experiences, and negative and intense reactions. Distinguished from *easy child* and *slow-to-warm-up child*. (p. 412)

discontinuous development The view that new ways of understanding and responding to the world emerge at specific times. Distinguished from *continuous development*. (p. 7)

disorganized/disoriented attachment The quality of insecure attachment characterizing infants who respond in a confused, contradictory fashion when reunited with the parent. This attachment pattern reflects the greatest insecurity. Distinguished from *secure, avoidant,* and *resistant attachment*. (p. 422)

distance curve A growth curve that plots the average size of a sample of children at each age. Indicates typical yearly progress toward maturity. (p. 172)

distributive justice Beliefs about how to divide materials goods fairly. (p. 502)

divergent thinking The generation of multiple and unusual possibilities when faced with a task or problem. Associated with creativity. Distinguished from *convergent thinking*. (p. 345)

divorce mediation A series of meetings between divorcing couples and a trained professional aimed at reducing family conflict, such as legal battles over property division and child custody. (p. 582)

dominance hierarchy A stable ordering of group members that predicts who will win when conflict arises. (p. 601)

dominant cerebral hemisphere The hemisphere of the cerebral cortex responsible for skilled motor action and where other important abilities are located. For right-handed individuals, language is usually housed with hand control in the left hemisphere. For left-handed individuals, motor and language skills are often shared between the hemispheres. (p. 185)

dominant–recessive inheritance A pattern of inheritance in which, under heterozygous conditions, the influence of only one allele is apparent. (p. 74)

dual representation Viewing a symbolic object as both an object in its own right and a symbol. (p. 235)

dynamic assessment An approach to testing consistent with Vygotsky's zone of proximal development in which an adult introduces purposeful teaching into the situation to find out what the child can attain with social support. (p. 337)

dynamic systems perspective A view that regards the child's mind, body, and physical and social worlds as a dynamic, integrated system. A change in any part of the system leads the child to reorganize his behavior so the components of the system work together again but in a more complex, effective way. (p. 29)

dynamic systems theory of motor development A theory that views new motor skills as reorganizations of previously mastered skills that lead to more effective ways of exploring and controlling the environment. Each new skill is a product of central nervous system development, movement possibilities of the body, the goal the child has in mind, and environmental supports for the skill. (p. 144)

E

easy child A child whose temperament is characterized by establishment of regular routines in infancy, general cheerfulness, and easy adaptation to new experiences. Distinguished from *difficult child* and *slow-to-warm-up child*. (p. 412)

ecological systems theory Bronfenbrenner's approach, which views the child as developing within a complex system of relationships affected by multiple levels of the surrounding environment, from immediate settings of family and school to broad cultural values and programs. (p. 26)

educational self-fulfilling prophecies The idea that children may adopt teachers' positive or negative views toward them and start to live up to those views. (p. 633)

effective strategy use Consistent use of a mental strategy that leads to improvement in performance. Distinguished from *production, control,* and *utilization deficiencies*. (p. 282)

effortful control The self-regulatory dimension of temperament that involves voluntarily suppressing a dominant response in order to plan and execute a more adaptive response. Variations in effortful control are evident in how effectively a child can focus and shift attention, inhibit impulses, and engage in problem solving to manage negative emotion. (p. 413)

egocentrism The failure to distinguish the symbolic viewpoints of others from one's own. (p. 236)

elaboration The memory strategy involving creating a relationship, or shared meaning, between two or more pieces of information that are not members of the same category. (p. 286)

embryo The prenatal organism from 2 to 8 weeks after conception, during which time the foundations of all body structures and internal organs are laid down. (p. 88)

emergent literacy Young children's active efforts to construct literacy knowledge through informal experiences. (p. 300)

emotion A rapid appraisal of the personal significance of a situation, which prepares the individual for action. (p. 396)

emotion-centered coping A strategy for managing emotion in which the child controls distress internally and privately when little can be done about an outcome. Distinguished from *problem-centered coping*. (p. 405)

emotional display rules Rules within a society that specify when, where, and how it is appropriate to express emotions. (p. 405)

emotional intelligence A set of abilities that includes accurately perceiving emotions, expressing emotion appropriately, understanding the causes and consequences of emotions, and managing one's own and others' feelings to facilitate thinking and social interaction. (p. 320)

emotional self-regulation Strategies for adjusting our emotional state to a comfortable level of intensity so we can accomplish our goals. (p. 403)

empathy The ability to take another's emotional perspective and to feel with that person, or respond emotionally in a similar way. (p. 409)

entity view of ability The view that ability is a fixed characteristic that cannot be improved through effort. Distinguished from *incremental view of ability*. (p. 453)

environmental cumulative deficit hypothesis The view that the effects of underprivileged rearing conditions intensify the longer children remain in them, causing early cognitive deficits to worsen and become increasingly difficult to overcome. (p. 326)

epigenesis Development resulting from ongoing, bidirectional exchanges between heredity and all levels of the environment. (p. 118)

epiphyses Special growth centers in the bones where new cartilage cells are produced and gradually harden. (p. 174)

episodic memory Memory for personally experienced events. (p. 290)

equilibration In Piaget's theory, the back-and-forth movement between equilibrium and disequilibrium that produces more effective schemes. (p. 221)

estrogens Hormones released by the ovaries that cause the breasts, uterus, and vagina to mature, the body to take on feminine proportions, and fat to accumulate. Estrogens also contribute to regulation of the menstrual cycle. (p. 178)

ethnic identity An enduring aspect of the self that includes a sense of ethnic group membership and attitudes and feelings associated with that membership. (p. 461)

ethnography A method by which the researcher attempts to understand the unique values and social processes of a culture or a distinct social group by living with its members and taking field notes for an extended period. (p. 49)

ethological theory of attachment A theory formulated by Bowlby that recognizes the infant's emotional tie to the caregiver as an evolved response that promotes survival. (p. 420)

ethology An approach concerned with the adaptive, or survival, value of behavior and its evolutionary history. (p. 24)

event sampling An observational procedure in which the researcher records all instances of a particular behavior during a specified time period. (p. 44)

evolutionary developmental psychology An approach that seeks to understand the adaptive value of species-wide cognitive, emotional, and social competencies as those competencies change with age. (p. 25)

exosystem In ecological systems theory, settings that do not contain children but that affect their experiences in immediate settings. Examples are parents' workplace, health and welfare services in the community, and parents' social networks. Distinguished from *microsystem, mesosystem, macrosystem,* and *chronosystem.* (p. 29)

expansions Adult responses that elaborate on a child's utterance, increasing its complexity. (p. 383)

experience-dependent brain growth Additional growth and refinement of established brain structures as a result of specific learning experiences that vary widely across individuals and cultures. Follows experience-expectant brain growth. (p. 188)

experience-expectant brain growth The young brain's rapidly developing organization, which depends on ordinary experiences, such as opportunities to see and touch objects, to hear language and other sounds, and to move about and explore the environment. Provides the foundation for experience-dependent brain growth. (p. 188)

experimental design A research design in which the investigator randomly assigns participants to two or more treatment conditions and studies the effect that manipulating an independent variable has on a dependent variable. Permits inferences about cause and effect. (p. 54)

expressive style A style of early language learning in which toddlers use language mainly to talk about people's feelings and needs. Initial vocabulary emphasizes social formulas and pronouns. Distinguished from *referential style.* (p. 372)

expressive traits Feminine-stereotyped personality traits that reflect warmth, caring, and sensitivity. Distinguished from *instrumental traits.* (p. 520)

extended-family household A household in which parent and child live with one or more adult relatives. (p. 573)

external validity The degree to which researchers' findings generalize to settings and participants outside the original study. Distinguished from *internal validity.* (p. 52)

extinction In classical conditioning, decline of the conditioned response (CR) as a result of presenting the conditioned stimulus (CS) enough times without the unconditioned stimulus (UCS). (p. 136)

F

factor analysis A complicated correlational procedure that identifies sets of test items that cluster together. Used to find out whether intelligence is one trait or an assortment of abilities. (p. 315)

fast-mapping Connecting a new word with an underlying concept after only a brief encounter. (p. 372)

fetal alcohol effects (FAE) The condition of children who display some but not all the defects of fetal alcohol syndrome. Usually their mothers drank alcohol in smaller quantities during pregnancy. (p. 96)

fetal alcohol syndrome (FAS) A set of defects that results when pregnant women consume large amounts of alcohol during most or all of pregnancy. Includes mental retardation; impaired motor coordination, attention, memory, language, planning, and problem solving; overactivity; slow physical growth; and facial abnormalities. (p. 96)

fetus The prenatal organism from the beginning of the third month to the end of pregnancy, during which completion of body structures and dramatic growth in size take place. (p. 89)

field experiment A research design in which participants are randomly assigned to treatment conditions in natural settings. (p. 54)

fluid intelligence In Cattell's theory, a form of intelligence that depends more heavily on basic information-processing skills than on accumulated knowledge and experience. Includes the ability to detect relationships among stimuli, the speed with which the individual can analyze information, and the capacity of working memory. Distinguished from *crystallized intelligence.* (p. 315)

Flynn effect An increase in IQ from one generation to the next. (p. 334)

formal operational stage Piaget's highest stage, in which adolescents develop the capacity for abstract, scientific thinking. Begins around age 11. (p. 246)

fraternal, or dizygotic, twins Twins resulting from the release and fertilization of two ova. They are genetically no more alike than ordinary siblings. Distinguished from *identical,* or *monozygotic, twins.* (p. 73)

friendship A close relationship involving companionship in which each partner wants to be with the other. (p. 604)

full inclusion An educational practice that places children with learning difficulties in regular classrooms full time. (p. 635)

functionalist approach to emotion A perspective emphasizing that the broad function of emotions is to energize behavior aimed at attaining personal goals and that emotions are central forces in all human endeavors. (p. 396)

fuzzy-trace theory A theory that proposes two types of encoding, one that automatically reconstructs information into a fuzzy version called a *gist,* which is especially useful for reasoning; and a second, verbatim version that is adapted for answering questions about specifics. (p. 289)

G

gametes Sperm and ova, which contain half as many chromosomes as a regular body cell. (p. 71)

gender consistency Kohlberg's final stage of gender understanding, in which children in the late preschool and early school years understand that sex is biologically based and remains the same even if a person decides to dress in "cross-gender" clothes or engage in nontraditional activities. (p. 539)

gender constancy A full understanding of the biologically based permanence of gender, which combines three understandings: gender labeling, gender stability, and gender consistency. (p. 538)

gender identity The perception of oneself as relatively masculine or feminine in characteristics. (p. 520)

gender intensification Increased stereotyping of attitudes and behavior and movement toward a more traditional gender identity. Often occurs in early adolescence. (p. 541)

gender labeling Kohlberg's first stage of gender understanding, in which children in the early preschool years can label their own sex and that of others. (p. 539)

gender roles The reflection of gender stereotypes in everyday behavior. (p. 520)

gender schema theory An information-processing approach to gender typing that combines social learning and cognitive-developmental features to explain how social pressures and cognition work together to affect stereotyping, gender identity, and gender-role adoption. (p. 541)

gender stability Kohlberg's second stage of gender understanding, in which preschoolers have a partial understanding of the permanence of sex; they grasp its stability over time. (p. 539)

gender-stereotype flexibility Belief that either gender can display a gender-stereotyped personality trait or activity. (p. 523)

gender stereotypes Widely held beliefs about characteristics deemed appropriate for males and females. (p. 520)

gender typing Broadly applied term that refers to any association of objects, activities, roles, or traits with biological sex in ways that conform to cultural stereotypes of gender. (p. 520)

gene A segment of a DNA molecule that contains hereditary instructions. (p. 70)

general growth curve A curve that represents overall changes in body size—rapid growth during infancy, slower gains in early and middle childhood, and rapid growth again during adolescence. (p. 181)

general intelligence, or "g" In Spearman's theory, a common underlying intelligence that influences, in varying degrees, all test items and that represents abstract reasoning capacity. Distinguished from *specific intelligence,* or *"s."* (p. 315)

generalized other A blend of what we imagine important people in our lives think of us. Contributes to a self-concept consisting of personality traits. (p. 447)

genetic counseling A communication process designed to help couples assess their chances of giving birth to a baby with a hereditary disorder and choose the best course of action in view of risks and family goals. (p. 80)

genetic–environmental correlation The idea that genes influence the environments to which individuals are exposed. (p. 117)

genetic imprinting A pattern of inheritance in which alleles are imprinted, or chemically marked, in such a way that one pair member is activated, regardless of its makeup. (p. 77)

genotype The genetic makeup of an individual. Distinguished from *phenotype.* (p. 69)

gifted Displaying exceptional intellectual strengths. Includes high IQ, creativity, and talent. (p. 344)

gist A vague, fuzzy representation of information that preserves essential content without details and is especially useful for reasoning. (p. 289)

glial cells Cells responsible for myelination of neural fibers. (p. 183)

goodness-of-fit model Thomas and Chess's model, which describes how temperament and environmental pressures can together produce favorable outcomes. Goodness of fit involves creating child-rearing environments that recognize each child's temperament while encouraging more adaptive functioning. (p. 417)

grammar The component of language concerned with *syntax,* the rules by which words are arranged into sentences, and *morphology,* the use of grammatical markers that indicate number, tense, case, person, gender, active or passive voice, and other meanings. (p. 354)

grammatical morphemes Small markers that change the meaning of sentences, as in "John's dog" and "he *is* eating." (p. 379)

growth hormone (GH) A pituitary hormone that affects development of all tissues except the central nervous system and the genitals. (p. 178)

guided participation Shared endeavors between more expert and less expert participants, without specifying the precise features of communication. A broader concept than *scaffolding*. (p. 261)

H

habituation A gradual reduction in the strength of a response due to repetitive stimulation. (p. 138)

heritability estimate A statistic that measures the extent to which individual differences in complex traits in a specific population are due to genetic factors. (p. 115)

heteronomous morality Piaget's first stage of moral development, in which children view rules as handed down by authorities, as having a permanent existence, as unchangeable, and as requiring strict obedience. (p. 485)

heterozygous Having two different alleles at the same place on a pair of chromosomes. Distinguished from *homozygous*. (p. 74)

hierarchical classification The organization of objects into classes and subclasses on the basis of similarities and differences. (p. 236)

Home Observation for Measurement of the Environment (HOME) A checklist for gathering information about the quality of children's home lives through observation and parental interview. Infancy, preschool, and middle childhood versions exist. (p. 339)

homozygous Having two identical alleles at the same place on a pair of chromosomes. Distinguished from *heterozygous*. (p. 74)

horizontal décalage Development within a Piagetian stage. Gradual mastery of logical concepts during the concrete operational stage is an example. (p. 244)

hostile aggression Aggression meant to harm another person. Distinguished from *instrumental aggression*. (p. 507)

human development An interdisciplinary field devoted to understanding all changes that human beings experience throughout the lifespan. (p. 4)

hypothalamus A structure located at the base of the brain that initiates and regulates pituitary secretions. (p. 178)

hypothesis A prediction drawn from a theory. (p. 42)

hypothetico-deductive reasoning A formal operational problem-solving strategy in which adolescents start with a *general theory* of all possible factors that might affect an outcome, *deducing* from it specific *hypotheses* (or predictions) about what might happen and testing these hypotheses in an orderly fashion to see which ones work in the real world. (p. 246)

I

I-self A sense of self as knower and actor. Includes self-awareness, self-continuity, self-coherence, and self-agency. Distinguished from *me-self*. (p. 441)

ideal reciprocity A standard of fairness based on mutuality of expectations, in which individuals express the same concern for the welfare of others as they would have others grant to them. Captured by the Golden Rule. (p. 486)

identical, or monozygotic, twins Twins that result when a zygote that has started to duplicate separates into two clusters of cells that develop into two individuals with the same genetic makeup. Distinguished from *fraternal*, or *dizygotic*, *twins*. (p. 73)

identity A well-organized conception of the self made up of values, beliefs, and goals to which the individual is solidly committed. (p. 438)

identity achievement The identity status of individuals who have explored and committed themselves to self-chosen values and goals. Distinguished from *identity moratorium*, *identity foreclosure*, and *identity diffusion*. (p. 456)

identity diffusion The identity status of individuals who lack both exploration and commitment to self-chosen values and goals. Distinguished from *identity achievement*, *identity moratorium*, and *identity foreclosure*. (p. 457)

identity foreclosure The identity status of individuals who lack exploration and, instead, are committed to ready-made values and goals that authority figures have chosen for them. Distinguished from *identity achievement*, *identity moratorium*, and *identity diffusion*. (p. 457)

identity moratorium The identity status of individuals who are exploring, but are not yet committed to, self-chosen values and goals. Distinguished from *identity achievement*, *identity foreclosure*, and *identity diffusion*. (p. 457)

illocutionary intent What a speaker means to say, even if the form of the utterance is not perfectly consistent with it. (p. 384)

imaginary audience Adolescents' belief that they are the focus of everyone else's attention and concern. (p. 248)

imitation Learning by copying the behavior of another person. Also called *modeling* or *observational learning*. (p. 141)

incremental view of ability The view that ability can be improved through effort. Distinguished from *entity view of ability*. (p. 457)

independent variable The variable the researcher expects to cause changes in another variable in an experiment. Distinguished from *dependent variable*. (p. 53)

individualistic societies Societies in which people think of themselves as separate entities and are largely concerned with their own personal needs. Distinguished from *collectivist societies*. (p. 34)

induction A type of discipline in which the adult helps the child notice others' feelings by pointing out the effects of the child's misbehavior on others, noting especially their distress and making clear that the child caused it. (p. 478)

infant mortality The number of deaths in the first year of life per 1,000 live births. (p. 112)

infantile amnesia The inability of most older children and adults to retrieve events that happened before age 3. (p. 293)

information processing An approach that views the human mind as a symbol-manipulating system through which information flows and that regards cognitive development as a continuous process. (p. 23)

informed consent The right of research participants, including children, to have explained to them, in language they can understand, all aspects of a study that may affect their willingness to participate. (p. 65)

inhibited, or shy, child A child whose temperament is characterized by negative reactions to and withdrawal from novel stimuli. Distinguished from *uninhibited*, or *sociable*, *child*. (p. 414)

inner self Awareness of the self's private thoughts and imaginings. (p. 453)

instrumental aggression Aggression in which children want an object, privilege, or space and, in trying to get it, push, shout at, or otherwise attack a person who is in the way. Distinguished from *hostile aggression*. (p. 507)

instrumental traits Masculine-stereotyped personality traits that reflect competence, rationality, and assertiveness. Distinguished from *expressive traits*. (p. 520)

intelligence quotient (IQ) A score that indicates the extent to which the raw score (number of items passed) on an intelligence test deviates from the typical performance of same-age individuals. (p. 324)

intentional, or goal-directed, behavior A sequence of actions in which schemes are deliberately combined to solve simple problems. (p. 223)

interactional synchrony A sensitively tuned "emotional dance," in which the caregiver responds to infant signals in a well-timed, rhythmic, appropriate fashion and both partners match emotional states, especially the positive ones. (p. 424)

intermodal perception Perception that combines information from more than one modality, or sensory system. (p. 160)

internal validity The degree to which conditions internal to the design of the study permit an accurate test of the researcher's hypothesis or question. Distinguished from *external validity*. (p. 52)

internal working model A set of expectations about the availability of attachment figures, their likelihood of providing support during times of stress, and the self's interaction with those figures. Becomes a vital part of personality, serving as a guide for all future close relationships. (p. 421)

internalization The process of adopting societal standards for right action as one's own. (p. 477)

intersubjectivity A process whereby two participants who begin a task with different understandings arrive at a shared understanding. (p. 260)

invariant features Features that remain stable in a constantly changing perceptual world. (p. 163)

investment theory of creativity Sternberg and Lubart's theory, in which investing in novel projects depends on diverse cognitive, personality, motivational, and environmental resources, each of which must be present to catalyze creativity. (p. 346)

J

joint attention A state in which the child and the caregiver attend to the same object or event and the caregiver offers verbal information. Supports language development. (p. 365)

joint custody Child custody arrangement following divorce in which the court grants both parents equal say in important decisions about their child's upbringing, as a means of encouraging both to remain involved in the child's life. (p. 582)

K

kinetic depth cues Depth cues created by movements of the body or of objects in the environment. (p. 154)

kinship studies Studies comparing the characteristics of family members to estimate the importance of heredity in complex human characteristics. (p. 115)

kwashiorkor A disease caused by a diet low in protein that usually appears after weaning, between 1 and 3 years of age. Symptoms include an enlarged belly, swollen feet, hair loss, skin rash, irritability, and listlessness. (p. 192)

L

laboratory experiment An experiment conducted in the laboratory, permitting the maximum possible control over treatment conditions. (p. 54)

language acquisition device (LAD) In Chomsky's theory, an innate system that permits children, as soon as they have acquired sufficient vocabulary, to combine words into grammatically consistent, novel utterances and to understand the meaning of sentences they hear. (p. 355)

lanugo A white, downy hair that covers the entire body of the fetus, helping the vernix stick to the skin. (p. 89)

lateralization Specialization of the two hemispheres of the cerebral cortex. (p. 184)

learned helplessness Attributions that credit success to external factors, such as luck, and failure to low ability. Leads to low expectancies of success and anxious loss of control in the face of challenging tasks. Distinguished from *mastery-oriented attributions*. (p. 453)

learning disability Great difficulty with one or more aspects of learning (usually reading), which causes the student's achievement to be considerably behind what would be expected on the basis of his or her IQ. (p. 635)

lexical contrast theory A theory that assumes that two principles govern semantic development: *conventionality*, children's natural desire to acquire the words and word meanings of their language community; and *contrast*, children's discovery of meanings by contrasting new words with words they know and assigning them to gaps in their vocabulary. (p. 376)

logical necessity A basic property of propositional reasoning, which specifies that the accuracy of conclusions drawn from premises rests on the rules of logic, not on real-world confirmation. (p. 250)

longitudinal design A research design in which one group of participants is studied repeatedly at different ages. Distinguished from *cross-sectional design*. (p. 57)

long-term memory The largest memory storage area of the information-processing system, which contains our permanent knowledge base. (p. 273)

M

macrosystem In ecological systems theory, cultural values, laws, customs, and resources that influence experiences and interactions at inner levels of the environment. Distinguished from *microsystem, mesosystem, exosystem,* and *chronosystem*. (p. 29)

mainstreaming Placement of students with learning difficulties in regular classrooms for part of the school day. (p. 635)

make-believe play A type of play in which children act out everyday and imaginary activities. (p. 224)

marasmus A disease usually appearing in the first year of life that is caused by a diet low in all essential nutrients. Leads to a wasted condition of the body. (p. 192)

mastery-oriented attributions Attributions that credit success to high ability and failure to insufficient effort. Lead to high expectancies of success and a willingness to approach challenging tasks. Distinguished from *learned helplessness*. (p. 453)

matching A research procedure in which participants are measured ahead of time on the factor in question, enabling investigators to assign participants with similar characteristics in equal numbers to each treatment condition in an experiment. Ensures that groups will be equivalent on factors likely to distort the results. (p. 54)

matters of personal choice Concerns that do not violate rights or harm others, are not socially regulated, and therefore are up to the individual. Distinguished from *moral imperatives* and *social conventions*. (p. 501)

maturation A genetically determined, naturally unfolding course of growth. (p. 12)

me-self A sense of self as object of knowledge and evaluation. Consists of all qualities that make the self unique, including material, psychological, and social characteristics. Distinguished from *I-self*. (p. 438)

meiosis The process of cell division through which gametes are formed and in which the number of chromosomes in each cell is halved. (p. 71)

memory span The longest sequence of items a person can recall; a measure of working-memory capacity. (p. 273)

menarche First menstruation. (p. 197)

mental representation Internal depictions of information that the mind can manipulate. The most powerful mental representations are images and concepts. (p. 221)

mental strategies Learned procedures that operate on and transform information, thereby increasing the efficiency and flexibility of thinking and the chances that information will be retained. (p. 272)

mesosystem In ecological systems theory, connections between microsystems. Distinguished from *microsystem, exosystem, macrosystem,* and *chronosystem*. (p. 28)

metacognition Awareness and understanding of various aspects of thought. (p. 296)

metalinguistic awareness Ability to think about language as a system. (p. 387)

microgenetic design A research design in which investigators present children with a novel task and follow their mastery over a series of closely spaced sessions. (p. 61)

microsystem In ecological systems theory, the activities and interaction patterns in the child's immediate surroundings. Distinguished from *mesosystem, exosystem, macrosystem,* and *chronosystem*. (p. 27)

mitosis The process of cell duplication, in which each new cell receives an exact copy of the original chromosomes. (p. 70)

model of strategy choice Siegler's evolutionary theory, in which children generate a variety of strategies when given challenging problems. Accurate, efficient strategies are selected and survive, whereas others die off, yielding adaptive problem-solving techniques. (p. 278)

modifier genes Genes that can enhance or dilute the effects of other genes. (p. 74)

moral imperatives Standards that protect people's rights and welfare. Distinguished from *social conventions* and *matters of personal choice*. (p. 500)

Moral Judgment Interview A clinical interviewing procedure for assessing moral understanding in which individuals resolve dilemmas that present conflicts between two moral values and justify their decisions. (p. 488)

moral self-regulation The ability to monitor one's own conduct, constantly adjusting it as circumstances present opportunities to violate inner standards. (p. 505)

moral self-relevance The degree to which morality is central to self-concept. (p. 496)

morphology The use of grammatical markers that indicate number, tense, case, person, gender, active or passive voice, and other meanings. (p. 354)

mutation A sudden but permanent change in a segment of DNA. (p. 78)

mutual exclusivity bias In the early phase of vocabulary growth, children's assumption that words refer to entirely separate (nonoverlapping) categories. (p. 376)

myelination The coating of neural fibers with an insulating fatty sheath (called *myelin*) that improves the efficiency of message transfer. (p. 183)

N

natural, or **quasi-, experiment** A research design in which the investigator studies already existing treatments in natural settings by carefully selecting groups of participants with similar characteristics. (p. 54)

natural, or **prepared, childbirth** An approach designed to reduce pain and medical intervention and to make childbirth a rewarding experience for parents. Includes three activities: classes providing information about the anatomy and physiology of labor and delivery, relaxation and breathing techniques to counteract the pain of contractions, and a labor coach who encourages and provides social support. (p. 106)

naturalistic observation A research method in which the investigator goes into the natural environment to observe the behavior of interest. Distinguished from *structured observation*. (p. 42)

nature–nurture controversy Disagreement among theorists about whether genetic or environmental factors are more important determinants of development and behavior. (p. 8)

neglected children Children who are seldom chosen, either positively or negatively, on sociometric measures of peer acceptance. Distinguished from *popular, rejected,* and *controversial children*. (p. 609)

Neonatal Behavioral Assessment Scale (NBAS) A test developed to assess the behavioral status of the newborn. Evaluates the baby's reflexes, state changes, responsiveness to physical and social stimuli, and other reactions. (p. 134)

neonatal mortality The rate of death within the first month of life. (p. 112)

neo-Piagetian theory A theory that reinterprets Piaget's stages within an information-processing framework. For example, in Case's theory, each major stage involves a distinct type of cognitive structure—in infancy, sensory input and physical actions; in early childhood, internal representations of events and actions; in middle childhood, simple transformations of representations; and in adolescence, complex transformations of representations. As children become more efficient cognitive processors, the amount of information they can hold and combine in working memory expands, making this sequence possible. (p. 276)

neurons Nerve cells that store and transmit information in the brain. (p. 182)

neurotransmitters Chemicals that are released by neurons that send messages across synapses. (p. 182)

niche-picking A type of genetic–environmental correlation in which individuals actively choose environments that complement their heredity. (p. 118)

noble savage Rousseau's view of the child as naturally endowed with a sense of right and wrong and with an innate plan for orderly, healthy growth. (p. 12)

non-rapid-eye-movement (NREM) sleep A "regular" sleep state in which the body is almost motionless and heart rate, breathing, and brain-wave activity are slow and regular. Distinguished from *rapid-eye-movement (REM) sleep*. (p. 130)

nonorganic failure to thrive A growth disorder that results from lack of parental love and that is usually present by 18 months of age. Infants who have it show all the signs of marasmus, but no organic (or biological) cause can be found. (p. 196)

nonshared environmental influences Environmental influences that make siblings living in the same home different from one another. Distinguished from *shared environmental influences*. (p. 339)

nonsocial activity Unoccupied, onlooker behavior and solitary play. (p. 599)

normal distribution A bell-shaped distribution that results when individual differences are measured in large samples. (p. 324)

normative approach An approach in which measures of behavior are taken on large numbers of individuals, and age-related averages are computed to represent typical development. (p. 14)

nuclear family unit A family unit consisting of parents and their dependent children living in one household. (p. 573)

O

obesity A body weight greater than 20 percent over the average body weight for the child's age, sex, and physical build. (p. 193)

object permanence The understanding that objects continue to exist when they are out of sight. (p. 223)

observer bias The tendency of observers who are aware of the purposes of a study to see and record what is expected rather than participants' actual behaviors. (p. 45)

observer influence The tendency of participants in a study to react to the presence of an observer and behave in unnatural ways. (p. 45)

operant conditioning A form of learning in which a spontaneous behavior is followed by a stimulus that changes the probability that the behavior will occur again. (p. 136)

operations In Piaget's theory, mental representations of actions that obey logical rules. (p. 236)

optical flow Visually detected movements in the surrounding environment, leading to postural adjustments so the body remains upright. (p. 150)

ordinality Order relationships between quantities. For example, three is more than two and two is more than one. (p. 302)

organization In *Piaget's theory*, a process that takes place internally, apart from direct contact with the environment, through which new schemes are formed, rearranged, and linked with other schemes to create a strongly interconnected cognitive system. In *information processing*, the memory strategy of grouping together related information. (pp. 221, 285)

overextension Applying a word to a broader collection of objects and events than is appropriate. Distinguished from *underextension*. (p. 374)

overregularization Extending a regular morphological rule to words that are exceptions. (p. 380)

P

parallel play A form of limited social participation in which a child plays near other children with similar materials but does not try to influence their behavior. Distinguished from *nonsocial activity, associative play,* and *cooperative play.* (p. 599)

peer acceptance Likeability, or the extent to which a child is viewed by a group of agemates (such as classmates) as a worthy social partner. (p. 609)

peer group An informal grouping of children that generates unique values and standards for behavior and a social structure of leaders and followers. (p. 613)

peer reputation Judgments by children and adolescents about whom most of their classmates admire, which assess peer acceptance in terms of *social prominence.* (p. 609)

peer victimization A destructive form of peer interaction in which certain children become frequent targets of verbal and physical attacks or other forms of abuse. (p. 611)

permissive child-rearing style A child-rearing style that is high in acceptance but overindulging or inattentive, low in control, and lenient rather than appropriate in autonomy granting. Distinguished from *authoritative, authoritarian,* and *uninvolved child-rearing styles.* (p. 565)

person perception The way individuals size up the attributes of people with whom they are familiar. (p. 462)

personal fable Adolescents' belief that they are special and unique. Leads them to conclude that others cannot possibly understand their thoughts and feelings. (p. 248)

perspective taking The capacity to imagine what other people may be thinking and feeling. (p. 465)

phenotype The individual's directly observable physical and behavioral characteristics, which are determined by both genetic and environmental factors. Distinguished from *genotype.* (p. 69)

phonemes The smallest sound unit that signals a change in meaning. (p. 363)

phonics approach An approach to beginning reading instruction that emphasizes simplified reading materials and training in the basic rules for translating written symbols into sounds. Distinguished from the *whole-language approach.* (p. 302)

phonological awareness The ability to reflect on and manipulate the sound structure of spoken language, as indicated by sensitivity to changes in sounds within words, to rhyming, and to incorrect pronunciation. A strong predictor of emergent literacy during early childhood and of later reading and spelling achievement. (p. 300)

phonological store A special part of working memory that permits us to retain speech-based information. Supports early vocabulary development. (p. 375)

phonology The component of language concerned with the rules governing the structure and sequence of speech sounds. (p. 354)

physical aggression A type of hostile aggression that harms others through physical injury. Includes pushing, hitting, kicking, punching, or destroying another's property. Distinguished from *verbal* and *relational aggression.* (p. 507)

pictorial depth cues Depth cues that artists use to make a painting look three-dimensional, including receding lines, texture changes, and overlapping objects. (p. 154)

pincer grasp The well-coordinated grasp emerging at the end of the first year, in which thumb and forefinger are used opposably. (p. 147)

pituitary gland A gland located at the base of the brain that releases hormones affecting physical growth. (p. 178)

placenta The organ that separates the mother's bloodstream from the embryo's or fetus's bloodstream but permits exchange of nutrients and waste products. (p. 87)

planning Thinking out a sequence of acts ahead of time and allocating attention accordingly to reach a goal. (p. 282)

polygenic inheritance A pattern of inheritance involving many genes that applies to characteristics that vary continuously among people. (p. 78)

popular children Children who get many positive votes on sociometric measures of peer acceptance. Distinguished from *rejected, controversial,* and *neglected children.* (p. 609)

popular-antisocial children A subgroup of popular children, apparent in late childhood and early adolescence, that consists of aggressive youngsters. Some are "tough" boys who are athletically skilled but are poor students who get into fights, cause trouble, and defy adult authority. Others are relationally aggressive boys and girls who use ignoring, excluding, and rumor-spreading to manipulate peer relationships in ways that enhance their own status. Distinguished from *popular-prosocial children.* (p. 610)

popular-prosocial children. A subgroup of popular children who combine academic and social competence. Distinguished from *popular-antisocial children.* (p. 610)

postconventional level Kohlberg's highest level of moral development, in which individuals define morality in terms of abstract principles and values that apply to all situations and societies. (p. 490)

practical intelligence Mental abilities apparent in the real world but not in testing situations. (p. 326)

practice effects Changes in participants' natural responses as a result of repeated testing. (p. 58)

pragmatics The component of language that refers to the rules for engaging in appropriate and effective communication. (p. 354)

preconventional level Kohlberg's first level of moral development, in which morality is externally controlled. Children accept the rules of authority figures and judge actions in terms of their consequences. (p. 489)

prenatal diagnostic methods Medical procedures that permit detection of developmental problems before birth. (p. 80)

preoperational stage Piaget's second stage, in which rapid growth in representation takes place but thought is not yet logical. Extends from about 2 to 7 years. (p. 231)

prereaching The well-aimed but poorly coordinated primitive reaching movements of newborn babies. (p. 146)

preterm infants Infants born several weeks or more before their due date. (p. 109)

primary sexual characteristics Physical features that involve the reproductive organs (ovaries, uterus, and vagina in females; penis, scrotum, and testes in males). Distinguished from *secondary sexual characteristics.* (p. 197)

private speech Self-directed speech that children use to guide their thinking and behavior. (p. 259)

problem-centered coping A strategy for managing emotion in which the child appraises the situation as changeable, identifies the difficulty, and decides what to do about it. Distinguished from *emotion-centered coping.* (p. 405)

production In language development, the words that children use. Distinguished from *comprehension.* (p. 370)

production deficiency The failure to produce a mental strategy when it could be helpful. Distinguished from *control* and *utilization deficiencies.* (p. 282)

programmed cell death Death of many surrounding neurons as neural fibers and their synapses increase rapidly, which makes room for these connective structures. (p. 182)

Project Head Start A U.S. federal program that provides low-SES children with a year or two of preschool education, along with nutritional and medical services, and that encourages parent involvement. (p. 342)

propositional thought A type of formal operational reasoning in which adolescents evaluate the logic of verbal statements without referring to real-world circumstances. (p. 247)

prosocial, or altruistic, behavior Actions that benefit another person without any expected reward for the self. (p. 409)

protection from harm The right of research participants to be protected from physical or psychological harm. (p. 63)

protodeclarative A preverbal gesture in which the baby touches an object, holds it up, or points to it while looking at others to make sure they notice. (p. 365)

protoimperative A preverbal gesture in which the baby gets another person to do something by reaching, pointing, and often making sounds at the same time. (p. 365)

proximodistal trend An organized pattern of physical growth and motor control that proceeds from the center of the body outward. (p. 143)

psychoanalytic perspective An approach to personality development introduced by Freud that assumes children move through a series of stages in which they confront conflicts between biological drives and social expectations. The way these conflicts are resolved determines the person's ability to learn, to get along with others, and to cope with anxiety. (p. 16)

psychological control Parental behaviors that intrude on and manipulate children's verbal expressions, individuality, and attachments to parents. (p. 565)

psychometric approach A product-oriented approach to cognitive development that focuses on the construction of tests to assess mental abilities. (p. 313)

psychophysiological methods Methods that measure the relationship between physiological processes and behavior. Among the most common are measures of autonomic nervous system activity (such as heart rate, respiration, and stress hormone levels) and measures of brain functioning (such as the electroencephalogram [EEG], event-related potentials [ERPs], and functional magnetic resonance imaging [fMRI]). (p. 47)

psychosexual theory Freud's theory, which emphasizes that the way parents manage their child's sexual and aggressive drives during the first few years is crucial for healthy personality development. (p. 16)

psychosocial dwarfism A growth disorder that usually appears between 2 and 15 years of age. Characterized by very short stature, decreased GH secretion, immature skeletal age, and serious adjustment problems, which help distinguish psychosocial dwarfism from normal shortness. Caused by emotional deprivation. (p. 197)

psychosocial theory Erikson's theory, which emphasizes that at each Freudian stage, individuals not only develop a unique personality but also acquire attitudes and skills that help them become active, contributing members of their society. Recognizes the lifespan nature of development and the impact of culture. (p. 16)

puberty Biological changes at adolescence that lead to an adult-sized body and sexual maturity (p. 197).

public policy Laws and government programs aimed at improving current conditions. (p. 31)

punishment In operant conditioning, either removing a desirable stimulus or presenting an unpleasant one to decrease the occurrence of a response. (p. 137)

R

random assignment An evenhanded procedure for assigning participants to treatment groups, such as drawing numbers out of a hat or flipping a coin. Increases the chances that participants' characteristics will be equally distributed across treatment conditions in an experiment. (p. 54)

range of reaction Each person's unique, genetically determined response to a range of environmental conditions. (p. 117)

rapid-eye-movement (REM) sleep An "irregular" sleep state in which brain-wave activity is similar to that of the waking state; eyes dart beneath the lids; heart rate, blood pressure, and breathing are uneven; and slight body movements occur. Distinguished from *non-rapid-eye-movement (NREM) sleep*. (p. 130)

realism A view of rules as external features of reality rather than as cooperative principles that can be modified at will. Characterizes Piaget's heteronomous stage of moral development. (p. 486)

recall A type of memory that involves generating a mental representation of an absent stimulus. Distinguished from *recognition*. (p. 287)

recasts Adult responses that restructure children's grammatically inaccurate speech into correct form. (p. 383)

reciprocal teaching A method of teaching based on Vygotsky's theory in which a teacher and two to four students form a cooperative group and take turns leading dialogues on the content of a text passage. Within these dialogues, group members apply four cognitive strategies: questioning, summarizing, clarifying, and predicting. Creates a zone of proximal development in which reading comprehension improves. (p. 263)

recognition The simplest form of memory, which involves noticing that a stimulus is identical or similar to one previously experienced. Distinguished from *recall*. (p. 287)

reconstruction A type of memory that involves recoding information while it is in the system or being retrieved. (p. 288)

recovery Following habituation, an increase in responsiveness to a new stimulus. (p. 138)

recursive thought The self-embedded form of perspective taking that involves thinking about what another person is thinking. (p. 467)

referential communication skills The ability to produce clear verbal messages and to recognize when the meaning of others' messages in unclear. (p. 385)

referential style A style of early language learning in which toddlers' vocabularies consist mainly of words that refer to objects. Distinguished from *expressive style*. (p. 372)

reflex An inborn, automatic response to a particular form of stimulation. (p. 126)

rehearsal The memory strategy of repeating information to oneself. (p. 285)

reinforcer In operant conditioning, a stimulus that increases the occurrence of a response. (p. 137)

rejected children Children who are actively disliked and get many negative votes on sociometric measures of peer acceptance. Distinguished from *popular, controversial*, and *neglected children*. (p. 609)

rejected-aggressive children A subgroup of rejected children who show severe conduct problems, such as high rates of conflict, physical and relational aggression, and hyperactive, inattentive, and impulsive behavior. Distinguished from *rejected-withdrawn children*. (p. 610)

rejected-withdrawn children A subgroup of rejected children who are passive and socially awkward. Distinguished from *rejected-aggressive children*. (p. 610)

relational aggression A form of hostile aggression that damages another's peer relationships through social exclusion, malicious gossip, or friendship manipulation. Distinguished from *physical* and *verbal aggression*. (p. 507)

reliability The consistency, or repeatability, of measures of behavior. (p. 51)

remembered self The life story, constructed from conversations with adults about the past, that leads to an autobiographical memory. (p. 440)

resilience The ability to adapt effectively in the face of threats to development. (p. 10)

resistant attachment The quality of insecure attachment characterizing infants who remain close to the parent before departure, are usually distressed when she leaves, and mix clinginess with angry, resistive behavior when she returns. Distinguished from *secure, avoidant*, and *disorganized/disoriented attachment*. (p. 422)

reticular formation A structure in the brain stem that maintains alertness and consciousness. (p. 187)

reversibility The ability to mentally go through a series of steps in a problem and then reverse direction, returning to the starting point. In Piaget's theory, part of every logical operation. (p. 236)

Rh factor incombatibility A condition that arises when the Rh protein, present in the fetus's blood but not in the mother's, causes the mother to build up antibodies. If these return to the fetus's system, they destroy red blood cells, reducing the oxygen supply to organs and tissues. (p. 108)

risks-versus-benefits ratio A comparison of the costs of a research study to participants in terms of inconvenience and possible psychological or physical injury against its value for advancing knowledge and improving conditions of life. Used in assessing the ethics of research. (p. 63)

rough-and-tumble play A form of peer interaction involving friendly chasing and play-fighting that, in our evolutionary past, may have been important for the development of fighting skill. (p. 600)

S

scaffolding A changing quality of support over a teaching session, in which the adult adjusts the assistance she provides to fit the child's current level of performance. As competence increases, the adult gradually withdraws support, turning responsibility over to the child. (p. 260)

scheme In Piaget's theory, a specific structure, or organized way of making sense of experience, that changes with age. (p. 221)

scripts General representations of what occurs and when it occurs in a particular situation. A basic means through which children organize and interpret repeated events. (p. 290)

secondary sexual characteristics Features visible on the outside of the body that serve as signs of sexual maturity but do not involve the reproductive organs (for example, breast development in females and the appearance of underarm and pubic hair in both sexes). Distinguished from *primary sexual characteristics*. (p. 197)

secular trends in physical growth Changes in body size and rate of growth from one generation to the next. (p. 180)

secure attachment The quality of attachment characterizing infants who use the parent as a secure base from which to explore and, when separated, are easily comforted by the parent when she returns. Distinguished from *avoidant, resistant,* and *disorganized/disoriented attachment*. (p. 422)

secure base The baby's use of the familiar caregiver as the point from which to explore the environment and to return to for emotional support. (p. 401)

selective attrition Selective loss of participants during an investigation, resulting in a biased sample. (p. 58)

self-care children Children who regularly look after themselves during after-school hours. (p. 587)

self-concept The set of attributes, abilities, attitudes, and values that an individual believes defines who he or she is. (p. 446)

self-conscious emotions Emotions that involve injury to or enhancement of the sense of self. Examples are shame, embarrassment, guilt, envy, and pride. (p. 402)

self-esteem The aspect of self-concept that involves judgments about one's own worth and the feelings associated with those judgments. (p. 449)

self-recognition Perception of the self as a separate being, distinct from other people and objects. (p. 440)

semantic bootstrapping Relying on semantics, or word meanings, to figure out sentence structure. (p. 382)

semantic memory The vast, taxonomically organized and hierarchically structured general knowledge system. (p. 290)

semantics The component of language involving the way underlying concepts are expressed in words and word combinations. (p. 354)

sensitive caregiving Responding promptly, consistently, and appropriately to infants and holding them tenderly and carefully. (p. 424)

sensitive period A time that is optimal for certain capacities to emerge and in which the individual is especially responsive to environmental influences. (p. 24)

sensorimotor stage Piaget's first stage, in which infants and toddlers "think" with their eyes, ears, hands, and other sensorimotor equipment. Spans the first 2 years of life. (p. 222)

sensory register The part of the information-processing system where sights and sounds are represented directly and stored briefly. (p. 272)

separation anxiety An infant's distressed reaction to the departure of the familiar caregiver. (p. 420)

sequential design A research design that combines longitudinal and cross-sectional strategies by following a sequence of samples (two or more age groups), collecting data on them at the same points in time. (p. 60)

seriation The ability to arrange items along a quantitative dimension, such as length or weight. (p. 243)

sex chromosomes The twenty-third pair of chromosomes, which determines the sex of the child. In females, this pair is called XX; in males, it is called XY. (p. 73)

shading A conversational strategy in which a change of topic is initiated gradually by modifying the focus of discussion. (p. 384)

shape constancy Perception of an object's shape as stable, despite changes in the shape of its retinal image when seen from different vantage points. (p. 158)

shared environmental influences Environmental influences that pervade the general atmosphere of the home and, therefore, similarly affect siblings living in it. Distinguished from *nonshared environmental influences*. (p. 339)

size constancy Perception of an object's size as stable, despite changes in the size of its retinal image caused by changes in its distance from the eye. (p. 158)

skeletal age A measure of development of the bones of the body. The best way of estimating a child's physical maturity. (p. 174)

slow-to-warm-up child A child whose temperament is characterized by inactivity; mild, low-key reactions to environmental stimuli; negative mood; and slow adjustment when faced with new experiences. Distinguished from *easy child* and *difficult child*. (p. 412)

small-for-date infants Infants whose birth weight is below normal when length of pregnancy is taken into account. May be full term or preterm. (p. 109)

social cognition Thinking about the characteristics of the self and of other people. (p. 437)

social comparisons Judgments of one's own abilities, behavior, and appearance in relation to those of others. (p. 446)

social-constructivist classroom A classroom based on Vygotsky's theory, in which children participate in a wide range of challenging activities with teachers and peers, with whom they jointly construct understandings. As children appropriate (take for themselves) the knowledge and strategies generated from working together, they advance in cognitive and social development and become competent, contributing members of their cultural community. Distinguished from *traditional* and *constructivist classrooms*. (p. 629)

social conventions Customs determined solely by consensus, such as table manners, dress styles, and rituals of social interaction. Distinguished from *moral imperatives* and *matters of personal choice*. (p. 500)

social learning theory A theory that emphasizes the role of modeling, or observational learning, in the development of behavior. Its most recent revision stresses the importance of thinking in social learning and is called *social-cognitive theory*. (p. 20)

social policy Any planned set of actions by a group, institution, or governing body directed at attaining a social goal. (p. 31)

social problem solving Resolving social conflicts in ways that are both acceptable to others and beneficial to the self. Involves encoding and accurately interpreting social cues, formulating goals that enhance relationships, generating and evaluating problem-solving strategies, and enacting a response. (p. 468)

social referencing Relying on another person's emotional reaction to appraise an uncertain situation. (p. 407)

social smile The smile evoked by the stimulus of the human face. First appears between 6 and 10 weeks. (p. 400)

social systems perspective A view of the family as a complex set of interacting relationships influenced by the larger social context. (p. 559)

sociocultural theory Vygotsky's theory, in which children acquire the ways of thinking and behaving that make up a community's culture through cooperative dialogues with more knowledgeable members of society. (p. 25)

sociodramatic play The make-believe play with other children that is under way by age 2½ and increases rapidly during the next few years. (p. 232)

socioeconomic status (SES) A measure of a family's social position and economic well-being that combines three interrelated, but not completely overlapping, variables: (1) years of education and (2) the prestige of and skill required by one's job, both of which measure social status; and (3) income, which measures economic status. (p. 328)

sociometric techniques Self-reports that measure peer acceptance in terms of *social preferences*—the extent to which children or adolescents like, or prefer to spend time with, particular peers. (p. 609)

Sociomoral Reflection Measure–Short Form (SRM–SF) A questionnaire for assessing moral understanding in which individuals rate the importance of moral values addressed by brief questions and explain their ratings. Does not require research participants to read and think about lengthy moral dilemmas. (p. 488)

specific intelligence, or "s" In Spearman's theory of intelligence, a mental ability factor that is unique to a task. Distinguished from *general intelligence, or "g."* (p. 315)

speech registers Language adaptations to social expectations. (p. 386)

spermarche First ejaculation. (p. 198)

stage A qualitative change in thinking, feeling, and behaving that characterizes a specific period of development. (p. 8)

standardization The practice giving a newly constructed test to a large, representative sample of individuals, which serves as the standard for interpreting individual scores. (p. 324)

Stanford-Binet Intelligence Scales, Fifth Edition An individually administered intelligence test, appropriate for individuals age 2 to adulthood, that is the modern descendent of Alfred Binet's first successful test for children. Measures general intelligence and five intellectual factors: fluid reasoning, quantitative reasoning, knowledge, visual-spatial processing, and working memory. (p. 322)

states of arousal Different degrees of sleep and wakefulness. (p. 128)

stereotype threat The fear of being judged on the basis of a negative stereotype, which can trigger anxiety that interferes with performance. (p. 336)

store model A model of the information-processing system that assumes that we hold, or store, information in three parts of the mental system for processing: the sensory register; working, or short-term, memory; and long-term memory. (p. 272)

Strange Situation A laboratory technique for assessing the quality of infant–caregiver attachment between 1 and 2 years of age that includes eight short episodes in which brief separations from and reunions with the parent occur in an unfamiliar playroom. (p. 421)

stranger anxiety The infant's expression of fear in response to unfamiliar adults. Appears in many babies after 6 months of age. (p. 401)

structured interview A method in which the researcher asks each participant the same questions in the same way. (p. 46)

structured observation A method in which the researcher sets up a laboratory situation that evokes the behavior of interest so every participant has an equal opportunity to display the response. Distinguished from *naturalistic observation*. (p. 44)

sudden infant death syndrome (SIDS) The unexpected death, usually during the night, of an infant under 1 year of age that remains unexplained after thorough investigation. (p. 132)

sympathy Feelings of concern or sorrow for another's plight. (p. 409)

synapse The gap between neurons, across which chemical messages are sent. (p. 182)

synaptic pruning Loss of synapses by seldom-stimulated neurons, thereby returning them to an uncommitted state so they can support future development. (p. 183)

syntactic bootstrapping The hypothesis that children discover many word meanings by observing how words are used in syntax, or the structure of sentences. (p. 376)

syntax The rules by which words are arranged into sentences. (p. 354)

T

tabula rasa Locke's view of the child as a "blank slate" whose character is shaped by experience. (p. 12)

talent Outstanding performance in one or a few related fields. (p. 346)

telegraphic speech Children's two-word utterances that, like a telegram, focus on high-content words and leave out smaller, less important ones. (p. 378)

television literacy An understanding of television's specialized symbolic code of conveying information. Has two parts: mastering the form of the message, and figuring out the content of the message. (p. 620)

temperament Early appearing, stable individual differences in reactivity and self-regulation. Reactivity refers to variations in quickness and intensity of emotional arousal, attention, and motor action. Self-regulation refers to strategies that modify reactivity. (p. 411)

teratogen Any environmental agent that causes damage during the prenatal period. (p. 91)

theory An orderly, integrated set of statements that describes, explains, and predicts behavior. (p. 6)

theory of mind A coherent understanding of people as mental beings, which children revise as they encounter new evidence. Includes knowledge of mental activity and awareness that people can have different perceptions, feelings, desires, and beliefs. (p. 296)

theory of multiple intelligences Gardner's theory, which identifies eight intelligences on the basis of distinct sets of processing operations applied in culturally valued activities: linguistic, logico-mathematical, musical, spatial, bodily-kinesthetic, naturalist, interpersonal, intrapersonal. (p. 318)

theory theory A theory that assumes that children draw on innate concepts to form naïve theories, or explanations of everyday events in each core domain of thought. Then they test their theory against experience, revising it when it cannot adequately account for new information. Preschoolers have naïve physical and biological theories and a psychological theory, or theory of mind. (p. 256)

three-stratum theory of intelligence Carroll's theory, which represents the structure of intelligence in three tiers, with "g" at the top; an array of biologically based abilities in the second tier; and, in the third tier, specific behaviors through which people display the second-tier factors. The most comprehensive factor-analytic classification of mental abilities to date. (p. 316)

thyroxine A hormone released by the thyroid gland that is necessary for brain development and for growth hormone (GH) to have its full impact on body size. (p. 178)

time out Removing children from the immediate setting—for example, by sending them to their rooms—until they are ready to act appropriately. (p. 482)

time sampling An observational procedure in which the researcher records whether certain behaviors occur during a sample of short intervals. (p. 45)

traditional classroom A classroom based on the educational philosophy that the teacher is the sole authority for knowledge, rules, and decision making. The student's role is relatively passive–consisting of listening, responding when called on, and completing teacher-assigned tasks. Children's progress is evaluated by how well they keep pace with a uniform set of standards for their grade. Distinguished from *constructivist* and *social-constructivist classrooms*. (p. 627)

transitive inference The ability to seriate—or arrange items along a quantitative dimension—mentally. (p. 243)

triarchic theory of successful intelligence Sternberg's theory, which states that intelligent behavior involves balancing analytical intelligence, creative intelligence, and practical intelligence to achieve success in life, according to one's personal goals and the requirements of one's cultural community. (p. 317)

turnabout A conversational strategy in which the speaker not only comments on what has just been said but also adds a request to get the partner to respond again. (p. 384)

U

ulnar grasp The clumsy grasp of the young infant, in which the fingers close against the palm. (p. 147)

umbilical cord The long cord connecting the prenatal organism to the placenta that delivers nutrients and removes waste products. (p. 88)

unconditioned response (UCR) In classical conditioning, a reflexive response that is produced by an unconditioned stimulus (UCS). (p. 135)

unconditioned stimulus (UCS) In classical conditioning, a stimulus that leads to a reflexive response. (p. 135)

underextension An early vocabulary error in which the child applies a word or words too narrowly, to a smaller number of objects or events than is appropriate. Distinguished from *overextension*. (p. 374)

uninhibited, or **sociable, child** A child whose temperament is characterized by positive emotion and approach to novel stimuli. Distinguished from *inhibited*, or *shy, child*. (p. 414)

uninvolved child-rearing style A parenting style that combines low acceptance and involvement with little control and general indifference to issues of autonomy. Distinguished from *authoritarian, authoritative,* and *permissive child-rearing styles*. (p. 565)

universal grammar In Chomsky's theory of language development, a built-in storehouse of grammatical rules that applies to all human languages. (p. 355)

utilization deficiency Consistent use of a mental strategy, with little or no improvement in performance. Distinguished from *production* and *control deficiencies*. (p. 282)

V

validity The extent to which methods in a research study accurately measure what the investigator set out to measure. (p. 51)

velocity curve A growth curve that plots the average amount of growth at each yearly interval for a sample of children. Reveals the exact timing of growth spurts. (p. 173)

verbal aggression A type of hostile aggression that harms others through threats of physical aggression, name-calling, or hostile teasing. Distinguished from *physical* and *relational aggression*. (p. 507)

vernix A white, cheese-like substance covering the fetus and preventing the skin from chapping due to constant exposure to the amniotic fluid. (p. 89)

violation-of-expectation method A method in which researchers habituate babies to a physical event and then determine whether they recover to (look longer at) an *expected event* (a variation of the first event that follows physical laws) or an *unexpected event* (a variation that violates physical laws). Recovery to the unexpected event suggests that the infant is "surprised" by a deviation from physical reality, as indicated by heightened attention and interest, and therefore is aware of that aspect of the physical world. (p. 224)

visual acuity Fineness of visual discrimination. (p. 152)

visual cliff An apparatus used to study depth perception in infants. Consists of a Plexiglas-covered table and a central platform, from which babies are encouraged to crawl. Checkerboard patterns placed beneath the glass create the appearance of a shallow and a deep side. (p. 154)

W

Wechsler Intelligence Scale for Children–IV (WISC–IV) An individually administered intelligence test, appropriate for ages 6 through 16, that includes a measure of general intelligence and four broad intellectual factors: verbal reasoning, perceptual reasoning, working memory, and processing speed. (p. 322)

Wernicke's area A language structure located in the left temporal lobe of the cerebral cortex that plays a role in comprehending word meaning. (p. 358)

whole-language approach An approach to beginning reading instruction that parallels natural language learning. Children are exposed to text in its complete form (stories, poems, letters, posters, and lists) so that they can appreciate the communicative function of written language. Distinguished from *phonics approach*. (p. 302)

working, or **short-term, memory** The part of the information-processing system where we "work" on a limited amount of information, actively applying mental strategies so the information will be retained. (p. 272)

X

X-linked inheritance A pattern of inheritance in which a recessive gene is carried on the X chromosome. Males are more likely to be affected. (p. 76)

Z

zone of proximal development In Vygotsky's theory, a range of tasks too difficult for the child to do alone but possible to do with the help of adults and more skilled peers. (p. 260)

zygote The union of sperm and ovum at conception. (p. 71)

REFERENCES

Abbott, S. (1992). Holding on and pushing away: Comparative perspectives on an eastern Kentucky child-rearing practice. *Ethos, 20,* 33–65.

Abikoff, H. B., Jensen, P. S., Arnold, L. L. E., Hoza, B., et al. (2002). Observed classroom behavior of children with ADHD: Relationship to gender and comorbidity. *Journal of Abnormal Child Psychology, 30,* 349–359.

Aboud, F. E. (2003). The formation of in-group favoritism and out-group prejudice in young children: Are they distinct attitudes? *Developmental Psychology, 39,* 48–60.

Aboud, F. E., & Amato, M. (2001). Developmental and socialization influences on intergroup bias. In R. Brown & S. Gaertner (Eds.), *Blackwell handbook of social psychology: Intergroup processes.* Oxford, UK: Blackwell.

Aboud, F. E., & Doyle, A. (1996). Parental and peer influences on children's racial attitudes. *International Journal of Intercultural Relations, 20,* 371–383.

Accutane Action Group Forum. (2003, October). General archive area. Retrieved from www.xsorbit1.com/users

Achenbach, T. M., Phares, V., Howell, C. T., Rauh, V. A., & Nurcombe, B. (1990). Seven-year outcome of the Vermont intervention program for low-birthweight infants. *Child Development, 61,* 1672–1681.

Acker, M. M., & O'Leary, S. G. (1996). Inconsistency of mothers' feedback and toddlers' misbehavior and negative affect. *Journal of Abnormal Child Psychology, 24,* 703–714.

Ackerman, B. P. (1978). Children's understanding of speech acts in unconventional frames. *Child Development, 49,* 311–318.

Ackerman, B. P. (1993). Children's understanding of the speaker's meaning in referential communication. *Journal of Experimental Child Psychology, 55,* 56–86.

Adams, M. (2003). *Fire and ice: The United States, Canada, and the myth of converging values.* Toronto: Penguin.

Adams, R., & Laursen, B. (2001). The organization and dynamics of adolescent conflict with parents and friends. *Journal of Marriage and the Family, 63,* 97–110.

Adler, P. A., & Adler, P. (1998). *Peer power.* New Brunswick, NJ: Rutgers University Press.

Adolph, K. E. (1997). Learning in the development of infant locomotion. *Monographs of the Society for Research in Child Development, 62*(3, Serial No. 251).

Adolph, K. E. (2000). Specificity of learning: Why infants fall over a veritable cliff. *Psychological Science, 11,* 290–295.

Adolph, K. E., & Eppler, M. A. (1998). Development of visually guided locomotion. *Ecological Psychology, 10,* 303–321.

Adolph, K. E., & Eppler, M. A. (1999). Obstacles to understanding: An ecological approach to infant problem solving. In E. Winograd, R. Fivush, & W. Hirst (Eds.), *Ecological approaches to cognition* (pp. 31–58). Mahwah, NJ: Erlbaum.

Adolph, K. E., Vereijken, B., & Denny, M. A. (1998). Learning to crawl. *Child Development, 69,* 1299–1312.

Adolph, K. E., Vereijken, B., & Shrout, P. E. (2003). What changes in infant walking and why. *Child Development, 74,* 475–497.

Aguiar, A., & Baillargeon, R. (1999). 2.5-month-old infants' reasoning about when objects should and should not be occluded. *Cognitive Psychology, 39,* 116–157.

Aguiar, A., & Baillargeon, R. (2002). Developments in young infants' reasoning about occluded objects. *Cognitive Psychology, 45,* 267–336.

Ahluwalia, I. B., Morrow, B., Hsia, J., & Grummer-Strawn, L. M. (2003). Who is breast-feeding? Recent trends from the pregnancy risk assessment and monitoring system. *Journal of Pediatrics, 142,* 486–491.

Ahmed, A., & Ruffman, T. (1998). Why do infants make A not B errors in a search task, yet show memory for the location of hidden objects in a nonsearch task? *Developmental Psychology, 34,* 441–453.

Ainsworth, M. D. S., Blehar, M., Waters, E., & Wall, S. (1978). *Patterns of attachment.* Hillsdale, NJ: Erlbaum.

Akers, J. F., Jones, R. M., & Coyl, D. D. (1998). Adolescent friendship pairs: Similarities in identity status development, behaviors, attitudes, and intentions. *Journal of Adolescent Research, 13,* 178–201.

Akhtar, N., & Montague, L. (1999). Early lexical acquisition: The role of cross-situational learning. *First Language, 19,* 347–358.

Akhtar, N., & Tomasello, M. (2000). The social nature of words and word learning. In R. Golinkoff & K. Hirsh-Pasek (Eds.), *Becoming a word learner: A debate on lexical acquisition.* Oxford, UK: Oxford University Press.

Akimoto, S. A., & Sanbonmatsu, D. M. (1999). Differences in self-effacing behavior between European and Japanese Americans: Effect on competence evaluations. *Journal of Cross-Cultural Psychology, 30,* 159–177.

Akshoomoff, N. A., Feroleto, C. C., Doyle, R. E., & Stiles, J. (2002). The impact of early unilateral brain injury on perceptual organization and visual memory. *Neuropsychologia, 40,* 539–561.

Alan Guttmacher Institute. (2001). *Can more progress be made? Teenager sexual and reproductive behavior in developed countries.* New York: Author. Retrieved from www.guttmacher.org

Alan Guttmacher Institute. (2002). Teen sex and pregnancy. Retrieved from www.agi-usa.org/pubs/ib_teensex.html

Alan Guttmacher Institute. (2004). Teen sexuality: Stats & facts. Retrieved from www.fotf.ca/familyfacts/issues/teensexuality/stats.html

Aldridge, M. A., Stillman, R. D., & Bower, T. G. R. (2001). Newborn categorization of vowel-like sounds. *Developmental Science, 4,* 220–232.

Alessandri, S. M., Bendersky, M., & Lewis, M. (1998). Cognitive functioning in 8- to 18-month-old drug-exposed infants. *Developmental Psychology, 34,* 565–573.

Alessandri, S. M., Sullivan, M. W., & Lewis, M. (1990). Violation of expectancy and frustration in early infancy. *Developmental Psychology, 26,* 738–744.

Alexander, J. M., Fabricius, W. V., Fleming, V. M., Zwahr, M., & Brown, S. A. (2003). The development of metacognitive causal explanations. *Learning and Individual Differences, 13,* 227–238.

Alexander, J. M., & Schwanenflugel, P. J. (1996). Development of metacognitive concepts about thinking in gifted and nongifted children: Recent research. *Learning and Individual Differences, 8,* 305–325.

Alexandre-Bidon, K. L., & Lett, D. (1997). *Les enfants au Moyen Age, Ve–XVe siecles.* Paris: Hachette.

Alfieri, T., Ruble, D. N., & Higgins, E. T. (1996). Gender stereotypes during adolescence: Developmental changes and the transition to junior high school. *Developmental Psychology, 32,* 1129–1137.

Ali, L., & Scelfo, J. (2002, December 9). Choosing virginity. *Newsweek,* pp. 60–65.

Alibali, M. W. (1999). How children change their minds: Strategy change can be gradual or abrupt. *Developmental Psychology, 35,* 127–145.

Alibali, M. W., & Goldin-Meadow, S. (1993). Gesture–speech mismatch and mechanisms of learning: What the hands reveal about a child's state of mind. *Cognitive Psychology, 25,* 468–523.

Allen, J. P., Philliber, S., Herrling, S., & Kuperminc, G. P. (1997). Preventing teen pregnancy and academic failure: Experimental evaluation of a developmentally based approach. *Child Development, 64,* 729–742.

Allen, M., & Burrell, N. (1996). Comparing the impact of homosexual and heterosexual parents on children: Meta-analysis of existing research. *Journal of Homosexuality, 32,* 19–35.

Allen, S. E. M. (1996). *Aspects of argument structure acquisition in Inuktitut.* Amsterdam: Benjamins.

Allen, S. E. M., & Crago, M. B. (1996). Early passive acquisition in Inukitut. *Journal of Child Language, 23,* 129–156.

Allison, B. N., & Schultz, J. B. (2004). Parent–adolescent conflict in early adolescence. *Adolescence, 39,* 101–119.

Alpert-Gillis, L. J., & Connell, J. P. (1989). Gender and sex-role influences on children's self-esteem. *Journal of Personality, 57,* 97–114.

Als, H., Duffy, F. H., McAnulty, G. B., Rivkin, M. J., Vajapeyam, S., & Mulkern, R. V. (2004). Early experience alters brain function and structure. *Pediatrics, 113,* 846–857.

Alsaker, F. D. (1995). Timing of puberty and reactions to pubertal changes. In M. Rutter (Ed.), *Psychosocial disturbances in young people* (pp. 37–82). New York: Cambridge University Press.

Amabile, T. M. (1982). Children's artistic creativity: Detrimental effects of competition in a field setting. *Personality and Social Psychology Bulletin, 8,* 573–578.

Amato, P. R. (2001). Children of divorce in the 1990s: An update of the Amato and Keith (1991) meta-analysis. *Journal of Family Psychology, 15,* 355–370.

Amato, P. R., & Booth, A. (2000). *A generation at risk: Growing up in an era of family upheaval.* Cambridge, MA: Harvard University Press.

Amato, P. R., & Fowler, F. (2002). Parenting practices, child adjustment, and family diversity. *Journal of Marriage and the Family, 64,* 703–716.

Ambert, A.-M. (2003). *Same-sex couples and same-sex-parent families: Relationships, parenting, and issues of marriage.* Ottawa, Canada: Vanier Institute of the Family. Retrieved from www.vifamily.ca

American Academy of Pediatrics. (1999). Contraception and adolescents. *Pediatrics, 104,* 1161–1166.

American Psychiatric Association. (1994). *Diagnostic and statistical manual of mental disorders* (4th ed.). Washington, DC: Author.

American Psychological Association. (2002). Ethical principles of psychologists and code of conduct. *American Psychologist, 57,* 1060–1073.

Ames, C. (1992). Classrooms: Goals, structures, and student motivation. *Journal of Educational Psychology, 84,* 261–271.

Ames, E. W., & Chisholm, K. (2001). Social and emotional development in children adopted from institutions. In D. B. Bailey, Jr., J. T. Bruer, F. J. Symons, & J. W. Lichtman (Eds.), *Critical thinking about critical periods* (pp. 129–148). Baltimore, MD: Brookes

Anand, S. S., Yusuf, S., Jacobs, R., Davis, A. D., Yi, Q., & Gerstein, H. (2001). Risk factors, arteriosclerosis, and cardiovascular disease among Aboriginal people in Canada: The study of health assessment and risk evaluation in Aboriginal peoples (SHARE-AP). *Lancet, 358,* 1147–1153.

Anaya, H. D., Cantwell, S. M., & Rothman-Borus, M. J. (2003). Sexual risk behaviors among adolescents. In A. Biglan & M. C. Wang (Eds.), *Preventing youth problems* (pp. 113–143). New York: Kluwer Academic.

Anderman, E. M., Eccles, J. S., Yoon, K. S., Roeser, R., Wigfield, A., & Blumenfeld, P. (2001). Learning to value mathematics and reading: Relations to mastery and performance-oriented instructional practices. *Contemporary Educational Psychology, 26,* 76–95.

Anderman, E. M., & Midgley, C. (1997). Changes in achievement goal orientations, perceived academic competence, and grades across the transition to middle-level schools. *Contemporary Educational Psychology, 22,* 269–298.

Andersen, E. (1992). *Speaking with style: The sociolinguistic skills of children.* New York: Routledge.

Andersen, E. (2000). Exploring register knowledge: The value of "controlled improvisation." In L. Menn & N. B. Ratner (Eds.), *Methods for studying language production* (pp. 225–248). Mahwah, NJ: Erlbaum.

Anderson, C. A., Berkowitz, L., Donnerstein, E., Huesmann, R., Johnson, J. D., Linz, D., Malamuth, N. M., & Wartella, E. (2003). The influence of media violence on youth. *Psychological Science in the Public Interest, 4*(3), 81–106.

Anderson, C. A., & Bushman, B. J. (2002). The effects of media violence on society. *Science, 295,* 2377–2379.

Anderson, D. M., Huston, A. C., Schmitt, K. L., Linebarger, D. L., & Wright, J. C. (2001). Early childhood television viewing and adolescent behavior. *Monographs of the Society for Research in Child Development, 66*(1, Serial No. 264).

Anderson, D. R., Bryant, J., Wilder, A., Santomero, A., Willams, M., & Crawley, A. M. (2000). Researching Blue's Clues: Viewing behavior and impact. *Media Psychology, 2,* 179–194.

Anderson, D. R., Collins, P. A., Schmitt, K. L., & Jacobvitz, R. S. (1996). Stressful life events and television viewing. *Communication Research, 23,* 243–260.

Anderson, G. C. (1999). Kangaroo care of the premature infant. In E. Goldson (Ed.), *Nurturing the premature infant: Developmental interventions in the neonatal intensive care nursery* (pp. 131–160). New York: Oxford University Press.

Anderson, J. L., Morgan, J. L., & White, K. S. (2003). A statistical basis for speech sound discrimination. *Language and Speech, 46,* 155–182.

Anderson, S. E., Dallal, G. E., & Must, A. (2003). Relative weight and race influence average age at menarche: Results from two nationally representative surveys of U.S. girls studied 25 years apart. *Pediatrics, 111,* 844–850.

Anderson, S. W., Bechara, A., Damasio, H., Tranel, D., & Damasio, A. R. (1999). Impairment of social and moral behavior related to early damage in human prefrontal cortex. *Nature Neuroscience, 2,* 1032–1037.

Andersson, B.-E. (1989). Effects of public day care—A longitudinal study. *Child Development, 60,* 857–866.

Andersson, B.-E. (1992). Effects of day-care on cognitive and socioemotional competence of thirteen-year-old Swedish schoolchildren. *Child Development, 63,* 20–36.

Andersson, H. (1996). The Fagan Test of Infant Intelligence: Predictive validity in a random sample. *Psychological Reports, 78,* 1015–1026.

Andersson, S. W., Bengtsson, C., Hallberg, L., Lapidus, L., Niklasson, A., Wallgren, A., & Huthén, L. (2001). Cancer risk in Swedish women: The relation to size at birth. *British Journal of Cancer, 84,* 1193–1198.

Andersson, T., & Magnusson, D. (1990). Biological maturation in adolescence and the development of drinking habits and alcohol abuse among young males: A prospective longitudinal study. *Journal of Youth and Adolescence, 19,* 33–41.

Andre, T., Whigham, M., Hendrickson, A., & Chambers, S. (1999). Competence beliefs, positive affect, and gender stereotypes of elementary students and their parents about science versus other school subjects. *Journal of Research in Science Teaching, 36,* 719–747.

Andrews, G., & Halford, G. S. (1998). Children's ability to make transitive inferences: The importance of premise integration and structural complexity. *Cognitive Development, 13,* 479–513.

Anglin, J. M. (1993). Vocabulary development: A morphological analysis. *Monographs of the Society for Research in Child Development, 58*(10, Serial No. 238).

Angold, A., & Rutter, M. (1992). Effects of age and pubertal status on depression in a large clinical sample. *Development and Psychopathology, 4,* 5–28.

Anhalt, K., & Morris, T. L. (1999). Developmental and adjustment issues of gay, lesbian, and bisexual adolescents: A review of the empirical literature. *Clinical Child Psychology and Psychiatry, 7,* 433–456.

Anisfeld, M., Turkewitz, G., Rose, S. A., Rosenberg, F. R., Shelber, F. J., Couturier-Fagan, D. A., Ger, J. S., & Sommer, I. (2001). No compelling evidence that newborns imitate oral gestures. *Infancy, 2,* 111–122.

Annett, M. (2002). *Handedness and brain asymmetry: The right shift theory.* Hove, UK: Psychology Press.

Antshel, K. M. (2003). Timing is everything: Executive functions in children exposed to elevated levels of phenylalanine. *Neuropsychology, 17,* 458–468.

Apgar, V. (1953). A proposal for a new method of evaluation in the newborn infant. *Current Research in Anesthesia and Analgesia, 32,* 260–267.

Aquilino, W. S., & Supple, A. J. (2001). Long-term effects of parenting practices during adolescence on well-being outcomes in young adulthood. *Journal of Family Issues, 22,* 289–308.

Archer, S. L. (1989). The status of identity: Reflections on the need for intervention. *Journal of Adolescence, 12,* 345–359.

Archer, S. L., & Waterman, A. S. (1990). Varieties of identity diffusions and foreclosures: An exploration of subcategories of the identity statuses. *Journal of Adolescent Research, 5,* 96–111.

Ardila-Rey, A., & Killen, M. (2001). Middle-class Colombian children's evaluations of personal, moral, and social-conventional interactions in the classroom. *International Journal of Behavioral Development, 25,* 246–255.

Armstrong, K. L., Quinn, R. A., & Dadds, M. R. (1994). The sleep patterns of normal children. *Medical Journal of Australia, 161,* 202–206.

Arnett, J. J. (1999). Adolescent storm and stress reconsidered. *American Psychologist, 54,* 317–326.

Arnett, J. J. (2000a). Emerging adulthood: A theory of development from the late teens through the twenties. *American Psychologist, 55,* 469–480.

Arnett, J. J. (2000b). High hopes in a grim world: Emerging adults' views of their futures and of "Generation X." *Youth and Society, 31,* 267–286.

Arnett, J. J. (2003). Conceptions of the transition to adulthood among emerging adults in American ethnic groups. In J. J. Arnett & N. L. Galambos (Eds.), *Exploring cultural conceptions of the transition to adulthood (New directions for child and adolescent development,* No. 100, pp. 63–75). San Francisco: Jossey-Bass.

Arnold, D. H., Fisher, P. H., Doctoroff, G. L., & Dobbs, J. (2002). Accelerating math development in Head Start classrooms. *Journal of Educational Psychology, 94,* 762–770.

Arnold, D. H., McWilliams, L., & Harvey-Arnold, E. (1998). Teacher discipline and child misbehavior in daycare: Untangling causality with correlational data. *Developmental Psychology, 34,* 276–287.

Arnold, L. E., Elliott, M., Sachs, L., Bird, H., Draemer, H. C., & Wells, K. C. (2003). Effects of ethnicity on treatment attendance, stimulant response/dose, and 14-month outcome in ADHD. *Journal of Consulting and Clinical Psychology, 71,* 713–727.

Arnold, P. (1999). Emotional disorders in deaf children. In V. L. Schwean & D. H. Saklofske (Eds.), *Handbook of psychosocial characteristics of exceptional children* (pp. 493–522). New York: Kluwer.

Arora, S., McJunkin, C., Wehrer, J., & Kuhn, P. (2000). Major factors influencing breastfeeding rates: Mother's perception of father's attitude and milk supply. *Pediatrics, 106,* e67.

Arriaga, X. B., & Foshee, V. A. (2004). Adolescent dating violence: Do adolescents follow in their friends' or their parents' footsteps? *Journal of Interpersonal Violence, 19,* 162–184.

Arterberry, M. E., Craton, L. G., & Yonas, A. (1993). Infants' sensitivity to motion-carried information for depth and object properties. In C. E. Granrud (Ed.), *Visual perception and cognition in infancy* (pp. 215–234). Hillsdale, NJ: Erlbaum.

Artman, L., & Cahan, S. (1993). Schooling and the development of transitive inference. *Developmental Psychology, 29,* 753–759.

Asakawa, K. (2001). Family socialization practices and their effects on the internationalization of educational values for Asian and white American adolescents. *Applied Developmental Science, 5,* 184–194.

Asendorpf, J. B., Warkentin, V., & Baudonniere, P. (1996). Self-awareness and other-awareness II: Mirror self-recognition, social contingency awareness, and synchronic imitation. *Developmental Psychology, 32,* 313–321.

Asher, S. R., & Rose, A. J. (1997). Promoting children's social-emotional adjustment with peers. In P. Salovey & D. J. Sluyter (Eds.), *Emotional development and emotional intelligence* (pp. 193–195). New York: Basic Books.

Aslin, R. N., Jusczyk, P. W., & Pisoni, D. B. (1998). Speech and auditory processing during infancy: Constraints on and precursors to language. In D. Kuhn & R. S. Siegler (Eds.), *Handbook of child psychology: Vol. 2. Cognition, perception, and language* (5th ed., pp. 147–198). New York: Wiley.

Astington, J. W. (1995). Commentary: Talking it over with my brain. In J. H. Flavell, F. L. Green, & E. R. Flavell, Young children's knowledge about thinking. *Monographs of the Society for Research in Child Development, 60*(1, Serial No. 243).

Astington, J. W., & Jenkins, J. M. (1995). Theory of mind development and social understanding. *Cognition and Emotion, 9,* 151–165.

Astington, J. W., Pelletier, J., & Homer, B. (2002). Theory of mind and epistemological development: The relation between children's second-order false belief understanding and their ability to reason about evidence. *New Ideas in Psychology, 20,* 131–144.

Astley, S. J., Clarren, S. K., Little, R. E., Sampson, P. D., & Daling, J. R. (1992). Analysis of facial shape in children gestationally exposed to marijuana, alcohol, and/or cocaine. *Pediatrics, 89,* 67–77.

Astuti, R., Solomon, G. E. A., & Carey, S. (2004). Constraints on conceptual development: A case study of the acquisition of folkbiological and folksociological knowledge in Madagascar. *Monographs of the Society for Research in Child Development, 69*(3, Serial No. 277).

Aten, M. J., Siegel, D. M., Enaharo, M., & Auinger, P. (2002). Keeping middle school students abstinent: Outcomes of a primary prevention intervention. *Journal of Adolescent Health, 31,* 70–78.

Atkins, R., Hart, D., & Donnelly, T.M. (2004). Moral identity development and school attachment. In D. Narvaez & D. Lapsley (Eds.), *Morality, self and identity* (pp. 65–82). Mahwah, NJ: Erlbaum.

Atkinson, J. (2000). *The developing visual brain.* Oxford: Oxford University Press.

Atkinson, R. C., & Shiffrin, R. M. (1968). Human memory: A proposed system and its control processes. In K. W. Spence & J. T. Spence (Eds.), *Advances in the psychology of learning and motivation* (Vol. 2, pp. 90–195). New York: Academic Press.

Atkinson-King, K. (1973). Children's acquisition of phonological stress contrasts. *UCLA Working Papers in Phonetics, 25.*

Attewell, P. (2001). The first and second digital divides. *Sociology of Education, 74,* 252–259.

Au, T. K., Dapretto, M., & Song, Y.-K. (1994). Input vs. constraints: Early word acquisition in Korean and English. *Journal of Memory and Language, 33,* 567–582.

Au, T. K., Sidle, A. L., & Rollins, K. B. (1993). Developing an intuitive understanding of conservation and contamination: Invisible particles as a plausible mechanism. *Developmental Psychology, 29,* 286–299.

Aunola, K., Stattin, H., & Nurmi, J.-E. (2000). Parenting styles and adolescents' achievement strategies. *Journal of Adolescence, 23,* 205–222.

Australian Bureau of Statistics. (2004). Divorce rates. Retrieved from www.abus.gov.au

Averhart, C. J., & Bigler, R. S. (1997). Shades of meaning: Skin tone, racial attitudes, and constructive memory in African-American children. *Journal of Experimental Child Psychology, 67,* 368–388.

Axia, G., Bonichini, S., & Benini, F. (1999). Attention and reaction to distress in infancy: A longitudinal study. *Developmental Psychology, 35,* 500–504.

Azar, S. T., & Wolfe, D. A. (1998). Child physical abuse and neglect. In E. J. Mash & R. A. Barkley (Eds.), *Treatment of childhood disorders* (2nd ed., pp. 501–504). New York: Guilford.

Azmitia, M. (1988). Peer interaction and problem solving: When are two heads better than one? *Child Development, 59,* 87–96.

Azmitia, M. (1996). Peer interactive minds: Developmental, theoretical, and methodological issues. In P. B. Baltes & U. M. Staudinger (Eds.), *Interactive minds: Life-span perspectives on the social foundations of cognition* (pp. 133–162). New York: Cambridge University Press.

Bacharach, V. R., & Baumeister, A. A. (1998). Direct and indirect effects of maternal intelligence, maternal age, income, and home environment on intelligence of preterm, low-birth-weight children. *Journal of Applied Developmental Psychology, 19,* 361–375.

Bach-y-Rita, P. (2001). Theoretical and practical considerations in the restoration of function after stroke. *Topics in Stroke Rehabilitation, 8,* 1–15.

Baddeley, A. (1993). Working memory and conscious awareness. In A. F. Collins, S. E. Gathercole, M. A. Conway, & P. E. Morris (Eds.), *Theories of memory* (pp. 11–28). Hove, UK: Erlbaum.

Baddeley, A. (2000). Short-term and working memory. In E. Tulving & R. I. M. Craik (Eds.), *The Oxford handbook of memory* (pp. 77–92). New York: Oxford University Press.

Baenninger, M., & Newcombe, N. (1995). Environmental input to the development of sex-related differences in spatial and mathematical ability. *Learning and Individual Differences, 7,* 363–379.

Baer, J. S., Sampson, P. D., Barr, H. M., Connor, P. D., & Streissguth, A. P. (2003). A 21-year longitudinal analysis of the effects of prenatal alcohol exposure on young adult drinking. *Archives of General Psychiatry, 60,* 377–385.

Bagwell, C. L., & Coie, J. D. (2004). The best friendships of aggressive boys: Relationship quality, conflict management, and rule-breaking behavior. *Journal of Experimental Child Psychology, 88,* 5–24.

Bagwell, C. L., Newcomb, A. F., & Bukowski, W. M. (1998). Preadolescent friendship and peer rejection as predictors of adult adjustment. *Child Development, 69,* 140–153.

Bagwell, C. L., Schmidt, M. E., Newcomb, A. F., & Bukowski, W. M. (2001). Friendship and peer rejection as predictors of adult adjustment. In D. W. Nangle & C. A. Erdley (Eds.), *The role of friendship in psychological adjustment* (pp. 25–49). San Francisco: Jossey-Bass.

Bahrick, L. E. (1992). Infants' perceptual differentiation of amodal and modality-specific audio-visual relations. *Journal of Experimental Child Psychology, 53,* 180–199.

Bahrick, L. E. (2001). Increasing specificity in perceptual development: Infants' detection of nested levels of multimodal stimulation. *Journal of Experimental Child Psychology, 79,* 253–270.

Bahrick, L. E. (2002). Generalization of learning in three-and-a-half-month-old infants on the basis of amodal relations. *Child Development, 73,* 667–681.

Bahrick, L. E., Flom, R., & Lickliter, R. (2003). Intersensory redundancy facilitates discrimination of tempo in 3-month-old infants. *Developmental Psychobiology, 41,* 352–363.

Bahrick, L. E., Gogate, L. J., & Ruiz, I. (2002). Attention and memory for faces and actions in infancy: The salience of actions over faces in dynamic events. *Child Development, 73,* 1629–1643.

Bahrick, L. E., Hernandez-Reif, M., & Pickens, J. N. (1997). The effect of retrieval cues on visual preferences and memory in infancy: Evidence for a four-phase attention function. *Journal of Experimental Child Psychology, 67,* 1–20.

Bahrick, L. E., Lickliter, R., & Flom, R. (2004). Intersensory redundancy guides the development of selective attention, perception, and cognition in infancy. *Current Directions in Psychological Science, 13,* 99–102.

Bahrick, L. E., Netto, D., & Hernandez-Reif, M. (1998). Intermodal perception of adult and child faces and voices by infants. *Child Development, 69,* 1263–1275.

Bahrick, L. E., & Pickens, J. N. (1995). Infant memory for object motion across a period of three months: Implications for a four-phase attention function. *Journal of Experimental Child Psychology, 59,* 343–371.

Bai, D. L., & Bertenthal, B. I. (1992). Locomotor status and the development of spatial search skills. *Child Development, 63,* 215–226.

Bailey, J. M., Bobrow, D., Wolfe, M., & Mikach, S. (1995). Sexual orientation of adult sons of gay fathers. *Developmental Psychology, 31,* 124–129.

Bailey, J. M., Dunne, M. P., & Martin, N. G. (2000). Genetic and environmental influences on sexual orientation and its correlates in an Australian twin sample. *Journal of Personality and Social Psychology, 78,* 524–536.

Bailey, R. C. (1990). Growth of African pygmies in early childhood. *New England Journal of Medicine, 323,* 1146.

Baillargeon, R. (1994). Physical reasoning in infancy. In M. S. Gazzaniga (Ed.), *The cognitive neurosciences* (pp. 181–204). Cambridge, MA: MIT Press.

Baillargeon, R. (2000). Reply to Bogartz, Shinskey, and Schilling; Schilling; and Cashon and Cohen. *Infancy, 1,* 447–462.

Baillargeon, R. (2004). Infants' reasoning about hidden objects: Evidence for event-general and event-specific expectations. *Developmental Science, 7,* 391–424.

Baillargeon, R., & DeVos, J. (1991). Object permanence in young infants: Further evidence. *Child Development, 62,* 1227–1246.

Bakeman, R., Adamson, L. B., Konner, M., & Barr, R. G. (1990). !Kung infancy: The social context of object exploration. *Child Development, 61,* 794–809.

Baker, D. P., & Jones, D. P. (1993). Creating gender equality: Cross-national gender stratification and mathematics performance. *Sociology of Education, 66,* 91–103.

Bakermans-Kranenburg, M. J., van IJzendoorn, M. H., & Juffer, F. (2003). Less is more: Meta-analyses of sensitivity and attachment interventions in early childhood. *Psychological Bulletin, 129,* 195–215.

Balaban, M. T., & Waxman, S. R. (1997). Do words facilitate object categorization in 9-month-old infants? *Journal of Experimental Child Psychology, 64,* 3–26.

Baldwin, J. M. (1895). *Mental development in the child and the race: Methods and processes.* New York: Macmillan.

Baldwin, J. M. (1897). *Social and ethnic interpretations in mental development: A study in social psychology.* New York: Macmillan.

Bandura, A. (1977). *Social learning theory.* Englewood Cliffs, NJ: Prentice-Hall.

Bandura, A. (1991). Social cognitive theory of moral thought and action. In W. M. Kurtines & J. L. Gewirtz (Eds.), *Handbook of moral behavior and development* (Vol. 1, pp. 45–103). Hillsdale, NJ: Erlbaum.

Bandura, A. (1992). Perceived self-efficacy in cognitive development and functioning. *Educational Psychologist, 28,* 117–148.

Bandura, A. (1999). Social cognitive theory of personality. In L. A. Pervin & O. P. John (Eds.), *Handbook of personality: Theory and research* (2nd ed., pp. 154–196). New York: Guilford.

Bandura, A. (2001). Social cognitive theory: An agentic perspective. *Annual Review of Psychology, 52,* 1–26.

Banish, M. T. (1998). Evolving perspectives on lateralization of function. *Current Directions in Psychological Science, 7,* 32–37.

Banish, M. T. (1998). Integration of information between the cerebral hemispheres. *Current Directions in Psychological Science, 7,* 32–37.

Banish, M. T., & Heller, W. (1998). Evolving perspectives on lateralization of function. *Current Directions in Psychological Science, 7,* 1–2.

Bank, L., Patterson, G. R., & Reid, J. B. (1996). Negative sibling interaction patterns as predictors of later adjustment problems in adolescent and young adult males. In G. H. Brody (Ed.), *Sibling relationships: Their causes and consequences* (pp. 197–229). Norwood, NJ: Ablex.

Banks, D. (2003). Proteomics: A frontier between genomics and metabolomics. *Chance, 16*(4), 6–7.

Banks, M. S. (1980). The development of visual accommodation during early infancy. *Child Development, 51,* 646–666.

Banks, M. S., & Ginsburg, A. P. (1985). Early visual preferences: A review and new theoretical treatment. In H. W. Reese (Ed.), *Advances in child development and behavior* (Vol. 19, pp. 207–246). New York: Academic Press.

Banks, M. S., & Salapatek, P. (1983). Infant visual perception. In M. M. Haith & J. J. Campos (Eds.), *Handbook of child psychology: Vol. 2. Infancy and developmental psychobiology* (4th ed., pp. 436–571). New York: Wiley.

Barber, B. K. (1996). Parental psychological control: Revisiting a neglected construct. *Child Development, 67,* 3296–3319.

Barber, B. K., & Harmon, E. L. (2002). Violating the self: Parental psychological control of children and adolescents. In B. K. Barber (Ed.), *Intrusive parenting: How psychological control affects children and adolescents* (pp. 15–52). Washington, DC: American Psychological Association.

Barber, B. K., & Olsen, J. A. (1997). Socialization in context: Connection, regulation, and autonomy in the family, school, and neighborhood, and with peers. *Journal of Adolescent Research, 12,* 287–315.

Bardwell, J. R., Cochran, S. W., & Walker, S. (1986). Relationship of parental education, race, and gender to sex role stereotyping in five-year-old kindergartners. *Sex Roles, 15,* 275–281.

Barenbaum, J., Ruchkin, V., & Schwab-Stone, M. (2004). The psychosocial aspects of children exposed to war: Practice and policy initiatives. *Journal of Child Psychology and Psychiatry, 45,* 41–62.

Barker, D. J. P. (2002). Fetal programming of coronary heart disease. *Trends in Endocrinology and Metabolism, 13,* 364.

Barker, D. J. P., Eriksson, J. G., Forsén, T., & Osmond, C. (2002). Fetal origins of adult disease: Strength of effects and biological basis. *International Journal of Epidemiology, 31,* 1235–1239.

Barker, R. G., & Gump, P. V. (1964). *Big school, small school: High school size and student behavior.* Stanford, CA: Stanford University Press.

Barkley, R. A. (2002a). Psychosocial treatments of attention-deficit/hyperactivity disorder in children. *Journal of Clinical Psychology, 63*(Suppl. 12), 36–43.

Barkley, R. A. (2002b). Major life activity and health outcomes associated with attention-deficit/hyperactivity disorder. *Journal of Clinical Psychiatry, 63*(Suppl. 12), 10–15.

Barkley, R. A. (2003a). Attention-deficit/hyperactivity disorder. In E. J. Mash & R. A. Barkley (Eds.), *Child psychopathology* (2nd ed., pp. 75–143). New York: Guilford Press.

Barkley, R. A. (2003b). Issues in the diagnosis of attention-deficit hyperactivity disorder in children. *Brain and Development, 25,* 77–83.

Barling, J., Rogers, K., & Kelloway, K. (1995). Some effects of teenagers' part-time employment: The quantity and quality of work make the differences. *Journal of Organizational Behavior, 16,* 143–154.

Barnes-Josiah, D., & Augustin, A. (1995). Secular trend in the age at menarche in Haiti. *American Journal of Human Biology, 7,* 357–362.

Barnet, B., Arroyo, C., Devoe, M., & Duggan, A. K. (2004). Reduced school dropout rates among adolescent mothers receiving school-based prenatal care. *Archives of Pediatric and Adolescent Medicine, 158,* 262–268.

Barnett, D., Ganiban, J., & Cicchetti, D. (1999). Maltreatment, negative expressivity, and the development of Type D attachments from 12 to 24 months of age. In J. I. Vondra & D. Barnett (Eds.), Atypical attachment in infancy and early childhood among children at developmental risk. *Monographs of the Society for Research in Child Development, 64*(3, Serial No. 258), 97–118.

Barnett, D., & Vondra, J. I. (1999). Atypical patterns of early attachment: Theory, research, and current directions. In J. I. Vondra & D. Barnett (Eds.), Atypical attachment in infancy and early childhood among children at developmental risk. *Monographs of the Society for Research in Child Development, 64*(3, Serial No. 258), 1–24.

Baron-Cohen, S. (2001). Theory of mind and autism: A review. In L. M. Glidden (Ed.), *International review of research in mental retardation: Autism* (Vol. 23, pp. 169–184). San Diego: Academic Press.

Baron-Cohen, S., Baldwin, D. A., & Crowson, M. (1997). Do children with autism use the speaker's direction of gaze strategy to crack the code of language? *ChildDevelopment, 68*, 48–57.

Barr, H. M., Streissguth, A. P., Darby, B. L., & Sampson, P. D. (1990). Prenatal exposure to alcohol, caffeine, tobacco, and aspirin: Effects on fine and gross motor performance in 4-year-old children. *Developmental Psychology, 26*, 339–348.

Barr, R. G. (2001). "Colic" is something infants do, rather than a condition they "have": A developmental approach to crying phenomena patterns, pacification and (patho)genesis. In R. G. Barr, I. St James-Roberts, & M. R. Keefe (Eds.), *New evidence on unexplained infant crying* (pp. 87–104). St. Louis: Johnson & Johnson Pediatric Institute.

Barr, R. G., & Gunnar, M. (2000). Colic: The 'transient responsivity' hypothesis. In R. G. Barr, B. Hopkins, & J. A. Green (Eds.), *Crying as a sign, a symptom, and a signal* (pp. 41–66). New York: Cambridge University Press.

Barr, R., & Hayne, H. (1999). Developmental changes in imitation from television during infancy. *Child Development, 70*, 1067–1081.

Barr, R., & Hayne, H. (2003). It's not what you know, it's who you know: Older siblings facilitate imitation during infancy. *International Journal of Early Years Education, 11*, 7–21.

Barrash, J., Tranel, D., & Anderson, S. W. (2000). Acquired personality disturbances associated with bilateral damage to the ventromedial prefrontal region. *Developmental Neuropsychology, 18*, 355–381.

Barratt, M. S., Roach, M. A., & Leavitt, L. A. (1996). The impact of low-risk prematurity on maternal behaviour and toddler outcomes. *International Journal of Behavioral Development, 19*, 581–602.

Barrett, J. L. (2002). Do children experience God as adults do? In J. Andresen (Ed.), *Religion in mind* (pp. 173–190). New York: Cambridge University Press.

Barrett, J. L., Richert, R. A., & Driesenga, A. (2001). God's beliefs versus mother's: The development of non-human agent concepts. *Child Development, 72*, 50–65.

Barrett, J. L., & Van Orman, B. (1996). The effects of the use of images in worship on God concepts. *Journal of Psychology and Christianity, 15*, 38–45.

Barrett, K. C. (1998). The origins of guilt in early childhood. In J. Bybee (Ed.), *Guilt and children* (pp. 75–90). San Diego: Academic Press.

Barrett, K. C., & Campos, J. J. (1987). Perspectives on emotional development II: A functionalist approach to emotions. In J. D. Osofsky (Ed.), *Handbook of infant development* (2nd ed., pp. 555–578). New York: Wiley.

Barriga, A. Q., Morrison, E. M., Liau, A. K., & Gibbs, J. C. (2001). Moral cognition: Explaining the gender difference in antisocial behavior. *Merrill-Palmer Quarterly, 47*, 532–562.

Barron, F. (1988). Putting creativity to work. In R. J. Sternberg (Ed.), *The nature of creativity: Contemporary psychological perspectives* (pp. 76–98). New York: Cambridge University Press.

Bartgis, J., Lilly, A. R., & Thomas, D. G. (2003). Event-related potential and behavioral measures of attention in 5-, 7-, and 9-year-olds. *Journal of General Psychology, 130*, 311–335.

Bartlett, F. C. (1932). *Remembering.* Cambridge: Cambridge University Press.

Barton, M. E., & Strosberg, R. (1997). Conversational patterns of two-year-old twins in mother–twin–twin triads. *Journal of Child Language, 24*, 257–269.

Barton, M. E., & Tomasello, M. (1991). Joint attention and conversation in mother-infant-sibling triads. *Child Development, 62*, 517–529.

Bartrip, J., Morton, J., & de Schonen, S. (2001). Responses to mother's face in 3-week to 5-month-old infants. *British Journal of Developmental Psychology, 19*, 219–232.

Bartsch, K., & London, K. (2000). Children's use of mental state information in selecting persuasive arguments. *Developmental Psychology, 36*, 352–365.

Bartsch, K., & Wellman, H. M. (1995). *Children talk about the mind.* New York: Oxford University Press.

Basinger, K. S., Gibbs, J. C., & Fuller, D. (1995). Context and the measurement of moral judgment. *International Journal of Behavioral Development, 18*, 537–556.

Basow, S. A., & Rubin, L. R. (1999). Gender influences on adolescent development. In N. G. Johnson & M. C. Roberts (Eds.), *Beyond appearance: A new look at adolescent girls* (pp. 25–52). Washington, DC: American Psychological Association.

Bates, E. (1999). Plasticity, localization, and language development. In S. H. Broman & J. M. Fletcher (Eds.), *The changing nervous system: Neurobehavioral consequences of early brain disorders* (pp. 214–247). New York: Oxford University Press.

Bates, E. (2004). Explaining and interpreting deficits in language development across clinical groups: Where do we go from here? *Brain and Language, 88*, 248–253.

Bates, E., & MacWhinney, B. (1987). Competition, variation, and language learning. In B. MacWhinney (Ed.), *Mechanisms of language acquisition* (pp. 157–193). Hillsdale, NJ: Erlbaum.

Bates, E., Marchman, V., Thal, D., Fenson, L., Dale, P., Reznick, J. S., Reilly, J., & Hartung, J. (1994). Developmental and stylistic variation in the composition of early vocabulary. *Journal of Child Language, 21*, 85–123.

Bates, E., Wilson, S. M., Saygin, A. P., Dick, F., Sereno, M. I., Knight, R. T., & Dronkers, N. F. (2003). Voxel-based lesion-symptom mapping. *Nature Neuroscience, 6*, 448–450.

Bates, J. E., Wachs, T. D., & Emde, R. N. (1994). Toward practical uses for biological concepts. In J. E. Bates & T. D. Wachs (Eds.), *Temperament: Individual differences at the interface of biology and behavior* (pp. 275–306). Washington, DC: American Psychological Association.

Bauer, P. J. (1997). Development of memory in early childhood. In N. Cowan (Ed.), *The development of memory in childhood* (pp. 83–111). Hove, UK: Psychology Press.

Bauer, P. J. (2002). Early memory development. In U. Goswami (Ed.), *Blackwell handbook of child cognitive development* (pp. 127–150). Malden, MA: Blackwell.

Bauer, P. J., Wiebe, S. A., Carver, L. J., Waters, J. M., & Nelson, C. A. (2003). Developments in long-term explicit memory late in the first year of life: Behavioral and electrophysiological indices. *Psychological Science, 14*, 629–635.

Baumeister, R. F. (1998). Inducing guilt. In J. Bybee (Ed.), *Guilt and children* (pp. 185–213). San Diego: Academic Press.

Baumeister, R. F., Campbell, J. D., Krueger, J. I., & Vohs, K. D. (2003). Does high self-esteem cause better performance, interpersonal success, happiness, or healthier lifestyles? *Psychological Science in the Public Interest, 4*(1), 1–44.

Baumeister, R. F., Smart, L., & Boden, J. M. (1996). Relation of threatened egotism to violence and aggression: The dark side of high self-esteem. *Psychological Review, 103*, 5–33.

Baumrind, D. (1971). Current patterns of parental authority. *Developmental Psychology Monograph, 4*(1, Pt. 2).

Baumrind, D. (1991). The influence of parenting style on adolescent competence and substance use. *Journal of Early Adolescence, 11*, 56–95.

Baumrind, D. (1997). Necessary distinctions. *Psychological Inquiry, 8*, 176–182.

Baumrind, D., & Black, A. E. (1967). Socialization practices associated with dimensions of competence in preschool boys and girls. *Child Development, 38*, 291–327.

Bauserman, R. (2002). Child adjustment in joint-custody versus sole-custody arrangements: A meta-analytic review. *Journal of Family Psychology, 16*, 91–102.

Baydar, N., Greek, A., & Brooks-Gunn, J. (1997). A longitudinal study of the effects of the birth of a sibling during the first 6 years of life. *Journal of Marriage and the Family, 59*, 939–956.

Bayley, N. (1969). *Bayley Scales of Infant Development.* New York: Psychological Corporation.

Bayley, N. (1993). *Bayley Scales of Infant Development* (2nd ed.). New York: Psychological Corporation.

Baynes, K., & Gazzaniga, M. S. (1988). Right hemisphere language: Insights into normal language mechanisms. In F. Plum (Ed.), *Language, communication, and the brain* (pp. 117–126). New York: Raven.

Beal, C. R. (1990). The development of text evaluation and revision skills. *Child Development, 61*, 247–258.

Beals, D. E. (2001). Eating and reading: Links between family conversations with preschoolers and later language literacy. In D. K. Dickinson & P. O. Tabors (Eds.), *Beginning literacy with language: Young children's learning at home and school* (pp. 75–92). Baltimore, MD: Paul H. Brookes.

Bearman, P. S., & Moody, J. (2004). Suicide and friendships among American adolescents. *American Journal of Public Health, 94*, 89–95.

Beatty, W. W. (1992). Gonadal hormones and sex differences in nonreproductive behaviors. In A. A. Gerall, H. Moltz, & I. L. Ward (Eds.), *Handbook of behavioral neurobiology: Vol. 11. Sexual differentiation* (pp. 85–128). New York: Plenum.

Beautrais, A. L. (2003). Life course factors associated with suicidal behaviors in young people. *American Behavioral Scientist, 46*, 1137–1156.

Becker, J. (1990). Processes in the acquisition of pragmatic competence. In G. Conti-Ramsden & C. Snow (Eds.), *Children's language* (Vol. 7, pp. 7–24). Hillsdale, NJ: Erlbaum.

Bedford, O. A. (2004). The individual experience of guilt and shame in Chinese culture. *Culture and Psychology, 10*, 29–52.

Begley, S. (1995, February 13). Surprising new lessons from the controversial science of race. *Newsweek*, pp. 67–68.

Behnke, M., Eyler, F. D., Garvan, C. W., & Wobie, K. (2001). The search for congenital malformations in newborns with fetal cocaine exposure. *Pediatrics, 107*, E74.

Behrman, R. E., Kliegman, R. M., & Arvin, A. M. (Eds.). (1996). *Nelson textbook of pediatrics* (15th ed.). Philadelphia: Saunders.

Behrman, R. E., Kliegman, R. M., & Jenson, H. B. (2000). *Nelson textbook of pediatrics* (16th ed.). Philadelphia: Saunders.

Beilin, H. (1992). Piaget's enduring contribution to developmental psychology. *Developmental Psychology, 28*, 191–204.

Beitel, A. H., & Parke, R. D. (1998). Paternal involvement in infancy: The role of maternal and paternal attitudes. *Journal of Family Psychology, 12*, 268–288.

Bell, A., Weinberg, M., & Hammersmith, S. (1981). *Sexual preference: Its development in men and women.* Bloomington: Indiana University Press.

Bell, J. H., & Bromnick, R. D. (2003). The social reality of the imaginary audience: A grounded theory approach. *Adolescence, 38*, 205–219.

Bell, K. L., Allen, J. P., Hauser, S. T., & O'Connor, T. G. (1996). Family factors and young adult transitions: Educational attainment and occupational prestige. In J. A. Graber, J. Brooks-Gunn, & A. C. Petersen (Eds.), *Transitions through adolescence: Interpersonal domains and contexts* (pp. 345–366). Mahwah, NJ: Erlbaum.

Bell, M. A. (1998). Frontal lobe function during infancy: Implications for the development of cognition and attention. In J. E. Richards (Ed.), *Cognitive neuroscience of attention: A developmental perspective* (pp. 327–362). Mahwah, NJ: Erlbaum.

Bell, M. A., & Fox, N. A. (1996). Crawling experience is related to changes in cortical organization during infancy: Evidence from EEG coherence. *Developmental Psychobiology, 29*, 551–561.

Bell, S. M., & Ainsworth, M. D. S. (1972). Infant crying and maternal responsiveness. *Child Development, 43*, 1171–1190.

Bell-Dolan, D. J., Foster, S. L., & Sikora, D. M. (1989). Effects of sociometric testing on children's behavior and loneliness in school. *Developmental Psychology, 25*, 306–311.

Bell-Dolan, D. J., & Wessler, A. E. (1994). Ethical administration of sociometric measures: Procedures in use and suggestions for impovement. *Professional Psychology—Research and Practice, 25*, 23–32.

Bellugi, U., Bihrle, A., Neville, H., Jernigan, T., & Doherty, S. (1992). Language, cognition, and brain organization in a neurodevelopmental disorder. In M. Gunnar & C. Nelson (Eds.), *Developmental behavioral neuroscience* (pp. 201–232). Hillsdale, NJ: Erlbaum.

Bellugi, U., Lichtenberger, L., Jones, W., Lai, Z., & St. George, M. (2000). The neurocognitive profile of Williams syndrome: A complex pattern of strengths and weaknesses. *Journal of Cognitive Neuroscience, 12*, 1–29.

Belsky, J. (1992). Consequences of child care for children's development: A deconstructionist view. In A. Booth (Ed.), *Child care in the 1990s: Trends and consequences* (pp. 83–85). Hillsdale, NJ: Erlbaum.

Belsky, J. (2001). Emanuel Miller Lecture: Developmental risks (still) associated with early child care. *Journal of Child Psychology and Psychiatry, 42*, 845–859.

Belsky, J., Campbell, S. B., Cohn, J. F., & Moore, G. (1996). Instability of infant–parent attachment security. *Developmental Psychology, 32*, 921–924.

Belsky, J., & Fearon, R. M. P. (2002). Early attachment security, subsequent maternal sensitivity, and later child development: Does continuity in development depend on caregiving? *Attachment and Human Development, 4*, 361–387.

Belsky, J., & Hsieh, K.-H. (1998). Patterns of marital change during the early childhood years: Parent personality, coparenting, and division-of-labor correlates. *Journal of Family Psychology, 12*, 511–528.

Bem, D. J. (1996). Exotic becomes erotic: A developmental theory of sexual orientation. *Psychological Review, 103*, 320–335.

Bem, S. L. (1977). On the utility of alternative procedures for assessing psychological androgyny. *Journal of Consulting and Clinical Psychology, 45*, 196–205.

Bem, S. L. (1993). *The lenses of gender: Transforming the debate on sexual inequality.* New Haven, CT: Yale University Press.

Bem, S. L. (1998). *An unconventional family.* New Haven, CT: Yale University Press.

Bempechat, J., & Drago-Severson, E. (1999). Cross-national differences in academic achievement: Beyond etic conceptions of children's understandings. *Review of Educational Research, 69*, 287–314.

Benbow, C. P., & Stanley, J. C. (1983). Sex differences in mathematical reasoning: More facts. *Science, 222*, 1029–1031.

Bendersky, M., & Lewis, M. (1994). Environmental risk, biological risk, and developmental outcome. *Developmental Psychology, 30*, 484–494.

Benenson, J. F., Apostoleris, N. H., & Parnass, J. (1997). Age and sex differences in dyadic and group interaction. *Developmental Psychology, 33*, 538–543.

Benenson, J. F., & Christakos, A. (2003). The greater fragility of females' versus males' closest same-sex friendships. *Child Development, 74*, 1123–1129.

Benenson, J. F., Nicholson, C., Waite, A., Roy, R., & Simpson, A. (2001). The influence of group size on children's competitive behavior. *Child Development, 72*, 921–928.

Bennett, M., Barrett, M., Karakozov, R., Kipiani, G., Lyons, E., Pavlenko, V., & Riazanova, T. (2004). Young children's evaluations of the ingroup and outgroups: A multi-national study. *Social Development, 13*, 124–141.

Benoit, D., & Parker, K. C. H. (1994). Stability and transmission of attachment across three generations. *Child Development, 65*, 1444–1456.

Berenbaum, S. A. (2001). Cognitive function in congenital adrenal hyperplasia. *Endocrinology and Metabolism Clinics of North America, 30*, 173–192.

Bergen, D., & Mauer, D. (2000). Symbolic play, phonological awareness, and literacy skills at three age levels. In K. A. Roskos & J. F. Christie (Eds.), *Play and literacy in early childhood: Research from multiple perspectives* (pp. 45–62). Mahwah, NJ: Erlbaum.

Bergin, C., Talley, S., & Hamer, L. (2003). Prosocial behaviours of young adolescents: A focus group study. *Journal of Adolescence, 26*, 13–32.

Berk, L. E. (1985). Relationship of caregiver education to child-oriented attitudes, job satisfaction, and behaviors toward children. *Child Care Quarterly, 14*, 103–129.

Berk, L. E. (1992). The extracurriculum. In P. W. Jackson (Ed.), *Handbook of research on curriculum* (pp. 1002–1043). New York: Macmillan.

Berk, L. E. (2001a). *Awakening children's minds: How parents and teachers can make a difference.* New York: Oxford University Press.

Berk, L. E. (2001b). Private speech and self-regulation in children with impulse-control difficulties: Implications for research and practice. *Journal of Cognitive Education and Psychology, 2*, 1–21.

Berk, L. E. (2003). Vygotsky, Lev. In L. Nadel (Ed.), *Encyclopedia of cognitive science* (Vol. 6). London: Macmillan.

Berk, L. E. (2004). *Conversations with children.* Normal, IL: Illinois State University.

Berk, L. E. (2005). Why parenting matters. In S. Olfman (Ed.), *Childhood lost: How American culture is failing our kids* (pp. 19–53). New York: Guilford.

Berk, L. E. (2005). Why parenting matters. In S. Olfman (Ed.), *Childhood lost: How American culture is failing our kids* (pp. 19–53). Westport, CT: Praeger.

Berk, L. E., & Spuhl, S. T. (1995). Maternal interaction, private speech, and task performance in preschool children. *Early Childhood Research Quarterly, 10*, 145–169.

Berk, L. E., & Winsler, A. (1995). *Scaffolding children's learning: Vygotsky and early childhood education.* Washington, DC: National Association for the Education of Young Children.

Berkey, C. S., Wang, X., Dockery, D. W., & Ferris, B. G., Jr. (1994). Adolescent height growth of U.S. children. *Annals of Human Biology, 21*, 435–442.

Berkowitz, C. M. (2004). *Talking to your kids about sex.* Somerville, NJ: Somerset Medical Center. Retrieved from www.somersetmedicalcenter.com/1817.cfm

Berkowitz, M. W., & Gibbs, J. C. (1983). Measuring the developmental features of moral discussion. *Merrill-Palmer Quarterly, 29*, 399–410.

Berman, P. (1980). Are women more responsive than men to the young? A review of developmental and situational variables. *Psychological Bulletin, 88*, 668–695.

Bermejo, V. (1996). Cardinality development and counting. *Developmental Psychology, 32*, 263–268.

Berndt, T. J., Cheung, P. C., Lau, S., Hau, K.-T., & Lew, W. J. F. (1993). Perceptions of parenting in mainland China, Taiwan, and Hong Kong: Sex differences and societal differences. *Developmental Psychology, 29*, 156–164.

Berndt, T. J., & Keefe, K. (1995). Friends' influence on adolescents' adjustment to school. *Child Development, 66*, 1312–1329.

Berndt, T. J., & Murphy, L. M. (2002). Influences of friends and friendships: Myths, truths, and research recommendations. In R. V. Kail (Ed.), *Advances in child development and behavior* (Vol. 30, pp. 275–310). San Diego, CA: Academic Press.

Bernier, J. C., & Siegel, D. H. (1994). Attention-deficit hyperactivity disorder: A family ecological systems perspective. *Families in Society, 75*, 142–150.

Berninger, V. W., Vermeulen, K., Abbott, R. D., McCutchen, D., Cotton, S., & Cude, J. (2003). Naming speed and phonological awareness as predictors of reading development. *Journal of Educational Psychology, 95*, 452–464.

Berry, G. L. (2003). Developing children and multicultural attitudes: The systemic psychosocial influences of television portrayals in a multimedia society. *Cultural Diversity and Ethnic Minority Psychology, 9*, 360–366.

Bertenthal, B. I. (1993). Infants' perception of biomechanical motions: Instrinsic image and knowledge-based constraints. In C. Granrud (Ed.), *Visual perception and cognition in infancy* (pp. 175–214). Hillsdale, NJ: Erlbaum.

Bertenthal, B. I., Campos, J. J., & Barrett, K. (1984). Self-produced locomotion: An organizer of emotional, cognitive, and social development in infancy. In R. Emde & R. Harmon (Eds.), *Continuities and discontinuities in development* (pp. 174–210). New York: Plenum.

Bertenthal, B. I., & Clifton, R. K. (1998). Perception and action. In D. Kuhn & R. S. Siegler (Eds.), *Handbook of child psychology: Vol. 2. Cognition, perception, and language* (pp. 51–102). New York: Wiley.

Bertenthal, B. I., Rose, J. L., & Bai, D. L. (1997). Perception–action coupling in the development of visual control of posture. *Journal of Experimental Psychology: Human Perception and Performance, 23*, 1631–1643.

Bertenthal, B., & von Hofsten, C. (1998). Eye, head and trunk control: The foundation for manual development. *Neuroscience and Biobehavioral Reviews, 22*, 515–520.

Berzonsky, M. D. (2004). Identity style, parental authority, and identity commitment. *Journal of Youth and Adolescence, 33*, 213–220.

Berzonsky, M. D., & Kuk, L. S. (2000). Identity status, identity processing style, and the transition to university. *Journal of Adolescent Research, 15*, 81–98.

Best, D. L. (2001). Gender concepts: Convergence in cross-cultural research and methodologies. *Cross-cultural Research: The Journal of Comparative Social Science, 35*, 23–43.

Betz, C. (1994). Beyond time-out: Tips from a teacher. *Young Children, 49*(3), 10–14.

Beyers, J. M., Bates, J. E., Pettit, G. S., & Dodge, K. A. (2003). Neighborhood structure, parenting processes, and the development of youths' externalizing behaviors: A multilevel analysis. *American Journal of Community Psychology, 31*, 35–53.

Beyth-Marom, R., & Fischhoff, B. (1997). Adolescents' decisions about risks: A cognitive perspective. In J. Schulenberg, J. L. Maggs, & K. Hurrelmann (Eds.), *Health risks and developmental transitions during adolescence* (pp. 110–135). New York: Cambridge University Press.

Bhandari, N., Bahl, R., Taneja, S., Strand, T., & Mølbak, K. (2002). Substantial reduction in severe diarrheal morbidity by daily zinc supplementation in young North Indian children. *Pediatrics, 109*, e86–e89.

Bhatt, R. S., Wilk, A., Hill, D., & Rovee-Collier, C. (2004). Correlated attributes and categorization in the first half-year of life. *Developmental Psychobiology, 44*, 103–115.

Bhutta, A. T., Cleves, M. A., Casey, P. H., Cradock, M. M., & Anand, K. J. S. (2002). Cognitive and behavioral outcomes of school-aged children who were born preterm. *Journal of the American Medical Association, 288*, 728–737.

Bialystok, E. (1986). Factors in the growth of linguistic awareness. *Child Development, 57*, 498–510.

Bialystok, E. (1999). Cognitive complexity and attentional control in the bilingual mind. *Child Development, 70*, 636–644.

Bialystok, E. (2001). *Bilingualism in development: Language, literacy, and cognition.* New York: Cambridge University Press.

Bialystok, E., & Herman, J. (1999). Does bilingualism matter for early literacy? *Language and Cognition, 2*, 35–44.

Bialystok, E., & Martin, M. M. (2003). Notation to symbol: Development in children's understanding of print. *Journal of Experimental Child Psychology, 86,* 223–243.

Bialystok, E., & Senman, L. (2004). Executive processes in appearance–reality tasks: The role of inhibition of attention and symbolic representation. *Child Development, 75,* 562–579.

Bianco, A., Stone, J., Lynch, L., Lapinski, R., Berkowitz, G., & Berkowitz, R. L. (1996). Pregnancy outcome at age 40 and older. *Obstetrics and Gynecology, 87,* 917–922.

Biederman, J., & Spencer, T. J. (2000). Genetics of childhood disorders: XIX. ADHD, part 3: Is ADHD a noradrenergic disorder? *Journal of the American Academy of Child and Adolescent Psychiatry, 39,* 1330–1333.

Bielinski, J., & Davison, M. L. (1998). Gender differences by item difficulty interactions in multiple-choice mathematics items. *American Educational Research Journal, 35,* 455–476.

Biernat, M. (1991). A multi-component, developmental analysis of sex-typing. *Sex Roles, 24,* 567–586.

Bigelow, A. (1992). Locomotion and search behavior in blind infants. *Infant Behavior and Development, 15,* 179–189.

Bigelow, A. E. (2003). The development of joint attention in blind infants. *Development and Psychopathology, 15,* 259–275.

Bigler, R. S. (1995). The role of classification skill in moderating environmental influences on children's gender stereotyping: A study of the functional use of gender in the classroom. *Child Development, 66,* 1072–1087.

Bigler, R. S., Brown, C. S., & Markell, M. (2001). When groups are not created equal: Effects of group status on the formation of intergroup attitudes in children. *Child Development, 72,* 1151–1162.

Bigler, R. S., & Liben, L. S. (1992). Cognitive mechanisms in children's gender stereotyping: Theoretical and educational implications of a cognitive-based intervention. *Child Development, 63,* 1351–1363.

Binet, A., & Simon, T. (1908). Le développement de l'intelligence chez les enfants. *L'Année Psychologique, 14,* 1–94.

Bioethics Consultative Committee. (2003). *Comparison of ethics legislation in Europe.* Retrieved from www.synapse .net.mt/bioethics/euroleg1.htm

Birch, E. E. (1993). Stereopsis in infants and its developmental relation to visual acuity. In K. Simons (Ed.), *Early visual development: Normal and abnormal* (pp. 224–236). New York: Oxford University Press.

Birch, L. L., & Fisher, J. A. (1995). Appetite and eating behavior in children. *Pediatric Clinics of North America, 42,* 931–953.

Birch, L. L., Fisher, J. O., & Davison, K. K. (2003). Learning to overeat: Maternal use of restrictive feeding practices promotes girls' eating in the absence of hunger. *American Journal of Clinical Nutrition, 78,* 215–220.

Birch, L. L., Zimmerman, S., & Hind, H. (1980). The influence of social-affective context on preschool children's food preferences. *Child Development, 51,* 856–861.

Birch, S. A. J., & Bloom, P. (2003). Children are cursed: An asymmetric bias in mental-state attribution. *Psychological Science, 14,* 283–285.

Birch, S. H., & Ladd, G. W. (1997). The teacher–child relationship and children's early school adjustment. *Journal of School Psychology, 35,* 61–79.

Birch, S. H., & Ladd, G. W. (1998). Children's interpersonal behaviors and the teacher–child relationship. *Developmental Psychology, 34,* 934–946.

Biringen, Z., Emde, R. N., Campos, J. J., & Appelbaum, M. I. (1995). Affective reorganization in the infant, the mother, and the dyad: The role of upright locomotion and its timing. *Child Development, 66,* 499–514.

Bischofshausen, S. (1985). Developmental differences in schema dependency for temporally ordered story events. *Journal of Psycholinguistic Research, 14,* 543–556.

Bishop, D., Aamodt-Leeper, G., Crewsell, C., McGurk, R., & Skuse, D. H. (2001). Individual differences in cognitive planning on the Tower of Hanoi task: Neuropsychological maturity or measurement error? *Journal of Child Psychology and Psychiatry and Allied Disciplines, 42,* 551–556.

Bjorklund, D. F. (1997). The role of immaturity in human development. *Psychological Bulletin, 122,* 153–169.

Bjorklund, D. F. (2004). *Children's thinking* (4th ed.). Belmont, CA: Wadsworth.

Bjorklund, D. F., & Coyle, T. R. (1995). Utilization deficiencies in the development of memory strategies. In F. E. Weinert & W. Schneider (Eds.), *Research on memory development: State of the art and future directions* (pp. 161–180). Hillsdale, NJ: Erlbaum.

Bjorklund, D. F., & Douglas, R. N. (1997). The development of memory strategies. In N. Cowan (Ed.), *The development of memory in childhood* (pp. 83–111). Hove, UK: Psychology Press.

Bjorklund, D. F., & Harnishfeger, K. K. (1995). The evolution of inhibition mechanisms and their role in human cognition and behavior. In M. L. Howe & R. Pasnak (Eds.), *Emerging themes in cognitive development: Vol. 1. Foundations* (pp. 141–173). New York: Springer-Verlag.

Bjorklund, D. F., & Pellegrini, A. D. (2000). Child development and evolutionary psychology. *Child Development, 71,* 1687–1708.

Bjorklund, D. F., & Pellegrini, A. D. (2002). *The origins of human nature: Evolutionary developmental psychology.* Washington, DC: American Psychological Association.

Bjorklund, D. F., Schneider, W., Cassel, W. S., & Ashley, E. (1994). Training and extension of a memory strategy: Evidence for utilization deficiencies in high- and low-IQ children. *Child Development, 65,* 951–965.

Bjorklund, D. F., Yunger, J. L., & Pellegrini, A. D. (2002). The evolution of parenting and evolutionary approaches to childrearing. In M. H. Bornstein (Ed.), *Handbook of parenting: Vol. 2. Biology and Ecology of Parenting* (2nd ed., pp. 3–30). Mahwah, NJ: Erlbaum.

Black, R. E., Williams, S. M., Jones, I. E., & Goulding, A. (2002). Children who avoid drinking cow milk have low dietary calcium intakes and poor bone health. *American Journal of Clinical Nutrition, 76,* 675–680.

Blake, J., & Boysson-Bardies, B. de (1992). Patterns in babbling: A cross-linguistic study. *Journal of Child Language, 19,* 51–74.

Blakemore, J. E. O. (2003). Children's beliefs about violating gender norms: Boys shouldn't look like girls, and girls shouldn't act like boys. *Sex Roles, 48,* 411–419.

Blanchard, M., & Main, M. (1979). Avoidance of the attachment figure and social-emotional adjustment in day-care infants. *Developmental Psychology, 15,* 445–446.

Blasi, A. (1994). Bridging moral cognition and moral action: A critical review of the literature. In B. Puka (Ed.), *Fundamental research in moral development: A compendium* (Vol. 2, pp. 123–167). New York: Garland.

Blasi, A. (1995). Moral understanding and the moral personality: The process of moral integration. In W. Kurtines & J. L. Gewirtz (Eds.), *Moral development: An introduction* (pp. 229–253). Boston: Allyn and Bacon.

Blasi, C. H., & Bjorklund, D. F. (2003). Evolutionary developmental psychology: A new tool for better understanding human ontogeny. *Human Development, 46,* 259–281.

Blass, E M. (1999). Savoring sucrose and suckling milk: Easing pain, saving calories, and learning about mother. In M. Lewis & D. Ramsay (Eds.), *Soothing and stress* (pp. 79–107). Mahwah, NJ: Erlbaum.

Blass, E. M., Ganchrow, J. R., & Steiner, J. E. (1984). Classical conditioning in newborn humans 2–48 hours of age. *Infant Behavior and Development, 7,* 223–235.

Blatchford, P., Bassett, P., Goldstein, H., & Martin, C. (2003). Are class size differences related to pupils' educational progress and classroom processes? Findings from the Institute of Education Class Size Study of Children Aged 5–7 years. *British Educational Research Journal, 29,* 709–730.

Blatchford, P., Edmonds, S., & Martin, C. (2003). Class size, pupil attentiveness, and peer relations. *British Journal of Educational Psychology, 7,* 15–36.

Blatchford, P., Moriarty, V., Edmonds, S., & Martin, C. (2002). Relationships between class size and teaching: A multimethod analysis of English infant schools. *American Educational Research Journal, 39,* 101–132.

Bleeker, M. M., & Jacobs, J. E. (2004). Achievement in math and science: Do mothers' beliefs matter 12 years later? *Journal of Educational Psychology, 96,* 97–109.

Blewitt, P. (1994). Understanding categorical hierarchies: The earliest levels of skill. *Child Development, 65,* 1279–1298.

Bliss, L. S., McCabe, A., & Miranda, A. E. (1998). Narrative assessment profile: Discourse analysis for school-age children. *Journal of Communication Disorders, 31,* 347–363.

Bloch, M. E. F., Solomon, G. E. A., & Carey, S. (2001). An understanding of what is passed on from parents to children: A cross-cultural investigation. *Journal of Cognition and Culture, 1,* 43–68.

Block, J., & Block, J. H. (1980). *The California Child Q-Set.* Palo Alto, CA: Consulting Psychologists Press.

Bloom, L. (1970). *Language development: Form and function in emerging grammars.* Cambridge, MA: MIT Press.

Bloom, L. (1991). *Language development from two to three.* New York: Cambridge University Press.

Bloom, L. (1998). Language acquisition in its developmental context. In D. Kuhn & R. S. Siegler (Eds.), *Handbook of child psychology: Vol. 2. Cognition, perception, and language* (5th ed., pp. 309–370). New York: Wiley.

Bloom, L. (2000). The intentionality model of language development: How to learn a word, any word. In R. Golinkoff, K. Hirsh-Pasek, N. Akhtar, L. Bloom, G. Hollich, L. Smith, M. Tomasello, & A. Woodward (Eds.), *Becoming a word learner: A debate on lexical acquisition.* New York: Oxford University Press.

Bloom, L., Lahey, M., Liften, K., & Fiess, K. (1980). Complex sentences: Acquisition of syntactic connections and the semantic relations they encode. *Journal of Child Language, 7,* 235–256.

Bloom, L., Margulis, C., Tinker E., & Fujita, N. (1996). Early conversations and word learning: Contributions from child and adult. *Child Development, 67,* 3154–3175.

Bloom, P. (1999). The role of semantics in solving the bootstrapping problem. In R. Jackendoff & P. Bloom (Eds.), *Language, logic, and concepts* (pp. 285–309). Cambridge, MA: MIT Press.

Blotner, R., & Bearison, D. J. (1984). Developmental consistencies in sociomoral knowledge: Justice reasoning and altruistic behavior. *Merrill-Palmer Quarterly, 30,* 349–367.

Bluestone, C., & Tamis-LeMonda, C. S. (1999). Correlates of parenting styles in predominantly working- and middle-class African-American mothers. *Journal of Marriage and the Family, 61,* 881–893.

Blumberg, M. S., & Lucas, D. E. (1996). A developmental and component analysis of active sleep. *Developmental Psychobiology, 29,* 1–22.

Bobo, N., Evert, A., Gallivan, J., Imperatore, G., Kelly, J., & Linder, B. (2004). An update on type 2 diabetes in youth from the National Diabetes Education Program. *Pediatrics, 114,* 259–263.

Bogaert, A. F. (2003). Number of older brothers and sexual orientation: New tests and the attraction/behavior distinction in two national probability samples. *Journal of Personality and Social Psychology, 84,* 644–652.

Bogartz, R. S., Shinskey, J. L., & Schilling, T. H. (2000). Object permanence in five-and-a-half-month-old infants. *Infancy, 1,* 403–428.

Bogin, B. (2001). *The growth of humanity.* New York: Wiley-Liss.

Bogin, B., Smith, P., Orden, A. B., Varela, S., & Loucky, J. (2002). Rapid change in height and body proportions of Maya American children. *American Journal of Human Biology, 14,* 753–761.

Bohannon, J. N., III, & Bonvillian, J. D. (2005). Theoretical approaches to language acquisition. In J. B. Gleason (Ed.), *The development of language* (6th ed., pp. 230–291). Boston: Allyn and Bacon.

Bohannon, J. N., III, & Stanowicz, L. (1988). The issue of negative evidence: Adult responses to children's language errors. *Developmental Psychology, 24,* 684–689.

Bohman, M. (1996). Predispositions to criminality: Swedish adoption studies in retrospect. In G. R. Bock & J. A. Goode (Eds.), *Genetics of criminal and antisocial behavior, Ciba Foundation Symposium 194* (pp. 99–114). Chichester, England: Wiley.

Bohman, M., & Sigvardsson, S. (1990). Outcome in adoption: Lessons from longitudinal studies. In D. M. Bordzkinsky & M. D. Schechter (Eds.), *The psychology of adoption* (pp. 93–106). New York: Oxford University Press.

Bohnert, A. M., Crnic, K., & Lim, K. G. (2003). Emotional competence and aggressive behavior in school-age children. *Journal of Abnormal Child Psychology, 31,* 79–91.

Boldizar, J. P. (1991). Assessing sex typing and androgyny in children: The children's sex role inventory. *Developmental Psychology, 27,* 505–515.

Boldizar, J. P., Perry, D. G., & Perry, L. C. (1989). Outcome values and aggression. *Child Development, 60,* 571–579.

Bolen, R. M. (2001). *Child sexual abuse.* New York: Kluwer Academic.

Bolger, K. E., & Patterson, C. J. (2001). Developmental pathways from child maltreatment to peer rejection. *Child Development, 72,* 549–568.

Boller, K., Grabelle, M., & Rovee-Collier, C. (1995). Effects of postevent information on infants' memory for a central target. *Journal of Experimental Child Psychology, 59,* 372–396.

Bono, M. A., & Stifter, C. A. (2003). Maternal attention-directing strategies and infant focused attention during problem solving. *Infancy, 4,* 235–250.

Bookstein, F. L., Sampson, P. D., Connor, P. D., & Streissguth, A. P. (2002). Midline corpus callosum is a neuroanatomical focus of fetal alcohol damage. *Anatomical Record, 269,* 162–174.

Boom, J., Brugman, D., & van der Heijden, P. G. M. (2001). Hierarchical structure of moral stages assessed by a sorting task. *Child Development, 72,* 535–548.

Borke, H. (1975). Piaget's mountains revisited: Changes in the egocentric landscape. *Developmental Psychology, 11,* 240–243.

Borkowski, J. G., & Muthukrisna, N. (1995). Learning environments and skill generalization: How contexts facilitate regulatory processes and efficacy beliefs. In F. Weinert & W. Schneider (Eds.), *Memory performances and competence: Issues in growth and development* (pp. 283–300). Hillsdale, NJ: Erlbaum.

Bornstein, M. H. (1989). Sensitive periods in development: Structural characteristics and causal interpretations. *Psychological Bulletin, 105,* 179–197.

Bornstein, M. H., & Arterberry, M. E. (2003). Recognition, discrimination, and categorization of smiling by 5-month-old infants. *Developmental Science, 6,* 585–599.

Bornstein, M. H., Haynes, O. M., Pascual, L., Painter, K. M., & Galperin, C. (1999). Play in two societies: Pervasiveness of process, specificity of structure. *Child Development, 70,* 317–331.

Bornstein, M. H., Selmi, A. M., Haynes, O. M., Painter, K. M., & Marx, E. S. (1999). Representational abilities and the hearing status of child/mother dyads. *Child Development, 70,* 833–852.

Bornstein, M. H., Tal, J., Rahn, C., Galperín, C. Z., Pàcheux, M., Lamour, M., Toda, S., Azuma, H., Ogino, M., & Tamis-LeMonda, C. S. (1992a). Functional analysis of the contents of maternal speech to infants of 5 and 13 months in four cultures: Argentina, France, Japan, and the United States. *Developmental Psychology, 28,* 593–603.

Bornstein, M. H., Vibbert, M., Tal, J., & O'Donnell, K. (1992b). Toddler language and play in the second year: Stability, covariation, and influences of parenting. *First Language, 12,* 323–338.

Bornstein, P., Duncan, P., D'Ari, A., Pieniadz, J., Fitzgerald, M., Abrams, C. L., Frankowski, B., Franco, O., Hunt, C., & Oh Cha, S. (1996). Family and parenting behaviors predicting middle school adjustment: A longitudinal study. *Family Relations, 45,* 415–425.

Borst, C. G. (1995). *Catching babies: The professionalization of childbirth, 1870–1920.* Cambridge, MA: Harvard University Press.

Bortolus, R., Parazzini, F., Chatenoud, L., Benzi, G., Bianchi, M. M., & Marini, A. (1999). The epidemiology of multiple births. *Human Reproduction Update, 5,* 179–187.

Bos, H. M. W., van Balen, F., & van den Boom, D. C. (2004). Experience of parenthood, couple relationship, social support, and child-rearing goals in planned lesbian mother families. *Journal of Child Psychology and Psychiatry, 25,* 755–764.

Bosacki, S. L., & Moore, C. (2004). Preschoolers' understanding of simple and complex emotions: Links with gender and language. *Sex Roles, 50,* 659–675.

Bosch, L., & Sebastian-Galles, N. (2001). Evidence of early language discrimination abilities in infants from bilingual environments. *Infancy, 2,* 29–49.

Botvinick, M. M., Braver, T. S., Barch, D. M., Carter, C. S., & Cohen, J. D. (2001). Conflict monitoring and cognitive control. *Psychological Review, 108,* 624–652.

Bouchard, T. J., Jr. (1997). IQ similarity in twins reared apart: Findings and responses to critics. In R. J. Sternberg & E. L. Grigorenko (Eds.), *Intelligence, heredity, and environment* (pp. 126–160). New York: Cambridge University Press.

Bouchard, T. J., Jr., & McGue, M. (1981). Familial studies of intelligence: A review. *Science, 212,* 1055–1058.

Bouchard, T. J., Jr., & McGue, M., (2003). Genetic and environmental influences on human psychological differences. *Journal of Neurobiology, 54,* 4–45.

Boukydis, C. F. Z., & Burgess, R. L. (1982). Adult physiological response to infant cries: Effects of temperament of infant, parental status and gender. *Child Development, 53,* 1291–1298.

Boukydis, C. F. Z., & Lester, B. M. (1998). Infant crying, risk status and social support in families of preterm and term infants. *Early Development and Parenting, 7,* 31–39.

Boulton, M. J. (1996). A comparison of 8- and 11-year-old girls' and boys' participation in specific types of rough-and-tumble play and aggressive fighting: Implications for functional hypotheses. *Aggressive Behavior, 22,* 271–287.

Boulton, M. J. (1999). Concurrent and longitudinal relations between children's playground behavior and social preference, victimization, and bullying. *Child Development, 70,* 944–954.

Boulton, M. J., & Smith, P. K. (1992). The social nature of play-fighting and play-chasing: Mechanisms and strategies underlying cooperation and compromise. In J. H. Barkow, L. Cosmides, & J. Tooby (Eds.), *The adapted mind* (pp. 429–444). New York: Oxford University Press.

Bowen, N. K., Bowen, G. L., & Ware, W. B. (2002). Neighborhood social disorganization, families, and the educational behavior of adolescents. *Journal of Adolescent Research, 17,* 468–490.

Bowerman, M. (1997). Argument structure and learnability: Is a solution in sight? *Proceedings of the Twenty-Second Annual Meeting of the Berkeley Linguistics Society, 22,* 454–468.

Bower-Russa, M. E., Knutson, J. F., & Winebarger, A. (2001). Disciplinary history, adult disciplinary attitudes, and risk for abusive parenting. *Journal of Community Psychology, 29,* 219–240.

Bowker, A. (2004). Predicting friendship stability during early adolescence. *Journal of Early Adolescence, 24,* 85–112.

Bowlby, J. (1969). *Attachment and loss: Vol. 1. Attachment.* New York: Basic Books.

Bowlby, J. (1980). *Attachment and loss: Vol. 3. Loss.* New York: Basic Books.

Bowman, S. A., Gortmaker, S. L., Ebbeling, C. B., Pereira, M. A., & Ludwig, D. S. (2004). Effects of fast-food consumption on energy intake and diet quality among children in a national household survey. *Pediatrics, 113,* 112–118.

Boyce, W., Doherty, M., Fortin, C., & MacKinnon, D. (2003). *Canadian youth, sexual health and HIV/AIDS study.* Toronto: Council of Ministers of Education, Canada.

Boyer, K., & Diamond, A. (1992). Development of memory for temporal order in infants and young children. In A. Diamond (Ed.), *Development and neural bases of higher cognitive function* (pp. 267–317). New York: New York Academy of Sciences.

Boyes, M. C., & Chandler, M. (1992). Cognitive development, epistemic doubt, and identity formation in adolescence. *Journal of Youth and Adolescence, 21,* 277–304.

Boysson-Bardies, B. de, & Vihman, M. M. (1991). Adaptation to language: Evidence from babbling and first words in four languages. *Language, 67,* 297–319.

Brackbill, Y., McManus, K., & Woodward, L. (1985). *Medication in maternity: Infant exposure and maternal information.* Ann Arbor: University of Michigan Press.

Bradford, K., Barber, B. K., Olsen, J. A., Maughan, S. L., Erickson, L. D., Ward, D., & Stolz, H. E. (2003). A multi-national study of interparental conflict, parenting, and adolescent functioning: South Africa, Bangladesh, China, India, Bosnia, Germany, Palestine, Colombia, and the United States. *Marriage and Family Review, 35,* 107–137.

Bradley, P. J., & Bray, K. H. (1996). The Netherlands' Maternal–Child Health Program: Implications for the United States. *Journal of Obstetric, Gynecologic, and Neonatal Nursing, 25,* 471–475.

Bradley, R. H. (1994). The HOME Inventory: Review and reflections. In H. W. Reese (Ed.), *Advances in child development and behavior* (Vol. 25, pp. 241–288). San Diego, CA: Academic Press.

Bradley, R. H., Caldwell, B. M., & Rock, S. L. (1988). Home environment and school performance: A ten-year follow-up and examination of three models of environmental action. *Child Development, 59,* 852–867.

Bradley, R. H., & Corwyn, R. F. (2003). Age and ethnic variations in family process mediators of SES. In M. H. Bornstein & R. H. Bradley (Eds.), *Socioeconomic status, parenting, and child development* (pp. 161–188). Mahwah, NJ: Erlbaum.

Bradley, R. H., Corwyn, R. F., McAdoo, H. P., & Garcia Coll, C. (2001). The home environments of children in the United States. Part I: Variations by age, ethnicity, and poverty status. *Child Development, 72,* 1844–1867.

Bradley, R. H., Whiteside, L., Mundfrom, D. J., Casey, P. H., Kelleher, K. J., & Pope, S. K. (1994). Contribution of early intervention and early caregiving experiences to resilience in low-birthweight, premature children living in poverty. *Journal of Clinical Child Psychology, 23,* 425–434.

Braet, C., & Crombez, G. (2003). Cognitive interference due to food cues in childhood obesity. *Journal of Clinical Child and Adolescent Psychology, 32,* 32–39.

Braine, L G., Schauble, L., Kugelmass, S., & Winter, A. (1993). Representation of depth by children: Spatial strategies and lateral biases. *Developmental Psychology, 29,* 466–479.

Braine, M. D. S. (1994). Is nativism sufficient? *Journal of Child Language, 21,* 1–23.

Brainerd, C. J. (2003). Jean Piaget, learning research, and American education. In B. J. Zimmerman (Ed.), *Educational psychology: A century of contributions* (pp. 251–287). Mahwah, NJ: Erlbaum.

Brainerd, C. J., & Gordon, L. L. (1994). Development of verbatim and gist memory for numbers. *Developmental Psychology, 30,* 163–177.

Brainerd, C. J., & Reyna, V. F. (1993). Memory independence and memory interference in cognitive development. *Psychological Review, 100,* 42–67.

Brainerd, C. J., & Reyna, V. F. (2001). Fuzzy-trace theory: Dual processes in memory, reasoning, and cognitive neuroscience. In H. W. Reese (Ed.), *Advances in child development and behavior* (Vol. 28). San Diego, CA: Academic Press.

Brainerd, C. J., Reyna, V. F., & Poole, D. A. (2000). Fuzzy-trace theory and false memory: Memory theory in the courtroom. In D. F. Bjorklund (Ed.), *Research and theory in false-memory* creation in children and adults (pp. 93–127). Mahwah, NJ: Erlbaum.

Brame, B., Nagin, D. S., & Tremblay, R. E. (2001). Developmental trajectories of physical aggression from school entry to late adolescence. *Journal of Child Psychology and Psychiatry, 42,* 503–512.

Branca, F., & Ferrari, M. (2002). Impact of micronutrient deficiencies on growth: The stunting syndrome. *Annals of Nutrition and Metabolism, 46*(Suppl. 1), 8–17.

Branje, S. J. T., van Lieshout, C. F. M., van Aken, M. A. G., & Haselager, G. J. T. (2004). Perceived support in sibling relationships and adolescent adjustment. *Journal of Child Psychology and Psychiatry, 45,* 1385–1396.

Braswell, G. S., & Callanan, M. A. (2003). Learning to draw recognizable graphic representations during mother–child interactions. *Merrill-Palmer Quarterly, 49,* 471–494.

Braungart, J. M., & Stifter, C. A. (1996). Infant responses to frustrating events: Continuity and change in reactivity and regulation. *Child Development, 67,* 1767–1779.

Braungart-Rieker, J., Courtney, S., & Garwood, M. M. (1999). Mother– and father–infant attachment: Families in context. *Journal of Family Psychology, 13,* 535–553.

Bray, J. H. (1999). From marriage to remarriage and beyond: Findings from the Developmental Issues in Stepfamilies Research Project. In E. M. Hetherington (Ed.), *Coping with divorce, single parenting, and remarriage: A risk and resiliency perspective* (pp. 295–319). Mahwah, NJ: Erlbaum.

Brazelton, T. B., Koslowski, B., & Tronick, E. Z. (1976). Neonatal behavior among urban Zambians and Americans. *Journal of the American Academy of Child Psychiatry, 15,* 97–107.

Brazelton, T. B., & Nugent, J. K. (1995). *Neonatal Behavioral Assessment Scale.* London: Mac Keith Press.

Brazelton, T. B., Nugent, J. K., & Lester, B. M. (1987). Neonatal Behavioral Assessment Scale. In J. D. Osofsky (Ed.), *Handbook of infant development* (2nd ed., pp. 780–817). New York: Wiley.

Bredekamp, S., & Copple, C. (Eds.). (1997). *Developmentally appropriate practice in early childhood programs* (rev. ed.). Washington, DC: National Association for the Education of Young Children.

Bremner, A. J., & Mareschal, D. (2004). Reasoning . . . what reasoning? *Developmental Science, 7,* 419–421.

Brendgen, M., Markiewicz, D, Doyle, A. B., & Bukowski, W. M. (2001). The relations between friendship quality, ranked-friendship preference, and adolescents' behavior with their friends. *Merrill-Palmer Quarterly, 47,* 395–415.

Brenes, M. E., Eisenberg, N., & Helmstadter, G. C. (1985). Sex role development of preschoolers from two-parent and one-parent families. *Merrill-Palmer Quarterly, 31,* 33–46.

Brennan, R. T., Kim, J., Wenz-Gross, M., & Siperstein, G. N. (2001). The relative equitability of high-stakes testing versus teacher-assigned grades: An analysis of the Massachusetts Comprehensive Assessment System

(MCAS). *Harvard Educational Review, 71,* 173–216.

Brennan, W. M., Ames, E. W., & Moore, R. W. (1966). Age differences in infants' attention to patterns of different complexities. *Science, 151,* 354–356.

Brenner, E., & Salovey, P. (1997). Emotion regulation during childhood: Developmental, interpersonal, and individual considerations. In P. Salovey & D. Sluyter (Eds.), *Emotional literacy and emotional development* (pp. 168–192). New York: Basic Books.

Brenner, R. A., Simons-Morton, B. G., Bhaskar, B., Revenis, M., Das, A., & Clemens, J. D. (2003). Infant–parent bed sharing in an inner-city population. *Archives of Pediatrics and Adolescent Medicine, 157,* 33–39.

Bretherton, I., Fritz, J., Zahn-Waxler, C., & Ridgeway, D. (1986). Learning to talk about emotions: A functionalist perspective. *Child Development, 57,* 529–548.

Bretherton, I., & Munholland, K. A. (1999). Internal working models in attachment relationships: A construct revisited. In J. Cassidy & P. R. Shaver (Eds.), *Handbook of attachment* (pp. 89–111). New York: Guilford.

Brewaeys, A., Ponjaert, I., Van Hall, E. V., & Golombok, S. (1997). Donor insemination: Child development and family functioning in lesbian mother families. *Human Reproduction, 12,* 1349–1359.

Brezina, T. (1999). Teenage violence toward parents as an adaptation to family strain: Evidence from a national survey of male adolescents. *Youth and Society, 30,* 416–444.

Bridges, L. J., & Moore, K. A. (2002). Religious involvement and children's well-being: What research tells us (and what it doesn't). *Child Trends Research Brief.* Retrieved from www.childtrends.org

Briefel, R. R., Reidy, K., Karwe, V., & Devaney, B. (2004). Feeding Infants and Toddlers Study: Improvements needed in meeting infant feeding recommendations. *Journal of the American Dietetic Association, 104*(Suppl. 1), s31–s37.

Briggs, F. (2000). *Children's view of the world.* Magill, Australia: University of South Australia.

Briggs, F. (2002). *To what extent can Keeping Ourselves Safe protect children?* Wellington, NZ: New Zealand Police.

British Columbia Reproductive Care Program. (2003). Guidelines for perinatal care manual: Perinatal cocaine use: Care of the newborn. Retrieved from http://mdm.ca/cpgsnew/cpgs-f/search/french/help/2bcrcp.htm

Broberg, A. G., Wessels, H., Lamb, M. E., & Hwang, C. P. (1997). Effects of day care on the development of cognitive abilities in 8-year-olds: A longitudinal study. *Developmental Psychology, 33,* 62–69.

Brody, G. H. (2004). Siblings' direct and indirect contributions to child development. *Current Directions in Psychological Science, 13,* 124–126.

Brody, G. H., & Flor, D. L. (1998). Maternal resources, parenting practices, and child competence in rural, single-parent African American families. *Child Development, 69,* 803–816.

Brody, G. H., Ge, X., Kim, S. Y., Murry, V. M., Simons, R. L., & Gibbons, F. X.

(2003). Neighborhood disadvantage moderates associations of parenting and older sibling problem attitudes and behavior with conduct disorders in African American children. *Journal of Consulting and Clinical Psychology, 71,* 211–222.

Brody, G. H., Graziano, W. G., & Musser, L. M. (1983). Familiarity and children's behavior in same-age and mixed-age peer groups. *Developmental Psychology, 19,* 568–576.

Brody, G. H., Stoneman, Z., & Flor, D. (1995). Linking family processes and academic competence among rural African American youths. *Journal of Marriage and the Family, 57,* 567–570.

Brody, G. H., Stoneman, Z., & Flor, D. (1996). Parental religiosity, family processes, and youth competence in rural, two-parent African American families. *Developmental Psychology, 32,* 696–706.

Brody, G. H., Stoneman, Z., & McCoy, J. K. (1992). Associations of maternal and paternal direct and differential behavior with sibling relationships: Contemporaneous and longitudinal analyses. *Child Development, 63,* 82–92.

Brody, G. H., Stoneman, Z., McCoy, J. K., & Forehand, R. (1992). Contemporaneous and longitudinal associations of sibling conflict with family relationship assessments and family discussions about sibling problems. *Child Development, 63,* 391–400.

Brody, L. (1999). *Gender, emotion, and the family.* Cambridge, MA: Harvard University Press.

Brody, L. R. (1997). Gender and emotion: Beyond stereotypes. *Journal of Social Issues, 53,* 369–393.

Brody, N. (1997). *Intelligence* (2nd ed.). San Diego: Academic Press.

Brody, N. (2000). History of theories and measurements of intelligence. In R. J. Sternberg (Ed.), *Handbook of intelligence* (pp. 17–33). Cambridge, UK: Cambridge University Press.

Broidy, L. M., Nagin, D. S., Tremblay, R. E., Bates, J. E., Brame, B., Dodge, K. A., Fergusson, D., Horwood, J. L., Loeber, R., Laird, R., Lynam, D. R., Moffitt, T. E., Pettit, G. S., & Vitaro, F. (2003). Developmental trajectories of childhood disruptive behaviors and adolescent delinquency: A six-site, cross-national study. *Developmental Psychology, 39,* 222–245.

Bronfenbrenner, U., & Evans, G. W. (2000). Developmental science in the 21st century: Emerging theoretical models, research designs, and empirical findings. *Social Development, 9,* 115–125.

Bronfenbrenner, U., & Morris, P. A. (1998). The ecology of developmental processes. In R. M. Lerner (Ed.), *Handbook of child psychology: Vol. 1. Theoretical models of human development* (5th ed., pp. 535–584). New York: Wiley.

Bronson, G. W. (1994). Infants' transitions toward adult-like scanning. *Child Development, 65,* 1243–1261.

Brooks, D., & Barth, R. P. (1999). Adult transracial and inracial adoptees: Effects of race, gender, adoptive family structure, and placement history on adjustment outcomes. *American Journal of Orthopsychiatry, 69,* 87–99.

Brooks, P. J., Hanauere, J. B., Padowska, B., & Rosman, H. (2003). The role of selective attention in preschoolers'

rule use in a novel dimensional card sort. *Cognitive Development, 18,* 195–215.

Brooks, P. J., & Tomasello, M. (1999). Young children learn to produce passives with nonce verbs. *Developmental Psychology, 35,* 29–44.

Brooks-Gunn, J. (1988). Antecedents and consequences of variations in girls' maturational timing. *Journal of Adolescent Health Care, 9,* 365–373.

Brooks-Gunn, J. (2003). Do you believe in magic? What we can expect from early childhood intervention programs. *Social Policy Report of the Society for Research in Child Development, 27*(1).

Brooks-Gunn, J., Han, W.-J., & Waldfogel, J. (2002). Maternal employment and child cognitive outcomes in the first three years of life: The NICHD study of early child care. *Child Development, 73,* 1052–1072.

Brooks-Gunn, J., Klebanov, P. K., Smith, J., Duncan, G. J., & Lee, K. (2003). The black–white test score gap in young children. Contributions of test and family characteristics. *Applied Developmental Science, 7,* 239–252.

Brooks-Gunn, J., & Ruble, D. N. (1980). Menarche: The interaction of physiology, cultural, and social factors. In A. J. Dan, E. A. Graham, & C. P. Beecher (Eds.), *The menstrual cycle: A synthesis of interdisciplinary research* (pp. 141–159). New York: Springer-Verlag.

Brooks-Gunn, J., & Ruble, D. N. (1983). The experience of menarche from a developmental perspective. In J. Brooks-Gunn & A. C. Peterson (Eds.), *Girls at puberty* (pp. 155–177). New York: Plenum.

Brooks-Gunn, J., Schley, S., & Hardy, J. (2002). Marriage and the baby carriage: Historical change and intergenerational continuity in early parenthood. In L. J. Crockett & R. K. Sibereisen (Eds.), *Negotiating adolescence in times of social change* (pp. 36–57). New York: Cambridge University Press.

Brown, A. L. (1997). Transforming schools into communities of thinking and learning about serious matters. *American Psychologist, 52,* 399–413.

Brown, A. L., & Campione, J. C. (1972). Recognition memory for perceptually similar pictures in preschool children. *Journal of Experimental Psychology, 95,* 55–62.

Brown, A. L., Smiley, S. S., Day, J. D., Townsend, M., & Lawton, S. Q. C. (1977). Intrusion of a thematic idea in children's recall of prose. *Child Development, 48,* 1454–1466.

Brown, A. L., Smiley, S. S., & Lawton, S. Q. C. (1978). The effects of experience on the selection of suitable retrieval cues for studying texts. *Child Development, 49,* 829–835.

Brown, A. M., & Miracle, J. A. (2003). Early binocular vision in human infants: Limitations on the generality of the Superposition Hypothesis. *Vision Research, 43,* 1563–1574.

Brown, A. S., & Susser, E. S. (2002). In utero infection and adult schizophrenia. *Mental Retardation and Developmental Disabilities Research Reviews, 8,* 51–57.

Brown, B. B., Feiring, C., & Furman, W. (1999). Missing the love boat: Why researchers have shied away from adolescent romance. In W. Furman, B. B. Bown, & C. Feiring (Eds.), *The development of romantic relationships in adolescence* (pp. 1–16). New York: Cambridge University Press.

Brown, B. B., Lohr, M. J., & McClenahan, E. L. (1986). Early adolescents' perceptions of peer pressure. *Journal of Early Adolescence, 6*, 139–154.

Brown, C. S., & Bigler, R. S. (2004). Children's perceptions of gender discrimination. *Developmental Psychology, 40*, 714–726.

Brown, J. R., Donelan-McCall, N., & Dunn, J. (1996). Why talk about mental states? The significance of children's conversations with friends, siblings and mothers. *Child Development, 67*, 836–849.

Brown, J. R., & Dunn, J. (1996). Continuities in emotion understanding from 3 to 6 years. *Child Development, 67*, 789–802.

Brown, R. (1973). *A first language: The early stages.* Cambridge, MA: Harvard University Press.

Brown, R. T., Reynolds, C. R., & Whitaker, J. S. (1999). Bias in mental testing since *Bias in Mental Testing. School Psychology Quarterly, 14*, 208–238.

Brown, R., & Hanlon, C. (1970). Derivational complexity and order of acquisition in child speech. In J. R. Hayes (Ed.), *Cognition and the development of language* (pp. 11–53). New York: Wiley.

Brown, S. S., & Eisenberg, L. (1995). (Eds.). *The best intentions.* Washington, DC: National Academy Press.

Brownell, C. A., & Carriger, M. S. (1990). Changes in cooperation and self-other differentiation during the second year. *Child Development, 61*, 1164–1174.

Browne, C. A., & Woolley, J. D. (2004). Preschoolers' magical explanations for violations of physical, social, and mental laws. *Journal of Cognition and Development, 5*, 239–260.

Bruce, D., Dolan, A., & Phillips-Grant, K. (2000). On the transition from childhood amnesia to recall of personal memories. *Psychological Science, 11*, 360–364.

Bruch, H. (2001). *The golden cage: The enigma of anorexia nervosa.* Cambridge, MA: Harvard University Press.

Bruck, M., & Ceci, S. J. (2004). Forensic developmental psychology: Unveiling four common misconceptions. *Current Directions in Psychological Science, 13*, 229–232.

Bruck, M., Ceci, S. J., & Hembrooke, H. (1998). Reliability and credibility of young children's reports. *American Psychologist, 53*, 136–151.

Bruer, J. T. (1999). *The myth of the first three years.* New York: Free Press.

Bruzzese, J.-M., & Fisher, C. B. (2003). Assessing and enhancing the research consent capacity of children and youth. *Applied Developmental Science, 7*, 13–26.

Bryant, P., & Nunes, T. (2002). Children's understanding of mathematics. In U. Goswami (Ed.), *Blackwell handbook of childhood cognitive development* (pp. 412–439). Malden, MA. Blackwell.

Buchanan, A. (1996). *Cycles of child maltreatment.* Chichester, UK: Wiley.

Buchanan, C. M., Eccles, J. S., & Becker, J. B. (1992). Are adolescents the victims of raging hormones? Evidence for activational effects of hormones on moods and behavior at adolescence. *Psychological Bulletin, 111*, 62–107.

Buchanan, C. M., & Holmbeck, G. N. (1998). Measuring beliefs about adolescent personality and behavior. *Journal of Youth and Adolescence, 27*, 609–629.

Buchanan, C. M., Maccoby, E. E., & Dornbusch, S. M. (1996). *Adolescents after divorce.* Cambridge, MA: Harvard University Press.

Buchanan-Barrow, E., & Barrett, M. (1998). Children's rule discrimination within the context of the school. *British Journal of Developmental Psychology, 16*, 539–551.

Budwig, N. (1995). *A developmental-functionalist approach to child language.* Mahwah, NJ: Erlbaum.

Bugental, D. B., Blue, J., Cortez, V., Fleck, K., & Rodriquez, A. (1992). Influences of a witnessed affect of information processing in children. *Child Development, 63*, 774–786.

Bugental, D. B., Ellerson, P. C., Lin, E. K., Rainey, B., & Kokotovic, A. (2002). A cognitive approach to child abuse prevention. *Journal of Family Psychology, 16*, 243–258.

Bugental, D. B., & Happaney, K. (2004). Predicting infant maltreatment in low-income families: The interactive effects of maternal attributions and child status at birth. *Developmental Psychology, 40*, 234–243.

Buhrmester, D. (1996). Need fulfillment, interpersonal competence, and the developmental contexts of early adolescent friendship. In W. M. Bukowski, A. F. Newcomb, & W. W. Hartup (Eds.), *The company they keep: Friendship during childhood and adolescence* (pp. 158–185). New York: Cambridge University Press.

Buhrmester, D. (1998). Need fulfillment, interpersonal competence, and the developmental contexts of early adolescent friendship. In W. M. Bukowski, A. F. Newcomb, & W. W. Hartup (Eds.), *The company they keep: Friendship in childhood and adolescence* (pp. 158–185). New York: Cambridge University Press.

Buhrmester, D., & Furman, W. (1990). Perceptions of sibling relationships during middle childhood and adolescence. *Child Development, 61*, 1387–1398.

Buhs, E. S., & Ladd, G. W. (2001). Peer rejection as antecedent of young children's school adjustment: An examination of mediating processes. *Developmental Psychology, 37*, 550–560.

Buiting, K., Gross, S., Lich, C., Gillessen-Kaesbach, G, el-Maarri, O., & Horsthemke, B. (2003). Epimutations in Prader-Willi and Angelman syndromes: A molecular study of 136 patients with an imprinting defect. *American Journal of Human Genetics, 72*, 571–577.

Bukowski, W. M. (2001). Friendship and the worlds of childhood. In D. W. Nangle & C. A. Erdley (Eds.), *The role of friendship in psychological adjustment* (pp. 93–105). San Francisco: Jossey-Bass.

Bukowski, W. M., Sippola, L. K., & Hoza, B. (1999). Same and other: Interdependency between participation in same- and other-sex friendships. *Journal of Youth and Adolescence, 28*, 439–459.

Bukowski, W. M., Sippola, L. K., & Newcomb, A. F. (2000). Variations in patterns of attraction of same- and other-sex peers during early adolescence. *Developmental Psychology, 36*, 147–154.

Bullock, M., & Lutkenhaus, P. (1990). Who am I? The development of self-understanding in toddlers. *Merrill-Palmer Quarterly, 36*, 217–238.

Burchinal, M. R., & Cryer, D. (2003). Diversity, child care quality, and developmental outcomes. *Early Childhood Research Quarterly, 18*, 401–426.

Burchinal, M. R., Peisner-Feinberg, E., Bryant, D. M., & Clifford, R. (2000). Children's social and cognitive development and child-care quality: Testing for differential associations related to poverty, gender, or ethnicity. *Applied Developmental Science, 4*, 149–165.

Burger, L. K., & Miller, P. J. (1999). Early talk about the past revisited: Affect in working-class and middle-class children's co-narrations. *Journal of Child Language, 26*, 133–162.

Burhans, K. K., & Dweck, C. S. (1995). Helplessness in early childhood: The role of contingent worth. *Child Development, 66*, 1719–1738.

Burts, D. C., Hart, C. H., Charlesworth, R., Fleege, P. O., Mosley, J., & Thomasson, R. H. (1992). Observed activities and stress behaviors of children in developmentally appropriate and inappropriate kindergarten classrooms. *Early Childhood Research Quarterly, 7*, 297–318.

Bushman, B. J., & Anderson, C. A. (2001). Media violence and the American public: Scientific facts versus media misinformation. *American Psychologist, 56*, 477–489.

Bushman, B. J., & Huesmann, L. R. (2001). Effects of televised violence on aggression. In D. G. Singer & J. L. Singer (Eds.), *Handbook of children and the media* (pp. 223–254). Thousand Oaks, CA: Sage.

Bushnell, E. W., & Boudreau, J. P. (1993). Motor development and the mind: The potential role of motor abilities as a determinant of aspects of perceptual development. *Child Development, 64*, 1005–1021.

Bushnik, T., Barr-Telford, L., & Bussiére, P. (2004). *In and out of high school: First results from the second cycle of the Youth in Transition Survey, 2002.* Ottawa, ON: Statistics Canada.

Bussey, K. (1992). Lying and truthfulness: Children's definitions, standards, and evaluative reactions. *Child Development, 63*, 129–137.

Bussey, K. (1999). Children's categorization and evaluation of different types of lies and truths. *Child Development, 70*, 1338–1347.

Bussey, K., & Bandura, A. (1992). Self-regulatory mechanisms governing gender development. *Child Development, 63*, 1236–1250.

Butler, R. (1998). Age trends in the use of social and temporal comparison for self-evaluation: Examination of a novel developmental hypothesis. *Child Development, 69*, 1054–1073.

Butler, R. (1999). Information seeking and achievement motivation in middle childhood and adolescence: The role of conceptions of ability. *Developmental Psychology, 35*, 146–163.

Butler, R., & Ruzany, N. (1993). Age and socialization effects on the development of social comparison motives and normative ability assessment in kibbutz and urban children. *Child Development, 64*, 532–543.

Byard, R. W., & Krous, H. F. (2003). Sudden infant death syndrome: Overview and update. *Perspectives on Pediatric Pathology, 6*, 112–127.

Bybee, J. (Ed.). (1998). *Guilt and children.* San Diego, CA: Academic Press.

Bybee, J., Merisca, R., & Velasco, R. (1998). The development of reactions to guilt-producing events. In J. Bybee (Ed.), *Guilt and children* (pp. 185–213). San Diego: Academic Press.

Bybee, J., & Slobin, D. (1982). Rules and schemes in the development and use of the English past tense. *Language, 58*, 265–289.

Byrnes, J. P. (2002). The development of decision-making. *Journal of Adolescent Health, 31*, 208–215.

Byrnes, J. P. (2003). Cognitive development during adolescence. In G. R. Adams & M. D. Berzonsky (Eds.), *Blackwell handbook of adolescence* (pp. 227–246). Malden, MA: Blackwell.

Cabrera, N. J., Tamis-LeMonda, C. S., Bradley, R. H., Hoferth, S., & Lamb, M. E. (2000). Fatherhood in the twenty-first century. *Child Development, 71*, 127–136.

Cain, K. M., & Dweck, C. S. (1995). The relation between motivational patterns and achievement cognitions through the elementary school years. *Merrill-Palmer Quarterly, 41*, 25–52.

Caine, N. (1986). Behavior during puberty and adolescence. In G. Mitchell & J. Erwin (Eds.), *Comparative primate biology: Vol. 2A. Behavior, conservation, and ecology* (pp. 327–361). New York: Alan R. Liss.

Cairns, R. B. (1992). The making of a developmental science: The contributions and intellectual heritage of James Mark Baldwin. *Developmental Psychology, 28*, 17–24.

Cairns, R. B. (1998). The making of developmental psychology. In R. M. Lerner (Ed.), *Handbook of child psychology: Vol. 1. Theoretical models of human development* (5th ed., pp. 25–105). New York: Wiley.

Cairns, R., Xie, H., & Leung, M.-C. (1998). The popularity of friendship and the neglect of social networks: Toward a new balance. In W. M. Bukowski & A. H. Cillessen (Eds.), *Sociometry then and now: Building on six decades of measuring children's experiences with the peer group* (pp. 25–53). San Francisco: Jossey-Bass.

Calderón, M. E., & Minaya-Rowe, L. (2003). *Designing and implementing two-way bilingual programs.* Thousand Oaks, CA: Corwin Press.

Caldwell, B. M., & Bradley, R. H. (1994). Environmental issues in developmental follow-up research. In S. L. Friedman & H. C. Haywood (Eds.), *Developmental follow-up* (pp. 235–256). San Diego: Academic Press.

Calkins, S. D. (2002). Does aversive behavior during toddlerhood matter? The effects of difficult temperament on maternal perceptions and behavior. *Infant Mental Health Journal, 23*, 381–402.

Calkins, S. D., & Fox, N. A. (2002). Self-regulatory processes in early personality development: A multilevel approach to the study of childhood social withdrawal and aggression. *Development and Psychopathology, 14*, 477–498.

Calkins, S. D., Fox, N. A., & Marshall, T. R. (1996). Behavioral and physiological antecedents of inhibited and uninhibited behavior. *Child Development, 67*, 523–540.

Calkins, S., & Johnson, M. C. (1998). Toddler regulation of distress to frustrating events: Temperamental and maternal correlates. *Infant Behavior and Development, 21*, 379–395.

Callaghan, T. C. (1999). Early understanding and production of graphic symbols. *Child Development, 70*, 1314–1324.

Callaghan, T. C., & Rankin, M. P. (2002). Emergence of graphic symbol functioning and the question of domain specificity: A longitudinal training study. *Child Development, 73*, 359–376.

Calle, E. E., Rodriguez, C., Walker-Thurmond, K., & Thun, M. J. (2003). Overweight, obesity, and mortality from cancer in a prospectively studied cohort of U.S. adults. *New England Journal of Medicine, 348*, 1625–1638.

Calvert, S. L., & Kotler, J. A. (2003). Lessons from children's television: The impact of the Children's Television Act on children's learning. *Applied Developmental Psychology, 24*, 275–335.

Calvert, S. L., Kotler, J. A., Zehnder, S. M., & Shockey, E. M. (2003). Gender stereotyping in children's reports about educational and informational television programs. *Media Psychology, 5*, 139–162.

Camara, K. A., & Resnick, G. (1988). Interparental conflict and cooperation: Factors moderating children's post-divorce adjustment. In E. M. Hetherington & J. D. Arasteh (Ed.), *Impact of divorce, single parenting, and stepparenting on children* (pp. 169–195). Hillsdale, NJ: Erlbaum.

Camarata, S., & Leonard, L. B. (1986). Young children pronounce object words more accurately than action words. *Journal of Child Language, 13*, 51–65.

Cameron, C. A., & Lee, K. (1997). The development of children's telephone communication. *Journal of Applied Developmental Psychology, 18*, 55–70.

Cameron, J. A., Alvarez, J. M., Ruble, D. N., & Fuligni, A. J. (2001). Children's lay theories about in-groups and out-groups: Reconceptualizing research on prejudice. *Personality and Social Psychology Review, 5*, 118–128.

Cameron, M. B., & Wilson, B. J. (1990). The effects of chronological age, gender, and delay of entry on academic achievement and retention: Implications for academic redshirting. *Psychology in the Schools, 27*, 260–263.

Cameron-Faulkner, T., Lieven, E., & Tomasello, M. (2003). A construction based analysis of child-directed speech. *Cognitive Science, 27*, 843–873.

Camodeca, M., Goossens, F. A., Meerum Terwogt, M., & Schuengel, C. (2002). Bullying and victimization among school-age children: Stability and links to proactive and reactive aggression. *Social Development, 11*, 332–345.

Campbell, F. A., Pungello, E. P., Miller-Johnson, S., Burchinal, M., & Ramey, C. T. (2001). The development of

cognitive and academic abilities: Growth curves from an early childhood educational experiment. *Developmental Psychology, 37*, 231–242.

Campbell, F. A., & Ramey, C. T. (1995). Cognitive and school outcomes for high-risk African-American students at middle adolescence: Positive effects of early intervention. *American Educational Research Journal, 32*, 743–772.

Campbell, F. A., Ramey, C. T., Pungello, E. P., Sparling, J., & Miller-Johnson, S. (2002). Early childhood education: Young adult outcomes from the Abecedarian Project. *Applied Developmental Science, 6*, 42–57.

Campbell, J. R., Hombo, C. M., & Mazzeo, J. (2000). *NAEP 1999: Trends in academic progress*. Washington, DC: U.S. Department of Education.

Campbell, R., & Sais, E. (1995). Accelerated metalinguistic (phonological) awareness in bilingual children. *British Journal of Developmental Psychology, 13*, 61–68.

Campos, J. J., Anderson, D. I., Barbu-Roth, M. A., Hubbard, E. M., Hertenstein, J. J., & Witherington, D. (2000). Travel broadens the mind. *Infancy, 1*, 149–219.

Campos, J. J., Frankel, C. B., & Camras, L. (2004). On the nature of emotion regulation. *Child Development, 75*, 377–394.

Campos, J. J., Kermoian, R., & Zumbahlen, M. R. (1992). Socioemotional transformation in the family system following infant crawling onset. In N. Eisenberg & R. A. Fabes (Eds.), *New directions for child development* (No. 55, pp. 25–40). San Francisco: Jossey-Bass.

Campos, R. G. (1989). Soothing pain-elicited distress in infants with swaddling and pacifiers. *Child Development, 60*, 781–792.

Camras, L. A. (1992). Expressive development and basic emotions. *Cognition and Emotion, 6*, 267–283.

Camras, L. A., Oster, H., Campos, J. J., & Bakeman, R. (2003). Emotional facial expressions in European-American, Japanese, and Chinese infants. *Annals of the New York Academy of Sciences, 1000*, 1–17.

Camras, L. A., Oster, H., Campos, J., Campos, R., Ujie, T., Miyake, K., Wang, L., & Meng, Z. (1998). Production of emotional and facial expressions in European American, Japanese, and Chinese infants. *Developmental Psychology, 34*, 616–628.

Camras, L. A., Oster, H., Campos, J. J., Miyake, K., & Bradshaw, D. (1992). Japanese and American infants' responses to arm restraint. *Developmental Psychology, 28*, 578–583.

Canada Campaign 2000. (2002). *Diversity or disparity? Early childhood education and care in Canada*. Retrieved from www.campaign2000.ca

Canada Campaign 2000. (2003a). *Diversity or disparity? Early childhood education and care in Canada (ECEC)*. Retrieved from www.campaign2000.ca

Canada Campaign 2000. (2003b). *Poverty amidst prosperity—building a Canada for all children: 2002 report card*. Ottawa, ON: Author.

Canada Campaign 2000. (2004). *The real facts about child poverty in Canada*. Ottawa, ON: Author. Retrieved from www.campaign2000.ca

Canadian Broadcast Standards Council. (2003). *Voluntary code regarding violence in television programming*. Retrieved from www.cbsc.ca/english/codes/violence/violence.htm

Canadian Fitness and Lifestyle Research Institute. (2003). A case for daily physical education. Retrieved from www.cflri.ca/cflri/tips/95/LT95_09.html

Canadian Fitness and Lifestyle Research Institute. (2004). Survey of physical activity in Canadian schools. Retrieved from www.cflri.ca/cflri/pa/surveys/2001survey/2001survey.html

Canadian Psychological Association. (2000). *Canadian code of ethics for psychologists*. Ottawa, ON: Author. Retrieved from www.cpa.ca/ethics2000.html

Candy-Gibbs, S., Sharp, K., & Petrun, C. (1985). The effects of age, object, and cultural/religious background on children's concepts of death. *Omega, 15*, 329–345.

Canetto, S. S., & Sakinofsky, I. (1998). The gender paradox in suicide. *Suicide and Life-Threatening Behavior, 28*, 1–23.

Canobi, K. H. (2004). Individual differences in children's addition and subtraction knowledge. *Cognitive Development, 19*, 81–93.

Canobi, K. H., Reeve, R. A., & Pattison, P. E. (1998). The role of conceptual understanding in children's addition problem solving. *Developmental Psychology, 34*, 882–891.

Canobi, K. H., Reeve, R. A., & Pattison, P. E. (2003). Patterns of knowledge in children's addition. *Developmental Psychology, 39*, 521–534.

Capaldi, D., DeGarmo, D., Patterson, G. R., & Forgatch, M. (2002). Contextual risk across the early life span and association with antisocial behavior. In J. B. Reid, G. R. Patterson, & J. Snyder (Eds.), *Antisocial behavior in children and adolescents* (pp. 123–145). Washington, DC: American Psychological Association.

Capelli, C. A., Nakagawa, N., & Madden, C. M. (1990). How children understand sarcasm: The role of context and intonation. *Child Development, 61*, 1824–1841.

Caplan, M., Vespo, J., Pedersen, J., & Hay, D. F. (1991). Conflict and its resolution in small groups of one- and two-year-olds. *Child Development, 62*, 1513–1524.

Caracciolo, E., Moderato, P., & Perini, S. (1988). Analysis of some concrete-operational tasks from an inter-behavioral standpoint. *Journal of Experimental Child Psychology, 46*, 391–405.

Carey, S. (1995). On the origins of causal understanding. In D. Sperber, D. Premack, & A. J. Premack (Eds.), *Causal cognition* (pp. 268–308). Oxford, UK: Clarendon Press.

Carey, S. (1999). Sources of conceptual change. In E. K. Scholnick, K. Nelson, S. A. Gelman, & P. H. Miller (Eds.), *Conceptual development: Piaget's legacy* (pp. 293–326). Mahwah, NJ: Erlbaum.

Carey, S., & Markman, E. M. (1999). Cognitive development. In B. M. Bly & D. E. Rumelhart (Eds.), *Cognitive science* (pp. 201–254). San Diego: Academic Press.

Carli, L. L. (1995). No: Biology does not create gender differences in personality. In M. R. Walsh (Ed.), *Women,*

men, and gender. New Haven, CT: Yale University Press.

Carlo, G., Koller, S. H., Eisenberg, N., Da Silva, M., & Frohlich, C. (1996). A cross-national study on the relations among prosocial moral reasoning, gender-role orientations, and prosocial behaviors. *Developmental Psychology, 32*, 231–240.

Carlson, C., Uppal, S., & Prosser, E. (2000). Ethnic differences in processes contributing to the self-esteem of early adolescent girls. *Journal of Early Adolescence, 20*, 44–67.

Carlson, C. I., Wilson, K. D., & Hargrave, J. L. (2003). The effect of school racial composition on Hispanic intergroup relations. *Journal of Social and Personal Relationships, 20*, 203–220.

Carlson, E. A. (1998). A prospective longitudinal study of attachment disorganization/disorientation. *Child Development, 4*, 1107–1128.

Carlson, S. M., & Moses, L. J. (2001). Individual differences in inhibitory control and children's theory of mind. *Child Development, 72*, 1032–1053.

Carlson, S. M., Moses, L. J., & Claxton, S. J. (2004). Individual differences in executive functioning and theory of mind: An investigation of inhibitory control and planning ability. *Journal of Experimental Child Psychology, 87*, 299–319.

Carlson, V. J., & Horwood, R. L. (2003). Attachment, culture, and the caregiving system: The cultural patterning of everyday experiences among Anglo and Puerto Rican mother–infant pairs. *Infant Mental Health Journal, 24*, 53–73.

Carlton, M. P., & Winsler, A. (1999). School readiness: The need for a paradigm shift. *School Psychology Review, 28*, 338–352.

Carmichael, S. L., & Shaw, G. M. (2000). Maternal life stress and congenital anomalies. *Epidemiology, 11*, 30–35.

Carolson, C., Uppal, S., & Prosser, E. C. (2000). Ethnic differences in processes contributing to the self-esteem of early adolescent girls. *Journal of Early Adolescence, 20*, 44–67.

Carpendale, J. I., & Chandler, M. J. (1996). On the distinction between false belief understanding and subscribing to an interpretive theory of mind. *Child Development, 67*, 1686–1706.

Carpenter, C. J. (1983). Activity structure and play: Implications for socialization. In M. Liss (Ed.), *Social and cognitive skills: Sex roles and children's play* (pp. 117–145). New York: Academic Press.

Carpenter, C. J., Huston, A. C., & Holt, W. (1986). Modification of preschool sex-typed behaviors by participation in adult-structured activities. *Sex Roles, 14*, 603–615.

Carpenter, M., Akhtar, N., & Tomasello, M. (1998). Fourteen- through 18-month-old infants differentially imitate intentional and accidental actions. *Infant Behavior and Development, 21*, 315–330.

Carpenter, T. P., Fennema, E., Fuson, K., Hiebert, J., Human, P., & Murray, H. (1999). Learning basic number concepts and skills as problem solving. In E. Fennema & T. A. Romberg (Eds.), *Mathematics classrooms that promote understanding: Studies in mathematical thinking and learning* series (pp. 45–61). Mahwah, NJ: Erlbaum.

Carr, J. (2002). Down syndrome. In P. Howlin & O. Udwin (Eds.), *Outcomes in neurodevelopmental and genetic disorders* (pp. 169–197). New York: Cambridge University Press.

Carr, M., & Jessup, D. L. (1997). Gender differences in first-grade mathematics strategy use: Social and metacognitive influences. *Journal of Educational Psychology, 89,* 318–328.

Carraher, T., Schliemann, A. D., & Carraher, D. W. (1988). Mathematical concepts in everyday life. In G. B. Saxe & M. Gearhart (Eds.), *New directions for child development* (Vol. 41, pp. 71–87). San Francisco: Jossey-Bass.

Carroll, J. B. (1993). *Human cognitive abilities: A survey of factor-analytic studies.* New York: Cambridge University Press.

Carroll, J. B. (1997). The three-stratum theory of cognitive abilities. In D. P. Flanagan, J. L. Genshaft, & P. Harrison (Eds.), *Contemporary intellectual assessment* (pp. 122–130). New York: Guilford.

Carskadon, M. A., Harvey, K., Duke, P., Anders, T. F., Litt, I. F., & Dement, W. C. (2002). Pubertal changes in daytime sleepiness. *Sleep, 25,* 525–605.

Carta, J. J., Atwater, J. B., Greenwood, C. R., McConnell, S. R., & McEvoy, M. A. (2001). Effects of cumulative prenatal substance exposure and environmental risks on children's developmental trajectories. *Journal of Clinical Psychology, 30,* 327–337.

Carver, K., Joyner, K., & Udry, J. R. (2003). National estimates of adolescent romantic relationships. In P. Florsheim (Ed.), *Adolescent romantic relations and sexual behavior: Theory, research, and practical implications* (pp. 23–56). Mahwah, NJ: Erlbaum.

Carver, P. R., Egan, S. K., & Perry, D. G. (2004). Children who question their heterosexuality. *Developmental Psychology, 40,* 43–53.

Casasola, M., Cohen, L. B., & Chiarello, E. (2003). Six-month-old infants' categorization of containment spatial relations. *Child Development, 74,* 679–693.

Case, R. (1992). *The mind's staircase.* Hillsdale, NJ: Erlbaum.

Case, R. (1996). Introduction: Reconceptualizing the nature of children's conceptual structures and their development in middle childhood. In R. Case & Y. Okamoto (Eds.), The role of central conceptual structures in the development of children's thought. *Monographs of the Society for Research in Child Development, 61*(1–2, Serial No. 246), pp. 1–26.

Case, R. (1998). The development of central conceptual structures. In D. Kuhn & R. Siegler (Eds.), *Handbook of child psychology: Vol. 2. Cognition, perception, and language* (5th ed., pp. 745–800). New York: Wiley.

Case, R., Griffin, S., & Kelly, W. M. (2001). Socioeconomic differences in children's early cognitive development and their readiness for schooling. In S. L. Golbeck (Ed.), *Psychological perspectives on early education* (pp. 37–63). Mahwah, NJ: Erlbaum.

Case, R., & Okamoto, Y. (Eds.). (1996). The role of central conceptual structures in the development of children's

thought. *Monographs of the Society for Research in Child Development, 61*(1–2, Serial No. 246).

Caselli, M. C., Bates, E., Casadio, P., Fenson, J., Fenson, L., Sanderl, L., & Weir, J. (1995). A cross-linguistic study of early lexical development. *Cognitive Development, 10,* 159–199.

Casey, B. J., Thomas, K. M., Davidson, M. C., Kunz, K., & Franzen, P. L. (2002). Dissociating striatal and hippocampal function developmentally with a stimulus-response compatibility task. *Journal of Cognitive Neuroscience, 22,* 8647–8652.

Casey, M. B., Nuttall, R. L., & Pezaris, E. (1997). Mediators of gender differences in mathematics college entrance test scores: A comparison of spatial skills with internalized beliefs and anxieties. *Developmental Psychology, 33,* 669–680.

Casey, M. B., Nuttall, R. L., & Pezaris, E. (2001). Spatial-mechanical reasoning skills versus mathematics self-confidence as mediators of gender differences on mathematics subtests using cross-national gender-based items. *Journal for Research in Mathematics Education, 32,* 28–57.

Cashon, C. H., & Cohen, L. B. (2000). Eight-month-old infants' perceptions of possible and impossible events. *Infancy, 1,* 429–446.

Casper, L. M., & Smith, K. E. (2002). Dispelling the myths: Self-care, class, and race. *Journal of Family Issues, 23,* 716–727.

Caspi, A. (1998). Personality development across the life course. In N. Eisenberg (Ed.), *Handbook of child psychology: Vol. 3. Social, emotional, and personality development* (5th ed., pp. 311–388). New York: Wiley.

Caspi, A. (2000). The child is father of the man: Personality continuities from childhood to adulthood. *Journal of Personality and Social Psychology, 78,* 158–172.

Caspi, A., Elder, G. H., Jr., & Bem, D. J. (1987). Moving against the world: Life-course patterns of explosive children. *Developmental Psychology, 23,* 308–313.

Caspi, A., Elder, G. H., Jr., & Bem, D. J. (1988). Moving away from the world: Life-course patterns of shy children. *Developmental Psychology, 24,* 824–831.

Caspi, A., Harrington, H., Milne, B., Amell, J. W., Theodore, R. F., & Moffitt, T. E. (2003). Children's behavioral styles at age 3 are linked to their adult personality traits at age 26. *Journal of Personality, 71,* 495–513.

Caspi, A., Lynam, D., Moffitt, T. E., & Silva, P. A. (1993). Unraveling girls' delinquency: Biological, dispositional, and contextual contributions to adolescent misbehavior. *Developmental Psychology, 29,* 19–30.

Caspi, A., Moffitt, T. E., Morgan, J., Rutter, M., Taylor, A., Kim-Cohen, J., & Polo-Tomas, M. (2004). Maternal expressed emotion predicts children's antisocial behavior problems: Using monozygotic-twin differences to identify environmental effects on behavioral development. *Developmental Psychology, 40,* 149–161.

Caspi, A., & Roberts, B. W. (2001). Personality development across the life course: The argument for change

and continuity. *Psychological Inquiry, 12,* 49–66.

Cassia, V. M., Simion, F., & Umiltá, C. (2001). Face preference at birth: The role of an orienting mechanism. *Developmental Science, 4,* 101–108.

Cassidy, J., & Berlin, L. J. (1994). The insecure/ambivalent pattern of attachment: Theory and research. *Child Development, 65,* 971–991.

Castellanos, F. X., Lee, P. P., Sharp, W., Jeffries, N. O., Greenstein, D. K., & Clasen, L. S. (2002). Developmental trajectories of brain volume abnormalities in children and adolescents with attention-deficit/hyperactivity disorder. *Journal of the American Medical Association, 288,* 1740–1748.

Castellanos, F. X., Sharp, W. S., Gottesman, R. F., Greenstein, D. K., Giedd, J. N., & Rapoport, J. L. (2003). Anatomic brain abnormalities in monozygotic twins discordant for attention-deficit hyperactivity disorder. *American Journal of Psychiatry, 160,* 1693–1695.

Castelli, F., Frith, C. D., Happé, F., & Frith, U. (2002). Autism, Asperger syndrome, and brain mechanisms for the attribution of mental states to animated shapes. *Brain, 125,* 1–11.

Catalano, R. A. (2003). Sex ratios in the two Germanies: A test of the economic stress hypothesis. *Human Reproduction, 18,* 1972–1975.

Caton, D., Corry, M. P., Frigoletto, F. D., Hokins, D. P., Liberman, E., & Mayberry, L. (2002). The nature and management of labor pain: Executive summary. *American Journal of Obstetrics and Gynecology, 186,* S1–S15.

Catsambis, S. (1994). The path to math: Gender and racial-ethnic differences in mathematics participation from middle school to high school. *Sociology of Education, 67,* 199–215.

Cattell, J. M. (1890). Mental tests and measurements. *Mind, 15,* 373–381.

Cattell, R. B. (1971). *Abilities: Their structure, growth and action.* Boston: Houghton Mifflin.

Cattell, R. B. (1987). *Intelligence: Its structure, growth and action.* Amsterdam: North-Holland.

Cavadini, C., Siega-Riz, A. M., & Popkin, B. M. (2000). U.S. adolescent food intake trends from 1965 to 1996. *Archives of Diseases in Childhood, 83,* 18–24.

Ceci, S. J. (1991). How much does schooling influence general intelligence and its cognitive components? A reassessment of the evidence. *Developmental Psychology, 27,* 703–722.

Ceci, S. J. (1999). Schooling and intelligence. In S. J. Ceci & W. M. Williams (Eds.), *The nature–nurture debate: The essential readings* (pp. 168–175). Oxford: Blackwell.

Ceci, S. J., & Bruck, M. (1998). Children's testimony: Applied and basic issues. In I. Sigel & K. A. Renninger (Eds.), *Handbook of child psychology: Vol. 4. Child psychology in practice* (5th ed., pp. 713–774). New York: Wiley.

Ceci, S. J., Bruck, M., & Battin, D. B. (2000). The suggestibility of children's testimony. In D. F. Bjorklund (Ed.), *False-memory creation in children and adults* (pp. 169–201). Mahwah, NJ: Erlbaum.

Ceci, S. J., Fitneva, S. A., & Gilstrap, L. L. (2003). Memory development and eyewitness testimony. In A. Slater &

G. Bremner (Eds.), *An introduction to developmental psychology* (pp. 283–310). Malden, MA: Blackwell.

Ceci, S. J., & Roazzi, A. (1994). The effects of context on cognition: Postcards from Brazil. In R. J. Sternberg (Ed.), *Mind in context* (pp. 74–101). New York: Cambridge University Press.

Ceci, S. J., Rosenblum, T. B., & Kumpf, M. (1998). The shrinking gap between high- and low-scoring groups: Current trends and possible causes. In U. Neisser (Ed.), *The rising curve* (pp. 287–302). Washington, DC: American Psychological Association.

Ceci, S. J., & Williams, W. M. (1997). Schooling, intelligence, and income. *American Psychologist, 52,* 1051–1058.

Center for Communication and Social Policy. (Ed.). (1998). *National television violence study* (Vol. 2). Newbury Park, CA: Sage.

Center for Effective Discipline. (2005). *Worldwide bans on corporal punishment.* Retrieved from www.stophitting.com/disatschool/facts.php

Cermak, S. A., & Daunhauer, L. A. (1997). Sensory processing in the post-institutionalized child. *American Journal of Occupational Therapy, 51,* 500–507.

Cernoch, J. M., & Porter, R. H. (1985). Recognition of maternal axillary odors by infants. *Child Development, 56,* 1593–1598.

Cervantes, C. A., & Callanan, M. A. (1998). Labels and explanations in mother–child emotion talk: Age and gender differentiation. *Developmental Psychology, 34,* 88–98.

Chalmers, J. B., & Townsend, M. A. R. (1990). The effects of training in social perspective taking on socially maladjusted girls. *Child Development, 61,* 178–190.

Chamberlain, P. (2003). Antisocial behavior and delinquency in girls. In P. Chamberlain (Ed.), *Treating chronic juvenile offenders* (pp. 109–127). Washington, DC: American Psychological Association.

Champion, T. B. (2003a). "A matter of vocabularly": Performances of low-income African-American Head Start children on the Peabody Picture Vocabulary Test. *Communication Disorders Quarterly, 24,* 121–127.

Champion, T. B. (2003b). *Understanding storytelling among African-American children: A journey from Africa to America.* Mahwah, NJ: Erlbaum.

Chan, R. W., Raboy, B., & Patterson, C. J. (1998). Psychosocial adjustment among children conceived via donor insemination by lesbian and heterosexual mothers. *Child Development, 69,* 443–457.

Chandler, M. J. (1973). Egocentrism and antisocial behavior: The assessment and training of social perspective-taking skills. *Developmental Psychology, 9,* 326–332.

Chandler, M. J., & Carpendale, J. I. (1998). Inching toward a mature theory of mind. In M. Ferrari & R. J. Sternberg (Eds.), *Self-awareness: Its nature and development* (pp. 148–190). New York: Guilford.

Chandra, R. K. (1991). Interactions between early nutrition and the immune system. In *Ciba Foundation Symposium* (No. 156, pp. 77–92). Chichester, UK: Wiley.

Chaney, C. (1992). Language development, metalinguistic skills, and print awareness in 3-year-old children. *Applied Psycholinguistics, 13,* 485–514.

Chang, L., Schwartz, D., Dodge, K. A., & McBride-Chang, C. (2003). Harsh parenting in relation to child emotion regulation and aggression. *Journal of Family Psychology, 17,* 598–606.

Chao, R. K. (1994). Beyond parental control and authoritarian parenting style: Understanding Chinese parenting through the cultural notion of training. *Child Development, 65,* 1111–1119.

Chapman, K. L., Leonard, L. B., & Mervis, C. B. (1986). The effect of feedback on young children's inappropriate word usage. *Journal of Child Language, 13,* 101–117.

Chapman, R. S. (2000). Children's language learning: An interactionist perspective. *Journal of Child Psychology and Psychiatry, 41,* 33–54.

Charman, T., Baron-Cohen, S., Swettenham, J., Baird, G., Cox, A., & Drew, A. (2001). Testing joint attention, imitation, and play as infancy precursors to language and theory of mind. *Cognitive Development, 15,* 481–498.

Chase-Lansdale, P. L., Brooks-Gunn, J., & Zamsky, E. S. (1994). Young African-American multigenerational families in poverty: Quality of mothering and grandmothering. *Child Development, 65,* 373–393.

Chase-Lansdale, P. L., Cherlin, A. J., & Kiernan, K. E. (1995). The long-term effects of parental divorce on the mental health of young children. *Child Development, 66,* 1614–1634.

Chase-Lansdale, P. L., Gordon, R., Brooks-Gunn, J., & Klebanov, P. K. (1997). Neighborhood and family influences on the intellectual and behavioral competence of preschool and early school-age children. In J. Brooks-Gunn, G. Duncan, & J. L. Aber (Eds.), *Neighborhood poverty: Context and consequences for development* (pp. 79–118). New York: Russell Sage Foundation.

Chassin, L., Ritter, J., Trim, R. S., & King, K. M. (2003). Adolescent substance use disorders. In E. J. Mash & R. A. Barkley (Eds.), *Child psychopathology* (2nd ed., pp. 199–230). New York: Guilford Press.

Chavajay, P., & Rogoff, B. (2002). Schooling and traditional collaborative social organization of problem solving by Mayan mothers and children. *Developmental Psychology, 38,* 55–66.

Chavous, T. M., Bernat, D. H., Schmeelk-Cone, K., Caldwell, C. H., Kohn-Wood, L., & Zimmerman, M. A. (2003). Racial identity and academic attainment among African-American adolescents. *Child Development, 74,* 1076–1090.

Checkley, W., Epstein, L. D., Gilman, R. H., Cabrera, L., & Black, R. E. (2003). Effects of acute diarrhea on linear growth in Peruvian children. *American Journal of Epidemiology, 157,* 166–175.

Chen, D. W., Fein, G. G., Killen, M., & Tam, H.-P. (2001). Peer conflicts of preschool children: Issues, resolution, incidence, and age-related patterns. *Early Education and Development, 12,* 523–544.

Chen, M. (2003). Wombs for rent: An examination of prohibitory and regulatory approaches to governing preconception arrangements. *Health Law in Canada, 23,* 33–50.

Chen, X. (2001). Growing up in a collectivistic culture: Socialization and socio-emotional development in Chinese children. In A. L. Comunian & U. P. Gielen (Eds.), *Human development in cross-cultural perspective.* Padua, Italy: Cedam.

Chen, X., Cen, G., Li, D., & He, Y. (2005). Social functioning and adjustment in Chinese children: The imprint of historical time. *Child Development, 76,* 182–195.

Chen, X., Hastings, P. D., Rubin, K. H., Chen, H., Cen, G., & Stewart, S. L. (1998). Child-rearing attitudes and behavioral inhibition in Chinese and Canadian toddlers: A cross-cultural study. *Developmental Psychology, 34,* 677–686.

Chen, X., Rubin, K. H., & Li, D. (1997). Relation between academic achievement and social adjustment: Evidence from Chinese children. *Developmental Psychology, 33,* 518–525.

Chen, X., Rubin, K. H., & Li, D. (1995). Social functioning and adjustment in Chinese children: A longitudinal study. *Developmental Psychology, 31,* 531–539.

Chen, X., Wu, H., Chen, H., Wang, L., & Cen, G. (2001). Parenting practices and aggressive behavior in Chinese children. *Parenting: Science and Practice, 1,* 159–184.

Chen, Y.-C., Yu, M.-L., Rogan, W., Gladen, B., & Hsu, C.-C. (1994). A 6-year follow-up of behavior and activity disorders in the Taiwan Yu-cheng children. *American Journal of Public Health, 84,* 415–421.

Chen, Y.-J., & Hsu, C.-C. (1994). Effects of prenatal exposure to PCBs on the neurological function of children: A neuropsychological and neurophysiological study. *Developmental Medicine and Child Neurology, 36,* 312–320.

Chen, Z., Sanchez, R. P., & Campbell, T. (1997). From beyond to within their grasp: The rudiments of analogical problem solving in 10- to 13-month-olds. *Developmental Psychology, 33,* 790–801.

Chen, Z., & Siegler, R. S. (2000). Across the great divide: Bridging the gap between understanding of toddlers' and older children's thinking. *Monographs of the Society for Research in Child Development, 65*(2, Serial No. 261).

Chesney-Lind, M. (2001). Girls, violence, and delinquency: Popular myths and persistent problems. In S. O. White (Ed.), *Handbook of youth and justice* (pp. 135–158). New York: Kluwer Academic.

Chess, S., & Thomas, A. (1984). *Origins and evolution of behavior disorders.* New York: Brunner/Mazel.

Chi, M. T. H. (1978). Knowledge structures and memory development. In R. S. Siegler (Ed.), *Children's thinking: What develops?* (pp. 73–96). Hillsdale, NJ: Erlbaum.

Child Care Advocacy Association of Canada. (2004). Family living costs in Manitoba, 2004, and cost of raising a child. Retrieved from www.action.web.ca/home/ccaac/alerts.shtml?x=67753

Child Trends. (2001). *Facts at a glance.* Washington, DC: Author.

Children's Defense Fund. (2004). *The state of America's children: Yearbook 2004.* Washington, DC: Author.

Children's Defense Fund. (2005). *The state of America's children 2005.* Washington, DC: Author.

Children's Television Act. (1990). Public Law No. 101-437, 104 Stat. 996-1000, codified at 47 USC Sections 303a, 303b, 394.

Chisholm, J. S. (1989). Biology, culture, and the development of temperament: A Navajo example. In J. K. Nugent, B. M. Lester, & T. B. Brazelton (Eds.), *Biology, culture, and development* (Vol. 1, pp. 341–364). Norwood, NJ: Ablex.

Chodirker, B., Cadrin, C., Davies, G., Summers, A., Wilson, R., Winsor, E., & Young, D. (2001). Genetic indications for prenatal diagnosis. *Journal of the Society of Obstetricians and Gynaecologists of Canada, 23,* 525–531.

Choi, J., & Silverman, I. (2003). Processes underlying sex differences in route-learning strategies in children and adolescents. *Personality and Individual Differences, 34,* 1153–1166.

Choi, S., & Gopnik, A. (1995). Early acquisition of verbs in Korean: A cross-linguistic study. *Journal of Child Language, 22,* 497–529.

Choi, S., McDonough, L., Bowerman, M., & Mandler, J. M. (1999). Early sensitivity to language-specific spatial categories in English and Korean. *Cognitive Development, 14,* 241–268.

Chomsky, C. (1969). *The acquisition of syntax in children from 5 to 10.* Cambridge, MA: MIT Press.

Chomsky, N. (1957). *Syntactic structures.* The Hague: Mouton.

Chomsky, N. (1976). *Reflections on language.* London: Temple Smith.

Chomsky, N. (1997). Language and mind: Current thoughts on ancient problems (Part 1). Retrieved from http://fccl.ksu.ru/papers/chomsky1.htm

Chouinard, M. M., & Clark, E. V. (2003). Adult reformulations of child errors as negative evidence. *Journal of Child Language, 30,* 637–669.

Christian, P. (2003). Micronutrients and reproductive health issues: An international perspective. *Journal of Nutrition, 133,* 1969S–1973S.

Christian, P., Khatry, S. K., Katz, J., Pradhan, E. K., LeClerq, S. C., & Shrestha, S. R. (2003). Effects of alternative maternal micronutrient supplements on low birth weight in rural Nepal: A double-blind randomized community trial. *British Medical Journal, 326,* 571–576.

Chumlea, W. C., Schubert, C. M., Roche, A. F., Kulin, H. E., Lee, P. A., Himes, J. H., & Sun, S. S. (2003). Age at menarche and racial comparisons in U.S. girls. *Pediatrics, 111,* 110–113.

Cicchetti, D. (2003). Neuroendocrine functioning in maltreated children. In D. Cicchetti & E. F. Walker (Eds.), *Neurodevelopmental mechanisms in psychopathology* (pp. 345–365). New York: Cambridge University Press.

Cicchetti, D., & Toth, S. L. (1998). The development of depression in children and adolescents. *American Psychologist, 53,* 221–241.

Cicchetti, D., & Toth, S. L. (2000). Developmental processes in maltreated children. In. D. J. Hansen (Ed.), *Nebraska Symposium on Motivation* (Vol. 46, pp. 85–160). Lincoln, NB: University of Nebraska Press.

Cicchetti, D., Toth, S. L., & Rogosch, F. A. (2004). Toddler–parent psychotherapy for depressed mothers and their offspring: Implications for attachment theory. In L. Atkinson & S. Goldberg (Eds.), *Attachment issues in psychotherapy and intervention* (pp. 229–275). Mahwah, NJ: Erlbaum.

Cillessen & Bellmore. (2004). Social skills and interpersonal perception in early and middle childhood. In P. K. Smith & C. H. Hart (Eds.), *Blackwell handbook of childhood social development* (pp. 355–374). Malden, MA: Blackwell.

Cillessen, A. H. N., & Mayeux, L. (2004). From censure to reinforcement: Developmental changes in the association between aggression and social status. *Child Development, 75,* 147–163.

Claes, M., Lacourse, E., Bouchard, C., & Perucchini, P. (2003). Parental practices in late adolescence, a comparison of three countries: Canada, France and Italy. *Journal of Adolescence, 26,* 387–399.

Clancy, P. (1985). Acquisition of Japanese. In D. I. Slobin (Ed.), *The crosslinguistic study of language acquisition: Vol. 1. The data* (pp. 323–524). Hillsdale, NJ: Erlbaum.

Clancy, P. (1989). Form and function in the acquisition of Korean wh- questions. *Journal of Child Language, 16,* 323–347.

Clapp, J. F., III, Kim, H., Burciu, B., Schmidt, S., Petry, K., & Lopez, B. (2002). Continuing regular exercise during pregnancy: Effect of exercise volume on fetoplacental growth. *American Journal of Obstetrics and Gynecology, 186,* 142–147.

Clark, E. V. (1983). Meanings and concepts. In P. H. Mussen (Ed.), *Handbook of child psychology: Vol. 3. Cognitive development* (pp. 787–840). New York: Wiley.

Clark, E. V. (1990). On the pragmatics of contrast. *Journal of Child Language, 17,* 417–431.

Clark, E. V. (1993). *The lexicon in acquisition.* Cambridge, UK: Cambridge University Press.

Clark, E. V. (1995). The lexicon and syntax. In J. L. Miller & P. D. Eimas (Eds.), *Speech, language, and communication* (pp. 303–337). San Diego: Academic Press.

Clark, K. E., & Ladd, G. W. (2000). Connectedness and autonomy support in parent–child relationships: Links to children's socioemotional orientation and peer relationships. *Developmental Psychology, 36,* 485–498.

Clark, L. A., Kochanska, G., & Ready, R. (2000). Mothers' personality and its interaction with child temperament as predictors of parenting. *Journal of Personality and Social Psychology, 79,* 701–719.

Clark, R., Hyde, J. S., Essex, M. J., & Klein, M. H. (1997). Length of maternity leave and quality of mother–infant interaction. *Child Development, 68,* 364–383.

Clarke-Stewart, A., Allhusen, V., & Goosens, F. (2001). Day care and the Strange Situation. In A. Göncu & E. L. Klein (Eds.), *Children in play, story, and school* (pp. 241–266). New York: Guilford.

Clarke-Stewart, K. A. (1998). Historical shifts and underlying themes in ideas about rearing young children in the United States: Where have we been? Where are we going? *Early Development and Parenting, 7*, 101–117.

Clarke-Stewart, K. A., & Hayward, C. (1996). Advantages of father custody and contact for the psychological well-being of school-age children. *Journal of Applied Developmental Psychology, 17*, 239–270.

Clarkson, T. W., Magos, L., & Myers, G. J. (2003). The toxicology of mercury—current exposures and clinical manifestations. *New England Journal of Medicine, 349*, 1731–1737.

Clausen, J. A. (1975). The social meaning of differential physical and sexual maturation. In S. E. Dragastin & G. H. Elder (Eds.), *Adolescence in the life cycle: Psychological change and the social context* (pp. 25–47). New York: Halsted.

Claxton, L. J., Keen, R., & McCarty, M. E. (2003). Evidence of motor planning in infant reaching behavior. *Psychological Science, 14*, 354–356.

Clements, D. H. (1990). Metacomponential development in a Logo programming environment. *Journal of Educational Psychology, 82*, 141–149.

Clements, D. H. (1995). Teaching creativity with computers. *Educational Psychology Review, 7*, 141–161.

Clements, D. H., & Nastasi, B. K. (1992). Computers and early childhood education. In M. Gettinger, S. N. Elliott, & T. R. Kratochwill (Eds.), *Advances in school psychology: Preschool and early childhood treatment directions* (pp. 187–246). Hillsdale, NJ: Erlbaum.

Clements, D. H., & Sarama, J. (2003). Young children and technology: What does the research say? *Young Children, 58*(6), 34–40.

Clifton, R. K., Muir, D. W., Ashmead, D. H., & Clarkson, M. G. (1993). Is visually guided reaching in early infancy a myth? *Child Development, 64*, 1099–1110.

Clifton, R. K., Rochat, P., Robin, D. J., & Berthier, N. E. (1994). Multimodal perception in the control of infant reaching. *Journal of Experimental Psychology: Human Perception and Performance, 20*, 876–886.

Clingempeel, W. G., & Henggeler, S. W. (2003). Aggressive juvenile offenders transitioning into emerging adulthood: Factors discriminating persistors and desistors. *American Journal of Orthopsychiatry, 73*, 310–323.

Cloud, N., Genesee, F., & Hamayan, E. (2000). *Dual language instruction: A handbook for enriched education.* Boston, MA: Heinle & Heinle.

Clutton-Brock, T. H. (1991). *The evolution of parental care.* Princeton, NJ: Princeton University Press.

Cohen, L. B. (2003). Commentary on Part I: Unresolved issues in infant categorization. In D. H. Rakison & L. M. Oakes (Eds.), *Early category and concept development: Making sense of the blooming, buzzing confusion* (pp. 193–209). New York: Oxford University Press.

Cohen, L. B., & Cashon, C. H. (2001). Infant object segregation implies information integration. *Journal of Experimental Child Psychology, 78*, 75–83.

Cohen, P., Kasen, S., Chen, H., Harmrk, C., & Gordon, K. (2003). Variations in patterns of developmental transitions in the emerging adulthood period. *Developmental Psychology, 39*, 657–669.

Cohn, J., & Tronick, E. Z. (1987). Mother–infant face-to-face interaction: The sequencing of dyadic states at 3, 6, and 9 months. *Developmental Psychology, 23*, 68–77.

Coholl, A., Kassotis, J., Parks, R., Vaughan, R., Bannister, H., & Northridge, M. (2001). Adolescents in the age of AIDS: Myths, misconceptions, and misunderstandings regarding sexually transmitted diseases. *Journal of the National Medical Association, 93*, 64–69.

Coie, J. D., & Dodge, K. A. (1998). Aggression and antisocial behavior. In N. Eisenberg (Ed.), *Handbook of child psychology: Vol. 3. Social, emotional, and personality development* (5th ed., pp. 779–862). New York: Wiley.

Coie, J. D., Dodge, K. A., & Coppotelli, H. (1982). Dimensions and types of social status: A cross-age perspective. *Developmental Psychology, 18*, 557–570.

Coie, J. D., & Krehbiel, G. (1984). Effects of academic tutoring on the social status of low-achieving, socially rejected children. *Child Development, 55*, 1465–1478.

Coie, J., Terry, R., Lenox, K., Lochman, J., & Hyman, C. (1995). Childhood peer rejection and aggression as predictors of stable patterns of adolescent disorder. *Development and Psychopathology, 7*, 697–713.

Colapinto, J. (2001). *As nature made him: The boy who was raised as a girl.* New York: Perennial.

Colby, A., & Damon, W. (1992). *Some do care: Contemporary lives of moral commitment.* New York: Free Press.

Colby, A., & Kohlberg, L. (1987). *The measurement of moral judgment: Theoretical foundations and research validation* (Vol. 1). Cambridge: Cambridge University Press.

Colby, A., Kohlberg, L., Gibbs, J. C., & Lieberman, M. (1983). A longitudinal study of moral judgment. *Monographs of the Society for Research in Child Development, 48*(1–2, Serial No. 200).

Cole, D. A., Martin, J. M., Peeke, L. A., Seroczynski, A. D., & Fier, J. (1999). Children's over- and underestimation of academic competence: A longitudinal study of gender differences, depression, and anxiety. *Child Development, 70*, 459–473.

Cole, D. A., Maxwell, S. E., Martin, J. M., Peeke, L. G., Seroczynski, A. D., & Tram, J. M. (2001). The development of multiple domains of child and adolescent self-concept: A cohort sequential longitudinal design. *Child Development, 72*, 1723–1746.

Cole, M. (1990). Cognitive development and formal schooling: The evidence from cross-cultural research. In L. C. Moll (Ed.), *Vygotsky and education* (pp. 89–110). New York: Cambridge University Press.

Cole, P. M., Bruschi, C. J., & Tamang, B. L. (2002). Cultural differences in children's emotional reactions to difficult situations. *Child Development, 73*, 983–996.

Cole, P. M., & Tamang, B. L. (1998). Nepali children's ideas about emotional displays in hypothetical challenges. *Developmental Psychology, 34*, 640–646.

Cole, T. J. (2000). Secular trends in growth. *Proceedings of the Nutrition Society, 59*, 317–324.

Coleman, P. K. (2003). Perceptions of parent–child attachment, social self-efficacy, and peer relationships in middle childhood. *Infant and Child Development, 12*, 351–368.

Coley, R. L. (1998). Children's socialization experiences and functioning in single-mother households: The importance of fathers and other men. *Child Development, 69*, 219–230.

Coley, R. L., & Chase-Lansdale, P. L. (1998). Adolescent pregnancy and parenthood: Recent evidence and future directions. *American Psychologist, 53*, 152–166.

Coley, R. L., Morris, J. E., & Hernandez, D. (2004). Out-of-school care and problem behavior trajectories among low-income adolescents: Individual, family, and neighborhood characteristics as added risks. *Child Development, 75*, 948–965.

Collie, R., & Hayne, H. (1999). Deferred imitation by 6- and 9-month-old infants: More evidence for declarative memory. *Developmental Psychobiology, 35*, 83–90.

Collins, M. A., & Amabile, T. M. (1999). Motivation and creativity. In R. J. Sternberg (Ed.), *Handbook of creativity* (pp. 297–312). Cambridge, UK: Cambridge University Press.

Collins, W. A. (1983). Children's processing of television content: Implications for prevention of negative effects. *Prevention in Human Services, 2*, 53–66.

Collins, W. A. (1997). Relationships and development during adolescence: Interpersonal adaptation to individual change. *Personal Relationships, 4*, 1–14.

Collins, W. A. (2003). More than myth: The developmental significance of romantic relationships during adolescence. *Journal of Research on Adolescence, 13*, 1–24.

Collins, W. A., Maccoby, E. E., Steinberg, L. D., Hetherington, E. M., & Bornstein, M. H. (2000). Contemporary research on parenting: The case for nature and nurture. *American Psychologist, 55*, 218–232.

Collins, W. A., Madsen, S. D., & Susman-Stillman, A. (2002). Parenting during middle childhood. In M. H. Bornstein (Ed.), *Handbook of parenting: Vol. 1. Children and Parenting* (2nd ed., pp. 73–101). Mahwah, NJ: Erlbaum.

Colombo, J. (2002). Infant attention grows up: The emergence of a developmental cognitive neuroscience perspective. *Current Directions in Psychological Science, 11*, 196–199.

Colombo, J., Shaddy, D. J., Richman, W. A., Maikranz, J. M., & Blaga, O. M. (2004). The developmental course of habituation in infancy and preschool outcome. *Infancy, 5*, 1–38.

Coltrane, S. (1990). Birth timing and the division of labor in dual-earner families. *Journal of Family Issues, 11*, 157–181.

Comings, D. E., Muhleman, D., Johnson, J. P., & MacMurray, J. P. (2002). Parent–daughter transmission of the androgen receptor gene as an explanation of the effect of father absence on age of menarche. *Child Development, 73*, 1046–1051.

Comstock, G. A., & Scharrer, E. (1999). *Television: What's on, who's watching, and what it means.* San Diego: Academic Press.

Comstock, G. A., & Scharrer, E. (2001). The use of television and other film-related media. In D. G. Singer & J. L. Singer (Eds.), *Handbook of children and the media* (pp. 47–72). Thousand Oaks, CA: Sage.

Comunian, A. L, & Gielan, U. P. (2000). Sociomoral reflection and prosocial and antisocial behavior: Two Italian studies. *Psychological Reports, 87*, 161–175.

Conger, R. D., & Conger, K. J. (2002). Resilience in Midwestern families: Selected findings from the first decade of a prospective, longitudinal study. *Journal of Marriage and the Family, 64*, 361–373.

Conner, D. B., & Cross, D. R. (2003). Longitudinal analysis of the presence, efficacy, and stability of maternal scaffolding during informal problem-solving interactions. *British Journal of Developmental Psychology, 21*, 315–334.

Connolly, J. A., & Doyle, A. B. (1984). Relations of social fantasy play to social competence in preschoolers. *Developmental Psychology, 20*, 797–806.

Connolly, J. A., & Goldberg, A. (1999). Romantic relationships in adolescence: The role of friends and peers in their emergence and development. In W. Furman, B. B. Brown, & C. Feiring (Eds.), *The development of romantic relationships in adolescence* (pp. 266–290). Cambridge, UK: Cambridge University Press.

Connolly, J., Craig, W., Goldberg, A., & Pepler, D. (2004). Mixed-gender groups, dating, and romantic relationships in early adolescence. *Journal of Research on Adolescence, 14*, 185–207.

Connolly, J., Furman, W., & Konarski, R. (2000). The role of peers in the emergence of romantic relationships in adolescence. *Child Development, 71*, 1395–1408.

Connor, P. D., Sampson, P. D., Bookstein, F. L., Barr, H. M., & Streissguth, A. P. (2001). Direct and indirect effects of prenatal alcohol damage on executive function. *Developmental Neuropsychology, 18*, 331–354.

Conti-Ramsden, G., & Pérez-Pereira, M. (1999). Conversational interactions between mothers and their infants who are congenitally blind, have low vision, or are sighted. *Journal of Visual Impairment and Blindness, 93*, 691–703.

Conyers, C., Miltenberger, R., Maki, A., Barenz, R., Jurgens, M., Sailer, A., Haugen, M., & Kopp, B. (2004). A comparison of response cost and differential reinforcement of other behaviors to reduce disruptive behavior in a preschool classroom. *Journal of Applied Behavior Analysis, 37*, 411–415.

Cooper, C. R. (1998). *The weaving of maturity: Cultural perspectives on adolescent development.* New York: Oxford University Press.

Cope-Farrar, K. M., & Kunkel, D. (2002). Sexual messages in teens' favorite prime-time television programs. In J. D. Brown, J. R. Steele, & K. Walsh-Childers (Eds.), *Sexual teens, sexual media* (pp. 59–78). Mahwah, NJ: Erlbaum.

Coplan, R. J., Barber, A. M., & Lagacé-Séquin, D. G. (1999). The role of child temperament as a predictor of early literacy and numeracy skills in preschoolers. *Early Childhood Research Quarterly, 14*, 537–553.

Coplan, R. J., Bowker, A., & Cooper, S. M. (2003). Parenting daily hassles, child temperament, and social adjustment in preschool. *Early Childhood Research Quarterly, 18*, 376–395.

Coplan, R. J., Gavinsky-Molina, M. H., Lagace-Seguin, D., & Wichmann, C. (2001). When girls versus boys play alone: Nonsocial play and adjustment in kindergarten. *Developmental Psychology, 37*, 464–474.

Coplan, R. J., Prakash, K., O'Neil, K., & Armer, M. (2004). Do you "want" to play? Distinguishing between conflicted shyness and social disinterest in early childhood. *Developmental Psychology, 40*, 244–258.

Corenblum, B. (2003). What children remember about ingroup and out-group peers: Effects of stereotypes on children's processing of information about group members. *Journal of Experimental Child Psychology, 86*, 32–66.

Corenblum, B., Annis, R., & Young, S. (1996). Effects of own group success or failure on judgments of task performance by children of different ethnicities. *European Journal of Social Psychology, 26*, 1996.

Cornelius, J. R., Maisto, S. A., Pollock, N. K., Martin, C. S., Salloum, I. M., Lynch, K. G., & Clark, D. B. (2003). Rapid relapse generally follows treatment for substance use disorders among adolescents. *Addictive Behaviors, 28*, 381–386.

Cornelius, M. D., Ryan, C. M., Day, N. L., Goldschmidt, L., & Willford, J. A. (2001). Prenatal tobacco effects on neuropsychological outcomes among preadolescents. *Developmental and Behavioral Pediatrics, 22*, 217–225.

Cosden, M., Peerson, S., & Elliott, K. (1997). Effects of prenatal drug exposure on birth outcomes and early child development. *Journal of Drug Issues, 27*, 525–539.

Costei, A. M., Kozer, E., Ho, T., Ito, S., & Koren, G. (2002). Perinatal outcome following third trimester exposure to paroxetine. *Archives of Pediatrics and Adolescent Medicine, 156*, 1129–1132.

Costello, E. J., & Angold, A. (1995). Developmental epidemiology. In D. Cicchetti & D. Cohen (Eds.), *Developmental psychopathology: Vol. 1. Theory and method* (pp. 23–56). New York: Wiley.

Costigan, C. L., Cox, M. J., & Cauce, A. M. (2003). Work–parenting linkages among dual-earner couples at the transition to parenthood. *Journal of Family Psychology, 17*, 397–408.

Costos, D., Ackerman, R., & Paradis, L. (2002). Recollections of menarche: Communication between mothers and daughters regarding menstruation. *Sex Roles, 46*, 49–59.

Coté, S., Zoccolillo, M., Tremblay, R., Nagin, D., & Vitaro, F. (2001). Predicting girls' conduct disorder in

adolescence from childhood trajectories of disruptive behaviors. *Journal of the American Academy of Child and Adolescent Psychiatry, 40*, 678–684.

Cotinot, C., Pailhoux, E., Jaubert, F., & Fellous, M. (2002). Molecular genetics of sex determination. *Seminars in Reproductive Medicine, 20*, 157–168.

Coulton, C. J., Korbin, J. E., & Su, M. (1999). Neighborhoods and child maltreatment: A multi-level study. *Child Abuse and Neglect, 23*, 1019–1040.

Courage, M. L., & Howe, M. L. (1998). The ebb and flow of infant attentional preferences: Evidence for long-term recognition memory in 3-month-olds. *Journal of Experimental Child Psychology, 18*, 98–106.

Courchesne, E., Carper, R., & Akshoomoff, N. (2003). Evidence of brain overgrowth in the first year of life in autism. *Journal of the American Medical Association, 290*, 337–344.

Covington, C. Y., Nordstrom-Klee, B., Ager, J., Sokol, R., & Delaney-Black, V. (2002). Birth to age 7 growth of children prenatally exposed to drugs: A prospective cohort study. *Neurotoxicology and Teratology, 24*, 489–496.

Cowan, C. P., & Cowan, P. A. (1995). Interventions to ease the transition to parenthood: Why they are needed and what they can do. *Family Relations, 44*, 412–423.

Cowan, C. P., & Cowan, P. A. (1997). Working with couples during stressful transitions. In S. Dreman (Ed.), *The family on the threshold of the 21st century* (pp. 17–47). Mahwah, NJ: Erlbaum.

Cowan, C. P., & Cowan, P. A. (2000). *When partners become parents.* Mahwah, NJ: Erlbaum.

Cowan, N. (2003). Comparisons of developmental modeling frameworks and levels of analysis in cognition: Connectionist and dynamic systems theories deserve attention. *Developmental Science, 6*, 440–447.

Cowan, N., Nugent, L. D., Elliott, E. M., Ponomarev, I., & Saults, J. S. (1999). The role of attention in the development of short-term memory: Age differences in the verbal span of apprehension. *Child Development, 70*, 1082–1097.

Cox, C. E., Kotch, J. B., & Everson, M. D. (2003). A longitudinal study of modifying influences in the relationship between domestic violence and child maltreatment. *Journal of Family Violence, 18*, 5–17.

Cox, M. J., Owen, M. T., Henderson, V. K., & Margand, N. A. (1992). Prediction of infant–father and infant–mother attachment. *Developmental Psychology, 28*, 474–483.

Cox, M. J., Paley, B., & Harter, K. (2001). Interparental conflict and parent–child relationships. In J. H. Grych & F. D. Fincham (Eds.), *Interparental conflict and child development: Theory, research, and applications* (pp. 249–272). New York: Cambridge University Press.

Cox, S. M., Hopkins, J., & Hans, S. L. (2000). Attachment in preterm infants and their mothers: Neonatal risk status and maternal representations. *Infant Mental Health Journal, 21*, 464–480.

Coyle, T. R., & Bjorklund, D. F. (1997). Age differences in, and consequences

of, multiple- and variable-strategy use on a multitrial sort-recall task. *Developmental Psychology, 33*, 372–380.

Crago, M. B., Annahatak, B., & Ningiuruvik, L. (1993). Changing patterns of language socialization in Inuit homes. *Anthropology and Education Quarterly, 24*, 205–223.

Craig, C. M., & Lee, D. N. (1999). Neonatal control of sucking pressure: Evidence for an intrinsic tau-guide. *Experimental Brain Research, 124*, 371–382.

Craig, W. (2005). Canadian Initiative for the Prevention of Bullying (CIPB). Retrieved from psyc.queensu.ca/~craigW/P1.htm

Craig, W. M., Pepler, D., & Atlas, R. (2000). Observations of bullying in the playground and in the classroom. *School Psychology International, 21*, 22-36.

Crair, M. C., Gillespie, D. C., & Stryker, M. P. (1998). The role of visual experience in the development of columns in the cat visual cortex. *Science, 279*, 566–570.

Cratty, B. J. (1986). *Perceptual and motor development in infants and children* (3rd ed.). Englewood Cliffs, NJ: Prentice-Hall.

Crawford, J. (1995). *Bilingual education: History, politics, theory, and practice.* Los Angeles: Bilingual Education Services.

Crawford, J. (1997). *Best evidence: Research foundations of the Bilingual Education Act.* Washington, DC: National Clearinghouse for Bilingual Education.

Creasey, G. L., Jarvis, P. A., & Berk, L. E. (1998). Play and social competence. In O. N. Saracho & B. Spodek (Eds.), *Multiple perspectives on play in early childhood education* (pp. 116–143). Albany: State University of New York Press.

Crick, N. R. (1996). The role of overt aggression, relational aggression, and prosocial behavior in the prediction of children's future social adjustment. *Child Development, 67*, 2317–2327.

Crick, N. R., & Dodge, K. A. (1994). A review and reformulation of social information-processing mechanisms in children's social adjustment. *Psychological Bulletin, 115*, 74–101.

Crick, N. R., Casas, J. F., & Mosher, M. (1997). Relational and overt aggression in preschool. *Developmental Psychology, 33*, 579–588.

Crick, N. R., Casas, J. F., & Nelson, D. A. (2002). Toward a more comprehensive understanding of peer maltreatment: Studies of relational victimization. *Current Directions in Psychological Science, 11*, 98–101.

Crick, N. R., & Nelson, D. A. (2002). Relational and physical victimization within friendships: Nobody told me there'd be friends like these. *Journal of Abnormal Child Psychology, 30*, 599–607.

Crick, N. R., Werner, N. E., Casas, J. F., O'Brien, K. M., Nelson, D. A., Grotpeter, J. K., & Markon, K. (1999). Childhood aggression and gender: A new look at an old problem. In D. Bernstein (Ed.), *Nebraska Symposia on Motivation* (Vol. 45, pp. 75–141). Omaha: University of Nebraska Press.

Crockenberg, S. C., & Leerkes, E. M. (2003a). Infant negative emotionality, caregiving, and family relationships. In A. C. Crouter & A. Booth (Eds.),

Children's influence on family dynamics (pp. 57–78). Mahwah, NJ: Erlbaum.

Crockenberg, S. C., & Leerkes, E. M. (2003b). Parental acceptance, postpartum depression, and maternal sensitivity: Mediating and moderating processes. *Journal of Family Psychology, 17*, 80–93.

Crosno, R., Kirkpatrick, M., & Elder, G. H., Jr. (2004). Intergenerational bonding in school: The behavioral and contextual correlates of student–teacher relationships. *Sociology of Education, 77*, 60–81.

Crouter, A. C., & Head, M. R. (2002). Parental monitoring and knowledge of children. In M. H. Bornstein (Ed.), *Handbook of parenting: Vol. 3. Being and Becoming a Parent* (2nd ed., pp. 461–483). Mahwah, NJ: Erlbaum.

Crouter, A. C., Manke, B. A., & McHale, S. M. (1995). The family context of gender intensification in early adolescence. *Child Development, 66*, 317–329.

Crowe, H. P., & Zeskind, P. S. (1992). Psychophysiological and perceptual responses to infant cries varying in pitch: Comparison of adults with low and high scores on the child abuse potential inventory. *Child Abuse and Neglect, 16*, 19–29.

Crowley, K., Callanan, M. A., Tenenbaum, H. R., & Allen, E. (2001). Parents explain more often to boys than to girls during shared scientific thinking. *Psychological Science, 12*, 258–261.

Csikszentmihalyi, M. (1999). Implications of a systems perspective for the study of creativity. In R. J. Sternberg (Ed.), *Handbook of creativity* (pp. 313–335). Cambridge, UK: Cambridge University Press.

Cuddy-Casey, M., & Orvaschel, H. (1997). Children's understanding of death in relation to child suicidality and homicidality. *Clinical Psychology Review, 17*, 33–45.

Cuijpers, P. (2002). Effective ingredients of school-based drug prevention programs: A systematic review. *Addictive Behaviors, 27*, 1009–1023.

Culbertson, F. M. (1997). Depression and gender: An international review. *American Psychologist, 52*, 25–51.

Culnane, M., Fowler, M. G., Lee, S. S., McSherry, G., Brady, M., & O'Donnell, K. (1999). Lack of long-term effects of in utero exposure to zidovudine among uninfected children born to HIV-infected women. *Journal of the American Medical Association, 281*, 151–157.

Cummings, E. M., & Davies, P. T. (1994). Maternal depression and child development. *Journal of Child Psychology and Psychiatry, 35*, 73–112.

Cummings, E. M., Iannotti, R. J., & Zahn-Waxler, C. (1985). Influence of conflict between adults on the emotions and aggression of young children. *Developmental Psychology, 21*, 495–507.

Cunningham, A. E., & Stanovich, K. E. (1998, Spring/Summer). What reading does for the mind. *American Educator*, 8–15.

Curtin, S. C., & Park, M. M. (1999). Trends in the attendant, place, and timing of births and in the use of obstetric interventions: United States, 1989–1997. *National Vital Statistics Report, 47*(27), 1–12.

Curtiss, S. (1977). *Genie: A psycholinguistic study of a modern-day "wild child."* New York: Academic Press.

Curtiss, S. (1989). The independence and task-specificity of language. In M. H. Bornstein & J. S. Bruner (Eds.), *Interaction in human development* (pp. 105–137). Hillsdale, NJ: Erlbaum.

Cutrona, C. E., Hessling, R. M., Bacon, P. L., & Russell, D. W. (1998). Predictors and correlates of continuing involvement with the baby's father among adolescent mothers. *Journal of Family Psychology, 12,* 369–387.

D'Agostino, J. A., & Clifford, P. (1998). Neurodevelopmental consequences associated with the premature neonate. *AACN Clinical Issues, 9,* 11–24.

D'Augelli, A. R. (2002). Mental health problems among lesbian, gay, and bisexual youths ages 14 to 21. *Clinical Child Psychology and Psychiatry, 7,* 433–456.

Dabrowska, E. (2000). From formula to schema: The acquisition of English questions. *Cognitive Linguistics, 11,* 1–20.

Dahl, R. E., & Lewin, D. S. (2002). Pathways to adolescent healthy sleep regulation and behavior. *Journal of Adolescent Health, 31,* 175–184.

Dahl, R. E., Scher, M. S., Williamson, D. E., Robles, N., & Day, N. (1995). A longitudinal study of prenatal marijuana use. Effects on sleep and arousal at age 3 years. *Archives of Pediatric and Adolescent Medicine, 149,* 145–150.

Dales, L., Hammer, S. J., & Smith, N. J. (2001). Time trends in autism and MMR immunization coverage in California. *Journal of the American Medical Association, 285,* 1183–1185.

Daley, K. C. (2004). Update on sudden infant death syndrome. *Current Opinion in Pediatrics, 16,* 227–232.

Daley, T. C., Whaley, S. E., Sigman, M. D., Espinosa, M. P., & Neumann, C. (2003). IQ on the rise: The Flynn effect in rural Kenyan children. *Psychological Science, 14,* 215–219.

Daly, M., & Wilson, M. (1988). *Homicide.* New York: Aldine de Gruyter.

Damasio, A. R. (1994). *Descartes' error: Emotion, reason, and the human brain.* New York: Putnam.

Damon, W. (1977). *The social world of the child.* San Francisco: Jossey-Bass.

Damon, W. (1988). *The moral child.* New York: Free Press.

Damon, W. (1990). Self-concept, adolescent. In R. M. Lerner, A. C. Petersen, & J. Brooks-Gunn (Eds.), *The encyclopedia of adolescence* (Vol. 2, pp. 67–91). New York: Garland.

Damon, W., & Hart, D. (1988). *Self-understanding in childhood and adolescence.* New York: Cambridge University Press.

Daniels, D. H. (1998). Age differences in concepts of self-esteem. *Merrill-Palmer Quarterly, 44,* 234–259.

Daniels, D. H., Kalkman, D. L., & McCombs, B. L. (2001). Young children's perspectives on learning and teacher practices in different classroom contexts: Implications for motivation. *Early Education and Development, 12,* 253–273.

Dannemiller, J. L., & Stephens, B. R. (1988). A critical test of infant pattern preference models. *Child Development, 59,* 210–216.

Dapretto, M., & Bjork, E. L. (2000). The development of word retrieval abilities in the second year and its relation to early vocabulary growth. *Child Development, 71,* 635–648.

Darnton-Hill, I., & Coyne, E. T. (1998). Feast and famine: Socioeconomic disparities in global nutrition and health. *Public Health and Nutrition, 1,* 23–31.

Daro, D., & Harding, K. (1999). Healthy Families America: Using research in going to scale. *Future of Children, 9,* 152–176.

Darroch, J. E., Frost, J. J., & Singh, S. (2001). *Teenage sexual and reproductive behavior in developed countries: Can more progress be made?* New York: Alan Guttmacher Institute.

Darwin, C. (1877). Biographical sketch of an infant. *Mind, 2,* 285–294.

Davidson, E., Levine, M., Malvern, J., Niebyl, J., & Tobin, M. (1993). A rebirth of obstetrical care. *Medical World News, 34*(5), 42–47.

Davidson, R. J. (1994). Asymmetric brain function, affective style, and psychopathology: The role of early experience and plasticity. *Development and Psychopathology, 6,* 741–758.

Davies, P. A., & Lindsay, L. L. (2004). Everyday marital conflict and child aggression. *Journal of Abnormal Child Psychology, 32,* 191–202.

Davis, H. A. (2003). Conceptualizing the role and influence of student–teacher relationships on children's social and cognitive development. *Educational Psychologist, 38,* 207–234.

Davis, K. F., Parker, K. P., & Montgomery, G. L. (2004). Sleep in infants and young children. Part 1: Normal sleep. *Journal of Pediatric Health Care, 18,* 65–71.

Davison, K. K., & Birch, L. L. (2002). Obesigenic families: Parents' physical activity and dietary intake patterns predict girls' risk of overweight. *International Journal of Obesity and Related Metabolic Disorders, 26,* 1186–1193.

Dawson, G., Ashman, S. B., Panagiotides, H., Hessl, D., Self, J., Yamada, E., & Embry, L. (2003). Preschool outcomes of children of depressed mothers: Role of maternal behavior, contextual risk, and children's brain activity. *Child Development, 74,* 1158–1175.

Dawson, G., Frey, K., Self, J., Panagiotides, H., Hessl, D., & Yamada, E. (1999). Frontal brain electrical activity in infants of depressed and nondepressed mothers: Relation to variations in infant behavior. *Development and Psychopathology, 11,* 589–605.

Dawson, T. L. (2002). New tools, new insights: Kohlberg's moral judgment stages revisited. *International Journal of Behavioral Development, 26,* 154–166.

Day, N. L., Leach, S. L., Richardson, G. A., Cornelius, M. D., Robles, N., & Larkby, C. (2002). Prenatal alcohol exposure predicts continued deficits in offspring size at 14 years of age. *Alcoholism: Clinical and Experimental Research, 26,* 1584–1591.

de Haan, M., & Johnson, M. H. (2003a). Introduction. In M. de Haan & M. H. Johnson (Eds.), *The cognitive neuroscience of development* (pp. xv–xx). New York: Psychology Press.

de Haan, M., & Johnson, M. H. (2003b). Mechanisms and theories of brain development. In M. de Haan & M. H. Johnson (Eds.), *The cognitive neuroscience of development* (pp. 1–18). Hove, U.K.: Psychology Press.

de León, L. (2000). The emergent participant: Interactive patterns in the socialization of Tzotzil (Mayan) infants. *Journal of Linguistic Anthropology, 8,* 131–161.

De Lisi, R., & Gallagher, A. M. (1991). Understanding gender stability and constancy in Argentinean children. *Merrill-Palmer Quarterly, 37,* 483–502.

de Muinck Keizer-Schrama, S. M. P. F., & Mul, D. (2001). Trends in pubertal development in Europe. *Human Reproduction Update, 7,* 287–291.

De Schipper, J. C., Tavecchio, L. W. C., van IJzendoorn, M. H., & van Zeijl, J. (2004). Goodness-of-fit in center day care: Relations of temperament, stability, and quality of care with the child's adjustment. *Early Childhood Research Quarterly, 19,* 257–272.

De Schipper, J. C., van IJzendoorn, M. H., & Tavecchio, L. W. C. (2004). Stability in center day care: Relations with children's well-being and problem behavior in day care. *Social Development, 13,* 531–550.

Deafness Research Foundation. (2003). Hear us: Incidence of deafness in newborns. Retrieved from www.hearinghealth.com

Deák, G. O. (2000). Hunting the fox of word learning: Why "constraints" fail to capture it. *Developmental Review, 20,* 29–80.

Deák, G. O., & Maratsos, M. (1998). On having complex representations of things: Preschoolers use multiple words for objects and people. *Developmental Psychology, 34,* 224–240.

Deák, G. O., Ray, S. D., & Brenneman, K. (2003). Children's perseverative appearance–reality errors are related to emerging language skills. *Child Development, 74,* 944–964.

Deák, G. O., Yen, L., & Pettit, J. (2001). By any other name: When will preschoolers produce several labels for a reference? *Journal of Child Language, 28,* 787–804.

Deary, I. J. (2001). *g* and cognitive elements of information processing: An agnostic view. In R. J. Sternberg & E. L. Grigorenko (Eds.), *The general factor of intelligence: How general is it?* (pp. 447–479). Mahwah, NJ: Erlbaum.

Deater-Deckard, K., Lansford, J. E., Dodge, K. A., Pettit, G. S., & Bates, J. E. (2003). The development of attitudes about physical punishment: An 8-year longitudinal study. *Journal of Family Psychology, 17,* 351–360.

Deater-Deckard, K., Pike, A., Petrill, S. A., Cutting, A. L., Hughes, C., & O'Connor, T. G. (2001). Nonshared environmental processes in social-emotional development: An observational study of identical twin differences in the preschool period. *Developmental Science, 4,* F1–F6.

Deater-Deckard, K., Scarr, S., McCartney, K., & Eisenberg, M. (1994). Paternal separation anxiety: Relationships with parenting stress, child-rearing attitudes, and maternal anxieties. *Psychological Science, 5,* 341–346.

Deaux, K. (1993). Commentary: Sorry, wrong number—A reply to Gentile's call. *Psychological Science, 4,* 125–126.

DeBerry, K. M., Scarr, S., & Weinberg, R. (1996). Family racial socialization and ecological competence: Longitudinal assessments of African-American transracial adoptees. *Child Development, 67,* 2375–2399.

Degirmencioglu, S. M., Urberg, K. A., Tolson, J. M., & Richard, P. (1998). Adolescent friendship networks: Continuity and change over the school year. *Merrill-Palmer Quarterly, 44,* 313–337.

Dejin-Karlsson, E., Hanson, B. S., Ostergren, P.-O., Sjoeberg, N.-O., & Marsal, K. (1998). Does passive smoking in early pregnancy increase the risk of small-for-gestational-age infants? *American Journal of Public Health, 88,* 1523–1527.

Deković, M., Noom, M. J., & Meeus, W. (1997). Expectations regarding development during adolescence: Parent and adolescent perceptions. *Journal of Youth and Adolescence, 26,* 253–271.

Delemarre-van de Waal, H. A. (2002). Regulation of puberty. *Best Practice and Research Clinical Endocrinology and Metabolism. 16,* 1–12.

Delemarre-van de Waal, H. A., van Coeverden, S. C., & Rotteveel, J. (2001). Hormonal determinants of pubertal growth. *Journal of Pediatric Endocrinology and Metabolism, 14,* 1521–1526.

Delgado-Gaitan, C. (1994). Socializing young children in Mexican-American families: An intergenerational perspective. In P. Greenfield & R. Cocking (Eds.), *Cross-cultural roots of minority child development* (p. 55–86). Hillsdale, NJ: Erlbaum.

Dell, D. L. (2001). Adolescent pregnancy. In N. L. Stotland & D. E. Stewart (Eds.), *Psychological aspects of women's health care* (pp. 95–116). Washington, DC: American Psychiatric Association.

DeLoache, J. S. (1987). Rapid change in symbolic functioning of very young children. *Science, 238,* 1556–1557.

DeLoache, J. S. (2002a). Early development of the understanding and use of symbolic artifacts. In U. Goswami (Ed.), *Blackwell handbook of child cognitive development* (pp. 206–226). Malden, MA: Blackwell.

DeLoache, J. S. (2002b). The symbol-mindedness of young children. In W. Hartup & R. A. Weinberg (Eds.), *Minnesota Symposia on Child Psychology* (Vol. 32, pp. 73–101). Mahwah, NJ: Erlbaum.

DeMarie-Dreblow, D., & Miller, P. H. (1988). The development of children's strategies for selective attention: Evidence for a transitional period. *Child Development, 59,* 1504–1513.

Demetriou, A., Christou, C., Spanoudis, G., & Platsidou, M. (2002). The development of mental processing: Efficiency, working memory, and thinking. *Monographs of the Society for Research in Child Development, 67*(1, Serial No. 268).

Demetriou, A., Efklides, A., Papadaki, M., Papantoniou, G., & Economou, A. (1993). Structure and development of causal–experimental thought: From early adolescence to youth. *Developmental Psychology, 29,* 480–497.

Demetriou, A., Pachaury, A., Metallidou, Y., & Kazi, S. (1996). Universals and specificities in the structure and development of quantitative-relational thought: A cross-cultural study in Greece and India. *International Journal of Behavioral Development, 19,* 255–290.

Dempster, F. N. (1995). Interference and inhibition in cognition: An historical perspective. In F. N. Dempster & C. J. Brainerd (Eds.), *Interference and inhibition in cognition* (pp. 3–26). San Diego: Academic Press.

Dempster, F. N., & Corkill, A. J. (1999). Interference and inhibition in cognition and behavior: Unifying themes for educational psychology. *Educational Psychology Review, 11,* 1–88.

Demuth, K. (1996). The prosodic structure of early words. In J. Morgan & K. Demuth (Eds.), *From signal to syntax* (pp. 171–184). Mahwah, NJ: Erlbaum.

Denham, S. A. (2005). Emotional competence counts: Assessment as support for school readiness. In K. Hirsh-Pasek, A. Kochanoff, N. S. Newcombe, & J. de Villiers (Eds.), *Using scientific knowledge to inform preschool assessment. Social Policy Report of the Society for Research in Child Development, 19*(No.1), 12.

Denham, S. A., Blair, K., Schmidt, M., & DeMulder, E. (2002). Compromised emotional competence: Seeds of violence sown early? *American Journal of Orthopsychiatry, 72,* 70–82.

Denham, S. A., & Burton, R. (2003). *Social and emotional prevention and intervention programming for preschoolers.* New York: Kluwer-Plenum.

Denham, S. A., & Kochanoff, A. T. (2002). Parental contributions to preschoolers' understanding of emotion. *Marriage and Family Review, 34,* 311–343.

Denham, S. A., von Salisch, M., Olthof, T., Kochanoff, A., & Caverly, S. (2004). Emotional and social development in childhood. In P. K. Smith & C. H. Hart (Eds.), *Blackwell handbook of childhood social development* (pp. 307–328). Malden, MA: Blackwell.

Dennis, W. (1960). Causes of retardation among institutionalized children: Iran. *Journal of Genetic Psychology, 96,* 47–59.

Department of Justice Canada. (2003). *Federal funding of provincial and territorial child support, support enforcement and child custody and access projects, 1997–2001.* Ottawa, ON: Author.

Department of Justice Canada. (2004). *Analysis of options for changes in the legal evaluation of child custody and access.* Retrieved from www.justice.gc .ca/en/ps/pad/reports/2001-FCY-2/ challenge4.html

Derom, C., Thiery, E., Vlietinck, R., Loos, R., & Derom, R. (1996). Handedness in twins according to zygosity and chorion type: A preliminary report. *Behavior Genetics, 26,* 407–408.

DeRosier, M. E., Cillessen, A. H. N., Coie, J. D., & Dodge, K. A. (1994). Group social context and children's aggressive behavior. *Child Development, 65,* 1068–1079.

DeRosier, M. E., & Thomas, J. M. (2003). Strengthening sociometric prediction: Scientific advances in the assessment of children's peer relations. *Child Development, 75,* 1379–1392.

Deutsch, W., & Pechmann, T. (1982). Social interaction and the development of definite descriptions. *Cognition, 11,* 159–184.

de Villiers, J. G. (2000). Language and theory of mind: What are the developmental relationships? In S. Baron-Cohen, H. Tager-Flusberg, & D. J. Cohen (Eds.), *Understanding other minds; Perspectives from developmental cognitive neuroscience* (2nd ed.). Oxford: Oxford University Press.

de Villiers, J. G., & de Villiers, P. A. (1973). A cross-sectional study of the acquisition of grammatical morphemes in child speech. *Journal of Psycholinguistic Research, 2,* 267–278.

de Villiers, J. G., & de Villiers, P. A. (1999). Language development. In M. H. Bornstein & M. E. Lamb (Eds.), *Developmental psychology: An advanced textbook* (4th ed., pp. 313–373). Mahwah, NJ: Erlbaum.

de Villiers, J. G., & de Villiers, P. A. (2000). Linguistic determinism and the understanding of false beliefs. In P. Mitchell & K. J. Riggs (Eds.), *Children's reasoning and the mind* (pp. 87–99). Hove, UK: Psychology Press.

de Waal, F. (1996). *Good natured: The origins of right and wrong in humans and other animals.* Cambridge, MA: Harvard University Press.

de Waal, F. B. M. (1993). Sex differences in chimpanzee (and human) behavior: A matter of social values? In M. Hechter, L. Nadel, & R. E. Michod (Eds.), *The origin of values* (pp. 285–303). New York: Aldine de Gruyter.

de Waal, F. B. M. (2001). *Tree of origin.* Cambridge, MA: Harvard University Press.

De Weerd, A. W., & van den Bossche, A. S. (2003). The development of sleep during the first months of life. *Sleep Medicine Reviews, 7,* 179–191.

De Weerth, C., van Hees, Y., & Buitelaar, J. K. (2003). Prenatal maternal cortisol levels and infant behvior during the first 5 months. *Early Human Development, 74,* 139–151.

De Wolff, M. S., & van IJzendoorn, M. H. (1997). Sensitivity and attachment: A meta-analysis on parental antecedents of infant attachment. *Child Development, 68,* 571–591.

Dewsbury, D. A. (1992). Comparative psychology and ethology: A reassessment. *American Psychologist, 47,* 208–215.

Diamond, A. (1991). Neuropsychological insights into the meaning of object concept development. In S. Carey & R. Gelman (Eds.), *The epigenesis of mind: Essays on biology and knowledge* (pp. 67–110). Hillsdale, NJ: Erlbaum.

Diamond, A. (2000). Close interrelation of motor development and cognitive development and of the cerebellum and prefrontal cortex. *Child Development, 71,* 44–56.

Diamond, A. Cruttenden, L., & Neiderman, D. (1994). AB with multiple wells: 1. Why are multiple wells sometimes easier than two wells? 2. Memory or memory + inhibition. *Developmental Psychology, 30,* 192–205.

Diamond, L. M. (1998). Development of sexual orientation among adolescent and young adult women. *Developmental Psychology, 34,* 1085–1095.

Diamond, L. M. (2003). Love matters: Romantic relationships among sexual-minority adolescents. In P. Florsheim (Ed.), *Adolescent romantic relations and sexual behavior* (pp. 85–108). Mahwah, NJ: Erlbaum.

Diamond, M., & Sigmundson, H. K. (1999). Sex reassignment at birth. In S. J. Ceci & W. M. Williams (Eds.), *The nature–nurture debate* (pp. 55–75). Malden, MA: Blackwell.

DiBiase, A., Gibbs, J. C., & Potter, G. B. (2005). *EQUIP for educators: Teaching youth (grades 5–8) to think and act responsibly.* Champaign, IL: Research Press.

DiCenso, A., Guyatt, G., Willan, A., & Griffith, L. (2002). Interventions to reduce unintended pregnancies among adolescents: Systematic review of randomized controlled trials. *British Medical Journal, 324,* 1426–1430.

Dick, D. M., Rose, R. J., Viken, R. J., & Kaprio, J. (2000). Pubertal timing and substance use: Associations between and within families across late adolescence. *Developmental Psychology, 36,* 180–189.

Dick, F., Dronkers, N. F., Pizzamiglio, L., Saygin, A. P., Small, S. L., & Wilson, S. (2004). Language and the brain. In M. Tomasello & D. I. Slobin (Eds.), *Beyond nature–nurture: Essays in honor of Elizabeth Bates* (pp. 237–260). Mahwah, NJ: Erlbaum.

Dickens, W. T., & Flynn, J. R. (2001). Heritability estimates versus large environmental effects: The IQ paradox resolved. *Psychological Review, 108,* 346–369.

Dickinson, D. K., & McCabe, A. (2001). Bringing it all together: The multiple origins, skills, and environmental supports of early literacy. *Learning Disabilities Research and Practice, 16,* 186–202.

Dickinson, D. K., McCabe, A., Anastasopoulos, L., Peisner-Feinberg, E. S., & Poe, M. D. (2003). The comprehensive language approach to early literacy: The interrelationships among vocabulary, phonological sensitivity, and print knowledge among preschool-age children. *Journal of Educational Psychology, 95,* 465–481.

Dick-Read, G. (1959). *Childbirth without fear.* New York: Harper & Brothers.

Dickson, K. L., Fogel, A., & Messinger, D. (1998). The development of emotion from a social process view. In M. F. Mascolo (Ed.), *What develops in emotional development?* (pp. 253–271). New York: Plenum.

Dickson, S. V., Collins, V. L., Simmons, D. C., & Kameenui, E. J. (1998). Meta-cognitive strategies: Research bases. In D. C. Simmons & E. J. Kameenui (Eds.), *What reading research tells us about children with diverse learning needs: Bases and basics* (pp. 295–360). Mahwah, NJ: Erlbaum.

Diener, M. L., Goldstein, L. H., & Mangelsdorf, S. C. (1995). The role of prenatal expectations in parents' reports of infant temperament. *Merrill-Palmer Quarterly, 41,* 172–190.

Dieticians of Canada, Canadian Paedictic Society, The College of Family Physicians of Canada, & Community Health Nurses Association of Canada. (2004). The use of growth charts for assessing and monitoring growth in Canadian infants and children. *Paediatrics and Child Health, 9,* 171–180.

Dietrich, K. N., Berger, O. G., & Succop, P. A. (1993). Lead exposure and the motor developmental status of urban six-year-old children in the Cincinnati Prospective Study. *Pediatrics, 91,* 301–307.

Dietz, T. L. (1998). An examination of violence and gender role portrayals in video games: Implications for gender socialization and aggressive behavior. *Sex Roles, 38,* 425–442.

DiLalla, L. F., Kagan, J., & Reznick, J. S. (1994). Genetic etiology of behavioral inhibition among 2-year-old children. *Infant Behavior and Development, 17,* 405–412.

Dildy, G. A., Jackson, G. M., Fowers, G. K., Oshiro, B. T., Varner, M. W., & Clark, S. L. (1996). Very advanced maternal age. Pregnancy after age 45. *American Journal of Obstetrics and Gynecology, 175,* 668–674.

DiMatteo, M. R., & Kahn, K. L. (1997). Psychosocial aspects of childbirth. In S. J. Gallant, G. P. Keita, & R. Royak-Schaler (Eds.), *Health care for women: Psychological, social, and behavioral influences* (pp. 175–186). Washington, DC: American Psychological Association.

DiPietro, J. A., Bornstein, M. H., Costigan, K. A., Pressman, E. K., Hahn, C.-S., & Painter, K. (2002). What does fetal movement predict about behavior during the first two years of life? *Developmental Psychobiology, 40,* 358–371.

DiPietro, J. A., Hodgson, D. M., Costigan, K. A., & Hilton, S. C. (1996). Fetal neurobehavioral development. *Child Development, 67,* 2553–2567.

Dirks, J. (1982). The effect of a commercial game on children's Block Design scores on the WISC-R test. *Intelligence, 6,* 109–123.

Dishion, T. J., Andrews, D. W., & Crosby, L. (1995). Antisocial boys and their friends in early adolescence: Relationship characteristics, quality, and interactional processes. *Child Development, 66,* 139–151.

Dishion, T. J., Poulin, F., & Burraston, B. (2001). Peer group dynamics associated with iatrogenic effects in group interventions with high-risk young adolescents. In D. W. Nangle & C. A. Erdley (Eds.), *The role of friendship in psychological adjustment* (pp. 79–92). San Francisco: Jossey-Bass.

Dixon, J. A., & Moore, C. F. (1990). The development of perspective taking: Understanding differences in information and weighting. *Child Development, 61,* 1502–1513.

Dodge, K. A., Pettit, G. S., McClaskey, C. L., & Brown, M. M. (1986). Social competence in children. *Monographs of the Society for Research in Child Development, 51*(2, Serial No. 213).

Dodge, K. A., & Price, J. M. (1994). On the relation between social information processing and socially competent behavior in early school-aged children. *Child Development, 65,* 1385–1397.

Doeker, N., Simic-Schleicher, A., Hauffa, B. P., & Andler, W. (1999). Psychosozialer Kleinwuchs maskiert als Wachstumshormonmangel. [Psychosocially stunted growth masked as growth hormone deficiency.] *Klinische Pädiatrie, 211,* 394–398.

Doherty, G., Lero, D. S., Goelmjan, H., Tougas, J., & LaGrange, A. (2000).

You bet I care! Caring and learning environments: Quality in regulated family child care across Canada. Guelph, ON: Centre for Families, Work and Well-Being, University of Guelph.

Dollaghan, C. (1985). Child meets word: "Fast mapping" in preschool children. *Journal of Speech and Hearing Research, 28,* 449–454.

Dombrowski, K. J., Lantz, P. M., & Freed, G. L. (2004). Risk factors for delay in age-appropriate vaccination. *Public Health Reports, 119,* 144–155.

Donahue, M. J., & Benson, P. L. (1995). Religion and the well-being of adolescents. *Journal of Social Issues, 51,* 145–160.

Dondi, M., Simion, F., & Caltran, G. (1999). Can newborns discriminate between their own cry and the cry of another newborn infant? *Developmental Psychology, 35,* 418–426.

Donnelly, P., & Kidd, B. (2004). *Realizing the expectations: Youth, character, and community in Canadian sport.* Ottawa: Canadian Centre for Ethics in Sport. Retrieved from www.cces.ca/pdfs/CCES-PAPER-Kidd-Donnelly-E.pdf

Donnerstein, E., Slaby, R. G., & Eron, L. D. (1994). The mass media and youth aggression. In L. D. Eron,

J. H. Gentry, & P. Schlegel (Eds.), *Reason to hope: A psychosocial perspective on violence and youth* (pp. 219–250). Washington, DC: American Psychological Association.

Donovan, W. L., Leavitt, L. A., & Walsh, R. O. (1997). Cognitive set and coping strategy affect mothers' sensitivity to infant cries: A signal detection approach. *Child Development, 68,* 760–772.

Donovan, W. L., Leavitt, L. A., & Walsh, R. O. (2000). Maternal illusory control predicts socialization strategies and toddler compliance. *Developmental Psychology, 36,* 402–411.

Dornbusch, S. M., & Glasgow, K. L. (1997). The structural context of family–school relations. In A. Booth & J. F. Dunn (Eds.), *Family–school links: How do they affect educational outcomes?* (pp. 35–55). Mahwah, NJ: Erlbaum.

Dornbusch, S. M., Glasgow, K. L., & Lin, I.-C. (1996). The social structure of schooling. *Annual Review of Psychology, 47,* 401–427.

Dorris, M. (1989). *The broken cord.* New York: Harper & Row.

Dougherty, T. M., & Haith, M. M. (1997). Infant expectations and reaction time as predictors of childhood speed of processing and IQ. *Developmental Psychology, 33,* 146–155.

Dowling, E. M., Gestsdottir, S., Anderson, P. M., von Eye, A., Almerigi, J., & Lerner, R. M. (2004). Structural relations among spirituality, religiosity, and thriving in adolescence. *Applied Developmental Psychology, 8,* 7–16.

Downs, A. C., & Fuller, M. J. (1991). Recollections of spermarche: An exploratory investigation. *Current Psychology: Research and Reviews, 10,* 93–102.

Downs, A. C., & Langlois, J. H. (1988). Sex typing: Construct and measurement issues. *Sex Roles, 18,* 87–100.

Dozier, M., Stovall, K. C., Albus, K. E., & Bates, B. (2001). Attachment for infants in foster care: The role of

caregiver state of mind. *Child Development, 72,* 1467–1477.

Drabman, R. S., Cordua, G. D., Hammer, D., Jarvie, G. J., & Horton, W. (1979). Developmental trends in eating rates of normal and overweight preschool children. *Child Development, 50,* 211–216.

Draper, P., & Cashdan, E. (1988). Technological change and child behavior among the !Kung. *Ethnology, 27,* 339–365.

Drew, L. M., Richard, M. H., & Smith, P. K. (1998). Grandparenting and its relationship to parenting. *Clinical Child Psychology and Psychiatry, 3,* 465–480.

Droege, K. L., & Stipek, D. J. (1993). Children's use of dispositions to predict classmates' behavior. *Developmental Psychology, 29,* 646–654.

Drotar, D., Overholser, J. C., Levi, R., Walders, N., Robinson, J. R., Palermo, T. M., & Riekert, K. A. (2000). Ethical issues in conducting research with pediatric and clinical child populations in applied settings. In D. Drotar (Ed.), *Handbook of research in pediatric and clinical child psychology* (pp. 305–326). New York: Kluwer.

Drotar, D., Pallotta, J., & Eckerle, D. (1994). A prospective study of family environments of children hospitalized for nonorganic failure-to-thrive. *Developmental and Behavioral Pediatrics, 15,* 78–85.

Dryburgh, H. (2001). Teenage pregnancy. *Health Reports, 12*(1), Statistics Canada, Cat. No. 82–003.

Dubé, E. M., Savin-Williams, R. C., & Diamond, L. M. (2001). Intimacy development, gender, and ethnicity among sexual-minority youths. In A. R. D'Augelli & C. J. Patterson (Eds.), *Lesbian, gay, and bisexual identities and youth* (pp. 129–152). New York: Oxford University Press.

DuBois, D. L., Burk-Braxton, C., Swenson, L. P., Tevendale, H. D., Lockerd, E. M., & Moran, B. L. (2002). Getting by with a little help from self and others: Self-esteem and social support as resources during early adolescence. *Developmental Psychology, 38,* 822–939.

DuBois, D. L., Felner, R. D., Brand, S., & George, G. R. (1999). Profiles of self-esteem in early adolescence: Identification and investigation of adaptive correlates. *American Journal of Community Psychology, 27,* 899–932.

Dubow, E. F., Tisak, J., Causey, D., Hryshko, A., & Reid, G. (1991). A two-year longitudinal study of stressful life events, social support, and social problem-solving skills: Contributions to children's behavioral and academic adjustment. *Child Development, 62,* 583–599.

Dueker, G. L., Modi, A., & Needham, A. (2003). 4.5-month-old infants' learning, retention and use of object boundary information. *Infant Behavior and Development, 26,* 588–605.

Duncan, G. J., & Brooks-Gunn, J. (2000). Family poverty, welfare reform, and child development. *Child Development, 71,* 188–196.

Duncan, G. J., & Magnuson, K. A. (2003). Off with Hollingshead: Socioeconomic resources, parenting, and child development. In M. H.

Bornstein & R. H. Bradley (Eds.), *Socioeconomic status, parenting, and child development* (pp. 83–106). Mahwah, NJ: Erlbaum.

Duncan, R. M., & Tarulli, D. (2003). Play as the leading activity of the preschool period: Insights from Vygotsky, Leont'ev, and Bakhtin. *Early Education and Development, 14,* 271–292.

Dunifon, R., Kalil, A., & Danziger, S. K. (2003). Maternal work behavior under welfare reform: How does the transition from welfare to work affect child development? *Children and Youth Services Review, 25,* 55–82.

Duniz, M., Scheer, P. J., Trojovsky, A., Kaschnitz, W., Kvas, E., & Macari, S. (1996). *European Child and Adolescent Psychiatry, 5,* 93–100.

Dunn, J. (1989). Siblings and the development of social understanding in early childhood. In P. G. Zukow (Ed.), *Sibling interaction across cultures* (pp. 106–116). New York: Springer-Verlag.

Dunn, J. (2002). Sibling relationships. In P. K. Smith & C. H. Hart (Eds.), *Blackwell handbook of childhood social development* (pp. 223–237). Malden, MA: Blackwell.

Dunn, J. (2004a). Annotation: Children's relationships with their nonresident fathers. *Journal of Child Psychology and Psychiatry, 45,* 659–671.

Dunn, J. (2004b). Sibling relationships. In P. K. Smith & C. H. Hart (Eds.), *Handbook of childhood social development* (pp. 223–237). *Malden, MA: Blackwell.*

Dunn, J., & Kendrick, C. (1982). *Siblings: Love, envy and understanding.* Cambridge, MA: Harvard University Press.

Dunn, J., Brown, J. R., & Maguire, M. (1995). The development of children's moral sensibility: Individual differences and emotion understanding. *Developmental Psychology, 31,* 649–659.

Dunn, J., Cheng, H., O'Connor, T. G., & Bridges, L. (2004). Children's perspectives on their relationships with their nonresident fathers: Influences, outcomes and implications. *Journal of Child Psychology and Psychiatry, 45,* 553–566.

Dunn, J., Slomkowski, C., & Beardsall, L. (1994). Sibling relationships from the preschool period through middle childhood and early adolescence. *Developmental Psychology, 30,* 315–324.

Durbin, D. L., Darling, N., Steinberg, L. D., & Brown, B. B. (1993). Parenting style and peer group membership among European-American adolescents. *Journal of Research on Adolescence, 3,* 87–100.

Durrant, J., Broberg, A., & Rose-Krasnor, L. (2000). Predicting use of physical punishment during mother-child conflicts in Sweden and Canada. In P. Hastings & C. Piotrowski (Eds.), *Conflict as a context for understanding maternal beliefs about child rearing and children's misbehavior: New directions for child development.* San Francisco: Jossey-Bass.

Durston, S., Pol, H. E. H., Schnack, H. G., Buitelaar, J. K., Steenhuis, M. P., & Minderaa, R. B. (2004). Magnetic resonance imaging of boys with attention-deficit/hyperactivity disorder and their unaffected siblings. *Journal*

of the American Academy of Child and Adolescent Psychiatry, 43, 332–340.

Dweck, C. S. (2002). Messages that motivate: How praise molds students' beliefs, motivation, and performance (in surprising ways). In J. Aronson (Ed.), *Improving academic achievement: Impact of psychological factors on education* (pp. 37–60). San Diego, CA: Academic Press.

Dworkin, J. B., Larson, R., & Hansen, D. (1993). Adolescents' accounts of growth experiences in youth activities. *Journal of Youth and Adolescence, 32,* 17–26.

Dye-White, E. (1986). Environmental hazards in the work setting: Their effect on women of child-bearing age. *American Association of Occupational Health and Nursing Journal, 34,* 76–78.

Eacott, M. J. (1999). Memory for the events of early childhood. *Current Directions in Psychological Science, 8,* 46–48.

East, P. L., & Felice, M. E. (1996). *Adolescent pregnancy and parenting: Findings from a racially diverse sample.* Mahwah, NJ: Erlbaum.

Ebeling, K. S., & Gelman, S. A. (1994). Children's use of context in interpreting "big" and "little." *Child Development, 65,* 1178–1192.

Eberhart-Phillips, J. E., Frederick, P. D., & Baron, R. C. (1993). Measles in pregnancy: A descriptive study of 58 cases. *Obstetrics and Gynecology, 82,* 797–801.

Eccles, J. S. (1994). Understanding women's educational and occupational choices: Applying the Eccles et al. model of achievement-related choices. *Psychology of Women Quarterly, 18,* 585–609.

Eccles, J. S., Barber, B., Jozefowicz, D., Malenchuk, O., & Vida, M. (1999). Self-evaluations of competence, task values, and self-esteem. In N. G. Johnson & M. C. Roberts (Eds.), *Beyond appearance: A new look at adolescent girls* (pp. 53–83). Washington, DC: American Psychological Association.

Eccles, J. S., Freedman-Doan, C., Frome, P., Jacobs, J., & Yoon, K. S. (2000). Gender-role socialization in the family: A longitudinal approach. In T. Eckes & H. M. Trautner (Eds.), *The developmental social psychology of gender* (pp. 333–360). Mahwah, NJ: Erlbaum.

Eccles, J. S., & Harold, R. D. (1991). Gender differences in sport involvement: Applying the Eccles' expectancy-value model. *Journal of Applied Sport Psychology, 3,* 7–35.

Eccles, J. S., Jacobs, J. E., & Harold, R. D. (1990). Gender-role stereotypes, expectancy effects, and parents' role in the socialization of gender differences in self-perceptions and skill acquisition. *Journal of Social Issues, 46,* 183–201.

Eccles, J. S., Templeton, J., Barber, B., & Stone, M. (2003). Adolescence and emerging adulthood: The critical passage ways to adulthood. In M. H. Bornstein, L. Davidson, C. L., Keyes, K. A. Moore, & the Center for Child Well-Being (Eds.), *Well-being: Positive development across the life course* (pp. 383–406). Mahwah, NJ: Erlbaum.

Eccles, J. S., Wigfield, A., Harold, R. D., & Blumfeld, P. B. (1993). Age and gender differences in children's self- and task perceptions during elementary school. *Child Development, 64,* 830–847.

Eccles, J. S., Wigfield, A., Midgley, C., Reuman, D., Mac Iver, D., & Feldlaufer, H. (1993b). Negative effects of traditional middle schools on students' motivation. *Elementary School Journal, 93,* 553–574.

Eccles, J. S., Wigfield, A., & Schiefele, U. (1998). Motivation to succeed. In N. Eisenberg (Ed.), *Handbook of child psychology: Vol. 3. Social, emotional, and personality development* (5th ed., pp. 1017–1095). New York: Wiley.

Eckerman, C. O., & Peterman, K. (2001). Peers and infant social/communicative development. In G. Bremner & A. Fogel (Eds.), *Blackwell handbook of infant development* (pp. 326–350). Malden, MA: Blackwell.

Eckerman, C. O., & Whitehead, H. (1999). How toddler peers generate coordinated action: A cross-cultural exploration. *Early Education and Development, 10,* 241–266.

Eder, R. A., & Mangelsdorf, S. C. (1997). The emotional basis of early personality development: Implications for the emergent self-concept. In R. Hogan, J. Johnson, & S. Briggs (Eds.), *Handbook of personality psychology* (pp. 209–240). San Diego, CA: Academic Press.

Edwards, C. P. (1978). Social experiences and moral judgment in Kenyan young adults. *Journal of Genetic Psychology, 133,* 19–30.

Egan, S. K., & Perry, D. G. (2001). Gender identity: A multidimensional analysis with implications for psychosocial adjustment. *Developmental Psychology, 37,* 451–463.

Egeland, B., Jacobvitz, D., & Sroufe, L. A. (1988). Breaking the cycle of abuse. *Child Development, 59,* 1080–1088.

Ehri, L. C., Nunes, S. R., Willows, D. M., Schuster, B. V., Yaghoub-Zadeh, Z., & Shanahan, T. (2001). Phonemic awareness instruction helps children learn to read: Evidence from the National Reading Panel's meta-analysis. *Reading Research Quarterly, 36,* 250–287.

Eichstedt, J. A., Serbin, L. A., Poulin-Dubois, D., & Sen, M. G. (2002). Of bears and men: Infants' knowledge of conventional and metaphorical gender stereotypes. *Infant Behavior and Development, 25,* 296–310.

Eiden, R. D., & Reifman, A. (1996). Effects of Brazelton demonstrations on later parenting: A meta-analysis. *Journal of Pediatric Psychology, 21,* 857–868.

Eisenberg, N. (1986). *Altruistic emotion, cognition, and behavior.* Hillsdale, NJ: Erlbaum.

Eisenberg, N. (2003). Prosocial behavior, empathy, and sympathy. In M. H. Bornstein & L. Davidson (Eds.), *Well-being: Positive development across the life course* (pp. 253–265). Mahwah, NJ: Erlbaum.

Eisenberg, N., Carlo, G., Murphy, B., & Van Court, P. (1995a). Prosocial development in late adolescence: A longitudinal study. *Child Development, 66,* 1179–1197.

Eisenberg, N., Cumberland, A., & Spinrad, T. L. (1998). Parental socialization of emotion. *Psychological Inquiry, 9,* 241–273.

Eisenberg, N., & Fabes, R. A. (1998). Prosocial development. In N. Eisenberg (Ed.), *Handbook of child psychology: Vol. 3. Social, emotional, and personality development* (5th ed., pp. 701–778). New York: Wiley.

Eisenberg, N., Fabes, R. A., Karbon, M., Murphy, B. C., Carlo, G., & Wosinski, M. (1996). Relations of school children's comforting behavior to empathy-related reactions and shyness. *Social Development, 5,* 330–351.

Eisenberg, N., Fabes, R. A., Murphy, B., Maszk, P., Smith, M., & Karbon, M. (1995b). The role of emotionality and regulation in children's social functioning: A longitudinal study. *Child Development, 66,* 1360–1384.

Eisenberg, N., Fabes, R., Murphy, B., Karbon, M., Smith, M., & Maszk, P. (1996). The relations of children's dispositional empathy-related responding to their emotionality, regulation, and social functioning. *Developmental Psychology, 32,* 195–209.

Eisenberg, N., Fabes, R. A., Shepard, S. A., Murphy, B. C., Jones, S., & Guthrie, I. K. (1998). Contemporaneous and longitudinal prediction of children's sympathy from dispositional regulation and emotionality. *Developmental Psychology, 34,* 910–924.

Eisenberg, N., Gershoff, E. T., Fabes, R. A., Shepard, S. A., Cumberland, A. J., & Losoya, S. H. (2001). Mothers' emotional expressivity and children's behavior problems and social competence: Mediation through children's regulation. *Developmental Psychology, 37,* 475–490.

Eisenberg, N., & McNally, S. (1993). Socialization and mothers' and adolescents' empathy-related characteristics. *Journal of Research on Adolescence, 3,* 171–191.

Eisenberg, N., Miller, P. A., Shell, R., McNalley, S., & Shea, C. (1991). Prosocial development in adolescence: A longitudinal study. *Developmental Psychology, 27,* 849–857.

Eisenberg, N., & Morris, A. S. (2002). Children's emotion-related regulation. In R. Kail (Ed.), *Advances in child development and behavior* (Vol. 30, pp. 190–229). San Diego, CA: Elsevier.

Eisenberg, N., Murphy, B. C., & Shepard, S. (1997). The development of empathic accuracy. In W. Ickes (Ed.), *Empathic accuracy* (pp. 73–116). New York: Guilford.

Eisenberg, N., Smith, C. L., Sadovsky, A., & Spinrad, T. L. (2004). Effortful control: Relations with emotion regulation, adjustment, and socialization in childhood. In R. Baumeister & K. D. Vohs (Eds.), *Handbook of self-regulation: Research, theory, and applications* (pp. 259–282). New York: Guilford.

Eisenberg, N., & Spinrad, T. L. (2004). Emotion-related regulation: Sharpening the definition. *Child Development, 75,* 334–339.

Eisenberg, N., Zhoe, Q., & Koller, S. (2001). Brazilian adolescents' prosocial moral judgment and behavior: Relations to sympathy, perspective taking, gender-role orientation, and demographic characteristics. *Child Development, 72,* 518–534.

Ekman, P. (2003). *Emotions revealed.* New York: Times Books.

Ekman, P., & Friesen, W. (1972). Constants across culture in the face of emotion. *Journal of Personality and Social Psychology, 17,* 124–129.

Elder, G. H., Jr. (1999). *Children of the Great Depression* (25th anniversary ed.). Boulder, CO: Westview Press.

Elder, G. H., Jr., & Caspi, A. (1988). Human development and social change: An emerging perspective on the life course. In N. Bolger, A. Caspi, G. Downey, & M. Moorehouse (Eds.), *Persons in context: Developmental processes* (pp. 77–113). Cambridge: Cambridge University Press.

Elder, G. H., Jr., & Hareven, T. K. (1993). Rising above life's disadvantage: From the Great Depression to war. In G. H. Elder, Jr., J. Modell, & R. D. Parke (Eds.), *Children in time and place* (pp. 47–72). Cambridge, UK: Cambridge University Press.

Elder, G. H., Jr., Liker, J. K., & Cross, C. E. (1984). Parent–child behavior in the Great Depression: Life course and intergenerational influences. In P. B. Baltes & O. G. Brim (Eds.), *Life-span development and behavior* (Vol. 6, pp. 109–158). New York: Academic Press.

Elder, G. H., Jr., Van Nguyen, T., & Caspi, A. (1985). Linking family hardship to children's lives. *Child Development, 56,* 361–375.

Elfenbein, D. S., & Felice, M. E. (2003). Adolescent pregnancy. *Pediatric Clinics of North America, 50,* 781–800.

Elias, C. L., & Berk, L. E. (2002). Self-regulation in young children: Is there a role for sociodramatic play? *Early Childhood Research Quarterly, 17,* 1–17.

Elias, G., & Broerse, J. (1996). Developmental changes in the incidence and likelihood of simultaneous talk during the first two years: A question of function. *Journal of Child Language, 23,* 201–217.

Elicker, J., Englund, M., & Sroufe, L. A. (1992). Predicting peer competence and peer relationships in childhood from early parent–child relationships. In R. D. Parke & G. W. Ladd (Eds.), *Family–peer relationships: Modes of linkage* (pp. 77–106). Hillsdale, NJ: Erlbaum.

Elkind, D. (1994). *A sympathetic understanding of the child: Birth to sixteen* (3rd ed.). Boston: Allyn and Bacon.

Elkind, D., & Bowen, R. (1979). Imaginary audience behavior in children and adolescence. *Developmental Psychology, 15,* 33–44.

Elliott, D. S. (1994). Serious violent offenders: Onset, developmental course, and termination. *Criminology, 32,* 1–21.

Elliott, D. S., Wilson, W. J., Huizinga, D., Sampson, R. J., Elliott, A., & Rankin, B. (1996). The effects of neighborhood disadvantage on adolescent development. *Journal of Research in Crime and Delinquency, 33,* 389–426.

Ellis, B. J., Bates, J. E., Dodge, K. A., Fergusson, D. M., Horwood, L. J., Pettit, G. S., & Woodward, L. (2003). Does father absence place daughters at special risk for early sexual activity and teenage pregnancy? *Child Development, 74,* 801–821.

Ellis, B. J., & Garber, J. (2000). Psychosocial antecedents of variation in girls' pubertal timing: Maternal depression, stepfather presence, and marital and family stress. *Child Development, 71,* 485–501.

Ellis, B. J., McFadyen-Ketchum, S., Dodge, K. A., Pettit, G. S., & Bates, J. E. (1999). Quality of early family relationships and individual differences in the timing of pubertal maturation in girls: A longitudinal test of an evolutionary model. *Journal of Personality and Social Psychology, 77,* 933–952.

Ellis, S., & Gauvain, M. (1992). Social and cultural influences on children's collaborative interactions. In L. T. Winegar & J. Valsiner (Eds.), *Children's development within social context* (Vol. 2, pp. 155–180). Hillsdale, NJ: Erlbaum.

Ellison, C. G., & Powers, D. A. (1994). The contact hypothesis and racial attitudes among black Americans. *Social Science Quarterly, 75,* 385–400.

Ellsworth, C. P., Muir, D. W., & Hains, S. M. J. (1993). Social competence and person-object differentiation: An analysis of the still-face effect. *Developmental Psychology, 29,* 63–73.

Elman, J. L. (2001). Connectionism and language acquisition. In M. Tomasello & E. Bates (Eds.), *Language development* (pp. 295–306). Oxford, UK: Blackwell.

Elsen, H. (1994). Phonological constraints and overextensions. *First Language, 14,* 305–315.

El-Sheikh, M., Cummings, E. M., & Reiter, S. (1996). Preschoolers' responses to ongoing interadult conflict: The role of prior exposure to resolved versus unresolved arguments. *Journal of Abnormal Child Psychology, 24,* 665–679.

Eltzschig, H. K., Lieberman, E. S., & Camann, W. R. (2003). Regional anesthesia and analgesia for labor and delivery. *New England Journal of Medicine, 384,* 319–332.

Ely, R. (2005). Language and literacy in the school years. In J. B. Gleason (Ed.), *The development of language* (6th ed., pp. 395–443). Boston: Allyn and Bacon.

Ely, R., & McCabe, A. (1994). The language play of kindergarten children. *First Language, 14,* 19–35.

Emde, R. N. (1992). Individual meaning and increasing complexity: Contributions of Sigmund Freud and René Spitz to developmental psychology. *Developmental Psychology, 28,* 347–359.

Emde, R. N., Bioringen, Z., Clyman, R. B., & Oppenheim, D. (1991). The moral self of infancy: Affective core and procedural knowledge. *Developmental Review, 11,* 251–270.

Emde, R. N., & Oppenheim, D. (1995). Shame, guilt, and the Oedipal drama: Developmental considerations concerning morality and the referencing of critical others. In J. P. Tangney & K. W. Fischer (Eds.), *Self-conscious emotions: The psychology of shame, guilt, embarrassment, and pride* (pp. 413–436). New York: Guilford.

Emde, R. N., Plomin, R., Robinson, J., Corley, R., DeFries, J., Fulker, D. W., Reznick, J. S., Campos, J., Kagan, J., & Zahn-Waxler, C. (1992). Temperament, emotion, and cognition at fourteen months: The MacArthur Longitudinal Twin Study. *Child Development, 63,* 1437–1455.

Emery, R. E. (2001). Interparental conflict and social policy. In J. H. Grych & F. D. Fincham (2001). *Interparental conflict and child development: Theory, research, and applications* (pp. 417–439). New York: Cambridge University Press.

Emery, R. E., & Laumann-Billings, L. (1998). An overview of the nature, causes, and consequences of abusive family relationships: Toward differentiating maltreatment and violence. *American Psychologist, 53,* 121–135.

Emery, R. E., Laumann-Billings, L., Waldron, M. C., Sbarra, D. A., & Dillon, P. (2001). Child custody mediation and litigation: Custody, contact, and coparenting 12 years after initial dispute resolution. *Journal of Consulting and Clinical Psychology, 69,* 323–332.

Emlen, S. T. (1995). An evolutionary theory of the family. *Proceedings of the National Academy of Sciences, 92,* 8092–8099.

Emmerich, W. (1981). Non-monotonic developmental trends in social cognition: The case of gender constancy. In S. Strauss (Ed.), *U-shaped behavioral growth* (pp. 249–269). New York: Academic Press.

Emory, E. K., Schlackman, L. J., & Fiano, K. (1996). Drug–hormone interactions on neurobehavioral responses in human neonates. *Infant Behavior and Development, 19,* 213–220.

Engle, R. A., & Conant, F. R. (2002). Guiding principles for fostering productive disciplinary engagement: Explaining an emergent argument in a community of learners classroom. *Cognition and Instruction, 20,* 399–483.

Enright, R. D., Lapsley, D. K., & Shukla, D. (1979). Adolescent egocentrism in early and late adolescence. *Adolescence, 14,* 687–695.

Epstein, J. L., & Sanders, M. G. (2002). Family, school, and community partnerships. In M. H. Bornstein (Ed.), *Handbook of parenting: Vol. 5. Practical issues in parenting* (2nd ed., pp. 407–437). Mahwah, NJ: Erlbaum.

Epstein, L. H., Roemmich, J. N., & Raynor, H. A. (2001). Behavioral therapy in the treatment of pediatric obesity. *Pediatric Clinics of North America, 48,* 981–983.

Erden, F., & Wolfgang, C. H. (2004). An exploration of the differences in prekindergarten, kindergarten, and first-grade teachers' beliefs related to discipline when dealing with male and female students. *Early Child Development and Care, 174,* 3–11.

Erdley, C. A., & Asher, S. R. (1999). A social goals perspective on children's social competence. *Journal of Emotional and Behavioral Disorders, 7,* 156–167.

Erikson, E. H. (1950). *Childhood and society.* New York: Norton.

Erikson, E. H. (1968). *Identity, youth, and crisis.* New York: Norton.

Ernst, M., Moolchan, E. T., & Robinson, M. L. (2001). Behavioral and neural consequences of prenatal exposure to nicotine. *Journal of the American Academy of Child and Adolescent Psychiatry, 40,* 630–641.

Espy, K. A., Kaufman, P. M., & Glisky, M. L. (1999). Neuropsychological function in toddlers exposed to cocaine in utero: A preliminary study. *Developmental Neuropsychology, 15,* 447–460.

Espy, K. A., Molfese, V. J., & DiLalla, L. F. (2001). Effects of environmental measures on intelligence in young children: Growth curve modeling of

longitudinal data. *Merrill-Palmer Quarterly, 47,* 42–73.

Ethier, K. A., Kershaw, T., Niccolai, L., Lewis, J. B., & Ickovics, J. R. (2003). Adolescent women underestimate their susceptibility to sexually transmitted infections. *Sexually Transmitted Infections, 79,* 408–411.

Evans, G. W. (2004). The environment of child poverty. *American Psychologist, 59,* 77–92.

Eveleth, P. B., & Tanner, J. M. (1990). *Worldwide variation in human growth* (2nd ed.). Cambridge, UK: Cambridge University Press.

Everman, D. B., & Cassidy, S. B. (2000). Genetics of childhood disorders: XII. Genomic imprinting: Breaking the rules. *Journal of the American Academy of Child and Adolescent Psychiatry, 38,* 386–389.

Fabes, R. A., Eisenberg, N., Hanish, L. D., & Spinrad, T. L. (2001). Preschoolers' spontaneous emotion vocabulary: Relations to likability. *Early Education and Development, 12,* 11–27.

Fabes, R. A., Eisenberg, N., Karbon, M., Troyer, D., & Switzer, G. (1994). The relations of children's emotion regulation to their vicarious emotional responses and comforting behavior. *Child Development, 65,* 1678–1693.

Fabes, R. A., Eisenberg, N., McCormick, S. E., & Wilson, M. S. (1988). Preschoolers' attributions of the situational determinants of others' naturally occurring emotions. *Developmental Psychology, 24,* 376–385.

Fabes, R. A., Martin, C. L., & Hanish, L. D. (2003). Young children's play qualities in same-, other-, and mixed-sex peer groups. *Child Development, 74,* 921–932.

Fabes, R. A., Shepard, S. A., Guthrie, I. K., & Martin, C. L. (1997). Roles of temperamental arousal and gender-segregated play in young children's social adjustment. *Developmental Psychology, 33,* 693–702.

Facchinetti, F., Battaglia, C., Benatti, R., Borella, P., & Genazzani, A. R. (1992). Oral magnesium supplementation improves fetal circulation. *Magnesium Research, 3,* 179–181.

Fagan, J. F., III. (1973). Infant's delayed recognition memory and forgetting. *Journal of Experimental Child Psychology, 16,* 424–450.

Fagan, J. F., III, & Detterman, D. K. (1992). The Fagan Test of Infant Intelligence: A technical summary. *Journal of Applied Developmental Psychology, 13,* 173–193.

Fagan, J. F., III, & Singer, L. T. (1983). Infant recognition memory as a measure of intelligence. In L. P. Lipsitt (Ed.), *Advances in infancy research* (Vol. 2, pp. 31–78). Norwood, NJ: Ablex.

Fagard, J., & Pezé, A. (1997). Age changes in interlimb coupling and the development of bimanual coordination. *Journal of Motor Behavior, 29,* 199–208.

Fagot, B. I. (1984). The child's expectations of differences in adult male and female interactions. *Sex Roles, 11,* 593–600.

Fagot, B. I. (1985a). Beyond the reinforcement principle: Another step toward understanding sex role development. *Developmental Psychology, 21,* 1097–1104.

Fagot, B. I. (1985b). Changes in thinking about early sex role development. *Developmental Review, 5,* 83–98.

Fagot, B. I., & Hagan, R. I. (1991). Observations of parent reactions to sex-stereotyped behaviors: Age and sex effects. *Child Development, 62,* 617–628.

Fagot, B. I., & Leinbach, M. D. (1989). The young child's gender schema: Environmental input, internal organization. *Child Development, 60,* 663–672.

Fagot, B. I., Leinbach, M. D., & O'Boyle, C. (1992). Gender labeling, gender stereotyping, and parenting behaviors. *Developmental Psychology, 28,* 225–230.

Fahrmeier, E. D. (1978). The development of concrete operations among the Hausa. *Journal of Cross-Cultural Psychology, 9,* 23–44.

Fairburn, C. G., Doll, H. A., Welch, S. L., Hay, P. J., Davies, B. A., & O'Conner, M. E. (1997). Risk factors for binge eating disorder: A community-based case control study. *Archives of General Psychiatry, 54,* 509–517.

Fairburn, C. G., & Harrison, P. J. (2003). Eating disorders. *Lancet, 361,* 407–416.

Falbo, T. (1992). Social norms and the one-child family: Clinical and policy implications. In F. Boer & J. Dunn (Eds.), *Children's sibling relationships* (pp. 71–82). Hillsdale, NJ: Erlbaum.

Falbo, T., & Poston, D. L., Jr. (1993). The academic, personality, and physical outcomes of only children in China. *Child Development, 64,* 18–35.

Falbo, T., Poston, D. L., Jr., Triscari, R. S., & Zhang, X. (1997). Self-enhancing illusions among Chinese school-children. *Journal of Cross-Cultural Psychology, 28,* 172–191.

Fantz, R. L. (1961). The origin of form perception. *Scientific American, 204,* 66–72.

Farrant, K., & Reese, E. (2000). Maternal style and children's participation in reminiscing: Stepping stones in children's autobiographical memory development. *Journal of Cognition and Development, 1,* 193–225.

Farrington, D. P. (1987). Epidemiology. In H. C. Quay (Ed.), *Handbook of juvenile delinquency* (pp. 33–61). New York: Wiley.

Farrington, D. P., & Loeber, R. (2000). Epidemiology of juvenile violence. *Juvenile Violence, 9,* 733–748.

Farver, J. M., & Branstetter, W. H. (1994). Preschoolers' prosocial responses to their peers' distress. *Developmental Psychology, 30,* 334–341.

Farver, J. M., Kim, Y. K., & Lee, Y. (1995). Cultural differences in Korean- and Anglo-American preschoolers' social interaction and play behaviors. *Child Development, 66,* 1088–1099.

Farver, J. M., & Wimbarti, S. (1995a). Indonesian toddlers' social play with their mothers and older siblings. *Child Development, 66,* 1493–1503.

Farver, J. M., & Wimbarti, S. (1995b). Paternal participation in toddlers' pretend play. *Social Development, 4,* 19–31.

Fasig, L. G. (2000). Toddlers' understanding of ownership: Implications for self-concept development. *Social Development, 9,* 370–382.

Fasouliotis, S. J., & Schenker, J. G. (2000). Ethics and assisted reproduction. *European Journal of Obstetrics,*

Gynecology, and Reproductive Biology, 90, 171–180.

Fattibene, P., Mazzei, R., Nuccetelli, C., & Risica, S. (1999). Prenatal exposure to ionizing radiation: Sources, effects, and regulatory aspects. *Acta Paediatrica, 88,* 693–702.

Federal Interagency Forum on Child and Family Statistics. (2003). *America's children: Key national indicators of well-being: 2003.* Washington, DC: U.S. Government Printing Office.

Fee, E. J. (1997). The prosodic framework for language learning. *Topics in Language Disorders, 17,* 53–62.

Feeney, J. A., Hohaus, L., Noller, P., & Alexander, R. P. (2001). *Becoming parents: Exploring the bonds between mothers, fathers, and their infants.* New York: Cambridge University Press.

Feinberg, M. E., & Hetherington, E. M. (2001). Differential parenting as a within-family variable. *Journal of Family Psychology, 51,* 22–37.

Feinberg, M. E., McHale, S. M., Crouter, A. C., & Cumsille, P. (2003). Sibling differentiation: Sibling and parent relationship trajectories in adolescence. *Child Development, 74,* 1261–1274.

Feingold, A. (1994). Gender differences in personality: A meta-analysis. *Psychological Bulletin, 116,* 429–456.

Feiring, C., & Taska, L. S. (1996). Family self-concept: Ideas on its meaning. In B. Bracken (Ed.), *Handbook of self-concept* (pp. 317–373). New York: Wiley.

Feiring, C., Taska, L. S., & Lewis, M. (1999). Age and gender differences in children's and adolescents' adaptation to sexual abuse. *Child Abuse and Neglect, 23,* 115–128.

Feldman, R. (2002). Parents' convergence on sharing and marital satisfaction, father involvement, and parent–child relationship in the transition to parenthood. *Infant Mental Health Journal, 21,* 176–191.

Feldman, R., & Eidelman, A. I. (2003). Skin-to-skin contact (kangaroo care) accelerates autonomic and neurobehavioral maturation in preterm infants. *Developmental Medicine and Child Neurology, 45,* 274–281.

Feldman, R., Eidelman, A., Sirota, L., & Weller, A. (2002). Comparison of skin-to-skin (kangaroo) and traditional care: Parenting outcomes and preterm infant development. *Pediatrics, 110,* 16–26.

Feldman, R., Greenbaum, C. W., & Yirmiya, N. (1999). Mother–infant affect synchrony as an antecedent of the emergence of self-control. *Developmental Psychology, 35,* 223–231.

Feldman, R., & Klein, P. S. (2003). Toddlers' self-regulated compliance to mothers, caregivers, and fathers: Implications for theories of socialization. *Developmental Psychology, 39,* 680–692.

Feldman, R., Weller, A., Sirota, L., & Eidelman, A. I. (2003). Testing a family intervention hypothesis: The contribution of mother–infant skin-to-skin contact (kangaroo care) to family interaction, proximity, and touch. *Journal of Family Psychology, 17,* 94–107.

Felner, R. D., Favazza, A., Shim, M., Brand, S., Gu, K., & Noonan, N. (2002). Whole school improvement and restructuring as prevention and promotion: Lessons from STEP and the Project on High Performance Learning Communities. *Journal of School Psychology, 39,* 177–202.

Felsman, D. E., & Blustein, D. L. (1999). The role of peer relatedness in late adolescent career development. *Journal of Vocational Behavior, 54,* 279–295.

Fennell, C. T., & Werker, J. F. (2003). Early word learners' ability to access phonetic detail in well-known words. *Language and Speech, 46,* 245–264.

Fennema, E., Carpenter, T. P., Jacobs, V. R., Franke, M. L., & Levi, L. W. (1998). A longitudinal study of gender differences in young children's mathematical thinking. *Educational Researcher, 27,* 6–11.

Fenson, L., Dale, P. S., Reznick, J. S., Bates, E., Thal, D. J., & Pethick, S. J. (1994). Variability in early communicative development. *Monographs of the Society for Research in Child Development, 59*(5, Serial No. 242).

Ferguson, R. F. (1998). Teachers' perceptions and expectations and the black–white test score gap. In C. Jencks & M. Phillips (Eds.), *The black–white test score gap* (pp. 273–317). Washington, DC: Brookings Institution.

Ferguson, T. J., Stegge, H., & Damhuis, I. (1991). Children's understanding of guilt and shame. *Child Development, 62,* 827–839.

Ferguson, T. J., Stegge, H., Miller, E. R., & Olsen, M. E. (1999). Guilt, shame, and symptoms in children. *Developmental Psychology, 35,* 347–357.

Fergusson, D. M., & Horwood, J. (2003). Resilience to childhood adversity: Results of a 21-year study. In S. S. Luthar (Ed.), *Resilience and vulnerability* (pp. 130–155). New York: Cambridge University Press.

Fergusson, D. M., & Woodward, L. J. (1999). Breast-feeding and later psychosocial adjustment. *Paediatric and Perinatal Epidemiology, 13,* 144–157.

Fergusson, D. M., & Woodward, L. J. (2000). Teenage pregnancy and female educational underachievement. *Journal of Marriage and the Family, 62,* 147–161.

Fergusson, D. M., Woodward, L. J., & Horwood, L. J. (2000). Risk factors and life processes associated with the onset of suicidal behaviour during adolescence and early adulthood. *Psychological Medicine, 30,* 23–39.

Fernald, A., & Morikawa, H. (1993). Common themes and cultural variations in Japanese and American mothers' speech to infants. *Child Development, 64,* 637–656.

Fernald, A., Pinto, J. P., Swingley, D., Weinberg, A., & McRoberts, G. W. (1998). Rapid gains in speed of verbal processing by infants in the 2nd year. *Psychological Science, 9,* 228–231.

Fernald, A., Swingley, D., & Pinto, J. P. (2001). When half a word is enough: Infants can recognize spoken words using partial phonetic information. *Child Development, 72,* 1003–1015.

Fernald, A., Taeschner, T., Dunn, J., Papousek, M., Boysson-Bardies, B., & Fukui, I. (1989). A cross-language study of prosodic modifications in mothers' and fathers' speech to preverbal infants. *Journal of Child Language, 16,* 477–502.

Fernald, L. C., & Grantham-McGregor, S. M. (1998). Stress response in school-age children who have been growth-retarded since early childhood. *American Journal of Clinical Nutrition, 68,* 691–698.

Ficca, G., Fagioli, I., Giganti, F., & Salzarulo, P. (1999). Spontaneous awakenings from sleep in the first year of life. *Early Human Development, 55,* 219–228.

Field, T. (2001). Massage therapy facilitates weight gain in preterm infants. *Current Directions in Psychological Science, 10,* 51–54.

Field, T., Hernandez-Reif, M., & Freedman, J. (2004). Stimulation programs for preterm infants. *Social Policy Report of the Society for Research in Child Development, 18*(1).

Field, T. M., Woodson, R., Greenberg, R., & Cohen, D. (1982). Discrimination and imitation of facial expressions by neonates. *Science, 218,* 179–181.

Fingerhut, L. A., & Christoffel, K. K. (2002). Firearm-related death and injury among children and adolescents. *Future of Children, 12,* 25–37.

Finkel, D., & Pedersen, N. L. (2001). Sources of environmental influence on cognitive abilities in adulthood. In E. L. Grigorenko & R. J. Sternberg (Eds.), *Family environment and intellectual functioning: A life-span perspective* (pp. 173–194). Mahwah, NJ: Erlbaum.

Finn, J. D., Pannozzo, G. M., & Achilles, C. M. (2003). The "why's" of class size: Student behavior in small classes. *Review of Educational Research, 73,* 321–368.

Finnilä, K., Mahlberga, N., Santtila, P., & Niemib, P. (2003). Validity of a test of children's suggestibility for predicting responses to two interview situations differing in degree of suggestiveness. *Journal of Experimental Child Psychology, 85,* 32–49.

Fins, A. I., & Wohlgemuth, W. K. (2001). Sleep disorders in children and adolescents. In H. Orvaschel & J. Faust (Eds.), *Handbook of conceptualization and treatment of child psychopathology* (pp. 437–448). Amsterdam: Pergamon.

Fisch, H., Hyun, G., Golden, R., Hensle, T. W., Olsson, C. A., & Liberson, G. L. (2003). The influence of paternal age on Down syndrome. *Journal of Urology, 169,* 2275–2278.

Fisch, S. M., Truglio, R. T., & Cole, C. (1999). The impact of Sesame Street on preschool children: A review and synthesis of 30 years' research. *Media Psychology, 1,* 165–190.

Fischer, K. W., & Bidell, T. R. (1998). Dynamic development of psychological structures in action and thought. In R. M. Lerner (Ed.), *Handbook of child psychology: Vol. 1. Theoretical models of human development* (5th ed., pp. 467–562). New York: Wiley.

Fischman, M. G., Moore, J. B., & Steele, K. H. (1992). Children's one-hand catching as a function of age, gender, and ball location. *Research Quarterly for Exercise and Sport, 63,* 349–355.

Fisher, C. B. (1993, Winter). Integrating science and ethics in research with high-risk children and youth. *Social Policy Report of the Society for Research in Child Development, 4*(4).

Fisher, C. B., Hoagwood, K., Boyce, C., Duster, T., Frank, D. A., & Grisso, T. (2002). Research ethics for mental health science involving ethnic minority children and youths. *American Psychologist, 57,* 1024–1040.

Fisher, J. O., Mitchell, D. S., Smiciklas-Wright, H., & Birch, L. L. (2001). Maternal milk consumption predicts the tradeoff between milk and soft drinks in young girls' diets. *Journal of Nutrition, 131,* 246–250.

Fisher, M., Barkley, R. A., Smallish, L., & Fletcher, K. (2002). Young adult follow-up of hyperactive children: Self-reported psychiatric disorders, comorbidity, and the role of childhood conduct problems and teen CD. *Journal of Abnormal Child Psychology, 39,* 463–475.

Fisher, P. A., Gunnar, M. R., Chamberlain, P., & Reid, J. B. (2000). Preventive intervention for maltreated preschool children: Impact on children's behavior, neuroendocrine activity, and foster parent functioning. *Journal of the American Academy of Child and Adolescent Psychiatry, 39,* 1356–1364.

Fitch, M., Huston, A. C., & Wright, J. C. (1993). From television forms to genre schemata: Children's perceptions of television reality. In G. L. Berry & J. K. Asamen (Eds.), *Children and television* (pp. 38–52). Newbury Park, CA: Sage.

FitzGerald, D. P., & White, K. J. (2003). Linking children's social worlds: Perspective-taking in parent–child and peer contexts. *Social Behavior and Personality, 31,* 509–522.

Fivush, R. (1989). Exploring sex differences in the emotional content of mother–child conversations about the past. *Sex Roles, 20,* 675–691.

Fivush, R., Haden, C., & Adam, S. (1995). Structure and coherence of preschoolers' personal narratives over time: Implications for childhood amnesia. *Journal of Experimental Child Psychology, 60,* 32–56.

Fivush, R., & Hamond, N. R. (1990). Autobiographical memory across the preschool years: Toward reconceptualizing childhood amnesia. In R. Fivush & J. A. Hudson (Eds.), *Knowing and remembering in young children* (pp. 223–248). New York: Cambridge University Press.

Fivush, R., & Reese, E. (2002). Reminiscing and relating: The development of parent–child talk about the past. In J. D. Webster & B. K. Haight (Eds.), *Critical advances in reminiscence work: From theory to application* (pp. 109–122). New York: Springer.

Flake, A. W. (2003). Surgery in the human fetus: The future. *Journal of Physiology, 547,* 45–51.

Flaks, D. K., Ficher, I., Masterpasqua, F., & Joseph, G. (1995). Lesbians choosing motherhood: A comparative study of lesbian and heterosexual parents and their children. *Developmental Psychology, 31,* 105–114.

Flanagan, C. A., & Faison, N. (2001). Youth civic development: Implications of research for social policy and programs. *Social Policy Report of the Society for Research in Child Development, 15*(1).

Flanagan, C. A., Jonsson, B., Botcheva, L., Csapo, B., Bowes, J., Macek, P., Averina, I., & Sheblanova, E. (1999). Adolescents and the social contract: Developmental roots of citizenship in seven countries. In M. Yates & J. Youniss (Eds.), *Roots of civic identity: International perspectives on community service and activism in youth* (pp. 135–155). New York: Cambridge University Press.

Flanagan, C. A., & Tucker, C. J. (1999). Adolescents' explanations for political issues: Concordance with their views of self and society. *Developmental Psychology, 35,* 1198–1209.

Flannery, K. A., & Liederman, J. (1995). Is there really a syndrome involving the co-occurrence of neurodevelopmental disorder, talent, nonright handedness and immune disorder among children? *Cortex, 31,* 503–515.

Flavell, J. H. (2000). Development of children's knowledge about the mental world. *International Journal of Behavioral Development, 24,* 15–23.

Flavell, J. H., Flavell, E. R., Green, F. L., & Korfmacher, J. E. (1990). Do young children think of television images as pictures or real objects? *Journal of Broadcasting and Electronic Media, 34,* 399–419.

Flavell, J. H., Green, F. L., & Flavell, E. R. (1987). Development of knowledge about the appearance–reality distinction. *Monographs of the Society for Research in Child Development, 51*(1, Serial No. 212).

Flavell, J. H., Green, F. L., & Flavell, E. R. (1993). Children's understanding of the stream of consciousness. *Child Development, 64,* 387–398.

Flavell, J. H., Green, F. L., & Flavell, E. R. (1995). Young children's knowledge about thinking. *Monographs of the Society for Research in Child Development, 60*(1, Serial No. 243).

Flavell, J. H., Green, F. L., & Flavell, E. R. (2000). Development of children's awareness of their own thoughts. *Journal of Cognition and Development, 1,* 97–112.

Flavell, J. H., Miller, P. H., & Miller, S. A. (2002). *Cognitive development* (4th ed.). Upper Saddle River, NJ: Prentice Hall.

Fleming, V., M., & Alexander, J. M. (2001). The benefits of peer collaboration: A replication with a delayed posttest. *Contemporary Educational Psychology, 26,* 588–601.

Fletcher, A. C., Nickerson, P., & Wright, K. L. (2003). Structured leisure activities in middle childhood: Links to well-being. *Journal of Community Psychology, 31,* 641–659.

Floccia, C., Christophe, A., & Bertoncini, J. (1997). High-amplitude sucking and newborns: The quest for underlying mechanisms. *Journal of Experimental Child Psychology, 64,* 175–198.

Flom, R., & Pick, A. D. (2003). Verbal encouragement and joint attention in 18-month-old infants. *Infant Behavior and Development, 26,* 121–134.

Florian, V., & Kravetz, S. (1985). Children's concepts of death: A cross-cultural comparison among Muslims, Druze, Christians, and Jews in Israel. *Journal of Cross-Cultural Psychology, 16,* 174–179.

Flynn, J. R. (1994). IQ gains over time. In R. J. Sternberg (Ed.), *The encyclopedia of human intelligence* (pp. 617–623). New York: Macmillan.

Flynn, J. R. (1999). Searching for justice: The discovery of IQ gains over time. *American Psychologist, 54,* 5–20.

Flynn, J. R. (2003). Movies about intelligence: The limitations of *g*. *Current Directions in Psychological Science, 12*, 95–99.

Fogel, A. (2000). Systems, attachment, and relationships. *Human Development, 43*, 314–320.

Fogel, A., Melson, G. F., Toda, S., & Mistry, T. (1987). Young children's responses to unfamiliar infants. *International Journal of Behavioral Development, 10*, 1071–1077.

Fomon, S. J., & Nelson, S. E. (2002). Body composition of the male and female reference infants. *Annual Review of Nutrition, 22*, 1–17.

Fonzi, A., Schneider, B. H., Tani, F., & Tomada, G. (1997). Predicting children's friendship status from their dyadic interaction in structured situations of potential conflict. *Child Development, 68*, 496–506.

Fordham, K., & Stevenson-Hinde, J. (1999). Shyness, friendship quality, and adjustment during middle childhood. *Journal of Child Psychology and Psychiatry, 40*, 757–768.

Forgatch, M. S., & DeGarmo, D. S. (1999). Parenting through change: An effective prevention program for single mothers. *Journal of Consulting and Clinical Psychology, 67*, 711–724.

Forsén, T., Eriksson, J., Tuomilehto, J., Reunanen, A., Osmond, C., & Barker, D. (2000). The fetal and childhood growth of persons who develop Type 2 diabetes. *Annals of Internal Medicine, 133*, 176–182.

Fowles, D. C., & Kochanska, G. (2000). Temperament as a moderator of pathways to conscience in children: The contribution of electrodermal activity. *Psychophysiology, 37*, 788–795.

Fox, N. A. (1991). If it's not left, it's right: Electroencephalograph asymmetry and the development of emotion. *American Psychologist, 46*, 863–872.

Fox, N. A., & Calkins, S. D. (2003). The development of self-control of emotion: Intrinsic and extrinsic influences. *Motivation and Emotion, 27*, 7–26.

Fox, N. A., & Card, J. A. (1998). Psychophysiological measures in the study of attachment. In J. Cassidy & P. Shaver (Eds.), *Handbook of attachment: Theory, research, and clinical applications* (pp. 226–245). New York: Guilford.

Fox, N. A., & Davidson, R. J. (1986). Taste-elicited changes in facial signs of emotion and the asymmetry of brain electrical activity in newborn infants. *Neuropsychologia, 24*, 417–422.

Fox, N. A., Schmidt, L. A., & Henderson, H. A. (2000). Developmental psychophysiology: Conceptual and methodological perspectives. In J. T. Cacioppo & L. G. Tassinary (Eds.), *Handbook of psychophysiology* (2nd ed., pp. 665–686). New York: Cambridge University Press.

Foy, J. G., & Mann, V. (2003). Home literacy environment and phonological awareness in preschool children: Differential effects for rhyme and phoneme awareness. *Applied Psycholinguistics, 24*, 59–88.

Franco, P., Danias, A. P., Akamine, E. H., Kawamoto, E. M., Fortes, Z. B., Scavone, C., & Tostes, R. C. (2002). Enhanced oxidative stress as a potential mechanism underlying the programming of hypertension in utero.

Journal of Cardiovascular Pharmacology, 40, 501–509.

Frank, D. A., Augustyn, M., Knight, W. G., Pell, T., & Zuckerman, B. (2001). Growth, development, and behavior in early childhood following prenatal cocaine exposure. *Journal of the American Medical Association, 285*, 1613–1625.

Frederiksen-Goldsen, K. I., & Sharlach, A. E. (2000). *Families and work: New directions in the twenty-first century.* New York: Oxford University Press.

Fredricks, J. A., & Eccles, J. S. (2002). Children's competence and value beliefs from childhood through adolescence: Growth trajectories in two male-sex-typed domains. *Developmental Psychology, 38*, 519–533.

Freedman, D. G., & Freedman, N. (1969). Behavioral differences between Chinese-American and European-American newborns. *Nature, 224*, 1227.

Freedman-Doan, C., Wigfield, A., Eccles, J. S., Blumenfeld, P., Arbreton, A., & Harold, R. D. (2000). What am I best at? Grade and gender differences in children's beliefs about ability improvement. *Journal of Applied Developmental Psychology, 21*, 379–402.

Freeman, D. (1983). *Margaret Mead and Samoa: The making and unmaking of an anthropological myth.* Cambridge, MA: Harvard University Press.

Freud, A., & Dann, S. (1951). An experiment in group upbringing. *Psychoanalytic Study of the Child, 6*, 127–168.

Freud, S. (1961). Some psychological consequences of the anatomical distinction between the sexes. In J. Strachey (Ed.), *Standard edition of the complete psychological works of Sigmund Freud* (Vol. 19, pp. 248–258). London: Hogarth Press. (Original work published 1925)

Freud, S. (1973). *An outline of psychoanalysis.* London: Hogarth. (Original work published 1938)

Freud, S. (1974). *The ego and the id.* London: Hogarth. (Original work published 1923)

Fried, P. A. (1993). Prenatal exposure to tobacco and marijuana: Effects during pregnancy, infancy, and early childhood. *Clinical Obstetrics and Gynecology, 36*, 319–337.

Fried, P. A. (2002a). Adolescents prenatally exposed to marijuana: Examination of facets of complex behaviors and comparisons with the influence of in utero cigarettes. *Journal of Clinical Pharmacology, 42*, 97S–102S.

Fried, P. A. (2002b). Conceptual issues in behavioral teratology and their application in determining long-term sequelae of prenatal marihuana exposure. *Journal of Child Psychology and Psychiatry, 43*, 81–102.

Fried, P. A., Watkinson, B., & Gray, R. (2003). Differential effects on cognitive functioning in 13- to 16-year-olds prenatally exposed to cigarettes and marijuana. *Neurotoxicology and Teratology, 25* 427–436.

Friedman, J. M. (1996). *The effects of drugs on the fetus and nursing infant: A handbook for health care professionals.* Baltimore: Johns Hopkins University Press.

Friedman, J. M., & Polifka, J. E. (1998). *The effects of neurologic and psychiatric drugs on the fetus and nursing*

infant. Baltimore, MD: Johns Hopkins University Press.

Friedrich, W. N., Grambusch, P., Damon, L., & Hewitt, S. K. (2001). Child sexual behavior inventory: Normative and clinical comparisons. *Child Maltreatment, 6*, 37–49.

Frijda, N. (2000). The psychologist's point of view. In M. Lewis & J. M. Haviland-Jones (Eds.), *Handbook of emotions* (pp. 59–74). New York: Guilford.

Frith, L. (2001). Gamete donation and anonymity: The ethical and legal debate. *Human Reproduction, 16*, 818–824.

Frith, U. (2003). *Autism: Explaining the enigma* (2nd ed.). Malden, MA: Blackwell.

Frosch, C. A., Mangelsdorf, S. C., & McHale, J. L. (2000). Marital behavior and security of preschooler–parent attachment relationships. *Journal of Family Psychology, 14*, 144–161.

Frost, J. L., Shin, D., & Jacobs, P. J. (1998). Physical environments and children's play. In O. N. Saracho & B. Spodek (Eds.), *Multiple perspectives on play in early childhood education* (pp. 255–294). Albany: State University of New York Press.

Fry, A. F., & Hale, S. (1996). Processing speed, working memory, and fluid intelligence: Evidence for a developmental cascade. *Psychological Science, 7*, 237–241.

Fuchs, I., Eisenberg, N., Hertz-Lazarowitz, R., & Sharabany, R. (1986). Kibbutz, Israeli city, and American children's moral reasoning about prosocial moral conflicts. *Merrill-Palmer Quarterly, 32*, 37–50.

Fuchs, L. S., Fuchs, D., Mathes, P. G., Martinez, E. A. (2002b). Preliminary evidence on the standing of students with learning disabilities in PALS and No-PALS classrooms. *Learning Disabilities Research and Practice, 17*, 205–215.

Fuchs, L. S., Fuchs, D., Yazkian, L., & Powell, S. R. (2002a). Enhancing first-grade children's mathematical development with peer-assisted learning strategies. *School Psychology Review, 31*, 569–583.

Fulhan, J., Collier, S., & Duggan, C. (2003). Update on pediatric nutrition: Breastfeeding, infant nutrition, and growth. *Current Opinion in Pediatrics, 15*, 323–332.

Fuligni, A. J. (1997). The academic achievement of adolescents from immigrant families: The roles of family background, attitudes, and behavior. *Child Development, 68*, 261–273.

Fuligni, A. J. (1998). Authority, autonomy, and parent–adolescent conflict and cohesion: A study of adolescents from Mexican, Chinese, Filipino, and European backgrounds. *Developmental Psychology, 34*, 782–792.

Fuligni, A. J. (2001). A comparative longitudinal approach to acculturation among children from immigrant families. *Harvard Educational Review, 71*, 566–578.

Fuligni, A. J., Yip, T., & Tseng, V. (2002). The impact of family obligation on the daily activities and psychological well-being of Chinese-American adolescents. *Child Development, 73*, 302–314.

Fuligni, A. J., & Yoshikawa, H. (2003). Socioeconomic resources, parenting, and child development among immigrant families. In M. H. Bornstein & R. H. Bradley (Eds.), *Socioeconomic status, parenting, ad child development* (pp. 107–124). Mahwah, NJ: Erlbaum.

Fung, H. (1999). Becoming a moral child: The socialization of shame among Chinese children. *Ethos, 27*, 180–209.

Furman, W. (2002). The emerging field of adolescent romantic relationships. *Current Directions in Psychological Science, 11*, 177–180.

Furman, W., & Buhrmester, D. (1992). Age and sex differences in perceptions of networks of personal relationships. *Child Development, 63*, 103–115.

Furman, W., & Shaffer, L. (2003). The role of romantic relationships in adolescent development. In P. Florsheim (Ed.), *Adolescent romantic relations and sexual behavior* (pp. 3–22). Mahwah, NJ: Erlbaum.

Furman, W., Simon, V. A., Shaffer, L., & Bouchey, H. A. (2002). Adolescents' working models and styles for relationships with parents, friends, and romantic partners. *Child Development, 73*, 241–255.

Furrow, J. L., King, P. E., & White, K. (2004). Religion and positive youth development: Identity, meaning, and prosocial concerns. *Applied Developmental Science, 8*, 17–26.

Furstenberg, F. F., Jr., & Harris, K. M. (1993). When and why fathers matter: Impact of father involvement on children of adolescent mothers. In R. I. Lerman & T. J. Ooms (Eds.), *Young unwed fathers* (pp. 117–138). Philadelphia: Temple University Press.

Fuson, K. C., & Burghard, B. H. (2003). Multidigit addition and subtraction methods invented in small groups and teacher support of problem solving and reflection. In A. J. Baroody & A. Dowker (Eds.), *The development of arithmetic concepts and skills* (pp. 267–304). Mahwah, NJ: Erlbaum.

Fuson, K. C., & Kwon, Y. (1992). Korean children's understanding of multidigit addition and subtraction. *Child Development, 63*, 491–506.

Gaillard, W., Sachs, B. C., Whitnah, J. R., Ahmad, Z., Balsamo, L. M., & Petrella, J. R. (2004). Developmental aspects of language processing: fMRI of verbal fluency in children and adults. *Human Brain Mapping, 18*, 176–185.

Galambos, N. L., Almeida, D. M., & Petersen, A. C. (1990). Masculinity, femininity, and sex role attitudes in early adolescence: Exploring gender intensification. *Child Development, 61*, 1904–1914.

Galambos, N. L., Leadbeater, B. J., & Barker, E. T. (2004). Gender differences in and risk factors for depression in adolescence: A 4-year longitudinal study. *International Journal of Behavioral Development, 28*, 16–25.

Galambos, N. L., & Maggs, J. L. (1991). Children in self-care: Figures, facts, and fiction. In J. V. Lerner & N. L. Galambos (Eds.), *Employed mothers and their children* (pp. 131–157). New York: Garland.

Galen, B. R., & Underwood, M. K. (1997). A developmental investigation of social aggression among children. *Developmental Psychology, 33*, 589–600.

Galler, J. R., Ramsey, C. F., Morley, D. S., Archer, E., & Salt, P. (1990). The long-term effects of early kwashiorkor compared with marasmus. IV. Performance on the National High School Entrance Examination. *Pediatric Research, 28*, 235–239.

Galler, J. R., Ramsey, F., & Solimano, G. (1985). A follow-up study of the effects of early malnutrition on subsequent development: I. Physical growth and sexual maturation during adolescence. *Pediatric Research, 19*, 518–523.

Galloway, J., & Thelen, E. (2004). Feet first: Object exploration in young infants. *Infant Behavior and Development, 27*, 107–112.

Galton, F. (1883). *Inquiries into human faculty and its development.* London: Macmillan.

Gandour, M. J. (1989). Activity level as a dimension of temperament in toddlers: Its relevance for the organismic specificity hypothesis. *Child Development, 60*, 1092–1098.

Gandy, J. (2004). Children explain God. Retrieved from www.geocities.com/jonathangandy.geo/childrendescribeGod.html

Ganger, J., & Brent, M. R. (2004). Reexamining the vocabulary spurt. *Developmental Psychology, 40*, 621–632.

Ganong, L. H., & Coleman, M. (1994). *Remarried family relationships.* Thousand Oaks, CA: Sage.

Garbarino, J., Andreas, J. B., & Vorrasi, J. A. (2002). Beyond the body count: Moderating the effects of war on children's long-term adaptation. In F. Jacobs, D. Wertlieb, & R. M. Lerner (Eds.), *Handbook of developmental science* (pp. 137–158). Thousand Oaks, CA: Sage.

Garbarino, J., & Bedard, C. (2001). *Parents under siege: Why you are the solution and not the problem in your child's life.* New York: Free Press.

Garbarino, J., & Kostelny, K. (1993). Neighborhood and community influences on parenting. In T. Luster & L. Okagaki (1993), *Parenting: An ecological perspective* (pp. 203–226). Hillsdale, NJ: Erlbaum.

Garcia, M. M., Shaw, D. S., Winslow, E. B., & Yaggi, K. E. (2000). Destructive sibling conflict and the development of conduct problems in young boys. *Developmental Psychology, 36*, 44–53.

García-Coll, C., & Magnuson, K. (1997). The psychological experience of immigration: A developmental perspective. In A. Booth, A. C. Crouter, & N. Landale (Eds.), *Immigration and the family* (pp. 91–131). Mahwah, NJ: Erlbaum.

Gardner, H. (1980). *Artful scribbles: The significance of children's drawings.* New York: Basic Books.

Gardner, H. (1983). *Frames of mind.* New York: Basic Books.

Gardner, H. (1993). *Multiple intelligences: The theory in practice.* New York: Basic Books.

Gardner, H. E. (1998a). Are there additional intelligences? The case of the naturalist, spiritual, and existential intelligences. In J. Kane (Ed.), *Educational information and transformation.* Upper Saddle River, NJ: Prentice-Hall.

Gardner, H. E. (1998b). Extraordinary cognitive achievements (ECA): A symbol systems approach. In W. Damon & R. M. Lerner (Eds.), *Handbook of*

child psychology: Vol. 1. Theoretical models of human development (5th ed., pp. 415–466). New York: Wiley.

Gardner, H. E. (2000). *Intelligence reframed: Multiple intelligences for the twenty-first century.* New York: Basic Books.

Garfinkel, I., & McLanahan, S. (1995). The effects of child support reform on child well-being. In P. L. Chase-Lansdale & J. Brooks-Gunn (Eds.), *Escape from poverty: What makes a difference for children?* (pp. 211–238). New York: Cambridge University Press.

Garmezy, N. (1993). Children in poverty: Resilience despite risk. *Psychiatry, 56*, 127–136.

Garner, P. W. (1996). The relations of emotional role taking, affective/moral attributions, and emotional display rule knowledge to low-income school-age children's social competence. *Journal of Applied Developmental Psychology, 17*, 19–36.

Garner, P. W. (2003). Child and family correlates of toddlers' emotional and behavioral responses to a mishap. *Infant Mental Health Journal, 24*, 580–596.

Gartstein, M. A., & Rothbart, M. K. (2003). Studying infant temperament via the revised infant behavior questionnaire. *Infant Behavior and Development, 26*, 64–86.

Gartstein, M. A., Slobodskaya, H. R., & Kinsht, I. A. (2003). Cross-cultural differences in temperament in the first year of life: United States of America (U.S.) and Russia. *International Journal of Behavioral Development, 27*, 316–328.

Garven, S., Wood, J. M., & Malpass, R. S. (2000). Allegations of wrongdoing: The effects of reinforcement on children's mundane and fantastic claims. *Journal of Applied Psychology, 85*, 38–49.

Garvey, C. (1974). Requests and responses in children's speech. *Journal of Child Language, 2*, 41–60.

Gasden, V. (1999). Black families in intergenerational and cultural perspective. In M. E. Lamb (Ed.), *Parenting and child development in "nontraditional" families* (pp. 221–246). Mahwah, NJ: Erlbaum.

Gash, H., & Morgan, M. (1993). School-based modifications of children's gender-related beliefs. *Journal of Applied Developmental Psychology, 14*, 277–287.

Gaskins, S. (1999). Children's daily lives in a Mayan village: A case study of culturally constructed roles and activities. In R. Göncü (Ed.), *Children's engagement in the world: Sociocultural perspectives* (pp. 25–61). Cambridge, UK: Cambridge University Press.

Gaskins, S. (2000). Children's daily activities in a Mayan village: A culturally grounded description. *Cross-Cultural Research, 34*, 375–389.

Gathercole, S. E. (1995). Is nonword repetition a test of phonological memory or long-term knowledge? It all depends on the nonwords. *Memory and Cognition, 23*, 83–94.

Gathercole, S. E., Hitch, G. J., Service, E., & Martin, A. J. (1997). Phonological short-term memory and new word learning in children. *Developmental Psychology, 33*, 966–979.

Gathercole, S. E., Service, E., Hitch, G. J., Adams, A., & Martin, A. J. (1999). Phonological short-term memory and vocabulary development: Further evidence on the nature of the relationship. *Applied Cognitive Psychology, 13*, 65–77.

Gathercole, V., Sebastián, E., & Soto, P. (1999). The early acquisition of Spanish verbal morphology: Across-the-board or piecemeal knowledge? *International Journal of Bilingualism, 3*, 133–182.

Gauvain, M. (2004). Bringing culture into relief: Cultural contributions to the development of children's planning skills. In R. V. Kail (Ed.), *Advances in child development and behavior* (pp. 39–71). San Diego, CA: Elsevier.

Gauvain, M., Ossa, J. L. de la, & Hurtado-Ortiz, M. T. (2001). Parental guidance as children learn to use cultural tools: The case of pictorial plans. *Cognitive Development, 16*, 551–575.

Gauvain, M., & Rogoff, B. (1989). Collaborative problem solving and children's planning skills. *Developmental Psychology, 25*, 139–151.

Gauze, C., Bukowski, W. M., Aquan-Assee, J., & Sippola, L. K. (1996). Interactions between family environment and friendship and associations with self-perceived well-being during early adolescence. *Child Development, 67*, 2201–2216.

Gazelle, H., & Ladd, G. W. (2002). Interventions for children victimized by peers. In P. A. Schewe (Ed.), *Preventing violence in relationships: Interventions across the life span* (pp. 55–78). Washington, DC: American Psychological Association.

Ge, X., Brody, G. H., Conger, R. D., Simons, R. L., & Murry, V. (2002). Contextual amplification of the effects of pubertal transition on African American children's deviant peer affiliation and externalized behavioral problems. *Developmental Psychology, 38*, 42–54.

Ge, X., Conger, R. D., & Elder, G. H., Jr. (1996). Coming of age too early: Pubertal influences on girls' vulnerability to psychological distress. *Child Development, 67*, 3386–3400.

Ge, X., Conger, R. D., & Elder, G. H., Jr. (2001a). Pubertal transition, stressful life events, and the emergence of gender differences in adolescent depressive symptoms. *Developmental Psychology, 37*, 404–417.

Ge, X., Conger, R. D., & Elder, G. H., Jr. (2001b). The relation between puberty and psychological distress in adolescent boys. *Journal of Research on Adolescence, 11*, 49–70.

Ge, X., Kim, I. J., Brody, G. H., Conger, R. D., & Simons, R. L. (2003). It's about timing and change: Pubertal transition effects on symptoms of major depression among African American youths. *Developmental Psychology, 39*, 430–439.

Geary, D. C. (1994). *Children's mathematical development.* Washington, DC: American Psychological Association.

Geary, D. C. (1998). *Male, female: The evolution of human sex differences.* Washington, DC: American Psychological Association.

Geary, D. C. (1999). Evolution and developmental sex differences. *Current Directions in Psychological Science, 8*, 115–120.

Geary, D. C. (2000). Evolution and proximate expression of human paternal investment. *Psychological Bulletin, 126*, 55–77.

Geary, D. C., & Bjorklund, D. F. (2000). Evolutionary developmental psychology. *Child Development, 71*, 57–65.

Geary, D. C., Bow-Thomas, C. C., Liu, F., & Siegler, R. S. (1996). Development of arithmetical competencies in Chinese and American children: Influence of age, language, and schooling. *Child Development, 67*, 2022–2044.

Geary, D. C., & Flinn, M. V. (2001). Evolution of human parental behavior and the human family. *Parenting Science and Practice, 1*, 5–61.

Gee, C. B., & Rhodes, J. E. (2003). Adolescent mothers' relationship with their children's biological fathers: Social support, social strain, and relationship continuity. *Journal of Family Psychology, 17*, 370–383.

Geerts, M., Steyaert, J., & Fryns, J. P. (2003). The XYY syndrome: A follow-up study on 38 boys. *Genetic Counseling, 14*, 267–279.

Gelman, R. (1972). Logical capacity of very young children: Number invariance rules. *Child Development, 43*, 75–90.

Gelman, R., & Koenig, M. A. (2003). Theory-based categorization in early childhood. In D. H. Rakison & L. M. Oakes (Eds.), *Early category and concept development* (pp. 330–359). New York: Oxford University Press.

Gelman, R., & Shatz, M. (1978). Appropriate speech adjustments: The operation of conversational constraints on talk to two-year-olds. In M. Lewis & L. A. Rosenblum (Eds.), *Interaction, conversation, and the development of language* (pp. 27–61). New York: Wiley.

Gelman, S. A. (2003). *The essential child: Origins of essentialism in everyday thought.* Oxford, UK: Oxford University Press.

Gelman, S. A., & Opfer, J. E. (2002). Development of the animate–inanimate distinction. In U. Goswami (Ed.), *Blackwell handbook of childhood cognitive development* (pp. 151–166). Malden, MA: Blackwell.

Gelman, S. A., Taylor, M. G., & Nguyen, S. P. (2004). Mother–child conversations about gender. *Monographs of the Society for Research in Child Development, 69*(1, Serial No. 275), pp. 1–127.

Genesee, F. (2001). Portrait of the bilingual child. In V. Cook (Ed.), *Portraits of the second language user.* Clevedon, UK: Multilingual Matters.

Gennetian, L. A., & Morris, P. A. (2003). The effects of time limits and make-work-pay strategies on the well-being of children: Experimental evidence from two welfare reform programs. *Children and Youth Services Review, 25*, 17–54.

Gerardi-Caulton, G. (2000). Sensitivity to spatial conflict and the development of self-regulation in children 24–36 months of age. *Developmental Science, 3*, 397–404.

Gergely, G., Bekkering, H., & Király, I. (2003). Rational imitation in preverbal infants. *Nature, 415*, 755.

Gergely, G., & Watson, J. (1999). Early socio-emotional development: Contingency perception and the social-biofeedback model. In P. Rochat (Ed.), *Early social cognition: Understanding others in the first months of life* (pp. 101–136). Mahwah, NJ: Erlbaum.

Gershoff, E. T. (2002a). Corporal punishment by parents and associated child behaviors and experiences: A meta-analytic and theoretical review. *Psychological Bulletin, 128,* 539–579.

Gershoff, E. T. (2002b). Corporal punishment, physical abuse, and the burden of proof: Reply to Baumrind, Larzelere, and Cowan (2002), Holden (2002), and Parke (2002). *Psychological Bulletin, 128,* 602–611.

Gershoff-Stowe, L., & Smith, L. B. (1997). A curvilinear trend in naming errors as a function of early vocabulary growth. *Cognitive Psychology, 34,* 37–71.

Gertner, S., Greenbaum, C. W., Sadeh, A., Dolfin, Z., Sirota, L., & Ben-Nun, Y. (2002). Sleep-wake patterns in preterm infants and 6 month's home environment: Implications for early cognitive development. *Early Human Development, 68,* 93–102.

Gervai, J., Turner, P. J., & Hinde, R. A. (1995). Gender-related behaviour, attitudes, and personality in parents of young children in England and Hungary. *International Journal of Behavioral Development, 18,* 105–126.

Geschwind, D. H., Boone, K. B., Miller, B. L., & Swerdloff, R. S. (2000). Neurobehavioral phenotype of Klinefelter syndrome. *Mental Retardation and Developmental Disabilities Research Reviews, 6,* 107–116.

Gesell, A. (1933). Maturation and patterning of behavior. In C. Murchison (Ed.), *A handbook of child psychology.* Worcester, MA: Clark University Press.

Gest, S. D., Graham-Bermann, S. A., & Hartup, W. W. (2001). Peer experience: Common and unique features of number of friendships, social network centrality, and sociometric status. *Social Development, 10,* 23–40.

Getchell, N., & Roberton, M. A. (1989). Whole body stiffness as a function of developmental level in children's hopping. *Developmental Psychology, 25,* 920–928.

Gettinger, M., Doll, B., & Salmon, D. (1994). Effects of social problem solving, goal setting, and parent training on children's peer relations. *Journal of Applied Developmental Psychology, 15,* 141–163.

Geurts, H. M., Verte, S., Oosterlaan, J., Roeyers, H., Sergeant, J. A., & Geurts, H. M. (2004). How specific are executive functioning deficits in attention-deficit hyperactivity disorder and autism? *Journal of Child Psychology and Psychiatry, 45,* 836–854.

Ghim, H. R. (1990). Evidence for perceptual organization in infants: Perception of subjective contours by young infants. *Infant Behavior and Development, 13,* 221–248.

Gibbons, A. (1998). Which of our genes make us human? *Science, 281,* 1432–1434.

Gibbons, R., Dugaiczyk, L. J., Girke, T., Duistermars, B., Zielinski, R., & Dugaiczyk, A. (2004). Distinguishing humans from great apes with AluYb8 repeats. *Journal of Molecular Biology, 339,* 721–729.

Gibbs, J. C. (1991). Toward an integration of Kohlberg's and Hoffman's theories

of morality. In W. M. Kurtines & J. L. Gewirtz (Eds.), *Handbook of moral behavior and development* (Vol. 1, pp. 183–222). Hillsdale, NJ: Erlbaum.

Gibbs, J. C. (1995). The cognitive developmental perspective. In W. M. Kurtines & J. L. Gewirtz (Eds.), *Moral development: An introduction* (pp. 27–48). Boston: Allyn and Bacon.

Gibbs, J. C. (2003). *Moral development and reality: Beyond the theories of Kohlberg and Hoffman.* Thousand Oaks, CA: Sage.

Gibbs, J. C. (2004). Moral reasoning training. In A. P. Goldstein, R. Nensen, B. Daleflod, & M. Kalt (Eds.), *New perspectives on aggression replacement training* (pp. 51–72). West Sussex, UK: Wiley.

Gibbs, J. C., Basinger, K. S., & Fuller, D. (1992). *Moral maturity: Measuring the development of sociomoral reflection.* Hillsdale, NJ: Erlbaum.

Gibbs, J. C., Basinger, K. S., & Grime, R. L. (2003). Moral judgment maturity: From clinical to standard measures. In S. J. Lopez & C. R. Snyder (Eds.), *Handbook of positive psychological assessment* (pp. 361–373). Washington, DC: American Psychological Association.

Gibbs, J. C., Basinger, K. S., & Grime, R. L. (2005, August). Cross-cultural research using the SRM–SF. In J. Comunian (Chair), *Cross-cultural research on morality using different assessment instruments.* Symposium conducted at the meeting of the American Psychological Association, Washington, DC.

Gibson, E. J. (1970). The development of perception as an adaptive process. *American Scientist, 58,* 98–107.

Gibson, E. J. (2000). Perceptual learning in development: Some basic concepts. *Ecological Psychology, 12,* 295–302.

Gibson, E. J. (2003). The world is so full of a number of things: On specification and perceptual learning. *Ecological Psychology, 15,* 283–287.

Gibson, E. J., & Walk, R. D. (1960). The "visual cliff." *Scientific American, 202,* 64–71.

Gibson, J. J. (1979). *The ecological approach to visual perception.* Boston: Houghton Mifflin.

Gilbert-Barnes, E. (2000). Maternal caffeine and its effect on the fetus. *American Journal of Medical Genetics, 93,* 253.

Gillies, R. M. (2000). The maintenance of cooperative and helping behaviours in cooperative groups. *British Journal of Educational Psychology, 70,* 97–111.

Gillies, R. M. (2003). The behaviors, interactions, and perceptions of junior high school students during small-group learning. *Journal of Educational Psychology, 95,* 137–147.

Gillies, R. M., & Ashman, A. F. (1996). Teaching collaborative skills to primary school children in classroom-based workgroups. *Learning and Instruction, 6,* 187–200.

Gilligan, C. F. (1982). *In a different voice.* Cambridge, MA: Harvard University Press.

Gilliom, M., Shaw, D. S., Beck, J. E., Schonberg, M. A., & Lukon, J. L. (2002). Anger regulation in disadvantaged preschool boys: Strategies, antecedents, and the development of self-control. *Developmental Psychology, 38,* 222–235.

Gimenez, M., & Harris, P. L. (2002). Understanding constraints on inheritance: Evidence for biological thinking in early childhood. *British Journal of Developmental Psychology, 20,* 307–324.

Ginsburg, H. P. (1997). *Entering the child's mind: The clinical interview in psychological research and practice.* New York: Cambridge University Press.

Gladwell, M. (1998, February 2). The Pima paradox. *The New Yorker,* pp. 44–57.

Gleason, T. R. (2002). Social provisions of real and imaginary relationships in early childhood. *Developmental Psychology, 38,* 979–992.

Gleason, T. R., Sebanc, A. M., & Hartup, W. W. (2000). Imaginary companions of preschool children. *Developmental Psychology, 36,* 419–428.

Gleitman, L. R. (1990). The structural sources of verb meanings. *Language Acquisition, 1,* 3–55.

Gleitman, L. R., & Gleitman, H. (1992). A picture is worth a thousand words, but that's the problem: The role of syntax in vocabulary acquisition. *Current Directions in Psychological Science, 1,* 31–35.

Gleitman, L., Gleitman, H., Landau, B., & Wanner, E. (1988). Where learning begins: Initial representations for language learning. In F. Newmeyer (Ed.), *Language: Psychological and biological aspects* (Vol. 3, pp. 150–193). Cambridge, UK: Cambridge University Press.

Glick, J. (1975). Cognitive development in cross-cultural perspective. In F. Horowitz (Ed.), *Review of child development research* (Vol. 4, pp. 595–654). Chicago: University of Chicago Press.

Glowinski, A. L., Madden, P. A. F., Bucholz, K. K., Lynskey, M. T., & Heath, A. C. (2003). Genetic epidemiology of self-reported lifetime DSM-IV major depressive disorder in a population-based twin sample of female adolescents. *Journal of Child Psychology and Psychiatry and Allied Disciplines, 44,* 988–996.

Gnepp, J. (1983). Children's social sensitivity: Inferring emotions from conflicting cues. *Developmental Psychology, 19,* 805–814.

Godfrey, K. M., & Barker, D. J. (2000). Fetal nutrition and adult disease. *American Journal of Clinical Nutrition, 71,* 1344S–1352S.

Godfrey, K. M., & Barker, D. J. (2001). Fetal programming and adult health. *Public Health Nutrition, 4,* 611–624.

Goelman, H. (1986). The language environments of family day care. In S. Kilmer (Ed.), *Advances in early education and day care* (Vol. 4, pp. 153–179). Greenwich, CT: JAI Press.

Goelman, H., Doherty, G., Lero, D. S., LaGrange, A., & Tougas, J. (2000). *You bet I care! Caring and learning environments: Quality in child care centres across Canada.* Guelph, ON: Centre for Families, Work and Well-Being, University of Guelph.

Goering, J. (Ed.). (2003). *Choosing a better life? How public housing tenants selected a HUD experiment to improve their lives and those of their children: The Moving to Opportunity Demonstration Program.* Washington, DC: Urban Institute Press.

Gogate, L. J., & Bahrick, L. E. (1998). Intersensory redundancy facilitates

learning of arbitrary relations between vowel sounds and objects in seven-month-old infants. *Journal of Experimental Child Psychology, 69,* 133–149.

Gogate, L. J., & Bahrick, L. E. (2001). Intersensory redundancy and 7-month-old infants' memory for arbitrary syllable–object relations. *Infancy, 2,* 219–231.

Gogate, L. J., Bahrick, L. E., & Watson, J. D. (2000). A study of multimodal motherese: The role of temporal synchrony between verbal labels and gestures. *Child Development, 71,* 878–894.

Goldbaum, S., Craig, W. M., Pepler, D., & Connolly, J. (2003). Developmental trajectories of victimization: Identifying risk and protective factors. *Journal of Applied School Psychology, 19,* 139–156.

Goldberg, A. E., & Perry-Jenkins, M. (2003). Division of labor and working-class women's well-being across the transition to parenthood. *Journal of Family Psychology, 18,* 225–236.

Goldberg, M. C., Maurer, D., & Lewis, T. L. (2001). Developmental changes in attention: The effects of endogenous cueing and of distracters. *Developmental Science, 4,* 209–219.

Goldberg, S., Benoit, D., Blokland, K., & Madigan, S. (2003). Atypical maternal behavior, maternal representations, and infant disorganized attachment. *Development and Psychopathology, 15,* 239–257.

Goldbloom, R. B. (2004). *Screening for hemoglobinopathies in Canada.* Hamilton, Ontario: McMaster University Medical Centre.

Goldenberg, C., Gallimore, R., Reese, L., & Garnier, H. (2001). Cause or effect? Immigrant Latino parents' aspirations and expectations, and their children's school performance. *American Educational Research Journal, 38,* 547–582.

Goldfield, B. A. (1987). The contributions of child and caregiver to referential and expressive language. *Applied Psycholinguistics, 8,* 267–280.

Goldfield, B. A. (2000). Nouns before verbs in comprehension vs. production: The view from pragmatics. *Journal of Child Language, 27,* 501–520.

Goldin-Meadow, S. (1999). The development of gesture with and without speech in hearing and deaf children. In L. S. Messing & R. Campbell (Eds.), *Gesture, speech, and sign* (pp. 117–132). New York: Oxford University Press.

Goldin-Meadow, S. (2002). Constructing communication by hand. *Cognitive Development, 17,* 1385–1405.

Goldin-Meadow, S. (2003). *The resilience of language.* New York: Psychology Press.

Goldin-Meadow, S., & Butcher, S. (2003). Pointing toward two-word speech in young children. In S. Kita (Ed.), *Pointing: Where language, culture, and cognition meet* (pp. 85–107). Mahwah, NJ: Erlbaum.

Goldin-Meadow, S., Butcher, C., Mylander, C., & Dodge, M. (1994). Nouns and verbs in a self-styled gesture system: What's in a name? *Cognitive Psychology, 27,* 259–319.

Goldin-Meadow, S., & Mylander, C. (1998). Spontaneous sign systems created by deaf children in two cultures. *Nature, 391,* 279–281.

Goldin-Meadow, S., Mylander, C., & Butcher, C. (1995). The resilience of combinatorial structure at the word level: Morphology in self-styled gesture systems. *Cognition, 56,* 88–96.

Goldin-Meadow, S., & Singer, M. A. (2003). From children's hands to adults' ears: Gesture's role in the learning process. *Developmental Psychology, 39,* 509–520.

Goldsmith, H. H., Lemery, K. S., Buss, K. A., & Campos, J. J. (1999). Genetic analyses of focal aspects of infant temperament. *Developmental Psychology, 35,* 972–985.

Goldsmith, L. T. (2000). Tracking trajectories of talent: Child prodigies growing up. In R. C. Friedman & B. M. Shore (Eds.), *Talents unfolding: Cognition and development* (pp. 89–122). Washington, DC: American Psychological Association.

Goleman, D. (1995). *Emotional intelligence.* New York: Bantam.

Goleman, D. (1998). *Working with emotional intelligence.* New York: Bantam.

Golomb, C. (2004). *The child's creation of a pictorial world* (2nd ed.). Mahwah, NJ: Erlbaum.

Golombok, S., & MacCallum, F. (2003). Practitioner review: Outcomes for parents and children following nontraditional conception: What do clinicians need to know? *Journal of Child Psychology and Psychiatry, 44,* 303–315.

Golombok, S., Perry, B., Burston, A., Murray, C., Mooney-Somers, J., Stevens, M., & Golding, J. (2003). Children with lesbian parents: A community study. *Developmental Psychology, 39,* 20–33.

Golombok, S., & Tasker, F. L. (1996). Do parents influence the sexual orientation of their children? Findings from a longitudinal study of lesbian families. *Developmental Psychology, 32,* 3–11.

Golub, M. S. (1996). Labor analgesia and infant brain development. *Pharmacology Biochemistry and Behavior, 55,* 619–628.

Gómez-Sanchiz, M., Canete, R., Rodero, I., Baeza, J. E., & Avilo, O. (2003). Influence of breast-feeding on mental and psychomotor development. *Clinical Pediatrics, 42,* 35–42.

Göncü, A. (1993). Development of intersubjectivity in the dyadic play of preschoolers. *Early Childhood Research Quarterly, 8,* 99–116.

Gonzales, N. A., Cauce, A. M., Friedman, R. J., & Mason, C. A. (1996). Family, peer, and neighborhood influences on academic achievement among African-American adolescents: One-year prospective effects. *American Journal of Community Psychology, 24,* 365–387.

Good, T. L., & Brophy, J. (2003). *Looking in classrooms* (9th ed.). Boston: Allyn and Bacon.

Goodall, J. (1990). *Through a window: My thirty years with the chimpanzees of Gombe.* Boston: Houghton Mifflin.

Goodlett, C. R., & Horn, K. H. (2001). Mechanisms of alcohol-induced damage to the developing nervous system. *Alcohol Research and Health, 25,* 175–191.

Goodlett, C. R., & Johnson, T. B. (1999). Temporal windows of vulnerability within the third trimester equivalent: Why "knowing when" matters. In J. H. Hannigan, L. P. Spear, N. P. Spear, &

C. R. Goodlet (Eds.), *Alcohol and alcoholism: Effects on brain and development* (pp. 59–91). Mahwah, NJ: Erlbaum.

Goodlin-Jones, B. L., Burnham, M. M., & Anders, T. F. (2000). Sleep and sleep disturbances: Regulatory processes in infancy. In A J. Sameroff, M. Lewis, & S. M. Miller (Eds.), *Handbook of developmental psychology* (2nd ed., pp. 309–325). New York: Kluwer.

Goodman, G. S., Hirschman, J. E., Hepps, D., & Rudy, L. (1991). Children's memory for stressful events. *Merrill-Palmer Quarterly, 37,* 109–158.

Goodman, G. S., Quas, J. A., Bulkley, J., & Shapiro, C. (1999). Innovations for child witnesses: A national survey. *Psychology, Public Policy,* and *Law, 5,* 255–281.

Goodman, S. H., Gravitt, G. W., Jr., & Kaslow, N. J. (1995). Social problem solving: A moderator of the relation between negative life stress and depression symptoms in children. *Journal of Abnormal Child Psychology, 23,* 473–485.

Goodwin, M. H. (1998). Games of stance: Conflict and footing in hopscotch. In S. Hoyle & C. T. Adger (Eds.), *Language practices of older children* (pp. 23–46). New York: Oxford University Press.

Gootman, E. (2005, January 16). New York City: The politics of promotion. *New York Times.* Retrieved from www.nytimes.com/2005/01/16/education/edlife/EDGOOT.html

Gopnik, A., & Choi, S. (1990). Do linguistic differences lead to cognitive differences? A cross-linguistic study of semantic and cognitive development. *First Language, 11,* 199–215.

Gopnik, A., & Choi, S. (1995). Names, relational words, and cognitive development in English and Korean speakers: Nouns are not always learned before verbs. In A. Gopnik & S. Choi (Eds.), *Beyond names for things: Children's acquisition of verbs* (pp. 63–80). Hillsdale, NJ: Erlbaum.

Gopnik, A., & Meltzoff, A. N. (1986). Relations between semantic and cognitive development in the one-word stage: The specificity hypothesis. *Child Development, 57,* 1040–1053.

Gopnik, A., & Meltzoff, A. N. (1987a). The development of categorization in the second year and its relation to other cognitive and linguistic developments. *Child Development, 58,* 1523–1531.

Gopnik, A., & Meltzoff, A. N. (1987b). Language and thought in the young child: Early semantic developments and their relationships to object permanence, means-ends understanding, and categorization. In K. Nelson & A. Van Kleeck (Eds.), *Children's language* (Vol. 6, pp. 191–212). Hillsdale, NJ: Erlbaum.

Gopnik, A., & Meltzoff, A. N. (1992). Categorization and naming: Basic-level sorting in eighteen-month-olds and its relation to language. *Child Development, 63,* 1091–1103.

Gopnik, A., & Nazzi, T. (2003). Words, kinds, and causal powers: A theory theory perspective on early naming and categorization. In D. H. Rakison & L. M. Oakes (Eds.), *Early category and concept development: Making sense of the blooming, buzzing*

confusion (pp. 303–329). New York: Oxford University Press.

Gopnik, A., & Wellman, H. M. (1994). The 'theory' theory. In L. A. Hirschfeld & S. A. Gelman (Eds.), *Mapping the mind: Domain specificity in cognition and culture* (pp. 257–293). Cambridge, UK: Cambridge University Press.

Gordon, B. N., Baker-Ward, L., & Ornstein, P. A. (2001). Children's testimony: A review of research on memory for past experiences. *Clinical Child and Family Psychology Review, 4,* 157–181.

Gordon, R. A., Chase-Lansdale, P. L., & Brooks-Gunn, J. (2004). Extended households and the life course of young mothers: Understanding the associations using a sample of mothers with premature, low-birth-weight babies. *Child Development, 75,* 1013–1038.

Gormally, S., Barr, R. G., Wertheim, L., Alkawaf, R., Calinoui, N., & Young, S. N. (2001). Contact and nutrient caregiving effects on newborn infant pain responses. *Developmental Medicine and Child Neurology, 43,* 28–38.

Gortmaker, S. L., Must, A., Perrin, J. M., Sobol, A. M., & Dietz, W. H., Jr. (1993). Social and economic consequences of overweight in adolescence and young adulthood. *New England Journal of Medicine, 329,* 1008–1012.

Goswami, U. (1996). Analogical reasoning and cognitive development. In H. Reese (Ed.), *Advances in child development and behavior* (Vol. 26, pp. 91–138). New York: Academic Press.

Goswami, U., & Brown, A. (1989). Melting chocolate and melting snowmen: Analogical reasoning and causal relations. *Cognition, 35,* 69–95.

Gott, V. L. (1998). Antoine Marfan and his syndrome: One hundred years later. *Maryland Medical Journal, 47,* 247–252.

Gottesman, I. I. (1963). Genetic aspects of intelligent behavior. In N. R. Ellis (Ed.), *Handbook of mental deficiency* (pp. 253–296). New York: McGraw-Hill.

Gottesman, I. I. (1991). *Schizophrenia genetics: The origins of madness.* New York: Freeman.

Gottfried, A. E. (1991). Maternal employment in the family setting: Developmental and environmental issues. In J. V. Lerner & N. L. Galambos (Eds.), *Employed mothers and their children* (pp. 63–84). New York: Garland.

Gottfried, A. E., Gottfried, A. W., & Bathurst, K. (2002). Maternal and dual-earner employment status and parenting. In M. H. Bornstein (Ed.), *Handbook of parenting: Vol. 3. Being and Becoming a Parent* (2nd ed., pp. 207–230). Mahwah, NJ: Erlbaum.

Gottlieb, G. (1992). *Individual development and evolution: The genesis of novel behavior.* New York: Oxford University Press.

Gottlieb, G. (1998). Normally occurring environmental and behavioral influences on gene activity: From central dogma to probabilistic epigenesis. *Psychological Review, 105,* 792–802.

Gottlieb, G. (2000). Environmental and behavioral influences on gene activity. *Current Directions in Psychological Science, 9,* 93–97.

Gottlieb, G. (2003). On making behavioral genetics truly developmental. *Human Development, 46,* 337–355.

Gottman, J. M., Katz, L. F., & Hooven, C. (1997). *Meta-emotion: How families*

communicate emotionally. Mahwah, NJ: Erlbaum.

Gould, E., Beylin, A., Tanapat, P., Reeves, A., & Shors, T. J. (1999). Learning enhances adult neurogenesis in the hippocampal formation. *Nature Neuroscience, 2,* 260–265.

Gould, J. L., & Keeton, W. T. (1996). *Biological science* (6th ed.). New York: Norton.

Gould, M., Jamieson, P., & Romer, D. (2003). Media contagion and suicide among the young. *American Behavioral Scientist, 46,* 1269–1284.

Government of Canada. (2004a). Action Plan for Official Languages. Retrieved from www.wd.gc.ca/rpts/strategies/ola/2004/1_e.asp

Government of Canada. (2004b). Food insecurity in Canada, 1998–May 2001. Retrieved from www11.sdc.gc.ca/en/cs/sp/arb/publications/research/2001-000066/page00.shtml

Goy, R. W., & Goldfoot, D. A. (1974). Experiential and hormonal factors influencing development of sexual behavior in the male rhesus monkey. In R. O. Schmitt & F. G. Worden (Eds.), *The neurosciences* (pp. 571–581). Cambridge, MA: MIT Press.

Graber, J. A. (2003). Puberty in context. In C. Hayward (Ed.), *Gender differences at puberty* (pp. 307–325). New York: Cambridge University Press.

Graber, J. A., Lewinsohn, P. M., Seeley, J. R., & Brooks-Gunn, J. (1997). Is psychopathology associated with the timing of pubertal development? *Journal of the American Academy of Child and Adolescent Psychiatry, 36,* 1768–1776.

Graber, J. A., Seeley, J. R., Brooks-Gunn, J., & Lewinsohn, P. M. (2004). Is pubertal timing associated with psychopathology in young adulthood? *Journal of the American Academy of Child and Adolescent Psychiatry, 43,* 718–726.

Graczyk, P. A., Weikssberg, R. P., Payton, J. W., Elias, M. J., Greenberg, M. T., & Zins, J. E. (2000). Criteria for evaluating the quality of school-based social and emotional learning programs. In R. Bar-On & J. D. A. Parker (Eds.), *Handbook of emotional intelligence* (pp. 391–410). San Francisco: Jossey-Bass.

Graham, Y. P., Heim, C., Goodman, S. H., Miller, A. H., & Nemeroff, C. B. (1999). The effects of neonatal stress on brain development: Implications for psychopathology. *Development and Psychopathology, 11,* 545–565.

Gralinski, J. H., & Kopp, C. B. (1993). Everyday rules for behavior: Mothers' requests to young children. *Developmental Psychology, 29,* 573–584.

Granger, R. C., & Cytron, R. (1999). Teenage parent programs: A synthesis of the long-term effects of the New Chance Demonstration, Ohio's Learning, Earning, and Parenting Program, and the Teenage Parent Demonstration. *Evaluation Review, 23,* 107–145.

Granic, I., Hollenstein, T., Dishion, T. J., & Patterson, G. R. (2003). Longitudinal analysis of flexibility and reorganization in early adolescence: A dynamic systems study of family interactions. *Developmental Psychology, 39,* 606–617.

Granot, M., Spitzer, A., Aroian, K. J., Ravid, C., Tamir, B., & Noam, R. (1996). Pregnancy and delivery practices and beliefs of Ethiopian immigrant women in Israel. *Western Journal of Nursing Research, 18,* 299–313.

Grant, H., & Dweck, C. S. (2001). Cross-cultural response to failure: Considering outcome attributions with different goals. In F. Salili & C. Chiu (Eds.), *Student motivation: The culture and context of learning* (pp. 203–219). New York: Plenum.

Grant, K., O'Koon, J., Davis, T., Roache, N., Poindexter, L., & Armstrong, M. (2000). Protective factors affecting low-income urban African American youth exposed to stress. *Journal of Early Adolescence, 20,* 388–418.

Grantham-McGregor, S., & Ani, C. (2001). A review of studies on the effect of iron deficiency on cognitive development in children. *Journal of Nutrition, 131,* 649S–668S.

Grantham-McGregor, S., Powell, C., Walker, S., Chang, S., & Fletcher, P. (1994). The long-term follow-up of severely malnourished children who participated in an intervention program. *Child Development, 65,* 428–439.

Grattan, M. P., De Vos, E., Levy, J., & McClintock, M. K. (1992). Asymmetric action in the human newborn: Sex differences in patterns of organization. *Child Development, 63,* 273–289.

Graue, M. E., & DiPerna, J. (2000). Redshirting and early retention: Who gets the "gift of time" and what are its outcomes? *American Educational Research Journal, 37,* 509–534.

Graves, S. B. (1993). Television, the portrayal of African Americans, and the development of children's attitudes. In G. L. Berry & J. K. Asamen (Eds.), *Children and television* (pp. 179–190). Newbury Park, CA: Sage.

Gray, J. (1997). *Mars and Venus on a date.* New York: HarperCollins.

Gray, M. R., & Steinberg, L. D. (1999). Unpacking authoritative parenting: Reassessing a multidimensional construct. *Journal of Marriage and the Family, 61,* 574–587.

Gray-Little, B., & Carels, R. (1997). The effects of racial and socioeconomic consonance on self-esteem and achievement in elementary, junior high, and high school students. *Journal of Research on Adolescence, 7,* 109–131.

Gray-Little, B., & Hafdahl, A. R. (2000). Factors influencing racial comparisons of self-esteem: A quantitative review. *Psychological Bulletin, 126,* 26–54.

Graziano, A. M., & Hamblen, J. L. (1996). Subabusive violence in child rearing in middle-class American families. *Pediatrics, 98,* 845–848.

Green, G. E., Irwin, J. R., & Gustafson, G. E. (2000). Acoustic cry analysis, neonatal status and long-term developmental outcomes. In R. G. Barr, B. Hopkins, & J. A. Green (Eds.), *Crying as a sign, a symptom, and a signal* (pp. 137–156). Cambridge, UK: Cambridge University Press.

Greenberger, E., Chen, C., Tallym, S. R., & Dong, Q. (2000). Family, peer, and individual correlates of depressive symptomology among U. S. and Chinese adolescents. *Journal of Consulting and Clinical Psychology, 68,* 209–219.

Greenberger, E., O'Neil, R., & Nagel, S. K. (1994). Linking workplace and home-place: Relations between the nature of adults' work and their parenting behaviors. *Developmental Psychology, 30,* 990–1002.

Greene, K., Krcmar, M., Walters, L. H., Rubin, D. L., Hale, J., & Hale, L. (2000). Targeting adolescent risk-taking behaviors: The contributions of egocentrism and sensation-seeking. *Journal of Adolescence, 23,* 439–461.

Greene, S. M., Anderson, E., Hetherington, E. M., Forgath, M. S., & DeGarmo, D. S. (2003). Risk and resilience after divorce. In R. Walsh (Ed.), *Normal family processes* (pp. 96–120). New York: Guilford.

Greenfield, P. (1992, June). *Notes and references for developmental psychology.* Conference on Making Basic Texts in Psychology More Culture-Inclusive and Culture-Sensitive, Western Washington University, Bellingham, WA.

Greenfield, P. M. (1994). Independence and interdependence as developmental scripts: Implications for theory, research, and practice. In P. M. Greenfield & R. R. Cocking (Eds.), *Cross-cultural roots of minority child development* (pp. 1–37). Hillsdale, NJ: Erlbaum.

Greenfield, P. M., Maynard, A. E., & Childs, C. P. (2000). History, culture, learning, and development. *Cross-Cultural Research, 34,* 351–374.

Greenfield, P. M., Quiroz, B., & Raeff, C. (2000). Cross-cultural conflict and harmony in the social construction of the child. In S. Harkness, C. Raeff, & C. M. Super (Eds.), *Variability in the social construction of the child* (pp. 93–108). San Francisco: Jossey-Bass.

Greenhill, L. L., Halperin, J. M., & Abikoff, H. (1999). Stimulant medications. *Journal of the American Academy of Child and Adolescent Psychiatry, 38,* 503–512.

Greenhoot, A. F. (2000). Remembering and understanding: The effects of changes in underlying knowledge on children's recollections. *Child Development, 71,* 1309–1328.

Greenough, W. T., & Black, J. E. (1992). Induction of brain structure by experience: Substrates for cognitive development. In M. R. Gunnar & C. A. Nelson (Eds.), *Minnesota Symposia on Child Psychology* (pp. 155–200). Hillsdale, NJ: Erlbaum.

Greenough, W. T., Wallace, C. S., Alcantara, A. A., Anderson, B. J., Hawrylak, N., Sirevaag, A. M., Weiler, I. J., & Withers, G. S. (1993). Development of the brain: Experience affects the structure of neurons, glia, and blood vessels. In N. J. Anastasiow & S. Harel (Eds.), *At-risk infants: Interventions, families, and research* (pp. 173–185). Baltimore: Paul H. Brookes.

Greenspan, S. I., & Shanker, S. G. (2004). *The first idea: How symbols, language, and intelligence evolved from our primate ancestors to modern humans.* Cambridge, MA: Da Capo Press.

Gregg, V., Gibbs, J. C., & Fuller, D. (1994). Patterns of developmental delay in moral judgment by male and female delinquents. *Merrill-Palmer Quarterly, 40,* 538–553.

Gresham, F. M., & MacMillan, D. L. (1997). Social competence and affective characteristics of students with mild disabilities. *Review of Educational Research, 67,* 377–415.

Grigorenko, E. L., & Sternberg, R. J. (1998). Dynamic testing. *Psychological Bulletin, 124,* 75–111.

Grigorenko, E. L., & Sternberg, R. J. (2001). Analytical, creative, and practical intelligence as predictors of self-reported adaptive functioning: A case study in Russia. *Intelligence, 29,* 57–73.

Grissmer, D., Flanagan, A., Kawata, J., & Williamson, S. (2000). *Improving student achievement: What do NAEP test scores tell us?* Santa Monica: RAND Corporation.

Grody, W. W. (1999). Cystic fibrosis: Molecular diagnosis, population screening, and public policy. *Archives of Pathology and Laboratory Medicine, 123,* 1041–1046.

Grolnick, W. S., Bridges, L. J., & Connell, J. P. (1996). Emotion regulation in two-year-olds: Strategies and emotional expression in four contexts. *Child Development, 67,* 928–941.

Grolnick, W. S., Kurowski, C. O., Dunlap, K. G., & Hevey, C. (2000). Parental resources and the transition to junior high. *Journal of Research on Adolescence, 10,* 465–488.

Gronau, R. C., & Waas, G. A. (1997). Delay of gratification and cue utilization: An examination of children's social information processing. *Merrill-Palmer Quarterly, 43,* 305–322.

Groome, L. J., Swiber, M. J., Atterbury, J. L., Bentz, L. S., & Holland, S. B. (1997). Similarities and differences in behavioral state organization during sleep periods in the perinatal infant before and after birth. *Child Development, 68,* 1–11.

Groome, L. J., Swiber, M. J., Holland, S. B., Bentz, L. S., Atterbury, J. L., & Trimm, R. F., III. (1999). Spontaneous motor activity in the perinatal infant before and after birth: Stability in individual differences. *Developmental Psychobiology, 35,* 15–24.

Gross, M. (1993). *Exceptionally gifted children.* London: Routledge.

Grossmann, K., Grossmann, K. E., Fremmer-Bombik, E., Kindler, H., Scheuerer-Englisch, H., & Zimmermann, P. (2002). The uniqueness of the child–father attachment relationship: Fathers' sensitive and challenging play as a pivotal variable in a 16-year longitudinal study. *Social Development, 11,* 307–331.

Grossmann, K., Grossmann, K. E., Spangler, G., Suess, G., & Unzner, L. (1985). Maternal sensitivity and newborns' orientation responses as related to quality of attachment in Northern Germany. In I. Bretherton & E. Waters (Eds.), *Growing points of attachment theory and research. Monographs of the Society for Research in Child Development, 50* (1–2, Serial No. 209).

Grotevant, H. D. (1978). Sibling constellations and sex-typing of interests in adolescence. *Child Development, 49,* 540–542.

Grotevant, H. D. (1998). Adolescent development in family contexts. In N. Eisenberg (Ed.), Handbook of child psychology: Vol. 3. Social, emotional, and personality development (5th ed., pp. 1097–1149). New York: Wiley.

Grotevant, H. D., & Cooper, C. R. (1998). Individuality and connectedness in adolescent development: Review and prospects for research on identity, relationships, and context. In E. Skoe & A. von der Lippe (Eds.), *Personality development in adolescence* (pp. 3–37). London: Routledge & Kegan Paul.

Grotevant, H. D., & Kohler, J. K. (1999). Adoptive families. In M. E. Lamb (Ed.), *Parenting and child development in "nontraditional" families* (pp. 161–190). Mahwah, NJ: Erlbaum.

Grow-Maienza, J., Hahn, D.-D., & Joo, C.-A. (2001). Mathematics instruction in Korean primary schools: Structures, processes, and a linguistic analysis of questioning. *Journal of Educational Psychology, 93,* 363–376.

Grusec, J. E. (1988). *Social development: History, theory, and research.* New York: Springer-Verlag.

Grusec, J. E., & Goodnow, J. J. (1994). Impact of parental discipline methods on the child's internalization of values: A reconceptualization of current points of view. *Developmental Psychology, 30,* 4–19.

Guay, F., LaRose, S., & Boivin, M. (2004). Academic self-concept and educational attainment level: A ten-year longitudinal study. *Self and Identity, 3,* 53–68.

Guay, F., Marsh, H. W., & Boivin, M. (2003). Academic self-concept and academic achievement: Developmental perspectives on their causal ordering. *Journal of Educational Psychology, 95,* 124–136.

Guerra, N. G., Attar, B., & Weissberg, R. P. (1997). Prevention of aggression and violence among inner-city youths. In D. M. Stoff, J. Breiling, & J. D. Maser (Eds.), *Handbook of antisocial behavior* (pp. 375–383). New York: Wiley.

Guerra, N. G., & Slaby, R. G. (1990). Cognitive mediators of aggression in adolescent offenders: 2. Intervention. *Developmental Psychology, 26,* 269–277.

Guilford, J. P. (1985). The structure-of-intellect model. In B. B. Wolman (Ed.), *Handbook of intelligence* (pp. 225–266). New York: Wiley.

Gullone, E. (2000). The development of normal fear: A century of research. *Clinical Psychology Review, 20,* 429–451.

Gunnar, M. R., Bruce, J., & Grotevant, H. D. (2000). International adoption of institutionally reared children: Research and policy. *Development and Psychopathology, 12,* 677–693.

Gunnar, M. R., & Cheatham, C. L. (2003). Brain and behavior interfaces: Stress and the developing brain. *Infant Mental Health Journal, 24,* 195–211.

Gunnar, M. R., Morison, S. J., Chisholm, K., & Schuder, M. (2001). Salivary cortisol levels in children adopted from Romanian orphanages. *Development and Psychopathology, 13,* 611–628.

Gunnar, M. R., & Nelson, C. A. (1994). Event-related potentials in year-old infants: Relations with emotionality and cortisol. *Child Development, 65,* 80–94.

Gunnoe, M. L., & Mariner, C. L. (1997). Toward a developmental-contextual model of the effects of parental spanking on children's aggression. *Archives of Pediatrics and Adolescent Medicine, 151,* 768–775.

Guo, G., & VanWey, L. K. (1999). Sibship size and intellectual development: Is the relationship causal? *American Sociological Review, 64,* 169–187.

Gurucharri, C., & Selman, F. L. (1982). The development of interpersonal understanding during childhood, preadolescence, and adolescence: A longitudinal follow-up study. *Child Development, 53,* 924–927.

Gustafson, G. E., Green, J. A., & Cleland, J. W. (1994). Robustness of individual identity in the cries of human infants. *Developmental Psychobiology, 27,* 1–9.

Gustafson, G. E., Wood, R. M., & Green, J. A. (2000). Can we hear the causes of infants' crying? In R. G. Barr, B. Hopkins, & J. A. Green (Eds.), *Crying as a sign, a symptom, and a signal* (pp. 8–22). New York: Cambridge University Press.

Gutman, L. M., Sameroff, A. J., & Cole, R. (2003). Academic growth curve trajectories from 1st grade to 12th grade: Effects of multiple social risk factors and preschool child factors. *Developmental Psychology, 39,* 777–790.

Gutman, L. M., Sameroff, A. J., & Eccles, J. S. (2002). The academic achievement of African-American students during early adolescence: An examination of multiple risk, promotive, and protective factors. *American Journal of Community Psychology, 39,* 367–399.

Gwiazda, J., & Birch, E. E. (2001). Perceptual development: Vision. In E. B. Goldstein (Ed.), *Blackwell handbook of perception* (pp. 636–668). Oxford: Blackwell.

Haas, L. (2003). Women in Sweden. In L. Walter (Ed.), *The Greenwood encyclopedia of women's issues worldwide: Europe.* Westport, CT: Greenwood Press.

Hack, M., Flannery, D. J., Schluchter, M., Cartar, L., Borawski, E., & Klein, N. (2002). Outcomes in young adulthood for very-low-birth-weight infants. *New England Journal of Medicine, 346,* 149–157.

Haden, C. A., Haine, R. A., & Fivush, R. (1997). Developing narrative structure in parent–child reminiscing across the preschool years. *Developmental Psychology, 33,* 295–307.

Hagekull, B., Bohlin, G., & Rydell, A. (1997). Maternal sensitivity, infant temperament, and the development of early feeding problems. *Infant Mental Health Journal, 18,* 92–106.

Hagerman, R. J., & Hagerman, P. J. (2002). Fragile X syndrome. In P. Howlin & O. Udwin (Eds.), *Outcomes in neurodevelopmental and genetic disorders* (pp. 198–219). New York: Cambridge University Press.

Haidt, J. (2001). The emotional dog and its rational tail: A social intuitionist approach to moral judgment. *Psychological Review, 108,* 814–834.

Haight, W. L., & Miller, P. J. (1993). *Pretending at home: Early development in a sociocultural context.* Albany, NY: SUNY Press.

Hainline, L. (1998). The development of basic visual abilities. In A. Slater (Ed.), *Perceptual development: Visual, auditory, and speech perception in infancy* (pp. 37–44). Hove, UK: Psychology Press.

Haith, M. M. (1994). Visual expectation as the first step toward the development

of future-oriented processes. In M. M. Haith, J. B. Benson, R. J. Roberts, Jr., & B. Pennington (Eds.), *The development of future-oriented processes* (pp. 11–38). Chicago: University of Chicago Press.

Haith, M. M. (1999). Some thoughts about claims for innate knowledge and infant physical reasoning. *Developmental Science, 2,* 153–156.

Haith, M. M., & Benson, J. B. (1998). Infant cognition. In D. Kuhn & R. S. Siegler (Eds.), *Handbook of child psychology: Vol. 2. Cognition, perception, and language* (5th ed., pp. 199–254). New York: Wiley.

Hakuta, K. (1999). The debate on bilingual education. *Developmental and Behavioral Pediatrics, 20,* 36–37.

Hakuta, K., Bialystok, E., & Wiley, E. (2003). Critical evidence: A test of the critical period hypothesis for second-language acquisition. *Psychological Science, 14,* 31–38.

Hale, C. M., & Tager-Flusberg, H. (2003). The influence of language on theory of mind: A training study. *Developmental Science, 6,* 346–359.

Hales, C. N., & Ozanne, S. E. (2003). The dangerous road of catch-up growth. *Journal of Physiology, 547,* 5–10.

Halfon, N., & McLearn, K. T. (2002). Families with children under 3: What we know and implications for results and policy. In N. Halfon & K. T. McLearn (Eds.), *Child rearing in America: Challenges facing parents with young children* (pp. 367–412). New York: Cambridge University Press.

Halford, G. S. (2002). Information-processing models of cognitive development. In U. Goswami (Ed.), *Blackwell handbook of childhood cognitive development* (pp. 555–574). Malden, MA: Blackwell.

Hall, C. M., Jones, J. A., Meyer-Bahlburg, H. F. L., Dolezal, C., Coleman, M., & Foster, P. (2004). Behavioral and physical masculinization are related to genotype in girls with congenital adrenal hyperplasia. *Journal of Clinical Endocrinology and Metabolism, 89,* 419–424.

Hall, D. G., & Graham, S. A. (1999). Lexical form class information guides word-to-object mapping in preschoolers. *Child Development, 70,* 78–91.

Hall, D. G., Lee, S. C., & Belanger, J. (2001). Young children's use of syntactic cues to learn proper names and count nouns. *Developmental Psychology, 37,* 298–307.

Hall, G. S. (1904). *Adolescence* (Vols. 1–2). New York: Appleton-Century-Crofts.

Halle, T. G. (2003). Emotional development and well-being. In M. H. Bornstein, L. Davidson, C. L. M. Keyes, K. A. Moore, & The Center for Child Well-Being (Eds.), *Well-being: Positive development across the life course* (pp. 125–138). Mahwah, NJ: Erlbaum.

Halle, T. G., Kurtz-Costes, B., & Mahoney, J. L. (1997). Family influences on school achievement in low-income, African-American children. *Journal of Educational Psychology, 89,* 527–537.

Hallett, M. (2000). Brain plasticity and recovery from hemiplegia. *Journal of Medical Speech-Language Pathology, 9,* 107–115.

Halliday, J. L., Watson, L. F., Lumley, J., Danks, D. M., & Sheffield, L. S.

(1995). New estimates of Down syndrome risks at chorionic villus sampling, amniocentesis, and live birth in women of advanced maternal age from a uniquely defined population. *Prenatal Diagnosis, 15,* 455–465.

Hallinan, M. T., & Kubitschek, W. N. (1999). Curriculum differentiation and high school achievement. *Social Psychology of Education, 3,* 41–62.

Halpern, C. T., Udry, J. R., & Suchindran, C. (1997). Testosterone predicts initiation of coitus in adolescent females. *Psychosomatic Medicine, 59,* 161–171.

Halpern, D. F. (1997). Sex differences in intelligence. *American Psychologist, 52,* 1091–1102.

Halpern, D. F. (2000). *Sex differences in cognitive abilities* (3rd ed.). Mahwah, NJ: Erlbaum.

Halpern, D. F. (2004). A cognitive-process taxonomy for sex differences in cognitive abilities. *Current Directions in Psychological Science, 13,* 135–139.

Halpern-Felsher, B. L., & Cauffman, E. (2001). Costs and benefits of a decision: Decision-making competence in adolescents and adults. *Journal of Applied Developmental Psychology, 22,* 257–273.

Hamer, D. H., Hu, S., Magnuson, V. L., Hu, N., & Pattatucci, A. M. L. (1993). A linkage between DNA markers on the X chromosome and male sexual orientation. *Science, 261,* 321–327.

Hamilton, C. E. (2000). Continuity and discontinuity of attachment from infancy through adolescence. *Child Development, 71,* 690–694.

Hamilton, S. F., & Hamilton, M. A. (2000). Research, intervention, and social change: Improving adolescents' career opportunities. In L. J. Crockett & R. K. Silbereisen (Eds.), *Negotiating adolescence in times of social change* (pp. 267–283). New York: Cambridge University Press.

Hamm, J. V. (2000). Do birds of a feather flock together? The variable bases for African American, Asian American, and European American adolescents' selection of similar friends. *Developmental Psychology, 36,* 209–219.

Hammes, B., & Laitman, C. J. (2003). Diethylstilbestrol (DES) update: Recommendations for the identification and management of DES-exposed individuals. *Journal of Midwifery and Women's Health, 48,* 19–29.

Hamre, B. K., & Pianta, R. C. (2001). Early teacher–child relationships and the trajectory of children's school outcomes through eighth grade. *Child Development, 72,* 625–638.

Han, J. J., Leichtman, M. D., & Wang, Q. (1998). Autobiographical memory in Korean, Chinese, and American children. *Developmental Psychology, 34,* 701–713.

Han, W.-J., & Waldfogel, J. (2003). Parental leave: The impact of recent legislation on parents' leave taking. *Demography, 40,* 191–200.

Hanawalt, B. A. (1993). *Growing up in medieval London: The experience of childhood in history.* New York: Oxford University Press.

Hanawalt, B. A. (2003). The child in the Middle Ages and the Renaissance. In W. Koops & M. Zuckerman (Eds.), *Beyond the century of childhood: Cultural history and developmental*

psychology. Philadelphia: University of Pennsylvania Press.

Handley, S. J., Capon, A., Beveridge, M., Dennis, I., & Evans, J. St. B. T. (2004). Working memory, inhibitory control and the development of children's reasoning. *Thinking and Reasoning, 10,* 175–195.

Hankin, B. I., Abramson, L. Y., Moffitt, T. E., Silva, P. A., & McGee, R. (1998). Development of depression from preadolescence to young adulthood: Emerging gender differences in a 10-year longitudinal study. *Journal of Abnormal Psychology, 107,* 128–140.

Hansen, M., Kurinczuk, J. J., Bower, C., & Webb, S. (2002). The risk of major birth defects after intracytoplasmic sperm injection and in vitro fertilization. *New England Journal of Medicine, 346,* 725–730.

Hanson, T. L. (1999). Does parental conflict explain why divorce is negatively associated with child welfare? *Social Forces, 77,* 1283–1316.

Hanvey, L., & Kunz, J. L. (2000). *Immigrant youth in Canada.* Toronto, ON: Canadian Council on Social Development.

Hardy, C. L., Bukowski, W. M., & Sippola, L. K. (2002). Stability and change in peer relationships during the transition to middle-level school. *Journal of Early Adolescence, 22,* 117–142.

Harley, B., & Jean, G. (1999). Vocabulary skills of French immersion students in their second language. *Zeitschrift für Interkulterellen Fremdsprachenunterricht, 4*(2). Retrieved from www.ualberta.ca

Harley, K., & Reese, E. (1999). Origins of autobiographical memory. *Developmental Psychology, 35,* 1338–1348.

Harlow, H. F. (1969). Age-mate or peer affectional system. In D. S. Lehrman, R. A. Hinde, & E. Shaw (Eds.), *Advances in the study of behavior* (Vol. 2, pp. 333–383). New York: Academic Press.

Harlow, H. F., & Zimmerman, R. (1959). Affectional responses in the infant monkey. *Science, 130,* 421–432.

Harold, G. T., Shelton, K. H., Goeke-Morey, M. C., & Cummings, E. M. (2004). Marital conflict, child emotional security about family relationships and child adjustment. *Social Development, 13,* 350–376.

Harris Poll. (2001). A 21st century juxtaposition: Grandma, grandpa, and high technology. *The Harris Poll #12.* Retrieved from www.harrisinteractive.com/harris_poll/index.asp?PID=207

Harris, G. (1997). Development of taste perception and appetite regulation. In G. Bremner, A. Slater, & G. Butterworth (Eds.), *Infant development: Recent advances* (pp. 9–30). East Sussex, UK: Erlbaum.

Harris, J. R. (1998). *The nurture assumption: Why children turn out the way they do.* New York: Free Press.

Harris, J. R. (2002). Beyond the nurture assumption: Testing hypotheses about the child's environment. In J. G. Borkowski & S. L. Ramey (Eds.), *Parenting and the child's world* (pp. 3–20). Mahwah, NJ: Erlbaum.

Harris, P. L., Brown, E., Marriott, C., Whitall, S., & Harmer, S. (1991). Monsters, ghosts and witches: Testing the limits of the fantasy–reality distinction in young children. *British Journal of Developmental Psychology, 9,* 105–123.

Harris, P. L., & Leevers, H. J. (2000). Reasoning from false premises. In P. Mitchell & K. J. Riggs (Eds.), *Children's reasoning and the mind* (pp. 67–99). Hove, UK: Psychology Press.

Harrison, A. O., Wilson, M. N., Pine, C. J., Chan, S. Q., & Buriel, R. (1994). Family ecologies of ethnic minority children. In G. Handel & G. G. Whitchurch (Eds.), *The psychosocial interior of the family* (pp. 187–210). New York: Aldine De Gruyter.

Harrison, Y. (2004). The relationship between daytime exposure to light and night-time sleep in 6–12-week-old infants. *Journal of Sleep Research, 13,* 345–352.

Harrist, A. W., Zaia, A. F., Bates, J. E., Dodge, K. A., & Pettit, G. S. (1997). Subtypes of social withdrawal in early childhood: Sociometric status and social–cognitive differences across four years. *Child Development, 68,* 278–294.

Hart, B. (2004). What toddlers talk about. *First Language, 24,* 91–106.

Hart, B., & Risley, T. R. (1995). *Meaningful differences in the everyday experience of young American children.* Baltimore: Paul H. Brookes.

Hart, C. H. (1999, November). *Combating the myth that parents don't matter.* Address presented at the World Congress of Families II, Geneva, Switzerland.

Hart, C. H., Burts, D. C., Durland, M. A., Charlesworth, R., DeWolf, M., & Fleege, P. O. (1998). Stress behaviors and activity type participation of preschoolers in more and less developmentally appropriate classrooms: SES and sex differences. *Journal of Research in Childhood Education, 13,* 176–196.

Hart, C. H., Nelson, D. A., Robinson, C. C., Olsen, S. F., & McNeilly-Choque, M. K. (1998). Overt and relational aggression in Russian nursery-school-age children: Parenting style and marital linkages. *Developmental Psychology, 34,* 687–697.

Hart, C. H., Newell, L. D., & Olsen, S. F. (2002). Parenting skills and social/communicative competence in childhood. In J. O. Greene & B. R. Burleson (Eds.), *Handbook of communication and social interaction skill.* Hillsdale, NJ: Erlbaum.

Hart, C. H., Newell, L. D., & Olsen, S. F. (2003). Parenting skills and social/communicative competence in childhood. In J. O. Greene & B. R. Burleson (Eds.), *Handbook of communication and social interaction* (pp. 753–797). Hillsdale, NJ: Erlbaum.

Hart, C. H., Newell, L. D., & Olsen, S. F. (2004). Parenting skills and social–communicative competence in childhood. In J. O. Greene & B. R. Burleson (Eds.), *Handbook of communication and social interaction skills* (pp. 753–797). Mahwah, NJ: Erlbaum.

Hart, C. H., Yang, C., Charlesworth, R., & Burts, D. C. (2003, April). *Kindergarten teaching practices: Associations with later child academic and social/emotional adjustment to school.* Paper presented at the biennial meeting of the Society for Research in Child Development, Tampa, FL.

Hart, C. H., Yang, C., Nelson, D. A., Jin, S., Bazarskaya, N., Nelson, L., Wu, X., & Wu, P. (1998). Peer contact patterns, parenting practices, and preschoolers' social competence in China, Russia, and the United States. In P. Slee & K. Rigby (Eds.), *Children's peer relations* (pp. 3–30). New York: Routledge.

Hart, C. H., Yang, C., Nelson, L. J., Robinson, C. C., Olsen, J. A., & Nelson, D. A. (2000). Peer acceptance in early childhood and subtypes of socially withdrawn behavior in China, Russia, and the United States. *International Journal of Behavioral Development, 24,* 73–81.

Hart, D., & Atkins, R. (2002). Civic competence in urban youth. *Applied Developmental Science, 6,* 227–236.

Hart, D., Atkins, R., & Ford, D. (1998). Urban America as a context for the development of moral identity in adolescence. *Journal of Social Issues, 54,* 513–530.

Hart, D., & Fegley, S. (1995). Prosocial behavior and caring in adolescence: Relations to self-understanding and social judgment. *Child Development, 66,* 1346–1359.

Hart, S., Field, T., & Roitfarb, M. (1999). Depressed mothers' assessments of their neonates' behaviors. *Infant Mental Health Journal, 20,* 200–210.

Harter, S. (1996). Developmental changes in self-understanding across the 5 to 7 shift. In A. J. Sameroff & M. M. Haith (Eds.), *The five to seven year shift* (pp. 207–236). Chicago: University of Chicago Press.

Harter, S. (1998). The development of self-representations. In N. Eisenberg (Ed.), *Handbook of child psychology: Vol. 3. Social, emotional, and personality development* (5th ed., pp. 553–618). New York: Wiley.

Harter, S. (1999). *The construction of self: A developmental perspective.* New York: Guilford.

Harter, S. (2003). The development of self-representations during childhood and adolescence. In M. R. Leary & J. P. Tangney (Eds.), *Handbook of self and identity* (pp. 610–642). New York: Guilford.

Harter, S., Waters, P., & Whitesell, N. R. (1998). Relational self-worth: Differences in perceived worth as a person across interpersonal contexts among adolescents. *Child Development, 69,* 756–766.

Harter, S., & Whitesell, N. R. (1989). Developmental changes in children's understanding of simple, multiple, and blended emotion concepts. In C. Saarni & P. Harris (Eds.), *Children's understanding of emotion* (pp. 81–116). Cambridge, UK: Cambridge University Press.

Harter, S., & Whitesell, N. R. (2003). Beyond the debate: Why some adolescents report stable self-worth over time and situation, whereas others report changes in self-worth. *Journal of Personality, 71,* 1027–1058.

Hartshorn, K., Rovee-Collier, C., Gerhardstein, P., Bhatt, R. S., Klein, P. J., Aaron, F., Wondoloski, T. L., & Wurtzel, N. (1998a). Developmental changes in the specificity of memory over the first year of life. *Developmental Psychobiology, 33,* 61–68.

Hartshorn, K., Rovee-Collier, C., Gerhardstein, P., Bhatt, R. S., Wondoloski, T. L., Klein, P., Gilch, J., Wurtzel, N., & Campos-de-Carvalho, M. (1998b). The ontogeny of long-term memory over the first year-and-a-half of life. *Developmental Psychobiology, 32,* 69–89.

Hartup, W. W. (1983). Peer relations. In E. M. Hetherington (Ed.), *Handbook of child psychology: Vol. 4. Socialization, personality, and social development* (4th ed., pp. 103–196). New York: Wiley.

Hartup, W. W. (1996). The company they keep: Friendships and their developmental significance. *Child Development, 67,* 1–13.

Hartup, W. W., & Abecassis, M. (2004). Friends and enemies. In P. K. Smith & C. H. Hart (Eds.), *Blackwell handbook of childhood social development* (pp. 285–306). Malden, MA: Blackwell.

Hartup, W. W., & Stevens, N. (1999). Friendships and adaptation across the life span. *Current Directions in Psychological Science, 8,* 76–79.

Harvey, E. (1999). Short-term and long-term effects of early parental employment on children of the National Longitudinal Survey of Youth. *Developmental Psychology, 35,* 445–459.

Haselager, J. T., Hartup, W. W., van Lieshout, C. F. M., & Riksen-Walraven, J. M. A. (1998). Similarities between friends and nonfriends in middle childhood. *Child Development, 69,* 1198–1208.

Haskett, M. E., Scott, S. S., Grant, R., Ward, C. S., & Robinson, C. (2003). Child-related cognitions and affective functioning of physically abusive and comparison parents. *Child Abuse and Neglect, 27,* 663–686.

Hastings, P. D., Zahn-Waxler, C., Usher, B., Robinson, J. L., & Bridges, D. (2000). The development of concern for others in children with behavior problems. *Developmental Psychology, 36,* 531–546.

Hatano, G. (1994). Introduction: Conceptual change—Japanese perspectives. *Human Development, 37,* 189–197.

Hatton, D. D., Bailey, D. B., Jr., Burchinal, M. R., & Ferrell, K. A. (1997). Developmental growth curves of preschool children with vision impairments. *Child Development, 68,* 788–806.

Hauck, F. R., Herman, S. M., Donovan, M., Iyasu, S., Merrick Moore, C., & Donoghue, E. (2003). Sleep environment and the risk of sudden infant death syndrome in an urban population: The Chicago Infant Mortality Study. *Pediatrics, 111,* 1207–1214.

Hausfather, A., Toharia, A., LaRoche, C., & Engelsmann, F. (1997). Effects of age of entry, day-care quality, and family characteristics on preschool behavior. *Journal of Child Psychology and Psychiatry, 38,* 441–448.

Hauth, J. C., Goldenberg, R. L., Parker, C. R., Cutter, G. R., & Cliver, S. P. (1995). Low-dose aspirin—lack of association with an increase in abruptio placentae or perinatal mortality. *Obstetrics and Gynecology, 85,* 1055–1058.

Hawkins, D. J., & Lam, T. (1987). Teacher practices, social development, and delinquency. In J. D. Burchard & S. N. Burchard (Eds.), *Prevention of delinquent behavior* (pp. 241–274). Newbury Park, CA: Sage.

Hawkins, J. N. (1994). Issues of motivation in Asian education. In H. F. O'Neil, Jr., & M. Drillings (Eds.), *Motivation: Theory and research* (pp. 101–115). Hillsdale, NJ: Erlbaum.

Hawley, P. A. (2003a). Prosocial and coercive configurations of resource control in early adolescence: A case for the well-adapted Machiavellian. *Merrill-Palmer Quarterly, 49,* 279–309.

Hawley, P. A. (2003b). Strategies of control, aggression, and morality in preschoolers: An evolutionary perspective. *Journal of Experimental Child Psychology, 85,* 213–235.

Hay, D. F., Pawlby, S., Angold, A., Harold, G. T., & Sharp, D. (2003). Pathways to violence in the children of mothers who were depressed postpartum. *Developmental Psychology, 39,* 1983–1094.

Hayne, H. (2004). Infant memory development: Implications for childhood amnesia. *Developmental Review, 24,* 33–73.

Hayne, H., Boniface, J., & Barr, R. (2000). The development of declarative memory in human infants: Age-related changes in deferred imitation. *Behavioral Neuroscience, 114,* 77–83.

Hayne, H., & Rovee-Collier, C. K. (1995). The organization of reactivated memory in infancy. *Child Development, 66,* 893–906.

Hayne, H., Rovee-Collier, C. K., & Perris, E. E. (1987). Categorization and memory retrieval by three-month-olds. *Child Development, 58,* 750–767.

Hayslip, B., Jr. (1994). Stability of intelligence. In R. J. Sternberg (Ed.), *Encyclopedia of human intelligence* (Vol. 2, pp. 1019–1026). New York: Macmillan.

Hazan, C., & Shaver P. R. (1994). Attachment as an organizational framework for research on close relationships. *Psychological Inquiry, 5,* 1–22.

Head Start Bureau. (2004). 2004 Head Start fact sheet. Retrieved from www.acf.dhhs.gov/programs/opa/facts/headst/htm

Head, E., & Lott, I. T. (2004). Down syndrome and beta-amyloid deposition. *Current Opinion in Neurology, 17,* 95–100.

Health Canada. (2000). *Paediatrics and Child Health: Canadian Report on Immunization.* Retrieved from www.hc-sc.gc.ca

Health Canada. (2001). *Prenatal and postpartum women and tobacco.* Ottawa: Tobacco Control Programme. Retrieved from www.hc-sc.gc.ca/hecs-sesc/tobacco/pdf/prenatal.pdf

Health Canada. (2002a). Breastfeeding. *Perinatal Surveillance System.* Retrieved from www.hc-sc.gc.ca/pphb-dgspsp/rhs-ssg/factshts/brstfd_e.html

Health Canada. (2002b). *Healthy Canadians: A federal report on comparable health indicators.* Retrieved from www.hc-sc.gc.ca/iacb-dgiac/arad-draa/english/accountability/indicators/html#high

Health Canada. (2002c). *Proceedings of a meeting of the Expert Advisory Group on Rubella in Canada.* Retrieved from www.hc-sc.gc.ca/pphb-dgspsp/publicat/ccdr-rmtc/02vol28/28s4

Health Canada. (2003a). *Acting on what we know: Preventing youth suicide in first nations.* Ottawa, Canada: Author.

Health Canada. (2003b). Alcohol and pregnancy. Retrieved from www.hc-sc.gc.ca/pphb-dgspsp/rhs-ssg/factshts/alcprg_e.html

Health Canada. (2003c). *Canadian peri-natal health report 2003.* Ottawa: Minister of Public Works and Government Services.

Health Canada. (2004a). *Aboriginal Head Start: Program overview.* Retrieved from www.phac-aspc.gc.ca/dca-dea/programs-mes/ahs_overview_e.html#allocation

Health Canada. (2004b). Canada Prenatal Nutrition Program (CPNP). Retrieved from www.phac-aspc.gc.ca/dca-dea/programs-mes/cpnp_main_e.html

Health Canada. (2004c). *Exclusive breast-feeding duration—2004 Health Canada recommendation.* Retrieved from www.hc-sc.gc.ca/hpfb-dgpsa/onpp-bppn/exclusive_breastfeeding_duration_e.html

Health Canada. (2004d). Women and HIV/AIDS in Canada. Retrieved from www.actoronto.org/website/home.nsf/pages/womenhivaidscanada

Hearold, S. (1986). A synthesis of 1,043 effects of television on social behavior. In G. Comstock (Ed.), *Public communications and behavior* (Vol. 1, pp. 65–133). New York: Academic Press.

Heath, S. B. (1982). Questioning at home and at school: A comparative study. In G. Spindler (Ed.), *Doing the ethnography of schooling: Educational anthropology in action* (pp. 102–127). New York: Holt.

Heath, S. B. (1989). Oral and literate traditions among black Americans living in poverty. *American Psychologist, 44,* 367–373.

Heath, S. B. (1990). The children of Trackton's children: Spoken and written language and social change. In J. Stigler, G. Herdt, & R. A. Shweder (Eds.), *Cultural psychology: Essays on comparative human development* (pp. 496–519). New York: Cambridge University Press.

Heckman, J. J., & Masterov, D. V. (2004). *The productivity argument for investing in young children.* Working Paper 5, Invest in Kids Working Group, Committee for Economic Development. Retrieved from jenni.uchicago.edu/Invest

Hedges, L. V., & Nowell, A. (1995). Sex differences in mental test scores: Variability and numbers of high-scoring individuals. *Science, 269,* 41–45.

Heinz, W. R. (1999a). Introduction: Transitions to employment in a cross-national perspective. In W. R. Heinz (Ed.), *From education to work: Cross-national perspectives* (pp. 1–21). New York: Cambridge University Press.

Heinz, W. R. (1999b). Job-entry patterns in a life-course perspective. In W. R. Heinz (Ed.), *From education to work: Cross-national perspectives* (pp. 214–231). New York: Cambridge University Press.

Helburn, S. W. (Ed.). (1995). *Cost, quality and child outcomes in child care centers.* Denver: University of Colorado.

Helms-Lorenz, M., Van de Vijver, F. J. R., & Poortinga, Y. H. (2003). Cross-lcultural differences in cognitive performance and Spearman's hypothesis: g or c? *Intelligence, 31,* 9–29.

Helwig, C. C. (1995). Adolescents' and young adults' conceptions of civil liberties: Freedom of speech and religion. *Child Development, 66,* 152–166.

Helwig, C. C., Arnold, M. L., Tan, D., & Boyd, D. (2003). Chinese adolescents'

reasoning about democratic and authority-based decision making in peer, family, and school contexts. *Child Development, 74,* 783–800.

Helwig, C. C., & Jasiobedzka, U. (2001). The relation between law and morality: Children's reasoning about socially beneficial and unjust laws. *Child Development, 72,* 1382–1393.

Helwig, C. C., & Kim, S. (1999). Children's evaluations of decision-making procedures in peer, family, and school contexts. *Child Development, 70,* 502–512.

Helwig, C. C., & Prencipe, A. (1999). Children's judgments of flags and flag-burning. *Child Development, 70,* 132–143.

Helwig, C. C., & Turiel, E. (2002). Civil liberties, autonomy, and democracy: Children's perspective. *International Journal of Law and Psychiatry, 25,* 253–270.

Helwig, C. C., Zelazo, P. D., & Wilson, M. (2001). Children's judgments of psychological harm in normal and non-canonical situations. *Child Development, 72,* 66–81.

Henderson, H. A., Marshall, P. J., Fox, N. A., & Rubin, K. H. (2004). Psychophysiological and behavioral evidence for varying forms and functions of nonsocial behavior in preschoolers. *Child Development, 75,* 251–263.

Hendrick, J., & Stange, T. (1991). Do actions speak louder than words? An effect of the functional use of language on dominant sex role behavior in boys and girls. *Early Childhood Research Quarterly, 6,* 565–576.

Hendricks, M., Guilford, J. P., & Hoepfner, R. (1969). *Measuring creative social intelligence.* (Reports from the Psychological Laboratory, University of Southern California No. 42).

Hennessy, K. D., Rabideau, G. J., & Cicchetti, D. (1994). Responses of physically abused and nonabused children to different forms of inter-adult anger. *Child Development, 65,* 815–828.

Henrich, C. C., Kuperminc, G. P., Sack, A., Blatt, S. J., & Leadbeater, B. J. (2000). Characteristics and homogeneity of early adolescent friendship groups: A comparison of male and female clique and nonclique members. *Applied Developmental Science, 4,* 15–26.

Henricsson, L., & Rydell, A.-M. (2004). Elementary school children with behavior problems: Teacher–child relations and self perception. A prospective study. *Merrill-Palmer Quarterly, 50,* 111–138.

Henry, B., Moffitt, T. E., Caspi, A., Langley, J., & Silva, P. A. (1994). On the "remembrance of things past": A longitudinal evaluation of the retrospective method. *Psychological Assessment, 6,* 92–101.

Hepper, P. G. (1997). Fetal habituation: Another Pandora's box? *Developmental Medicine and Child Neurology, 39,* 274–278.

Herdt, G., & Boxer, A. M. (1993). *Children of horizons: How gay and lesbian teens are leading a new way out of the closet.* Boston: Beacon Press.

Herman, L. M., & Uyeyama, R. K. (1999). The dolphin's grammatical competency: Comments on Kako. *Animal Learning and Behavior, 27,* 18–23.

Herman, M. R. (2004). Forced to choose: Some determinants of racial identification in multiracial adolescents. *Child Development, 75,* 730–748.

Herman, M. R., Dornbusch, S. M., Herron, M. C., & Herting, J. R. (1997). The influence of family regulation, connection, and psychological autonomy on six measures of adolescent functioning. *Journal of Adolescent Research, 12,* 34–67.

Hernandez, D. J. (1994, Spring). Children's changing access to resources: A historical perspective. *Social Policy Report of the Society for Research in Child Development, 8* (1).

Hernandez, F. D., & Carter, A. S. (1996). Infant response to mothers and fathers in the still-face paradigm. *Infant Behavior and Development, 19,* 502.

Herrera, E., Reissland, N., & Shepherd, J. (2004). Maternal touch and maternal child-directed speech: Effects of depressed mood in the postnatal period. *Journal of Affective Disorders, 81,* 29–39.

Herrnstein, R. J., & Murray, C. (1994). *The bell curve: Intelligence and class structure in American life.* New York: Free Press.

Hespos, S. J., & Baillargeon, R. (2001). Reasoning about containment events in very young infants. *Cognition, 78,* 207–245.

Hesse, E., & Main, M. (2000). Disorganized infant, child, and adult attachment: Collapse in behavioral and attentional strategies. *Journal of the American Psychoanalytic Association, 48,* 1097–1127.

Hetherington, E. M. (1995, April). *The changing American family and the well-being of children.* Master lecture presented at the biennial meeting of the Society for Research in Child Development, Indianapolis.

Hetherington, E. M. (1999). Social capital and the development of youth from nondivorced, divorced, and remarried families. In A. Collins (Ed.), *Minnesota Symposia on Child Psychology* (Vol. 29, pp. 177–209). Mahwah, NJ: Erlbaum.

Hetherington, E. M. (2003). Social support and the adjustment of children in divorced and remarried families. *Childhood, 10,* 237–254.

Hetherington, E. M., Henderson, S. H., & Reiss, D. (1999). Adolescent siblings in stepfamilies: Family functioning and adolescent adjustment. *Monographs of the Society for Research in Child Development, 64*(4, Serial No. 259).

Hetherington, E. M., & Jodl, K. M. (1994). Stepfamilies as settings for child development. In A. Booth & J. Dunn (Eds.), *Stepfamilies: Who benefits? Who does not?* (pp. 55–79). Hillsdale, NJ: Erlbaum.

Hetherington, E. M., & Kelly, J. (2002). *For better or worse: Divorce reconsidered.* New York: Norton.

Hetherington, E. M., & Stanley-Hagan, M. (1999). The adjustment of children with divorced parents: A risk and resiliency perspective. *Journal of Child Psychology and Psychiatry, 40,* 129–140.

Hetherington, E. M., & Stanley-Hagan, M. (2000). Diversity among stepfamilies. In D. H. Demo, K. R. Allen, & M. A. Fine (Eds.), *Handbook of family diversity* (pp. 173–196). New York: Oxford University Press.

Hetherington, E. M., & Stanley-Hagan, M. (2002). Parenting in divorced and remarried families. In M. H. Bornstein (Ed.), *Handbook of parenting: Vol. 3. Being and Becoming a Parent* (2nd ed., pp. 287–315). Mahwah, NJ: Erlbaum.

Hewlett, B. S. (1992). Husband–wife reciprocity and the father–infant relationship among Aka pygmies. In B. S. Hewlett (Ed.), *Father– child relations: Cultural and biosocial contexts* (pp. 153–176). New York: Aldine De Gruyter.

Hewlett, S. (2003). *Creating a life.* New York: Miramax.

Hewstone, M. (1996). Contact and categorization: Social psychological interventions to change intergroup relations. In C. N. Macrae, C. Stangor, & M. Hewstone (Eds.), *Stereotypes and stereotyping* (pp. 323–368). New York: Guilford.

Heyman, G. D., & Dweck, C. S. (1998). Children's thinking about traits: Implications for judgments of the self and others. *Child Development, 69,* 391–403.

Heyman, G. D., Dweck, C. S., & Cain, K. M. (1992). Young children's vulnerability to self-blame and helplessness: Relationship to beliefs about goodness. *Child Development, 63,* 401–415.

Heyman, G. D., & Gelman, S. A. (1999). The use of trait labels in making psychological inferences. *Child Development, 70,* 604–619.

Heyman, G. D., & Legare, C. H. (2004). Children's beliefs about gender differences in the academic and social domains. *Sex Roles, 50,* 227–239.

Hibell, B. (2001). *European School Survey Project on Alcohol and Drugs.* Stockholm: Swedish Council for Information on Alcohol and Other Drugs.

Hickling, A. K., & Wellman, H. M. (2001). The emergence of children's causal explanations and theories: Evidence from everyday conversation. *Developmental Psychology, 37,* 668–683.

Higley, J. D., Hopkins, W. D., Thompson, W. W., Byrne, E. A., Hirsch, R. M., & Suomi, S. J. (1992). Peers as primary attachment sources in yearling rhesus monkeys (*Macaca mulatta*). *Developmental Psychology, 28,* 1163–1171.

Hildreth, K., & Rovee-Collier, C. (2002). Forgetting functions of reactivated memories over the first year of life. *Developmental Psychobiology, 41,* 277–288.

Hildreth, K., Sweeney, B., & Rovee-Collier, C. (2003). Differential memory-preserving effects of reminders at 6 months. *Journal of Experimental Child Psychology, 84,* 41–62.

Hill, J. L., Brooks-Gunn, J., & Waldfogel, J. (2003). Sustained effects of high participation in an early intervention for low-birth-weight premature infants. *Developmental Psychology, 39,* 730–744.

Hill, N. E., Bush, K. R., & Roosa, M. W. (2003). Parenting and family socialization strategies and children's mental health: Low-income Mexican-American and Euro-American mothers and children. *Child Development, 74,* 189–204.

Hill, N. E., & Taylor, L. C. (2004). Parental school involvement and children's academic achievement: Pragmatics and issues. *Current Directions in Psychological Science, 13*, 161–164.

Hillis, S. D., Anda, R. F., Dube, S. R., Felitti, V. J., Marchbanks, P. A., & Marks, J. S. (2004). The association between adverse childhood experiences and adolescent pregnancy, long-term psychosocial consequences, and fetal death. *Pediatrics, 113*, 320–327.

Hinde, R. A. (1989). Ethological and relationships approaches. In R. Vasta (Ed.), *Annals of child development* (Vol. 6, pp. 251–285). Greenwich, CT: JAI Press.

Hines, M. (2003). Sex steroids and human behavior: Prenatal androgen exposure and sex-typical play behavior in children. *Annals of the New York Academy of Sciences, 1007*, 272–282.

Hines, M. (2004). *Brain gender.* New York: Oxford University Press.

Hines, M., Brook, C., & Conway, G. S. (2004). Androgen and psychosexual development: Core gender identity, sexual orientation, and recalled childhood gender role behavior in women and men with congenital adrenal hyperplasia (CAH). *Journal of Sex Research, 41*, 75–81.

Hines, M., & Green, R. (1991). Human hormonal and neural correlates of sex-typed behaviors. *Review of Psychiatry, 10*, 536–555.

Hinojosa, T., Sheu, C.-F., & Michel, G. F. (2003). Infant hand-use preference for grasping objects contributes to the development of a hand-use preference for manipulating objects. *Developmental Psychobiology, 43*, 328–334.

Hirschfeld, L. A. (1995). Do children have a theory of race? *Cognition, 54*, 209–252.

Hirschfeld, L. A. (1996). *Race in the making: Cognition, culture, and the child's construction of human kinds.* Cambridge, MA: MIT Press.

Hirsh-Pasek, K., & Golinkoff, R. M. (2003). *Einstein never used flash cards.* New York: Rodale.

Hock, H. S., Park, C. L., & Bjorklund, D. F. (1998). Temporal organization in children's strategy formation. *Journal of Experimental Child Psychology, 70*, 187–206.

Hodges, E. V. E., Boivin, M., Vitaro, F., & Bukowski, W. M. (1999). The power of friendship: Protection against an escalating cycle of peer victimization. *Developmental Psychology, 35*, 94–101.

Hodges, J., & Tizard, B. (1989). Social and family relationships of ex-institutional adolescents. *Journal of Child Psychology and Psychiatry, 30*, 77–97.

Hodges, R. M., & French, L. A. (1988). The effect of class and collection labels on cardinality, class-inclusion, and number conservation tasks. *Child Development, 59*, 1387–1396.

Hoff, E. (2003a). Causes and consequences of SES-related differences in parent-to-child speech. In M. H. Bornstein & R. H. Bradley (Eds.), *Socioeconomic status, parenting, and child development* (pp. 147–160). Mahwah, NJ: Erlbaum.

Hoff, E. (2003b). The specificity of environmental influence: Socioeconomic status affects early vocabulary development via maternal speech. *Child Development, 74*, 1368–1378.

Hoff, E. (2004). The specificity of environmental influence: Socioeconomic status affects early vocabulary development via maternal speech. *Child Development, 74*, 1368–1378.

Hoff, E., Laursen, B., & Tardiff, T. (2002). Socioeconomic status and parenting. In M. H. Bornstein (Ed.), *Handbook of parenting: Vol. 2. Biology and ecology of parenting* (2nd ed., 231–252). Mahwah, NJ: Erlbaum.

Hoff, E., & Naigles, L. (2002). How children use input to acquire a lexicon. *Child Development, 73*, 418–433.

Hofferth, S. L., & Anderson, K. G. (2003). Are all dads equal? Biology versus marriage as a basis for paternal investment. *Journal of Marriage and the Family, 65*, 213–232.

Hofferth, S., & Sandberg, J. (1999). *Family life changes in American children's time, 1981–1997.* Retrieved from www.fourhcouncil.edu/Revolution/Resources/Family_Life_Changes.asp

Hoffman, L. W. (2000). Maternal employment: Effects of social context. In R. D. Taylor & M. C. Wang (Eds.), *Resilience across contexts: Family, work, culture, and community* (pp. 147–176). Mahwah, NJ: Erlbaum.

Hoffman, L. W., & Youngblade, L. M. (1999). *Mothers at work: Effects on children's well-being.* New York: Cambridge University Press.

Hoffman, M. L. (2000). *Empathy and moral development.* New York: Cambridge University Press.

Hoffman, S., & Hatch, M. C. (1996). Stress, social support and pregnancy outcome: A reassessment based on research. *Paediatric and Perinatal Epidemiology, 10*, 380–405.

Hoffmann, W. (2001). Fallout from the Chernobyl nuclear disaster and congenital malformations in Europe. *Archives of Environmental Health, 56*, 478–483.

Hoffner, C., & Badzinski, D. M. (1989). Children's integration of facial and situational cues to emotion. *Child Development, 60*, 411–422.

Hofstadter, M., & Reznick, J. S. (1996). Response modality affects human infant delayed-response performance. *Child Development, 67*, 646–658.

Hogan, J. D. (2003). G. Stanley Hall: Educator, organizer, and pioneer developmental psychologist. In G. A. Kimble & M. Wertheimer (Eds.), *Portraits of pioneers in psychology* (Vol. 5, pp. 19–35). Mahwah, NJ: Erlbaum.

Hogan, R. T., Harkness, A. R., & Lubinski, D. (2000). Personality and individual differences. In K. Pawlik & M. R. Rosensweig (Eds.), *International handbook of psychology* (pp. 283–304). London: Sage.

Hokoda, A., & Fincham, F. D. (1995). Origins of children's helpless and mastery achievement patterns in the family. *Journal of Educational Psychology, 87*, 375–385.

Holden, G. W., Coleman, S. M., & Schmidt, K. L. (1995). Why 3-year-old children get spanked: Determinants as reported by college-educated mothers. *Merrill-Palmer Quarterly, 41*, 431–452.

Holden, G. W., & Zambarano, R. J. (1992). Passing the rod: Similarities between parents and their young children in orientation toward physical punishment. In I. E. Sigel, A. V. McGillicuddy-DeLisi, & J. J. Goodnow (Eds.), *Parental belief systems: The psychological consequences for children* (2nd ed., pp. 143–172). Hillsdale, NJ: Erlbaum.

Hollich, G. J., Hirsh-Pasek, K., & Golinkoff, R. M. (2000). Breaking the language barrier: An emergentist coalition model for the origins of word learning. *Monographs of the Society for Research in Child Development, 65*(3, Serial No. 262).

Holliday, R. E. (2003). Reducing misinformation effects in children with cognitive interviews: Dissociating recollection and familiarity. *Child Development, 74*, 728–751.

Holmbeck, G. N. (1996). A model of family relational transformations during the transition to adolescence: Parent–adolescent conflict and adaptation. In J. A. Graber, J. Brooks-Gunn, & A. C. Petersen (Eds.), *Transitions through adolescence* (pp. 167–199). Mahwah, NJ: Erlbaum.

Holmes, W. C., & Slap, G. B. (1998). Sexual abuse of boys: Definition, prevalence, correlates, sequelae, and management. *Journal of the American Medical Association, 280*, 1855–1862.

Holobow, N., Genesee, F., & Lambert, W. (1991). The effectiveness of a foreign language immersion program for children from different ethnic and social class backgrounds: Report 2. *Applied Psycholinguistics, 12*, 179–198.

Holowka, S., Brosseau-Lapré, F., & Petitto, L. A. (2002). Semantic and conceptual knowledge underlying bilingual babies' first signs and words. *Language Learning, 52*, 205–262.

Holsen, I., Kraft, P., & Vittersø, J. (2000). Stability in depressed mood in adolescence. *Journal of Youth and Adolescence, 29*, 61–78.

Honein, M. A., Paulozzi, L. J., & Erickson, J. D. (2001). Continued occurrence of Accutane-exposed pregnancies. *Teratology, 64*, 142–147.

Hong, Z.-R., Veach, P. M., & Lawrenz, F. (2003). An investigation of the gender stereotyped thinking of Taiwanese secondary school boys and girls. *Sex Roles, 48*, 495–504.

Honzik, M. P., Macfarlane, J. W., & Allen, L. (1948). The stability of mental test performance between two and eighteen years. *Journal of Experimental Education, 17*, 309–329.

Hood, B. M. (2004). Is looking good enough or does it beggar belief? *Developmental Science, 7*, 415–417.

Hope, S., Power, C., & Rodgers, B. (1999). Does financial hardship account for elevated psychological distress in lone mothers? *Social Science and Medicine, 29*, 381–389.

Hopkins, B., & Butterworth, G. (1997). Dynamical systems approaches to the development of action. In G. Bremner, A. Slater, & G. Butterworth (Eds.), *Infant development: Recent advances* (pp. 75–100). East Sussex, UK: Psychology Press.

Hopkins, B., & Westra, T. (1988). Maternal handling and motor development: An intracultural study. *Genetic, Social and General Psychology Monographs, 14*, 377–420.

Hopkins-Golightly, T., Raz, S., & Sander, C. J. (2003). Influence of slight to moderate risk for birth hypoxia on acquisition of cognitive and language function in the preterm infant: A cross-sectional comparison with preterm-birth controls. *Neuropsychology, 17*, 3–13.

Horgan, D. (1978). The development of the full passive. *Journal of Child Language, 5*, 65–80.

Horn, J. L. (1994). Theory of fluid and crystallized intelligence. In R. J. Sternberg (Ed.), *Encyclopedia of intelligence* (pp. 443–451). New York: Macmillan.

Horn, J. L., & Noll, J. (1997). Human cognitive capabilities: Gf-Gc theory. In D. P. Flanagan & J. L. Genshaft (Eds.), *Contemporary intellectual assessment: Theories, tests, and issues* (pp. 53–91). New York: Guilford.

Horner, T. M. (1980). Two methods of studying stranger reactivity in infants: A review. *Journal of Child Psychology and Psychiatry, 21*, 203–219.

Horowitz, F. D. (1992). John B. Watson's legacy: Learning and environment. *Developmental Psychology, 28*, 360–367.

Hort, B. E., Leinbach, M. D., & Fagot, B. I. (1991). Is there coherence among the cognitive components of gender acquisition? *Sex Roles, 24*, 195–207.

Hotz, V. J., McElroy, S. W., & Sanders, S. G. (1997). The costs and consequences of teenage childbearing for mothers. In R. A. Maynard (Ed.), *Kids having kids* (pp. 55–94). Washington, DC: Urban Institute.

Hoven, C. W., Mandell, D., & Duarte, C. S. (2003). Mental health of New York City public school children after 9/11: An epidemiologic investigation. In S. W. Coates & J. L. Rosenthal (Eds.), *September 11: Trauma and human bonds* (pp. 51–74). Hillsdale, NJ: Analytic Press.

Howard, D. E., & Wang, M. Q. (2004). Multiple sexual-partner behavior among sexually active U.S. adolescent girls. *American Journal of Health Behavior, 28*, 3–12.

Howe, M. L. (2003). Memories from the cradle. *Current Directions in Psychological Science, 12*, 62–65.

Howe, M. L. (2004). The role of conceptual recoding in reducing children's retroactive interference. *Developmental Psychology, 40*, 131–139.

Howe, N., Aquan-Assee, J., & Bukowski, W. M. (2001). Predicting sibling relations over time: Synchrony between maternal management styles and sibling relationship quality. *Merrill-Palmer Quarterly, 47*, 121–141.

Howes, C. (1998). The earliest friendships. In W. M. Bukowski, A. F. Newcomb, & W. W. Hartup (Eds.), *The company they keep: Friendship in childhood and adolescence* (pp. 66–86). New York: Cambridge University Press.

Howes, C., & Farver, J. (1987). Social pretend play in 2-year-olds: Effects of age of partner. *Early Childhood Research Quarterly, 2*, 305–314.

Howes, C., & James, J. (2002). Children's social development within the socialization context of child care and early childhood education. In P. Smith & C. H. Hart (Eds.), *Handbook of childhood social development.* New York: Blackwell.

Howes, C., & Matheson, C. C. (1992). Sequences in the development of competent play with peers: Social and social pretend play. *Developmental Psychology, 28*, 961–974.

Hu, Y., Wood, J. F., Smith, V., & Westbrook, N. (2004). Friendships through IM: Examining the relationship between instant messaging and intimacy. *Journal of Computer-Mediated Communication, 10*(1). Retrieved from jcmc.indiana.edu/vol10/issue1

Hubbard, F. O. A., & van IJzendoorn, M. H. (1991). Maternal unresponsiveness and infant crying across the first 9 months: A naturalistic longitudinal study. *Infant Behavior and Development, 14*, 299–312.

Hudson, J. A., & Fivush, R. (1991). As time goes by: Sixth graders remember a kindergarten experience. *Applied Cognitive Psychology, 5*, 347–360.

Hudson, J. A., Fivush, R., & Kuebli, J. (1992). Scripts and episodes: The development of event memory. *Applied Cognitive Psychology, 6*, 483–505.

Hudson, J. A., Sosa, B. B., & Shapiro, L. R. (1997). Scripts and plans: The development of preschool children's event knowledge and event planning. In S. L. Friedman & E. K. Scholnick (Eds.), *The developmental psychology of planning: Why, how, and when do we plan?* (pp. 77–102). Mahwah, NJ: Erlbaum.

Huesmann, L. R. (1986). Psychological processes promoting the relation between exposure to media violence and aggressive behavior by the viewer. *Journal of Social Issues, 42*, 125–139.

Huesmann, L. R., Moise-Titus, J., Podolski, C., & Eron, L. D. (2003). Longitudinal relations between children's exposure to TV violence and their aggressive and violent behavior in young adulthood: 1977–1992. *Developmental Psychology, 39*, 201–221.

Huey, S. J., Jr., & Henggeler, S. W. (2001). Effective community-based interventions for antisocial and delinquent adolescents. In J. N. Hughes & A. M. La Greca (Eds.), *Handbook of psychological services for children and adolescents* (pp. 301–322). London: Oxford University Press.

Hughes, C., & Dunn, J. (1998). Understanding mind and emotion: Longitudinal associations with mental-state talk between young friends. *Developmental Psychology, 34*, 1026–1037.

Hughes, D. C., & Ng, S. (2003). Reducing health disparities among children. *Future of Children, 13*, 153–167.

Hughes, F. P. (1998). Play in special populations. In O. N. Saracho & B. Spodek (Eds.), *Multiple perspectives on play in early childhood education* (pp. 171–193). Albany: State University of New York Press.

Hughes, J. N., Cavell, T. A., & Grossman, P. B. (1997). A positive view of self: Risk or protection for aggressive children? *Development and Psychopathology, 9*, 75–94.

Humphrey, L. T. (1998). Growth patterns in the modern human skeleton. *American Journal of Physical Anthropology, 105*, 57–72.

Humphrey, T. (1978). Function of the nervous system during prenatal life. In U. Stave (Ed.), *Perinatal physiology* (pp. 651–683). New York: Plenum.

Hunnius, S., & Geuze, R. H. (2004a). Developmental changes in visual scanning of dynamic faces and abstract stimuli in infants: A longitudinal study. *Infancy, 6*, 231–255.

Hunnius, S., & Geuze, R. H. (2004b). Gaze shifting in infancy: A longitudinal study using dynamic faces and abstract stimuli. *Infant Behavior and Development, 27*, 397–416.

Hunsberger, B., Pratt, M., & Pancer, S. M. (2001). Adolescent identity formation: Religious exploration and commitment. *Identity, 1*, 365–386.

Hura, S. L., & Echols, C. H. (1996). The role of stress and articulatory difficulty in children's early productions. *Developmental Psychology, 32*, 165–176.

Hurewitz, F., Brown-Schmidt, S., Thorpe, K., Gleitman, L. R., & Trueswell, J. C. (2000). One frog, two frog, red frog, blue frog: Factors affecting children's syntactic choices in production and comprehension. *Journal of Psycholinguistic Research, 29*, 597–626.

Hursti, U. K. (1999). Factors influencing children's food choice. *Annals of Medicine, 31*, 26–32.

Husain, G., Thompson, W. F., & Schellenberg, E. G. (2002). Effects of musical tempo and mode on arousal, mood, and spatial abilities. *Music Perception, 20*, 151–171.

Huston, A. C., & Alvarez, M. M. (1990). The socialization context of gender role development in early adolescence. In R. Montemayor, G. R. Adams, & T. P. Gullotta (Eds.), *From childhood to adolescence: A transitional period?* (pp. 156–179). Newbury Park, CA: Sage.

Huston, A. C., Donnerstein, E., Fairchild, H., Feshbach, N. D., Katz, P. A., & Murray, J. P. (1992). *Big world, small screen: The role of television in American society.* Lincoln: University of Nebraska Press.

Huston, A. C., Wright, J. C., Marquis, J., & Green, S. B. (1999). How young children spend their time: Television and other activities. *Developmental Psychology, 35*, 912–925.

Huttenlocher, P. R. (1994). Synaptogenesis in human cerebral cortex. In G. Dawson & K. W. Fischer (Eds.), *Human behavior and the developing brain* (pp. 137–152). New York: Guilford.

Huttenlocher, P. R. (2002). *Neural plasticity: The effects of environment on the development of the cerebral cortex.* Cambridge, MA: Harvard University Press.

Hyde, J. S., Essex, M. J., Clark, R., & Klein, M. H. (2001). Maternity leave, women's employment, and marital incompatibility. *Journal of Family Psychology, 15*, 476–491.

Hyde, J. S., Klein, M. H., Essex, M. J., & Clark, R. (1995). Maternity leave and women's mental health. *Psychology of Women Quarterly, 19*, 257–285.

Hyde, K. E. (1990). *Religion in childhood and adolescence.* Birmingham, AL: Religious Education Press.

Hymel, S., LeMare, L., Ditner, E., & Woody, E. Z. (1999). Assessing selfconcept in children: Variations across self-concept domains. *Merrill-Palmer Quarterly, 45*, 602–623.

Hymel, S., Vaillancourt, T., McDougall, P., & Renshaw, P. D. (2004). Peer acceptance and rejection in childhood. In P. K. Smith & C. H. Hart (Eds.), *Blackwell handbook of childhood social development* (pp. 265–284). Malden, MA: Blackwell.

Hyppönen, E., Power, C., & Smith, G. D. (2003). Prenatal growth, BMI, and risk of type 2 diabetes by early midlife. *Diabetes Care, 26*, 2512–2517.

Iglowstein, I., Jenni, O. G., Molinari, L., & Largo, R. H. (2003). Sleep duration from infancy to adolescence: Reference values and generational trends. *Pediatrics, 111*, 302–307.

Imai, M., & Haryu, E. (2001). Learning proper nouns and common nouns without clues from syntax. *Child Development, 72*, 787–802.

Inagaki, K. (1997). Emerging distinctions between naïve biology and naïve psychology. In H. M. Wellman & K. Inagaki (Eds.), *The emergence of core domains of thought: New directions for child development #75*, (pp. 27–44). San Francisco: Jossey-Bass.

Inagaki, K., & Hantano, G. (2002). *Young children's naïve thinking about the biological world.* New York: Psychology Press.

Ingram, D. (1986). Phonological development: Production. In P. Fletcher & M. Garman (Eds.), *Language acquisition* (2nd ed., pp. 223–239). Cambridge: Cambridge University Press.

Ingram, D. (1999). Phonological acquisition. In M. Barrett (Ed.), *The development of language* (pp. 73–97). Philadelphia: Psychology Press/Taylor & Francis.

Inhelder, B., & Piaget, J. (1958). *The growth of logical thinking from childhood to adolescence: An essay on the construction of formal operational structures.* New York: Basic Books. (Original work published 1955)

Inoff-Germain, G., Arnold, G. S., Nottelman, E. D., Susman, E. J., Cutler, G. B., Jr., & Crousos, G. P. (1988). Relations between hormone levels and observational measures of aggressive behavior of young adolescents in family interactions. *Developmental Psychology, 24*, 129–139.

International Human Genome Sequencing Consortium. (2004). Finishing the euchromatic sequence of the human genome. *Nature, 21*, 931–945.

Intons-Peterson, M. J. (1988). *Gender concepts of Swedish and American youth.* Hillsdale, NJ: Erlbaum.

Irvine, J. J. (1986). Teacher–student interactions: Effects of student race, sex, and grade level. *Journal of Educational Psychology, 78*, 14–21.

Isabella, R. A. (1993). Origins of attachment: Maternal interactive behavior across the first year. *Child Development, 64*, 605–621.

Isabella, R. A., & Belsky, J. (1991). Interactional synchrony and the origins of infant–mother attachment: A replication study. *Child Development, 62*, 373–384.

Iverson, J. M., Capirci, O., & Caselli, M. C. (1994). From communication to language in two modalities. *Cognitive Development, 9*, 23–43.

Izard, C. E. (1979). *The maximally discriminative facial movement scoring system.* Unpublished manuscript, University of Delaware.

Izard, C. E., & Ackerman, B. P. (2000). Motivational, organizational, and regulatory functions of discrete emotions. In M. Lewis & J. M. Haviland-Jones (Eds.), *Handbook of emotions* (2nd ed., pp. 253–264). New York: Guilford.

Izard, C. E., Hembree, E. A., & Huebner, R. R. (1987). Infants' emotion expressions to acute pain. *Developmental Psychology, 23*, 105–113.

Jaakkola, J. J., & Gissler, M. (2004). Maternal smoking in pregnancy, fetal development, and childhood asthma. *American Journal of Public Health, 94*, 136–140.

Jaccard, J., Dittus, P., & Gordon, V. V. (2000). Parent–adolescent congruency in reports of adolescent sexual behavior and in communications about sexual behavior. *Child Development, 69*, 247–261.

Jaccard, J., Dodge, T., & Dittus, P. (2002). Parent–adolescent communication about sex and birth control: A conceptual framework. In S. S. Feldman & D. A. Rosenthal (Eds.), *Talking sexuality: Parent–adolescent communication* (pp. 9–41). San Francisco: Jossey-Bass.

Jaccard, J., Dodge, T., & Dittus, P. (2003). Maternal discussions about pregnancy and adolescents' attitudes toward pregnancy. *Journal of Adolescent Health, 33*, 84–87.

Jackson, P. W. (1968). *Life in classrooms.* New York: Holt, Rinehart & Winston.

Jackson, R. A., Gibson, K. A., & Wu, Y. W. (2004). Perinatal outcomes in singletons following in vitro fertilization: A meta-analysis. *Obstetrics and Gynecology, 103*, 551–563.

Jacobs, J. E., & Eccles, J. S. (1992). The impact of mothers' gender-role stereotypic beliefs on mothers' and children's ability perceptions. *Journal of Personality and Social Psychology, 63*, 932–944.

Jacobs, J. E., & Klaczynski, P. A. (2002). The development of judgment and decision making during childhood and adolescence. *Current Directions in Psychological Science, 11*, 145–149.

Jacobs, J. E., Lanza, S., Osgood, D. W., Eccles, J. S., & Wigfield, A. (2002). Changes in children's self-competence and values: Gender and domain differences across grades one through twelve. *Child Development, 73*, 509–527.

Jacobs, J. E., & Weisz, V. (1994). Gender stereotypes: Implications for gifted education. *Roeper Review, 16*, 152–155.

Jacobson, J. L., & Jacobson, S. W. (2003). Prenatal exposure to polychlorinated biphenyls and attention at school age. *Journal of Pediatrics, 143*, 780–788.

Jacobson, J. L., Jacobson, S. W., Fein, G., Schwartz, P. M., & Dowler, J. (1984). Prenatal exposure to an environmental toxin: A test of the multiple effects model. *Developmental Psychology, 20*, 523–532.

Jacobson, K. C., & Crockett, L. J. (2000). Parental monitoring and adolescent adjustment: An ecological perspective. *Journal of Research on Adolescence, 10*, 65–97.

Jacquet, P. (2004). Sensitivity of germ cells and embryos to ionizing radiation. *Journal of Biological Regulators and Homeostatic Agents, 18*, 106–114.

Jadack, R. A., Hyde, J. S., Moore, C. F., & Keller, M. L. (1995). Moral reasoning about sexually transmitted diseases. *Child Development, 66*, 167–177.

Jaffe, J., Beebe, B., Feldstein, S., Crown, C. L., & Jasnow, M. D. (2001). Rhythms of dialogue in infancy. *Monographs of the Society for Research in Child Development, 66*(2, Serial No. 265).

Jaffee, S. R., Caspi, A., Moffitt, T. E., Belsky, J., & Silva, P. (2001). Why are children born to teen mothers at risk for adverse outcomes in young adulthood? Results of a 20-year longitudinal study. *Development and Psychopathology, 13,* 377–397.

Jaffee, S. R., & Hyde, J. S. (2000). Gender differences in moral orientation: A meta-analysis. *Psychological Bulletin, 126,* 703–706.

Jaffee, S. R., Moffitt, T. E., Caspi, A., & Taylor, A. (2003). Life with (or without) father: The benefits of living with two biological parents depend on the father's antisocial behavior. *Child Development, 74,* 109–126.

Jain, A., Concat, J., & Leventhal, J. M. (2002). How good is the evidence linking breastfeeding and intelligence? *Pediatrics, 109,* 1044–1053.

Jambunathan, S., Burts, D. C., & Pierce, S. (2000). Comparisons of parenting attitudes among five ethnic groups in the United States. *Journal of Comparative Family Studies, 31,* 395–406.

James, D. (1998). Recent advances in fetal medicine. *British Medical Journal, 316,* 1580–1583.

James, W. (1963). *Psychology.* New York: Fawcett. (Original work published 1890)

Jameson, S. (1993). Zinc status in pregnancy: The effect of zinc therapy on perinatal mortality, prematurity, and placental ablation. *Annals of the New York Academy of Sciences, 678,* 178–192.

Jamieson, J. R. (1995). Interactions between mothers and children who are deaf. *Journal of Early Intervention, 19,* 108–117.

Jang, S. J., & Johnson, B. R. (2001). Neighborhood disorder, individual religiosity, and adolescent use of illicit drugs: A test of multilevel hypotheses. *Criminology, 39,* 109–143

Jankowski, J. J., Rose, S. A., & Feldman, J. F. (2001). Modifying the distribution of attention in infants. *Child Development, 72,* 339–351.

Jansen, A., Theunissen, N., Slechten, K., Nederkoorn, C., Boon, B., Mulkens, S., & Roefs, A. (2003). Overweight children overeat after exposure to food cues. *Eating Behaviors, 4,* 197–209.

Janssen, P. A., Lee, S. K., Ryan, E. M., Etches, D. J., Farquharson, D. F., & Peacock, D. (2002). Outcomes of planned home births versus planned hospital births after regulation of midwifery in British Columbia. *Canadian Medical Association Journal, 166,* 315–323.

Jarrold, C., Baddeley, A. D., & Hewes, A. K. (1998). Verbal and nonverbal abilities in the Williams syndrome phenotype: Evidence for diverging developmental trajectories. *Journal of Child Psychology and Psychiatry, 39,* 511–523.

Jayakody, R., & Kalil, A. (2002). Social fathering in low-income, African-American families with preschool children. *Journal of Marriage and the Family, 64,* 504–516.

Jeffrey, J. (2004, November). Parents often blind to their kids' weight. *British Medical Journal Online, 1.* Retrieved from http://content.health.msn.com/content/article/97/104292.htm

Jenkins, J. M., & Astington, J. W. (1996). Cognitive factors and family structure associated with theory of mind development in young children. *Developmental Psychology, 32,* 70–78.

Jenkins, J. M., & Astington, J. W. (2000). Theory of mind and social behavior: Causal models tested in a longitudinal study. *Merrill-Palmer Quarterly, 46,* 203–220.

Jenkins, J. M., Rasbash, J., & O'Connor, T. G. (2003). The role of the shared family context in differential parenting. *Developmental Psychology, 39,* 99–113.

Jenkins, J. M., Turrell, S. L., Kogushi, Y., Lollis, S., & Ross, H. S. (2003). A longitudinal investigation of the dynamics of mental state talk in families. *Child Development, 74,* 905–920.

Jensen, A. R. (1969). How much can we boost IQ and scholastic achievement? *Harvard Educational Review, 39,* 1–123.

Jensen, A. R. (1974). Cumulative deficit: A testable hypothesis. *Developmental Psychology, 10,* 996–1019.

Jensen, A. R. (1980). *Bias in mental testing.* New York: Free Press.

Jensen, A. R. (1985). The nature of the black–white difference on various psychometric tests: Spearman's hypothesis. *Behavioral and Brain Sciences, 8,* 193–219.

Jensen, A. R. (1998). *The g factor: The science of mental ability.* New York: Praeger.

Jensen, A. R. (2001). Spearman's hypothesis. In J. M. Collis & S. Messick (Eds.), *Intelligence and personality: Bridging the gap in theory and measurement* (pp. 3–24). Mahwah, NJ: Erlbaum.

Jensen, A. R. (2002). Galton's legacy to research on intelligence. *Journal of Biosocial Science, 34,* 145–172.

Jensen, A. R., & Figueroa, R. A. (1975). Forward and backward digit-span interaction with race and IQ: Predictions from Jensen's theory. *Journal of Educational Psychology, 67,* 882–893.

Jensen, A. R., & Reynolds, C. R. (1982). Race, social class and ability patterns on the WISC-R. *Personality and Individual Differences, 3,* 423–438.

Jiao, S., Ji, G., & Jing, Q. (1996). Cognitive development of Chinese urban only children and children with siblings. *Child Development, 67,* 387–395.

Joe, S., & Marcus, S. C. (2003). Datapoints: Trends by race and gender in suicide attempts among U.S. adolescents. *Psychiatric Services, 54,* 454.

Johnson, A., Bowler, U., Yudkin, P., Hockley, C., Wariyar, U., Gardner, F., & Mutch, L. (2003). Health and school performance of teenagers born before 29 weeks gestation. *Archives of Diseases of Childhood, 88,* F190–F198.

Johnson, D. E. (2000). Medical and developmental sequelae of early childhood institutionalization in Eastern European adoptees. In C. A. Nelson (Ed.), *Minnesota Symposia on Child Psychology* (Vol. 31, pp. 113–162). Mahwah, NJ: Erlbaum.

Johnson, D. E. (2002). Adoption and the effect on children's development. *Early Human Development, 68,* 39–54.

Johnson, J. G., Cohen, P., Smailes, E. M., Kasen, S., & Brook, J. S. (2002). Television viewing and aggressive behavior during adolescence and adulthood. *Science, 295,* 2468–2471.

Johnson, J., Im-Bolter, N., & Pascual-Leone, J. (2003). Development of mental attention in gifted and mainstream children: The role of mental capacity, inhibition, and speed of processing. *Child Development, 74,* 1594–1614.

Johnson, M. H. (1998). The neural basis of cognitive development. In D. Kuhn & R. S. Siegler (Ed.), *Handbook of child psychology: Vol. 2. Cognition, perception, and language* (5th ed., pp. 1–49). New York: Wiley.

Johnson, M. H. (1999). Ontogenetic constraints on neural and behavioral plasticity: Evidence from imprinting and face processing. *Canadian Journal of Experimental Psychology, 55,* 77–90.

Johnson, M. H. (2001a). The development and neural basis of face recognition: Comment and speculation. *Infant and Child Development, 10,* 31–33.

Johnson, M. H. (2001b). Functional brain development in humans. *Nature Reviews, 2,* 475–483.

Johnson, M. H., & Mareschal, D. (2001). Cognitive and perceptual development during infancy. *Current Opinion in Neurobiology, 11,* 213–218.

Johnson, S. P. (1996). Habituation patterns and object perception in young infants. *Journal of Reproductive and Infant Psychology, 14,* 207–218.

Johnson, S. P. (1997). Young infants' perception of object unity: Implications for development of attentional and cognitive skills. *Current Directions in Psychological Science, 6,* 5–11.

Johnson, S. P. (2004). Development of perceptual completion in infancy. *Psychological Science, 15,* 769–775.

Johnson, S. P., Amso, D., & Slemmer, J. A. (2003). Development of object concepts in infancy: Evidence for early learning in an eye-tracking paradigm. *Proceedings of the National Academy of Sciences, 100,* 10568–10753.

Johnson, S. P., Bremner, J. G., Slater, A. M., Mason, U. C., & Foster, K. (2002). Young infants' perception of unity and form in occlusion displays. *Journal of Experimental Child Psychology, 81,* 358–374.

Johnson, S. P., Bremner, J. G., Slater, A., Mason, U., Foster, K., & Cheshire, A. (2003). Infants' perception of object trajectories. *Child Development, 74,* 94–108.

Johnson, S. P., Slemmer, J. A., & Amso, D. (2004). Where infants look determines how they see: Eye movements and object perception performance in 3-month-olds. *Infancy, 6,* 185–201.

John-Steiner, V., & Mahn, H. (1996). Sociocultural approaches to learning and development: A Vygotskian framework. *Educational Psychologist, 3,* 191–206.

Johnston, J. R., & Slobin, D. I. (1979). The development of locative expressions in English, Italian, Serbo-Croatian, and Turkish. *Journal of Child Language, 16,* 531–547.

Johnston, M. V., Nishimura, A., Harum, K., Pekar, J., & Blue, M. E. (2001). Sculpting the developing brain. *Advances in Pediatrics, 48,* 1–38.

Jones, C. M., Braithwaite, V. A., & Healy, S. D. (2003). The evolution of sex differences in spatial ability. *Behavioral Neuroscience, 117,* 403–411.

Jones, D. C., Abbey, B. B., & Cumberland, A. (1998). The development of display rule knowledge: Linkages with family expressiveness and social competence. *Child Development, 69,* 1209–1222.

Jones, E. F., & Thomson, N. R. (2001). Action perception and outcome valence: Effects on children's inferences of intentionality and moral and liking judgments. *Journal of Genetic Psychology, 162,* 154–166.

Jones, F. (2003). Religious commitment in Canada, 1997 and 2000. *Religious Commitment Monograph No. 3.* Ottawa, Canada: Christian Commitment Research Institute.

Jones, G. P., & Dembo, M. H. (1989). Age and sex role differences in intimate friendships during childhood and adolescence. *Merrill-Palmer Quarterly, 35,* 445–462.

Jones, G., Ritter, F. E., & Wood, D. J. (2000). Using a cognitive architecture to examine what develops. *Psychological Science, 11,* 93–100.

Jones, J., Lopez, A., & Wilson, M. (2003). Congenital toxoplasmosis. *American Family Physician, 67,* 2131–2137.

Jones, L. B., Rothbart, M. K., & Posner, M. I. (2003). Development of executive attention in preschool children. *Developmental Science, 6,* 498–504.

Jones, M. C. (1965). Psychological correlates of somatic development. *Child Development, 36,* 899–911.

Jones, M. C., & Mussen, P. H. (1958). Self-conceptions, motivations, and interpersonal attitudes of early- and late-maturing girls. *Child Development, 29,* 491–501.

Jones, N. A., Field, T., & Davalos, M. (2000). Right frontal EEG asymmetry and lack of empathy in preschool children of depressed mothers. *Child Psychiatry and Human Development, 30,* 189–204.

Jones, N. A., Field, T., Fox, N. A., Lundy, B., & Davalos, M. (1997). EEG activation in 1-month-old infants of depressed mothers. *Development and Psychopathology, 9,* 491–505.

Jones, S. S., & Raag, T. (1989). Smile production in older infants: The importance of a social recipient for the facial signal. *Child Development, 60,* 811–818.

Jones, W., Bellugi, U., Lai, Z., Chiles, M., Reilly, J., Lincoln, A., & Adolphs, R. (2000). Hypersociability in Williams syndrome. *Journal of Cognitive Neuroscience, 12,* 30–46

Jongbloet, P. H., Zielhuis, G. A., Groenewoud, H. M., & Paster-De Jong, P. C. (2001). The secular trends in male:female ratio at birth in postwar industrialized countries. *Environmental Health Perspectives, 109,* 749–752.

Jordan, B. (1993). *Birth in four cultures.* Prospect Heights, IL: Waveland.

Jorgensen, K. M. (1999). Pain assessment and management in the newborn infant. *Journal of PeriAnesthesia Nursing, 14,* 349–356.

Joseph, R. (2000). Fetal brain behavior and cognitive development. *Developmental Review, 20,* 81–98.

Joseph, R. M., & Tager-Flusberg, H. (2004). The relationship of theory of mind and executive functions to symptom type and severity in children with autism. *Development and Psychopathology, 16,* 137–155.

Josselson, R. (1992). *The space between us.* San Francisco: Jossey-Bass.

Josselson, R. (1994). The theory of identity development and the question of intervention. In S. L. Archer (Ed.), *Interventions for adolescent identity development* (pp. 12–25). Thousand Oaks, CA: Sage.

Jouen, F., & Lepecq, J.-C. (1989). Sensitivity to optical flow in neonates. *Psychologie Française, 34,* 13–18.

Joyner, M. H., & Kurtz-Costes, B. (1997). Metamemory development. In W. Schneider & F. E. Weinert (Eds.), *Memory performance and competencies: Issues in growth and development* (pp. 275–300). Hillsdale, NJ: Erlbaum.

Jusczyk, P. W. (1995). Language acquisition: Speech sounds and phonological development. In J. L. Miller & P. D. Eimas (Eds.), *Handbook of perception and cognition: Vol. 11. Speech, language, and communication* (pp. 263–301). Orlando, FL: Academic Press.

Jusczyk, P. W. (2001). In the beginning, was the word ... In F. Lacerda & C. von Hofsten (Eds.), *Emerging cognitive abilities in early infancy* (pp. 173–192). Mahwah, NJ: Erlbaum.

Jusczyk, P. W. (2002). Some critical developments in acquiring native language sound organization. *Annals of Otology, Rhinology and Laryngology, 189,* 11–15.

Jusczyk, P. W. (2003). The role of speech perception capacities in early language acquisition. In M. T. Banich & M. Mack (Eds.), *Mind, brain, and language: Multidisciplinary perspectives* (pp. 61–83). Mahwah, NJ: Erlbaum.

Jusczyk, P. W., & Hohne, E. A. (1997). Infants' memory for spoken words. *Science, 277,* 1984–1986.

Jusczyk, P. W., Houston, D. M., & Newsome, M. (1999). The beginnings of word segmentation in English-learning infants. *Cognitive Psychology, 39,* 159–207.

Jusczyk, P. W., Johnson, S. P., Spelke, E. S., & Kennedy, L. J. (1999). Synchronous change and perception of object unity: Evidence from adults and infants. *Cognition, 71,* 257–288.

Justice for Children and Youth. (2003). *Corporal punishment.* Toronto: Canadian Foundation for Children, Youth, and the Law. Retrieved from www.jfcy.org/corporalp/corporalp.html

Justice, E. M. (1986). Developmental changes in judgments of relative strategy effectiveness. *British Journal of Developmental Psychology, 4,* 75–81.

Justice, E. M., Baker-Ward, L., Gupta, S., & Jannings, L. R. (1997). Means to the goal of remembering: Developmental changes in awareness of strategy use–performance relations. *Journal of Experimental Child Psychology, 65,* 293–314.

Kagan, J. (1998). Biology and the child. In N. Eisenberg (Ed.), *Handbook of child psychology: Vol. 3. Social, emotional, and personality development* (5th ed., pp. 177–236). New York: Wiley.

Kagan, J. (2003). Behavioral inhibition as a temperamental category. In R. J. Davidson, K. R. Scherer, & H. H. Goldsmith (Eds.), *Handbook of affective science* (pp. 320–331). New York: Oxford University Press.

Kagan, J., Arcus, D., Snidman, N., Feng, W. Y., Hendler, J., & Greene, S. (1994). Reactivity in infants: A cross-national comparison. *Developmental Psychology, 30,* 342–345.

Kagan, J., Kearsley, R. B., & Zelazo, P. R. (1978). *Infancy: Its place in human development.* Cambridge, MA: Harvard University Press.

Kagan, J., & Saudino, K. J. (2001). Behavioral inhibition and related

temperaments. In R. N. Emde & J. K. Hewitt (Eds.), *Infancy to early childhood: Genetic and environmental influences on developmental change* (pp. 111–119). New York: Oxford University Press.

Kagan, J., & Snidman, N. (1991). Temperamental factors in human development. *American Psychologist, 46,* 856–862.

Kagan, J., Snidman, N., Zentner, M., & Peterson, E. (1999). Infant temperament and anxious symptoms in school-age children. *Development and Psychopathology, 11,* 209–224.

Kahn, P. H., Jr. (1992). Children's obligatory and discretionary moral judgments. *Child Development, 63,* 416–430.

Kail, R. (1988). Developmental functions for speeds of cognitive processes. *Journal of Experimental Child Psychology, 45,* 339–364.

Kail, R. (1991). Processing time declines exponentially during childhood and adolescence. *Developmental Psychology, 27,* 259–266.

Kail, R. (1993). The role of a global mechanism in developmental change in speed of processing. In M. L. Howe & R. Pasnak (Eds.), *Emerging themes in cognitive development: Vol. 1. Foundations.* New York: Springer-Verlag.

Kail, R. (1997). Processing time, imagery, and spatial memory. *Journal of Experimental Child Psychology, 64,* 67–78.

Kail, R. V. (2003). Information processing and memory. In M. H. Bornstein, L. Davidson, C. L. M. Keyes, K. A. Moore, and The Center for Child Well-Being (Eds.), *Well-being: Positive development across the life course* (pp. 269–280). Mahwah, NJ: Erlbaum.

Kail, R., Hall, L. K., & Caskey, B. J. (1999). Processing speed, exposure to print, and naming speed. *Applied Psycholinguistics, 20,* 303–314.

Kail, R., & Park, Y. (1992). Global developmental change in processing time. *Merrill-Palmer Quarterly, 38,* 525–541.

Kaitz, M., Meirov, H., Landman, I., & Eidelman, A. I. (1993). Infant recognition by tactile cues. *Infant Behavior and Development, 16,* 333–341.

Kalil, A., Schweingruber, H., & Seefeldt, K. (2001). Correlates of employment among welfare recipients: Do psychological characteristics and attitudes matter? *American Journal of Community Psychology, 29,* 701–723.

Kallós, D., & Broman, I. T. (1997). Swedish child care and early childhood education in transition. *Early Education and Development, 8,* 265–284.

Kaltiala-Heino, R., Kosunen, E., & Rimpelä, M. (2003). Pubertal timing, sexual behaviour and self-reported depression in middle adolescence. *Journal of Adolescence, 26,* 531–545.

Kamerman, S. B. (1993). International perspectives on child care policies and programs. *Pediatrics, 91,* 248–252.

Kamerman, S. B. (2000). From maternity to parental leave policies: Women's health, employment, and child and family well-being. *Journal of the American Medical Women's Association, 55,* 96–99.

Kandall, S. R., Gaines, J., Habel, L., Davidson, G., & Jessop, D. (1993). Relationship of maternal substance abuse to subsequent sudden infant death syndrome in offspring. *Journal of Pediatrics, 123,* 120–126.

Kane, C. M. (2000). African-American family dynamics as perceived by family members. *Journal of Black Studies, 30,* 691–702.

Kao, G. (2000). Psychological well-being and educational achievement among immigrant youth. In D. J. Hernandez (Ed.), *Children of immigrants: Health, adjustment, and public assistance.* Washington, DC: National Academy Press.

Kao, G., & Tienda, M. (1995). Optimism and achievement: The educational performance of immigrant youth. *Social Science Quarterly, 76,* 1–19.

Kaprio, J., Rimpela, A., Winter, T., Viken, R. J., Pimpela, M., & Rose, R. J. (1995). Common genetic influence on BMI and age at menarche. *Human Biology, 67,* 739–753.

Karadsheh, R. (1991, March). *This room is a junkyard! Children's comprehension of metaphorical language.* Paper presented at the biennial meeting of the Society for Research in Child Development, Seattle, WA.

Karafantis, D. M., & Levy, S. R. (2004). The role of children's lay theories about the malleability of human attributes in beliefs about volunteering for disadvantaged groups. *Child Development, 75,* 236–250.

Karmiloff-Smith, A. (1999). The connectionist infant: Would Piaget turn in his grave? In A. Slater & D. Muir (Eds.), *The Blackwell reader in developmental psychology* (pp. 43–52). Malden, MA: Blackwell.

Karmiloff-Smith, A., Brown, J. H., Grice, S., & Paterson, S. (2003). Dethroning the myth: Cognitive dissociations and innate modularity in Williams syndrome. *Developmental Neuropsychology, 23,* 227–242.

Karmiloff-Smith, A., Grant, J., Berthoud, I., Davies, M., Howlin, P., & Udwin, O. (1997). Language and Williams syndrome: How intact is "intact"? *Child Development, 68,* 246–262.

Karmiloff-Smith, A., Grant, J., Sims, K., Jones, M., & Cuckle, P. (1996). Rethinking metalinguistic awareness: Representing and accessing knowledge about what counts as a word. *Cognition, 58,* 197–219.

Karmiloff-Smith, A., Tyler, L. K., Voice, K., Sims, K., Udwin, O., Howlin, P., & Davies, M. (1998). Linguistic dissociations in Williams syndrome: Evaluating receptive syntax in on-line and off-line tasks. *Neuropsychologia, 36,* 343–351.

Karpati, A. M., Rubin, C. H., Kieszak, S. M., Marcus, M., & Troiano, R. P. (2002). Stature and pubertal stage assessment in American boys: The 1988–1994 Third National Health and Nutrition Examination Survey. *Journal of Adolescent Health, 30,* 205–212.

Kashani, J. H., & Shepperd, J. A. (1990). Aggression in adolescents: The role of social support and personality. *Canadian Journal of Psychiatry, 35,* 311–315.

Kato, I., Franco, P., Groswasser, J., Scaillet, S., Kelmanson, I., Togari, H., & Kahn, A. (2003). Incomplete arousal processes in infants who were victims of sudden death. *American Journal of Respiratory and Critical Care, 168,* 1298–1303.

Katz, L. F., & Windecker-Nelson, B. (2004). Parental meta-emotion philosophy

in families with conduct-problem children: Links with peer relations. *Journal of Abnormal Child Psychology, 32,* 385–398.

Katz, P. A., & Kofkin, J. A. (1997). Race, gender, and young children. In S. S. Luthar, J. A. Burack, D. Cicchetti, & J. Weisz (Eds.), *Developmental psychopathology: Perspectives on adjustment, risk, and disorder* (pp. 51–74). Cambridge, UK: Cambridge University Press.

Kaufman, A. S., Kamphaus, R. W., & Kaufman, N. L. (1985). New directions in intelligence testing: The Kaufman Assessment Battery for Children (K-ABC). In B. B. Wolman (Ed.), *Handbook of intelligence* (pp. 663–698). New York: Wiley.

Kaufman, A. S., & Lichtenberger, E. O. (2002). *Assessing adolescent and adult intelligence* (2nd ed.). Boston: Allyn and Bacon.

Kaufman, J., & Charney, D. (2001). Effects of early stress on brain structure and function: Implications for understanding the relationship between child maltreatment and depression. *Development and Psychopathology, 13,* 451–471.

Kaufman, J., & Charney, D. (2003). The neurobiology of child and adolescent depression: Current knowledge and future directions. In D. Cicchetti & E. Walker (Eds.), *Neurodevelopmental mechanisms in psychopathology* (pp. 461–490). New York: Cambridge University Press.

Kavanaugh, R. D., & Engel, S. (1998). The development of pretense and narrative in early childhood. In O. N. Saracho & B. Spodek (Eds.), *Multiple perspectives on play in early childhood education* (pp. 80–99). Albany: State University of New York Press.

Kaye, K., & Marcus, J. (1981). Infant imitation: The sensory-motor agenda. *Developmental Psychology, 17,* 258–265.

Kazdin, A. E. (2000). Treatments for aggressive and antisocial children. *Child and Adolescent Psychiatric Clinics of North America, 9,* 841–858.

Kazdin, A. E., & Whitley, M. K. (2003). Treatment of parental stress to enhance therapeutic change among children referred for aggressive and antisocial behavior. *Journal of Consulting and Clinical Psychology, 71,* 504–515.

Kearins, J. M. (1981). Visual spatial memory in Australian aboriginal children of desert regions. *Cognitive Psychology, 13,* 434–460.

Keating, D. (1979). Adolescent thinking. In J. Adelson (Ed.), *Handbook of adolescent psychology* (pp. 211–246). New York: Wiley.

Keating, D. (1990). Adolescent thinking. In S. S. Feldman & G. R. Elliott (Eds.), *At the threshold* (pp. 54–89). Cambridge, MA: Harvard University Press.

Keating, D., & Clark, L. V. (1980). Development of physical and social reasoning in adolescence. *Developmental Psychology, 16,* 23–30.

Keats, D. M., & Fang, F.-X. (1992). The effect of modification of the cultural content of stimulus materials on social perspective taking ability in Chinese and Australian children. In S. Iwawaki, & Y. Kashina (Eds.), *Innovations in cross-cultural psychology* (pp. 319–327). Amsterdam: Swets & Zeitlinger.

Keil, F. C. (1986). Conceptual domains and the acquisition of metaphor. *Cognitive Development, 1,* 72–96.

Keil, F. C., & Lockhart, K. L. (1999). Explanatory understanding in conceptual development. In E. K. Scholnick, K. Nelson, S. A. Gelman, & P. H. Miller (Eds.), *Conceptual development: Piaget's legacy* (pp. 103–130). Mahwah, NJ: Erlbaum.

Keith, T. Z., Keith, P. B., Quirk, K. J., Sperduto, J., Santillo, S., & Killings, S. (1998). Longitudinal effects of parent involvement on high school grades: Similarities and differences across gender and ethnic groups. *Journal of School Psychology, 36,* 335–363.

Kelley, M. L., Power, T. G., & Wimbush, D. D. (1992). Determinants of disciplinary practices in low-income black mothers. *Child Development, 63,* 573–582.

Kelley, S. A., Brownell, C. A., & Campbell, S. B. (2000). Mastery motivation and self-evaluative affect in toddlers: Longitudinal relations with maternal behavior. *Child Development, 71,* 1061–1071.

Kelley, S. S., Borawski, E. A., Flocke, S. A., & Keen, K. J. (2003). The role of sequential and concurrent sexual relationships in the risk of sexually transmitted diseases among adolescents. *Journal of Adolescent Health, 32,* 296–305.

Kelly, F. W., Terry, R., & Naglieri, R. (1999). A review of alternative birthing positions. *Journal of the American Osteopathic Association, 99,* 470–474.

Kelly, S. D., Singer, M., Hicks, J., & Goldin-Meadow, S. (2002). A helping hand in assessing children's knowledge: Instructing adults to attend to gesture. *Cognition and Instruction, 20,* 1–26.

Kelly, S. J., Day, N., & Streissguth, A. P. (2000). Effects of prenatal alcohol exposure on social behavior in humans and other species. *Neurotoxicology and Teratology, 22,* 143–149.

Kemeny, M. E. (2003). The psychobiology of stress. *Current Directions in Psychological Science, 12,* 124–129.

Kempe, C. H., B. F., Steele, P. W., Droegemueller, P. W., & Silver, H. K. (1962). The battered-child syndrome. *Journal of the American Medical Association, 181,* 17–24.

Kendler, K. S., Thornton, L. M., Gilman, S. E., & Kessler, R. C. (2000). Sexual orientation in a U.S. national sample of twin and non-twin sibling pairs. *American Journal of Psychiatry, 157,* 1843–1846.

Kennell, J., Klaus, M., McGrath, S., Robertson, S., & Hinkley, C. (1991). Continuous emotional support during labor in a U.S. hospital. *Journal of the American Medical Association, 265,* 2197–2201.

Kenyon, B. L. (2001). Current research in children's conceptions of death: A critical review. *Omega, 43,* 63–91.

Kerckhoff, A. C. (2002). The transition from school to work. In J. T. Mortimer & R. Larson (Eds.), *The changing adolescent experience* (pp. 52–87). New York: Cambridge University Press.

Kerestes, M., & Youniss, J. E. (2003). Rediscovering the importance of religion in adolescent development.

In R. M. Lerner, F. Jacobs, & D. Wertlieb (Eds.), *Handbook of applied developmental science* (Vol. 1, pp. 165–184). Thousand Oaks, CA: Sage.

Kerestes, M., Youniss, J., & Metz, E. (2004). Longitudinal patterns of religious perspective and civic integration. *Applied Developmental Science, 8,* 39–46.

Kerig, P. K., Cowan, P. A., & Cowan, C. P. (1993). Marital quality and gender differences in parent–child interactions. *Developmental Psychology, 29,* 931–939.

Kernis, M. H. (2002). Self-esteem as a multifaceted construct. In T. M. Brinthaupt & R. P. Lipka (Eds.), *Understanding early adolescent self and identity* (pp. 57–88). Albany, NY: State University of New York Press.

Kerr, D. C. R., Lopez, N. L., Olson, S. L., & Sameroff, A. J. (2004). Parental discipline and externalizing behavior problems in early childhood: The roles of moral regulation and child gender. *Journal of Abnormal Child Psychology, 32,* 369–383.

Kessen, W. (1967). Sucking and looking: Two organized congenital patterns of behavior in the human newborn. In H. W. Stevenson, E. H. Hess, & H. L. Rheingold (Eds.), *Early behavior: Comparative and developmental approaches* (pp. 147–179). New York: Wiley.

Kihlstrom, J. F., & Cantor, N. (2000). Social intelligence. In R. J. Sternberg (Ed.), *Handbook of intelligence* (pp. 359–379). Cambridge: Cambridge University Press.

Killen, M., Lee-Kim, J., McGlothlin, H., & Stangor, C. (2002). How children and adolescents evaluate gender and racial exclusion. *Monographs of the Society for Research in Child Development, 67*(4, Serial No. 271).

Killen, M., & Nucci, L. P. (1995). Morality, autonomy, and social conflict. In M. Killen & D. Hart (Eds.), *Morality in everyday life: Developmental perspectives* (pp. 52–86). Cambridge: Cambridge University Press.

Killen, M., & Stangor, M. (2001). Children's social reasoning about inclusion and exclusion in gender and race peer group contexts. *Child Development, 72,* 174–186.

Kilpatrick, S. W., & Sanders, D. M. (1978). Body image stereotypes: A developmental comparison. *Journal of Genetic Psychology, 132,* 87–95.

Kim, J. M. (1998). Korean children's concepts of adult and peer authority and moral reasoning. *Developmental Psychology, 34,* 947–955.

Kim, J. M., & Turiel, E. (1996). Korean children's concepts of adult and peer authority. *Social Development, 5,* 310–329.

Kim, K. J., Conger, R. D., Lorenz, F. O., & Elder, G. H., Jr. (2001). Parent–adolescent reciprocity in negative affect and its relation to early adult social development. *Developmental Psychology, 37,* 775–790.

Kim, M., McGregor, K. K., & Thompson, C. K. (2000). Early lexical development in English- and Korean-speaking children: Language-general and language-specific patterns. *Journal of Child Language, 27,* 225–254.

Kim, W. J. (2002). Benefits and risks of intercountry adoption. *Lancet, 360,* 423–424.

Kimm, S. Y. S., Barton, B. A., Obarzanek, E., McMahon, R. P., Kronsberg, S., & Waclawiw, M. A. (2002). Obesity development during adolescence in a biracial cohort: The NHLBI Growth and Health Study. *Pediatrics, 110,* e54–e58.

King, P. E., & Furrow, J. L. (2004). Religion as a resource for positive youth development: Religion, social capital, and moral outcomes. *Developmental Psychology, 40,* 703–713.

Kinney, D. (1999). From "headbangers" to "hippies": Delineating adolescents' active attempts to form an alternative peer culture. In J. A. McLellan & M. J. V. Pugh (Eds.), *The role of peer groups in adolescent social identity: Exploring the importance of stability and change* (pp. 21–35). San Francisco: Jossey-Bass.

Kinney, H. C., Randall, L. L., Sleeper, L. A., Willinger, M., Belliveau, R. A., & Zec. N. (2003). Serotonergic brainstem abnormalities in Northern Plains Indians with the sudden infant death syndrome. *Journal of Neuropathology and Experimental Neurology, 62,* 1178–1191.

Kirby, D. (2002a). Antecedents of adolescent initiation of sex, contraceptive use, and pregnancy. *American Journal of Health Behavior, 26,* 473–485.

Kirby, D. (2002b). Effective approaches to reducing adolescent unprotected sex, pregnancy, and childbearing. *Journal of Sex Research, 39,* 51–57.

Kirby, D. (2002c). The impact of schools and school programs upon adolescent sexual behavior. *Journal of Sex Research, 39,* 27–33.

Kirk, K. M., Bailey, J. M., Dunne, M. P., & Martin, N. G. (2000). Measurement models for sexual orientation in a community twin sample. *Behavior Genetics, 30,* 345–356.

Kirkham, N. Z., Slemmer, J. A., & Johnson, S. P. (2002). Visual statistical learning in infancy: Evidence for a domain general learning mechanism. *Cognition, 83,* B35–B42.

Kirkman, M., Rosenthal, D. A., & Feldman, S. S. (2002). Talking to a tiger: Fathers reveal their difficulties in communicating about sexuality with adolescents. In S. S. Feldman & D. A. Rosenthal (Eds.), *Talking sexuality: Parent–adolescent communication* (pp. 57–74). San Francisco: Jossey-Bass.

Kisilevsky, B. S., Hains, S. M. J., Lee, K., Muir, D. W., Xu, F, Fu, G., Zhao, Z. Y., & Yang, R. L. (1998). The still-face effect in Chinese and Canadian 3- to 6-month-old infants. *Developmental Psychology, 34,* 629–639.

Kitzmann, K. M., Cohen, R., & Lockwood, R. L. (2002). Are only children missing out? Comparison of the peer-related social competence of only children and siblings. *Journal of Social and Personal Relationships, 19,* 299–316.

Klaczynski, P. A. (1997). Bias in adolescents' everyday reasoning and its relationships with intellectual ability, personal theories, and self-serving motivation. *Developmental Psychology, 33,* 273–283.

Klaczynski, P. A. (2001). Analytic and heuristic processing influences on adolescent reasoning and decision-making. *Child Development, 72,* 844–861.

Klaczynski, P. A., & Narasimham, G. (1998a). Development of scientific reasoning biases: Cognitive versus ego-protective explanations. *Developmental Psychology, 34,* 175–187.

Klaczynski, P. A., & Narasimham, G. (1998b). Representations as mediators of adolescent deductive reasoning. *Developmental Psychology, 34,* 865–881.

Klaczynski, P. A., Schuneman, M. J., & Daniel, D. B. (2004). Theories of conditional reasoning: A developmental examination of competing hypotheses. *Developmental Psychology, 40,* 559–571.

Klahr, D., & MacWhinney, B. (1998). Information processing. In D. Kuhn & R. S. Siegler (Eds.), *Information processing.* In D. Kuhn & R. S. Siegler (Eds.), *Handbook of child psychology: Vol. 2. Cognition, perception, and language* (5th ed., pp. 631–678). New York: Wiley.

Klahr, D., & Nigam, M. (2004). The equivalence of learning paths in early science instruction: Effects of direct instruction and discovery learning. *Psychological Science, 15,* 661–667.

Klaw, E. L., Rhodes, J. E., & Fitzgerald, L. F. (2003). Natural mentors in the lives of African-American adolescent mothers: Tracking relationships over time. *Journal of Youth and Adolescence, 32,* 223–232.

Klebanoff, M. A., Levine, R. J., Clemens, J. D., & Wilkins, D. G. (2002). Maternal serum caffeine metabolites and small-for-gestational-age birth. *American Journal of Epidemiology, 155,* 32–37.

Klebanov, P. K., Brooks-Gunn, J., McCarton, C., & McCormick, M. C. (1998). The contribution of neighborhood and family income to developmental test scores over the first three years of life. *Child Development, 69,* 1420–1436.

Klein, P. J., & Meltzoff, A. N. (1999). Long-term memory, forgetting, and deferred imitation in 12-month-old infants. *Developmental Science, 2,* 102–113.

Klenberg, L., Korkman, M., & Lahti-Nuuttila, P. (2001). Differential development of attention and executive functions in 3- to 12-year-old Finnish children. *Developmental Neuropsychology, 20,* 407–428.

Klesges, L., M., Johnson, K. C., Ward, K. D., & Barnard, M. (2001). Smoking cessation in pregnant women. *Obstetrics and Gynecology Clinics of North America, 28,* 269–282.

Kliewer, W., Fearnow, M. D., & Miller, P. A. (1996). Coping socialization in middle childhood: Tests of maternal and paternal influences. *Child Development, 67,* 2339–2357.

Klimes-Dougan, B., & Kistner, J. (1990). Physically abused preschoolers' responses to peers' distress. *Developmental Psychology, 26,* 599–602.

Klineberg, O. (1963). Negro–white differences in intelligence test performance: A new look at an old problem. *American Psychologist, 18,* 198–203.

Klingner, J. K., Vaughn, S., Hughes, M. T., Schumm, J. S., & Elbaum, B. (1998). Outcomes for students with and without learning disabilities in inclusive classrooms. *Learning Disabilities Research and Practice, 13,* 153–161.

Klump, K. L., Kaye, W. H., & Strober, M. (2001). The evolving foundations of eating disorders. *Psychiatric Clinics of North America, 24,* 215–225.

Knecht, S., Draeger, B., Deppe, M., Bobe, L., Lohmann, H., Floeel, A., Ringelstein, E.-B., & Henningsen, H. (2000). Handedness and hemispheric language dominance in healthy humans. *Brain, 123,* 2512–2518.

Knight, N., Sousa, P., Barrett, J. L., & Atran, S. (2004). Children's attributions of beliefs to humans and God: Cross-cultural evidence. *Cognitive Science, 28,* 117–126.

Knobloch, H., & Pasamanick, B. (Eds.). (1974). *Gesell and Amatruda's Developmental Diagnosis.* Hagerstown, MD: Harper & Row.

Knoers, N., van den Ouweland, A., Dreesen, J., Verdijk, M., Monnens, L. S., & van Oost, B. A. (1993). Nephrogenic diabetes insipidus: Identification of the genetic defect. *Pediatric Nephrology, 7,* 685–688.

Knudsen, K., & Waerness, K. (2003). National context, individual characteristics, and attitudes on mothers' employment: A comparative analysis of Great Britain, Sweden, and Norway. *Acta Sociologica, 44,* 67–97.

Kobayashi, T., Kazuo, H., Ryoko, M., & Hasegawa, T. (2004). Baby arithmetic: One object plus one tone. *Cognition, 91,* B23–B34.

Kochanska, G. (1991). Socialization and temperament in the development of guilt and conscience. *Child Development, 62,* 1379–1392.

Kochanska, G. (1993). Toward a synthesis of parental socialization and child temperament in early development of conscience. *Child Development, 64,* 325–347.

Kochanska, G. (1997a) Multiple pathways to conscience for children with different temperaments: From toddlerhood to age 5. *Developmental Psychology, 33,* 228–240.

Kochanska, G. (1997b) Mutually responsive orientation between mothers and their young children: Implications for early socialization. *Child Development, 68,* 94–112.

Kochanska, G. (1998). Mother–child relationship, child fearfulness, and emerging attachment: A short-term longitudinal study. *Developmental Psychology, 34,* 480–490.

Kochanska, G., Aksan, N., & Nichols, K. E. (2003). Maternal power assertion in discipline and moral discourse contexts: Commonalities, differences, and implications for children's moral conduct and cognition. *Developmental Psychology, 39,* 949–963.

Kochanska, G., Aksan, N., Knaack, A., & Rhines, H. M. (2004). Maternal parenting and children's conscience: Early security as moderator. *Child Development, 75,* 1229–1242.

Kochanska, G., Forman, D. R., & Coy, K. C. (1999). Implications of the mother–child relationship in infancy for socialization in the second year of life. *Infant Behavior and Development, 22,* 249–265.

Kochanska, G., Gross, J. N., Lin, M.-H., & Nichols, K. E. (2002). Guilt in young children: Development, determinants, and relations with broader system standards. *Child Development, 73,* 461–482.

Kochanska, G., & Knaack, A. (2003). Effortful control as a personality characteristic of young children: Antecedents, correlates, and consequences. *Journal of Personality, 71,* 1087–1112.

Kochanska, G., & Murray, K. T. (2000). Mother–child mutually responsive orientation and conscience development: From toddler to early school age. *Child Development, 71,* 417–431.

Kochanska, G., Murray, K. T., & Harlan, E. T. (2000). Effortful control in early childhood: Continuity and change, antecedents, and implications for social development. *Developmental Psychology, 36,* 220–232.

Kochenderfer-Ladd, B. (2003). Identification of aggressive and asocial victims and the stability of their peer victimization. *Merrill-Palmer Quarterly, 49,* 401–425.

Kochenderfer-Ladd, B., & Wardrop, J. L. (2001). Chronicity and instability of children's peer victimization experiences as predictors of loneliness and social satisfaction trajectories. *Child Development, 72,* 134–151.

Koelsch, S., Gunter, T., von Cramon, D., Zysset, S., Lohmann, G., & Friederici, A. (2002). Bach speaks: A cortical "language-network" serves the processing of music. *NeuroImage, 17,* 956–966.

Koestner, R., Franz, C., & Weinberger, J. (1990). The family origins of empathic concern: A 26-year longitudinal study. *Journal of Personality and Social Psychology, 58,* 709–717.

Kohen, D. E., Brooks-Gunn, J., Leventhal, T., & Hertzman, C. (2002). Neighborhood income and physical and social disorder in Canada: Associations with young children's competencies. *Child Development, 73,* 1844–1860.

Kohen, D., Hunter, T., Pence, A., & Goelman, H. (2000). The Victoria Day Care Research Project: Overview of a longitudinal study of child care and human development in Canada. *Canadian Journal of Research in Early Childhood Education, 8,* 49–54.

Kohlberg, L. (1958). *The development of modes of moral thinking and choice in the years ten to sixteen.* Unpublished doctoral dissertation, University of Chicago.

Kohlberg, L. (1966). A cognitive-developmental analysis of children's sex-role concepts and attitudes. In E. E. Maccoby (Ed.), *The development of sex differences* (pp. 82–173). Stanford, CA: Stanford University Press.

Kohlberg, L. (1969). Stage and sequence: The cognitive-developmental approach to socialization. In D. A. Goslin (Ed.), *Handbook of socialization theory and research* (pp. 347–480). Chicago: Rand McNally.

Kohlberg, L. (1976). Moral stages and moralization: The cognitive-developmental approach. In T. Lickona (Ed.), *Moral development and behavior: Theory, research, and social issues* (pp. 31–53). New York: Holt.

Kohlberg, L., & Diessner, R. (1991). A cognitive-developmental approach to moral attachment. In W. M. Kurtines (Ed.), *Intersections with attachment* (pp. 229–246). Hillsdale, NJ: Erlbaum.

Kohlberg, L., Levine, C., & Hewer, A. (1983). *Moral stages: A current formulation and a response to critics.* Basel: Karger.

Kolb, B., & Gibb, R. (2001). Early brain injury, plasticity, and behavior. In C. A. Nelson & M. Luciana (Eds.), *Handbook of developmental cognitive neuroscience* (pp. 175–190). Cambridge, MA: MIT Press.

Kolominsky, Y., Igumnov, S., & Drozdovitch, V. (1999). The psychological development of children from Belarus exposed in the prenatal period to radiation from the Chernobyl atomic power plant. *Journal of Child Psychology and Psychiatry, 40,* 299–305.

Kolvin, I., & Trowell, J. (1996). Child sexual abuse. In I. Rosen (Ed.), *Sexual deviation* (3rd ed., pp. 337–360). Oxford, UK: Oxford University Press.

Kopp, C. B. (1994). Infant assessment. In C. B. Fisher & R. M. Lerner (Eds.), *Applied developmental psychology* (pp. 265–293). New York: McGraw-Hill.

Kopp, C. B., & Neufeld, S. J. (2003). Emotional development during infancy. In R. Davidson, K. R. Scherer, & H. H. Goldsmith (Eds.), *Handbook of affective sciences* (pp. 347–374). Oxford, UK: Oxford University Press.

Korkman, M., Kettunen, S., & Autti-Raemoe, I. (2003). Neurocognitive impairment in early adolescence following prenatal alcohol exposure of varying duration. *Child Neurology, 9,* 117–128.

Kornhaber, M., Orfield, G., & Kurlaender, M. (2001). *Raising standards or raising barriers? Inequality and high-stakes testing in public education.* New York: Century Foundation Press.

Kouvonen, A., & Kivivuori, J. (2001). Part-time jobs, delinquency, and victimization among Finnish adolescents. *Journal of Scandinavian Studies in Criminology and Crime Prevention, 2,* 191–212.

Kovacs, D. M., Parker, J. G., & Hoffman, L. W. (1996). Behavioral, affective, and social correlates of involvement in cross-sex friendship in elementary school. *Child Development, 67,* 2269–2286.

Kowalski, K., & Lo, Y. (1999, April). *The influence of perceptual features and sociocultural information on the development of ethnic/racial bias in young children.* Paper presented at the biennial meeting of the Society for Research in Child Development, Albuquerque, NM.

Kozulin, A. (Ed.). (2003). *Vygotsky's educational theory in cultural context.* Cambridge, U.K.: Cambridge University Press.

Kraemer, H.C., Yesavage, J. A., Taylor, J. L., & Kupfer, D. (2000). How can we learn about dvelopmental processes from cross-sectional studies, or can we? *American Journal of Psychiatry, 157,* 163–171.

Krafft, K., & Berk, L. E. (1998). Private speech in two preschools: Significance of open-ended activities and make-believe play for verbal self-regulation. *Early Childhood Research Quarterly, 13,* 637–658.

Kramer, M. S., Guo, T., Platt, R. W., Sevkovskaya, Z., Dzikovich, I., & Collet, J. P. (2003). Infant growth and health outcomes associated with 3 compared with 6 mo. of exclusive breastfeeding. *American Journal of Clinical Nutrition, 78,* 291–295.

Kramer, M. S., Guo, T., Platt, R. W., Shapiro, S., Collet, J. P., & Chalmers, B. (2002). Breastfeeding and infant growth: Biology or bias? *Pediatrics, 110,* 343–347.

Kramer, M. S., & Kakuma, R. (2002). Optimal duration of exclusive breastfeeding. *Cochrane Database of Systematic Reviews, 2002*(4). Retrieved from www.cochrane.org/cochrane/revabstr/ab003517.htm

Krascum, R. M., & Andrews, S. (1998). The effects of theories on children's acquisition of family-resemblance categories. *Child Development, 69,* 333–346.

Krebs, D., & Gillmore, J. (1982). The relationship among the first stages of cognitive development, role-taking abilities, and moral development. *Child Development, 53,* 877–886.

Krebs, N. F., & Jacobson, M. S. (2003). Prevention of pediatric overweight and obesity. *Pediatrics, 112,* 424–430.

Krevans, J., & Gibbs, J. C. (1996). Parents' use of inductive discipline: Relations to children's empathy and prosocial behavior. *Child Development, 67,* 3263–3277.

Kroger, J. (1995). The differentiation of "firm" and "developmental" foreclosure identity statuses: A longitudinal study. *Journal of Adolescent Research, 10,* 317–337.

Kroger, J. (2000). *Identity development: Adolescence through adulthood.* Thousand Oaks, CA: Sage.

Kroger, J. (2001). What transits in an identity status transition: A rejoinder to commentaries. *Identity, 3,* 291–304.

Kruger, A. C. (1993). Peer collaboration: Conflict, cooperation, or both? *Social Development, 2,* 165–182.

Krumhansl, C. L., & Jusczyk, P. W. (1990). Infants' perception of phrase structure in music. *Psychological Science, 1,* 70–73.

Kubik, M. Y., Lytle, L. A., Hannan, P. J., Perry, C. L., & Story, M. (2003). The association of the school food environment with dietary behaviors of young adolescents. *American Journal of Public Health, 93,* 1168–1173.

Kuczynski, L. (1984). Socialization goals and mother–child interaction: Strategies for long-term and short-term compliance. *Developmental Psychology, 20,* 1061–1073.

Kuczynski, L. (2003). Beyond bidirectionality. In L. Kuczynski (Ed.), *Handbook of dynamics in parent–child relations* (pp. 3–24). Thousand Oaks, CA: Sage.

Kuczynski, L., & Hildebrandt, N. (1997). Models of conformity and resistance in socialization theory. In J. E. Grusec & L. Kuczynski (Eds.), *Parenting and children's internalization of values* (pp. 227–256). New York: Wiley.

Kuczynski, L., & Lollis, S. (2002). Four foundations for a dynamic model of parenting. In J. R. M. Gerris (Eds.), *Dynamics of parenting.* Hillsdale, NJ: Erlbaum.

Kuebli, J., Butler, S., & Fivush, R. (1995). Mother–child talk about past emotions: relations of maternal language and child gender over time. *Cognition and Emotion, 9,* 265–283.

Kuhl, P. K. (2000). A new view of language acquisition. *Proceedings of the National Academy of Sciences, 97,* 11850–11857.

Kuhl, P. K., Williams, K. A., Lacerda, F., Stevens, K. N., & Lindblom, B. (1992). Linguistic experience alters phonetic perception in infants by 6 months of age. *Science, 255,* 606–608.

Kuhn, D. (1989). Children and adults as intuitive scientists. *Psychological Review, 96,* 674–689.

Kuhn, D. (1993). Connecting scientific and informal reasoning. *Merrill-Palmer Quarterly, 39,* 74–103.

Kuhn, D. (1995). Microgenetic study of change: What has it told us? *Psychological Science, 6,* 133–139.

Kuhn, D. (1999). Metacognitive development. *Current Directions in Psychological Science, 9,* 178–181.

Kuhn, D. (2000). Why development does (and does not) occur: Evidence from the domain of inductive reasoning. In R. Siegler & J. McClelland (Eds.), *Mechanisms of cognitive development* (pp. 221–249). Mahwah, NJ: Erlbaum.

Kuhn, D. (2002). What is scientific thinking, and how does it develop? In U. Goswami (Ed.), *Blackwell handbook of childhood cognitive development* (pp. 371–393). Malden, MA: Blackwell.

Kuhn, D., Amsel, E., & O'Loughlin, M. (1988). *The development of scientific thinking* skills. Orlando, FL: Academic Press.

Kuhn, D., & Dean, D., Jr. (2004). Connecting scientific reasoning and causal inference. *Journal of Cognition and Development, 5,* 261–288.

Kuhn, D., & Pearsall, S. (2000). Developmental origins of scientific thinking. *Journal of Cognition and Development, 1,* 113–129.

Kuklinski, M. R., & Weinstein, R. S. (2001). Classroom and developmental differences in a path model of teacher expectancy effects. *Child Development, 72,* 1554–1578.

Kumar, S., & O'Brien, A. (2004). Recent developments in fetal medicine. *British Medical Journal, 328,* 1002–1006.

Kumpfer, K. L., & Alvarado, R. (2003). Family-strengthening approaches for the prevention of youth problem behaviors. *American Psychologist, 58,* 457–465.

Kunkel, D. (2001). Children and television advertising. In D. G. Singer & J. L. Singer (Eds.), *Handbook of children and the media* (pp. 375–393). Thousand Oaks, CA: Sage.

Kunnen, E. S., & Bosma, H. A. (2003). Fischer's skill theory applied to identity development: A response to Kroger. *Identity, 3,* 247–270.

Kunzinger, E. L., III. (1985). A short-term longitudinal study of memorial development during early grade school. *Developmental Psychology, 21,* 642–646.

Kurdek, L. A., & Fine, M. A. (1994). Family acceptance and family control as predictors of adjustment in young adolescents: Linear, curvilinear, or interactive effects? *Child Development, 65,* 1137–1146.

Kyratzis, A., & Guo, J. (2001). Preschool girls' and boys' verbal conflict strategies in the United States and China. *Research on Language and Social Interaction, 34,* 45–74.

Lackey, P. N. (1989). Adults' attitudes about assignments of household chores to male and female children. *Sex Roles, 20,* 271–281.

Lacourse, E., Nagin, D., Tremblay, R. E., Vitaro, F., & Claes, M. (2003). Developmental trajectories of boys' delinquent group membership and facilitation of violent behaviors during adolescence. *Development and Psychopathology, 15,* 183–197.

Ladd, G. W. (1999). Peer relationships and social competence during early and middle childhood. *Annual Review of Psychology, 50,* 333–359.

Ladd, G. W., Birch, S. H., & Buhs, E. S. (1999). Children's social and scholastic lives in kindergarten: Related spheres of influence? *Child Development, 70,* 1373–1400.

Ladd, G. W., Buhs, E. S., & Seid, M. (2000). Children's initial sentiments about kindergarten: Is school liking an antecedent of early classroom participation and achievement? *Merrill-Palmer Quarterly, 46,* 255–279.

Ladd, G. W., & Burgess, K. B. (1999). Charting the relationship trajectories of aggressive, withdrawn, and aggressive/withdrawn children during early grade school. *Child Development, 70,* 910–929.

Ladd, G. W., Kochenderfer, B. J., & Coleman, C. C. (1997). Classroom peer acceptance, friendship, and victimization: Distinct relational systems that contribute uniquely to children's school adjustment? *Child Development, 68,* 1181–1197.

Ladd, G. W., LeSieur, K., & Profilet, S. M. (1993). Direct parental influences on young children's peer relations. In S. Duck (Ed.), *Learning about relationships* (Vol. 2, pp. 152–183). London: Sage.

Ladd, G. W., & Pettit, G. S. (2002). Parenting and the development of children's peer relationships. In M. Bornstein (Ed.), *Handbook of parenting* (2nd ed.). Mahwah, NJ: Erlbaum.

Ladd, G. W., & Price, J. M. (1987). Predicting children's social and school adjustment following the transition from preschool to kindergarten. *Child Development, 58,* 1168–1189.

Ladd, G. W., & Troop-Gordon, W. (2003). The role of chronic peer difficulties in the development of children's psychological adjustment problems. *Child Development, 74,* 1344–1367.

LaFontana, K. M., & Cillessen, A. H. N. (1999). Children's interpersonal perceptions as a function of sociometric and peer perceived popularity. *Journal of Genetic Psychology, 160,* 225–242.

Lagattuta, K. H., Wellman, H. M., & Flavell, J. H. (1997). Preschoolers' understanding of the link between thinking and feeling: Cognitive cuing and emotional change. *Child Development, 68,* 1081–1104.

Lagercrantz, H., & Slotkin, T. A. (1986). The "stress" of being born. *Scientific American, 254,* 100–107.

Lagnado, L. (2001, November 2). Kids confront Trade Center trauma. *The Wall Street Journal,* pp. B1, B6.

La Greca, A. M., Prinstein, M. J., & Fetter, M. D. (2001). Adolescent peer crowd affiliation: Linkages with health-risk behaviors and close friendships. *Journal of Pediatric Psychology, 26,* 131–143.

Laible, D. J., & Thompson, R. A. (1998). Attachment and emotional understanding in preschool children. *Developmental Psychology, 34,* 1038–1045.

Laible, D. J., & Thompson, R. A. (2002). Mother–child conflict in the toddler years: Lessons in emotion, morality, and relationships. *Child Development, 73,* 1187–1203.

Laing, E., Butterworth, G., Ansari, D., Gsödl, M., Longhi, E., Panagiotaki, G., Paterson, S., & Karmiloff-Smith, A. (2002). Atypical development of language and social communication in toddlers with Williams syndrome. *Developmental Science, 5,* 233–246.

Laird, J. (2003). Lesbian and gay families. In F. Walsh (Ed.), *Normal family processes* (pp. 176–209). New York: Guilford.

Laird, R. D., Jordan, K. Y., Dodge, K. A., Pettit, G. S., & Bates, J. E. (2001). Peer rejection in childhood, involvement with antisocial peers in early adolescence, and the development of externalizing behavior problems. *Development and Psychopathology, 13,* 337–354.

Laird, R. D., Pettit, G. S., Bates, J. E., & Dodge, K. A. (2003). Parents' monitoring-relevant knowledge and adolescents' delinquent behavior: Evidence of correlated developmental changes and reciprocal influences. *Child Development, 74,* 752–768.

Lamaze, F. (1958). *Painless childbirth.* London: Burke.

Lamb, M. E. (1987). *The father's role: Cross-cultural perspectives.* Hillsdale, NJ: Erlbaum.

Lamb, M. E. (1997). The development of father–infant relationships. In M. E. Lamb (Ed.), *The role of the father in child development* (3rd ed., pp. 104–120). New York: Wiley.

Lamb, M. E. (1998). Nonparental child care: Context, quality, correlates, and consequences. In I. E. Sigel & K. A. Renninger (Eds.), *Handbook of child psychology: Vol. 4. Child psychology in practice* (5th ed., pp. 73–133). New York: Wiley.

Lamb, M. E., & Oppenheim, D. (1989). Fatherhood and father–child relationships: Five years of research. In S. H. Cath, A. Gurwitt, & L. Gunsberg (Eds.), *Fathers and their families* (pp. 11–26). Hillsdale, NJ: Erlbaum.

Lamb, M. E., Sternberg, K. J., & Prodromidis, M. (1992). Nonmaternal care and the security of infant–mother attachment: A reanalysis of the data. *Infant Behavior and Development, 15,* 71–83.

Lamb, M. E., Thompson, R. A., Gardner, W., Charnov, E. L., & Connell, J. P. (1985). *Infant– mother attachment: The origins and developmental significance of individual differences in Strange Situation behavior.* Hillsdale, NJ: Erlbaum.

Lamborn, S. D., Mounts, N. S., Steinberg, L. D., & Dornbusch, S. M. (1991). Patterns of competence and adjustment among adolescents from authoritative, authoritarian, indulgent, and neglectful families. *Child Development, 62,* 1049–1065.

Lammers, C., Ireland, M., Resnick, M., & Blum, R. (2000). Influences on adolescents' decisions to postpone onset of sexual intercourse: A survival analysis of virginity among youths aged 13 to 18 years. *Journal of Adolescent Health, 26,* 43–48.

Lancaster, J. B., & Whitten, P. (1980). Family matters. *The Sciences, 20,* 10–15.

Landry, S. H., Smith, K. E., Swank, P. R., & Miller-Loncar, C. L. (2000). Early maternal and child influences on children's later independent cognitive and social functioning. *Child Development, 71,* 358–375.

Langer, J., Gillette, P., & Arriaga, R. I. (2003). Toddlers' cognition of adding and subtracting objects in action and in perception. *Cognitive Development, 18,* 233–246.

Lansford, J. E., Criss, M. M., Pettit, G. S., Dodge, K. A., & Bates, J. E. (2003). Friendship quality, peer group affiliation, and peer antisocial behavior as moderators of the link between negative parenting and adolescent externalizing behavior. *Journal of Research on Adolescence, 13,* 161–184.

Lansford, J. E., Deater-Deckard, K., Dodge, K. A., Bates, J. E., & Pettit, G. S. (2004). Ethnic differences in the link between physical discipline and later adolescent externalizing behaviors. *Journal of Child Psychology and Psychiatry, 45,* 801–812.

Lapsley, D. K., Jackson, S., Rice, K., & Shadid, G. (1988). Self-monitoring and the "new look" at the imaginary audience and personal fable: An ego-developmental analysis. *Journal of Adolescent Research, 3,* 17–31.

Larson, R. W. (2001). How U.S. children and adolescents spend time: What it does (and doesn't) tell us about their development. *Current Directions in Psychological Science, 10,* 160–164.

Larson, R. W., & Ham, M. (1993). Stress and "storm and stress" in early adolescence: The relationship of negative events with dysphoric affect. *Developmental Psychology, 29,* 130–140.

Larson, R. W., & Lampman-Petraitis, C. (1989). Daily emotional states as reported by children and adolescents. *Child Development, 60,* 1250–1260.

Larson, R. W., Moneta, G., Richards, M. H., & Wilson, S. (2002). Continuity, stability, and change in daily emotional experience across adolescence. *Child Development, 73,* 1151–1165.

Larson, R. W., & Richards, M. (1998). Waiting for the weekend: Friday and Saturday night as the emotional climax of the week. In A. C. Crouter & R. Larson (Eds.), *Temporal rhythms in adolescence: Clocks, calendars, and the coordination of daily life* (pp. 37–51). San Francisco: Jossey-Bass.

Larson, R. W., Richards, M. H., Moneta, G., Holmbeck, G., & Duckett, E. (1996). Changes in adolescents' daily interactions with their families from ages 10 to 18: Disengagement and transformation. *Developmental Psychology, 32,* 744–754.

Larson, R. W., Richards, M. H., Sims, B., & Dworkin, J. (2001). How urban African-American young adolescents spend their time: Time budgets for locations, activities, and companionship. *American Journal of Community Psychology, 29,* 565–597.

Larzelere, R. E., Schneider, W. N., Larson, D. B., & Pike, P. L. (1996). The effects of discipline responses in delaying toddler misbehavior recurrences. *Child and Family Behavior Therapy, 18,* 35–57.

Lasoya, S. H., & Eisenberg, N. (2001). Affective empathy. In J. A. Hall & F. A. Bernieri (Eds.), *Interpersonal sensitivity: Theory and measurement* (pp. 21–43). Mahwah, NJ: Erlbaum.

Latz, S., Wolf, A. W., & Lozoff, B. (1999). Sleep practices and problems in young children in Japan and the United States. *Archives of Pediatric and Adolescent Medicine, 153,* 339–346.

Laucht, M., Esser, G., & Schmidt, M. H. (1997). Developmental outcome of infants born with biological and psychosocial risks. *Journal of Child Psychology and Psychiatry, 38,* 843–853.

Lauer, J. A., Betrán, A. P., Victora, C. G., de Onís, M., & Barros, A. J. (2004). Breastfeeding patterns and exposure to suboptimal breastfeeding among children in developing countries: Review and analysis of nationally representative surveys. *BMC Medicine, 2,* 26.

Laupa, M. (1995). "Who's in charge?" Preschool children's concepts of authority. *Early Childhood Research Quarterly, 9,* 1–7.

Laursen, B., Coy, K. C., & Collins, W. A. (1998). Reconsidering changes in parent–child conflict across adolescence: A meta-analysis. *Child Development, 69,* 817–832.

Law, K. L., Stroud, L. R., Niaura, R., LaGasse, L. L., Liu, J., & Lester, B. M. (2003). Smoking during pregnancy and newborn neurobehavior. *Pediatrics, 111,* 1318–1323.

Law, K. S., Wong, C.-S., & Song, L. J. (2004). The construct and criterion validity of emotional intelligence and its potential utility for management studies. *Journal of Applied Psychology, 89,* 483–496.

Lawrence, K., Kuntsi, J., Coleman, M., Campbell, R., & Skuse, D. (2003). Face and emotion recognition deficits in Turner syndrome: A possible role for X-linked genes in amygdala development. *Neuropsychology, 17,* 39–49.

Lazar, I., & Darlington, R. (1982). Lasting effects of early education: A report from the Consortium for Longitudinal Studies. *Monographs of the Society for Research in Child Development, 47*(2–3, Serial No. 195).

Lazarus, R. S., & Lazarus, B. N. (1994). *Passion and reason.* New York: Oxford University Press.

Leadbeater, B. J., Kuperminc, G. P., Blatt, S. J., & Hertzog, C. (1999). A multivariate model of gender differences in adolescents' internalizing and externalizing problems. *Developmental Psychology, 35,* 1268–1282.

Leaper, C. (1994). Exploring the correlates and consequences of gender segregation: Social relationships in childhood, adolescence, and adulthood. In C. Leaper (Ed.), *New directions for child development* (No. 65, pp. 67–86). San Francisco: Jossey-Bass.

Leaper, C. (2000). Gender, affiliation, assertion, and the interactive context of parent–child play. *Developmental Psychology, 36,* 381–393.

Leaper, C. (2002). Parenting girls and boys. In M. H. Bornstein (Ed.), *Handbook of parenting: Vol. 1. Children and Parenting* (pp. 127–152). Mahwah, NJ: Erlbaum.

Leaper, C., Anderson, K. J., & Sanders, P. (1998). Moderators of gender effects on parents' talk to their children: A meta-analysis. *Developmental Psychology, 34,* 3–27.

Leaper, C., Tenenbaum, H. R., & Shaffer, T. G. (1999). Communication patterns of African-American girls and boys from low-income, urban backgrounds. *Child Development, 70,* 1489–1503.

Learning Partnership. (2003). *The quality of public education in Canada.* Retrieved from www.cprn.com/en/doc.cfm?doc=224

Lederer, J. M. (2000). Reciprocal teaching of social studies in inclusive elementary classrooms. *Journal of Learning Disabilities, 33,* 91–106.

Lee, K., Cameron, C., Xu, F., Fu, G., & Board, J. (1997). Chinese and Canadian children's evaluations of lying and truth telling: Similarities and differences in the context of pro- and antisocial behaviors. *Child Development, 68,* 924–934.

Lee, V. E., Smerdon, B. A., Alfeld-Liro, C., & Brown, S. L. (2000). Inside large and small high schools: Curriculum and social relations. *Educational Evaluation and Policy Analysis, 22,* 147–171.

Leech, S. L., Day, N. L., Richardson, G. A., & Goldschmidt, L. (2003). Predictors of self-reported delinquent behavior in a sample of young adolescents. *Journal of Early Adolescence, 23,* 78–106.

Leeman, L. W., Gibbs, J. C., & Fuller, D. (1993). Evaluation of a multi-component group treatment program for juvenile delinquents. *Aggressive Behavior, 19,* 281–292.

Lefkowitz, E. S., Boone, T. L., Sigman, M., & Au, T. K. (2002). He said, she said: Gender differences in mother–adolescent conversations about sexuality. *Journal of Research on Adolescence, 12,* 217–242.

Lefkowitz, E. S., Sigman, M., & Au, T. K. (2000). Helping mothers discuss sexuality and AIDS with adolescents. *Child Development, 71,* 1383–1394.

Legerstee, M. (1991). The role of people and objects in early imitation. *Journal of Experimental Child Psychology, 51,* 423–433.

Legerstee, M., Barna, J., & DiAdamo, C. (2000). Precursors to the development of intention at 6 months: Understanding people and their actions. *Developmental Psychology, 36,* 627–634.

Lehman, D. R., & Nisbett, R. E. (1990). A longitudinal study of the effects of undergraduate training on reasoning. *Developmental Psychology, 26,* 952–960.

Lehman, E. B., Steier, A., Guidash, K. M., & Wanna, S. Y. (2002). Predictors of compliance in toddlers: Child temperament, maternal personality, and emotional availability. *Early Child Development and Care, 172,* 301–310.

Leiferman, J. A., & Evenson, K. R. (2003). The effect of regular leisure physical activity on birth outcomes. *Maternal and Child Health Journal, 7,* 59–64.

Leinbach, M. D., Hort, B. E., & Fagot, B. I. (1997). Bears are for boys: Metaphorical associations in young children's gender stereotypes. *Cognitive Development, 12,* 107–130.

Lemery, K. S., Goldsmith, H. H., Klinnert, M. D., & Mrazek, D. A. (1999). Developmental models of infant and childhood temperament. *Developmental Psychology, 35,* 189–204.

Lempert, H. (1990). Acquisition of passives: The role of patient animacy, salience, and lexical accessibility. *Journal of Child Language, 17,* 677–696.

Lengua, L. J., Wolchik, S., Sandler, I. N., & West, S. G. (2000). The additive and interactive effects of parenting and temperament in predicting problems of children of divorce. *Journal of Clinical Psychology, 29,* 232–244.

Lenneberg, E. H. (1967). *Biological foundations of language.* New York: Wiley.

Leon, K. (2003). Risk and protective factors in young children's adjustment to parental divorce: A review of the research. *Family Relations, 52,* 258–270.

Lerner, R. M., Fisher, C. B., & Weinberg, R. A. (2000). Toward a science for and of the people: Promoting civil society through the application of developmental science. *Child Development, 71,* 11–20.

Lerner, R. M., Rothbaum, F., Boulos, S., & Castellino, D. R. (2002). Developmental systems perspective on parenting. In M. H. Bornstein (Ed.), *Handbook of parenting: Vol. 2. Biology and Ecology of Parenting* (2nd ed., pp. 315–344). Mahwah, NJ: Erlbaum.

Leslie, A. M. (2004). Who's for learning? *Developmental Science, 7,* 417–419.

Lester, B. M. (1985). Introduction: There's more to crying than meets the ear. In B. M. Lester & C. F. Z. Boukydis (Eds.), *Infant crying* (pp. 1–27). New York: Plenum.

Lester, B. M. (2000). Prenatal cocaine exposure and child outcome: A model for the study of the infant at risk. *Israel Journal of Psychiatry and Related Sciences, 37,* 223-235.

Lester, B. M., ElSohly, M., Wright, L. L., Smeriglio, V. L., Verter, J., & Bauer, C. R. (2001). The maternal lifestyle study: Drug use by meconium toxicology and maternal self-report. *Pediatrics, 107,* 309–317.

Lester, B. M., Kotelchuck, M., Spelke, E., Sellers, M. J., & Klein, R. E. (1974). Separation protest in Guatemalan infants: Cross-cultural and cognitive findings. *Developmental Psychology, 10,* 79–85.

Lester, B. M., LaGasse, L., Seifer, R., Tronick, E. Z., Bauer, C., & Shankaran, S. (2003). The maternal lifestyle study (MLS): Effects of prenatal cocaine and/or opiate exposure on auditory brain response at one month. *Journal of Pediatrics, 142,* 279–285.

Lester, D. (2003). Adolescent suicide from an international perspective. *American Behavioral Scientist, 46,* 1157–1170.

Lett, D. (1997). *L'enfant des miracles: Enfance et société au Moyen Ages, XIIe–XIIIe siecles.* Paris: Aubier.

LeVay, S. (1993). *The sexual brain.* Cambridge, MA: MIT Press.

Leventhal, T., & Brooks-Gunn, J. (2003). Children and youth in neighborhood contexts. *Current Directions in Psychological Science, 12,* 27–31.

Levin, I., & Bus, A. G. (2003). How is emergent writing based on drawing? Analyses of children's products and their sorting by children and mothers. *Developmental Psychology, 39,* 891–905.

Levine, L. E. (1983). Mine: Self-definition in 2-year-old boys. *Developmental Psychology, 19,* 544–549.

Levine, L. J. (1995). Young children's understanding of the causes of anger and sadness. *Child Development, 66,* 697–709.

LeVine, R. A., Dixon, S., LeVine, S., Richman, A., Leiderman, P. H., Keefer, C. H., & Brazelton, T. B. (1994). *Child care and culture: Lessons from Africa.* New York: Cambridge University Press.

Levine, S. C., Huttenlocher, J., Taylor, A., & Langrock, A. (1999). Early sex differences in spatial skill. *Developmental Psychology, 35,* 940–949.

Levine, S. C., Huttenlocher, P., Banish, M. T., & Duda, E. (1987). Factors affecting cognitive functioning of hemiplegic children. *Developmental Medicine and Child Neurology, 29,* 27–35.

Levtzion-Korach, O., Tennenbaum, A., Schnitzer, R., & Ornoy, A. (2000). Early motor development of blind children. *Journal of Paediatric and Child Health, 36,* 226–229.

Levy, G. D., Taylor, M. G., & Gelman, S. A. (1995). Traditional and evaluative aspects of flexibility in gender roles, social conventions, moral rules, and physical laws. *Child Development, 66,* 515–531.

Levy, S. R., & Dweck, C. S. (1999). The impact of children's static vs. dynamic conceptions of people on stereotype formation. *Child Development, 70,* 1163–1180.

Levy, Y. (1996). Modularity of language reconsidered. *Brain and Language, 55,* 240–263.

Levy-Shiff, R. (2001). Psychological adjustment of adoptees in adulthood: Family environment and adoption-related correlates. *International Journal of Behavioral Development, 25,* 97–104.

Levy-Shiff, R., & Israelashvili, R. (1988). Antecedents of fathering: Some further exploration. *Developmental Psychology, 24,* 434–440.

Lew, A. R., & Butterworth, G. (1997). The development of hand–mouth coordination in 2- to 5-month-old infants: Similarities with reaching and grasping. *Infant Behavior and Development, 20,* 59–69.

Lewis, C., Freeman, N. H., Kyriadidou, C., Maridakikassotaki, K., & Berridge, D. M. (1996). Social influences on false belief access—specific sibling influences or general apprenticeship? *Child Development, 67,* 2930–2947.

Lewis, M. (1992). *Shame: The exposed self.* New York: Free Press.

Lewis, M. (1994). Myself and me. In S. T. Parker, R. W. Mitchell, & M. L. Boccia (Eds.), *Self-awareness in animals and humans: Developmental perspectives* (pp. 20–34). New York: Cambridge University Press.

Lewis, M. (1995). Cognition-emotion feedback and the self-organization of developmental paths. *Human Development, 38,* 71–102.

Lewis, M. (1997). *Altering fate: Why the past does not predict the future.* New York: Guilford.

Lewis, M. (1998). Emotional competence and development. In D. Pushkar, W. M. Bukowski, A. E. Schwartzman, E. M. Stack, & D. R. White (Eds.), *Improving competence across the lifespan* (pp. 27–36). New York: Plenum.

Lewis, M. (1999). The role of the self in cognition and emotion. In T. Dalgleish & M. J. Power (Eds.), *Handbook of cognition and emotion* (pp. 125–142). Chichester, UK: Wiley.

Lewis, M. D. (2000). The promise of dynamic systems approaches for an integrated account of human development. *Child Development, 71,* 36–43.

Lewis, M., Alessandri, S. M., & Sullivan, M. W. (1992). Differences in shame and pride as a function of children's gender and task difficulty. *Child Development, 63,* 630–638.

Lewis, M., & Brooks-Gunn, J. (1979). *Social cognition and the acquisition of self.* New York: Plenum.

Lewis, M., Ramsay, D. S., & Kawakami, K. (1993). Differences between Japanese infants and Caucasian American infants in behavioral and cortisol response to inoculation. *Child Development, 64,* 1722–1731.

Lewis, M., Sullivan, M. W., & Ramsay, D. S. (1992). Individual differences in anger and sad expressions during extinction: Antecedents and consequences. *Infant Behavior and Development, 15,* 443–452.

Lewis, M., Sullivan, M. W., Stanger, C., & Weiss, M. (1989). Self development and self-conscious emotions. *Child Development, 60,* 146–156.

Lewis, M., Sullivan, M. W., & Vasen, A. (1987). Making faces: Age and emotion differences in the posing of emotional expressions. *Developmental Psychology, 23,* 690–697.

Lewontin, R. (1995). *Human diversity.* New York: Freeman.

Lewontin, R. (2003). *Race: The power of an illusion.* Alexandria, VA: Public Broadcasting System. Retrieved from www.pbs.org/race

Lewontin, R. C. (1976). Race and intelligence. In N. J. Block & G. Dworkin (Eds.), *The IQ controversy* (pp. 78–92). New York: Pantheon Books.

Liau, A. K., Barriga, A. Q., & Gibbs, J. C. (1998). Relations between self-serving cognitive distortion and overt vs. covert antisocial behavior in adolescents. *Aggressive Behavior, 24,* 335–346.

Liben, L. S. (1999). Developing an understanding of external spatial representations. In I. E. Sigel (Ed.), *Development of mental representation* (pp. 297–321). Mahwah, NJ: Erlbaum.

Liben, L. S., & Bigler, R. S. (2002). The developmental course of gender differentiation: Conceptualizing, measuring, and evaluating constructs and pathways. *Monographs of the Society for Research in Child Development, 67*(2, Serial No. 269).

Liben, L. S., Bigler, R. S., & Krogh, H. R. (2001). Pink and blue collar jobs: Children's judgments of job status and job aspirations in relation to sex of worker. *Journal of Experimental Child Psychology, 79,* 346–363.

Liben, L. S., Bigler, R. S., & Krogh, H. R. (2002). Language at work: Children's gendered interpretations of occupational titles. *Child Development, 73,* 810–828.

Liben, L. S., & Downs, R. M. (1993). Understanding person-space-map relations: Cartographic and developmental perspectives. *Developmental Psychology, 29,* 739–752.

Liben, L. S., & Signorella, M. L. (1993). Gender-schematic processing in children: The role of initial interpretations of stimuli. *Developmental Psychology, 29,* 141–149.

Lickliter, R., & Bahrick, L. E. (2000). The development of infant intersensory perception: Advantages of a comparative convergent-operations approach. *Psychological Bulletin, 126,* 260–280.

Lickliter, R., Bahrick, L. E., & Honeycutt, H. (2002). Intersensory redundancy facilitates prenatal perceptual learning in bobwhite quail (*Colinus virginianus*) embryos. *Developmental Psychology, 38,* 15–23.

Lickona, T. (1976). Research on Piaget's theory of moral development. In T. Lickona (Ed.), *Moral development and behavior* (pp. 219–240). New York: Holt, Rinehart & Winston.

Lidz, C. S. (2001). Multicultural issues and dynamic assessment. In L. A. Suzuki & J. G. Ponterotto (Eds.), *Handbook of multicultural assessment: Clinical, psychological, and educational applications* (2nd ed., pp. 523–539). San Francisco: Jossey-Bass.

Lieven, E., Pine, J., & Baldwin, G. (1997). Lexically based learning and early grammatical development. *Journal of Child Language, 24,* 187–220.

Light, P., & Perret-Clermont, A. (1989). Social context effects in learning and testing. In A. R. H. Gellatly, D. Rogers, & J. Sloboda (Eds.), *Cognition and social worlds* (pp. 99–112). Oxford: Clarendon Press.

Lillard, A. S. (1998). Playing with a theory of mind. In O. N. Saracho & B. Spodek (Eds.), *Multiple perspectives on play in early childhood education* (pp. 11–33). Albany: State University of New York Press.

Lillard, A. S. (2001). Pretending, understanding pretense, and understanding minds. In S. Reifel (Ed.), *Theory in contect and out: Play and culture studies, Vol. 3* (pp. 233–254). Westport, CT: Ablex.

Lin, C. C., Hsiao, C. K., & Chen, W. J. (1999). Development of sustained attention assessed using the continuous performance test among children 6–15 years. *Journal of Abnormal Child Psychology, 27,* 403–412.

Lindsay-Hartz, J., de Rivera, J., & Mascolor, M. F. (1995). Differentiating guilt and shame and their effects on motivation. In J. P. Tangney & K. W. Fischer (Eds.), *Self-conscious emotions* (pp. 274–300). New York: Guilford.

Lindsey, D., & Martin, S. K. (2003). Deepening child poverty: The not so good news about welfare reform. *Children and Youth Services Review, 25,* 165–173.

Lindsey, E. W., & Colwell, M. J. (2003). Preschoolers' emotional competence: Links to pretend and physical play. *Child Study Journal, 33,* 39–52.

Lindsey, E. W., & Mize, J. (2000). Parent–child physical and pretense play: Links to children's social competence. *Merrill-Palmer Quarterly, 46,* 565–591.

Linn, M. C., & Petersen, A. C. (1985). Emergence and characterization of sex differences in spatial ability: A meta-analysis. *Child Development, 56,* 1479–1498.

Linn, S. (2004). *Consuming kids: The hostile takeover of childhood.* New York: New Press.

Linn, S. (2005). The commercialization of childhood. In S. Olfman (Ed.), *Childhood lost: How American culture is failing our kids* (pp. 107–122). Westport, CT: Praeger.

Lipman, E. L., Boyle, M. H., Dooley, M. D., & Offord, D. R. (2002). Child well-being in single-mother families. *Journal of the American Academy of Child and Adolescent Psychiatry, 41,* 75–82.

Lipsitt, L. P. (2003). Crib death: A biobehavioral phenomenon? *Psychological Science, 12,* 164–170.

Lipton, J. S., & Spelke, E. S. (2003). Origins of number sense: Large-number discrimination in human infants. *Psychological Science, 14,* 396–401.

Litovsky, R. Y., & Ashmead, D. H. (1997). Development of binaural and spatial hearing in infants and children. In R. H. Gilkey & T. R. Anderson (Eds.), *Binaural and spatial hearing in real and virtual environments* (pp. 571–592). Mahwah, NJ: Erlbaum.

Liu, J., Raine, A., Venables, P. H., Dalais, C., & Mednick, S. A. (2003). Malnutrition at age 3 years and lower cognitive ability at age 11 years. *Archives of Paediatric and Adolescent Medicine, 157,* 593–600.

Lloyd, L. (1999). Multi-age classes and high ability students. *Review of Educational Research, 69,* 187–212.

Lochman, J. E., & Dodge K. A. (1998). Distorted perceptions in dyadic interactions of aggressive and nonaggressive boys: Effects of prior expectations, context, and boys' age. *Development and Psychopathology, 10,* 495–512.

Locke, J. (1892). Some thoughts concerning education. In R. H. Quick (Ed.), *Locke on education* (pp. 1–236). Cambridge, UK: Cambridge University Press. (Original work published 1690)

Lockhart, R. S., & Craik, F. I. M. (1990). Levels of processing: A retrospective commentary on a framework for memory research. *Canadian Journal of Psychology, 44,* 87–112.

Loeb, S., Fuller, B., Kagan, S. L., & Carrol, B. (2004). Child care in poor communities: Early learning effects of type, quality, and stability. *Child Development, 75,* 47–65.

Loeber, R. L., Farrington, D. P., Stouthamer-Loeber, M., Moffitt, T. E., & Caspi, A. (1999). The development of male offending: Key findings from the first decade of the Pittsburgh Youth Study. *Studies on Crime and Crime Prevention, 8,* 245–263.

Loehlin, J. C. (2000). Group differences in intelligence. In R. J. Sternberg (Ed.), *Handbook of intelligence* (pp. 176–193). New York: Cambridge University Press.

Loehlin, J. C., Horn, J. M., & Willerman, L. (1997). Heredity, environment, and IQ in the Texas Adoption Project. In R. J. Sternberg & E. L. Grigorenko (Eds.), *Intelligence, heredity, and environment* (pp. 105–125). New York: Cambridge University Press.

Loganovskaja, T. K., & Loganovsky, K. N. (1999). EEG, cognitive and psychopathological abnormalities in children irradiated in utero. *International Journal of Psychophysiology, 34,* 211–224.

Lohman, D. F. (2000). Measures of intelligence: Cognitive theories. In A. E. Kazdin (Ed.), *Encyclopedia of psychology: Vol. 5* (pp. 147–150). Washington, DC: American Psychological Association.

Lonigan, C. J., & Whitehurst, G. J. (1998). Relative efficacy of parent and teacher involvement in a shared-reading intervention for preschool children from low-income backgrounds. *Early Childhood Research Quarterly, 13,* 263–290.

Looker, D., & Thiessen, V. (2003). *The digital divide in Canadian schools: Factors affecting student access to and use of information technology.* Ottawa: Canadian Education Statistics Council.

Loots, G., & Devise, I. (2003). The use of visual–tactile communication strategies by deaf and hearing fathers and mothers of deaf infants. *Journal of Deaf Studies and Deaf Education, 8,* 31–42.

Lorenz, K. Z. (1943). Die angeborenen Formen möglicher Erfahrung. *Zeitschrift für Tierpsychologie, 5,* 235–409.

Lorenz, K. Z. (1983). *So Kam der Mensch auf den Hund.* Munich: DTV.

Losey, K. M. (1995). Mexican-American students and classroom interaction: An overview and critique. *Review of Educational Research, 65,* 283–318.

Louie, V. (2001). Parents' aspirations and investment: The role of social class in the educational experiences of 1.5- and second generation Chinese Americans. *Harvard Educational Review, 71,* 438–474.

Louis, J., Cannard, C., Bastuji, H., & Challamel, M.-J. (1997). Sleep ontogenesis revisited: A longitudinal 24-hour home polygraphic study on 15 normal infants during the first two years of life. *Sleep, 20,* 323–333.

Lourenco, O. (2003). Making sense of Turiel's dispute with Kohlberg: The case of the child's moral competence. *New Ideas in Psychology, 21,* 43–68.

Love, J. M., Harrison, L., Sagi-Schwartz, A., van IJzendoorn, M. H., Ross, C., & Ungerer, J. A. (2003). Child care quality matters: How conclusions may vary with context. *Child Development, 74,* 1021–1033.

Lozoff, B., Klein, N. K., Nelson, E. C., McClish, D. K., Manuel, M., & Chacon, M. E. (1998). Behavior of infants with iron-deficiency anemia. *Child Development, 69,* 24–36.

Lubart, T. I. (2003). In search of creative intelligence. In R. J. Sternberg, J. Lautrey, & T. I. Lubart (Eds.), *Models of intelligence: International perspectives* (pp. 279–292). Washington, DC: American Psychological Association.

Lubinski, D., & Benbow, C. P. (1994). The study of mathematically precocious youth: The first three decades of a planned 50-year study of intellectual talent. In R. F. Subotnik & K. D. Arnold (Eds.), *Beyond Terman: Contemporary longitudinal studies of giftedness and talent* (pp. 255–281). Norwood, NJ: Ablex.

Lucariello, J. (1998). Together wherever we go: The ethnographic child and the developmentalist. *Child Development, 69,* 355–358.

Lucariello, J., Kyratzis, A., & Nelson, K. (1992). Taxonomic knowledge: What kind and when? *Child Development, 63,* 978–998.

Lucas, S. R., & Behrends, M. (2002). Sociodemographic diversity, correlated achievement, and de facto tracking. *Sociology of Education, 75,* 328–348.

Luciana, M., Sullivan, J., & Nelson, C. A. (2001). Associations between phenylalanine-to-tyrosine ratios and performance on tests of neuropsychological function in adolescents treated early and continuously for phenylketonuria. *Child Development, 72,* 1637–1652.

Ludemann, P. M. (1991). Generalized discrimination of positive facial expressions by seven- and ten-month-old infants. *Child Development, 62,* 55–67.

Lueptow, L. B., Garovich, L., & Lueptow, M. B. (2001). Social change and the persistnce of sex typing: 1974–1997. *Social Forces, 80,* 1–36.

Luna, B., Garvger, K. E., Urban, T. A., Lazar, N. A., & Sweeney, J. A. (2004). Maturation of cognitive processes from late childhood to adulthood. *Child Development, 75,* 1357–1372.

Luna, B., Thulborn, K. R., Monoz, D. P., Merriam, E. P., Garver, K. E., Minshew, N. J., Keshavan, M. S., Genovese, C. R., Eddy, W. F., & Sweeney, J. A. (2001). Maturation of widely distributed brain function subserves cognitive development. *Neuroimage, 13,* 786–793.

Luria, A. R. (1976). *Cognitive development: Its cultural and social foundations.* Cambridge, MA: Harvard University Press.

Lussier, G., Deater-Deckard, K., Dunn, J., & Davies, L. (2002). Support across two generations: Children's closeness to grandparents following parental divorce and remarriage. *Journal of Family Psychology, 16,* 363–376.

Luster, T., & Dubow, E. (1992). Home environment and maternal intelligence as predictors of verbal intelligence: A comparison of preschool and school-age children. *Merrill-Palmer Quarterly, 38,* 151–175.

Luster, T., & McAdoo, H. (1996). Family and child influences on educational attainment: A secondary analysis of the High/Scope Perry Preschool data. *Developmental Psychology, 32,* 26–39.

Luthar, S. S., & Becker, B. E. (2002). Privileged but pressured: A study of affluent youth. *Child Development, 73,* 1593–1610.

Luthar, S. S., & Latendresse, S. J. (2005a). Children of the affluent: Challenges to well-being. *Current Directions in Psychological Science, 14,* 49–53.

Luthar, S. S., & Latendresse, S. J. (2005b). Comparable "risks" at the socioeconomic status extremes: Preadolescents' perceptions of parenting. *Development and Psychopathology, 17,* 207–230.

Luthar, S. S., & Sexton, C. (2004). The high price of affluence. In R. V. Kail (Ed.), *Advances in child development* (Vol. 32, pp. 126–162). San Diego, CA: Academic Press.

Lutz, D. J., & Sternberg, R. J. (1999). Cognitive development. In M. H. Bornstein & M. E. Lamb (Eds.), *Developmental psychology: An advanced textbook* (4th ed., pp. 275–311). Mahwah, NJ: Erlbaum.

Lutz, S. E., & Ruble, D. N. (1995). Children and gender prejudice: Context, motivation, and the development of gender conception. In R. Vasta (Ed.), *Annals of child development* (Vol. 10, pp. 131–166). London: Jessica Kingsley.

Lynch, M., & Cicchetti, D. (1998). An ecological-transactional analysis of children and contexts: The longitudinal interplay among child maltreatment, community violence, and children's symptomatology. *Development and Psychopathology, 10,* 235–257.

Lyon, G. R., Fletcher, J. M., & Barnes, M. C. (2002). Learning disabilities. In E. J. Mash & R. A. Barkley (Eds.), *Child psychopathology* (2nd ed., pp. 520–586). New York: Guilford.

Lyon, T. D., & Flavell, J. H. (1994). Young children's understanding of "remember" and "forget." *Child Development, 65,* 1357–1371.

Lyons-Ruth, K. (1996). Attachment relationships among children with aggressive behavior problems: The role of disorganized early attachment patterns. *Journal of Consulting and Clinical Psychology, 64,* 64–73.

Lyons-Ruth, K., Bronfman, E., & Parsons, E. (1999). Maternal frightened, frightening, or atypical behavior and disorganized infant attachment patterns. *Monographs of the Society for Research in Child Development, 64*(3, Serial No. 258), 67–96.

Lyons-Ruth, K., Easterbrooks, A., & Cibelli, C. (1997). Infant attachment strategies, infant mental lag, and maternal depressive symptoms: Predictors of internalizing and externalizing problems at age 7. *Developmental Psychology, 33,* 681–692.

Lytton, H., & Romney, D. M. (1991). Parents' sex-related differential socialization of boys and girls: A meta-analysis. *Psychological Bulletin, 109,* 267–296.

Maccoby, E. E. (1984). Socialization and developmental change. *Child Development, 55,* 317–328.

Maccoby, E. E. (1998). *The two sexes: Growing up apart, coming together.* Cambridge, MA: Belknap/Harvard University Press.

Maccoby, E. E. (2000a). Parenting and its effects on children: On reading and misreading behavior genetics. *Annual Review of Psychology, 51,* 1–27.

Maccoby, E. E. (2000b). Perspectives on gender development. *International Journal of Behavioral Development, 24,* 398–406.

Maccoby, E. E. (2002). Gender and group process: A developmental perspective. *Current Directions in Psychological Science, 11,* 54–58.

Maccoby, E. E., & Jacklin, C. N. (1987). Gender segregation in childhood. In E. H. Reese (Ed.), *Advances in child development and behavior* (Vol. 20, pp. 239–287). New York: Academic Press.

Maccoby, E. E., & Martin, J. A. (1983). Socialization in the context of the family. In E. M. Hetherington (Ed.), *Handbook of Child Psychology: Vol. 4. Socialization, personality, and social development* (pp. 1–101). New York: Wiley.

Mackey, K., Arnold, M. L., & Pratt, M. W. (2001). Adolescents' stories of decision making in more and less authoritative families: Representing the voices of parents in narrative. *Journal of Adolescent Research, 16,* 243–268.

MacLean, K. (2003). The impact of institutionalization on child development. *Development and Psychopathology, 15,* 853–884.

MacWhinney, B. (Ed.). (1999). *The emergence of language.* Mahwah, NJ: Erlbaum.

Madon, S., Jussim, L., & Eccles, J. (1997). In search of the powerful self-fulfilling prophecy. *Journal of Personality and Social Psychology, 72,* 791–809.

Magnuson, K. A., & Duncan, G. J. (2002). Parents in poverty. In M. H. Bornstein (Ed.), *Handbook of parenting: Vol. 4. Social Conditions and Applied Parenting* (2nd ed., pp. 95–122). Mahwah, NJ: Erlbaum.

Mahalingham, R. (1999). Essentialism, power, and representation of caste: A developmental study. *Dissertation Abstracts International, 60*(2–B), 856.

Mahon, M. M., Goldberg, E. Z., & Washington, S. K. (1999). Concept of death in a sample of Israeli kibbutz children. *Death Studies, 23,* 43–59.

Mahoney, J. L. (2000). Participation in school extracurricular activities as a moderator in the development of antisocial patterns. *Child Development, 71,* 502–516.

Mahoney, J. L., & Cairns, R. B. (1997). Do extracurricular activities protect against early school dropout? *Developmental Psychology, 33,* 241–253.

Mahoney, J. L., & Magnuson, D. (2001). Parent participation in community activities and the persistence of criminality. *Development and Psychopathology, 13,* 123–139.

Mahoney, J. L., Schweder, A. E., & Stattin, H. (2002). Structured after-school activities as a moderator of depressed mood for adolescents with detached relations to their parents. *Journal of Community Psychology, 30,* 69–86.

Mahoney, J. L., Stattin, H., & Magnusson, D. (2001). Youth recreation centre participation and criminal offending: A 20-year longitudinal study of Swedish boys. *International Journal of Behavioral Development, 25,* 509–520.

Main, M. (2000). The organized categories of infant, child, and adult attachment: Flexible vs. inflexible attention under attachment-related stress. *Journal of the American Psychoanalytic Association, 48,* 1055–1096.

Main, M., & Goldwyn, R. (1994). *Interview-based adult attachment classifications: Related to infant–mother and infant–father attachment.* Unpublished manuscript, University of California, Berkeley.

Main, M., & Goldwyn, R. (1998). *Adult attachment classification system.* London: University College.

Main, M., & Solomon, J. (1990). Procedures for identifying infants as disorganized/disoriented during the Ainsworth Strange Situation. In M. Greenberg, D. Cicchetti, & M. Cummings (Eds.), *Attachment in the preschool years: Theory, research, and intervention* (pp. 121–160). Chicago: University of Chicago Press.

Major, B., Spencer, S., Schmader, T., Wolfe, C., & Crocker, J. (1998). Coping with negative stereotypes about intellectual performance: The role of psychological disengagement. *Personality and Social Psychology Bulletin, 24,* 34–50.

Makin, J. W., Fried, P. A., & Watkinson, B. (1991). A comparison of active and passive smoking during pregnancy: Long-term effects. *Neurotoxicology and Teratology, 13,* 5–12.

Malatesta, C. Z., Grigoryev, P., Lamb, C., Albin, M., & Culver, C. (1986). Emotion socialization and expressive development in preterm and full-term infants. *Child Development, 57,* 316–330.

Malina, R. M., & Bouchard, C. (1991). *Growth, maturation, and physical activity.* Champaign, IL: Human Kinetics.

Mandler, J. M. (2004). *The foundations of mind: Origins of conceptual thought.* New York: Oxford University Press.

Mandler, J. M., & McDonough, L. (1993). Concept formation in infancy. *Cognitive Development, 8,* 291–318.

Mandler, J. M., & McDonough, L. (1998). On developing a knowledge base in infancy. *Developmental Psychology, 34,* 1274–1288.

Mandler, J. M., & Robinson, C. A. (1978). Developmental changes in picture recognition. *Journal of Experimental Child Psychology, 26,* 122–136.

Mange, E. J., & Mange, A. P. (1998). *Basic human genetics* (2nd ed.). Sunderland, MA: Sinauer Associates.

Mangelsdorf, S. C., Schoppe, S. J., & Burr, H. (2000). The meaning of parental reports: A contextual approach to the study of temperament and behavior problems. In V. J. Molfese & D. L. Molfese (Eds.), *Temperament and personality across the life span* (pp. 121–140). Mahwah, NJ: Erlbaum.

Manlove, J., Ryan, S., & Franzetta, K. (2003). Patterns of contraceptive use within teenagers' first sexual relationships. *Perspectives on Sexual and Reproductive Health, 35,* 246–255.

Mann, T., Braswell, G., & Berk, L. E. (2005, April). *A community children's museum as a context for parent–child engagement.* Poster presented at the biennial meeting of the Society for Research in Child Development, Atlanta, GA.

Mant, C. M., & Perner, J. (1988). The child's understanding of commitment. *Developmental Psychology, 24,* 343–351.

Maqsud, M. (1977). The influence of social heterogeneity and sentimental credibility on moral judgments of Nigerian Muslim adolescents. *Journal of Cross-Cultural Psychology, 8,* 113–122.

Maratsos, M. (1998). The acquisition of grammar. In D. Kuhn & R. S. Siegler (Eds.), *Handbook of child psychology: Vol. 2. Cognition, perception and language* (5th ed., pp. 421–466). New York: Wiley.

Maratsos, M. (2000). More overregularizations after all: New data and discussion on Marcus, Pinker, Ullman, Hollander, Rosen, & Xu. *Journal of Child Language, 27,* 183–212.

Maratsos, M. P., & Chalkley, M. A. (1980). The internal language of children's syntax: The ontogenesis and representation of syntactic categories. In K. Nelson (Ed.), *Children's language* (Vol. 2, pp. 127–214). New York: Gardner Press.

March of Dimes. (2004). Use of vitamins containing folic acid among women of childbearing age—United States, 2004. *Morbidity and Mortality Weekly Report, 53,* 847–850.

Marchman, V. A., & Thal, D. J. (2005). Words and grammar. In M. Tomasello & D. I. Slobin (Eds.), *Beyond nature-nurture: Essays in honor of Elizabeth Bates* (pp. 141–164). Mahwah, NJ: Erlbaum.

Marcia, J. E. (1966). Development and validation of ego-identity status. *Journal of Personality and Social Psychology, 3,* 551–558.

Marcia, J. E. (1980). Identity in adolescence. In J. Adelson (Ed.), *Handbook of adolescent psychology* (pp. 159–187). New York: Wiley.

Marcia, J. E., Waterman, A. S., Matteson, D. R., Archer, S. L., & Orlofsky, J. L. (1993). *Ego identity: A handbook for psychosocial research.* New York: Springer-Verlag.

Marcon, R. A. (1999a). Differential impact of preschool models on development and early learning of inner-city children: A three-cohort study. *Developmental Psychology, 35,* 358–375.

Marcon, R. A. (1999b). Positive relationships between parent–school involvement and public school inner-city preschoolers' development and academic performance. *School Psychology Review, 28,* 395–412.

Marcus, G. F., Pinker, S., Ullman, M., Hollander, M., Rosen, T. J., & Xu, F. (1992). Overregularization in language acquisition. *Monographs of the Society for Research in Child Development, 57*(4, Serial No. 228).

Marcus, G. F., Vijayan, S., Rao, S. B., & Vishton, P. M. (1999). Rule learning by seven-month-old infants. *Science, 283,* 77–80.

Mareschal, D. (2003). The acquisition and use of implicit categories in early development. In D. H. Rakison & L. M. Oakes (Eds.), *Early category and concept development* (pp. 360–383). New York: Oxford University Press.

Markman, E. M. (1992). Constraints on word learning: Speculations about their nature, origins, and domain specificity. In M. R. Gunnar & M. P. Maratsos (Eds.), *Minnesota Symposia on Child Psychology* (Vol. 25, pp. 59–101). Hillsdale, NJ: Erlbaum.

Markman, E. M., Wasow, J. L., & Hansen, M. B. (2003). Use of the mutual exclusivity assumption by young word learners. *Cognitive Psychology, 47,* 241–275.

Markovits, H., Benenson, J., & Dolensky, E. (2001). Evidence that children and adolescents have internal models of peer interactions that are gender differentiated. *Child Development, 72,* 879–886.

Markovits, H., Fleury, M. L., Quinn, S., & Venet, M. (1998). The development of conditional reasoning and the structure of semantic memory. *Child Development, 69,* 742–755.

Markovits, H., Schleifer, M., & Fortier, L. (1989). Development of elementary deductive reasoning in young children. *Developmental Psychology, 25,* 787–793.

Marks, N. F., & Lambert, J. D. (1998). Marital status continuity and change among young and midlife adults. *Journal of Family Issues, 19,* 652–686.

Markson, L., & Bloom, P. (1997). Evidence against a dedicated system for word learning in children. *Nature, 385,* 813–815.

Markstrom-Adams, C., & Adams, G. R. (1995). Gender, ethnic group, and grade differences in psychosocial functioning during middle adolescence? *Journal of Youth and Adolescence, 24,* 397–417.

Markus, H. R., & Kitayama, S. (1991). Culture and the self: Implications for cognition, emotion, and motivation. *Psychological Review, 98,* 224–253.

Marlier, L., & Schaal, B. (1997). La perception de la familiarité olfactive chez le nouveau-né: Influence différentielle du mode d'alimentation? [The perception of olfactory familiarity in the neonate: Differential influence of the mode of feeding] *Enfance, 1,* 47–61.

Marlier, L., Schaal, B., & Soussignan, R. (1998). Neonatal responsiveness to the odor of amniotic and lacteal fluids: A test of perinatal chemosensory continuity. *Child Development, 69,* 611–623.

Marsh, D. T., Serafica, F. C., & Barenboim, C. (1981). Interrelationships among perspective taking, interpersonal problem solving, and interpersonal functioning. *Journal of Genetic Psychology, 138,* 37–48.

Marsh, H. W. (1990). The structure of academic self-concept: The Marsh/Shavelson model. *Journal of Educational Psychology, 82,* 623–636.

Marsh, H. W., & Ayotte, V. (2003). Do multiple dimensions of self-concept become more differentiated with age? The differential distinctiveness hypothesis. *Journal of Educational Psychology, 95,* 687–706.

Marsh, H. W., Craven, R., & Debus, R. (1998). Structure, stability, and development of young children's self-concepts: A multicohort-multioccasion study. *Child Development, 69,* 1030–1053.

Marsh, H. W., Ellis, L. A., & Craven, R. G. (2002). How do preschool children feel about themselves? Unraveling measurement and multidimensional self-concept structure. *Developmental Psychology, 38,* 376–393.

Marsh, H. W., & Hau, K.-T. (2003). Big-fish–little-pond effect on academic self-concept: A cross-cultural (26-country) test of the negative effects of academically selective schools. *American Psychologist, 58,* 364–376.

Marsh, H. W., & Kleitman, S. (2005). Consequences of employment during high school: Character building, subversion of academic goals, or a threshold? *American Educational Research Journal, 42,* 331–369.

Marsh, J. S., & Daigneault, J. P. (1999). The young athlete. *Current Opinion in Pediatrics, 11,* 84–88.

Marsh, M. W., Parada, R. H., & Ayotte, V. (2004). A multidimensional perspective of relations between self-concept (Self Description Questionnaire II) and adolescent mental health (Youth Self Report). *Psychological Assessment, 16,* 27–41.

Marshall-Baker, A., Lickliter, R. & Cooper, R. P. (1998). Prolonged exposure to a visual pattern may promote behavioral organization in preterm infants. *Journal of Perinatal and Neonatal Nursing, 12,* 50–62.

Martin, C. L. (1989). Children's use of gender-related information in making social judgments. *Developmental Psychology, 25,* 80–88.

Martin, C. L., Eisenbud, L., & Rose, H. (1995). Children's gender-based reasoning about toys. *Child Development, 66,* 1453–1471.

Martin, C. L., & Fabes, C. A. (2001). The stability and consequences of young children's same-sex peer interactions. *Developmental Psychology, 37,* 431–446.

Martin, C. L., Fabes, R. A., Evans, S. M., & Wyman, H. (1999). Social cognition on the playground: Children's beliefs about playing with girls versus boys and their relations to sex segregated play. *Journal of Social and Personal Relationships, 16,* 751–771.

Martin, C. L., & Halverson, C. F., Jr. (1987). The role of cognition in sex role acquisition. In D. B. Carter (Ed.), *Current conceptions of sex roles and sex typing: Theory and research* (pp. 123–137). New York: Praeger.

Martin, C. L., & Little, J. K. (1990). The relation of gender understanding to children's sex-typed preferences and gender stereotypes. *Child Development, 61,* 1427–1439.

Martin, C. L., & Ruble, D. (2004). Children's search for gender cues. *Current Directions in Psychological Science, 13,* 67–70.

Martin, C. L., Ruble, D. N., & Szkrybalo, J. (2002). Cognitive theories of early gender development. *Psychological Bulletin, 128,* 903–933.

Martin, J. A. (1981). A longitudinal study of the consequences of early mother-infant interaction: A microanalytic approach. *Monographs of the Society for Research in Child Development, 46*(3, Serial No. 190).

Martin, J. A., Hamilton, B. E., Ventura, S. J., Menacker, F., & Park, M. M. (2003). Births: Final data for 2002. *National Vital Statistics Reports, 52*(10), 1–113. Hyattsville, MD: National Center for Health Statistics.

Martin, R. P., Olejnik, S., & Gaddis, L. (1994). Is temperament an important contributor to schooling outcomes in elementary school? Modeling effects of temperament and scholastic ability on academic achievement. In W. B. Carey & S. C. McDevitt (Eds.), *Prevention and early intervention* (pp. 59–68). New York: Brunner/Mazel.

Martinez, C. R., & Forgatch, M. S. (2002). Adjusting to change: Linking family structure transitions with parenting and boys' adjustment. *Journal of Family Psychology, 16,* 107–117.

Martins, C., & Gaffan, E. A. (2000). Effects of maternal depression on patterns of infant–mother attachment: A meta-analytic investigation. *Journal of Child Psychology and Psychiatry, 41,* 737–746.

Martlew, M., & Connolly, K. J. (1996). Human figure drawings by schooled and unschooled children in Papua New Guinea. *Child Development, 67,* 2743–2762.

Martyn, C. N., Barker, D. J. P., & Osmond, C. (1996). Mothers' pelvic size, fetal growth, and death from stroke and coronary heart disease in men in the UK. *Lancet, 348,* 1264–1268.

Marzolf, D. P., & DeLoache, J. S. (1994). Transfer in young children's understanding of spatial representations. *Child Development, 65,* 1–15.

Masataka, N. (1996). Perception of motherese in a signed language by 6-month-old deaf infants. *Developmental Psychology, 32,* 874–879.

Mason, M. G., & Gibbs, J. C. (1993a). Role-taking opportunities and the transition to advanced moral judgment. *Moral Education Forum, 18,* 1–12.

Mason, M. G., & Gibbs, J. C. (1993b). Social perspective taking and moral judgment among college students. *Journal of Adolescent Research, 8,* 109–123.

Masten, A. S. (2001). Ordinary magic: Resilience processes in development. *American Psychologist, 56,* 227–238.

Masten, A. S., & Coatsworth, J. D. (1998). The development of competence in favorable and unfavorable environments: Lessons from research on successful children. *American Psychologist, 53,* 205–220.

Masten, A. S., Coatsworth, J. D., Neemann, J., Gest, S. D., Tellegen, A., & Garmezy, N. (1995). The structure and coherence of competence from childhood through adolescence. *Child Development, 66,* 1635–1659.

Masten, A. S., Hubbard, J. J., Gest, S. D., Tellegen, A., Garmezy, N., & Ramirez, M. (1999). Adaptation in the context of adversity: Pathways to resilience and maladaptation from childhood to late adolescence. *Development and Psychopathology, 11,* 143–169.

Masten, A. S., & Powell, J. L. (2003). A resilience framework for research, policy, and practice. In S. S. Luthar (Ed.), *Resilience and vulnerability* (pp. 1–25). New York: Cambridge University Press.

Masten, A. S., & Reed, M. J. (2002). Resilience in development. In C. R. Snyder & S. J. Lopez (Eds.), *Handbook of positive psychology* (pp. 74–88). New York: Oxford University Press.

Mastropieri, D., & Turkewitz, G. (1999). Prenatal experience and neonatal responsiveness to vocal expressions of emotion. *Developmental Psychobiology, 35,* 204–214.

Masur, E. F., McIntyre, C. W., & Flavell, J. H. (1973). Developmental changes in apportionment of study time among items in a multi-trial free recall task. *Journal of Experimental Child Psychology, 15,* 237–246.

Masur, E. F., & Rodemaker, J. E. (1999). Mothers' and infants' spontaneous vocal, verbal, and action imitation during the second year. *Merrill-Palmer Quarterly, 45,* 392–412.

Matas, L., Arend, R., & Sroufe, L. A. (1978). Continuity of adaptation in the second year: The relationship between quality of attachment and later competence. *Child Development, 49,* 547–556.

Matheny, A. P., Jr. (1989). Temperament and cognition: Relations between temperament and mental test scores. In G. A. Kohnstamm, J. E. Bates, & M. K. Rothbart (Eds.), *Temperament in childhood* (pp. 263–282). New York: Wiley.

Matheson, G. O. (2001). The dark side of kids' sports. *Physician and Sportsmedicine, 29.* Retrieved from www.physsportsmed.com/journal.htm

Mathews, F., Yudkin, P., & Neil, A. (1999). Influence of maternal nutrition on outcome of pregnancy: Prospective cohort study. *British Medical Journal, 319,* 339–343.

Maticka-Tyndale, E. (2001). Sexual health and Canadian youth: How do we measure up? *Canadian Journal of Human Sexuality, 10*(1–2), 1–17.

Matsuba, M. K., & Walker, L. J. (1998). Moral reasoning in the context of ego functioning. *Merrill-Palmer Quarterly, 44,* 464–483.

Matsuda, Y., Maeda, T., & Kouno, S. (2003). Comparison of neonatal outcome including cerebral palsy between placenta abruptio and placenta previa. *European Journal of Obstetrics, Gynecology, and Reproductive Biology, 106,* 125–129.

Mattson, S. N., Riley, E. P., Delis, D. C., & Jones, K. L. (1998). Neuropsychological comparison of alcohol-exposed children with or without physical features of fetal alcohol syndrome. *Neuropsychology, 12,* 146–153.

Matute-Bianchi, M. E. (1986). Ethnic identities and patterns of school success and failure among Mexican-descent and Japanese-American students in a California high school: An ethnographic analysis. *American Journal of Education, 95,* 233–255.

Mayberry, R. I. (1994). The importance of childhood to language acquisition: Evidence from American Sign Language. In J. C. Goodman & H. C. Nusbaum (Eds.), *The development of speech perception: The transition from speech sounds to spoken words* (pp. 57–90). Cambridge, MA: MIT Press.

Mayeux, L., & Cillessen, A. H. N. (2003). Development of social problem solving in early childhood: Stability, change, and associations with social competence. *Journal of Genetic Psychology, 164,* 153–173.

Mayer, J. D., Caruso, D., & Salovey, P. (1999). Emotional intelligence meets traditional standards for an intelligence. *Intelligence, 27,* 267–298.

Mayer, J. D., Salovey, P., & Caruso, D. R. (2000). Selecting a measure of emotional intelligence: The case for ability scales. In R. Bar-On & J. D. A. Parker (Eds.), *Handbook of emotional intelligence* (pp. 320–342). San Francisco: Jossey-Bass.

Mayer, J. D., Salovey, P., & Caruso, D. R. (2003). *Mayer–Salovey–Caruso Emotional Intelligence Test (MSCEIT): User's Manual.* Toronto, Canada: Multi-Health Systems.

Mayes, L. C. (1999). Reconsidering the concept of vulnerability in children using the model of prenatal cocaine exposure. In T. B. Cohen & E. M. Hossein (Eds.), *The vulnerable child* (Vol. 3, pp. 35–54). Madison, CT: International Universities Press.

Mayes, L. C., & Zigler, E. (1992). An observational study of the affective concomitants of mastery in infants. *Journal of Child Psychology and Psychiatry, 33,* 659–667.

Maynard, A. E. (2002). Cultural teaching: The development of teaching skills in Maya sibling interactions. *Child Development, 73,* 969–982.

Maynard, A. E., & Greenfield, P. M. (2003). Implicit cognitive development in cultural tools and children: Lessons from Maya Mexico. *Cognitive Development, 18,* 489–510.

McBride-Chang, C., & Kail, R. V. (2002). Cross-cultural similarities in the predictors of reading acquisition. *Child Development, 73,* 1392–1407.

McCabe, A. (1997). Developmental and cross-cultural aspects of children's narration. In M. Bamberg (Ed.), *Narrative development: Six approaches* (pp. 137–174). Mahwah, NJ: Erlbaum.

McCabe, A., & Peterson, C. (1988). A comparison of adults' versus children's spontaneous use of *because* and *so.*

Journal of Genetic Psychology, 149, 257–268.

McCall, R. B. (1977). Childhood IQs as predictors of adult educational and occupational status. *Science, 197,* 482–483.

McCall, R. B. (1993). Developmental functions for general mental performance. In D. K. Detterman (Ed.), *Current topics in human intelligence* (Vol. 3, pp. 3–29). Norwood, NJ: Ablex.

McCall, R. B., Appelbaum, M. I., & Hogarty, P. S. (1973). Developmental changes in mental performance. *Monographs of the Society for Research in Child Development, 38*(3, Serial No. 150).

McCall, R. B., & Carriger, M. S. (1993). A meta-analysis of infant habituation and recognition memory performance as predictors of later IQ. *Child Development, 64,* 57–79.

McCartney, K., Harris, M. J., & Bernieri, F. (1990). Growing up and growing apart: A developmental meta-analysis of twin studies. *Psychological Bulletin, 107,* 226–237.

McCarton, C. (1998). Behavioral outcomes in low birth weight infants. *Pediatrics, 102,* 1293–1297.

McCarty, M. E., & Ashmead, D. H. (1999). Visual control of reaching and grasping in infants. *Developmental Psychology, 35,* 620–631.

McClelland, J. L., & Siegler, R. S. (Eds.). (2001). *Mechanisms of cognitive development: Behavioral and neural perspectives.* Mahwah, NJ: Erlbaum.

McConaghy, M. J. (1979). Gender permanence and the genital basis of gender: Stages in the development of constancy of gender identity. *Child Development, 50,* 1223–1226.

McConaghy, N., & Silove, D. (1992). Do sex-linked behaviors in children influence relationships with their parents? *Archives of Sexual Behavior, 21,* 469–479.

McCune, L. (1993). The development of play as the development of consciousness. In M. H. Bornstein & A. O'Reilly (Eds.), *New directions for child development* (No. 59, pp. 67–79). San Francisco: Jossey-Bass.

McDaniel, J., Purcell, D., & D'Augelli, A. R. (2001). The relationship between sexual orientation and risk for suicide: Research findings and future directions for research and prevention. *Suicide and Life-Threatening Behavior, 31,* 84–105.

McDonough, L. (1999). Early declarative memory for location. *British Journal of Developmental Psychology, 17,* 381–402.

McDowell, D. J., & Parke, R. D. (2000). Differential knowledge of display rules for positive and negative emotions: Influences from parents, influences on peers. *Social Development, 9,* 415–432.

McDowell, D. J., Parke, R. D., & Wang, S. J. (2004). Differences between mothers' and fathers' advice-giving style and content: Relations with social competence and psychological functioning in middle childhood. *Merrill-Palmer Quarterly, 49,* 55–76.

McGee, G. (1997). Legislating gestation. *Human Reproduction, 12,* 407–408.

McGee, G. (1997). Legislating gestation. *Human Reproduction, 12,* 407–408.

McGee, L. M., & Richgels, D. J. (2004). *Literacy's beginnings* (4th ed.). Boston: Allyn and Bacon.

McGillicuddy-De Lisi, A. V., Watkins, C., & Vinchur, A. J. (1994). The effect of relationship on children's distributive justice reasoning. *Child Development, 65,* 1694–1700.

McGrath, J. E., & Johnson, B. A. (2003). Methodology makes meaning: How both qualitative and quantitative paradigms shape evidence and its interpretation. In P. M. Camic, J. E. Rhodes, & L. Yardley (Eds.), *Qualitative research in psychology* (pp. 31–48). Washington, DC: American Psychological Association.

McGue, M., Bouchard, T. J., Jr., Iacono, W. G., & Lykken, D. T. (1993). Behavioral genetics of cognitive ability: A life-span perspective. In R. Plomin & G. E. McClearn (Eds.), *Nature, nurture, and psychology* (pp. 59–76). Washington, DC: American Psychological Association.

McGuffin, P., & Sargeant, M. P. (1991). Major affective disorder. In P. McGuffin & R. Murray (Eds.), *The new genetics of mental illness* (pp. 165–181). London: Butterworth-Heinemann.

McHale, J. P., Lauretti, A., Talbot, J., & Pouquette, C. (2002). Retrospect and prospect in the psychological study of coparenting and family group process. In J. P. McHale & W. S. Grolnick (Eds.), *Retrospect and prospect in the psychological study of families* (pp. 127–165). Mahwah, NJ: Erlbaum.

McHale, S. M., Bartko, W. T., Crouter, A. C., & Perry-Jenkins, M. (1990). Children's housework and psychosocial functioning: The mediating effects of parents' sex-role behaviors and attitudes. *Child Development, 61,* 68–81.

McHale, S. M., Crouter, A. C., & Whiteman, S. D. (2003). The family contexts of gender development in childhood and adolescence. *Social Development, 12,* 125–148.

McHale, S. M., Updegraff, K. A., Helms-Erikson, H., & Crouter, A. C. (2001). Sibling influences on gender development in middle childhood and early adolescence: A longitudinal study. *Developmental Psychology, 37,* 115–125.

McIntyre, T. M., & Ventura, M. (2003). Children of war: Psychosocial sequelae of war trauma in Angolan adolescents. In S. Krippner & T. M. McIntyre (Eds.), *The psychological impact of war trauma on civilians: An international perspective* (pp. 39–53). Westport, CT: Praeger.

McKelvie, P., & Low, J. (2002). Listening to Mozart does not improve children's spatial ability: Final curtains for the Mozart effect. *British Journal of Developmental Psychology, 20,* 241–258.

McKenna, J. J. (2001). Why we never ask "Is it safe for infants to sleep alone?" *Academy of Breast Feeding Medicine News and Views, 7*(4), 32, 38.

McKenna, J. J. (2002, September/October). Breastfeeding and bedsharing still useful (and important) after all these years. *Mothering, 114.* Retrieved from www.mothering.com/articles/new_baby/sleep/mckenna.html

McKeown, R. E., Garrison, C. Z., Cuffe, S. P., Waller, J. L., Jackson, K. L., & Addy, C. L. (1998). Incidence and predictors of suicidal behaviors in a

longitudinal sample of young adolescents. *Journal of the American Academy of Child and Adolescent Psychiatry, 37,* 612–619.

McKown, C., & Weinstein, R. S. (2002). Modeling the role of child ethnicity and gender in children's differential response to teacher expectations. *Journal of Applied Social Psychology, 32,* 159–184.

McKown, C., & Weinstein, R. S. (2003). The development and consequences of stereotype consciousness in middle childhood. *Child Development, 74,* 498–515.

McKusick, V. A. (1998). *Mendelian inheritance in man: A catalog of human genes and genetic disorders.* Baltimore: Johns Hopkins University Press.

McLanahan, S. (1999). Father absence and the welfare of children. In E. M. Hetherington (Ed.), *Coping with divorce, single parenting, and remarriage: A risk and resiliency perspective* (pp. 117–145). Mahwah, NJ: Erlbaum.

McLean, D. F., Timajchy, K. H., Wingo, P. A., & Floyd, R. L. (1993). Psychosocial measurement: Implications of the study of preterm delivery in black women. *American Journal of Preventive Medicine, 9,* 39–81.

McLoyd, V. C., & Smith, J. (2002). Physical discipline and behavior problems in African-American, European-American, and Hispanic children: Emotional support as a moderator. *Journal of Marriage and the Family, 64,* 40–53.

McMahon, R. J. (1999). Parent training. In S. W. Russ & T. H. Ollendick (Eds.), *Handbook of psychotherapies with children and families* (pp. 153–180). New York: Kluwer Academic.

McManus, I. C., Sik, G., Cole, D. R., Mellon, A. F., Wong, J., & Kloss, J. (1988). The development of handedness in children. *British Journal of Developmental Psychology, 6,* 257–273.

McNamee, S., & Peterson, J. (1986). Young children's distributive justice reasoning, behavior, and role taking: Their consistency and relationship. *Journal of Genetic Psychology, 146,* 399–404.

MCR Vitamin Study Research Group. (1991). Prevention of neural tube defects: Results of the Medical Research Council Vitamin Study. *Lancet, 338,* 131–137.

Mead, G. H. (1934). *Mind, self, and society.* Chicago: University of Chicago Press.

Mead, M. (1928). *Coming of age in Samoa.* Ann Arbor, MI: Morrow.

Mead, M., & Newton, N. (1967). Cultural patterning of perinatal behavior. In S. Richardson & A. Guttmacher (Eds.), *Childbearing: Its social and psychological aspects* (pp. 142–244). Baltimore: Williams & Wilkins.

Mebert, C. J. (1991). Dimensions of subjectivity in parents' ratings of infant temperament. *Child Development, 62,* 352–361.

Media Awareness Network. (2001). Parental awareness of Canadian children's Internet use. Retrieved from www.media-awareness,ca

Meehan, B. T., Hughes, J. N., & Cavell, T. A. (2003). Teacher–student relationships as compensatory resources for aggressive children. *Child Development, 74,* 1145–1157.

Meeus, W. (1996). Studies on identity development in adolescence: An overview of research and some new data. *Journal of Youth and Adolescence, 25,* 569–598.

Meeus, W., Iedema, J., Helsen, M., & Vollebergh, W. (1999). Patterns of adolescent identity development: Review of literature and longitudinal analysis. *Developmental Review, 19,* 419–461.

Meeus, W., Oosterwegel, A., & Vollebergh, W. (2002). Parental and peer attachment and identity development in adolescence. *Journal of Adolescence, 25,* 93–106.

Mehlmadrona, L., & Madrona, M. M. (1997). Physician- and midwife-attended home births—effects of breech, twin, and post-dates outcome data on mortality rates. *Journal of Nurse-Midwifery, 42,* 91–98.

Meins, E., Fernyhough, C., Russell, J., & Clark-Carter, D. (1998). Security of attachment as a predictor of symbolic and mentalizing abilities: A longitudinal study. *Social Development, 7,* 1–24.

Meins, E., Fernyhough, C., Wainwright, R., Clark-Carter, D., Gupta, M. D., Fradley, E., & Tucker, M. (2003). Pathways to understanding mind: Construct validity and predictive validity of maternal mind-mindedness. *Child Development, 74,* 1194–1211.

Meins, E., Fernyhough, C., Wainwright, R., Gupta, M. D., Fradley, E., & Tukey, M. (2002). Maternal mind-mindedness and attachment security as predictors of theory of mind understanding. *Child Development, 73,* 1715–1726.

Meisels, S. J., Dichtelmiller, M., & Liaw, F. R. (1993). A multidimensional analysis of early childhood intervention programs. In C. H. Zeanah (Ed.), *Handbook of infant mental health* (pp. 361–385). New York: Guilford.

Meltzoff, A. N. (1995). Understanding the intentions of others: Re-enactment of intended acts by 18-month-old children. *Developmental Psychology, 31,* 838–850.

Meltzoff, A. N., & Decety, J. (2003). What imitation tells us about social cognition: A rapprochement between developmental psychology and cognitive neuroscience. *Philosophical Transactions of the Royal Society of London, Series B, Biological Sciences, 358,* 491–500.

Meltzoff, A. N., & Kuhl, P. K. (1994). Faces and speech: Intermodal processing of biologically relevant signals in infants and adults. In D. J. Lewkowicz & R. Lickliter (Eds.), *The development of intersensory perception: Comparative perspectives* (pp. 335–369). Hillsdale, NJ: Erlbaum.

Meltzoff, A. N., & Moore, M. K. (1977). Imitation of facial and manual gestures by human neonates. *Science, 198,* 75–78.

Meltzoff, A. N., & Moore, M. K. (1994). Imitation, memory, and the representation of persons. *Infant Behavior and Development, 17,* 83–99.

Meltzoff, A. N., & Moore, M. K. (1999). Persons and representations: Why infant imitation is important for theories of human development. In J. Nadel & G. Butterworth (Eds.), *Imitation in infancy* (pp. 9–35). Cambridge, UK: Cambridge University Press.

Menn, L., & Stoel-Gammon, C. (2005). Phonological development: Learning sounds and sound patterns. In J. B. Gleason (Ed.), *The development of language* (pp. 62–111). Boston: Allyn and Bacon.

Mennella, J. A., & Beauchamp, G. K. (1998). Early flavor experiences: Research update. *Nutrition Reviews, 56,* 205–211.

Ment, L. R., Vohr, B., Allan, W., Katz, K. H., Schneider, K. C., Westerveld, M., Cuncan, C. C., & Makuch, R. W. (2003). Change in cognitive function over time in very low-birth-weight infants. *Journal of the American Medical Association, 289,* 705–711.

Menyuk, P., Liebergott, J. W., & Schultz, M. C. (1995). *Early language development in full-term and premature infants.* Hillsdale, NJ: Erlbaum.

Meredith, N. V. (1978). *Human body growth in the first ten years of life.* Columbia, SC: State Printing.

Mervis, C. B., Pani, J. R., & Pani, A. M. (2003). Transaction of child cognitive-linguistic abilities and adult input in the acquisition of lexical categories at the basic and subordinate levels. In D. H. Rakison & L. M. Oakes (Ed.), *Early category and concept development* (pp. 242–274). New York: Oxford University Press.

Mervis, C. B., & Robinson, B. F. (2000). Expressive vocabulary ability of toddlers with Williams syndrome or Down syndrome: A comparison. *Developmental Neuropsychology, 17,* 111–126.

Metcalfe, J., & Mischel, W. (1999). A hot/cool system analysis of delay of gratification: Dynamics of willpower. *Psychological Review, 106,* 3–19.

Metz, E., McLellan, J., & Youniss, J. (2003). Types of voluntary service and adolescents' civic development. *Journal of Adolescent Research, 18,* 188–203.

Meyer-Bahlburg, H. F. L., Dolezal, C., Baker, S. W., Carlson, A. D., Obeid, J. S., & New, M. I. (2004). Prenatal androgenization affects gender-related behavior but not gender identity in 5- to 12-year-old girls with congenital adrenal hyperplasia. *Archives of Sexual Behavior, 33,* 97–104.

Meyer-Bahlburg, H. F. L., Ehrhardt, A. A., Rosen, L. R., Gruen, R. S., Veridiano, N. P., Vann, F. H., & Neuwalder, H. F. (1995). Prenatal estrogens and the development of homosexual orientation. *Developmental Psychology, 31,* 12–21.

Meyers, C., Adam, R., Dungan, J., & Prenger, V. (1997). Aneuploidy in twin gestations: When is maternal age advanced? *Obstetrics and Gynecology, 89,* 248–251.

Miceli, P. J., Whitman, T. L., Borkowski, J. G., Braungart-Riekder, J., & Mitchell, D. W. (1998). Individual differences in infant information processing: The role of temperamental and maternal factors. *Infant Behavior and Development, 21,* 119–136.

Michael, R. T., Gagnon, J. H., Laumann, E. O., & Kolata, G. (1994). *Sex in America.* Boston: Little, Brown.

Michels, K. B., Trichopoulos, D., Robins, J. M., Rosner, B. A., Manson, J. E., & Hunter, D. J. (1996). Birth weight as a risk factor for breast cancer. *Lancet, 348,* 1542–1546.

Milberger, S., Biederman, J., Faraone, S. V., Guite, J., & Tsuang, M. T. (1997). Pregnancy, delivery and infancy complications and attention deficit hyperactivity disorder: Issues of gene–environment interaction. *Biological Psychiatry, 41,* 65–75.

Miles, C. (1935). Sex in social psychology. In C. Murchison (Ed.), *Handbook of social psychology* (pp. 699–704). Worcester, MA: Clark University Press.

Miller, B. C., Fan, X., Christensen, M., Grotevant, H. D., & van Dulmen, M. (2000). Comparisons of adopted and nonadopted adolescents in a large, nationally representative sample. *Child Development, 71,* 1458–1473.

Miller, B., Cummings, J., Mishkin, F., Boone, K., Prince, F., Ponton, M., & Cotman, C. (1998). Emergence of artistic talent in frontotemporal dementia. *Neurology, 51,* 978–982.

Miller, J. G. (1997). Culture and self: Uncovering the cultural grounding of psychological theory. In J. G. Snodgrass & R. L. Thompson (Eds.), *Annals of the New York Academy of Sciences* (Vol. 18, pp. 217–231). New York: New York Academy of Sciences.

Miller, J. G., & Bersoff, D. M. (1995). Development in the context of everyday family relationships: Culture, interpersonal morality, and adapation. In M. Killen & D. Hart (Eds.), *Morality in everyday life: Developmental perspectives* (pp. 259–282). Cambridge, UK: Cambridge University Press.

Miller, K. S., Forehand, R., & Kotchick, B. (1999). Adolescent sexual behavior in two ethnic minority samples: The role of family variables. *Journal of Marriage and the Family, 61,* 85–98.

Miller, L. T., & Vernon, P. A. (1992). The general factor in short-term memory, intelligence, and reaction time. *Intelligence, 16,* 5–29.

Miller, P. A., Eisenberg, N., Fabes, R. A., & Shell, R. (1996). Relations of moral reasoning and vicarious emotion to young children's prosocial behavior toward peers and adults. *Developmental Psychology, 32,* 210–219.

Miller, P. H. (2000). How best to utilize a deficiency. *Child Development, 71,* 1013–1017.

Miller, P. H., & Bigi, L. (1979). The development of children's understanding of attention. *Merrill-Palmer Quarterly, 25,* 235–250.

Miller, P. H., Haynes, V. F., DeMarie-Dreblow, D., & Woody-Ramsey, J. (1986). Children's strategies for gathering information in three tasks. *Child Development, 57,* 1429–1439.

Miller, P. J., Fung, H., & Mintz, J. (1996). Self-construction through narrative practices: A Chinese and American comparison of early socialization. *Ethos, 24,* 1–44.

Miller, P. J., Hengst, J. A., & Wang, S. (2003). Ethnographic methods: Applications from developmental cultural psychology. In P. M. Camic & J. E. Rhodes (Eds.), *Qualitative research in psychology* (pp. 219–242). Washington, DC: American Psychological Association.

Miller, P. H., Kessel, F. S., & Flavell, J. H. (1970). Thinking about people thinking about people thinking about . . . : A study of social cognitive development. *Child Development, 41,* 613–623.

Miller, P. J., Wang, S., Sandel, T., & Cho, G. E. (2002). Self-esteem as folk theory: A comparison of European American and Taiwanese mothers' beliefs. *Parenting: Science and Practice, 2,* 209–239.

Miller, P. J., Wiley, A. R., Fung, H., & Liang, C.-H. (1997). Personal storytelling as a medium of socialization in Chinese and American families. *Child Development, 68,* 557–568.

Miller, R. B. (2000). Do children make a marriage unhappy? *Family Science Review, 13,* 60–73.

Miller, S. A. (1998). *Developmental research methods* (2nd ed.). Englewood Cliffs, NJ: Prentice-Hall.

Miller, S. A., & Davis, T. L. (1992). Beliefs about children: A comparative study of mothers, teachers, peers, and self. *Child Development, 63,* 1251–1265.

Miller, S. A., Hardin, C. A., & Montgomery, D. E. (2003). Young children's understanding of the conditions for knowledge acquisition. *Journal of Cognition and Development, 4,* 325–356.

Mills, D. L., Coffey-Corina, S., & Neville, H. J. (1997). Language comprehension and cerebral specialization from 13 to 20 months. *Developmental Neuropsychology, 13,* 397–445.

Mills, R. S. L. (2005). Taking stock of the developmental literature on shame. *Developmental Review, 25,* 26–63.

Mills, R., & Grusec, J. E. (1989). Cognitive, affective, and behavioral consequences of praising altruism. *Merrill-Palmer Quarterly, 35,* 299–326.

Minami, M., (1996). Japanese preschool children's narrative development. *First Language, 16,* 339–363.

Minde, K. (2000). Prematurity and serious medical conditions in infancy: Implications for development, behavior, and intervention. In C. H. Zeanah, Jr. (Ed.), *Handbook of infant mental health* (pp. 176–194). New York: Guilford.

Mischel, H. N., & Liebert, R. M. (1966). Effects of discrepancies between observed and imposed reward criteria on their acquisition and transmission. *Journal of Personality and Social Psychology, 3,* 45–53.

Mischel, H. N., & Mischel, W. (1983). The development of children's knowledge of self-control strategies. *Child Development, 54,* 603–619.

Mischel, W. (1996). From good intentions to willpower. In P. M. Gollwitzer & J. A. Bargh (Eds.), *The psychology of action* (pp. 197–218). New York: Guilford.

Mischel, W., & Ayduck, O. (2004). Willpower in a cognitive–affective processing system: The dynamics of delay of gratification. In R. F. Baumeister & K. D. Vohs (Eds.), *Handbook of self-regulation* (pp. 99–129). New York: Guilford.

Mischel, W., & Baker, N. (1975). Cognitive appraisals and transformations in delay behavior. *Journal of Personality and Social Psychology, 31,* 254–261.

Mischel, W., Shoda, Y., & Peake, P. K. (1988). The nature of adolescent competencies predicted by preschool delay of gratification. *Journal of Personality and Social Psychology, 54,* 687–696.

Mishna, F., Antle, B. J., & Regehr, C. (2004). Tapping the perspectives of children. *Qualitative Social Work, 3,* 449–468.

Mistry, J. (1997). The development of remembering in cultural context. In N. Cowan (Ed.), *The development of memory in childhood* (pp. 343–368). Hove, UK: Psychology Press.

Mitchell, A., & Boss, B. J. (2002). Adverse effects of pain on the nervous systems of newborns and young children: A review of the literature. *Journal of Neuroscience Nursing, 34,* 228–235.

Miura, I. T., & Okamoto, Y. (2003). Language supports for mathematics understanding and performance. In A. J. Baroody & A. Dowker (Eds.), *The development of arithmetic concepts and skills* (pp. 229–242). Mahwah, NJ: Erlbaum.

Mize, J., & Pettit, G. S. (1997). Mothers' social coaching, mother–child relationship style, and children's peer competence: Is the medium the message? *Child Development, 68,* 312–332.

Moerk, E. L. (1992). *A first language taught and learned.* Baltimore: Paul H. Brookes.

Moffitt, T. E., Caspi, A., Dickson, N., Silva, P., & Stanton, W. (1996). Childhood-onset versus adolescent-onset antisocial conduct problems in males: Natural history from ages 3 to 18 years. *Development and Psychopathology, 8,* 399–424.

Moll, I. (1994). Reclaiming the natural line in Vygotsky's theory of cognitive development. *Human Development, 37,* 333–342.

Monastersky, R. (2005, March 4). Primed for numbers: Are boys born better at math? Experts try to divide the influences of nature and nurture. *Chronicle of Higher Education.* pp. A1, A12–A14.

Mondloch, C. J., Lewis, T., Budreau, D. R., Maurer, D., Dannemiller, J. L., Stephens, B. R., & Kleiner-Gathercoal, K. A. (1999). Face perception during early infancy. *Psychological Science, 10,* 419–422.

Monk, C., Myers, M. M., Sloan, R. P., Ellman, L. M., & Fifer, W. P. (2003). Effects of women's stress-elicited physiological activity and chronic anxiety on fetal heart rate. *Journal of Developmental and Behavioral Pediatrics, 24,* 32–38.

Montague, D. P. F., & Walker-Andrews, A. S. (2001). Peekaboo: A new look at infants' perception of emotion expressions. *Developmental Psychology, 37,* 826–838.

Montemayor, R., & Eisen, M. (1977). The development of self-conceptions from childhood to adolescence. *Developmental Psychology, 13,* 314–319.

Montgomery, D. E. (1993). Young children's understanding of interpretive diversity between different-aged listeners. *Developmental Psychology, 29,* 337–345.

Moon, C., Cooper, R. P., & Fifer, W. P. (1993). Two-day-old infants prefer their native language. *Infant Behavior and Development, 16,* 495–500.

Moon, S. M., & Feldhusen, J. F. (1994). The Program for Academic and Creative Enrichment (PACE): A follow-up study ten years later. In R. F. Subotnik & K. D. Arnold (Eds.), *Beyond Terman: Contemporary longitudinal studies of giftedness and talent* (pp. 375–400). Norwood, NJ: Ablex.

Moore, D. R., & Florsheim, P. (2001). Interpersonal processes and psychopathology among expectant and nonexpectant adolescent couples. *Journal of Consulting and Clinical Psychology, 69,* 101–113.

Moore, D. S., Spence, M. J., & Katz, G. S. (1997). Six-month-olds' categorization of natural infant-directed utterances. *Developmental Psychology, 33,* 980–989.

Moore, E. G. J. (1986). Family socialization and the IQ test performance of traditionally and trans- racially adopted black children. *Developmental Psychology, 22,* 317–326.

Moore, G. A., Cohn, J. E., & Campbell, S. B. (2001). Infant affective responses to mother's still face at 6 months differentially predict externalizing and internalizing behaviors at 18 months. *Developmental Psychology, 37,* 706–714.

Moore, K. A., Morrison, D. R., & Greene, A. D. (1997). Effects on the children born to adolescent mothers. In R. A. Maynard (Ed.), *Kids having kids* (pp. 145–180). Washington, DC: Urban Institute.

Moore, K. A., Myers, D. E., Morrison, D. R., Nord, C. W., Brown, B., & Edmonston, B. (1993). Age at first childbirth and later poverty. *Journal of Research on Adolescence, 3,* 393–422.

Moore, K. L., & Persaud, T. V. N. (2003). *Before we are born* (6th ed.). Philadelphia: Saunders.

Moore, M. K., & Meltzoff, A. N. (1999). New findings on object permanence: A developmental difference between two types of occlusion. *British Journal of Developmental Psychology, 17,* 563–584.

Moore, M. K., & Meltzoff, A. N. (2004). Object permanence after a 24-hr delay and leaving the locale of disappearance: The role of memory, space, and identity. *Developmental Psychology, 40,* 606–620.

Morales, M., Mundy, P., Delgado, C. E. F., Yale, M., Messinger, D., Neal, R., & Schwartz, H. K. (2000). Responding to joint attention across the 6- through 24-month age period and early language acquisition. *Journal of Applied Developmental Psychology, 21,* 283–298.

Moran, G. F., & Vinovskis, M. A. (1986). The great care of godly parents: Early childhood in Puritan New England. In A. B. Smuts & J. W. Hagen (Eds.), History and research in child development. *Monographs of the Society for Research in Child Development, 50*(4–5, Serial No. 211), pp. 24–37.

Morelli, G. A., Rogoff, B., & Angelillo, C. (2003). Cultural variation in young children's access to work or involvement in specialized child-focused activities. *International Journal of Behavioral Development, 27,* 264–274.

Morelli, G. A., Rogoff, B., Oppenheim, D., & Goldsmith, D. (1992). Cultural variation in infants' sleeping arrangements: Questions of independence. *Developmental Psychology, 28,* 604–613.

Morford, J. P., & Goldin-Meadow, S. (1997). From here and now to there and then: The development of displaced reference in homesign and English. *Child Development, 68,* 420–435.

Morgan, B., Maybery, M., & Durkin, K. (2003). Weak central coherence, poor joint attention, and low verbal ability: Independent deficits in early autism. *Developmental Psychology, 28,* 604–613.

Morgane, P. J., Austin-LaFrance, R., Bronzino, J., Tonkiss, J., Diaz-Cintra, S., Cintra, L., Kemper, T., & Galler, J. R. (1993). Prenatal malnutrition and development of the brain. *Neuroscience and Biobehavioral Reviews, 17,* 91–128.

Morris, J. F., Balsam, K. F., & Rothblum, E. D. (2001). Lesbian and bisexual mothers and nonmothers: Demographics and the coming-out process. *Journal of Family Psychology, 16,* 144–156.

Morrongiello, B. A., Fenwick, K. D., & Chance, G. (1998). Crossmodal learning in newborn infants: Inferences about properties of auditory-visual events. *Infant Behavior and Development, 21,* 543–554.

Morton, J. (1993). Mechanisms in infant face processing. In B. de Boysson-Bardies, S. de Schonen, P. Jusczyk, P. McNeilage, & J. Morton (Eds.), *Developmental neurocognition: Speech and face processing in the first year of life* (pp. 93–102). London: Kluwer.

Mosby, L., Rawls, A. W., Meehan, A. J., Mays, E., & Pettinari, C. J. (1999). Troubles in interracial talk about discipline: An examination of African American child rearing narratives. *Journal of Comparative Family Studies, 30,* 489–521.

Mosely-Howard, G. S., & Evans, C. B. (2000). Relationships and contemporary experiences of the African-American family: An ethnographic case study. *Journal of Black Studies, 30,* 428–451.

Moses, L. J., Baldwin, D. A., Rosicky, J. G., & Tidball, G. (2001). Evidence for referential understanding in the emotions domain at twelve and eighteen months. *Child Development, 72,* 718–735.

Moshman, D. (1998). Cognitive development beyond childhood. In D. Kuhn & R. S. Siegler (Eds.), *Handbook of child psychology: Vol. 2. Cognition, perception, and language* (5th ed., pp. 947–978). New York: Wiley.

Moshman, D. (1999). *Adolescent psychological development: Rationality, morality, and identity.* Mahwah, NJ: Erlbaum.

Moshman, D., & Franks, B. A. (1986). Development of the concept of inferential validity. *Child Development, 57,* 153–165.

Mosko, S., Richard, C., & McKenna, J. J. (1997a). Infant arousals during mother–infant bed sharing: Implications for infant sleep and sudden infant death syndrome research. *Pediatrics, 100,* 841–849.

Mosko, S., Richard, C., & McKenna, J. J. (1997b). Maternal sleep and arousals during bedsharing with infants. *Sleep, 20,* 142–150.

Mosteller, F. (1995). The Tennessee Study of Class Size in the Early School Grades. *Future of Children, 5*(2), 113–127.

Motl, R. W., Dishman, R. K., Saunders, R. P., Dowda, M., Felton, G., Ward, D. S., & Pate, R. R. (2002). Examining social–cognitive determinants of intention and physical activity among black and white adolescent girls using structural equation modeling. *Health Psychology, 21,* 459–467.

Mounts, N. S., & Steinberg, L. D. (1995). An ecological analysis of peer influence on adolescent grade point average and drug use. *Developmental Psychology, 31,* 915–922.

Mrug, S., Hoza, B., & Gerdes, A. C. (2001). Children with attention-deficit/hyperactivity disorder: Peer relationships and peer-oriented interventions. In D. W. Nangle & C. A. Erdley (Eds.), *The role of friendship in psychological adjustment* (pp. 51–77). San Francisco: Jossey-Bass.

Mueller, C. M., & Dweck, C. S. (1998). Intelligence praise can undermine motivation and performance. *Journal of Personality and Social Psychology, 75,* 33–52.

Mueller, R. A., Rothermel, R., Behen, M., Muzik, O., Mangner, T., & Chugani, H. (1998). Differential patterns of language and motor reorganization following early left hemisphere injury. *Archives of Neurology, 55,* 1113–1119.

Mulder, E. J. H., Robles de Medina, P. G., Huizink, A. C., Van den Bergh, B. R. H., Buitelaar, J. K., & Visser, G. H. A. (2002). Prenatal maternal stress: Effects on pregnancy and the (unborn) child. *Early Human Development, 70,* 3–14.

Muller, F., Rebiffe, M., Taillandier, A., Oury, J.-F., & Mornet, E. (2000). Parental origin of the extra chromosome in prenatally diagnosed fetal trisomy. *Human Genetics, 106,* 340–344.

Müller, U., Overton, W. F., & Reese, K. (2001). Development of conditional reasoning: A longitudinal study. *Journal of Cognition and Development, 2,* 27–49.

Mumme, D. L., Fernald, A., & Herrera, C. (1996). Infants' responses to facial and vocal emotional signals in a social referencing paradigm. *Child Development, 67,* 3219–3237.

Munakata, Y. (2000). Challenges to the violation-of-expectation paradigm: Throwing the conceptual baby out with the perceptual processing bathwater? *Infancy, 1,* 471–477.

Munakata, Y., Casey, B. J., & Diamond, A. (2004). Developmental cognitive neuroscience: Progress and potential. *Trends in Cognitive Sciences, 8,* 122–128.

Munakata, Y., & McClelland, J. L. (2003). Connectionist models of development. *Developmental Science, 6,* 413–429.

Mundy, P. (2003). The neural basis of social impairments in autism: The role of the dorsal medial-frontal cortex and anterior cingulate system. *Journal of Child Psychology and Psychiatry and Allied Disciplines, 44,* 793–809.

Mundy, P., & Stella, J. (2000). Joint attention, social orienting, and nonverbal communication in autism. In A. M. Wetherby & B. M. Prizant (Eds.), *Autism spectrum disorders* (Vol. 9, pp. 55–77). Baltimore, MD: Paul H. Brookes.

Munson, B. (2001). Phonological pattern frequency and speech production in adults and children. *Journal of Speech, Language, and Hearing Research, 44,* 778–792.

Murata, A. (2004). Paths to learning ten-structured understandings of teen sums: Addition solution methods of Japanese grade 1 students. *Cognition and Instruction, 22,* 185–218.

Murett-Wagstaff, S., & Moore, S. G. (1989). The Hmong in America: Infant behavior and rearing practices. In J. K. Nugent, B. M. Lester, & T. B. Brazelton (Eds.), *Biology, culture, and development* (Vol. 1, pp. 319–339). Norwood, NJ: Ablex.

Murray, A. D. (1985). Aversiveness is in the mind of the beholder. In B. M. Lester & C. F. Z. Boukydis (Eds.), *Infant crying* (pp. 217–239). New York: Plenum.

Murray, A. D., Johnson, J., & Peters, J. (1990). Fine-tuning of utterance length to preverbal infants: Effects on later language development. *Journal of Child Language, 17,* 511–525.

Mussen, P. H., & Eisenberg-Berg, N. (1977). *Roots of caring, sharing, and helping.* San Francisco: Freeman.

Mustillo, S., Worthman, C., Erkanli, A., Keeler, G., Angold, A., & Costello, E. J. (2003). Obesity and psychiatric disorder: Developmental trajectories. *Pediatrics, 111,* 851–859.

Myers, M. G., Brown, S. A., Tate, S., Abrantes, A., & Tomlinson, K. (2001). *Adolescents, alcohol, and substance abuse* (pp. 275–296). New York: Guilford.

Myowa-Yamakoshi, M., Tomonaga, M., Tanaka, M., & Matsuzawa, T. (2004). Imitation in neonatal chimpanzees *(Pan troglodytes). Developmental Science, 7,* 437–442.

Nagin, D., & Tremblay, R. E. (1999). Trajectories of boys' physical aggression, opposition, and hyperactivity on the path to physically violent and nonviolent juvenile delinquency. *Child Development, 70,* 1181–1196.

Nagy, W. E., & Scott, J. A. (2000). Vocabulary processes. In M. L. Kamil & P. B. Mosenthal (Eds.), *Handbook of reading research* (Vol. 3, pp. 269–284). Mahwah, NJ: Erlbaum.

Naigles, L. G., & Gelman, S. A. (1995). Overextensions in comprehension and production revisited: Preferential-looking in a study of dog, cat, and cow. *Journal of Child Language, 22,* 19–46.

Naito, M., & Miura, H. (2001). Japanese children's numerical competencies: Age- and schooling-related influences on the development of number concepts and addition skills. *Developmental Psychology, 37,* 217–230.

Nakamura, K. (2001). The acquisition of polite language by Japanese children. In K. E. Nelson, A. Aksu-Koc, & C. E. Johnson (Eds.), *Children's language: Vol. 10. Developing narrative and discourse competence* (pp. 93–112). Mahwah, NJ: Erlbaum.

Namy, L. L., & Waxman, S. R. (1998). Words and gestures: Infants' interpretations of different forms of symbolic reference. *Child Development, 69,* 295–308.

Nánez, J., Sr., & Yonas, A. (1994). Effects of luminance and texture motion on infant defensive reactions to optical collision. *Infant Behavior and Development, 17,* 165–174.

Nastasi, B. K., & Clements, D. H. (1994). Effectance motivation, perceived scholastic competence, and higher-order thinking in two cooperative computer environments. *Journal of Educational Computing Research, 10,* 249–275.

National Association for the Education of Young Children. (1998). *Accreditation criteria and procedures of the National Academy of Early Childhood Programs* (2nd ed.). Washington, DC: Author.

National Center for Juvenile Justice. (2004, September). Juvenile arrests 2002. *Juvenile Justice Bulletin.* Washington, DC: Author.

National Council of Teachers of Mathematics. (2000). *Principles and standards for school mathematics.* Retrieved from www.nctm.org/standards

National Council of Youth Sports. (2002). *Report on trends and participation in youth sports.* Stuart, FL: Author.

National Federation of State High School Associations. (2004). *High school athletic participation survey.* Kansas City, MO: Author.

National Forum on Welfare to Work. (2004). *Welfare to work: The next generation. A national forum.* St. John's, Newfoundland: Author. Retrieved from www.envision.ca

National Institutes of Health. (2004). *Genes and disease.* Retrieved from www.ncbi.nlm.nih.gov/books/bv.fcgi?call=bv.View.ShowSection&rid=gnd

Navarrete, C., Martinez, I., & Salamanca, F. (1994). Paternal line of transmission in chorea of Huntington with very early onset. *Genetic Counseling, 5,* 175–178.

Needham, A. (2001). Object recognition and object segregation in 4.5-month-old infants. *Journal of Experimental Child Psychology, 78,* 3–24.

Neff, K. D., & Helwig, C. C. (2002). A constructivist approach to understanding the development of reasoning about rights and authority within cultural contexts. *Cognitive Development, 17,* 1429–1450.

Neisser, U., Boodoo, G., Bouchard, T. J., Jr., Boykin, A. W., Brody, N., Ceci, S. J., Halpern, D. F., Loehlin, J. C., Perloff, R., Sternberg, R. J., & Urbina, S. (1996). Intelligence: Knowns and unknowns. *American Psychologist, 51,* 77–101.

Neitzel, C., & Stright, A. D. (2003). Mothers' scaffolding of children's problem solving: Establishing a foundation of academic self-regulatory competence. *Journal of Family Psychology, 17,* 147–159.

Nelson, C. A. (2000). Neural plasticity and human development: The role of early experience sculpting memory systems. *Developmental Science, 3,* 115–130.

Nelson, C. A. (2001). The development and neural bases of face recognition. *Infant and Child Development, 10,* 3–18.

Nelson, C. A. (2002). Neural development and lifelong plasticity. In R. M. Lerner, F. Jacobs, & D. Wertlieb (Eds.), *Handbook of applied developmental science* (Vol. 1, pp. 31–60). Thousand Oaks, CA: Sage.

Nelson, C. A., & Bosquet, M. (2000). Neurobiology of fetal and infant development: Implications for infant mental health. In C. H. Zeanah, Jr. (Ed.), *Handbook of infant mental health* (2nd ed., pp. 37–59). New York: Guilford.

Nelson, D. A., Nelson, L. J., Hart, C. H., Yang, C., & Jin, S. (2005). Parenting and peer-group behavior in cultural context. In X. Chen, B. Schneider, & D. French (Eds.), *Peer relations in cultural context.* New York Cambridge University Press.

Nelson, D. A., Robinson, C. C., & Hart, C. H. (2000). Relational and physical aggression of preschool-age children: Peer status linkages across informants. *Early Education and Development, 16,* 115–139.

Nelson, E. A. S., Schiefenhoevel, W., & Haimerl, F. (2000). Child care practices in nonindustrialized societies. *Pediatrics, 105,* e75.

Nelson, E. E., & Panksepp, J. (1998). Brain substrates of infant–mother attachment: Contributions of opioids, oxytocin, and norepinephrine. *Neuroscience and Biobehavioral Reviews, 22,* 437–452.

Nelson, G., Westhues, A., & MacLeod, J. (2003). A meta-analysis of longitudinal research on preschool prevention programs for children. *Prevention and Treatment, 6.* Retrieved from www.apa.org

Nelson, K. (1973). Structure and strategy in learning to talk. *Monographs of the Society for Research in Child Development, 38*(1–2, Serial No. 149).

Nelson, K. (1993). The psychological and social origins of autobiographical memory. *Psychological Science, 1,* 1–8.

Nelson, K. (2003). Narrative and the emergence of a consciousness of self. In G. D. Fireman & T. E. McVay, Jr. (2003). *Narrative and consciousness: Literature, psychology, and the brain* (pp. 17–36). London: Oxford University Press.

Nelson, K., & Fivush, R. (2004). The emergence of autobiographical memory: A social cultural developmental theory. *Developmental Review, 111,* 486–511.

Nelson, W. E. (Ed.). (1996). *Nelson textbook of pediatrics.* Philadelphia: Saunders.

Nesdale, D., Durkin, K., Maass, A., & Griffiths, J. (2004). Group status, out-group ethnicity, and children's ethnic attitudes. *Applied Developmental Psychology, 25,* 237–251.

Nesse, R. M. (1990). Evolutionary explanations of emotions. *Human Nature, 1,* 261–289.

Neuman, S. B. (1999). Books make a difference: A study of access to literacy. *Reading Research Quarterly, 34,* 286–311.

Neumark-Sztainer, D., Hannan, P. J., Story, M., Croll, J., & Perry, C. (2003). Family meal patterns: Associations with sociodemographic characteristics and improved dietary intake among adolescents. *Journal of the American Dietetic Association, 103,* 317–322.

Neville, H. J., & Bavelier, D. (1998). Neural organization and plasticity of language. *Current Opinion in Neurobiology, 8,* 254–258.

Neville, H. J., & Bruer, J. T. (2001). Language processing: How experience affects brain organization. In D. B. Bailey, Jr., J. T. Bruer, F. J. Symons, & J. W. Lichtman (Eds.), *Critical thinking about critical periods* (pp. 151–172). Baltimore: Paul H. Brookes.

Newborg, J., Stock, J. R., & Wnek, L. (1984). *Batelle Developmental Inventory.* Allen, TX: LINC Associates.

Newcomb, A. F., & Bagwell, C. (1995). Children's friendship relations: A meta-analytic review. *Psychological Bulletin, 117,* 306–347.

Newcomb, A. F., Bukowski, W. M., & Pattee, L. (1993). Children's peer relations: A meta-analytic review of popular, rejected, neglected, controversial, and average sociometric status. *Psychological Bulletin, 113,* 99–128.

Newcombe, N. (1982). Development of spatial cognition and cognitive development. In R. Cohen (Ed.), *Children's conceptions of spatial relationships* (pp. 65–81). San Francisco: Jossey-Bass.

Newcombe, N., & Fox, N. A. (1994). Infantile amnesia: Through a glass darkly. *Child Development, 65,* 31–40.

Newcombe, N., & Huttenlocher, J. (1992). Children's early ability to solve perspective-taking problems. *Developmental Psychology, 28,* 635–643.

Newman, A. J., Bavelier, D., Corina, D., Jezzard, P., & Neville, H. J. (2001). A critical period for right hemisphere recruitment in American Sign Language processing. *Nature Neuroscience, 5,* 76–80.

Newman, C., Atkinson, J., & Braddick, O. (2001). The development of reaching and looking preferences in infants to objects of different sizes. *Developmental Psychology, 37,* 561–572.

Newman, L. S. (1990). Intentional and unintentional memory in young children: Remembering vs. playing. *Journal of Experimental Child Psychology, 50,* 243–258.

Newnham, J. P., Evans, S. F., Michael, C. A., Stanley, F. J., & Landau, L. I. (1993). Effects of frequent ultrasound during pregnancy: A randomized controlled trial. *Lancet, 342,* 887–890.

Newport, E. L. (1991). Contrasting conceptions of the critical period for language. In S. Carey & R. Gelman (Eds.), *The epigenesis of mind: Essays on biology and cognition* (pp. 111–130). Hillsdale, NJ: Erlbaum.

Newport, E. L., & Aslin, R. N. (2000). Innately constrained learning: Blending old and new approaches to language acquisition. In S. C. Howell, S. A. Fish, & T. Keith-Lucas (Eds.), *Proceedings of the 24th Annual Boston University Conference on Language Development* (pp. 1–21). Somerville, MA: Cascadilla Press.

Newson, J., & Newson, E. (1975). Intersubjectivity and the transmission of culture: On the social origins of symbolic functioning. *Bulletin of the British Psychological Society, 28,* 437–446.

Nguyen, S. P., & Murphy, G. L. (2003). An apple is more than just a fruit: Cross-classification in children's concepts. *Child Development, 74,* 1783–1806.

Ni, Y. (1998). Cognitive structure, content knowledge, and classificatory reasoning. *Journal of Genetic Psychology, 159,* 280–296.

Niccolai, L. M., Ethier, K. A., Kershaw, T. S., Lewis, J. B., Meade, C. S., & Ickovics, J. R. (2004). New sex partner acquisition and sexually transmitted disease risk among adolescent females. *Journal of Adolescent Health, 34,* 216–223.

NICHD (National Institute for Child Health and Development) Early Child Care Research Network. (1997). The effects of infant child care on infant–mother attachment security: Results of the NICHD Study of Early Child Care. *Child Development, 68,* 860–879.

NICHD (National Institute for Child Health and Development) Early Child Care Research Network. (1999). Child care and mother–child interaction in the first 3 years of life. *Developmental Psychology, 35,* 1399–1413.

NICHD (National Institute for Child Health and Development) Early Child Care Research Network. (2000b). The relation of child care to cognitive and language development. *Child Development, 71,* 960–980.

NICHD (National Institute for Child Health and Development) Early Child Care Research Network. (2001, April). *Early child care and children's development prior to school entry.* Symposium presented at the biennial meeting of the Society for Research in Child Development, Minneapolis, MN.

NICHD (National Institute of Child Health and Development) Early Child Care Research Network. (2004b). Trajectories of physical aggression from toddlerhood to middle childhood. *Monographs of the Society for Research in Child Development, 69*(4, Serial No. 278).

NICHD (National Institute of Child Health and Development) Early Child Care Research Network. (2004a). Does class size in first grade relate to children's academic and social performance or observed classroom processes? *Developmental Psychology, 40,* 651–664.

NICHD (National Institute of Child Health and Human Development) Early Child Care Research Network. (2004c). Type of child care and children's development at 54 months. *Early Childhood Research Quarterly, 19,* 203–230.

NICHD (National Institute of Child Health and Human Development) Early Child Care Research Network. (2002a). Child-care structure → process → outcome: Direct and indirect effects of child-care quality on young children's development. *Psychological Science, 13,* 199–206.

NICHD (National Institute of Child Health and Human Development) Early Child Care Research Network. (2002b). The interaction of child care and family risk in relation to child development at 24 and 36 months. *Applied Developmental Science, 6,* 144–156.

NICHD (National Institute of Child Health and Human Development) Early Child Care Research Network. (2003a). Does amount of time spent in child care predict socioemotional adjustment during the transition to kindergarten? *Child Development, 74,* 976–1005.

NICHD (National Institute of Child Health and Human Development) Early Child Care Research Network. (2003b). Does quality of child care affect child outcomes at age 4½? *Developmental Psychology, 39,* 451–469.

NICHD (National Institute of Child Health and Human Development) Early Child Care Research Network. (2001). Before Head Start: Income and ethnicity, family characteristics, child care experiences, and child development. *Early Education and Development, 12,* 545–575.

NICHD (National Institute of Child Health and Human Development) Early Child Care Research Network. (2000). Characteristics and quality of child care for toddlers and preschoolers. *Applied Developmental Science, 4,* 116–135.

Nicholls, A. L., & Kennedy, J. M. (1992). Drawing development: From similarity of features to direction. *Child Development, 63,* 227–241.

Niehaus, M. D., Moore, S. R., Patrick, P. D., Derr, L. L., Lorntz, B., Lima, A. A., & Gurerrant, R. L. (2002). Early childhood diarrhea is associated with diminished cognitive function 4 to 7 years later in children in a northeast Brazilian shantytown. *American Journal of Tropical Medicine and Hygiene, 66,* 590–593.

Nilsson, L., & Hamberger, L. (1990). *A child is born.* New York: Delacorte.

Nippold, M. A. (2000). Language development in the adolescent years: Aspects of pragmatics, syntax, and semantics. *Topics in Language Disorders, 20,* 15–28.

Nippold, M. A., Allen, M. M., & Kirsch, D. I. (2001). Proverb comprehension as a function of reading proficiency in preadolescents. *Language, Speech and Hearing Services in the Schools, 32,* 90–100.

Nippold, M. A., Taylor, C. L., & Baker, J. M. (1996). Idiom understanding in Australian youth: A cross-cultural comparison. *Journal of Speech and Hearing Research, 39,* 442–447.

Nisbett, R. E. (1998). Race, genetics, and IQ. In C. Jencks & M. Phillips (Eds.), *The black–white test score gap* (pp. 86–102). Washington, DC: Brookings Institution.

Niu, W., & Sternberg, R. (2001). Cultural influence of artistic creativity and its evaluation. *International Journal of Psychology, 36,* 225–241.

Niu, W., & Sternberg, R. J. (2003). Societal and school influences on student creativity: The case of China. *Psychology in the Schools, 40,* 103–114.

Nix, R. L., Pinderhughes, E. E., Dodge, K. A., Bates, J. E., Pettit, G. S., & McFadyen-Ketchum, S. A. (1999). The relation between mothers' hostile attribution tendencies and children's externalizing behavior problems: The mediating role of mothers' harsh discipline practices. *Child Development, 70,* 896–909.

Nolen-Hoeksema, S. (2002). Gender differences in depression. In I. H. Gotlib & C. L. Hammen (Eds.), *Handbook of depression* (pp. 492–509). New York: Guilford.

Noterdaeme, M., Mildenberger, K., Minow, F., & Amorosa, H. (2002). Evaluation of neuromotor deficits in children with autism and children with a specific speech and language disorder. *European Child and Adolescent Psychiatry, 11,* 219–225.

Nucci, L. P. (1996). Morality and the personal sphere of action. In E. Reed, E. Turiel, & T. Brown (Eds.), *Values and knowledge* (pp. 41–60). Hillsdale, NJ: Erlbaum.

Nucci, L. P. (2002). The development of moral reasoning. In U. Goswami (Ed.), *Blackwell handbook of childhood cognitive development* (pp. 303–325). Malden, MA: Blackwell.

Nucci, L. P., Camino, C., & Sapiro, C. M. (1996). Social class effects on Northeastern Brazilian children's conceptions of areas of personal choice and social regulation. *Child Development, 67,* 1223–1242.

Nucci, L. P., & Weber, E. (1995). Social interactions in the home and the development of young children's conceptions of the personal. *Child Development, 66,* 1438–1452.

Nuckolls, K. B., Cassel, J., & Kaplan, B. H. (1972). Psychosocial assets, life crisis, and the prognosis of pregnancy. *American Journal of Epidemiology, 95,* 431–441.

Nurmi, J.-E., Poole, M. E., & Kalakoski, V. (1996). Age differences in adolescent identity exploration and commitment in urban and rural environments. *Journal of Adolescence, 19,* 443–452.

Nye, B., Hedges, L. V., & Konstantopoulos, S. (2001). Are effects of small classes cumulative? Evidence from a Tennessee experiment. *Journal of Educational Research, 94,* 336–345.

Oakes, L. M., & Madole, K. L. (2003). Principles of developmental change in infants' category formation. In D. H. Rakison & L. M. Oakes (Eds.), *Early category and concept development: Making sense of the blooming, buzzing confusion* (pp. 132–158). New York: Oxford University Press.

Oakes, L. M., Coppage, D. J., & Dingel, A. (1997). By land or by sea: The role of perceptual similarity in infants' categorization of animals. *Developmental Psychology, 33,* 396–407.

O'Callaghan, M. J., Burn, Y. R., Mohay, H. A., Rogers, Y., & Tudehope, D. I. (1993). The prevalence and origins of left hand preference in high-risk infants, and its implications for intellectual, motor, and behavioral performance at four and six years. *Cortex, 29,* 617–627.

Ochs, E. (1988). *Culture and language development: Language acquisition and language socialization in a Samoan village.* Cambridge, UK: Cambridge University Press.

O'Connor, T. G., & Croft, C. M. (2001). A twin study of attachment in preschool children. *Child Development, 72,* 1501–1511.

O'Connor, T. G., Deater-Deckard, K., Fulker, D., Rutter, M., & Plomin, R. (1998). Genotype–environment correlations in late childhood and early adolescence: Antisocial behavioral problems and coercive parenting. *Developmental Psychology, 34,* 970–981.

O'Connor, T. G., Heron, J., Golding, J., Beveridge, M., & Glover, V. (2002). Maternal antenatal anxiety and children's behavioural/emotional problems at 4 years: Report from the Avon Longitudinal Study of Parents and Children. *British Journal of Psychiatry, 180,* 502–508.

O'Connor, T. G., Marvin, R. S., Rutter, M., Olrich, J. T., Britner, P. A., & The English and Romanian Adoptees Study Team. (2003). Child–parent attachment following early institutional deprivation. *Development and Psychopathology, 15,* 19–38.

O'Connor, T. G., Rutter, M., Beckett, C., Keaveney, L., Dreppner, J. M., & the English and Romanian Adoptees Study Team. (2000). The effects of global severe privation on cognitive competence: Extension and longitudinal follow-up. *Child Development, 71,* 376–390.

Ogbu, J. U. (1997). Understanding the school performance of urban blacks: Some essential background knowledge. In H. J. Walberg, O. Reyes, & R. P. Weissberg (Eds.), *Children and youth: Interdisciplinary perspectives* (pp. 190–222). Thousand Oaks, CA: Sage.

Ogbu, J. U. (2003). *Black American students in an affluent suburb: A study of academic disengagement.* Mahwah, NJ: Erlbaum.

Ohgi, S., Arisawa, K., Takahashi, T., Kusumoto, T., Goto, Y., Akiyama, T., & Saito, H. (2003a). Neonatal Behavioral Assessment Scale as a predictor of later developmental disabilities of low-birth-weight and/or premature infants. *Brain and Development, 25,* 313–321.

Ohgi, S., Takahashi, T., Nugent, J. K., Arisawa, K., & Akiyama, T. (2003b). Neonatal behavioral characteristics and later behavioral problems. *Clinical Pediatrics, 42,* 679–686.

Okagaki, L. (2001). Parental beliefs, parenting style, and children's intellectual development. In E. L. Grigorenko & R. J. Sternberg (Eds.), *Family environment and intellectual functioning: A life-span perspective* (pp. 141–172). Mahwah, NJ: Erlbaum.

Okagaki, L., & Frensch, P. A. (1996). Effects of video game playing on measures of spatial performance: Gender effects in late adolescence. In P. M. Greenfield & R. R. Cocking (Eds.), *Interacting with video* (pp. 115–140). Norwood, NJ: Ablex.

Okagaki, L., & Frensch, P. A. (1998). Parenting and children's school achievement: A multi-ethnic perspective. *American Educational Research Journal, 35,* 123–144.

Okagaki, L., & Sternberg, R. J. (1993). Parental beliefs and children's school performance. *Child Development, 64,* 36–56.

Okami, P., Weisner, T., & Olmstead, R. (2002). Outcome correlates of parent–child bedsharing: An eighteen-year longitudinal study. *Developmental and Behavioral Pediatrics, 23,* 244–253.

O'Keefe, M. J., O'Callaghan, M., Williams, G. M., Najman, J. M., & Bor, W. (2003). Learning, cognitive, and attentional problems in adolescents born small for gestational age. *Pediatrics, 112,* 301–307.

Olafson, E., & Boat, B. W. (2000). Long-term management of the sexually abused child: Considerations and challenges. In R. M. Reece (Ed.), *Treatment of child abuse: Common ground for mental health, medical, and legal practitioners* (pp. 14–35). Baltimore: Johns Hopkins University Press.

Ollendick, T. H., Yang, B., King, N. J., Dong, Q., & Akande, A. (1996). Fears in American, Australian, Chinese, and Nigerian children and adolescents: A cross-cultural study. *Journal of Child Psychology and Psychiatry, 37,* 213–220.

Oller, D. K. (2000). *The emergence of the speech capacity.* Mahwah, NJ: Erlbaum.

Oller, D. K., Eilers, R. E., Urbano, R., & Cobo-Lewis, A. B. (1997). Development of precursors to speech in infants exposed to two languages. *Journal of Child Language, 24,* 407–425.

Olsen, S. F., Yang, C. M., Hart, C. H., Robinson, C. C., Wu, P., Nelson, D. A., Nelson, L. J., Jin, S., & Wo, J. (2002). Maternal psychological control and preschool children's behavioral outcomes in China, Russia, and the United States. In B. Barber (Ed.), *Intrusive parenting: How psychological control affects children and adolescents* (pp. 235–262). Washington, DC: American Psychological Association.

Olson, S. L., Bates, J. E., Sandy, J. M., & Lantheir, R. (2000). Early development precursors of externalizing behavior in middle childhood and adolescence. *Journal of Abnormal Child Psychology, 28,* 119–133.

Olweus, D., Mattison, A., Schalling, D., & Low, H. (1988). Circulating testosterone levels and aggression in adolescent males: A causal analysis. *Psychosomatic Medicine, 50,* 261–272.

O'Mahoney, J. F. (1989). Development of thinking about things and people: Social and nonsocial cognition during adolescence. *Journal of Genetic Psychology, 150,* 217–224.

Omar, H., McElderry, D., & Zakharia, R. (2003). Educating adolescents about puberty: What are we missing? *International Journal of Adolescent Medicine and Health, 15,* 79–83.

Ondrusek, N., Abramovitch, R., Pencharz, P., & Koren, G. (1998). Empirical examination of the ability of children to consent to clinical research. *Journal of Medical Ethics, 24,* 158–165.

O'Neil, R., Welsh, M., Parke, R. D., Wang, S., & Strand, C. (1997). A longitudinal assessment of the academic correlates of early peer acceptance and rejection. *Journal of Clinical Child Psychology, 26,* 290–303.

Ong, W., Allison, J., & Haladyna, T. M. (2000). Student achievement of third graders in comparable single-age and multiage classrooms. *Journal of Research in Childhood Education, 14,* 205–215.

Oosterwegel, A., & Oppenheimer, L. (1993). *The self-system: Developmental changes between and within self-concepts.* Hillsdale, NJ: Erlbaum.

Oostra, B. A., & Willemsen, R. (2002). The X chromosome and fragile X mental retardation. *Cytogenetic and Genome Research, 99,* 257–264.

O'Rahilly, R., & Müller, F. (2001). *Human embryology and teratology.* New York: Wiley-Liss.

Orbio de Castro, B., Veerman, J. W., Koops, W., Bosch, J. D., & Monshouwer, H. J. (2002). Hostile attribution of intent and aggressive behavior: A meta-analysis. *Child Development, 73,* 916–934.

O'Reilly, A. W., & Bornstein, M. H. (1993). Caregiver–child interaction in play. In M. H. Bornstein & A. W. O'Reilly (Eds.), *New directions for child development* (No. 59, pp. 55–66). San Francisco: Jossey-Bass.

Ornstein, P. A., Shapiro, L. R., Clubb, P. A., & Follmer, A. (1997). The influence of prior knowledge on children's memory for salient medical experiences. In N. Stein, P. A. Ornstein, C. J. Brainerd, & B. Tversky (Eds.), *Memory for everyday and emotional events* (pp. 83–112). Hillsdale, NJ: Erlbaum.

Osborne, J. (1994). Academics, self-esteem, and race: A look at the underlying assumption of the disidentification hypothesis. *Personality and Social Psychology Bulletin, 21,* 449–455.

Osherson, D. N., & Markman, E. M. (1975). Language and the ability to evaluate contradictions and tautologies. *Cognition, 2,* 213–226.

Oshima-Takane, Y., Goodz, E., & Derevensky, J. (1996). Birth order effects on early language development: Do children learn from overheard speech? *Child Development, 67,* 621–634.

Oshima-Takane, Y., & Robbins, M. (2003). Linguistic environment of secondborn children. *First Language, 23,* 21–40.

Osmond, C., & Barker, D. J. (2000). Fetal, infant, and childhood growth are predictors of coronary heart disease, diabetes, and hypertension in adult men and women. *Environmental Health Perspectives, 108,* 545–553.

OSSTF (Ontario Secondary School Teachers' Federation). (2005). *Grade 10 literacy test continues to take its toll on students.* Retrieved from www.newswire.ca/en/releases/archive/April2004/29/c6966.html

O'Sullivan, M., Guilford, J. P., & deMille, R. (1965). The measurement of social intelligence (Reports from the Psychological Laboratory, University of Southern California No. 34).

Ovando, C. J., & Collier, V. P. (1998). *Bilingual and ESL classrooms: Teaching in multicultural contexts.* Boston: McGraw-Hill.

Owen, M. T., & Cox, M. J. (1997). Marital conflict and the development of infant–parent attachment relationships. *Journal of Family Psychology, 11,* 152–164.

Owens, R. E. (2005). *Language development: An introduction* (6th ed.). Boston: Allyn and Bacon.

Pagani, L., Boulerice, B., Vitaro, F., & Tremblay, E. (1999). Effects of poverty on academic failure and delinquency in boys: A change and process model approach. *Journal of Child Psychology and Psychiatry, 40,* 1209–1219.

Pagani, L., Tremblay, R. E., Vitaro, F., Boulerice, B., & McDuff, P. (2001). Effects of grade retention on academic performance and behavioral development. *Development and Psychopathology, 13,* 297–315.

Paladino, J., & Berk, L. E. (2005, September). *Development and functional significance of private speech in children with autism.* Paper presented at the First International Society for Cultural and Activity Research, Seville, Spain.

Palincsar, A. S. (2003). Advancing a theoretical model of learning and instruction. In B. J. Zimmerman (Ed.), *Educational psychology: A century of contributions* (pp. 459–475). Mahwah, NJ: Erlbaum.

Palincsar, A. S., & Klenk, L. (1992). Fostering literacy learning in supportive contexts. *Journal of Learning Disabilities, 25,* 211–225.

Palmer, J. R., Hatch, E. E., Rao, R. S., Kaufman, R. H., Herbst, A. L., & Noller, K. L. (2001). Infertility among women exposed prenatally to diethylstilbestrol. *American Journal of Epidemiology, 154,* 316–321.

Pan, B. A., & Snow, C. E. (1999). The development of conversation and discourse skills. In M. Barrett (Ed.), *The development of language* (pp. 229–249). Hove, UK: Psychology Press.

Pan, H. W. (1994). Children's play in Taiwan. In J. L. Roopnarine, J. E. Johnson, & F. H. Hooper (Eds.), *Children's play in diverse cultures* (pp. 31–50). Albany, NY: SUNY Press.

Parameswaran, G. (2003). Experimenter instructions as a mediator in the effects of culture on mapping one's neighborhood. *Journal of Environmental Psychology, 23,* 409–417.

Parent, A., Teilmann, G., Juul, A., Skakkebaek, N. E., Toppari, J., & Bourguignon, J. (2003). The timing of normal puberty and the age limits of sexual precocity: Variations around the world, secular trends, and changes after migration. *Endocrine Reviews, 24,* 668–693.

Parer, J. T. (1998). Effects of fetal asphyxia on brain cell structure and function: Limits of tolerance. *Comparative Biochemistry and Physiology, 119A,* 711–716.

Parke, R. D. (1996). *Fatherhood.* Cambridge, MA: Cambridge University Press.

Parke, R. D., & Buriel, R. (1998). Socialization in the family: Ethnic and ecological perspectives. In N. Eisenberg (Ed.), *Handbook of child psychology: Vol. 3. Social, emotional, and personality development* (5th ed., pp. 463–552). New York: Wiley.

Parke, R. D., & Kellam, S. G. (Eds.) (1994). *Exploring family relationships with other social contexts.* Hillsdale, NJ: Erlbaum.

Parke, R. D., Simpkins, S. D., McDowell, D. J., Kim, M., Killian, C., Dennis, J., Flyr, M. L., Wild, M., & Rah, Y. (2004). Relative contributions of families and peers to children's social development. In P. K. Smith & C. H. Hart (Eds.), *Blackwell handbook of childhood social development* (pp. 156–177). Malden, MA: Blackwell.

Parker, F. L., Boak, A. Y., Griffin, K. W., Ripple, C., & Peay, L. (1999). Parent–child relationship, home learning environment, and school readiness. *School Psychology Review, 28,* 413–425.

Parker, J. G., & Asher, S. R. (1987). Peer relations and later personal adjustment: Are low-accepted children at risk? *Psychological Bulletin, 102,* 357–389.

Parker, J. G., & Asher, S. R. (1993). Friendship and friendship quality in middle childhood: Links with peer group acceptance and feelings of loneliness and social dissatisfaction. *Developmental Psychology, 29,* 611–621.

Parten, M. (1932). Social participation among preschool children. *Journal of Abnormal and Social Psychology, 27,* 243–269.

Pascalis, O., de Haan, M., & Nelson, C. A. (1998). Long-term recognition memory for faces assessed by visual paired comparison in 3- and 6-month-old infants. *Journal of Experimental Psychology: Learning, Memory, and Cognition, 24,* 249–260.

Pate, R. R., Trost, S. G., Levin, S., & Dowda, M. (2000). Sports participation and health-related behaviors among U.S. youth. *Archives of Pediatric and Adolescent Medicine, 154,* 904–911.

Patel, D. R., Pratt, H. D., & Greydanus, D. E. (2003). Treatment of adolescents with anorexia nervosa. *Journal of Adolescent Research, 18,* 244–260.

Patrick, E., & Abravanel, E. (2000). The self-regulatory nature of preschool children's private speech in a naturalistic setting. *Applied Psycholinguistics, 21,* 45–61.

Patterson, C. J. (2001). *Lesbian and gay parenting.* [On-line]. Available: www.apa.org/pi/parent.html

Patterson, C. J. (2002). Lesbian and gay parenthood. In M. H. Bornstein (Ed.), *Handbook of parenting: Vol. 3. Being and becoming a parent* (2nd ed., pp. 317–338). Mahwah, NJ: Erlbaum.

Patterson, G. R. (1995). Coercion—A basis for early age of onset for arrest. In J. McCord (Ed.), *Coercion and punishment in long-term perspective* (pp. 81–105). New York: Cambridge University Press.

Patterson, G. R. (1997). Performance models for parenting: A social interactional perspective. In J. E. Grusec & L. Kuczynski (Eds.), *Parenting and children's internalization of values* (pp. 193–226). New York: Wiley.

Patterson, G. R., DeBaryshe, B. D., & Ramsey, E. (1989). A developmental perspective on antisocial behavior. *American Psychologist, 44,* 329–335.

Patterson, G. R., & Fisher, P. A. (2002). Recent developments in our understanding of parenting: Bidirectional effects, causal models, and the search for parsimony. In M. H. Bornstein (Ed.), *Handbook of parenting: Vol. 5. Practical issues in parenting* (2nd ed., pp. 59–88). Mahwah, NJ: Erlbaum.

Patterson, G. R., & Forgatch, M. (1995). Predicting future clinical adjustment from treatment outcome and process variables. *Psychological Assessment, 7,* 275–285.

Patterson, G. R., & Yoerger, K. (2002). A developmental model for early- and late-onset delinquency. In J. B. Reid & G. R. Patterson (Eds.), *Antisocial behavior in children and adolescents* (pp. 147–172). Washington, DC: American Psychological Association.

Patton, G. C., Selzer, R., Coffey, C., Carlin, J. B., & Wolfe, R. (1999). Onset of adolescent eating disorders: Population based cohort study over 3 years. *British Medical Journal, 318,* 765–768.

Paul, J. J., & Cillessen, A. H. N. (2003). Dynamics of peer victimization in early adolescence: Results from a four-year longitudinal study. *Journal of Applied School Psychology, 19,* 25–43.

Payne, R. J. (1998). *Getting beyond race: The changing American culture.* Boulder, CO: Westview.

Peake, P. K., Hebl, M., & Mischel, W. (2002). Strategic attention deployment for delay of gratification in working and waiting situations. *Developmental Psychology, 38,* 313–326.

Pebody, R. G., Edmunds, W. J., Conyn-van Spaendonck, M., Olin, P., Berbers, G., & Rebiere, I. (2000). The sero-epidemiology of rubella in western Europe. *Epidemiology and Infections, 125,* 347–357.

Pederson, D. R., Gleason, K. E., Moran, G., & Bento, S. (1998). Maternal attachment representations, maternal sensitivity, and the infant–mother attachment relationship. *Developmental Psychology, 34,* 925–933.

Pederson, D. R., & Moran, G. (1995). A categorical description of infant–mother relationships in the home and its relation to Q-sort measures of infant–mother interaction. In E. Waters, B. E. Vaughn, G. Posada, & K. Kondo-Ikemura (Eds.), Caregiving, cultural, and cognitive perspectives on secure-base behavior and working models: New growing points of attachment theory and research. *Monographs of the Society for Research in Child Development, 60*(2–3, Serial No. 244).

Pederson, D. R., & Moran, G. (1996). Expressions of the attachment relationship outside of the Strange Situation. *Child Development, 67,* 915–927.

Pedlow, R., Sanson, A., Prior, M., & Oberklaid, F. (1993). Stability of maternally reported temperament from infancy to 8 years. *Developmental Psychology, 29,* 998–1007.

Peiser-Feinberg, E. S., Burchinal, M. R., Clifford, R. M., Culkin, M. L., Howes, C., Kagan, S. L., & Yazijian, N. (2001). The relation of preschool child-care quality to children's cognitive and social developmental trajectories through second grade. *Child Development, 72,* 1534–1553.

Pellegrini, A. D. (2003). Perceptions and functions of play and real fighting in early adolescence. *Child Development, 74,* 1522–1533.

Pellegrini, A. D. (2004). Rough-and-tumble play from childhood through adolescence: Development and possible functions. In P. K. Smith & C. H. Hart (Eds.), *Blackwell handbook of childhood social development* (pp. 438–453). Malden, MA: Blackwell.

Pellegrini, A. D., & Smith, P. K. (1998). Physical activity play: The nature and function of a neglected aspect of play. *Child Development, 69,* 577–598.

Peoples, C. E., Fagan, J. F., III, & Drotar, D. (1995). The influence of race on 3-year-old children's performance on the Stanford-Binet: Fourth Edition. *Intelligence, 21,* 69–82.

Peplau, L. A., Garnets, L. D., Spalding, L. R., Conley, T. D., & Venigas, R. C. (1998). A critique of Bem's "exotic becomes erotic" theory of sexual orientation. *Psychological Review, 105,* 387–394.

Pepler, D., Craig, W., Yuile, A., & Connolly, J. (2004). Girls who bully: A developmental and relational perspective. In M. Putallaz & K. L. Bierman (Eds.), *Aggression, antisocial behavior, and violence among girls: A developmental perspective* (pp. 90–109). New York: Guilford.

Pepperberg, I. M. (2000). *The Alex studies: Cognitive and communicative abilities of grey parrots.* Cambridge, MA: Harvard University Press.

Peralta de Mendoza, O. A., & Salsa, A. M. (2003). Instruction in early comprehension and use of a symbol–referent relation. *Cognitive Development, 18,* 269–284.

Perez, B. (2004). *Becoming biliterate: A study of two-way bilingual immersion education.* Mahwah, NJ: Erlbaum.

Perie, M., Sherman, J. D., Phillips, G., & Riggan, M. (2000). Elementary and secondary education: An international perspective. *Education Statistics Quarterly* . Retrieved from http://nces.ed.gov/pubs2000/quarterly/summer/5int/q51.html

Perlman, M., & Ross, H. S. (1997). The benefits of parent intervention in children's disputes: An examination of concurrent changes in children's fighting styles. *Child Development, 64,* 690–700.

Perlmutter, M. (1984). Continuities and discontinuities in early human memory: Paradigms, processes, and performances. In R. V. Kail, Jr., & N. R. Spear (Eds.), *Comparative perspectives on the development of memory* (pp. 253–287). Hillsdale, NJ: Erlbaum.

Perner, J. (1988). Higher-order beliefs and intentions in children's understanding of social interaction. In J. W. Astington, P. L. Harris, & D. R. Olson (Eds.), *Developing theories of mind* (pp. 271–294). New York: Cambridge University Press.

Perry, D. G., Perry, L. C., & Rasmussen, P. (1986). Cognitive social learning mediators of aggression. *Child Development, 57,* 700–711.

Perry, D. G., Perry, L. C., & Weiss, R. J. (1989). Sex differences in the consequences that children anticipate for aggression. *Developmental Psychology, 25,* 171–184.

Perry, M. (2000). Explanations of mathematical concepts in Japanese, Chinese, and U.S. first- and fifth-grade classrooms. *Cognition and Instruction, 18,* 181–207.

Peshkin, A. (1978). *Growing up American: Schooling and the survival of the community.* Chicago: University of Chicago Press.

Peshkin, A. (1997). *Places of memory: Whiteman's schools and native American communities.* Mahwah, NJ: Erlbaum.

Peters, R. D., Petrunka, K., & Arnold, R. (2003). The Better Beginnings, Better Futures Project: A universal, comprehensive, community-based prevention approach for primary school children and their families. *Journal of Clinical Child and Adolescent Psychology, 32,* 215–227.

Peterson, C. (1999). Children's memory for medical emergencies 2 years later. *Developmental Psychology, 35,* 1493–1506.

Peterson, C., & McCabe, A. (1983). *Developmental psycholinguistics: Three ways of looking at a child's narrative.* New York: Plenum.

Peterson, C., & Rideout, R. (1998). Memory for medical emergencies experienced by 1- and 2-year-olds. *Developmental Psychology, 34,* 1059–1072.

Peterson, C., & Roberts, C. (2003). Like mother, like daughter: Similarities in narrative style. *Developmental Psychology, 39,* 551–562.

Peterson, C. C. (2001). Influence of siblings' perspectives on theory of mind. *Cognitive Development, 15,* 435–455.

Peterson, C. C., Peterson, J. L., & Seeto, D. (1983). Developmental changes in ideas about lying. *Child Development, 54,* 1529–1535.

Petitto, L. A., Holowka, S., Sergio, L. E., & Ostry, D. (2001). Language rhythms in babies' hand movements. *Nature, 413,* 35–36.

Petitto, L. A., Holowka, S., Sergio, L. E., Levy, B., & Ostry, D. J. (2004). Baby hands that move to the rhythm of language: Hearing babies acquiring sign languages babble silently on the hands. *Cognition, 93,* 43–73.

Petitto, L. A., & Marentette, P. F. (1991). Babbling in the manual mode: Evidence for the ontogeny of language. *Science, 251,* 1493–1496.

Petrovich, O. (1997). Understanding non-natural causality in children and adults: The case against artificialism. *Psyche en Geloof, 8,* 151–165.

Pettigrew, T. (1998). Intergroup contact theory. *American Review of Psychology, 49,* 65–85.

Pettit, G. S. (2004). Violent children in developmental perspective. *Current Directions in Psychological Science, 13,* 194–197.

Pettit, G. S., Bates, J. E., & Dodge, K. A. (1997). Supportive parenting, ecological context, and children's adjustment: A seven-year longitudinal study. *Child Development, 68,* 908–923.

Pettit, G. S., Brown, E. G., Mize, J., & Lindsey, E. (1998). Mothers' and fathers' socializing behaviors in three contexts: Links with children's peer competence. *Merrill-Palmer Quarterly, 44,* 173–193.

Pettit, G. S., Laird, R. D., Dodge, K. A., Bates, J. E., & Criss, M. M. (2001). Antecedents and behavior-problem outcomes of parental monitoring and psychological control in early adolescents. *Child Development, 72,* 583–598.

Phillips, M. (1997). What makes schools effective? A comparison of the relationships of communitarian climate and academic climate to mathematics achievement and attendance during middle school. *American Educational Research Journal, 34,* 633–662.

Phillipsen, L. C. (1999). Associations between age, gender, and group acceptance and three components of friendship quality. *Journal of Early Adolescence, 19,* 438–464.

Phinney, J. S., & Chavira, V. (1995). Parental ethnic socialization and adolescent outcomes in ethnic minority families. *Journal of Research on Adolescence, 5,* 31–53.

Phinney, J. S., Horenczyk, G., Liebkind, K., & Vedder, P. (2001a). Ethnic identity, immigration, and well-being: An interactional perspective. *Journal of Social Issues, 57,* 493–510.

Phinney, J. S., & Kohatsu, E. L. (1997). Ethnic and racial identity development and mental health. In J. Schulenberg, J. L. Maggs, & K. Hurrelmann (Eds.), *Health risks and developmental transitions during adolescence* (pp. 420–443). Cambridge, UK: Cambridge University Press.

Phinney, J. S., Ong, A., & Madden, T. (2000). Cultural values and intergenerational value discrepancies in immigrant and non-immigrant families. *Child Development, 71,* 528–539.

Phinney, J. S., Romero, I., Nava, M., & Huang, D. (2001b). The role of language, parents, and peers in ethnic identity among adolescents in immigrant families. *Journal of Youth and Adolescence, 30,* 135–153.

Piaget, J. (1926). *The language and thought of the child.* New York: Harcourt, Brace & World. (Original work published 1923)

Piaget, J. (1928). *Judgment and reasoning in the child.* New York: Harcourt, Brace & World. (Original work published 1926)

Piaget, J. (1930). *The child's conception of the world.* New York: Harcourt, Brace & World. (Original work published 1926)

Piaget, J. (1951). *Play, dreams, and imitation in childhood.* New York: Norton. (Original work published 1945)

Piaget, J. (1952). *The origins of intelligence in children.* New York: International Universities Press. (Original work published 1936)

Piaget, J. (1965). *The moral judgment of the child.* New York: Free Press. (Original work published 1932)

Piaget, J. (1967). *Six psychological studies.* New York: Vintage.

Piaget, J. (1971). *Biology and knowledge.* Chicago: University of Chicago Press.

Piaget, J., & Inhelder, B. (1956). *The child's conception of space.* London: Routledge & Kegan Paul. (Original work published 1948)

Piaget, J., Inhelder, B., & Szeminska, A. (1960). *The child's conception of geometry.* New York: Basic Books. (Original work published 1948)

Pianta, R. C., Egeland, B., & Erickson, M. F. (1989). The antecedents of maltreatment: Results of the Mother–Child Interaction Research Project. In D. Cicchetti & V. Carlson (Eds.), *Child maltreatment* (pp. 203–253). New York: Cambridge University Press.

Pianta, R. C., Hamre, B., & Stuhlman, M. (2003). Relationships between teachers and children. In W. M. Reynolds & G. E. Miller (Eds.), *Handbook of psychology: Educational psychology* (Vol. 7, pp. 199–234). New York: Wiley.

Pickens, J., Field, T., & Nawrocki, T. (2001). Frontal EEG asymmetry in response to emotional vignettes in preschool age children. *International Journal of Behavioral Development, 25,* 105–112.

Pierce, K. M., Hamm, J. V., & Vandell, D. L. (1999). Experiences in after-school programs and children's adjustment in first-grade classrooms. *Child Development, 70,* 756–767.

Pierce, S. H., & Lange, G. (2000). Relationships among metamemory, motivation and memory performance in young school-age children. *British Journal of Developmental Psychology, 18,* 121–135.

Pierce, W. D., & Epling, W. F. (1995). *Behavior analysis and learning.* Englewood Cliffs, NJ: Prentice-Hall.

Pinderhughes, E. E., Dodge, K. A., Bates, J. E., Pettit, G. S., & Zelli, A. (2000). Discipline responses: Influences of parents' socioeconomic status, ethnicity, beliefs about parenting, stress, and cognitive-emotional processes. *Journal of Family Psychology, 14,* 380–400.

Pine, D. S. (2001). Functional magnetic resonance imaging in children and adolescents: Implications for research on emotion. In J. M. Morihisa (Ed.), *Advances in brain imaging* (pp. 53–82). Washington, DC: American Psychiatric Publishing.

Pinker, S. (1989). *Learnability and cognition.* Cambridge, MA: MIT Press.

Pinker, S. (1994). *The language instinct: How the mind creates language.* New York: William Morrow.

Pinker, S. (1999). *Words and rules: The ingredients of language.* New York: Basic Books.

Pinker, S., Lebeaux, D. S., & Frost, L. A. (1987). Productivity and constraints in the acquisition of the passive. *Cognition, 26,* 195–267.

Pinker. S., & Ullman, M. (2002). The past and future of the past tense. *Trends in Cognitive Sciences, 6,* 456–463.

Pipp, S., Easterbrooks, M. A., & Brown, S. R. (1993). Attachment status and complexity of infants' self- and other-knowledge when tested with mother and father. *Social Development, 2,* 1–14.

Pipp, S., Easterbrooks, M. A., & Harmon, R. J. (1992). The relation between attachment and knowledge of self and mother in one-year-old infants to three-year-old infants. *Child Development, 63,* 738–750.

Pitts, V. P. (1976). Drawing the invisible: Children's conceptualization of God. *Character Potential, 8,* 12–24.

Pivarnik, J. M. (1998). Potential effects of maternal physical activity on birth weight: Brief review. *Medicine and Science in Sports and Exercise, 30,* 407–414.

Plantin, L., Mansson, S.-A., & Kearney, J. (2003). Talking and doing fatherhood: On fatherhood and masculinity in Sweden and England. *Fathering, 1,* 3–26.

Plomin, R. (1994). *Genetics and experience: The interplay between nature and nurture.* Thousand Oaks, CA: Sage.

Plomin, R. (2003). General cognitive ability. In R. Plomin & J. C. DeFries (Eds.), *Behavioral genetics in the postgenomic era* (pp. 183–201). Washington, DC: American Psychological Association.

Plomin, R., DeFries, J. C., McClearn, G. E., & McGuffin, P. (2001). *Behavioral genetics* (4th ed.). New York: Worth.

Plomin, R., Fulker, D. W., Corley, R., & DeFries, J. C. (1997). Nature, nurture and cognitive development from 1 to 16 years: A parent–offspring study. *Psychological Science, 8,* 442–447.

Plomin, R., & Spinath, F. M. (2004). Intelligence: Genetics, genes, and genomics. *Journal of Personality and Social Psychology, 86,* 112–129.

Plumert, J. M., Pick, H. L., Jr., Marks, R. A., Kintsch, A. S., & Wegesin, D. (1994). Locating objects and communicating about locations: Organizational differences in children's searching and direction-giving. *Developmental Psychology, 30,* 443–453.

Plunkett, K. (1998). Connectionism and development. In M. Sabourin & F. Craik (Eds.), *Advances in psychological science* (Vol. 2, pp. 581–600). Hove, UK: Psychology Press.

Plunkett, K., Karmiloff-Smith, A., Bates, E., Elman, J. L., & Johnson, M. H. (1997). Connectionism and developmental psychology. *Journal of Child Psychology and Psychiatry, 38,* 53–80.

Pohl, R. (2002). *Poverty in Canada.* Ottowa: Innercity Ministries.

Polka, L., & Sundara, M. (2003). Word segmentation in monolingual and bilingual infant learners of English and French. In *Proceedings of the 15th International Congress of Phonetic Sciences* (Vol. 1, pp. 1021–1024). Barcelona, Spain: University Autonoma Barcelona.

Polka, L., & Werker, J. F. (1994). Developmental changes in perception of non-native vowel contrasts. *Journal of Experimental Psychology: Human Perception and Performance, 20,* 421–435.

Pollitt, E. (1996). A reconceptualization of the effects of undernutrition on children's biological, psychosocial, and behavioral development. *Social Policy Report of the Society for Research in Child Development, 10*(5).

Pollock, L. (1987). *A lasting relationship: Parents and children over three centuries.* Hanover, NH: University Press of New England.

Pomerantz, E. M., & Eaton, M. M. (2000). Developmental differences in children's conceptions of parental control: "They love me, but they make me feel incompetent." *Merrill-Palmer Quarterly, 46,* 140–167.

Pomerantz, E. M., & Ruble, D. N. (1998a). The multidimensional nature of control: Implications for the development of sex differences in self-evaluation. In J. Heckhausen & C. S. Dweck (Eds.), *Motivation and self-regulation across the life span* (pp. 159–184). New York: Cambridge University Press.

Pomerantz, E. M., & Ruble, D. N. (1998b). The role of maternal control in the development of sex differences in child self-evaluative factions. *Child Development, 69,* 458–478.

Pomerantz, E. M., & Saxon, J. L. (2001). Conceptions of ability as stable and self-evaluative processes: A longitudinal examination. *Child Development, 72,* 152–173.

Pomerleau, A., Scuccimarri, C., & Malcuit, G. (2003). Mother–infant behavioral interactions in teenage and adult mothers during the first six months postpartum: Relations with infant development. *Infant Mental Health Journal, 24,* 495–509.

Pons, F., Lawson, J., Harris, P. L., & de Rosnay, M. (2003). Individual differences in children's emotion understanding: Effects of age and language. *Scandinavian Journal of Psychology, 44,* 347–353.

Poole, D. A., & Lindsay, D. S. (2001). Children's eyewitness reports after exposure to misinformation from parents. *Journal of Experimental Psychology: Applied, 7,* 27–50.

Porter, R. H., Makin, J. W., Davis, L. B., & Christensen, K. M. (1992). An assessment of the salient olfactory environment of formula-fed infants. *Physiology and Behavior, 50,* 907–911.

Porter-Stevens, C., Raz, S., & Sander, C. J. (1999). Peripartum hypoxic risk and cognitive outcome: A study of term and preterm birth children at early school age. *Neuropsychology, 13,* 598–608.

Posada, G., Carbonell, O. A., Alzate, G., & Plata, S. J. (2004). Through Colombian lenses: Ethnographic and conventional analyses of maternal care and their associations with secure base behavior. *Developmental Psychology, 40,* 508–518.

Posada, G., Jacobs, A., Richmond, M. K., Carbonell, O. A., Alzate, G., Bustamante, M. R., & Quiceno, J. (2002). Maternal caregiving and infant security in two cultures. *Developmental Psychology, 38,* 67–78.

Posner, J. K., & Vandell, D. L. (1994). Low-income children's after-school care: Are there beneficial effects of after-school programs? *Child Development, 64,* 440–456.

Posner, J. K., & Vandell, D. L. (1999). After-school activities and the development of low-income urban children: A longitudinal study. *Developmental Psychology, 35,* 868–879.

Potter, G. B., Gibbs, J. C., & Goldstein, A. P. (2001). *EQUIP implementation guide.* Champaign, IL: Research Press.

Poulin-Dubois, D., Serbin, L. A., Eichstedt, J. A., Sen, M. G., & Beissel, C. F. (2002). Men don't put on make-up.: Toddlers' knowledge of the gender stereotypes of household activities. *Social Development, 11,* 166–181.

Poulton, R., Caspi, A., Milne, B. J., Thomson, W. M., Taylor, A., Sears, M. R., & Moffitt, T. E. (2002). Association between children's experience of socioeconomic disadvantage and adult health: A life-course study. *Lancet, 360,* 1640–1645.

Povinelli, D. J. (2001). The self: Elevated in consciousness and extended in time. In C. Moore & K. Lemmon (Eds.), *The self in time: Developmental perspectives* (pp. 75–95). Mahwah, NJ: Erlbaum.

Powlishta, K. K. (2000). The effect of target age on the activation of gender stereotypes. *Sex Roles, 42,* 271–282.

Powlishta, K. K., Sen, M. G., Serbin, L. A., Poulin-Dubois, D., & Eichstedt, J. A. (2001). From infancy through middle childhood: The role of cognitive and social factors in becoming gendered. In R. K. Unger (Ed.), *Handbook of the psychology of women and gender* (pp. 116–132). New York: Wiley.

Powlishta, K. K., Serbin, L. A., & Moller, L. C. (1993). The stability of individual differences in gender typing: Implications for understanding gender segregation. *Sex Roles, 29,* 723–737.

Powlishta, K. K., Serbin, L. A., Doyle, A., & White, D. R. (1994). Gender, ethnic, and body type biases: The generality of prejudice in childhood. *Developmental Psychology, 30,* 526–536.

Powls, A., Botting, N., Cooke, R. W. I., & Marlow, N. (1996). Handedness in very-low-birthweight (VLBW) children at 12 years of age: Relation to perinatal and outcome variables. *Developmental Medicine and Child Neurology, 38,* 594–602.

Pratt, M. W., Skoe, E. E., & Arnold, M. L. (2004). Care reasoning development and family socialization patterns in later adolescence: A longitudinal analysis. *International Journal of Behavioral Development, 28,* 139–147.

Prechtl, H. F. R. (1958). Problems of behavioral studies in the newborn infant. In D. S. Lehrmann, R. A. Hinde, & E. Shaw (Eds.), *Advances in the study of behavior* (Vol. 1, pp. 75–98). New York: Academic Press.

Prechtl, H. F. R., & Beintema, D. (1965). *The neurological examination of the full-term newborn infant.* London: William Heinemann Medical Books.

Preisler, G. M. (1991). Early patterns of interaction between blind infants and their sighted mothers. *Child: Care, Health and Development, 17,* 65–90.

Preisler, G. M. (1993). A descriptive study of blind children in nurseries with sighted children. *Child: Care, Health and Development, 19,* 295–315.

Preissler, M. A., & Carey, S. (2004). Do both pictures and words function as symbols for 18- and 24-month-old children? *Journal of Cognition and Development, 5,* 185–212.

Pressley, M. (1995). More about the development of self-regulation: Complex, long-term, and thoroughly social. *Educational Psychologist, 30,* 207–212.

Pressley, M., Wharton-McDonald, R., Raphael, L. M., Bogner, K., & Roehrig, A. (2002). Exemplary first-grade teaching. In B. M. Taylor & P. D. Pearson (Eds.), *Teaching reading: Effective schools, accomplished teachers* (pp. 73–88). Mahwah, NJ: Erlbaum.

Previc, F. H. (1991). A general theory concerning the prenatal origins of cerebral lateralization. *Psychological Review, 98,* 299–334.

Preyer, W. (1888). *The mind of the child* (2 vols.). New York: Appleton. (Original work published 1882)

Primus, W., Rawlings, L., Larin, K., & Porter, K. (1999). *Initial impacts of welfare reform on the incomes of single-mother families.* Washington, DC: Center on Budget and Policy Priorities.

Prinstein, M. J., Boergers, J., & Spirito, A. (2001). Adolescents' and their friends' health-risk behavior: Factors that alter or add to peer influence. *Journal of Pediatric Psychology, 26,* 287–298.

Prinstein, M. J., Boergers, J., & Vernberg, E. M. (2001). Overt and relational aggression in adolescents: Social–psychological adjustment of aggressors and victims. *Journal of Clinical Child Psychology, 30,* 479–491.

Prinstein, M. J., & Cillessen, A. H. N. (2003). Forms and functions of adolescent peer aggression associated with high levels of peer status. *Merrill-Palmer Quarterly, 49,* 310–342.

Prinstein, M. J., & La Greca, A. M. (2002). Peer crowd affiliation and internalizing distress in childhood and adolescence: A longitudinal follow-back study. *Journal of Research on Adolescence, 12,* 325–351.

Prinstein, M. J., & La Greca, A. M. (2004). Childhood peer rejection and aggression as predictors of adolescent girls' externalizing and health risk behaviors: A 6-year longitudinal study. *Journal of Consulting and Clinical Psychology, 72,* 103–112.

Prior, M., Smart, D., Sanson, A., & Oberklaid, F. (2000). Does shy-inhibited temperament in childhood lead to anxiety problems in adolescence? *Journal of the American Academy of Child and Adolescent Psychiatry, 39,* 461–468.

Proctor, M. H., Moore, L. L., Gao, D., Cupples, L. A., Bradlee, M. L., Hood, M. Y., & Ellison, R. C. (2003). Television viewing and change in body fat from preschool to early adolescence: The Framingham Children's Study. *International Journal of Obesity, 27,* 827–833.

Programme for International Student Assessment. (2000). *Messages from Programme for International Student Assessment 2000.* Retrieved from www.pisa.oecd.org

Programme for International Student Assessment. (2003). *Learning for tomorrow's world: First results from Program for International Student Assessment 2003.* Retrieved from www.pisa.oecd.org

Programme for International Student Assessment. (2005). *School factors related to quality and equity.* Retrieved from www.pisa.oecd.org

Provins, K. A. (1997). Handedness and speech: A critical reappraisal of the role of genetic and environmental factors in the cerebral lateralization of function. *Psychological Review, 104,* 554–571.

Pruett, M. K., Williams, T. Y., Insabella, G., & Little, T. D. (2003). Family and legal indicators of child adjustment to divorce among families with young children. *Journal of Family Psychology, 17,* 169–180.

Pryor, J., & Rodgers, B. (2001). *Children in changing families: Life after parental separation.* Oxford, UK: Blackwell.

Prysak, M., Lorenz, R. P., & Kisly, A. (1995). Pregnancy outcome in nulliparous women 35 years and older. *Obstetrics and Gynecology, 85,* 65–70.

Public Agenda. (2002). *A lot easier said than done: Parents talk about raising children in today's America.* Retrieved from www.publicagenda.org/specials/parents/parents.htm

Pungello, E. P., & Kurtz-Costes, B. (1999). Why and how working women choose child care: A review with a focus on infancy. *Developmental Review, 19,* 31–96.

Purcell-Gates, V. (1996). Stories, coupons, and the TV Guide: Relationships between home literacy experiences and emergent literacy knowledge. *Reading Research Quarterly, 31,* 406–428.

Putnam, F. W. (2003). Ten-year research update review: Child sexual abuse. *Journal of the American Academy of Child and Adolescent Psychiatry, 42,* 269–278.

Putnam, S. P., Samson, A. V., & Rothbart, M. K. (2000). Child temperament and parenting. In V. J. Molfese & D. L. Molfese (Eds.), *Temperament and personality across the life span* (pp. 255–277). Mahwah, NJ: Erlbaum.

Pyeritz, R. E. (1998). Sex: What we make of it. *Journal of the American Medical Association, 279,* 269.

Quatman, T., Sokolik, E., & Smith, K. (2000). Adolescent perception of peer success: A gendered perspective over time. *Sex Roles, 43,* 61–84.

Quillian, L., & Campbell, M. E. (2003). Beyond black and white: The present and future of multiracial friendship segregation. *American Sociological Review, 68,* 540–566.

Quinn, C. T., Rogers, Z. R., & Buchanan, G. R. (2004). Survival of children with sickle cell disease. *Blood, 103,* 4023–4027.

Quinn, P. C., & Eimas, P. D. (1996). Perceptual organization and categorization in young infants. In C. Rovee-Collier & L. P. Lipsitt (Eds.), *Advances in infancy research* (Vol. 10, pp. 1–36). Norwood, NJ: Ablex.

Quint, J. C., Box, J. M., & Polit, D. F. (1997, July). *New chance: Final report on a comprehensive program for disadvantaged young mothers and their children.* New York: Manpower Demonstration Research Corporation.

Quist, J. R., & Kennedy, J. L. (2001). Genetics of childhood disorders: XXIII. ADHD, part 7: The serotonin system. *Journal of the American Academy of Child and Adolescent Psychiatry, 40,* 253–256.

Quyen, G. T., Bird, H. R., Davies, M., Hoven, C., Cohen, P., Jensen, P. S., & Goodman, S. (1998). Adverse life events and resilience. *Journal of the American Academy of Child and Adolescent Psychiatry, 37,* 1191–1200.

Radecki, C. M., & Jaccard, J. (1995). Perceptions of knowledge, actual knowledge, and information search behavior. *Journal of Experimental Social Psychology, 31,* 107–138.

Radelet, M. A., Lephart, S. M., Rubinstein, E. N., & Myers, J. B. (2002). Survey of the injury rate for children in community sports. *Pediatrics, 110,* e28.

Radin, N. (1994). Primary caregiving fathers in intact families. In A. E. Gottfried & A. W. Gottfried (Eds.), *Redefining families: Implications for children's development* (pp. 11–54). New York: Plenum.

Radke-Yarrow, M., & Kochanska, G. (1990). Anger in young children. In N. L. Stein, B. Leventhal, & T. Trabasso (Eds.), *Psychological and behavioral approaches to emotion* (pp. 297–310). Hillsdale, NJ: Erlbaum.

Raffaeli, M., Bogenschneider, K., & Flood, M. F. (1998). Parent–teen communication about sexual topics. *Journal of Family Issues, 19,* 315–333.

Rahman, Q., & Wilson, G. D. (2003). Born gay? The psychobiology of human sexual orientation. *Personality and Individual Differences, 34,* 1337–1382.

Raine, A. (1997). Antisocial behavior and psychophysiology: A biosocial perspective and a prefrontal dysfunction hypothesis. In D. M. Stoff, J. Breiling, & J. D. Maser (Eds.), *Handbook of antisocial behavior* (pp. 289–304). New York: Wiley.

Rakoczy, H., Tomasello, M., & Striano, T. (2004). Young children know that trying is not pretending: A test of the "behaving-as-if" construal of children's early concept of pretense. *Developmental Psychology, 40,* 388–399.

Ramey, S. L. (1999). Head Start and preschool education: Toward continued improvement. *American Psychologist, 54,* 344–346.

Ramey, S. L., & Ramey, C. T. (1999). Early experience and early intervention for children "at risk" for developmental delay and mental retardation. *Mental Retardation and Developmental Disabilities, 5,* 1–10.

Ramos, E., Frontera, W. R., Llorpart, A., & Feliciano, D. (1998). Muscle strength and hormonal levels in adolescents: Gender related differences. *International Journal of Sports Medicine, 19,* 526–531.

Ramsey, P. G. (1991). Young children's awareness and understanding of social class differences. *Journal of Genetic Psychology, 152,* 71–82.

Ramsey, P. G. (1995, September). Growing up with the contradictions of race and class. *Young Children, 50*(6), 18–22.

Rank, M. R. (2000). Socialization of socioeconomic status. In W. C. Nichols & M. A. Pace-Nichols (Eds.), *Handbook of family development and intervention* (pp. 129–142). New York: Wiley.

Rasmussen, C., Ho, E., & Bisanz, J. (2003). Use of the mathematical principle of inversion in young children. *Journal of Experimental Child Psychology, 85,* 89–102.

Rasmussen, E. R., Neuman, R. J., Heath, A. C., Levy, F., Hay, D. A., & Todd, R. D. (2004). Familial clustering of latent class and *DSM-IV* defined attention-deficit hyperactivity disorder (ADHD) subtypes. *Journal of Child Psychology and Psychology, 45,* 589–598.

Rast, M., & Meltzoff, A. N. (1995). Memory and representation in young children with Down syndrome: Exploring deferred imitation and object permanence. *Development and Psychopathology, 7,* 393–407.

Rauscher, F. H., Shaw, G. L., & Ky, K. N. (1993). Music and spatial task performance. *Nature, 365,* 611.

Raver, C. C. (2003). Does work pay psychologically as well as economically? The role of employment in predicting depressive symptoms and parenting among low-income families. *Child Development, 74,* 1720–1736.

Ray, O. (2004). How the mind hurts and heals the body. *American Psychologist, 59,* 29–40.

Rayner, K., & Pollatsek, A. (1989). *The psychology of reading.* Englewood Cliffs, NJ: Prentice-Hall.

Rayner, K., Pollatsek, A., & Starr, M. S. (2003). Reading. In A. F. Healy & R. W. Proctor (Eds.), (2003). *Handbook of psychology: Experimental psychology* (Vol. 4, pp. 549–574). New York: Wiley.

Raz, S., Shah, F., & Sander, C. J. (1996). Differential effects of perinatal hypoxic risk on early developmental outcome: A twin study. *Neuropsychology, 10,* 429–436.

Reese, E., Haden, C. A., & Fivush, R. (1996). Mothers, fathers, daughters and sons: Gender differences in autobiographical reminiscing. *Research on Language and Social Interaction, 29*(1), 27–56.

Regnerus, M., Smith, C., & Fritsch, M. (2003). *Religion in the lives of American adolescents: A review of the literature.* Chapel Hill, NC: National Study of Youth and Religion.

Reid, P. T., & Trotter, K. H. (1993). Children's self-presentations with infants: Gender and ethnic comparisons. *Sex Roles, 29,* 171–181.

Reifman, A., Villa, L. C., Amans, J. A., Rethinam, V., & Telesca, T. Y. (2001). Children of divorce in the 1990s: A meta-analysis. *Journal of Divorce and Remarriage, 36,* 27–36.

Reilly, J. S., Bates, E. A., & Marchman, V. A. (1998). Narrative discourse in children with early focal brain injury. *Brain and Language, 61,* 335–375.

Reilly, T. P., Hasazi, J. E., & Bond, L. A. (1983). Children's concepts of death and personal mortality. *Journal of Paediatric Psychology, 8,* 21–31.

Reis, O., & Youniss, J. (2004). Patterns in identity change and development in relationships with mothers and friends. *Journal of Adolescent Research, 19,* 31–44.

Reisman, J. E. (1987). Touch, motion, and proprioception. In P. Salapatek & L. Cohen (Eds.), *Handbook of infant perception: Vol. 1. From sensation to perception* (pp. 265–303). Orlando, FL: Academic Press.

Reiss, A. L., & Dant, C. C. (2003). The behavioral neurogenetics of fragile X syndrome: Analyzing gene–brain–behavior relationships in child developmental psychopathologies. *Development and Psychopathology, 15,* 927–968.

Reiss, D. (2003). Child effects on family systems: Behavioral genetic strategies. In A. C. Crouter & A. Booth (Eds.), *Children's influence on family dynamics: The neglected side of family relationships* (pp. 3–36). Mahwah, NJ: Erlbaum.

Relph, K., Harrington, K., & Pandha, H. (2004). Recent developments and current status of gene therapy using viral vectors in the United Kingdom. *British Medical Journal, 329,* 839–842.

Renninger, K. A. (1998). Developmental psychology and instruction: Issues from and for practice. In I. Sigel & K. A. Renninger (Eds.), *Handbook of child psychology: Vol. 4. Child psychology and practice* (pp. 211–274). New York: Wiley.

Renzetti, C. M., & Curran, D. J. (1998). *Living sociology.* Boston: Allyn and Bacon.

Repacholi, B. M. (1998). Infants' use of attentional cues to identify the referent of another person's emotional expression. *Developmental Psychology, 34,* 1017–1025.

Repacholi, B. M., & Gopnik, A. (1997). Early reasoning about desires: Evidence from 14- and 18-month-olds. *Developmental Psychology, 33,* 12–21.

Resnick, M. B., Gueorguieva, R. V., Carter, R. L., Ariet, M., Sun, Y., Roth, J., Bucciarelli, R. L., Curran, J. S., & Mahan, C. S. (1999). The impact of low birth weight, perinatal conditions, and sociodemographic factors on educational outcome in kindergarten. *Pediatrics, 104,* e74.

Rest, J. R. (1979). *Development in judging moral issues.* Minneapolis: University of Minnesota Press.

Rest, J. R. (1986). *Moral development: Advances in research and theory.* New York: Praeger.

Reyna, V. F., & Kiernan, B. (1994). Development of gist versus verbatim memory in sentence recognition: Effects of lexical familiarity, semantic content, encoding instructions, and retention interval. *Developmental Psychology, 30,* 178–191.

Reynolds, A. J., & Robertson, D. L. (2003). School-based early intervention and later child maltreatment in the Chicago Longitudinal Study. *Child Development, 74,* 3–26.

Reynolds, A. J., & Temple, J. A. (1998). Extended early childhood intervention and school achievement: Age thirteen findings from the Chicago Longitudinal Study. *Child Development, 69,* 231–246.

Reynolds, A. J., Temple, J. A., Robertson, D. L., & Mann, E. A. (2001). Long-term effects of an early childhood intervention on educational achievement and juvenile arrest. *Journal of the American Medical Association, 285,* 2339–2346.

Reynolds, C. R., & Kaiser, S. M. (1990). Test bias in psychological assessment. In T. B. Gutkin & C. R. Reynolds (Eds.), *The handbook of school psychology* (pp. 487–525). New York: Wiley.

Reynolds, M. A., Schieve, L. A., Martin, J. A., Meng, G., & Macaluso, M. (2003). Trends in multiple births conceived using assisted reproductive technology, United States, 1997–2000. *Pediatrics, 111,* 1159–1162.

Reznick, J. S., & Goldfield, B. A. (1992). Rapid change in lexical development in comprehension and production. *Developmental Psychology, 28,* 406–413.

Rholes, W. S., Newman, L. S., & Ruble, D. N. (1990). Understanding self and others: Developmental and motivational aspects of perceiving persons in terms of invariant dispositions. In E. Higgins & R. Sorrentino (Eds.),

Handbook of motivation and cognition: Foundations of social behavior (Vol. 2, pp. 369–407). New York: Guilford.

Ricard, M., & Kamberk-Kilicci, M. (1995). Children's empathic responses to emotional complexity. *International Journal of Behavioral Development, 18,* 211–225.

Rice, M. L. (1990). Preschoolers' QUIL: Quick incidental learning of words. In G. Conti-Ramsden & C. E. Snow (Eds.), *Children's language* (Vol. 7, pp. 171–195). Hillsdale, NJ: Erlbaum.

Richards, J. E., & Holley, F. B. (1999). Infant attention and the development of smooth pursuit tracking. *Developmental Psychology, 35,* 856–867.

Richardson, G. A., Hamel, S. C., Goldschmidt, L., & Day, N. L. (1996). The effects of prenatal cocaine use on neonatal neurobehavioral status. *Neurotoxicology and Teratology, 18,* 519–528.

Rich-Edwards, J. W., Colditz, G. A., Stampfer, M. J., Willett, W. C., Gillman, M. W., Hennekens, C. H., Speizer, F. E., & Manson, J. E. (1999). Birthweight and the risk for type 2 diabetes mellitus in adult women. *Annals of Internal Medicine, 130,* 278–284.

Richmond, L. J. (2004). When spirituality goes awry: Students in cults. *Professional School Counseling, 7,* 367–375.

Riegle-Crumb, C. (2000). *International gender inequality in math and science education.* Unpublished doctoral dissertation, University of Chicago.

Rietvelt, M. J. H., Hudziak, J. J., Bartels, M., van Beijsterveldt, C. E. M., & Boomsma, D. I. (2004). Heritability of attention problems in children: Longitudinal results from a study of twins, age 3 to 12. *Journal of Child Psychology and Psychiatry, 45,* 577–588.

Rigby, K. (2004). Bullying in childhood. In P. K. Smith & C. H. Hart (Eds.), *Blackwell handbook of childhood social development* (pp. 549–568). Malden, MA: Blackwell.

Riggs, K. J., & Peterson, D. M. (2000). Counterfactual thinking in preschool children: Mental state and causal inferences. In P. Mitchell & K. J. Riggs (Eds.), *Children's reasoning and the mind* (pp. 87–99). Hove, UK: Psychology Press.

Rijsdijk, F. V., & Boomsma, D. I. (1997). Genetic mediation of the correlation between peripheral nerve conduction velocity and IQ. *Behavior Genetics, 27,* 87–98.

Ripple, C. H., & Zigler, E. (2003). Research, policy, and the federal role in prevention initiatives for children. *American Psychologist, 58,* 482–490.

Riva, D., & Giorgi, C. (2000). The cerebellum contributes to higher functions during development: Evidence from a series of children surgically treated for posterior fossa tumours. *Brain, 123,* 1051–1061.

Rivera, S. M., Wakeley, A., & Langer, J. (1999). The drawbridge phenomenon: Representational reasoning or perceptual preference? *Developmental Psychology, 35,* 427–435.

Robb, A. S., & Dadson, M. J. (2002). Eating disorders in males. *Child and Adolescent Psychiatric Clinics of North America, 11,* 399–418.

Roberton, M. A. (1984). Changing motor patterns during childhood. In J. R. Thomas (Ed.), *Motor development during childhood and adolescence* (pp. 48–90). Minneapolis: Burgess Publishing.

Roberts, D. F., Foehr, U. G., & Rideout, V. (2005). *Generation M: Media in the lives of 8–18 year olds.* Menlo Park, CA: Henry J. Kaiser Family Foundation.

Roberts, J. E., Burchinal, M. R., & Durham, M. (1999). Parents' report of vocabulary and grammatical development of American preschoolers: Child and environment associations. *Child Development, 70,* 92–106.

Roberts, R. J., Jr., & Aman, C. J. (1993). Developmental differences in giving directions: Spatial frames of reference and mental rotation. *Child Development, 64,* 1258–1270.

Robin, D. J., Berthier, N. E., & Clifton, R. K. (1996). Infants' predictive reaching for moving objects in the dark. *Developmental Psychology, 32,* 824–835.

Robins, R. W., Tracy, J. L., Trzesniewski, K., Potter, J., & Gosling, S. D. (2001). Personality correlates of self-esteem. *Journal of Research in Personality, 35,* 463–482.

Robinson, B. F., Mervis, C. B., & Robinson, B. W. (2003). The roles of verbal short-term memory in the acquisition of grammar by children with Williams syndrome. *Developmental Neuropsychology, 23,* 13–31.

Robinson, C. C., Anderson, G. T., Porter, C. L., Hart, C. H., & Wouden-Miller, M. (2003). Sequential transition patterns of preschoolers' social interactions during child-initiated play: Is parallel-aware play a bi-directional bridge to other play states? *Early Childhood Research Quarterly, 18,* 3–21.

Rochat, P. (1989). Object manipulation and exploration in 2- to 5-month-old infants. *Developmental Psychology, 25,* 871–884.

Rochat, P. (1998). Self-perception and action in infancy. *Experimental Brain Research, 123,* 102–109.

Rochat, P. (2001). *The infant's world.* Cambridge, MA: Harvard University Press.

Rochat, P. (2003). Five levels of self-awareness as they unfold early in life. *Consciousness and Cognition, 12,* 717–731.

Rochat, P., & Goubet, N. (1995). Development of sitting and reaching in 5- to 6-month-old infants. *Infant Behavior and Development, 18,* 53–68.

Rochat, P., & Hespos, S. J. (1997). Differential rooting response by neonates: Evidence for an early sense of self. *Early Development and Parenting, 6,* 105–112.

Rochat, P., Querido, J. G., & Striano, T. (1999). Emerging sensitivity to the timing and structure of protoconversation. *Developmental Psychology, 35,* 950–957.

Rochat, P., & Striano, T. (2002). Who's in the mirror? Self–other discrimination in specular images by four- and

nine-month-old infants. *Infant and Child Development, 11,* 289–303.

Rochat, P., Striano, T., & Blatt, L. (2002). Differential effects of happy, neutral, and sad still-faces on 2-, 4-, and 6-month-old infants. *Infant and Child Development, 11,* 289–303.

Rodgers, J. L. (2001). The confluence model: An academic "tragedy of the commons"? In E. L. Grigorenko & R. J. Sternberg (Eds.), *Family environment and intellectual functioning: A life-span perspective* (pp. 71–95). Mahwah, NJ: Erlbaum.

Rodgers, J. L., Cleveland, H. H., van den Oord, E., & Rowe, D. C. (2000). Resolving the debate over birth order, family size, and intelligence. *American Psychologist, 55,* 599–612.

Rodkin, P. C., Farmer, T. W., Pearl, R., & Van Acker, R. (2000). Resolving the debate over birth order, family size, and intelligence. *American Psychologist, 55,* 599–612.

Rodriguez, M. L., Mischel, W., & Shoda, Y. (1989). Cognitive and personality variables in the delay of gratification of older children at risk. *Journal of Personality and Social Psychology, 57,* 358–367.

Roebers, C. M., & Schneider, W. (2001). Individual differences in children's eyewitness recall: The influence of intelligence and shyness. *Applied Developmental Science, 5,* 9–20.

Roelfsema, N. M., Hop, W. C., Boito, S. M., & Wladimiroff, J. W. (2004). Three-dimensional sonographic measurement of normal fetal brain volume during the second half of pregnancy. *American Journal of Obstetrics and Gynecology, 190,* 275–280.

Roeser, R. W., Eccles, J. S., & Freedman-Doan, C. (1999). Academic functioning and mental health in adolescence: Patterns, progressions, and routes from childhood. *Journal of Adolescent Research, 14,* 135–174.

Roeser, R. W., Eccles, J. S., & Sameroff, A. J. (2000). School as a context of early adolescents' academic and social-emotional development: A summary of research findings. *Elementary School Journal, 100,* 443–471.

Roffwarg, H. P., Muzio, J. N., & Dement, W. C. (1966). Ontogenetic development of the human sleep-dream cycle. *Science, 152,* 604–619.

Rogers, L., Resnick, M. D., Mitchell, J. E., & Blum, R. W. (1997). The relationship between socioeconomic status and eating disordered behaviors in a community sample of adolescent girls. *International Journal of Eating Disorders, 22,* 15–23.

Roggman, L. A., Langlois, J. H., Hubbs-Tait, L., & Rieser-Danner, L. A. (1994). Infant day-care, attachment, and the "file drawer problem." *Child Development, 65,* 1429–1443.

Rogler, L. H. (2002). Historical generations and psychology. *American Psychologist, 57,* 1013–1023.

Rogoff, B. (1998). Cognition as a collaborative process. In D. Kuhn & R. S. Siegler (Eds.), *Handbook of child psychology: Vol. 2. Cognition, perception, and language* (5th ed., pp. 679–744). New York: Wiley.

Rogoff, B. (2003). *The cultural nature of human development.* New York: Oxford University Press.

Rogoff, B., & Chavajay, P. (1995). What's become of research on the cultural basis of cognitive development? *American Psychologist, 50,* 859–877.

Rogoff, B., & Mistry, J. (1985). Memory development in cultural context. In M. Pressley & C. Brainerd (Eds.), *Cognitive learning and memory in children* (pp. 117–142). New York: Springer-Verlag.

Rogoff, B., Paradise, R., Arauz, R. M., Correa-Chávez, M., & Angelillo, C. (2003). Firsthand learning through intent participation. *Annual Review of Psychology, 54,* 175–203.

Rogoff, B., & Waddell, K. J. (1982). Memory for information organized in a scene by children from two cultures. *Child Development, 53,* 1224–1228.

Rogol, A. D., Roemmich, J. N., & Clark, P. A. (2002). Growth at puberty. *Journal of Adolescent Health, 31,* 192–200.

Rohner, R. P., & Brothers, S. A. (1999). Perceived parental rejection, psychological maladjustment, and borderline personality disorder. *Journal of Emotional Abuse, 1,* 81–95.

Rohner, R. P., & Veneziano, R. A. (2001). The importance of father love: History and contemporary evidence. *Review of General Psychology, 5,* 382–405.

Roid, G. (2003). *The Stanford-Binet Intelligence Scales, Fifth Edition, Interpretive Manual.* Itasca, IL: Riverside Publishing.

Roizen, N. J., & Patterson, D. (2003). Down's syndrome. *Lancet, 361,* 1281–1289.

Romans, S. E., Martin, M., Gendall, K., & Herbison, G. P. (2003). Age of menarche: The role of some psychosocial factors. *Psychological Medicine, 33,* 933–939.

Rome-Flanders, T., & Cronk, C. (1995). A longitudinal study of infant vocalizations during mother–infant games. *Journal of Child Language, 22,* 259–274.

Romero, A. J., & Roberts, R. E. (2003). The impact of multiple dimensions of ethnic identity on discrimination and adolescents' self-esteem. *Journal of Applied Social Psychology, 33,* 2288–2305.

Rönnqvist, L., & Hopkins, B. (1998). Head position preference in the human newborn: A new look. *Child Development, 69,* 13–23.

Roopnarine, J. L., Hossain, Z., Gill, P., & Brophy, H. (1994). Play in the East Indian context. In J. L. Roopnarine, J. E. Johnson, & F. H. Hooper (Eds.), *Children's play in diverse cultures* (pp. 9–30). Albany, NY: SUNY Press.

Roopnarine, J. L., Talukder, E., Jain, D., Joshi, P., & Srivastave, P. (1990). Characteristics of holding, patterns of play, and social behaviors between parents and infants in New Delhi, India. *Developmental Psychology, 26,* 667–673.

Rosander, K., & von Hofsten, C. (2004). Infants' emerging ability to represent occluded object motion. *Cognition, 91,* 1–22.

Rose, A. J. (2002). Co-rumination in the friendships of girls and boys. *Child Development, 73,* 1830–1843.

Rose, A. J., & Asher, S. R. (1999). Children's goals and strategies in response to

conflicts within a friendship. *Developmental Psychology, 35,* 69–79.

Rose, A. J., Swenson, L. P., & Waller, E. M. (2004). Overt and relational aggression and perceived popularity: Developmental differences in concurrent and prospective relations. *Developmental Psychology, 40,* 378–387.

Rose, J. L., & Bertenthal, B. I. (1995). A longitudinal study of the visual control of posture in infancy. In B. G. Bardy, R. J. Bootsma, & Y. Guiard (Eds.), *Studies in perception and action* (pp. 251–253). Mahwah, NJ: Erlbaum.

Rose, S. A., Jankowski, J. J., & Senior, G. J. (1997). Infants' recognition of contour-deleted figures. *Journal of Experimental Psychology: Human Perception and Performance, 23,* 1206–1216.

Rosen, A. B., & Rozin, P. (1993). Now you see it, now you don't: The preschool child's conception of invisible particles in the context of dissolving. *Developmental Psychology, 29,* 300–311.

Rosen, D. (2003). Eating disorders in children and young adolescents: Etiology, classification, clinical features, and treatment. *Adolescent Medicine: State of the Art Reviews, 14,* 49–59.

Rosenberg, D. R., Sweeney, J. A., Gillen, J. S., Kim, J., Varanelli, M. J., O'Hearn, K. M., & Erb, P. A. (1997). Magnetic resonance imaging of children without sedation: Preparation with simulation. *Journal of the American Academy of Child and Adolescent Psychiatry, 36,* 853–859.

Rosengren, K. S., & Hickling, A. K. (2000). The development of children's thinking about possible events and plausible mechanisms. In K. S. Rosengren, C. N. Johnson, & P. L. Harris (Eds.), *Imagining the impossible* (pp. 75–98). Cambridge, UK: Cambridge University Press.

Rosenshine, B., & Meister, C. (1994). Reciprocal teaching: A review of nineteen experimental studies. *Review of Educational Research, 64,* 479–530.

Ross, H. S., Conant, C., Cheyne, J. A., & Alevizos, E. (1992). Relationships and alliances in the social interactions of kibbutz toddlers. *Social Development, 1,* 1–17.

Roth, J., Brooks-Gunn, J., Murray, L., & Foster, W. (1998). Promoting healthy adolescents: Synthesis of youth development program evaluations. *Journal of Research on Adolescence, 8,* 423–459.

Rothbart, M. K. (2003). Temperament and the pursuit of an integrated developmental psychology. *Merrill-Palmer Quarterly, 50,* 492–505.

Rothbart, M. K. (2004). Emotion-related regulation: Sharpening the definition. *Child Development, 75,* 334–339.

Rothbart, M. K., Ahadi, S. A., & Evans, D. E. (2000). Temperament and personality: Origins and outcome. *Journal of Personality and Social Psychology, 78,* 122–135.

Rothbart, M. K., & Bates, J. E. (1998). Temperament. In N. Eisenberg (Ed.), *Handbook of child psychology: Vol. 3. Social, emotional, and personality development* (5th ed., pp. 105–176). New York: Wiley.

Rothbart, M. K., Ellis, L. K., Rueda, M. R., & Posner, M. I. (2003). Developing mechanisms of temperamental effortful control. *Journal of Personality, 71,* 1113–1143.

Rothbart, M. K., & Mauro, J. A. (1990). Questionnaire approaches to the study of infant temperament. In J. W. Fagen & J. Colombo (Eds.), *Individual differences in infancy: Reliability, stability, and prediction* (pp. 411–429). Hillsdale, NJ: Erlbaum.

Rothbaum, F., Pott, M., Azuma, H., Miyake, K., & Weisz, J. (2000b). The development of close relationships in Japan and the United States: Paths of symbiotic harmony and generative tension. *Child Development, 71,* 1121–1142.

Rothbaum, F., Weisz, J., Pott, M., Miyake, K., & Morelli, G. A. (2000a). Attachment and culture: Security in the United States and Japan. *American Psychologist, 55,* 1093–1104.

Rousseau, J. J. (1955). *Emile.* New York: Dutton. (Original work published 1762)

Rovee-Collier, C. K. (1999). The development of infant memory. *Current Directions in Psychological Science, 8,* 80–85.

Rovee-Collier, C. K., & Bhatt, R. S. (1993). Evidence of long-term memory in infancy. *Annals of Child Development, 9,* 1–45.

Rovee-Collier, C., & Barr, R. (2001). Infant learning and memory. In G. Bremner & A. Fogel (Eds.), *Blackwell handbook of infant development* (p. 139–168). Oxford, UK: Blackwell.

Rovet, J., Netley, C., Keenan, M., Bailey, J., & Stewart, D. (1996). The psycho-educational profile of boys with Klinefelter syndrome. *Journal of Learning Disabilities, 29,* 180–196.

Rowe, D. C. (1994). *The limits of family influence: Genes, experience, and behavior.* New York: Guilford.

Rowe, S., & Wertsch, J. V. (2002). Vygotsky's model of cognitive development. In G. Bremner & A. Fogel (Eds.), *Blackwell handbook of infant development* (pp. 538–554). Oxford, U.K.: Blackwell.

Rowland, C., & Pine, J. M. (2000). Subject-auxiliary inversion errors and wh-question acquisition: "What children do know?" *Journal of Child Language, 27,* 157–181.

Rubin, K. H., Bukowski, W., & Parker, J. G. (1998). Peer interactions, relationships, and groups. In N. Eisenberg (Ed.), *Handbook of child psychology: Vol. 3. Social, emotional, and personality development* (5th ed., pp. 619–700). New York: Wiley.

Rubin, K. H., Burgess, K. B., & Coplan, R. (2002). Social withdrawal and shyness. In P. K. Smith & C. H. Hart (Eds.), *Blackwell handbook of child social development* (pp. 329–352). Oxford, UK: Blackwell.

Rubin, K. H., Burgess, K. B., & Hastings, P. D. (2002). Stability and social-behavioral consequences of toddlers' inhibited temperament and parenting behaviors. *Child Development, 73,* 483–495.

Rubin, K. H., Burgess, K. B., Dwyer, K. M., & Hastings, P. D. (2003). Predicting preschoolers' externalizing behaviors

from toddler temperament, conflict, and maternal negativity. *Developmental Psychology, 39,* 164–176.

Rubin, K. H., & Coplan, R. J. (1998). Social and nonsocial play in childhood: An individual differences perspective. In O. N. Saracho & B. Spodek (Eds.), *Multiple perspectives on play in early childhood education* (pp. 144–170). Albany, NY: State University of New York Press.

Rubin, K. H., Fein, G. G., & Vandenberg, B. (1983). Play. In E. M. Hetherington (Ed.), *Handbook of child psychology: Vol. 4. Socialization, personality, and social development* (4th ed., pp. 693–744). New York: Wiley.

Rubin, K. H., Hastings, P. D., Stewart, S. L., Henderson, H. A., & Chen, X. (1997). The consistency and concomitants of inhibition: Some of the children, all of the time. *Child Development, 68,* 467–483.

Rubin, K. H., Stewart, S. L., & Coplan, R. J. (1995). Social withdrawal in childhood: Conceptual and empirical perspectives. In T. H. Ollendick & R. J. Prinz (Eds.), *Advances in clinical child psychology* (Vol. 17, pp. 157–196). New York: Plenum.

Rubin, K. H., Watson, K. S., & Jambor, T. W. (1978). Free-play behaviors in preschool and kindergarten children. *Child Development, 49,* 534–536.

Ruble, D. N., Alvarez, J., Bachman, M., Cameron, J., Fuligni, A., Garcia Coll, C., & Rhee, E. (2004). The development of a sense of "we": The emergence and implications of children's collective identity. In M. Bennett & F. Sani (Eds.), *The development of the social self* (pp. 29–76). Hove, UK: Psychology Press.

Ruble, D. N., & Dweck, C. S. (1995). Self-conceptions, person conceptions, and their development. In N. Eisenberg (Ed.), *Social development* (pp. 109–139). Thousand Oaks, CA: Sage.

Ruble, D. N., & Flett, G. L. (1988). Conflicting goals in self-evaluative information seeking: Developmental and ability level analyses. *Child Development, 59,* 97–106.

Ruble, D. N., & Martin, C. L. (1998). Gender development. In N. Eisenberg (Ed.), *Handbook of child psychology: Vol. 3. Social, emotional, and personality development* (5th ed., pp. 933–1016). New York: Wiley.

Rudolph, D. K., & Heller, T. L. (1997). Interpersonal problem solving, externalizing behavior, and social competence in preschoolers: A knowledge-performance discrepancy? *Journal of Applied Developmental Psychology, 18,* 107–117.

Rudolph, D. K., Lambert, S. F., Clark, A. G., & Kurlakowsky, K. D. (2001). Negotiating the transition to middle school: The role of self-regulatory processes. *Child Development, 72,* 929–946.

Ruff, H. A., & Capozzoli, M. C. (2003). Development of attention and distractibility in the first 4 years of life. *Developmental Psychology, 39,* 877–890.

Ruff, H. A., & Rothbart, M. K. (1996). *Attention in early development.* New York: Oxford University Press.

Ruff, H. A., Saltarelli, L. M., Capozzoli, M., & Dubiner, K. (1992). The differentiation of activity in infants' exploration of objects. *Developmental Psychology, 28,* 851–861.

Ruffman, T. (1999). Children's understanding of logical inconsistency. *Child Development, 70,* 872–886.

Ruffman, T., & Langman, L. (2002). Infants' reaching in a multi-well A not B task. *Infant Behavior and Development, 25,* 237–246.

Ruffman, T., Perner, J., Olson, D. R., & Doherty, M. (1993). Reflecting on scientific thinking: Children's understanding of the hypothesis– evidence relation. *Child Development, 64,* 1617–1636.

Rumbaut, R. G. (1997). Ties that bind: Immigration and immigrant families in the United States. In A. Booth, A. C. Crouter, & N. Landale (Eds.), *Immigration and the family: Research and policy on U.S. immigrants* (pp. 3–46). Mahwah, NJ: Erlbaum.

Runco, M. A. (1992a). Children's divergent thinking and creative ideation. *Developmental Review, 12,* 233–264.

Runco, M. A. (1992b). The evaluative, valuative, and divergent thinking of children. *Journal of Creative Behavior, 25,* 311–319.

Runco, M. A. (1993). Divergent thinking, creativity, and giftedness. *Gifted Child Quarterly, 37,* 16–22.

Runco, M. A., & Okuda, S. M. (1988). Problem, discovery, divergent thinking, and the creative process. *Journal of Youth and Adolescence, 17,* 211–220.

Rushton, J. L., Forcier, M., & Schectman, R. M. (2002). Epidemiology of depressive symptoms in the National Longitudinal Study of Adolescent Health. *Journal of the American Academy of Child and Adolescent Psychiatry, 41,* 199–205.

Rushton, J. P., & Jensen, A. R. (2003). African–white IQ differences from Zimbabwe on the Wechsler Intelligence Scale for Children–Revised are mainly on the g factor. *Personality and Individual Differences, 34,* 177–183.

Russell, A., Mize, J., & Bissaker, K. (2004). Parent–child relationships. In P. K. Smith & C. H. Hart (Eds.), *Blackwell handbook of childhood social development* (pp. 204–222). Malden, MA: Blackwell.

Russell, A., Pettit, G. S., & Mize, J. (1998). Horizontal qualities in parent–child relationships: Parallels with and possible consequences for children's peer relationships. *Developmental Review, 18,* 313–352.

Russell, J. A. (1990). The preschooler's understanding of the causes and consequences of emotion. *Child Development, 61,* 1872–1881.

Russell, R. B., Petrini, J. R., Damus, K., Mattison, D. R., & Schwarz, R. H. (2003). The changing epidemiology of multiple births in the United States. *Obstetrics and Gynecology, 101,* 129–135.

Rust, J., Golombok, S., Hines, M., Johnston, K., Golding, J., & the ALSPAC Study Team. (2000). The role of brothers and sisters in the gender development of preschool children. *Journal of Experimental Child Psychology, 77,* 292–303.

Rutter, M. (1996). Maternal deprivation. In M. H. Bornstein (Ed.), *Handbook of parenting: Vol. 4. Applied and practical parenting* (pp. 3–31). Mahwah, NJ: Erlbaum.

Rutter, M. (2002). Nature, nurture, and development: From evangelism through science toward policy and practice. *Child Development, 73,* 1–21.

Rutter, M., & the English and Romanian Adoptees Study Team. (1998). Developmental catch-up, and deficit, following adoption after severe global early privation. *Journal of Child Psychology and Psychiatry, 39,* 465–476.

Rutter, M., O'Connor, T. G., and the English and Romanian Adoptees Study Team. (2004). Are there biological programming effects for psychological development? Findings from a study of Romanian adoptees. *Developmental Psychology, 40,* 81–94.

Rutter, M., Pickles, A., Murray, R., & Eaves, L. (2001). Testing hypotheses on specific environmental causal effects on behavior. *Psychological Bulletin, 127,* 291–324.

Saarni, C. (1999). *The development of emotional competence.* New York: Guilford.

Saarni, C. (2000). Emotional competence: A developmental perspective. In R. Bar-On & J. D. A. Parker (Eds.), *Handbook of emotional intelligence* (pp. 68–91). San Francisco: Jossey-Bass.

Saarni, C., Mumme, D. L., & Campos, J. J. (1998). Emotional development: Action, communication, and understanding. In N. Eisenberg (Ed.), *Handbook of child psychology: Vol. 3. Social, emotional, and personality development* (5th ed., pp. 237–309). New York: Wiley.

Sacks, P. (1999). *Standardized minds: The high price of America's testing culture and what we can do to change it.* Cambridge, MA: Perseus.

Sadeh, A. (1997). Sleep and melatonin in infants: A preliminary study. *Sleep, 20,* 185–191.

Sadler, T. W. (2000). *Langman's medical embryology* (8th ed.). Baltimore: Williams & Wilkins.

Saenger, P. (2003). Dose effects of growth hormone during puberty. *Hormone Research, 60*(Suppl. 1), 52–57.

Saffran, J. R., Aslin, R. N., & Newport, E. L. (1996). Statistical learning by 8-month-old infants. *Science, 274,* 1926–1928.

Saffran, J. R., & Thiessen, E. D. (2003). Pattern induction by infant language learners. *Developmental Psychology, 39,* 484–494.

Salbe, A. D., Weyer, C., Harper, I., Lindsay, R. S., Ravussin, E., & Tataranni, P. A. (2002b). Assessing risk factors for obesity between childhood and adolescence: II. Energy metabolism and physical activity. *Pediatrics, 110,* 307–314.

Salbe, A. D., Weyer, C., Lindsay, R. S., Ravussin, E., & Tataranni, P. A. (2002a). Assessing risk factors for obesity between childhood and adolescence: I. Birth weight, childhood adiposity, parental obesity, insulin, and leptin. *Pediatrics, 110,* 299–306.

Salerno, M., Micillo, M., Di Maio, S., Capalbo, D., Ferri, P., & Lettiero, T. (2001). Longitudinal growth, sexual maturation and final height in patients with congenital hypo-thyroidism detected by neonatal screening. *European Journal of Endocrinology, 145,* 377–383.

Salguero, R. A. T., & Morán, R. M. B. (2003). Measuring problem video game playing in adolescents. *Addiction, 97,* 1601–1606.

Salidis, J., & Johnson, J. S. (1997). The production of minimal words: A longitudinal case study of phonological development. *Language Acquisition, 6,* 1–36.

Salihu, H. M., Shumpert, M. N., Slay, M., Kirby, R. S., & Alexander, G. R. (2003). Childbearing beyond maternal age 50 and fetal outcomes in the United States. *Obstetrics and Gynecology, 102,* 1006–1014.

Salmela-Aro, K., Nurmi, J.-E., Saisto, T., & Halmesmaki, E. (2000). Women's and men's personal goals during the transition to parenthood. *Journal of Family Psychology, 14,* 171–186.

Salmivalli, C., Kaukiainen, A., & Lagerspetz, K. (2000). Aggression and sociometric status of adolescents' self-concept and its relation to their social behavior. *Journal of Research on Adolescence, 8,* 333–354.

Salmivalli, C., & Voeten, M. (2004). Connections between attitudes, group norms, and behaviour in bullying situations. *International Journal of Behavioral Development, 28,* 246–258.

Salovey, P., & Pizzaro, D. A. (2003). The value of emotional intelligence. In R. J. Sternberg, J. Lautrey, & T. I. Lubart (Eds.), *Models of intelligence: International perspectives* (pp. 263–278). Washington, DC: American Psychological Association.

Salter, D., McMillan, D., Richards, M., Talbot, T., Hodges, J., Bentovim, A., & Hastings, R. (2003). Development of sexually abusive behavior in sexually victimized males: A longitudinal study. *Lancet, 361,* 471–476.

Samenow, S. E. (1984). *Inside the criminal mind.* New York: Random House.

Sameroff, A. J., & MacKenzie, M. J. (2003). Research strategies for capturing transactional models of development: The limits of the possible. *Development and Psychopathology, 15,* 613–640.

Sameroff, A. J., Seifer, R., Baldwin, A., & Baldwin, C. (1993). Stability of intelligence from preschool to adolescence: The influence of social and family risk factors. *Child Development, 64,* 80–97.

Samuels, M. (2003). Viruses and sudden infant death. *Peaediatric Respiratory Review, 4,* 178–183.

Sandnabba, N. K., & Ahlberg, C. (1999). Parents' attitudes and expectations about children's cross-gender behavior. *Sex Roles, 40,* 249–263.

Sandqvist, K. (1992). Sweden's sex-role scheme and commitment to gender equality. In S. Lewis, D. N. Izraeli, & H. Hottsmans (Eds.), *Dual-earner families: International perspectives.* London: Sage.

Sandstrom, M. J., & Cillessen, A. H. N. (2003). Sociometric status and children's peer experiences: Use of the daily diary method. *Merrill-Palmer Quarterly, 49,* 427–452.

Sandstrom, M. J., & Coie, J. D. (1999). A developmental perspective on peer rejection: Mechanisms of stability and change. *Child Development, 70,* 955–966.

Sansavini, A., Bertoncini, J., & Giovanelli, G. (1997). Newborns discriminate the rhythm of multisyllabic stressed words. *Developmental Psychology, 33,* 3–11.

Sanson, A., Hemphill, S. A., & Smart, D. (2004). Connections between temperament and social development: A review. *Social Development, 13,* 142–170.

Santoloupo, S., & Pratt, M. (1994). Age, gender, and parenting style variations in mother–adolescent dialogues and adolescent reasoning about political issues. *Journal of Adolescent Research, 9,* 241–261.

Sapp, F., Lee, K., & Muir, D. (2000). Three-year-olds' difficulty with the appearance–reality distinction: Is it real or is it apparent? *Developmental Psychology, 36,* 547–560.

Sarason, I. G. (1980). *Test anxiety: Theory, research, and applications.* Hillsdale, NJ: Erlbaum.

Sarnecka, B. W., & Gelman, S. A. (2004). Six does not just mean a lot: Preschoolers see number words as specific. *Cognition, 92,* 329–352.

Sarrazin, G. (1999). *WISC-III, Échelle d'intelligence de Wechs pour Enfants troisième édition, adaptation canadienne-française, Manuel d'administration.* Toronto, Canada: Psychological Corporation.

Satcher, D. S. (2001, January). DHHS blueprint for action on breastfeeding. *Public Health Reports.* Retrieved from www.findarticles.com/p/articles/ mi_m0835/is_1_116/ai_78785176

Saucier, J. F., Sylvestre, R., Doucet, H., Lambert, J., Frappier, J. Y., Charbonneau, L., & Malus, M. (2002). Cultural identity and adaptation to adolescence in Montreal. In F. J. C. Azima & N. Grizenko (Eds.), *Immigrant and refugee children and their families: Clinical, research, and training issues* (pp. 133–154). Madison, WI: International Universities Press.

Saudino, K. J. (2003). Parent ratings of infant temperament: Lessons from twin studies. *Infant Behavior and Development, 26,* 100–107.

Saudino, K. J., & Cherny, S. S. (2001). Sources of continuity and change in observed temperament. In R. N. Emde & J. K. Hewitt (Eds.), *Infancy to early childhood: Genetic and environmental influences on developmental change* (pp. 89–110). New York: Oxford University Press.

Saudino, K. J., & Plomin, R. (1997). Cognitive and temperamental mediators of genetic contributions to the home environment during infancy. *Merrill-Palmer Quarterly, 43,* 1–23.

Sauls, D. J. (2002). Effects of labor support on mothers, babies, and birth outcomes. *Journal of Obstetric, Gynecologic, and Neonatal Nursing, 31,* 733–741.

Savage, A. R., Petersen, M. B., Pettay, D., Taft, L., Allran, K., Freeman, S. B., Karadima, G., Avramopoulos, D., Torfs, C., Mikkelsen, M., & Hassold, T. J. (1998). Elucidating the mechanisms of paternal non-disjunction of chromosome 21 in humans. *Human Molecular Genetics, 7,* 1221–1227.

Savage-Rumbaugh, E. S. (2001). *Apes, language, and the human mind.* New York: Oxford University Press.

Savage-Rumbaugh, E. S., Murphy, J., Sevcik, R. A., Brakke, K. E., Williams, S. L., & Rumbaugh, D. M. (1993). Language comprehension in ape and child. *Monographs of the Society for Research in Child Development, 58*(3–4, Serial No. 233).

Savage-Rumbaugh, S., & Shanker, S. (1998). *Apes, language, and the human mind.* New York: Oxford University Press.

Savin-Williams, R. C. (2000). A critique of research on sexual-minority youths. *Journal of Adolescence, 24,* 5–13.

Savin-Williams, R. C. (2003). Lesbian, gay, and bisexual youths' relationships with their parents. In L. D. Garnets & D. C. Kimmel (Eds.), *Psychological perspectives on lesbian, gay, and bisexual experiences* (2nd ed., pp. 299–326). New York: Columbia University Press.

Savin-Williams, R. C., & Berndt, T. J. (1990). Friendship and peer relations. In S. S. Feldman & G. R. Elliott (Eds.), *At the threshold: The developing adolescent* (pp. 277–307). Cambridge, MA: Harvard University Press.

Savin-Williams, R. C., & Ream, G. L. (2003a). Suicide attempts among sexual-minority male youth. *Journal of Clinical Child and Adolescent Psychology, 32,* 509–522.

Savin-Williams, R. C., & Ream, G. L. (2003b). Sex variations in the disclosure to parents of same-sex attractions. *Journal of Family Psychology, 17,* 429–438.

Sawaguchi, T., Particia, F., Kadhim, H., Groswasser, J., Sottiaux, M., & Nishida, H. (2003). The presence of TATA-binding protein in the brainstem, correlated with sleep apnea in SIDS victims. *Early Human Development, 75,* S109–S118.

Saxe, G. B. (1988, August–September). Candy selling and math learning. *Educational Researcher, 17*(6), 14–21.

Saygin, A. P., Wilson, S. M., Dronkers, N. F., & Bates, E. (2004). Action comprehension in aphasia: Linguistic and non-linguistic deficits and their lesion correlates. *Neuropsychologia, 42,* 1788–1804.

Saylor, C. F., Cowart, B. L., Lipovsky, J. A., Jackson, C., & Finch, A. J., Jr. (2003). Media exposure to September 11: Elementary school students' experiences and posttraumatic symptoms. *American Behavioral Scientist, 46,* 1622–1642.

Saylor, M. M., Baldwin, D. A., & Sabbagh, M. A. (2005). Word learning: A complex product. In G. Hall & S. Waxman (Eds.), *Weaving a lexicon.* Cambridge, MA: MIT Press.

Saylor, M. M., & Sabbagh, M. A. (2004). Different kinds of information affect word learning in the preschool years: The case of part-term learning. *Child Development, 75,* 395–408.

Saylor, M. M., Sabbagh, M. A., & Baldwin, D. A. (2002). Children use whole–part juxtaposition as a pragmatic cue to word meaning. *Developmental Psychology, 38,* 993–1003.

Saywitz, K. J., Goodman, G. S., & Lyon, T. D. (2002). Interviewing children in and out of court: Current research and practice implications. In J. E. B. Myers & L. Berliner (Eds.), *The APSAC handbook on child maltreatment* (2nd ed., pp. 349–377). Thousand Oaks, CA: Sage.

Scarr, S. (1997). Behavior-genetic and socialization theories of intelligence: Truce and reconciliation. In R. J. Sternberg & E. L. Grigorenko (Eds.), *Intelligence, heredity, and environment* (pp. 3–41). New York: Cambridge University Press.

Scarr, S., & McCartney, K. (1983). How people make their own environments: A theory of genotype environment effects. *Child Development, 54,* 424–435.

Scarr, S., & Weinberg, R. A. (1983). The Minnesota Adoption Studies: Genetic differences and malleability. *Child Development, 54,* 260–267.

Schaal, B., Marlier, L., & Soussignan, R. (2000). Human foetuses learn odours from their pregnant mother's diet. *Chemical Senses, 25,* 729–737.

Scharrer, E., & Comstock, G. (2003). Entertainment televisual media: Content patterns and themes. In E. L. Palmer & B. M. Young (Eds.), *The faces of televisual media: Teaching, violence, selling to children* (pp. 161–193). Mahwah, NJ: Erlbaum.

Schellenberg, E. G. (2004). Music lessons enhance IQ. *Psychological Science, 15,* 511–514.

Scher, A., Epstein, R., & Tirosh, E. (2004). Stability and changes in sleep regulation: A longitudinal study from 3 months to 3 years. *International Journal of Behavioral Development, 28,* 268–274.

Scher, A., Tirosh, E., Jaffe, M., Rubin, L., Sadeh, A., & Lavie, P. (1995). Sleep patterns of infants and young children in Israel. *International Journal of Behavioral Development, 18,* 701–711.

Schlagmüller, M., & Schneider, W. (2002). The development of organizational strategies in children: Evidence from a microgenetic longitudinal study. *Journal of Experimental Child Psychology, 81,* 298–319.

Schlegel, A., & Barry, H., III. (1991). *Adolescence: An anthropological inquiry.* New York: Free Press.

Schmid, R. G., Tirsch, W. S., & Scherb, H. (2002). Correlation between spectral EEG parameters and intelligence test variables in school-age children. *Clinical Neurophysiology, 113,* 1647–1656.

Schmidt, U. (2000). Eating disorders. In D. Kohen (Ed.), *Women and mental health* (pp. 174–197). London: Routledge.

Schmitt, K. L., & Anderson, D. R. (2002). Television and reality: Toddlers' use of visual information from video to guide behavior. *Media Psychology, 4,* 51–76.

Schmitz, M. K. H., & Jeffery, R. W. (2000). Public health interventions for the prevention and treatment of obesity. *Medical Clinics of North America, 84,* 491–512.

Schmitz, S., Fulker, D. W., Plomin, R., Zahn-Waxler, C., Emde, R. N., & DeFries, J. C. (1999). Temperament and problem behaviour during early childhood. *International Journal of Behavioural Development, 23,* 333–355.

Schneider, B. H., Atkinson, L., & Tardif, C. (2001). Child–parent attachment and children's peer relations: A quantitative review. *Developmental Psychology, 37,* 86–100.

Schneider, W. (1986). The role of conceptual knowledge and metamemory in the development of organizational processes in memory. *Journal of Experimental Child Psychology, 42,* 218–236.

Schneider, W. (2002). Memory development in childhood. In U. Goswami (Ed.), *Blackwell handbook of childhood cognitive development* (pp. 236–256). Malden, MA: Blackwell.

Schneider, W., & Bjorklund, D. F. (1992). Expertise, aptitude, and strategic remembering. *Child Development, 63,* 461–473.

Schneider, W., & Bjorklund, D. F. (1998). Memory. In D. Kuhn & R. S. Siegler (Eds.), *Handbook of child psychology: Vol. 2. Cognition, perception, and language* (5th ed., pp. 467–521). New York: Wiley.

Schneider, W., Perner, J., Bullock, M., Stefanek, J., & Ziegler, A. (1999). Development of intelligence and thinking. In F. E. Weinert & W. Schneider (Eds.), *Individual development from 3 to 12: Findings from the Munich Longitudinal Study* (pp. 9–28). Cambridge, UK: Cambridge University Press.

Schneider, W., & Pressley, M. (1997). *Memory development between two and twenty* (2nd ed.). Mahwah, NJ: Erlbaum.

Schnoert-Reichel, K. A. (1999). Relations of peer acceptance, friendship adjustment, and social bhavior to moral reasoning during early adolescence. *Journal of Early Adolescence, 19,* 249–279.

Scholl, B. J., & Leslie, A. M. (2000). Minds, modules, and meta-analysis. *Child Development, 72,* 696–701.

Scholl, T. O., Heidiger, M. L., & Belsky, D. (1996). Prenatal care and maternal health during adolescent pregnancy: A review and meta-analysis. *Journal of Adolescent Health, 15,* 444–456.

Scholnick, E. K. (1995, Fall). Knowing and constructing plans. *SRCD Newsletter,* pp. 1–2, 17.

Schott, J. M., & Rossor, M. N. (2003). The grasp and other primitive reflexes. *Journal of Neurological and Neurosurgical Psychiatry, 74,* 558–560.

Schuengel, G., Bakermans-Kranenburg, M. J., & van IJzendoorn, M. H. (1999). Attachment and loss: Frightening maternal behavior linking unresolved loss and disorganized infant attachment. *Journal of Consulting and Clinical Psychology, 67,* 54–63.

Schull, W. J. (2003). The children of atomic bomb survivors: A synopsis. *Journal of Radiological Protection, 23,* 369–384.

Schulman, J. D., & Black, S. H. (1997). Screening for Huntington disease and certain other dominantly inherited disorders: A case for preimplantation genetic testing. *Journal of Medical Screening, 4,* 58–59.

Schunk, D. H., & Zimmerman, B. J. (2003). Self-regulation and learning. In W. M. Reynolds & G. E. Miller (Eds.), *Handbook of psychology* (Vol. 7, pp. 59–78). New York: Wiley.

Schuster, B., Ruble, D. N., & Weinert, F. E. (1998). Causal inferences and the positivity bias in children: The role of the covariation principle. *Child Development, 69,* 1577–1596.

Schwanenflugel, P. J., Fabricius, W. V., & Noyes, C. R. (1996). Developing organization of mental verbs: Evidence for the development of a constructivist theory of mind in middle childhood. *Cognitive Development, 11,* 265–294.

Schwanenflugel, P. J., Henderson, R. L., & Fabricius, W. V. (1998). Develping organisation of mental verbs and theory of mind in middle childhood: Evidence from extensions. *Developmental Psychology, 34,* 514–524.

Schwartz, C. E., Snidman, N., & Kagan, J. (1999). Adolescent social anxiety as an outcome of inhibited temperament in childhood. *Journal of the American Academy of Child and Adolescent Psychiatry, 38,* 1008–1015.

Schwartz, C. E., Wright, C. I., Shin, L. M., Kagan, J., & Raugh, S. L. (2003). Inhibited and uninhibited infants "grown up": Adult amygdalar response to novelty. *Science, 300,* 1952–1953.

Schwartz, D., Proctor, L. J., & Chien, D. H. (2001). The aggressive victim of bullying: Emotional and behavioral dysregulation as a pathway to victimization by peers. In J. Juonen & S. Graham (Eds.), *Peer harassment in school: The plight of the vulnerable and victimized* (pp. 147–174). New York: Guilford.

Schwartz, L. L. (2003). A nightmare for King Solomon: The new reproductive technologies. *Journal of Family Psychology, 17,* 229–237.

Schwarz, N. (1999). Self-reports: How the questions shape the answers. *American Psychologist, 54,* 93–105.

Schweinhart, L. J., Montie, J., Xiang, Z., Barnett, W. S., & Belfield, C. R. (2004). *Lifetime effects: The High/Scope Perry Preschool Study through age 40.* Boston, MA: Strategies for Children. Retrieved from www.highscope.org/Research/PerryProject/perrymain.htm

Schwimmer, J. B., Burwinkle, T. M., & Varni, J. W. (2003). Health-related quality of life of severely obese children and adolescents. *Journal of the American Medical Association, 289,* 1813–1819.

Scott, K. D., Berkowitz, G., & Klaus, M. (1999). A comparison of intermittent and continuous support during labor: A meta-analysis. *American Journal of Obstetrics and Gynecology, 180,* 1054–1059.

Scrimsher, S., & Tudge, J. (2003). The teaching/learning relationship in the first years of school: Some revolutionary implications of Vygotsky's theory. *Early Education and Development, 14,* 293–312.

Sebanc, A. (2003). The friendship features of preschool children: Links with prosocial behavior and aggression. *Social Development, 12,* 249–268.

Seccombe, K. (2002). "Beating the odds" versus "changing the odds": Poverty, resilience, and family policy. *Journal of Marriage and the Family, 64,* 384–394.

Seginer, R. (1998). Adolescents' perceptions of relationships with older siblings in the context of other close relationships. *Journal of Research on Adolescence, 8,* 287–308.

Seidenberg, M. S., & Petitto, L. A. (1987). Communication, symbolic communication, and language: Comment on Savage-Rumbaugh, McDonald, Sevcik, Hopkins, and Rupert. *Journal of Experimental Psychology: General, 116,* 279–287.

Seidman, E., Aber, J. L., & French, S. E. (2004). Assessing the transitions to middle and high school. *Journal of Adolescent Research, 19,* 3–30.

Seidman, E., Lambert, L. E., Allen, L., & Aber, J. L. (2003). Urban adolescents' transition to junior high school and protective family transactions. *Journal of Early Adolescence, 23,* 166–193.

Seifer, R. (2000). Temperament and goodness of fit: Implications for developmental psychopathology. In A. J. Sameroff & M. Lewis (Eds.), *Handbook of developmental psychopathology* (2nd ed., pp. 257–276). New York: Kluwer.

Seifer, R., & Schiller, M. (1995). The role of parenting sensitivity, infant temperament, and dyadic interaction in attachment theory and assessment. In E. Waters, B. E. Vaughn, G. Posada, & K. Kondo-Ikemura (Eds.), *Caregiving, cultural, and social perspectives on secure-base behavior and working models: New growing points of attachment theory and research. Monographs of the Society for Research in Child Development, 60*(2–3, Serial No. 244).

Seiffge-Krenke, I. (2003). Testing theories of romantic development from adolescence to young adulthood: Evidence of a developmental sequence. *International Journal of Behavioral Development, 27,* 519-531.

Seinhausen, H. (2002). The outcome of anorexia nervosa in the 20th century. *American Journal of Psychiatry, 159,* 1284–1293.

Seitz, V., & Apfel, N. H. (1993). Adolescent mothers and repeated childbearing: Effects of a school-based intervention program. *American Journal of Orthopsychiatry, 63,* 572–581.

Seitz, V., & Apfel, N. H. (1994). Effects of a school for pregnant students on the incidence of low-birthweight deliveries. *Child Development, 65,* 666–676.

Selman, R. L. (1976). Social-cognitive understanding: A guide to educational and clinical practice. In T. Lickona (Ed.), *Moral development and behavior: Theory, research, and social issues* (pp. 299–316). New York: Holt, Rinehart & Winston.

Selman, R. L. (1980). *The growth of interpersonal understanding.* New York: Academic Press.

Selman, R. L., & Byrne, D. F. (1974). A structural-developmental analysis of levels of role taking in middle childhood. *Child Development, 45,* 803–806.

Sen, M. G., Yonas, A., & Knill, D. C. (2001). Development of infants' sensitivity to surface contour information for spatial layout. *Perception, 30,* 167–176.

Senechal, M., & LeFevre, J. (2002). Parental involvement in the development of children's reading skill: A five-year longitudinal study. *Child Development, 73,* 445–460.

Senghas, A., & Coppola, M. (2001). Children creating language: How Nicaraguan sign language acquired a spatial grammar. *Psychological Science, 12,* 323–328.

Serbin, L. A., Connor, J. M., & Citron, C. C. (1978). Environmental control of independent and dependent behaviors in preschool girls and boys: A model for early independence training. *Sex Roles, 4,* 867–875.

Serbin, L. A., Connor, J. M., & Iler, I. (1979). Sex-stereotyped and non-stereotyped introductions of new toys in the preschool classroom: An observational study of teacher behavior and its effects. *Psychology of Women Quarterly, 4,* 261–265.

Serbin, L. A., Poulin-Dubois, D., Colburne, K. A., Sen, M. G., & Eichstedt, J. A. (2001). Gender stereotyping in infancy: Visual preferences for and knowledge of gender-stereotyped toys in the second year. *International Journal of Behavioral Development, 25,* 7–15.

Serbin, L. A., Powlishta, K. K., & Gulko, J. (1993). The development of sex typing in middle childhood. *Monographs of the Society for Research in Child Development, 58*(2, Serial No. 232).

Sermon, K., Van Steirteghem, A., & Liebaers, I. (2004). Preimplantation genetic diagnosis. *Lancet, 363,* 1633–1641.

Serpell, R., Sonnenschein, S., Baker, L., & Ganapathy, H. (2002). Intimate culture of families in the early socialization of literacy. *Journal of Family Psychology, 16,* 391–405.

Servin, A., Nordenström, A., Larssonk, A., & Bohlin, G. (2003). Prenatal androgens and gender-typed behavior: A study of girls with mild and severe forms of congenital hyperplasia. *Developmental Psychology, 39,* 440–450.

Sesame Workshop. (2005). Sesame workshop. Retrieved from www.sesameworkshop.org

Sethi, A., Mischel, W., Aber, J. L., Shoda, Y., & Rodriguez, M. L. (2000). The role of strategic attention deployment in development of self-regulation: Predicting preschoolers' delay of gratification from mother–toddler interactions. *Developmental Psychology, 36,* 767–777.

Seward, R. R., Yeats, D. E., & Zottarelli, L. K. (2002). Parental leave and father involvement in child care: Sweden and the United States. *Journal of Comparative Family Studies, 33,* 387–399.

Seymour, S. C. (1999). *Women, family, and child care in India.* Cambridge, UK: Cambridge University Press.

Shafer, V. L., Shucard, D. W., & Jaeger, J. J. (1999). Electrophysiological indices of cerebral specialization and the role of prosody in language acquisition in 3-month-old infants. *Developmental Neuropsychology, 15,* 73–109.

Shahar, S. (1990). *Childhood in the Middle Ages.* London: Routledge & Kegan Paul.

Shainess, N. (1961). A re-evaluation of some aspects of femininity through a study of menstruation: A preliminary report. *Comparative Psychiatry, 2,* 20–26.

Shanahan, M. L., Mortimer, J. T., & Krüger, H. (2002). Adolescence and adult work in the twenty-first century. *Journal of Research on Adolescence, 12,* 99–120.

Shanker, S. G., Savage-Rumbaugh, S., & Taylor, T. J. (1999). Kanzi: A new beginning. *Animal Learning and Behavior, 27,* 24–25.

Shann, M. H. (2001). Students' use of time outside school: A case for after school programs for urban middle school youth. *Urban Review, 33,* 339–356.

Shapiro, A. F., Gottman, J. M., & Carrere, S. (2000). The baby and the marriage: Identifying factors that buffer against decline in marital satisfaction after the first baby arrives. *Journal of Family Psychology, 14,* 59–70.

Sharma, S. K., & Leveno, K. J. (2003). Regional analgesia and progress of labor. *Clinical Obstetrics and Gynecology, 46,* 633–645.

Shaver, P., Furman, W., & Buhrmester, D. (1985). Transition to college: Network changes, social skills, and loneliness. In S. Duck & D. Perlman (Eds.), *Understanding personal relationships: An interdisciplinary approach* (pp. 193–219). London: Sage.

Shaver, P. R., Wu, S., & Schwartz, J. C. (1992). Cross-cultural similarities and differences in emotion and its representation: A prototype approach. In M. S. Clark (Ed.), *Review of personality and social psychology* (Vol. 13, pp. 175–212). Newbury Park, CA: Sage.

Shaw, D. S., Gilliom, M., Ingoldsby, E. M., & Nagin, D. S. (2003). Trajectories leading to school-age conduct problems. *Developmental Psychology, 39,* 189–200.

Shaw, D. S., Winslow, E. B., & Flanagan, C. (1999). A prospective study of the effects of marital status and family relations on young children's adjustment among African-American and European-American families. *Child Development, 70,* 742–755.

Shedler, J., & Block, J. (1990). Adolescent drug use and psychological health: A longitudinal inquiry. *American Psychologist, 45,* 612–630.

Sheehy, A., Gasser, T., Molinari, L., & Largo, R. H. (1999). An analysis of variance of the pubertal and mid-growth spurts for length and width. *Annals of Human Biology, 26,* 309–331.

Sherrill, C. L., & Pinderhughes, E. E. (1999). Conceptions of family and adoption among older adoptees. *Adoption Quarterly, 2,* 21–48.

Sherry, B., McDivitt, J., Birch, L. L., Cook, F. H., Sanders, S., Prish, J. L., Francis, L. A., & Scanlon, K. S. (2004). Attitudes, practices, and concerns about child feeding and child weight status among socioeconomically diverse white, Hispanic, and African-American mothers. *Journal of the American Dietetic Association, 104,* 215–221.

Shields, A., Dickstein, S., Siefer, R., Giusti, L., Magee, K. D., & Spritz, B.

(2001). Emotional competence and early school adjustment: A study of preschoolers at risk. *Early Education and Development, 12,* 73–96.

Shields, A., Ryan, R. M., & Cicchetti, D. (2001). Narrative representations of caregivers and emotion dysregulation as predictors of maltreated children's rejection by peers. *Developmental Psychology, 37,* 321–337.

Shiller, V., Izard, C. E., & Hembree, E. A. (1986). Patterns of emotion expression during separation in the Strange Situation. *Developmental Psychology, 22,* 378–382.

Shiloh, S. (1996). Genetic counseling: A developing area of interest for psychologists. *Professional Psychology: Research and Practice, 27,* 475–486.

Shimizu, H. (2001). Japanese adolescent boys' senses of empathy (omoiyari) and Carol Gilligan's perspectives on the morality of care: A phenomenological approach. *Culture and Psychology, 7,* 453–475.

Shinn, M. W. (1900). *The biography of a baby.* Boston: Houghton Mifflin.

Shipman, K. L., Zeman, J., Nesin, A. E., & Fitzgerald, M. (2003). Children's strategies for displaying anger and sadness: What works with whom? *Merrill-Palmer Quarterly, 49,* 100–122.

Shoda, Y., Mischel, W., & Peake, P. K. (1990). Predicting adolescent cognitive and self-regulatory competencies from preschool delay of gratification: Identifying diagnostic conditions. *Developmental Psychology, 26,* 978–986.

Shonk, S. M., & Cicchetti, D. (2001). Maltreatment, competency deficits, and risk for academic and behavioral maladjustment. *Developmental Psychology, 37,* 3–17.

Shonkoff, J., & Phillips, D. (Eds.). (2001). *Neurons to neighborhoods: The science of early childhood development.* Washington, DC: National Academy Press.

Shulman, S., Elicker, J., & Sroufe, L. A. (1994). Stages of friendship growth in preadolescence as related to attachment history. *Journal of Social and Personal Relationships, 11,* 341–361.

Shulman, S., & Kipnis, O. (2001). Adolescent romantic relationships: A look from the future. *Journal of Adolescence, 24,* 337–351.

Shure, M. B. (2001). I Can Problem Solve (ICPS): An interpersonal cognitive problem solving program for children. *Residential Treatment for Children and Youth, 18,* 3–14.

Shweder, R. A. (1996). True ethnography: The lore, the law, and the lure. In R. Jessor, A. Colby, & R. A. Shweder (Eds.), *Ethnography and human development* (pp. 15–52). Chicago: University of Chicago Press.

Shweder, R. A., Goodnow, J., Hatano, G., LeVine, R. A., Markus, H., & Miller, P. (1998). The cultural psychology of development: One mind, many mentalities. In R. M. Lerner (Ed.), *Handbook of child psychology: Vol. 1. Theoretical models of human development* (5th ed., pp. 865–937). New York: Wiley.

Shweder, R. A., Mahapatra, M., & Miller, J. G. (1990). Culture and moral development. In J. Stigler, R. A.

Shweder, & G. Herdt (Eds.), *Cultural psychology: Essays on comparative human development* (pp. 130–204). New York: Cambridge University Press.

Sidebotham, P., Heron, J., & The ALSPAC Study Team. (2003). Child maltreatment in the "children of the nineties": The role of the child. *Child Abuse and Neglect, 27,* 337–352.

Siegel, B. (1996, Spring). Is the emperor wearing clothes? Social policy and the empirical support for full inclusion of children with disabilities in the preschool and early elementary school grades. *Social Policy Report of the Society for Research in Child Development, 10*(2–3), 2–17.

Siegler, R. S. (1996). *Emerging minds: The process of change in children's thinking.* New York: Oxford University Press.

Siegler, R. S. (1998). *Children's thinking* (3rd ed.). Upper Saddle River, NJ: Prentice-Hall.

Siegler, R. S. (2002). Microgenetic studies of self-explanation. In N. Granott & J. Parziale (Eds.), *Microdevelopment: Transition processes in development and learning* (pp. 31–58). New York: Cambridge University Press.

Siegler, R. S., & Booth, J. L. (2004). Development of numerical estimation in young children. *Child Development, 75,* 428–444.

Siegler, R. S., & Crowley, K. (1991). The microgenetic method: A direct means for studying cognitive development. *American Psychologist, 46,* 606–620.

Siegler, R. S., & Ellis, S. (1996). Piaget on childhood. *Psychological Science, 7,* 211–215.

Siegler, B. S., & Jenkins, E. (1989). *How children discover new strategies.* Hillsdale, NJ: Erlbaum.

Siegler, R. S., & Richards, D. D. (1980). *College students' prototypes of children's intelligence.* Paper presented at the annual meeting of the American Psychological Association, New York.

Siervogel, R. M., Maynard, L. M., Wisemandle, W. A., Roche, A. F., Guo, S. S., Chumlea, W. C., & Towne, B. (2000). Annual changes in total body fat and fat-free mass in children from 8 to 18 years in relation to changes in body mass index: The Fels Longitudinal Study. *Annals of the New York Academy of Sciences, 904,* 420–423.

Sigman, M. (1999). Developmental deficits in children with Down syndrome. In H. Tager-Flusberg (Ed.), *Neurodevelopmental disorders: Developmental cognitive neuroscience* (pp. 179–195). Cambridge, MA: MIT Press.

Sigman, M., Cohen, S. E., & Beckwith, L. (1997). Why does infant attention predict adolescent intelligence? *Infant Behavior and Development, 20,* 133–140.

Signorella, M. L., Bigler, R. S., & Liben, L. S. (1993). Developmental differences in children's gender schemata about others: A meta-analytic review. *Developmental Review, 13,* 147–183.

Signorelli, N. (1993). Television, the portrayal of women, and children's attitudes. In G. L. Berry & J. K. Asamen (Eds.), *Children and television: Images in a changing socio-cultural world* (pp. 229–242). Newbury Park, CA: Sage.

Signorielli, N. (2001). Television's gender-role images and contribution to stereotyping. In D. G. Singer & J. L. Singer (Eds.), *Handbook of children and the media* (pp. 341–358). Thousand Oaks, CA: Sage.

Silberg, J., Rutter, M., D'Onofrio, B., & Eaves, L. (2003). Genetic and environmental risk factors in adolescent substance use. *Journal of Child Psychology and Psychiatry and Allied Disciplines, 44,* 664–676.

Silk, J. S., Morris, A. S., Kanaya, T., & Steinberg, L. D. (2003). Psychological control and autonomy granting: Opposite ends of a continuum or distinct constructs? *Journal of Research on Adolescence, 13,* 113–128.

Silk, J. S., Sessa, F. M., Morris, A. S., & Steinberg, L. D. (2004). Neighborhood cohesion as a buffer against hostile maternal parenting. *Journal of Family Psychology, 18,* 135–146.

Silvén, M. (2001). Attention in very young infants predicts learning of first words. *Infant Behavior and Development, 24,* 229–237.

Silverman, B. E., Goodine, W. M., Ladouceur, M. G., & Quinn, J. (2001). Learning needs of nurses working in Canada's First Nations communities. *Journal of Continuing Education in Nursing, 32,* 38–45.

Sim, T. N. (2000). Adolescent psychosocial competence: The importance and role of regard for parents. *Journal of Research on Adolescence, 10,* 49–64.

Sim, T. N., & Koh, S. F. (2003). A domain conceptualization of adolescent susceptibility to peer pressure. *Journal of Research on Adolescence, 13,* 57–80.

Simcock, G., & Hayne, H. (2002). Breaking the barrier? Children fail to translate their preverbal memories into language. *Psychological Science, 13,* 225–231.

Simcock, G., & Hayne, H. (2003). Age-related changes in verbal and nonverbal memory during early childhood. *Developmental Psychology, 39,* 805–814.

Simion, F., Cassia, V. M., Turati, C., & Valenza, E. (2001). The origins of face perception: Specific versus non-specific mechanisms. *Infant and Child Development, 10,* 59–65.

Simmons, R. (2002). *Odd girl out: The hidden culture of aggression in girls.* New York: Harcourt.

Simmons, R. G., & Blyth, D. A. (1987). *Moving into adolescence.* New York: Aldine De Gruyter.

Simoneau, M., & Markovits, H. (2003). Reasoning with premises that are not empirically true: Evidence for the role of inhibition and retrieval. *Developmental Psychology, 39,* 964–975.

Simons, R. L., & Chao, W. (1996). Conduct problems. In R. L. Simons & Associates (Eds.), *Understanding differences between divorced and intact families* (pp. 125–143). Thousand Oaks, CA: Sage.

Simons, R. L., Whitbeck, L. B., Conger, R. D., & Chyi-In, W. (1991). Intergenerational transmission of harsh parenting. *Developmental Psychology, 27,* 159–171.

Simons-Morton, B. G., & Haynie, D. L. (2003). Growing up drug free: A developmental challenge. In M. H. Bornstein, L. Davidson, C. L. M. Keyes, K. A. Moore, & the Center for Child Well-Being (Eds.), *Well-being: Positive development across the life course* (pp. 109–122). Mahwah, NJ: Erlbaum.

Simonton, D. K. (1999). Creativity and genius. In L. Pervin & O. John (Eds.), *Handbook of personality theory and research* (2nd ed., pp. 629–652). New York: Guilford.

Simonton, D. K. (2000). Creativity: Cognitive, personal, developmental, and social aspects. *American Psychologist, 55,* 151–158.

Simpkins, S. D., & Parke, R. D. (2001). The relations between parental friendships and children's friendships: Self-reports and observational analysis. *Child Development, 72,* 569–582.

Simpson, J. A., Rholes, W. S., Campbell, L., Tran, S., & Wilson, C. L. (2003). Adult attachment, the transition to parenthood, and depressive symptoms. *Journal of Personality and Social Psychology, 84,* 1172–1187.

Simpson, J. L., de la Cruz, F., Swerdloff, R. S., Samango-Sprouse, C., Skakkebaek, N. E., & Graham, J. M., Jr. (2003). Klinefelter syndrome: Expanding the phenotype and identifying new research directions. *Genetic Medicine, 5,* 460–468.

Simpson, J. M. (2001). Infant stress and sleep deprivation as an aetiological basis for the sudden infant death syndrome. *Early Human Development, 61,* 1–43.

Singer, D. G. (1999). Imaginative play and television: Factors in a child's development. In J. A. Singer & P. Salovey (Eds.), *At play in the fields of consciousness: Essays in honor of Jerome L. Singer* (pp. 303–326). Mahwah, NJ: Erlbaum.

Singer, D. G., & Singer, J. L. (2005). *Imagination and play in the electronic age.* Cambridge, MA: Harvard University Press.

Singer, L. T., Arendt, R., Minnes, S., Farkas, K., Salvator, A., Kirchner, H. L., & Kliegman, R. (2002a). Cognitive and motor outcomes of cocaine-exposed infants. *Journal of the American Medical Association, 287,* 1952–1960.

Singer, L. T., Salvator, A., Arendt, R., Minnes, S., Farkas, K., & Kliegman, R. (2002b). Effects of cocaine/polydrug exposure and maternal psychological distress on infant birth outcomes. *Neurotoxicology and Teratology, 24,* 127–135.

Singh, S., & Darroch, J. E. (2000). Adolescent pregnancy and childbearing: Levels and trends in developed countries. *Family Planning Perspectives, 32,* 14–23.

Singleton, J. L., & Newport, E. L. (2004). When learners surpass their models: The acquisition of American Sign Language from inconsistent input. *Cognitive Psychology, 49,* 370–407.

Sippola, L., Bukowski, W. M., & Noll, R. B. (1997). Age differences in children's and early adolescents' liking for same-sex and other-sex peers. *Merrill-Palmer Quarterly, 43,* 547–561.

Sitskoorn, M. M., & Smitsman, A. W. (1995). Infants' perception of dynamic relations between objects: Passing through or support? *Developmental Psychology, 31,* 437–447.

Skinner, B. F. (1957). *Verbal behavior.* New York: Appleton-Century-Crofts.

Skinner, E. A., Zimmer-Gembeck, M. J., & Connell, J. P. (1998). Individual differences and the development of perceived control. *Monographs of the Society for Research in Child Development, 63*(2–3, Serial No. 254).

Skoe, E. E., & Diessner, R. (1994). Ethic of care, justice, identity and gender: An extension and replication. *Merrill-Palmer Quarterly, 40,* 102–119.

Skoe, E. E. A. (1998). The ethic of care: Issues in moral development. In E. E. A. Skoe & A. L. von der Lippe (Eds.), *Personality development in adolescence* (pp. 143–171). London: Routledge.

Slaby, R. G., & Frey, K. S. (1975). Development of gender constancy and selective attention to same-sex models. *Child Development, 46,* 849–856.

Slade, A., Belsky, J., Aber, J. L., & Phelps, J. L. (1999). Mothers' representations of their relationships with their toddlers: Links to adult attachment and observed mothering. *Developmental Psychology, 35,* 611–619.

Slater, A. (2001). Visual perception. In G. Bremner & A. Fogel (Eds.), *Blackwell handbook of infant development* (pp. 5–34). Malden, MA: Blackwell.

Slater, A., & Johnson, S. P. (1999). Visual sensory and perceptual abilities of the newborn: Beyond the blooming, buzzing confusion. In A. Slater & S. P. Johnson (Eds.), *The development of sensory, motor and cognitive capacities in early infancy* (pp. 121–141). Hove, UK: Sussex Press.

Slater, A., & Quinn, P. C. (2001). Face recognition in the newborn infant. *Infant and Child Development, 10,* 21–24.

Slater, A., Bremner, G., Johnson, S. P., Sherwood, P., Hayes, R., & Brown, E. (2000). Newborn infants' preference for attractive faces: The role of internal and external facial features. *Infancy, 1,* 265–274.

Slaughter, V., Jaakkola, R., & Carey, S. (1999). Constructing a coherent theory: Children's biological understanding of life and death. In M. Siegel & C. C. Petersen (Eds.), *Children's understanding of biology and health* (pp. 71–96). Cambridge, UK: Cambridge University Press.

Slaughter, V., & Lyons, M. (2003). Learning about life and death in early childhood. *Cognitive Psychology, 46,* 1–30.

Slicker, E. K., & Thornberry, I. (2002). Older adolescent well-being and authoritative parenting. *Adolescent and Family Health, 3,* 9–10.

Slobin, D. I. (1982). Universal and particular in the acquisition of language. In L. R. Gleitman & H. E. Wanner (Eds.), *Language acquisition: The state of the art* (pp. 128–170). Cambridge, UK: Cambridge University Press.

Slobin, D. I. (1985). Crosslinguistic evidence for the language-making capacity. In D. I. Slobin (Ed.), *The crosslinguistic study of language acquisition: Vol. 2. Theoretical issues* (pp. 1157–1256). Hillsdale, NJ: Erlbaum.

Slobin, D. I. (Ed.). (1997). *The cross-linguistic study of language acquisition: Vol. 5. Expanding the contexts* (pp. 265–324). Mahwah, NJ: Erlbaum.

Small, M. (1998). *Our babies, ourselves.* New York: Anchor.

Smetana, J. G. (1981). Preschool children's conceptions of moral and social rules. *Child Development, 52,* 1333–1336.

Smetana, J. G. (1985). Preschool children's conceptions of transgressions: Effects of varying moral and conventional domain-related attributes. *Developmental Psychology, 21,* 18–29.

Smetana, J. G. (1995). Morality in context: Abstractions, ambiguities and applications. In R. Vasta (Ed.), *Annals of child development* (Vol. 10, pp. 83–130). Philadelphia: Jessica Kingsley.

Smetana, J. G. (2002). Culture, autonomy, and personal jurisdiction in adolescent–parent relationships. In R. V. Kail & H. W. Reese (Eds.), *Advances in child development and behavior* (Vol. 29, pp. 51–87). San Diego, CA: Academic Press.

Smetana, J. G., & Asquith, P. (1994). Adolescents' and parents' conceptions of parental authority and adolescent autonomy. *Child Development, 65,* 1147–1162.

Smith, A. E., Jussim, L., Eccles, J., VanNoy, M., Madon, S., & Palumbo, P. (1998). Self-fulfilling prophecies, perceptual biases, and accuracy at the individual and group levels. *Journal of Experimental Social Psychology, 34,* 530–561.

Smith, C. L., & Tager-Flusberg, H. (1982). Metalinguistic awareness and language development. *Journal of Experimental Child Psychology, 34,* 449–468.

Smith, E. P., Walker, K., Fields, L., Brookins, C. C., & Seay, R. C. (1999). Ethnic identity and its relationship to self-esteem, perceived efficacy, and prosocial attitudes in early adolescence. *Journal of Adolescence, 22,* 867–880.

Smith, J. R., Brooks-Gunn, J., Kohen, D., & McCarton, C. (2001). Transitions on and off AFDC: Implications for parenting and children's cognitive development. *Child Development, 72,* 1512–1533.

Smith, J., Duncan, G. J., & Lee, K. (2003). The black–white test score gap in young children: Contributions of test and family characteristics. *Applied Developmental Science, 7,* 239–252.

Smith, K. E., Landry, S. H., Swank, P. R., Baldwin, C. D., Denson, S. E., & Wildin, S. (1996). The relation of medical risk and maternal stimulation with preterm infants' development of cognitive, language and daily living skills. *Journal of Child Psychology and Psychiatry, 37,* 855–864.

Smith, L. B., Quittner, A. L., Osberger, M. J., & Miyamoto, R. (1998). Audition and visual attention: The developmental trajectory in deaf and hearing populations. *Developmental Psychology, 34,* 840–850.

Smith, L. B., Thelen, E., Titzer, R., & McLin, D. (1999b). Knowing in the

context of acting: The task dynamics of the A-not-B error. *Psychological Review, 106,* 235–260.

Smith, P. K. (2003). Play and peer relations. In A. Slater & G. Bremner (Eds.), *An introduction to developmental psychology* (pp. 311–333). Malden, MA: Blackwell.

Smith, P. K., Ananiadou, K., & Cowie, H. (2003). Interventions to reduce school bullying. *Canadian Journal of Psychiatry, 48,* 591–599.

Smith, P., Perrin, S., Yule, W., & Rabe-Hesketh, S. (2001). War exposure and maternal reactions in the psychological adjustment of children from Bosnia-Hercegovina. *Journal of Child Psychology and Psychiatry and Allied Disciplines, 42,* 395–404.

Smith, S. L., & Atkin, C. (2003). Television advertising and children: Examining the intended and unintended effects. In E. L. Palmer & B. M. Young (Eds.), *The faces of televisual media: Teaching, violence, selling to children* (pp. 301–326). Mahwah, NJ: Erlbaum.

Smylie, J. (2001). A guide for health professionals working with Aboriginal peoples. *Journal of the Society of Obstetricians and Gynaecologists of Canada, 100,* 2–15.

Snarey, J. R. (1995). In a communitarian voice: The sociological expansion of Kohlbergian theory, research, and practice. In W. M. Kurtines & J. L. Gewirtz (Eds.), *Moral development: An introduction* (pp. 109–134). Boston: Allyn and Bacon.

Snarey, J. R., & Bell, D. (2003). Distinguishing structural and functional models of human development: A response to "What transits in an identity status transition?" *Identity, 3,* 221–230.

Snarey, J. R., Reimer, J., & Kohlberg, L. (1985). The development of social-moral reasoning among kibbutz adolescents: A longitudinal cross-cultural study. *Developmental Psychology, 20,* 3–17.

Snidman, N., Kagan, J., Riordan, L., & Shannon, D. C. (1995). Cardiac function and behavioral reactivity. *Psychophysiology, 32,* 199–207.

Snow, C. E., Pan, B. A., Imbens-Bailey, A., & Herman, J. (1996). Learning how to say what one means: A longitudinal study of children's speech act use. *Social Development, 5,* 56–84.

Snyder, J., Brooker, M., Patrick, M. R., Snyder, A., Schrepferman, L., & Stoolmiller, M. (2003). Observed peer victimization during early elementary school: Continuity, growth, and relation to risk for child antisocial and depressive behavior. *Child Development, 74,* 1881–1898.

So, L. K. H., & Dodd, B. J. (1995). The acquisition of phonology by Cantonese-speaking children. *Journal of Child Language, 22,* 473–495.

Society for Research in Child Development. (1993). Ethical standards for research with children. In *Directory of Members* (pp. 337–339). Ann Arbor, MI: Author.

Soderstrom, M., Seidl, A., Nelson, D. G. K., & Jusczyk, P. W. (2003). The prosodic bootstrapping of phrases: Evidence from prelinguistic infants. *Journal of Memory and Language, 49,* 249–267.

SOGC (Society of Obstetricians and Gynaecologists of Canada). (2003).

Multiple births. Retrieved from www.sogc.org/multiple/facts_e.shtml

Sokol, R. J., Delaney-Black, V., & Nordstrom, B. (2003). Fetal alcohol spectrum disorder. *Journal of the American Medical Association, 290,* 2996–2999.

Solomon, G. B., & Bredemeier, B. J. L. (1999). Children's moral conceptions of gender stratification in sport. *International Journal of Sport Psychology, 30,* 350–368.

Solomon, G. E. A., Johnosn, S. C., Zaitchik, D., & Carey, S. (1996). Like father, like son: Children's understanding of how and why offspring resemble their parents. *Child Development, 67,* 151–171.

Sondergaard, C., Henriksen, T. B., Obel, C., & Wisborg, K. (2002). Smoking during pregnancy and infantile colic. *Journal of the American Academy of Child and Adolescent Psychiatry, 41,* 147.

Sontag, C. W., Baker, C. T., & Nelson, V. L. (1958). Mental growth and personality development: A longitudinal study. *Monographs of the Society for Research in Child Development, 23*(2, Serial No. 68).

Sophian, C. (1995). Representation and reasoning in early numerical development: Counting, conservation, and comparisons between sets. *Child Development, 66,* 559–577.

Sørensen, T. I., Holst, C., & Stunkard, A. J. (1998). Adoption study of environmental modifications of the genetic influences on obesity. *International Journal of Obesity and Related Metabolic Disorders, 22,* 73–81.

Sosa, R., Kennell, J., Klaus, M., Robertson, S., & Urrutia, J. (1980). The effect of a supportive companion on perinatal problems, length of labor, and mother–infant interaction. *New England Journal of Medicine, 303,* 597–600.

Sowell, E. R., Thompson, P. M., Welcome, S. E., Henkenius, A. L., Toga, A. W., & Peterson, B. S. (2003). Cortical abnormalities in children and adolescents with attention-deficit hyperactivity disorder. *Lancet, 362,* 1699–1707.

Sowell, E. R., Trauner, D. A., Camst, A., & Jernigan, T. (2002). Development of cortical and subcortical brain structures in childhood and adolescence: A structural MRI study. *Developmental Medicine and Child Neurology, 44,* 4–16.

Spear, L. P. (2003). Neurodevelopment during adolescence. In D. Cicchetti & E. Walker (Eds.), *Neurodevelopmental mechanisms in psychopathology* (pp. 62–83). New York: Cambridge University Press.

Spearman, C. (1927). *The abilities of man: Their nature and measurement.* New York: Macmillan.

Speece, M. W., & Brent, S. B. (1996). The development of children's understanding of death. In C. A. Corr & D. M. Corr (Eds.), *Handbook of childhood death and bereavement* (pp. 29–50). New York: Springer.

Speicher, B. (1994). Family patterns of moral judgment during adolescence and early adulthood. *Developmental Psychology, 30,* 624–632.

Spelke, E. (2000). Core knowledge. *American Psychologist, 55,* 1233–1242.

Spelke, E. S., Breinlinger, K., Macomber, J., & Jacobson, K. (1992). Origins of knowledge. *Psychological Review, 99,* 605–632.

Spelke, E. S., & Hermer, L. (1996). Early cognitive development: Objects and space. In R. Gelman & T. K. Au (Eds.), *Perceptual and cognitive development* (pp. 71–114). San Diego: Academic Press.

Spelke, E. S., & Newport, E. L. (1998). Nativism, empiricism, and the development of knowledge. In R. M. Lerner (Ed.), *Handbook of child psychology: Vol. 1. Theoretical models of human development* (5th ed., pp. 199–254). New York: Wiley.

Spence, M. J., & DeCasper, A. J. (1987). Prenatal experience with low-frequency maternal voice sounds influences neonatal perception of maternal voice samples. *Infant Behavior and Development, 10,* 133–142.

Spencer, J. P., & Schöner, G. (2003). Bridging the representational gap in the dynamic systems approach to development. *Developmental Science, 6,* 392–412.

Spencer, J. P., Verejiken, B., Diedrich, F. J., & Thelen, E. (2000). Posture and the emergence of manual skills. *Developmental Science, 3,* 216–233.

Spencer, M. B., Fegley, S. G., & Harpalani, V. (2003). A theoretical and empirical examination of identity as coping: Linking coping resources to the self processes of African American youth. *Applied Developmental Science, 7,* 181–188.

Spencer, P. (2001, November). I want that. *Woman's Day,* p. 162.

Spencer, P. E. (2000). Looking without listening: Is audition a prerequisite for normal development of visual attention in infancy? *Journal of Deaf Studies and Education, 5,* 291–302.

Spencer, P. E., & Lederberg, A. (1997) Different modes, different models: Communication and language of young deaf children and their mothers. In L. B. Adamson & M. Romski (Eds.), *Communication and language acquisition: Discoveries from atypical development* (pp. 203–230). Baltimore, MD: Paul H. Brookes.

Spencer, P. E., & Meadow-Orlans, K. P. (1996). Play, language, and maternal responsiveness: A longitudinal study of deaf and hearing infants. *Child Development, 67,* 3176–3191.

Spere, K. A., Schmidt, L. A., Theall-Honey, L. A., & Martin-Chang, S. (2004). Expressive and receptive language skills of temperamentally shy preschoolers. *Infant and Child Development, 13,* 123–133.

Spirito, A., Valeri, S., Boergers, J., & Donaldson, D. (2003). Predictors of continued suicidal behavior in adolescents following a suicide attempt. *Journal of Clinical Child and Adolescent Psychology, 32,* 284–289.

Spitz, R. A. (1946). Anaclitic depression. *Psychoanalytic Study of the Child, 2,* 313–342.

Spock, B., & Needlman, R. (2004). *Dr. Spock's baby and child care* (8th ed.). New York: Pocket.

Sport Canada. (2003). *Reconnecting Government with Youth Survey (2003): Youth Participation in Sport.* Retrieved from www.pch.gc.ca/progs/sc/info-fact/youth_e.cfm

Sprott, J. B., & Doob, R. N. (2003). It's all in the denominator: Trends in the processing of girls in Canada's youth courts. *Canadian Journal of Criminology and Criminal Justice, 45,* 73–80.

Spruijt-Metz, D., Lindquist, C. H., Birch, L. L., Fisher, J. O., & Goran, M. I. (2002). Relation between mothers' child-feeding practices and children's adiposity. *American Journal of Clinical Nutrition, 75,* 581–586.

Sridhar, D., & Vaughn, S. (2001). Social functioning of students with learning disabilities. In D. P. Hallahan & B. K. Keogh (Eds.), *Research and global perspectives in learning disabilities* (pp. 65–91). Mahwah, NJ: Erlbaum.

Sroufe, L. A. (1979). The ontogenesis of emotion. In J. D. Osofsky (Ed.), *Handbook of infant development* (pp. 462–516). New York: Wiley.

Sroufe, L. A. (1985). Attachment classification from the perspective of infant–caregiver relationships and infant temperament. *Child Development, 56,* 1–14.

Sroufe, L. A., Egeland, B., & Kreutzer, T. (1990). The fate of early experience following developmental change: Longitudinal approaches to individual adaptation. *Child Development, 61,* 1363–1373.

Sroufe, L. A., & Waters, E. (1976). The ontogenesis of smiling and laughter: A perspective on the organization of development in infancy. *Psychological Review, 83,* 173–189.

Sroufe, L. A., & Wunsch, J. P. (1972). The development of laughter in the first year of life. *Child Development, 43,* 1324–1344.

St James-Roberts, I., Goodwin, J., Peter, B., Adams, D., & Hunt, S. (2003). Individual differences in responsivity to a neurobehavioural examination predict crying patterns of 1-week-old infants at home. *Developmental Medicine and Child Neurology, 45,* 400–407.

St James-Roberts, I., & Halil, T. (1991). Infant crying patterns in the first year: Normal community and clinical findings. *Journal of Child Psychology and Psychiatry, 32,* 951–968.

Stacey, J., & Biblarz, T. (2001). (How) Does the sexual orientation of parents matter? *American Sociological Review, 66,* 159–183.

Stack, D. M., & Muir, D. W. (1992). Adult tactile stimulation during face-to-face interactions modulates five-month-olds' affect and attention. *Child Development, 63,* 1509–1525.

Stager, C. L., & Werker, J. F. (1997). Infants listen for more phonetic detail in speech perception than in word-learning tasks. *Nature, 388,* 381–382.

Stams, G. J. M., Juffer, R., & van IJzendoorn, M. H. (2002). Maternal sensitivity, infant attachment, and temperament in early childhood predict adjustment in middle childhood: The case of adopted children and their biologically unrelated

parents. *Developmental Psychology, 38,* 806–821.

Standley, J. M. (1998). The effect of music and multimodal stimulation on responses of premature infants in neonatal intensive care. *Pediatric Nursing, 24,* 532–538.

Stanley, C., Murray, L., & Stein, A. (2004). The effect of postnatal depression on mother–infant interaction, infant response to the still-face perturbation, and performance on an instrumental learning task. *Development and Psychopathology, 16,* 1–18.

Stanovich, K. E. (2004). *How to think straight about psychology* (7th ed.). Boston: Allyn and Bacon.

Stark, L. J., Allen, K. D., Hurst, M., Nash, D. A., Rigney, B., & Stokes, T. F. (1989). Distraction: Its utilization and efficacy with children undergoing dental treatment. *Journal of Applied Behavior Analysis, 22,* 297–307.

Starkey, P. (1992). The early development of numerical reasoning. *Cognition, 43,* 93–126.

Statistics Canada. (2000). Immigrant youth in Canada. *Juristat, 22*(6). Retrieved from www.statcan.ca

Statistics Canada. (2002, October 29). Computer access at school and at home. *The Daily.* Retrieved from www.statcan.ca/english/edu/feature/computer/htm

Statistics Canada. (2002a). *Family studies kit.* Retrieved from www.statcan.ca/english/kits/Family/pdf/ch3_3e.pdf

Statistics Canada. (2002b). Language composition of Canada, 2001. Census. Retrieved from www.statcan.ca/english/IPS/Data/97F007XCB20010000.htm

Statistics Canada. (2003a). Crime statistics in Canada. *Juristat, 24,* No. 6. Retrieved from www.statcan.ca

Statistics Canada. (2003b). The gap in achievement between boys and girls. Retrieved from www.statcan.ca/english/freepub/81-004-XIE/200410/mafe.htm

Statistics Canada. (2003c). *National Longitudinal Survey of Children and Youth: Challenges of late adolescence.* Retrieved from www.statcan.ca/Daily/English/030616/d030616a.htm

Statistics Canada. (2003d, March 31). University enrolment by field of study. *The Daily.* Retrieved from www.statcan.ca/Daily/English/030331/d030331b.htm

Statistics Canada. (2003e). Women in Canada: Work chapter updates. Retrieved from www.statcan.ca/cgi-bin/downpub/freepub.cgi

Statistics Canada. (2004a). Canadian vital statistics, births. Retrieved from www.statcan.ca/english/freepub/84F0210XIE/free.htm

Statistics Canada. (2004b). *Divorces.* Retrieved from www.statcan.ca

Statistics Canada. (2004c, July 8). Household Internet Use Survey. *The Daily.* Retrieved from www.statcan.ca/Daily/English/040708/d040708a.htm

Statistics Canada. (2004d). Infant mortality rates. Retrieved from www.statcan.ca/english/Pgdb/health21.htm

Statistics Canada. (2004e, June 16). Youth in Transition Survey: Education and labor market pathways of young adults. *The Daily.* Retrieved from

www.statcan.ca/Daily/English/040616/d040616b.htm

Statistics Canada. (2005a, February 7). Child care. *The Daily.* Retrieved from www.statcan.ca/Daily/English/050207/d050207b.htm

Statistics Canada. (2005b). *Statistics Canada data bank and analysis of television viewing in Canada.* Retrieved from www.statcan.ca/english/freepub/87-008-GIE/sect/tvmain.htm

Stattin, H., & Kerr, M. (2000). Parental monitoring: A reinterpretation. *Child Development, 71,* 1072–1085.

Stattin, H., & Magnusson, D. (1990). *Pubertal maturation in female development.* Hillsdale, NJ: Erlbaum.

Staub, F. C., & Stern, E. (2002). The nature of teachers' pedagogical content beliefs matters for students' achievement gains: Quasi-experimental evidence from elementary mathematics. *Journal of Educational Psychology, 94,* 344–355.

Steele, C. M. (1997). A threat in the air: How stereotypes shape intellectual identity and performance. *American Psychologist, 52,* 613–629.

Steele, C. M., & Aronson, J. (1995). Stereotype threat and the intellectual test performance of African Americans. *Journal of Personality and Social Psychology, 69,* 797–811.

Steele, H., Steele, M., & Fonagy, P. (1996). Associations among attachment classifications of mothers, fathers, and their infants. *Child Development, 67,* 541–555.

Steele, J. (2003). Children's gender stereotypes about math: The role of stereotype stratification. *Journal of Applied Social Psychology, 33,* 2587–2606.

Steele, J., Joseph, R. M., & Tager-Flusberg, H. (2003). Developmental change in theory of mind abilities in children with autism. *Journal of Austism and Developmental Disorders, 33,* 461–467.

Stehr-Green, P., Tull, P., Stellfeld, M., Mortenson, P. B., & Simpson, D. (2003). Autism and thimerosal-containing vaccines: Lack of consistent evidence for an association. *American Journal of Preventive Medicine, 25,* 101–106.

Stein, J. H., & Reiser, L. W. (1994). A study of white middle-class adolescent boys' responses to "semenarche" (the first ejaculation). *Journal of Youth and Adolescence, 23,* 373–384.

Stein, N., & Levine, L. J. (1999). The early emergence of emotional understanding and appraisal: Implications for theories of development. In T. Dalgleish & M. J. Power (Eds.), *Handbook of cognition and emotion* (pp. 383–408). Chichester, UK: Wiley.

Stein, Z., Susser, M., Saenger, G., & Marolla, F. (1975). *Famine and human development: The Dutch hunger winter of 1944–1945.* New York: Oxford University Press.

Steinberg, L. D. (1986). Latchkey children and susceptibility to peer pressure: An ecological analysis. *Developmental Psychology, 22,* 433–439.

Steinberg, L. D. (2001). We know some things: Parent–adolescent relationships in retrospect and prospect.

Journal of Research on Adolescence, 11, 1–19.

Steinberg, L. D. (2004). *The ten basic principles of good parenting.* New York: Simon & Schuster.

Steinberg, L. D., Darling, N. E., & Fletcher, A. C. (1995). Authoritative parenting and adolescent development: An ecological journey. In P. Moen, G. H. Elder, & K. Luscher (Eds.), *Examining lives in context* (pp. 423–466). Washington, DC: American Psychological Association.

Steinberg, L. D., Fegley, S., & Dornbusch, S. (1993). Negative impact of part-time work on adolescent adjustment: Evidence from a longitudinal study. *Developmental Psychology, 29,* 171–180.

Steinberg, L. D., & Morris, A. S. (2001). Adolescent development. *Annual Review of Psychology, 52,* 83–110.

Steinberg, L. D., & Silk, J. S. (2002). Parenting adolescents. In M. H. Bornstein (Ed.), *Handbook of parenting: Vol. 1. Children and Parenting* (2nd ed., pp. 103–134). Mahwah, NJ: Erlbaum.

Steinberg, L. D., & Silverberg, S. (1986). The vicissitudes of autonomy in early adolescence. *Child Development, 57,* 841–851.

Steinberg, S., & Bellavance, F. (1999). Characteristics and treatment of women with antenatal and postpartum depression. *International Journal of Psychiatry and Medicine, 29,* 209–233.

Steiner, J. E. (1979). Human facial expression in response to taste and smell stimulation. In H. W. Reese & L. P. Lipsitt (Eds.), *Advances in child development and behavior* (Vol. 13, pp. 257–295). New York: Academic Press.

Steiner, J. E., Glaser, D., Hawilo, M. E., & Berridge, D. C. (2001). Comparative expression of hedonic impact: Affective reactions to taste by human infants and other primates. *Neuroscience and Biobehavioral Review, 25,* 53–74.

Stenberg, C., & Campos, J. (1990). The development of anger expressions in infancy. In N. Stein, B. Leventhal, & T. Trabasso (Eds.), *Psychological and biological approaches to emotion* (pp. 247–282). Hillsdale, NJ: Erlbaum.

Stenberg, C., Campos, J., & Emde, R. (1983). The facial expression of anger in seven-month-old infants. *Child Development, 54,* 178–184.

Stenberg, G. (2003). Effects of maternal inattentiveness on infant social referencing. *Infant and Child Development, 12,* 399–419.

Stern, M., & Karraker, K. H. (1989). Sex stereotyping of infants: A review of gender labeling studies. *Sex Roles, 20,* 501–522.

Sternberg, R. J. (1997). *Successful intelligence.* New York: Plume.

Sternberg, R. J. (2001). Beyond g: The theory of successful intelligence. In R. J. Sternberg & E. L. Grigorenko (Eds.), *The general factor of intelligence: How general is it?* (pp. 447–479). Mahwah, NJ: Erlbaum.

Sternberg, R. J. (2002). Intelligence is not just inside the head: The theory of successful intelligence. In J. Aronson (Ed.), *Improving academic achieve-*

ment (pp. 227–244). San Diego, CA: Academic Press.

Sternberg, R. J. (2003a). A broad view of intelligence: The theory of successful intelligence. *Consulting Psychology Journal: Practice and Research, 55,* 139–154.

Sternberg, R. J. (2003b). The development of creativity as a decision-making process. In R. K. Sawyer, V. John-Steiner, S. Moran, R. J. Sternberg, D. H. Feldman, J. Nakamura, & M. Csikszentmihalyi (Eds.), *Creativity and development* (pp. 91–138). New York: Oxford University Press.

Sternberg, R. J., Castejaon, J. L., Prieto, M. D., Hautaméaki, J., & Grigorenko, E. L. (2001). Confirmatory factor analysis of the Sternberg Triarchic Abilities Test (multiple-choice items) in three international samples: An empirical test of the triarchic theory of intelligence. *European Journal of Psychological Assessment, 17,* 1–16.

Sternberg, R. J., & Detterman, D. K. (1986). *What is intelligence?* Norwood, NJ: Ablex.

Sternberg, R. J., Forsythe, G. B., Hedlund, J., Horvath, J. A., Wagner, R. K., Williams, W. M., Snook, S. A., & Grigorenko, E. L. (2000). *Practical intelligence in everyday life.* Cambridge, UK: Cambridge University Press.

Sternberg, R. J., & Grigorenko, E. L. (2002). *Dynamic testing.* New York: Cambridge University Press.

Sternberg, R. J., Grigorenko, E. L., Ferrari, M., & Clinkenbeard, P. (1999). A triarchic analysis of an aptitude-treatment interaction. *European Journal of Psychological Assessment, 15,* 1–11.

Sternberg, R. J., & Jarvin, L. (2003). Alfred Binet's contributions as a paradigm for impact in psychology. In R. J. Sternberg (Ed.), *The anatomy of impact: What makes the great works of psychology great?* (pp. 89–107). Washington, DC: American Psychological Association.

Sternberg, R. J., & Lubart, T. I. (1991). An investment theory of creativity and its development. *Human Development, 34,* 1–31.

Sternberg, R. J., & Lubart, T. I. (1996). Investing in creativity. *American Psychologist, 51,* 677–688.

Stetsenko, A., Little, T. D., Gordeeva, T., Grassof, M., & Oettingen, G. (2000). Gender effects in children's beliefs about school performance: A cross-cultural study. *Child Development, 71,* 517–527.

Stevenson, H. W., Lee, S., & Mu, X. (2000). Successful achievement in mathematics: China and the United States. In C. F. M. van Lieshout & P. G. Heymans (Eds.), *Developing talent across the lifespan* (pp. 167–183). Philadelphia: Psychology Press.

Stevenson, R., & Pollitt, C. (1987). The acquisition of temporal terms. *Journal of Child Language, 14,* 533–545.

Steward, D. K. (2001). Behavioral characteristics of infants with nonorganic failure to thrive during a play interaction. *American Journal of Maternal Child Nursing, 26,* 79–85.

Stewart, P., Reihman, J., Lonky, E., Darvill, T., & Pagano, J. (2000). Prenatal PCB exposure and neonatal behavioral assessment scale (NBAS) performance. *Neurotoxicology and Teratology, 22,* 21–29.

Stewart, R. B., Jr. (1990). *The second child: Family transition and adjustment.* Newbury Park, CA: Sage.

Stifter, C. A., Coulehan, C. M., & Fish, M. (1993). Linking employment to attachment: The mediating effects of maternal separation anxiety and interactive behavior. *Child Development, 64,* 1451–1460.

Stiles, J. (2001a). Neural plasticity in cognitive development. *Developmental Neuropsychology, 18,* 237–272.

Stiles, J. (2001b). Spatial cognitive development. In C. A. Nelson & M. Luciana (Eds.), *Handbook of developmental cognitive neuroscience* (pp. 399–414). Cambridge, MA: MIT Press.

Stiles, J., Bates, E. A., Thal, D., Trauner, D. A., & Reilly, J. (2002). Linguistic and spatial cognitive development in children with pre- and perinatal focal brain injury: A ten-year overview from the San Diego longitudinal project. In M. H. Johnson & Y. Munakata (Eds.), *Brain development and cognition: A reader* (2nd ed., pp. 272–291). Malden, MA: Blackwell.

Stiles, J., Moses, P., Roe, K., Akshoomoff, N. A., Trauner, D., & Hesselink, J. (2003). Alternative brain organization after prenatal cerebral injury: Convergent fMRI and cognitive data. *Journal of the International Neuropsychological Society, 9,* 604–622.

Stipek, D. (1995). The development of pride and shame in toddlers. In J. P. Tangney & K. W. Fischer (Eds.), *Self-conscious emotions* (pp. 237–252). New York: Guilford.

Stipek, D. (2002). At what age should children enter kindergarten? A question for policy makers and parents. *Social Policy Report of the Society for Research in Child Development, 16*(3).

Stipek, D. J., & Byler, P. (1997). Early childhood education teachers: Do they practice what they preach? *Early Childhood Research Quarterly, 12,* 305–326.

Stipek, D. J., & Byler, P. (2001). Academic achievement and social behaviors associated with age of entry into kindergarten. *Journal of Applied Developmental Psychology, 22,* 175–189.

Stipek, D. J., Gralinski, J. H., & Kopp, C. B. (1990). Self-concept development in the toddler years. *Developmental Psychology, 26,* 972–977.

Stipek, D. J., Recchia, S., & McClintic, S. (1992). Self-evaluation in young children. *Monographs of the Society for Research in Child Development, 57*(1, Serial No. 226).

Stoch, M. B., Smythe, P. M., Moodie, A. D., & Bradshaw, D. (1982). Psychosocial outcome and CT findings after growth undernourishment during infancy: A 20-year developmental study. *Developmental Medicine and Child Neurology, 24,* 419–436.

Stocker, C. M., & Dunn, J. (1994). Sibling relationships in childhood and adolescence. In J. C. DeFries, R. Plomin, & D. W. Fulker (Eds.), *Nature and nurture in middle childhood* (pp. 214–232). Cambridge, MA: Blackwell.

Stoll, S. (1998). The role of Aktionsart in the acquisition of Russian aspect. *First Language, 18,* 351–378.

Stone, M. R., & Brown, B. B. (1999). Identity claims and projections: Descriptions of self and crowds in secondary school. In J. A. McLellan & M. J. V. Pugh (Eds.), *The role of peer groups in adolescent social identity: Exploring the importance of stability and change* (pp. 7–20). San Francisco: Jossey-Bass.

Stoneman, Z., Brody, G. H., & MacKinnon, C. E. (1986). Same-sex and cross-sex siblings: Activity choices, roles, behavior, and gender stereotypes. *Sex Roles, 15,* 495–511.

Storch, S. A., & Whitehurst, G. J. (2001). The role of family and home in the literacy development of children from low-income backgrounds. In P. R. Britto & J. Brooks-Gunn (Eds.), *New directions for child and adolescent development* (No. 92, pp. 53–71). San Francisco: Jossey-Bass.

Stormshak, E. A., Bellanti, C. J., Bierman, K. L., & Conduct Problems Prevention Research Group. (1996). The quality of sibling relationships and the development of social competence and behavioral control in aggressive children. *Developmental Psychology, 32,* 79–89.

Stormshak, E. A., Bierman, K. L., Bruschi, C., Dodge, K. A., & Coie, J. D. (1999). The relation between behavior problems and peer preference in different classroom contexts. *Child Development, 70,* 169–182.

Stormshak, E. A., Bierman, K. L., McMahon, R. J., Lengua, L. J., and the Conduct Problems Prevention Research Group. (2000). Parenting practices and child disruptive behavior problems in early elementary school. *Journal of Clinical Child Psychology, 29,* 17–29.

Strachan, T., & Read, A. (2004). *Human molecular genetics* (3rd ed.). New York: Garland Science.

Strapp, C. M., & Federico, A. (2000). Imitations and repetitions: What do children say following recasts? *First Language, 20,* 273–290.

Straus, M. A., & Stewart, J. H. (1999). Corporal punishment by American parents: National data on prevalence, chronicity, severity, and duration in relation to child and family characteristics. *Clinical Child and Family Psychology Review, 2,* 55–70.

Strauss, R. S., & Pollack, H. A. (2003). Social marginalization of overweight children. *Archives of Pediatric and Adolescent Medicine, 157,* 746–752.

Strauss, S. (1998). Cognitive development and science education: Toward a middle level model. In I. E. Sigel & K. Renninger (Eds.), *Handbook of child psychology: Vol. 4. Child psychology in practice* (5th ed., pp. 357–399). New York: Wiley.

Strayer, J., & Roberts, W. (2004). Children's anger, emotional expressiveness, and empathy: Relations with parents' empathy, emotional expressiveness, and parenting practices. *Social Development, 13,* 229–254.

Streissguth, A. P., Barr, H. M., Sampson, P. D., & Bookstein, F. L. (1994). Prenatal alcohol and offspring development: The first fourteen years. *Drug and Alcohol Dependence, 36,* 89–99.

Streissguth, A. P., Treder, R., Barr, H. M., Shepard, T., Bleyer, W. A., Sampson, P. D., & Martin, D. (1987). Aspirin and acetaminophen use by pregnant women and subsequent child IQ and attention decrements. *Teratology, 35,* 211–219.

Strelau, J., Zawadzki, B., & Piotrowska, A. (2001). Temperament and intelligence: A psychometric approach to the links between both phenomena. In J. M. Collis & Messick (Eds.), *Intelligence and personality* (pp. 61–78). Mahwah, NJ: Erlbaum.

Streri, A., Lhote, M., & Dutilleul, S. (2000). Haptic perception in newborns. *Developmental Science, 3,* 319–327.

Striano, T., & Rochat, P. (2000). Emergence of selective social referencing in infancy. *Infancy, 1,* 253–264.

Striano, T., Tomasello, M., & Rochat, P. (2001). Social and object support for early symbolic play. *Developmental Science, 4,* 442–455.

Stright, A. D., Neitzel, C., Sears, K. G., & Hoke-Sinex, L. (2002). Instruction begins in the home: Relations between parental instruction and children's self-regulation in the classroom. *Journal of Educational Psychology, 93,* 456–466.

Stromswold, K. (2000). The cognitive neuroscience of language acquisition. In M. S. Gazzaniga (Ed.), *The new cognitive neurosciences* (pp. 909–932). Boston: MIT Press.

Strouse, D. L. (1999). Adolescent crowd orientations: A social and temporal analysis. In J. A. McLellan & M. J. V. Pugh (Eds.), *The role of peer groups in adolescent social identity: Exploring the importance of stability and change* (pp. 37–54). San Francisco: Jossey-Bass.

Stryer, B. K., Tofler, I. R., & Lapchick, R. (1998). A developmental overview of child and youth sports in society. *Child and Adolescent Psychiatric Clinics of North America, 7,* 697–724.

Styne, D. M. (2003). The regulation of pubertal growth. *Hormone Research, 60*(Suppl.1), 22–26.

Suárez-Orozco, C., & Suárez-Orozco, M. M. (2001). *Children of immigration.* Cambridge, MA: Harvard University Press.

Subbotsky, E. V. (1994). Early rationality and magical thinking in preschoolers: Space and time. *British Journal of Developmental Psychology, 12,* 97–108.

Subbotsky, E. V. (2004). Magical thinking in judgments of causation: Can anomalous phenomena affect ontological causal beliefs in children and adults? *British Journal of Developmental Psychology, 22,* 123–152.

Subrahmanyam, K., & Greenfield, P. M. (1996). Effect of video game practice on spatial skills in girls and boys. In P. M. Greenfield & R. R. Cocking (Eds.), *Interacting with video* (pp. 95–114). Norwood, NJ: Ablex.

Subrahmanyam, K., Greenfield, P., Kraut, R., & Gross, E. (2001). The impact of computer use on children's and adolescents' development. *Applied Developmental Psychology, 22,* 7–30.

Suddendorf, T. (2003). Early representational insight: Twenty-four-month-olds can use a photo to find an object in the world. *Child Development, 74,* 896–904.

Sullivan, H. S. (1953). *The interpersonal theory of psychiatry.* New York: Norton.

Sullivan, M. W., & Lewis, M. (2003). Contextual determinants of anger and other negative expressions in young infants. *Developmental Psychology, 39,* 693–705.

Sundell, H. (2001). Why does maternal smoke exposure increase the risk of sudden infant death syndrome? *Acta Paediatrica, 90,* 718–720.

Super, C. M. (1981). Behavioral development in infancy. In R. H. Monroe, R. L. Monroe, & B. B. Whiting (Eds.), *Handbook of cross-cultural human development* (pp. 181–270). New York: Garland.

Sureau, C. (1997). Trials and tribulations of surrogacy: From surrogacy to parenthood. *Human Reproduction, 12,* 410–411.

Sutcliffe, A. G. (2002). Health risks in babies born after assisted reproduction. *British Medical Journal, 325,* 117–118.

Sutton, M. J., Brown, J. D., Wilson, K. M., & Klein, J. D. (2002). Shaking the tree of forbidden fruit: Where adolescents learn about sexuality and contraception. In J. D. Brown, J. R. Steele, & K. Walsh-Childers (Eds.), *Sexual teens, sexual media* (pp. 25–55). Mahwah, NJ: Erlbaum.

Suzuki, L. A., & Valencia, R. R. (1997). Race–ethnicity and measured intelligence. *American Psychologist, 52,* 1103–1114.

Svensson, A. (2000). Computers in school: Socially isolating or a tool to promote collaboration? *Journal of Educational Computing Research, 22,* 437–453.

Swendsen, J. D., & Mazure, C. M. (2000). Life stress as a risk factor for postpartum depression: Current research and methodological issues. *Clinical Psychology—Science and Practice, 7,* 17–31.

Swingley, D. (2005). Statistical clustering and the contents of the infant vocabulary. *Cognitive Psychology, 50,* 86–132.

Swingley, D., & Aslin, R. N. (2002). Lexical neighborhoods and the word-form representations of 14-month-olds. *Psychological Science, 13,* 480–484.

Symons, D. K. (2001). A dyad-oriented approach to distress and mother–child relationship outcomes in the first 24 months. *Parenting: Science and Practice, 1,* 101–122.

Symons, D. K. (2004). Mental state discourse, theory of mind, and the internalization of self–other understanding. *Developmental Review, 24,* 159–188.

Szepkouski, G. M., Gauvain, M., & Carberry, M. (1994). The development of planning skills in children with and without mental retardation. *Journal of Applied Developmental Psychology, 15,* 187–206.

Szkrybalo, J., & Ruble, D. N. (1999). "God made me a girl": Sex-category constancy judgments and explanations revisited. *Developmental Psychology, 35,* 392–402.

Tacon, A., & Caldera, Y. (2001). Attachment and parental correlates in late adolescent Mexican American women. *Hispanic Journal of Behavioral Sciences, 23,* 71–88.

Tager-Flusberg, H. (2005). Putting words together: Morphology and syntax in the preschool years. In J. B. Gleason (Ed.), *The development of language* (5th ed., pp. 148–190). Boston: Allyn and Bacon.

Takahashi, K. (1990). Are the key assumptions of the "Strange Situation" procedure universal? A view from Japanese research. *Human Development, 33,* 23–30.

Tam, C. W., & Stokes, S. F. (2001). Form and function of negation in early developmental Cantonese. *Journal of Child Language, 28,* 373–391.

Tamis-LeMonda, C. S., Bornstein, M. H., & Baumwell, L. (2001). Maternal responsiveness and children's achievement of language milestones. *Child Development, 72,* 748–767.

Tammelin, T., Näyhä, S., Hills, A. P., & Järvelin, M. (2003). Adolescent participation in sports and adult physical activity. *American Journal of Preventive Medicine, 24,* 22–28.

Tamminen, K. (1991). *Religious development in childhood and youth.* Helsinki, Finland: Gummerus Kirjapaino Oy.

Tangney, J. P. (2001). Constructive and destructive aspects of shame and guilt. In A. C. Bohart & D. J. Stipek (Eds.), *Constructive and destructive behavior* (pp. 127–145). Washington, DC: American Psychological Association.

Taniguchi, H. (1999). The timing of childbearing and women's wages. *Journal of Marriage and the Family, 61,* 1008–1019.

Tanner, J. M. (1990). *Foetus into man* (2nd ed.). Cambridge, MA: Harvard University Press.

Tanner, J., M., Healy, M., & Cameron, N. (2001). *Assessment of skeletal maturity and prediction of adult height (TW3 method)* (3rd ed.). Philadelphia: Saunders.

Tardif, T., Gelman, S. A., & Xu, F. (1999). Putting the "noun bias" in context: A comparison of English and Mandarin. *Child Development, 70,* 620–635.

Tasbihsazan, R., Nettelbeck, T., & Kirby, N. (2003). Predictive validity of the Fagan Test of Infant Intelligence. *British Journal of Developmental Psychology, 21,* 585–597.

Tauber, M. A. (1979). Parental socialization techniques and sex differences in children's play. *Child Development, 50,* 225–234.

Taylor, E. (2004). ADHD is best understood as a cultural construct: Against, *British Journal of Psychiatry, 184,* 9.

Taylor, J. H., & Walker, L. J. (1997). Moral climate and the development of moral reasoning: The effects of dyadic discussions between young offenders. *Journal of Moral Education, 26,* 21–43.

Taylor, M. (1996). The development of children's beliefs about the social and biological aspects of gender differences. *Child Development, 67,* 1555–1571.

Taylor, M. (1999). *Imaginary companions and the children who create them.* New York: Oxford University Press.

Taylor, M., & Carlson, S. M. (1997). The relation between individual differences in fantasy and theory of mind. *Child Development, 68,* 436–455.

Taylor, M., & Carlson, S. M. (2000). The influence of religious beliefs on parental attitudes about children's fantasy behavior. In K. S. Rosengren, C. N. Johnson, & P. L. Harris (Eds.), *Imagining the impossible* (pp. 247–268). New York: Cambridge University Press.

Taylor, M., Esbensen, B. M., & Bennett, R. T. (1994). Children's understanding of knowledge acquisition: The tendency for children to report that they have always known what they have just learned. *Child Development, 65,* 1581–1604.

Taylor, M. C., & Hall, J. A. (1982). Psychological androgyny: Theories, methods, and conclusions. *Psychological Bulletin, 92,* 347–366.

Taylor, R. D., & Roberts, D. (1995). Kinship support and maternal and adolescent well-being in economically disadvantaged African-American families. *Child Development, 66,* 1585–1597.

Taylor, R. L. (2000). Diversity within African-American families. In D. H. Demo & K. R. Allen (Eds.), *Handbook of family diversity* (pp. 232–251). New York: Oxford University Press.

Teller, D. Y. (1998). Spatial and temporal aspects of infant color vision. *Vision Research, 38,* 3275–3282.

Tellings, A. (1999). Psychoanalytical and genetic-structuralistic approaches of moral development: Incompatible views? *Psychoanalytic Review, 86,* 903–914.

Temple, C. M., & Carney, R. A. (1995). Patterns of spatial functioning in Turner's syndrome. *Cortex, 31,* 109–118.

Templeton, A. R. (2002). The genetic and evolutionary significance of human races. In J. M. Fish (Ed.), *Race and intelligence* (pp. 31–56). Mahwah, NJ: Erlbaum.

Templeton, L. M., & Wilcox, S. A. (2000). A tale of two representations: The misinformation effect and children's developing theory of mind. *Child Development, 71,* 402–416.

Tenenbaum, H. R., & Leaper, C. (2002). Are parents' gender schemas related to their children's gender-related cognitions? A meta-analysis. *Developmental Psychology, 38,* 615–630.

Tenenbaum, H. R., & Leaper, C. (2003). Parent–child conversations about science: The socialization of gender inequities? *Developmental Psychology, 39,* 34–47.

Tepper, C. A., & Cassidy, K. W. (1999). Gender differences in emotional language in children's picture books. *Sex Roles, 40,* 265–280.

Terman, L., & Oden, M. H. (1959). *Genetic studies of genius: Vol. 4. The gifted group at midlife.* Stanford, CA: Stanford University Press.

Terwel, J., Gillies, R. M., van den Eeden, P., & Hoek, D. (2001). Cooperative learning processes of students: A longitudinal multilevel perspective. *British Journal of Educational Psychology, 71,* 619–645.

Teti, D. M., Gelfand, D. M., Messinger, D. S., & Isabella, R. (1995). Maternal depression and the quality of early attachment: An examination of infants, preschoolers, and their mothers. *Developmental Psychology, 31,* 364–376.

Teti, D. M., Saken, J. W., Kucera, E., & Corns, K. M. (1996). And baby makes four: Predictors of attachment security among preschool-age firstborns during the transition to siblinghood. *Child Development, 67,* 579–596.

Teyber, E. (2001). *Helping children cope with divorce* (rev. ed.). San Francisco: Jossey-Bass.

Thapar, A., Fowler, T., Rice, F., Scourfield, J., van den Bree, M., Thomas, H., Harold, G., & Hay, D. (2003). Maternal smoking during pregnancy and attention deficit hyperactivity disorder symptoms in offspring. *American Journal of Psychiatry, 160,* 1985–1989.

Tharpar, N., & Sanderson, I. R. (2004). Diarrhea in children: An interface between developing and developed countries. *Lancet, 363,* 641–653.

Tharpe, A. M., & Ashmead, D. H. (2001). A longitudinal investigation of infant auditory sensitivity. *American Journal of Audiology, 10,* 104–112.

Thatcher, R. W., Lyon, G. R., Rumsey, J., & Krasnegor, J. (1996). *Developmental neuroimaging.* San Diego, CA: Academic Press.

Thatcher, R. W., Walker, R. A., & Guidice, S. (1987). Human cerebral hemispheres develop at different rates and ages. *Science, 236,* 1110–1113.

Thelen, E. (1989). The (re)discovery of motor development: Learning new things from an old field. *Developmental Psychology, 25,* 946–949.

Thelen, E. (2001). Dynamic mechanisms of change in early perceptual–motor development. In J. L. McClelland & R. S. Siegler (Eds.), *Mechanisms of cognitive development: Behavioral and neural perspectives* (pp. 161–184). Mahwah, NJ: Erlbaum.

Thelen, E., & Adolph, K. E. (1992). Arnold Gesell: The paradox of nature and nurture. *Developmental Psychology, 28,* 368–380.

Thelen, E., & Bates, E. (2003). Connectionism and dynamic systems: Are they really different? *Developmental Science, 6,* 378–391.

Thelen, E., & Corbetta, D. (2002). Microdevelopment and dynamic systems: Applications to infant motor development. In N. Granott & J. Parziale (Eds.), *Microdevelopment: Transition processes in development and learning* (pp. 59–79). New York: Cambridge University Press.

Thelen, E., Corbetta, D., & Spencer, J. P. (1996). Development of reaching during the first year: Role of movement speed. *Journal of Experimental Psychology: Human Perception and Performance, 22,* 1059–1076.

Thelen, E., Corbetta, D., Kamm, K., Spencer, J. P., Schneider, K., & Zernicke, R. F. (1993). The transition to reaching: Mapping intention and intrinsic dynamics. *Child Development, 64,* 1058–1098.

Thelen, E., Fisher, D. M., & Ridley-Johnson, R. (1984). The relationship between physical growth and a newborn reflex. *Infant Behavior and Development, 7,* 479–493.

Thelen, E., & Smith, L. B. (1998). Dynamic systems theories. In R. M. Lerner (Ed.), *Handbook of child psychology: Vol. 1. Theoretical models of human development* (5th ed., pp. 563–634). New York: Wiley.

Thierry, K. L., & Spence, M. J. (2002). Source-monitoring training facilitates preschoolers' eyewitness memory performance. *Developmental Psychology, 38,* 428–437.

Thiessen, E. D., & Saffran, J. R. (2003). When cues collide: Use of stress and statistical cues to word boundaries by 7- to 9-month-old infants. *Developmental Psychology, 39,* 706–716.

Thoman, E. B., & Ingersoll, E. W. (1993). Learning in premature infants. *Developmental Psychology, 29,* 692–700.

Thomas, A., & Chess, S. (1977). *Temperament and development.* New York: Brunner/Mazel.

Thomas, A., Chess, S., & Birch, H. G. (1968). *Temperament and behavior disorders in children.* New York: New York University Press.

Thomas, K. M., & Casey, B. J. (2003). Methods for imaging the developing brain. In M. de Haan & M. H. Johnson (Eds.), *The cognitive neuroscience of development* (pp. 19–41). Hove, U.K.: Psychology Press.

Thomas, R. M. (2000). *Comparing theories of child development* (5th ed.). Belmont, CA: Wadsworth.

Thompson, A., Hollis, C., & Richards, D. (2003). Authoritarian parenting attitudes as a risk for conduct problems: Results of a British national cohort study. *European Child and Adolescent Psychiatry, 12,* 84–91.

Thompson, L. A., Goodman, D. C., & Little, G. A. (2002). Is more neonatal intensive care always better? Insights from a cross-national comparison of reproductive care. *Pediatrics, 109,* 1036–1043.

Thompson, P. M., Giedd, J. N., Woods, R. P., MacDonald, D., Evans, A. C., & Toga, A. W. (2000). Growth patterns in the developing brain detected by using continuum mechanical tensor maps. *Nature, 404,* 190–192.

Thompson, R. A. (1990a). On emotion and self-regulation. In R. A. Thompson (Ed.), *Nebraska Symposium on Motivation* (Vol. 36, pp. 383–483). Lincoln: University of Nebraska Press.

Thompson, R. A. (1990b). Vulnerability in research: A developmental perspective on research risk. *Child Development, 61,* 1–16.

Thompson, R. A. (1992). Developmental changes in research risk and benefit: A changing calculus of concerns. In B. Stanley & J. E. Sieber (Eds.), *Social research on children and adolescents: Ethical issues* (pp. 31–64). Newbury Park, CA: Sage.

Thompson, R. A. (1998). Early socio-personality development. In N. Eisenberg (Ed.), *Handbook of child psychology: Vol. 3. Social, emotional, and personality development* (5th ed., pp. 25–104). New York: Wiley.

Thompson, R. A. (2000). The legacy of early attachments. *Child Development, 71,* 145–152.

Thompson, R. A., Easterbrooks, M. A., & Padilla-Walker, L. M. (2003). Social and emotional development in infancy. In R. M. Lerner & M. A. Easterbrooks (Eds.), *Social and emotional development in infancy* (pp. 91–112). New York: Wiley.

Thompson, R. A., & Leger, D. W. (1999). From squalls to calls: The cry as a developing socioemotional signal. In B. Lester, J. Newman, & F. Pedersen, (Eds.), *Biological and social aspects of infant crying.* New York: Plenum.

Thompson, R. A., & Limber, S. (1991). "Social anxiety" in infancy: Stranger wariness and separation distress. In H. Leitenberg (Ed.), *Handbook of social and evaluation anxiety* (pp. 85–137). New York: Plenum.

Thompson, R. A., & Nelson, C. A. (2001). Developmental science and the media: Early brain development. *American Psychologist, 56,* 5–15.

Thompson, R. A., & Raikes, H. A. (2003). Toward the next quarter-century: Conceptual and methodological challenges for attachment theory. *Development and Psychopathology, 15,* 691–718.

Thompson, W. F., Schellenberg, E. G., & Husain, G. (2001). Arousal, mood and the Mozart effect. *Psychological Science, 12,* 248–251.

Thornberry, T., & Krohn, M. D. (2001). The development of delinquency: An interactional perspective. In S. O. White (Ed.), *Handbook of youth and justice* (pp. 289–305). Dordrecht, Netherlands: Kluwer.

Thornton, S. (1999). Creating conditions for cognitive change: The interaction between task structures and specific strategies. *Child Development, 70,* 588–603.

Thurstone, L. L. (1938). *Primary mental abilities.* Chicago: University of Chicago Press.

Tienari, P., Wynne, L. C., Laksy, K., Moring, J., Nieminen, P., & Sorri, A. (2003). Genetic boundaries of the schizophrenia spectrum: Evidence from the Finnish adoptive family study of schizophrenia. *American Journal of Psychiatry, 160,* 1587–1594.

Tienari, P., Wynne, L. C., Moring, J., & Lahti, I. (1994). The Finnish adoptive family study of schizophrenia: Implications for family research. *British Journal of Psychiatry, 164,* 20–26.

Tietjen, A., & Walker, L. (1985). Moral reasoning and leadership among men in a Papua, New Guinea village. *Developmental Psychology, 21,* 982–992.

Tinbergen, N. (1973). *The animal in its world: Explorations of an ethologist, 1932–1972.* Cambridge, MA: Harvard University Press.

Tincoff, R., & Jusczyk, P. W. (1999). Some beginnings of word comprehension in 6-month-olds. *Psychological Science, 10,* 172–175.

Tisak, M. S. (1995). Domains of social reasoning and beyond. In R. Vasta (Ed.), *Annals of child development* (Vol. 11, pp. 95–130). London: Jessica Kingsley.

Tizard, B., & Rees, J. (1975). The effect of early institutional rearing on the behaviour problems and affectional relationships of four-year-old children. *Journal of Child Psychology and Psychiatry, 16,* 61–73.

Tocci, S. (2000). *Down syndrome.* New York: Franklin Watts.

Tofler, I. R., Knapp, P. K., & Drell, M. J. (1998). The achievement by proxy spectrum in youth sports: Historical perspective and clinical approach to pressured and high-achieving children and adolescents. *Adolescent Psychiatric Clinics of North America, 7,* 803–820.

Tolson, J. M., & Urberg, K. A. (1993). Similarity between adolescent best friends. *Journal of Adolescent Research, 8,* 274–288.

Tomasello, M. (1992). *First verbs: A case study of early grammatical development.* New York: Cambridge University Press.

Tomasello, M. (1999). Having intentions, understanding intentions, and understanding communicative intentions. In P. D. Zelazo, J. W. Astington, & J. Wilde (Eds.), *Developing theories of intention: Social understanding and self-control* (pp. 63–75). Mahwah, NJ: Erlbaum.

Tomasello, M. (2000). Do young children have adult syntactic competence? *Cognition, 74,* 209–253.

Tomasello, M. (2003). *Constructing a language: A usage-based theory of language acquisition.* Cambridge, MA: Harvard University Press.

Tomasello, M., & Akhtar, N. (1995). Two-year-olds use pragmatic cues to differentiate reference to objects and actions. *Cognitive Development, 10,* 201–224.

Tomasello, M., Akhtar, N., Dodson, K., & Rekau, L. (1997). Differential productivity in young children's use of nouns and verbs. *Journal of Child Language, 24,* 373–387.

Tomasello, M., & Brooks, P. (1999). Early syntactic development: A construction grammar approach. In M. Barrett (Ed.), *The development of language* (pp. 161–190). London: UCL Press.

Tomasello, M., Call, J., & Hare, B. (2003). Chimpanzees understand psychological states—the question is which ones and to what extent. *Trends in Cognitive Sciences, 7,* 153–156.

Tomasello, M., & Rakoczy, H. (2003). What makes human cognition unique? From individual to shared to collective intentionality. *Mind and Language, 18,* 121–147.

Toomela, A. (2002). Drawing as a verbally mediated activity: A study of relationships between verbal, motor, visuospatial skills and drawing in children. *International Journal of Behavioral Development, 26,* 234–247.

Torff, B., & Gardner, H. (1999). The vertical mind—The case for multiple intelligences. In M. Anderson (Ed.), *The development of intelligence* (pp. 139–159). Hove, UK: Psychology Press.

Torney-Purta, J. (2002). The school's role in developing civic engagement: A study of adolescents in twenty-eight countries. *Applied Developmental Science, 6,* 203–212.

Torrance, E. P. (1988). The nature of creativity as manifest in its testing. In R. J. Sternberg (Ed.), *The nature of creativity: Contemporary psychological perspectives* (pp. 43–75). New York: Cambridge University Press.

Torrey, E. F., Bower, A. E., Taylor, E. H., & Gottesman, I. I. (1994). *Schizophrenia and manic-depressive disorder: The biological roots of mental illness as revealed by the landmark study of identical twins.* New York: Basic Books.

Toth, J. F., & Xu, X. (1999). Ethnic and cultural diversity in fathers' involvement: A racial/ethnic comparison of African-American, Hispanic, and white fathers. *Youth and Society, 31,* 76–99.

Touwen, B. C. L. (1984). Primitive reflexes—conceptual or semantic problem? In H. F. R. Prechtl (Ed.), *Continuity of neural functions from prenatal to postnatal life* (Clinics in Developmental Medicine, No. 94, pp. 115–125). Philadelphia: Lippincott.

Trahms, C. M., & Pipes, P. L. (1997). *Nutrition in infancy and childhood* (6th ed.). New York: McGraw-Hill.

Trautner, H. M., Gervai, J., & Nemeth, R. (2003). Appearance–reality distinction and development of gender constancy understanding in children. *International Journal of Behavioral Development, 27,* 275–283.

Treffert, D. A., & Wallace, G. L. (2002, June). Islands of genius. *Scientific American,* pp. 76–85.

Trehub, S. E. (2001). Musical predispositions in infancy. *Annals of the New York Academy of Sciences, 930,* 1–16.

Tremblay, R. E. (2000). The development of aggressive behaviour during childhood: What have we learned in the past century? *International Journal of Behavioral Development, 24,* 129–141.

Tremblay, R. E. (2002). Prevention of injury by early socialization of aggressive behavior. *Injury Prevention, 8*(Suppl. IV), 17–21.

Tremblay, R. E., Japel, C., Perusse, D., Voivin, M., Zoccolillo, M., Montplaisir, J., & McDuff, P. (1999). The search for the age of "onset" of physical aggression: Rousseau and Bandura revisited. *Criminal Behavior and Mental Health, 9,* 8–23.

Tremblay, R. E., Schaal, B., Boulerice, B., Arseneault, L., Soussignan, R., & Perusse, D. (1997). Male physical aggression, social dominance, and testosterone levels at puberty: A developmental perspective. In A. Raine & P. A. Brennan (Eds.), *Biosocial bases of violence. NATO ASI Series: Series A: Life sciences* (Vol. 292, pp. 271–291). New York: Plenum.

Trent, K., & Harlan, S. L. (1994). Teenage mothers in nuclear and extended households. *Journal of Family Issues, 15,* 309–337.

Trevarthen, C. (2003). Infant psychology is an evolving culture. *Human Development, 46,* 233–246.

Triandis, H. C. (1995). *Individualism and collectivism.* Boulder, CO: Westview Press.

Triandis, H. C. (1998, May). *Cross-cultural versus cultural psychology: A synthesis?* Colloquium presented at Illinois Wesleyan University, Bloomington, IL.

Trickett, P. K., Noll, J., Reiffman, A., & Putnam, F. (2001). Variants of intrafamilial sexual abuse experiences: Implications for short- and long-term development. *Development and Psychopathology, 13,* 1001–1019.

Trickett, P. K., & Putnam, F. W. (1998). Developmental consequences of child sexual abuse. In P. K. Trickett & C. J. Schellenbach (Eds.), *Violence against children in the family and community* (pp. 39–56). Washington, DC: American Psychological Association.

Trivers, R. L. (1971). The evolution of reciprocal altruism. *Quarterly Review of Biology, 46,* 35–57.

Trocomé, N., & Wolfe, D. (2002). *Child maltreatment in Canada: The Canadian Incidence Study of Reported Child Abuse and Neglect.* Retrieved from www.hc-sc.gc.ca/pphb-dgspsp/cm-vee

Tronick, E. Z., Morelli, G. A., & Ivey, P. (1992). The Efe forager infant and toddler's pattern of social relationships: Multiple and simultaneous. *Developmental Psychology, 28,* 568–577.

Tronick, E. Z., Thomas, R. B., & Daltabuit, M. (1994). The Quechua manta pouch: A caretaking practice for buffering the Peruvian infant against the multiple stressors of high altitude. *Child Development, 65,* 1005–1013.

True, M. M., Pisani, L., & Oumar, F. (2001). Infant–mother attachment among the Dogon of Mali. *Child Development, 72,* 1451–1466.

Truglio, R. (2000, April). *Research guides "Sesame Street."* Public lecture presented as part of the Consider the Children program, Illinois State University, Normal, IL.

Trzesniewski, K. H., Donnellan, M. B., & Robins, R. W. (2003). Stability of self-esteem across the life span. *Journal of Personality and Social Psychology, 84,* 205–220.

Tucker, C. J., McHale, S. M., & Crouter, A. C. (2001). Conditions of siblings support in adolescence. *Journal of Family Psychology, 15,* 254–271.

Tucker, C. J., McHale, S. M., & Crouter, A. C. (2003). Dimensions of mothers' and fathers' differential treatment of siblings: Links with adolescents' sex-typed personal qualities. *Family Relations, 52,* 82–89.

Tudge, J. R. H., Hogan, D. M., Snezhkova, I. A., Kulakova, N. N., & Etz, K. E. (2000). Parents' child-rearing values and beliefs in the United States and Russia: The impact of culture and social class. *Infant and Child Development, 9,* 105–121.

Tudge, J. R. H., and Scrimsher, S. (2003). Lev S. Vygotsky on education: A cultural-historical, interpersonal, and individual approach to development. In B. J. Zimmerman & D. H. Schunk (Eds.), *Educational psychology: A century of contributions* (pp. 207–228). Mahwah, NJ: Erlbaum.

Tudge, J. R. H., & Winterhoff, P. A. (1993). Vygotsky, Piaget, and Bandura: Perspectives on the relations between the social world and cognitive development. *Human Development, 36,* 61–81.

Turati, C. (2004). Why faces are not special to newborns: An account of the face preference. *Current Directions in Psychological Science, 13,* 5–8.

Turiel, E. (1998). The development of morality. In N. Eisenberg (Ed.), *Handbook of child psychology: Vol. 3. Social, emotional, and personality development* (Vol. 3, pp. 863–932). New York: Wiley.

Turiel, E., Smetana, J. G., & Killen, M. (1991). Social contexts in social cognitive development. In W. M. Kurtines & J. L. Gewirtz (Eds.), *Handbook of moral behavior and development* (Vol. 2, pp. 307–332). Hillsdale, NJ: Erlbaum.

Turkheimer, E. (2003). Socioeconomic status modifies heritability of IQ in young children. *Psychological Science, 14,* 623–628.

Turkheimer, E., Haley, A., Waldron, M., D'Onofrio, B., & Gottesman, I. I. (2003). Socioeconomic status modifies heritability of IQ in young children. *Psychological Science, 14,* 623–628.

Turkle, S. (1995). *Life on the screen: Identity in the age of the Internet.* New York: Simon & Schuster.

Turnbull, M., Hart, D., & Lapkin, S. (2003). Grade 6 French immersion students' performance on large-scale reading, writing, and mathematics tests: Building explanations. *Alberta Journal of Educational Research, 49,* 6–23.

Turner, P. J., & Gervai, J. (1995). A multidimensional study of gender typing in preschool children and their parents: Personality, attitudes, preferences, behavior, and cultural differences. *Developmental Psychology, 31,* 759–772.

Turner, P. J., Gervai, J. & Hinde, R. A. (1993). Gender typing in young children: Preferences, behaviour and cultural differences. *British Journal of Developmental Psychology, 11,* 323–342.

Turner-Bowker, D. M. (1996). Gender stereotyped descriptors in children's picture books: Does "Curious Jane" exist in the literature? *Sex Roles, 35,* 461–488.

Tuss, P., Zimmer, J., & Ho, H.-Z. (1995). Causal attributions of underachieving fourth-grade students in China, Japan, and the United States. *Journal of Cross-Cultural Psychology, 26,* 408–425.

Tuyen, J. M., & Bisgard, K. (2003). Community setting: Pertussis outbreak. Atlanta, GA: U.S. Centers for Disease Control and Prevention. Retrieved from www.cdc.gov/nip/publications/pertussis/chapter10.pdf

Twenge, J. M., & Campbell, W. K. (2001). Age and birth cohort differences in self-esteem: A cross-temporal meta-analysis. *Personality and Social Psychology Review, 5,* 321–344.

Twenge, J. M., & Crocker, J. (2002). Race and self-esteem: Meta-analyses comparing whites, blacks, Hispanics, Asians, and America Indians and comment on Gray-Little and Hafdahl (2000*). Psychological Bulletin, 128,* 371–408.

Tychsen, L. (2001). Critical periods for development of visual acuity, depth perception, and eye tracking. In D. B. Bailey, Jr., J. T. Bruer, F. J. Symons, & J. W. Lichtman (Eds.), *Critical thinking about critical periods* (pp. 67–82). Baltimore: Paul H. Brookes.

Tyrka, A. R., Graber, J. A., & Brooks-Gunn, J. (2000). The development of disordered eating: Correlates and predictors of eating problems in the context of adolescence. In A. J. Sameroff & M. Lewis (Eds.), *Handbook of developmental psychopathology* (2nd ed., pp. 607–624). New York: Kluwer.

Tzuriel, D. (2001). *Dynamic assessment of young children.* New York: Kluwer Academic.

Tzuriel, D., & Kaufman, R. (1999). Mediated learning and cognitive modifiability: Dynamic assessment of young Ethiopian immigrant children to Israel. *Journal of Cross-Cultural Psychology, 30,* 359–380.

Underwood, M. K. (2003). *Social aggression among girls.* New York: Guilford.

Underwood, M. K., Galen, B. R., & Paquette, J. (2001). Top ten challenges for understanding aggression and gender: Why can't we all just get along? *Social Development, 10,* 248–266.

Unger, B., Kemp, J. S., Wilkins, D., Psara, R., Ledbetter, T., & Graham, M. (2003). Racial disparity and modifiable risk factors among infants dying suddenly and unexpectedly. *Pediatrics, 111,* E127–E131.

UNICEF (United Nations Children's Fund). (2000). Child poverty in rich nations. *Innocenti Report Card No. 1.* Florence, Italy: UNICEF Innocenti Research Center.

UNICEF (United Nations Children's Fund). (2001). Teenage births in rich nations. *Innocenti Report Card No. 3.* Florence, Italy: UNICEF Innocenti Research Center.

UNICEF (United Nations Children's Fund). (2004). Statistics: Malnutrition. Retrieved from www.childinfo.org/eddb/malnutrition

UNICEF (United Nations Children's Fund). (2005). *Children under threat.* New York: Author.

United Nations. (2001). *World social situation.* New York: Author.

United Nations. (2002). *Human Development Report 2001.* New York: Author.

United Nations. (2004a). Women, girls, HIV and AIDS. Retrieved from www.un.org/events/aids

United Nations. (2004b). *World population prospects: The 2003 revision.* Retrieved from www.unpopulation.org

United Nations Development Programme. (2002). *Human development report 2002.* New York: Author.

U.S. Census Bureau. (2004a). International data base. Retrieved from www.census.gov/ipc/www/idbnew.html

U.S. Census Bureau. (2004b). *Statistical abstract of the United States* (124th ed.). Washington, DC: U.S. Government Printing Office.

U.S. Department of Agriculture. (2003). *Food insecurity in households with children.* Washington, DC: Author.

U.S. Department of Agriculture. (2004a). *Expenditures on children by families, 2004.* Retrieved from www.cnpp.usda.gov

U.S. Department of Agriculture. (2004b). Frequently asked questions about the Special Supplemental Nutrition Program for Women, Infants, and Children (WIC). Retrieved from www.ers.usda.gov/Briefing/WIC

U.S. Department of Education. (2003a). *The Nation's Report Card: National Assessment of Educational Progress: 2003 results.* Retrieved from nces.ed.gov/nationsreportcard/mathematics

U.S. Department of Education. (2003b). *The Nation's Report Card: Reading.* Retrieved from nces.ed.gov/nationsreportcard

U.S. Department of Education. (2004a). *The condition of education 2004.* Washington, DC: U.S. Government Printing Office.

U.S. Department of Education. (2004b). *Digest of education statistics 2003.* Washington, DC: U.S. Government Printing Office.

U.S. Department of Health and Human Services. (2000). 2000 CDC growth charts. Retrieved from www.cdc.gov/growthcharts

U.S. Department of Health and Human Services. (2001). *CDC School Health Policies and Programs Study, 2000.* Retrieved from www.cdc.gov/nccdphp/dash/shpps/factsheets/fs00–pe.htm

U.S. Department of Health and Human Services. (2003a). Fetal alcohol syndrome. Retrieved from www.cdc.gov/ncbddd/fas/fasask.htm

U.S. Department of Health and Human Services. (2003b). National, state, and urban area vaccination levels among children aged 19 to 35 months: United States 2002. *Morbidity and Mortality Weekly Report, 52,* 728–732.

U.S. Department of Health and Human Services. (2003c). Prenatal care. Retrieved from www.cdc.gov/nchs/fastats/prenatal.htm

U.S. Department of Health and Human Services. (2004a). Birth defects. Retrieved from www.cdc.gov/ncbddd

U.S. Department of Health and Human Services. (2004b). Births: Final data for 2003. *National Vital Statistics Report, 53*(11). Retrieved from www.cdc.gov/nchs

U.S. Department of Health and Human Services. (2004c). *Cases of HIV infection and AIDS in the United States, 2002. HIV/AIDS surveillance Report, 14.* Retrieved from www.cdc.gov/hiv/stats/hasr1402.htm

U.S. Department of Health and Human Services. (2004d). *Health United States and Injury Chartbook.* Washington, DC: U.S. Government Printing Office.

U.S. Department of Health and Human Services. (2004e). *Monitoring the Future: National results on adolescent drug use: Overview of key findings, 2004.* Bethesda, MD: National Institute on Drug Abuse.

U.S. Department of Health and Human Services. (2004f). Youth risk behavior surveillance. *Morbidity and Mortality Weekly Report, 53*(No. SS-2). Atlanta, GA: Centers for Disease Control and Prevention.

U.S. Department of Health and Human Services. (2005). *Child maltreatment 2004: Summary of key findings.* Washington, DC: National Clearinghouse on Child Abuse and Neglect Information.

U.S. Department of Justice. (2004). *Crime in the United States.* Washington, DC: U.S. Government Printing Office.

Updegraff, K. A., McHale, S. M., & Crouter, A. C. (1996). Gender roles in marriage: What do they mean for girls' and boys' school achievement? *Journal of Youth and Adolescence, 25,* 73–88.

Uribe, F. M. T., LeVine, R. A., & LeVine, S. E. (1994). Maternal behavior in a Mexican community: The changing environments of children. In P. M. Greenfield & R. R. Cocking (Eds.), *Cross-cultural roots of minority child development* (pp. 41–54). Hillsdale, NJ: Erlbaum.

Usmiani, S., & Daniluk, J. (1997). Mothers and their adolescent daughters: Relationship between self-esteem, gender role identity, and body image. *Journal of Youth and Adolescence, 26,* 45–60.

Uttal, D. H., Gregg, V. H., Tan, L. S., Chamberlin, M. H., & Sines, A. (2001). Connecting the dots: Children's use of a systematic figure to facilitate mapping and search. *Developmental Psychology, 37,* 338–350.

Vaidyanathan, R. (1988). Development of forms and functions of interrogatives in children: A language study of Tamil. *Journal of Child Language, 15,* 533–549.

Vaidyanathan, R. (1991). Development of forms and functions of negation in the early stages of language acquisition: A study of Tamil. *Journal of Child Language, 18,* 51–66.

Vaillancourt, T., Brendgen, M., Boivin, M., & Tremblay, R. E. (2003). A longitudinal confirmatory factor analysis of indirect physical aggression: Evidence of two factors over time? *Child Development, 74,* 1628–1638.

Vaillancourt, T., Hymel, S., & McDougall, P. (2003). Bullying is power: Implications for school-based intervention strategies. *Journal of Applied Social Psychology, 19,* 157–176.

Vaish, A., & Striano, T. (2004). Is visual reference necessary? Contributions of facial versus vocal cues in 12-month-olds' social referencing behavior. *Developmental Science, 7,* 261–269.

Valdés, G. (1998). The world outside and inside schools: Language and immigrant children. *Educational Researcher, 27*(6), 4–18.

Valentine, J. C., DuBois, D. L., & Cooper, H. (2004). The relation between self-beliefs and academic achievement: A meta-analytic review. *Educational Psychologist, 39,* 111–133.

Valian, V. (1999). Input and language acquisition. In W. C. Ritchie & T. K. Bhatia (Eds.), *Handbook of child language acquisition* (pp. 497–530). San Diego: Academic Press.

Valian, V. V. (1991). Syntactic subjects in the early speech of American and Italian children. *Cognition, 40,* 21–81.

Van den Bergh, B. R. H., & De Rycke, L. (2003). Measuring the multidimensional self-concept and global self-worth of 6- to 8-year-olds. *Journal of Genetic Psychology, 164,* 201–225.

van den Boom, D. C. (2002). First attachments: Theory and research. In G. Bremner & A. Fogel (Eds.), *Blackwell handbook of infant development* (pp. 296–325). Oxford, U.K.: Blackwell.

van den Boom, D. C., & Hoeksma, J. B. (1994). The effect of infant irritability on mother–infant interaction: A growth-curve analysis. *Developmental Psychology, 30,* 581–590.

van der Meer, A. L. H., van der Weel, F. R., & Lee, D. N. (1995). The functional significance of arm movements in neonates. *Science, 267,* 693–695.

van der Woerd, K. A., & Cox, D. N. (2001, August). *Assessing academic competence and the well-being of Aboriginal students in British Columbia.* Poster presented at the annual meeting of the American Psychological Association, Atlanta.

Van Goozen, S. H. M., Cohen-Kettenis, P. T., Gooren, I. J. G., Frijda, N. H., & Van De Poll, N. E. (1995). Gender differences in behaviour: Activating effects of cross-sex hormones. *Psychoneuroendocrinology, 20,* 171–177.

van Hoof, A., & Raaijmakers, Q. A. W. (2003). The search for the structure of identity formation. *Identity, 3,* 271–289.

van IJzendoorn, M. H. (1995). Adult attachment representations, parental responsiveness, and infant attachment: A meta-analysis on the predictive validity of the adult attachment interview. *Psychological Bulletin, 117,* 387–403.

van IJzendoorn, M. H. (1995). Adult attachment representations, parental responsiveness, and infant attachment: A meta-analysis on the predictive validity of the Adult Attachment Interview. *Psychological Bulletin, 117,* 411–415.

van IJzendoorn, M. H., & De Wolff, M. S. (1997). In search of the absent father—meta-analyses of infant-father attachment: A rejoinder to our discussants. *Child Development, 68,* 604–609.

van IJzendoorn, M. H., Goldberg, S., Kroonenberg, P. M., & Frenkel, O. J. (1992). The relative effects of maternal and child problems on the quality of attachment: A meta-analysis of attachment in clinical samples. *Child Development, 63,* 840–858.

van IJzendoorn, M. H., & Hubbard, F. O. A. (2000). Are infant crying and maternal responsiveness during the first year related to infant–mother attachment at 15 months? *Attachment and Human Development, 2,* 371–391.

van IJzendoorn, M. H., & Kroonenberg, P. M. (1988). Cross-cultural patterns of attachment: A meta-analysis of the Strange Situation. *Child Development, 59,* 147–156.

van IJzendoorn, M. H., & Sagi, A. (1999). Cross-cultural patterns of attachment. In J. Cassidy & P. R. Shaver (Eds.), *Handbook of attachment: Theory, research, and clinical applications* (pp. 713–734). New York: Guilford.

van IJzendoorn, M. H., Schuengel, C., & Bakermans-Kranenburg, M. J. (1999). Disorganized attachment in early childhood: Meta-analysis of precursors, concomitants, and sequelae. *Development and Psychopathology, 11,* 225–249.

van IJzendoorn, M. H., Vereijken, C. M. J. L., Bakermans-Kranenburg, M. J., & Riksen-Walraven, J. M. (2004). Assessing attachment security with the Attachment Q-Sort: Meta-analytic evidence for the validity of the observer AQS. *Child Development, 75,* 1188–1213.

Van Keer, H. (2004). Fostering reading comprehension in fifth grade by explicit instruction in reading strategies and peer tutoring. *British Journal of Educational Psychology, 74,* 37–70.

Vandell, D. L. (1999). When school is out: Analysis and recommendations. *The Future of Children, 9*(2). [Online]. Available: www.futureofchildren.org

Vandell, D. L., & Mueller, E. C. (1995). Peer play and friendships during the first two years. In H. C. Foot, A. J. Chapman, & J. R. Smith (Eds.), *Friendship and social relations in children* (pp. 181–208). New Brunswick, NJ: Transaction.

Vandell, D. L., & Posner, J. K. (1999). Conceptualization and measurement of children's after-school environments. In S. L. Friedman & T. D. Wachs (Eds.), *Measuring environment across the life span* (pp. 167–196). Washington, DC: American Psychological Association.

Vandell, D. L., & Shumow, L. (1999). After-school child care programs. *Future of Children, 9*(2), 64–80.

Vandenberg, B. (1998). Real and not real: A vital developmental dichotomy: In O. N. Saracho & B. Spodek (Eds.), *Multiple perspectives on play in early childhood education* (pp. 295–305). Albany: State University of New York.

Vandivere, S., Gallagher, M., & Moore, K. A. (2004). *Changes in children's well-being and family environments. Snapshots of America's Families III,* No. 18. New York: Urban Institute. Retrieved from www.urban.org/url.cfm?ID=310912

Vanier Institute of the Family. (2004). *Profiling Canada's families: II.* Ottawa, ON: Author.

Varendi, H., Christensson, K., Porter, R. H., & Winberg, J. (1998). Soothing effect of amniotic fluid smell in newborn infants. *Early Human Development, 51,* 47–55.

Varendi, H., & Porter, R. H. (2001). Breast odour as the only maternal stimulus elicits crawling toward the odour source. *Acta Paediactrica, 90,* 372–375.

Vartanian, L. R. (1997). Separation–individuation, social support, and adolescent egocentrism: An exploratory study. *Journal of Early Adolescence, 17,* 245–270.

Vartanian, L. R., & Powlishta, K. K. (1996). A longitudinal examination of the social-cognitive foundations of adolescent egocentrism. *Journal of Early Adolescence, 16,* 157–178.

Vasudev, J., & Hummel, R. C. (1987). Moral stage sequence and principled reasoning in an Indian sample. *Human Development, 30,* 105–118.

Vatten, L. J., Maehle, B. O., Lund, N. T., Treti, S., Hsieh, C. C., Trichopoulos, D., & Stuver, S. O. (2002). Birth weight as a predictor of breast cancer: A case-control study in Norway. *British Journal of Cancer, 86,* 89–91.

Vaughn, B. E., & Bost, K. K. (1999). Attachment and temperament: Redundant, independent, or interacting influences on interpersonal adaptation and personality development? In J. Cassidy & P. Shaver (Eds.), *Handbook of attachment: Theory, research, and clinical applications* (pp. 265–286). New York: Guilford.

Vaughn, B. E., Colvin, T. N., Azria, M. R., Caya, L., & Krzysik, L. (2001). Dyadic analyses of friendship in a sample of preschool-age children attending Head Start: Correspondence between measures and implications for social competence. *Child Development, 72,* 862–878.

Vaughn, B. E., Kopp, C. B., & Krakow, J. B. (1984). The emergence and consolidation of self-control from eighteen to thirty months of age: Normative trends and individual differences. *Child Development, 55,* 990–1004.

Vaughn, S., & Klingner, J. K. (1998). Students' perceptions of inclusion and resource room settings. *Journal of Special Education, 32,* 79–88.

Vazsonyi, A. T., Hibbert, J. R., & Snider, J. B. (2003). Exotic enterprise no more? Adolescent reports of family and parenting processes from youth in four countries. *Journal of Research on Adolescence, 13,* 129–160.

Vedam, S. (2003). Home birth versus hospital birth: Questioning the quality of the evidence on safety. *Birth, 30,* 57–63.

Venet, M., & Markovits, H. (2001). Understanding uncertainty with abstract conditional premises. *Merrill-Palmer Quarterly, 47,* 74–99.

Veneziano, R. A. (2003). The importance of paternal warmth. *Cross-Cultural Research, 37,* 265–281.

Ventura, S. J., Hamilton, B. E., Mathews, T. J., & Chandra, A. (2003). Trends and variations in smoking during pregnancy and low birth weight: Evidence from the birth certificate, 1990–2000. *Pediatrics, 111,* 1176–1180.

Vernon, P. A., Wickett, J. C., Bazana, G., & Stelmack, R. M. (2001). The neuropsychology and psychophysiology of human intelligence. In R. J. Sternberg (Ed.), *Handbook of intelligence* (pp. 245–264). Cambridge, UK: Cambridge University Press.

Videon, T. M., & Manning, C. K. (2003). Influences on adolescent eating patterns: The importance of family meals. *Journal of Adolescent Health, 32,* 365–373.

Vihman, M. M. (1996). *Phonological development.* London: Blackwell.

Vik, T., Bakketeig, L. S., Trygg, K. U., Lund-Larsen, K., & Jacobsen, G. (2003). High caffeine consumption in the third trimester of pregnancy: Gender-specific effects on fetal growth. *Paediatric and Perinatal Epidemiology, 17,* 324–331.

Vinden, P. G. (1996). Junín Quechua children's understanding of mind. *Child Development, 67,* 1707–1716.

Vinden, P. G. (2002). Understanding minds and evidence for belief: A study of Mofu children in Cameroon. *International Journal of Behavioral Development, 26,* 445–452.

Visher, E. B., Visher, J. S., & Pasley, K. (2003). Remarriage families and stepparenting. In F. Walsh (Ed.), *Normal family processes* (pp. 153–175). New York: Guilford.

Vitaro, F., Brendgen, M., & Tremblay, R. E. (2000). Influence of deviant friends on delinquency: Searching for moderator variables. *Journal of Abnormal Child Psychology, 28,* 313–325.

Vogel, D. A., Lake, M. A., Evans, S., & Karraker, H. (1991). Children's and adults' sex-stereotyped perceptions of infants. *Sex Roles, 24,* 605–616.

Volling, B. L. (2001). Early attachment relationships as predictors of preschool children's emotion regulation with a distressed sibling. *Early Education and Development, 12,* 185–207.

Volling, B. L., & Belsky, J. (1992). Contribution of mother–child and father–child relationships to the quality of sibling interaction: A longitudinal study. *Child Development, 63,* 1209–1222.

Volling, B. L., McElwain, N. L., & Miller, A. L. (2002). Emotion regulation in context: The jealousy complex between young siblings and its relations with child and family characteristics. *Child Development, 73,* 581–600.

von Hofsten, C. (1982). Eye–hand coordination in the newborn. *Developmental Psychology, 18,* 450–461.

von Hofsten, C. (1993). Prospective control: A basic aspect of action development. *Human Development, 36,* 253–270.

von Hofsten, C. (2004). An action perspective on motor development. *Trends in Cognitive Sciences, 8,* 266–272.

von Hofsten, C., & Rosander, K. (1998). The establishment of gaze control in early infancy. In S. Simion & G. Butterworth (Eds.), *The development of sensory, motor and cognitive capacities in early infancy* (pp. 49–66). Hove, UK: Psychology Press.

Vondra, J. I., Hommerding, K. D., & Shaw, D. S. (1999). Stability and change in infant attachment in a low-income sample. In J. I Vondra & D. Barnett (Eds.), *Atypical attachment in infancy and early childhood among children at developmental risk. Monographs of the Society for Research in Child Development, 64*(3, Serial No. 258), 119–144.

Vondra, J. I., Shaw, D. S., Searingen, L., Cohen, M., & Owens, E. B. (2001). Attachment stability and emotional and behavioral regulation from infancy to preschool age. *Development and Psychopathology, 13,* 13–33.

Vonk, R., & Ashmore, R. D. (2003). Thinking about gender types: Cognitive organization of female and male types. *British Journal of Social Psychology, 42,* 257–280.

Voss, L. D., Mulligan, J., & Betts, P. R. (1998). Short stature at school entry—an index of social deprivation? (The Wessex Growth Study). *Child: Care, Health and Development, 24,* 145–156.

Votruba-Drzal, E., Coley, R. L., & Chase-Lansdale, P. L. (2004). Child care and low-income children's development: Direct and moderated effects. *Child Development, 75,* 296–312.

Vouloumanos, A., & Werker, J. F., (2004). Tuned to the signal: The privileged status of speech for young infants. *Developmental Science, 7,* 270–276.

Voyer, D., Voyer, S., & Bryden, M. P. (1995). Magnitude of sex differences in spatial abilities: A meta-analysis and consideration of critical variables. *Psychological Bulletin, 117,* 250–270.

Vurpillot, E. (1968). The development of scanning strategies and their relation to visual differentiation. *Journal of Experimental Child Psychology, 6,* 632–650.

Vygotsky, L. S. (1978). *Mind in society: The development of higher mental processes.* Cambridge, MA: Harvard University Press. (Original works published 1930, 1933, and 1935)

Vygotsky, L. S. (1986). *Thought and language* (A. Kozulin, Trans.). Cambridge, MA: MIT Press. (Original work published 1934)

Vygotsky, L. S. (1987). Thinking and speech. In R. W. Rieber, A. S. Carton (Eds.), & N. Minick (Trans.), *The collected works of L. S. Vygotsky: Vol. 1. Problems of general psychology* (pp. 37–285). New York: Plenum. (Original work published 1934)

Wachs, T. D. (1999). The what, why, and how of temperament: A piece of the action. In L. Balter & C. S. Tamis-LeMonda (Eds.), *Child psychology: A handbook of contemporary issues* (pp. 23–44). Philadelphia: Psychology Press.

Wachs, T. D., & Bates, J. E. (2001). Temperament. In G. Bremner & A. Fogel (Eds.), *Blackwell handbook of infant development* (pp. 465–501). Oxford, UK: Blackwell.

Waddington, C. H. (1957). *The strategy of the genes.* London: Allen and Unwin.

Wadhwa, P. D., Sandman, C. A., & Garite, T. J. (2001). The neurobiology of stress in human pregnancy: Implications for prematurity and development of the fetal central nervous system. *Progress in Brain Research, 133,* 131–142.

Wagner, B. M., Silverman, M. A. C., & Martin, C. E. (2003). Family factors in youth suicidal behaviors. *American Behavioral Scientist, 46,* 1171–1191.

Wagner, R. K. (2000). Practical intelligence. In R. J. Sternberg (Ed.), *Handbook of intelligence* (pp. 380–395). Cambridge, UK: Cambridge University Press.

Wahlsten, D. (1994). The intelligence of heritability. *Canadian Psychology, 35,* 244–259.

Wainryb, C. (1997). The mismeasure of diversity: Reflections on the study of cross-cultural differences. In H. D. Saltzstein (Ed.), *New directions for child development* (No. 76, pp. 51–65). San Francisco: Jossey-Bass.

Wainryb, C., & Ford, S. (1998). Young children's evaluations of acts based on beliefs different from their own. *Merrill-Palmer Quarterly, 44,* 484–503.

Wakeley, A., Rivera, S., & Langer, J. (2000). Can young infants add and subtract? *Child Development, 71,* 1477–1720.

Walberg, H. J. (1986). Synthesis of research on teaching. In M. C. Wittrock (Ed.), *Handbook of research on teaching* (3rd ed., pp. 214–229). New York: Macmillan.

Waldfogel, J. (2001). International policies toward parental leave and child care. *Future of Children 11,* 52–61.

Waldman, I. D., Weinberg, R. A., & Scarr, S. (1994). Racial-group differences in IQ in the Minnesota Transracial Adoption Study: A reply to Levin and Lynn. *Intelligence, 19,* 29–44.

Walker, A., Rosenberg, M., & Balaban-Gil, K. (1999). Neurodevelopmental and neurobehavioral sequelae of selected substances of abuse and psychiatric medications in utero. *Neurological Disorders: Developmental and Behavioral Sequelae, 8,* 845–867.

Walker, L. J. (1980). Cognitive and perspective-taking prerequisites for moral development. *Child Development, 51,* 131–139.

Walker, L. J. (1989). A longitudinal study of moral reasoning. *Child Development, 60,* 157–166.

Walker, L. J. (1995). Sexism in Kohlberg's moral psychology? In W. M. Kurtines & J. L. Gewirtz (Eds.), *Moral development: An introduction* (pp. 83–107). Boston: Allyn and Bacon.

Walker, L. J. (2004). Progress and prospects in the psychology of moral development. *Merrill-Palmer Quarterly, 50,* 546–557.

Walker, L. J., & Hennig, K. H. (1997). Moral development in the broader context of personality. In S. Hala (Ed.), *The development of social cognition* (pp. 297–327). Hove, UK: Psychology Press.

Walker, L. J., & Moran, T. J. (1991). Moral reasoning in a communist Chinese society. *Journal of Moral Education, 20,* 139–155.

Walker, L. J., Pitts, R. C., Hennig, K. H., & Matsuba, M. K. (1995). Reasoning about morality and real-life moral problems. In M. Killen & D. Hart (Eds.), *Morality in everyday life* (pp. 37–407). New York: Cambridge University Press.

Walker, L. J., Pitts, R. C., Hennig, K. H., & Matsuba, M. K. (1999). Reasoning about morality and real-life moral problems. In M. Killen & D. Hart (Eds.), *Morality in everyday life* (pp. 371–407). New York: Cambridge University Press.

Walker, L. J., & Taylor, J. H. (1991a). Family interactions and the development of moral reasoning. *Child Development, 62,* 264–283.

Walker, L. J., & Taylor, J. H. (1991b). Stage transitions in moral reasoning: A longitudinal study of developmental processes. *Developmental Psychology, 27,* 330–337.

Walker-Andrews, A. S. (1997). Infants' perception of expressive behaviors: Differentiation of multimodal information. *Psychological Bulletin, 121,* 437–456.

Walkowiak, J., Wiener, J., Fastabend, A., Heinzow, B., Krämer, U., & Schmidt, E. (2001). Environmental exposure to polychlorinated biphenyls and quality of the home environment: Effects on psychodevelopment in early childhood. *Lancet, 358,* 1602–1607.

Wallace, J. M., Jr., Bachman, J. G., O'Malley, P. M., Schulenberg, J. E., Cooper, S. M., & Johnston, L. D. (2003). Gender and ethnic differences in smoking, drinking, and illicit drug use among American 8th, 10th, and 12th grade students, 1976–2000. *Addiction, 98,* 225–234.

Wang, Q. (2003). Infantile amnesia reconsidered: A cross-cultural analysis. *Memory, 11,* 65–80.

Wang, S., Baillargeon, R., & Paterson, S. (2005). Detecting continuity violations in infancy: A new account and new evidence from covering and tube events. *Cognition, 95,* 129–173.

Wanska, S. K., & Bedrosian, J. L. (1985). Conversational structure and topic performance in mother–child interaction. *Journal of Speech and Hearing Research, 28,* 579–584.

Wark, G. R., & Krebs, D. L. (1996). Gender and dilemma differences in real-life moral judgment. *Developmental Psychology, 32,* 220–230.

Warnock, F., & Sandrin, D. (2004). Comprehensive description of newborn distress behavior in response to acute pain (newborn male circumcision). *Pain, 107,* 242–255.

Warren, A. R., & Tate, C. S. (1992). Egocentrism in children's telephone conversations. In R. M. Diaz & L. E. Berk (Eds.), *Private speech: From social interaction to self-regulation* (pp. 245–264). Hillsdale, NJ: Erlbaum.

Warren, D. H. (1994). *Blindness and children: An individual difference approach.* New York: Cambridge University Press.

Waschbusch, D. A., Daleiden, E., & Drabman, R. S. (2000). Are parents accurate reporters of their child's cognitive abilities? *Journal of Psychopathology and Behavioral Assessment, 22,* 61–77.

Wasik, B. A., & Bond, M. A. (2001). Beyond the pages of a book: Interactive book reading and language development in preschool classrooms. *Journal of Educational Psychology, 93,* 243–250.

Wasserman, G., Graziano, J. H., Factor-Litvak, P., Popovac, D., Morina, N., & Musabegovic, A. (1994). Consequences of lead exposure and iron supplementation on childhood development at age 4 years. *Neurotoxicology and Teratology, 16,* 233–240.

Watamura, S. E., Donzella, B., Alwin, J., & Gunnar, M. R. (2003). Morning-to-afternoon increases in cortisol concentrations for infants and toddlers at child care: Age differences and behavioral correlates. *Child Development, 74,* 1006–1020.

Waters, E., & Cummings, E. M. (2000). A secure base from which to explore close relationships. *Child Development, 71,* 164–172.

Waters, E., Merrick, S., Treboux, D., Crowell, J., & Albersheim, L. (2000). Attachment security in infancy and early adulthood: A twenty-year longitudinal study. *Child Development, 71,* 684–689.

Waters, E., Vaughn, B. E., Posada, G., & Kondo-Ikemura K. (Eds.). (1995). Caregiving, cultural, and cognitive perspectives on secure-base behavior and working models: New growing points of attachment theory and research. *Monographs of the Society for Research in Child Development, 60*(2–3, Serial No. 244).

Watson, A. C., Nixon, C. L., Wilson, A., & Capage, L. (1999). Social interaction skills and theory of mind in young children. *Developmental Psychology, 35,* 386–391.

Watson, D. J. (1989). Defining and describing whole language. *Elementary School Journal, 90,* 129–141.

Watson, J. B., & Raynor, R. (1920). Conditioned emotional reactions. *Journal of Experimental Psychology, 3,* 1–14.

Watson, M. (1990). Aspects of self development as reflected in children's role playing. In D. Cicchetti & M. Beeghly (Eds.), *The self in transition: Infancy to childhood* (pp. 281–307). Chicago: University of Chicago Press.

Waxman, S. R. (2003). Links between object categorization and naming: Origins and emergence in human infants. In D. H. Rakison & L. M. Oakes (Eds.), *Early category and concept development: Making sense of the blooming, buzzing confusion* (pp. 193–209). New York: Oxford University Press.

Waxman, S. R., & Markow, D. B. (1998). Object properties and object kind: Twenty-one-month-old infants' extension of novel adjectives. *Child Development, 69,* 1313–1329.

Waxman, S. R., & Senghas, A. (1992). Relations among word meanings in early lexical development. *Developmental Psychology, 28,* 862–873.

Webb, N. M., Nemer, K. M., & Chizhik, A. W. (1998). Equity issues in collaborative group assessment: Group composition and performance. *American Educational Research Journal, 35,* 607–651.

Webb, N. M., Troper, J., & Fall, R. (1995). Constructive activity and learning in collaborative small groups. *Journal of Educational Psychology, 87,* 406–423.

Webb, S. J., Monk, C. S., & Nelson, C. A. (2001). Mechanisms of postnatal neurobiological development: Implications for human development. *Developmental Neuropsychology, 19,* 147–171.

Weber, C., Hahne, A., Friedrich, M., & Friederici, A. (2004). Discrimination of word stress in early infant perception: Electrophysiological evidence. *Cognitive Brain Research, 18,* 149–161.

Webster-Stratton, C., Reid, J., & Hammond, M. (2001). Social skills and problem-solving training for children with early-onset conduct problems: Who benefits? *Journal of Child Psychology and Psychiatry, 42,* 943–952.

Wechsler, D. (1996). *Canadian supplement manual for the WISC-III.* Toronto: Psychological Corporation.

Wechsler, D. (2002). *WPPSI-III: Wechsler Preschool and Primary Scale of Intelligence* (3rd ed.). San Antonio, TX: Psychological Corporation.

Wechsler, D. (2003). *WISC-IV: Wechsler Intelligence Scale for Children* (4th ed.). San Antonio, TX: Psychological Corporation.

Wehren, A., De Lisi, R., & Arnold, M. (1981). The development of noun definition. *Journal of Child Language, 8,* 165–175.

Weikart, D. P. (1998). Changing early childhood development through educational intervention. *Preventive Medicine, 27,* 233–237.

Weinberg, M. K., & Tronick, E. Z. (1994). Beyond the face: An empirical study of infant affective configurations of facial, vocal, gestural, and regulatory behaviors. *Child Development, 65,* 1503–1515.

Weinberg, M. K., Tronick, E. Z., Cohn, J. F., & Olson, K. L. (1999). Gender differences in emotional expressivity and self-regulation during early infancy. *Developmental Psychology, 35,* 175–188.

Weinberg, R., Tenenbaum, G., McKenzie, A., Jackson, S., Anshel, M., Grove, R., & Fogarty, G. (2000). Motivation for youth participation in sport and physical activity: Relationships to culture, self-reported activity levels, and gender. *International Journal of Sport Psychology, 31,* 321–346.

Weiner, A. (1988). *The Trobrianders of Papua New Guinea.* New York: Holt.

Weiner, J., & Tardif, C. (2004). Social and emotional functioning of children with learning disabilities: Does special education placement make a difference? *Learning Disabilities Research and Practice, 19,* 20–32.

Weinert, F. E., & Hany, E. A. (2003). The stability of individual differences in intellectual development: Empirical evidence, theoretical problems, and new research questions. In R. J. Sternberg, J. Lautrey, & T. I. Lubart (Eds.), *Models of intelligence: International perspectives* (pp. 169–181). Washington, DC: American Psychological Association.

Weinert, F. E., & Schneider, W. (Eds.). (1999). *Individual development from 3 to 12: Findings from the Munich Longitudinal Study.* Cambridge, UK: Cambridge University Press.

Weinfield, N. S., Sroufe, L. A., & Egeland, B. (2000). Attachment from infancy to early adulthood in a high-risk sample: Continuity, discontinuity, and their correlates. *Child Development, 71,* 695–702.

Weinfield, N. S., Whaley, G. J. L., & Egeland, B. (2004). Continuity, discontinuity, and coherence in attachment from infancy to late adolescence: Sequelae of organization and disorganization. *Attachment and Human Development, 6,* 73–97.

Weinraub, M., Clemens, L. P., Sockloff, A., Ethridge, T., Gracely, E., & Myers, B. (1984). The development of sex-role stereotypes in the third year: Relationships to gender labeling, gender identity, sex-typed toy preference, and family characteristics. *Child Development, 55,* 1493–1503.

Weinstein, R. S. (2002). *Reaching higher: The power of expectations in schooling.* Cambridge, MA: Harvard University Press.

Weinstock, H., Berman, S., & Cates, W., Jr. (2004). Sexually transmitted diseases among American youth: Incidence and prevalence estimates, 2000. *Perspectives on Sexual and Reproductive Health, 36,* 6–10.

Weisberg, R. W. (1993). *Creativity: Beyond the myth of genius.* New York: Freeman.

Weisfeld, G. E. (1997). Puberty rites as clues to the nature of human adolescence. *Cross-Cultural Research, 31,* 27–54.

Weisner, T. S., & Wilson-Mitchell, J. E. (1990). Nonconventional family lifestyles and sex typing in six-year-olds. *Child Development, 61,* 1915–1933.

Weissman, M. D., & Kalish, C. (1999). The inheritance of desired characteristics: Children's view of the role of intention in parent–offspring resemblance. *Quarterly Journal of Experimental Child Psychology, 73,* 245–265.

Weisz, A. N., & Black, B. M. (2002). Gender and moral reasoning: African American youths respond to dating dilemmas. *Journal of Human Behavior in the Social Environment, 6,* 17–34.

Weizman, Z. O., & Snow, C. E. (2001). Lexical output as related to children's vocabulary acquisition: Effects of sophisticated exposure and support for meaning. *Developmental Psychology, 37,* 265–279.

Wekerle, C., & Avgoustis, E. (2003). Child maltreatment, adolescent dating, and adolescent dating violence. In P. Florsheim (Ed.), *Adolescent romantic relations and sexual behavior: Theory, research, and practical implications* (pp. 213–242). Mahwah, NJ: Erlbaum.

Wekerle, C., & Wolfe, D. A. (2003). Child maltreatment. In E. J. Mash & R. A. Barkley (Eds.), *Child psychopathology* (2nd ed., pp. 632–684). New York: Guilford.

Wellman, H. M. (1990). *The child's theory of mind.* Cambridge, MA: MIT Press.

Wellman, H. M. (2002). Understanding the psychological world: Developing a theory of mind. In U. Goswami (Ed.), *Blackwell handbook of child cognitive development* (pp. 167–187). Malden, MA: Blackwell.

Wellman, H. M., & Gelman, S. A. (1998). Knowledge acquisition in foundational domains. In D. Kuhn & R. S. Siegler (Eds.), *Handbook of child psychology: Vol. 2. Cognition, perception, and language* (5th ed., pp. 523–630). New York: Wiley.

Wellman, H. M., Cross, D., & Watson, J. (2001). Meta-analysis of theory-of-mind development: The truth about false belief. *Child Development, 72,* 655–684.

Wellman, H. M., & Hickling, A. K. (1994). The mind's "I": Children's conception of the mind as an active agent. *Child Development, 65,* 1564–1580.

Wellman, H. M., Hickling, A. K., & Schultz, C. A. (1997). Young children's psychological, physical, and biological explanations. In H. M. Wellman & K. Inagaki (Eds.), *The emergence of core domains of thought: New directions for child development #75* (pp. 7–25). San Francisco: Jossey-Bass.

Wellman, H. M., Phillips, A. T., & Rodriquez, T. (2000). Young children's understanding of perception, desire, and emotion. *Child Development, 71,* 895–912.

Wellman, H. M., Somerville, S. C., & Haake, R. J. (1979). Development of search procedures in real-life spatial environments. *Developmental Psychology, 15,* 530–542.

Wendland-Carro, J., Piccinini, C. A., & Millar, W. S. (1999). The role of an early intervention on enhancing the quality of mother–infant interaction. *Child Development, 70,* 713–721.

Wentworth, N., Benson, J. B., & Haith, M. M. (2000). The development of infants' reaches for stationary and moving targets. *Child Development, 71,* 576–601.

Wentworth, N., & Haith, M. M. (1998). Infants' acquisition of spatiotemporal expectations. *Developmental Psychology, 24,* 247–257.

Wentzel, K. R., Barry, C. M., & Caldwell, K. A. (2004). Friendships in middle school: Influences on motivation and school adjustment. *Journal of Educational Psychology, 96,* 195–203.

Werker, J. F., Pegg, J. E., & McLeod, P. (1994). A cross-language investigation of infant preference for infant-directed communication. *Infant Behavior and Development, 17,* 323–333.

Werker, J. F., & Tees, R. C. (1999). Influences on infant speech processing: Toward a new synthesis. *Annual Review of Psychology, 50,* 509–535.

Werner, E. E. (1989). Children of the Garden Island. *Scientific American, 260*(4), 106–111.

Werner, E. E. (2001). Journeys from childhood to midlife: Risk, resilience, and recovery. Ithaca, NY: Cornell University Press.

Werner, E. E., & Smith, R. S. (1982). *Vulnerable but invincible.* New York: McGraw-Hill.

Werner, E. E., & Smith, R. S. (1992). *Overcoming the odds: High risk children from birth to adulthood.* Ithaca, NY: Cornell University Press.

Werner, N. E., & Crick, N. R. (2004). Maladaptive peer relationships and the development of relational and physical aggression during middle childhood. *Social Development, 13,* 495–514.

Westen, D., & Gabbard, G. O. (1999). Psychoanalytic approaches to personality. In L. A. Pervin & O. P. John (Eds.), *Handbook of personality: Theory and research* (2nd ed., pp. 57–101). New York: Guilford.

Wheeler, T., Barker, D. J. P., & O'Brien, P. M. S. (1999). *Fetal programming: Influences on development and disease in later life.* London: RCOG Press.

Wheeler, W. (2002). Youth leadership for development: Civic activism as a component of youth development programming and a strategy for strengthening civil society. In R. M. Lerner, F. Jacobs, & D. Wertlieb (Eds.), *Handbook of applied developmental science: Vol. 2* (pp. 491–506). Thousand Oaks, CA: Sage.

White, B., & Held, R. (1966). Plasticity of sensorimotor development in the human infant. In J. F. Rosenblith & W. Allinsmith (Eds.), *The causes of behavior* (pp. 60–70). Boston: Allyn and Bacon.

White, L., & Gilbreth, J. G. (2001). When children have two fathers: Effects of relationships with stepfathers and noncustodial fathers on adolescent outcomes. *Journal of Marriage and the Family, 63,* 155–167.

White, S. H. (1992). G. Stanley Hall: From philosophy to developmental psychology. *Developmental Psychology, 28,* 25–34.

Whitehurst, G. J., Arnold, D. S., Epstein, J. N., Angell, A. L., Smith, M., & Fischel, J. E. (1994). A picture book reading intervention in day care and home for children from low-income families. *Developmental Psychology, 30,* 679–689.

Whiteside-Mansell, L., Bradley, R. H., Owen, M. T., Randolph, S. M., & Cauce, A. M. (2003). Parenting and children's behavior at 36 months: Equivalence between African-American and European-American mother–child dyads. *Parenting: Science and Practice, 3,* 197–234.

Whiting, B., & Edwards, C. P. (1988a). *Children of different worlds.* Cambridge, MA: Harvard University Press.

Whiting, B., & Edwards, C. P. (1988b). A cross-cultural analysis of sex differences in the behavior of children aged 3 through 11. In G. Handel (Ed.), *Childhood socialization* (pp. 281–297). New York: Aldine De Gruyter.

Whitington, V., & Ward, C. (1999). Intersubjectivity in caregiver–child communication. In L. E. Berk (Ed.), *Landscapes of development* (pp. 109–120). Belmont, CA: Wadsworth.

Whitley, B. E. (1983). Sex role orientation and self-esteem: A critical meta-analytic review. *Journal of Personality and Social Psychology, 44,* 765–778.

Wichmann, C., Coplan, R. J., & Daniels, T. (2004). The social cognitions of socially withdrawn children. *Social Development, 13,* 377–392.

Wichstrøm, L. (1999). The emergence of gender difference in depressed mood during adolescence: The role of intensified gender socialization. *Developmental Psychology, 35,* 232–245.

Wickham, S. (1999, Summer). Homebirth: What are the issues? *Midwifery Today, 50,* 16–18.

Wideen, M. F., O'Shea, T., Pye, I., & Ivany, G. (1997). High-stakes testing and the teaching of science. *Canadian Journal of Education, 22,* 428–444.

Wierenga, K. J., Hambleton, I. R., & Lewis, N. A. (2001). Survival estimates for patients with homozygous sickle-cell disease in Jamaica: A clinic-based population study. *Lancet, 357,* 680–683.

Wigfield, A., & Eccles, J. S. (1994). Children's competence beliefs, achievement values, and general self-esteem change across elementary and middle school. *Journal of Early Adolescence, 14,* 107–138.

Wigfield, A., Eccles, J. S., Yoon, K. S., Harold, R. D., Arbreton, A. J., Freedman-Doan, C., & Blumenfeld, P. C. (1997). Changes in children's competence beliefs and subjective task values across the elementary school years: A three-year study. *Journal of Educational Psychology, 89,* 451–469.

Wilcox, A. J., Weinberg, C. R., & Baird, D. D. (1995). Timing of sexual intercourse in relation to ovulation: Effects on the probability of conception, survival of the pregnancy, and sex of the baby. *New England Journal of Medicine, 333,* 1517–1519.

Wildes, J. E., Emery, R. E., & Simons, A. D. (2001). The roles of ethnicity and culture in the development of eating disturbance and body dissatisfaction: A meta-analytic review. *Clinical Psychology Review, 21,* 521–551.

Wilkinson, K., Ross, E., & Diamond, A. (2003). Fast mapping of multiple words: Insights into when "the information provided" does and does not equal "the information perceived." *Applied Developmental Psychology, 24,* 739–762.

Willatts, P. (1999). Development of means–end behavior in young infants: Pulling a support to retrieve a distant object. *Developmental Psychology, 35,* 651–667.

Wille, D. E. (1991). Relation of preterm birth with quality of infant–mother attachment at one year. *Infant Behavior and Development, 14,* 227–240.

Wille, M. C., Weitz, B., Kerper, P., & Frazier, S. (2004). Advances in preconception genetic counseling. *Journal of Perinatal and Neonatal Nursing, 18,* 28–40.

Williams, E., Radin, N., & Allegro, T. (1992). Sex-role attitudes of adolescents reared primarily by their fathers: An 11-year follow-up. *Merrill-Palmer Quarterly, 38,* 457–476.

Williams, G. C. (1997). Review of *Adaptation*, edited by Michael R. Rose and George V. Lauder. *Copeia*, No. 3, 645–647.

Williams, J. E., & Best, D. L. (1990). *Measuring sex stereotypes: A multination study.* Newbury Park, CA: Sage.

Williams, K., Haywood, K. I., & Painter, M. (1996). Environmental versus biological influences on gender differences in the overarm throw for force: Dominant and nondominant arm throws. *Women in Sport and Physical Activity Journal, 5,* 29–48.

Williams, P. E., Weiss, L. G., & Rolfhus, E. (2003). *WICS-IV: Theoretical model and test blueprint.* San Antonio, TX: Psychological Corporation.

Williams, S. C., Lochman, J. E., Phillips, N. C., & Barry, T. D. (2003). Aggressive and nonaggressive boys' physiological and cognitive processes in response to peer provocations. *Journal of Clinical Child and Adolescent Psychology, 32,* 568–576.

Williams, T. M. (1986). *The impact of television: A natural experiment in three communities.* Orlando, FL: Academic Press.

Williams, W. M. (1998). Are we raising smarter children today? School- and home-related influences on IQ. In U. Neisser (Ed.), *The rising curve: Long-term gains in IQ and related measures* (pp. 125–154). Washington, DC: American Psychological Association.

Willinger, M., Ko, C. W., Hoffman, H. J., Kessler, R. C., & Corwin, M. J. (2003). Trends in infant bed sharing in the United States, 1993–2000: The National Infant Sleep Position Study. *Archives of Pediatric and Adolescent Medicine, 157,* 43–49.

Willms, J. D., Tremblay, M. S., & Katzmarzyk, P. T. (2003). Geographic and demographic variation in the prevalence of overweight Canadian children. *Obesity Research, 11,* 668–673.

Willoughby, J., Kupersmidt, J. B., & Bryant, D. (2001). Overt and covert dimensions of antisocial behavior. *Journal of Abnormal Child Psychology, 29,* 177–187.

Wilson, E. O. (1975). *Sociobiology: The new synthesis.* Cambridge, MA: Harvard University Press.

Wilson, R., & Cairns, E. (1988). Sex-role attributes, perceived competence, and the development of depression in adolescence. *Journal of Child Psychology and Psychiatry, 29,* 635–650.

Winner, E. (1986, August). Where pelicans kiss seals. *Psychology Today, 20* (8), 25–35.

Winner, E. (1988). *The point of words: Children's understanding of metaphor and irony.* Cambridge, MA: Harvard University Press.

Winner, E. (1996). *Gifted children: Myths and realities.* New York: Basic Books.

Winner, E. (1997). Exceptionally high intelligence and schooling. *American Psychologist, 52,* 1070–1081.

Winner, E. (2000). The origins and ends of giftedness. *American Psychologist, 55,* 159–169.

Winner, E. (2003). Creativity and talent. In M. H. Bornstein, L. Davidson, C. L. M. Keyes, K. A. Moore, & The Center for Child Well-Being (Eds.), *Well-being: Positive development across the life course* (pp. 371–380). Mahwah, NJ: Erlbaum.

Winsler, A., Diaz, R. M., & Montero, I. (1997). The role of private speech in the transition from collaborative to independent task performance in young children. *Early Childhood Research Quarterly, 12,* 59–79.

Winsler, A., & Naglieri, J. (2003). Overt and covert verbal problem-solving strategies: Developmental trends in use, awareness, and relations with task performance in children aged 5 to 17. *Child Development, 74,* 659–678.

Witherington, D. C., von Hofsten, C., Rosander, K., Robinette, A., Woollacott, M. H., & Bertenthal, B. I. (2002). The development of anticipatory postural adjustments in infancy. *Infancy, 3,* 495–517.

Wolak, J., Mitchell, K. J., & Finkelhor, D. (2003). Escaping or connecting? Characteristics of youth who form close online relationships. *Journal of Adolescence, 26,* 105–119.

Wolchik, S. A., Sandler, I. N., Millsap, R. E., Plummer, B. A., Greene, S. M., & Anderson, E. R. (2003). Six-year follow-up of preventive interventions for children of divorce: A randomized controlled trial. *Journal of the American Medical Association, 288,* 1874–1881.

Wolchik, S. A., Wilcox, K. L., Tein, J.-Y., & Sandler, I. N. (2000). Maternal acceptance and consistency of discipline as buffers of divorce stressors on children's psychological adjustment problems. *Journal of Abnormal Child Psychology, 28,* 87–102.

Wolfe, D. A. (1999). *Child abuse* (2nd ed.). Thousand Oaks, CA: Sage.

Wolfe, D. A., Scott, K., Wekerle, C., & Pittman, A. (2001). Child maltreatment: Risk of adjustment problems and dating violence in adolescence. *Journal of the American Academy of Child and Adolescent Psychiatry, 40,* 282–289.

Wolfelt, A. D. (1997). Death and grief in the school setting. In T. N. Fairchild (Ed.), *Crisis intervention strategies for school-based helpers* (2nd ed., pp. 199–244). Springfield, IL: Charles C. Thomas.

Wolff, P. H. (1966). The causes, controls and organization of behavior in the neonate. *Psychological Issues, 5*(1, Serial No. 17).

Wolff, P. H., & Fesseha, G. (1999). The orphans of Eritrea: A five-year follow-up study. *Journal of Child Psychology and Psychiatry and Allied Disciplines, 40,* 1231–1237.

Wolfinger, N. H. (2000). Beyond the intergenerational transmission of divorce: Do people replicate the patterns of marital instability they grew up with? *Journal of Family Issues, 21,* 1061–1086.

Wolpe, J., & Plaud, J. J. (1997). Pavlov's contributions to behavior therapy: The obvious and not so obvious. *American Psychologist, 52,* 966–972.

Wong, C. A., Eccles, J. S., & Sameroff, A. (2003). The influence of ethnic discrimination and ethnic identification on African American adolescents' school and socioemotional adjustment. *Journal of Personality, 71,* 1197–1232.

Wood, E., Desmarais, S., & Gugula, S. (2002). The impact of parenting experience on gender stereotyped toy play of children. *Sex Roles, 47,* 39–49.

Wood, J. J., Emmerson, N. A., & Cowan, P. A. (2004). Is early attachment security carried forward into relationships with preschool peers? *British Journal of Developmental Psychology, 22,* 245–253.

Wood, S. (2001). Interview. *Frontline.* Retrieved from: www.pbs.org/wgbh/pages/frontline/shows/fertility/interviews/wood.html

Woodhouse, B. B. (2001). Children's rights. In S. O. White (Ed), *Handbook of youth and justice* (pp. 377–410). New York: Kluwer Academic.

Woodward, A. L., & Markman, E. M. (1998). Early word learning. In D. Kuhn & R. S. Siegler (Eds.), *Handbook of child psychology: Vol. 2. Cognition, perception, and language* (5th ed., pp. 371–420). New York: Wiley.

Woodward, J. (2004). Mathematics education in the United States: Past to present. *Journal of Learning Disabilities, 37,* 16–31.

Woodward, J., & Ono, Y. (2004). Mathematics and academic diversity in Japan. *Journal of Learning Disabilities, 37,* 74–82.

Woodward, L. J., & Fergusson, D. M. (1999). Childhood peer relationship problems and psychosocial adjustment in late adolescence. *Journal of Abnormal Child Psychology, 27,* e87.

Woody-Dorning, J., & Miller, P. H. (2001). Children's individual differences in capacity: Effects on strategy production and utilization. *British Journal of Developmental Psychology, 19,* 543–557.

Woody-Ramsey, J., & Miller, P. H. (1988). The facilitation of selective attention in preschoolers. *Child Development, 59,* 1497–1503.

Woolley, J. D. (2000). The development of beliefs about direct mental–physical causality in imagination, magic, and religion. In K. S. Rosengren, C. N. Johnson, & P. L. Harris (Eds.), *Imagining the impossible* (pp. 99–129). New York: Cambridge University Press.

Woolley, J. D., Phelps, K. E., Davis, D. L., & Mandell, D. J. (1999). Where theories of mind meet magic: The development of children's beliefs about wishing. *Child Development, 70,* 571–587.

Wooster, D. M. (1999). Assessment of nonorganic failure to thrive. *Infant-Toddler Intervention, 9,* 353–371.

Wooster, D. M. (2000). Intervention for nonorganic failure to thrive. *Transdisciplinary Journal, 10,* 37–45.

World Education Services. (2005). World education database. Retrieved from www.wes.org

World Health Organization. (2003). *The world health report, 2003.* Geneva, Switzerland: Author.

World Press Review. (2004). *Obesity: A worldwide issue.* Retrieved from www.worldpress.org/Africa/1961.cfm

Wright, B. C., & Dowker, A. D. (2002). The role of cues to differential absolute size in children's transitive inferences. *Journal of Experimental Child Psychology, 81,* 249–275.

Wright, J. C., Huston, A. C., Murphy, K. C., St. Peters, M., Pinon, M., Scantlin, R., & Kotler, J. (2001). The relations of early television viewing to school readiness and vocabulary of children from low-income families: The Early Window Project. *Child Development, 72,* 1347–1366.

Wright, J. C., Huston, A. C., Reitz, A. L., & Piemyat, S. (1994). Young children's perceptions of television reality: Determinants and developmental differences. *Developmental Psychology, 30,* 229–239.

Wright, V. C., Schieve, L. A., Reynolds, M. A., Jeng, G., & Kissin, D. (2004). Assisted reproductive technology surveillance—United States 2001. *Morbidity and Mortality Weekly Report, 53,* 1–20.

Wrotniak, B. H., Epstein, L. H., Raluch, R. A., & Roemmich, J. N. (2004). Parent weight change as a predictor of child weight change in family-based behavioral obesity treatment. *Archives of Pediatric and Adolescent Medicine, 158,* 342–347.

Wu, L. L., Bumpass, L. L., & Musick, K. (2001). Historical and life course trajectories of nonmarital childbearing. In L. L. Wu & B. Wolfe (Eds.), *Out of wedlock: Causes and consequences of nonmarital fertility* (pp. 3–48). New York: Russell Sage Foundation.

Wu, P., Robinson, C. C., Yang, C., Hart, C. H., Olsen, S. F., Porter, C. L., Jin, S., Wo, J., & Wu, X. (2002). Similarities and differences in mothers' parenting of preschoolers in China and the United States. *International Journal of Behavioral Development, 26,* 481–491.

Wu, T., Mendola, P., & Buck, G. M. (2002). Ethnic differences in the presence of secondary sex characteristics and menarche among U.S. girls: The Third National Health and Nutrition Examination Survey, 1988–1994. *Pediatrics, 110,* 752–757.

Wyatt, J. M., & Carlo, G. (2002). What will my parents think? Relations among adolescents' expected parental reactions, prosocial moral reasoning and prosocial and antisocial behaviors. *Journal of Adolescent Research, 17,* 646–666.

Wynn, K. (1992). Addition and subtraction by human infants. *Nature, 358,* 749–750.

Wynn, K. (1998). Psychological foundations of number: Numerical competence in human infants. *Trends in Cognitive Sciences, 2,* 296–303.

Wynn, K. (2002). Do infants have numerical expectations or just perceptual preferences? Comment. *Developmental Science, 5,* 207–209.

Xu, F., & Spelke, E. S. (2000). Large number discrimination in 6-month-old infants. *Cognition, 74,* B1–B11.

Xu, X., & Peng, L. (2001). Reflection on parents' educational beliefs in the new century. *Theory and Practice of Education, 21,* 62–63.

Xue, Y., & Meisels, S. J. (2004). Early literacy instruction and learning in kindergarten: Evidence from the early childhood longitudinal study—kindergarten class of 1998–1999. *American Educational Research Journal, 41,* 191–229.

Yale, M. E., Messinger, D. S., Cobo-Lewis, A. B., Oller, D. K., & Eilers, R. E. (1999). An event-based analysis of the coordination of early infant vocalizations and facial actions. *Developmental Psychology, 35,* 505–513.

Yan, J., & Smetana, J. G. (2003). Conceptions of moral, social-conventional, and personal events among Chinese preschoolers in Hong Kong. *Child Development, 74,* 647–658.

Yang, B., Ollendick, T. H., Dong, Q., Xia, Y., & Lin, L. (1995). Only children and children with siblings in the People's Republic of China: Levels of fear, anxiety, and depression. *Child Development, 66,* 1301–1311.

Yang, C., Hart, C. H., Nelson, D. A., Porter, C. L., Olsen, S. F., Robinson, C. C., & Jin, S. (2003). Fathering in a Beijing Chinese sample: Associations with boys' and girls' negative emotionality and aggression. In R. D. Day & M. E. Lamb (Eds.), *Conceptualizing and measuring father involvement* (pp. 185–215). Mahwah, NJ: Erlbaum.

Yang, C.-K., & Hahn, H.-M. (2002). Cosleeping in young Korean children. *Developmental and Behavioral Pediatrics, 23,* 151–157.

Yarrow, M. R., Campbell, J. D., & Burton, R. V. (1970). Recollections of childhood: A study of the retrospective method. *Monographs of the Society for Research in Child Development, 35*(5, Serial No. 138).

Yarrow, M. R., Scott, P. M., & Waxler, C. Z. (1973). Learning concern for others. *Developmental Psychology, 8,* 240–260.

Yates, W. R., Cadoret, R. J., & Troughton, E. P. (1999). The Iowa adoption studies: Methods and results. In M. C. LaBuda & E. L. Grigorenko (Eds.), *On the way to individuality: Current methodological issues in behavioral genetics* (pp. 95–125). Commack, NY: Nova Science Publishers.

Yeates, K. O., Schultz, L. H., & Selman, R. L. (1991). The development of interpersonal negotiation strategies in thought and action: A social-cognitive link to behavioral adjustment and social status. *Merrill-Palmer Quarterly, 37,* 369–405.

Yeh, H.-C., & Lempers, J. D. (2004). Perceived sibling relationships and adolescent development. *Journal of Youth and Adolescence, 33,* 133–147.

Yirmiya, N., Erel, O., Shaked, M., & Solomonica-Levi, D. (1998). Meta-analyses comparing theory of mind abilities of individuals with autism, individuals with mental retardation, and normally developing individuals. *Psychological Bulletin, 124,* 283–307.

Yirmiya, N., & Shulman, C. (1996). Seriation, conservation, and theory of mind abilities in individuals with autism, individuals with mental retardation, and normally developing children. *Child Development, 67,* 2045–2059.

Yirmiya, N., Solomonica-Levi, D., & Shulman, C. (1996). The ability to manipulate behavior and to understand manipulation of beliefs: A comparison of individuals with autism, mental retardation, and normal development. *Developmental Psychology, 32,* 62–69.

Yogman, M. W. (1981). Development of the father–infant relationship. In H. Fitzgerald, B. Lester, & M. W. Yogman (Eds.), *Theory and research in behavioral pediatrics* (Vol. 1, pp. 221–279). New York: Plenum.

Yonas, A., Granrud, E. C., Arterberry, M. E., & Hanson, B. L. (1986). Infants' distance perception from linear perspective and texture gradients. *Infant Behavior and Development, 9,* 247–256.

Yoshinaga-Itano, C. (2003). Early intervention after universal neonatal hearing screening: Impact on outcomes. *Mental Retardation and Developmental Disabilities Research Reviews, 9,* 252–266.

Young, J. F., & Mroczek, D. K. (2003). Predicting intraindividual self-concept trajectories during adolescence. *Journal of Adolescence, 26,* 589–603.

Young, K. T. (1990). American conceptions of infant development from 1955 to 1984: What the experts are telling parents. *Child Development, 61,* 17–28.

Young, S. K., Fox, N. A., & Zahn-Waxler, C. (1999). The relations between temperament and empathy in 2-year-olds. *Developmental Psychology, 35,* 1189–1197.

Youngblade, L. M., & Dunn, J. (1995). Individual differences in young children's pretend play with mother and sibling: Links to relationships and understanding of other people's feelings and beliefs. *Child Development, 66,* 1472–1492.

Younger, B. A. (1985). The segregation of items into categories by ten-month-old infants. *Child Development, 56,* 1574–1583.

Younger, B. A. (1993). Understanding category members as "the same sort of thing": Explicit categorization in ten-month infants. *Child Development, 64,* 309–320.

Youngstrom, E., Wolpaw, J. M., Kogos, J. L., Schoff, K., Ackerman, B., & Izard, C. (2000). Interpersonal problem solving in preschool and first grade: Developmental change and ecological validity. *Journal of Clinical Child Psychology, 29,* 589–602.

Youniss, J., McLellan, J. A., & Yates, M. (1997). What we know about engendering civic identity. *American Behavioral Scientist, 40,* 620–631.

Youniss, J., McLellan, J., & Yates, M. (1999). Religion, community service, and identity in American youth. *Journal of Adolescence, 22,* 243–253.

Yu, R. (2002). On the reform of elementary school education in China. *Educational Exploration, 129,* 56–57.

Yu, Y., & Nelson, K. (1993). Slot-filler and conventional category organization in young Korean children. *International Journal of Behavioral Development, 16,* 1–14.

Yuill, N., & Pearson, A. (1998). The developmental bases for trait attribution: Children's understanding of traits as causal mechanisms based on desire. *Developmental Psychology, 34,* 574–576.

Yunger, J. L., Carver, P. R., & Perry, D. G. (2004). Does gender identity influence children's psychological well-being? *Developmental Psychology, 40,* 572–582.

Zach, T., Pramanik, A., & Ford, S. P. (2001). Multiple births. *eMedicine.* Retrieved from mypage.direct.ca/c/csamson/multiples/2twinningrates.html

Zafeiriou, D. I. (2000). Plantar grasp reflex in high-risk infants during the first year of life. *Pediatric Neurology, 22,* 75–76.

Zahn-Waxler, C. (1991). The case for empathy: A developmental review. *Psychological Inquiry, 2,* 155–158.

Zahn-Waxler, C., Cole, P. M., & Barrett, K. C. (1991). Guilt and empathy: Sex differences and implications for the development of depression. In J. Garber & K. A. Dodge (Eds.), *The development of emotion regulation and dysregulation* (pp. 243–272). Cambridge, UK: Cambridge University Press.

Zahn-Waxler, C., Kochanska, G., Krupnick, J., & McKnew, D. (1990). Patterns of guilt in children of depressed and well mothers. *Developmental Psychology, 26,* 51–59.

Zahn-Waxler, C., & Radke-Yarrow, M. (1990). The origins of empathic concern. *Motivation and Emotion, 14,* 107–130.

Zahn-Waxler, C., Radke-Yarrow, M., & King, R. M. (1979). Childrearing and children's prosocial initiations toward victims of distress. *Child Development, 50,* 319–330.

Zahn-Waxler, C., & Robinson, J. (1995). Empathy and guilt: Early origins of feelings of responsibility. In J. P. Tangney & K. W. Fischer (Eds.),

Self-conscious emotions (pp. 143–173). New York: Guilford.

Zahn-Waxler, C., Schiro, K., Robinson, J. L., Emde, R. N., & Schmitz, S. (2001). Empathy and prosocial patterns in young MZ and DZ twins: Development and genetic and environmental influences. In R. N. Emde & J. K. Hewitt (Eds.), *Infancy to early childhood: Genetic and environmental influences on developmental change* (pp. 141–162). New York: Oxford University Press.

Zeifman, D. M. (2003). Predicting adult responses to infant distress: Adult characteristics associated with perceptions, emotional reactions, and timing of intervention. *Infant Mental Health Journal, 24*, 597–612.

Zelazo, N. A., Zelazo, P. R., Cohen, K. M., & Zelazo, P. D. (1993). Specificity of practice effects on elementary neuromotor patterns. *Developmental Psychology, 29*, 686–691.

Zelazo, P. D., Frye, D., & Rapus, T. (1996). An age-related dissociation between knowing rules and using them. *Cognitive Development, 11*, 37–63.

Zeskind, P. S., & Barr, R. G. (1997). Acoustic characteristics of naturally occurring cries of infants with "colic." *Child Development, 68*, 394–403.

Zeskind, P. S., & Lester, B. M. (2001). Analysis of infant crying. In L. T. Singer & P. S. Zeskind (Eds.), *Biobehavioral assessment of the infant* (pp. 149–166). New York: Guilford.

Zeskind, P. S., & Ramey, C. T. (1978). Fetal malnutrition: An experimental study of its consequences on infant development in two caregiving environments. *Child Development, 49*, 1155–1162.

Zeskind, P. S., & Ramey, C. T. (1981). Preventing intellectual and interactional sequelae of fetal malnutrition: A longitudinal, transactional, and synergistic approach to development. *Child Development, 52*, 213–218.

Zhou, M., & Bankston, C. L. (1998). *Growing up American: How Vietnamese children adapt to life in the United States.* New York: Russell Sage Foundation.

Zhou, Q., Eisenberg, N., Lousoya, S. H., Fabes, R. A., Reiser, M., Guthrie, I. K., Murphy, B. C., Cumberland, A. J., & Shepard, S. A. (2002). The relations of parental warmth and positive expressiveness to children's empathy-related responding and social functioning: A longitudinal study. *Child Development, 73*, 893–915.

Zigler, E. F., & Finn-Stevenson, M. (1999). Applied developmental psy-

chology. In M. H. Bornstein & M. E. Lamb (Eds.), *Developmental psychology: An advanced textbook* (4th ed., pp. 555–598). Mahwah, NJ: Erlbaum.

Zigler, E. F., & Gilman, E. (1998). The legacy of Jean Piaget. In G. A. Kimble & M. Wertheimer (Eds.), *Portraits of pioneers in psychology* (Vol. 3, pp. 145–160). Washington, DC: American Psychological Association.

Zigler, E. F., & Hall, N. W. (2000). *Child development and social policy: Theory and applications.* New York: McGraw-Hill.

Zigler, E., & Styfco, S. J. (2001). Can early childhood intervention prevent delinquency? A real possibility. In A. C. Bohart & D. J. Stipek (Eds.), *Constructive and destructive behavior: Implications for family, school, and society* (pp. 231–248). Washington, DC: American Psychological Association.

Zimmer-Gembeck, M. J., Siebenbruner, J., & Collins, W. A. (2001). Diverse aspects of dating: Associations with psychosocial functioning from early to middle adolescence. *Journal of Adolescence, 24*, 313–336.

Zimmerman, B. J., & Risemberg, R. (1997). Self-regulatory dimensions of academic learning and motiva-

tion. In G. D. Phye (Ed.), *Handbook of academic learning: Construction of knowledge* (pp. 105–125). San Diego: Academic Press.

Zimmerman, P., & Becker-Stoll, F. (2002). Stability of attachment representations during adolescence: The influence of ego-identity status. *Journal of Adolescence, 25*, 107–124.

Ziv, M., & Frye, D. (2003). The relation between desire and false belief in children's theory of mind: No satisfaction? *Developmental Psychology, 39*, 859–876.

Zucker, K. J. (2001). Biological influences on psychosexual differentiation. In R. K. Unger (Ed.), *Handbook of the psychology of women and gender* (pp. 101–115). New York: Wiley.

Zuckerman, B., Frank, D. A., & Mayes, L. (2002). Cocaine-exposed infants and developmental outcomes: "Crack kids" revisited. *Journal of the American Medical Association, 287*, 1990–1991.

Zukow-Goldring, P. (2002). Sibling caregiving. In M. H. Bornstein (Ed.), *Handbook of parenting: Vol. 3* (2nd ed., pp. 253–286). Hillsdale, NJ: Erlbaum.

Zur, O., & Gelman, R. (2004). Young children can add and subtract by predicting and checking. *Early Childhood Research Quarterly, 19*, 121–137.

NAME INDEX

Italic "n" following page number indicates caption or note accompanying figure, illustration, or table.